TRUEMAN'S *Specific* Series®

NTA UGC-NET/SET

HRM

TRUEMAN'S *Specific* Series®

NTA UGC-NET/SET

For JRF and Eligibility Test for Assistant Professor (and Ph.D Entrance Exams)

HRM

Code No. : 55

Labour Welfare and Industrial Relations, Labour and Social Welfare, Human Resource Management

NEW SYLLABUS with Previous Years' Papers

By
REETU DOGRA
&
SUNIL KUSHWAHA

Authentic & Dependable

Produced and Published by
Danika Publishing Company
(Publishers of Trueman's *Specific* Series)
4352/4C, Ansari Road,
Daryaganj, New Delhi - 110002
Ph.: 011-23242482, 41501988
e-mail: danikabooks@yahoo.com

Can be had from
Invincible Publishers
2nd Floor, SAS Tower, Medicity, Sector 38,
Gurugram (Haryana)

ISBN : 9788189301316

New Edition : 2025

Price : Rs. 650/-

Data Processing :
Inhouse

Printed at :
Dhruv Printers
New Delhi.

PUBLISHERS' NOTE

The present work is a humble attempt to satisfy the needs of students appearing for UGC NET/SET Examinations. Syllabus and Guidelines for Paper II have been given in the book. After theory and MCQs, model papers are provided for practice. We have also incorporated questions asked in previous NET examinations. The book in the present form shall serve as a reliable evocative book for those preparing for NET/SET examinations.

Any suggestions for the improvement shall be thankfully acknowledged.

— With Best Wishes

CONTENTS

Guidelines and Syllabus

UNIT 1. Principles and Practices of Management 1

UNIT 2. Human Resource Management 85

UNIT 3. Human Resource Development 191

UNIT 4. Organisational Behaviour 255

UNIT 5. Industrial Relations 361

UNIT 6. Industrial Disputes 467

UNIT 7. Labour Legislation 511

UNIT 8. Wages 553

UNIT 9. Labour Welfare 617

UNIT 10. Labour Market 661

Additional Multiple Choice Questions 701

Model Papers (Set I & Set II) 759

Previous Years' Papers 783

UNIT 1

PRINCIPLES AND PRACTICES OF MANAGEMENT

Syllabus

- Development of management Thought, Contributions of Taylor, Fayol, Mayo, Mary Parker Follett and C.I. Barnard.
- Behavioural Approach, Systems Approach, Quantitative Approach and Contingency Approach.
- **Function of Management:** Planning and Decision Making, Organising, Staffing, Directing, Controlling, Coordinating.

DEVELOPMENT OF MANAGEMENT THOUGHT

Meaning of Management

Management is an individual or a group of individuals that accept responsibilities to run an organisation. They Plan, Organise, Direct and Control all the essential activities of the organisation. Management does not do the work themselves. They motivate others to do the work and co-ordinate (*i.e.*, bring together) all the work for achieving the objectives of the organisation.

Management brings together all **Six Ms** *i.e.*, Men and Women, Money, Machines, Materials, Methods and Markets. They use these resources for achieving the objectives of the organisation such as high sales, maximum profits, business expansion, etc.

Management is the process of conducting a set of functions (planning, organising, staffing, directing and controlling) to get the work done in an efficient and effective manner.

Management is the art of knowing what you want to do and then seeing that they do it in the best and the cheapest way.

In other words, *"Management is the process of planning, organising, leading, and controlling the efforts of organisation members and of using all other organisational resources to achieve stated organisational goals"*.

Management focuses on the entire organisation from both a short and a long-term perspective. Management aims to increase the effectiveness of organisations. It's about making the most of the resources entrusted to you, and making sure the expectations of customers, employees and shareholders are met.

According to **Theo Heimann**, management has three different meanings, viz.,

1. **Management as a Noun.** refers to a Group of Managers.
2. **Management as a Process.** refers to the Functions of Management *i.e.*, Planning, Organising, Directing, Controlling, etc.
3. **Management as a Discipline.** refers to the Subject of Management.

Definition of Management

- According to **D.J. Clough,** "Management is the art and Science of decision-making and leadership."
- According to **Henry L. Sisk,** "Management is the coordination of all resources through the process of planning, organising, directing and controlling in order to attain stated goals."
- According to **George R. Terry,** "Management is a distinct process consisting of planning, organising, actuating and controlling performed to determine and accomplish stated objectives by the use of human being and other resources."
- According to **C.W. Wilson,** "Management is a process of releasing and directing human energies towards attaining a definite goal.
- According to **B.O. Wheeler,** "Business management is a human activity which directs and controls the organisation and operations of business enterprise."
- According to **Mary Parker Follet,** "Management is the art of getting things done through people."
- According to **Peter F. Drucker,** "Management is a multi-purpose organ that manages business and manages managers and manages workers and work." This definition of management was given by Peter Drucker in his book *"The Principles of Management"*.

UGC-NET NEW SYLLABUS

The Test will consist of two papers as given below:

Paper	Marks	Number of Questions	MCQs	Duration
I	100	50	The questions will be generic in nature, intending to assess the teaching/research aptitude of the candidate. It will primarily be designed to test reasoning ability, comprehension, divergent thinking and general awareness of the candidate.	03 hours All the questions will be compulsory.
II	200	100	This will be based on the subject selected by the candidate.	

The Test will be conducted in Computer Based Test (CBT) mode only, and will be held on different dates at various centres in India.

Syllabus for all NET Subjects can be downloaded from the UGC website: **https://www.ugcnetonline.in/syllabus-new.php.**

SYLLABUS

UNIT-I PRINCIPLES AND PRACTICES OF MANAGEMENT

Development of management Thought, Contributions of Taylor, Fayol, Mayo, Mary Parker Follett and C.I. Barnard.

Behavioural Approach, Systems Approach, Quantitative Approach and Contingency Approach.

Function of Management: Planning and Decision Making, Organising, Staffing, Directing, Controlling, Coordinating.

UNIT-II HUMAN RESOURCE MANAGEMENT

Conceptual framework, Human Resource Planning, Job Analysis, Recruitment, Selection, Placement, Induction, Training and Development, Performance Management, Job Evaluation, Compensation Management, Employee Benefits and Incentives, Managing Career.

New Trends in HRM: Changing environment of HRM and contemporary challenges, Emerging HRM Concepts.

UNIT-III HUMAN RESOURCE DEVELOPMENT (HRD)

Concepts, Assumptions, Values, HRD Mechanisms, Action – research Model, HRD Culture and Climate, HRD Interventions, HR Accounting and Audit, Consultant – client relationship, Knowledge Management, Human Resource Information System.

International Human Resource Management (IHRM): Organisational context of IHRM, IHRM and Sustainable Business, Functions of IHRM, Cross – Cultural Studies, Cultural Diversity, Transnational Organisations, IHRM models.

UNIT-IV ORGANISATIONAL BEHAVIOUR

Concept, Scope, Nature of human behavior, Personality, Perception, Learning, Attitude, Motivation, Interpersonal Behaviour, Group Dynamics, Leadership, Communication, Power and Authority, Stress, Organisational Change and Development.

UNIT-V **INDUSTRIAL RELATIONS**

Concept, Scope, Evolution, Approaches, Actors and Models, Conflict and cooperation, Bi-partitism, Tri-partitism, Collective Bargaining, Workers' Participation in Management, Grievance Handling and Disciplinary Action, Code of Conduct, Industrial Relations in changing scenario, Employers' organisations.

Trade Unions: Concepts, Evolution, Problems of trade unions in India, Recognition, The Trade Unions Act, 1926. Emerging role of trade unions in India.

UNIT-VI **INDUSTRIAL DISPUTES**

Factors, Forms, Trends, Prevention and Settlement, Role of State and Central Labour Administration, Strikes and Lockouts. The Industrial Employment (Standing Orders) Act, 1946. The Industrial Disputes Act, 1947.

UNIT-VII **LABOUR LEGISLATION**

Objectives, Principles, Classification and Evolution. International Labour Organisation, Social Justice and Labour Legislation, Indian Constitution and Labour Laws.

- The Factories Act, 1948.
- The Mines Act, 1952.
- The Inter-state Migrant Workmen (Regulation of employment and conditions of service) Act, 1979.
- The Contract Labour (Regulation and Abolition) Act, 1970.
- The Building and other Construction workers (Regulation of employment and conditions of service) Act, 1996.
- The Child Labour (Prohibition and Regulation) Act, 1986.

UNIT-VIII **WAGES**

Concept, Types, Factors influencing wages, Wage Theories and Wage Differentials

- The Minimum Wages Act, 1948.
- The Payment of Wages Act, 1936.
- The Payment of Bonus Act, 1965.
- The Equal Remuneration Act, 1976.
- The Payment of Gratuity Act, 1972.
- The Employees' Provident Fund and Miscellaneous Provisions Act, 1952.

UNIT-IX **LABOUR WELFARE**

Concept, Scope, Types, Theories and Principles, Industrial Health and Hygiene, Industrial Accidents and safety, Occupational Diseases

Social Security: Concept and Scope, Social Assistance and Social assurance.

UNIT-X **LABOUR MARKET**

Features, Demand and Supply of Labour, Nature and Composition of Indian Labour Force, Unemployment and Underemployment, Types of Labour Market,

Characteristics of Indian Labour Market, New Dynamics of Labour Market in India, Economic Systems and Labor Market, Problems of Labour in India.

- According to **Harold Koontz**, "Management is the art of getting things done through and with people in formally organised groups." Harold Koontz gave this definition of management in his book "*The Management Theory Jungle*".
- According to **Henry Fayol**, "To manage is to forecast and to plan, to organise, to command, to co-ordinate and to control." Henry Fayol gave this definition of management in his book "*Industrial and General Administration*".

Features of Management

FEATURES OF MANAGEMENT	
1.	Continuous and Never Ending process.
2.	Art of Getting Work Done from people.
3.	Is Result- Oriented.
4.	Multidisciplinary in Nature.
5.	Group and Not an Individual Activity.
6.	Follows Established Principles or Rules.
7.	Aided but Not Replaced by Computers.
8.	Situational in Nature.
9.	Separate from Ownership.
10.	Is All Pervasive.
11.	Intangible but its Impact is Felt.
12.	Dynamic in Nature.

1. **Continuous and never ending process.** Management is a Process. It includes four main functions, viz., Planning, Organising, Directing and Controlling. The manager has to Plan and Organise all the activities. He had to give proper Directions to his subordinates. He also has to Control all the activities. The manager has to perform these functions continuously. Therefore, management is a continuous and never ending process.
2. **Getting things done through people.** The managers do not do the work themselves. They get the work done through the workers. The workers should not be treated like slaves. They should not be tricked, threatened or forced to do the work. A favorable work environment should be created and maintained
3. **Result oriented science and art.** Management is result oriented because it gives a lot of importance to "**Results**". Examples of Results like, increase in market share increase in profits, etc. Management always wants to get the best results at all times.
4. **Multi-disciplinary in nature.** Management has to get the work done through people. It has to manage people. This is a very difficult job because different people have different emotions, feelings, aspirations, etc. Similarly, the same person may have different emotions at different times. So, management is a very complex job. Therefore, management uses knowledge from many different subjects such as Economics, Information Technology, Psychology, Sociology, etc. Therefore, it is Multi-disciplinary in nature.
5. **A group and not an individual activity.** Management is not an individual activity. It is a group activity. It uses group (employees) efforts to achieve group (owners) objectives. It tries to satisfy the needs and wants of a group (consumers). Nowadays, importance is given to the team (group) and not to individuals
6. **Follows established principles or rules.** Management follows established principles, such as division of work, discipline, unity of command, etc. These principles help to prevent and solve the problems in the organisation.
7. **Aided but not replaced by computers.** Now-a-days, all managers use computers. Computers help the managers to take accurate decisions. However, computers can only help management. Computers cannot replace management. This is because management takes the final responsibility. Thus Management is aided (helped) but not replaced by computers.
8. **Situational in nature.** Management makes plans, policies and decisions according to the situation. It changes its style according to the situation. It uses different plans, policies, decisions

and styles for different situations. The manager first studies the full present situation. Then he draws conclusions about the situation. Then he makes plans, decisions, etc., which are best for the present situation. This is called **Situational** Management.

9. **Need not be ownership.** In small organisations management and ownership are one and the same. However, in large organisations, management is separate from ownership. The managers are highly qualified professionals who are hired from outside. The owners are the shareholders of the company.
10. **Management is all pervasive.** Management is necessary for running a business. It is also essential for running business, educational, charitable and religious institutions. Management is a must for all activities, and therefore, it is all pervasive.
11. **Management is intangible.** Management is intangible, *i.e.,* it cannot be seen and touched, but it can be felt and realised by its results. The success or failure of management can be judged only by its results. If there is good discipline, good productivity, good profits, etc., then the management is successful and vice-versa.
12. **Dynamic in nature.** Management is dynamic in nature. That is, management is creative and innovative. An organisation will survive and succeed only if it is dynamic. It must continuously bring in new and creative ideas, new products, new product features, new ads, new marketing techniques, etc.

Objectives of Management

Objectives of management can be broadly divided into the following three categories:

- **Organisational Objectives.** It refers to ascertain objectives for the whole organisation which are survival, profit and growth:
  - (i) **Survival.** Every business wants to survive for long. So, management by taking positive decisions with regard to different business activities should ensure that business survives for long.
  - (ii) **Profit.** Profit plays an important role in facing business hazards and successful running of business activities. So, it must be ensured that adequate profit is earned by the business.
  - (iii) **Growth.** Every business wants to grow. Management must ensure growth of business. Growth can be measured by sales, number of employees, products, capital investment, etc. If all these show increasing trend then it can be concluded that business is heading towards growth.
- **Social Objectives.** It refers to assure health, safety and price control to the society.

  Main social objectives of management are included in the following list:
  - (i) To save environment from getting polluted.
  - (ii) To contribute in improving living standard.
  - (iii) To make available good quality products at a reasonable price.
- **Personal Objectives.** It refers to ascertainment of the objectives in reference to the employees. While ascertaining personal objectives, care must be taken that in no way there is a clash between organisational and personal objectives.

Main objectives of management towards employees are as follows: (i) To give deserving remuneration. (ii) To provide good working environment. (iii) To provide a share in profit. (iv) Importance of Management

AIMS AND OBJECTIVES OF MANAGEMENT
■ Maximum utilization of resources
■ Increasing Profit
■ Customer Satisfaction
■ Improves employee's welfare
■ Improves employer & employee relation
■ Ensure a regular supply of goods
■ Minimising Risk
■ Aims at research & improving Business growth

In short, the importance of management is explained through the following facts:

- **Management helps in the Development of Society.** Management has some responsibility towards society. Managers by fulfilling their social responsibilities helps in the development of society. These responsibilities are to provide employment opportunities, to prevent environment from getting pollution, to make available good quality products at a reasonable price, etc.
- **Management Creates a Dynamic Organisation.** Every organisation works in an ever changing environment. To face the changing environment, many changes need to be made in the organisation as well. But people resist changes. Manager creates a favorable environment through introducing employees to the benefits arising by adapting changes.
- **Management Increases Efficiency.** A manager increases efficiency through the optimum utilisation of all the resources, such as, Man, Machine, Material and Money.
- **Management helps in achieving Group Goals.** It is the most important characteristic of management that it is goal-oriented activity. A manager achieves these goals by giving the common direction to the efforts of all individuals.
- **Management helps in achieving Personal Objectives.** Every employee wants to get suitable remuneration, a share in profit, participation in management, promotion, etc. in the form of his personal objectives. This objective can only be achieved, if they work while using their full abilities. Managers make employees able through motivation, good leadership and open communication. As a result, they attain their individual objectives.

Level of Management

Two leaders may serve as managers within the same company but have very different titles and purposes. Large organisations, in particular, may break down management into different levels because so many more people need to be managed. Typical management levels fall into the following categories:

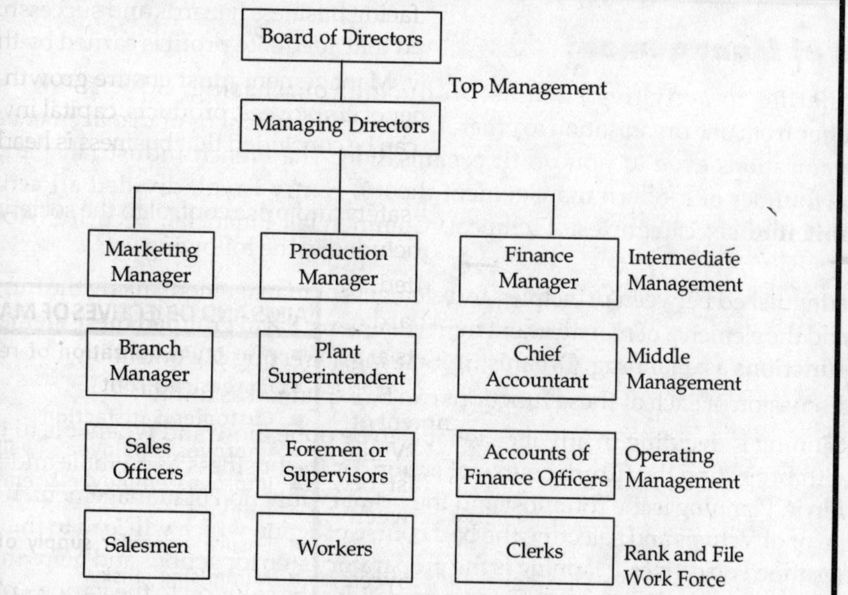

Level of Management

- **Top level.** Managers at this level ensure that major performance objectives are established and accomplished. Common job titles for top managers include chief executive officer (CEO), chief operating officer (COO), president, and vice president. These senior managers are considered executives, responsible for the performance of an organisation as a whole or for one of its significant parts.
- **Middle level.** Middle managers report to top managers and are in charge of relatively large departments or divisions consisting of several smaller units. Examples of middle managers include clinic directors in hospitals; deans in universities; and division managers, plant managers, and branch sales managers in businesses. Middle managers develop and implement action plans consistent with company objectives, such as increasing market presence.
- **Low level.** The initial management job that most people attain is typically a **first-line management** position, such as a team leader or supervisor – a person in charge of smaller work units composed of hands-on workers. Job titles for these first-line managers vary greatly, but include such designations as department head, group leader, and unit leader. First-line managers ensure that their work teams or units meet performance objectives, such as producing a set number of items at a given quality, that are consistent with the plans of middle and top management.

Difference Between Top, Middle and Lower Level of Management

Basis of Difference	Top Level Management	Middle Level Management	Lower Level Management
Skills	Creative skills are required.	Persuasive skills are required.	Operative skills are required
Persons	Very less number of persons	Moderate number of persons	Relatively high number of persons
Function	Policy formulation	Policy Interpretation	Policy Implementation
Nature	Administrative	Executive	Operative
Period	Long period is covered	Intermediate range is covered	Short period is covered

Functions of Management

Functions relating to activities such as producing, purchasing, advertising, selling and accounting differ from one organisation to other. However, the functions of management are common to all the organisations even to non-profit organisation. The French Industrialist and popularly known as the founder of modern management theory, **Henry Fayol, divided all activities of an industrial unit into six categories:** Technical, Commercial, Financial, Security, Accounting &, Managerial

Fayol distinguished between principles and elements of management, using the former for rules and guides, and the elements of management for its functions. **Fayol grouped these elements into five managerial functions as:** Planning, Organising, Staffing, Directing & Controlling

A brief discussion of each of these functions can be explained as follow:

Planning. Planning is deciding in advance what is to be done, how and when it is to be done. It is concerned with projecting the future course of action for the business as a whole and the different sections within it. Planning is the foremost and the primary function of management. It involves the determination of objectives and selecting the best course of action which will lead to the achievement of the predetermined objectives. Planning is the preparatory step for actions and helps in bridging the gap between the present and the future. Planning provides the solution to the various problems like:

- What are the necessary actions for the achievements of the predetermined objectives?
- What are the reasons for these necessary actions?

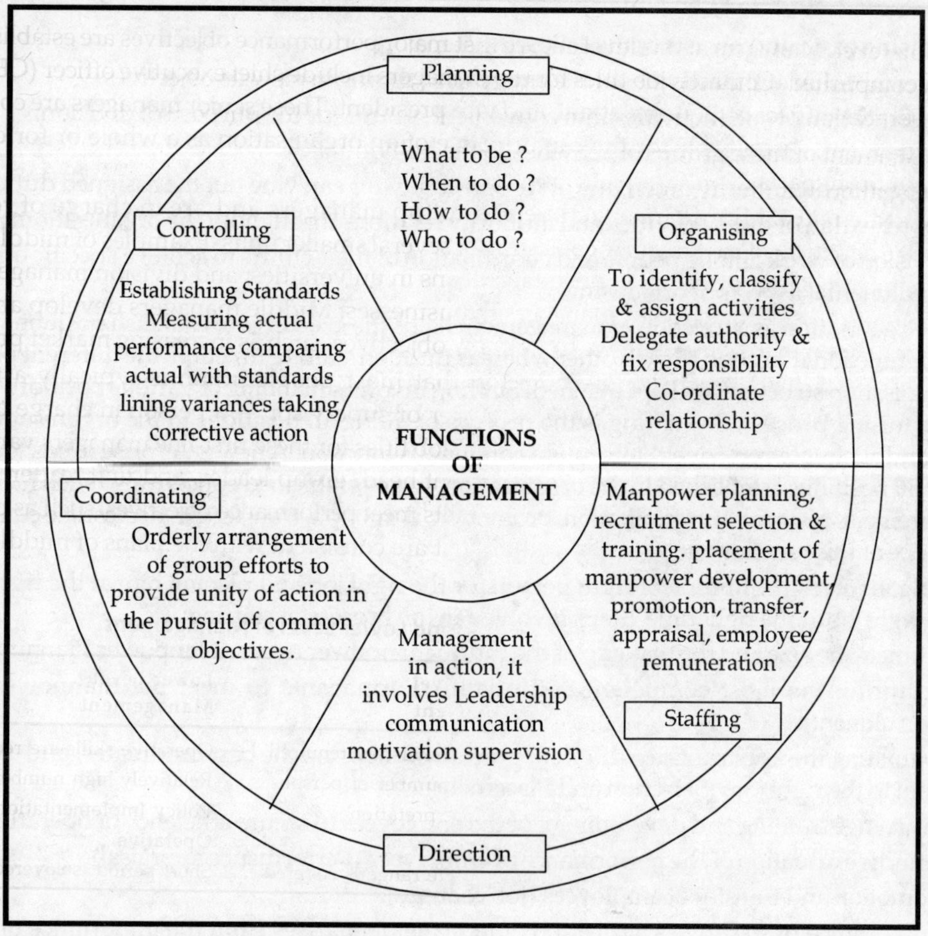

- When will these actions take place?
- How will these actions take place?
- Who should be made responsible for these actions?

Basically planning is concerned with the determination of the following: Objectives, Policies, Procedures, Rules, Programme, Budget & Strategies

The process of planning includes the following steps:

- Determination of the objectives of the organisation
- Forecasting or anticipating the future courses of actions
- Choosing the best course of action or decision making
- Formulation of policies, programmes, budget etc. for the achievement of the predetermined objectives.
- Laying down the procedures and standards of performance.

Organising. To divide the work, rights, and liability among the personnel engaged in the achievement of the objectives and establishing the formal relationship among them is called organising. It is concerned with development of a structure of authority and responsibility among the personnel, so that they can effectively perform their work. Thus, Organising is the process of establishing harmonious relationship among the members of the enterprise.

Organising basically consists of the following steps:

- Determination of the activities of the enterprise keeping in view its objectives.
- Classification of such activities into convenient groups for the purpose of division.
- Assignment of these groups of activities to the individuals.
- Delegation of authority and fixing of responsibility for carrying out the assigned duties.
- Coordination of these activities and authority relations throughout the organisation.

So, division of work among people and coordination of their efforts to achieve specific objectives are the fundamental aspects of organising.

Staffing. Organisation as a function of management helps the executive to establish positions and lay down their functional relation to each other whereas through staffing function, the different positions in the organisation structure are kept manned. Staffing involves manning of various positions created by the organising process. So staffing is the process of filling all positions in the organisation with qualified and adequate personnel. Staffing is a continuous function. A new enterprise needs to employ people to fill positions established in the organisation. In an established concern also such factors like death, retirement, resignation, termination, promotion, demotion, transfer etc. necessitate continuous performance of this function.

Staffing involves the finding of right person for the right job and placing him at the right place, doing the right job at the right time. Steps involved in the process of staffing:

- Estimate the size and the makeup of the future manpower needs (Manpower Planning).
- Acquiring the most competent and qualified applicants to meet the manpower needs (Recruitment).
- Evaluating the applicants for different positions, choosing the best candidates, and assigning them to the right jobs (Selection and Placement).
- To arrange training and development of the employees to secure efficiency of operation.
- Periodic evaluation of the performance of employees (Performance appraisal).
- Promotion and transfer of employees (Job changes).

The importance of staffing as a function of management arises from the importance of human resources in an organisation. Staffing involves manning the organisation structure through proper and effective recruitment, selection, training, development and appraisal of personnel to fill the roles designed into structure. Staffing ensures the availability of the required human resources at all times.

Directing. In addition to planning, organising and staffing every manager must also direct his subordinates. Directing is thus the initiating function of management that actuates plans and the organisation. Directing is an important function of management which involves communicating and providing leadership to the subordinates and motivating them to continue to the best of their capability for the achievement of organisational objectives. It is concerned with influencing the behaviour of human resources for the accomplishment of organisational objectives. It is therefore the life spark of an organisation as it is through directing that actual performance of the employees is guided towards common goals.

Important elements of Directing. The main elements of directing are :

- *Supervision:* Supervision is the main element of directing. The term supervision is made up of two words super and vision which means expert overseeing of employees at work. It involves direct personal contact with the subordinates. Supervision converts plans into action. Further the supervisor serves as a link between the workers and the management. It is necessary at all levels of management and throughout the chain of command; each superior supervises the work performance of his subordinates.

- *Motivation:* Motivation is an impulse drive or urge to move in specific direction to reduce a need. It is an act of understanding the motives and satisfying them to direct and sustain behaviour towards the accomplishment of organisational goals. Thus, motivation is an act of stimulating people to get desired course of action. Motivation is a psychological concept. It is concerned with the intrinsic forces operating within an individual which impel him to act or not to act in a particular way.
- *Communication:* Communication is an important element of direction. In fact superior subordinate relationship cannot thrive without effective and meaningful communication. Effective communication is defined as the exchange of thoughts, facts, opinions, or information by two or more persons so as to bring mutual understanding or confidence. Communication can be done through words, symbols, letters, or actions. So communication is the transfer of information or understanding from one person to another.
- *Leadership:* Leadership is one of the important aspects of managing. It is an interpersonal process of influencing the behaviour of individual and the group so that defined objectives are accomplished willingly and enthusiastically. A leader is the individual with the major influence in the group and whose main role is to get others to the organisational goals. A leader directs and motivates members of the group. He also represents the group to the outside world and the outside world to the group.

Controlling. Control is a fundamental function of management that usually follows the other functions. It is a continuing process of management. Controlling means the measurement and correction of performance of activities of subordinates in order to ensure that predetermined objectives can be achieved. So control guides the activities of the employees towards the predetermined goals. It is the process of ensuring that events confirm to the plans as closely as possible. It is the application of corrective measures to remove the deviations if actual performance does not meet the standards.

Controlling is the last but the most important function of management. Objective of every organisation is to use scarce resources in a best possible way. Plans are framed to achieve better results. Control is the process of checking whether the plans are being adhered to or not, keeping a record of progress, then taking corrective measures, if there is any deviation. Control is one of the important managerial functions which bring the actual results closer to the desired results.

Following steps are included in the process of controlling:

- Setting of goals and standards.
- Appraisal of performance.
- Determining the reasons of deviations.
- Taking Corrective Action.

Thus controlling is the process under which actual performance is compared with the fixed standards, deviations are discovered, the reasons are analyzed, and corrective action is taken so that repetition of such mistakes in future can be avoided.

SCHOOL OF MANAGEMENT THOUGHT

Stages in the History of Development of Management Thought

I. **The Classical Approach**

1. Bureaucratic model introduced by Max Weber around 1900.
2. Scientific management concepts introduced by F.W. Taylor around 1910.
3. Functional and administrative theory advanced by Henry Fayol around 1910.

II. **The Neo Classical Approach**

1. Human relation movement was propagated by Elton Mayo and Roethlisberger around 1930.
2. Behavioural Sciences movement was introduced by A. Maslow, McGregor around 1940.

III. **The Modern Approach**

1. Quantitative approach or operation research analysis.
2. System approach was propounded by Boulding, Johnson and others after 1950.
3. Contingency Approach was developed by Lorsch, Lawrence and others.

THE CLASSICAL APPROACH

Classical Scientific Management

The **classical management theory,** developed during the Industrial Revolution when new problems related to the factory system began to appear. Managers were unsure of how to train employees (many of them non-English speaking immigrants) or deal with increased labour dissatisfaction, so they began to test solutions.

As a result, the classical management theory developed from efforts to find the "one best way" to perform and manage tasks. This school of thought is made up of two branches: classical scientific and classical administrative, described in the following sections.

The **classical scientific branch** arose because of the need to increase productivity and efficiency. The emphasis was on trying to find the best way to get the most work done by examining how the work process was actually accomplished and by scrutinising the skills of the workforce.

The classical scientific school owes its roots to several major contributors, including Fredrick Taylor, Henry Gantt, Frank and Lillian Gilbert.

Meaning of Scientific Management

The concept of scientific management was introduced by Fredrick Winslow Taylor in U.S.A in the beginning of 20th Century. This concept was further carried on by Frank and Lillian, Edward Fellen etc. Scientific management was basically concerned with the improvement in the operational efficiency of the shop floor workers.

In a broad sense, scientific management implies the application of scientific methods of study and analysis to the problems of management. It is a systematic and thoughtful approach to the job of management as compared to the rule-of-thumb, or hit and miss, or trial and error approaches. It is concerned with the scientific bent of mind and is more than merely a set of techniques for improving efficiency. It implies substitution of exact scientific investigation and knowledge for individual judgement or opinion in all matters undertaken in the establishment.

Definition of Scientific Management

- According to **F.W. Taylor**, "Scientific management is concerned with knowing exactly what you want men to do and then see in that they do it in the best and cheapest way".
- According to **Drucker**, "The cost of scientific management is the organised study of work, the analysis of work into its simplest elements and the systematic management of the workers, performance of each element".

Taylor pointed out that the objective of management should be to secure the maximum prosperity for both the employer and the employee. Therefore, every employee should be developed to his/her greatest efficiency. Taylor provided the scientific approach to management comprising of observation, measurement, experimentation, and inference for eliminating the waste and inefficiency. Taylor had emphasized on the scientific decision making for the managers. He stated that the managers should resort to the scientific research for every work and decision. According to him the managers should make important decisions on the basis of the collected facts instead of giving directions without proper deliberations. A manager should not take any action on any matters until all facts are collected and scientific analysis is made on them. On the basis of this data decisions can be verified and the matters can be decided in the right prospects.

Principles of Scientific Management

Taylor's philosophy consists of the following principles which constitute the cornerstone of scientific management:

1. **Science, not rule of thumb.** According to this principle, scientific investigation should be applied in the scientific management, which will replace the rule of thumb. Taylor had made study of every job and fixed the method and timing for performing the job so that the worker should know that what, when, and how is required to perform the job. This principle is the starting point that distinguishes scientific management with the traditional management. Further, this principle eliminates the trend of go on trying, failing, wasting the resources, and finally perfecting the job. For this purpose Taylor had developed the various studies like; method study, time study, motion study etc.

> **FOUR PRINCIPLES OF SCIENTIFIC MANAGEMENT**
>
> **Frederick Taylor.** The father of Scientific Management who was influenced by Wilson's essay.
>
> - Adopt scientific measurements to break jobs into series of small, related tasks.
> - Use systematic methods for selecting workers and training them for specific jobs.
> - Establish clear division of responsibility between management and workers, where management sets goals, plans, and supervises, and the workers execute the required tasks.
> - Establish a discipline where management sets the objectives and the workers cooperate in achieving them.

2. **Harmony, not discord.** This principle states that there should be cooperation between the management and the workers. In order to achieve the best possible results from the business operations, it is essential that there should be harmonious relations between the management and the workers. According to this principle, attempts should be made to obtain the harmony in the group action rather than discord. Workers should have sense of belongingness towards the organisation.
3. **Mental Revolution.** The technique of Mental revolution involves a change in the attitude of workers and management towards each other. Both should realise the importance of each other and should work with full cooperation. Management as well as the workers should aim to increase the profits of the organisation.

   For this the workers should put in their best efforts so that the company makes profit and on the other hand management should share part of profits with the workers. Thus, mental revolution requires a complete change in the outlook of both management and workers. There should be a spirit of togetherness between workers and management.
4. **Cooperation, Not Individualism.** This principle is an extension of principle of 'Harmony, not discord' and lays stress on mutual cooperation between workers and the management. Cooperation, mutual confidence, sense of goodwill should prevail among both, managers as well as workers. The intention is to replace internal competition with cooperation.
5. **Development of each and every person to his or her greatest efficiency and prosperity.** According to this principle the right men is placed on the right job. The jobs are determined first

for which the workers are required and then the qualifications required for the job are determined. On the basis of these standards the employees are selected. So procedure for the selection of the members is designed scientifically. Further, management is responsible for the development and training of the workers. In scientific management, all workers should be developed to the fullest extent possible for their own as well as for the company's prosperity.

Techniques of Scientific Management

1. **Functional Foremanship.** Functional foremanship involves the supervision of the workers by several specialist foremen. Taylor evolved the concept of functional foremanship on the basis of specialisation and provided the importance to the supervision. He advocated the appointment of specialist foreman for the specific jobs. In this system eight persons are involved to direct the activities of the workers at the job. These eight persons are divided in two:

   Production department : Four persons
   - ***Speed boss.*** Maintaining the planned speed of production.
   - ***Inspector.*** Matching that work done is according to the standards.
   - ***Maintenance Foreman.*** Maintenance of machines and equipments.
   - ***Gang Boss.*** Making arrangement of machines, material, and men for the job.

   Planning department : Four persons
   - ***Route Clerk.*** Determine the process of job.
   - ***Instruction Card Clerk.*** Laying down the instructions for the workers.
   - ***Time and Cost Clerk.*** Setting the time table and cost budget for the job.
   - ***Disciplinarian.*** Maintaining proper discipline in the factory.

2. **Motion Study.** Motion study is designed to eliminate unnecessary motions and to reinforce necessary motions. It is a close observation of analyzing the body movements of the worker performing the job. This study helps in analyzing that if any element of the job can be eliminated or not. This study helps in:
   - Finding and eliminating the unnecessary motions of the workers on the job.
   - Increasing the efficiency of the workers by reducing the fatigue and manual labour.
   - Increasing the production and the productivity of the worker.

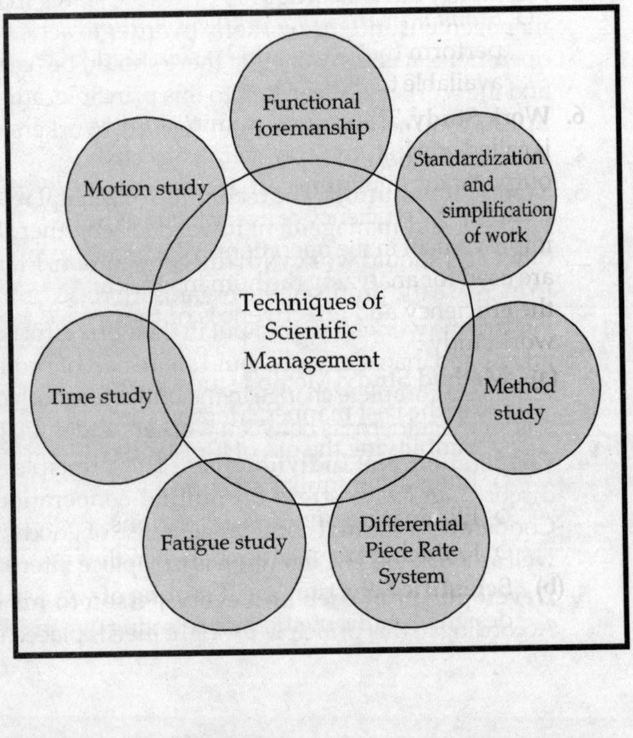

3. **Time study.** This study helps in determining the time required by an average skill worker to efficiently perform a particular job. Time study helps in determining the standard time for the job. This standard time is then fixed for the workers for performing the job. So, time study is used to measure precisely the time required in doing every element of a job with the purpose of deciding the fair day's work.

This study helps in:

- Determine scientifically the standard time required to perform the job.
- Creating time consciousness among the workers.
- Measuring the efficiency of the workers.
- Restricting the carelessness of the employees.
- Differentiating between efficient and inefficient workers.

4. **Differential Piece Wage System.** According to the Taylor, the efficient worker should be paid more than the inefficient one. Financial incentives motivate the workers to put their maximum efforts and according to Taylor are the provision exists in the company to earn higher wages by putting the extra effort, worker will be motivated to work more. Based on this Taylor evolved the Differential Piece Rate System. Under this system there are two piece rates:
   - Higher piece rate for those who produce standard quantity or more.
   - Lower piece rate for those who produce less than standard quantity.
5. **Standardisation.** Taylor emphasized that standardisation should be maintained in respect of product, raw material, machines, equipments, methods, and working conditions. These things should be planned in advance on the basis of job analysis and the elements of cost that involved in the performance of the job. So according to Taylor the maximum objectives can be achieved only when the labour, raw material, machine etc. should be standardised and not to be left on hit and trial. Standardisation is required for:
   - ***Standardisation of raw material.*** Raw material used in the production of the product should be standardised and also predetermined.
   - ***Standardisation of product.*** Product produced should also be standardised in their design, weight, shape, and size.
   - ***Standardisation of machines and equipments.*** Machines and equipments on which the job is performed by the workers should also be standardised.
   - ***Standardisation of methods.*** Method and the techniques of production should be determined in advance after proper job analysis and the research.
   - ***Standardisation of working conditions.*** Working conditions under which the worker has to perform the job should be standardised and all the requirements for the job to be made available to the workers.
6. **Work Study.** The critical examination of efficiency of the various operations in an organisation is called work study. The overall objective of the scientific management is to achieve maximum output at the minimum cost. For the purpose of the achievement of this objective it is required to examine the efficiency of every factor which affects the production for the purpose of bringing improvement in the operations. Work study is the generic term given to those techniques which are used for analyzing the human work and systematic investigation of all factors which affect the efficiency and effectiveness of the operations. The following studies are included in the work study :

   (a) **Method Study.** Method study is conducted to know the standardised method of doing the job in the best manner. Method study helps in efficiently performing the job by:
   - Simplifying the use of tools and equipments.
   - Integrating similar activities.
   - Eliminating unnecessary actions.
   - Reducing the distance between the place of storing and consumption of raw material.

   (b) **Scientific Selection and Training of workers.** According to Taylor, management should design scientific method for selecting the suitable workers, and for determining the training needs of the workers. Further, worker should be given work for which the worker is competent and suitable. Proper emphasis should be given on the training of the workers to make them efficient for the job, which they have to perform.

(c) **Fatigue Study.** When a worker works continuously his efficiency in the work goes on diminishing and he becomes tired. So fatigue in the work is natural and obvious. Fatigue has an adverse effect on the ability and efficiency of the worker. Scientific management determines the standard time of the job and the time after which the worker will require the rest. Fatigue study helps in

- Reducing the fatigue among the workers
- Increasing the efficiency of the worker.
- Maintains the operational efficiency of the worker.

(d) **Mental Revolution.** Taylor emphasized the mutual cooperation between the workers and the management as the human element comprising of worker and management is essentially a very sensitive factor of production. The basic idea behind the mental revolution is to change the mental attitude of the workers and the management towards each other. Mental revolution requires that there should be perfect cooperation and coordination between the efforts of labour and the management. The basic objectives of mental revolution are:

- To encourage the workers to put maximum efforts for the increase in production.
- Creation of mutual trust and confidence.
- Making the relations between the management and workers harmonious.
- Developing the scientific attitude towards the business problems and issues.
- Relationship between Fayol's and Taylor's Principles of Management.

Advantages of Scientific Management

Scientific Management provide the following advantages to the management:

1. Enhanced production
2. Ability to control
3. Decreased inaccuracy
4. Decreased autocracy
5. Cost of production is reduced
6. Pay system
7. Quick decision making
8. Benefit to customers
9. Efficiency increased
10. Best use of resources and development
11. Beneficial to the nation
12. Less production time
13. Work is carried out in a systematic manner
14. A proper atmosphere for working and conditions
15. Beneficial for owners and investors
16. Avoids labour and management disputes.

Disadvantages of Scientific Management

Following are the limitations of scientific management:

1. Requires huge capital
2. Management takes control
3. Planning reduces productivity
4. Demotivating approach
5. Overly bureaucratic
6. Mechanistic
7. Not suitable for teams
8. Work division
9. Avoids bargaining
10. Loss
11. Unemployment
12. Adverse effects
13. Stress
14. Wrong assumption
15. Follows narrow application
16. Time consuming.

Classical Administrative School (Bureaucratic Model)

Whereas scientific management focused on the productivity of individuals, the classical administrative approach concentrates on the total organisation. The emphasis is on the development of managerial principles rather than work methods.

Contributors to this school of thought include Max Weber, Henri Fayol, Mary Parker Follett, and Chester I. Barnard. These theorists studied the flow of information within an organisation and emphasized the importance of understanding how an organisation operated.

In the late 1800s, **Max Weber** disliked that many European organisations were managed on a "personal" family-like basis and that employees were loyal to individual supervisors rather than to the organisation. He believed that organisations should be managed impersonally and that a formal organisational structure, where specific rules were followed, was important. In other words, he didn't think that authority should be based on a person's personality. He thought authority should be something that was part of a person's job and passed from individual to individual as one person left and another took over. This no personal, objective form of organisation was called a **bureaucracy.**

Max Weber's Theory

Features of Bureaucracy Structure	
1. Division Labour	Complex work broke down into simple jobs
2. Hierarchy of Authority	Accepted chain of command to direct individual's effort towards organisational goal accomplishment
3. Framework of Rules	Effort directed and coordinated by rules
4. Impersonality	Hiring and promoting people on the basis of objective merit rather than favoritism (on the basis of what the know, and not who they know)
5. Formal Selection	Technical competence members selected accordingly on the basis of training, qualification, education etc.

Elements of Bureaucracy

Weber has provided a number of features in bureaucratic organisation. These are given below :

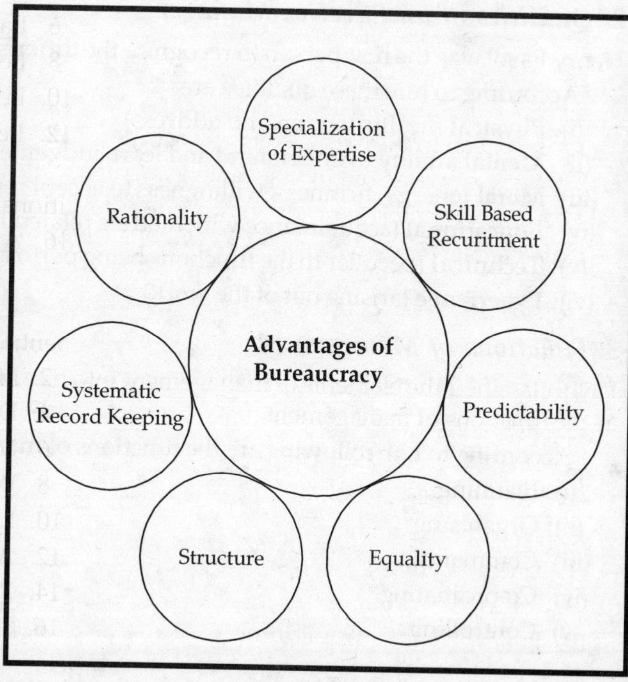

- **Hierarchy.** Hierarchy is a way of ranking positions in descending order from top to bottom of an organisation. All positions within a bureaucracy are structured in a way that permits the higher positions to supervise and control the lower positions. This clear chain of command facilitates control and order throughout the organisation.
- **Rules, regulations and procedures.** Standard operating procedures govern all organisational activities to provide certainty and facilitate coordination.

- **Division of work.** All responsibilities in an organisation are specialised so that each employee has the necessary expertise to do a particular task.
- **Impersonal relationships.** Managers should maintain an impersonal relationship with employees so that favouritism and personal prejudice do not influence decisions.
- **Competence.** Competence, not "who you know," should be the basis for all decisions made in hiring, job assignments, and promotions in order to foster ability and merit as the primary characteristics of a bureaucratic organisation.
- **Records.** Proper records have to be kept for everything. A bureaucracy needs to maintain complete files regarding all its activities.

Functional and Administrative Management

Henry Fayol (1841-1925) started his career as a junior engineer in a coal mine company in France and become its general manager in 1880. He not only saved a large coal and steel company from bankruptcy, but also led to crowning success.

His ideas on management have been summed up as the **Administrative Management Theory,** which later evolved into the management process school. Fayol contribution to management can be discussed under the following heads:

1. *Division of Industrial Activities*

Fayol observed the organisational functioning from manager's point of view

He found that all activities of the industrial enterprise could be divided into six groups :

(i) Technical (relating to production)
(ii) Commercial (buying, selling and exchange)
(iii) Financial (Search for capital and its optimum use)
(iv) Security (protection of property and person)
(v) Accounting (preparation of various statements, accounts, return etc.) and
(vi) Managerial (Planning, organisation, command, coordination and control)

2. *Qualities of an Effective Manager*

Henry Fayol was the first person to recognise the different qualities for managers.

According to him these qualities are :

(i) **Physical** (health, vigour, and address)
(ii) **Mental** (ability to understand and learn judgement, mental vigour, and adaptability)
(iii) **Moral** (energy, firmness, willingness to accept responsibility)
(iv) **Educational** (acquaintance with matters related to general functioning)
(v) **Technical** (peculiar to the functions being performed)
(vi) **Experience** (arising out of the work)

3. *Functions of Management*

Fayol classified the elements of management into five and all such elements were considered by him as the functions of management.

According to him following are the functions of management:

(i) Planning
(ii) Organising
(iii) Commanding
(iv) Co-ordinating
(v) Controlling

4. *Principles of Management*

Henri Fayol, a French mining engineer, developed 14 principles of management based on his management experiences. These principles provide modern-day managers with general guidelines on how a supervisor should organise her department and manage her staff. Although later research has created controversy over many of the following principles, they are still widely used in management theories.

- **Division of Work.** Division of work in the management process produces more and better work with the same effort. Various functions of management like planning, organising, directing and controlling cannot be performed efficiently by a single proprietor or by a group of directors. They must be entrusted to specialists in related fields.
- **Authority and Responsibility.** As the management consists of getting the work done through others, it implies that the manager should have the right to give orders and power to exact obedience. A manager may exercise formal authority and also personal power. Formal authority is derived from his official position, while personal power is the result of intelligence, experience, moral worth, ability to lead, past service, etc. Responsibility is closely related to authority and it arises wherever authority is exercised. An individual who is willing to exercise authority, must also be prepared to bear responsibility to perform the work in the manner desired. However, responsibility is feared as much as authority is sought after.
- **Discipline.** Discipline is absolutely essential for the smooth running of business. By discipline we mean, the obedience to authority, observance of the rules of service and norms of performance, respect for agreements, sincere efforts for completing the given job, respect for superiors, etc. The best means of maintaining discipline are (a) good supervisors at all levels, (b) clear and fair agreements between the employees and the employer, and (c) judicious application of penalties. In fact, discipline is what leaders make it.
- **Unity of Command.** This principle requires that each employee should receive instructions about a particular work from one superior only. Fayol believed that if an employee was to report to more than one superior, he would be confused due to conflict in instructions and also it would be difficult to pinpoint responsibility to him.
- **Unity of Direction.** It means that there should be complete identity between individual and organisational goals on the one hand and between departmental goals *inter se* on the other. They should not pull in different directions.
- **Subordination of Individual Interest to General Interest.** In a business concern, an individual is always interested in maximising his own satisfaction through more money, recognition, status, etc. This is very often against the general interest which lies in maximising production. Hence the need to subordinate the individual interest to general interest.
- **Remuneration.** The remuneration paid to the personnel of the firm should be fair. It should be based on general business conditions, cost of living, productivity of the concerned employees and the capacity of the firm to pay. Fair remuneration increases workers" efficiency and morale and fosters good relations between them and the management.
- **Centralisation.** If subordinates are given more role and importance in the management and organisation of the firm, it is decentralisation. The management must decide the degree of centralisation or decentralisation of authority on the basis of the nature of the circumstances, size of the undertaking, the type of activities and the nature of organisational structure. The objective to pursue should be the optimum utilisation of all faculties of the personnel.
- **Scalar Chain.** Scalar chain means the hierarchy of authority from the highest executive to the lowest one for the purpose of communication. It states superior-subordinate relationship and the authority of superiors in relation to subordinates at various levels. As per this principle, the orders or communications should pass through the proper channels of authority along the

scalar chain. But in case there is need for swift action, the proper channels of authority may be short-circuited by making direct contact (called gang plank) with the concerned authority.

CRITICISM OF ADMINISTRATIVE MANAGEMENT

- Gave more attention to function aspect and neglected structural aspect.
- For Peter Drucker, Fourteen principles have a great deal of overlapping.
- His theory is more applicable for manufacturing company rather than big public organizations.
- Unity of command and coordination may conflict.
- For Barnard and Simon, the informal side of organization and social-psychological or emotion needs of the employees were ignored.

- **Order.** To put things in an order needs effort. Disorder does not need any effort. It evolves by itself. Management should obtain orderliness in work through suitable organisation of men and materials. The principle of "right place for everything and for every man" should be observed by the management. To observe this principle, there is need for scientific selection of competent personnel, correct assignment of duties to personnel and good organisation.
- **Equity.** Equity means equality of fair treatment. Equity results from a combination of kindness and justice. Employees expect management to be equally just to everybody. It requires managers to be free from all prejudices, personal likes or dislikes. Equity ensures healthy industrial relations between management and labour which is essential for the successful working of the enterprise.
- **Stability of Tenure of Personnel.** In order to motivate workers to do more and better work, it is necessary that they should be assured security of job by the management. If they have fear of insecurity of job, their morale will be low and they cannot give more and better work. Further, they will not have any sense of attachment to the firm and they will always be on the lookout for a job elsewhere.
- **Initiative.** Initiative means freedom to think out and execute a plan. The zeal and energy of employees are augmented by initiative. Innovation which is the hallmark of technological progress is possible only where the employees are encouraged to take initiative. According to Fayol. Initiative is one of the keenest satisfactions for an intelligent man to experience, and hence, he advises managers to give their employees sufficient scope to show their initiative. Employees should be encouraged to make all kinds of suggestions to conceive and carry out their plans, even when some mistakes result.

Differences between Fayol and Taylor Contribution

Both Taylor and Fayol wanted to improve the efficiency of work through the systematic approach to management problems. At this stage, it may be worthwhile to establish the relationship between Taylor's and Fayol's point of view as both of them attempted to develop the rational approach to management. Both of them had practical experience and had systematically developed the management principles. After analyzing deeply we find that both are complimentary to each other and there exist lot of similarity between the both points of views. Similarities between Taylor's and Fayol's point of view:

Following are the points of similarities between both points of views:

- Point of views of both has systematically attempted to overcome the managerial problems.
- Principles of both can be applied in solving the managerial problems.
- Both have concluded that sound principles are required for the effective management decisions.
- Both have emphasized that training is necessary for developing the managerial qualities among the personnel's.
- For the achievement of organisational goals both have emphasized the cooperation and mutual trust among the workers and the management.

Basis	Henry Fayol	F.W Taylor
Place	France	America
Period	1841-1925	1856-1915
Level	Higher Management Level	Shop Floor Level
Scope	Wider as principles are applicable to all types of management.	Narrower, as is applied to factory level only.
Emphasizes	Overall efficiency can be achieved by observing principles.	Efficiency through work simplification and standardisation.
Results	Personal experiences translated into universal truths.	Scientific observation and measurement.
Concern	Efficiency of managers	Asks, workers, and supervisors
Achievement	Administrative management	Scientific management
Status	Father of modern management	Father of scientific management
Orientation	Managerial functions	Production and engineering

Mary Parker Follett stressed the importance of an organisation establishing common goals for its employees. However, she also began to think somewhat differently than the other theorists of her day, discarding command-style hierarchical organisations where employees were treated like robots. She began to talk about such things as ethics, power, and leadership. She encouraged managers to allow employees to participate in decision making. She stressed the importance of people rather than techniques — a concept very much before her time. As a result, she was a pioneer and often not taken seriously by management scholars of her time. But times change and innovative ideas from the past suddenly take on new meanings. Much of what managers do today is based on the fundamentals that Follett established more than 80 years ago.

Chester Barnard, who was president of New Jersey Bell Telephone Company, introduced the idea of the **informal organisation** — *cliques* (exclusive groups of people) that naturally form within a company. He felt that these informal organisations provided necessary and vital communication functions for the overall organisation and that they could help the organisation accomplish its goals.

Barnard felt that it was particularly important for managers to develop a sense of common purpose where a willingness to cooperate is strongly encouraged. He is credited with developing the **acceptance theory of management,** which emphasizes the willingness of employees to accept that managers have legitimate authority to act. Barnard felt that four factors affected the willingness of employees to accept authority:

- The employees must understand the communication.
- The employees accept the communication as being consistent with the organisation's purposes.
- The employees feel that their actions will be consistent with the needs and desires of the other employees.

THE NEOCLASSICAL APPROACH

Behavioural School

Behavioural management theory was developed in response to the need to account for employee behaviour and motivation. The shift moved management from a production orientation (classical leadership theory) to a leadership style focussed on the workers, human need for work related satisfaction and good working conditions.

The **behavioural science approach** developed as a natural evolution from the Hawthrone experiment. The behavioural science approach applies the knowledge of the behavioural science – psychology, sociology, and anthropology –to managing people.

The **behavioural management theory** is often called the human relations movement because it addresses the human dimension of work. Behavioural theorists believed that a better understanding of human behaviour at work, such as motivation, conflict, expectations, and group dynamics, improved productivity. The theorists who contributed to this school viewed employees as individuals, resources, and assets to be developed and worked with —-not as machines, as in the past. Several individuals and experiments contributed to this theory.

Elton Mayo's contributions came as part of the *Hawthorne studies,* a series of experiments that rigorously applied classical management theory only to reveal its shortcomings. The Hawthorne experiments consisted of two studies conducted at the Hawthorne Works of the Western Electric Company in Chicago from 1924 to 1932. The first study was conducted by a group of engineers seeking to determine the relationship of lighting levels to worker productivity. Surprisingly enough, they discovered that worker productivity increased as the lighting levels decreased – that is, until the employees were unable to see what they were doing, after which performance naturally declined.

A few years later, a second group of experiments began. Harvard researchers Mayo and F. J. Roethlisberger supervised a group of five women in a bank wiring room. They gave the women special privileges, such as the right to leave their workstations without permission, take rest periods, enjoy free lunches, and have variations in pay levels and workdays. This experiment also resulted in significantly increased rates of productivity.

BEHAVIOURAL THEORY

"The behavioural theory is a perspective on management that emphasises the importance of attempting to understand the various factors that affect human behaviour in organisations".

The employees behavior was not affected by job conditions alone there were internal reactions to the job situation also that affect their behaviour.

In this case, Mayo and Roethlisberger concluded that the increase in productivity resulted from the supervisory arrangement rather than the changes in lighting or other associated worker benefits. Because the experimenters became the primary supervisors of the employees, the intense interest they displayed for the workers was the basis for the increased motivation and resulting productivity. Essentially, the experimenters became a part of the study and influenced its outcome. This is the origin of the term *Hawthorne effect,* which describes the special attention researchers give to a study's subjects and the impact that attention has on the study's findings.

The general conclusion from the Hawthorne studies was that human relations and the social needs of workers are crucial aspects of business management. This principle of human motivation helped revolutionise theories and practices of management.

The Following are the important aspect of the behavioural science approach:

(i) **Communication.** Communication plays a vital role in human behaviour school. A better understanding develops between the management and workers, because of the reduced channel of communication in an organisation.

(ii) **Employee development.** It is concerned with the continued upgrading of employee skill and managerial skill.

(iii) **Leadership.** This school also underlines the role of the personal leadership of management. The scope of this school includes study of human relations and how the managers can grasp their implication, study of managers as a leaders and the way he should lead and study of successful and unsuccessful managerial behaviour.

(iv) **Employee motivation.** This includes a determination of the factors that lead to high productivity and high morale.

(v) **Organisation as social system.** It includes the study of role, status symbol as well as the function of the informal organisation.

Contributions of Behavioural Scientists

Abraham Maslow, James March and Herbert Simon, Douglas McGregor, Victor Vroom, Fredrick Herzberg, Chester Barnard, etc., made important contributions to the behavioural science approach.

Contributions of Behavioural Thinkers to Management Thought

Name	Period	Contribution
Mary Parker Follet	1868-1933	Advocated the concept of 'power sharing' and integration
Elton Mayo	1868-1933	foundation for the Human Relations Movement;
Abraham Maslow	1908-1970	motivated by a hierarchy of needs
Douglas McGregor	1906-1964	Theory X and Theory Y personalities
Chris Argyris	–	Classified organisations based on the employees set of values

Assumptions of Behavioural Science Approach

Basic assumptions and **propositions** of Behavioural Science Approach are :

1. In an organisation conflicts are unavoidable.
2. Different people have different perceptions, attitudes, needs and values. These differences must be found out and recognised by management.
3. Personal goals and Organisational goals must be joined together.
4. Work and interpersonal behaviour of people in the organisation is influenced by many factors.
5. Organisations are socio-technical systems. The management must integrate both the systems.
6. Employees are motivated not only by physiological needs but also by social and psychological needs.

Abraham Maslow's Hierarchy of need Theory

Abraham Maslow. A practising psychologist, developed one of the most widely recognised **need theories,** a theory of motivation based upon a consideration of human needs. His theory of human needs had three assumptions:

- Human needs are never completely satisfied.
- Human behaviour is purposeful and is motivated by the need for satisfaction.
- Needs can be classified according to a hierarchical structure of importance, from the lowest to highest.

Maslow divided hierarchy of needs into five specific areas:

- **Physiological needs.** Maslow grouped all physical needs necessary for maintaining basic human well-being, such as food and drink, into this category. After the need is satisfied, however, it is no longer a motivator.
- **Safety needs.** These needs include the need for basic security, stability, protection, and freedom from fear. A normal state exists for an individual to have all these needs generally satisfied. Otherwise, they become primary motivators.

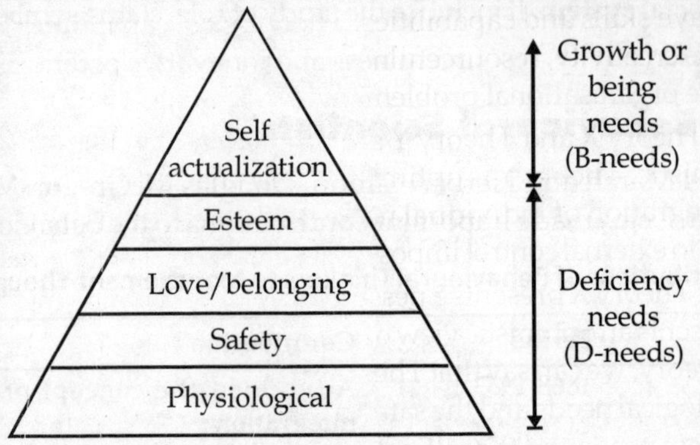

(Maslow's Motivation Model)

- **Belonging and love needs.** After the physical and safety needs are satisfied and are no longer motivators, the need for belonging and love emerges as a primary motivator. The individual strives to establish meaningful relationships with significant others.
- **Esteem needs.** An individual must develop self-confidence and wants to achieve status, reputation, fame, and glory.
- **Self-actualisation needs.** Assuming that all the previous needs in the hierarchy are satisfied, an individual feels a need to find himself.

Douglas McGregor's (1906-1964) Theories X and Y

In 1960, Douglas McGregor formulated Theory X and Theory Y suggesting two aspects of human behaviour at work, or in other words, two different views of individuals (employees): one of which is negative, called as Theory X and the other is positive, so called as Theory Y. According to McGregor, the perception of managers on the nature of individuals is based on various assumptions.

Assumptions of Theory X

- An average employee intrinsically does not like work and tries to escape it whenever possible.
- Since the employee does not want to work, he must be persuaded, compelled, or warned with punishment so as to achieve organisational goals. A close supervision is required on part of managers. The managers adopt a more dictatorial style.
- Many employees rank job security on top, and they have little or no aspiration/ ambition.
- Employees generally dislike responsibilities.
- Employees resist change.
- An average employee needs formal direction.

Assumptions of Theory Y

- Employees can perceive their job as relaxing and normal. They exercise their physical and mental efforts in an inherent manner in their jobs.
- Employees may not require only threat, external control and coercion to work, but they can use self-direction and self-control if they are dedicated and sincere to achieve the organisational objectives.
- If the job is rewarding and satisfying, then it will result in employees' loyalty and commitment to organisation.
- An average employee can learn to admit and recognise the responsibility. In fact, he can even learn to obtain responsibility.

- The employees have skills and capabilities. Their logical capabilities should be fully utilised. In other words, the creativity, resourcefulness and innovative potentiality of the employees can be utilised to solve organisational problems.

The assumptions in Theory X and Theory Y are fundamentally distinct. Theory X is static, rigid, conservative and pessimistic. Theory Y is optimistic, dynamic, flexible and progressive. It suggests self direction and the integration of individual needs with organisational needs. On the other hand, more importance is given to external control imposed by the superior on the subordinate in the Theory X.

Thus, we can say that Theory X presents a pessimistic view of employees' nature and behaviour at work, while Theory Y presents an optimistic view of the employees' nature and behaviour at work. If correlate it with Maslow's theory, we can say that Theory X is based on the assumption that the employees emphasize on the physiological needs and the safety needs; while Theory X is based on the assumption that the social needs, esteem needs and the self-actualisation needs dominate the employees.

McGregor views Theory Y to be more valid and reasonable than Theory X. Thus, he encouraged cordial team relations, responsible and stimulating jobs, and participation of all in decision-making process.

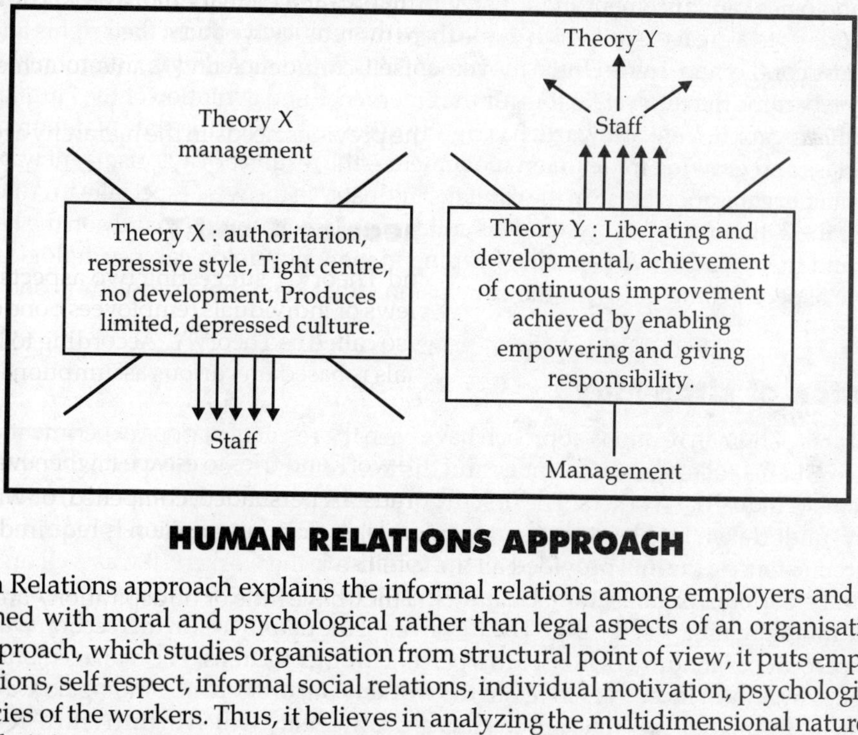

HUMAN RELATIONS APPROACH

The Human Relations approach explains the informal relations among employers and employees and concerned with moral and psychological rather than legal aspects of an organisation. Unlike Classical approach, which studies organisation from structural point of view, it puts emphasis upon human relations, self respect, informal social relations, individual motivation, psychological feelings and tendencies of the workers. Thus, it believes in analyzing the multidimensional nature of human beings and their interactions for understanding the working of organisations.

An approach is a way of gaining access to the understanding of a subject or a discipline. It refers to a particular manner of dealing with the problem. Several approaches to the study of Public Administration – Classical, Scientific Management, Bureaucratic, Human Relations, Behavioural, System and Ecological – have been developed since the inception of the subject as an independent field of study by Woodrow Wilson in 1887. Among these, Human Relations Approach occupies a significant place in the understanding of the comparatively newly emerged discipline of public administration as a science.

The human relations approach is also known as New Classical approach. Elton Mayo termed it Clinical approach. It attempts to explain the informal relations among employers and employees are concerned with moral and psychological rather than legal aspects of an organisation. The approach considers worker not only one of the means of production system but as a man'.

The credit for shaping this approach goes to Elton Mayo and his associates such as F. J. Roethlisberger, William J. Dickson, T. North Whitehead, E Warne, W. Lloyd and L. J. Henderson.

Emergence of Human Relations Approach

Human Relations approach emerged after 1920 to explain the informal aspect of an organisation. It emerged as a reaction to the Taylor's Scientific Management approach–an offshoot of broad Classical approach – which became popular in the beginning of the 20th century. As a result of the Scientific Management approach whole human culture was influenced by material and mechanical environment. In industries emphasis was on increasing production. Resultantly, labor became a commodity and human being cog in the wheel. Main problems before workers were low wages, more hours of work, unhealthy working conditions and labors' exploitation. Managers were ignoring psychological needs of labors and social aspects of work. All these factors made workers apathetic towards their work. Besides, technological advancement in industry increased the educational level and professional skills of the workers to a great extent which made them more assertive about their rights and interests. Further, the class conflict and Trade Union movement in U.S.A. coupled with Communist Revolution in Soviet Union became the catalyst factors for the emergence and evolution of the Human Relations approach. In this regard B. Venkateswarlu has rightly observed, given the state of dehumanisation of the working class and growing trade union movement – the results of Taylorism – new problems of management and organisation arose in the capitalist industry in the west especially in America, in the first decade of the 20th century...Mayo and his colleagues, concentrating mainly on the behaviour of the workers and their productive capacity, keeping in view physiological, psychological, physical and economic aspects, came out with the conclusion...that the whole problem is one of human relations.'

Contribution of Elton Mayo

The basic features of human relations approach have been the result of various experiments conducted by Elton Mayo and his colleagues in twenties and thirties' of the last century focusing their attention on the problems of industrial workers. The first major research study which came to be known as The First Enquiry undertaken by Mayo was in a textile mill in 1923 near Philadelphia. Under the then prevailing circumstances, the mill provided all the facilities to the workers. It was well organised and considered to be a model organisation. Despite this, it faced some serious problems in one of the sections – the mule spinning – of the mill. The turnover of the employees in this section was estimated to nearly 250 percent per annum as against 5 to 6 percent in other sections. The management introduced several schemes by way of incentives to retain the workers but of no avail. Finding no way out of this ticklish problem, the matter was referred to Harvard University which in turn entrusted it to Elton Mayo.

Mayo studied the problem from various perspectives i.e. social, physical and psychological and started experiments with the permission of the management. In the very beginning, he studied the problem of physical fatigue. In order to overcome this problem he introduced rest periods of ten minutes each in the morning and afternoon for every worker of the mule section. Finding positive and encouraging results of this exercise, the scheme was extended to all other sections. Consequently, the symptoms of fatigue disappeared and the labor turnover almost came to an end as the workers started taking interest in work. The overall production level increased and the morale of the workers boosted. Further, Mayo suggested certain measures whereby workers had to earn their rest periods and bonus by producing more than a certain percentage. While these privileges made the workers happy but not liked by the supervisors as the same were not available to them. Keeping this fact in mind Mayo introduced a new scheme of shutting down whole of the spinning department for ten minutes, four times a day. This brought a new change in the outlook of supervisors and employees as all of them were satisfied with this new work culture. Besides, he placed the control of rest periods purely in the hands of workers which led to mutual consultations among them giving rise to the process of social interaction. Thus a new awakening began whereby the assumptions of rabble hypothesis' which assumes mankind a horde of unorganised individuals actuated by self- interest', was questioned and replaced by group interest.

Hawthorne Experiments

Hawthorne Experiments of Elton Mayo are considered as the bedrock of human relations movement in the management. These experiments were conducted in the Hawthorne plant of the Western Electric Company from 1924 to 1932. It may be pointed out that these experiments were initiated by the National Research Council of the National Academy of Sciences along with George Pennock, supervisor of the company, and his associates. Thus, Mayo was involved in the experiments after some initial probing by the research team especially when it failed to come to any definite conclusions. The main objective of these experiments was to know and understand the factors affecting efficiency and productivity of workers.

THE MODERN APPROACH

System Approach

The word **System** is taken from a Greek language which means to bring together or to combine. A system is a set of inter-related parts, which work together to achieve certain goals.

Ludwig von Bertalanffy is called the Father of the Systems Approach.

Definition

According to Ludwig von Bertalanffy, "In order to understand an organised whole, we must know both the parts as well as the relation between them."

Concepts of System Approach to Management

A system approach has the following key concepts:

1. **Open or Closed Systems.** Systems may be either open or closed. An open system is one, which depends on the outside environment for survival. A closed system does not interact with the environment.
2. **Sub-system.** The full system is made up of many parts. Each part is called sub-systems. A system may be a sub-system of a larger system. For e.g. A department is a sub-system of a plant. A plant is a sub-system of a company.
3. **Synergy.** Synergy means that the whole is greater than the sum of its parts. In an organisation, when different departments co-operate and interact, they become more productive. This is called synergy.
4. **Defined boundaries.** Each system has a boundary that separates it from its environment. In case of a closed system, the system boundary is rigid. However, in an open system, the boundary is flexible. A business organisation has boundaries with many external systems like creditors, suppliers, customers, government agencies, etc. The system is inside the boundary, the environment is outside the boundary.

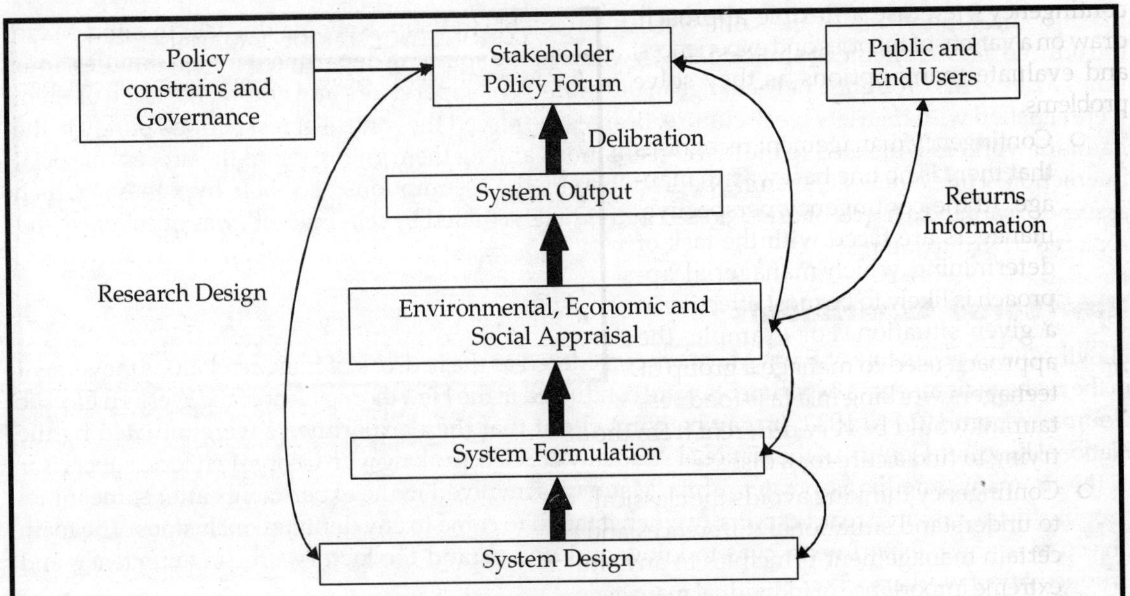

SYSTEM APPROACH FRAMEWORK (SAF)

5. **Feedback mechanism.** A system can adjust itself to the changing environment through the feedback mechanism. Feedback helps the system to find out and correct its mistakes.
6. **Multi-disciplinary.** Management system uses information from many fields such as psychology, sociology, ecology, economics, mathematics, statistics, operations research, systems analysis, etc. Therefore, it is Multi-disciplinary.
7. **Consideration of whole system.** No part of the system can be fully studied and understood without understanding all its parts. So instead of dealing separately with different parts of one organisation, the manager must study the organisation as a whole. For example, in order to understand the working of the finance or production or marketing departments, he must understand the company as a whole. It is because the activity of any one part of the company affects the activity of every other part.
8. **Input output system.** A business organisation is an input-output system. Inputs consist of human, physical and financial resources obtained from the environment. These resources are converted into outputs of products and services.

Contributions of Systems Approach to Management

- Under systems approach, managers have a good view of the organisation.
- It gives importance to interdependence of the different parts of an organisation and its environment.
- It forecasts consequences and plans actions.
- Systems' thinking warns managers against adopting piecemeal approach to the problem-solving.

CONTINGENCY SCHOOL OF MANAGEMENT

The contingency school of management can be summarised as an "it all depends" approach. The appropriate management actions and approaches depend on the situation. Managers with a contingency view use a flexible approach, draw on a variety of theories and experiences, and evaluate many options as they solve problems.

> **CONTINGENCY SCHOOL OF MANAGEMENT**
>
> - The contingency school of management can be summarized as an "it all depends" approach.
> - The appropriate management actions and approaches depend on the situation.
> - Managers with a contingency view use a flexible approach, draw on a variety of theories and experiences, and evaluate many options as they solve problems.
> - Contingency management recognizes that there is no one best way to manage.

- Contingency management recognises that there is no one best way to manage. In the contingency perspective, managers are faced with the task of determining which managerial approach is likely to be most effective in a given situation. For example, the approach used to manage a group of teenagers working in a fast-food restaurant would be very different from the approach used to manage a medical research team trying to find a cure for a disease.
- Contingency thinking avoids the classical "one best way" arguments and recognises the need to understand situational differences and respond appropriately to them. It does not apply certain management principles to any situation. Contingency theory is a recognition of the extreme importance of individual manager performance in any given situation. The contingency approach is highly dependent on the experience and judgement of the manager in a given organisational environment.

QUANTITATIVE SCHOOL OF MANAGEMENT

During World War II, mathematicians, physicists, and other scientists joined together to solve military problems. The quantitative school of management is a result of the research conducted during World War II. The **quantitative approach** to management involves the use of quantitative techniques, such as statistics, information models, and computer simulations, to improve decision making. This school consists of several branches, described in the following sections.

> **THE QUANTITATIVE MANAGEMENT PERSPECTIVE**
>
> - **Quantitative Management Uses**
>   - Helped World War II Allied forces manage logistical problems.
>   - Focuses on decision making, economic effectiveness, mathematical models, and the use of computers to solve quantitative problems.
> - **Management Science**
>   - Focuses on the development of representative mathematical models to assist with decisions.
> - **Operations Management**
>   - The practical application of management science to efficiently manage the production and distribution of products and services.

Management Science

The management science school emerged to treat the problems associated with global warfare. Today, this view encourages managers to use mathematics, statistics, and other quantitative techniques to make management decisions. Managers can use computer models to figure out the best way to do something — saving both money and time. Managers use several science applications.

- Mathematical forecasting helps to make projections that are useful in the planning process.
- Inventory modelling helps control inventories by mathematically establishing how and when to order a product.
- Queuing theory helps allocate service personnel or workstations to minimise customer waiting and service cost.

Operation Management

Operations management is a narrow branch of the quantitative approach to management. It focuses on managing the process of transforming materials, labour, and capital into useful goods and/or services. The product outputs can be either goods or services; effective operations management is a concern for both manufacturing and service organisations. The resource inputs, or factors of production, include the wide variety of raw materials, technologies, capital information, and people needed to create finished products. The transformation process, in turn, is the actual set of operations or activities through which various resources are utilised to produce finished goods or services of value to customers or clients. Operations management today pays close attention to the demands of quality, customer service, and competition. The process begins with attention to the needs of customers: What do they want? Where do they want it? When do they want it? Based on the answers to these questions, managers line up resources and take any action necessary to meet customer expectations.

Management Information System

Management information systems (MIS) is the most recent subfield of the quantitative school. A management information system organises past, present, and projected data from both internal and external sources and processes it into usable information, which it then makes available to managers at all organisational levels. The information systems are also able to organise data into usable and accessible formats. As a result, managers can identify alternatives quickly, evaluate alternatives by using a spreadsheet program, pose a series of "what-if" questions, and finally, select the best alternatives based on the answers to these questions.

Quality School of Management

The quality school of management is a comprehensive concept for leading and operating an organisation, aimed at continually improving performance by focusing on customers while addressing the needs of all stakeholders. In other words, this concept focuses on managing the total organisation to deliver high quality to customers.

QUALITY SCHOOL OF MANAGEMENT
■ Quality school is the most current and is world-wide.
■ Its roots are in the behavioural, quantitative, management theory.
■ People are key to commitments and performance.
■ What is done must be evaluated qualitatively.

The quality school of management considers the following in its theory:

- **Organisation makeup.** Organisations are made up of complex systems of customers and suppliers. Every individual, executive, manager, and worker functions as both a supplier and a customer.
- **Quality of goods and services.** Meeting the customers' requirements is a priority goal and presumed to be a key to organisational survival and growth.
- **Continuous improvement in goods and services.** Recognising the need to pinpoint internal and external requirements and continuously strive to improve. It is an idea that says, "the company is good, but it can always become better."
- **Employees working in teams.** These groups are primary vehicles for planning and problem solving.
- **Developing openness and trust.** Confidence among members of the organisation at all levels is an important condition for success.

Quality management involves employees in decision making as a way to prevent quality problems. The **Kaizen** (pronounced *ky*-zen) approach uses incremental, continuous improvement for people, products, and processes. The re-engineering approach focuses on sensing the need to change, seeing change coming, and reacting effectively to it when it comes.

MARY PARKER FOLLETT (1868-1933)

Follett defined management as: "the art of getting things done through people".

Her ideas are contradictory to the idea of scientific management, as she believed that managers and subordinates should fully collaborate. Power is central to her ideas. Power is created and organised by organisations, and according to her it is legitimate and inevitable. Regarding to power Follett used the term "integration," to refer to non-coercive power-sharing based on the use of her concept of "power with" rather than "power over."

Her ideas were formulated in three principles:

1. Functions are specific task areas within organisations. The appropriate degree of authority and responsibility should be allocated to them so tasks can be accomplished.
2. Responsibility is expressed in terms of an empirical duty: People should manage their responsibility on the basis of evidence and should integrate this effectively with the functions of others.
3. Authority flows from an entitlement to exercise power, which is based upon legitimate authority.

CHESTER BARNARD (1886-1961)

Chester Irving Barnard was a tele-communication Executive and the most important, he is the author of 'Functions of The Executives'. Which means, he presented a theory of organisation and the functions of executives in organisations.

He has developed two concepts in **Management Theory**.

1. Strategic Planning
   - the formulation of major plan or strategies to pursuit of major objectives.
   - three top functions:
     (i) establish and maintain an effective communication system.
     (ii) hire the experienced and suitable personnel.
     (iii) motivate those personnel.
2. Acceptance Theory of Authority
   - managers have more authority than employees. It suggested that authority flows downward but depends on acceptance by the subordinate.
   - it depends on 4 conditions:-
     (i) employees can and do understand the communication.
     (ii) employees must be able to follow any instruction given by a Manager.
     (iii) employees must think that the directive is in keeping with organisational objectives.
     (iv) employees must think that the directive is not contrary to their personal goals.

When Chester Barnard retired as the CEO of New Jersey Bell Telephone, he has recorded his theories about management in his book, 'Functions of The Executive'. His main objective is to discuss the functions of the executive which means that everyone must have their own perspective and not to deriving them from a conception of co-operative systems based on previous concepts.

'The Functions of the Executive', by Chester Barnard.

Three essential elements in an organisation:

1. Communication.
2. Persons willing to contribute action.
3. A common purpose (function).

If existence is dependent on these factors, continued existence is dependent on organisational effectiveness or efficency. Organisation is an impersonal system of coordinated human efforts.

1. **Willingness to Cooperate**
   - **Definition.** 'self-abnegation, which means the surrender of control of personal conduct and the depersonalization of personal action.
   - causes cohesion of effort. Willingness ranges in intensity among the individuals in the organisation.
   - personal willingness is constantly fluctuating, therefore agregate willingness in organisation is unstable.
2. **Purpose**
   - Willingness is unable to develop with a purpose which is accepted by all those in the organisation.
   - Two views of purpose : (1) the cooperative aspect: what the action asked of the individual means in the context of the organisation as a whole and (2) subjective aspect : what the action means , personally, to the individual.
3. **Communication**
   - catalyst for those with common purpose to realize potentialities. 'communication technique shapes the form and the internal economy of organisation'.
4. **Organisational Effeciency**
   - Survival depends on ability to carry out purpose. Destroys itself by accomplishing its purpose, hence may require adoption of new purpose.
   - Effeciency definition: 'effeciency relative to the securing of necessary personal contributions to the cooperative system.'
   - Barnard says material inducements insufficient over extended time. Attempt to maintain non-economic inducements: pride of craft/accomplishment, ect.

Barnard was not an academic; his theories were put together painstakingly from decades of organisational experience. In this aspect, he is rather unique among management scholars of the twentieth century. However, during the last several years, Barnard's stature in the realm of management theory and practice has gradually waned. Although his book is required reading in the occasional Doctoral curriculum, it has more or less disappeared from the mainstream of management literature. He is infrequently cited, and credited with originating the "Acceptance Theory of Authority", but not much else.

Roles Performed by Managers

A manager wears many hats. Not only is a manager a team leader, but he or she is also a planner, organiser, cheerleader, coach, problem solver, and decision maker — all rolled into one. And these are just a few of a manager's roles.

In his classic book, ***The Nature of Managerial Work,*** **Henry Mintzberg** describes a set of ten roles that a manager fills. These roles fall into three categories:

- **Interpersonal.** This role involves human interaction.
- **Informational.** This role involves the sharing and analyzing of information.
- **Decisional.** This role involves decision making.

Table contains a more in-depth look at each category of roles that help managers carry out all five functions described in the preceding "Functions of Managers" section.

Mintzberg's Set of Ten Roles

Category	Role	Activity
Informational	Monitor	Seek and receive information; scan periodicals and reports; maintain personal contact with stakeholders.
	Disseminator	Forward information to organisation members via memos, reports, and phone calls.
	Spokesperson	Transmit information to outsiders via reports, memos, and speeches.
Interpersonal	Figurehead	Perform ceremonial and symbolic duties, such as greeting visitors and signing legal documents.
	Leader	Direct and motivate subordinates; counsel and communicate with subordinates.
	Liaison	Maintain information links both inside and outside organisation via mail, phone calls, and meetings.
Decisional	Entrepreneur	Initiate improvement projects; identify new ideas and delegate idea responsibility to others.
	Disturbance handler	Take corrective action during disputes or crises; resolve conflicts among subordinates; adapt to environments.
	Resource allocator	Decide who gets resources; prepare budgets; set schedules and determine priorities.
	Negotiator	Represent department during negotiations of union contracts, sales, purchases, and budgets.

Skills Needed by Managers

Not everyone can be a manager. Certain **skills,** or abilities to translate knowledge into action that results in desired performance, are required to help other employees become more productive. These skills fall under the following categories:

- **Technical Skills.** This skill requires the ability to use a special proficiency or expertise to perform particular tasks. Accountants, engineers, market researchers, and computer scientists, as examples, possess technical skills. Managers acquire these skills initially through formal education and then further develop them through training and job experience. Technical skills are most important at lower levels of management.
- **Human Skills.** This skill demonstrates the ability to work well in cooperation with others. Human skills emerge in the workplace as a spirit of trust, enthusiasm, and genuine involvement in interpersonal relationships. A manager with good human skills has a high degree of self-awareness and a capacity to understand or empathise with the feelings of others. Some managers are naturally born with great human skills, while others improve their skills through classes or experience. No matter how human skills are acquired, they're critical for all managers because of the highly interpersonal nature of managerial work.

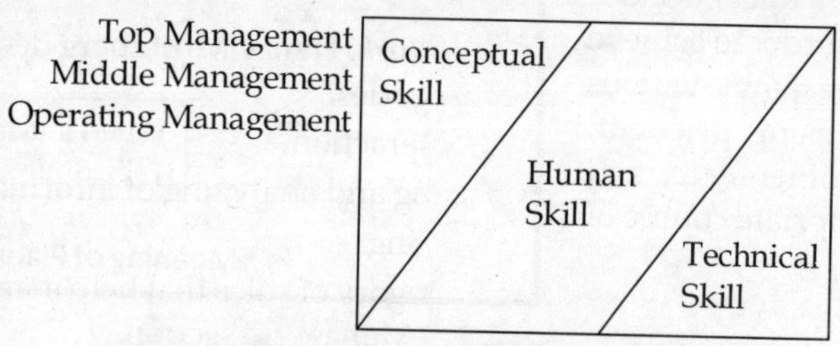

MANAGERIAL SKILLS AT VARIOUS LEVELS

- **Conceptual Skills.** This skill calls for the ability to think analytically. Analytical skills enable managers to break down problems into smaller parts, to see the relations among the parts, and to recognise the implications of any one problem for others. As managers assume ever-higher responsibilities in organisations, they must deal with more ambiguous problems that have long-term consequences. Again, managers may acquire these skills initially through formal education and then further develop them by training and job experience. The higher the management level, the more important conceptual skills become. Although all three categories contain skills essential for managers, their relative importance tends to vary by level of managerial responsibility.

Business and management educators are increasingly interested in helping people acquire technical, human, and conceptual skills, and develop specific competencies, or specialised skills that contribute to high performance in a management job. Following are some of the skills and personal characteristics :

- **Leadership** – ability to influence others to perform tasks
- **Self-objectivity** – ability to evaluate yourself realistically
- **Analytic thinking** – ability to interpret and explain patterns in information
- **Behavioural flexibility** – ability to modify personal behaviour to react objectively rather than subjectively to accomplish organisational goals
- **Oral communication** – ability to express ideas clearly in words
- **Written communication** – ability to express ideas clearly in writing
- **Personal impact** – ability to create a good impression and instil confidence
- **Resistance to stress** – ability to perform under stressful conditions
- **Tolerance for uncertainity** – ability to perform in ambiguous situation

FUNCTION OF MANAGEMENT

PLANNING

Meaning. A plan is a course of action to be taken in future. It is a predecided course of action. Planning is the process of deciding in advance what is to be done, how it is to be done, where, when and by whom. It involves determination of objectives to be achieved as well as the activities required to achieve the objectives. For example, a trader decides to increase his sales. In order to achieve this objective he should examine various alternatives e.g. advertising, price cut, better service to customers, etc. and choose the most appropriate course of action.

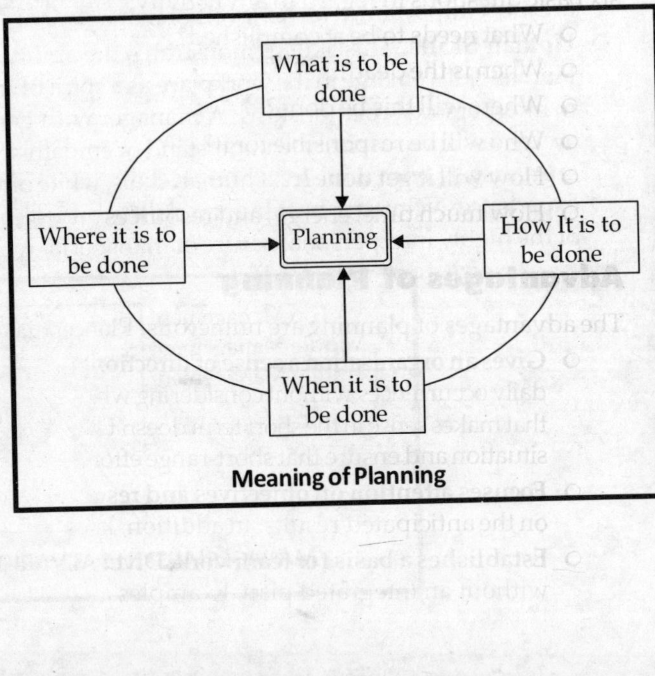

Meaning of Planning

Definition

- According to **Koontz & O'Donnell,** "Planning is deciding in advance what to do, how to do and who is to do it. Planning bridges the gap between where we are to, where we want to go. It makes possible things to occur which would not otherwise occur".
- According to **L.F. Urwick,** "Planning is fundamentally a mental predisposition to do things in an orderly way, to think before acting and to act in the light of the facts rather than of guesses."
- According to **Alfred and Beatty**, "Planning is the thinking process, the organised foresight, the vision based on facts and experience that is required for intellient action."
- According to **M.E. Hurley**, "Planning is deciding in advance what is to be done. It involves the selection of objectives, policies, procedures and programmes from among alternatives."

The Five management functions are – planning, organising, staffing, leading and controlling – planning is the most fundamental. All other functions stem from planning. However, planning doesn't always get the attention that it deserves; when it does, many managers discover that the planning process isn't as easy as they thought it would be — or that even the best-laid plans can go awry. Before a manager can tackle any of the other functions, he or she must first devise a plan. A **plan** is a blueprint for goal achievement that specifies the necessary resource allocations, schedules, tasks, and other actions.

> A ***goal*** is a desired future state that the organisation attempts to realise. Goals are important because an organisation exists for a purpose, and goals define and state that purpose. Goals specify future ends; plans specify today's means.

The word **planning** incorporates both ideas: It means determining the organisation's goals and defining the means for achieving them. Planning allows managers the opportunity to adjust to the environment instead of merely reacting to it. Planning increases the possibility of survival in business by actively anticipating and managing the risks that may occur in the future.

In short, planning is preparing for tomorrow, today. It's the activity that allows managers to determine what they want and how they will achieve it.

Not only does planning provide direction and a unity of purpose for organisations, it also answers six basic questions in regard to any activity:

- What needs to be accomplished?
- When is the deadline?
- Where will this be done?
- Who will be responsible for it?
- How will it get done?
- How much time, energy, and resources are required to accomplish this goal?

Advantages of Planning

The advantages of planning are numerous. Planning fulfils the following objectives:

- **Gives an organisation a sense of direction.** Without plans and goals, organisations merely react to daily occurrences without considering what will happen in the long run. For example, the solution that makes sense in the short term doesn't always make sense in the long term. Plans avoid this drift situation and ensure that short-range efforts will support and harmonise with future goals.
- **Focuses attention on objectives and results.** Plans keep the people who carry them out focused on the anticipated results. In addition, keeping sight of the goal also motivates employees.
- **Establishes a basis for teamwork.** Diverse groups cannot effectively cooperate in joint projects without an integrated plan. Examples are numerous: Plumbers, carpenters, and electricians

cannot build a house without blueprints. In addition, military activities require the coordination of Army, Navy, and Air Force units.

- **Planning involved forecasting.** When management plans, it can help forecast future problems and make any necessary changes up front to avoid them. Planning for these potential problems helps to minimise mistakes and reduce the "surprises" that inevitably occur.
- **Provides guidelines for decision making.** Decisions are future-oriented. If management doesn't have any plans for the future, they will have few guidelines for making current decisions. If a company knows that it wants to introduce a new product three years in the future, its management must be mindful of the decisions they make now. Plans help both managers and employees keep their eyes on the big picture.
- **Serves as a prerequisite to employing all other management functions.** Planning is primary, because without knowing what an organisation wants to accomplish, management can't intelligently undertake any of the other basic managerial activities: organising, staffing, leading, and/or controlling.

Criteria for Effective Goals

To make sure that goal setting benefits the organisation, managers must adopt certain characteristics and guidelines. The following describes these criteria:

- **Goals must be specific and measurable.** When possible, use quantitative terms, such as increasing profits by two percent or decreasing student enrollment by one percent, to express goals.
- **Goals should cover key result areas.** Because goals cannot be set for every aspect of employee or organisational performance, managers should identify a few key result areas. These key areas are those activities that contribute most to company performance – for example, customer relations or sales.
- **Goals should be challenging but not too difficult.** When goals are unrealistic, they set employees up for failure and lead to low employee morale. However, if goals are too easy, employees may not feel motivated. Managers must be sure that goals are determined based on existing resources and are not beyond the team's time, equipment, and financial resources.
- **Goals should specify the time period over which they will be achieved.** Deadlines give team members something to work toward and help ensure continued progress. At the same time, managers should set short-term deadlines along the way so that their subordinates are not overwhelmed by one big, seemingly un-accomplishable goal. It would be more appropriate to provide a short term goal such as, "Establish a customer database by June 30."
- **Goals should be linked to rewards.** People who attain goals should be rewarded with something meaningful and related to the goal. Not only will employees feel that their efforts are valued, but they will also have something tangible to motivate them in the future.

Coordination of Goals

All the different levels of management should have plans that work together to accomplish the organisation's purpose. The plans of the top, middle, and first-level managers of an organisation should work together to achieve the main goal.

All managers plan basically the same way, but the kinds of plans they develop and the amount of time they spend on planning vary. Here are some examples:

- Top-level managers are concerned with longer time periods and with plans for larger organisational units. Their planning includes developing the mission for the organisational units, the organisational objective, and major policy areas. These goals are called *strategic* goals or objectives.

- Middle-level managers' planning responsibilities centre on translating broad objectives of top-level management into more specific goals for work units. These goals are called *tactical* goals or objectives.
- First-level managers are involved in day-to-day plans, such as scheduling work hours, deciding what work will be done and by whom, and developing structures to reach these goals. These goals are called *operational* goals or objectives.

If a first-level manager develops a set of plans that contradicts that of a middle-level manager, conflicts will result. Therefore, all managers must work together when planning their activities and the activities of others.

Types of Planning

1. **Corporate Planning.** Drucker has defined corporate planning as the continuous process of making present risk-taking decision systematically and with the greatest knowledge of their futurity: organising systematically the efforts needed to carry out these decision, and measuring the result of these decision against the expectations through organised and systematic feedback.

   The corporate planning activities are carried out at the top level because they are vital for the success of the whole organisation. The top management are responsible for such plan and are prepared according to the inputs that are given to them either from the environment or the lower level in the organisational hierarchy. The plans are long term in nature and are broad based.

2. **Strategic Planning.** A **strategic planning** is an outline of steps designed with the goals of the entire organisation as a whole in mind, rather than with the goals of specific divisions or departments. Strategic planning begins with an organisation's mission.

   Strategic plans look ahead over the next two, three, five, or even more years to move the organisation from where it currently is to where it wants to be. Requiring multilevel involvement, these plans demand harmony among all levels of management within the organisation. Top-level management develops the directional objectives for the entire organisation, while lower levels of management develop compatible objectives and plans to achieve them. Top management's strategic plan for the entire organisation becomes the framework and sets dimensions for the lower level planning.

3. **Tactical Planning Or Operational Planning.** Operational planning is defined as the process of deciding the most effective use of the resources already located and to develop a control mechanism to assure effective implementation to the desired action.

   A tactical planning is concerned with what the lower level units within each division must do, how they must do it, and who is in charge at each level. Tactics are the means needed to activate a strategy and make it work.

   An operational plan is annual work plan. Tactical plans are concerned with shorter time frames and narrower scopes than are strategic plans. These plans usually span one year or less because they are considered short-term goals. Long-term goals, on the other hand, can take several years or more to accomplish. Normally, it is the middle manager's responsibility to take the broad strategic plan and identify specific tactical actions.

4. **Functional Planning.** The planning that is carried out to ensure smooth working of the organisation taking into consideration the requirement of each and every department. The goal of functional planning is to promote standardised management practice for corporate function in the department decentralised corporate management structure.

5. **Proactive and Reactive Planning. Proactive planning** is based on the anticipation of the future outcomes and state of affairs that would affect the working in an organisation. Such a planning has to be broad based, highly flexible and creative in nature.

   Reactive planning as the name suggest the reactive planning is not based on the anticipation of the future outcomes but becomes active only when the problem is confronted and occurred.

6. **Formal And Informal.** Formal planning exists in the formal hierarchy of the organisation and always carried out in the step wise process. This type of planning is done at large scale and is based on logical thinking.

   On the other hand the informal planning is usually carried out in very small organisation where the formal organisation structure may or may not exist. The planning is usually intuitive in nature and short term.

7. **Contingency Plans.** Intelligent and successful management depends upon a constant pursuit of adaptation, flexibility, and mastery of changing conditions. Strong management requires a "keeping all options open" approach at all times — that's where contingency planning comes in.

> **Contingency planning** involves identifying alternative courses of action that can be implemented if and when the original plan proves inadequate because of changing circumstances. Keep in mind that events beyond a manager's control may cause even the most carefully prepared alternative future scenarios to go awry. Unexpected problems and events frequently occur. When they do, managers may need to change their plans. Anticipating change during the planning process is best in case things don't go as expected. Management can then develop alternatives to the existing plan and ready them for use when and if circumstances make these alternatives appropriate.

Steps in Planning Process

Planning function of management involves following steps:

1. **Establishment of objectives**
   - Planning requires a systematic approach.
   - Planning starts with the setting of goals and objectives to be achieved.
   - Objectives provide a rationale for undertaking various activities as well as indicate direction of efforts.
   - Moreover objectives focus the attention of managers on the end results to be achieved.
   - As a matter of fact, objectives provide nucleus to the planning process. Therefore, objectives should be stated in a clear, precise and unambiguous language. Otherwise the activities undertaken are bound to be ineffective.
   - As far as possible, objectives should be stated in quantitative terms. For example, Number of men working, wages given, units produced, etc. But such an objective cannot be stated in quantitative terms like performance of quality control manager, effectiveness of personnel manager.
   - Such goals should be specified in qualitative terms.
   - Hence objectives should be practical, acceptable, workable and achievable.
2. **Establishment of Planning Premises**
   - Planning premises are the assumptions about the lively shape of events in future.
   - They serve as a basis of planning.
   - Establishment of planning premises is concerned with determining where one tends to deviate from the actual plans and causes of such deviations.

- It is to find out what obstacles are there in the way of business during the course of operations.
- Establishment of planning premises is concerned to take such steps that avoid these obstacles to a great extent.
- Planning premises may be internal or external. Internal includes capital investment policy, management labour relations, philosophy of management, etc. Whereas external includes socio- economic, political and economical changes.
- Internal premises are controllable whereas external are non- controllable.

3. Choice of alternative course of action

- When forecast are available and premises are established, a number of alternative course of actions have to be considered.
- For this purpose, each and every alternative will be evaluated by weighing its pros and cons in the light of resources available and requirements of the organisation.
- The merits, demerits as well as the consequences of each alternative must be examined before the choice is being made.
- After objective and scientific evaluation, the best alternative is chosen.
- The planners should take help of various quantitative techniques to judge the stability of an alternative.

4. Formulation of derivative plans

- Derivative plans are the sub plans or secondary plans which help in the achievement of main plan.
- Secondary plans will flow from the basic plan. These are meant to support and expedited the achievement of basic plans.
- These detail plans include policies, procedures, rules, programmes, budgets, schedules, etc. For example, if profit maximisation is the main aim of the enterprise, derivative plans will include sales maximisation, production maximisation, and cost minimisation.
- Derivative plans indicate time schedule and sequence of accomplishing various tasks.

5. Securing Co-operation

- After the plans have been determined, it is necessary rather advisable to take subordinates or those who have to implement these plans into confidence.
- The purposes behind taking them into confidence are :
  i. Subordinates may feel motivated since they are involved in decision making process.
  ii. The organisation may be able to get valuable suggestions and improvement in formulation as well as implementation of plans.
  iii. Also the employees will be more interested in the execution of these plans.

6. Follow up/Appraisal of plans

- After choosing a particular course of action, it is put into action.
- After the selected plan is implemented, it is important to appraise its effectiveness.
- This is done on the basis of feedback or information received from departments or persons concerned.
- This enables the management to correct deviations or modify the plan.
- This step establishes a link between planning and controlling function.
- The follow up must go side by side the implementation of plans so that in the light of observations made, future plans can be made more realistic.

Characteristics of Planning

1. **Planning is goal-oriented.**
   - Planning is made to achieve desired objective of business.
   - The goals established should general acceptance otherwise individual efforts & energies will go misguided and misdirected.
   - Planning identifies the action that would lead to desired goals quickly & economically.
   - It provides sense of direction to various activities. E.g. Maruti Udhyog is trying to capture once again Indian Car Market by launching diesel models.
2. **Planning is looking ahead.**
   - Planning is done for future.
   - It requires peeping in future, analyzing it and predicting it.
   - Thus planning is based on forecasting.
   - A plan is a synthesis of forecast.
   - It is a mental predisposition for things to happen in future.
3. **Planning is an intellectual process.**
   - Planning is a mental exercise involving creative thinking, sound judgement and imagination.
   - It is not a mere guesswork but a rotational thinking.
   - A manager can prepare sound plans only if he has sound judgement, foresight and imagination.
   - Planning is always based on goals, facts and considered estimates.
4. **Planning involves choice & decision making.**
   - Planning essentially involves choice among various alternatives.
   - Therefore, if there is only one possible course of action, there is no need planning because there is no choice.
   - Thus, decision making is an integral part of planning.
   - A manager is surrounded by no. of alternatives. He has to pick the best depending upon requirements & resources of the enterprises.
5. **Planning is the primary function of management / Primacy of Planning.**
   - Planning lays foundation for other functions of management.
   - It serves as a guide for organising, staffing, directing and controlling.
   - All the functions of management are performed within the framework of plans laid out.
   - Therefore planning is the basic or fundamental function of management.
6. **Planning is a Continuous Process.**
   - Planning is a never ending function due to the dynamic business environment.
   - Plans are also prepared for specific period of time and at the end of that period, plans are subjected to revaluation and review in the light of new requirements and changing conditions.
   - Planning never comes into end till the enterprise exists issues, problems may keep cropping up and they have to be tackled by planning effectively.
7. **Planning is all Pervasive.**
   - It is required at all levels of management and in all departments of enterprise.
   - Of course, the scope of planning may differ from one level to another.

- The top level may be more concerned about planning the organisation as a whole whereas the middle level may be more specific in departmental plans and the lower level plans implementation of the same.

8. **Planning is designed for efficiency.**
   - Planning leads to accomplishment of objectives at the minimum possible cost.
   - It avoids wastage of resources and ensures adequate and optimum utilisation of resources.
   - A plan is worthless or useless if it does not value the cost incurred on it.
   - Therefore planning must lead to saving of time, effort and money.
   - Planning leads to proper utilisation of men, money, materials, methods and machines.
9. **Planning is Flexible.**
   - Planning is done for the future.
   - Since future is unpredictable, planning must provide enough room to cope with the changes in customer's demand, competition, govt. policies etc.
   - Under changed circumstances, the original plan of action must be revised and updated to make it more practical.

Types of Plans

1. **Standing Plan or Strategic Plan** are put to use again and again over long periods of time. Once established, they continue to apply until they are modified or abandoned. Standing plan developed for activities that recur regularly over a period of time.
   - **Objective.** The first and primary step in planning is to set objectives (goal, target) of an enterprise. Objectives decide the end points to which an individual or organisation wants to move. All activities of the undertaking are aimed at these goals. They specify the destination where we want to go. Objectives are the open ended result that needs to be achieved in the definite time period.

     According to Allen, "objectives are goals established to guide the efforts of the company and each of its components.
   - **Policies.** A policy is a basic statement that guides decision making. Its tell people what they may or may not do. It directs the way in which activities are to be achieved. It is concerned with "how" of administrative action. Policies decide the limits within which management can take decisions.

     According to Koontz and O'Donnell, "a policy is a guide to thinking and action of those who take decision"
   - **Procedure.** A procedure is a well thought out course of action. It describes the specific ways in which a piece of work is to be done. Procedure is called action guidelines. Where policy define a broad field, procedure shows the sequences of activities within that area. The emphasis is an chronological, step by step sequences of required actions.

     Koontz and O'Donnell, "procedures are plans that establish required methods of handling"
   - **Methods.** Methods is a subunits of procedure. They show clearly as to how a step of procedure should be performed. They indicated the techniques to be employed to make a procedure effective. Methods indicate the simplified and standardised techniques to be employed (to find the best way doing a piece of work) to carry out (one step of a procedure) a task.
   - **Rules.** A rule is very specific and detailed guide to action. It is established to direct and restrict action in a fairly narrow manner. "Rules spell out either specific required action or no action, allowing no discretion. For example "No Smoking" is a rule which allow no discretion or deviation on the part of anybody in the organisation.

2. **Single use or Operational Plan** are non recurring in nature and deal with problems that probably will not be repeated in the same form in future.
   - **Projects.** A project is temporary endeavour undertaken to create a unique product or service. Temporary means that the projects has an end date. Unique means that the projects end result is different then the result of the other function of the organisation. Every objective have specific objectives that need to be achieved in a definite time periods
   - **Budgets.** Budget is financial statement of estimated revenues or income and expenses for a given period of time, usually a year. Budget may be different types depending on their usage rate and the end result that are required for them.
   - **Targets.** These are the end result formulated for each facility department and operation of the organisation to track progress towards achieving goal. Targets are quantifiable in nature so that the measurement and the comparison become easier.
   - **Programmes.** Programme is a sequence of activities undertaken for the implementation of the policies and achieving the objectivities of the business enterprise.

Advantages of Planning

1. **Planning facilitates management by objectives.**
   - Planning begins with determination of objectives.
   - It highlights the purposes for which various activities are to be undertaken.
   - In fact, it makes objectives more clear and specific.
   - Planning helps in focusing the attention of employees on the objectives or goals of enterprise.
   - Without planning an organisation has no guide.
   - Planning compels manager to prepare a Blue-print of the courses of action to be followed for accomplishment of objectives.
   - Therefore, planning brings order and rationality into the organisation.
2. **Planning minimise uncertainties.**
   - Business is full of uncertainties.
   - There are risks of various types due to uncertainties.
   - Planning helps in reducing uncertainties of future as it involves anticipation of future events.
   - Although future cannot be predicted with cent percent accuracy but planning helps management to anticipate future and prepare for risks by necessary provisions to meet unexpected turn of events.
   - Therefore with the help of planning, uncertainties can be forecasted which helps in preparing standbys as a result, uncertainties are minimised to a great extent.
3. **Planning facilitate co-ordination.**
   - Planning revolves around organisational goals.
   - All activities are directed towards common goals.
   - There is an integrated effort throughout the enterprise in various departments and groups.
   - It avoids duplication of efforts. In other words, it leads to better co-ordination.
   - It helps in finding out problems of work performance and aims at rectifying the same.
4. **Planning improves employee's moral.**
   - Planning creates an atmosphere of order and discipline in organisation.
   - Employees know in advance what is expected of them and therefore conformity can be achieved easily.
   - This encourages employees to show their best and also earn reward for the same.

- Planning creates a healthy attitude towards work environment which helps in boosting employees moral and efficiency.

5. **Planning helps in achieving economies.**
   - Effective planning secures economy since it leads to orderly allocation of resources to various operations.
   - It also facilitates optimum utilisation of resources which brings economy in operations.
   - It also avoids wastage of resources by selecting most appropriate use that will contribute to the objective of enterprise. For example, raw materials can be purchased in bulk and transportation cost can be minimised. At the same time it ensures regular supply for the production department, that is, overall efficiency.
6. **Planning facilitate controlling.**
   - Planning facilitates existence of certain planned goals and standard of performance.
   - It provides basis of controlling.
   - We cannot think of an effective system of controlling without existence of well thought out plans.
   - Planning provides pre-determined goals against which actual performance is compared.
   - In fact, planning and controlling are the two sides of a same coin. If planning is root, controlling is the fruit.
7. **Planning provide competitive edge.**
   - Planning provides competitive edge to the enterprise over the others which do not have effective planning. This is because of the fact that planning may involve changing in work methods, quality, quantity designs, extension of work, redefining of goals, etc.
   - With the help of forecasting not only the enterprise secures its future but at the same time it is able to estimate the future motives of its competitor which helps in facing future challenges.
   - Therefore, planning leads to best utilisation of possible resources, improves quality of production and thus the competitive strength of the enterprise is improved.
8. **Planning encourage innovations.**
   - In the process of planning, managers have the opportunities of suggesting ways and means of improving performance.
   - Planning is basically a decision making function which involves creative thinking and imagination that ultimately leads to innovation of methods and operations for growth and prosperity of the enterprise.

Disadvantages of Planning

Internal Limitations. There are several limitations of planning. Some of them are inherit in the process of planning like rigidity and other arise due to shortcoming of the techniques of planning and in the planners themselves.

1. **Rigidity**
   - Planning has tendency to make administration inflexible.
   - Planning implies prior determination of policies, procedures and programmes and a strict adherence to them in all circumstances.
   - There is no scope for individual freedom.
   - The development of employees is highly doubted because of which management might have faced lot of difficulties in future.

- Planning therefore introduces inelasticity and discourages individual initiative and experimentation.

2. **Misdirected Planning**
   - Planning may be used to serve individual interests rather than the interest of the enterprise.
   - Attempts can be made to influence setting of objectives, formulation of plans and programmes to suit ones own requirement rather than that of whole organisation.
   - Machinery of planning can never be freed of bias. Every planner has his own likes, dislikes, preferences, attitudes and interests which is reflected in planning.
3. **Time consuming**
   - Planning is a time consuming process because it involves collection of information, its analysis and interpretation thereof. This entire process takes a lot of time specially where there are a number of alternatives available.
   - Therefore planning is not suitable during emergency or crisis when quick decisions are required.
4. **Probability in planning**
   - Planning is based on forecasts which are mere estimates about future.
   - These estimates may prove to be inexact due to the uncertainty of future.
   - Any change in the anticipated situation may render plans ineffective.
   - Plans do not always reflect real situations in spite of the sophisticated techniques of forecasting because future is unpredictable.
   - Thus, excessive reliance on plans may prove to be fatal.
5. **False sense of security**
   - Elaborate planning may create a false sense of security to the effect that everything is taken for granted.
   - Managers assume that as long as they work as per plans, it is satisfactory.
   - Therefore they fail to take up timely actions and an opportunity is lost.
   - Employees are more concerned about fulfillment of plan performance rather than any kind of change.
6. **Expensive**
   - Collection, analysis and evaluation of different information, facts and alternatives involves a lot of expense in terms of time, effort and money
   - According to Koontz and O'Donell, 'Expenses on planning should never exceed the estimated benefits from planning.'

External Limitations of Planning

1. **Policies of competitors.** e.g., Policies of Coca Cola and Pepsi.
2. **Changes in demand and prices.** Change in fashion, change in tastes, change in income level, demand falls, price falls, etc.
3. **Natural Calamities.** Earthquakes and floods.
4. **Political Climate.** Change of government from Congress to BJP, etc.
5. **Technological changes.** Modern techniques and equipments, computerisation.
6. **Labour Union.** Strikes, lockouts, agitations.

Organising

Organising, the second of the universal management functions, is the process of establishing the orderly use of resources by assigning and coordinating tasks. The organising process transforms plans into reality through the purposeful deployment of people and resources within a decision-making framework known as the organisational structure. The organisational structure is defined as

- The set of formal tasks assigned to individuals and departments.
- The formal reporting relationships, including lines of authority, decision responsibility, number of hierarchical levels, and span of managerial control.
- The design of systems to ensure effective coordination of employees across departments.

The organisational structure provides a framework for the hierarchy, or *vertical structure,* of the organisation. An **organisational chart** is the visual representation of this vertical structure.

DEFINITION OF ORGANISING

- According to **Henri Fayal**, "To organise a business means to provide it everything useful to its functioning–raw materials, tools, capital & personnel."
- According to **George R. Terry**, "Organising is the process of establishing effective authority relationship among selected works, persons and work places in order for the group to work together efficiently."
- According to **Haney**, "Organisation is harmonious adjustment of the specialised parts for the accomplishment of some common purpose or purposes."
- According to **Mc Farland**, "An identifiable group of people contributing their efforts for the attainment of the common goals is called organisation."
- According to **Urwick,** "To determine the activities necessary to complete any work and distribution of those activities among persons is called organisation."

The Organisation Process

Organising, like planning, must be a carefully worked out and applied process. This process involves determining what work is needed to accomplish the goal, assigning those tasks to individuals, and arranging those individuals in a decision-making framework (organisational structure). The end result of the organising process is an **organisation** — a whole consisting of unified parts acting in harmony to execute tasks to achieve goals, both effectively and efficiently.

A properly implemented organising process should result in a work environment where all team members are aware of their responsibilities. If the organising process is not conducted well, the results may yield confusion, frustration, loss of efficiency, and limited effectiveness.

In general, the organisational process consists of six steps (a flowchart of these steps shown in Figure):

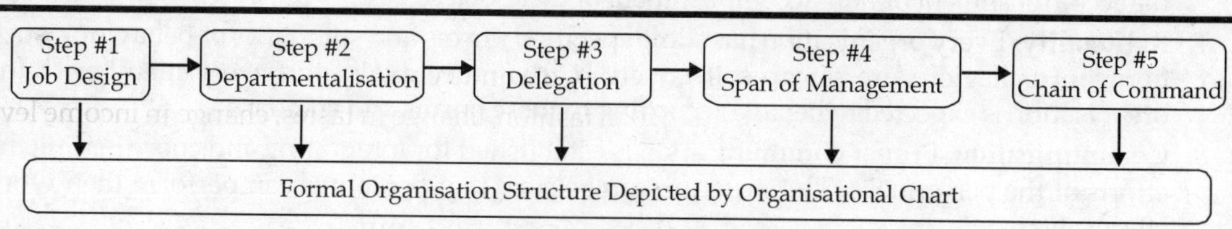

The organisational process.

- **Clearly defined objectives.** Objectives are the specific activities that must be completed to achieve goals. Plans shape the activities needed to reach those goals. Managers must examine plans initially and continue to do so as plans change and new goals are developed.

- **Determine the work activities.** Although this task may seem overwhelming to some managers, it doesn't need to be. Managers simply list and analyze all the tasks that need to be accomplished in order to reach organisational goals.
- **Assigning duties.** A manager can group activities based on four models of departmentalisation: functional, geographical, product, and customer.
- **Delegate authority.** Managers assign the defined work activities to specific individuals. Also, they give each individual the authority (right) to carry out the assigned tasks.
- **Providing physical facilities and right environment.** The success of an organisation depends upon the providing physical facilities and right environment. Whereas its important right person in the right job. It is equally important to have right working environment.
- **Design a hierarchy of relationships.** A manager should determine the vertical (decision-making) and horizontal (coordinating) relationships of the organisation as a whole. Next, using the organisational chart, a manager should diagram the relationships.

Features of Organising

Organisation has the following features:

1. **Group of Persons.** Organisation is concerned with the group of persons working together for the achievement of the common objectives. This group can be large or small. Further, cooperative relationship between two or more persons is known as organisation.
2. **Division of Work.** Organisation follows the Fayol's principle of division of work. An organisation comes into existence when the total work is divided among the different employees. This is not because that one person cannot perform the whole task but due to the reason it's the only way of ensuring specialisation in business.
3. **Common Objectives.** Every organisation has common objectives separated from the personal objectives of the individuals in the organisation. Organisation is directed towards the achievement of the common goals which is the basis of cooperation among the members.
4. **Cooperative Effort.** For the achievement of the common goals cooperative relationships are established both vertically and horizontally among different departments of the organisation. The members of the organisation help each other for the achievement of the common goals.
5. **Central and Top Authority.** There is a central and top authority in every organisation and this authority controls and directs the efforts of the groups or departments for the achievement of the organisational objectives. Further the chain of command is also established, which defines the authority and responsibility of every individual in the organisation.
6. **Purposive Creation.** The organisation is a purposive creation that is all the organisations have some objectives or set of objectives. The success and failure of the organisation depends upon the accomplishment or non-accomplishment of these objectives.
7. **Rationality.** Every organisation has some specified norms and standards of behaviour, such norms of behaviour are set up collectively by the individuals, and every member of the organisation is expected to behave according to these norms and standards.
8. **Communication.** Proper communication is established for integrating and coordinating the efforts of the personnel's. The structure can be such that personnel can perform their work effectively.

Formal and Informal Organisation

Organisation integrates the individual efforts and leads to the achievement of the common goals. Relationship between individuals working in the organisation can be classified into formal and informal organisation.

Formal Organisation

Formal organisations are created deliberately by assigning duties and responsibilities and delegating authority. A formal organisation is the structure of consciously coordinated relationships between two or more persons working for the common objectives.

According to Barnard, "Any organisation shall be considered formal at the stage when the activities of two or more persons are coordinated consciously to achieve the definite objective."

FEATURES OF FORMAL ORGANISATION

1. It is absolutely non-individual.
2. It is predetermined and deliberately created.
3. It is created on the basis of delegation of authority.
4. Rights, authorities, and responsibilities of the employees are clearly defined.
5. The jobs are not performed according to the individuals to whom they are entrusted.
6. It does not consider the emotional aspect.
7. Division of labour and specialisation becomes possible.
8. Organisation charts are followed.

Advantages of the Formal Organisation

1. **Reduces Confusion.** The work is allocated efficiently by clearly defining the rights, duties, and accountability. So formal organisation reduces confusions, and brings clarity in the working.
2. **Ensures Specialisation.** Formal organisations allow the employees to perform the tasks in which they have specialisation so that they can properly concentrate on their work.
3. **Fixing of Responsibility.** Formalised activities and detailed specifications of duties help in finding employee performance and fixing his responsibility for the tasks performed by him.
4. **Help in Achievement of Objectives.** Systematic allocation of duties and responsibilities is the only means for the achievement of the objectives of the organisation.
5. **Provide Stability to the Firm.** With the help of formal organisation, the firm can keep operating inspite of changes in the work force.
6. **Increases Organisational Efficiency.** Formal organisation help in optimum utilisation of the resources and reducing the wastage to the minimum. This increases the efficiency of the enterprise.

Disadvantages of the Formal Organisation

1. **Reduced Initiatives.** Mechanical functions being involved in formal organisations lead to the reduction in initiatives of the person working in the enterprise.
2. **Lack of Match between Objectives.** Generally, congruence is not found in the individual and organisational objectives. This means the personal objectives of the employees and organisational objectives did not match with each other.
3. **Problem due to Informal Relations.** On account of formal organisation, hurdles arise in the development of informal relations and communication system. Sometimes due to the informal relations, working of the formal organisations is interrupted.
4. **Disturbance in Relations.** This organisation gives both the vices like jealousy and hopelessness among the persons engaged with the enterprise.
5. **Delay in Work.** Every activity is performed according to the rules and regulations prescribed for it, this leads to the delay in working of the organisation

Informal Organisation

Informal organisations are formed on the basis of individual relations, communication, general knowledge, etc. Informal organisation is all pervasive as it is found at all levels of management.

According to J.L. Massie, "Informal organisation is any human group interactions that occur spontaneously and naturally over long period of time."

FEATURES OF INFORMAL ORGANISATION

1. It is supplement to the formal organisation.
2. The informal relationships are established spontaneously.
3. These organisations are found at each level of management.
4. The informal relationships are based on the personal preferences and understanding.
5. It reflects human relationships.
6. Such organisations have no place in the charts of organisation.

Advantages of Informal Organisation

1. **Cooperation.** Spirit of cooperation is found more in informal organisations. An informal organisation has strong group attitudes and a manager can increase his effectiveness by winning the cooperation of informal groups.
2. **Sense of Belongingness.** Informal organisations fill the sense of belonging by stressing each member's individual personality. Each member feels that he is somebody.
3. **Communication.** Informal organisations develop their own communication system to keep its members informed of what is going on in the organisation. This informal communication is very fast as compared to the formal communication.
4. **Aid on the Job.** Members of the informal organisation usually help one another in case of accidents, illness, etc. They protect each other from the arbitrary actions.

Disadvantages of Informal Organisation

1. **Resistance to Change.** Informal organisation has its own culture and traditions. Sometimes the demands made by the management are not accepted by the informal groups and they resist the changes demanded by the management.
2. **Clash in Interest.** The interests of formal and informal groups may clash leading to a confrontation making the job of the managers difficult.
3. **Rumour.** Informal communication is very much affected by the rumours. The original story is filtered and becomes distorted when people add the details of their own interest to the message

Differences Between Formal and Informal Organisation

Basis	Formal Organisation	Informal Organisation
Origination	It is originated with delegation of authority.	It originates automatically due to social relations.
Objectives	These are formed for organisational objectives.	These are formed for social satisfaction.
Relations	Members of these organisations have formal relations.	Members of these organisations have personal relations.
Structure	It has a well-defined structure.	It does not have a well-defined and clear cut structure.

Basis	Formal Organisation	Informal Organisation
Authority	Authority flows from top to bottom.	Authority flows from down to top or horizontally.
Period	These are long-term and enduring organisations.	These are short-term and instable organisations.
Dynamism	More rigid	More flexible
Leadership	Managers are leaders	Leaders are voluntarily chosen.
Nature	It is official organisation	It is sentimental organisation.
Communication	Communication is slow due to the following the chain of command.	Communication is quick and fast.
Examples	Committees, Project teams	Players, Travellers

Concepts of Organising. The working relationships — vertical and horizontal associations between individuals and groups — that exist within an organisation affect how its activities are accomplished and coordinated. Effective organising depends on the mastery of several important concepts: work specialisation, chain of command, authority, delegation, span of control, and centralisation versus decentralisation. Many of these concepts are based on the principles developed by Henri Fayol.

Work specialisation. One popular organisational concept is based on the fundamental principle that employees can work more efficiently if they're allowed to specialise. **Work specialisation,** sometimes called division of labour, is the degree to which organisational tasks are divided into separate jobs. Employees within each department perform only the tasks related to their specialised function.

When specialisation is extensive, employees specialise in a single task, such as running a particular machine in a factory assembly line. Jobs tend to be small, but workers can perform them efficiently. By contrast, if a single factory employee built an entire automobile or performed a large number of unrelated jobs in a bottling plant, the results would be inefficient.

Despite the apparent advantages of specialisation, many organisations are moving away from this principle. With too much specialisation, employees are isolated and perform only small, narrow, boring tasks. In addition, if that person leaves the company, his specialised knowledge may disappear as well. Many companies are enlarging jobs to provide greater challenges and creating teams so that employees can rotate among several jobs.

Chain of Command

The **chain of command** is an unbroken line of authority that links all persons in an organisation and defines who reports to whom. This chain has two underlying principles: unity of command and scalar principle.

- **Unity of command.** This principle states that an employee should have one and only one supervisor to whom he or she is directly responsible. No employee should report to two or more people. Otherwise, the employee may receive conflicting demands or priorities from several supervisors at once, placing this employee in a no-win situation.
- Sometimes, however, an organisation deliberately breaks the chain of command, such as when a project team is created to work on a special project. In such cases, team members report to their immediate supervisor and also to a team project leader. Another example is when a sales representative reports to both an immediate district supervisor and a marketing specialist, who is coordinating the introduction of a new product, in the home office.
- **Scalar principle.** The scalar principle refers to a clearly defined line of authority that includes all employees in the organisation. The classical school of management suggests that there

should be a clear and unbroken chain of command linking every person in the organisation with successively higher levels of authority up to and including the top manager. When organisations grow in size, they tend to get taller, as more and more levels of management are added. This increases overhead costs, adds more communication layers, and impacts understanding and access between top and bottom levels. It can greatly slow decision making and can lead to a loss of contact with the client or customer.

Authority

Authority is the formal and legitimate right of a manager to make decisions, issue orders, and allocate resources to achieve organisationally desired outcomes. A manager's authority is defined in his or her job description.

Organisational authority has three important underlying principles:

- Authority is based on the organisational position, and anyone in the same position has the same authority.
- Authority is accepted by subordinates. Subordinates comply because they believe that managers have a legitimate right to issue orders.
- Authority flows down the vertical hierarchy. Positions at the top of the hierarchy are vested with more formal authority than are positions at the bottom.

Authority Comes in Three Types

- **Line authority** gives a manager the right to direct the work of his or her employees and make many decisions without consulting others. Line managers are always in charge of essential activities such as sales, and they are authorised to issue orders to subordinates down the chain of command.
- **Staff authority** supports line authority by advising, servicing, and assisting, but this type of authority is typically limited. For example, the assistant to the department head has staff authority because he or she acts as an extension of that authority. These assistants can give advice and suggestions, but they don't have to be obeyed. The department head may also give the assistant the authority to act, such as the right to sign off on expense reports or memos. In such cases, the directives are given under the line authority of the boss.
- **Functional authority** is authority delegated to an individual or department over specific activities undertaken by personnel in other departments. Staff managers may have functional authority, meaning that they can issue orders down the chain of command within the very narrow limits of their authority. For example, supervisors in a manufacturing plant may find that their immediate bosses have line authority over them, but that someone in corporate headquarters may also have line authority over some of their activities or decisions.

Delegation

Delegation of Authority. To delegate is to give, offer, confer, and allot a part of authority to subordinates. Large scale and complex nature are the important features of the modern organisations. Due to this management cannot perform all its tasks and thus they share their work with their subordinates. So this shared task along with the corresponding authority is called delegation of authority. Delegation of authority is the essence of management. It is one of the important factors in the process of organising and facilitates the existence of the formal organisation. With the help of the delegation manager calls his subordinates to render their help in accomplishing the organisational objectives. So, the practice of granting authority to a subordinate for getting things done from him is known as delegation of authority.

Elements of Delegation of Authority

Following are the elements of delegation of authority:

1. **Responsibility.** The basic essence of the responsibility is obligation. Responsibility is the obligation of the subordinate to complete the work which is assigned to him. The responsibility is always in relation to a person and in relation to a thing and the basis of responsibility is the superior-subordinate relationship that exists in the organisation. So the duty to perform the assigned organisational tasks, functions, and assignments is called responsibility.

   According to Haimann, "Responsibility is the obligation of a subordinate to perform the duty as required by his superior."

   According to Koontz, "Responsibility may be defined as the obligation of a subordinate to whom the duty has been assigned to perform."

2. **Authority.** Authority is the term packed with variety of meanings by theorists and management practitioners. In everyday life authority is commonly understood as rightful power or right to command. Authority is the attribute of the job and not of man. Thus, Mr. A, as office superintendent derives authority over his subordinates not because he is Mr. A but because he is office superintendent. Authority gives the legitimate right to the superior to command over his subordinates and get the work done from them.

   According to Henry Fayol, "Authority is the right to give orders to and the power to extract obedience from the subordinates."

   According to Allen, "Authority is the sum of powers and rights entrusted to make possible the performance of the work delegated."

3. **Accountability.** Accountability denotes answerability for the accomplishment of the task assigned by the superior to his subordinates. It is to be noted that the process of delegation is not at all complete with just assigning the duty and delegating appropriate authority for the accomplishment of the task. The process of delegation becomes complete only by making the delegate answerable to the superior for his functioning. For example if the publicity manager of a company is assigned with the task of formulating and implementing a mass publicity plan for a new product, he is answerable for its effectiveness. So accountability is the obligation of an individual to keep his superior informed of his use of authority and accomplishment of the assigned tables

Basis	Authority	Responsibility
Meaning	It is the right of the manager to command his subordinates.	It is the obligation of the subordinate to complete the assigned work.
Origin	It arises due to the position of superior.	It arises due to superior-subordinate relationship.
Flow	It flows from top to bottom.	It flows from bottom to top.
Period	It has longer period as compared to responsibility.	It gets completed with the completion of the task so has the shorter period.
Nature	Authority is power.	Responsibility is the duty.
Delegation	Authority can be delegated to others.	Responsibility cannot be delegated.

According to Peterson, "To be accountable is to be answerable for one's conduct in respect to obligation fulfilled or unfulfilled."

Process of Delegation

Irrespective of the level at which authority is passed on to subordinates; delegation can be conceived as a four-step process as follows:

- **Allocation of Duties.** Duties are the tasks and activities that a superior desires to have someone else to do. Before the authority can be delegated, therefore, the duties over which the authority relates must be allocated to subordinates. So the top officer assigns certain definite work to his subordinate. This work should be assigned after thorough examination of the ability, efficiency, and the self confidence of subordinates.
- **Granting of Authority.** The essence of granting the authority is to empower another person to act for the manager. It is passing of formal rights to act on behalf of another. So the adequate authority is hence delegated to the subordinates to make them able to perform the assigned the task but these rights should be according to the allocated duty.
- **Assignment of Responsibility.** When authority is delegated one must assign responsibility. That is when one is given rights then one must be assigned corresponding obligation to perform. Here the parity between authority and responsibility should be considered.
- **Creation of Accountability.** To complete the delegation process, the manager must create accountability; so the subordinates should be made answerable for the discharge of the duties assigned and for the proper use of delegated authority. Accountability originates because the manager has the right to require an accounting for the authority delegated and task assigned to subordinates.

Thus, duties, authority, and obligation constitute three important ingredients of delegation of authority.

Span of Control

Span of control (sometimes called span of management) refers to the number of workers who report to one manager. For hundreds of years, theorists have searched for an ideal span of control. When no perfect number of subordinates for a manager to supervise became apparent, they turned their attention to the more general issue of whether the span should be wide or narrow.

A wide span of management exists when a manager has a large number of subordinates. Generally, the span of control may be wide when

- The manager and the subordinates are very competent.
- The organisation has a well-established set of standard operating procedures.
- Few new problems are anticipated.

A narrow span of management exists when the manager has only a few subordinates. The span should be narrow when

- Workers are located far from one another physically.
- The manager has a lot of work to do in addition to supervising workers.
- A great deal of interaction is required between supervisor and workers.
- New problems arise frequently.

Centralisation & Decentralisation

A **centralised organisation** systematically works to concentrate authority at the upper levels. In a **decentralised organisation,** management consciously attempts to spread authority to the lower organisation levels.

Decentralisation. Decentralisation is basically concerned with attitude and philosophy of the organisation and management. It is not merely a process of handing over the part of the authority to the subordinates. Decentralisation of authority means dispersal of decision-making power to the lower level of the organisation. It is the wider form of delegation of authority. So, when the rights permanently and relatively in more quantum are delegated by any superior to his subordinates, this process of delegation of rights is called decentralisation. For example, if the superior of any department, delegates authority to recruit personnel of his department to any head of that department, it is called delegation of authority. On the other hand, if the authority to recruit personnel is delegated to the heads of all the departments it is called decentralisation.

The general pattern of authority throughout an organisation determines the extent to which that organisation is centralised or decentralised.

According to Henry Fayol, "Everything that goes to increase the importance of the subordinates is decentralisation, anything that gives to reduce it, is called centralisation."

Direction

Directing is said to be a process in which the managers instruct, guide and oversee the performance of the workers to achieve predetermined goals. Directing is said to be the heart of management process. Planning, organising, staffing have got no importance if direction function does not take place.

Directing initiates action and it is from here actual work starts. Direction is said to be consisting of human factors. In simple words, it can be described as providing guidance to workers is doing work. In field of management, direction is said to be all those activities which are designed to encourage the subordinates to work effectively and efficiently. According to Human, "Directing consists of process or technique by which instruction can be issued and operations can be carried out as originally planned" Therefore, Directing is the function of guiding, inspiring, overseeing and instructing people towards accomplishment of organisational goals.

Importance of Directing Function

Directing or Direction function is said to be the heart of management of process and therefore, is the central point around which accomplishment of goals take place. A few philosophers call Direction as "*Life spark of an enterprise*". It is also called as on actuating function of management because it is through direction that the operation of an enterprise actually starts. Being the central character of enterprise, it provides many benefits to a concern which are as follows:-

- **It Initiates Actions.** Directions is the function which is the starting point of the work performance of subordinates. It is from this function the action takes place, subordinates understand their jobs and do according to the instructions laid. Whatever are plans laid, can be implemented only once the actual work starts. It is there that direction becomes beneficial.
- **It Integrates Efforts.** Through direction, the superiors are able to guide, inspire and instruct the subordinates to work. For this, efforts of every individual towards accomplishment of goals are required. It is through direction the efforts of every department can be related and integrated with others. This can be done through persuasive leadership and effective communication. Integration of efforts bring effectiveness and stability in a concern.
- **Means of Motivation.** Direction function helps in achievement of goals. A manager makes use of the element of motivation here to improve the performances of subordinates. This can be done by providing incentives or compensation, whether monetary or non - monetary, which serves as a "Morale booster" to the subordinates Motivation is also helpful for the subordinates to give the best of their abilities which ultimately helps in growth.
- **It Provides Stability.** Stability and balance in concern becomes very important for long term sun survival in the market. This can be brought upon by the managers with the help of four tools or elements of direction function – judicious blend of persuasive leadership, effective communication, strict supervision and efficient motivation. Stability is very important since that is an index of growth of an enterprise. Therefore a manager can use of all the four traits in him so that performance standards can be maintained.
- **Coping up with the changes.** It is a human behaviour that human beings show resistance to change. Adaptability with changing environment helps in sustaining planned growth and becoming a market leader. It is directing function which is of use to meet with changes in

environment, both internal as external. Effective communication helps in coping up with the changes. It is the role of manager here to communicate the nature and contents of changes very clearly to the subordinates. This helps in clarifications, easy adoptions and smooth running of an enterprise. For example, if a concern shifts from handlooms to power looms, an important change in technique of production takes place. The resulting factors are less of manpower and more of machinery. This can be resisted by the subordinates. The manager here can explain that the change was in the benefit of the subordinates. Through more mechanisation, production increases and thereby the profits. Indirectly, the subordinates are benefited out of that in form of higher remuneration.

- **Efficient Utilisation of Resources.** Direction finance helps in clarifying the role of every subordinate towards his work. The resources can be utilised properly only when less of wastages, duplication of efforts, overlapping of performances, etc. doesn't take place. Through direction, the role of subordinates become clear as manager makes use of his supervisory, the guidance, the instructions and motivation skill to inspire the subordinates. This helps in maximum possible utilisation of resources of men, machine, materials and money which helps in reducing costs and increasing profits.

Elements of Direction Includes

Elements of Direction includes: (a) Supervision, (b) Leadership, (c) Motivation, (d) Communication

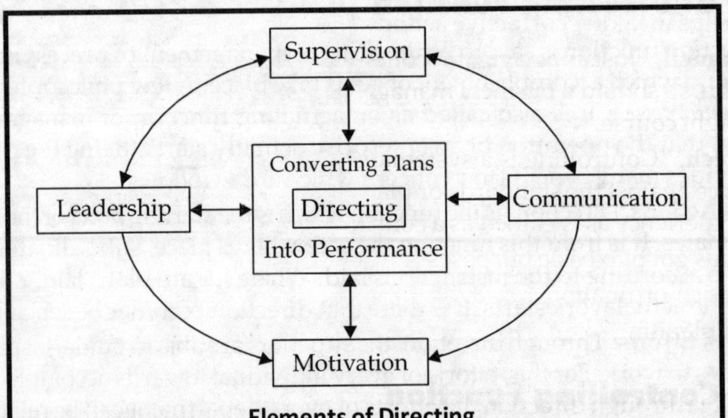

Elements of Directing

Supervision. *"Guiding and directing efforts of employees and other resources to accomplish stated work outputs"* **- *Terry and Franklin.***

Supervision is an element of direction. *"Day-to-day relationship between an executive and his immediate assistant and covers training, direction, motivation, coordination, maintenance of discipline, etc."* **- *Newman and Warren.***

Supervision denotes the functions performed by the supervisors.

Motivation. *"Motivation is the complex force starting and keeping a person at work in an organisation. Motivation is something that moves the person to action, and continues him in the course of action already initiates."* **- *Dubin.***

Motivation is the core of management. Technically, the term motivation can be traced to the Latin word movere, which means 'to move'. Motivating is a term which implies that one person induces another, to engage in action by ensuring that a channel to satisfy the motive becomes available to the individual. Motive is energizer of action, motivating is the channelisation and activation of motives, motivation is the work behaviour itself. Motivation depends on motives and motivating. It is a complex process.

Leadership. *"Leadership is essentially a continuous process of influencing behaviour. A leader breathes life into the group and motivates it towards goals. The lukewarm desires for achievement are transformed into burning passion for accomplishment"*

- George R. Terry.

Leadership is the process of influencing the behaviour of others to work willingly and enthusiastically for achieving predetermined goals. It is an essential ingredient for successful organisation. The successful organisation has one major attribute that sets it apart from unsuccessful organisation that is dynamic and effective leadership.

Communication. *"Communication is the transfer of information from one person to another person. It is a way of reaching others by transmitting ideas, facts, thoughts, feeling sand values."* **- Newstrom and Davis.**

Communication is regarded as basic to the functioning of the organisation, in its absence; the organisation would cease to exist. It is the process through which two or more persons come to exchange ideas and understanding among themselves.

Controlling

Concept and Definition

Controlling consists of verifying whether everything occurs in conformities with the plans adopted, instructions issued and principles established. Controlling ensures that there is effective and efficient utilisation of organisational resources so as to achieve the planned goals. Controlling measures the deviation of actual performance from the standard performance, discovers the causes of such deviations and helps in taking corrective actions.

According to Donnell, "Just as a navigator continually takes reading to ensure whether he is relative to a planned action, so should a business manager continually take reading to assure himself that his enterprise is on right course."

According to Brech, "Controlling is a systematic exercise which is called as a process of checking actual performance against the standards or plans with a view to ensure adequate progress and also recording such experience as is gained as a contribution to possible future needs."

Controlling has got two basic purposes

1. It facilitates co-ordination
2. It helps in planning

Features of Controlling Function

Following are the characteristics of controlling function of management :

1. **Controlling is a dynamic process.** Since controlling requires taking reviewable methods, changes have to be made wherever possible.
2. **Controlling is forward looking.** Because effective control is not possible without past being controlled. Controlling always look to future so that follow-up can be made whenever required.
3. **Controlling is related with planning.** Planning and Controlling are two inseparable functions of management. Without planning, controlling is a meaningless exercise and without controlling, planning is useless. *Planning presupposes controlling* and *controlling succeeds planning.*
4. **Controlling is an end function.** A function which comes once the performances are made in conformities with plans.
5. **Controlling is a pervasive function.** which means it is performed by managers at all levels and in all type of concerns.

The Control Process

The control process involves carefully collecting information about a system, process, person, or group of people in order to make necessary decisions about each. Managers set up control systems that consist of four key steps:

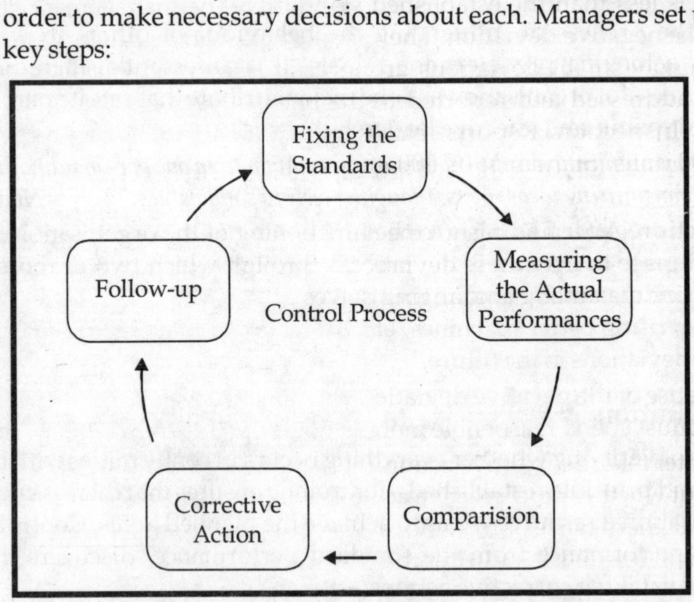

1. **Fixing the Control Standards.** A standard is a criterion (base) which is used to measure the performance of the subordinates. Standards may be of two types, *i.e.,* Quantitative Standards and Qualitative Standards. **Quantitative Standard** can be easily defined and measured. For e.g. number of products, number of customers, cost, net profit, time limits, etc. **Qualitative Standard** cannot be easily defined and measured. For e.g. measurement of morale, measurement of job satisfaction, measurement of effect of a training programme, advertisement programme, etc. It is better to have quantitative standards because they are measurable. However, today there are many new techniques for measuring qualitative standards. The standards should be as clear as possible. It should be easily understood by both superiors and subordinates. The responsibility of each individual should also be clearly defined *i.e.,* everyone should be responsible for achieving a particular goal, objective, target, etc. For e.g. The marketing department fixes a standard – *"We will sell 2,000 units of product X in one month"*. So here the standard is 2,000 units.
2. **Measuring the Actual Performances.** The second major step in controlling is to measure the performance. Finding out deviations becomes easy through measuring the actual performance. Performance levels are sometimes easy to measure and sometimes difficult. Measurement of tangible standards is easy as it can be expressed in units, cost, money terms, etc. Quantitative measurement becomes difficult when performance of manager has to be measured. Performance of a manager cannot be measured in quantities. It can be measured only by :
   a. Attitude of the workers,
   b. Their morale to work,
   c. The development in the attitudes regarding the physical environment, and
   d. Their communication with the superiors.

   It is also sometimes done through various reports like weekly, monthly, quarterly, yearly reports.
3. **Comparison of actual and standard performance.** The actual performances of the subordinates are compared with established standards, and then the deviations are found out. The deviations which are found out may be positive or negative.

Positive Deviation means that the actual performances are better than the established standards. Positive deviations should be appreciated. Negative Deviation means that the actual performance is less than the established standards. The management should pay special attention to the negative deviation. They should find out the causes of negative deviations. Generally, minor (small) deviations are ignored. However, major deviations should be immediately addressed and reported to the top management. PERT, Budgetary Control, Observation, Inspection, Reports, etc. are some of the methods used for comparison. For e.g. 10,000 units (Standard) - 9,000 units (Actual Performance) = 1,000 units (Negative Deviation).

4. **Corrective Action.** After finding out the negative deviations and their causes, the managers should take steps to correct these deviations. Corrective actions should be taken promptly. Corrective action may include, changing the standards, providing better motivation, giving better training, using better machines, etc. The management should take essential steps to prevent these deviations in the future.
   For e.g. The cause of the negative deviation was less advertising and untrained salesmen. So, the company must spend reasonable money on advertising and training.
5. **Follow-up.** After taking corrective action, the management must do a follow-up. Follow-up is done to find out whether the corrective actions are taken properly. It also finds out whether the deviations and their causes are removed. If follow-up is done properly, then the actual performance will be equal to or better than the established standards.

Types of Organisational Control

These types of controls are formally called feed forward, concurrent, and feedback, respectively.

- **Feed forward controls,** sometimes called preliminary or preventive controls, attempt to identify and prevent deviations in the standards before they occur. Feed forward controls focus on human, material, and financial resources within the organisation. These controls are evident in the selection and hiring of new employees. For example, organisations attempt to improve the likelihood that employees will perform up to standards by identifying the necessary job skills and by using tests and other screening devices to hire people with those skills.
- **Concurrent controls** monitor ongoing employee activity to ensure consistency with quality standards. These controls rely on performance standards, rules, and regulations for guiding employee tasks and behaviours. Their purpose is to ensure that work activities produce the desired results. As an example, many manufacturing operations include devices that measure whether the items being produced meet quality standards. Employees monitor the measurements; if they see that standards are not being met in some area, they make a correction themselves or let a manager know that a problem is occurring.

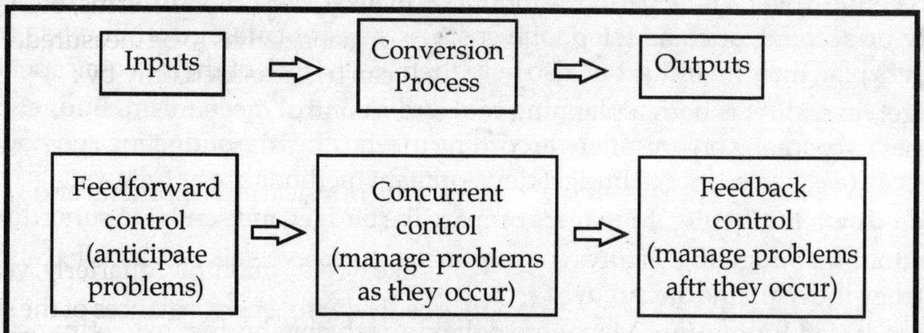

Three Types of Control

- **Feedback controls** involve reviewing information to determine whether performance meets established standards. For example, suppose that an organisation establishes a goal of increasing its profit by 12 percent next year. To ensure that this goal is reached, the organisation must monitor its profit on a monthly basis. After three months, if profit has increased by 3 percent, management might assume that plans are going according to schedule.

Organisational Control Techniques

Control techniques provide managers with the type and amount of information they need to measure and monitor performance. The information from various controls must be tailored to a specific management level, department, unit, or operation.

To ensure complete and consistent information, organisations often use standardised documents such as financial, status, and project reports. Each area within an organisation, however, uses its own specific control techniques, described in the following sections.

1. **Financial controls.** After the organisation has strategies in place to reach its goals, funds are set aside for the necessary resources and labour. As money is spent, statements are updated to reflect how much was spent, how it was spent, and what it obtained. Managers use these financial statements, such as an income statement or balance sheet, to monitor the progress of programs and plans. **Financial statements** provide management with information to monitor financial resources and activities. The **income statement** shows the results of the organisation's operations over a period of time, such as revenues, expenses, and profit or loss. The *balance sheet* shows what the organisation is worth (assets) at a single point in time, and the extent to which those assets were financed through debt (liabilities) or owner's investment (equity).

   Financial audits, or formal investigations, are regularly conducted to ensure that financial management practices follow generally accepted procedures, policies, laws, and ethical guidelines. Audits may be conducted internally or externally. **Financial ratio analysis** examines the relationship between specific figures on the financial statements and helps explain the significance of those figures:
   - **Liquidity ratios** measure an organisation's ability to generate cash.
   - **Profitability ratios** measure an organisation's ability to generate profits.
   - **Debt ratios** measure an organisation's ability to pay its debts.
   - **Activity ratios** measure an organisation's efficiency in operations and use of assets.

   In addition, *financial responsibility centres* require managers to account for a unit's progress toward financial goals within the scope of their influences. A manager's goals and responsibilities may focus on unit profits, costs, revenues, or investments.
2. **Budget controls.** A budget depicts how much an organisation expects to spend (expenses) and earn (revenues) over a time period. Amounts are categorised according to the type of business activity or account, such as telephone costs or sales of catalogues. Budgets not only help managers plan their finances, but also help them keep track of their overall spending.

   A budget, in reality, is both a planning tool and a control mechanism. Budget development processes vary among organisations according to who does the budgeting and how the financial resources are allocated. Some budget development methods are as follows:
   - **Top-down budgeting.** Managers prepare the budget and send it to subordinates.
   - **Bottom-up budgeting.** Figures come from the lower levels and are adjusted and coordinated as they move up the hierarchy.
   - **Zero-based budgeting.** Managers develop each new budget by justifying the projected allocation against its contribution to departmental or organisational goals.

- **Flexible budgeting.** Any budget exercise can incorporate flexible budgets, which set "meet or beat" standards that can be compared to expenditures.

3. **Marketing controls. Marketing controls** help monitor progress toward goals for customer satisfaction with products and services, prices, and delivery. The following are examples of controls used to evaluate an organisation's marketing functions:
   (i) **Market research** gathers data to assess customer needs—information critical to an organisation's success. Ongoing market research reflects how well an organisation is meeting customers' expectations and helps anticipate customer needs. It also helps identify competitors.
   (ii) **Test marketing** is small-scale product marketing to assess customer acceptance. Using surveys and focus groups, test marketing goes beyond identifying general requirements and looks at what (or who) actually influences buying decisions.
   (iii) **Marketing statistics** measure performance by compiling data and analyzing results. In most cases, competency with a computer spreadsheet program is all a manager needs. Managers look at *marketing ratios,* which measure profitability, activity, and market shares, as well as *sales quotas,* which measure progress toward sales goals and assist with inventory controls.

   Unfortunately, scheduling a regular evaluation of an organisation's marketing program is easier to recommend than to execute. Usually, only a crisis, such as increased competition or a sales drop, forces a company to take a closer look at its marketing program. However, more regular evaluations help minimise the number of marketing problems.

4. **Human resource controls.** Human resource controls help managers regulate the quality of newly hired personnel, as well as monitor current employees' developments and daily performances.

   On a daily basis, managers can go a long way in helping to control workers' behaviours in organisations. They can help direct workers' performances toward goals by making sure that goals are clearly set and understood. Managers can also institute policies and procedures to help guide workers' actions. Finally, they can consider past experiences when developing future strategies, objectives, policies, and procedures.

   Common control types include performance appraisals, disciplinary programs, observations, and training and development assessments. Because the quality of a firm's personnel, to a large degree, determines the firm's overall effectiveness, controlling this area is very crucial.

5. **Computers and information controls.** Almost all organisations have confidential and sensitive information that they don't want to become general knowledge. Controlling access to computer databases is the key to this area. Increasingly, computers are being used to collect and store information for control purposes. Many organisations privately monitor each employee's computer usage to measure employee performance, among other things. Some people question the appropriateness of computer monitoring. Managers must carefully weigh the benefits against the costs—both human and financial—before investing in and implementing computerised control techniques.

6. **Management Audit.** Management Audit is an evaluation of the management as a whole. It critically examines the full management process, *i.e.,* planning, organising, directing, and controlling. It finds out the efficiency of the management. To check the efficiency of the management, the company's plans, objectives, policies, procedures, personnel relations and systems of control are examined very carefully. Management auditing is conducted by a team of experts. They collect data from past records, members of management, clients and employees. The data is analysed and conclusions are drawn about managerial performance and efficiency

7. **Management Information System (MIS).** In order to control the organisation properly the management needs accurate information. They need information about the internal working of the organisation and also about the external environment. Information is collected continuously to identify problems and find out solutions. MIS collects data, processes it and provides it to the managers. MIS may be manual or computerised. With MIS, managers can delegate authority to subordinates without losing control.
8. **PERT and CPM Techniques.** Programme Evaluation and Review Technique (PERT) and Critical Path Method (CPM) techniques were developed in USA in the late 50's. Any programme consists of various activities and sub-activities. Successful completion of any activity depends upon doing the work in a given sequence and in a given time.
   CPM / PERT can be used to minimise the total time or the total cost required to perform the total operations. Importance is given to identifying the critical activities. Critical activities are those which have to be completed on time otherwise the full project will be delayed. So, in these techniques, the job is divided into various activities / sub-activities. From these activities, the critical activities are identified. More importance is given to completion of these critical activities. So, by controlling the time of the critical activities, the total time and cost of the job is minimised.
9. **Self-Control.** Self-Control means self-directed control. A person is given freedom to set his own targets, evaluate his own performance and take corrective measures as and when required. Self-control is especially required for top level managers because they do not like external control. The subordinates must be encouraged to use self-control because it is not good for the superior to control each and everything. However, self-control does not mean no control by the superiors. The superiors must control the important activities of the subordinates.
10. **Break Even Analysis.** Break Even Analysis or Break Even Point is the point of no profit, no loss. For e.g. When an organisation sells 50K cars it will break even. It means that, any sale below this point will cause losses and any sale above this point will earn profits. The Break-even analysis acts as a control device. It helps to find out the company's performance. So the company can take collective action to improve its performance in the future. Break-even analysis is a simple control tool.
11. **Return on Investment (ROI).** Investment consists of fixed assets and working capital used in business. Profit on the investment is a reward for risk taking. If the ROI is high then the financial performance of a business is good and vice-versa. ROI is a tool to improve financial performance. It helps the business to compare its present performance with that of previous years' performance. It helps to conduct inter-firm comparisons. It also shows the areas where corrective actions are needed.

Coordination

Meaning

Coordination as a function of the management refers to the tasks of integrating the activity of separate units of an organisation to accomplish the goals efficiently. It permeates all levels and all department of the management hence it is regarded as the essence of the management.

Features of Coordination

1. **Function.** Coordination is not a separate function of management. It is the part and essence of management.
2. **Responsibility.** Coordination is the basic responsibility of all managers and it can be only achieved through managerial function. This cannot be avoided by any manager and whenever

people work together for the common objective, coordination is required.

3 **Unity.** The main aspect of coordination is the unity of effort and action, which includes the predetermining the timing and method of the performance of the various activities so that efforts of individual are blended into group efforts.

4. **Requirement.** Coordination is required in the group efforts and not in the individual efforts. It is not required when an individual works alone but when the group is working for the common objective then their efforts needs to be coordinated.

5. **Integration.** Higher the degree of integration higher the coordination is required, further lower the degree of integration, lower level of coordination is required.

6. **Continuous and dynamic.** Coordination is a continuous and dynamic process. It is continuous as it is achieved through the performance of functions. It is dynamic as it changes with the changes in the functions.

7. **Purpose.** Coordination has the purpose to achieve the organisational objectives.

8. **Elements.** Balancing, timing, and integration are the three main elements of the coordination.

DEFINITION OF COORDINATION

- **According to the Mcfarland,** "Coordination is the process whereby an executive develops an orderly pattern of group efforts among his subordinate and secure unity of the action in the pursuit of a common purpose".
- **According to E.F.L Breach,** "Coordination is the balancing and keeping together, the team by ensuring a suitable allocation of tasks to various members and seeing that the tasks are performed with due harmony among the members themselves".
- **According to Henry Fayol,** "To coordinate is to harmonise all the activities of a concern so as to facilitate its working and its success".
- **According to George terry,** "The orderly synchronisation of efforts to provide the proper amount timing and directly of execution resulting harmonious and unified action to stated objectives".
- **According to Haimann,** "Coordination is not a separate activity of management. It is the organ of all other managerial functions like – planning, organising, staffing, directing, and controlling".
- **According to Mooney and Railey,** "Coordination is the achievement or group efforts and the unity of action of the pursuit of a common purpose".

Difference Between Coordination and Cooperation

Basis	Coordination	Cooperation
Scope	It has the wider scope and cooperation is the part of it.	It has limited scope and it is the part of the coordination.
Nature	It is practical and professional in nature.	It is emotional in nature.
Principle	Direct Contact and Continuity of efforts	Voluntary association
Relationship	Formal and informal both	Informal only
Objective	Synchronisation of efforts of individual.	Protecting the interest of members.

Types of Coordination

Coordination can be classified into following categories:

- **Vertical Coordination.** Vertical coordination exists between the departments where the department heads are asked to coordinate the work of the employees principles of coordination.
- **Horizontal Coordination.** Horizontal coordination takes place sideways. It exists between different departments such as production, sales, purchasing, finance etc.

- **Internal Coordination.** Coordination among the employees of the same department or section and among the employees at different levels is called internal coordination.
- **External Coordination.** Coordination with the outside parties with whom the organisation has the business connections like government, suppliers, customers etc. is called external coordination.

Following are the Principles of Coordination

- **Principle of early introduction.** Coordination must be visualised right from the early stages of planning and policy-making. At the time of preparation of the plan, mutual cooperation, consultation, give and take become the necessity. In case the plan is prepared without coordination then it becomes difficult to supply the required materials or results in the misallocation of the duties.
- **Principle of continuity.** According to this principle, coordination should be followed in the organisation on continuous basis and it should be taken as a regular activity. Managers should treat coordination as the never ending exercise.
- **Principle of Direct Contact.** According to the principle of direct contact, coordination can only be established through the direct contact of the parties whose activities are to be coordinated. As through direct contact the parties can discuss the methods, plans, actions, activities and work for the achievement of overall organisational goals.
- **Principle of mutual relation.** This principle states that every employee should understand the problems faced by the other employees and try to solve them. For the purpose of coordination, there should be perfect adjustment and sense of fellow feeling among the employees placed under them.

MULTIPLE CHOICE QUESTIONS

1. Who is considered the father of scientific management?
   (1) Frederick Taylor
   (2) Henri Fayol
   (3) Elton Mayo
   (4) Mary Parker Follett
2. Which of the following is NOT a principle of scientific management?
   (1) Division of labour
   (2) Time and motion studies
   (3) Employee empowerment
   (4) Standardisation of work
3. Who is known for developing the administrative theory of management?
   (1) Frederick Taylor
   (2) Henri Fayol
   (3) Elton Mayo
   (4) Mary Parker Follett
4. Which of the following is NOT a function of management, according to Henri Fayol?
   (1) Planning
   (2) Organising
   (3) Leading
   (4) Evaluating
5. Who is known for developing the human relations school of management?
   (1) Frederick Taylor
   (2) Henri Fayol
   (3) Elton Mayo
   (4) Mary Parker Follett
6. Which of the following is a key component of the Hawthorne studies?
   (1) Time and motion studies
   (2) Employee motivation
   (3) Division of labour
   (4) Employee empowerment
7. Who is known for developing the theory of organisation and leadership?
   (1) Frederick Taylor
   (2) Henri Fayol
   (3) Elton Mayo
   (4) Mary Parker Follett
8. Which of the following is NOT a principle of Mary Parker Follett's management philosophy?
   (1) Coordination of effort
   (2) Conflict resolution
   (3) Power and authority
   (4) Hierarchy of needs
9. Who is known for developing the systems theory of management?
   (1) Frederick Taylor
   (2) Henri Fayol
   (3) Elton Mayo
   (4) C.I. Barnard
10. Which of the following is a key component of the contingency approach to management?
    (1) One best way of management
    (2) Universal principles of management
    (3) Matching management style to the situation
    (4) Division of labour
11. Who is known for developing the theory of bureaucratic management?
    (1) Frederick Taylor
    (2) Henri Fayol
    (3) Max Weber
    (4) Mary Parker Follett
12. Which of the following is a key component of Max Weber's theory of bureaucracy?
    (1) Employee empowerment
    (2) Personal relationships

(3) Rules and procedures
(4) Division of labour

13. Who is known for developing the situational leadership model?
(1) Frederick Taylor
(2) Henri Fayol
(3) Paul Hersey and Kenneth Blanchard
(4) Mary Parker Follett

14. Which of the following is a key component of Maslow's hierarchy of needs?
(1) Safety and security needs
(2) Esteem needs
(3) Self-actualisation needs
(4) All of the above

15. Who is known for developing the theory of total quality management?
(1) Frederick Taylor
(2) W. Edwards Deming
(3) Elton Mayo
(4) Mary Parker Follett

16. Which of the following is NOT a principle of total quality management?
(1) Customer focus
(2) Continuous improvement
(3) Autocratic leadership
(4) Employee empowerment

17. Who is known for developing the contingency theory of leadership?
(1) Frederick Taylor
(2) Henri Fayol
(3) Fred Fiedler
(4) Mary Parker Follett

18. Which of the following is a key component of the path-goal theory of leadership?
(1) Employee empowerment
(2) Motivation
(3) Goal setting
(4) All of the above

19. Who is known for developing the theory of transformational leadership?
(1) Frederick Taylor
(2) James MacGregor Burns
(3) Elton Mayo
(4) Mary Parker Follett

20. Which of the following is a key component of transformational leadership?
(1) Charisma
(2) Inspiration
(3) Intellectual stimulation
(4) All of the above

21. Who is known for developing the theory of emotional intelligence?
(1) Howard Gardner
(2) Daniel Goleman
(3) Robert Sternberg
(4) Mary Parker Follett

22. Which of the following is NOT a component of emotional intelligence, according to Daniel Goleman?
(1) Self-awareness
(2) Self-regulation
(3) Social skills
(4) Division of labour

23. Who is known for developing the theory of the learning organisation?
(1) Peter Senge
(2) Edgar Schein
(3) Chris Argyris
(4) Mary Parker Follett

24. Which of the following is a key component of the learning organisation?
(1) Continuous learning and improvement
(2) Employee empowerment
(3) Command and control leadership
(4) Division of labour

25. Who is known for developing the concept of the balanced scorecard?
(1) Robert Kaplan and David Norton
(2) Frederick Taylor
(3) Henri Fayol
(4) Mary Parker Follett

26. Which is the correct sequence of the stages of group development, according to Tuckman's model?
(1) Forming, storming, norming, performing, adjourning
(2) Forming, storming, norming, adjourning, performing

(3) Storming, forming, norming, performing, adjourning
(4) Storming, norming, forming, adjourning, performing

27. Which of the following is NOT a type of power, according to French and Raven's model of power?
(1) Expert power
(2) Legitimate power
(3) Charismatic power
(4) Coercive power

28. Who is known for developing the concept of reinventing organisations?
(1) Peter Drucker
(2) Frederic Laloux
(3) Michael Porter
(4) Gary Hamel

29. Which of the following is NOT a characteristic of a learning organisation, according to Peter Senge?
(1) Systems thinking
(2) Shared vision
(3) Employee empowerment
(4) Centralised decision-making

30. Who is known for developing the contingency model of organisational design?
(1) Tom Burns and G.M. Stalker
(2) Jay Galbraith
(3) James Thompson
(4) Joan Woodward

31. Who is known for developing the concept of evidence-based management?
(1) Tom Peters
(2) Jeffrey Pfeffer
(3) Rosabeth Moss Kanter
(4) Michael Hammer

32. Which of the following is NOT a key principle of evidence-based management?
(1) Diverse perspectives
(2) Best available evidence
(3) Rigorous research methods
(4) Intuition and guesswork

33. Who is known for developing the concept of implicit bias?
(1) Daniel Kahneman
(2) Mahzarin Banaji and Anthony Greenwald
(3) Richard Thaler
(4) Amos Tversky

34. Which of the following is NOT a component of the balanced scorecard?
(1) Financial perspectives
(2) Customer perspectives
(3) Learning perspectives
(4) Division of labour perspectives

35. Who is known for developing the concept of servant leadership?
(1) Robert Greenleaf
(2) Stephen Covey
(3) Ken Blanchard
(4) Peter Drucker

36. Which of the following is a key component of servant leadership?
(1) Follower empowerment
(2) Leader charisma
(3) Goal setting
(4) Division of labour

37. Who is known for developing the concept of mindful leadership?
(1) Ellen Langer
(2) Jon Kabat-Zinn
(3) Richard Boyatzis
(4) Peter Senge

38. What is the main goal of servant leadership?
(1) To maximise shareholder value
(2) To empower followers and serve their needs
(3) To maximise productivity
(4) To minimise costs

39. Which of the following is NOT a principle of mindful leadership?
(1) Focusing on the present moment
(2) Non-judgmental awareness
(3) Autocratic decision-making
(4) Compassionate action

40. Who is known for developing the concept of charismatic leadership?
(1) Max Weber

(2) Robert House
(3) Frederic Avolio
(4) Bass and Avolio

41. Which of the following is a key component of charismatic leadership?
(1) Inspirational communication
(2) Rational persuasion
(3) Process control
(4) Division of labour

42. Who is known for developing the concept of transactional leadership?
(1) Max Weber
(2) Robert House
(3) Frederic Avolio
(4) Bass and Avolio

43. Which of the following is a key component of transactional leadership?
(1) Transformational communication
(2) Laissez-faire management
(3) Contingent reward
(4) Division of labour

44. Who is known for developing the concept of behavioural management theory?
(1) Frederick Taylor
(2) Henri Fayol
(3) Elton Mayo
(4) Douglas McGregor

45. Which of the following is a key component of Douglas McGregor's theory of management?
(1) Theory X management
(2) Theory Y management
(3) Command and control leadership
(4) Division of labour

46. Who is known for developing the concept of the learning organisation?
(1) Peter Senge
(2) Edgar Schein
(3) Chris Argyris
(4) Mary Parker Follett

47. Which of the following is a key component of the learning organisation?
(1) Continuous learning and improvement
(2) Employee empowerment
(3) Command and control leadership
(4) Division of labour

48. Who is known for developing the concept of organisational culture?
(1) Edgar Schein
(2) Peter Senge
(3) Frederick Taylor
(4) Henri Fayol

49. Which of the following is NOT a component of organisational culture, according to Edgar Schein?
(1) Shared values
(2) Shared assumptions
(3) Charismatic leadership
(4) Shared artifacts

50. Who is known for developing the concept of organisational learning?
(1) Peter Senge
(2) Chris Argyris
(3) Edgar Schein
(4) Mary Parker Follett

51. Which of the following is NOT a key principle of organisational learning?
(1) Continuous learning and improvement
(2) Employee empowerment
(3) Autocratic leadership
(4) Systems thinking

52. Who is known for developing the concept of strategic management?
(1) Michael Porter
(2) Peter Drucker
(3) Tom Peters
(4) Gary Hamel

53. Which of the following is a key component of the strategic management process?
(1) Goal setting
(2) Decision-making
(3) Planning
(4) All of the above

54. Who is known for developing the concept of complexity theory in management?
(1) Eric Trist (2) Ralph Stacey
(3) Herbert Simon
(4) W. Edwards Deming

55. Which of the following is NOT a principle of complexity theory in management?
(1) Non-linear relationships
(2) Self-organisation
(3) Reductionism
(4) Emergence

56. Who is known for developing the concept of social network analysis?
(1) Mark Granovetter
(2) Robert Putnam
(3) Daniel Kahneman
(4) Amos Tversky

57. Which of the following is NOT a key principle of social network analysis?
(1) Centrality
(2) Cohesion
(3) Division of labour
(4) Cliques

58. Who is known for developing the concept of stakeholder management?
(1) Edward Freeman
(2) Rosabeth Moss Kanter
(3) Michael Porter
(4) Gary Hamel

59. Which of the following is a key component of stakeholder management?
(1) Maximising shareholder value
(2) Identifying and managing relationships with key stakeholders
(3) Minimising costs
(4) Division of labour

60. Who is known for developing the concept of strategic human resource management?
(1) Jeffrey Pfeffer
(2) David Ulrich
(3) Rosabeth Moss Kanter
(4) Michael Porter

61. Which of the following is a key component of strategic human resource management?
(1) Recruitment and selection
(2) Employee training and development
(3) Performance management
(4) All of the above

62. Assertion: Coordination is focused on establishing effective communication channels between employees and management.
Reason: Communication is a key element of both coordination and delegation in the workplace.
(1) Both assertion and reason are true and the reason is the correct explanation of the assertion.
(2) Both assertion and reason are true, but the reason is not the correct explanation of the assertion.
(3) Assertion is true but reason is false.
(4) Assertion is false but reason is true.

63. Assertion: Effective delegation involves transferring responsibility and authority while retaining accountability.
Reason: Effective delegation enhances control and authority over employees.
(1) Both assertion and reason are true and the reason is the correct explanation of the assertion.
(2) Both assertion and reason are true, but the reason is not the correct explanation of the assertion.
(3) Assertion is true but reason is false.
(4) Assertion is false but reason is true.

64. Who is known for developing the concept of the "psychological contract" in organisations?
(1) Edgar Schein
(2) Chris Argyris
(3) Denise Rousseau
(4) Mary Parker Follett

65. Which of the following is NOT a key principle of organisational justice?
(1) Distributive justice
(2) Procedural justice
(3) Interactional justice
(4) Division of labour

66. Who is known for developing the concept of ethical leadership?
(1) Robert Sternberg
(2) James MacGregor Burns
(3) Linda Trevino and Michael Brown
(4) Max Weber

67. Which approach of management emphasizes the importance of understanding people's behaviour in organisations?
(1) Behavioural Approach
(2) Systems Approach
(3) Quantitative Approach
(4) Contingency Approach

68. Which approach of management views organisations as complex systems with interdependent parts?
(1) Behavioural Approach
(2) Systems Approach
(3) Quantitative Approach
(4) Contingency Approach

69. Which approach of management uses mathematical models and statistical analysis to solve management problems?
(1) Behavioural Approach
(2) Systems Approach
(3) Quantitative Approach
(4) Contingency Approach

70. Which approach of management proposes that there is no one right way to manage organisations?
(1) Behavioural Approach
(2) Systems Approach
(3) Quantitative Approach
(4) Contingency Approach

71. Which approach of management focuses on the situation, rather than a one-size-fits-all solution?
(1) Behavioural Approach
(2) Systems Approach
(3) Quantitative Approach
(4) Contingency Approach

72. Which approach of management was pioneered by Mary Parker Follett?
(1) Behavioural Approach
(2) Systems Approach
(3) Quantitative Approach
(4) Contingency Approach

73. Who developed the theory of motivation known as ERG theory?
(1) Abraham Maslow
(2) Frederick Herzberg
(3) Clayton Alderfer
(4) Peter Drucker

74. Who is known for developing the Hawthorne studies?
(1) Frederick Taylor
(2) Henri Fayol
(3) Elton Mayo
(4) Mary Parker Follett

75. Which of the following is NOT a key principle of the behavioural approach to management?
(1) Employee empowerment
(2) Understanding individual behaviour
(3) Autocratic decision-making
(4) Motivation and job satisfaction

76. Who developed the theory of organisational culture?
(1) Edgar Schein
(2) Peter Senge
(3) Chris Argyris
(4) Mary Parker Follett

77. Which of the following is NOT a component of organisational culture, according to Edgar Schein?
(1) Shared values
(2) Shared assumptions
(3) Division of labour
(4) Shared artifacts

78. Who developed the contingency theory of leadership?
(1) Tom Burns and G.M. Stalker
(2) Jay Galbraith
(3) James Thompson
(4) Joan Woodward

79. Which of the following is NOT a key principle of the contingency approach to management?
(1) One best way of management
(2) Universal principles of management
(3) Matching management style to the situation
(4) Division of labour

80. Who developed the systems theory of management?

(1) Frederick Taylor (2) Henri Fayol
(3) Elton Mayo (4) C.I. Barnard

81. Which of the following is NOT a key principle of the systems approach to management?
(1) Interdependence
(2) Synergy
(3) Division of labour
(4) Holism

82. Which of the following is NOT a key principle of the quantitative approach to management?
(1) Use of mathematical models
(2) Use of statistical analysis
(3) Use of intuition and guesswork
(4) Objective decision-making

83. Who developed the decision theory approach to management?
(1) Peter Drucker
(2) Herbert Simon
(3) Mary Parker Follett
(4) Max Weber

84. Who developed the game theory approach to management?
(1) Peter Drucker (2) Herbert Simon
(3) John Nash (4) Max Weber

85. Which of the following is NOT a key principle of the game theory approach to management?
(1) Strategic thinking
(2) Cooperation
(3) Division of labour
(4) Competitive behaviour

86. Who developed the quality control approach to management?
(1) W. Edwards Deming
(2) Henri Fayol
(3) Elton Mayo
(4) Mary Parker Follett

87. Which of the following is NOT a key principle of the quality control approach to management?
(1) Continuous improvement
(2) Employee empowerment
(3) Command and control leadership
(4) Customer focus

88. Who developed the portfolio analysis approach to management?
(1) Peter Drucker
(2) Frederic Laloux
(3) Igor Ansoff
(4) Boston Consulting Group

89. Which of the following is NOT a key principle of the portfolio analysis approach to management?
(1) Focus on high-growth markets
(2) Focus on high-market share products
(3) Division of labour
(4) Evaluation of performance

90. Who developed the resource-based view of the firm?
(1) C.K. Prahalad and Gary Hamel
(2) Michael Porter
(3) Peter Drucker
(4) Frederick Herzberg

91. Which of the following is NOT a key principle of the resource-based view of the firm?
(1) Evaluation of internal resources
(2) Acquisition of external resources
(3) Division of labour
(4) Sustainable competitive advantage

92. How does the behavioural approach to management differ from the classical approach?
(1) The behavioural approach emphasizes the importance of understanding people's behaviour in organisations, while the classical approach emphasizes the importance of division of labour and command and control.
(2) The behavioural approach emphasizes the importance of matching management style to the situation, while the classical approach emphasizes the importance of a one-size-fits-all solution.
(3) The behavioural approach emphasizes the importance of employee empowerment and motivation, while the classical approach emphasizes the importance of production efficiency.

(4) The behavioural approach and the classical approach are essentially the same.

93. How does the systems approach to management differ from the contingency approach?

(1) The systems approach sees organisations as complex systems with interdependent parts, while the contingency approach sees organisations as collections of independent variables.

(2) The systems approach emphasizes the importance of interdependence and synergy, while the contingency approach emphasizes the importance of matching management style to the situation.

(3) The systems approach and the contingency approach are essentially the same.

(4) The contingency approach emphasizes the importance of interdependence and synergy, while the systems approach emphasizes the importance of matching management style to the situation.

94. How does the quantitative approach to management differ from the decision theory approach?

(1) The quantitative approach uses mathematical models and statistical analysis to solve management problems, while the decision theory approach uses logic and rationality.

(2) The quantitative approach emphasizes objective decision-making, while the decision theory approach emphasizes subjective decision-making.

(3) The quantitative approach and the decision theory approach are essentially the same.

(4) The decision theory approach uses mathematical models and statistical analysis to solve management problems, while the quantitative approach uses logic and rationality.

95. How does the contingency approach to management differ from the resource-based view of the firm?

(1) The contingency approach emphasizes the importance of matching management style to the situation, while the resource-based view of the firm emphasizes the importance of evaluation of internal resources.

(2) The contingency approach emphasizes the importance of interdependence and synergy, while the resource-based view of the firm emphasizes the importance of sustainable competitive advantage.

(3) The contingency approach and the resource-based view of the firm are essentially the same.

(4) The resource-based view of the firm emphasizes the importance of matching management style to the situation, while the contingency approach emphasizes the importance of evaluation of internal resources.

96. How does the behavioural approach to management differ from the quality control approach?

(1) The behavioural approach emphasizes the importance of employee motivation and empowerment, while the quality control approach emphasizes the importance of customer focus and continuous improvement.

(2) The behavioural approach emphasizes the importance of understanding individual behaviour, while the quality control approach emphasizes the importance of objective decision-making.

(3) The behavioural approach and the quality control approach are essentially the same.

(4) The quality control approach emphasizes the importance of understanding individual behaviour, while the behavioural approach emphasizes the importance of customer focus and continuous improvement.

97. Interdependence and synergy

(1) Behavioural Approach

(2) Systems Approach

(3) Quantitative Approach

(4) Contingency Approach

98. Use of mathematical models and statistical analysis

(1) Behavioural Approach
(2) Systems Approach
(3) Quantitative Approach
(4) Contingency Approach

99. Sustainable competitive advantage
(1) Behavioural Approach
(2) Systems Approach
(3) Quantitative Approach
(4) Contingency Approach

100. Employee empowerment and motivation
(1) Behavioural Approach
(2) Systems Approach
(3) Quantitative Approach
(4) Contingency Approach

101. One-size-fits-all management solution
(1) Behavioural Approach
(2) Systems Approach
(3) Quantitative Approach
(4) Contingency Approach

102. **Assertion:** Collaboration is a critical element of effective coordination in the workplace.
Reason: Collaboration enhances communication and transparency and improves problem-solving capabilities.
(1) Both assertion and reason are true and the reason is the correct explanation of the assertion.
(2) Both assertion and reason are true, but the reason is not the correct explanation of the assertion.
(3) Assertion is true but reason is false.
(4) Assertion is false but reason is true.

103. Customer focus and continuous improvement
(1) Behavioural Approach
(2) Systems Approach
(3) Quantitative Approach
(4) Contingency Approach

104. Matching management style to the situation
(1) Behavioural Approach
(2) Systems Approach
(3) Quantitative Approach
(4) Contingency Approach

105. **Assertion:** The contingency approach emphasizes the importance of matching management style to the situation.
Reason: The contingency approach proposes that there is no one right way to manage organisations.
(1) Both assertion and reason are true and the reason is the correct explanation of the assertion.
(2) Both assertion and reason are true but the reason is not the correct explanation of the assertion.
(3) Assertion is true but reason is false.
(4) Assertion is false but reason is true.

106. **Assertion:** The behavioural approach to management emphasizes the importance of employee empowerment and motivation.
Reason: The behavioural approach proposes that people's behaviour in organisations can be understood and controlled.
(1) Both assertion and reason are true and the reason is the correct explanation of the assertion.
(2) Both assertion and reason are true but the reason is not the correct explanation of theassertion.
(3) Assertion is true but reason is false.
(4) Assertion is false but reason is true.

107. **Assertion:** Assertion: The systems approach to management emphasizes the importance of interdependence and synergy.
Reason: The systems approach proposes that organisations are collections of independent variables.
(1) Both assertion and reason are true and the reason is the correct explanation of the assertion.
(2) Both assertion and reason are true but the reason is not the correct explanation of the assertion.
(3) Assertion is true but reason is false.
(4) Assertion is false but reason is true.

108. **Assertion:** The quality control approach to management emphasizes the importance of customer focus and continuous improvement.

Reason: The quality control approach proposes that production efficiency is the most important factor in managing organisations.

(1) Both assertion and reason are true and the reason is the correct explanation of the assertion.
(2) Both assertion and reason are true but the reason is not the correct explanation of the assertion.
(3) Assertion is true but reason is false.
(4) Assertion is false but reason is true.

109. Assertion: The resource-based view of the firm emphasizes the importance of sustainable competitive advantage.

Reason: The resource-based view of the firm proposes that external factors are the most important determinants of a firm's success.

(1) Both assertion and reason are true and the reason is the correct explanation of the assertion.
(2) Both assertion and reason are true but the reason is not the correct explanation of the assertion.
(3) Assertion is true but reason is false.
(4) Assertion is false but reason is true.

110. What is the first function of management?
(1) Controlling (2) Organising
(3) Planning (4) Leading

111. What is the purpose of planning?
(1) To establish goals and objectives
(2) To allocate resources
(3) To forecast future events
(4) All of the above

112. What is a common tool used in planning?
(1) SWOT analysis
(2) Financial statement analysis
(3) Performance appraisal
(4) Gantt chart

113. What is the process of evaluating alternatives and choosing a course of action?
(1) Planning
(2) Controlling
(3) Decision making
(4) Leading

114. What is the difference between a strategy and a tactic?
(1) A strategy is long-term, while a tactic is short-term
(2) A strategy is reactive, while a tactic is proactive
(3) A strategy is focused on details, while a tactic is focused on the big picture
(4) A strategy is individualistic, while a tactic involves collaboration

115. What is the purpose of a contingency plan?
(1) To provide an alternative course of action if the original plan fails
(2) To prepare for a specific event that is expected to occur
(3) To establish long-term goals for the organisation
(4) To evaluate the performance of employees

116. What is the difference between a goal and an objective?
(1) A goal is specific, while an objective is abstract
(2) A goal is measurable, while an objective is intangible
(3) A goal is broad, while an objective is narrow
(4) A goal is short-term, while an objective is long-term

117. What is the difference between a mission and a vision?
(1) A mission is long-term, while a vision is short-term
(2) A mission is focused on the organisation, while a vision is focused on the customer
(3) A mission is a statement of purpose, while a vision is a statement of future direction
(4) A mission is broad, while a vision is narrow

118. What is the purpose of a budget?
(1) To monitor the performance of employees
(2) To allocate resources

(3) To establish long-term goals for the organisation
(4) All of the above

119. What is the difference between a fixed budget and a flexible budget?
(1) A fixed budget is adjusted for changes in sales, while a flexible budget is not
(2) A fixed budget is used for short-term planning, while a flexible budget is used for long-term planning
(3) A fixed budget is based on a single level of sales, while a flexible budget adjusts for changes in sales
(4) A fixed budget is focused on sales, while a flexible budget is focused on expenses

120. What is strategic planning?
(1) Planning that focuses on the day-to-day operations of the organisation
(2) Planning that involves the entire organisation in decision making
(3) A long-term planning process that focuses on achieving the organisation's mission and vision
(4) A short-term planning process that focuses on a specific objective

121. What is tactical planning?
(1) Planning that focuses on the day-to-day operations of the organisation
(2) Planning that involves the entire organisation in decision making
(3) A long-term planning process that focuses on achieving the organisation's mission and vision
(4) A short-term planning process that focuses on a specific objective

122. What is operational planning?
(1) Planning that focuses on the day-to-day operations of the organisation
(2) Planning that involves the entire organisation in decision making
(3) A long-term planning process that focuses on achieving the organisation's mission and vision
(4) A short-term planning process that focuses on a specific objective

123. What is the purpose of a contingency plan?
(1) To provide an alternative course of action if the original plan fails
(2) To prepare for a specific event that is expected to occur
(3) To establish long-term goals for the organisation
(4) To evaluate the performance of employees

124. What is the decision-making process?
(1) A process that involves evaluating alternatives and choosing a course of action
(2) A process that involves setting goals and objectives
(3) A process that involves monitoring the performance of employees
(4) A process that involves allocating resources

125. Establishing goals and objectives
(1) Planning (2) Organising
(3) Leading (4) Controlling

126. Allocating resources
(1) Planning (2) Organising
(3) Leading (4) Controlling

127. Directing and motivating employees
(1) Planning (2) Organising
(3) Leading (4) Controlling

128. Monitoring performance and making corrections
(1) Planning (2) Organising
(3) Leading (4) Controlling

129. Creating a structure of authority and responsibility
(1) Planning
(2) Organising
(3) Leading
(4) Controlling

130. **Assertion:** One of the primary goals of coordinating work activities in the workplace is to optimise the use of resources and minimise waste.

Reason: Coordination is focused on ensuring all work activities are aligned towards achieving shared organisational objectives.

(1) Both assertion and reason are true and the reason is the correct explanation of the assertion.
(2) Both assertion and reason are true, but the reason is not the correct explanation of the assertion.
(3) Assertion is true but reason is false.
(4) Assertion is false but reason is true.

131. Setting standards and measuring performance
(1) Planning (2) Organising
(3) Leading (4) Controlling

132. Establishing policies and procedures
(1) Planning (2) Organising
(3) Leading (4) Controlling

133. Motivating and training employees
(1) Planning (2) Organising
(3) Leading (4) Controlling

134. Evaluating employee performance
(1) Planning (2) Organising
(3) Leading (4) Controlling

135. Assertion: The purpose of planning is to establish goals and objectives.
Reason: Planning involves allocating resources and monitoring employee performance.
(1) Both assertion and reason are true and the reason is the correct explanation of the assertion.
(2) Both assertion and reason are true but the reason is not the correct explanation of the assertion.
(3) Assertion is true but reason is false.
(4) Assertion is false but reason is true.

136. Assertion: A contingency plan provides an alternative course of action if the original plan fails.
Reason: A contingency plan is focused on short-term goals and objectives.
(1) Both assertion and reason are true and the reason is the correct explanation of the assertion.
(2) Both assertion and reason are true but the reason is not the correct explanation of the assertion.
(3) Assertion is true but reason is false.
(4) Assertion is false but reason is true.

137. Assertion: Decision making involves evaluating alternatives and choosing a course of action.
Reason: Decision making is the same as planning.
(1) Both assertion and reason are true and the reason is the correct explanation of the assertion.
(2) Both assertion and reason are true but the reason is not the correct explanation of the assertion.
(3) Assertion is true but reason is false.
(4) Assertion is false but reason is true.

138. Assertion: Operational planning is focused on the day-to-day operations of the organisation.
Reason: Operational planning involves setting long-term goals and objectives.
(1) Both assertion and reason are true and the reason is the correct explanation of the assertion.
(2) Both assertion and reason are true but the reason is not the correct explanation of the assertion.
(3) Assertion is true but reason is false.
(4) Assertion is false but reason is true.

139. Assertion: Strategic planning is a long-term planning process that focuses on achieving the organisation's mission and vision.
Reason: Strategic planning involves only top-level management in decision making.
(1) Both assertion and reason are true and the reason is the correct explanation of the assertion.
(2) Both assertion and reason are true but the reason is not the correct explanation of the assertion.
(3) Assertion is true but reason is false.
(4) Assertion is false but reason is true.

140. What is the purpose of organising?
(1) To establish goals and objectives
(2) To allocate resources
(3) To create a structure of authority and responsibility
(4) To make decisions

141. What is the difference between a formal and informal organisation?
(1) A formal organisation is created by the employees, while an informal organisation is created by management
(2) A formal organisation is focused on the day-to-day operations, while an informal organisation is focused on long-term planning
(3) A formal organisation is created by management, while an informal organisation is created by the employees
(4) A formal organisation involves collaboration, while an informal organisation involves individual contributions

142. What is a common tool used in organising?
(1) SWOT analysis
(2) Financial statement analysis
(3) Flowchart
(4) Gantt chart

143. What is the process of dividing work into specific jobs and tasks?
(1) Delegation (2) Job analysis
(3) Job design
(4) Performance appraisal

144. What is the difference between centralisation and decentralisation?
(1) Centralisation involves decision making at the lower levels of the organisation, while decentralisation involves decision making at the top levels of the organisation
(2) Centralisation involves decision making at the top levels of the organisation, while decentralisation involves decision making at the lower levels of the organisation
(3) Centralisation involves collaboration, while decentralisation involves individual contributions
(4) Centralisation is focused on short-term goals, while decentralisation is focused on long-term goals

145. What is the purpose of a job description?
(1) To evaluate the performance of employees
(2) To allocate resources
(3) To define the responsibilities and requirements of a job
(4) To establish long-term goals for the organisation

146. What is the process of assigning tasks to employees?
(1) Job analysis
(2) Job design
(3) Job assignment
(4) Performance appraisal

147. What is the difference between a line and staff function?
(1) A line function is focused on day-to-day operations, while a staff function is focused on planning and strategy
(2) A line function involves direct production activities, while a staff function provides support to line functions
(3) A line function is focused on long-term planning, while a staff function is focused on short-term planning
(4) A line function involves collaboration, while a staff function involves individual contributions

148. What is the process of grouping jobs based on similarities in tasks and skills?
(1) Job analysis
(2) Job design
(3) Job classification
(4) Performance appraisal

149. What is the difference between a functional and divisional structure?
(1) A functional structure is focused on specific products or services, while a divisional structure is focused on departments within the organisation
(2) A functional structure groups jobs based on similarities in tasks and skills, while a divisional structure groups jobs by geographic location
(3) A functional structure involves direct production activities, while a divisional structure provides support to line functions

(4) A functional structure is focused on long-term planning, while a divisional structure is focused on short-term planning

150. What is the purpose of a span of control?

(1) To determine the level of authority within the organisation
(2) To evaluate the performance of employees
(3) To identify the number of subordinates that can be effectively managed by a supervisor
(4) To establish long-term goals for the organisation

151. What is the difference between a tall and flat organisation?

(1) A tall organisation has a wide span of control, while a flat organisation has a narrow span of control
(2) A tall organisation has many levels of management, while a flat organisation has few levels of management
(3) A tall organisation is focused on long-term planning, while a flat organisation is focused on short-term planning
(4) A tall organisation is centralised, while a flat organisation is decentralised

152. What is the process of preparing employees for new responsibilities or promotions?

(1) Training
(2) Job design
(3) Job classification
(4) Performance appraisal

153. What is the purpose of a hierarchy of authority?

(1) To determine the level of authority within the organisation
(2) To evaluate the performance of employees
(3) To establish chain of command and unity of direction
(4) To allocate resources

154. What is the difference between a mechanistic and organic organisation?

(1) A mechanistic organisation is decentralised, while an organic organisation is centralised
(2) A mechanistic organisation has a narrow span of control, while an organic organisation has a wide span of control
(3) A mechanistic organisation is focused on long-term planning, while an organic organisation is focused on short-term planning
(4) A mechanistic organisation is flexible, while an organic organisation is rigid

155. Delegating responsibilities

(1) Planning (2) Organising
(3) Leading (4) Controlling

156. Creating a structure of authority and responsibility

(1) Planning (2) Organising
(3) Leading (4) Controlling

157. Job analysis

(1) Planning (2) Organising
(3) Leading (4) Controlling

158. Job assignments

(1) Planning (2) Organising
(3) Leading (4) Controlling

159. Job classification

(1) Planning (2) Organising
(3) Leading (4) Controlling

160. Training and development

(1) Planning (2) Organising
(3) Leading (4) Controlling

161. Span of control

(1) Planning (2) Organising
(3) Leading (4) Controlling

162. Hierarchy of authority

(1) Planning (2) Organising
(3) Leading (4) Controlling

163. Mechanistic organisation

(1) Planning (2) Organising
(3) Leading (4) Controlling

164. Organic organisation

(1) Planning (2) Organising
(3) Leading (4) Controlling

165. Assertion: Job design is the process of assigning tasks to employees.

Reason: Job design involves breaking down a job into its component parts.

(1) Both assertion and reason are true and the reason is the correct explanation of the assertion.
(2) Both assertion and reason are true but the reason is not the correct explanation of the assertion.
(3) Assertion is true but reason is false.
(4) Assertion is false but reason is true.

166. Assertion: A job description defines the requirements and responsibilities of a job.

Reason: A job description is the same as a job design.

(1) Both assertion and reason are true and the reason is the correct explanation of the assertion.
(2) Both assertion and reason are true but the reason is not the correct explanation of the assertion.
(3) Assertion is true but reason is false.
(4) Assertion is false but reason is true.

167. Assertion: A tall organisation has many levels of management.

Reason: A tall organisation is designed to be flexible.

(1) Both assertion and reason are true and the reason is the correct explanation of the assertion.
(2) Both assertion and reason are true but the reason is not the correct explanation of the assertion.
(3) Assertion is true but reason is false.
(4) Assertion is false but reason is true.

168. Assertion: A mechanistic organisation is rigid.

Reason: A mechanistic organisation is designed to be flexible.

(1) Both assertion and reason are true and the reason is the correct explanation of the assertion.
(2) Both assertion and reason are true but the reason is not the correct explanation of the assertion.
(3) Assertion is true but reason is false.
(4) Assertion is false but reason is true.

169. Assertion: Decentralisation involves decision making at the lower levels of the organisation.

Reason: Decentralisation is the same as a tall organisation.

(1) Both assertion and reason are true and the reason is the correct explanation of the assertion.
(2) Both assertion and reason are true but the reason is not the correct explanation of the assertion.
(3) Assertion is true but reason is false.
(4) Assertion is false but reason is true.

170. What is staffing?

(1) The process of determining the wealth of an organisation
(2) The process of recruiting and selecting employees
(3) The process of establishing goals and objectives
(4) The process of allocating resources

171. What is the purpose of staffing?

(1) To establish a structure of authority
(2) To create a culture of innovation
(3) To ensure that the organisation is staffed with qualified individuals
(4) To allocate resources

172. What is the difference between recruitment and selection?

(1) Recruitment involves advertising job openings, while selection involves evaluating and choosing candidates
(2) Recruitment involves evaluating and choosing candidates, while selection involves advertising job openings
(3) Recruitment is the same as selection
(4) Recruitment and selection are not related to staffing

173. What is the purpose of job analysis?

(1) To evaluate the performance of employees
(2) To create a structure of authority
(3) To define the responsibilities and requirements of a job

(4) To establish long-term goals for the organisation

174. What is the difference between internal and external recruitment?

(1) Internal recruitment involves recruiting candidates from outside the organisation, while external recruitment involves recruiting candidates within the organisation

(2) Internal recruitment involves promoting or transferring employees from within the organisation, while external recruitment involves recruiting candidates from outside the organisation

(3) Internal and external recruitment are the same

(4) Internal recruitment is focused on short-term goals, while external recruitment is focused on long-term goals

175. What is the difference between a structured and unstructured interview?

(1) A structured interview involves pre-determined questions, while an unstructured interview involves random questions

(2) A structured interview involves random questions, while an unstructured interview involves pre-determined questions

(3) A structured interview is standardised and formal, while an unstructured interview is informal

(4) A structured interview involves collaboration, while an unstructured interview involves individual contributions

176. What is the purpose of a selection test?

(1) To evaluate the performance of employees

(2) To assess the skills and abilities of candidates

(3) To establish long-term goals for the organisation

(4) To allocate resources

177. What is the difference between a cognitive and personality test?

(1) A cognitive test assesses personality traits, while a personality test assesses cognitive abilities

(2) A cognitive test assesses cognitive abilities, while a personality test assesses personality traits

(3) A cognitive test and a personality test are the same

(4) A cognitive test and a personality test are not related to staffing

178. What is the difference between a reference check and a background check?

(1) A reference check involves verifying a candidate's work history, while a background check involves verifying a candidate's criminal record

(2) A reference check involves verifying a candidate's criminal record, while a background check involves verifying a candidate's work history

(3) A reference check and a background check are the same

(4) A reference check and a background check are not related to staffing

179. What is the purpose of an orientation program?

(1) To evaluate the performance of employees

(2) To provide training and development opportunities

(3) To familiarise new employees with the organisation and its culture

(4) To allocate resources

180. What is the difference between internal and external equity?

(1) Internal equity involves equal pay for equal work within the organisation, while external equity involves equal pay for equal work with other organisations

(2) Internal equity involves equal pay for equal work with other organisations, while external equity involves equal pay for equal work within the organisation

(3) Internal equity and external equity are the same

(4) Internal equity is focused on long-term goals, while external equity is focused on short-term goals

181. What is the difference between a job specification and a job description?

(1) A job specification defines the responsibilities and requirements of a job, while a job description defines the qualifications and skills of a candidate
(2) A job specification and a job description are the same
(3) A job specification focuses on long-term goals, while a job description focuses on short-term goals
(4) A job specification focuses on salary and compensation, while a job description focuses on job duties

182. What is the purpose of a career development program?
(1) To evaluate the performance of employees
(2) To provide training and development opportunities that prepare employees for future roles and opportunities within the organisation
(3) To establish long-term goals for the organisation
(4) To allocate resources

183. What is the difference between a promotion and a transfer?
(1) A promotion involves moving an employee to a different department, while a transfer involves moving an employee to a higher position within the same department
(2) A promotion involves moving an employee to a higher position within the same department, while a transfer involves moving an employee to a different department
(3) A promotion and a transfer are the same
(4) A promotion is focused on short-term goals, while a transfer is focused on long-term goals

184. What is the purpose of a performance appraisal?
(1) To allocate resources
(2) To evaluate the performance of employees
(3) To establish long-term goals for the organisation
(4) To provide training and development opportunities

185. Assertion: The main purpose of staffing is to create a culture of innovation within the organisation.
Reason: Staffing focuses on recruiting and selecting employees.
(1) Both assertion and reason are true and the reason is the correct explanation of the assertion.
(2) Both assertion and reason are true but the reason is not the correct explanation of the assertion.
(3) Assertion is true but reason is false.
(4) Assertion is false but reason is true.

186. Assertion: Job analysis is the process of assigning tasks to employees.
Reason: Job analysis involves breaking down a job into its component parts.
(1) Both assertion and reason are true and the reason is the correct explanation of the assertion.
(2) Both assertion and reason are true but the reason is not the correct explanation of the assertion.
(3) Assertion is true but reason is false.
(4) Assertion is false but reason is true.

187. Assertion: A structured interview is informal.
Reason: A structured interview involves predetermined questions.
(1) Both assertion and reason are true and the reason is the correct explanation of the assertion.
(2) Both assertion and reason are true but the reason is not the correct explanation of the assertion.
(3) Assertion is true but reason is false.
(4) Assertion is false but reason is true.

188. Assertion: External recruitment involves recruiting candidates within the organisation.
Reason: External recruitment involves promoting or transferring employees from within the organisation.

(1) Both assertion and reason are true and the reason is the correct explanation of the assertion.
(2) Both assertion and reason are true but the reason is not the correct explanation of the assertion.
(3) Assertion is true but reason is false.
(4) Assertion is false but reason is true.

189. Assertion: Performance appraisal is the process of allocating resources.
Reason: Performance appraisal involves evaluating the performance of employees.
(1) Both assertion and reason are true and the reason is the correct explanation of the assertion.
(2) Both assertion and reason are true but the reason is not the correct explanation of the assertion.
(3) Assertion is true but reason is false.
(4) Assertion is false but reason is true.

190. Which of the following is not a function of directing?
(1) Delegation (2) Coordination
(3) Planning (4) Supervision

191. Which of the following is not an element of leadership?
(1) Vision (2) Responsibility
(3) Control (4) Inspiration

192. Which of the following is not a step in the controlling process?
(1) Setting standards
(2) Measuring performance
(3) Adjusting systems
(4) Setting goals

193. Which of the following is not a type of control?
(1) Feedback control
(2) Feedforward control
(3) Concurrent control
(4) Prediction control

194. Which of the following best describes the function of directing?
(1) Planning and organising work activities
(2) Selecting employees for specific positions
(3) Motivating and leading employees to accomplish organisational objectives
(4) Measuring and evaluating job performance

195. What is the primary focus of motivating employees?
(1) Encouraging teamwork
(2) Enhancing creativity
(3) Increasing engagement and productivity
(4) Optimising technological tools and systems

196. What is the essence of effective delegation?
(1) Keeping control over all tasks and decision-making
(2) Micro-managing employees to avoid errors
(3) Transferring responsibility and authority while retaining accountability
(4) Avoiding communication and collaboration with employees

197. Which of the following is not a key element of effective communication?
(1) Clear and concise messaging
(2) Active listening
(3) Avoiding feedback and follow-up
(4) Understanding the audience

198. Which of the following is not a key trait of effective leaders?
(1) Integrity and ethical behaviour
(2) Autocratic decision-making
(3) Vision and foresight
(4) Empathy and emotional intelligence

199. What is the primary aim of controlling in management?
(1) To exert power and authority over employees
(2) To maximise profits at all costs
(3) To regulate and monitor performance against established standards
(4) To create a culture of secrecy and mistrust

200. Which of the following is not a basic step in the control process?
(1) Establishing standards
(2) Collecting data
(3) Forecasting performance
(4) Taking corrective action

201. Which of the following is not an advantage of feedforward control?
(1) Early detection of problems
(2) Enhanced problem-solving capabilities
(3) Reduced costs and increased efficiency
(4) Increased motivation and morale

202. Which of the following is not a primary goal of feedback control?
(1) To identify deviations from planned performance
(2) To take corrective action as needed
(3) To enhance employee skills and abilities
(4) To maintain established standards of performance

203. What is the main advantage of concurrent control?
(1) Enhanced collaboration and teamwork
(2) Increased motivation and job satisfaction
(3) Swift identification and correction of problems
(4) Improved communication and transparency

204. What is the primary goal of prediction control?
(1) To forecast long-term trends and future performance
(2) To optimise the use of technology and systems
(3) To eliminate the need for feedback control
(4) To establish effective performance standards

205. Which of the following is not a key attribute of effective delegation?
(1) Recognising employee strengths and abilities
(2) Clearly communicating expectations and outcomes
(3) Retaining all decision-making and control over tasks
(4) Ensuring accountability at all levels

206. Which of the following is not a benefit of effective communication?
(1) Increased employee engagement and satisfaction
(2) Enhanced teamwork and collaboration
(3) Greater clarity and understanding of expectations
(4) Improved productivity and performance

207. What is the main disadvantage of autocratic leadership?
(1) Reduced employee engagement and motivation
(2) Inadequate control over employee behaviour
(3) Lack of effective decision-making and prioritisation
(4) Decreased employee satisfaction and morale

208. Which of the following is not a primary goal of effective leadership?
(1) Encouraging diversity and inclusion
(2) Fostering a culture of innovation
(3) Maximising profits at all costs
(4) Aligning employee goals with organisational objectives

209. What is the main advantage of using data in the controlling process?
(1) Enhanced decision-making capabilities
(2) Increased employee engagement and productivity
(3) Reduced need for feedback and follow-up
(4) Improved communication and collaboration

210. Which of the following is not a primary element of the directing function?
(1) Delegation (2) Coordination
(3) Controlling (4) Planning

211. Which of the following is not a critical step in the motivating process?

(1) Recognition and reward
(2) Establishing clear goals and expectations
(3) Fostering a positive work culture
(4) Encouraging employee feedback and input

212. What is the primary goal of coordination in management?
(1) To establish effective communication channels
(2) To optimise the use of technology and systems
(3) To ensure all activities and efforts are aligned towards achieving organisational objectives
(4) To exert control and authority over employees

213. What is the primary goal of the controlling function?
(1) To control and regulate employee behaviour
(2) To forecast future trends and opportunities
(3) To monitor and adjust performance against established standards
(4) To establish broad-based organisational goals and objectives

214. What is the main disadvantage of autocratic leadership?
(1) Decreased employee satisfaction and motivation
(2) Increased employee engagement and productivity
(3) Enhanced decision-making capabilities
(4) Reduced need for feedback and follow-up

215. Assertion: One of the primary goals of directing is to motivate and inspire employees to achieve organisational objectives.
Reason: Effective leadership is essential in communicating organisational goals and expectations to employees and fulfills a critical role in the directing function.
(1) Both assertion and reason are true and the reason is the correct explanation of the assertion.
(2) Both assertion and reason are true but the reason is not the correct explanation of the assertion.
(3) Assertion is true but reason is false.
(4) Assertion is false but reason is true.

216. Assertion: The directing function is primarily focused on establishing effective communication channels between employees and management.
Reason: Effective communication is critical to ensure that employees understand their roles and objectives and are motivated and equipped to achieve them.
(1) Both assertion and reason are true and the reason is the correct explanation of the assertion.
(2) Both assertion and reason are true but the reason is not the correct explanation of the assertion.
(3) Assertion is true but reason is false.
(4) Assertion is false but reason is true.

217. Assertion: The main disadvantage of autocratic leadership is decreased employee satisfaction and motivation.
Reason: Autocratic leaders tend to retain control over decision-making processes and tend not to consider the input of employees in decision-making processes.
(1) Both assertion and reason are true and the reason is the correct explanation of the assertion.
(2) Both assertion and reason are true but the reason is not the correct explanation of the assertion.
(3) Assertion is true but reason is false.
(4) Assertion is false but reason is true.

218. Assertion: The controlling function is focused on regulating and monitoring performance against established standards.
Reason: The controlling function is comprised of four stages - setting standards, measuring performance, taking corrective action, and adjusting systems.
(1) Both assertion and reason are true and the reason is the correct explanation of the assertion.

(2) Both assertion and reason are true but the reason is not the correct explanation of the assertion.
(3) Assertion is true but reason is false.
(4) Assertion is false but reason is true.

219. **Assertion:** The main goal of feedforward control is to take corrective action in response to deviations from planned performance.
Reason: Feedforward control is focused on predicting potential problems and taking action to prevent them before they occur.
(1) Both assertion and reason are true and the reason is the correct explanation of the assertion.
(2) Both assertion and reason are true but the reason is not the correct explanation of the assertion.
(3) Assertion is true but reason is false.
(4) Assertion is false but reason is true.

220. Which of the following is not a key element of the coordinating function of management?
(1) Collaboration
(2) Communication
(3) Delegation
(4) Planning

221. What is the primary goal of coordinating work activities in the workplace?
(1) To ensure all employees are working equally hard
(2) To optimise the use of resources and minimise waste
(3) To eliminate the need for feedback and follow-up
(4) To exert control and authority over employees

222. What is the main advantage of effective collaboration in the workplace?
(1) Enhanced use of technological tools and systems
(2) Increased employee engagement and motivation
(3) Improved communication and transparency
(4) Increased control and authority over employees

223. Which of the following is not a key element of effective delegation?
(1) Setting clear expectations and goals
(2) Ensuring accountability at all levels
(3) Retaining all decision-making and control over tasks
(4) Recognising employee strengths and abilities

224. What is the primary goal of the coordination function in management?
(1) To establish effective communication channels
(2) To optimise the use of resources and minimise waste
(3) To ensure all work activities are aligned towards achieving organisational objectives
(4) To exert control and authority over employees

225. What is the main disadvantage of poor coordination in the workplace?
(1) Decreased employee engagement and motivation
(2) Increased waste and inefficiency
(3) Enhanced communication and transparency
(4) Increased control and authority over employees

226. What is the primary goal of effective communication in management?
(1) To establish clear expectations and goals
(2) To exert control and authority over employees
(3) To eliminate the need for feedback and follow-up
(4) To optimise the use of technological tools and systems

227. Which of the following is not a benefit of effective collaboration in the workplace?
(1) Enhanced communication and transparency
(2) Increased employee engagement and motivation
(3) Increased waste and inefficiency
(4) Improved problem-solving capabilities

228. What is the primary goal of effective delegation in the workplace?
(1) Retaining all decision-making and control over tasks
(2) Recognising employee strengths and abilities
(3) Transferring responsibility and authority while retaining accountability
(4) Reducing the need for collaboration and teamwork

229. What is the main disadvantage of poor communication in the workplace?
(1) Decreased employee engagement and motivation
(2) Enhanced communication and transparency
(3) Increased waste and inefficiency
(4) Increased control and authority over employees

230. Which of the following is not a key ingredient of successful collaboration in the workplace?
(1) Trust and mutual respect
(2) Active listening
(3) Micro-managing employees to avoid errors
(4) Recognition of individual strengths and abilities

231. Which of the following is not a primary goal of the coordinating function of management?
(1) Establishing effective communication channels
(2) Ensuring alignment of work activities towards achieving organisational objectives
(3) Maximising profits at all costs
(4) Optimising the use of resources and minimising waste

232. What is the primary focus of effective communication in the workplace?
(1) Establishing clear expectations and goals
(2) Exerting control and authority over employees
(3) Eliminating the need for feedback and follow-up
(4) Optimising the use of technological tools and systems

233. Which of the following is not a benefit of effective delegation in the workplace?
(1) Increased employee engagement and motivation
(2) Improved teamwork and collaboration
(3) Enhanced control and authority over employees
(4) Reduced need for feedback and follow-up

234. What is the primary goal of effective collaboration in the workplace?
(1) Optimising the use of technological tools and systems
(2) Minimising waste and inefficiency
(3) Achieving shared organisational objectives
(4) Exerting control and authority over employees

235. Which of the following is not a key element of effective management of work activities?
(1) Collaboration
(2) Communication
(3) Micro-managing employees to avoid errors
(4) Planning

236. What is the primary focus of effective delegation in the workplace?
(1) Maintaining control and authority over employees
(2) Recognising employee strengths and abilities
(3) Transferring responsibility and authority while retaining accountability
(4) Eliminating the need for feedback and follow-up

237. Which of the following is not a benefit of effective coordination in the workplace?
(1) Minimising waste and inefficiency
(2) Enhancing problem-solving capabilities
(3) Decreasing employee engagement and motivation
(4) Establishing effective communication channels

238. What is the main advantage of effective communication in the workplace?

(1) Increased control and authority over employees
(2) Enhanced teamwork and collaboration
(3) Improved productivity and performance
(4) Reduced need for feedback and follow-up

239. Which of the following is not a benefit of effective delegation in the workplace?

(1) Increased employee engagement and motivation
(2) Improved decision-making capabilities
(3) Retaining all control and decision-making over tasks
(4) Ensuring accountability at all levels

240. What is the primary goal of the coordinating function in management?

(1) Enhancing employee engagement and motivation
(2) Minimising waste and inefficiency
(3) Ensuring all work activities are aligned towards achieving organisational objectives
(4) Exerting control and authority over employees

241. What is the primary goal of effective communication in the workplace?

(1) Establishing clear expectations and goals
(2) Exerting control and authority over employees
(3) Eliminating the need for feedback and follow-up
(4) Optimising the use of technological tools and systems

242. Which of the following is not a key element of effective delegation in the workplace?

(1) Setting clear expectations and goals
(2) Ensuring accountability at all levels
(3) Micro-managing employees to avoid errors
(4) Recognising employee strengths and abilities

243. What is the main disadvantage of poor collaboration in the workplace?

(1) Increased employee engagement and motivation
(2) Increased waste and inefficiency
(3) Enhanced communication and transparency
(4) Increased control and authority over employees

244. What is the primary goal of effective coordination in management?

(1) Maximising profits at all costs
(2) Achieving shared organisational objectives
(3) Exerting control and authority over employees
(4) Optimising the use of resources and minimising waste

ANSWER KEY

1. (1) **2.** (4) **3.** (2) **4.** (4) **5.** (3) **6.** (4) **7.** (4) **8.** (4) **9.** (4) **10.** (3)
11. (3) **12.** (3) **13.** (3) **14.** (4) **15.** (2) **16.** (4) **17.** (3) **18.** (4) **19.** (2) **20.** (4)
21. (2) **22.** (4) **23.** (1) **24.** (4) **25.** (1) **26.** (1) **27.** (3) **28.** (2) **29.** (4) **30.** (2)
31. (2) **32.** (4) **33.** (2) **34.** (4) **35.** (1) **36.** (4) **37.** (1) **38.** (2) **39.** (4) **40.** (4)
41. (4) **42.** (2) **43.** (4) **44.** (4) **45.** (2) **46.** (1) **47.** (4) **48.** (1) **49.** (4) **50.** (2)
51. (4) **52.** (1) **53.** (4) **54.** (2) **55.** (3) **56.** (1) **57.** (4) **58.** (1) **59.** (2) **60.** (2)
61. (4) **62.** (1) **63.** (1) **64.** (3) **65.** (4) **66.** (3) **67.** (1) **68.** (2) **69.** (3) **70.** (4)
71. (4) **72.** (1) **73.** (3) **74.** (3) **75.** (4) **76.** (1) **77.** (4) **78.** (2) **79.** (3) **80.** (4)
81. (4) **82.** (3) **83.** (2) **84.** (3) **85.** (4) **86.** (1) **87.** (4) **88.** (4) **89.** (4) **90.** (1)
91. (4) **92.** (3) **93.** (2) **94.** (2) **95.** (2) **96.** (3) **97.** (2) **98.** (3) **99.** (4) **100.** (1)
101. (4) **102.** (1) **103.** (4) **104.** (4) **105.** (1) **106.** (1) **107.** (4) **108.** (1) **109.** (1) **110.** (3)
111. (4) **112.** (4) **113.** (3) **114.** (1) **115.** (1) **116.** (3) **117.** (3) **118.** (4) **119.** (3) **120.** (3)
121. (1) **122.** (1) **123.** (1) **124.** (1) **125.** (1) **126.** (2) **127.** (1) **128.** (4) **129.** (2) **130.** (1)
131. (4) **132.** (2) **133.** (3) **134.** (4) **135.** (1) **136.** (1) **137.** (1) **138.** (3) **139.** (1) **140.** (3)
141. (3) **142.** (3) **143.** (3) **144.** (2) **145.** (3) **146.** (3) **147.** (2) **148.** (3) **149.** (2) **150.** (3)
151. (2) **152.** (1) **153.** (3) **154.** (2) **155.** (3) **156.** (2) **157.** (2) **158.** (2) **159.** (2) **160.** (3)
161. (2) **162.** (2) **163.** (2) **164.** (2) **165.** (1) **166.** (1) **167.** (4) **168.** (3) **169.** (1) **170.** (2)
171. (3) **172.** (1) **173.** (3) **174.** (2) **175.** (3) **176.** (2) **177.** (2) **178.** (1) **179.** (3) **180.** (2)
181. (1) **182.** (2) **183.** (2) **184.** (2) **185.** (4) **186.** (4) **187.** (4) **188.** (2) **189.** (3) **190.** (4)
191. (4) **192.** (4) **193.** (4) **194.** (3) **195.** (3) **196.** (3) **197.** (4) **198.** (4) **199.** (3) **200.** (4)
201. (4) **202.** (3) **203.** (3) **204.** (4) **205.** (4) **206.** (3) **207.** (4) **208.** (4) **209.** (4) **210.** (4)
211. (2) **212.** (3) **213.** (3) **214.** (1) **215.** (1) **216.** (1) **217.** (1) **218.** (1) **219.** (3) **220.** (2)
221. (2) **222.** (3) **223.** (3) **224.** (3) **225.** (2) **226.** (1) **227.** (3) **228.** (3) **229.** (1) **230.** (3)
231. (3) **232.** (1) **233.** (3) **234.** (3) **235.** (d) **236.** (3) **237.** (3) **238.** (3) **239.** (3) **240.** (3)
241. (1) **242.** (3) **243.** (2) **244.** (2)

UNIT 2

HUMAN RESOURCE MANAGEMENT

Syllabus

- Conceptual framework, Human Resource Planning, Job Analysis, Recruitment, Selection, Placement, Induction, Training and Development, Performance Management, Job Evaluation, Compensation Management, Employee Benefits and Incentives, Managing Career.
- **New Trends in HRM:** Changing environment of HRM and contemporary challenges, Emerging HRM Concepts.

HUMAN RESOURCE DEVELOPMENT

The emphasis on proper and effective human resources management has increased in the recent times. It has been identified as an important factor in the successful management of an organisation.

Human resource development in the organisational context is a process by which the employees of an organisation are helped in a continuous, planned way to:

(1) Acquire or sharpen capabilities required to perform various functions associated with their present or expected future roles.

(2) Develop their general capabilities as individuals and discover and exploit their own inner potentials for their own and organisational development purpose.

(3) Develop an organisational culture in which supervisor – subordinate relationship, team work and collaboration among sub-units are strong and contribute to the professional well being, motivation and pride of employees.

(4) Develop technical, managerial and behavioural knowledge, skills and abilities, and mould the values, beliefs, attitude necessary to perform present and future roles by realizing highest human potential with a view to contribute positively to the organisational, group, individual and social goals.

Concept of Human Resource Management

The term 'human resources' may be defined as the total knowledge, talents and aptitudes of an organisation's workforce, as well as the values, attitudes, approaches and beliefs of the individuals involved in the affairs of the organisation. It is the sum, total or aggregate of inherent abilities, acquired knowledge and skills represented by the talents and aptitudes of the persons employed in an organisation.

Several terms have been used by various management thinkers to represent human resources. These includes 'personnel', 'people at work', 'human resource', 'staff' and 'employees'. Whatever may be the term used, the human resources of an organisation include all individuals engaged in various organisational activities at different levels. Leon C. Megginson says, "From the national point of view, human resources may be defined as the knowledge, skills, creative abilities, talents and aptitudes obtained in the population; whereas from the viewpoint of the individual enterprise, they represent the total of the inherent abilities, acquired knowledge and skills as exemplified in the talents and aptitudes of its employees". HRM is a process, which consists of four main activities, namely acquisitions, development, motivation, as well as maintenance of human resources.

According to the Institute of Personnel Management (U.K.), "Personnel management is an integral but distinctive part of management, concerned with people at work and their relationships within the enterprise. It seeks to bring together into an effective organisation the men and women who staff the enterprise, enabling each to make his/her best contribution to its success, both as a member of a working group and as an individual. It seeks to provide relationships within the enterprise that are conducive both to effective work and human satisfaction."

According to Flippo, "Personnel management is the planning, organising, compensation, integration and maintenance of people for the purpose of contributing to organisational, individual and societal goals.

According to Breach, "Personnel Management is that part which is primarily concerned with human resource of organisation.

Perspectives of Human Resource Management

The growth of human resource management in United State of America was evolutionary in nature. It took place because of the voluntary efforts of the employers. But in countries like India, human resource management grew because of compulsions made by the Government. In 1931, the Royal Commission on Labour recommended the abolition of Jobber system and the appointment of labour officers in the industries to look after recruitment and welfare of employees. In 1948, the Factories Act made it obligatory for certain industrial enterprises to appoint welfare officers.

The scope of human resource management has expanded considerably throughout the world. Over the last forty years or so, new techniques axnd styles of managing the human resources have been developed as a result of the researches and experiences in the field. The task of the human manager is not confined only to the recruitment of workers, but also to looking after their welfare and handling their grievances.

Under the influence of technological development, organisational complexities are growing. The impact on the work, working methods, work rules, tools, equipment, etc. is inevitable. Jobs have become more complex and need specialised skills and professionals. As a result of this, emphasis is being given to the training and development aspects. In order to meet the growing needs of such human resources, management institutes, universities and other bodies have started training and executive development programmes.

Human management is no longer restricted only to the wage earners in the factories. It has become equally important in offices, sales organisations, hospitals, research and development institutions and in the ranks of management itself. Human management is not needed by private industry alone. No-profit institutions, government departments and armed services also need human management for better employer-employee relations.

The other terms used frequently in discussion of personnel problems and techniques are "labour relations" and "industrial relations". Sometimes, these are used interchangeably with "personnel management or administration", but it is useful to distinguish between them. The term "labour relations" refers primarily to the relations between management and unionised labour. The subject matter of labour relations includes the negotiation of contracts with unions and day-to-day relations with union leaders and business agents in the handling of differences arising under the contract, arbitration and government regulations of the terms and conditions of employment.

The use of the term 'industrial relations' as synonymous with 'human resource/personnel management' has been very common in United States of America.

In India, the field of personnel management has three branches, viz. (i) personnel administration, (ii) industrial relations and (iii) labour welfare. Personnel administration deals with the administrative aspects of personnel functions such as recruitment, selection, placement, promotion, transfer, wages and incentives, etc. Industrial relations deals broadly with employer-employee relationship, negotiations and collective bargaining, settlement of grievance and disputes, joint consultation. Labour welfare programmes seek to improve the working and living conditions of the employees by the provision of facilities such as crèches, canteen, housing, recreation, education etc.

NATURE OF HUMAN RESOURCE MANAGEMENT

The nature of the human resource management has been highlighted in its following features :

(1) Inherent part of management
(2) Pervasive function
(3) Basic to all functional areas
(4) People centred
(5) Personal activities of functions
(6) Continuous process
(7) Based on human relations

In the Indian context, these three areas have developed some kind of identity of their own and have been recognised as integral parts of the broad field of personnel management. However, these three are not watertight compartments. This kind of division has facilitated convenient grouping of personnel functions. It is worth noting that these three groups of personnel functions have been generally dealt with by officers with three different sets of designations. The first have been usually dealt with by officers designated as personnel officers, while the second and third are handled generally by those with designations of labour officer and welfare officer respectively.

Objectives

The objectives of Human Resource Management are :

(a) To provide attractive, equitable incentives, rewards, benefits, social security measures, to ensure retention of competent employees.
(b) To provide, create, utilise and motivate employees to accomplish organisational goals.
(c) To maintain high morale, encourage value system and create environment of trust, mutuality of interests.
(d) To create opportunities, to provide facilities, necessary motivation to individuals and groups for their growth with the growth of the organisation by training and development.
(e) To secure integration of individuals and groups in securing organisational effectiveness.
(f) To ensure that, there is no threat of unemployment, inequalities, adopting a policy recognising merit and employee contribution and conditions for stability of employment.
(g) To provide opportunities for communication, expression, participation, appreciation, recognition and provide fair efficient leadership.
(h) To create a sense and feeling of belongingness, team spirit and encourage suggestions from employees.
(i) To develop dyadic relationship between each employee and every supervisor.
(j) To develop the overall health and self renewing capabilities.

Scope

All major activities in the working life of the employee from the time of his entry into the organisation until he leaves, come under the purview of human resource management.

The most important activities undertaken are :

(1) **Planning**, job design, job analysis, procurement, recruitment, selection, induction, placement, training and development.
(2) **Compensation**, rewards, benefits, retrial benefits, medical and health care.
(3) **Motivation.** Motivational aids, bonus, incentives, career development, growth, decision making, delegation of authority and power, promotion etc.
(4) **Employee Relations.** Grievance handling, participation, collective bargaining and other aspects of cordial relations conducive to mutual understanding and trust.
(5) Employee evaluation and performance improvement, Human Resource Audit and Human Resource Accounting.
(6) Appraisal of performance of employees and taking corrective steps such as transfer from one job to another.
(7) Social security and welfare of employees.

HUMAN RESOURCE PLANNING

Human Resource Planning is the process by which a management determines how an organisation should move from its current human resource position to its desired human resource position. Through planning, a management strives to have the right number and the right kind of people at the right places, at the right time, to do things which result in both the organisation and the individual receiving the maximum long range benefits. Of all the "M.S." in management (*i.e.*, the management of materials, machines, methods, money, motive power) the most important is "M" for men or human resources. It is the most valuable asset of an organisation. It is in fact an important economic resource, covering all human resources – organised or unorganised, employed or capable of employment, working at all levels – supervisors, executives; government employees, 'blue' and 'white' collar workers, managerial, scientific, engineering, technical, skilled or unskilled persons, who are employed in creating, designing, developing, managing and operating productive and service enterprises and other economic activities.

1. **Coleman** has defined Human Resource Planning as "the process of determining manpower requirements and the mans for meeting those requirements in order to carry out the integrated plan of the organisation.
2. According to **Wikstrom**, Human Resource Planning consists of a series of activities, viz.
   (a) Forecasting future manpower requirements, either in terms of mathematical projections of trends in the economic environment and developments in industry, or in terms of judgemental estimates based upon the specific future plans of a company;
   (b) Making an inventory of present manpower resources and assessing the extent to which these resources are employed optimally;
   (c) Anticipating manpower problems by projecting present resources into the future and comparing them with the forecast of requirements to determine their adequacy, both quantitatively and qualitatively; and
   (d) Planning the necessary programmes of requirements, selection, training, development, utilisation, transfer, promotion, motivation and compensation to ensure that future manpower requirements are properly met.

Human resource planning is an important tool of Human Resources Management as it helps in the following ways :

1. Human resource planning results in reduced labour costs as it helps the management to anticipate shortages and / or surpluses of human resource and correct these imbalances before they become unmanageable and expensive.
2. It is a better basis for planning employee development that is designed to make optimum use of workers skills within the organisation.
3. It enables identification of the gaps of the existing human resource so that corrective training could be imparted. Thus, the training programme becomes more effective.
4. It leads to improvement in the overall business planning process.
5. It helps in formulating managerial succession plan as a part of the replacement planning process which is necessitated when job change plans for managers are formulated. Besides, this exercise would provide enough lead time for identifying and developing managers to move up the corporate ladder.
6. It leads to a greater awareness of the importance of sound human resource management throughout the organisation.
7. It serves as a tool to evaluate the effect of alternative human resource actions and policies.
8. It formulate transfer and promotion policies.

Process of Human Resource Planning

The process of human resource planning is one of the most crucial, complex and continuing managerial functions which embraces organisational development, management development, career planning and succession planning. The process has gained importance in India with the increase in the size of business enterprises, complex production technology and the adoption of professional management technique.

The process of human resource planning involves the following steps :

(1) Determination of objectives of human resource planning
(2) Current human resource inventory
(3) Demand forecasting
(4) Job requirement
(5) Employment plan
(6) Training and development programme
(7) Appraisal of human resource planning

Human resource planning is a continuous process. The manager responsible for human resource planning has to be concerned with all the steps at all times. He may have to revise employment plan and training and development plan and training and development programme from time to time depending upon the changes in circumstances such as sudden changes in volume of production, unexpected high rate of labour turnover, obsolescence of existing skills and so on. A brief explanation of the steps in the Human Resource Planning process is given below :

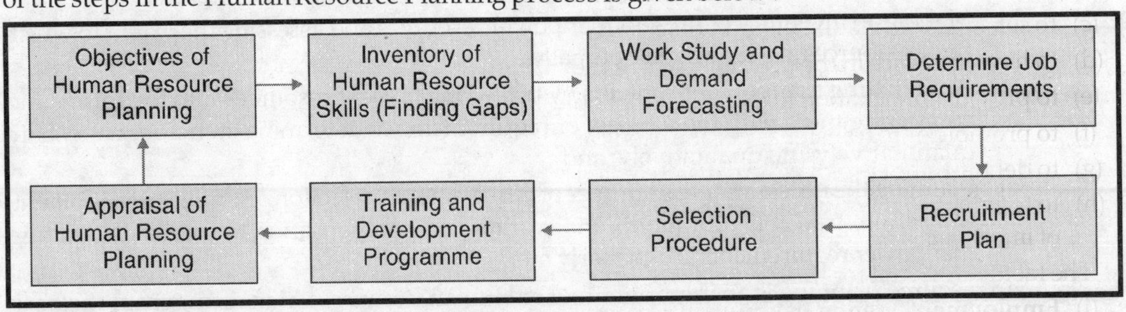

(1) Determination of Objectives of Human Resource Planning

Human resources planning fulfils individual, organisational and national goals, but the ultimate mission or purpose is to relate future human resources to future enterprise needs so as to maximise the future return on investment in human resources. In effect, the main purpose is one of matching or fitting employee abilities to enterprise requirements, with an emphasis on future instead of present arrangements. The future organisation structure and job design should be made clear and changes in the organisation structure should be examined so as to anticipate its manpower requirements. The objectives may be laid down for a short term (*i.e.*, for one year). For example, the short-term objective may be to hire 25 persons from Scheduled Tribes or Backward Classes for purpose of training. The long-term objective may be to start a new industry, to expand the market, to produce a new product, to develop its own sales force rather than depend on distributors, or to have minority group members eventually in position of middle and upper management cadres.

(2) Current Human Resource Inventory

Analysis of current human resource supply may be undertaken by department, by function, by occupation, or by level of skill or qualifications. Appropriate adjustments in these would need to be made in the light of an foreseeable change in weekly hours of work, holidays, leave entitlements, etc.

It may be noted that assessment of demand for the operative personnel presents less problems of uncertainty and current human resource supply can be adjusted accordingly. But projections of human resource requirements for supervisory and managerial levels present a complex problem because the required talents are not available at a short notice. This explains the need to ascertain the present human resource inventory in the enterprise. This will also help in drawing recruitment and development plans to meet the needs of certain skills in the future.

Systematic steps must be taken in order to ensure that a reservoir of talent is available when vacancies occur. The search for talented employees in the organisation must be continuous. To be sure that available talent has been included, the inventory of various skills in the enterprise should be indexed. Detailed bio-data of each individual included in the human resource inventory must be obtained separately for the purpose of human resource planning. This record will provide the foundation for a programme of individual development. It will also reveal the scarcity or non-availability of certain talents for which outside sources of human resource may be adopted.

(3) Demand Forecasting

Forecasting human resource demand is the process of estimating the future human resource requirement of right quality and right number. A proper forecast of human resources required in the future (say, after one year, two years, three years and so on) must be attempted.

The main steps involved in HRP process are :

(a) to determine and to identify present and prospective needs of human resource,
(b) to discover and recruit the recruit the required number of persons,
(c) to select the right number and type from the available people,
(d) to hire and place in the positions which they are qualified,
(e) to provide information to the selected people about the nature of work assigned to than,
(f) to promote or to transfer as per the needs and the performance of employees.
(g) to denote if the employees are disinterested or their performance is not upto the mark.
(h) to terminate if they are not needed or their performance is below standard and shows no hopes of improvement.

The factors relevant for human resource forecasting are as follows :

(i) **Employment Trends.** The human resource planning committee at the corporate level should make an examination of number of the employees on the payroll during the past five years to know the trend within each group. With the help of this, it would be possible to determine whether a particular group has been stable or unstable and whether it has been expanding or contracting.

(ii) **Replacement Needs.** The need for replacement arises due to death, retirement, resignation and termination of employees. The examination of replacement needs may relate to specific human resource groups: supervisory, skilled, clerical, unskilled, etc. For some groups like managerial or supervisory, it is very difficult to predict the needs. One of the major difficulties involved in predicting the need for managerial skill is that the management development cycle takes a long time. So the needs for managerial human resource should be anticipated sufficiently in advance. Forecasts of human resource may be based to a great extent on the analysis of historical data. It is presumed that the factors causing past occurrences will also play a similar role in the future. But these data must be adjusted in the light of other known information about the future. Certain losses of key personnel can be predicted with a substantial degree of accuracy. These include losses from retirement, physical disabilities and cases of sub-standard performance. But retirement is the most common type of anticipated separation which gives rise to the need for replacement. This category would include all employees who will reach the normal retirement age during the period under consideration. In the same way, losses from known physical disabilities and for substandard performance can be predicted. There will, of course, be other losses of personnel. This estimate may also be based upon past experience. An examination of the number of deaths, discharges, releases and quits during the last five years may provide a basis for projecting the need for replacement in the future because of these reasons. Another important factor influencing the replacement needs is transfer of some employees to other departments of the organisation or promotion of some employees to higher jobs. This number can be estimated on the basis of a review of the persons promoted or transferred during the previous years and the records of performance of various employees during the past years.

(iii) **Productivity.** An important area to which the human resource planning is related is the improvement in productivity. Gains in productivity add to the growth potential of the organisation and can make possible healthy wage increase. Gains in productivity will also influence the requirements of human resource.

Planning for productivity gains has several aspects. The first and the important one relates to affecting gains by improvements in existing human resource utilisation. Current levels of utilisation and indications about the needed improvement can be obtained by the application of various analytical techniques of industrial engineering or work study such as activity charts, flow charts, multiple activity charts, and activity sampling studies and so on. Methods improvement techniques help reduce work content. Conceptually, similar approaches aimed at upgrading management performance help secure productivity gains at the managerial level.

The second aspect relates to installation of more productive tools, equipments or processes. Any anticipated change due to the introduction of automation will affect human resource needs in the plants as well as in the divisional offices. The human resource planning experts should attempt to learn about such changes with sufficient time to appraise their possible impact on the number and kinds of employees required in the future.

The last aspect relates to the matching of skills with the requirements of the jobs. Job analysis techniques facilitate a clear specification of the skills and experience requirements of jobs. The immediate products of this analysis are job description and job specification.

(iv) **Growth and Expansion.** Another aspect relevant for human resource planning is personnel requirements for growth and expansion of the organisation. The expansion plans of various plants and divisions should be carefully reviewed to assess their probable effects on the number of employees required in each group. The accuracy with which such human resource requirements can be forecast will depend, among other things, on the degree of accuracy which can be achieved in relation to the expansion programme. Where the expansion programme is less specific and the time perspective is larger, uncertainties will also be greater.

A going concern is a living and growing organism. It is not contended with the exiting level of production or profits. It also wants to grow and increase its share in the total activities of industry. One of the basic aspirations of most business managers is to perpetuate the enterprise in which they are engaged. In this world of competition, perpetuation would mean that every organisation has its plans ahead of its activities and aims at a better growth rate and at diversification of its activities and at a better image of itself. All these aims and aspirations result in expansion and growth creating numerous positions for work-force at various levels. These aims and aspirations can be fulfilled if there are a sufficient number of capable persons to handle various positions in the organisation.

A good organisation always tries to adapt itself to change in the methods and techniques of production. Developments in scientific world like the emergence of space science, nuclear science, electronics, computer science (e-commerce) etc. has considerably opened up new avenues of business investment and has also introduced great complexities in the management of companies. Some technological changes may completely throw out of gear the capacity and ability of existing employees to meet the new situations unless they are adequately educated and trained. Human resource planners should take all these factors into account while studying the impact of various business expansion plans on human resource requirements.

(v) **Absenteeism.** It means a situation when a person fails to come for work when he is scheduled to work. The rate of absenteeism can be calculated by the following formula:

$$\text{Absenteeism} = \frac{\text{Man - days lost}}{\text{Man - days worked} + \text{Man - days lost}}$$

There are certain employees who are more prone to absenteeism in any organisation. 10 to 20 per cent of such employees may account for 70 to 80 per cent of absences. It should be noted that excessive absenteeism (more than the irreducible minimum, say 3% to 5%) involves a considerable cost to the firm even when the absent employees receive no pay. Work schedules are upset leading to overtime work which in turn leads to increase in cost of production. The management should go into the causes of absenteeism and attempt to reduce the absenteeism as far as possible. The human resource planning experts will have to consider the known rate of absenteeism in their decision regarding estimation of human resource requirements.

(vi) **Work Study.** Work study technique can be used when it is possible to apply work measurement to know how long operations should take and the amount of labour required. This is also known as 'Workload analysis'. On the basis of the work-load of each plant during the forthcoming years, workforce analysis is done considering the rates of absenteeism and labour turnover.

(4) Job Requirements

Job analysis is the qualitative aspect of human resource requirement since it determines the demands of a job in terms of responsibilities and duties and then translates these demands in terms of skills, qualities and other human attributes. It helps in determining the number and kinds of jobs and qualifications needed to fill these jobs because with the help of job analysis it is known that what is the quantum of work which an average person can do in a day. It facilitates the division of work into different jobs. Thus, it is an essential element of effective human resource planning. At managerial levels, accurate job descriptions help in preparation of inventories of executive talent.

(5) Employment Plans

This phase deals with planning how the organisation can obtain the required number of right type of personnel as reflected by the personnel forecasts. In other words, there is a need to prepare programmes of recruitment, selection, training, transfer and promotion so that personnel needs of various departments of the organisation are met.

(6) Training and Development Programmes

The preparation of skill inventory helps in identifying the training and development needs of the organisation. Training is necessary not only for new employees, but also for old employees. Executive development programmes have to be devised for the development of managerial personnel. No enterprise has a choice of whether to provide training or not, the only choice is that of method or technique. All types of jobs usually require some sort of training for their efficient performance even when the persons appointed have some job experience, they must be given some training to renew their knowledge and skills and to tell them what they are expected to do. The talents of the employees are not fully productive without a systematic programme of training and development.

(7) Appraisal of Human resource Planning

After the employment and training programmes have been implemented, an appraisal must be made of the effectiveness of human resource planning. Deficiencies in the programme should be pointed out and the catalogue of human resource inventory should be updated periodically. Corrective actions should also be taken wherever it is necessary to remove the deficiencies in human resource planning. An appraisal of the existing human resource plans will also serve as a guide in the future human resource planning. Human resource planning is closely linked to the goals of human resource management and those of the organisation. Shortage or surplus of human resources in any department or at any level should be minimised. Human Resource Planning programme will be effective if it can anticipate the deficiencies of various skills well in time so that steps are initiated for recruitment of required human resources. Similarly, if some types of personnel are surplus, they should be adjusted after giving them appropriate training. If it is not possible, they may be phased out through voluntary retirement scheme.

Types of Human Resource Planning

In most developing countries the development of human resources has been regarded as one amongst many objectives of long-term economic growth. The following have been the prime concerns of governments in developing countries.

(i) How to cope with the phenomenal explosion in population?

(ii) How to provide productive employment to the already unemployed and to those who are entering the labour market?

(iii) What supplementary programmes to initiate for specific target group (rural/urban poor, socially disadvantaged groups like the scheduled castes/tribes, backward classes, minorities, women, children, physically handicapped, etc.) for employment creation, income generation and poverty alleviation?

(iv) What pro-active measures to take up to meet the skill shortages so that there is no problem in realising plan targets due to shortage in critical skills at various levels and in various trades/disciplines?

(v) How to upgrade technical, administrative and managerial skills in different sectors of the economy to sustain and improve productivity and further the pace of economic development?

(vi) How to cope with the growing imbalances in the supply and demand side of human resources in an uncertain and turbulent environment within and outside the country in an increasingly interdependent world?

Techniques of Human Resource Planning

The quantitative aspects of human resource planning involve demand forecasting and supply forecasting.

Demand Forecasting

It is the process of estimating the requirement of different kinds of personnel in future. The basis of human resource forecasts should be the annual budget and long-term corporate plan translated into activity levels for each function and department. In a manufacturing company, the sales budget would be translated into a manufacturing plan giving the number and types of products to be made in each period. From this information, the number of man-hours by skill categories to make the quota for each period would be computed. In an insurance company, forecasts of new business would be translated into the number of proposals that would have to be processed by the underwriting department. In a mail order company, forecasts would be made of the number of orders that might have to be processed, assembled and dispatched.

There are three basic demand forecasting methods:

1. Managerial judgement
2. Work study techniques
3. Statistical techniques

In many cases, a combination of methods, say managerial judgement and statistical techniques might be more useful. A brief description of these methods is given below.

1. Managerial Judgement

The most typical method of forecasting used in smaller companies, or those who do not have access to work study data, is managerial judgment. This approach is applied by small as well as large organisations. This simply requires managers to sit down, think about their future workloads and decide how many people they need. This technique involves two types of approaches, i.e., 'bottom-up approach' and 'top-down approach.' Under the 'bottom-up approach', line managers send their departmental requirement of human resources to top management. Top management ultimately forecasts the human resource requirement for the overall organisation on the basis of proposals of departmental heads. Under the 'Top-down approach', top management forecasts the human resource requirement for the entire organisation and various departments. This information is supplied to various departmental heads for their review and approval. However, a combination of both the approaches, i.e. 'Participative approach', should be applied for demand forecasting. Under this approach, top management and departmental heads meet and decide about the future human resource requirement. So, demand of human resources can be forecasted with unanimity under this approach.

Perhaps the best way of using managerial judgement is to adopt both the 'bottom-up' and 'top-down' approach. Guidelines for departmental managers should be prepared which indicate broad company assumptions about future activity levels which will affect their departments. Targets are also set, whenever necessary. Armed with these guidelines, departmental managers prepare their forecasts in a laid-down format. They are encouraged to seek help at this stage from personnel, O&M, or work study departments. Meanwhile, the personnel department in conjunction, as necessary, with planning, O&M or work study departments, prepares a company human resource forecast. The two sets of forecasts are then reviewed by a human resource head. A committee reconciles with departmental managers any discrepancies between the two forecasts and submits the final amended forecast to top management for approval. This is sometimes called the 'right-angle method'.

2. Work Study Technique or Workload Forecasting

Work study technique can be used when it is possible to apply work measurement to know how long operations should take and the amount of labour required. This is also known as 'workload analysis'. On the basis of the work-load of each plant during the forthcoming years, workforce analysis is done considering the rates of absenteeism and labour turnover. Under this method, estimated total production and activities for a specific future period are predicted.

In work-load analysis, the human resource planning expert needs to find out sales forecasts, work schedules and thus determine the human resource required per unit of product. The sales forecasts are translated into work performance for the various departments of the enterprise. In a manufacturing enterprise, one shall first find out the master schedule and then departmental schedules. The departmental work-loads are converted into man-hours in terms of different skills required. Work loads analysis is used to determine how many employees of various types are required to achieve total production target. Similarly, plans are made concerning the amount of work that all other departments (marketing department, purchase department, etc.) of the organisation are expected to accomplish during the coming year. It is essential to determine the work-load in some tangible units so that they may be translated into man-hours required per unit. Past experience can, of course, be utilised for translating workloads into man-hours required.

The following example gives clear idea about this technique :

Let us assume that the estimated production of an organisation is 3,00,000 units. The standard man-hours required to produce each unit are 2 hours. The part experiences show that the work ability of each employee in man-hours is 1500 hrs. per annum. The work load and demand of human resources can be calculated as under :

- Estimated total annual production = 3,00,000 units (a).
- Standard man-hours needed to produce each unit = 2 hrs (b).
- Estimated man-hours needed to meet estimated annual production (a × b) = 600000 hrs. (c).
- Work ability / contribution per employee in terms of man-hours = 1500 units (d).
- Estimated no. of workers needed $\left(\frac{c}{d}\right) = \frac{600000}{1500}$

$= 400$ units.

The above example clearly show that 400 workers are needed for the year.

Further, absenteeism rate, rate of labour turnover, resignations, deaths, machine break-down, strikes, power-failure etc., should also be taken into consideration while estimating future demand of human resources/manpower.

3. Statistical Techniques

The earlier techniques are only a rough approximation of the number of employees required and are suitable only for short range demand forecasting. Long range personnel forecasting is more amenable to statistical and mathematical techniques. This has been particularly true in recent years as new mathematical techniques have been developed and computers are used to rapidly analyse large amount of personnel planning data. Some of the important statistical tools for forecasting are discussed as under:

(a) **Ratio and Trend Analysis.** Under this method, the main emphasis is on the ratios which are calculated for the past data relating to number of employees of each category, of production level, sales level, activity level/workload level, and direct employees and indirect employees. Future production level, sales level activity level/work load are estimated with an allowance for changes in organisation, methods and job. Future ratios are also estimated when changes are expected in the organisation of human resources. Then future human resource requirements are calculated the basis of established ratios.

These techniques, although crude, are easy to understand and use. Their value depends upon accurate records and realistic estimates of future activity levels and the effect of improved performance or changed methods.

The following example will help in clearly understanding this technique :

Estimated production for next year = 1,40,000 units

Estimated no. of workers needed (on the basis of ratio-trend of 1 : 200) will be = 700.

(b) **Econometric Models.** To build an econometric model for human resource planning purposes, it is necessary to analyse past statistical data and to describe the relationship between a number of variables in a mathematical formula. The variables affecting human resource requirement may be identified under headings such as investment, sales or the complexity of the product line. The formula could then be applied to forecasts of movements in these variables to produce a human resource forecast. This is a complex process which is suitable for large organisations.

(c) **Regression Analysis.** This technique is used to estimate the human resource requirements of an organisation at a future point of time, based upon factors such as sales, output, services rendered, etc. Regression analysis is used when dependent and independent variables are functionally related to each other. Computers are used to solve the regression equations and forecast the demand for personnel.

(d) **Bureks-Smith Model.** Elmer H. Bureks and Robert D. Smith have developed a mathematical model for personnel forecasting based on selected key variables that affect the organisation's overall human resource needs. The basic equation of the formula is

$$E_n = \frac{(Lagg + G)1/X}{Y}$$

Where,

- E_n is estimated level of personnel demand in n planning period (e.g., year).
- Lagg is the overall turnover or aggregate level of current business activity in rupees.
- G is the total growth in business activity anticipated through period n in terms of rupees.
- X is the average productivity improvement anticipated from today through planning period n (e.g. if X=1.08, it means an average productivity improvement of 8%).

Y is conversion figure relating today's overall activity to personnel required (total level of today's business activity by the current number of persons). It reflects the level of business activity per person.

The application of this forecasting model depends heavily on obtaining accurate estimates of total growth (G), average productivity improvement (X) and conversion rates (Y). In order to obtain these parameters, separate statistical techniques may be used.

The accuracy of prediction of results by various statistical models is dependent upon the strength of relationships, how accurately these relationships are captured by the model and the degree to which the relationships remain true in the future. Prediction based on poor or loose relationships, inaccurate representation of relationships, or of relationships that will not remain true in future will be inaccurate. The application of any model in highly complex situations becomes even difficult because of the large number of factors (variables) which must be considered.

The use of any quantitative model requires knowledge of the underlying assumptions and limitations. Besides this, persons attempting to take a quantitative approach to personnel should have strong background in statistics, operations research, management science, and computer science. Equally important, the quality of information used to generate estimates and predictions from quantitative models must be timely, accurate and carefully collected.

4. Delphi Technique

Delphi technique is also very important technique used for estimating demand of human resources. This technique takes into consideration human resources requirements given by a group of experts i.e., managers. The human resource experts collect the manpower needs, summarises the various responses and prepare a report. This process is continued until all experts agree on estimated human resources requirement.

Supply Forecasting

Supply forecasting is concerned with the estimate of supply of human resources given the analysis of current resources and future availability. Here the personnel planner must consider both the external supply (employees available for higher position in the organisation's geographic work force) and the internal supply (organisation's current employees). External supply of personnel is important for two reasons. First, the normal separation of employees through voluntary turnover, retirements, illness death and discharge may require that the organisation look to employment agencies, colleges and universities and other sources to replenish lost personnel. Second, organisational growth and diversification require the use of external sources to obtain additional numbers and types of employees.

The internal supply of personnel is influenced by the following factors:

(a) existing human resources;
(b) potential losses to existing resources through labour wastage;
(c) potential changes to exiting resources through internal promotions;
(d) effect of changing conditions of work and absenteeism;
(e) sources of supply from the firm.

External supply of human resource depends on some factors mentioned below :

(a) Supply and demand of jobs.
(b) Literacy rate of nation.
(c) Rate of population.
(d) Industry and expected growth rate and levels.
(e) Technological development.
(f) Compensation system based on education, experience, skill and age.

Based on the above information, the following techniques may be used to anticipate the supply of human resources:

(i) **Markov Analysis.** This method uses historical information on the movement of personnel that takes place during a typical plan period. Data are collected and reviewed for a number of years in order to estimate the likelihood that persons in a particular job remain in that job or be transferred, promoted, demoted, terminated or retired. These historical flows of personnel through the organisation are represented by probabilities. The probabilities are arranged in a 'transition matrix' and future personnel flows are estimated on the basis of the matrix.

(ii) **Simulation.** Based on Markov analysis, the simulation technique considers alternative flows which are examined for effects on future human resource supplies. Alternative flows reflect the anticipated results of policy or programme changes concerning voluntary and involuntary turn over, retirement, promotion, etc.

(iii) **Renewal Analysis.** The technique estimates future flows and supplies of human resources by calculating (a) Vacancies created by the organisation and (b) The results of decision rules governing the filling of vacancies. Alterative models may assess the effect of changes in growth estimates, turnover, promotions, etc.

(iv) **Goal Programming.** It is an operational research technique under which the planner tends to optimise goal. In this case, the goal to optimise is the desired staffing pattern subject to a set of constraints concerning such factors as the upper limits of flows, the percentage of new recruits permitted and total salary budget.

JOB ANALYSIS

Job analysis is a procedure by which pertinent information is obtained about a job, i.e., it is a detailed and systematic study of information relating to the operation and responsibilities of a specific job. An authority has defined job analysis as "the process of determining, by observation and study, and reporting pertinent information relating to the nature of a specific job... "It is the determination of the tasks which comprise the job and of the skills, knowledge, abilities and responsibilities required of the worker for a successful performance and which differentiate one job from all others".

Job analysis is a part of overall work planning also known as 'work design' which involves analysis, measurement, control, design and redesign of different jobs in the organisation. It is a primary tool in personnel management.

A job may be defined as a, "collection or aggregation of tasks, duties and responsibilities which as a whole, are regarded as a regular assignment to individual employees" and which is different from other assignments. In other words, when the total work to be done is divided and grouped into packages, we call it a "job". And when some information is required about this job, then job analysis comes into existence.

Purpose of Job Analysis

Job Analysis plays an important role in recruitment and selection, job evaluation, job designing, deciding compensation and benefits packages, performance appraisal, analyzing training and development needs, assessing the worth of a job and increasing personnel as well as organisational productivity.

- **Recruitment and Selection.** Job Analysis helps in determining what kind of person is required to perform a particular job. It points out the educational qualifications, level of experience and technical, physical, emotional and personal skills required to carry out a job in desired fashion. The objective is to fit a right person at a right place.
- **Performance Analysis.** Job analysis is done to check if goals and objectives of a particular job are met or not. It helps in deciding the performance standards, evaluation criteria and individual's output. On this basis, the overall performance of an employee is measured and he or she is appraised accordingly.

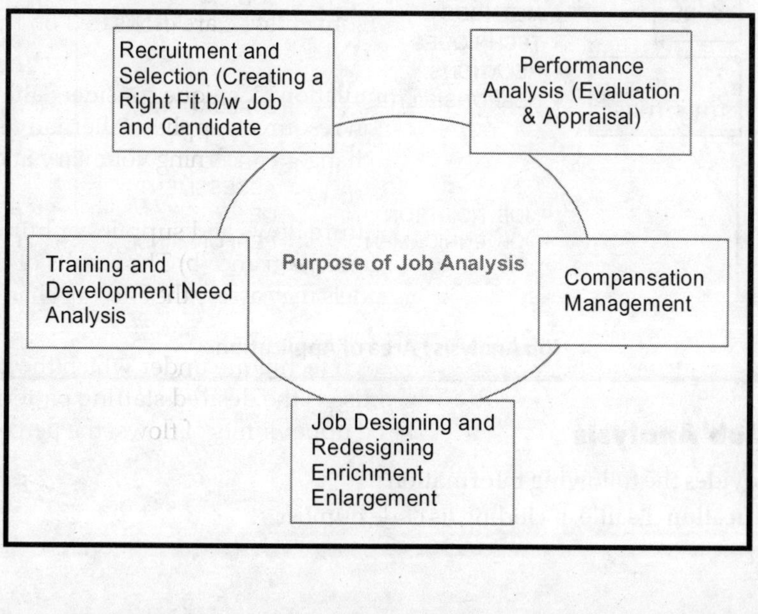

- **Training and Development.** Job Analysis can be used to assess the training and development needs of employees. The difference between the expected and actual output determines the level of training that need to be imparted to employees. It also helps in deciding the training content, tools and equipments to be used to conduct training and methods of training.
- **Compensation Management.** Of course, job analysis plays a vital role in deciding the pay packages and extra perks and benefits and fixed and variable incentives of employees. After all, the pay package depends on the position, job title and duties and responsibilities involved in a job. The process guides HR managers in deciding the worth of an employee for a particular job opening.
- **Job designing and Redesigning.** The main purpose of job analysis is to streamline the human efforts and get the best possible output. It helps in designing, redesigning, enriching, evaluating and also cutting back and adding the extra responsibilities in a particular job. This is done to enhance the employee satisfaction while increasing the human output. Therefore, job analysis is one of the most important functions of an HR manager or department. This helps in fitting the right kind of talent at the right place and at the right time.

After a job has been defined, it is analyzed *i.e.* each task is described in detail. Job analysis is a procedure and a tool for determining the specified tasks, operations and requirements of each job. In the process of getting information about jobs, especially, what the worker does, how he gets it done; why he does it, skill, education and training is required; relationship to other jobs; physical demands; environmental conditions. In other words, it refers to the anatomy of the job. It is a complete study of the job, embodying every known and determinable factor including the duties and responsibilities involved in its performance, the nature of the task, the qualities required in the worker, and such conditions of employment as pay, opportunities and privileges. It also emphasises the relation of one job to others in the organisation.

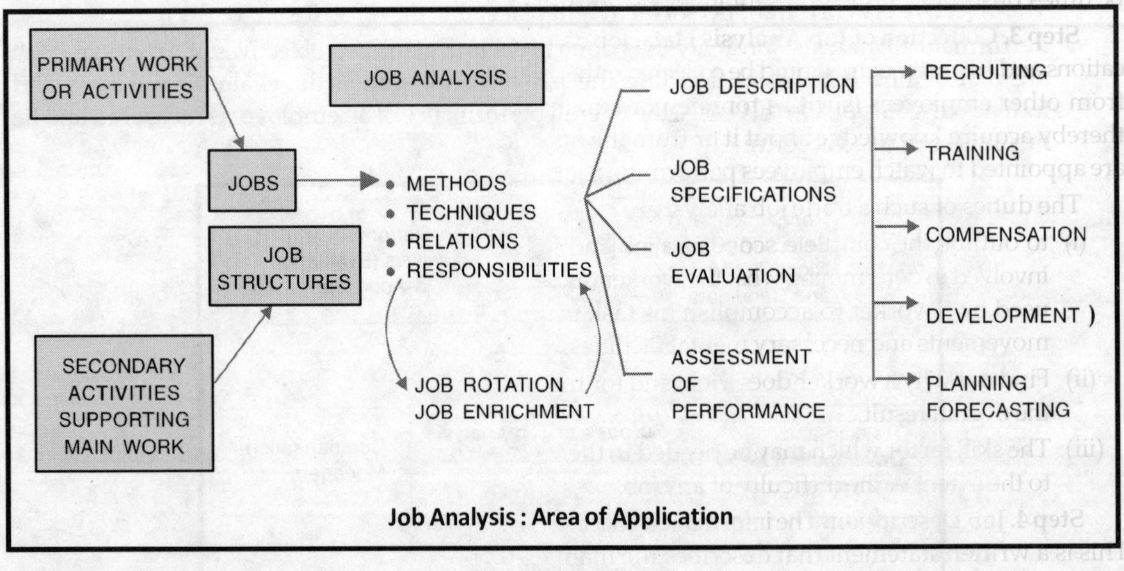

Job Analysis : Area of Application

Contents of Job Analysis

A job analysis provides the following information :

(i) **Job identification.** Its title, including its code number.

(ii) **Significant characteristics of a job.** Its location, physical setting, supervision, union jurisdiction, hazards and discomforts.

(iii) **What the typical worker does.** Specific operation and tasks that make up an assignment, their relative timings and importance, their simplicity, routine or complexity, the responsibility or safety of others for property, funds, confidence and trust.

(iv) **Which materials and equipments a worker uses.** Metals, plastics, grains, yarns, milling machines, punch presses and micrometres; etc.

(v) **How a job is performed.** Nature of operation – lifting, handling, cleaning, washing, feeding, removing, drilling, driving, setting up and many others.

(vi) **Required personnel attributes.** Experience, training, apprenticeship, physical strength, co-ordination or dexterity, physical demands, mental capabilities, aptitudes, social skills.

(vii) **Job relationship.** Experience required, opportunities for advancement, patterns of promotions, essential co-operation, direction or leadership from and for a job.

The Steps in Job Analysis

There are five basic steps required for doing a job analysis, *viz.*,

Step 1. Collection of Background Information. The information about the job can be had by reviewing available background information such as organisation charts (which show how the job in question relates to other jobs and where they fit into the overall organisation); class specifications (which describes the general requirements of the class of job to which the job under analysis belongs); and the existing *job descriptions* which provide a starting point from which to build the revised job description.

Step 2. Selection of Representative Position to be Analysed. Since the analysis of all jobs would be time-consuming, flow representative positions should be analysed.

Step 3. Collection of Job Analysis Data. Job data on features of the job, required employee qualifications and requirements, should be collected either from the employees who actually perform a job; or from other employees (such as foremen or supervisors) who watch the workers doing a job and thereby acquire knowledge about it or from the outside persons, known as the *trade job analysts* who are appointed to watch employees performing a job.

The duties of such a trade job analyst are :

(i) to outline the complete scope of a job and to consider all the physical and mental activities involved in determining what the worker does. For this purpose, he studies the physical methods used by a worker to accomplish his task including the use of machinery, tools and his own movements and necessary mental facilities.

(ii) Find out why a worker does a job; and for this purpose he studies why each task is essential for the overall result.

(iii) The skill factor which may be needed in the worker to differentiate between jobs and establish to the extent of the difficulty of any job.

Step 4. Job Description. The information collected is to be developed in the form of a job description. This is a written statement that describes the main features of the job, as well as the qualifications/ activities which the job incumbents must possess.

Step 5. Developing Job Specification. The last step is to convert the Job Description statement into Job Specifications *i.e.*, to specifically mention what personal qualities, traits, skills and background is necessary for getting the job done.

Techniques of Job Analysis Data

(i) **Personal Observation.** The materials and equipments used, the working conditions and probable hazards, and an understanding of what the work involves are the facts which should be known by an analyst. Direct observation is especially useful in jobs that consist primarily of physical ability like the jobs of draftsmen, mechanic, spinner.

(ii) **Sending Out Questionnaires.** The method is usually employed by engineering consultants. Properly drafted questionnaires are sent out to job-holders for completion and are returned to supervisors. However, the information received is often unorganised and incoherent. The idea in issuing questionnaire is to elicit the necessary information from job-holders so that any error may first be discussed with the employee and, after due corrections, may be submitted to the job analyst.

(iii) **Maintenance of Log Records.** The employee maintains a daily diary record of duties he performs, marking the time at which each task is started and finished. But, this system is incomplete, for it does not give us any desirable data on supervisor relationship, the equipment used, and working conditions. Moreover, it is time-consuming.

(iv) **Personnel Interviews.** May be held by the analyst with the employees and answers to relevant questions may be recorded.

(v) **Critical incidents.** In this method, job holder are asked to describe incidents concerning the job based on the past experiences. The incidents are so collected are analysed and classified according to the job areas described. A fairly clear picture of actual job requirement can be obtained by distinguishing between effective and ineffective behaviour of the job. The analyst requires the high degree of skill to analyses the content of descriptions given by the workers.

Quantitative Methods

1. **Position Analysis Questionnaire Model.** PAQ represents Position Analysis Questionnaire. This well-known and commonly used technique is used to analyze a job by getting the questionnaires filled by job incumbents and their superiors. Designed by a trained and experienced job analyst, the process involves interviewing the subject matter experts and employees and evaluating the questionnaires on those bases. The PAQ contain 194 items, each of which represent a basic elements that may or may not play an important role on the job. The job analyst decided Whether each item play a role on the job, if so to that extent.

   194 job elements covered by PAQ are grouped into six section.

   (i) Information input
   (ii) Mental processes
   (iii) Work output
   (iv) relationship
   (v) Job context
   (vi) Other job characteristics

2. **Management position analysis questionnaire (MPDQ).** MPDQ is a standardised instrument designed by specifically for use in analysing managerial jobs. The 274 items questionnaire contains 15 sections. It would take 2 ½ hours to complete the questionnaire .in most cases the respondent are asked to state how each item is to the positions

3. **Functional Job Analysis Model.** FJA is a worker oriented job analysis techniques that attempts to describe the whole person on the job .its tries to examine the fundamental components of data, people and thing.

   Functional Job Analysis and helps in collecting and recording job-related data to a deeper extent. It is used to develop task-related statements. Developed by Sidney Fine and his colleagues, the technique helps in determining the complexity of duties and responsibilities involved in a specific job. This work-oriented technique works on the basis of relatedness of job-data where complexity of work is determined on a scale of various scores given to a particular job. The lower scores represent greater difficulty.

Job Description

'Job description' is an important document which is basically descriptive in nature and contains a statement of job analysis. It provides both organisational information (location in structure, authority, etc.) and functional information (what the work is). It describes the scope of job activities, major responsibilities and positioning of the job in the organisation. It provides the worker, analyst and supervisor with a clear idea of what the worker must do to meet the demands of the job. Though job description is not assessment, it provides an important basis for establishing assessment standards and objectives.

Purpose of Job Description

1. The main purpose of job description is to collect job-related data in order to advertise for a particular job. If helps in attracting, targeting, recruiting and selecting the right candidate for the right job.
2. It is done to determine what needs to be delivered in a particular job. It clarifies what employees are supported to do if selected for that particular job opening.
3. It gives recruiting staff, a clear view what kind of candidate is required by a particular department or division to perform a specific task or job. It also clarifies who will report to whom.

Components or Content of Job Description

A job description contains the following data:

1. **Job identification, or Organisational Position** which includes the job title, alternate department, division, plant and code number of the job. The job title identifies and designates the job properly. The department, division etc., indicate the name of the department where it is situated – whether it is the maintenance department, mechanical shop etc. The location gives the name of the place. The portion of job description gives answer to two important questions : to what higher level job is this job accountable; and who is supervised directly ?
2. **Job Summary** serves two important purposes. *First*, it provides a short definition which is useful as an additional identification information when a job title is not adequate. *Second*, it serves as a summary to orient the reader towards an understanding of detailed information which follows. It gives the reader a "quick capsule explanation" of the content of a job usually in one or two sentences.
3. **Job duties and responsibilities** give a comprehensive listing of the duties together with some indication of the frequency of occurrence or percentage of time devoted to each major duty. *It is regarded as the heart of a job.* It tells us What needs to be done ?, How it should be done ? and Why it should be done ? It also describes the responsibilities related to the custody of money, the supervision of workers and the training of subordinates.
4. **Relation to other jobs.** This helps to locate the job in the organisation by indicating the job immediately below or above it in the job hierarchy. It also gives an idea of the vertical relationships of work flow and procedures.

5. **Supervision.** Under it is given the number of persons to be supervised alongwith their job titles and the extent of supervision involved – general, intermediate or close supervision.
6. **Machine, tools and equipments** define each major type or trade name of the machines and tools and the raw materials used.
7. **Working conditions** usually give us information about the environment in which a job holder must work. These include cold, heat, dust, wetness, moisture, fumes, odour, oily conditions etc. existing inside the organisation.
8. **Hazards** give us the nature of risks to life and limb, their possibilities of occurrence etc.

Information about jobs can be had from :

(i) Observation of employees while an work,
(ii) Study of specially maintained diaries,
(iii) A review of critical incidents, and
(iv) Discussions with departmental heads and outside experts or consultants.

Uses of Job Description

Job description has several uses, such as:

(i) Preliminary drafts can be used as a basis for productive group discussions, particularly if the process starts at the executive level.
(ii) It aids in the development of job specifications, which are useful in planning, recruitment, in training and in hiring people with required skills.
(iii) It can be used to orient new employees towards basic responsibilities and duties.
(iv) It is a basic document used in developing performance standards.
(v) It can be used for job evaluation, and as a wage and salary administration technique.

A job description enables the manager to frame suitable questions to be asked during an interview. It is particularly helpful when the application form is used as a tool for eliminating the unfit personnel. It helps in:

(i) Job grading and classification.
(ii) Transfer and promotions.
(iii) Redressal of grievances.
(iv) Defining and outflowing promotional steps.
(v) Establishing a common understanding of a job between employers and employees.
(vi) Averting accidents.
(vii) Indicating faulty work procedures or duplication of papers.
(viii) Maintaining, operating and adjusting machinery.
(ix) Time and motion studies.
(x) Defining the limits of authority.
(xi) Indicating case of personnel merit.
(xii) Facilitating job placements.
(xiii) Studies of health and fatigue.
(xiv) Scientific guidance.
(xv) Determining job suitable for receptional therapy.
(xvi) Providing hiring specifications.
(xvii) Providing performance indication.

Developing Job Descriptions or Guidelines for writing a Job Description

Opinions differ on how to write job descriptions. Job descriptions are written by Personnel Department or its representatives. Although there is no set way of writing a job description, the following pattern are used by many companies.

(i) A photograph is allocated to each major task of responsibility
(ii) Paragraphs are numbered and arranged in a logical orders, task sequence or importance.
(iii) Sentences are begun with an active verb, e.g. "types letters", "interview the candidates", "collects, sorts out, sorts and distributes mail."
(iv) Accuracy and simplicity are emphasised rather than an elegant style.
(v) Brevity is usually considered to be important but is largely conditioned by the type of job being analyzed and the need for accuracy
(vi) Examples of work performed are often quoted and are useful in making the job description explicit.
(vii) Job descriptions, particularly when they are used as bases for training, often incorporate details of the faults which may be encountered in operator tasks and safety check-points.
(viii) Statements of opinions, such as 'dangerous situations are encountered', should be avoided.
(ix) When job descriptions are written for supervisly jobs, the main factors (such as manning, cost control etc.) are identified and listed. Each factor is then broken down into a series of elements with a note on the supervisor's responsibility.

SELECTING HUMAN RESOURCES

The selection procedure is concerned with securing relevant information about an applicant. The objective of selection process is to determine whether an applicant meets the qualifications for a specific job and to choose the applicant who is most likely to perform well in that job. It is a long process, commencing from the preliminary interview of the applicants and ending with the contract of employment.

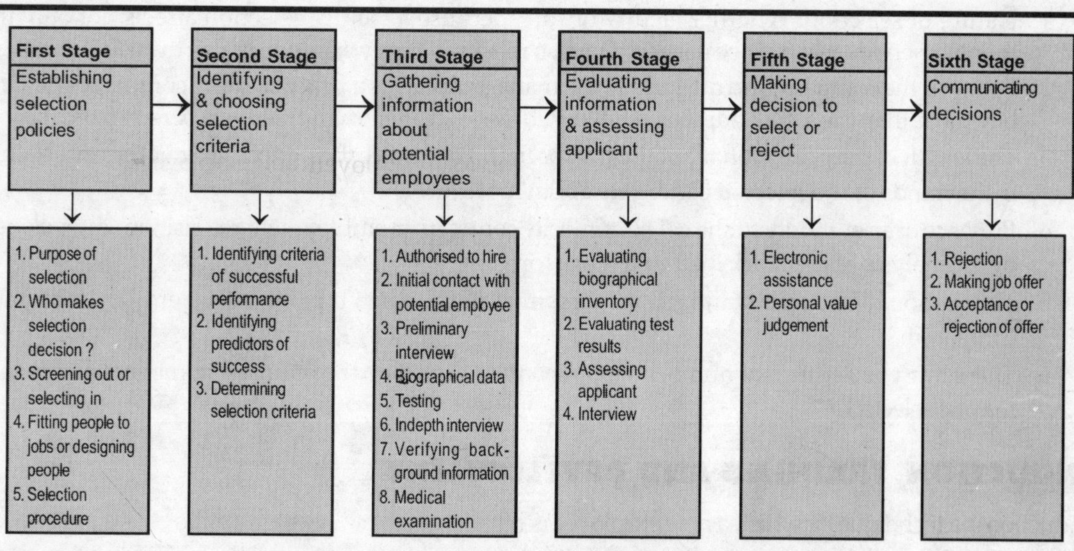

Model Procedure for Effective Personnel Selection

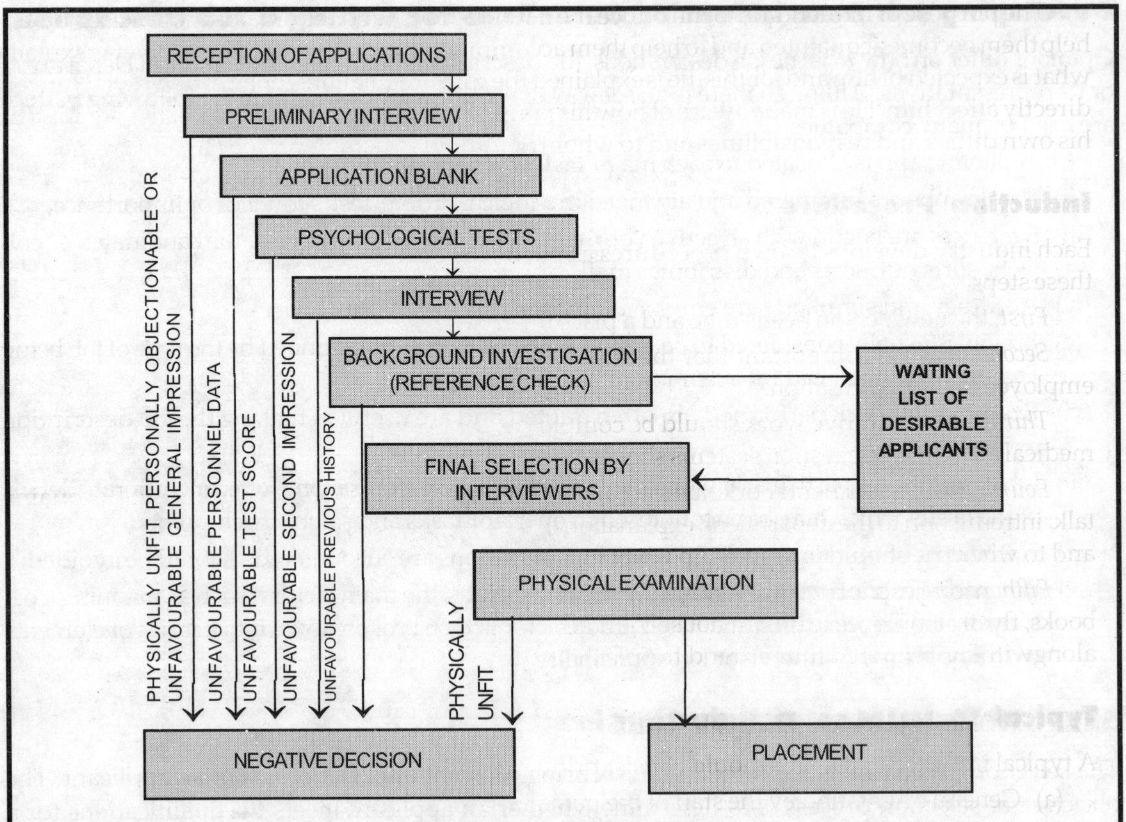

Steps in Selection Procedure

Essentials of Selection Procedure

1. Nature of selection. Whether faculty or safe, because a faculty selection affects not only the training periods that may be needed, but also results in heavy expenditure on the new employee.
2. Policy of the company and attitude of the management. As a practice some companies usually hire more than the actual number needed with a view to removing the unfit person from the job.
3. The length of the probationary of the trial period. The longer the period, greater the uncertainty in the minds of the selected candidate about his future.
4. Presence of an authority for hire. The authority comes from employment requisition as developed by an analysis of the work load and work force.
5. There should be some standard or personnel with which a prospective employer may be compared.
6. There must be a sufficient number of applicants from whom the required number of employees may be selected.

INDUCTION, TRAINING AND DEVELOPMENT

Induction is a technique by which a new employee is rehabilitated into his surroundings and introduced to the practices, policies and purposes of the organisation. In other words, the idea is to welcome a newcomer, make him feel at home and generate in him a feeling that his own job, however small, is meaningful and has a significance as a part of the total organisation.

The purpose of induction is to introduce the new employee and the organisation to each other, to help them become acquainted and to help them accommodate each other. The newcomer is explained what is expected of him and for this, he is explained the rules, regulations, policies and procedures that directly affect him. He is made aware of how his job fits into the overall operation of the organisation, his own duties and responsibilities and to whom he should look for when he has any problem.

Induction Procedure

Each industry develops its own procedures as per its needs. The procedure should basically follow these steps :

First, the new person needs time and a place to report to work.

Second, it is very important that the supervisor or the immediate boss meet and welcome the employee to the organisation.

Third, administrative work should be completed. Such items as vacations, probationary period, medical absences, suggestion systems should be covered.

Fourth, the departmental orientation can be conducted. This should include a get – acquainted talk, introduction to the department, explanation of the functions of the department, and job instruction and to whom he should look for help when he has any problem.

Fifth, verbal explanations are supplemented by a wide variety of printed material, employee hand books, flyers, employee manuals, house-journals, picture stories, comics and cartoons, pamphlets, etc. alongwith short guided tour around the plant.

Typical Techniques of Induction Programs

A typical induction program should consist primarily of three steps :

(a) General orientation by the staff of the personnel department;

(b) Specific orientation by the job supervisor, or his representative; and

(c) Follow-up orientation by either the personnel department or the supervisor.

The first phase of the programme should ordinarily be conducted by the personnel department. This type of induction is general, because it gives the necessary general information about the history and operations of the firm - *the purpose of which is to help an employee to build up some pride and interest in the organisation*. Information is also given on specific employee services, such as pension, health and welfare plans, safety programmes etc. *The better policy is not to give everything in one day, but to administer smaller doses over a long period.*

At the second stage, induction should be conducted by the job supervisor. *Induction is specific and requires skill on the part of the foreman.* The employee is shown the department and his place of work, introduced to other employees, informed of the locations of the bathrooms, lavatories, canteens and time clock; and told about the organisation's specific practices and customs. The *purpose of specific induction is to enable an employee to adjust himself to his work and environment.*

Follow-up induction takes place within one week to six months from the time of the initial hiring and orientation. It is conducted either by a foreman or a specialist. *Its purpose is to find out whether the employee is reasonably well-satisfied with him.*

Training and Development

In a rapidly changing society, employee's training and development are not only an activity that is desirable but also an activity that an organisation must commit resources to if it is to maintain a viable and knowledgeable work force.

Training is a process of learning a sequence of programmed behaviour. It is application of knowledge. It gives people an awareness of the rules and procedures to guide their behaviour. It attempts to improve their performance on the current job or prepare them for an intended job. *Development* is a related process. It covers not only those activities which improve job performance but also those which bring about growth of their personality; help individuals in the progress towards maturity and actualisation of their potential capacities. In organisational terms, it is intended to equip persons to earn promotion and hold greater responsibility. Training a person for a bigger and higher job is development.

Training has been defined by different scholars of management. Some important definitions of training are as under:

- According to **Dale.S.Beach**, "Training is the organised procedure in which people learn knowledge and skill for definite purpose".
- According to **Jucius**, "The term training is used here to indicate only process by which the aptitudes, skill and abilities of employees to perform specific jobs are increased".
- In the words of **Michael J. Jucius**, "Training is a process by which the aptitudes, skills and abilities of employees to perform specific jobs are increased."
- In the words of **Dale S. Beach**, "Training is the organised procedure by which people learn knowledge and Improve skill for a definite purpose."

Distinction Between Training and Development

"*Training*" is short-term process utilising a systematic and organised procedure by which non-managerial personnel learn technical knowledge and skills for a definite purpose.... On the other hand Development is a long-term educational process utilising a systematic and organised procedure by which managerial personnel learn conceptual and theoretical knowledge for general purpose.

"*Training*" refers only to instruction in technical and mechanical operations, while "development" refers to philosophical and theoretical educational concepts. Training is designed for non-managers, while development involves managerial personnel.

Differences Between Training and Development

Basis	Training	Development
Meaning	Training means learning skills and knowledge for the particular job.	Development means growth of an employee in all aspects
Use	Training is used for imparting specific Skills.	Development is used for the overall growth of the executives.
Nature	It is job related in nature.	It is career oriented in nature.
Perspective	It has short term perspective.	It has long term perspective.
Aim	The best possible performance on the specific job by the employee.	The best possible utilization of the employee capability.
Scope	Training is limited in scope and is the part of development.	Development is wider term and includes education, learning, and training.
Level of involved persons	It is imparted to lower level employees or junior managers.	The level of development is higher and concerns with senior managers.
Depth of knowledge	Deep Knowledge is provided.	Development does not provide deep knowledge and simply facilitates growth.
Initiative in learning	Initiative of learning is not on the employee and is on the organisation.	Initiative of learning is on the employee and not on the organisation.
Duration	It is imparted for the fixed period.	It is an unending practice in the company.

Steps in Training Programs

CHARACTERISTICS OR FEATURES OF TRAINING
1. Job related
2. Continuous
3. Provides benefit to employee and employer.
4. Training is different from development.
5. Training is different from education.
6. Training is needed at all levels.
7. All types of employees need training.

1. Discovering or Identifying Training Needs

A training program should be established only when it is felt that it would assist in the solution of specific operational problems. The most important step, in the first place, is to make a thorough analysis of the entire organisation, its operations and human resource resources available in order to find out "The trouble spots" where training may be needed.

2. Getting Ready for the Job

Under this step, it is to be decided who is to be trained – the newcomer or the older employee, or the supervisory staff or all of them selected from different departments.

The trainer has to be prepared for the job, for he is the key figure in the entire program.

3. Preparation of the Learner

This step consists : (i) In putting the learner at ease; (ii) in stating the importance and ingredients of the job and its relationship to work flow; (iii) in explaining why he is being taught; (iv) in creating interest and encouraging questions. Finding out what the learner already knows about his job or other jobs; (v) in explaining the 'why' of the whole job and relating it to some other job, the worker already knows; (vi) in placing the learner as close to his normal working position as possible; and (vii) in familiarising him with the equipments, materials, tools and trade terms.

4. Presentation of Operation and Knowledge

The trainer should clearly *tell show, illustrate* and *question* in order to put over the new knowledge and operations. The learner should be told of the sequence of the entire job and why each step in its performance is necessary. Instructions should be given clearly, completely and patiently; there should be an emphasis on key points, and one point should be explained at a time. For this purpose, the trainer should demonstrate or make use of audio-visual aids and should ask the trainee to repeat the operations. He should also be encouraged to ask questions in order to indicate that he really knows and understands the job.

5. Performance Try Out

Under this, the trainee is asked to go through the job several times slowly, explaining him each step. Mistakes are corrected and if necessary, some complicated steps are done for the trainee the first time. The trainee is asked to do the job, gradually building up skill and speed. As soon as the trainee demonstrates that he can do the job in a right way, he is put on his own, but not abandoned.

6. Follow-up

This step is undertaken with a view to testing the effectiveness of training efforts.

This consists in :

(a) Putting a trainee "on his own."

(b) Checking frequently to be sure that he has followed instructions; and

(c) Tapering off extra supervision and close follow-up until he is qualified to work with normal supervision.

Elements of Training

1. Trainee

The proper selection of trainers is of major importance of permanent and gainful results are to be obtained. A trainee should be trained for the kind of job he likes and is suitable to perform. In respect of this, training is closely related to the selection of personnel. Careful screening of conditions for training raises the effectiveness of the training work.

While giving training to an employer the first step is to place him at ease as most people are generally nervous when approaching an unfamiliar task. The trainee must be given the proper background information before he starts learning the new job skills and knowledge.

In case of suspensory training, it is better to include all suspensions and other employers considered suitable for promotion. Excluding the employers who do not need training or who are already doing their work satisfactorily is poor policy. The presence of outstanding persons benefits the less competent persons and they benefit themselves too.

2. Trainer

The trainer is the key figure in an effective training programme. Qualified instructions may be got from inside or outside the organisation. He must be able to divide the job into logical parts, so that he may teach one part at a time without losing the perspective of the whole. He must be tolerant and patient.

Training has to be based on the needs of the organisation and the trainer must have a clear cut idea about the requirements of the organisation. Very often training occurs in vacuums i.e. trainers organise courses which seem to be interesting or an agenda is developed in terms of some preconceived notion of what constitutes a body of useful information.

3. Training Period

The length of the training period depends upon the skill to be acquired, the trainers learning capacity and the training media used. The use of effective visual material usually helps to reduce the training time.

To maintain interest and to secure maximum accomplishment, no single session should last longer than two hours. The alternative to giving training during working hours which may effect production and the organisation, will have to compensate the time, is to organise training after the working hours when the employer may not be able to make full the use of training.

4. Training Methods

There are many methods and techniques for importing training among trainers. The choice of any method will depend upon

- cost
- time available
- number of trainees
- depth of knowledge required
- background of the trainers

Various Training Techniques

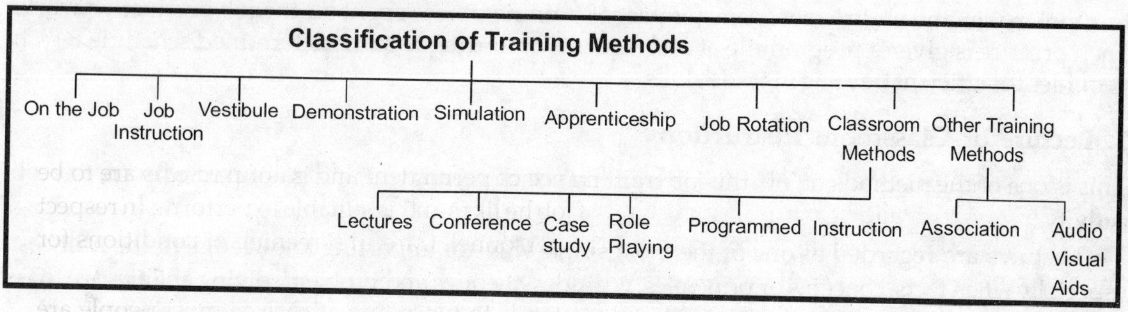

1. On-The-Job-Training

This is the most common and widely used, accepted form of training and is also the most necessary one. Trainers learn as they work under mechanic or craftsman, they receive immediate feedback, practice in the actual work environment and associate with the very same people they will work with after training. Under this training, an employee is placed in a new job and is told how it is performed.

2. Job Instruction Training

This method is very popular for preparing supervisors to train operatives. The instruction and training method requires skilled trainers, extensive job analysis, training schedules and prior assignment of the trainees job knowledge. This method is also known as 'training through step-by-step learning.' It involves listing all necessary steps in the job. This shows what is to be done, alongside is listed the corresponding 'key point' which shows how and why it is done.

3. Vestibule Training

It is a classroom training which is often imparted with the help of equipment and machines which are identical to those used at the place of work. This technique enables the trainee to concentrate on learning the new skill rather than on performing on actual job. Theoretical training is given in the class room, while the practical work is conducted on the production time.

4. Demonstrations and Examples

In this method the trainee describes and displays something by actually performing the activity himself and by going through on step by step explanation of why and what he is doing.

Demonstration are very effective in teaching because it is much easier to show a person how to do a job than to tell him or ask him to gather instruction from the reading material. Demonstrations are often used in combination with lectures, pictures, text materials and discussions.

Teaching by example is effective in mechanical operations or interpersonal relationships for job duties and responsibilities for informal group standards, supervisory explanations and the like.

5. Simulation

Simulation is a technique which duplicates as nearly as possible the actual conditions encountered on a job. The vestibule training method or the business game method are examples of business simulation.

6. Apprenticeship

For training in crafts, trades and in technical areas, this is the oldest and most commonly used method especially when proficiency in a job is the result of a relatively long training period of 2-3 years. The field in which apprenticeship training is offered are numerous and range from the job of a mechanist to a tool maker and electricians. A major part of training time is spent on-the-job productive work. Each practice is given a programme of assignments according to a pre-determined schedule which provides for efficient training in trade skills.

7. Lecture or Classroom Instruction

This is one of the methods of 'off-the-job training which means training is not part of everyday job activity.'

Lectures are regarded as one of the most single ways of imparting knowledge to the trainees, especially when facts, concepts or principles, attitudes, theories and problem solving abilities are to be taught. Lectures are formal organised talks by training specialists.

8. Conference Method

In this method the participating individuals confer to discuss points of common interest to each other. A conference is basic to most participative group centred methods of development. Its a formal meeting conducted in accordance with an organised plan in which the leader seeks to develop knowledge and understanding by obtaining a considerable amount of oral participation from the trainers. It lays stress on small group discussions, on organised subject matter and on active participation of members involved.

There are three types of conferences.

(i) **Directed discussions.** Where the trainee guides the discussion by explaining the facts, principles or concepts.

(ii) **Training conference.** Where the instruction gets the group to pool its knowledge and brings different parts of view to bear on the problem.

(iii) **Seminar conference.** The answer is bound to question or solution of a problem. Here the instructor defines the problem, encourages and ensures full participation.

9. Seminar or Team Discussion

This is an established way for training. A seminar can be conducted in many ways :

(i) It may be based on a paper prepared by one or more trainees on a subject selected in consultation with the person in charge of the seminar. The trainees read their papers and this is followed by a critical discussion. The chairman of the seminar summarises the contents of the paper and the discussions.

(ii) It may be based on a statement made by the person in charge of the seminar or on a document prepared by an expert who is invited to participate in the discussion.

(iii) The person in charge of the seminar distributes in advance the material to be analyzed in the form of required readings. The seminar compares the reactions of trainees, encourage discussion, defines the general trends and guides the participant to certain conclusions.

(iv) Valuable working material may be provided to the trainees by actual files. The trainees may consult the files and bring these to the seminar where they may study in detail the various aspects, specifications and complexities of a particular job or work or task.

10. Case Studies

This method was first developed in the 1880's by Christopher Langdell. The objective of this is to help students learn by themselves by independent thinking and by discovering principles and ideas which have lasting validity and general applicability. The object is to help them, develop skills in using their knowledge.

The case study is based on the belief that management competence can best be attained through the study, contemplation and discussion of concrete cases. The 'case' is a set of data written or oral miniature description and summary of such data that presents issues and problems calling for solutions or action on part of trainer. The trainees are given cases to analyse, they are asked to identify the problems and to recommend solutions.

In the case study the trainee is expected to:

(i) Master the facts and become acquainted with the content of the case.
(ii) Define the objectives sought in dealing with the issues of the case.
(iii) Identify the problems in case and uncover their probable causes.
(iv) Develop alternative courses of action
(v) Screen the alternatives using the objectives as criteria
(vi) Select the alternative that is most in keeping with the stated objectives.
(vii) Define the controls needed to make the action effective.
(viii) To role play the action, to test its effectiveness and find conditions that may limit it.

11. Role Playing

The method is also called as 'Role reversal', socio-drama or psychodrama, emphasises on learning human relation skills through practice and insight into ones own behaviour and its effect on others. It has been defined as, 'a method of human interactions which involves realistic behaviour in imaginary situations.' A role playing experience demonstrates the gap between thinking and doing. The idea of role playing involves action, doing and practice.

Role playing primarily involves employee-employer relationships – hiring, filling, discussing grievance procedure, conducting a post appraisal interview, disciplinary or a sales marketing situation.

12. Programmed Instruction

Also referred to as teaching by the machine method, it involves a sequence of steps which are often set up through the control panel of an electronic computer as it guides in the performance of a desired operation or series of operation. It incorporates a 'pre-arranged, proposed or desired course of proceedings pertaining to the learning or acquisition of some specific skills or general knowledge. A programmed instruction involves creating information down into meaningful units and then arranging these in a proper way to form a logical and sequential learning programme or package.

13. T-Group Training

Also called 'sensitivity training'. The aim is to improve the trainers in dealing with people. This method has a two fold function.

(a) to help the trainers learn how groups actually work.
(b) to give each member of the group a chance to discover how other people interpret and are affected by their own behaviour.

This training mainly consists of sitting around a table discussing for hours. A trainer usually a psychologist merely guides the discussion. As the member are free to criticise the behaviour of each other, thereby giving feedback which may be positive or negative.

14. Retraining

Retraining programmes are generally arranged for employers who have long been in the services of the organisation. The retraining programme may be necessitated by the following facts :

(a) Some employers are engaged in a confined phase of a particular task and lose their all around skills in a particular trade. To represent them active in are around skills, training is needed.

(b) During prolonged lay offs, employers on certain highly skilled jobs are given retraining when called back to work.

(c) Technological changes may make a particular job unnecessary and its beneficial to retrain the employer than discharging him.

(d) An employee due to illness, accident or incapacity may no longer be able to do his share of work which he performed when in normal health.

(e) Economic depression or cyclic variations in production create conditions in which employment stabilisation may be achieved by having a versatile force capable of performing more than one job.

15. Job Rotation

In this method the trainee moves from one job to another, so that he can know to work on all the seats. This type of training is common for the employees of general management positions. Under this method trainee understand the problems of the other seats while working on that seat. Such movement may be for the period ranging from 6 months to 2 years before a person is established in a particular job or department.

16. Internship Training

The training is basically provided to bring the balance between the theoretical knowledge and the practical skills required to do the job. This training is the combined effort of the educational institutions and business organisations. In this theoretical knowledge is imparted by educational institutions and practical knowledge is imparted through business organisations.

Career Development

Career development is the process of improving an individual's abilities in anticipation of future opportunities for achieving career objectives. A formal approach taken by an organisation to help its people acquire the skills and experiences needed to perform current and future jobs is termed as career development. Company's policies especially policies regarding promotion, counselling the employees, opportunities to excel in future help employees to develop their career. Career development consists of skills, education and experiences as well as behavioural modification and refinement techniques that allow individuals to work better and add value.

Career development is an ongoing organised and formalised effort that recognises people as a vital organisational resource. It differs from training in that it has a wider focus, longer time frame, and broader scope. The goal of training is improvement in performance; the goal of development is enrichment and more capable workers.

Recently, career development has come to be seen as a means for meeting both organisational and employee needs, as opposed to solely meeting the needs of the organisation as it had done in the past. Now, organisations see career development as a way of preventing job burnout, providing career information to employees, improving the quality of work lives and meeting affirmative action goals. That is, career development must be seen as a key business strategy if an organisation wants to survive in an increasingly competitive and global business environment.

Meeting the Challenges of Effective Career Development

Creative decision making is a must in designing and implementing an effective development program. The three phases of development often blend together in a real life program. These three phases include the assessment phase, the direction phase, and the development phase.

A. **The Assessment Phase.** The assessment phase involves activities ranging from self-assessment to organisationally provided assessment. The goal of both of these types of assessment is to identify employees' strengths and weaknesses.

B. **The Direction Phase.** This involves determining the type of career that employees want and the steps they must take to make their career goals a reality. It involves:
   - Individual career counseling
   - Information services

C. **The Development Phase.** The development phase is taking actions to create and increase skills to prepare for future job opportunities and is meant to foster this growth and self-improvement. The methods are:
   1. ***Mentoring & Coaching.*** It has become increasingly clear over the years that employees who aspire to higher management levels in the organisation often need the assistance and advocacy of someone higher up in the organisation. When senior employee takes an active role in guiding another individual, we refer to this activity as mentoring and coaching. This can occur at any level and can be most effective when the two individuals do not have any type of reporting relationship.
   2. ***Job Rotation.*** Involves moving employees from one job to another for the purpose of providing them with broader experience.
   3. ***Tuition Assistance Programs.*** To help individuals plan their careers, organisations try to provide additional information in order to have better choice of the career.

EXIT POLICY AND IMPLICATIONS

The Govt. of India adopted a new economic policy and one of the important aspects of the liberalised economic policy in the Exit Policy.

Under this policy, the govt. has allowed business and industrial establishment, to reduce their excess staff and employers. The reduction of excess staff is a result of restructuring of organisations due to modernising, applying new technology and new methods of operation, so that the industrial organisations could operate economically and withstand the competition with companies and organisations which have accepted foreign collaborations, innovative methods and technology upgradation, rendering some employees' services.

THE REASONS FOR PROPOSING V.R.S.
1. Recession in business.
2. Intense competition which makes the establishment unviable unless downsizing is resorted to.
3. Changes in technology, production process, innovation, new product line .
4. Realignment of business - due to market conditions.
5. Joint-ventures with foreign collaborations.
6. Takeovers and mergers.
7. Business re-engineering process.
8. Product/Technology out-of-date.

Exit Policy

Voluntary Retirement Schemes - have been legally found to be giving no problem to employers, employees and their unions. The essence of the voluntary retirement scheme which is approved by the Government - involves voluntary separation of employees who are above the age of 40 years or have served the company or establishment for minimum 10 years. The company, may offer different separation benefits to employees in different age groups subject to overall benefits which are tax exempted upto a limit of Rs. 5 lacks. Public sector undertakings, however, have to obtain prior approval of the government before offering and implementing the voluntary retirement schemes.

Procedure for voluntary Retirement Scheme

The employer has to issue a circular communicating of his decisions to offer voluntary retirement scheme - mentioning therein.

(a) The reasons for downsising
(b) Eligibility *i.e.*, who are eligible to apply for voluntary retirement.
(c) The age limit and the minimum service period of employees who can apply (Employees who are 40 and above and those who have completed minimum 10 years of service in the establishment).
(d) The benefits that are offered.
(e) The right of an employer to accept or reject any application for voluntary retirement.
(f) The date upto which the scheme is open and applications are received for consideration by the employer.
(g) The circular may indicate income tax incidence on any voluntary retirement benefits which are in excess of Rs. 5 lacs, which is maximum tax free benefit under such schemes.
(h) It should also indicate that those employees who opt for voluntary retirement and accept the benefits under such scheme shall not be eligible in future for employment in the establishment.

Steps to be taken for Introducing and Implementing Voluntary Retirement Scheme

1. If the company is public sector undertaking, obtain approval of the government.
2. Identify departments/employees to whom V.R.S. is to be offered (Target group of employees - age above 40 years and employees with more than 10 years service in the company).
3. If there is a union of employees in the establishment, involve the union by communicating to them the reasons, the target group and the benefits to be offered to those who opt for the scheme.
4. Formulate the terms of V.R.S. and benefits to be offered are to be mentioned in the circular and decide the period during which the scheme is to be kept open.
5. Motivate the managers through counselling.
6. Counselling employees is an essential part of implementing the scheme. The counselling should include what the retiring employee can do in future *i.e.*, rehabilitation, how to manage the funds received under the scheme.
7. After receipt of applications for accepting V.R.S., scrutinise, decide whose applications are to be accepted and those whose are not to be accepted.
8. For those whose applications are to be accepted prepare a worksheet showing the benefits, each will receive including other dues like provident fund, gratuity and earned leave wages for the balance unveiled, earned leave and tax incidence if the V.R.S. amount exceed Rs. 5 lakhs.

PERFORMANCE APPRAISAL AND EVALUATION

Performance appraisal is a process of evaluating an employee's performance for a job in terms of its requirements.

According to Mc Gregor, "*Formal Performance appraisal plans are designed to meet three needs*, one of the organisation and the other two of the individual, namely :

(i) They provide systematic judgements to back up salary increases, transfers, demotions or terminations.

(ii) They are means of telling a subordinate how he is doing and suggesting needed changes in his behavioural attitudes, skills or job knowledge. They let him know 'where he stands' with the boss.

(iii) They are used as a base for coaching and counselling the individual by the superior.

Definitions

Performance appraisal has been defined by different scholars in various ways. Some of the important definitions are as follows:

- **Heyel,** "It is the process of evaluating the performance and qualifications of the employees in terms of the requirements of the job for which he is employed, for purposes of administration including placement, selection for promotions, providing financial rewards and other actions which require differential treatment among the members of a group as distinguished from actions affecting all members equally."
- **Dale S. Beach,** "Performance appraisal is systematic evaluation of the individual with respect to his or her performance on the job and his or her potential for development".
- **Dale Yoder,** "Performance appraisal includes all formal procedures used to evaluated personalities and contributions and potentials of group members in a working organisation. It is a continuous process to secure information necessary for making correct and objective decisions on employees."
- **Randall S. Schuler,** "Performance appraisal is a formal, structured system of measuring and evaluating an employee's job, related behaviour and outcomes to discover how and why the employee is presently perfuming on the job and how the employee can perform more effectively in the future so that the employee, organisation, and society all benefit."

What should be Rated ?

The seven criteria for assessing performance are:

1. **Quality.** The degree to which the process or result of carrying out an activity approaches perfection.
2. **Quantity.** The amount produced, expressed in monetary terms, number of units, or number of completed activity cycles.
3. **Timeliness.** The degree to which an activity or a result produced.
4. **Cost Effectiveness.** The degree to which the use of the organisation's resources (*e.g.*, human, monetary, technology, material) is maximised in the sense of getting the highest gain.
5. **Need for Supervision.** The degree to which a job performer can carry out a job function without supervisory assistance.
6. **Interpersonal Impact.** The degree to which a performer promotes feelings of self-esteem, goodwill and co-operation among co-workers and subordinates.
7. **Training.** Need for training for improving his skill's knowledge.

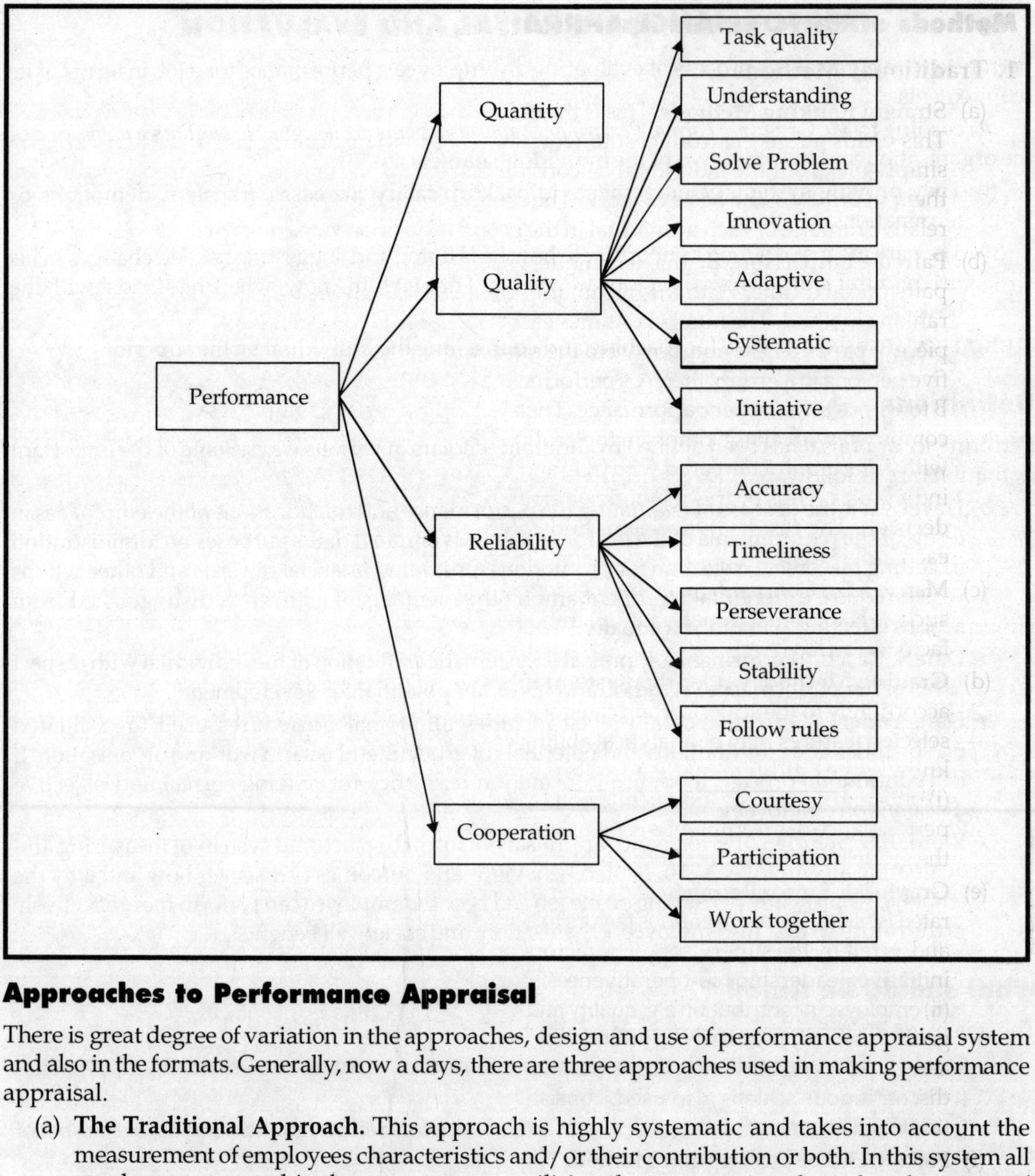

Approaches to Performance Appraisal

There is great degree of variation in the approaches, design and use of performance appraisal system and also in the formats. Generally, now a days, there are three approaches used in making performance appraisal.

(a) **The Traditional Approach.** This approach is highly systematic and takes into account the measurement of employees characteristics and/or their contribution or both. In this system all employees are rated in the same manner utilising the same approach so that the rating of separate personnel can be compared.

(b) **The Causal Approach.** This is an unsystematic use and often haphazard appraisal system which was commonly used in the past, but now it has given a place to more formal method, the main basis being seniority or quantitative measures of quantity and quality of output for rank and file personnel.

(c) **The Behavioural or Modern Approach.** This approach is based upon mutual goal setting and appraisal of progress by both appraisor and appraise. This lays emphasis on behavioural values of fundamental trust in goodness, capability and responsibility of human beings.

Methods of Performance Appraisal

1. Traditional Methods

(a) **Straight Ranking Methods.** This is the oldest and simplest method of performance appraisal. This yields a ranking from best to worst of all individuals comprising the group. The rater simply picks out the individual he considers best, the one he thinks next best etc. and ranks them in order on the basis of work. The ranks assigned by rater are then averaged and then relative ranking of each individual in the group are assigned/determined.

(b) **Paired Comparison.** By this technique, each employee is compared with all the persons in pairs one at a time. With this technique, the judgement is easier and simpler than ordinary ranking method. The number of times each individual is compared with another is tallied on a piece of paper. These numbers yield the rank order of the entire group. For example, if there are five persons in a group, then A's performance is compared to B's and a decision is arrived at A, B to whose is the better performance. Then A is compared to C, D and E in that order. Next B is compared with all the others in the group individually. Since he has already been compared with A, he is only compared with C, D and E. Similar comparison is made with respect to all the individuals. Thus by this method, we arrive at ten decisions and only two are involved in each decision. The results of decisions and comparisons are tabulated and a rank is assigned to each individual.

(c) **Man to Man Comparison.** In this method, certain factors are selected for the purpose of analysis such as leadership, dependability, initiative etc. and a scale is designed by the rater for each factor awarded.

(d) **Grading Method.** Under this system, the rater considers certain features and marks them accordingly to the scale. Certain categories of worth are carefully established and defined. The selected features may be analytical ability, co-operativeness, dependability, self experience job knowledge, judgement, leadership and organising ability etc. These may be rated (i) outstanding (ii) very good, (iii) good/average (iv) fair, (v) poor or any other scale. The actual performance of an employee is then compared with these grade definitions and he is allotted the grade which best describes his performance.

(e) **Graphic or Linear Rating Scale.** Under this system a printed form, one for each employee to be rated is filled. There are various factors to be checked and rated as per the performance and ability and as felt by the supervisors. The factors are of two type i.e. (i) Employer characteristics such initiative, leadership, co-operativeness, dependability, attitude, enthusiasm, loyalty etc. and (ii) employee's contribution e.g. quality and quantity of work, the responsibilities assumed, specific goals achieved, regularity of attendance, leadership offered, attitudes towards superiors and associates versatility etc. These traits are evaluated on a continuous scale or sometime a discontinuous scale is also used, consisting of appropriate boxes or squares which are to be ticked off.

(f) **Forced Choice Description Method.** This rating form prepares a series of item or statements which usually describe the degree of proficiency. The rater then chooses among the member of each group in terms of how will be believes the statements describing the individual being rated on various arrangements of items employed.

(g) **Check List.** Under this system, the rater does not evaluate an employer's performance. He supplies report information about it and the final rating is done by the personnel department. A series of questions are presented concerning an employee to his behaviour. The rater then checks to indicate if the answer to a question about an employee is positive or negative. The value of each question may be valued/weighed equally or certain questions may be weighed heavily than others.

The following are some of the sample questions in the check list

Is the employee really interested in the task assigned?	Yes/No
Is he respected by his colleagues (Co-workers)	Yes/No
Does he give respect to his superiors?	Yes/No
Does he follow instructions properly?	Yes/No
Does he make mistakes frequently?	Yes/No.

(h) **Free Essay Method.** In this method, the supervisor makes a free form, open ended appraisal of an employer in his own words and puts down his impression about the employer. The following factors are taken into account by supervisor.

(i) Relation with fellow supervisor and personnel assigned to him.
(ii) General organisation and planning ability
(iii) Job knowledge and potentials
(iv) Employee characteristics and attitudes
(v) Understanding and application of company policies and procedures
(vi) Production, quality and cost control
(vii) Physical conditions.
(viii) Development needs for future.

(i) **Critical Incident Method.** The basis of the method is the principle that 'there are certain significant acts in each employee's behaviour and performance which make all the difference between success and failure on the job'. The supervisor keeps a written record of the events that can be easily recalled/referred and used in the course of periodical or formal appraisal. Feedback is provided about the incidents during performance review session.

This method provides an objective basis for conducting a thorough discussion of an employee's performance. This method avoids recency bias (most recent incidents get too much emphasis). Most frequently, the critical incidents technique of evaluation is applied to evaluate the performance of superiors rather than of peers of subordinates.

(j) **Group Appraisal Method.** Under this, employees are rated by an appraisal group, consisting of their supervisors and three or four supervisors who have some knowledge of employee's performance. The supervisor explains to the group the nature of his subordinate's job, the actual performance of job holder, the causes of their particular level of performance and offers suggestions for future improvement.

(k) **Field Review Method.** Under this method, a trained employer from personnel department interviews the line supervisor to evaluate their respective subordinates. The appraiser is fully equipped with definite test questions, usually memorised in advance, which he puts to supervisors. The supervisor is required to give his opinion about the progress of his subordinates, the level of performance of each subordinate, his weaknesses, his good points, outstanding ability, promotability and possible plans of action in cases requiring further consideration. The appraisal takes detailed notes of the answers, which are then approved by the supervisors and placed in employee's personal file.

2. Modern Methods of Appraisal

(a) **Appraisal by Results or Management by Objectives (MBO).** This has been evolved by Peter Drucker. MBO has been defined as a 'process where by superior and subordinate managers of an organisation jointly identify the goals which are common, define each individual's major area of responsibility and set the targets and results which are expected of them and use these as guide for unit operations and assessing, the contribution of each of its members.'

Some features of MBO are :

- MBO emphasizes participatively set goals that are tangible, verifiable and measurable.
- MBO focuses attention on what must be accomplished (goals) rather than how it is to be accomplished (Methods).
- MBO, by concentrating on key result areas translates the abstract philosophy of management into concrete phraseology. The technique can be put to general use (non specialist technique). Further it is a dynamic system which seeks to integrate the company's need to clarify and achieve its profit and growth targets with the manager's need to contribute and develop himself.'
- MBO is a systematic and rational technique that allows management to attain maximum results from available resources by focussing on achievable goals. It allows the subordinate plenty of room to make creative decisions on his own.

This process emphasises the value of present and the future instead of past and focuses attention on the results that are accomplished and not on personal traits.

(b) **Assessment Centre Method.** Under this method many evaluators join together to judge employee's performance in several situations with the use of a variety of criteria. The assessments are made/done with the help of couple of employees and involves a par and pencil test, interviews and situational exercises such as in basket exercise, business game, a role playing incident and leaderless group discussions.

(c) **Human Assets Accounting Method.** This method refers to the activity devoted to attaching money estimates to the nature of a firm's internal human organisation and the external customer goodwill. If able and will trained personnel leave the firm, the human organisation is worthless, if they join it, its human assets increase. If distrust and conflict prevails the human enterprise is devalued. If team work and high morale prevails, the human organisation is a very valuable asset.

(d) **Behaviourally Anchored Rating Scales.** The procedure for BARS is usually five stepped.

(i) Generate critical incidents
(ii) Develop performance dimensions
(iii) Reallocate incidents
(iv) Scale of incidents
(v) Develop final instrument

GUIDELINES FOR EFFECTIVE PERFORMANCE APPRAISAL

- The contingency school of management can be summarized as an "it all depends" approach.
- The appropriate management actions and approaches depends on the situation.
- Managers with a contingency view use a 'flexible approach, draw on a variety of theories and experiences, and evaluate many options as they solve problems.
- Contingency management recongnizes that there is no one best way to manage.

POTENTIAL ASSESSMENT

In most Indian organisations, people earn promotions on the basis of their past performance. The performance is considered a good indicator of future job success. This could be true, if the jobs to played by the promotee are similar. However, in actual practice, the roles that a role holder played in the past may not be the same that he is expected to play if he assumes a different job after his transfer or promotion to a new position. Past performance, therefore, may not be a good indicator of the suitability of an indicator for a higher role.

To overcome this inadequacy, organisations must think of a new system called potential appraisal. The objective of potential appraisal is to identify the potential of a given employee to occupy higher positions in the organisation hierarchy and under take higher responsibilities.

Potential assessment is required to :

(i) Inform employees about their future prospects;
(ii) Help the organisation chalk out of a suitable succession plan;
(iii) Update training efforts from time to time;
(iv) Advice employees about what they must do to improve their career prospects.

Steps to be followed while introducing a Good Potential Assessment System

The following are some of the steps required to be followed while introducing a potential assessment system:

- **Role Description.** Organisational roles and functions must be defined. To this end, job descriptions must be prepared for each job.
- **Qualities needed to Perform the Roles.** Bases on job descriptions, the roles to be played by people must be prepared (i.e., technical, managerial jobs and behavioural dimensions).
- **Rating Mechanism.** Besides listing the functions and qualities, the potential assessment system must list mechanisms of judging the qualities of employees such as:
  1. ***Rating by others.*** The potential of a candidate could be rated by the immediate supervisor who is acquainted with the candidate's work in the past, especially his technical capabilities.
  2. ***Test.*** Managerial and behavioural dimensions can be measured through a battery of psychological tests.
  3. ***Games.*** Simulation games and exercise (assessment centre, business games, in basket, role play etc.) could be used to uncover the potential of a candidate.
  4. ***Records.*** Performance records and ratings of a candidate on his previous jobs could be examined carefully on various dimensions such as initiative, creativity, risk taking ability, etc., which might play a key role in discharging his duties in a new job.
- **Organising the System.** After covering the above preliminaries, he must set up a system that will allow the introduction of the scheme smoothly giving answers to some puzzling questions:
  (i) How much weightage to merit in place of seniority in promotions?
  (ii) How much weightage to each of the performance dimensions – technical, managerial, behavioural qualities.
  (iii) What are the mechanisms of assessing the individual on different indicators of his potential and with what reliability?
- **Feedback.** The system must provide an opportunity for every employee to know the results of his assessment. "He should be helped to understand the qualities actually required for performing the role for which he thinks he has the potential, the mechanisms used by the organisations to appraise his potential and the results of such an appraisal".

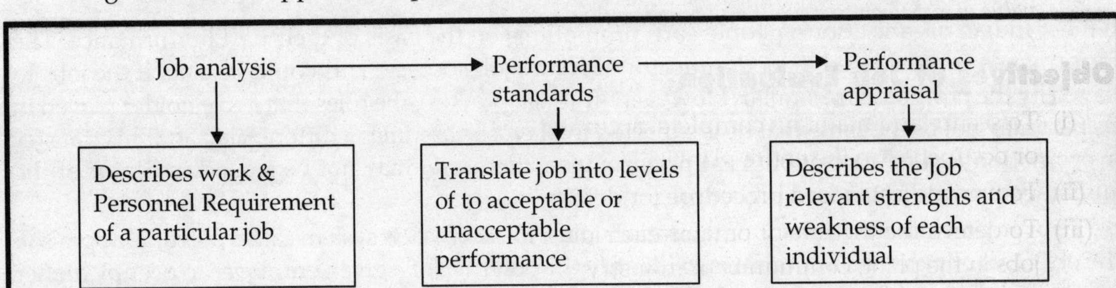

JOB EVALUATION

Job evaluation is an attempt to determine and compare demands which the normal performance of a particular job makes on normal workers without taking into account the individual abilities or performance of the workers concerned.

The evaluation may be achieved through the assignment of points or the use of some other systematic methods for essential job requirements, such as skills, experience and responsibility.

It does not set the price of a job; it merely fixes its relative worth. It presents an effort to determine the relative value of every job in a plant and to determine what the fair basic wage for such a job should be. It is not evaluating the merit of the worker who is doing the work. It rates the job and not the qualities of the individual worker on the job, which is the task of employee rating.

Definitions of Job Evaluations

Below are given some important definitions of job analysis:

Job Evaluation involves determination of relative worth of each job for the purpose of establishing wage and salary differentials. Relative worth is determined mainly on the basis of Job Description and Job Specification only. Job Evaluation helps to determine wages and salary grades for all jobs. Employees need to be compensated depending on the grades of jobs they perform. Remuneration must be based on the relative worth of each job. Ignoring this basic principle results in inequitable compensation and attendant ill effects on employees' morale. A perception of inequity is a sure way of De-motivating an employee.

- In the words of **Dale Yoder,** *"Job evaluation is a practice which seeks to provide a degree of objectivity in measuring the comparative value of jobs within an organisation and among similar organisations."*
- According to **Bethel, Atwater and Smith et at,** *"Job evaluation as a personal term has both a specific and genetic meaning specifically, it means job rating or the grading of occupations in terms of duties ; generally it means the entire field of wages and salary administration along modern lines"*
- According to **Bureau of Labour Statistics,** *"Job evaluation is the evaluation or rating of job to determine their position in job hierarchy. The evaluation may be achievement through assignment of points or the use of some other systematic rating method for essential job requirements such as skill, experience and responsibility."*
- In the words of **Edwin B. Flippo.** *"Job evaluation is a systematic and orderly process of determining the worth of a job in relation to other jobs."*
- According to **International Labour Organisation,** *"Job evaluation may be defined as an attempt to determine and compare the demands which the normal performance of particular job makes on normal workers without taking account of the individual abilities or performance of the workers concerned."*
- According to **Kimball and Kimball Jr.,** *"Job evaluation represents an effort to determine the relative value of every job in a plant and to determine what the fair basic wage for such a job should be."*

Objectives of Job Evaluation

(i) To secure and maintain complete, accurate and impersonal descriptions of each distinct job or occupation in the entire plant;

(ii) To provide a standard procedure for determining the relative worth of each job in a plant;

(iii) To determine the rate of pay for each job which is fair and equitable with relation to other jobs in the plant, community or industry;

(iv) To ensure that like wages are paid to all qualified employees for advancement and transfer;

(v) To promote a fair and accurate consideration of all employees for advancement and transfer;

(vi) To provide a factual basis for the consideration of wage rates for similar jobs in a community and in an industry; and

(vii) To provide information for 'work organisation, employees' selection, placement, training and numerous other similar problems.

Procedure of Job Evaluation

(i) **Analyse and Prepare Job Description.** This requires the preparation of a job description and also an analysis of job requirements for successful performance.

(ii) **Select and Prepare a Job Evaluation Plan.** This means that a job must be broken down into its component parts, *i.e.*, it should involve the selection of factors, elements needed for the performance of all jobs for which money is paid, determining their value and preparing written instructions for evaluation.

(iii) **Classify Jobs.** This requires grouping for arranging jobs in a correct sequence in terms of value to the firm and relating them to the money terms in order to ascertain their relative value.

(iv) **Install the Program.** This involves explaining it to employees and putting it into operation.

(v) **Maintain the Program.** Jobs cannot continue without updating new jobs and job changes in obedience to changing conditions and situations.

Methods of Job Evaluation

A. Non-Quantitative Methods or Qualitative Methods.

1. Ranking Method. Under this system all the jobs are arranged or ranked in order of their importance from simplest to the hardest order, each job being higher than the previous one in the sequence. A committee of several executives is constituted, which evaluated the job descriptions and ranks them in order of importance. The committee does not have specific factors before it but the things like nature of job, working conditions, supervision needed, responsibilities involved etc. are kept in mind while ranking the job. These factors are not assigned any weight or points. Following steps are taken in ranking.

(a) **Preparation of Job Description.** The first step in job evaluation process is the preparation of job description. Though it is not essential to prepare job description under ranking system but it is better and helpful in this system. If more than one person is assigned the job of ranking then they will give different ranking to the jobs.

(b) **Selection of Raters.** The second step in the process of ranking is the selection of raters. The jobs may be ranked department wise or in cluster (factory jobs, clerical jobs, menial jobs). Factory jobs should not be compared with clerical jobs or menial jobs because of their different nature. Generally, a committee of raters is used for the purpose.

(c) **Selection of Rates and Key Jobs.** First of all certain key jobs are selected and then other jobs are compared with them. The key jobs are selected from major departments or main functions.

(d) **Ranking of All Jobs.** Each job is then compared with the other similar job to establish its exact ranking in the scale. All the jobs are then ranked from lowest to highest or vice-versa.

Advantages

- **Simple.** The system is quite simple. A company does not face any difficulty in installing this system.

- **Easy.** As the workers understand the process there is no problem in administering this system.
- **Less time.** Less time is taken in evaluating the jobs.
- **Suitable for smaller concern.** This system is suitable for smaller organisation where the rates are fully acquainted with all the existing jobs in the enterprise.

Disadvantages

- **No scientific approach.** As there is no standard for an analysis of the whole job position, different bases of comparison may occur. Importance of the job may be arbitrarily ranked resulting in differences in similar jobs and may be resented by the employees.
- **No fair judgement.** This method decides the ranks of the jobs on the basis of their importance but does not tell the reasons. So ranks judgements are subjective and the fairness of the judgement cannot be advocated.
- **Difficult for large organisation.** In a complex industrial organisation, it is not possible to be familiar with all the jobs and thus general description will not enable correct assessment of the relative importance of the jobs.

2. Job Grading Method. Under this system, a number of pre-determined grades or classifications are decided by the committee and each job is assigned to one of the grades of classes. With the help of job analysis, information about different jobs is collected and they are put under different grades as per their nature and importance. For each grade or class there is different rate of wage. The jobs may be graded as skilled, unskilled, clerical, administrative etc.

The following steps are involved in grading system.

(a) **Preparation of Grade Descriptions.** The first thing to be done in this method is to prepare grade description to evolve classifications of jobs. A number of grades, different from each other, are selected. The grading should be done by considering the nature of duties of the job, supervising responsibilities etc. Each job is then, attached to an appropriate grade. For grade description, information about various jobs is collected through job description.

(b) **Selection of Grades and Key Jobs.** A number of jobs are graded, normally between 10 to 20, are selected. Key jobs are selected from important functions and major departments.

(c) **Grading the key jobs.** Key jobs are assigned to an appropriate grade level and their relationship to each other studied.

(d) All the jobs are put in relevant grades or classification. For e.g., all menial jobs, put in one class, clerical jobs in another class, technical jobs in still other class and so on. The jobs in one class receive the same wage rates.

Following table is a brief description of such a classification in an office:

Grade	Description of Job-Classification
I. Grade Unskilled	This generally covers the jobs of clerical nature, which requires accuracy, reliability etc. So special training is required.
II. Grade Skilled	This also covers the job with the nature of clerical work. But under this personnel require training programmes. This may include: ***draftsman, ledger man, laboratory assistant etc.***
III. Grade Interpretative	This requires a special skill to perform the jobs. These may be of clerical or non-clerical nature. This includes: ***foremans, layout draftsman etc.*** This is also of non-supervisory nature.
IV. Grade Creative	This involves a high degree of creativity and special knowledge. This covers ***engineers, salesman, staff supervisor, designers etc.***

Grade	Description of Job-Classification
V. Grade Executive	This is related to the supervisory and creative jobs category. This generally covers the ***managers of all different departments.***
VI. Grade Administrative	This is related with a little bit policy formulation and implementation. They have to work with great sense of responsibility. This may include: ***division manager, district sales managers, works engineers and treasurer etc.***
VII. Grade Policy	Their position is of the top in a concern. They have to formulate the policies of a company. This cover the top management posts like ***directors, managers etc.***

3. Point System. It involves quantitative and analytical approach to the measurement of job worth. A number of important factors to be considered in each job are determined. The degree of each factor is also determined for assigning points. Various factors are assigned points and sum of them gives us an index for the relative significance of the jobs that are rated. The point system is based on these assumptions that important factors of each job can be determined for evaluating it. The point of different jobs are, later on, converted into money value or wage rates.

Following steps are taken for job evaluation :

(a) **Type of jobs to be evaluated.** There are a number of jobs in every organisation and these may range from top executive to unskilled one. Similar jobs should be put in the same category for evaluation purpose. There should be separate evaluation programme for each class because the factors influencing them will be different. The job requirement of supervisor will be different from that of an unskilled worker.

(b) **Number of factors to be used.** It is very difficult to select the number of factors to be used for evaluating a job. The number of factors should be such that all aspects of a job are evaluated. The number of factors to be used varies from company to company, ranking from 3 to as many as 50. The common factors to be selected are education, training, skills, physical ability, mental requirement, suspensibility, job conditions etc.

(c) **Determination of Degree.** Each factor if evaluation should be further sub-divided into degrees for example, experience which is commonly used factor in each job may be sub-divided into five degrees. The first degree may have experience of 3 to 6 months with 5 points, second degree points having experience from 6 months to 1 year with 10 points, 15 for experience between 1 to 2 years, 20 points for experience of 2 to 4 years and 25 points for experience of over 4 years.

(d) **Assigning of Weights.** Each factor may be assigned a weight as per as its importance. For executives, mental requirements will have more weight than physical requirements.

(e) **Assigning Money Values to points.** The points assigned to each factor are added up for finding out the value of job. The values of jobs are translated into terms of money with a pre-determined formula. The following types of formula may be used:

Point Range	Pay Scale Rs.	Grade
50–100	700–1600	1
100–150	1200–2000	2
150–250	1500–2500	3
200–250	2500–4000	4
250–300	3000–5000	5

4. Factor Comparison Method. This method is a combination of ranking and point system of job evaluation. Under this method the relative rank of the jobs is evacuated in relation of monetary scale. Some key jobs are selected at the first instance and then ranked by considering one factor at a time. In this method five factors are generally evaluated for each job; mental requirements, skill, physical requirements, responsibilities and working conditions.

Following steps are taken under factor comparison method.

(a) **Selecting factors to be used.** The first thing to be done under this method is the selection of factors to be used this method is the selection of factors to be used for evaluation. The persons writing job descriptions should be given the proper definitions of these factors. The universally used factors are

(i) mental requirements
(ii) physical requirements
(iii) skill requirements
(iv) stop ousibility
(v) working conditions.

The number of factors may be more than five. Pay will be assigned in this method by compaining the weights of the factor required for each job, i.e., the present wages paid for key jobs may be divided among the factors weighted by importance. So the wages are assigned to the job in comparison to its ranking on each job factor.

(b) **Selection of key jobs.** They are to be taken as a standard and all other jobs are to be compared with key jobs evaluation. All key jobs should be exact and will understood and there should be no conflict between management and employees about them. The jobs so selected should cover the range from lowest to the lightest paid ones. Generally, 10 to 25 jobs are picked up as key jobs.

(c) **Ranking of key jobs.** All the members of job evaluation committee rank various jobs given earlier. A meeting of the committee is called to evolve a consensus on each job.

(d) **Valuing the factors.** Each factor of key job is then allocated a basic pay. The pay for such jobs should range from the lowest to the highest.

(e) **Comparison of jobs.** All jobs are compared with key job factor to determine their relative importance and position in the scale of jobs. The money value of jobs is also determined with this comparison.

(f) **Establishing wage structure.** By assigning money value to each factor of various jobs, a wage structure is determined by summing up these values.

COMPENSATION MANAGEMENT

Compensation Management and Benefits (Human Resource Management)

Compensation management and benefits is vital function of human resource managing team of companies who operate at international level. It is very important to compensate employees for their contribution in business process of company. Compensation is explained as all forms of financial rewards received by employees. It begins from their employment. It occupies a significant position in the employee's personal and official life. It has a substantial cost to the managers. Compensation is major human resource tools that organizations utilize to manage their employees. For an organization to get its money worth and encourage and hold skilled employees, it needs to guarantee that its compensation system is not an island by itself. It is important for firm to link compensation to its general goals and strategies as well as its compensation system to align with its HR strategy.

Compensation Management is an organized practice that involves balancing the work-employee relation by providing monetary and non-monetary benefits to employees. Compensation includes payments such as bonuses, profit sharing, overtime pay, recognition rewards and sales commission. Compensation can also include non-monetary perks such as a company-paid car, company-paid housing and stock options. Compensation assists to motivate the employees and enhances organizational effectiveness. Compensation displeasure can lead to absenteeism, turnover, job dissatisfaction, low performance, strikes and grievances.

Importance of Compensation Management

Many studies have demonstrated that good compensation is essential for every industry and helps to give proper return to the workers for their contributions to the organization. It communicates a positive control on the competence of workers and encourages them to give their best and accomplish the specific standards. It forms a basis of pleasure and satisfaction for the workers that minimizes the labour turnover and presents a steady organization. It increases the job evaluation process which consecutively helps in establishing more realistic and achievable standards. It is planned to obey with the various labour acts and therefore does not result in disagreement between the worker union and the management. This builds up a peaceable relationship between the employer and the employees. It creates an environment of self-esteem, efficiency and cooperation among the workers and provides satisfaction to the workers. It motivates the employees to increase efficiency and show their excellence. It provides growth and development opportunities to the deserving employees.

Deluca (1993) and Rajkumar (1996) described that "compensation is defined as pay, reward, remuneration, or salary and wage management". These terms are often used interchangeably in organization. In an organization standpoint, compensation is as an important human resource management function where it emphasizes planning, organizing, and controlling various types of pay systems. For instance, direct and indirect payments, monetary and non-monetary rewards and cash and non-cash payments, those compensation is used for rewarding employees who perform in their work or service. In this study, compensation can be seen as a measure of justice. Normally, it is the major source of employees' financial security.

Benefits is defined as the part of the total compensation package provided to the employee in whole or in part by payments from the employer and it does not comprise of the pay for time spent on work. Moreover, benefits are group membership rewards that give security for workforce and their family member. Benefits are a non-compensation paid to employees. Some benefits are mandated by law, for example social security, unemployment compensation and worker compensation. Employees' benefits include pension, health insurance, fringe benefits, welfare etc. Benefits are a vital part of an employee's total compensation package. Benefits packages became accepted after World War II, when wage controls made it more complex to give competitive salaries. Benefits can be treated as the payment or entitlement, such as one makes under an insurance policy or employment agreement, or public assistance program or more generally, something of value or utility. Benefits may also be considered as an expression of justice in society.

Carter (2008) explained that "benefits are forms of value, other than payment, that are provided to the employee in return for their contribution to the organization, which is for doing their work". Employee's benefit includes disability income protection, retirement benefits, work-life balance (for example, sick leave, vacation, jury duty and etc), allowances (for example, dental, insurance, medical, transportation, housing, mobile phone and etc.). Carter (2002) anticipated that benefits are increasingly costly for businesses to provide to employees, so the range and options of benefits are varying quickly to include, such as flexible benefits plan. For employers, they use benefits to catch the attention and retain good and capable workers. For employees, they rely on benefits for example, medical subsidies, vacations, and retirement, to secure their financial status. By linking benefits such as, pension and holidays to seniority, workers will be unwilling to change jobs. Lee, Hsu and Lien (2006) said that benefits are planned to uphold employees and their family against problems due to sickness, accidents or retirements. There are many components of benefits to bring out its effect of employees. Work life balance such as temporal flexibility, leave benefits, and interpersonal relationships has the potential to decrease or increase strain on workers with life responsibilities. The condition of work life balance strategies can provide a positive and direct effect on an employee's choice to stay with an employer. Milkovich & Newman (2008) stated that income protection assists to guard employees from the financial risks inbuilt in daily life. It serves as a support to employees' salaries in the event that an employee is sick, disabled, or no longer able to work. Workers allowances are extremely needed for employees. It helps to lessen the financial burden of employees and also can be treated as extra sum of salaries indeed. Therefore, a benefit has great consequence to the whole organizations.

It has been seen that major labour management clashes relate to compensation. Compensation is the extrinsic that employees receive in exchange for their work. It is composed of the base wage or salary and incentives or bonuses and benefit. Compensation is a key factor to attract and keep the best employees and ensuring that the organization has the competitive edge in a progressively more competitive world. The Compensation Management factor enables to distinguish between the payments strategies and those of competitors while still allowing flexibility, control and cost effectiveness. It provides a toolset for strategic remuneration planning that reveals the organization culture and pay strategies, and it makes powerful line managers within a framework of flexible budget control. Compensation management permit to control bottom line expenditures and competitive and motivating compensation, be it fixed pay, variable pay, stock options, merit increases, or promotion in other words, total compensation.

An employee's total compensation comprises of four components. The relative proportion of each constituent in the total compensation varies form firm to firm. The first and generally the major component is base compensation which means the fixed pay an employee receives on a regular basis, either in the form of a salary or as wages. The second component is allowances such as house rent allowance (HRA), dearness allowance (DA) and city compensatory allowance (CCA). The third component is incentive pay planned to reward employees for good performance, such as performance linked bonus, share in profit, etc. The fourth component is benefits or indirect compensation or perquisites such as company accommodation, company car, paid holiday, club membership, stock options. Compensation is evenly important for the employee as it determines life standard and position in society. In other words, compensation has great impact on employees economically, socially and psychologically.

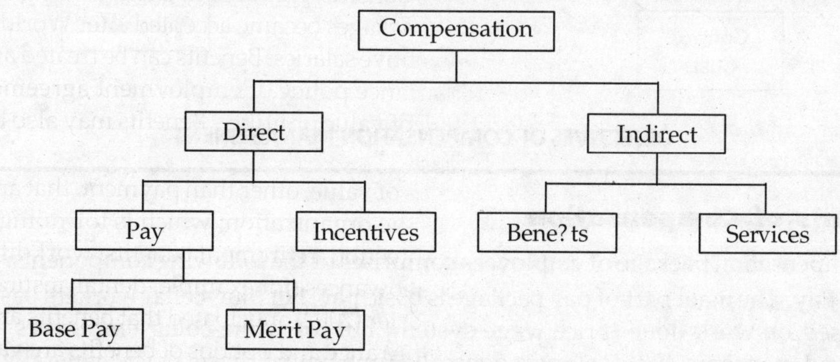

TYPE OF COMPENSATION

Compensation management consists of designing the lowest cost pay structure that will attract, keep, and stimulate the capable employees and which is perceived as fair by the employee satisfaction.

The major purposes of compensation management are as follows:

1. A perfect compensation system will have positive impact on the competence and results produced by employees. It will encourage the employees to perform better and achieve the standards fixed.
2. Compensation will raise the confidence, efficiency and cooperation among the workers. Being just and fair will provide satisfaction to the workers.
3. Good compensation and Rewards system bring harmony in the relationship of manager and employees, collective bargaining generally focus on compensation issues.
4. The ideal compensation system provides stand for cheerful and satisfied personnel. This minimizes the labour turnover. The organization becomes stable in marketplace.
5. The industry can devise compensation strategy and growth if it has the support of skilful, talented and happy workforce.
6. The effective compensation system is characteristic of organization success and wealth.
7. The success and constancy of the organization is measured with pay-package it provides to its employees.

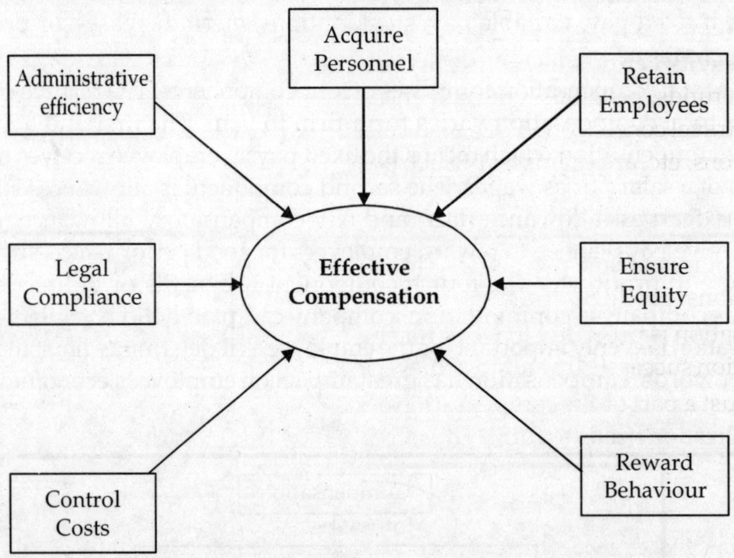

OBJECTIVES OF COMPENSATION MANAGEMENT

Components of Compensation

Financial compensation package of employees comprises of the following components:

1. **Basic Pay.** The main part of pay package is basic pay. For blue-collar workers basic wage may be based on work done (price wage system) but for white-collar employees, supervisory staff and managers, basic salary is generally time bound. Basic pay is generally determined through job evaluation which is the process of systematically ascertaining the relative worth of a job.

2. **Allowances.** Several allowances are paid in addition to basic pay. Some of these allowances are given below:
   - ***Dearness Allowance.*** This allowance is given to protect real income against inflation. Generally, dearness allowance (DA) is paid as a percentage of basic pay.
   - ***House Rent Allowance.*** Employers who do not provide living accommodation and pay house rent allowance (HRA) to employees. This allowance is calculated as a percentage of basic pay (Percentage varies according to Class of city from 10% to 35% of basic pay in case of government employees).
   - ***City Compensatory Allowance.*** This allowance is paid generally to employees in metros and other big cities where cost of living is comparatively high. City compensatory allowance (CCA) is generally a fixed amount per month.
   - ***Transport Allowance/Conveyance Allowance.*** Some employers pay transport allowance (TA) to their employees. A fixed sum is paid every month to cover a part of traveling charges.

   In some cases, medical allowance, education allowance for children, Tiffin allowance are also paid.
3. **Incentives.** Incentive compensation is performance-linked remuneration paid with the aim to encourage employees to work more and perform better. Both individual incentives and group incentives are used. Bonus, profit-sharing, commissions on sales are some examples of incentive compensation.
4. **Fringe Benefits/Perquisites.** Different types of benefits are paid particularly to senior managers. Provident funds, pensions, gratuity, encashment of earned leave, company house, company car, leave travel concession (LTC), medical aid, interest free loan, holiday homes, entertainment, stock options, etc. are examples of such benefits.

Needs of Compensation Management

1. A good compensation package is significant to stimulate the employees to increase the organizational productivity.
2. Compensation is provided to work for the organization. Compensation helps in running an organization successfully and to achieve its goals.
3. Salary is just a part of the compensation system, the employees have other psychological and self-actualization needs to fulfil. Thus, compensation serves the purpose.

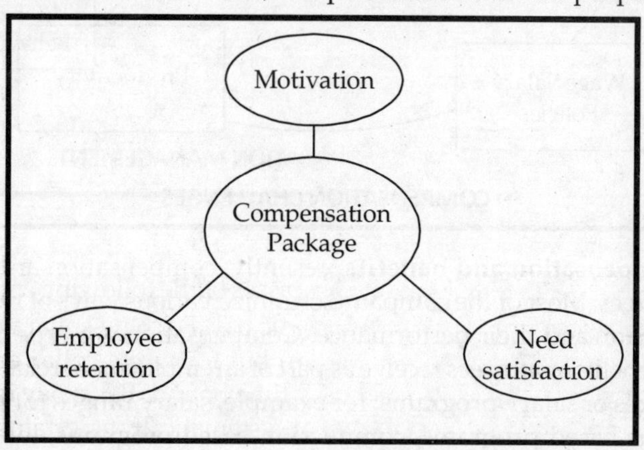

Major Phases of Compensation Management

Compensation management consists of four phases which are shown with the help of diagram given below:

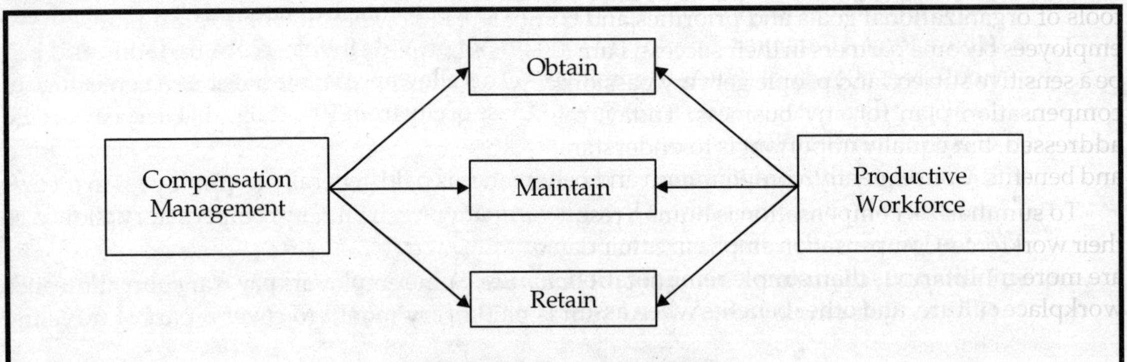

COMPENSATION MANAGEMENT

Compensation challenges. HR experts in most of the companies have major compensation-related concerns. Most specifically, the problem is money. Compensation structures are major issue for human resources departments in all types of organizations. Another problem for HR professionals is a compensation budget and salery. Key issues are depicted in below figure.

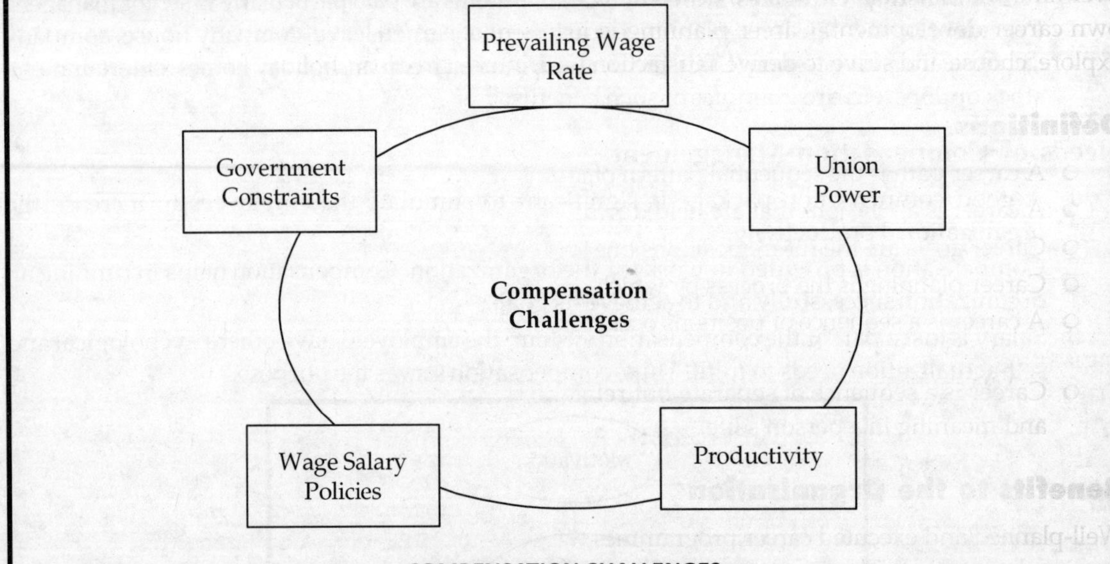

COMPENSATION CHALLENGES

Relation between compensation and benefit. presently, compensation and benefits are growing fields in Human Resources. Most of the company scrutinize various ways of rewarding employees to boost their job satisfaction and their performance. Compensation is a type of financial return and concrete services and benefits employees receive as part of an employment relationship, which includes topics in regard to wages or salary programs; for example, salary ranges for job descriptions, merit based programs, bonus based programs, commission based programs, long term or short terms incentives programs. Employee's benefit comprises of the allowances, income protection, life insurances, life balance, and vacation. Benefits are forms of value, other than payment, that are given to the employee in return for their work to the organization. Employers must design a suitable compensation and benefits system to their workers. This is because unsuitable compensation and benefits will have unhelpful effect to employee job satisfaction. Compensation and benefits is dominant tools of organizational goals and priorities and companies that expect to be successful must make employees become partners in their success. Pam (2007) scrutinized that employee compensation can be a sensitive subject, and people get very passionate when trying to determine the most appropriate compensation plan for any business. Today, many human resources related issues need to be addressed, but equally important is to understand the financial aspects of employee compensation and benefits. Consequently, compensation and benefits is major part of an organization.

To summarize, compensation is human resource mechanism that organizations use to manage their workforce. Compensation emphasizes fair day pay for fair day work. Compensation and benefits are more multifarious than simple remuneration. Many staff considers professional development, workplace culture, and other benefits when assessing workplace satisfaction.

MANAGING CAREER

Meaning and Definitions of Careers

Career is viewed as a sequence of position occupied by a person during the course of his lifetime. Career may also be viewed as amalgam of changes in value, attitude and motivation that occur, as a person grows older. The implicit assumption is that an individual can make a different in his destiny over time and can adjust in ways that would help him to enhance and optimize the potential for his own career development. Career planning is important because it would help the individual to explore, choose and strive to derive satisfaction with one's career object.

Definitions

- A career path is the sequential pattern of jobs that form a career.
- A career is all the jobs that are held during one's working life.
- Career goals are the future positions one strives a part of career.
- Career planning is the process by which one selects career goals and the path to these goals.
- A career is a sequence of positions occupied by a person during the course of a lifetime.
  – Decenzo & Robbins
- Career is a sequence of separate but related work activities that provides continuity, order and meaning in a person's life.
  – Edwin Flippo

Benefits to the Organisation

Well-planned and executed career programmes will benefit both the organisation and the employees in a number of ways. These include the following:

- **Staffing inventories.** Effective career management will help ensure a continuous supply of professional, technical and managerial talent so that future organisational goals may be achieved.
- **Staffing from within.** Because of the many potential advantages of promotion from within, most organisations like to promote employees when positions become available. But recruitment from within requires a strong career management programme to guarantee that employees can perform effectively in their new jobs. Promoting employees before they are ready

to assume their new jobs will result in unsatisfactory performance, as predicted by the Peter Principle. Peter Principle: Observation that in an hierarchy people tend to rise to "their level of incompetence." Thus, as people are promoted, they become progressively less-effective because good performance in one job does not guaranty similar performance in another. Named after the Canadian researcher Dr. Laurence J. Peter (1910-90) who popularized this observation in his 1969 book 'The Peter Principle.'

- **Solving staffing problems.** Certain staffing problems may be remedied through effective career management. First, a high rate of employee turnover may be caused, at least in part, by a feeling that little opportunity exists within the organisation. Second, recruiting new employees may be easier if applicants realise that the company develops its employees and provides career opportunities.
- **Satisfying employee needs.** The current generation of employees are very different from those of generations past. Higher levels of education have raised career expectations. And many workers hold their employers responsible for providing opportunities so that those expectations may be realised.
- **Enhanced motivation.** Because progression along the career path is directly related to job performance, an employee is likely to be motivated to perform at peak levels so that career goals may be accomplished.
- **Employment equity.** Guidelines demand fair and equitable recruiting, selection and placement policies and the elimination of discriminatory practices concerning promotions and career mobility- Many affirmative action programmes contain formal provisions to enhance the career mobility of women and other formerly excluded groups, including the development of career paths and the design of formal T&D activities.

Meaning & Definitions of Career Planning

Career planning is an ongoing process through which an individual sets career goals and identifies the means to achieve them. The process by which individuals plan their life's work is referred to as career planning.

"Career planning is a process of systematically matching career goals and individual capabilities with opportunities for their fulfillment." ***(Schermerhorn: 2002)***

"Career Planning is a deliberate process of becoming aware of self, opportunities, constraints, choices, and consequences; identifying career-related goals; and "career pathing" or programming work, education, and related developmental experiences to provide the direction, timing, and sequence of steps to attain a specific career goal." ***(McMahon and Merman: 1987)***

Career Anchors

Career anchors denote the basic drives that create the urge to take up a certain type of a career. These drives are as follows:

- **Managerial Competence.** Person having this drive seeks managerial positions that provide opportunities for higher responsibility, decision making, control and influence over others.
- **Technical Competence.** People having this anchor seek to make career choices based on the technical or functional content of the work. It provide continuous learning and updating one's expertise in a technical or specialised area such as quality control, engineering, accounting, advertising, public relations etc.

- **Security.** If one's career anchor is security than he is willing to do what is required to maintain job security (through compliance with organisational prescriptions), a decent income and a stable future.
- **Creativity.** This drive provides entrepreneurial and innovative opportunities to the people. People are driven by an overwhelming desire to do something new that is totally of their own making.
- **Autonomy.** These people seek a career that provides freedom of action and independence.
- Career planning facilitates the employees to develop not only their career goals but also the ways to achieve these goals.
- It helps individuals to remain competitive in the labour market by constantly upgrading competences as part of goal fulfillment efforts.
- It acts as the basis or standard for tracing the career progression achieved by an employee throughout his work life.
- It forms the basis for succession planning in the organisation. It helps the organisation in its preparation for the future by identifying and developing people for critical positions.
- Through career planning, an organisation can attract and retain its best people for a relatively longer period of time.
- Career planning is viewed as an effective technique by the organisation to limit the labour turnover and achieve better employee efficiency and commitment.
- It provides an opportunity for the organisation to assess the strengths and weaknesses and also the area of development of the employees for the purpose of *career* planning and development.
- It forms the basis for determining the training and development requirements of each employee in the organisation.

The main purpose of career planning is to integrate individuals' and organisational growth needs.

- It helps to develop individuals and groups, provides opportunities and challenges and strengthens work cultures.
- To increase managerial competence.
- To attract competent person and retain them in the organisation.
- To provide suitable promotional opportunities.
- To enable the employees to develop and make them ready to meet the future challenges.
- To increase the utilization of managerial reserves within an organisation.
- To correct employee placement.
- To reduce employee dissatisfaction and turnover.
- To improve motivation and morale.

Nature of Career Planning

The following are the salient features of career planning:

- **A Process.** Career planning is a process of developing human resources rather than an event.
- **Upward movement.** It involve upward movement in the organisational hierarchy, or special assignments, project work which require abilities to handle recurring problems, human relations issued and so on.

- **Mutuality of Interest.** The individual's interest is served as his needs and aspirations are met to a great extent and the organisation's interest is served as each of its human resources is provided an opportunity to develop and contribute to the organisational goals and objectives to the optimum of its ability and confidence.
- **Dynamic.** Career planning is dynamic in nature due to an ever changing environment.

Functions of Career Planning

The following are the functions performed by career planning:

(i) It helps in determining the career paths for different types of employees.

(ii) Create positions of self-development for employees in an organisation.

(iii) Provide such career planning information system which works as a database of career path, promotions and replacement.

(iv) To boost up morale of the employees and remove frustration from their minds.

(v) To develop such an internal environment in which employees can develop their talents and give them a fair chance to go up and contribute the organisation.

(vi) To establish such career paths on which employee can promote himself.

(vii) To enable employees to discover, develop and use their full potential for the organisation.

Career Planning Process

The possibility of conflict between the individual and organisation objectives calls for career planning efforts which can help to identify areas of conflict and initiate such actions as necessary to resolve the conflict. Career planning, thus, involves matching of rewards and incentives offered by the career path and career structure with hopes and aspirations of different categories of employees regarding their own concept of progression. A general approach to career planning would involve the following steps:

(i) **Analysis of the characteristics of the rewards and incentives** offered by the prevailing career system needs to be done and made known to employees. Many individuals may not be aware of their own career progression paths as such information may be confined to only a selected group of managers.

(ii) **Analysis of the characteristics of the hopes and aspirations** of different categories of employees including identification of their career anchors must be done through objective assessment. Most organisations assume the career aspirations of individual employees which need not be in tune with the reality. The individuals may not have a clear idea of their short and long-term career and life goals, and may not be aware of their aspirations and career anchors.

(iii) **Mechanisms for identifying congruence between individual career aspirations** and organisational career systems must be developed so as to enable the organisation to discuss cases of mismatch or incongruence. On the basis of above analyses, it will be necessary to compare and identify specific areas of match and mismatch for different category of employees.

(iv) **Alternative strategies for dealing with mismatch** will have to be formulated.

Some of the strategies adopted by several organisations include the following:

(a) **Changes in the career system** by creating new career paths, new incentives, new rewards, by providing challenges through job redesign opportunities for lateral movement and the like.

(b) **Change in the employees' hopes** and aspirations by creating new needs, new goals, new aspirations or by helping the employees to scale down goals and aspirations that are unrealistic or unattainable for one reason or the other.

(c) **Seek new basis of integration**, compromise or other forms of mutual change on the part of both employees and organisation through problem-solving, negotiations or other devices.

The Need for Carrier Planning

Organisations can hope to achieve high quality of work from their employees and foster positive attitudes and loyalty among workers through career planning. Career planning ensures that goals of individuals and organisations are in synergy and consequently tries to keep the motivation of managers high. This implies that once the individual becomes aware of his capabilities and opportunities within the organisation, he chooses to develop himself in a direction that improves his chances of being able to handle new responsibilities.

Organisational Career Planning

Following activities should be included:

1. **Human Resource Forecasting and Planning.** This helps in identifying the number of people to be hired. Second, the organisations will be able to coordinate their selection procedure with the overall strategic goals.
2. **Career information.** This should he shared with employees and includes promotional policy and career paths. Role directions and critical attributes could he made available to employees for identifying possible career paths and competency requirements.
3. **Career Counselling.** Senior executives should have periodic discussions with their subordinates and offer career counselling to them.
4. **Career Patching.** Organisations nowadays plan job sequences for their employees by which transfers and promotions are done more systematically.
5. **Skill Assessment Training.** Three types of analysis should be performed – organisational analysis, job analysis and job manpower requirement analysis. Organisational analysis and job analysis are the first steps in the training process.
6. **Succession Planning.** Here organisations assure that competent candidates are available in succession for critical positions. HR subsystems like promotions, terminations, transfers, retirements, etc. also make succession planning necessary.

Limitations of Career Planning

Though career planning helps an organisation in numerous ways, it has a few limitations that undermine the importance and relevance of career planning.

These are:

- **Time Factor.** Career planning is usually a long-term and time-consuming process. It is based on the logic of suffering short-term pain to get long-term gains. However, organisations may not be ready to spend a lot of time and resources on a process that would prove beneficial only in the long term.
- **Unsuitable for Large Workforce.** It may not be possible for organisations with a large workforce to develop individual career plans breach and every employee of the organisation. This is because the career plan process requires an in-depth analysis of each employee's strengths and weaknesses on a sustained basis.

- **Lack of Objectivity.** Only those organisations which believe in strict observance of objectivity in promotion and transfers can succeed in career planning. In contrast, favoritism and nepotism in promotions often make career planning an unsuccessful exercise.
- **External Interventions.** Government rules and regulations can also affect the Grieve planning options of an organisation.
- **Lack of Knowledge and Awareness.** Career planning by an employee is essentially a self-management process. It requires the employees to be aware of the basics of career planning and management activities. However, the employees at the lower levels of the organisational hierarchy may not be familiar with the career planning process.
- **Lack of Flexibility.** Many organisations treat career planning as a ritualistic, rigid exercise. They often fail to consider the uncertainties caused to the career planning activities by the changes in the situation. In fact, the absence of dynamic career planning programmes may limit the applicability of the career plans in uncertain and changing situations.

Different Phases in the Career of an Employee

Most working people go through career stages and it has been found that individual's needs and expectations change as the individual moves through these stages.

1. **Exploration Stage.** This is the stage where an individual builds expectations about his career. Some of them are realistic and some are not. But the fact is that these could be a result of the individual's ambitions.
2. **Establishment Stage.** This could be at the stage where the individual gets his first job, gets accepted by his peers, learns in this job, and also gains the first tangible evidence of success or failure. The establishment/advancement stage tends to occur between ages 25 and 44. In this stage, the individual has made his or her career choice and is concerned with achievement, performance and advancement. This stage is marked by high employee productivity and career growth, as the individual is motivated to succeed in the organisation and in his or her chosen occupation. Opportunities for job challenge and use of special competencies are desired in this stage. The employee strives for creativity and innovation through new job assignments. Employees also need a certain degree of autonomy in this stage so that they can experience feelings of individual achievement and personal success.
3. **Mid-Career Stage.** The individual's performance levels either continue to improve, or levels, or even deteriorates.
4. **Late Career.** This is regarded as a pleasant phase, where one is allowed to relax and play the role of an elderly statesman in the organisation.
5. **Decline.** The stage, where the individual is heading towards retirement.

The Career Development Action are:

- **Job performance**. Employee must prove that their performance on the job is to the level of standards established, if they want career development.
- **Exposure.** They should expose their skills, knowledge, qualifications, achievements, performance etc. to those who take the decision about the career progress.
- **Resignation.** Employee may resign the present job, if they find career opportunities elsewhere are better than those of the present organisation.
- **Change the job.** Employees who put organisational loyalty above career loyalty may change the job in the same organisation if they find that career opportunities in other jobs in the same organisation are better than those of present job.

- **Career guidance.** Counselling provides, information, advice and encouragement to switch over to other career or organisation, where career opportunities are better.
- So, there are two types of mobility in career development actions – internal and external mobility.

Effective organisational career development techniques include:

- Challenging initial job
- Dissemination of career option information
- Job postings
- Assessment centers
- Career development workshops
- Continuing education and training
- Periodic job change
- Sabbaticals

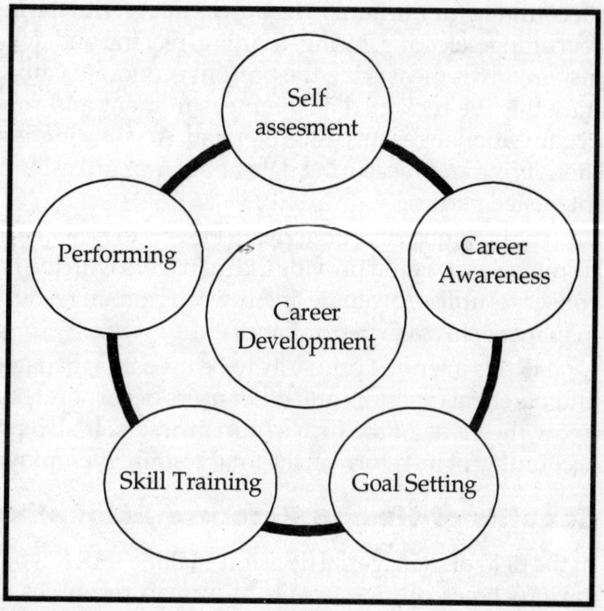

Individual career development is a three-step self-assessment process:

- Identification and organisation- Identify and organise your skills, interests, work-related needs, and values.
- Conversion into general fields and a specific goal- Convert these inventories into general career fields and specific job goals.
- Testing against realities – Test these possibilities against the realities of the organisation or the job market.

Career Paths

Career paths have historically® focused on upward mobility within a particular occupation. One of four types of career paths may be used: traditional, network, lateral, and dual.

A. **Traditional Career Path.** An employee progresses vertically upward in the organisation from one specific job to the next.

B. **Network Career Path.** A method of career pathing that contains both a vertical sequence of jobs and a series of horizontal opportunities.

C. **Lateral Skill Path.** traditionally, a career path was viewed as moving upward to higher levels of management in the organisation. The availability of the previous two options has diminished considerably in recent years. But this does not mean that an individual has to remain in the same job for life. There are often lateral moves within the firm that can be taken to allow an employee to become revitalized and find new challenges.

D. **Dual-Career Path.** A career-path method, that recognizes that technical specialists can and should be allowed to continue to contribute their expertise to a company without having to become managers.

NEW TRENDS IN HRM

CHANGING ENVIRONMENT OF HRM

Human Resource Accounting (HRA)

Accounting for the human resources deals with the measurement of costs which are associated with recruiting, selecting, hiring, training, placing and developing the employers of an organisation. This also involves measuring the present economic value of human resources to an organisation. HRA may then be reckoned as the measurement and reporting of the cost and value of the people as organisational resources. American Accounting Association has defined HRA as a process of identifying and measuring data about human resources and communicating this information to the interested parties.

The basic objective underlying HRA is to facilitate the effective and efficient management of human resources as it would provide the managers with the information needed to acquire, develop, allocate, conserve, utilise, evaluate and reward human resources. Besides, HRA also provides feedback to a manager of his own performance.

HRA is intended primarily to be used as a managerial tool. It also has a significant use for present and potential investors and other users of corporate financial statements who would be interested to know the value of the firm's human assets. It also provides the organisation with a more accurate accounting of its return on the total resources employed.

Benefits of Human Resource Accounting

In the field of managerial decision-making, HRA would help in making meaningful choices between various types of investments in human resources and other assets. It would assist the manager particularly with regard to :

(i) Direct recruitment vs. promotion
(ii) Transfer vs. retention.
(iii) Retrenchment or relieving vs. retention.
(iv) Utility of cost reduction programme in view of the possible impact on human relations.
(v) Impact of budgetary control on human relations and organisational behaviour.
(vi) New dimension added to capital budgeting process which includes human resource investment costs.
(vii) Consideration for an adequate return on investment in human assets and also a more useful interpretation of return on capital employed.
(viii) Decision on relocating factories, developing overseas subsidiaries, closing down or streamlining existing units.

EMERGING HR CONCEPTS

Advantages/Benefits/Significance/Importance/Need of HRM

Human Resource Management becomes significant for business organisation due to the following reasons.

- **Objective.** Human Resource Management helps a company to achieve its objective from time to time by creating a positive attitude among workers. Reducing wastage and making maximum use of resources etc.
- **Facilitates professional growth.** Due to proper Human Resource policies employees are trained well and this makes them ready for future promotions. Their talent can be utilised not only in

the company in which they are currently working but also in other companies which the employees may join in the future.

- **Better relations between union and management.** Healthy Human Resource Management practices can help the organisation to maintain co-ordinal relationship with the unions. Union members start realising that the company is also interested in the workers and will not go against them therefore chances of going on strike are greatly reduced.
- **Helps an individual to work in a team/group.** Effective Human Resource practices teach individuals team work and adjustment. The individuals are now very comfortable while working in team thus team work improves.
- **Identifies person for the future.** Since employees are constantly trained, they are ready to meet the job requirements. The company is also able to identify potential employees who can be promoted in the future for the top level jobs. Thus one of the advantages of HRM is preparing people for the future.
- **Allocating the jobs to the right person.** If proper recruitment and selection methods are followed, the company will be able to select the right people for the right job. When this happens the number of people leaving the job will reduce as the will be satisfied with their job leading to decrease in labour turnover.

Benchmarking

Any organisation which aims at grand success in a competitive world can learn a lot from the management practices of excellent corporations. Such practices serve as the benchmarks. Benchmarking is a continuous search for an application of significantly better practices that lead to superior competitive performance. It Ps much more than simply copying. *According to Robert C. Camp,* "Benchmarking is the search for industry's best practices that lead to superior performance."

It is the practice of measuring and comparing key aspects of an organisation with those in other organisations, to establish measures of relative performance and discover areas for improvement.

In the words of David Kearns of Xerox Corporation, "Benchmarking is the continuous process of measuring products, services and practices against the toughest competitors or those companies recognised as industry leaders."

It is a systematic way to identifying the superior products, services, processes and practices that can be adapted to an organisation to reduce costs, improve quality, cut inventory and provide greater satisfaction to customers.

Benchmarking is the process of comparing one's business processes and performance matches to industry bests or best practices from other industries. Dimensions typically measured are quality, time and cost. In the process of benchmarking, management identifies the best firms in their industry, or in another industry where similar processes exist, and compare the results and processes of those studied (the "targets") to one's own results and processes. In this way, they learn how well the targets perform and, more importantly, the business processes that explain why these firms are successful.

Benchmarking is used to measure performance using a specific indicator (cost per unit of measure, productivity per unit of measure, cycle time of x per unit of measure or defects per unit of measure) resulting in a metric of performance that is then compared to others.

Also referred to as "best practice benchmarking" or "process benchmarking", this process is used in management and particularly strategic management, in which organisations evaluate various aspects of their processes in relation to best practice companies' processes, usually within a peer group defined for the purposes of comparison. This then allows organisations to develop plans on how to make improvements or adapt specific best practices, usually with the aim of increasing some aspect of performance. Benchmarking may be a one-off event, but is often treated as a continuous process in which organisations continually seek to improve their practices.

Types of Benchmarking

- **Process benchmarking** - the initiating firm focuses its observation and investigation of business processes with a goal of identifying and observing the best practices from one or more benchmark firms. Activity analysis will be required where the objective is to benchmark cost and efficiency; increasingly applied to back-office processes where outsourcing may be a consideration.
- **Financial benchmarking** - performing a financial analysis and comparing the results in an effort to assess your overall competitiveness and productivity.
- **Benchmarking from an investor perspective**- extending the benchmarking universe to also compare to peer companies that can be considered alternative investment opportunities from the perspective of an investor.
- **Performance benchmarking** - allows the initiator firm to assess their competitive position by comparing products and services with those of target firms.
- **Product benchmarking** - the process of designing new products or upgrades to current ones. This process can sometimes involve reverse engineering which is taking apart competitors products to find strengths and weaknesses.
- **Strategic benchmarking** - involves observing how others compete. This type is usually not industry specific, meaning it is best to look at other industries.
- **Functional benchmarking** - a company will focus its benchmarking on a single function to improve the operation of that particular function. Complex functions such as Human Resources, Finance and Accounting and Information and Communication Technology are unlikely to be directly comparable in cost and efficiency terms and may need to be disaggregated into processes to make valid comparison.
- **Best-in-class benchmarking** - involves studying the leading competitor or the company that best carries out a specific function.
- **Operational benchmarking** - embraces everything from staffing and productivity to office flow and analysis of procedures performed.
- **Energy benchmarking** - process of collecting, analysing and relating energy performance data of comparable activities with the purpose of evaluating and comparing performance between or within entities. Entities can include processes, buildings or companies. Benchmarking may be internal between entities within a single organisation, or - subject to confidentiality restrictions - external between competing entities.

Benchmarking Process Benefits

1. **Competitive Advantage** the main benefit is to identify where you are at the moment in comparison to your main competitors and the reasons of why your business is behind others; by identifying the factors that are holding you back; this will give you an opportunity for process improvement and the opportunity to be the best in your market.
2. **Understanding of the External Environment** by analysing other companies within the same sector; this will let you know if the external problems you are having are the same being faced by your competitor; example: lack of reliable providers.
3. **Process Improvement** understanding the external environment will provide some of the tools needed to achieve competitive advantage; however, without process improvements; this will not be feasible; improving the areas where you are behind will put you on a different level.
4. **Clear and Concise Objectives** it will set objectives and clear targets to improve operations, processes and even performance of people. The importance of clear objectives relies in the motivational effect that has in the people responsible for providing results.
5. **Personnel Retention.** More companies nowadays are also performing personnel benchmarking in terms of salaries, benefits and satisfaction; this will allow to reward the

staff depending on what the average market does; this is especially important for key people in the organisation.

Pitfalls of Benchmarking

(i) Lack of focus and priority.
(ii) Lack of commitment on the part of management
(iii) Incompetent leadership.
(iv) Failure to consider customer requirements
(v) Lack of proper planning
(vi) Not involving the staff in the programme.
(vii) Lack of adequate resources and facilities.

Requirement of Successful Benchmarking

(i) Select the best companies for benchmarking.
(ii) Focus on the best practices.
(iii) Understand your own company's processes and practices thoroughly.
(iv) Be willing to change.
(v) Use benchmarking regularly.

Six Sigma

Organisations practicing Six Sigma create special levels for employees within the organisation. Such levels are called as: "Green belts", "Black belts" and so on. Individuals certified with any of these belts are often experts in six sigma process. **According to Six Sigma any process which does not lead to customer satisfaction is referred to as a defect and has to be eliminated from the system to ensure superior quality of products and services**. Every organisation strives hard to maintain excellent quality of its brand and the process of six sigma ensures the same by removing various defects and errors which come in the way of customer satisfaction. The process of Six Sigma originated in manufacturing processes but now it finds its use in other businesses as well. Proper budgets and resources need to be allocated for the implementation of Six Sigma in organisations.

Following are the two Six Sigma methods:

- DMAIC
- DMADV

DMAIC focuses on improving existing business practices. DMADV, on the other hand focuses on creating new strategies and policies.

DMAIC has Five Phases

D - Define the Problem. In the first phase, various problems which need to be addressed to are clearly defined. Feedbacks are taken from customers as to what they feel about a particular product or service. Feedbacks are carefully monitored to understand problem areas and their root causes.

M - Measure and find out the key points of the current process. Once the problem is identified, employees collect relevant data which would give an insight into current processes.

A - Analyze the data. The information collected in the second stage is thoroughly verified. The root cause of the defects are carefully studied and investigated as to find out how they are affecting the entire process.

I - Improve the current processes based on the research and analysis done in the previous stage. Efforts are made to create new projects which would ensure superior quality.

C - Control the processes so that they do not lead to defects.

DMADV Method

D - Design strategies and processes which ensure hundred percent customer satisfaction.

M - Measure and identify parameters that are important for quality.

A - Analyze and develop high level alternatives to ensure superior quality.

D - Design details and processes.

V - Verify various processes and finally implement the same.

Kaizen

Kaizen process aims at continuous improvement of processes not only in manufacturing sector but all other departments as well. Implementing Kaizen tools is not the responsibility of a single individual but involves every member who is directly associated with the organisation. Every individual, irrespective of his/her designation or level in the hierarchy needs to contribute by incorporating small improvements and changes in the system. Following are the main elements of Six Sigma:

- Teamwork
- Personal Discipline
- Improved Morale
- Quality Circles
- Suggestions for Improvement

Five S of Kaizen

"Five S" of Kaizen is a systematic approach which leads to foolproof systems, standard policies, rules and regulations to give rise to a healthy work culture at the organisation. You would hardly find an individual representing a Japanese company unhappy or dissatisfied. Japanese employees never speak ill about their organisation. Yes, the process of Kaizen plays an important role in employee satisfaction and customer satisfaction through small continuous changes and eliminating defects. Kaizen tools give rise to a well organised workplace which results in better productivity and yield better results. It also leads to employees who strongly feel attached towards the organisation.

Let us understand the five S in Detail:

1. **SEIRI.** SEIRI stands for Sort Out. According to Seiri, employees should sort out and organise things well. Label the items as "Necessary", "Critical", "Most Important", "Not needed now", "Useless and so on. Throw what all is useless. Keep aside what all is not needed at the moment. Items which are critical and most important should be kept at a safe place.
2. **Seition.** Seition means to Organise. Research says that employees waste half of their precious time searching for items and important documents. Every item should have its own space and must be kept at its place only.
3. **SEISO.** The word "SEISO" means shine the workplace. The workplace ought to be kept clean. De-clutter your workstation. Necessary documents should be kept in proper folders and files. Use cabinets and drawers to store your items.
4. **SEIKETSU-SEIKETSU** refers to Standardisation. Every organisation needs to have certain standard rules and set policies to ensure superior quality.
5. **SHITSUKE or Self Discipline.** Employees need to respect organisation's policies and adhere to rules and regulations. Self discipline is essential. Do not attend office in casuals. Follow work procedures and do not forget to carry your identity cards to work. It gives you a sense of pride and respect for the organisation.

Quality of Work Life

Quality of work life refers to the favorableness or unfavourableness of the job environment of an organisation for its employees. It is generic term which covers a person's feelings about every dimension of his work e.g. economic incentives and rewards, job security, working conditions, organisational and interpersonal relationships etc. The term QWL has different meanings for different people. A few important definitions of QWL are as follows:

- According to Harrison: "**Quality of Work Life** is the degree to which work in an organisation contributes to material and psychological well being of its members."
- According to D.S. Cohan "**Quality of Work Life** is a process of joint decision making, collaborations and building mutual respect between management and employees."
- According to the American Society of Training and Development "**Quality of Work Life** is a process of work organisation which enables its members at all levels to participate actively and effectively in shaping the organisations' environment, methods and outcomes. It is a value based process which is aimed towards meeting the twin goals of enhanced effectiveness of the organisation and improved quality of life at work for the employees".

Principles of QWL

According to N.Q. Herrick and M. Maccoby there are four basic principles, which will humanise work and improve the Quality of Work Life:

1. **The Principle of Security.** Quality of work cannot be improved until employees are relieved of the anxiety, fear and loss of future employment. The working conditions must be safe and fear of economic want should be eliminated. Job security and safety against occupational hazards is an essential precondition of humanisation of work.
2. **The Principle of Equity.** There should be a direct and positive relation between effort and reward. All types of discrimination between people doing similar work and with same level of performance must be eliminated. Equity also requires sharing the profits of the organisation.
3. **The Principle of individualism.** Employees differ in terms of their attitudes, skills, potentials etc. Therefore, every individual should be provided the opportunities for development of his personality and potential. Humanisation of work requires that employees are able to decide their own pace of activities and design of work operations.
4. **The Principle of Democracy.** This means greater authority and responsibility to employees. Meaningful participation in decision making process improves the quality of work life.

The Mckinsey 7s Framework

How do you go about analyzing how well your organisation is positioned to achieve its intended objective? This is a question that has been asked for many years, and there are many different answers. Some approaches look at internal factors, others look at external ones, some combine these perspectives, and others look for congruence between various aspects of the organisation being studied. Ultimately, the issue comes down to which factors to study. While some models of organisational effectiveness go in and out of fashion, one that has persisted is the McKinsey 7s framework. Developed in the early 1980s by Tom Peters and Robert Waterman, two consultants working at the McKinsey & Company consulting firm, the basic premise of the model is that there are seven internal aspects of an organisation that need to be aligned if it is to be successful.

The 7s model can be used in a wide variety of situations where an alignment perspective is useful, for example to help you:

- Improve the performance of a company.
- Examine the likely effects of future changes within a company.
- Align departments and processes during a merger or acquisition.
- Determine how best to implement a proposed strategy.

The Seven Elements

The McKinsey 7s model involves seven interdependent factors which are categorised as either "hard" or "soft" elements:

Hard Elements	Soft Elements
Strategy	Shared Values
Structure	Skills
Systems	Style
	Staff

"Hard" elements are easier to define or identify and management can directly influence them: These are strategy statements; organisation charts and reporting lines; and formal processes and IT systems.

"Soft" elements, on the other hand, can be more difficult to describe, and are less tangible and more influenced by culture. However, these soft elements are as important as the hard elements if the organisation is going to be successful. The way the model is presented in Figure below depicts the interdependency of the elements and indicates how a change in one affects all the others.

Let's look at each of the elements specifically:

- **Strategy** the plan devised to maintain and build competitive advantage over the competition.
- **Structure** the way the organisation is structured and who reports to whom.
- **Systems** the daily activities and procedures that staff members engage in to get the job done.
- **Shared Values** called "superordinate goals" when the model was first developed, these are the core values of the company that are evidenced in the corporate culture and the general work ethic.
- **Style** the style of leadership adopted.
- **Staff** the employees and their general capabilities.
- **Skills** the actual skills and competencies of the employees working for the company.

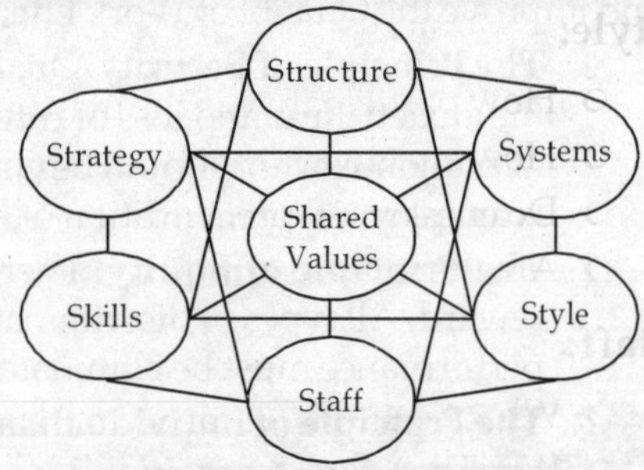

THE MCKINSEY 7S MODEL.

7s Checklist Questions

Here are some of the questions that you'll need to explore to help you understand your situation in terms of the 7s framework. Use them to analyse your current (Point A) situation first, and then repeat the exercise for your proposed situation (Point B).

Strategy:

- What is our strategy?
- How do we intend to achieve our objectives?
- How do we deal with competitive pressure?
- How are changes in customer demands dealt with?
- How is strategy adjusted for environmental issues?

Structure:

- How is the company / team divided?
- What is the hierarchy?
- How do the various departments coordinate activities?
- How do the team members organise and align themselves?
- Is decision making and controlling centralised or decentralised? Is this as it should be, given what we're doing?
- Where are the lines of communication? Explicit and implicit?

Systems:

- What are the main systems that run the organisation? Consider financial and HR systems as well as communications and document storage.
- Where are the controls and how are they monitored and evaluated?
- What internal rules and processes does the team use to keep on track?

Shared Values:

- What are the core values?
- What is the corporate/team culture?
- How strong are the values?
- What are the fundamental values that the company/team was built on?

Style:

- How participative is the management/leadership style?
- How effective is that leadership?
- Do employees/team members tend to be competitive or cooperative?
- Are there real teams functioning within the organisation or are they just nominal groups?

Staff:

- What positions or specialisations are represented within the team?
- What positions need to be filled?
- Are there gaps in required competencies?

Skills:

- What are the strongest skills represented within the company/team?
- Are there any skills gaps?
- What is the company/team known for doing well?
- Do the current employees/team members have the ability to do the job?
- How are skills monitored and assessed?

Business Process Re-engineering

Hammer and Champy's concept of Business Process Re-Engineering depends on harnessing technology to optimise processes as its main driver. To understand why technology is imperative for BPR, let's first review what BPR does. "BPR is the fundamental rethinking and radical redesign of business processes to achieve dramatic improvements in critical contemporary measures of performance, such as cost, quality, service, and speed." Instead of starting with an activity flowchart, corporations are advised to start with a clean slate. They are then told to look into why they perform the tasks the way they do. A Process Engineer will look at the activities to be performed and how they can be engineered to invest minimum resources and get maximum returns. To illustrate the point, let us consider the example of Apple iPod. Apple rethought the way music ought to be made available to the consumers. The changes it brought were:

- **Radical.** While all other music labels were selling music via brick and mortar stores, Apple developed its iTunes software to sell music digitally. (Napster had made digital music available through a P2P platform earlier, but was sued by music labels for copyright violation)
- **Fundamental.** Apple sold single tracks as opposed to whole albums being sold at brick and mortar shops. Apple just kept in mind the end need of the consumer and reconsidered whether conventions were required.

Business process re-engineering is required in two cases:

1. The organisation has discovered some breakthrough methodology which will revolutionise its processes to give it more productivity and efficiency and therefore the entire process needs to be changes.
2. The organisation has failed to keep up to date with the changing technologies. Since it did not continuously innovate, it is now faced with a "change or die" situation and business process re-engineering which helps integrate latest best practices into the processes are the only way to save the business.

Information Availability. To fundamentally redesign a process, one must know the details involved. Details from internal and external sources must be captured and provided to the relevant people in the required time duration. This helps them to identify the bottlenecks and work around better ways of reaching the desired end.

Information Sharing. A BPR project is usually facilitated by a cross functional team. Most of the times, teams are spread across different geographic locations. Information needs to be successfully shared amongst various people to ensure the re-engineering goes as planned and without hiccups.

Technology as the Solution. The new processes that are developed as a result of BPR initiatives deploy the latest technology to achieve the desired end results. Usually it is e-Commerce, automation or another technology driven solution that is implemented.

Business Process Re-engineering has become a very important buzzword in the BPM lexicon. Many corporations who were late in realising the power and importance of BPM have to undergo re-engineering initiatives to ensure that they are still relevant to the marketplace. Re-engineering initiatives are however expensive and may require certain downtime. This is the reason they are resented by many corporations.

NEW CHALLENGES OF HRM

1. Retaining your best talent – Make it your top priority

Gone are the days where recruiting good talent was enough, retaining that good talent is also imperative. Especially those employees who possess greater professional and technical knowledge are much in demand in the job market as such employees have the ability to keep their company ahead in the race. Such employees are invaluable assets for any company. Employee development and engagement, health and safety, recognition, flexible work timings, work-life balance are some examples of novel approaches that you could use to retain your employees.

2. Ensuring better employee productivity to maximise your profits

Maximizing profit and minimizing cost is the core of every business. Higher the in case it is due to inefficient employee, training the employee of eve staff could be a solution of finding alternative resources for sufficient inadequate resources are the case. HRM should manage on-site as was training for employees. Providing training and support to employees benefits the company but also helps the employees who take this round they are a vital part of the business.

3. Managing a diverse workforce : Unity in diversity is the new business

Composition of workforce is getting diverse at present situation. Divided and created by age, gender, educational background and religion but also personality and background of workers. However, with a more diversed some usual issues such as harassment of discrimination may arise. To instances, a company must formulate and implement strict rules.

4. Dealing with the 'New normal' – Globalization

We live in a global world today. In fact, mergers, acquisitions, collaborate takeovers are a common phenomenon. While internationalization of a firm is sign of success, it is also a challenge as with globalization, you also several challenges related to different language, work culture, manage approach, culture and tradition. You are also required to handle various such as scheduling meetings, managing holidays and outsourcing of overcome these challenges.

5. Resistance to change–What if i am replaced by a machine in the future?

This is a common fear which plagues the mind of many employees. Especially the ones who consider change to be a threat and think that their roles within the company will be replaced by a machine or computer that can do the job cheaper or faster.

As with any change in the workplace, changes in technology could cause anxiety or even resistance among your employees. The role of the human resource manager would be to develop strategies to combat this resistance to change which begins by assuring employees of their worth for the business. They must be able to perceive the technology as an aid not an obstacle to their work.

6. Maintaining privacy and managing vital business information

As the technology within an organization advances, so do the privacy and security concerns connected with those technical changes. Ensuring that your employees are well trained in securing data and hence preventing privacy breaches Providing employee training on how to secure data and preventing any breach of privacy thus ensuring the safety of sensitive business information is a key challenge for human resources. Communicating with technology vendors and keeping up-to-date with the technical aspects of the company are some more ways for human resources managers to recognize and confront this challenge.

7. Maintaining discipline and ensuring successful achievement of business goals

Discipline is one of the key issues, lack of which can cause various problems impacting the productivity of the company. For instance, if discipline is not maintained; employees may neglect their tasks and duties or even procrastinate their tasks and misbehave with co-workers. The ultimate result of these activities is decreased productivity of your company.

You need to make your policies clear and inform every employee about your disciplinary procedures as well as let them know who they can appeal to. You must follow different processes depending on the severity of the employee's actions. There is a need to ascertain whether discipline is due to employee performance issue or if it is misconduct.

8. Embrace technology or get extinct

Any company must consider technological changes as the present day worlod demands every firm to move with the change, or else be left behind Technological changes influence the overall nature of work and businesses need to find employees that are able to adjust with the change.

During this process, unemployment as well as employment opportunities arise, creating new challenges for HRM. With new developments in technology as well as with the use of new tools, such as talent networks and internal social networks, there is the promise of increased flexibility and productivity.

9. Leadership Development and Succession Planning

Leadership development is one of the biggest challenges for human resource management. It needs to be a critical strategic initiative. HR professionals are expected to provide the essential structure, processes and tools to select the best and develop the future leaders of the organization.

Most such initiatives can also be successfully conducted with the use of a scientific approach through customised assessments. With online assessments on identifying the best talent, predicting success at your workplace as well as building the next set of leaders by evaluating them through this approach can be the best next steps.

Main Differences Between Personnel Management and HRM (HRM Vs Personnel Management)

Dimensions		Personnel and IR	HRM
Beliefs and assumptions			
1.	Contract	Careful delineation of written contracts	Aim to go beyond contract
2.	Rules	Importance of devising clear rules/mutually	'Can-do' outlook; Impatience with 'rule'
3.	Guide to management action	Procedures	Business-need'
4.	Behaviour referent	Norms/custom and practice	Values/mission
5.	Managerial task vis-a-vis labour	Monitoring	Nurturing
6.	Nature of relations	Pluralist	Unitarist
7.	Conflict	Institutionalised	De-emphasised
Strategic aspects			
8.	Key relations	Labour management	Customer
9.	Initiatives	Piecemeal	Integrated
10.	Corporate plan	Marginal	Central
11.	Speed of decision	Slow	Fast
Line management			
12.	Management role	Transactional	Transformational leadership
13.	Key managers	Personnel/ IR specialists	General/business/line managers
14.	Communication	Indirect	Direct
15.	Standardisation	High (e.g. 'parity' an issue)	Low (e.g. 'parity' not seen as relevant)
16.	Prized management skills	Negotiation	Facilitation
Key levers			
17.	Selection	Separate, marginal task	Integrated, key task
18.	Pay	Job evaluation (fixed grades)	Performance-related

HRM has a long history of growing from a simple welfare and maintenance function to that of a board level activity of the companies. In recent years, the focus on people management from human capital/intellectual capital perspective is also shaping firmly. However, the hard fact is that this growth can be generally witnessed in management literature and rarely in practice. Peripheral observation of people management in organisation can mislead the observers since, hardly there could be any organisation that is yet to rename its old fashioned title of industrial relations/ personnel/welfare/administration department into HRM department. But, in practice, these organisations continue to handle the people management activities the way they had been handling earlier. The reasons for this could be many and varied. Among them, the potential reason is lack of clear understanding about the differences between personnel/IR and HRM.

MULTIPLE CHOICE QUESTIONS

1. Which of the following is not a key function of human resource management?
(1) Recruitment and selection
(2) Compensation and benefits
(3) Inventory and supply chain management
(4) Training and development

2. Which of the following is not a benefit of effective human resource planning?
(1) Improved organisational performance and productivity
(2) Increased employee satisfaction and engagement
(3) Minimising legal and regulatory risks
(4) Reducing the need for employee feedback and communication

3. What is the primary goal of effective workforce management?
(1) Maximising individual employee potential
(2) Minimising employee turnover and attrition
(3) Optimising the use of organisational resources and capabilities
(4) Exerting control and authority over employees

4. Which of the following is not a key element of effective human resource management?
(1) Strategic planning and decision-making
(2) Compensation and benefits administration
(3) Vertical alignment with organisational values and objectives
(4) Employee training and development

5. What is the primary focus of effective human resource planning?
(1) Exerting control and authority over employees
(2) Optimising the use of organisational resources and capabilities
(3) Minimising legal and regulatory risks
(4) Maximising employee engagement and satisfaction

6. What is the primary goal of effective recruitment and selection?
(1) Maximising employee potential and performance
(2) Minimising employee turnover and attrition
(3) Exerting control and authority over employees
(4) Reducing the need for employee feedback and communication

7. Which of the following is not a benefit of effective compensation and benefits management?
(1) Enhanced employee loyalty and engagement
(2) Minimising legal and compliance risks
(3) Increased employee turnover and attrition
(4) Attracting and retaining top talent

8. What is the primary goal of effective performance management?
(1) Exerting control and authority over employees
(2) Maximising individual employee potential and performance
(3) Reducing the need for employee feedback and communication
(4) Minimising employee turnover and attrition

9. Which of the following is not a key element of effective employee training and development?
   (1) Strategic planning and decision-making
   (2) Alignment with organisational values and objectives
   (3) Enhancing employee loyalty and engagement
   (4) Developing key job skills and competencies

10. What is the primary focus of effective compensation and benefits management?
   (1) Minimising legal and compliance risks
   (2) Attracting and retaining top talent
   (3) Optimising employee performance and potential
   (4) Minimising organisational costs

11. Which of the following is not a benefit of effective employee training and development?
   (1) Reducing legal and regulatory risks
   (2) Maximising employee potential and performance
   (3) Enhancing employee job satisfaction and engagement
   (4) Minimising employee turnover and attrition

12. What is the primary goal of effective employee engagement and satisfaction management?
   (1) Minimising employee turnover and attrition
   (2) Optimising the use of organisational resources and capabilities
   (3) Maximising individual employee potential and performance
   (4) Enhancing employee loyalty and commitment to the organisation

13. What is the primary focus of effective human resource management?
   (1) Maximising individual employee potential and performance
   (2) Decreasing employee engagement and satisfaction
   (3) Minimising organisational costs
   (4) Exerting control and authority over employees

14. What is the primary goal of effective performance appraisal?
   (1) Maximising employee potential and performance
   (2) Minimising employee turnover and attrition
   (3) Enhancing employee loyalty and engagement
   (4) Providing feedback to employees and in turn improving their performance

15. Which of the following is not a benefit of effective employee engagement and satisfaction management?
   (1) Improved organisational performance and productivity
   (2) Enhanced employee loyalty and commitment to the organisation
   (3) Maximising the use of organisational resources and capabilities
   (4) Decreased employee turnover and attrition

16. What is the primary focus of effective employee retention management?
   (1) Attracting and retaining top talent
   (2) Minimising legal and regulatory risks
   (3) Exerting control and authority over employees
   (4) Minimising employee feedback and communication

17. Which of the following is not a key element of effective succession planning?
   (1) Strategic decision-making and planning
   (2) Identifying and developing key employee competencies and skills
   (3) Minimising legal and regulatory risks
   (4) Ensuring smooth transitions and continuity of organisational leadership

18. What is the primary goal of effective employee engagement and satisfaction management?

(1) Maximisng employee potential and individual performance
(2) Enhancing employee loyalty and commitment to the organisation
(3) Decreasing employee turnover and attrition
(4) Minimising legal and regulatory risks

19. Which of the following is not a benefit of effective employee retention?
(1) Attracting and retaining top talent
(2) Maximising individual employee potential and performance
(3) Minimising legal and compliance risks
(4) Enhancing employee loyalty and commitment to the organisation

20. What is the primary focus of effective employee performance management?
(1) Exerting control and authority over employees
(2) Providing feedback to employees to improve their performance
(3) Minimising employee feedback and communication
(4) Maximising employee potential and individual performance

21. What is the primary goal of effective employee job analysis?
(1) Identifying key employee competencies and skills
(2) Providing feedback to employees to improve their performance
(3) Enhancing employee loyalty and commitment to the organisation
(4) Ensuring clear and accurate job descriptions

22. Which of the following is not a key element of effective staffing management?
(1) Recruitment and selection
(2) Succession planning
(3) Ensuring diversity and inclusion in the workplace
(4) Exerting control and authority over employees

23. What is the primary focus of effective employee development?
(1) Maximising individual employee potential and performance
(2) Minimising employee engagement and satisfaction
(3) Optimising the use of organisational resources and capabilities
(4) Ensuring effective communication channels

24. Which of the following is not a benefit of effective employee job analysis?
(1) Ensuring clear and accurate job descriptions
(2) Optimising the use of organisational resources and capabilities
(3) Identifying key employee competencies and skills
(4) Supporting effective workforce planning and decision-making

25. What is the primary goal of effective employee engagement management?
(1) Maximising employee potential and individual performance
(2) Enhancing employee loyalty and commitment to the organisation
(3) Minimising legal and compliance risks
(4) Attracting and retaining top talent

26. **Assertion:** Effective employee training and development is focused on developing key job skills and competencies.
Reason: Employee training and development involves providing feedback to employees to improve their performance.
(1) Both assertion and reason are true and the reason is the correct explanation of the assertion.
(2) Both assertion and reason are true, but the reason is not the correct explanation of the assertion.
(3) Assertion is true but reason is false.
(4) Assertion is false but reason is true.

27. **Assertion:** Performance appraisal is one of the key elements of effective employee management.

Reason: Performance appraisal involves providing feedback to employees to improve their performance.

(1) Both assertion and reason are true and the reason is the correct explanation of the assertion.
(2) Both assertion and reason are true, but the reason is not the correct explanation of the assertion.
(3) Assertion is true but reason is false.
(4) Assertion is false but reason is true.

28. **Assertion:** Human resource planning involves Optimising the use of organisational resources and capabilities.

Reason: Effective human resource planning requires alignment with organisational values and objectives.

(1) Both assertion and reason are true and the reason is the correct explanation of the assertion.
(2) Both assertion and reason are true, but the reason is not the correct explanation of the assertion.
(3) Assertion is true but reason is false.
(4) Assertion is false but reason is true.

29. **Assertion:** Performance management is focused on effectively communicating organisational values and objectives to employees.

Reason: Performance management involves providing feedback to employees to improve their performance.

(1) Both assertion and reason are true and the reason is the correct explanation of the assertion.
(2) Both assertion and reason are true, but the reason is not the correct explanation of the assertion.
(3) Assertion is true but reason is false.
(4) Assertion is false but reason is true.

30. **Assertion:** Effective employee retention is focused on Minimising legal and regulatory risks.

Reason: Employee retention enhances organisational performance and productivity.

(1) Both assertion and reason are true and the reason is the correct explanation of the assertion.
(2) Both assertion and reason are true, but the reason is not the correct explanation of the assertion.
(3) Assertion is true but reason is false.
(4) Assertion is false but reason is true

31. Which of the following is not a key function of human resource management?

(1) Recruitment and selection
(2) Compensation and benefits
(3) Inventory and supply chain management
(4) Training and development

32. What is the primary goal of effective human resource planning?

(1) Exerting control and authority over employees
(2) Optimising the use of organisational resources and capabilities
(3) Minimising legal and regulatory risks
(4) Maximising employee engagement and satisfaction

33. What is the primary focus of effective workforce management?

(1) Maximising individual employee potential
(2) Minimising employee turnover and attrition
(3) Optimising the use of organisational resources and capabilities
(4) Exerting control and authority over employees

34. Which of the following is not a key element of effective human resource management?

(1) Strategic planning and decision-making
(2) Compensation and benefits administration
(3) Vertical alignment with organisational values and objectives
(4) Employee training and development

35. Which of the following is not a benefit of effective human resource planning?

(1) Improved organisational performance and productivity
(2) Increased employee satisfaction and engagement
(3) Minimising legal and regulatory risks
(4) Reducing the need for employee feedback and communication

36. What is the primary focus of effective recruitment and selection?
(1) Maximising individual employee potential and performance
(2) Minimising employee turnover and attrition
(3) Exerting control and authority over employees
(4) Reducing the need for employee feedback and communication

37. What is the primary goal of effective compensation and benefits management?
(1) Enhanced employee loyalty and engagement
(2) Minimising legal and compliance risks
(3) Attracting and retaining top talent
(4) All of the above

38. Which of the following is not a benefit of effective performance management?
(1) Maximising individual employee potential and performance
(2) Reducing the need for employee feedback and communication
(3) Enhancing employee loyalty and commitment to the organisation
(4) Minimising employee turnover and attrition

39. What is the primary focus of effective employee engagement and satisfaction management?
(1) Minimising employee turnover and attrition
(2) Optimising the use of organisational resources and capabilities
(3) Maximising individual employee potential and performance
(4) Enhancing employee loyalty and commitment to the organisation

40. Which of the following is not a key element of effective employee training and development?
(1) Strategic planning and decision-making
(2) Alignment with organisational values and objectives
(3) Enhancing employee loyalty and engagement
(4) Developing key job skills and competencies

41. Which of the following is not a benefit of effective compensation and benefits management?
(1) Attracting and retaining top talent
(2) Increased employee loyalty and engagement
(3) Minimising legal and compliance risks
(4) Minimising employee morale and job satisfaction

42. What is the primary goal of effective employee retention management?
(1) Maximising individual employee potential and performance
(2) Minimising legal and regulatory risks
(3) Attracting and retaining top talent
(4) Exerting control and authority over employees

43. What is the primary focus of effective employee performance management?
(1) Exerting control and authority over employees
(2) Maximising employee potential and individual performance
(3) Reducing the need for employee feedback and communication
(4) Minimising employee turnover and attrition

44. What is the primary goal of effective employee job analysis?
(1) Ensuring clear and accurate job descriptions

(2) Identifying key employee competencies and skills
(3) Providing feedback to employees to improve their performance
(4) Enhancing employee loyalty and commitment to the organisation

45. Which of the following is not a benefit of effective employee job analysis?
(1) Supporting effective workforce planning and decision-making
(2) Ensuring clear and accurate job descriptions
(3) Identifying key employee competencies and skills
(4) Optimising the use of organisational resources and capabilities

46. What is the primary goal of effective succession planning?
(1) Strategic decision-making and planning
(2) Ensuring smooth transitions and continuity of organisational leadership
(3) Identifying and developing key employee competencies and skills
(4) Minimising legal and regulatory risks

47. Which of the following is not a key element of effective staffing management?
(1) Recruitment and selection
(2) Succession planning
(3) Ensuring diversity and inclusion in the workplace
(4) Exerting control and authority over employees

48. Which of the following is not a benefit of effective employee retention?
(1) Enhanced employee loyalty and commitment to the organisation
(2) Attracting and retaining top talent
(3) Minimising legal and compliance risks
(4) Maximising individual employee potential and performance

49. What is the primary focus of effective employee engagement management?
(1) Enhancing employee loyalty and commitment to the organisation
(2) Exerting control and authority over employees
(3) Minimising legal and compliance risks
(4) Attracting and retaining top talent

50. What is the primary goal of effective employee engagement and satisfaction management?
(1) Maximising individual employee potential and performance
(2) Enhancing employee loyalty and commitment to the organisation
(3) Decreasing employee turnover and attrition
(4) Minimising legal and regulatory risks

51. Which of the following is not a benefit of effective workforce management?
(1) Increased employee satisfaction and engagement
(2) Minimising employee turnover and attrition
(3) Optimising the use of organisational resources and capabilities
(4) Exerting control and authority over employees

52. What is the primary focus of effective succession planning?
(1) Ensuring smooth transitions and continuity of organisational leadership
(2) Minimising legal and regulatory risks
(3) Optimising the use of organisational resources and capabilities
(4) Enhancing employee loyalty and commitment to the organisation

53. Which of the following is not a benefit of effective performance appraisal?
(1) Enhancing employee loyalty and commitment to the organisation
(2) Maximising individual employee potential and performance
(3) Providing feedback to employees to improve their performance
(4) Minimising employee turnover and attrition

54. What is the primary goal of effective staffing management?
(1) Ensuring diversity and inclusion in the workplace
(2) Exerting control and authority over employees
(3) Recruitment and selection
(4) All of the above

55. What are the primary components of the HRM conceptual framework?
(1) Strategic alignment, agility, and performance management
(2) Employee development, succession planning, and workforce management
(3) Strategic alignment, employee development, and performance management
(4) None of the above

56. What is the primary goal of strategic alignment in HRM?
(1) Minimising employee feedback and communication
(2) Ensuring effective communication channels
(3) Aligning HRM practices with organisational values and objectives
(4) Exerting control and authority over employees

57. What is the purpose of human resource planning?
(1) Exerting control and authority over employees
(2) Optimising the use of organisational resources and capabilities
(3) Maximising employee engagement and satisfaction
(4) All of the above

58. Which of the following is not a key element of effective workforce management?
(1) Developing job descriptions and specifications
(2) Providing employee feedback and communication
(3) Minimising employee morale and job satisfaction
(4) Ensuring effective communication channels

59. What is the purpose of employee training and development?
(1) Exerting control and authority over employees
(2) Developing key job skills and competencies
(3) Minimising employee turnover and attrition
(4) All of the above

60. What is the goal of HRM?
(1) Exerting control and authority over employees
(2) Optimising the use of organisational resources and capabilities
(3) Maximising employee engagement and satisfaction
(4) All of the above

61. What are the key components of effective human resource planning?
(1) Strategic alignment, workforce management, and employee development
(2) Recruitment and selection, compensation and benefits, and performance management
(3) Workforce management, employee performance management, and employee engagement management
(4) None of the above

62. What is the goal of effective employee development?
(1) Maximising individual employee potential and performance
(2) Ensuring effective communication channels
(3) Exerting control and authority over employees
(4) Minimising employee feedback and communication

63. What is the purpose of effective staffing management?
(1) Exerting control and authority over employees

(2) Ensuring diversity and inclusion in the workplace
(3) Recruitment and selection
(4) All of the above

64. What is the purpose of effective succession planning?
(1) Providing feedback to employees to improve their performance
(2) Ensuring smooth transitions and continuity of organisational leadership
(3) Minimising legal and regulatory risks
(4) Ensuring effective communication channels

65. What is the primary focus of effective HRM?
(1) Developing key job skills and competencies
(2) Exerting control and authority over employees
(3) Optimising the use of organisational resources and capabilities
(4) Providing feedback to employees to improve their performance

66. What is the primary focus of effective HR planning?
(1) Optimising the use of organisational resources and capabilities
(2) Developing job descriptions and specifications
(3) Minimising employee morale and job satisfaction
(4) Exerting control and authority over employees

67. What is HRM?
(1) A function that concentrates on the recruitment, compensation and benefits, training, job analysis and evaluation of employees in the organisation
(2) A function that concentrates on the management of organisational resources
(3) A function that focuses on the production of goods and services
(4) A function that ensures the safety and security of the organisation

68. What is the role of job analysis in HR management?
(1) To guide recruitment and selection
(2) To perform performance appraisals
(3) To assess the market value of a job
(4) All of the above

69. What is the goal of recruitment and selection?
(1) To identify the best set of candidates for the job
(2) To hire as many people as possible
(3) To exclude certain groups from the selection process
(4) To ensure that candidates are not overqualified for the job

70. What is human resource development?
(1) The promotion of employees to higher levels of responsibility
(2) Activities intended to enhance the quality of people in the workforce and contribute to organisational success
(3) The advancement of technology to better manage organizations
(4) All of the above

71. What is the difference between human resource planning and human resource development?
(1) HR planning is concerned with recruitment, selection and job analysis; HR development deals with training and development
(2) HR planning is concerned with workforce planning, job evaluation and compensation; HR development deals with performance management and career development
(3) HR planning is concerned with operations in the HR department; HR development deals with operations in the rest of the organisation
(4) There is no difference between HR planning and HR development

72. What is the primary goal of workforce planning?

(1) To manage employee turnover
(2) To ensure that the company has the right number of employees with the right skills in the right place at the right time
(3) To reduce costs by not hiring when there is little demand for products and services
(4) To ensure that a company is staffed as efficiently as possible

73. What is the difference between employee training and employee development?
(1) Employee training is job-specific; employee development is career-oriented
(2) Employee training involves learning new skills; employee development involves enhancing existing skills
(3) Employee training is not mandatory; employee development is mandatory
(4) Employee training is formal; employee development is informal

74. What is the goal of succession planning?
(1) To attract top talent to the organisation
(2) To Maximise individual employee potential and performance
(3) To ensure that high-potential employees are identified and developed for future leadership roles
(4) All of the above

75. What is the primary goal of effective staffing?
(1) To reduce employee turnover rates
(2) To ensure that the company has the best available employees
(3) To make sure that each employee is in the right job
(4) All of the above

76. What is the difference between work analysis and job analysis?
(1) Work analysis is a broader concept that includes job analysis
(2) Job analysis is a broader concept that includes work analysis
(3) There is no difference between work analysis and job analysis

77. What is the goal of job evaluation?
(1) To determine the market value of a job
(2) To match the salary of employees to the duties of their job
(3) To ensure that employees are compensated fairly for the work they do
(4) To ensure that salaried employees are classified correctly

78. What is the primary goal of effective compensation management?
(1) To ensure that the company is compliant with legal requirements
(2) To attract and retain skilled and motivated employees
(3) To ensure that employees are compensated appropriately for their work
(4) To reduce employee turnover and attrition rates

79. What is the key element of effective employee benefits management?
(1) Ensuring compliance with legal requirements
(2) Attracting and retaining top talent
(3) Enhancing employee loyalty and engagement
(4) All of the above

80. Which of the following is not a key element of job analysis?
(1) Identifying the tasks and duties of a job
(2) Developing job descriptions and specifications
(3) Conducting employee performance appraisals
(4) Assessing the knowledge, skills, and abilities required for a job

81. What is the primary goal of job analysis?
(1) Identifying the tasks and duties of a job
(2) Assessing the knowledge, skills, and abilities required for a job
(3) Developing job descriptions and specifications
(4) Conducting employee performance appraisals

82. Which of the following is not a benefit of effective job analysis?
(1) Improved workforce planning and decision-making
(2) Reduced employee turnover and attrition
(3) Decreased legal and regulatory risks
(4) Increased employee morale and job satisfaction

83. What is the primary focus of effective job analysis?
(1) Identifying the tasks and duties of a job
(2) Assessing the knowledge, skills, and abilities required for a job
(3) Developing job descriptions and specifications
(4) Conducting employee performance appraisals

84. What is the purpose of a job analysis questionnaire?
(1) To assess the knowledge, skills, and abilities required for a job
(2) To identify the tasks and duties of a job
(3) To develop job descriptions and specifications
(4) To conduct employee performance appraisals

85. Which of the following is not a key element of effective recruitment?
(1) Developing clear job descriptions and specifications
(2) Effective job advertising and marketing
(3) Providing performance feedback to candidates
(4) Conducting effective candidate screening

86. Which of the following is not a key element of effective selection?
(1) Developing clear job descriptions and specifications
(2) Effective candidate screening
(3) Effective performance feedback to candidates
(4) Developing effective selection criteria and tests

87. What is the primary goal of effective selection?
(1) Exerting control and authority over employees
(2) Developing clear job descriptions and specifications
(3) Hiring the most qualified candidate for the job
(4) Conducting effective performance appraisals

88. Which of the following is not a benefit of effective selection?
(1) Attracting and hiring top talent
(2) Improved workforce planning and decision-making
(3) Increased employee turnover and attrition
(4) Hiring the most qualified candidate for the job

89. What is the purpose of effective employee placement?
(1) To place employees in the most appropriate job or role
(2) To develop clear job descriptions and specifications
(3) To exert control and authority over employees
(4) To conduct effective performance appraisals

90. Which of the following is an example of internal employee placement?
(1) Job advertising and marketing
(2) Job fairs and networking events
(3) Performance appraisals and evaluations
(4) Internal job transfers and promotions

91. What is the primary goal of effective induction?
(1) Exerting control and authority over employees
(2) Providing employees with the resources and training to be successful in their new role
(3) Developing clear job descriptions and specifications

(4) Conducting effective performance appraisals

92. Which of the following is a benefit of effective induction?
(1) Increased employee turnover and attrition
(2) Decreased legal and regulatory risks
(3) Providing employees with the resources and training to be successful in their new role
(4) Exerting control and authority over employees

93. Assertion: Job analysis is the process of defining a job in terms of its tasks, responsibilities, and duties.
Reason: Job analysis helps ensure that jobs are designed in a way that is both efficient and effective.
(1) Both assertion and reason are true and the reason is the correct explanation of the assertion.
(2) Both assertion and reason are true but the reason is not the correct explanation of the assertion.
(3) Assertion is true but reason is false.
(4) Assertion is false but reason is true.

94. Assertion: The primary focus of effective recruitment is to attract and hire top talent.
Reason: Effective recruitment involves developing clear job descriptions and specifications.
(1) Both assertion and reason are true and the reason is the correct explanation of the assertion.
(2) Both assertion and reason are true but the reason is not the correct explanation of the assertion.
(3) Assertion is true but reason is false.
(4) Assertion is false but reason is true.

95. Assertion: Effective selection involves developing clear selection criteria and tests.
Reason: Effective selection helps ensure that the most qualified candidate is hired for the job.
(1) Both assertion and reason are true and the reason is the correct explanation of the assertion.
(2) Both assertion and reason are true but the reason is not the correct explanation of the assertion.
(3) Assertion is true but reason is false.
(4) Assertion is false but reason is true.

96. Assertion: The primary goal of effective placement is to place employees in the most appropriate job or role.
Reason: Effective placement involves developing clear job descriptions and specifications.
(1) Both assertion and reason are true and the reason is the correct explanation of the assertion.
(2) Both assertion and reason are true but the reason is not the correct explanation of the assertion.
(3) Assertion is true but reason is false.
(4) Assertion is false but reason is true.

97. Assertion: Induction involves providing employees with the resources and training to be successful in their new role.
Reason: Effective induction helps ensure that employees are compliant with legal and regulatory requirements.
(1) Both assertion and reason are true and the reason is the correct explanation of the assertion.
(2) Both assertion and reason are true but the reason is not the correct explanation of the assertion.
(3) Assertion is true but reason is false.
(4) Assertion is false but reason is true.

98. Which of the following is not a benefit of effective job analysis?
(1) Effective employee selection and placement
(2) Improved workforce planning and decision-making
(3) Increased employee morale and job satisfaction
(4) Increased employee turnover

99. What is the primary focus of job analysis?
(1) Conducting employee performance appraisals
(2) Identifying the tasks and duties of a job
(3) Assessing the knowledge, skills, and abilities required for a job
(4) Exerting control and authority over employees

100. What is the purpose of a job analysis interview?
(1) To develop clear job descriptions and specifications
(2) To identify the tasks and duties of a job
(3) To develop effective selection criteria and tests
(4) All of the above

101. Who typically conducts the job analysis process?
(1) Human resource professionals
(2) Job incumbents and supervisors
(3) Senior management
(4) External consultants

102. What is the primary outcome of effective job analysis?
(1) Improved employee performance appraisals
(2) Reduced legal and regulatory risks
(3) Clear job descriptions and specifications
(4) Increased employee turnover

103. What is the purpose of developing effective job descriptions and specifications?
(1) To attract and hire top talent
(2) To exert control and authority over employees
(3) To conduct effective employee performance appraisals
(4) To decrease legal and regulatory risks

104. Which of the following is not a key element of effective recruitment communications?
(1) Clarity and transparency
(2) Effective marketing and advertising techniques
(3) Overpromising and overstating the job benefits and responsibilities
(4) Engaging and interactive platforms

105. Who is involved in the effective recruitment process?
(1) Human resource professionals and senior management
(2) Job incumbents and supervisors
(3) Hiring managers and recruiters
(4) External consultants

106. What is the purpose of effective candidate screening?
(1) To hire the most qualified candidate for the job
(2) To conduct employee performance appraisals
(3) To develop clear job descriptions and specifications
(4) To exert control and authority over employees

107. What is the primary outcome of effective selection?
(1) Reduced legal and regulatory risks
(2) Clear selection criteria and tests
(3) Improved employee morale and job satisfaction
(4) Increased employee turnover

108. Who is involved in the effective selection process?
(1) Human resource professionals and senior management
(2) Job incumbents and supervisors
(3) Hiring managers and recruiters
(4) All of the above

109. **Assertion:** Effective job analysis is essential to developing clear job descriptions and specifications.
Reason: Job analysis helps identify the tasks and duties required for a job and the knowledge, skills, and abilities needed to perform those tasks.
(1) Both assertion and reason are true and the reason is the correct explanation of the assertion.

(2) Both assertion and reason are true but the reason is not the correct explanation of the assertion.
(3) Assertion is true but reason is false.
(4) Assertion is false but reason is true.

110. Assertion: The primary focus of effective recruitment is to attract and hire top talent.

Reason: Effective recruitment involves developing clear job descriptions and specifications.

(1) Both assertion and reason are true and the reason is the correct explanation of the assertion.
(2) Both assertion and reason are true but the reason is not the correct explanation of the assertion.
(3) Assertion is true but reason is false.
(4) Assertion is false but reason is true.

111. Assertion: Effective employee placement involves placing employees in the most appropriate job or role.

Reason: Effective placement helps reduce employee turnover and increases job satisfaction.

(1) Both assertion and reason are true and the reason is the correct explanation of the assertion.
(2) Both assertion and reason are true but the reason is not the correct explanation of the assertion.
(3) Assertion is true but reason is false.
(4) Assertion is false but reason is true.

112. Assertion: The primary goal of effective employee induction is to establish control over new employees.

Reason: Effective employee induction provides new employees with the resources, training, and support necessary to be successful in their new role.

(1) Both assertion and reason are true and the reason is the correct explanation of the assertion.
(2) Both assertion and reason are true but the reason is not the correct explanation of the assertion.
(3) Assertion is true but reason is false.
(4) Assertion is false but reason is true.

113. Assertion: Effective candidate screening involves assessing the knowledge, skills, and abilities required for a job.

Reason: Effective candidate screening helps ensure that the most qualified candidate is hired for the job.

(1) Both assertion and reason are true and the reason is the correct explanation of the assertion.
(2) Both assertion and reason are true but the reason is not the correct explanation of the assertion.
(3) Assertion is true but reason is false.
(4) Assertion is false but reason is true.

114. Which of the following is a common training method?
(1) Job analysis
(2) Performance appraisal
(3) On-the-job training
(4) Recruitment

115. What is the primary goal of a training needs assessment?
(1) To identify employee weaknesses
(2) To recommend promotion opportunities
(3) To identify areas where training is needed
(4) To evaluate employee performance

116. Which of the following is most useful for tracking employee training progress?
(1) Performance appraisals
(2) Training evaluations
(3) Job analysis
(4) Recruitment efforts

117. Which of the following is a benefit of e-learning as a training method?
(1) It allows for personalized training content
(2) It offers real-time feedback
(3) It provides face-to-face interaction
(4) It requires specialized software

118. Which of the following is a disadvantage of on-the-job training?

(1) It is expensive to implement
(2) It requires specialized trainers
(3) It can be disruptive to the work environment
(4) It can be inconsistent across trainers and trainees

119. What is the primary focus of performance management?
(1) Recruiting top talent
(2) Setting salary and benefits packages
(3) Improving employee performance
(4) Conducting employee training

120. What is the difference between performance appraisal and performance management?
(1) Performance appraisal refers to the overall process of managing employee performance.
(2) Performance management focuses on setting goals and measuring employee progress.
(3) Performance appraisal is focused on compensation and benefits.
(4) Performance management is part of the recruitment process.

121. What is the primary purpose of a performance appraisal?
(1) To evaluate employee performance
(2) To train and develop employees
(3) To recruit top talent
(4) To set salary and benefits packages

122. What is the purpose of a 360-degree feedback system?
(1) To provide overall performance evaluations for employees
(2) To measure the effectiveness of training and development programs
(3) To involve multiple perspectives in employee performance evaluations
(4) To track employee attendance and productivity

123. What is the advantage of using performance metrics?
(1) They allow for a more objective evaluation of employee performance
(2) They save time by eliminating the need for employee performance appraisals
(3) They provide standardized evaluations across all job types
(4) They eliminate the need for continuous employee training and development

124. Who is responsible for setting performance goals and objectives?
(1) Senior management
(2) Human resource professionals
(3) Employees and their supervisors
(4) External consultants

125. What is the primary benefit of setting clear performance goals and objectives?
(1) Improved employee morale and motivation
(2) Increased employee turnover
(3) Reduced legal and regulatory risks
(4) Improved employee performance

126. What is the purpose of a performance improvement plan?
(1) To identify top-performing employees
(2) To set performance goals and objectives
(3) To address areas of employee performance that need improvement
(4) To measure the effectiveness of training programs

127. Which of the following is a common method for measuring employee productivity?
(1) Performance appraisals
(2) Time and attendance tracking
(3) 360-degree feedback
(4) Training evaluations

128. What is the primary goal of performance feedback?
(1) To provide an opportunity for employees to vent their frustrations
(2) To evaluate the effectiveness of the performance appraisal system
(3) To help employees improve their performance
(4) To establish control over employees

129. What is the primary goal of performance recognition and reward programs?

(1) To improve employee morale and motivation
(2) To eliminate the need for performance evaluations
(3) To reduce legal and regulatory risks
(4) To exert control over employees

130. Which of the following is a common method for rewarding employee performance?
(1) Providing negative feedback
(2) Offering additional vacation time
(3) Offering promotions and pay raises
(4) Reducing employee workload

131. What is the purpose of effective employee coaching and support?
(1) To train and develop employees
(2) To address areas of employee performance that need improvement
(3) To provide an opportunity for employees to vent their frustrations
(4) To establish control over employees

132. Who is responsible for providing effective employee coaching and support?
(1) Senior management
(2) Human resource professionals
(3) Employees and their supervisors
(4) External consultants

133. **Assertion:** On-the-job training is a common training method that involves learning through experience and observation.
Reason: On-the-job training is an expensive and time-consuming method that is not suitable for most employees.
(1) Both assertion and reason are true and the reason is the correct explanation of the assertion.
(2) Both assertion and reason are true but the reason is not the correct explanation of the assertion.
(3) Assertion is true but reason is false.
(4) Assertion is false but reason is true.

134. **Assertion:** The primary goal of a performance appraisal is to evaluate employee performance.
Reason: Performance appraisals help identify areas where employee training is needed.
(1) Both assertion and reason are true and the reason is the correct explanation of the assertion.
(2) Both assertion and reason are true but the reason is not the correct explanation of the assertion.
(3) Assertion is true but reason is false.
(4) Assertion is false but reason is true.

135. **Assertion:** The purpose of a performance improvement plan is to identify areas of employee performance that need improvement.
Reason: Performance improvement plans are used to recognize top-performing employees.
(1) Both assertion and reason are true and the reason is the correct explanation of the assertion.
(2) Both assertion and reason are true but the reason is not the correct explanation of the assertion.
(3) Assertion is true but reason is false.
(4) Assertion is false but reason is true.

136. **Assertion:** Performance feedback is intended to help employees improve their performance.
Reason: Performance feedback is used to establish control over employees.
(1) Both assertion and reason are true and the reason is the correct explanation of the assertion.
(2) Both assertion and reason are true but the reason is not the correct explanation of the assertion.
(3) Assertion is true but reason is false.
(4) Assertion is false but reason is true.

137. **Assertion:** Employee coaching and support is the responsibility of senior management.
Reason: Effective coaching and support can help address areas of employee performance that need improvement.
(1) Both assertion and reason are true and the reason is the correct explanation of the assertion.

(2) Both assertion and reason are true but the reason is not the correct explanation of the assertion.
(3) Assertion is true but reason is false.
(4) Assertion is false but reason is true.

138. Assertion: The primary goal of performance recognition and reward programs is to establish control over employees.

Reason: Performance recognition and reward programs eliminate the need for performance evaluations.

(1) Both assertion and reason are true and the reason is the correct explanation of the assertion.
(2) Both assertion and reason are true but the reason is not the correct explanation of the assertion.
(3) Assertion is true but reason is false.
(4) Assertion is false but reason is true.

139. Assertion: Employee engagement initiatives are designed to improve employee morale and motivation.

Reason: Employee engagement initiatives provide opportunities for employees to vent their frustrations.

(1) Both assertion and reason are true and the reason is the correct explanation of the assertion.
(2) Both assertion and reason are true but the reason is not the correct explanation of the assertion.
(3) Assertion is true but reason is false.
(4) Assertion is false but reason is true.

140. Assertion: A training needs assessment is conducted to identify areas where employee training is needed.

Reason: Training needs assessments are no longer used in modern human resource management practices.

(1) Both assertion and reason are true and the reason is the correct explanation of the assertion.
(2) Both assertion and reason are true but the reason is not the correct explanation of the assertion.
(3) Assertion is true but reason is false.
(4) Assertion is false but reason is true.

141. Assertion: Performance metrics provide standardized evaluations across all job types.

Reason: Performance metrics eliminate the need for performance appraisals.

(1) Both assertion and reason are true and the reason is the correct explanation of the assertion.
(2) Both assertion and reason are true but the reason is not the correct explanation of the assertion.
(3) Assertion is true but reason is false.
(4) Assertion is false but reason is true.

142. Assertion: Effective performance management involves setting clear performance goals and objectives.

Reason: Clear performance goals and objectives help establish control over employees.

(1) Both assertion and reason are true and the reason is the correct explanation of the assertion.
(2) Both assertion and reason are true but the reason is not the correct explanation of the assertion.
(3) Assertion is true but reason is false.
(4) Assertion is false but reason is true.

143. What is the primary role of job evaluation within human resource management?

(1) To determine the qualifications required for each job
(2) To assess employee performance and productivity
(3) To determine the relative worth of each job within an organisation
(4) To determine the salary for each employee

144. Which of the following is an example of a factor that may be considered in job evaluation?

(1) Physical fitness
(2) Employee attendance
(3) Education and training
(4) Personal relationships

145. What is the primary goal of compensation management within human resource management?
(1) To ensure all employees are paid the same salary
(2) To ensure employee salaries are in line with the industry average
(3) To attract, retain, and motivate employees through competitive compensation packages
(4) To reduce overall labor costs for the organisation

146. Which of the following is an example of indirect compensation?
(1) Base salary
(2) Performance bonuses
(3) Health insurance
(4) Paid time off

147. Which of the following is an example of direct compensation?
(1) Retirement benefits
(2) Life insurance
(3) Base salary
(4) Stock options

148. What is the purpose of a salary survey?
(1) To determine employee performance and productivity
(2) To assess the level of employee engagement and satisfaction
(3) To compare salaries and compensation packages with other companies in the same industry
(4) To identify areas for improvement within the organisation

149. What is the definition of a pay grade?
(1) A specific salary range associated with a particular job
(2) The average salary for a particular industry
(3) The maximum salary an employee can earn within an organisation
(4) The minimum salary an employee must earn in order to be considered for a particular job

150. Which of the following factors may be considered when determining an employee's salary within a pay grade?
(1) Qualifications and experience
(2) Performance and productivity
(3) Market competitiveness
(4) All of the above

151. What is the primary goal of a job analysis?
(1) To assess employee performance and productivity
(2) To identify the qualifications and responsibilities associated with each job
(3) To determine the market value of each job within an organisation
(4) To develop performance improvement plans for employees

152. What is the definition of a job description?
(1) A summary of the qualifications and responsibilities associated with a particular job
(2) An assessment of employee performance and productivity
(3) A list of employee benefits and compensation packages
(4) An evaluation of employee experience and education

153. What is the primary function of a job evaluation committee?
(1) To assess employee performance and productivity
(2) To develop performance improvement plans
(3) To determine the relative worth of each job within an organisation
(4) To determine employee salaries based on personal relationships

154. What is the definition of a benchmark job?
(1) A job that is assigned to new employees with no experience or qualifications
(2) A job that is used as a reference point for job evaluations and compensation management
(3) A job that is considered less important or valuable within an organisation

(4) A job that is only available to employees with a certain level of education or experience

155. What is the primary goal of a variable pay program?
(1) To provide all employees with the same salary increase each year
(2) To reward employees for achieving specific goals or objectives
(3) To reduce overall labor costs for the organisation
(4) To align employee salaries with the industry average

156. Which of the following is an example of a variable pay program?
(1) Base salary
(2) Performance bonuses
(3) Health insurance
(4) Retirement benefits

157. What is the definition of a job family?
(1) A group of jobs with similar qualifications and responsibilities
(2) An assessment of employee performance and productivity
(3) A list of employee benefits and compensation packages
(4) An evaluation of employee experience and education

158. Which of the following is an example of a non-monetary reward?
(1) Base salary
(2) Commission
(3) Recognition and praise
(4) Retirement benefits

159. What is the primary goal of a salary review?
(1) To determine employee performance and productivity
(2) To assess the level of employee engagement and satisfaction
(3) To ensure that employee salaries are in line with the industry average
(4) To identify areas for improvement within the organisation

160. What is the definition of employee benefits?
(1) Compensation and rewards in addition to base salary, such as health insurance and retirement plans
(2) Employee performance evaluations and feedback
(3) The qualifications and experience required for a particular job
(4) The number of hours an employee works per week

161. What is the primary goal of a benefits analysis?
(1) To assess employee performance and productivity
(2) To compare employee benefits with other companies in the same industry
(3) To assess the level of employee engagement and satisfaction
(4) To identify areas for improvement within the organisation

162. Which of the following is an example of a flexible benefit plan?
(1) An employee pension plan
(2) A health insurance plan with few options for coverage
(3) An online portal where employees can select their own benefits based on their needs and preferences
(4) A performance bonus for achieving predetermined objectives

163. What is the definition of a cafeteria-style benefit plan?
(1) A benefit plan with a limited number of options for coverage
(2) A benefit plan where employees can select benefits based on their needs and preferences
(3) A benefit plan where all employees receive the same coverage
(4) A benefit plan where the employer selects the benefits for each employee

164. Who is responsible for administering employee benefits within an organisation?
(1) Human resources department

(2) Accounting department
(3) Sales department
(4) Marketing department

165. What is the primary impact of employee benefits on employee retention and motivation?
(1) Increased job satisfaction and loyalty
(2) Decreased job satisfaction and increased absenteeism
(3) Reduced overall labor costs for the organisation
(4) Increased competition for top talent among industry competitors

166. What is the definition of a salary increase?
(1) An increase in base salary provided to all employees within an organisation
(2) An increase in base salary provided to individual employees based on performance or market forces
(3) A one-time payment provided to employees as part of a company-wide bonus program
(4) A reduction in base salary provided to individual employees based on performance evaluations

167. What is the primary goal of a salary negotiation?
(1) To ensure that employee salaries are in line with the industry average
(2) To reduce overall labor costs for the organisation
(3) To achieve a fair and equitable salary for both the employee and employer
(4) To retain valuable employees through salary increases and bonuses

168. What is the definition of a merit-based pay system?
(1) A system where all employees receive the same salary increase each year
(2) A system where salaries are determined based on market competitiveness
(3) A system where salaries are determined based on individual employee performance and productivity
(4) A system where salaries are determined based on employee seniority and experience

169. Which of the following is an example of a performance reward?
(1) Base salary
(2) Commission
(3) Stock options
(4) Profit sharing

170. What is the definition of profit sharing?
(1) A bonus program where all employees receive the same payment
(2) A bonus program where payment is based on individual employee performance
(3) A bonus program where payment is based on the organisation's profitability
(4) A bonus program where payment is based on employee seniority and experience

171. What is the primary goal of a benefits evaluation?
(1) To assess employee performance and productivity
(2) To compare employee benefits with other companies in the same industry
(3) To identify areas where employee benefits can be improved
(4) To identify areas for improvement within the organisation

172. What is the definition of a compensable factor?
(1) A factor that can be used to assess employee performance and productivity
(2) A factor that can be used to determine the relative worth of each job within an organisation
(3) A factor that can be used to evaluate employee experience and qualifications
(4) A factor that can be used to determine employee compensation

173. What is the primary goal of a compensation analysis?

(1) To assess employee performance and productivity
(2) To compare employee compensation with other companies in the same industry
(3) To identify areas where employee compensation can be reduced
(4) To identify areas where employee benefits can be improved

174. What is the definition of a salary survey?
(1) An assessment of employee performance and productivity
(2) A comparison of employee salaries with other companies in the same industry
(3) An evaluation of employee experience and qualifications
(4) An analysis of employee turnover rates and absenteeism

175. What is the definition of a job grade?
(1) A specific salary range based on market competitiveness
(2) A specific salary range based on individual employee performance and productivity
(3) A specific salary range associated with a particular job
(4) A specific salary range that varies based on employee experience and qualifications

176. What is the primary impact of employee compensation on employee retention and motivation?
(1) Increased job satisfaction and loyalty
(2) Decreased job satisfaction and increased absenteeism
(3) Reduced overall labor costs for the organisation
(4) Increased competition for top talent among industry competitors

177. Who is responsible for establishing salary ranges and compensation packages within an organisation?
(1) Human resources department
(2) Accounting department
(3) Sales department
(4) Marketing department

178. What is the definition of a merit raise?
(1) A salary increase provided to all employees within an organisation
(2) A salary increase provided to individual employees based on performance evaluations
(3) A one-time payment provided to employees as part of a company-wide bonus program
(4) A reduction in base salary provided to individual employees based on performance evaluations

179. What is the primary purpose of a variable pay program?
(1) To provide employees with a fixed bonus payment each year
(2) To reward employees for achieving specific goals or objectives
(3) To adjust employee salaries based on market competitiveness
(4) To provide employees with a standard pay increase each year

180. What is the definition of a lump-sum payment?
(1) A bonus payment provided to individual employees based on performance evaluations
(2) A bonus payment provided to all employees within an organisation
(3) A one-time payment provided to employees
(4) A reduction in base salary provided to individual employees based on performance evaluations

181. What is the primary impact of the Affordable Care Act on employee benefits?
(1) Reduced availability of employee benefits
(2) Increased cost of employee benefits
(3) Increased availability and affordability of healthcare coverage
(4) Decreased competition for top talent among industry competitors

182. What is the definition of a defined benefit plan?
(1) A retirement plan where employees contribute a fixed amount each month
(2) A retirement plan where employees receive a fixed payment each month after retirement
(3) A retirement plan where employees receive a lump sum payment at retirement
(4) A retirement plan where employees receive a percentage of their salary at retirement

183. What is the definition of a defined contribution plan?
(1) A retirement plan where employees receive a fixed payment each month after retirement
(2) A retirement plan where employees contribute a fixed amount each month
(3) A retirement plan where employees receive a lump sum payment at retirement
(4) A retirement plan where employees receive a percentage of their salary at retirement

184. Who is responsible for ensuring compliance with employee benefits regulations and laws?
(1) Human resources department
(2) Accounting department
(3) Sales department
(4) Marketing department

185. What is the primary impact of employee turnover on an organisation?
(1) Increased labor costs and reduced productivity
(2) Increased competition for top talent among industry competitors
(3) Decreased need for new hires
(4) Decreased employee morale and motivation

186. What is the definition of a pay-for-performance program?
(1) A program designed to reduce overall labor costs for the organisation
(2) A program that rewards employees for achieving specific goals or objectives
(3) A program that adjusts employee salaries based on market competitiveness
(4) A program that provides employees with a standard pay increase each year

187. What is the definition of a base salary?
(1) An employee's total compensation package, including benefits and bonuses
(2) The salary an employee is paid before any bonuses or other compensation are added
(3) The minimum salary an employee must earn in order to be considered for a particular job
(4) The maximum salary an employee can earn within an organisation

188. What is the primary purpose of a total rewards package?
(1) To reduce overall labor costs for the organisation
(2) To provide employees with a comprehensive and competitive compensation package
(3) To assess the level of employee engagement and satisfaction
(4) To identify areas for improvement within the organisation

189. What is the definition of a job reference?
(1) A list of qualifications and experience required for a particular job
(2) A list of job duties and responsibilities associated with a particular job
(3) A list of individuals who can provide feedback on an employee's job performance
(4) A list of past employers and jobs held by an employee

190. What is the primary purpose of a benefits survey?
(1) To identify areas for improvement within employee benefits packages
(2) To compare employee benefits with other companies in the same industry

(3) To assess the level of employee engagement and satisfaction
(4) To identify areas where employee benefits can be reduced

191. What is the definition of a performance improvement plan?
(1) A plan designed to reward employees for achieving specific goals or objectives
(2) A plan designed to help employees improve their job performance
(3) A plan designed to reduce overall labor costs for the organisation
(4) A plan designed to increase employee engagement and satisfaction

192. What is the definition of a salary increase guideline?
(1) A specific percentage salary increase recommended for all employees within an organisation
(2) A set of criteria used to determine individual employee salary increases
(3) A list of qualifications and experience required for a particular job
(4) A list of job duties and responsibilities associated with a particular job

193. Which of the following is an example of a qualified benefit plan?
(1) A cafeteria-style benefit plan
(2) A 401(k) retirement plan
(3) A lump-sum payment
(4) A defined benefit plan

194. Who is responsible for developing compensation policies and procedures within an organisation?
(1) Human resources department
(2) Accounting department
(3) Sales department
(4) Marketing department

195. What is the definition of a performance-based pay plan?
(1) A plan that rewards employees for achieving specific goals or objectives
(2) A plan that provides all employees with the same salary increase each year
(3) A plan that adjusts employee salaries based on market competitiveness
(4) A plan that reduces overall labor costs for the organisation

196. What is the primary goal of a compensation plan?
(1) To reduce overall labor costs for the organisation
(2) To attract, retain, and motivate employees through competitive compensation packages
(3) To assess employee performance and productivity
(4) To provide a uniform salary increase for all employees within an organisation

197. What is the definition of salary compression?
(1) A situation where new employees are paid more than current employees for the same position
(2) A situation where current employees are paid more than new employees for the same position
(3) A situation where employee salaries are compressed into a smaller salary range
(4) A situation where employee salaries are not adjusted for inflation

198. What is the primary goal of a compensation survey?
(1) To reduce overall labor costs for the organisation
(2) To compare employee compensation with other companies in the same industry
(3) To assess employee performance and productivity
(4) To identify areas for improvement within employee compensation packages

199. What is the definition of an equity adjustment?
(1) An adjustment made to employee salaries based on market competitiveness
(2) An adjustment made to employee salaries to correct salary compression issues

(3) An adjustment made to employee salaries based on individual employee performance and productivity
(4) An adjustment made to employee salaries to reduce overall labor costs for the organisation

200. What is the primary goal of an incentive program?
(1) To reward employees for achieving specific goals or objectives
(2) To reduce overall labor costs for the organisation
(3) To adjust employee salaries based on market competitiveness
(4) To provide a uniform salary increase for all employees within an organisation

201. Which of the following is an example of a perk?
(1) Paid time off
(2) Health insurance
(3) Free meals or snacks
(4) Base salary

202. What is the definition of a flexible benefit plan?
(1) A benefit plan with a limited number of options for coverage
(2) A benefit plan where employees can select benefits based on their needs and preferences
(3) A benefit plan where all employees receive the same coverage
(4) A benefit plan where the employer selects the benefits for each employee

203. What is the primary impact of employee benefits on an organisation's bottom line?
(1) Increased labor costs
(2) Decreased labor costs
(3) Increased competition for top talent among industry competitors
(4) Decreased need for new hires

204. What is the definition of a range penetration?
(1) The percentage of employee salaries within a salary range
(2) The percentage of employee salaries above the maximum of a salary range
(3) The percentage of employee salaries below the minimum of a salary range
(4) The percentage of employee salaries outside of the salary range

205. What is the primary goal of a wage and hour audit?
(1) To assess employee performance and productivity
(2) To identify areas for improvement within the organisation
(3) To ensure that the organisation is complying with federal and state wage and hour laws
(4) To assess the level of employee engagement and satisfaction

206. What is the primary impact of employee compensation on an organisation's bottom line?
(1) Increased labor costs
(2) Decreased labor costs
(3) Increased competition for top talent among industry competitors
(4) Increased employee engagement and satisfaction

207. Assertion: The primary goal of a compensation plan is to ensure that all employees are paid the same salary.
Reason: Standardizing salaries across the organisation promotes fairness and equality.
(1) Both assertion and reason are false.
(2) Assertion is true but reason is false.
(3) Both assertion and reason are true but the reason is not the correct explanation of the assertion.
(4) Both assertion and reason are true and the reason is the correct explanation of the assertion.

208. Assertion: A pay-for-performance program rewards all employees within an organisation equally.

Reason: A pay-for-performance program is designed to reward employees for achieving specific goals or objectives.

(1) Both assertion and reason are true but the reason is not the correct explanation of the assertion.
(2) Both assertion and reason are true and the reason is the correct explanation of the assertion.
(3) Assertion is true but reason is false.
(4) Both assertion and reason are false.

209. Assertion: A cafeteria-style benefit plan allows employees to select their own benefits based on their needs and preferences.

Reason: A cafeteria-style benefit plan offers a limited number of options for coverage.

(1) Both assertion and reason are true but the reason is not the correct explanation of the assertion.
(2) Assertion is true but reason is false.
(3) Both assertion and reason are false.
(4) Both assertion and reason are true and the reason is the correct explanation of the assertion.

210. Assertion: A job analysis is designed to identify the qualifications and responsibilities associated with each job.

Reason: A job analysis is a relatively modern tool used by human resource managers.

(1) Both assertion and reason are true but the reason is not the correct explanation of the assertion.
(2) Both assertion and reason are false.
(3) Assertion is true but reason is false.
(4) Both assertion and reason are true and the reason is the correct explanation of the assertion.

211. Assertion: Employee benefits have a significant impact on an organisation's bottom line.

Reason: Employee benefits are often the most expensive part of an organisation's compensation package.

(1) Both assertion and reason are true and the reason is the correct explanation of the assertion.
(2) Both assertion and reason are true but the reason is not the correct explanation of the assertion.
(3) Assertion is true but reason is false.
(4) Both assertion and reason are false.

212. What is the primary goal of job evaluation?

(1) To assess employee performance and productivity
(2) To determine the relative value of each job to the organisation
(3) To identify areas for improvement within the organisation
(4) To assess the level of employee engagement and satisfaction

213. What is the definition of a job description?

(1) A summary of an employee's past job performance
(2) A profile of an organisation's ideal job candidate
(3) A document outlining the duties and responsibilities of a job
(4) A performance appraisal tool used to assess employees

214. Which of the following is a method of job evaluation?

(1) Position evaluation
(2) Market analysis
(3) Job ranking
(4) All of the above

215. What is the primary impact of job evaluation on an organisation's compensation strategy?

(1) Increased labor costs
(2) Decreased labor costs
(3) Improved fairness and consistency in pay decisions
(4) Decreased competition for top talent among industry competitors

216. What is the definition of a pay grade?

(1) A range of pay levels assigned to each job class based on market analysis
(2) The minimum and maximum pay levels for a specific job

(3) A group of jobs with similar responsibilities and pay grades
(4) The range of pay levels offered within an organisation

217. What is the definition of a wage survey?
(1) A study of employee satisfaction and engagement levels
(2) An analysis of employee turnover rates and absenteeism
(3) A survey of wages and salaries offered by competing organisations in the same industry
(4) An evaluation of employee experience and qualifications

218. What is the definition of a pay range?
(1) The minimum pay level for a specific job
(2) A set of pay grades assigned to each job class based on market analysis
(3) The range of pay levels assigned to a specific job based on performance and experience
(4) The maximum pay level for a specific job

219. What is the primary impact of employee compensation on an organisation's bottom line?
(1) Increased labor costs
(2) Decreased labor costs
(3) Increased competition for top talent among industry competitors
(4) Increased employee engagement and satisfaction

220. What is the definition of a merit increase?
(1) An increase in pay based on an employee's level of experience
(2) An increase in pay based on an employee's seniority within the organisation
(3) An increase in pay based on an employee's individual performance
(4) An increase in pay given to all employees at the same time

221. What is the definition of a bonus?
(1) An additional payment given to all employees at the same time
(2) An additional payment given to employees based on their level of experience
(3) An additional payment given to employees as a reward for achieving specific goals or objectives
(4) An additional payment given to employees based on their seniority within the organisation

222. What is the definition of a commission?
(1) A fixed payment given to employees without any additional bonuses or incentives
(2) A percentage of a sale given to employees as a reward for making the sale
(3) A bonus given to employees based on their individual performance
(4) A payment given to employees based on the organisation's overall financial performance

223. What is the primary goal of a wage and hour audit?
(1) To assess employee performance and productivity
(2) To identify areas for improvement within the organisation
(3) To ensure that the organisation is complying with federal and state wage and hour laws
(4) To assess the level of employee engagement and satisfaction

224. What is the definition of a wage structure?
(1) A set of pay grades and ranges based on job evaluations and market data
(2) An assessment of employee performance and productivity
(3) An analysis of employee turnover rates and absenteeism
(4) An evaluation of employee experience and qualifications

225. What is the definition of a wage compression?
(1) A situation where the difference in pay between employees at different levels within the organisation is too small

(2) A situation where the difference in pay between new hires and existing employees is too small
(3) A situation where the difference in pay between employees with different levels of experience or qualifications is too small
(4) A situation where the difference in pay between employees in different job classes is too small

226. What is the primary impact of employee benefits on an organisation's bottom line?
(1) Increased labor costs
(2) Decreased labor costs
(3) Increased competition for top talent among industry competitors
(4) Decreased need for new hires

227. What is the definition of a flexible benefit plan?
(1) A benefit plan with a limited number of options for coverage
(2) A benefit plan where employees can select benefits based on their needs and preferences
(3) A benefit plan where all employees receive the same coverage
(4) A benefit plan where the employer selects the benefits for each employee

228. What is the definition of a range penetration?
(1) The percentage of employee salaries within a salary range
(2) The percentage of employee salaries above the maximum of a salary range
(3) The percentage of employee salaries below the minimum of a salary range
(4) The percentage of employee salaries outside of the salary range

229. What is the definition of reinforcement theory?
(1) A theory that suggests that employees are motivated by their perceived level of equity or fairness in the workplace
(2) A theory that suggests that employees are motivated by their level of extrinsic rewards
(3) A theory that suggests that employees are motivated by the consequences of their behaviour in the workplace
(4) A theory that suggests that employees are motivated by their personal goals and values

230. What is the definition of a compensation philosophy?
(1) A document outlining an organisation's overall approach to compensation and benefits
(2) A set of employee performance metrics used to assess compensation
(3) A document outlining an employee's specific compensation package
(4) A set of guidelines used to assess employee promotions and career development opportunities

231. What is the definition of a cost-of-living adjustment (COLA)?
(1) An adjustment made to employee salaries based on the cost of consumer goods and services
(2) An adjustment made to employee salaries based on their level of experience
(3) An adjustment made to employee salaries based on the market rates for similar jobs
(4) An adjustment made to employee salaries based on their level of performance

232. What is the definition of a merit pool?
(1) A pool of funds set aside for use in a bonus program
(2) A pool of funds set aside for use in a commission program
(3) A pool of funds set aside for base salary increases based on employee performance
(4) A pool of funds set aside for special project or initiative bonuses

233. What is the primary advantage of using surveys to gather market data for compensation decisions?
(1) Surveys are a cost-effective way to gather data

(2) Surveys provide an objective source of data
(3) Surveys provide detailed information on employee performance
(4) Surveys provide detailed information on employee benefits

234. What is the primary disadvantage of using surveys to gather market data for compensation decisions?
(1) Surveys are a time-consuming way to gather data
(2) Surveys provide an objective source of data
(3) Surveys provide limited information on the specific jobs being evaluated
(4) Surveys provide limited information on employee benefits

235. What is the definition of a lump-sum merit increase?
(1) An increase in pay given to an employee in a single payment as opposed to being added to their base salary
(2) An increase in pay given to an employee over a period of time as opposed to being added to their base salary
(3) An increase in pay given to all employees at the same time
(4) An increase in pay based on an employee's level of experience

236. What is the primary advantage of using pay-for-performance systems for compensation decisions?
(1) Pay-for-performance systems are a cost-effective way to improve employee engagement
(2) Pay-for-performance systems are a way to standardize salaries across the organisation
(3) Pay-for-performance systems provide a clear link between individual employee performance and compensation
(4) Pay-for-performance systems are a way to reduce labor costs

237. What is the definition of a job family?
(1) A group of employees who have similar job titles and responsibilities
(2) A group of jobs with similar responsibilities and qualifications that are grouped together for pay and classification purposes
(3) A group of employees who have similar levels of experience and education
(4) A group of employees who have similar performance metrics

238. What is the definition of a comparator group?
(1) A group of employees who have similar job titles and responsibilities
(2) A group of organisations used as benchmarks for compensation decisions
(3) A group of employees who have similar levels of experience and education
(4) A group of employees who have similar performance metrics

239. What is the definition of a market pay policy line?
(1) A line drawn on a graph to show the relationship between job values and salaries paid in the external market
(2) A line drawn on a graph to show the relationship between job values and salaries paid within the organisation
(3) A line drawn on a graph to show the relationship between employee seniority and bonuses paid within the organisation
(4) A line drawn on a graph to show the relationship between employee performance and commissions paid within the organisation

240. What is the definition of a total rewards program?
(1) A program that provides employees with total control over their benefits and compensation packages
(2) A program that includes all of the rewards and incentives an organisation offers to employees

(3) A program that provides employees with unlimited sick and vacation time
(4) A program that provides employees with unlimited access to all of an organisation's resources

241. What is the definition of a salary schedule?
(1) A document outlining the specific compensation package for each employee
(2) A document outlining the minimum and maximum pay levels for each job
(3) A document outlining the qualifications and responsibilities of each job
(4) A document outlining employee performance metrics

242. What is the definition of a flex-time schedule?
(1) A schedule that allows employees to work from home
(2) A schedule that allows employees to work a certain number of hours per week rather than a set schedule
(3) A schedule that allows employees to choose their own hours within certain limits
(4) A schedule that allows employees to take time off whenever they want

243. What is the primary goal of a job family analysis?
(1) To assess employee performance and productivity
(2) To update job descriptions and qualifications
(3) To group jobs with similar responsibilities and qualifications for pay and classification purposes
(4) To assess the level of employee engagement and satisfaction

244. What is the definition of an exempt employee?
(1) An employee who is paid an hourly wage and is eligible for overtime pay
(2) An employee who is paid a salary and is not eligible for overtime pay
(3) An employee who is paid a salary and is eligible for overtime pay
(4) An employee who is paid an hourly wage and is not eligible for overtime pay

245. What is the definition of a non-exempt employee?
(1) An employee who is paid an hourly wage and is eligible for overtime pay
(2) An employee who is paid a salary and is not eligible for overtime pay
(3) An employee who is paid a salary and is eligible for overtime pay
(4) An employee who is paid an hourly wage and is not eligible for overtime pay

246. What is the primary goal of executive compensation?
(1) To promote fairness and equality within the organisation
(2) To provide executives with pay packages that reflect their level of experience and qualifications
(3) To attract and retain top executive talent
(4) To reduce labor costs by standardizing salaries across the organisation

247. What is the definition of a total direct compensation package?
(1) A package that includes all of the compensation and benefits an organisation offers to employees
(2) A package that includes only an employee's base salary
(3) A package that includes an employee's base salary, bonuses, commissions, and any other direct financial compensation
(4) A package that includes only an employee's indirect compensation, such as benefits

248. What is the definition of a total indirect compensation package?
(1) A package that includes all of the compensation and benefits an organisation offers to employees
(2) A package that includes only an employee's base salary

(3) A package that includes an employee's base salary, bonuses, commissions, and any other direct financial compensation
(4) A package that includes only an employee's indirect compensation, such as benefits

249. What is the definition of a compression ratio?
(1) The ratio of employee salaries within a salary range
(2) The ratio of employee salaries below the minimum of a salary range
(3) The ratio of employee salaries above the maximum of a salary range
(4) The ratio of employee salaries outside of the salary range

250. What is the primary goal of compensation communication?
(1) To promote fairness and equality within the organisation
(2) To ensure that employees understand their compensation packages and how they are determined
(3) To reduce labor costs by standardizing salaries across the organisation
(4) To attract and retain top talent among industry competitors

251. What is the definition of a salary survey percentile?
(1) A percentage of employee salaries within a salary range
(2) A percentage of employee salaries above the minimum of a salary range
(3) A percentage of employee salaries below the maximum of a salary range
(4) The percentage of competing organisations that pay similar salaries for a specific job

252. What is the primary disadvantage of using purely external market data for compensation decisions?
(1) External market data may not accurately reflect the organisation's internal needs and goals
(2) External market data is often too expensive to obtain
(3) External market data is often not specific enough to be useful
(4) External market data may differ significantly from the organisation's own salary structure

253. What is the definition of a pay-for-knowledge system?
(1) A compensation system based on an employee's seniority within the organisation
(2) A compensation system that rewards employees for gaining new knowledge and skills
(3) A compensation system that rewards employees for achieving specific goals or objectives
(4) A compensation system that is linked to stock options and other financial incentives

254. What is the primary goal of a job evaluation committee?
(1) To assess employee performance and productivity
(2) To determine the relative value of each job to the organisation
(3) To evaluate and update job descriptions and qualifications
(4) To make recommendations on compensation and classification decisions

255. What is the primary goal of a salary range penetration analysis?
(1) To assess employee performance and productivity
(2) To evaluate the quality and effectiveness of a compensation plan
(3) To determine the percentage of employee salaries above or below a specific salary range
(4) To assess the level of employee engagement and satisfaction

256. What is the definition of a severance package?

(1) A package of benefits and compensation offered to employees who are leaving the organisation due to a layoff or termination
(2) A package of benefits and compensation offered to new employees as an incentive to join the organisation
(3) A package of benefits and compensation offered to employees as a reward for achieving specific goals or objectives
(4) A package of benefits and compensation offered to high-performing employees

257. What is the definition of a clawback provision?
(1) A provision in an employment contract that allows employees to claw back any bonuses or other compensation if they fail to meet specific performance targets
(2) A provision in an employment contract that allows the organisation to take back bonus payments or other compensation in specific circumstances
(3) A provision in an employment contract that provides employees with the right to suethe organisation for wrongful termination
(4) A provision in an employment contract that provides employees with the right to request a salary increase

258. What is the primary goal of a compensation audit?
(1) To assess employee performance and productivity
(2) To ensure that the organisation is complying with federal and state wage and hour laws
(3) To evaluate the effectiveness of the organisation's compensation plan
(4) To identify and correct any discrepancies or inconsistencies in the organisation's compensation practices

259. What is the definition of a total compensation statement?
(1) A document outlining an employee's base salary and benefits
(2) A document outlining an employee's total compensation, including salary, benefits, and other incentives
(3) A document outlining an employee's qualifications and experience
(4) A document outlining an employee's performance metrics

260. What is the primary goal of a salary compression analysis?
(1) To assess employee performance and productivity
(2) To identify areas for improvement within the organisation
(3) To determine the extent of salary compression within the organisation and potential remedies
(4) To assess the level of employee engagement and satisfaction.

261. Which of the following is not a common employee benefit?
(1) Health insurance
(2) Retirement plan
(3) Job title
(4) Paid time off

262. Which of the following is a type of non-monetary incentive?
(1) Bonuses
(2) Stock options
(3) Employee recognition programs
(4) Pay raises

263. Which of the following is a type of financial incentive?
(1) Paid time off
(2) Employee stock purchase plan
(3) Employee discounts
(4) Employee recognition programs

264. Which of the following is a type of retirement plan?
(1) 401(k) (2) IRA
(3) Mutual fund (4) Bond fund

265. What is the primary benefit of offering employee benefits and incentives?
(1) Reduced labor costs
(2) Increased employee engagement and satisfaction
(3) Increased competition for top talent among industry competitors
(4) Reduced competition for top talent among industry competitors

266. What is the definition of an employee recognition program?
(1) A program that provides employees with bonuses based on their individual performance
(2) A program that provides employees with discounts on their purchases from the company
(3) A program that rewards employees for their achievements and contributions to the organisation
(4) A program that provides employees with paid time off and other non-monetary incentives

267. What is the definition of a wellness program?
(1) A program that provides employees with opportunities for career growth and development
(2) A program that provides employees with discounts on health and wellness products
(3) A program that promotes healthy behaviours among employees and may include activities such as exercise classes and health screenings
(4) A program that provides employees with paid time off for medical reasons

268. What is the definition of a flexible spending account (FSA)?
(1) A savings account that allows employees to set aside pre-tax dollars to pay for eligible healthcare expenses
(2) A special account that allows employees to earn interest on their retirement savings
(3) A savings account that allows employees to set aside pre-tax dollars to pay for eligible education expenses
(4) A special account that allows employees to set aside pre-tax dollars to pay for their children's education expenses

269. What is the definition of a 401(k) plan?
(1) A traditional retirement savings account where employees contribute pre-tax dollars and the employer matches a portion of the contribution
(2) An investment account where employees can buy and sell stocks and bonds
(3) A savings account where employees can set aside pre-tax dollars to pay for eligible healthcare expenses
(4) A savings account where employees can set aside pre-tax dollars to pay for eligible education expenses

270. What is the definition of a stock option?
(1) The right to buy company stock at a specified price in the future
(2) The right to sell company stock at a specified price in the future
(3) A bonus paid to employees based on their level of experience
(4) A salary increase based on an employee's individual performance

271. What is the definition of a vesting period?
(1) The period of time after which an employee can sell their stock options
(2) The period of time after which an employee is eligible for retirement benefits
(3) The period of time after which an employee's contributions to their retirement plan are fully vested
(4) The period of time after which an employee becomes eligible for paid time off

272. What is the definition of a defined benefit plan?
(1) A retirement plan where the employer promises to pay the employee a set amount of money after they retire
(2) A retirement plan where the employee contributes a set amount of money and

the employer matches a portion of the contribution

(3) A retirement plan where the employee is responsible for choosing how their contributions are invested

(4) A retirement plan where the employee can choose how the employer matches their contributions

273. What is the definition of a defined contribution plan?

(1) A retirement plan where the employer promises to pay the employee a set amount of money after they retire

(2) A retirement plan where the employee contributes a set amount of money and the employer matches a portion of the contribution

(3) A retirement plan where the employee is responsible for choosing how their contributions are invested

(4) A retirement plan where the employee can choose how the employer matches their contributions

274. What is the definition of a pension plan?

(1) A retirement plan where the employer promises to pay the employee a set amount of money after they retire

(2) A retirement plan where the employee contributes a set amount of money and the employer matches a portion of the contribution

(3) A retirement plan where the employer is solely responsible for funding and managing the plan

(4) A retirement plan where the employee is solely responsible for funding and managing the plan

275. What is the definition of a career path?

(1) A series of jobs within an organisation that typically lead to higher levels of responsibility and compensation

(2) The specific job duties and responsibilities outlined in a job description

(3) A document outlining the required skills and qualifications for a specific position

(4) A document outlining the employee's individual performance metrics and goals

276. What is the definition of career development?

(1) A process where employees are evaluated and provided with feedback on their job performance

(2) A process where employees are provided with opportunities for education, training, and other professional development activities

(3) A process where employees are provided with incentives and bonuses for achieving specific goals

(4) A process where employees are promoted to higher levels of responsibility and compensation

277. What is the definition of job enrichment?

(1) A process where employees are provided with opportunities for education, training, and other professional development activities

(2) A process where employees are given more responsibility and autonomy in their jobs

(3) A process where employees are promoted to higher levels of responsibility and compensation

(4) A process where employees are evaluated and provided with feedback on their job performance

278. What is the definition of a mentorship program?

(1) A program that provides employees with opportunities for education, training, and other professional development activities

(2) A program that matches employees with experienced professionals who can provide guidance and support

(3) A program that provides employees with bonuses based on their individual performance

(4) A program that provides employees with paid time off and other non-monetary incentives

279. What is the definition of a career counselor?
(1) A professional who provides employees with guidance and support related to their career development
(2) A professional who evaluates and provides feedback on employee performance
(3) A professional who manages employee benefits and compensation
(4) A professional who is responsible for recruiting and hiring new employees

280. What is the primary benefit of offering career development opportunities to employees?
(1) Reduced labor costs
(2) Increased employee engagement and job satisfaction
(3) Increased competition for top talent among industry competitors
(4) Reduced competition for top talent among industry competitors

281. What is the definition of skills training?
(1) A process where employees are given more responsibility and autonomy in their jobs
(2) A process where employees are provided with opportunities to learn new skills that are relevant to their job or career goals
(3) A process where employees are promoted to higher levels of responsibility and compensation
(4) A process where employees are evaluated and provided with feedback on their job performance

282. What is the definition of a career ladder?
(1) A process where employees are provided with opportunities for education, training, and other professional development activities
(2) A series of promotions within an organisation that typically lead to higher levels of responsibility and compensation
(3) A document outlining the required skills and qualifications for a specific position
(4) A document outlining the employee's individual performance metrics and goals

283. What is the definition of job rotation?
(1) A process where employees are given more responsibility and autonomy in their jobs
(2) A process where employees move between different jobs or departments within the organisation
(3) A process where employees are promoted to higher levels of responsibility and compensation
(4) A process where employees are evaluated and provided with feedback on their job performance

284. What is the primary benefit of offering job rotation opportunities to employees?
(1) Reduced labor costs
(2) Increased employee engagement and job satisfaction
(3) Increased employee skill development and knowledge
(4) Reduced competition for top talent among industry competitors

285. What is the definition of a job share arrangement?
(1) A process where two or more employees share the responsibilities of a single job
(2) A process where employees rotate between different jobs or departments within the organisation
(3) A process where employees are given more responsibility and autonomy in their jobs
(4) A process where employees are promoted to higher levels of responsibility and compensation

286. What is the definition of a performance appraisal?
(1) A process where employees are provided with opportunities for education,

training, and other professional development activities
(2) A process where employees are evaluated and provided with feedback on their job performance
(3) A process where employees are promoted to higher levels of responsibility and compensation
(4) A process where employees are given more responsibility and autonomy in their jobs

287. What is the primary goal of a performance appraisal?
(1) To provide feedback and recognition for good performance
(2) To identify problem areas and areas for improvement
(3) To determine employee compensation and benefits
(4) To reduce labor costs and increase efficiency

288. What is the definition of a career goal?
(1) The specific job duties and responsibilities outlined in a job description
(2) The employee's overall career objectives, aspirations, and desired outcomes
(3) The employee's individual performance metrics and goals
(4) The skills and qualifications required for a specific position

289. What is the definition of a career plan?
(1) A document outlining the employee's individual performance metrics and goals
(2) A document outlining the specific job duties and responsibilities for a particular position
(3) A document outlining the employee's career goals and the steps he or she plans to take to achieve them
(4) A document outlining the required skills and qualifications for a specific position.

290. Which of the following is a contemporary challenge facing HRM?
(1) Changing work ethics
(2) Technological advancements
(3) Globalization
(4) All of the above

291. Which of the following is a key factor driving changes in the environment of HRM?
(1) Diversity and inclusion
(2) Changes in technology
(3) Workforce demographics
(4) All of the above

292. Which of the following is a component of the external environment that affects HRM?
(1) Legislation and regulations
(2) Employee attitudes
(3) Organisational culture
(4) Workforce diversity

293. What is the role of HRM in managing change within an organisation?
(1) To resist change in order to maintain the status quo
(2) To support and facilitate change
(3) To ignore change and focus on traditional HR practices
(4) To place the responsibility of change management on employees

294. Which of the following is an example of a contemporary HRM practice?
(1) Traditional recruitment and selection
(2) Telecommuting
(3) Strict hierarchical management structure
(4) Top-down decision making

295. What is the purpose of talent management in HRM?
(1) To identify and develop the skills of employees
(2) To manage the performance of employees
(3) To ensure that the organisation has the talent it needs to achieve its strategic objectives
(4) To reduce employee turnover and improve retention rates

296. Which of the following HRM practices is related to diversity and inclusion?
(1) Payroll and benefits administration
(2) Talent management
(3) Affirmative action
(4) Performance appraisal

297. What is the primary focus of strategic HRM?
(1) Administrative tasks
(2) Day-to-day management of employees
(3) Aligning HR practices with the strategic objectives of the organisation
(4) Compliance with labor laws and regulations

298. What is the role of HRM in managing employee engagement?
(1) To provide employees with a high salary and benefits
(2) To create a positive work environment and culture
(3) To support employees in achieving their career goals
(4) All of the above

299. What is the purpose of a competency framework in HRM?
(1) To identify the specific skills required for each job in the organisation
(2) To ensure that employees are trained and developed in the areas they need to improve
(3) To align employee skills and abilities with the strategic objectives of the organisation
(4) To assess employee performance in relation to pre-determined criteria

300. Why is employee retention important for HRM?
(1) It reduces recruitment and training costs
(2) It provides job security for existing employees
(3) It increases employee motivation and job satisfaction
(4) It improves productivity and performance

301. Which of the following is a key trend in HRM?
(1) Decreased focus on employee engagement
(2) Increased focus on diversity and inclusion
(3) Decreased focus on retention and turnover
(4) Increased focus on top-down decision making

302. What is the primary goal of HR analytics?
(1) To improve employee productivity
(2) To reduce employee turnover
(3) To use data to improve HR practices and decision making
(4) To automate HR processes

303. Which of the following is a contemporary HRM challenge related to technology?
(1) Cybersecurity threats
(2) Resistance from employees to adopt new technology
(3) Decreased efficiency and productivity
(4) Lack of available technology solutions

304. What is the concept of strategic talent management?
(1) The identification, development, and retention of top talent in an organisation to achieve strategic objectives
(2) A traditional approach to recruitment and selection
(3) A focus on employee engagement and motivation
(4) A top-down approach to HRM

305. What is the concept of the gig economy?
(1) A workforce that is composed of temporary or short-term workers who work on a project-by-project basis
(2) A traditional workforce that is composed of full-time employees
(3) A workforce that is composed of remote employees
(4) A workforce that is composed of highly skilled and talented workers

306. What is the concept of total rewards?
(1) A focus on providing employees with a high salary and benefits package
(2) A focus on providing employees with a wide range of rewards and benefits that meet their individual needs and preferences
(3) A focus on providing employees with opportunities for career advancement
(4) A focus on compliance with labor laws and regulations

307. What is the concept of employee experience?
(1) A focus on employees as individuals and their unique experiences within the organisation
(2) A focus on traditional HR practices
(3) A focus on top-down decision making
(4) A focus on employee productivity and efficiency

308. What is the concept of emotional intelligence in HRM?
(1) The ability of employees to manage their emotions and the emotions of others in the workplace
(2) The ability of HR professionals to make decisions based on data and analytics
(3) The ability of employees to adapt and change in response to new environments
(4) The ability of employees to think creatively and come up with innovative ideas

309. What is the concept of employer branding?
(1) The process of creating a positive image of the organisation to attract and retain top talent
(2) The process of managing employee performance
(3) The process of creating a diverse and inclusive workplace
(4) The process of providing employees with opportunities for career growth and development

310. What is the concept of job crafting?
(1) The process of designing jobs to meet the unique needs and preferences of individual employees
(2) The process of reducing the complexity of jobs to improve efficiency
(3) The process of eliminating non-essential job duties
(4) The process of providing employees with flexibility in their work schedules

311. What is the concept of HR outsourcing?
(1) The process of hiring external vendors to manage HR functions
(2) The process of reducing the number of HR staff in an organisation
(3) The process of automating HR processes
(4) The process of providing employees with opportunities for career growth and development

312. What is the concept of employee wellness?
(1) A focus on providing employees with a high salary and benefits package
(2) A focus on helping employees achieve and maintain physical and emotional health
(3) A focus on employee productivity and efficiency
(4) A focus on compliance with labor laws and regulations

313. What is the concept of flexible work arrangements?
(1) The process of eliminating non-essential job duties
(2) The process of providing employees with opportunities for career advancement
(3) The process of providing employees with a flexible work schedule or the ability to work from home
(4) The process of providing employees with a diverse and inclusive workplace

314. What is the concept of employee engagement?
(1) A focus on providing employees with a high salary and benefits package

(2) A focus on creating a positive work environment that promotes employee motivation and job satisfaction
(3) A focus on reducing employee turnover
(4) A focus on compliance with labor laws and regulations

315. What is the concept of work-life balance?
(1) The process of balancing work responsibilities with family and personal responsibilities
(2) The process of reducing the number of hours that employees work
(3) The process of providing employees with opportunities for career advancement
(4) The process of providing employees with a diverse and inclusive workplace

316. What is the concept of knowledge management?
(1) The process of managing and sharing knowledge within an organisation
(2) The process of automating HR processes
(3) The process of managing employee performance
(4) The process of providing employees with a high salary and benefits package

317. What is the concept of employee empowerment?
(1) The process of providing employees with the skills and resources they need to take control of their work and make decisions
(2) The process of managing employee performance
(3) The process of eliminating non-essential job duties
(4) The process of providing employees with a high salary and benefits package

318. What is the concept of agile HR?
(1) The process of adapting HR practices to respond to changing business needs
(2) The process of eliminating non-essential job duties
(3) The process of providing employees with opportunities for career growth and development
(4) The process of providing employees with a diverse and inclusive workplace

319. **Assertion:** Employee experience is a concept that focuses on employees as individuals and their unique experiences within the organisation.
Reason: Employee experience is related to the concept of customer experience and is designed to provide employees with the same level of service and attention that customers receive.
(1) Both assertion and reason are true and the reason is the correct explanation of the assertion.
(2) Both assertion and reason are true but the reason is not the correct explanation of the assertion.
(3) Assertion is true but reason is false.
(4) Assertion is false but reason is true.

320. **Assertion:** Employer branding is the process of creating a positive image of the organisation to attract and retain top talent.
Reason: Employer branding is focused solely on attracting new employees to the organisation.
(1) Assertion is true but reason is false.
(2) Assertion is false but reason is true.
(3) Both assertion and reason are true but the reason is not the correct explanation of the assertion.
(4) Both assertion and reason are true and the reason is the correct explanation of the assertion.

321. **Assertion:** HR outsourcing is the process of hiring external vendors to manage HR functions.
Reason: HR outsourcing is a cost-effective alternative to having an internal HR department.
(1) Both assertion and reason are true and the reason is the correct explanation of the assertion.

(2) Both assertion and reason are true but the reason is not the correct explanation of the assertion.
(3) Assertion is true but reason is false.
(4) Assertion is false but reason is true.

322. Assertion: Knowledge management is the process of managing and sharing knowledge within an organisation.

Reason: Knowledge management is focused solely on capturing and storing information and does not involve sharing or collaboration.

(1) Assertion is true but reason is false.
(2) Assertion is false but reason is true.
(3) Both assertion and reason are true but the reason is not the correct explanation of the assertion.
(4) Both assertion and reason are true and the reason is the correct explanation of the assertion.

323. Assertion: Work-life balance is the process of balancing work responsibilities with family and personal responsibilities.

Reason: Work-life balance is focused solely on reducing the number of hours that employees work.

(1) Assertion is true but reason is false.
(2) Assertion is false but reason is true.
(3) Both assertion and reason are true but the reason is not the correct explanation of the assertion.
(4) Both assertion and reason are true and the reason is the correct explanation of the assertion.

324. Assertion: Talent management is the identification, development, and retention of top talent in an organisation to achieve strategic objectives.

Reason: Talent management is focused solely on recruitment and selection.

(1) Assertion is true but reason is false.
(2) Assertion is false but reason is true.
(3) Both assertion and reason are true but the reason is not the correct explanation of the assertion.
(4) Both assertion and reason are true and the reason is the correct explanation of the assertion.

325. Assertion: Flexible work arrangements provide employees with a flexible work schedule or the ability to work from home.

Reason: Flexible work arrangements are designed to reduce employee workload and increase efficiency.

(1) Assertion is true but reason is false.
(2) Assertion is false but reason is true.
(3) Both assertion and reason are true but the reason is not the correct explanation of the assertion.
(4) Both assertion and reason are true and the reason is the correct explanation of the assertion.

326. Assertion: Agile HR is the process of adapting HR practices to respond to changing business needs.

Reason: Agile HR is focused solely on reducing labor costs and increasing efficiency.

(1) Assertion is true but reason is false.
(2) Assertion is false but reason is true.
(3) Both assertion and reason are true but the reason is not the correct explanation of the assertion.
(4) Both assertion and reason are true and the reason is the correct explanation of the assertion.

327. Assertion: Employee empowerment is the process of providing employees with the skills and resources they need to take control of their work and make decisions.

Reason: Employee empowerment is focused solely on reducing employee turnover and improving retention rates.

(1) Assertion is true but reason is false.
(2) Assertion is false but reason is true.
(3) Both assertion and reason are true but the reason is not the correct explanation of the assertion.
(4) Both assertion and reason are true and the reason is the correct explanation of the assertion.

328. **Assertion:** Emotional intelligence is the ability of employees to manage their emotions and the emotions of others in the workplace.

Reason: Emotional intelligence is focused solely on improving employee productivity and performance.

(1) Assertion is true but reason is false.
(2) Assertion is false but reason is true.
(3) Both assertion and reason are true but the reason is not the correct explanation of the assertion.
(4) Both assertion and reason are true and the reason is the correct explanation of the assertion.

329. **Assertion:** Competency frameworks are designed to assess employee performance in relation to pre-determined criteria.

Reason: Competency frameworks are designed to identify the specific skills required for each job in the organisation.

(1) Assertion is true but reason is false.
(2) Assertion is false but reason is true.
(3) Both assertion and reason are true but the reason is not the correct explanation of the assertion.
(4) Both assertion and reason are true and the reason is the correct explanation of the assertion.

330. **Assertion:** Strategic HRM is focused solely on compliance with labor laws and regulations.

Reason: Strategic HRM is a focus on aligning HR practices with the strategic objectives of the organisation.

(1) Assertion is true but reason is false.
(2) Assertion is false but reason is true.
(3) Both assertion and reason are true but the reason is not the correct explanation of the assertion.
(4) Both assertion and reason are true and the reason is the correct explanation of the assertion.

ANSWER KEY

1. (4)	**2.** (4)	**3.** (3)	**4.** (3)	**5.** (4)	**6.** (1)	**7.** (3)	**8.** (2)	**9.** (3)	**10.** (4)
11. (3)	**12.** (4)	**13.** (3)	**14.** (4)	**15.** (4)	**16.** (1)	**17.** (3)	**18.** (2)	**19.** (3)	**20.** (2)
21. (4)	**22.** (4)	**23.** (1)	**24.** (2)	**25.** (2)	**26.** (1)	**27.** (1)	**28.** (1)	**29.** (1)	**30.** (2)
31. (4)	**32.** (2)	**33.** (3)	**34.** (3)	**35.** (4)	**36.** (1)	**37.** (4)	**38.** (4)	**39.** (4)	**40.** (3)
41. (4)	**42.** (3)	**43.** (2)	**44.** (1)	**45.** (4)	**46.** (2)	**47.** (4)	**48.** (3)	**49.** (1)	**50.** (2)
51. (4)	**52.** (1)	**53.** (3)	**54.** (4)	**55.** (3)	**56.** (3)	**57.** (4)	**58.** (3)	**59.** (4)	**60.** (4)
61. (3)	**62.** (1)	**63.** (4)	**64.** (2)	**65.** (3)	**66.** (1)	**67.** (1)	**68.** (4)	**69.** (1)	**70.** (2)
71. (2)	**72.** (2)	**73.** (1)	**74.** (3)	**75.** (4)	**76.** (2)	**77.** (3)	**78.** (3)	**79.** (4)	**80.** (3)
81. (3)	**82.** (4)	**83.** (1)	**84.** (2)	**85.** (4)	**86.** (4)	**87.** (3)	**88.** (4)	**89.** (1)	**90.** (4)
91. (2)	**92.** (3)	**93.** (1)	**94.** (1)	**95.** (1)	**96.** (4)	**97.** (3)	**98.** (4)	**99.** (2)	**100.** (4)
101. (2)	**102.** (3)	**103.** (1)	**104.** (3)	**105.** (3)	**106.** (1)	**107.** (2)	**108.** (4)	**109.** (1)	**110.** (1)
111. (1)	**112.** (3)	**113.** (1)	**114.** (3)	**115.** (3)	**116.** (2)	**117.** (2)	**118.** (4)	**119.** (3)	**120.** (2)
121. (1)	**122.** (3)	**123.** (1)	**124.** (3)	**125.** (4)	**126.** (3)	**127.** (2)	**128.** (3)	**129.** (1)	**130.** (3)
131. (2)	**132.** (3)	**133.** (3)	**134.** (4)	**135.** (3)	**136.** (3)	**137.** (4)	**138.** (3)	**139.** (3)	**140.** (2)
141. (1)	**142.** (3)	**143.** (3)	**144.** (3)	**145.** (3)	**146.** (3)	**147.** (3)	**148.** (3)	**149.** (1)	**150.** (4)
151. (1)	**152.** (1)	**153.** (3)	**154.** (2)	**155.** (2)	**156.** (2)	**157.** (1)	**158.** (3)	**159.** (3)	**160.** (1)
161. (2)	**162.** (3)	**163.** (2)	**164.** (1)	**165.** (1)	**166.** (2)	**167.** (3)	**168.** (3)	**169.** (4)	**170.** (3)
171. (3)	**172.** (4)	**173.** (2)	**174.** (2)	**175.** (3)	**176.** (1)	**177.** (1)	**178.** (2)	**179.** (2)	**180.** (3)
181. (3)	**182.** (2)	**183.** (2)	**184.** (1)	**185.** (1)	**186.** (2)	**187.** (2)	**188.** (2)	**189.** (3)	**190.** (2)
191. (2)	**192.** (2)	**193.** (2)	**194.** (1)	**195.** (1)	**196.** (2)	**197.** (3)	**198.** (2)	**199.** (2)	**200.** (1)
201. (3)	**202.** (2)	**203.** (1)	**204.** (2)	**205.** (3)	**206.** (1)	**207.** (4)	**208.** (2)	**209.** (4)	**210.** (4)
211. (1)	**212.** (2)	**213.** (3)	**214.** (4)	**215.** (3)	**216.** (3)	**217.** (3)	**218.** (3)	**219.** (3)	**220.** (3)
221. (3)	**222.** (2)	**223.** (3)	**224.** (1)	**225.** (3)	**226.** (1)	**227.** (2)	**228.** (2)	**229.** (3)	**230.** (1)
231. (1)	**232.** (3)	**233.** (2)	**234.** (3)	**235.** (1)	**236.** (3)	**237.** (2)	**238.** (2)	**239.** (1)	**240.** (2)
241. (2)	**242.** (2)	**243.** (3)	**244.** (2)	**245.** (1)	**246.** (3)	**247.** (3)	**248.** (1)	**249.** (1)	**250.** (2)
251. (4)	**252.** (1)	**253.** (2)	**254.** (4)	**255.** (3)	**256.** (1)	**257.** (2)	**258.** (4)	**259.** (2)	**260.** (3)
261. (3)	**262.** (3)	**263.** (3)	**264.** (1)	**265.** (2)	**266.** (3)	**267.** (3)	**268.** (1)	**269.** (1)	**270.** (1)
271. (3)	**272.** (1)	**273.** (2)	**274.** (3)	**275.** (1)	**276.** (2)	**277.** (2)	**278.** (2)	**279.** (1)	**280.** (2)
281. (2)	**282.** (2)	**283.** (2)	**284.** (3)	**285.** (1)	**286.** (2)	**287.** (1)	**288.** (2)	**289.** (3)	**290.** (2)
291. (4)	**292** (1)	**293.** (1)	**294.** (2)	**295.** (3)	**296.** (3)	**297.** (3)	**298.** (4)	**299.** (3)	**300.** (1)
301. (2)	**302.** (3)	**303.** (1)	**304.** (1)	**305.** (1)	**306.** (2)	**307.** (1)	**308.** (1)	**309.** (1)	**310.** (1)
311. (1)	**312.** (2)	**313.** (3)	**314.** (2)	**315.** (1)	**316.** (1)	**317.** (1)	**318.** (1)	**319.** (1)	**320.** (4)
321. (1)	**322.** (4)	**323.** (4)	**324.** (4)	**325.** (4)	**326.** (4)	**327.** (4)	**328.** (4)	**329.** (4)	**330.** (4)

UNIT 3

HUMAN RESOURCE DEVELOPMENT

Syllabus

- Concepts, Assumptions, Values, HRD Mechanisms, Action – research Model, HRD Culture and Climate, HRD Interventions, HR Accounting and Audit, Consultant – client relationship, Knowledge Management, Human Resource Information System.
- **International Human Resource Management (IHRM):** Organisational context of IHRM, IHRM and Sustainable Business, Functions of IHRM, Cross – Cultural Studies, Cultural Diversity, Transnational Organisations, IHRM models.

HUMAN RESOURCE DEVELOPMENT (HRD)

CONCEPT OF HUMAN RESOURCE DEVELOPMENT (HRD)

Human Resource Development (HRD) is the framework for helping employees develop their personal and organisational skills, knowledge and abilities. Human Resource Development includes such opportunities as employee training employee career development, performance management and development, coaching, mentoring, succession planning, key employee identification & organisation development.

HRD is mainly concerned with developing the skills, knowledge and competencies of people and it is people-oriented concept. The concept of HRD is not yet well conceived by various authors though they have defined the term from their approach as it is of recent origin and still is in the conceptualizing stage. Many personnel managers and organisations view HRD as synonymous to training and development. The concept was formally introduced by **Leonard Nadler in 1969** as "those learning experiences which are organised for a specific time and designed to bring about the possibility of behavioural change."

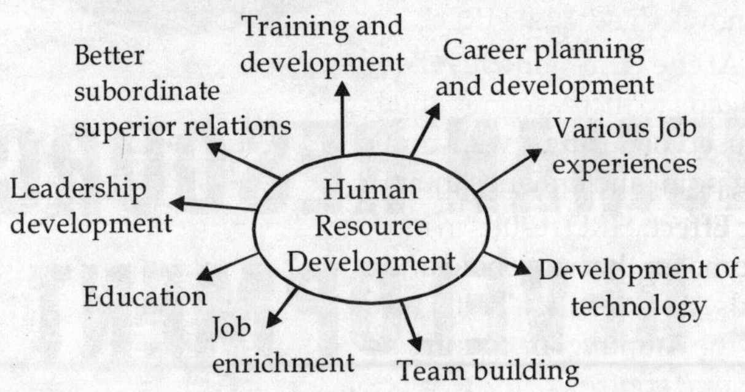

(Concept of HRD)

HRD from organisational point of view is a process in which the employees of an organisation are helped/motivated to acquire and develop technical, managerial and behavioural knowledge, skills and abilities, and mould the values, beliefs, attitude necessary to perform present and future roles by realizing highest human potential with a view to contribute positively to the organisational, group, individual and social goals.

Importance of HRD

Human resource development (HRD) is an essential component for growth and economic development. It can occur at both the nationwide level and the firm-wide level. The enhancement of HRD of a country is dependent on the government and national policies, while at the firm or micro level HRD can happen through training and efficient utilization of resources. Resources are efficiently utilised to support HRD when the maximum benefit is created at the lowest possible cost.

1. **Economic Development.** As the human resources of a country develop, the country progresses and the benefits spread all over the country. Better skilled and well-trained human resources attract a larger foreign direct investment into the country and improve the brand image of the country internationally. HRD for an economy is dependent on the economic policy of the government and the effort by the institutions in the economy to actively participate in the development process.

2. **Increase in Entrepreneurial Activity.** Human resource development may occur as a result of better education, training or development of vocational skills for individuals. This activity results in an increase in entrepreneurial activity due to the creative process that is encouraged by HRD. Moreover, even in an economy faced by high levels of unemployment, vocational training can generate substantial number of entrepreneurs who look for self-employment. Thus, HRD opens more options and wider avenues of success for individuals.
3. **Increase in Productivity.** HRD leads to better and efficient utilization of the available resources. The same numbers of individuals are able to improve their performance through training or learning of more productive skills. This leads to an increase in productivity in the same company at the firm-wide level and to an increase in the overall value of goods produced at the country-wide level. An increase in productivity of employees generates high economic progress for the country.
4. **Counteracting Social Taboos.** HRD can lead to a change in social perception of many people and can result in the development of the society. Better educated and skilled workers can think and act more constructively and result in a change of the social environment. Improved education leads to self-awareness and prevents individuals from embracing superstitions.
5. **Human Rights.** A better trained and educated workforce is well aware of its rights and is better able to protect against human rights violations. Workplace environments improve and workers rights are acknowledged with HRD.
6. **Profitability At the firm-wide level**, HRD leads to increased productivity and better client service. This leads to increased revenues at reduced costs for the company. Most companies today are focused on hiring a well-trained and competitive workforce in order to develop a unique selling point and enhance their profitability.
7. **Demographic Effect.** HRD results in more households with two working parents. This provides enhanced income for the household and at the same time reduces the time available to parents for raising kids. As a result, a better educated workforce results in a smaller increase in the population of the country. For countries like India, HRD can help prevent the population from increasing beyond control.

Objectives of HRD

1. To provide a comprehensive framework for the overall personality of each and every person on the organisation.
2. To develop the constructive mind and overall personality of each and every person in the organisation.
3. To develop the capabilities of each individual in relation to his present and extend the future roles.
4. To develop and maintain high level of motivation of employees.
5. To develop dyadic relationship between each employee and every supervisor.
6. To develop the sense of team spirit, team work and inter team collaboration in the organisation.
7. To develop the overall health and self renewing capabilities.
8. To generate systematic information about human resource for the purpose of manpower planning, placement, succession planning and the like.

Organisation of HRD Functions

1. **Training and development.** Training and development is aimed at improving or changing the knowledge skills and attitudes of the employees. While training involves providing the knowledge and skills required for doing a particular job to the employees, developmental

activities focus on preparing the employees for future job responsibilities by increasing the capabilities of an employee which also helps him to perform his present job in a better way. These activities start when an employee joins an organisation in the form of orientation and skills training. After the employee becomes proficient, the HR activities focus on the development of the employee through methods like coaching and counseling.

2. **Organisation development.** OD is the process of increasing the effectiveness of an organisation along with the well being of its members with the help of planned interventions that use the concepts of behavioural science. Both micro and macro changes are implemented to achieve organisation development. While the macro changes are intended to improve the overall effectiveness of the organisation the micro changes are aimed at individuals of small groups. Employee involvement programmes requiring fundamental changes in work expectation, reporting, procedures and reward systems are aimed at improving the effectiveness of the organisation. The human resource development professional involved in the organisation development intervention acts as an agent of change. He often consults and advising the line manager in strategies that can be adopted to implement the required changes and sometimes becomes directly involve in implementing these strategies.
3. **Career development.** It is a continuous process in which individual progresses through different stages of career each having a relatively unique set of issues and tasks. Career development comprises of two distinct processes. Career Planning and career management. Whereas career planning involves activities to be performed by the employee, often with the help of counselor and others, to assess his capabilities and skills in order to frame realistic career plan. Career management involves the necessary steps that need to be taken to achieve that plan. Career management generally focus more on the steps that an organisation that can take to foster the career development of the employees.

Features of HRD

1. **Planned and systematic Approach.** HRD is a systematic and planned approach for the development of individuals in order to achieve organisational, group and individual goals. HRD is a continuous process for the development of technical, managerial, behavioural and conceptual skills and knowledge HRD develops the skills and knowledge not only at the individual but also at dyadic level, group level and organisational level.
2. **HRD is Inter-disciplinary Approach.** It draws inputs from Engineering, Technology, Psychology, Anthropology, management, Commerce, Economics, Medicine etc. HRD is embodied with techniques and processes HRD is essential not only for manufacturing and service industry but also for information technology industry.
3. **HRD Recruiting** the employees within the dimensions and possibilities for developing human resources Selecting those employees having potentialities for development to meet the present and future organisational needs. Analysing, appraising and developing performance of employees as individuals, members of a group and organisations with a view to develop them by identifying the gaps in skills and knowledge.
4. **HRD Changes in Economic Policies.** Changing job requirements Need for Multi-skilled Human Resources Organisational viability and transformation process Technological Advances Organisational complexity, and Human Relations.
5. **HRD is Continuous Process.** HRD is a continuous and dynamic process which believes in the need for continues development of personnel to face the innumerable challenge in the functioning of an organisation. It is based on the belief that there is no end to the development of an individual and the learning process can continue throughout the life.

6. **Both macro and micro aspects.** HRD, at the macro level, HRD is described as the core of all the development activities in the sense of improvement of the quality of work life of a nation. At the micro level, HRD involves the improvement the quality of managers and workers so as to achieve greater quality of managers and workers so as to achieve greater quality of productivity.

ASPECT OF HRD
■ Systematic approach ■ Continuous process ■ Multi-disciplinary subject ■ All pervasive ■ Techniques
SCOPE OF HRD
1. Recruitment and selection of employees for meeting the present and future requirements of an organization. 2. Performance appraisal of the employees in order to understand their capabilities and improving them through additional training. 3. Offering the employees performance counselling and performance interviews from the superiors.

Functions of Human Resource Development

HRD at Macro and Micro Level. HRD as stated earlier is mainly concerned with developing the competencies of people. When we all see it as a people oriented concept then several questions come to the mind like should the people be developed in the larger and national context or in the smaller institutional context? Are they different at the macro level and micro level? As things stand now, HRD applies to both institutional (micro) as well as national (macro issues). The main objective however is to develop the newer capabilities in people so as to enable them to tackle both present and future challenges while realizing organisational goals. However, it is useful both at macro and micro levels.

1. **Macro level.** At the macro level HRD is concerned with the development of people for the nation's well being. It takes health capabilities skills, attitudes of people which are more useful to the development of the nation as a whole. While calculating the national income and economic growth the prospective HRD concept examines the individual's potentialities, their attitudes, aspirations, skills, knowledge etc. and establishes a concrete base for economic planning. However, HRD's contribution at macro level has not gained popularity as yet.
2. **Micro Levels.** HRD is concern for development in the organisations at the grass root level. Small wonder then, that HRD was well received by companies and managements as they realized its importance and foresaw its future contribution for the individual and organisational development. Generally HRD at micro level talks of the organisations' manpower, planning, selection, training, performance appraisal, development, potential appraisal, compensation, organisational development etc. HRD's involvement in all these areas is mainly with an objective to develop certain new capabilities in people concerned to equip them to meet the present job challenges and to accept future job requirements.

Differences Between HRD and Personnel

Personnel Function

(1) Maintenance oriented.
(2) An independent function with independent sub functions.
(3) Reactive functions responding to events as and when they take place.
(4) Exclusive responsibility of personnel department.
(5) Emphases is put on monetary rewards.
(6) Improved performances is the result of improved satisfaction and morale.
(7) Tries to improve the efficiency of people and administration.

Points of distinction: (i) Orientation (ii) Structure (iii) Philosophy (iv) Responsibility (v) Motivators (vi) Outcomes (vii) AIMS

Human resources development

(1) Development oriented.
(2) Consists of inter dependent parts.
(3) Proactive function, trying to anticipate and get ready with appropriate responses.
(4) Responsibility of all managers in the organisation.
(5) Emphasis is on higher order needs such as – how to design jobs with stretch pull and challenge how to improve creativity and problem solving skills, how to empower people in all respects etc.
(6) Better use of human resources leads to improved satisfaction and morale.
(7) It tries to develop the organisation and its culture as a whole.

DIFFERENCE BETWEEN HRM AND PERSONNEL MANAGEMENT

S.No.	Dimension	PM	HRM
1.	Employment contract	Careful dimensions of written contract	Aim to go beyond contract
2.	Rules	Importance of devising clear rules	Impatience with rules
3.	Guide to management action	Procedures	Business need
4.	Behaviour referent	Norms/customs & practices	Values/mission
5.	Managerial task vis-a-vis labour	Monitoring	Nurturing
6.	Key relations	Labour	Customer
7.	Initiatives	Piecerneal	Integrated
8.	Speed of decision	slow	fast
9.	Management role	Transactional	Transformational
10.	Communication	Indirect	Direct
11.	Management skill	Negotiation	Facilitation
12.	Selection	Separate	Integrated
13.	Pay	Job Evaluation	Performance related
14.	Conditions	Separately negotiated	Harmonisation
15.	Labour management	Collective bargaining contracts	Individual contracts
16.	Jab categories and grades	Many	Few
17.	Job design	Division of labour	Team work.

HRD MECHANISMS

1. **Performance Appraisal.** Performance appraisal have become increasingly important tools for organisations to use in managing and improving the performance of employees, in making timely and accurate staffing decisions and improving the overall quality of the firms products and services. The appraisal process is the formal way of evaluating the employee's performance. Its purpose is to provide an accurate picture of post and future employee's performance. To meet this performance appraisal are set. The targets are based on job related criteria that best determine successful job performance. Where possible actual performance is measured directly and objectively. Using a wide variety of techniques, specialists select an appropriate method to

measure an employee's actual performance against the previously set targets. The process is used to strengthen the effort performance linkage. Appraisals help an organisation communicate its expectations regarding performance and connection between performance and reward to employees. They increase employees' confidence and employees' feedback that their efforts are being adequately rewarded. The feedback is offered through an evaluation interview. Here the rater tries to give both positive and negative sides of the employee performance. To be useful, raters or supervisors should use HRD orientated appraisals as a mechanism to:

- Uncover difficulties faced by the subordinate while handling assigned task and try to remove these hurdles.
- Understand the strengths and weaknesses of subordinates and help the subordinates overcome the obstacles in the way.
- Encourage subordinates to meet problems head-on, accept responsibilities and face challenges with confidence and courage.
- Plan for effective utilization of the talents of subordinates.

2. **Potential Appraisal.** The term 'potential' refers to the abilities possessed by an employee but not put to use currently or the abilities to assume challenging responsibilities in future assignments. The term 'performance' refers to one's skills, abilities in meeting the requirements of the job which one is holding currently. Potential appraisal is different from performance appraisal which shows an employee's current performance in his existing role. If the employee is required to play a completely different set of roles at the higher levels, potential appraisal needs to be carried out at regular intervals. "The objective of potential appraisal is to identify the potential of a given employee to occupy higher positions in the organisational hierarchy and undertaken higher technologies." The appraisal is carried out on the basis of (i) supervisor's observations; (ii) performance data relating to various previous roles played by an employee; (iii) performance on roles in simulating to a new position. A good potential appraisal system helps management to pick up a suitable candidate for a given job and offer additional training, if necessary.

3. **Career Planning.** A career is a sequence of positions held by a person in the course of a lifetime. Career planning is a process of integrating the employees' needs and aspirations with organisational needs. Career programmes and HR programmes are linked to the degree that they help each individual meet individual and organisation requirements.

   In the HRD system, the long term growth plans of a company are not kept secret. They are made known to the employees. Major changes are discussed at all levels to promote understanding and commitment among employees. The immediate concern of employees would be to find out where do stand in such a road map. Do they have any chance to grow while building the organisation brick by brick? Since managers have information about the growth plans of the company, they need to transmit their information to their subordinates. The subordinates should be assisted in planning their careers within the company. It is, however, not necessary that each one of them would scale new heights every year but at least they are aware of the opportunities and get ready for greater challenges ahead. Career planning doesn't guaranty success. But without it, employees are rarely prepared to encase the opportunities that come their way.

4. **Training and Employee Development.** Training has gained importance in present day environment where jobs are change rapidly. Training is a learning experience designed to achieve a relatively permanent change in an individual that will improve the ability to perform on the job. Employee development on the other hand is a future oriented training process, focusing on the personal growth of the employee. Both training and development focus on learning. Training programmes should not be designed as quick fixes for organisational

problems, nor should they depend on faddish techniques just because they are popular now and are followed by our next door neighbour. Instead, training should be planned to meet the specific needs of the organisation and its employees. To survive and grow in a competitive environment, organisations have to motivate their employees to get ready for all kinds of future challenges.

5. **Organisation Development.** Organisations are never perfectly static. They keep on changing. Employees' skills and abilities, therefore, require continual upgrading. The future is uncertain when full of surprises. It is not easy to fight the force of change without adequate preparation and training. A systematic planned way of managing this change is through the process of OD. OD may be defined as a change effort that is planned, focused on an entire organisation or a large subsystem, managed from the top, aimed at enhancing organisational health and effectiveness and based on planned interventions made with the help of change agent or third party who is well versed in the behavioural science.
6. **Rewards.** People do what they do to satisfy needs. They choose to behave in way which will maximize their rewards. The most obvious reward is pay but there are many others. Intrinsic rewards come from their job itself such as feelings of achievement, pride in doing a job etc. Extrinsic rewards come from a source outside the job including pay, promotion and benefits offered by management. Reward could be linked to performance as well to motivate high achievers to do well. If rewards are allocated completely on non-performance factors such as seniority, job titles etc. then employees are likely to reduce their efforts. Now a days organisations also use team based rewards to motivate empowered work teams to exceed established targets.
7. **Employee welfare & quality of work life (QWL).** The term employee welfare means "the efforts to make life worth living for workmen". It includes various services, facilities & benefits offered to employees by the employers, unions & govt. The purpose is to improve the living standards of workers & thereby improve the quality of work life. Employees voluntarily extend a number of benefits to employees in the hope that these indirect compensation plans motivate employees to perform better. Over the years, the types of benefits offered have been expanding in line with competitive pressures, changing job market trends, employee expectations, union demands & legislative requirements.

   Quality of work life (QWL) efforts are systematic efforts by organisations to give workers a greater opportunity to affect the way they do their jobs & the contributions they make to the organisation's overall effectiveness. It is a way of empowering employees by giving them a greater 'say' in the decision making process. QWL means having good working conditions, good wages & benefits, good leadership & interesting, challenging jobs. QWL efforts include the following:

   - **Suggestion programme.** It is a formal method for generating, evaluating & implementing employee ideas.
   - **Socio-technical systems.** These are interventions in the work situation that redesign the work, the workgroups & the relationship between workers and the technologies they use to perform their jobs.
   - **Co-determination.** In this method, representatives of workers meet management in a formal way to discuss & vote important decisions that affect the lives of workers.
   - HRD system focuses on employee welfare & QWL by continually examining employee needs & meeting them to the best possible extent.
   - **Self-managed work teams.** These are employee groups (also called autonomous workgroups) with a high degree of decision-making, responsibility & behavioural control for completing their work. The team is usually given the responsibility for producing an entire product or service.

- **Quality circles.** These are small group of employees who meet regularly to find, analyze & solve quality & other work-related problems of a particular department/ section/ area.
- **Open door policies.** Where open door policies exist, employees are free to walk into any manager's office with their problems & seek solutions to such problems.
- **Employee involvement.** Here employees are given the opportunity to participate in the decisions that affect them & their relationship in the company.

8. **Human resource information systems.** Human resource information system (HRIS) is a method by which an organisation collects, maintains & reports information on people & jobs, the information is generally stored in a central human resource data bank, preferably in a computer containing the following details:
   - ***Personal data.*** Identification, education, reserved category, place of origin, etc.;
   - ***Recruitment data.*** Entry date, grade in aptitude tests, grade in leadership tests;
   - ***Experience data.*** Placement history, promotions, tasks performed grade wise;
   - ***Appraisal data.*** Appraisal on each job, ratings of behaviours in a group, commitment to overall goals, etc.;
   - ***Training data.*** Nature of training received at each level, current training assignment, etc.;
   - ***Miscellaneous.*** Health status, personal problems, security needs, record of incentives received, absence & sickness data, etc.;

   This information is put to use whenever there is a need to identify employees for certain special assignments.
9. **Job Rotation.** The work task should be rotated among the employees so as broaden their field of specialization as well as their knowledge about the organisation operation as a whole, the work tasks, therefore, should be rotated one in a years among the various employees depending upon their qualification and suitability to perform new roles.
10. **Human resource planning.** It is the process aimed at ensuring that the organisation will have adequate number of qualified person, available at proper time, performing jobs which would meet the need of the organisation and also prove the satisfaction for the individual involved. It is endeavour to match the demand and supply for various types of human skill in the organisation.
11. **Recruitment, selection and placement.** Recruitment is generation of application for specific position for anticipated vacancies, the idols recruitment efforts will be generate adequate numbers of suitable candidate, selection is the process of ascertaining the qualification, experience skill knowledge, etc. of applicant with a view to appraising their suitability for a job. Placement is the process of assigning the selected candidate with the most suitable job. It underlines the need for placing the right men at the right job so that best result could be utilized.
12. **Building morale and motivation among the employees.** The organisation must give the constant evidence to the belief that human resource in the organisation are the key of development. This requires the proper motivation of the employees which provides the base for the management function of planning and organising. A climate of creativity must be developed by the management so that performance level come up to the mark and growth become the way of life.
13. **Development of team work.** The HRD section must try to develop a habit of the team work among human resource, team work requires among others things, that the member have an image of their own team mates, coincides as precisely as possible with reality.
14. **Developing emotional intelligence.** Human resources are considered greatest assets in any organisation. It is thus essential to understand the role of emotional intelligence in enhancing the productivity of the human resources to achieve the overall goal and success.

The Contribution of Subsystems to HRD Goals

The Contribution of HRD Subsystem to Development Dimension

Development dimensions	HRD subsystems Mechanism		
Individual	Training	Career planning	Potential appraisal and development
	Feedback and coaching performance	Rewards	
Individual in the present role	Performance appraisal	Training Rewards	Feedback and performance coaching
Individual in regard to likely future roles	Potential appraisal and development	Training	Performance appraisal Feedback and performance coaching
Dyadic relationships	Feedback and performance coaching	Performance appraisal	Training
Teams & teamwork	Organisation development	Training	Team rewards
Collaboration among different units/teams	Organisation development	Training	
Self-renewing capability and health of organisation	Performance appraisal	Organisation development	Training

The subsystems described already, contributes to the achievement of overall HRD goals performance appraisal helps an individual to develop his current role capabilities. Potential appraisal focuses on identifying the employee's likely future roles within the organisation. Training helps an employee to improve his job knowledge and skills. It enables an employee to do his current job more efficiently and prepare himself for a higher level job. It bridges the gap between job requirements and employee's skills, knowledge and behaviour. Feedback and performance coaching helps the development of the individual as well as interpersonal relationships. Organisation development aims at developing team spirit and self-renewing skills. Welfare amenities, rewards and incentives improve the quality of life of employees and make the work place a stimulating one for employees. The contribution of these HRD subsystems to various development dimensions is shown in the table of previous page.

HRD MATRIX

The HRD matrix shows the interrelationship between HRD instruments, processes, outcomes and organisational effectiveness.

1. **HRD Instruments.** These include performance appraisal, counselling, role analysis, potential development, training, communication policies, job rotations, rewards, job enrichment programme, etc. These instruments may vary depending on the size of the organisation, the internal environment, the support and commitment of the top management, the competitive policies etc.
2. **HRD Processes.** The HRD instruments lead to the generation of HRD processes like role clarity, performance planning, development climate, risk-taking, dynamism in employees. Such HRD processes should result in more competent, satisfied and committed people that would make the organisation grow by contributing their best to it.
3. **HRD Outcomes.** HRD instruments and processes make people more committed and satisfied, where they tend to give their best to the organisation enthusiastically.
4. **Organisational Effectiveness.** The HRD outcomes influence the organisational effectiveness, which in turn, depends on a number of variables like environment, technology, competitors, etc.

A Schematic Presentation of Linkages between HRD Instruments, Processes, Outcomes and Organisational Effectiveness

HRD Climate. The HRD climate of an organisation plays a very important role in ensuring the competency, motivation and development of its employees. The HRD climate can be created using appropriate HRD systems and leadership styles of top management. The HRD climate is both a means to an end as well as an end in itself. In the recent past simple instruments have been developed to measure the HRD climate in organisations. These instruments are being widely used to assess periodically the climate, maintain profiles and design interventions to further improve it. This unit presents a detailed conceptual background of the HRD climate, various research studies available on HRD climate and discusses an instrument to measure HRD climate that is being used by different organisations. By the end of the unit the reader should be able to use the HRD climate survey questionnaire to measure the HRD climate of his own organisation. Reader also will get an overview of the HRD climate existing in different organisations.

HRD Climate and organisational climate. The conventional connotation with which the term 'climate' has been used in literature is 'Organisational Climate'. The concept of climate with specific reference to HRD context, *i.e.*, HRD climate, has been recently introduced by Rao and Abraham (1986). Perhaps it could be due to this reason that there is hardly any research work available in published literature.

HRD climate is an integral part of organisational climate. It can be defined as perceptions the employee can have on the developmental environment of an organisation. This developmental climate will have the following characteristics (Rao and Abraham, 1986):

- A tendency at all levels starting from top management to the lowest level to treat the people as the most important resources.
- A perception that developing the competencies in the employees is the job of every manager/ supervisor.
- Faith in the capability of employees to change and acquire new competencies at any stage of life.
- A tendency to be open in communications and discussions rather than being secretive (fairly free expression of feeling).
- Encouraging risk taking and experimentation.
- Making efforts to help employees recognize their strengths and weaknesses through feedback
- A general climate of trust.
- A tendency on the part of employees to be generally helpful to each other and collaborate with each other.
- Tendency to discourage stereotypes and favoritism.
- Supportive – Supportive HRD practices including performance appraisal, training, reward management, potential development, job-rotation, career planning, etc.

  Organisations differ in the extent to which they have these tendencies. Some organisations may have some of these tendencies, some others may have only a few of these and few may have most of these. It is possible to work out the profile of an organisation on the basis of these tendencies.
- HRD climate contributes to the organisations' overall health and self-renewing capabilities which in turn, increase the enabling capabilities of individual, dyads, team and the entire organisation.

ACTION - RESEARCH MODEL

The term "action research" is contested and has various meanings in different settings. Additionally, several related terms overlap in some ways (e.g., participatory research, participatory action research, practitioner research, action science). Approaches to action research could be placed in each of Burrell and Morgan's four paradigms. In fact, the primary differences between action research approaches are easiest to understand by using a rubric such as that presented by Burrell and Morgan.

In the U.S., action research continued mainly as a problem solving technique within organisations and schools. The earlier approaches of Collier and Lewin, which emphasized examinations of social issues, were now transformed into largely apolitical activities. In HRD, action research continues to be seen as an organisation development (OD) tool that is primarily centered around the role of the OD/ HRD consultant. Most perceptions of action research within HRD and organisational studies place it primarily within the functionalist paradigm. However, there are exceptions. William Foote Whyte (e.g., 1991) worked for decades in the area of participatory action research (PAR). Whyte's form of PAR was largely centered around a democratic sociocultural approach. Similarly, Eric Trist worked from a democratic sociotechnical approach for most of his life, until he died in 1993 . Currently, approaches such as appreciative inquiry, dialogue conferences, and storytelling conferences emphasize the transformative effects of dialogue in action research. These approaches are increasingly becoming more popular within organisations and have the potential of moving further away from the functionalist paradigm. However, approaches like these emphasize widespread participation, but not an examination of deeper social problems. For that reason, work like this is better classified as *humanistic* than *critical*. In other words, this work seeks milder humanistic aims, but does not seek to understand the underlying sources of social problems. Another continuing stream of PAR is seen in adult education, particularly with the work of Paulo Freire, the Brazilian adult educator (starting in the 1960s). Freire's literacy education work among poor Brazilians aimed to help students conduct their own research, which resulted in social action and the questioning of societal norms and injustices (Anderson et al., 1994). In the U.S., the community development work of the Highlander Center in Tennessee is widely used as an example of PAR. Highlander heavily advocates critical approaches in its work with rural communities in Appalachia.

How Does Action Research Relate to Critical HRD?

Aristotle described three types of knowledge: *episteme*, *techne*, and *phronesis* knowledge. Most social science research focuses on *episteme* knowledge (i.e., predictive, theoretical knowledge), which is combined with *techne* knowledge (i.e., practical technical knowledge). Habermas, an influential member of the Frankfurt School of critical theory, believed strongly in Aristotle's concept of *phronesis*, which integrates practical and moral knowledge. In other words, Habermas advocated inquiry that does not neglect the practical day-to-day concerns, but integrates those practical concerns with larger moral and societal issues. Additionally, Habermas rejected the linear notion that theory should drive practice. Instead, he advocated the integration of theory into the everyday lives of practitioners (McNiff, 2000). Action research is a natural fit with Habermas' ideas of critical theory and has long been used for emancipatory purposes and community action. The principles behind critical action research have a long history beyond the functionalist problem solving methods that we often see in HRD action research. Functionalist approaches to action research surely have a place in our field, but critical approaches also provide an opportunity to utilize Aristotle's ideas of phronesis by integrating moral and societal issues with everyday practical concerns.

Individual, Group, and Large-Scale Action Research

As most types of social research, action research occurs at the individual, group, and organisation/ large-scale levels. Reason and Bradbury (2001) conclude that action research is most beneficial when it occurs at all three levels. Action research may begin as an individual project and evolve into a small group effort, which could lead to an organisation-wide effort. Alternatively, it could begin as a small group effort or a large-scale effort. On the other hand, others are wary of moving beyond the individual or group levels, for fear that action research will become another tool for social engineering. There is a fear that organisation sponsorship or cooption of action research dilutes its political and emancipatory nature. Involvement at the large-scale level by an organisation could thwart the critical nature of action research, especially within a company or other employing organisation. On the other hand, it would be more viable for a critical action research project to be taken to a large-scale level by a labor union or non-profit advocacy group. In such a case, there may be less risk of action research losing its critical edge. However, large-scale projects are often controlled through means of technical rationality, which would certainly go against democratic aims.

HRD can learn from the emerging field of practitioner action research in K-12 education. In these conceptions of action research, it often occurs at the individual or small group levels. The role of university researchers and consultants is oftentimes de-emphasized in favor of grass roots efforts. Individual or small group sponsorship is favored over organisation/large-scale projects.

Principles in Designing HRD System

There have been many queries regarding the principles of Human Resource development. Many a times we get confused between principles and functions of HRD however there is a clear cut distinction between the two. The main functions of HRD are Training, Personal development, Organisational development, Career planning and development and Change Management. The principles therefore are not the functions.

HRD systems must be designed differently for different organisations. Although the basic principles may remain the same, the specific components, their relationships, the processes involved in each, the phasing, and so on, may differ from one organisation to another organisation. Designing an integrated HRD system requires a thorough understanding of the principles and models of human resource development and a diagnosis of the organisation culture, existing HRD practices in the organisation, employee perceptions of these practices, and the developmental climate within the organisation.

The following principles related to focus, structure, and functioning should be considered when designing integrated HRD systems.

- **Focus on enabling capabilities.** The primary purpose of HRD is to help the organisation to increase its "enabling" capabilities. These include development of human resources, development of organisational health, improvement of problem solving capabilities, development of diagnostic ability (so that problems can be located quickly and effectively), and increased employee productivity and commitment.
- **Balancing adaptation and change in the organisational culture.** Although HRD systems are designed to suit the organisational culture, the role of HRD may be to modify that culture to increase the effectiveness of the organisation. There always has been a controversy between those who believe that HRD should be designed to suit the culture and those who believe that HRD should be able to change the culture. Both positions seem to be extreme. HRD should take the organisation forward, and this can be done only if its design anticipates change and evolution in the future.
- **Attention to contextual factors.** What is to be included in the HRD systems, how is it to be sub-divided, what designations and titles will be used, and similar issues should be settled after consideration of the various contextual factors of the organisation—its culture and tradition, size, technology, levels of existing skills, available support for the function, availability of outside help and so on.

- **Building linkages with other functions.** Human resource development systems should be designed to strengthen other functions in the company such as long-range corporate planning, budgeting and finance, marketing, production, and other similar functions. These linkages are extremely important.
- **Balancing specialization and diffusion of the function.** Although HRD involves specialised functions, line people should be involved in various aspects of HRD. Action is the sole responsibility of the line people, and HRD should strengthen their roles.
- **Ensuring respectability for the function.** In many companies, the personnel function does not have much credibility because it is not perceived as a major function within the organisation. It is necessary that HRD be instituted at a very high level in the organisation and that the head of the HRD department is classified as a senior manager. Both the credibility and usefulness of HRD depend on this.
- **Balancing differentiation and integration.** The human resource development function often includes personnel administration, human resource development and training, and industrial relations. These three functions have distinct identities and requirements and should be differentiated within the HRD department. One person may be responsible for OD, another for training, another for potential appraisal and assessment, etc. At the same time, these roles should be integrated through a variety of mechanisms. For example, inputs from manpower planning should be available to line managers for career planning and HRD units for potential appraisal and development. Data from recruitment should be fed into the human resources information system. If salary administration and placement are handled separately, they should be linked to performance appraisals. Differentiation as well as integration mechanisms are essential if the HRD system is to function well.
- **Establishing linkage mechanisms.** HRD has linkages with outside systems as well as with internal sub-systems. It is wise to establish specific linkages to be used to manage the system. Standing committees for various purposes (with membership from various parts and levels of the organisation), task groups, and ad hoc committees' for specific tasks are useful mechanisms.
- **Developing monitoring mechanisms.** The HRD function is always evolving. It therefore requires systematic monitoring to review the progress and level of effectiveness of the system and to plan for its next step. A thorough annual review reappraisal every three years will be invaluable in reviewing and planning the system. It may be helpful to include persons from other functions in the organisation in the HRD assessment effort.

HRD Culture and Climate

The elements of HRD climate can be grouped into three broad categories — general climate, OCTAPAC culture and HRD mechanism. The general climate items deal with the importance given to human resources development in general by the top management and line manager The OCTAPAC items deal with the extent to which Openness, Confrontation. Trust, Autonomy, Proactively, Authenticity and Collaboration are valued and promoted in the organisation. The items dealing with HRD mechanisms measure the extent to which HRD mechanisms are implemented seriously. These three groups were taken with following assumption :

(a) **A general supportive climate** is important for HRD if it has to be implemented effectively. Such supportive climate consists of not only top management line management's commitment but good personnel policies and positive attitudes towards development.

(b) **Successful implementation of HRD** involves an integrated look at HRD and efforts to use as many HRD mechanisms as possible. These mechanisms include: performance appraisal, potential appraisal, career planning, performance rewards feedback and counselling, training, employee welfare for quality work life, Job-rotation, etc.

(c) **OCTAPAC culture** is essential for facilitating HRD. Openness is there when: employees feel free to discuss their ideas, activities and feelings with each other. Confrontation is bringing out problems and issues into the open with a view to solving them rather than hiding them for fear of hurting or getting hurt. Trust is taking people at their face value and believing what they say. Autonomy is giving freedom to let people work independently with responsibility. Proactively is encouraging employees to take initiative and risks. Authenticity is the tendency on the part of people to do what they say. Collaboration is to accept interdependencies, to be helpful to each other and work as teams.

The following factors may be considered as contributing to HRD climate:

(1) **Top Management Style and Philosophy.** A developmental style a belief in the capability of people participative approach openness and receptivity to suggestions from the subordinates are some of the dimensions that contribute to the creation of a positive HRD climate.

(2) **Personnel Policies.** Personnel policies that show high concern for employees, that emphasize equity and objectivity in appraisals policies that emphasize sufficient resource allocation for welfare and developmental activities, policies that emphasize a collaborative attitude and trust among the people go a long way in creating the HRD climate.

(3) **HRD Instruments and Systems.** A number of HRD instruments have been found to generate a good HRD climate. Particularly open systems of appraisal with emphasis of counselling, career development systems, informal training mechanisms, potential development systems etc. contribute to HRD climate.

(4) **Self-renewal Mechanisms.** Organisations that have built in self-renewal mechanisms are likely to generate a positive HRD climate.

(5) **Attitudes of Personnel and URD Staff.** A helpful and supportive attitude on the part of HRD and personnel people plays a very critical role in generating the HRD climate. If the personal behaviour of any of these agents is not supportive, the HRD climate is likely to be vitiated.

(6) **Commitment or Line Managers.** The commitment of line managers to the development of their subordinates is a very important determiner of HRD climate.

HRD Intervention

The designer of the training program needs to understand each of the methods and the delivery system to determine the best method for meeting training objectives, given the organisational constraints. Instructional methods differ in their ability to influence knowledge, skills and attitudes, so the training designer must be able to evaluate a method's strengths and weaknesses to make good decisions about its use. Although the method's effectiveness in meeting the learning objective should be the major criterion for selection, other consideration are costs, time needed to develop material, and the time allotted for training session.

Selecting Training Methods and Media

A 2003 survey conducted by Raining magazine revealed that, contrary to popular belief, classroom programs were still the most popular instructional method (see Table).

ORGANISATIONS MAKING FREQUENT USE OF VARIOUS TRAINING METHODS AND MEDIA AND ITS PERCENTAGE SHARE

Methods	Percent
Instructor-led Classroom Programs	91
Self-Study, Web-based	44
Job-based Performance Support	44
Public Seminars	42
Case Studies	40
Role Plays	35
Games or Simulations, Non-computer-based	25
Self-Study, Non-computer-based	23
Virtual Classroom, with Instructor	21
Games or Simulations, Computer-based	10
Experiential Programs	6
Virtual Reality Programs	3
Media	
Workbooks/Manuals	79
Internet/Intranet/Extranet	63
CD-ROM/DVD/Diskettes	55
Videotapes	52
Teleconferencing	24
Video conferencing	23
Satellite/Broadcast TV	12
Audiocassettes	4

Adopted from Werner & DeSimone (2007). Human Resource Development, 4e. Thomson South-Western.

The survey indicated that 91 percent of organisations use the classroom format "always" or "often" to deliver at least some of their training. There has been considerable recent growth in web-based self-study programs and work-based performance support programs. More general public seminars continue to remain popular as well. Workbooks and manuals continue to be widely used, though there has been a substantial recent increase in the use of the Internet/company intranets and CD-ROM/DVDs for provide training.

Computer applications, orientation, management development, technical training, communication skills, and sexual harassment were the topics most frequently offered.

An ASTD survey revealed that, in 2002, organisations surveyed reported using instructor-led classroom training for 72 percent of their training, with 19 percent of training being delivered via learning technologies such as computer-based training, multimedia, CD-ROMs, and company intranets. For organisations identified as training investment leaders, the figures for delivery via classroom versus learning technologies were 62 percent and 29 percent, respectively.

One way of classifying the training is by the degree of activity expected or required from the trainees. On one end, the lecture method and videotapes are generally the least active (or most passive) form of training. At the other extreme, highly experiential methods such as outdoor training, role-playing exercises, games, and simulations demand the greatest amount of activity or action from trainees. Other approaches such as computer-based instruction or videoconferencing fall somewhere in between.

Training approaches can also be grouped into two broad categories: on-the-job methods, which typically occur in the employee's normal work setting, and class¬room methods, which typically take place away from the job (such as in a conference room or lecture hall). This categorization is not definitive, as some training methods have multiple applications. Computer-based training (CBT), for example, can be implemented using a computer at an employee's desk or workstation, in a company classroom, or even at an employee's home.

With such an array of training methods and media available (as seen in Table), how does a HRD professional choose as to which approach is most appropriate for maximum learning? Several factors should be considered:

1. **The objectives of the program.** This factor is paramount. As will be clear, some approaches are more appropriate for achieving particular objectives than others. For example, if the objective is to improve interpersonal skills, then more active approaches such as videotaping, role playing, or behaviour modeling would be better choices than the lecture or computer-based training methods.
2. **Time and money available.** In an ideal world, we would have all the time and money needed to accomplish our goals. Unfortunately, in many organisations, managers often ask the HRD department to design and implement programs quickly, while spending as little money as possible. Competing needs may also force HRD professionals to select certain approaches because of its low cost. For example, when designing a program to train mechanics to repair a complicated mechanical system, an interactive, computer-based program may be appropriate, but because of its cost, the HRD professional may have to accept for a combination of traditional classes (using lecture, discussion, and reference books) and on-the-job training.
3. **Availability of other resources.** Some methods require highly trained trainers and specialized equipment and facilities to be delivered effectively. Again, trade-offs are likely to be made by choosing alternative approaches with less cost resources.
4. **Trainee characteristics and preferences.** The issues here are on both the trainee's readiness and the diversity of the target population. Methods such as computer-based training require a fairly high level of literacy. If literacy or fluency is a problem, either a less reading-and writing-intensive method (such as videotape) may be used, or literacy training must be done first. Similarly, because individuals have different learning styles, some training methods may be more appropriate than others.

In the end, the selection of training methods and media requires that program designers have the knowledge of different HRD techniques, and then use sound judgment in their decision making. HRD professionals should investigate all available methods, and when in doubt, consult experienced colleagues, instructional designers, and consultants.

HR Accounting and Audit

Human resource accounting is the procedure to recognize and report the investments made in the Human Resources of an Organisation that are currently not accounted for in the conventional accounting practices. It is an expansion of the Accounting Principles of matching the costs and revenues and of organising data to converse significant information. Normally, human resource Accounting (HRA) engages accounting for the organisation's management and employees as human capital that provides future benefits. In the human resource accounting approach, expenditures associated with human resources are reported as assets on the balance sheet in contrast to the conventional accounting approach which treats costs related to a company's human resources as expenses on the income statement that decrease profit.In the decade of 1960, many researchers developed procedures of accounting for organisational human resource asset. It is based on the established notion that all expenditure of human capital formation is regarded as a charge against the revenue of the period as it does not create any physical asset. But this concept has changed and the cost incurred on any asset (as human resources) should be capitalized as it yields benefits quantifiable in financial terms. Human Resource Accounting indicates accounting for people as the organisational resources. It is the measurement of the cost and value of people to organisation. It involves measuring costs incurred by private firms and public sectors to recruit, select, employ, train and develop employees and judge their economic value to the organisation. Human resource accounting is a complicated way to determine in financial terms the effectiveness of the personal manager activities and the use of people in an organisation. It is process of accounting people as an organisation resource. It attempts to place a value on the organisational human resources as assets and not as expenses. This method demonstrates the investment made by organisation in the people and how the value of these people changes over a time. The possession of employee is compared with the substitute cost from time to time.

According to American accounting association committee, Human Resource Accounting is the process of identifying and measuring data about human resource and identifying and measuring data about human resource and communicating this information to interested parties. Likert (1971) explained that Human Resource Accounting serves several purposes in an organisation. It provides cost/value information for taking management decisions about acquiring, allocating, developing, and maintaining human resources in order to attain cost-effectiveness. It permits management employees to scrutinize effectively the use of human resources. Jasrotia (2004) emphasized the need for human resource accounting on India. The investigator concentrated on the remarkable shift from manufacturing to service rendering in the Indian economy where success of organisations depends on the knowledge and intellectual capabilities of personnel. The suggestion from the research was that Indian government should make the accounting and reporting of human resources mandatory for every organisation just like as it is adopted in Denmark from the year 2015. HRA provides effective basis of human asset control, that is, whether the asset is appreciated, depleted or conserved. It assists in the development of management principles by classifying the financial consequences of various practices. Main goals of Human Resource Accounting is to provide cost value information about acquiring, developing, allocating and maintaining Reallocating and maintaining HR, enable management to effectively monitor the use of HR, enable management to effectively monitor the use of HR, find whether human asset is appreciating or depreciating, find whether human asset is appreciating or depreciating over a period of time, assist in the development of effective management practices, to motivate individual persons in the organisation, increase their worth by training, in planning physical resource. The human resource accounting is done to provide cost value information for making appropriate and effective management decisions about acquiring, allocating, developing and maintaining human resources in order to achieve cost effective organisational objectives. Leading management scholar, Flamholtz (1979) explains the human resource accounting model as "psycho-technical systems" (PTS) approach to organisational measurement. This approach indicated that, the two functions of measurement are process functions in the process of measurement and numerical information from the numbers themselves. Therefore important role of human resource accounting is to present numerical measures. The HRA measurement process facilitates to increase recognition that human capital is vital to the organisation's short and long-term productivity and expansion.

Grojer and Johansson stated that human resource accounting is a political tool used to demonstrate mismanagement of human resource. It works as a pedagogical instrument for analyzing and structuring, and used as a decision making aid to ensure that decision on HR are more rational from the management point of view.

There is several advantage of using human resource accounting. These include foresee the changes, provides different methods of testing , Increase productivity, brings high return, helps individual employee to aspire, provides scope for advancement, throws light on the strength and weaknesses of existing workforce and helps potential investors to judge a company.

Consultant-Client Relationship

Consultants are expected to maintain professional and ethical standards when dealing with their clients. This can take the form of maintaining arm's length relationships, not intervening in the internal affairs and politics of the client's organisations, keeping confidential information away from interested parties looking for insider knowledge, and reporting any violations in the conduct (financial, operational, and behavioural) by the client's organisation to the regulators. This is the code of conduct that is usually prescribed for consulting firms whenever they take on work from client organisations.

However, this is rarely followed in practice as evidenced by the large numbers of corporate scandals that have emerged in the last decade or so where the consultant was found to be aiding and even abetting the malfeasance conducted by the client. For instance, the Enron scandal manifested itself because the consulting firm was in cahoots with the client in cooking the books. Indeed, in this case, it was found that the consulting firm's partners went beyond collaboration and were indeed one of the culprits.

Similarly, the Satyam scandal in India was also found to be a case where the consultants (or some of them) knew about the goings-on in the company and were in breach of the code of conduct and even legal aspects since they did not report the matter to the regulators. However, the saving grace in this case was that when the malfeasance became too big and too hot to handle, it was the new consulting firm that had been roped in for another purpose that blew the whistle on the scam.

These examples indicate that the consultants have to walk a thin line between fulfilling professional obligations and reporting unethical behaviour. Since the client is the one who pays them, it is often the case that the consultants are reluctant to report malfeasance to the regulators. Further, considering the extremely competitive nature of the market wherein there are several consulting firms competing for the same client, money talks and hence, consultants are often found to go along with the client. There are no easy answers when one considers all the aspects and it would be indeed a brave and conscientious consultant who would be the whistleblower.

Having said that, there are some solutions that have emerged in recent years about the course of action to be taken by the consulting firms. For instance, after the Enron scandal, the SEC (Securities and Exchange Commission) and other regulators ensured that new rules separating consulting and investment banking so that the same consulting firm which was also advising the client in financial matters would now be two different firms. While this was intended to reduce the conflict of interest since it was thought that when consultants and investment bankers represent two firms they would automatically be in a position to wink at malfeasance, it is debatable as to how far this law succeeded given the Global Economic Crisis of 2008 wherein several case of malfeasance came to light.

Finally, above everything the maintenance of normative consultant client relations depends on the institutional structures, the incentives for good behaviour as well as the incentives for moral hazard, the role of the regulators and how strictly they enforce the law, and the individuals themselves considering that they are the ones who are either benefiting or losing out when the scandal breaks. It is also about human nature since it is hard to resist the temptations of money and power and at the same time be true to the professional obligations and the observance of the code of conduct.

KNOWLEDGE MANAGEMENT

Knowledge management (KM) is the process of creating, sharing, using and managing the knowledge and information of an organisation. It refers to a multidisciplinary approach to achieving organisational objectives by making the best use of knowledge.

An established discipline since 1991, KM includes courses taught in the fields of business administration, information systems, management, library, and information sciences. Other fields may contribute to KM research, including information and media, computer science, public health and public policy. Several universities offer dedicated master's degrees in knowledge management.

Many large companies, public institutions and non-profit organisations have resources dedicated to internal KM efforts, often as a part of their business strategy, IT, or human resource management departments. Several consulting companies provide advice regarding KM to these organisations.

Knowledge management efforts typically focus on organisational objectives such as improved performance, competitive advantage, innovation, the sharing of lessons learned, integration and continuous improvement of the organisation. These efforts overlap with organisational learning and may be distinguished from that by a greater focus on the management of knowledge as a strategic asset and on encouraging the sharing of knowledge. KM is an enabler of organisational learning.

Knowledge management efforts have a long history, including on-the-job discussions, formal apprenticeship, discussion forums, corporate libraries, professional training, and mentoring programs. With increased use of computers in the second half of the 20th century, specific adaptations of technologies such as knowledge bases, expert systems, information repositories, group decision support systems, intranets, and computer-supported cooperative work have been introduced to further enhance such efforts.

In 1999, the term personal knowledge management was introduced; it refers to the management of knowledge at the individual level.

In the enterprise, early collections of case studies recognised the importance of knowledge management dimensions of strategy, process and measurement. Key lessons learned include people and the cultural norms which influence their behaviours are the most critical resources for successful knowledge creation, dissemination and application; cognitive, social and organisational learning processes are essential to the success of a knowledge management strategy; and measurement, benchmarking and incentives are essential to accelerate the learning process and to drive cultural change. In short, knowledge management programs can yield impressive benefits to individuals and organisations if they are purposeful, concrete and action-orientated.

KM emerged as a scientific discipline in the early 1990s. It was initially supported by individual practitioners, when Skandia hired Leif Edvinsson of Sweden as the world's first Chief Knowledge Officer (CKO).Hubert Saint-Onge (formerly of CIBC, Canada), started investigating KM long before that. The objective of CKOs is to manage and maximise the intangible assets of their organisations. Gradually, CKOs became interested in practical and theoretical aspects of KM, and the new research field was formed. The KM idea has been taken up by academics, such as Ikujiro Nonaka (Hitotsubashi University), Hirotaka Takeuchi (Hitotsubashi University), Thomas H. Davenport (Babson College) and Baruch Lev (New York University).

In 2001, Thomas A. Stewart, former editor at Fortune magazine and subsequently the editor of Harvard Business Review, published a cover story highlighting the importance of intellectual capital in organisations. The KM discipline has been gradually moving towards academic maturity. First, is a trend toward higher cooperation among academics; single-author publications are less common. Second, the role of practitioners has changed. Their contribution to academic research declined from 30% of overall contributions up to 2002, to only 10% by 2009. Third, the number of academic knowledge management journals has been steadily growing, currently reaching 27 outlets.

Multiple KM disciplines exist; approaches vary by author and school. As the discipline matured, academic debates increased regarding theory and practice, including:

- Techno-centric with a focus on technology, ideally those that enhance knowledge sharing and creation.

- Organisational with a focus on how an organisation can be designed to facilitate knowledge processes best.
- Ecological with a focus on the interaction of people, identity, knowledge, and environmental factors as a complex adaptive system akin to a natural ecosystem.

Regardless of the school of thought, core components of KM roughly include people/culture, processes/structure and technology. The details depend on theperspective.KM perspectives include:

- community of practice
- social network analysis
- intellectual capital
- information theory
- complexity science
- constructivism

The practical relevance of academic research in KM has been questioned with action research suggested as having more relevance and the need to translate the findings presented in academic journals to a practice.

Strategies

Knowledge may be accessed at three stages: before, during, or after KM-related activities. Organisations have tried knowledge capture incentives, including making content submission mandatory and incorporating rewards into performance measurement plans. Considerable controversy exists over whether such incentives work and no consensus has emerged.

One strategy to KM involves actively managing knowledge (push strategy). In such an instance, individuals strive to explicitly encode their knowledge into a shared knowledge repository, such as a database, as well as retrieving knowledge they need that other individuals have provided (codification).

Another strategy involves individuals making knowledge requests of experts associated with a particular subject on an ad hoc basis (pull strategy). In such an instance, expert individual(s) provide insights to requestor (personalisation).

Hansen et al. defined the two strategies. Codification focuses on collecting and storing codified knowledge in electronic databases to make it accessible. Codification can therefore refer to both tacit and explicit knowledge. In contrast, personalisation encourages individuals to share their knowledge directly. Information technology plays a less important role, as it is only facilitates communication and knowledge sharing.

Other knowledge management strategies and instruments for companies include:

- Knowledge sharing (fostering a culture that encourages the sharing of information, based on the concept that knowledge is not irrevocable and should be shared and updated to remain relevant)
- Make knowledge-sharing a key role in employees' job description
- Inter-project knowledge transfer
- Intra-organisational knowledge sharing
- Inter-organisational knowledge sharing
- Proximity & architecture (the physical situation of employees can be either conducive or obstructive to knowledge sharing)
- Storytelling (as a means of transferring tacit knowledge)
- Cross-project learning
- After-action reviews
- Knowledge mapping (a map of knowledge repositories within a company accessible by all)
- Communities of practice
- Expert directories (to enable knowledge seeker to reach to the experts)
- Expert systems (knowledge seeker responds to one or more specific questions to reach knowledge in a repository)

- Best practice transfer
- Knowledge fairs
- Competence management (systematic evaluation and planning of competences of individual organisation members)
- Master-apprentice relationship, Mentor-mentee relationship, job shadowing
- Collaborative software technologies (wikis, shared bookmarking, blogs, social software, etc.)
- Knowledge repositories (databases, bookmarking engines, etc.)
- Measuring and reporting intellectual capital (a way of making explicit knowledge for companies)
- Knowledge brokers (some organisational members take on responsibility for a specific "field" and act as first reference on a specific subject)

Motivations

Multiple motivations lead organisations to undertake KM. Typical considerations include:

- Making available increased knowledge content in the development and provision of products and services
- Achieving shorter development cycles
- Facilitating and managing innovation and organisational learning
- Leveraging expertises across the organisation
- Increasing network connectivity between internal and external individuals
- Managing business environments and allowing employees to obtain relevant insights and ideas appropriate to their work
- Solving intractable or wicked problems
- Managing intellectual capital and assets in the workforce (such as the expertise and know-how possessed by key individuals or stored in repositories)

Knowledge management (KM) technology can be categorised:

- Groupware – Software that facilitates collaboration and sharing of organisational information. Such applications provide tools for threaded discussions, document sharing, organisation-wide uniform email, and other collaboration-related features.
- Workflow systems – Systems that allow the representation of processes associated with the creation, use and maintenance of organisational knowledge, such as the process to create and utilise forms and documents.
- Content management and document management systems – Software systems that automate the process of creating web content and/or documents. Roles such as editors, graphic designers, writers and producers can be explicitly modeled along with the tasks in the process and validation criteria. Commercial vendors started either to support documents or to support web content but as the Internet grew these functions merged and vendors now perform both functions.
- Enterprise portals – Software that aggregates information across the entire organisation or for groups such as project teams.
- eLearning – Software that enables organisations to create customised training and education. This can include lesson plans, monitoring progress and online classes.
- Planning and scheduling software – Software that automates schedule creation and maintenance. The planning aspect can integrate with project management software.
- Telepresence – Software that enables individuals to have virtual "face-to-face" meetings without assembling at one location. Videoconferencing is the most obvious example.

HUMAN RESOURCE INFORMATION SYSTEM

The Human Resource Information System (HRIS) is a software or online solution for the data entry, data tracking, and data information needs of the Human Resources, payroll, management, and accounting functions within a business. It is useful for all processes that you want to track and from which you hope to gather useful and purposeful data.

Normally packaged as a database, hundreds of companies sell some form of HRIS and every HRIS has different capabilities. Pick your HRIS carefully based on the capabilities you need in your company. As HRIS have become increasingly sophisticated, the choice has become enough to practically paralyze an HR department.

Watching a technology company, where computer experts exist, go through three different HRIS systems in ten years before finally settling on their current system, was an education in their complexity. This is why choosing an HRIS is a major undertaking for a business.

Key Considerations as You Look at Your HRIS Options

The selection of an HRIS is a stressful situation as so many options exist. Picking the options that are best for your needs at your company is challenging. Wading through the information provided by each system is challenging, too.

The salespeople are often commissioned salespeople who verbally may tell you that the system will meet your needs. Make sure you check this out with multiple sources including current customers, online discussion groups, LinkedIn, other SHRM members, and Google reviews.

These are the other factors to consider as you select your HRIS.

- Remember that even if your company is only a few people today, it may have twice that many or even 10 times that many employees in the future, so pick a system that can grow with your business.
- Another key factor that you must consider is that many HRIS are able to accomplish only part of what you need automation to accomplish. In these cases, you will want to make certain that the components of any add-ons or additional systems work together flawlessly. Again, don't take the salesperson's word about the systems working together. Do your research.
- Check also to see what kinds of training and ongoing support are available for your staff. You should also ensure that the sales consultant's promises about training and follow-up following the purchase are written right into your contract to purchase the HRIS. And, check with other organisations to make certain that your selected company has a track record of ongoing, helpful support.

Typically, the better Human Resource Information Systems (HRIS) provide overall:

Management of all employee information. Data such as names, titles, addresses, and salaries are a basic start. Salary and position history, reporting structures, performance appraisal histories, and other critical employee information.

Company-related documents. This includes such items as employee handbooks, emergency evacuation procedures, and safety guidelines.

Benefits administration. You will want benefits administration including enrollment, status changes, and personal information updating. In an ideal system, you can allow employees to look up and review their own information, including vacation tracking.

Complete integration with payroll. This integration will also include other company financial software and accounting systems. When these are connected, you can ensure that paychecks are correct. There is never a disconnect between what the official pay rate is and the information that payroll has. If the systems don't integrate, it's easy to update a salary in one system and not in the other.

Applicant tracking and resume management. When your system is seamless, the recruiter can click a hired button and all of the information from the applicant is transferred to the employee side of things. This saves so much time because your data entry and paperwork practically disappear.

If an applicant puts in his own information when applying, you can ensure accuracy. If the offer letter is generated out of the same system as the payroll system, the salary will match perfectly and there is no misunderstanding.

Performance development plans. It's not just enough to have plans if they are recorded in a central system, then they can easily follow the employee from position to position. Senior leadership can run reports to see where people are and what their individual bosses are planning in terms of succession planning for their futures.

Disciplinary Actions. It's important to keep track of who has been suspended, demoted, or had other negative actions taken against them noted—even after the employee leaves your organisation. When a company calls and asks for a former employee reference, it's easy for an admin in the HR department to look up and report back whether or not the person is eligible for rehire.

Training records. This is especially critical in a company where certifications and licenses are required. In other companies, training records may not have that level of importance, but you may still find that having the information is useful as you develop your employees, a key factor that they want from work.

In summary, the HRIS that most effectively serves companies tracks this information:

- attendance and PTO use,
- pay grades and positions held,
- training received,
- personal employee information, and occasionally,
- management and key employee succession plans,
- high potential employee identification, and
- applicant tracking, interviewing, and selection.
- pay raises and history,
- performance development plans,
- disciplinary action received,

INTERNATIONAL HUMAN RESOURCE MANAGEMENT (IHRM)

IHRM can be defined as set of activities aimed at managing organisational human resources at international level to achieve organisational objectives and achieve competitive advantage over competitors at national and international level. IHRM includes typical HRM functions such as recruitment, selection, training and development, performance appraisal and dismissal done at international level and additional activities such as global skills management, expatriate management and so on.

In simple terms, IHRM is concerned about managing human resources at Multinational Companies (MNC) and it involves managing 03 types of employees namely,

1. Home country employees. Employees belonging to home country of the firm where the corporate head quarter is situated.
2. Host country employees. Employees belonging to the nation in which the subsidiary is situated.
3. Third country employees. These are the employees who are not from home country/host country but are employed at subsidiary or corporate head quarters. As an example a American MNC which has a subsidiary at India may employ a French person as the CEO to the subsidiary. The Frenchman employed is a third country employee.

Differences between domestic HRM and International HRM (IHRM) are summarized below:

- Domestic HRM is done at national level and IHRM is done at international level.

- Domestic HRM is concerned with managing employees belonging to one nation and IHRM is concerned with managing employees belonging to many nations (Home country, host country and third country employees)
- Domestic HRM is concerned with managing limited number of HRM activities at national level and IHRM has concerned with managing additional activities such as expatriate management.
- Domestic HRM is less complicated due to less influence from the external environment. IHRM is very complicated as it is affected heavily by external factors such as cultural distance and institutional factors.

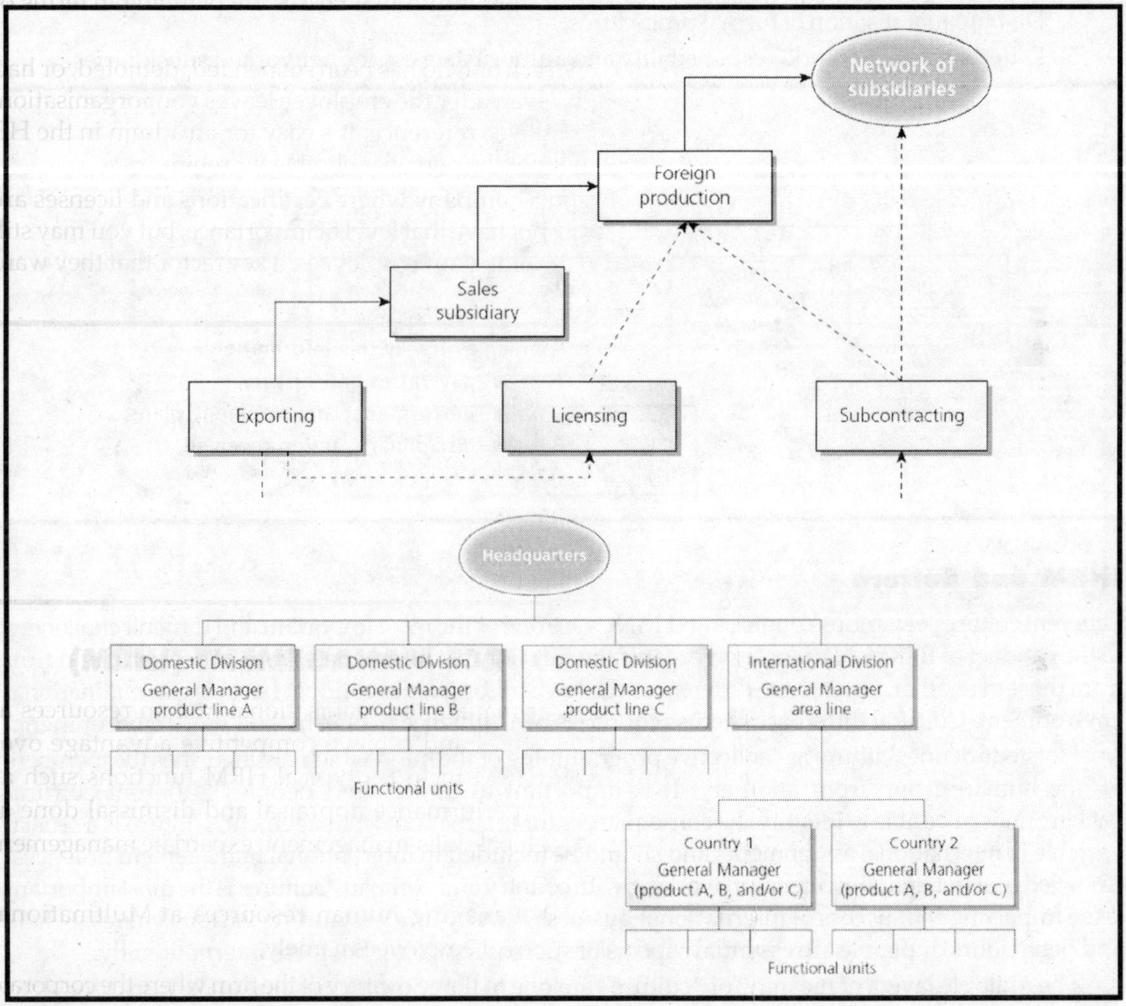

Organisational Context

Organisational structures of IHRMs change due to:

1. Strain imposed due to growth and geographical spread
2. The need for improved coordination and control across business units.
3. The constrains imposed by host-government regulations and ownership and equity.

International matrix is unmanageable because of:

1. Dual reporting, which leads to conflict and confusion.

2. The proliferation of communication channels which creates informational logjams.
3. Overlapping responsibilities, which produces turf battles and a loss of accountability.
4. The barriers of distance, language, time, culture, which often make it very difficult for managers to resolve conflicts and clarify confusion.

International Management involves less hierarchal structure and features five dimensions:

1. Delegation of decision making authority to appropriate units and levels.
2. Geographical dispersa of key functions across units in different countries.
3. Delayering of organisational levels.
4. De-bureaucratisation of formal procedures.
5. Differentiation of work, responsibility and authority across the networked subsidiaries.

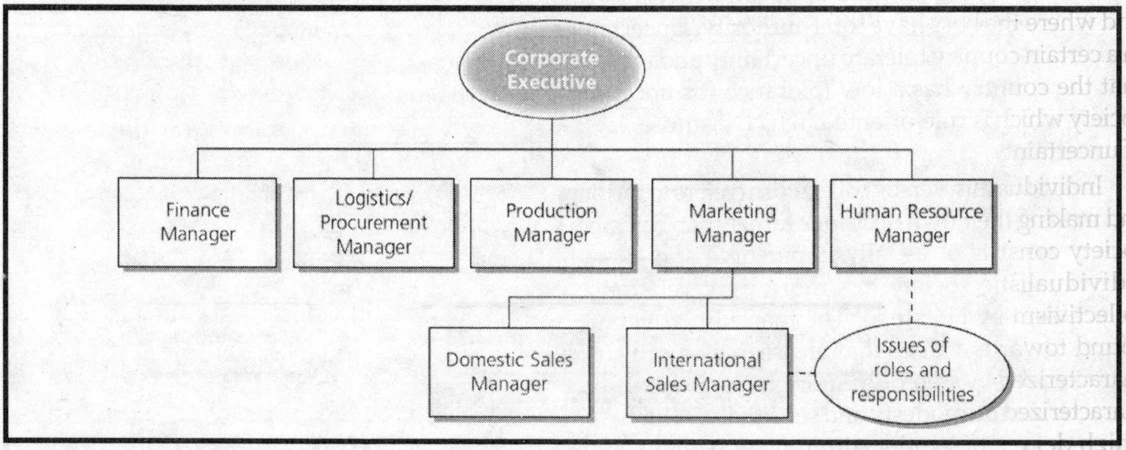

IHRM and Culture

Different cultures of various countries and MNCs are one of the most important and difficult challenges to the conduct of IHRM. National and organisational cultures differentiate from one country and firm from those of another. Often these differences clash when companies conduct business in multinational environment. Cultural differences across countries can influence people in their work environment.

Hofstede defines culture as "collective programming of the mind which distinguishes the members of one human group from another". It is important to understand peoples' different cultural backgrounds to be able to identify the consequences for international management. Culture is a crucial variable in international assignments and should be included in international management practices. Knowledge about and competency in working with country and company cultures is the most important issue impacting the success of international business activity, understanding various values, beliefs and behaviours of people are essential aspects of success for doing business internationally.

The multiple layers of meaning of "culture" are one of the complexities that make it so difficult to manage. There are a large number of readily observable characteristics (such as food, art, clothing, greetings and historical landmarks) that differ obviously from other countries or operations. Sometimes these are referred as manifestations of underlying values and assumptions which are much less obvious.

One way to understand this complexity is explained by the layers of culture model. The model represents culture as a series of layers. Moving from outside to inside, each layer represents less and less explicit values and assumptions while the values and assumptions become more important in determining the attitudes and behaviours. The outermost layer, which is called the surface layer, corresponds to readily visible values and assumptions, like dress, body language and food. The middle layer or the hidden culture layer corresponds to religions, values and philosophies concerning for example what is right and wrong. The invisible layer at the core represents one culture's universal truths, which is most difficult for foreigners to understand. There exist different cultural dimension among different cultures. These cultural dimensions have been identified and one frequently cited work from a well-known researcher within this cultural dimension field is Geert Hofstede.

Hofstede have identified five cultural dimensions for which each country could be classified in. These five dimensions are power distance, uncertainty avoidance, individualism versus collectivism, masculinity versus femininity, and long-term versus short-term orientation. Power distance indicates the level of inequality in institutions and organisations. A country with large power distance is characterized by formal hierarchies and by subordinates who have little influence in their own work and where the boss have total authority. Uncertainty avoidance focuses on the level in which people in a certain country tolerate uncertainty and ambiguity within the society. High uncertainty indicates that the country has a low tolerance for uncertainty and ambiguity. This will inevitably create a society which is rule-oriented, which institutes laws, regulations and controls to diminish the amount of uncertainty.

Individualism versus collectivism refers to the degree where people prefer to take care of themselves, and making their own decisions rather than being bound to groups or families. A highly individualistic society consists of usually impersonal and loose relationships between individuals, while a low individualistic society has more tight relationships between individuals, hence referred to as collectivism by Hofstede. The masculinity versus femininity dimension describes if a culture are bound towards values that are seen as more similar to women's or men's values. Masculinity is characterized by stereotype adjectives such as assertiveness and competitive, while the femininity is characterized by modesty and sensitivity. A high masculinity ranking indicates the country experiences a high degree of gender differences, usually favoring men rather than women. The fifth and last cultural dimension is long-term versus short-term orientation. A long-term oriented society emphasize on building a future oriented perspective in contrast to the short-term oriented society which values the present and past.

IHRM - Sustainability and Strategy

Under the global context, understanding how multinational Corporations (MNCs) can operate more effectively becomes more important than ever. This links a MNC with the need of an internationalized strategy which can direct its subsidiaries' operation not only in the home country, but also in different parts of the world. There are several reasons to develop IHRM strategy:

1. at any level, HRM is important to strategy implementation;
2. major strategic components of multinational enterprises have a major influence on international management issues, functions, and policies and practices;
3. the attainment of the concerns and goals of MNCs can be influenced by many of these characteristics of IHRM;
4. the study of IHRM is challenging and important because there are a wide variety of factors making the relationship between MNCs and IHRM complex. Strategic IHRM is defined as human resource management issues, functions and policies and practices that result from the strategic activities of multinational enterprises and that impact the international concerns and goals of those enterprises.

Two major strategic components of MNCs that influence Strategic IHRM are pointed out: inter-unit linkages and internal operations. Regarding inter-unit linkages, multinational enterprises are concerned with how to effective operate their various world-wide operating units. In particular, the key objectives appear to be how these operating units are to be differentiated and integrated, controlled and coordinated. For strategic IHRM, the issues associated with integrating and coordinating an MNC's units represent a major influence on strategic IHRM issues, policies and practices. With respect to internal operations, they require the same attention as the linkage of the units, since they all influence MNC effectiveness. Each unit has to be operated as effectively as possible relative to the competitive strategy of the MNC and the unit itself.

It has been argued that the success of strategic IHRM in a MNC is largely influenced by the quality of its human resources and how effectively the corporation's employees are managed. There are three approaches which describe how multinational companies manage the human resources and their overseas subsidiaries: ethnocentric, polycentric and geocentric.

1. **Ethnocentric Approach:** This practice usually happens in the early stage of a firm's internationalization involvement. With this approach, strategic decisions are all made by the headquarters and the management practices are transferred to the subsidiaries. Most important positions are filled by parent-country nationals (PCNs).As a result, little autonomy is given to overseas operating units. During this stage, home country expatriates exercise tight control.
2. **Polycentric Approach:** When the strategy becomes polycentric, there is a marked decline in the number of PCNs sending abroad and their role changes into communication and coordination of strategic objectives. Host-country nationals (HCNs) are recruited to manage the operating units in their own country because local managers know more about the local circumstances and are more familiar with local business ethics. More autonomy is given to local managers to develop their own management practices appropriate for the subsidiary.
3. **Geocentric Approach:** This approach relates most closely to the global or transnational strategy. Selection of employees is based on competency rather than nationality. The best of headquarter and local practices are combined by MNCs in order to come up with a global-implemented HR strategy.

Most MNCs take the IHRM strategy as a guideline and implement it locally. It is therefore the HR managers' responsibilities to provide the proper international HR strategy to prepare and manage the employees in their home country or an international assignment.

IHRM Case Study Module

This research project explains how the International Human Resource theories are used in Coca Cola as a multinational organisation. Moreover it clarifies the IHRM theoretical side and how the company uses it in its practices. Also it explains both of the strength and weak points of the practical methods. Coca cola is an example of Multinational enterprises (MNEs) as it operates its business in more than 200 countries.

Introduction

Local Human Resource Management practices are different of international Human Resource Practices, because the core different in the organisational structure. The structure of a Multinational organisation as Coca Cola should be different of another American local organisation. These differences come from the significant role and senior strategies of the company. This should cause some significant change in the HR practices and functions.

Since Coca Cola is a company operates its business around a huge number of countries around the world it began to respond to both of local and international needs. Environment, culture and political differences exist from a region to another.

Globalization is the most important factor of the multinational enterprises phenomenon. Coca Cola one of the American companies became a multinational company to take the benefits of new markets and to minimize the labour costs. Haile (2002) mentioned that Bernadin and Russell (1998) and Robbins (1997) all stated that Coca-Cola and Pepsi receive more than half of their revenues from operations outside the United States. These reasons and more encourage the company to operate its business outside the boundaries. While the company started its operations outside USA it considered the environmental, cultural and political change. Also it considered the differences among the multinational employees. Therefore it started to find the methods and the practices which help to avoid any obstacles since the IHRM has new concepts were developed internationally. As a core point, the international human resource practices should be aligned with the predefined strategic business goals.

Company's Background

Coca Cola was invested in May 1886 by Dr. John S. Pemberton in Atlanta, Georgia. Currently, its operations are in more than 200 countries, and with diverse work force of approximately 55,000 employees.

Global Strategy

The strategic vision of the company is to achieve five strategic goals: Profit, people, value, partners and planet.

One of the above strategic is people, which is the most important element in Coca Cola as people are the workforce which operates the whole work. Moreover the company gives its attention to the HRM to control the human functions and roles and to be aligning with the company's senior strategy. In line with the higher objectives of the company, human resources management seriously seeking to get the best management achieve the objectives of the company. For these reasons, IHRM should define know the structure of the company as a global.

(The Times Newspaper, 2005, P. 2)

The company's structure

The home country of Coca Cola is USA it controls both of centralization and localization's functions. Senior decisions at The Coca Cola Company are made by an Executive Committee of 12 company Officers. This committee helped to shape the strategic priorities. The chair of the executive committee acts as a head for the company and chairs the board meetings. He is also the Chief Executive Officer (CEO) and as such he is the senior decision maker. Other executives are responsible either for the major regions (e.g. Africa) or have an important business specialization for example the Chief Financial Officer.

(The Times Newspaper, 2005, P. 3)

There are seven main regions where Coca Cola operates in:

North America, Africa, Asia, Europe, Eurasia, Middle East, Latin America. Each region has divided into countries and each country has its own structure the following figure explains the structure of Coca Cola in Great Britain.

(The Times Newspaper, 2005, P. 3)

IHRM concepts in Coca Cola's practices and reasons to transfer employees to the host countries

Staff selection, international assignments, international training and development, international compensation, and IHRM in the host Country context are some key concepts of the international practices which Coca Cola's HRM is responsible to deal with. And it is important to know the reason of transferring people from a region to another among Coca Cola parent company, host countries and subsidiaries.

The reason of sending staff for international assignment in Coca Cola is to achieve three major goals within short and long terms: to fill positions, develop the management and to fulfil Coca Cola's development. (Hartono 2009)

The following table shows the reasons of transferring staff from the parent country of Coca Cola to the host countries (e.g. china).

Why does Coca Cola transfer staff from the parent country (USA) to the host countries

Transfer of technical or Managerial knowledge, training of subsidiary managers, or lack of qualified local personal

(Position Filling)

- Level of education in host country is low
- Subsidiary is young
- Subsidiary is Greenfield establishment
- Gain international experience develop global awareness (Management Development)
- MNC is more internationalized
- MNC is large
- Control and coordination of subsidiary operations (Organisational Development)
- Uncertainly avoidance in home country is high
- Level of cultural distance between home country and host country is high
- Level of political risk in host country is high
- Subsidiary is large
- Subsidiary is majority-owned
- Subsidiary is higher in corporate reporting chain Subsidiary is young
- Subsidiary is under-performing
- Improvement of communication channels between head quarter and subsidiary (Organisational Development)
- Level of cultural distance between home and host country is high
- Level of political risk in host country is high
- Subsidiary is young
- Selecting staff for global assignments in Coca Cola

Hartono (2009) argued that studies explained that selecting employees for global tasks to achieve international specific jobs is difficult. Also wrong selection may lead to significant problems. Therefore Coca Cola developed its own system for careful selecting employees, in this system the company determines carefully the appropriate persons for each assignment. (Slavenski 2003)

In Coca Cola they always give enough time to assess employees they wish to go for an international assignment. First step is to receive applications from the employees who find that he is qualified for the task. Then conduct five hours assessment for all the applicants to identify the following nine skills:

1. Organising and planning
2. Perception and analysis
3. Decision making
4. Oral communication
5. Decisiveness
6. Adaptability
7. Interpersonal skills
8. Written communication
9. Perseverance

Second step is to determine the best applicants who have succeed in the first assessment and ask them to return next day for the organisational orientation, also there is three days of training for the line managers who are responsible for this selection. In Coca Cola usually the third step is an interview to select one of three applicants to do the international assignment.

Comparing with the old approach of selecting staff to do a global task there are a significant change in the way and technique used currently in Coca Cola. According to Slavenski (2003) he stated that These results indicate that the new method of interviewing is more effective than traditional interviewing. Hence, the assessment/hiring ratio was lowered from 3: 1 to 2:1. T hat is, for every two people assessed in the centre, one could be selected. The cost savings amounted to about $48,000 per centre or $4,000 per candidate.

IHRM MODELS

Matching Model

- Models of IHRM Matching Model.
- Highlights the resource aspect of HRM.
- Emphasize on efficient utilization of human resources to meet organisational objectives.
- Right fit between organisational strategies, organisational structure and HRM systems will result in success.

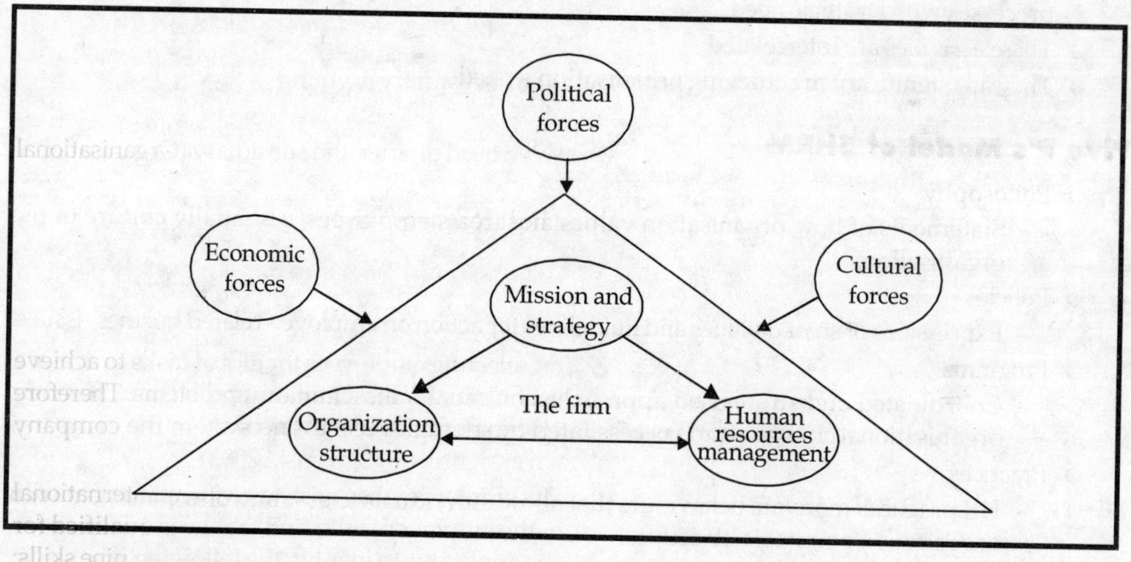

Harvard Model

- Focuses on Human, Soft aspect of HRM.
- It emphasizes in employee-employer relationship.
- Also highlights the interests of different stakeholders of organisation-shareholders, management, employee groups, government, community, unions.
- How these interests can be related to objectives of management?
- The model illustrates the influence of situational factors on stake-holder interests, and their impact on human resource policy choices which are destined to deliver a raft of predetermined human resource outcomes such as commitment, competence, congruence and cost-effectiveness.
- These outcomes consequently produce long-term and sustainable benefits for the individual, the organisation and society.

- This is a highly prescriptive model of HRM which emphasizes a number of presumed long-term benefits of acting on stakeholder interests and situational factors, assuming that there is a set of predetermined and 'superior' human resource policy choices
- The Matching and Harvard models were often compared and contrasted in terms of their approaches to the use of human resources.
- While the Matching model focuses on the strategic resource aspect of human resources, the Harvard model emphasizes the human element in the human resource formulations.

Contextual Model

- Organisations may follow a number of different means to achieve same results.
- This is due to existence of linkage between external environment context-Socioeconomic, technological, political-legal and competitive, and internal organisational context-culture, structure, leadership, task, technology, and business output.
- The linkage will determine content of organisation's HRM
- 5-P Model
- Links five human resource activities-philosophies, policies, programmes, practices, and processes with strategic needs.
- These activities are Interrelated
- They are significant in achieving organisation's needs.

Five P's Model of SHRM

- Philosophy
  - Statements of how organisation values and treats employees; essentially culture of the organisation.
- Policies
  - Expressions of shared values and guidelines for action on employee-related business issues.
- Programs
  - Coordinated and strategised approaches to initiate, disseminate, and sustain strategic organisational change efforts necessitated by strategic business needs.
- Practices
  - HR practices motivate behaviours that allow individuals to assume roles consistent with organisation's strategic objectives.
  - Three categories of roles:
    a. Leadership
    b. Managerial
    c. Operational
- Processes
  - Continuum of participation by all employees in specific activities to facilitate formulation and implementation of other activities.

European Model

- It is based on the argument that European organisations are constrained at both international (European Union) and national level by national culture and legislation.

- They are also constrained at the organisational level by patterns of ownership and at the HRM level by trade union involvement and consultative arrangements.
- All the constraints need to be considered for forming a HR system.

Model of SHRM in Multinational Companies

- Successful SHRM efforts begin with identification of strategic needs.
- Employee participation is critical to linking strategy and HR practices.
- Strategic HR depends on systematic and analytical mindset.
- Corporate HR departments can have impact on organisation's efforts to launch strategic initiatives.

Evolution of MNE's

Three Stages of Evolution

1. **Export stage**
   initial inquiries => firms rely on export agents
   expansion of export sales
   further expansion þ foreign sales branch or assembly operations (to save transport cost)
2. **Foreign Production Stage.** There is a limit to foreign sales (tariffs, NTBs)
   DFI versus Licensing. Once the firm chooses foreign production as a method of delivering goods to foreign markets, it must decide whether to establish a foreign production subsidiary or license the technology to a foreign firm.
   Licensing. Licensing is usually first experience (because it is easy)
   e.g.: Kentucky Fried Chicken in the U.K.
   it does not require any capital expenditure
   it is not risky
   payment = a fixed % of sales
   Problem: the mother firm cannot exercise any managerial control over the licensee (it is independent)
   The licensee may transfer industrial secrets to another independent firm, thereby creating a rival.
   Direct Investment. It requires the decision of top management because it is a critical step.
   It is risky (lack of information) (US -> Canada)plants are established in several countries licensing is switched from independent producers to its subsidiaries, export continues
3. **Multinational Stage.** The company becomes a multinational enterprise when it begins to plan, organise and coordinate production, marketing, R&D, financing, and staffing. For each of these operations, the firm must find the best location.
   Rule of Thumb. A company whose foreign sales are 25% or more of total sales. This ratio is high for small countries, but low for large countries, e.g. Nestle (98%: Dutch), Phillips (94%: Swiss).
   Motives for Direct Foreign Investment. New MNCs do not pop up randomly in foreign nations. It is the result of conscious planning by corporate managers. Investment flows from regions of low anticipated profits to those of high returns. Growth motive A company may have reached a plateau satisfying domestic demand, which is not growing. Looking for new markets.
   Protection in the importing countries. Foreign direct investment is one way to expand bypassing protective instruments in the importing country.

European Community: imposed common external tariff against outsiders. US companies circumvented these barriers by setting up subsidiaries.

Japanese corporations located auto assembly plants in the US, to bypass VERs.

Market competition. The most certain method of preventing actual or potential competition is to acquire foreign businesses.

GM purchased Monarch (GM Canada) and Opel (GM Germany). It did not buy Toyota, Datsun (Nissan) and Volkswagen. They later became competitors.

Cost reduction. United Fruit has established banana-producing facilities in Honduras.

Cheap foreign labor. Labor costs tend to differ among nations. MNCs can hold down costs by locating part of all their productive facilities abroad. (Maquildoras)

Supplying Products to Foreign Buyers

Export versus Direct Foreign Investment

MES is the minimum rate of output at which Average Cost (AC) is minimized. If minimum efficient scale (MES) is not achieved, then export.

MULTIPLE CHOICE QUESTIONS

1. What is the goal of Human Resource Development (HRD)?
   (1) To improve job satisfaction for employees
   (2) To increase sales for the organisation
   (3) To develop the skills and knowledge of employees
   (4) To achieve compliance with labor laws and regulations
2. What is the role of HRD in an organisation?
   (1) To monitor employee performance
   (2) To manage employee benefits
   (3) To facilitate employee development and training
   (4) To ensure payroll is accurate and on time
3. Which of the following is not a component of the HRD process?
   (1) needs assessment
   (2) learning and development
   (3) performance management
   (4) employee discipline
4. Which of the following is an assumption of HRD?
   (1) Employees are not interested in personal development
   (2) Learning is not a continuous process
   (3) Employees have the potential for growth and development
   (4) Employment is a temporary arrangement
5. Which of the following is a value of HRD?
   (1) Autonomy and independence for employees
   (2) Compliance with organisational policy
   (3) Respect and recognition of employee needs
   (4) Centralized decision-making
6. Which of the following is a goal of performance management in HRD?
   (1) To identify strengths and weaknesses of employees
   (2) To punish employees for poor performance
   (3) To assign employees to specific job roles
   (4) To reduce employee turnover
7. What is the role of feedback in the HRD process?
   (1) To provide employees with negative criticism
   (2) To measure employee performance
   (3) To provide employees with constructive feedback to enhance their development
   (4) To compare employee performance to benchmarks
8. What is the role of mentoring in the HRD process?
   (1) To discipline employees
   (2) To provide employees with emotional support
   (3) To provide employees with guidance and professional development
   (4) To assess employee performance
9. Which of the following is a form of informal learning in the HRD process?
   (1) Self-directed learning
   (2) Classroom-based learning
   (3) On-the-job training
   (4) E-learning
10. Which of the following is a benefit of e-learning in the HRD process?
    (1) Decreased flexibility for employees
    (2) Increased engagement for employees
    (3) Limited access to learning resources
    (4) Decreased accessibility for employees with disabilities

11. What is the role of diversity and inclusion in HRD?
(1) To limit opportunities for underrepresented groups
(2) To enhance organisational culture through differing perspectives
(3) To provide a homogenous workforce
(4) To limit the potential for bias in the workplace

12. What is the purpose of a competency model in HRD?
(1) To assess employee performance
(2) To predict employee turnover
(3) To align employee skills with organisational goals
(4) To determine employee salary

13. What is the goal of a career planning and development program in HRD?
(1) To limit employee choices
(2) To prepare employees for their next role
(3) To assess employee knowledge and skills
(4) To enhance employee retention and motivation

14. Which of the following is a component of organisational learning in HRD?
(1) Capacity building
(2) Employee discipline
(3) Compliance with labor laws
(4) Salary and compensation management

15. What is the role of the HRD function in organisational change?
(1) To resist change and maintain the status quo
(2) To support change and facilitate employee development
(3) To ignore change and focus on traditional HR practices
(4) To place the responsibility of change management on employees

16. Which of the following is a contemporary challenge facing HRD?
(1) Decreasing reliance on technology
(2) Globalization
(3) Limited access to learning resources
(4) Limited access to e-learning resources

17. Which of the following is a key factor driving changes in HRD?
(1) Technological advancements
(2) Demographic shifts
(3) Globalization
(4) All of the above

18. What is the role of HRD in talent management?
(1) To limit opportunities for high-performing employees
(2) To manage employee benefits
(3) To identify and develop talent to achieve strategic business goals
(4) To ignore employee growth and development

19. Which of the following is an emerging trend in HRD?
(1) Increased focus on traditional classroom-based learning
(2) Decreased focus on diversity and inclusion
(3) Increased focus on informal learning
(4) Decreased focus on performance management

20. What is the purpose of a learning management system in HRD?
(1) To manage employee discipline
(2) To facilitate the delivery and tracking of learning and development activities
(3) To reduce employee turnover
(4) To automate payroll and benefits administration

21. Which of the following is a benefit of HRD for employees?
(1) Stagnation in job roles
(2) Limited access to learning opportunities
(3) Personal and professional growth and development
(4) Limited access to career planning resources

22. What is the role of needs assessment in the HRD process?
(1) To manage employee performance
(2) To assess employee skills and knowledge
(3) To identify learning and development needs of employees
(4) To determine employee salary

23. What is the role of coaching in the HRD process?
(1) To discipline employees
(2) To reward employees for good performance
(3) To provide employees with feedback and guidance
(4) To assign employees to specific job roles

24. Which of the following is a goal of diversity and inclusion in HRD?
(1) To limit opportunities for underrepresented groups
(2) To limit access to learning opportunities
(3) To enhance organisational culture through differing perspectives
(4) To discriminate against certain employees

25. What is the role of HRD in employee engagement?
(1) To provide employees with negative feedback
(2) To reduce employee motivation
(3) To create a positive work environment that promotes employee motivation and job satisfaction
(4) To limit employee access to learning opportunities

26. What is the purpose of a performance improvement plan in HRD?
(1) To discipline employees
(2) To reduce employee motivation
(3) To provide employees with an opportunity to improve their performance
(4) To eliminate non-essential job duties

27. What is the role of a job analysis in the HRD process?
(1) To assess employee performance
(2) To identify specific job duties and responsibilities
(3) To determine employee salary
(4) All of the above

28. What is the role of on-the-job training in the HRD process?
(1) To discipline employees
(2) To provide employees with feedback and guidance
(3) To provide hands-on learning opportunities
(4) To limit employee access to learning opportunities

29. What is the role of needs analysis in HRD?
(1) To develop a strategic HR plan
(2) To assess employee skills and knowledge
(3) To determine the learning and development needs of employees
(4) To assign employees to specific job roles

30. Which of the following is a benefit of informal learning in the HRD process?
(1) Increased impact on employee behaviour and performance
(2) Limited access to learning resources
(3) Decreased flexibility for employees
(4) Decreased accessibility for employees with disabilities

31. What is the goal of a training and development program in HRD?
(1) To limit employee access to learning opportunities
(2) To assess employee performance
(3) To enhance employee knowledge and skills
(4) To limit employee promotions

32. Which of the following is a benefit of a competency-based approach to HRD?
(1) Increased focus on compliance with labor laws
(2) Increased assessment of job duties and responsibilities
(3) Increased alignment of employee skills with organisational goals
(4) Decreased employee empowerment

33. What is the role of leadership development in HRD?

(1) To limit opportunities for leadership advancement
(2) To assess employee performance
(3) To provide employees with the skills and knowledge necessary for leadership roles
(4) To eliminate non-essential job duties

34. What is the role of a learning organisation in HRD?

(1) To resist change and maintain the status quo
(2) To support change and facilitate employee development
(3) To create a culture of continuous learning and improvement
(4) To ignore employee growth and development

35. What is the purpose of a training needs analysis in HRD?

(1) To assess employee performance
(2) To identify learning and development needs of employees
(3) To determine employee salary
(4) To assign employees to specific job roles

36. What is the role of a development plan in the HRD process?

(1) To assess employee performance
(2) To provide employees feedback and guidance
(3) To provide employees with a structured approach to achieving their career goals
(4) To limit employee access to learning opportunities

37. Which of the following is a benefit of a mentorship program in HRD?

(1) Decreased engagement for employees
(2) Increased assessment of job duties and responsibilities
(3) Increased guidance and support for employee development
(4) Decreased employee access to learning opportunities

38. What is the role of employee engagement in HRD?

(1) To reduce employee motivation
(2) To create a positive work environment that promotes employee motivation and job satisfaction
(3) To provide employees with negative feedback
(4) To limit employee access to learning opportunities

39. What is the role of professional development in HRD?

(1) To eliminate non-essential job duties
(2) To provide employees with opportunities to develop their skills and knowledge
(3) To assess employee performance
(4) All of the above

40. Which of the following is a benefit of a job rotation program in HRD?

(1) Increased assessment of job duties and responsibilities
(2) Increased opportunities for employee motivation and job satisfaction
(3) Decreased access to learning opportunities
(4) Decreased employee autonomy

41. What is the purpose of a staying plan in HRD?

(1) To assess employee performance
(2) To limit employee career choices
(3) To enhance employee retention and prevent turnover
(4) To reduce employee access to learning opportunities

42. What is the role of a succession plan in HRD?

(1) To limit opportunities for employee advancement
(2) To develop a plan for leadership transition and development
(3) To discipline employees
(4) To eliminate non-essential job duties

43. What is the purpose of a learning contract in HRD?

(1) To limit employee access to learning opportunities
(2) To provide employees feedback and guidance
(3) To outline employee roles and expectations during the learning process
(4) To assess employee performance

44. What is the role of job enrichment in HRD?
(1) To eliminate non-essential job duties
(2) To provide employees with more challenging and meaningful work
(3) To limit employee promotions
(4) To reduce employee motivation

45. What is the purpose of a talent review in HRD?
(1) To assess employee performance
(2) To identify high-potential employees for development and advancement
(3) To limit employee access to learning opportunities
(4) To assign employees to specific job roles

46. **Assertion:** The role of HRD is to manage employee benefits and payroll.
Reason: The role of HRD is to provide employees with opportunities for growth and development.
(1) Both assertion and reason are true and the reason is the correct explanation of the assertion.
(2) Both assertion and reason are true but the reason is not the correct explanation of the assertion.
(3) Assertion is true but reason is false.
(4) Assertion is false but reason is true.

47. **Assertion:** The goal of HRD is to assess employee performance.
Reason: The goal of HRD is to develop the skills and knowledge of employees.
(1) Assertion is false but reason is true.
(2) Assertion is true but reason is false.
(3) Both assertion and reason are true but the reason is not the correct explanation of the assertion.
(4) Both assertion and reason are true and the reason is the correct explanation of the assertion.

48. **Assertion:** Performance management in HRD is focused solely on assigning employees to specific job roles.
Reason: Performance management in HRD is focused on identifying employee strengths and weaknesses.
(1) Assertion is false but reason is true.
(2) Assertion is true but reason is false.
(3) Both assertion and reason are true but the reason is not the correct explanation of the assertion.
(4) Both assertion and reason are true and the reason is the correct explanation of the assertion.

49. **Assertion:** Coaching in the HRD process is focused solely on discipline.
Reason: Coaching in the HRD process is focused on providing employees with feedback and guidance.
(1) Assertion is false but reason is true.
(2) Assertion is true but reason is false.
(3) Both assertion and reason are true but the reason is not the correct explanation of the assertion.
(4) Both assertion and reason are true and the reason is the correct explanation of the assertion.

50. **Assertion:** Informal learning in the HRD process is focused on classroom-based training.
Reason: Informal learning in the HRD process is focused on self-directed learning.
(1) Assertion is false but reason is true.
(2) Assertion is true but reason is false.
(3) Both assertion and reason are true but the reason is not the correct explanation of the assertion.
(4) Both assertion and reason are true and the reason is the correct explanation of the assertion.

51. **Assertion:** Diversity and inclusion in HRD is focused on limiting opportunities for under-represented groups.
Reason: Diversity and inclusion in HRD is focused on enhancing organisational culture through differing perspectives.
(1) Assertion is false but reason is true.

(2) Assertion is true but reason is false.
(3) Both assertion and reason are true but the reason is not the correct explanation of the assertion.
(4) Both assertion and reason are true and the reason is the correct explanation of the assertion.

52. Assertion: A competency model in HRD is focused on assessing employee performance.
Reason: A competency model in HRD is focused on aligning employee skills with organisational goals.
(1) Assertion is false but reason is true.
(2) Assertion is true but reason is false.
(3) Both assertion and reason are true but the reason is not the correct explanation of the assertion.
(4) Both assertionand reason are true and the reason is the correct explanation of the assertion.

53. Assertion: Career planning and development programs in HRD are designed to limit employee choices.
Reason: Career planning and development programs in HRD are designed to prepare employees for their next role.
(1) Assertion is false but reason is true.
(2) Assertion is true but reason is false.
(3) Both assertion and reason are true but the reason is not the correct explanation of the assertion.
(4) Both assertion and reason are true and the reason is the correct explanation of the assertion.

54. Assertion: Organisational learning in HRD includes compliance with labour laws.
Reason: Organisational learning in HRD is focused on capacity building.
(1) Assertion is true but reason is false.
(2) Assertion is false but reason is true.
(3) Both assertion and reason are true but the reason is not the correct explanation of the assertion.
(4) Both assertion and reason are true and the reason is the correct explanation of the assertion.

55. Assertion: The HRD function plays no role in organisational change.
Reason: The HRD function plays a role in facilitating employee development during organisational change.
(1) Assertion is true but reason is false.
(2) Assertion is false but reason is true.
(3) Both assertion and reason are true but the reason is not the correct explanation of the assertion.
(4) Both assertion and reason are true and the reason is the correct explanation of the assertion.

56. What is the relationship between HRD culture and climate?
(1) They are the same thing
(2) Culture is a subset of climate
(3) Climate is a subset of culture
(4) They are unrelated

57. Which of the following factors can contribute to a positive HRD climate?
(1) Strong organisational hierarchy
(2) Strict adherence to rules and regulations
(3) Support for continuous learning and development
(4) Limited opportunities for employee empowerment

58. Which of the following is a characteristic of a positive HRD climate?
(1) Encourages conformity to norms and values
(2) Limits opportunities for personal growth and development
(3) Promotes employee engagement and job satisfaction
(4) Places emphasis on individual goals and self-interest

59. Which of the following best defines HRD culture?
(1) Set of shared norms, values, and beliefs related to learning and development within an organisation
(2) A formal organisational policy related to promotions

(3) The standard operating procedures for HRD interventions

(4) The collective knowledge and skills of employees within an organisation

60. Which of the following is not a factor that influences HRD culture and climate?

(1) Organisational leadership style

(2) Corporate social responsibility

(3) Employee ethnicity

(4) Organisational structure

61. Which of the following is an implication of a positive HRD culture?

(1) Decreased employee engagement

(2) Increased employee turnover

(3) Improved motivation and organisational performance

(4) Decreased organisational agility and innovation

62. Which of the following is a barrier to developing a positive HRD culture?

(1) Employee resistance to change

(2) Lack of technological resources

(3) Limited training and development opportunities

(4) Dominance of a traditional management style

63. Which of the following best defines HRD climate?

(1) The attitude and perception of employees towards learning and development within an organisation

(2) An organisation's formal policy regarding diversity and inclusion

(3) An individual employee's learning and development goals

(4) The collective knowledge and skills of employees within an organisation

64. Which of the following are benefits of a positive HRD culture and climate?

(1) Increased employee turnover

(2) Decreased employee engagement

(3) Enhanced organisational agility and innovation

(4) Limited opportunities for employee growth and development

65. Which of the following is a goal of HRD culture?

(1) To limit opportunities for organisational growth

(2) To promote and support employee learning and development

(3) To eliminate diversity and inclusion initiatives

(4) To decrease employee engagement and motivation

66. Which of the following is a benefit of a positive HRD climate?

(1) Increased emphasis on individual goals and self-interest

(2) Decreased organisational performance

(3) Enhanced employee motivation and engagement

(4) Limited opportunities for employee empowerment

67. Which of the following is a factor that can impact HRD climate?

(1) Employee ethnicity

(2) Organisational history

(3) National taxation policy

(4) Organisational leadership style

68. How does a positive HRD culture and climate benefit an organisation?

(1) By limiting opportunities for employee growth and development

(2) By increasing employee turnover

(3) By improving job satisfaction and motivation

(4) By limiting organisational agility and innovation

69. What is the role of HRD in promoting a positive organisational culture and climate?

(1) To limit employee access to learning and development opportunities

(2) To provide a structured framework to meet organisational goals

(3) To promote a culture that emphasizes learning and development

(4) To enforce organisational policies and procedures

70. What is the role of leadership in establishing a positive HRD culture and climate?
(1) To limit opportunities for employee empowerment
(2) To provide a framework for HRD interventions
(3) To create and promote an organisational culture that values learning and development
(4) To enforce compliance with organisational policies and procedures

71. Which of the following is a characteristic of a positive HRD culture?
(1) Emphasis on traditional learning methods
(2) Limited opportunities for employee empowerment
(3) Support for continuous learning and development
(4) Adherence to formal organisational procedures

72. What is the relationship between HRD culture and employee job satisfaction?
(1) There is no relationship
(2) They are negatively related
(3) They are positively related
(4) HRD culture has no impact on employee job satisfaction

73. What is the role of culture in promoting employee motivation?
(1) Culture has no impact on employee motivation
(2) Culture provides a framework for motivation
(3) A positive culture can enhance employee motivation
(4) Culture is unrelated to employee motivation

74. What is the role of HRD climate in promoting employee performance?
(1) HRD climate has no impact on employee performance
(2) A positive HRD climate can enhance employee performance
(3) HRD climate can only impact employee performance negatively
(4) A negative HRD climate is necessary for high employee performance

75. How does HRD culture contribute to organisational development?
(1) By limiting opportunities for employee growth and development
(2) By promoting a culture that values learning and development
(3) By enforcing compliance with organisational policies and procedures
(4) By limiting organisational agility and innovation

76. **Assertion:** HRD interventions are designed to improve organisational performance through the development and enhancement of employee knowledge and skills.
Reason: HRD interventions are a one-time training event that does not require ongoing evaluation and updating.
(1) Both assertion and reason are false.
(2) Both assertion and reason are true but the reason is not the correct explanation of the assertion.
(3) Assertion is true but reason is false.
(4) Both assertion and reason are true and the reason is the correct explanation of the assertion .

77. **Assertion:** The goal of HRD interventions is to identify and solve organisational problems through the development and enhancement of employee knowledge and skills.
Reason: HRD interventions can take many forms, including training programs, coaching, and mentoring.
(1) Both assertion and reason are true and the reason is the correct explanation of the assertion .
(2) Both assertion and reason are true but the reason is not the correct explanation of the assertion.
(3) Assertion is true but reason is false.
(4) Both assertion and reason are false.

78. **Assertion:** Assessment is a critical component of HRD interventions.

Reason: HRD interventions require assessment of employee knowledge and skills before and after any intervention.

(1) Both assertion and reason are true and the reason is the correct explanation of the assertion .

(2) Both assertion and reason are true but the reason is not the correct explanation of the assertion.

(3) Assertion is true but reason is false.

(4) Both assertion and reason are false.

79. **Assertion:** HRD interventions can only be initiated by the HR department within an organisation.

Reason: HRD interventions can be initiated by any organisational unit with the goal of improving employee knowledge and skills.

(1) Both assertion and reason are false.

(2) Both assertion and reason are true but the reason is not the correct explanation of the assertion.

(3) Assertion is true but reason is false.

(4) Both assertion and reason are true and the reason is the correct explanation of the assertion .

80. **Assertion:** HRD interventions should be designed based on the personal experiences of employees.

Reason: HRD interventions should be designed based on the specific needs of an organisation and the objectives of an intervention.

(1) Both assertion and reason are false.

(2) Both assertion and reason are true but the reason is not the correct explanation of the assertion.

(3) Assertion is false but reason is true.

(4) Assertion is true but reason is false .

81. **Assertion:** HRD interventions can take many forms, including coaching, mentoring, and e-learning programs.

Reason: HRD interventions are limited to in-person classroom training sessions.

(1) Both assertion and reason are false.

(2) Both assertion and reason are true but the reason is not the correct explanation of the assertion.

(3) Assertion is true but reason is false.

(4) Both assertion and reason are true and the reason is the correct explanation of the assertion .

82. **Assertion:** The success of HRD interventions can be measured through performance evaluations and assessments.

Reason: The success of HRD interventions can only be measured through self-reporting techniques.

(1) Both assertion and reason are false.

(2) Both assertion and reason are true but the reason is not the correct explanation of the assertion.

(3) Assertion is true but reason is false.

(4) Both assertion and reason are true and the reason is the correct explanation of the assertion .

83. **Assertion:** HRD interventions are designed to improve organisational performance through the development of employee knowledge and skills.

Reason: HRD interventions have no impact on organisational performance.

(1) Both assertion and reason are false.

(2) Both assertion and reason are true but the reason is not the correct explanation of the assertion.

(3) Assertion is false but reason is true.

(4) Assertion is true but reason is false .

84. **Assertion:** HRD interventions are necessary for organisational development and success.

Reason: HRD interventions can only be initiated by the HR department within an organisation.

(1) Both assertion and reason are false.

(2) Both assertion and reason are true but the reason is not the correct explanation of the assertion.

(3) Assertion is true but reason is false.

(4) Both assertion and reason are true and the reason is the correct explanation of the assertion .

85. **Assertion:** HRD interventions can be initiated by any organisational unit with the goal of improving employee knowledge and skills.

Reason: HRD interventions should be based on the personal experiences of employees.

(1) Both assertion and reason are false.

(2) Both assertion and reason are true but the reason is not the correct explanation of the assertion.

(3) Assertion is false but reason is true.

(4) Assertion is true but reason is false .

86. **Assertion:** E-learning programs are a commonly used HRD intervention.

Reason: E-learning programs are only effective for developing technical skills.

(1) Both assertion and reason are false.

(2) Both assertion and reason are true but the reason is not the correct explanation of the assertion.

(3) Assertion is true but reason is false.

(4) Both assertion and reason are true and the reason is the correct explanation of the assertion .

87. **Assertion:** HRD interventions are designed to provide a one-time training event with no follow-up evaluation or updating required.

Reason: HRD interventions require ongoing evaluation and updating to ensure continued effectiveness.

(1) Both assertion and reason are false.

(2) Both assertion and reason are true but the reason is not the correct explanation of the assertion.

(3) Assertion is true but reason is false.

(4) Both assertion and reason are true and the reason is the correct explanation of the assertion .

88. **Assertion:** HRD interventions are necessary for organisational growth and development.

Reason: HRD interventions are only effective for enhancing individual performance.

(1) Both assertion and reason are false.

(2) Both assertion and reason are true but the reason is not the correct explanation of the assertion.

(3) Assertion is true but reason is false.

(4) Both assertion and reason are true and the reason is the correct explanation of the assertion .

89. **Assertion:** Coaching and mentoring are commonly used HRD interventions for improving employee performance.

Reason: Coaching and mentoring are only effective for developing technical skills.

(1) Both assertion and reason are false.

(2) Both assertion and reason are true but the reason is not the correct explanation of the assertion.

(3) Assertion is true but reason is false.

(4) Both assertion and reason are true and the reason is the correct explanation of the assertion .

90. **Assertion:** HRD interventions are necessary for enhancing organisational performance and addressing the changing needs of an organisation.

Reason: HRD interventions can be used to address both individual and systemic issues within an organisation.

(1) Both assertion and reason are true and the reason is the correct explanation of the assertion .

(2) Both assertion and reason are true but the reason is not the correct explanation of the assertion.

(3) Assertion is true but reason is false.

(4) Both assertion and reason are false.

91. What is HR accounting?

(1) A process for gauging the monetary value of human resources

(2) An accounting process to estimate employee expenses

(3) An accounting process for recording employee salaries

(4) A process for managing employee pensions and retirement benefits

92. What are the types of HR accounting?
(1) Historical cost and current cost
(2) Annual cost and bi-annual cost
(3) Future cost and retrospective cost
(4) Historical cost, current cost and future cost

93. What is the objective of HR accounting?
(1) To evaluate the monetary value of employees
(2) To evaluate the performance of individual employees
(3) To evaluate the performance of the HR department
(4) To evaluate the monetary value of employee benefits

94. Which of the following is an advantage of HR accounting?
(1) It provides a complete accounting of employee expenses
(2) It helps in providing long term employee benefits
(3) It helps in identifying which employee to be replaced
(4) It enables the organisation to make more informed decisions regarding its human resources

95. What is HR audit?
(1) A process for investigating employee complaints
(2) A review and evaluation of HR policies and practices
(3) A process for measuring employee motivation
(4) A process for measuring employee performance

96. Which of the following is the primary goal of HR audit?
(1) To evaluate the performance of individual employees
(2) To evaluate the performance of the HR department
(3) To ensure HR policies and practices are legally compliant and effective
(4) To determine employee salaries

97. Which of the following is an advantage of HR audit?
(1) It provides a complete accounting of employee expenses
(2) It helps in providing long term employee benefits
(3) It identifies areas of potential risk and non-compliance
(4) It identifies which employee to be replaced

98. Which of the following is a component of HR audit?
(1) Financial audit
(2) Performance audit
(3) Legal compliance audit
(4) All of the above

99. What is the purpose of a legal compliance audit in HR audit?
(1) To evaluate the performance of individual employees
(2) To evaluate the performance of the HR department
(3) To ensure HR policies and practices are in compliance with labor laws and regulations
(4) To determine employee salaries

100. Which of the following is an outcome of HR audit?
(1) Identification of potential areas of risk and non-compliance
(2) Increased employee turnover
(3) Decreased employee engagement
(4) Improved employee performance without any cost incurred

101. What is the role of HR accounting in organisational decision making?
(1) To enable more informed decisions regarding human resources
(2) To limit employee access to benefits
(3) To limit employee career opportunities
(4) To limit the use of HR metrics for managing human resources

102. What is the role of HR audit in organisational decision making?

(1) To limit employee career opportunities
(2) To limit the use of HR metrics for managing human resources
(3) To enable more informed decisions regarding human resources
(4) To decrease employee engagement

103. Which of the following is a benefit of HR audit?
(1) It enables more informed decision-making regarding human resources
(2) It facilitates strategic downsizing of employee benefits
(3) It limits the use of HR metrics for managing human resources
(4) It limits employee career opportunities

104. What is the role of HR accounting in ensuring employee retention?
(1) To eliminate employee benefits
(2) To limit employee career opportunities
(3) To evaluate the monetary value of retention strategies
(4) To evaluate the monetary value of employee benefits and retention strategies

105. What is the role of HR audit in ensuring compliance with labor laws and regulations?
(1) To limit employee career opportunities
(2) To limit the use of HR metrics for managing human resources
(3) To facilitate compliance with labor laws and regulations
(4) To limit employee access to benefits

106. **Assertion:** HR accounting is a process for assessing the monetary value of an organisation's human resources.
Reason: HR accounting is limited to assessing the value of an organisation's employees and does not take into account other assets or liabilities.
(1) Both assertion and reason are true and the reason is the correct explanation of the assertion .
(2) Both assertion and reason are true but the reason is not the correct explanation of the assertion.
(3) Assertion is true but reason is false.
(4) Both assertion and reason are false.

107. **Assertion:** HR audit is a process for evaluating the effectiveness of an organisation's HR policies and practices.
Reason: HR audit is focused solely on identifying potential legal compliance issues.
(1) Both assertion and reason are false.
(2) Both assertion and reason are true but the reason is not the correct explanation of the assertion.
(3) Assertion is true but reason is false.
(4) Both assertion and reason are true and the reason is the correct explanation of the assertion .

108. **Assertion:** HR accounting is focused solely on the financial aspects of an organisation's human resources.
Reason: HR accounting takes into account both financial and non-financial aspects of an organisation's human resources.
(1) Both assertion and reason are false.
(2) Both assertion and reason are true but the reason is not the correct explanation of the assertion.
(3) Assertion is true but reason is false.
(4) Both assertion and reason are true and the reason is the correct explanation of the assertion .

109. **Assertion:** HR audit is a one-time process that does not need to be repeated.
Reason: HR audit is an ongoing evaluation of an organisation's HR policies and practices.
(1) Both assertion and reason are false.
(2) Both assertion and reason are true but the reason is not the correct explanation of the assertion.
(3) Assertion is false but reason is true.
(4) Both assertion and reason are true and the reason is the correct explanation of the assertion .

110. **Assertion:** HR accounting is a tool for measuring and evaluating the monetary value of an organisation's human resources.

Reason: HR accounting can be used to assess the non-financial value of an organisation's human resources, such as employee satisfaction and engagement.

(1) Both assertion and reason are true and the reason is the correct explanation of the assertion .

(2) Both assertion and reason are true but the reason is not the correct explanation of the assertion.

(3) Assertion is true but reason is false.

(4) Both assertion and reason are false.

111. What is the primary goal of a consultant-client relationship?

(1) To impose the consultant's ideas on the client

(2) To create a long-term partnership based on mutual trust and collaboration

(3) To maintain a professional distance between the consultant and the client

(4) To ensure the consultant's profit margin

112. What is the role of the consultant in a consulting engagement?

(1) To provide expert advice and guidance to the client

(2) To dictate the client's course of action

(3) To limit the client's access to resources

(4) To act as a substitute for the client's management team

113. What is the role of the client in a consulting engagement?

(1) To blindly follow the consultant's recommendations

(2) To actively engage with the consultant and collaborate in the consulting process

(3) To resist change and maintain the status quo

(4) To limit the consultant's access to organisational resources

114. What is the importance of communication in a consultant-client relationship?

(1) Communication is not necessary in a consultant-client relationship

(2) Good communication is necessary for building a strong consultant-client relationship

(3) Communication is solely the responsibility of the consultant

(4) Communication is solely the responsibility of the client

115. What is the importance of trust in a consultant-client relationship?

(1) Trust is not necessary in a consultant-client relationship

(2) Trust is crucial for building a strong and effective consultant-client relationship

(3) Trust is solely the responsibility of the consultant

(4) Trust is solely the responsibility of the client

116. What is the importance of knowledge management in organisations?

(1) To stifle innovation and creativity

(2) To maintain the status quo

(3) To ensure the effective creation, sharing, and use of knowledge within an organisation

(4) To limit employee access to information

117. What is the process of knowledge management?

(1) Restricting access to information

(2) Disseminating information only to select employees

(3) Creating, sharing, and using knowledge effectively within an organisation

(4) Keeping knowledge within a select group of decision-makers

118. Which of the following is not a process of knowledge management?

(1) Knowledge capture

(2) Knowledge sharing

(3) Knowledge hoarding

(4) Knowledge utilization

119. What is the role of a knowledge management system in an organisation?

(1) To restrict access to information

(2) To facilitate the creation, sharing, and use of knowledge within an organisation
(3) To limit employee access to information
(4) To waste organisational resources on unnecessary information management tools

120. What is the importance of sharing knowledge within an organisation?
(1) To maintain the status quo
(2) To promote a culture of secrecy
(3) To facilitate innovation and improve organisational performance
(4) To limit employee access to information

121. What is the purpose of a Human Resource Information System (HRIS)?
(1) To limit employee access to information
(2) To automate HR processes
(3) To maintain employee records and data
(4) To promote a culture of secrecy

122. What are the benefits of an HRIS for an organisation?
(1) Improved efficiency and accuracy of HR processes
(2) Increased employee engagement and satisfaction
(3) Improved decision-making based on accurate data
(4) All of the above

123. What is the role of an HRIS in recruitment and selection?
(1) To limit employee access to information
(2) To automate job postings and applications
(3) To manage candidate information and data
(4) To discourage employee retention

124. What is the role of an HRIS in employee training and development?
(1) To limit employee access to information
(2) To support the planning and management of employee training and development programs
(3) To automate the training and development process
(4) To discourage employee participation in training and development programs

125. What is the role of an HRIS in performance management?
(1) To limit employee access to information
(2) To support the planning and management of performance appraisal processes
(3) To automate the performance management process
(4) To discourage employee participation in performance appraisal processes

126. What is the importance of accuracy in an HRIS?
(1) Accuracy is not important in an HRIS
(2) An accurate HRIS is critical for effective decision-making and workforce planning
(3) Inaccurate data can support strategic planning and decision-making
(4) Inaccurate data can improve employee engagement and satisfaction

127. What is the importance of data security in an HRIS?
(1) Data security is not important in an HRIS
(2) Data security is critical for protecting employee data and maintaining compliance
(3) Data security can limit employee productivity and engagement
(4) Data security is solely the responsibility of the IT department

128. What is the role of an HRIS in succession planning and talent management?
(1) To limit employee access to information
(2) To support the planning and management of succession planning and talent management initiatives
(3) To automate the succession planning and talent management process

(4) To discourage employee participation in succession planning and talent management initiatives

129. What is the role of an HRIS in compensation and benefits management?
(1) To limit employee access to information
(2) To manage employee compensation and benefits data
(3) To automate the compensation and benefits management process
(4) To discourage employee participation in compensation and benefits management initiatives

130. What is the importance of data analysis in an HRIS?
(1) Data analysis is not important in an HRIS
(2) Accurate data analysis can support strategic planning and decision-making
(3) Inaccurate data analysis can support strategic planning and decision-making
(4) Data analysis is solely the responsibility of the IT department

131. **Assertion:** The goal of a consultant-client relationship is to impose the consultant's ideas on the client.
Reason: Consulting engagements are focused solely on generating revenue for the consultant.
(1) Both assertion and reason are false.
(2) Both assertion and reason are true but the reason is not the correct explanation of the assertion.
(3) Assertion is false but reason is true.
(4) Both assertion and reason are true and the reason is the correct explanation of the assertion.

132. **Assertion:** The role of the consultant in a consulting engagement is to provide expert advice and guidance to the client.
Reason: The role of the client in a consulting engagement is to blindly follow the consultant's recommendations.
(1) Both assertion and reason are false.
(2) Both assertion and reason are true but the reason is not the correct explanation of the assertion.
(3) Assertion is true but reason is false.
(4) Both assertion and reason are true and the reason is the correct explanation of the assertion.

133. **Assertion:** Communication is not necessary in a consultant-client relationship.
Reason: A strong and effective consultant-client relationship does not depend on communication.
(1) Both assertion and reason are false.
(2) Both assertion and reason are true but the reason is not the correct explanation of the assertion.
(3) Assertion is false but reason is true.
(4) Both assertion and reason are true and the reason is the correct explanation of the assertion.

134. **Assertion:** Trust is not necessary in a consultant-client relationship.
Reason: A strong and effective consultant-client relationship does not depend on trust.
(1) Both assertion and reason are false.
(2) Both assertion and reason are true but the reason is not the correct explanation of the assertion.
(3) Assertion is false but reason is true.
(4) Both assertion and reason are true and the reason is the correct explanation of the assertion.

135. **Assertion:** A consultant must maintain a professional distance from the client in a consulting engagement.
Reason: Collaboration and partnership between the consultant and client are unimportant in a consulting engagement.
(1) Both assertion and reason are false.
(2) Both assertion and reason are true but the reason is not the correct explanation of the assertion.
(3) Assertion is true but reason is false.
(4) Both assertion and reason are true and the reason is the correct explanation of the assertion.

136. **Assertion:** Knowledge management is only concerned with the creation and storage of information in an organisation.
Reason: The primary goal of knowledge management is to promote knowledge sharing and utilization within an organisation.
(1) Both assertion and reason are false.
(2) Both assertion and reason are true but the reason is not the correct explanation of the assertion.
(3) Assertion is false but reason is true.
(4) Both assertion and reason are true and the reason is the correct explanation of the assertion.

137. **Assertion:** The process of knowledge management involves restricting access to information.
Reason: Openness and transparency are not important in an effective knowledge management process.
(1) Both assertion and reason are false.
(2) Both assertion and reason are true but the reason is not the correct explanation of the assertion.
(3) Assertion is true but reason is false.
(4) Both assertion and reason are true and the reason is the correct explanation of the assertion.

138. **Assertion:** Knowledge hoarding is a beneficial practice in knowledge management.
Reason: The value of knowledge is determined by its scarcity and limited access.
(1) Both assertion and reason are false.
(2) Both assertion and reason are true but the reason is not the correct explanation of the assertion.
(3) Assertion is false but reason is true.
(4) Both assertion and reason are true and the reason is the correct explanation of the assertion.

139. **Assertion:** An effective knowledge management system can improve an organisation's ability to innovate and adapt to changing circumstances.
Reason: Knowledge management systems limit access to information and resources.
(1) Both assertion and reason are false.
(2) Both assertion and reason are true but the reason is not the correct explanation of the assertion.
(3) Assertion is true but reason is false.
(4) Both assertion and reason are true and the reason is the correct explanation of the assertion.

140. **Assertion:** A culture of openness and transparency is important in an effective knowledge management system.
Reason: Collaboration and sharing are critical components of an effective knowledge management system.
(1) Both assertion and reason are true and the reason is the correct explanation of the assertion.
(2) Both assertion and reason are true but the reason is not the correct explanation of the assertion.
(3) Assertion is false but reason is true.
(4) Both assertion and reason are false.

141. **Assertion:** The role of an HRIS is limited to automating HR processes.
Reason: An HRIS is not designed to support HR decision-making and strategic planning.
(1) Both assertion and reason are false.
(2) Both assertion and reason are true but the reason is not the correct explanation of the assertion.
(3) Assertion is false but reason is true.
(4) Both assertion and reason are true and the reason is the correct explanation of the assertion.

142. **Assertion:** An HRIS can improve the efficiency and accuracy of HR processes.
Reason: An HRIS limits the ability of HR personnel to manage employee data and information.
(1) Both assertion and reason are false.
(2) Both assertion and reason are true but the reason is not the correct explanation of the assertion.

(3) Assertion is true but reason is false.
(4) Both assertion and reason are true and the reason is the correct explanation of the assertion.

143. Assertion: Accurate data analysis is not important in an HRIS.
Reason: Inaccurate data can result in poor decision-making and strategic planning.
(1) Both assertion and reason are false.
(2) Both assertion and reason are true but the reason is not the correct explanation of the assertion.
(3) Assertion is false but reason is true.
(4) Both assertion and reason are true and the reason is the correct explanation of the assertion.

144. Assertion: An HRIS can improve an organisation's ability to manage employee performance and development.
Reason: An HRIS provides tools and resources for creating and managing training and development programs.
(1) Both assertion and reason are true and the reason is the correct explanation of the assertion.
(2) Both assertion and reason are true but the reason is not the correct explanation of the assertion.
(3) Assertion is false but reason is true.
(4) Both assertion and reason are false.

145. Assertion: Data security is solely the responsibility of the IT department in an organisation.
Reason: An HRIS does not contain sensitive employee data or confidential information.
(1) Both assertion and reason are false.
(2) Both assertion and reason are true but the reason is not the correct explanation of the assertion.
(3) Assertion is false but reason is true.
(4) Both assertion and reason are true and the reason is the correct explanation of the assertion.

146. International Human Resource Management (IHRM) involves which of the following?
(1) Managing employees who work in different locations and/or countries
(2) Managing employees with diverse cultural backgrounds
(3) Managing employees with different legal and regulatory requirements
(4) All of the above

147. Which of the following is an important consideration in the organisational context of IHRM?
(1) The size and structure of the organisation
(2) The degree of internationalization of the organisation
(3) The organisational culture and values
(4) All of the above

148. What is the importance of IHRM in sustainable business practices?
(1) IHRM promotes environmental sustainability through employee practices
(2) IHRM supports social sustainability through equality and diversity initiatives
(3) IHRM promotes sustainable economic practices through global talent management
(4) IHRM has no direct impact on sustainable business practices

149. What is the role of IHRM in managing a diverse workforce?
(1) To promote a homogenous culture within the organisation
(2) To manage cultural differences and promote understanding and respect
(3) To limit diversity in the organisation
(4) To discourage employee participation in diversity initiatives

150. What is the importance of IHRM in managing global talent?
(1) To limit employee mobility and access to global business markets

(2) To facilitate the recruitment, development, and retention of talent on a global scale

(3) To limit the transfer of knowledge and expertise across the organisation

(4) To promote insular business practices

151. What is the role of IHRM in managing expatriates?

(1) To impose the organisation's policies and practices on the expatriate

(2) To provide support for the expatriate to facilitate success in the host country

(3) To limit the expatriate's access to resources

(4) To discourage the use of expatriates in international business operations

152. Which of the following is a challenge to IHRM in managing a global workforce?

(1) Managing cultural differences and diversity

(2) Adapting to different legal and regulatory environments

(3) Balancing global and local business needs

(4) All of the above

153. What is the importance of IHRM in managing a global workforce?

(1) To limit employee mobility and access to global business markets

(2) To facilitate global business operations and promote organisational effectiveness

(3) To discourage diversity and cultural differences within the organisation

(4) To impose homogeneity and uniformity in all business practices

154. What is the importance of IHRM in managing employee recruitment and selection for overseas assignments?

(1) To limit employee access to global business markets

(2) To ensure the right employees are recruited for overseas assignments

(3) To discourage employee participation in overseas assignments

(4) To prioritize local talent over global talent

155. What is the role of IHRM in managing employee development and training for global assignments?

(1) To limit employee access to global business markets

(2) To prioritize local talent over global talent

(3) To facilitate the development and training of employees for successful global assignments

(4) To discourage employee participation in global assignments

156. What is the importance of IHRM in managing logistics and support for employees on global assignments?

(1) To limit employee access to global business markets

(2) To prioritize local talent over global talent

(3) To support employees on global assignments through logistics and support services

(4) To discourage employee participation in global assignments

157. What is the role of IHRM in managing employee compensation on global assignments?

(1) To limit employee access to global business markets

(2) To prioritize local talent over global talent

(3) To provide fair and equitable compensation for employees on global assignments

(4) To discourage employee participation in global assignments

158. What is the importance of IHRM in managing employee repatriation?

(1) To limit employee access to global business markets

(2) To prioritize local talent over global talent

(3) To facilitate the successful transition of employees from global assignments to domestic operations
(4) To discourage employee participation in global assignments

159. What is the role of IHRM in managing employee retention on global assignments?
(1) To limit employee access to global business markets
(2) To prioritize local talent over global talent
(3) To promote employee retention through effective management of global assignments
(4) To discourage employee participation in global assignments

160. What is the importance of IHRM in managing workforce planning on a global scale?
(1) To limit employee access to global business markets
(2) To prioritize local talent over global talent
(3) To facilitate effective workforce planning for global business operations
(4) To discourage employee participation in global assignments

161. What is the role of IHRM in promoting diversity and inclusion in the workplace?
(1) To promote a homogenous culture within the organisation
(2) To manage cultural differences and promote understanding and respect
(3) To promote diversity and inclusion through policies and practices
(4) To discourage diversity and cultural differences within the organisation

162. What is the importance of IHRM in developing global leadership in an organisation?
(1) To limit employee access to global business markets
(2) To prioritize local talent over global talent
(3) To facilitate the development of global leadership competencies and skills
(4) To discourage employee participation in global assignments

163. What is the role of IHRM in promoting ethical business practices on a global scale?
(1) To promote insular business practices
(2) To facilitate understanding and respect for diverse cultural and regulatory environments
(3) To promote ethical business practices through policies and practices
(4) To discourage the development and implementation of ethical business practices

164. What is the importance of IHRM in promoting social responsibility in an organisation?
(1) To limit employee access to global business markets
(2) To prioritize local talent over global talent
(3) To promote social responsibility through policies and practices
(4) To discourage the development and implementation of social responsibility initiatives

165. What is the role of IHRM in promoting sustainable business practices on a global scale?
(1) To promote insular business practices
(2) To facilitate sustainable business practices through global talent management
(3) To discourage the development and implementation of sustainable business practices
(4) To limit employee participation in sustainability initiatives

166. Which of the following is an important consideration in the organisational context of IHRM?
(1) The size and structure of the organisation
(2) The degree of internationalization of the organisation
(3) The organisational culture and values
(4) All of the above

167. What is the role of IHRM in managing social and environmental sustainability in an organisation?
(1) To limit employee participation in sustainability initiatives
(2) To develop policies and practices that promote social and environmental sustainability
(3) To promote insular business practices
(4) To prioritize profitability over sustainability

168. What is the importance of IHRM in managing diversity in an organisation?
(1) To promote a homogenous culture within the organisation
(2) To manage cultural differences and foster understanding and respect
(3) To discourage diversity in the organisation
(4) To limit employee participation in diversity initiatives

169. What is the role of IHRM in promoting global talent management in an organisation?
(1) To limit employee mobility and access to global business markets
(2) To facilitate the recruitment, development, and retention of talent on a global scale
(3) To limit the transfer of knowledge and expertise across the organisation
(4) To promote insular business practices

170. What is the importance of IHRM in managing a diverse workforce?
(1) To promote a homogenous culture within the organisation
(2) To manage cultural differences and promote understanding and respect
(3) To limit diversity in the organisation
(4) To discourage employee participation in diversity initiatives

171. Assertion: The organisational context of IHRM involves consideration of the size and structure of the organisation.

Reason: The size and structure of the organisation can impact the effectiveness of IHRM practices.
(1) Both assertion and reason are true and the reason is the correct explanation of the assertion.
(2) Both assertion and reason are true but the reason is not the correct explanation of the assertion.
(3) Assertion is true but reason is false.
(4) Both assertion and reason are false.

172. Assertion: IHRM plays an important role in promoting long-term sustainability in an organisation.

Reason: IHRM promotes sustainability through effective management of social, environmental, and economic factors.
(1) Both assertion and reason are true and the reason is the correct explanation of the assertion.
(2) Both assertion and reason are true but the reason is not the correct explanation of the assertion.
(3) Assertion is true but reason is false.
(4) Both assertion and reason are false.

173. Assertion: IHRM is solely concerned with managing legal and regulatory requirements in different countries.

Reason: IHRM does not involve managing employees with diverse cultural backgrounds.
(1) Both assertion and reason are false.
(2) Both assertion and reason are true but the reason is not the correct explanation of the assertion.
(3) Assertion is false but reason is true.
(4) Both assertion and reason are true and the reason is the correct explanation of the assertion.

174. Assertion: The role of IHRM is limited to managing employee diversity within an organisation.

Reason: Effective IHRM practices involve managing employees with diverse cultural backgrounds, regulatory environments, and legal requirements.

(1) Both assertion and reason are true and the reason is the correct explanation of the assertion.
(2) Both assertion and reason are true but the reason is not the correct explanation of the assertion.
(3) Assertion is true but reason is false.
(4) Both assertion and reason are false.

175. Assertion: IHRM plays a limited role in business sustainability and social responsibility.

Reason: IHRM is solely concerned with managing employee mobility and access to global business markets.

(1) Both assertion and reason are false.
(2) Both assertion and reason are true but the reason is not the correct explanation of the assertion.
(3) Assertion is true but reason is false.
(4) Both assertion and reason are true and the reason is the correct explanation of the assertion.

176. Assertion: The success of IHRM practices is dependent upon the structure and size of the organisation.

Reason: IHRM practices can be successful regardless of the structure and size of the organisation.

(1) Both assertion and reason are false.
(2) Both assertion and reason are true but the reason is not the correct explanation of the assertion.
(3) Assertion is true but reason is false.
(4) Both assertion and reason are true and the reason is the correct explanation of the assertion.

177. Assertion: The role of IHRM in managing global talent is limited to recruitment and selection.

Reason: Effective management of global talent involves development, retention, and succession planning.

(1) Both assertion and reason are true and the reason is the correct explanation of the assertion.
(2) Both assertion and reason are true but the reason is not the correct explanation of the assertion.
(3) Assertion is true but reason is false.
(4) Both assertion and reason are false.

178. Assertion: IHRM plays an important role in managing employee logistics and support on global assignments.

Reason: IHRM is not involved in managing employee logistics and support on global assignments.

(1) Both assertion and reason are false.
(2) Both assertion and reason are true but the reason is not the correct explanation of the assertion.
(3) Assertion is true but reason is false.
(4) Both assertion and reason are true and the reason is the correct explanation of the assertion.

179. Assertion: IHRM is solely concerned with managing employee recruitment and selection for global assignments.

Reason: Effective management of global assignments involves managing employee compensation, development, and repatriation.

(1) Both assertion and reason are true and the reason is the correct explanation of the assertion.
(2) Both assertion and reason are true but the reason is not the correct explanation of the assertion.
(3) Assertion is true but reason is false.
(4) Both assertion and reason are false.

180. Assertion: IHRM plays a limited role in managing global employee retention.

Reason: Employee retention on global assignments is solely dependent on employee motivation and performance.

(1) Both assertion and reason are false.
(2) Both assertion and reason are true but the reason is not the correct explanation of the assertion.

(3) Assertion is true but reason is false.
(4) Both assertion and reason are true and the reason is the correct explanation of the assertion.

181. Which of the following is a primary function of IHRM?
(1) Employee retention
(2) Employee selection
(3) Employee development
(4) All of the above

182. What is the role of IHRM in employee recruitment?
(1) To develop policies and procedures for recruitment
(2) To attract and select the right candidates for the job
(3) To minimize employee turnover
(4) To limit employee diversity

183. What is the importance of IHRM in employee retention?
(1) To limit employee mobility and access to global business markets
(2) To retain employees with critical skills and knowledge
(3) To discourage diversity and cultural differences within the organisation
(4) To discourage employee participation in diversity initiatives

184. What is the role of IHRM in employee development?
(1) To discourage employee participation in professional development activities
(2) To provide opportunities for employee development and growth
(3) To limit access to employee development opportunities
(4) To impose an authoritative management style

185. How does IHRM facilitate employee performance management?
(1) By providing adequate resources and support
(2) By setting performance targets and goals
(3) By providing feedback and coaching
(4) All of the above

186. What is the role of IHRM in global workforce planning?
(1) To limit employee access to global business markets
(2) To plan and manage a diverse global workforce
(3) To discourage diversity and cultural differences within the organisation
(4) To impose uniformity in all business practices

187. What is the importance of IHRM in global talent management?
(1) To limit employee mobility and access to global business markets
(2) To facilitate the recruitment, development, and retention of talent on a global scale
(3) To discourage diversity and cultural differences within the organisation
(4) To discourage employee participation in diversity initiatives

188. What is the role of IHRM in employee compensation and benefits?
(1) To limit compensation and benefits for employees
(2) To provide fair and equitable compensation and benefits for employees
(3) To discourage employee participation in compensation and benefits initiatives
(4) To prioritize profitability over employee satisfaction

189. How does IHRM facilitate employee career management?
(1) By providing opportunities for career development and advancement
(2) By limiting access to career development opportunities
(3) By discouraging employee participation in career development activities
(4) By imposing an authoritative management style

190. What is the importance of IHRM in managing employee relations?
(1) To limit employee mobility and access to global business markets
(2) To foster positive and productive employee relations
(3) To discourage diversity and cultural differences within the organisation
(4) To impose uniformity in all business practices

191. What is the importance of cross-cultural studies in IHRM?
(1) To limit employee access to global business markets
(2) To manage employees with diverse cultural backgrounds and values
(3) To impose a homogenous culture within the organisation
(4) To discourage cultural diversity within the organisation

192. What is the role of cross-cultural studies in managing employee performance?
(1) To limit employee access to global business markets
(2) To promote cultural understanding and respect
(3) To impose a uniform management style
(4) To limit employee participation in employee performance initiatives

193. What is the importance of cross-cultural studies in facilitating communication and teamwork among employees?
(1) To promote a homogenous culture within the organisation
(2) To promote cultural understanding and respect
(3) To discourage diversity and cultural differences within the organisation
(4) To limit employee participation in teamwork activities

194. What is the role of cross-cultural studies in managing employee development?
(1) To promote cultural assimilation
(2) To promote cultural understanding and respect for diverse backgrounds and perspectives
(3) To discourage diversity and cultural differences within the organisation
(4) To discourage employee participation in professional development activities

195. What is the importance of cross-cultural studies in managing diversity and inclusion in the workplace?
(1) To promote a homogenous culture within the organisation
(2) To promote cultural understanding and respect for diverse backgrounds and perspectives
(3) To discourage employee participation in diversity initiatives
(4) To discourage diversity and cultural differences within the organisation

196. What is the importance of cultural diversity in managing a global workforce?
(1) To promote a homogenous culture within the organisation
(2) To manage cultural differences and foster understanding and respect
(3) To discourage diversity and cultural differences within the organisation
(4) To limit employee participation in diversity initiatives

197. What is the role of cultural diversity in managing employee motivation and performance?
(1) To limit employee access to global business markets
(2) To promote employee motivation and performance through understanding and respect for diverse cultural backgrounds
(3) To discourage employee participation in employee performance initiatives
(4) To impose a uniform management style

198. What is the importance of cultural diversity in developing effective cross-cultural communication?

(1) To promote a homogenous culture within the organisation
(2) To manage cultural differences and foster understanding and respect
(3) To discourage diversity and cultural differences within the organisation
(4) To limit employee participation in communication initiatives

199. What is the role of cultural diversity in managing employee development?
(1) To discourage employee participation in professional development activities
(2) To provide opportunities for employee development and growth in diverse cultural environments
(3) To limit access to employee development opportunities
(4) To impose an authoritative management style

200. What is the importance of cultural diversity in promoting innovation and creativity in an organisation?
(1) To promote a homogenous culture within the organisation
(2) To foster understanding and respect for diverse perspectives and ideas
(3) To discourage employee participation in innovation initiatives
(4) To limit exposure to diverse perspectives and ideas

201. What is the role of cultural diversity in managing a diverse global workforce?
(1) To limit employee access to global business markets
(2) To manage cultural differences and foster understanding and respect
(3) To discourage diversity and cultural differences within the organisation
(4) To impose a homogenous culture within the organisation

202. What is the importance of cultural diversity in managing employee motivation and performance?
(1) To promote a homogenous culture within the organisation
(2) To promote employee motivation and performance through understanding and respect for diverse cultural backgrounds
(3) To discourage employee participation in employee performance initiatives
(4) To impose a uniform management style

203. What is the role of cultural diversity in developing effective cross-cultural communication?
(1) To limit employee access to global business markets
(2) To manage cultural differences and foster understanding and respect
(3) To discourage diversity and cultural differences within the organisation
(4) To impose a homogenous communication style

204. What is the importance of cultural diversity in managing employee development?
(1) To discourage employee participation in professional development activities
(2) To provide opportunities for employee development and growth in diverse cultural environments
(3) To limit access to employee development opportunities
(4) To impose an authoritative management style

205. What is the role of cultural diversity in promoting innovation and creativity in an organisation?
(1) To promote a homogenous culture within the organisation
(2) To foster understanding and respect for diverse perspectives and ideas
(3) To discourage employee participation in innovation initiatives
(4) To limit exposure to diverse perspectives and ideas

206. Assertion: Cross-cultural communication skills are essential for effective IHRM.

Reason: Global organisations are typically comprised of employees with diverse cultural backgrounds and values.

(1) Both assertion and reason are true and the reason is the correct explanation of the assertion.

(2) Both assertion and reason are true but the reason is not the correct explanation of the assertion.

(3) Assertion is true but reason is false.

(4) Both assertion and reason are false.

207. Assertion: Cultural diversity is not an important consideration for IHRM.

Reason: A homogenous organisational culture is necessary for effective IHRM.

(1) Both assertion and reason are false.

(2) Both assertion and reason are true but the reason is not the correct explanation of the assertion.

(3) Assertion is false but reason is true.

(4) Both assertion and reason are true and the reason is the correct explanation of the assertion.

208. Assertion: An organisation's success in managing a diverse global workforce is dependent upon its management practices.

Reason: Effective management practices promote understanding and respect for diverse cultural backgrounds.

(1) Both assertion and reason are true and the reason is the correct explanation of the assertion.

(2) Both assertion and reason are true but the reason is not the correct explanation of the assertion.

(3) Assertion is true but reason is false.

(4) Both assertion and reason are false.

209. Assertion: Cultural diversity is a hindrance to effective employee motivation and performance.

Reason: A homogenous organisational culture is necessary for effective employee motivation and performance.

(1) Both assertion and reason are false.

(2) Both assertion and reason are true but the reason is not the correct explanation of the assertion.

(3) Assertion is false but reason is true.

(4) Both assertion and reason are true and the reason is the correct explanation of the assertion.

210. Assertion: Cultural diversity has no impact on global talent management.

Reason: Global talent management is predominantly concerned with recruitment and selection.

(1) Both assertion and reason are false.

(2) Both assertion and reason are true but the reason is not the correct explanation of the assertion.

(3) Assertion is true but reason is false.

(4) Both assertion and reason are true and the reason is the correct explanation of the assertion.

211. Which of the following is a defining characteristic of a transnational organisation?

(1) Operates in multiple countries

(2) Operates in a single country

(3) Has a centralized organisational structure

(4) Has a homogenous organisational culture

212. What is the purpose of a transnational organisation?

(1) To limit operations to a single country

(2) To expand operations globally

(3) To impose a homogenous culture within the organisation

(4) To discourage diversity and cultural differences within the organisation

213. What is the role of a transnational organisation in global business markets?

(1) To limit access to global business markets

(2) To operate with flexibility and agility in a dynamic and complex global business environment

(3) To impose uniformity in all business practices
(4) To prioritize profitability over social responsibility

214. What is the importance of a transnational organisation in managing political and economic risks?
(1) To limit access to global business markets
(2) To operate with flexibility and agility in a dynamic and complex global business environment, including managing political and economic risks
(3) To impose a uniform management style
(4) To impose a homogenous culture within the organisation

215. What is the role of a transnational organisation in managing cultural diversity and social responsibility?
(1) To impose a homogenous culture within the organisation
(2) To manage cultural differences and foster understanding and respect
(3) To prioritise profitability over social responsibility
(4) To discourage employee participation in social responsibility initiatives

216. What is the purpose of a transnational organisation's global strategy?
(1) To limit operations to a single country
(2) To expand operations globally and achieve competitive advantage through a globally coordinated approach
(3) To impose uniformity in all business practices
(4) To prioritize profitability over social responsibility

217. What is the role of a transnational organisation in promoting innovation and creativity?
(1) To limit exposure to diverse perspectives and ideas
(2) To foster understanding and respect for diverse perspectives and ideas
(3) To impose a uniform management style
(4) To promote a homogenous culture within the organisation

218. What is the importance of a transnational organisation's ethical and social responsibility?
(1) To prioritise profitability over social responsibility
(2) To promote ethical behaviour and demonstrate social responsibility
(3) To promote a homogenous culture within the organisation
(4) To discourage employee participation in social responsibility initiatives

219. Which IHRM model is characterised by standardised policies and practices across all countries?
(1) The ethnocentric model
(2) The geocentric model
(3) The polycentric model
(4) The regiocentric model

220. Which IHRM model is characterised by adapting policies and practices to local country requirements?
(1) The ethnocentric model
(2) The geocentric model
(3) The polycentric model
(4) The regiocentric model

221. Which IHRM model is characterized by a mix of both centralized and decentralized decision-making?
(1) The ethnocentric model
(2) The geocentric model
(3) The polycentric model
(4) The regiocentric model

222. What is the focus of the ethnocentric IHRM model?
(1) To centralize decision-making at the headquarters
(2) To adapt policies and practices to local country requirements
(3) To heavily rely on home-country employees for senior global positions

(4) To encourage employee mobility and career advancement opportunities

223. What is the focus of the polycentric IHRM model?

(1) To centralize decision-making at the headquarters
(2) To adapt policies and practices to local country requirements
(3) To heavily rely on home-country employees for senior global positions
(4) To encourage employee mobility and career advancement opportunities

224. What is the focus of the geocentric IHRM model?

(1) To centralize decision-making at the headquarters and heavily rely on home-country employees for senior global positions
(2) To adapt policies and practices to local country requirements
(3) To encourage employee mobility and career advancement opportunities for all employees regardless of nationality
(4) To impose a homogenous culture within the organisation

225. What is the focus of the regiocentric IHRM model?

(1) To centralize decision-making at the headquarters
(2) To adapt policies and practices to local country requirements within specific regions
(3) To encourage employee mobility and career advancement opportunities for all employees regardless of nationality
(4) To impose a homogenous culture within the organisation

226. What is the role of the ethnocentric IHRM model in managing cultural diversity?

(1) To promote cultural understanding and respect for diverse backgrounds and perspectives
(2) To centralize decision-making and impose a homogenous organisational culture
(3) To adapt policies and practices to local country requirements
(4) To promote a mix of both centralized and decentralized decision-making

227. What is the role of the geocentric IHRM model in managing cultural diversity?

(1) To promote cultural assimilation
(2) To promote cultural understanding and respect for diverse backgrounds and perspectives through a global organisational culture
(3) To centralize decision-making and impose a homogenous organisational culture
(4) To adapt policies and practices to local country requirements

228. What is the role of the polycentric IHRM model in managing cultural diversity?

(1) To promote cultural understanding and respect for diverse backgrounds and perspectives through a global organisational culture
(2) To adapt policies and practices to local country requirements
(3) To centralize decision-making and impose a homogenous organisational culture
(4) To promote a mix of both centralized and decentralized decision-making

229. What is the role of the regiocentric IHRM model in managing cultural diversity?

(1) To promote cultural understanding and respect for diverse backgrounds and perspectives through a global organisational culture
(2) To adapt policies and practices to local country requirements within specific regions
(3) To centralize decision-making and impose a homogenous organisational culture
(4) To promote a mix of both centralized and decentralized decision-making

230. What is the role of the ethnocentric IHRM model in managing global talent?

(1) To heavily rely on home-country employees for senior global positions
(2) To prioritize local talent development opportunities
(3) To promote equal career opportunities for all employees regardless of nationality
(4) To encourage employee mobility and career advancement opportunities

231. What is the role of the geocentric IHRM model in managing global talent?
(1) To centralize decision-making and impose a homogenous organisational culture
(2) To prioritize local talent development opportunities
(3) To encourage employee mobility and career advancement opportunities for all employees regardless of nationality
(4) To impose a uniform management style

232. What is the role of the polycentric IHRM model in managing global talent?
(1) To rely on local talent for senior global positions
(2) To prioritize local talent development opportunities
(3) To encourage employee mobility and career advancement opportunities for all employees regardless of nationality
(4) To impose a uniform management style

233. What is the role of the regiocentric IHRM model in managing global talent?
(1) To encourage employee mobility and career advancement opportunities
(2) To prioritize local talent development opportunities within specific regions
(3) To impose a homogenous organisational culture
(4) To rely on home-country employees for senior global positions

234. Assertion: The ethnocentric IHRM model is best suited for organisations operating in multiple countries.
Reason: The ethnocentric model involves adapting policies and practices to local country requirements.
(1) Both assertion and reason are false.
(2) Both assertion and reason are true but the reason is not the correct explanation of the assertion.
(3) Assertion is true but reason is false.
(4) Both assertion and reason are true and the reason is the correct explanation of the assertion.

235. Assertion: The geocentric IHRM model promotes equal career opportunities for all employees, regardless of nationality.
Reason: The geocentric model involves adapting policies and practices to local country requirements.
(1) Both assertion and reason are true and the reason is the correct explanation of the assertion.
(2) Both assertion and reason are true but the reason is not the correct explanation of the assertion.
(3) Assertion is true but reason is false.
(4) Both assertion and reason are false.

236. Assertion: The polycentric IHRM model involves standardizing policies and practices across all countries.
Reason: The polycentric model involves adapting policies and practices to local country requirements.
(1) Both assertion and reason are false.
(2) Both assertion and reason are true but the reason is not the correct explanation of the assertion.
(3) Assertion is false but reason is true.
(4) Both assertion and reason are true and the reason is the correct explanation of the assertion.

237. Assertion: The regiocentric IHRM model is best suited for organisations operating in a single country.
Reason: The regiocentric model focuses on adapting policies and practices to local country requirements within specific regions.

(1) Both assertion and reason are false.
(2) Both assertion and reason are true but the reason is not the correct explanation of the assertion.
(3) Assertion is true but reason is false.
(4) Both assertion and reason are true and the reason is the correct explanation of the assertion.

238. Assertion: The ethnocentric IHRM model is best suited for managing cultural diversity within a global workforce.
Reason: The ethnocentric model involves adapting policies and practices to local country requirements.
(1) Both assertion and reason are false.
(2) Both assertion and reason are true but the reason is not the correct explanation of the assertion.
(3) Assertion is true but reason is false.
(4) Both assertion and reason are true and the reason is the correct explanation of the assertion.

239. Assertion: The polycentric IHRM model is best suited for managing global talent within a global workforce.
Reason: The polycentric model involves relying on local talent for senior global positions.
(1) Both assertion and reason are true and the reason is the correct explanation of the assertion.
(2) Both assertion and reason are true but the reason is not the correct explanation of the assertion.
(3) Assertion is true but reason is false.
(4) Both assertion and reason are false.

240. Assertion: The geocentric IHRM model is best suited for global organisations.
Reason: The geocentric model involves adapting policies and practices to local country requirements, while also facilitating global coordination and integration.
(1) Both assertion and reason are true and the reason is the correct explanation of the assertion.
(2) Both assertion and reason are true but the reason is not the correct explanation of the assertion.
(3) Assertion is true but reason is false.
(4) Both assertion and reason are false.

ANSWER KEY

1. (3)	**2.** (3)	**3.** (1)	**4.** (3)	**5.** (3)	**6.** (1)	**7.** (3)	**8.** (3)	**9.** (1)	**10.** (2)
11. (2)	**12.** (3)	**13.** (4)	**14.** (1)	**15.** (2)	**16.** (2)	**17.** (4)	**18.** (3)	**19.** (3)	**20.** (2)
21. (3)	**22.** (3)	**23.** (3)	**24.** (3)	**25.** (3)	**26.** (3)	**27.** (4)	**28.** (3)	**29.** (3)	**30.** (1)
31. (3)	**32.** (3)	**33.** (3)	**34.** (3)	**35.** (2)	**36.** (3)	**37.** (3)	**38.** (2)	**39.** (4)	**40.** (2)
41. (3)	**42.** (2)	**43.** (3)	**44.** (2)	**45.** (2)	**46.** (1)	**47.** (4)	**48.** (3)	**49.** (3)	**50.** (4)
51. (3)	**52.** (3)	**53.** (2)	**54.** (3)	**55.** (4)	**56.** (3)	**57.** (3)	**58.** (3)	**59.** (1)	**60.** (4)
61. (3)	**62.** (4)	**63.** (4)	**64.** (3)	**65.** (2)	**66.** (3)	**67.** (4)	**68.** (3)	**69.** (3)	**70.** (3)
71. (3)	**72.** (3)	**73.** (3)	**74.** (2)	**75.** (2)	**76.** (4)	**77.** (1)	**78.** (1)	**79.** (4)	**80.** (4)
81. (4)	**82.** (4)	**83.** (4)	**84.** (4)	**85.** (4)	**86.** (4)	**87.** (4)	**88.** (4)	**89.** (4)	**90.** (1)
91. (1)	**92.** (4)	**93.** (1)	**94.** (4)	**95.** (2)	**96.** (3)	**97.** (3)	**98.** (4)	**99.** (3)	**100.** (1)
101. (1)	**102.** (3)	**103.** (1)	**104.** (4)	**105.** (3)	**106.** (1)	**107.** (4)	**108.** (4)	**109.** (4)	**110.** (1)
111. (2)	**112.** (1)	**113.** (2)	**114.** (2)	**115.** (2)	**116.** (3)	**117.** (3)	**118.** (4)	**119.** (2)	**120.** (3)
121. (3)	**122.** (3)	**123.** (3)	**124.** (2)	**125.** (2)	**126.** (2)	**127.** (2)	**128.** (2)	**129.** (2)	**130.** (2)
131. (4)	**132.** (4)	**133.** (4)	**134.** (4)	**135.** (4)	**136.** (4)	**137.** (4)	**138.** (4)	**139.** (4)	**140.** (1)
141. (4)	**142.** (4)	**143.** (4)	**144.** (1)	**145.** (4)	**146.** (4)	**147.** (4)	**148.** (3)	**149.** (2)	**150.** (2)
151. (2)	**152.** (2)	**153.** (2)	**154.** (2)	**155.** (3)	**156.** (3)	**157.** (3)	**158.** (3)	**159.** (3)	**160.** (3)
161. (3)	**162.** (3)	**163.** (3)	**164.** (3)	**165.** (2)	**166.** (4)	**167.** (2)	**168.** (2)	**169.** (2)	**170.** (2)
171. (1)	**172.** (1)	**173.** (4)	**174.** (1)	**175.** (4)	**176.** (4)	**177.** (1)	**178.** (4)	**179.** (1)	**180.** (4)
181. (4)	**182.** (2)	**183.** (2)	**184.** (2)	**185.** (4)	**186.** (2)	**187.** (2)	**188.** (2)	**189.** (1)	**190.** (2)
191. (2)	**192.** (2)	**193.** (2)	**194.** (2)	**195.** (2)	**196.** (2)	**197.** (2)	**198.** (2)	**199.** (2)	**200.** (2)
201. (2)	**202.** (2)	**203.** (2)	**204.** (2)	**205.** (2)	**206.** (1)	**207.** (4)	**208.** (1)	**209.** (4)	**210.** (4)
211. (1)	**212.** (2)	**213.** (2)	**214.** (2)	**215.** (2)	**216.** (2)	**217.** (2)	**218.** (2)	**219.** (1)	**220.** (3)
221. (4)	**222.** (3)	**223.** (2)	**224.** (3)	**225.** (2)	**226.** (2)	**227.** (2)	**228.** (2)	**229.** (2)	**230.** (1)
231. (3)	**232.** (2)	**233.** (2)	**234.** (4)	**235.** (1)	**236.** (4)	**237.** (4)	**238.** (4)	**239.** (1)	**240.** (1)

UNIT 4

ORGANISATIONAL BEHAVIOUR

Syllabus

- Concept, Scope, Nature of human behavior, Personality, Perception, Learning, Attitude, Motivation, Interpersonal Behaviour, Group Dynamics, Leadership, Communication, Power and Authority, Stress, Organisational Change and Development.

ORGANISATIONAL BEHAVIOUR

Organisation is an essential part of human life. We are born in organisations, educated in organisations and spend most of our lives working for organisations.

DEFINITION OF ORGANISATION

According to Gary Johns, "Organisations are social inventions for accomplishing goals through group efforts". This definition covers wide variety of groups such as businesses, schools, hospitals, fraternal groups, religious bodies, government agencies and so on. There are three significant aspects in the above definition, which require further analysis. They are as follows:

1. **Social Inventions.** The word "social" as a derivative of society basically means gathering of people. It is the people that primarily make up an organisation.
2. **Accomplishing Goals.** All organisations have reasons for their existence. These reasons are the goals towards which all organisational efforts are directed. While the primary goal of any commercial organisation is to make money for its owners, this goal is inter-related with many other goals. Accordingly, any organisational goal must integrate in itself the personal goals of all individuals associated with the organisation.
3. **Group Effort.** People, both as members of the society at large and as a part of an organisation interact with each other and are inter-dependent. Individuals in themselves have physical and intellectual limitations and these limitations can only be overcome by group efforts.

Concept and Definition of Organisational Behaviour

Organisational behaviour is concerned with people's thoughts, feelings, emotions and actions in setting up a work. Understanding an individual behaviour is in itself a challenge, but understanding group behaviour in an organisational environment is a monumental managerial task.

1. "**Organisational behaviour** is a field of study that investigates the impact that individuals, groups and structure have on behaviour within organisation for the purpose of applying such knowledge toward improving organisation effectiveness." *– Stephen P. Robbins*
2. "**Organisational behaviour** is the study and application at knowledge about the how people - as individuals and a groups - act within organisation. It strives to identify ways in which people can act more effectively." *– Keith Davis*
3. "**Organisational behaviour** can be defined as the understanding, prediction and management of the human behaviour affect the performance of the organisations." *– Luthans*

As Nadler and Tushman put it, "Understanding one individual's behaviour is challenging in and of itself; understanding a group that is made up of different individuals and comprehending the many relationships among those individuals is even more complex. Ultimately, the organisation's work gets done through people, individually or collectively, on their own or in collaboration with technology. Therefore, the management of organisational behaviour is central to the management task – a task that involves the capacity to "understand" the behaviour patterns of individuals, groups and organisations, to "predict'" what behavioural responses will be elicited by various managerial actions and finally to use this understanding and these predictions to achieve "control".

Organisational behaviour can then be defined as: "The study of human behaviour in organisational settings, the interface between human behaviour and the organisational context, and the organisation itself." The above definition has three parts – the individual behaviour, the organisation and the interface between the two. Each individual brings to an organisation a unique set of beliefs, values, attitudes and other personal characteristics and these characteristics of all individuals must interact with each other in order to create organisational settings. The organisational behaviour is specifically concerned with work-related behaviour, which takes place in organisations.

In addition to understanding; the on-going behavioural processes involved, in their own jobs, managers must understand the basic human element of their work. Organisational behaviour offers three major ways of understanding this context; people as organisations, people as resources and people as people.

Above all, organisations are people; and without people there would be no organisations. Thus, if managers are to understand the organisations in which they work, they must first understand the people who make up the organisations.

As resources, people are one of the organisation's most valuable assets. People create the organisation, guide and direct its course, and vitalise and revitalise it. People make the decisions, solve the problems, and answer the questions. As managers increasingly recognise the value of potential contributions by their employees, it will become more and more important for managers and employees to grasp the complexities of organisational behaviour.

Finally, there are people as people – an argument derived from the simple notion of humanistic management. People spend a large part of their lives in organisational settings, mostly as employees. They have a right to expect something in return beyond wages and benefits. They have a right to expect satisfaction and to learn new skills. An understanding of organisational behaviour can help the manager better appreciate the variety of individual needs and expectations.

Fundamental Concepts of Organisational Behaviour

Organisational behaviour starts with the following six fundamental concepts revolving around the nature of people and organisations:

The nature of people

- Individual differences
- A whole person
- Motivated behaviour
- Value of the person

The nature of organisation

- Social system
- Mutual interest

The Nature of People

1. **Individual Differences.** Individuals are different in their physical and mental traits. They are different not only in the physical appearance such as sex, age, height, weight, complexion and so on but also different in their psychological trait such as intelligence, attitude, motivation and perception. This belief that each person is different from all others is typically called the 'Law of Individual Differences'. Individual differences mean that the management has to treat them differently to get the best out of them.
2. **A Whole Person.** Though the organisation may feel that they are employing only the individual's skill or intelligence, in fact, they employ the 'whole person'. This means that individual does not have only the skill and intelligence but he has a personal life, needs and desires as well. In other words, his personal life cannot be separated from his work life since people function as total human beings.

   When management practices organisational behaviour, it is not only trying to develop a better employee but it also wants to develop a 'better person' in terms of all round growth and development. The benefit will extend beyond the firm into the larger society in which each employee lives.
3. **Motivated behaviour.** It is the urge of the individual to satisfy a particular need that motivates him to do an act. The motivation could be positive or negative. Motivation is essential for the

proper functioning of organisations. The organisation can show to its employees how certain actions will increase their need fulfilment.

4. **Value of the Person.** It is more an ethical philosophy. It stresses that people are to be treated with respect and dignity. Every job, however simple, entitles the people who do it to proper respect and recognition of their unique aspirations and abilities. Since organisational behaviour involves people, ethical philosophy is involved in one way or the other.

Elements of Organisational Behaviour

The key elements in the organisational behaviour are people, structure, technology and the environment in which the organisation operates.

- **People.** People make up the internal and social system of the organisation. They consist of individuals and groups. The groups may be big or small; formal or informal; official or unofficial. Groups are dynamic and they work in the organisation to achieve their objectives.
- **Structure.** Structure defines the formal relationships of the people in organisations. Different people in the organisation are performing different type of jobs and they need to be (elated in some structural way so that their work can be effectively co-ordinated.

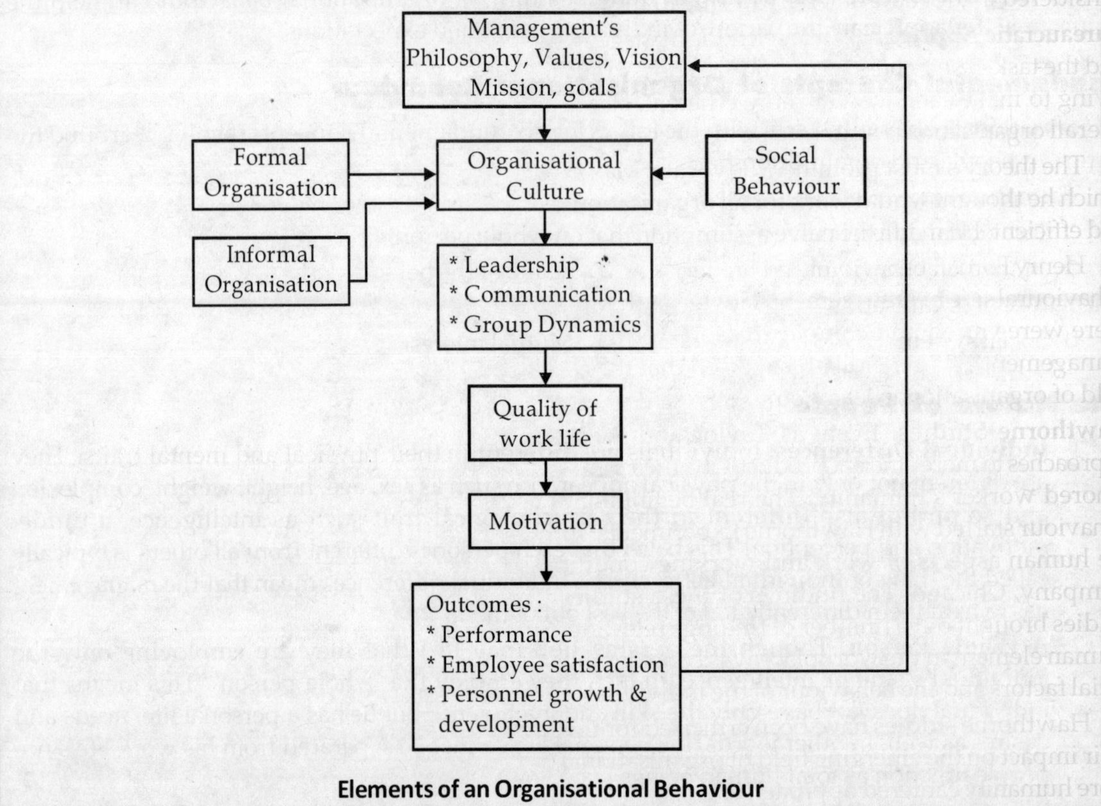

Elements of an Organisational Behaviour

- **Technology.** Technology such as machines and work processes provide the resources with which people work and affects the tasks that they perform. The technology used has a significant influence on working relationships. It allows people to do more and work better but it also restricts' people in various ways.

- **Environment.** All organisations operate within an external environment. It is the part of a larger system that contains many other elements such as government, family and other organisations. All of these mutually influence each other in a complex system that creates a context for a group of people.

Evolution or Historical Background for Modern Organisational Behaviour

Scientific Management Approach. Scientific management approach was developed by F.W. Taylor at the beginning of the 20th century. This theory supported the use of certain steps in scientifically studying each element of a job, selecting and training the best workers for the job arid making sure that the workers follow the prescribed method of doing the job. It provided a scientific rationale for job specialisation and mass production. His assumption was that employees are motivated largely by money. To increase the output, Taylor advised managers to pay monetary incentives to efficient workers.

Yet, his theory was criticised by many employers and workers. Workers objected to the pressure of work as being harder and faster. Critics worried that the methods took the humanity out of labour, reducing workers to machines responding to management incentives. Therefore, Taylor's view is now considered inadequate and narrow due to the points given by the critics.

Bureaucratic Approach. While scientific management was focusing on the interaction between workers and the task, researchers were studying how to structure the organisation more effectively. Instead of trying to make each worker more efficient, classical organisation theory sought the most effective overall organisational structure for workers and managers.

The theory's most prominent advocate, Max Weber, proposed a 'bureaucratic form' of structure, which he thought would work for all organisations. Weber's idea! Bureaucracy was , logical, rational and efficient. He made the naive assumption that one structure would work best for all organisations.

Henry Ford, Henry Fayol and Frederick W. Taylor, the early management pioneers, recognised the behavioural side of management. However, they did not emphasize the human dimensions. Although there were varied and complex reasons for the emerging importance of behavioural approach to management, it is generally recognised that the Hawthorne studies mark the historical roots for the field of organisational behaviour.

Hawthorne Studies. Even, as Taylor and Weber brought attention with their rational, logical approaches to more efficient productivity; their views were criticised on the ground that both approaches ignored worker's humanity. The real beginning of applied research in the area of organisational behaviour started with Hawthorne Experiments. In 1924, a group of professors began an enquiry into the human aspects of work and working conditions at the Hawthorne plant of Western Electric Company, Chicago. The findings of these studies were given a new name 'human relations' the studies brought out a number of findings relevant to understanding human behaviour at work. The Human element in the workplace was considerably more important. The workers are influenced by social factors and the behaviour of the individual worker is determined by the group.

Hawthorne studies have been criticised for their research methods and conclusions drawn. But their impact on the emerging field of organisational behaviour was dramatic. They helped usher in a more humanity cantered approach to work.

Importance of Organisational Behaviour

Organisational behaviour offers several ideas to management as to how human factor should be properly emphasised to achieve organisational objectives. Barnard has observed that an organisation is a conscious interaction of two or more people. This suggests that since an organisation is the interaction of persons, they should be given adequate importance in managing the organisation. Organisational behaviour provides opportunity to management to analyse human behaviour and prescribe means for shaping it to a particular direction.

Understanding Human Behaviour Organisational behaviour provides under-standing the human behaviour in all directions in which the human beings interact. Thus, organisational behaviour can be understood at the individual level, interpersonal level, group level and inter-group level.

Main Features of Organisational Behaviour

- OB provides a good map to our lives in organisations.
- OB uses scientific research to understand and make organisation life, as it helps to predict what people will do under conditions.
- It helps to influence organisational events – to understand and predict events.
- If helps individual understand herself / himself in better fashion.
- It helps manager to manage human resources effectively e.g. motivation.
- If helps organisations for maintaining cordial industrial relations.
- It is also useful in the field marketing.

Organisational behaviour helps to analyse 'why' and 'how' an individual behaves in a particular way. Human behaviour is a complex phenomenon and is affected by a large number of factors including the psychological, social and cultural implications. Organisational behaviour integrates these factors to provide simplicity in understanding the human behaviour.

1. **Interpersonal Level.** Human behaviour can be understood at the level of interpersonal interaction. Organisational behaviour provides means for understanding the interpersonal relationships in an organisation. Analysis of reciprocal relationships, role analysis and transactional analysis are some of the common methods, which provide such understanding.
2. **Group Level.** Though people interpret anything at their individual level, they are often modified by group pressures, which then become a force in shaping human behaviour, Thus, individuals should be studied in groups also. Research in group dynamics has contributed vitally to organisational behaviour and shows how a group behaves in its norms, cohesion, goals, procedures, communication pattern and leadership. These research results are advancing managerial knowledge of understanding group behaviour, which is very important for organisational morale and productivity.
3. **Inter-group Level.** The organisation is made up of many groups that develop complex relationships to build their process and substance. Understanding the effect of group relationships is important for managers in today's organisation. Inter-group relationship may be in the form of co-operation or competition.

   The co-operative relationships help the organisation in achieving its objectives. Organisational behaviour provides means to understand and achieve co-operative group relationships through interaction, rotation of members among groups, avoidance of win-lose situation and focussing on total group objectives.
4. **Controlling and Directing Behaviour.** After understanding the mechanism of human behaviour, managers are required to control and direct the behaviour so that it conforms to the standards required for achieving the organisational objectives. Thus, managers are required to control and direct the behaviour at all levels of individual interaction. Therefore, organisational behaviour helps managers in controlling and directing in different areas such as use of power and sanction, leadership, communication and building organisational climate favourable for better interaction.

5. **Use of Power and Sanction.** The behaviours can be controlled and directed by the use of power and sanction, which are formally defined by the organisation. Power is referred to as the capacity of an individual to take certain action and may be utilised in many ways. Organisational behaviour explains how various means of power and sanction can be utilised so that both organisational and individual objectives are achieved simultaneously.
6. **Leadership.** Organisational behaviour brings new insights and understanding to the practice and theory of leadership. It identifies various leadership styles available to a manager and analyses which style is more appropriate in a given situation. Thus, managers can adopt styles keeping in view the various dimensions of organisations, individuals and situations.
7. **Communication.** Communication helps people to come in contact with each other. To achieve organisational objectives, the communication must be effective. The communication process and its work in inter-personal dynamics have been evaluated by organisational behaviour.
8. **Organisational Climate.** Organisational climate refers to the total organisational situations affecting human behaviour. Organisational climate takes a system perspective that affect human behaviour. Besides improving the satisfactory working conditions and adequate compensation, organisational climate includes creation of an atmosphere of effective supervision; the opportunity for the realisation of personal goals, congenial relations with others at the work place and a sense of accomplishment.
9. **Organisational Adaptation.** Organisations, as dynamic entities are characterised by pervasive changes. Organisations have to adapt themselves to the environmental changes by making suitable, internal arrangements such as convincing employees who normally have the tendency of resisting any changes.

The Roles, in the Context of Organisational Behaviour, are as follows:

Managers perform four major functions such as planning, organising, directing and controlling. In addition to these functions there are ten managerial roles, which can be defined as organised set of behaviours identified with the position. These roles are developed by Henry Mintzberg in 1960s after a careful study of executives at work. All these roles, in one form or other deal with people and their behaviour. These ten managerial roles are divided into three categories. The first category called the interpersonal roles arises directly from the manager's position and the formal authority given to him. The second category, the informational role arises as a direct result of the interpersonal roles and these two categories give rise to the third category called decisional roles.

1. **Interpersonal Roles.** In every organisation managers spend a considerable amount of time in interacting with other people both within their own organisations as well as outside. These people include peers, subordinates, superiors, suppliers, customers, government officials and community leaders. All these interactions require an understanding of interpersonal behaviour. Studies show that interacting with people takes up nearly 80% of a manager's time. These interactions involve the following three major interpersonal roles:
   - *Figure/lead Role.* Managers act as symbolic figureheads performing social or legal obligations. These duties include greeting visitors, signing legal documents, taking important customers to lunch, attending a subordinate's wedding and speaking at functions in schools and churches. All these, primarily, are duties of a ceremonial nature but are important for the smooth functioning of an organisation.
   - *Leadership Role.* The influence of the manager is most clearly seen in the leadership role as a leader of a unit or an organisation. Since he is responsible for the activities of his subordinates therefore he must lead and coordinate their activities in meeting task-related goals and motivate them to perform better. He must be an ideal leader so that his subordinates follow his directions and guidelines with respect and dedication.

- *Liaison Role.* The managers must maintain a network of outside contacts. In addition, they need to have a constant contact with their own subordinates, peers and superiors in order to assess the external environment of competition, social changes or changes in governmental rules and regulations. In this role, the managers build up their own external information system. This can be achieved by attending meetings and professional conferences, personal phone calls, trade journals and informal personal contacts with outside agencies.

2. **Informational Roles.** A manager, by virtue of his interpersonal contacts, emerges as a source of information about a variety of issues concerning an organisation. In this capacity of information processing, a manager executes the following three roles.
   - *Monitor Role.* The managers are constantly monitoring and scanning their internal and external environment, collecting and studying information regarding their organisation. This can be done by reading reports and periodicals, interrogating their liaison contacts and through gossip, hearsay and speculation.
   - *Information Disseminator Role.* The managers must transmit the information regarding changes in policies or other matters to their subordinates, their peers and to other members of an organisation. This can be done through memos, phone calls, individual meetings and group meetings.
   - *Spokesman Role.* A manager has to be a spokesman for his unit and represent his unit in either sending relevant information to people outside his unit or making some demands on behalf of his unit.

3. **Decisional Roles.** A manager must make decisions and solve organisational problems on the basis of the environmental information received. In that respect, a manager plays four important roles.
   - **Entrepreneur Role.** Managers, as entrepreneurs are constantly involved in improving their units and facing the dynamic technological challenges. They are constantly on the lookout for new ideas for product improvement or product addition. They initiate feasibility studies, arrange capital for new products and ask for suggestions from the employees to improve organisation. This can be achieved through suggestion boxes, holding strategy meetings with project managers and R&D personnel.
   - **Conflict Handling Role.** The managers are constantly involved as judge in solving conflicts among the employees and between employees and management. Managers must anticipate such problems and take preventive action and take corrective action once the problem arises. These problems may involve labour disputes, customer complaints, employee grievances, machine breakdowns, cash flow shortages and interpersonal conflicts.
   - **Resource Allocation Role.** The managers establish priorities among various projects or programs and make budgetary allocations to different activities of an organisation based on these priorities.
   - **Negotiator Role.** The managers in their negotiator role represent their organisation in negotiating deals and agreements within and outside of an organisation. They negotiate contracts with the unions. Sales managers may negotiate prices with prime customers. Purchasing managers may negotiate prices with vendors.

SCOPE OF ORGANISATIONAL BEHAVIOUR

The three internal organisational elements viz., people, technology and structure and the fourth element, i.e., external social systems may be taken as the scope of O.B.

1. People

The people constitute the internal social system of the organisation. They consist of individuals and groups. Groups may be large or small, formal or informal, official or unofficial. They are dynamic. They form, change and disband. Human organisation changes everyday. Today, it is not the same as it was yesterday. It may change further in the coming days. People are living, thinking and feeling being who created the organisation and try to achieve the objectives and goals. Thus, organisations exist to serve the people and not the people exist to serve the organisation.

2. Structure

Structure defines the sole relationship of people in an organisation. Different people in an organisation are given different roles and they have certain relationship with others. It leads to division of labour so that people can perform their duties or work to accomplish the organisational goal. Thus, everybody cannot be an accountant or a clerk. Work is complex and different duties are to be performed by different people. Some may be accountant, others may be managers, clerks, peons or workers. All are so related to each other to accomplish the goal in a co-ordinated manner. Thus, structure relates to power and duties. One has the authority and others have a duty to obey him.

3. Technology

Technology imparts the physical and economic conditions within which people work. With their bare hands people can do nothing so they are given assistance of buildings, machines, tools, processes and resources. The nature of technology depends very much on the nature of the organisation and influences the work or working conditions. Thus, technology brings effectiveness and at the same restricts people in various ways.

4. Social System

Social system provides external environment which the organisation operates. A single organisation cannot exist also. It is a part of the whole. One organisation cannot give everything and therefore, there are many other organisations. All these organisations influence each other. It influences the attitudes of people, their working conditions and above all provides competition for resources and power.

O.B. is the study of human behaviour at work in organisations. Accordingly, the scope of O.B. includes the study of individuals, groups and organisation/structure. Let us briefly reflect on what aspects each of these three cover.

Individuals

Organisations are the associations of individuals. Individuals differ in many respects. The study of individuals, therefore, includes aspects such as personality, perception, attitudes, values, job satisfaction, learning and motivation.

Groups of Individuals

Groups include aspects such as group dynamics, group conflicts, communication, leadership, power and politics and the like.

PERSONALITY

The word personality is derived from a Greek word *"persona"* which means "to speak through." Personality is the combination of characteristics or qualities that forms a person's unique identity. It signifies the role which a person plays in public. Every individual has a unique, personal and major determinant of his behaviour that defines his/her personality.

Personality trait is basically influenced by two major features:

- Inherited characteristics
- Learned characteristics

Inherited Characteristics

The features an individual acquires from their parents or forefathers, in other words the gifted features an individual possesses by birth is considered as inherited characteristics. It consists of the following features :

- Colour of a person's eye
- Religion/Race of a person
- Shape of the nose
- Shape of earlobes

Learned Characteristics

Nobody learns everything by birth. First, our school is our home, then our society, followed by educational institutes. The characteristics an individual acquires by observing, practicing, and learning from others and the surroundings is known as learned characteristics.

Learned characteristics includes the following features :

- **Perception.** Result of different senses like feeling, hearing etc.
- **Values.** Influences perception of a situation, decision making process.
- **Personality.** Patterns of thinking, feeling, understanding and behaving.
- **Attitude.** Positive or negative attitude like expressing one's thought.

Traits of Personality

Personality traits are the enduring features that define an individual's behaviour. A personality trait is a unique feature in an individual. Psychologists resolved that there are five major personality traits and every individual can be categorised into at least one of them. These five personality traits are:

- Extrovert
- Neurotic
- Open
- Agreeable
- Conscientious

Major Personality Attributes

Following are the five major personality attributes that influence OB :

Locus of Control

Locus of control is the center of control of an individual's code of conduct. People can be grouped into two categories i.e., internals and externals respectively.

People who consider themselves as the masters of their own fates are known as internals, while, those who affirm that their lives are controlled by outside forces known as externals.

Before making any decision, internals actively search for information, they are achievement driven, and want to command their environment. Thus, internals do well on jobs that craves complex information processing, taking initiative and independent action.

Externals, on the other hand, are more compliant, more willing to follow instructions, so, they do well in structured, routine jobs.

Machiavellianism

Machiavellianism is being practical, emotionally distant, and believing that ends justify means.

Machiavellians are always wanting to win and are great persuaders. Here are the significant features of a high-mach individuals:

- High-Machs prefer precise interactions rather than beating about the bush.
- High-Machs tend to improvise; they do not necessarily abide by rules and regulations all the time.
- High-Machs get distracted by emotional details that are irrelevant to the outcome of a project.

Self-esteem

It is the extent up to which people either like or dislike themselves. Self-Esteem is directly related to the expectations of success and on-the-job satisfaction.

Individuals with high self-esteem think that they have what it takes to succeed. So, they take more challenges while selecting a job.

On the other hand, individuals with low self-esteem are more susceptible to external distractions. So, they are more likely to seek the approval of others and to adapt the beliefs and behaviours of those they respect.

Self-monitoring

Self-monitoring is the capability of regulating one's behaviour according to social situations. Individuals with high self-monitoring skill easily adjust their behaviour according to external, situational factors. Their impulsive talents allow them to present public personae which are completely different from their private personalities.

However, people with low self-monitoring skills cannot cover themselves. Regardless of any situation, they are always themselves. They have an attitude of, "what you see is what you get."

Risk Taking

Generally, managers are reluctant on taking risks. However, individual risk-taking inclination affects the bulk of information required by the managers and how long it takes them to make decisions.

Thus, it is very important to recognise these differences and align risk-taking propensity with precise job demands that can make sense.

Theories of Personality

A theory is a simple model of reality that helps us understand, explain, predict and deal with reality. We have some theories that explain an individual's personality.

Sigmund Freud's Psychoanalytic Theory

This theory is based on the belief that man is encouraged more by unforeseen forces than the conscious and logical thought. Freud believed that most of the things in life are not present at the conscious level but they are present at an unconscious level.

The features of Freud's theory include three attributes : Id, Ego, and Superego.

- **Id.** It defines the innate component of personality. It is the impulsive and unconscious part of mind that seeks immediate satisfaction. *Example.* A hungry baby cries till he/she is fed.

- **Ego.** It is derived from Id and assists in dealing with the external world. It also helps in translating the inner needs into expressions. It deals with practical and rational thinking process. *Example.* We have a fight with our friend and expect the friend to talk first, even though both of us want to talk.
- **Superego.** It is different from ego and is partially unconscious. It includes the traditional values of society as interpreted by our parents. It also helps in the integral vision of punishment. *Example.* Ram came late today so he is grounded for a week.

Erikson's Theory

This theory states that personality is groomed throughout lifetime. He presents eight distinct stages each with two possible outcomes. Successful completion of each stage leads to a healthy personality. These stages are:

- **Infancy.** It is the period between 0-1 years of age. In this stage, children learn the ability to trust others depending on their caregivers. Unsuccessful completion in this stage results in anxiety and insecurity. *Example.* Children of this age are more comfortable with those faces they see more often and not with strangers.
- **Early Childhood.** It is the period between 1-3 years of age. In this stage, children learn to be independent. If given support, they become more confident else they become dependent over others. *Example.* Children in this age are taught how to walk, how to talk etc.
- **Play Age.** It is the period between 3-6 years of age. In this stage, children assert themselves frequently. The failure leads to development of a sense of guilt among them. *Example.* Children in this age group, need to be taught how to behave and should be taught to be focused.
- **School Age.** It is the period between 6 years of age till puberty. In this stage, children become more innovative. They feel confident and want to achieve their goals. If not encouraged they may feel inferior. *Example.* Teenagers should be protected and parents need to understand them and should handle them patiently.
- **Adolescence.** This stage is a transformation from childhood to adulthood. Here children find their own identity and should be guided and supported in order to help them choose the right direction. *Example.* Decision such as which stream to choose science or commerce etc. happens during this stage.
- **Young Childhood.** This stage is also known as young adulthood. Here, they begin to open up and become more intimate with others. *Example.* Making close friends.
- **Adulthood.** In this stage, they focus on establishing career and settling down with relationships that are important. *Example.* Applying for jobs.
- **Mature Adulthood.** In this stage, a person is old and thus in this stage the productivity slows down. *Example.* Taking care of the family.

Sheldon's Physiognomy Theory

This theory was proposed by William Sheldon. He presents personalities by classifying individuals into convenient categories based on their body shapes. They are:

Endomorphs

In this category, the body is soft and spherical. People with this kind of personality love comfort, eat a lot, like to be around people and desire affection. Some common endomorph features are large amount of fat accumulation, insatiable appetite, larger frame etc.

Some endomorph personalities are John Goodman, Jack Black etc.

Mesomorphs

In this category, the body is hard and rectangular physique. People with this kind of personality like to take risk, are courageous and have power. Some common mesomorph features are wide shoulders, small waist, low body fat.

Some mesomorph personalities are Jennifer Garner, Tina Turner etc.

Ectomorphs

In this category, the body is fragile, flat chest and delicate body. People with this kind of personality are anxious, ambitious and dedicated. Some common ectomorph features are narrow frame, low body fat, etc.

Some notable ectomorph personalities are Brad Pitt, Bruce Lee etc.

PERCEPTION

Perception is an intellectual process of transforming sensory stimuli to meaningful information. It is the process of interpreting something that we see or hear in our mind and use it later to judge and give a verdict on a situation, person, group etc.

It can be divided into six types:

- **Of sound.** The ability to receive sound by identifying vibrations.
- **Of speech.** The competence of interpreting and understanding the sounds of language heard.
- **Touch.** Identifying objects through patterns of its surface by touching it.
- **Taste.** The ability to receive flavor of substances by tasting it through sensory organs known as taste buds.
- **Other senses.** They approve perception through body, like balance, acceleration, pain, time, sensation felt in throat and lungs etc.
- **Of the social world.** It permits people to understand other individuals and groups of their social world. ***Example.*** Priya goes to a restaurant and likes their customer service, so she will perceive that it is a good place to hang out and will recommend it to her friends, who may or may not like it. Priya's perception about the restaurant is good.

Perceptual Process

Perceptual process are the different stages of perception we go through. The different stages are:

Receiving

Receiving is the first and most important stage in the process of perception. It is the initial stage in which a person collects all information and receives the information through the sense organs.

Selecting

Selecting is the second stage in the process. Here a person doesn't receive the data randomly but selectively. A person selects some information out of all in accordance with his interest or needs. The selection of data is dominated by various external and internal factors.

- **External factors.** The factors that influence the perception of an individual externally are intensity, size, contrast, movement, repetition, familiarity, and novelty.
- **Internal factors.** The factors that influence the perception of an individual internally are psychological requirements, learning, background, experience, self-acceptance, and interest.

Organising

Keeping things in order or say in a synchronised way is organising. In order to make sense of the data received, it is important to organise them.

We can organise the data by:

- Grouping them on the basis of their similarity, proximity, closure, continuity.
- Establishing a figure ground is the basic process in perception. Here by figure we mean what is kept as main focus and by ground we mean background stimuli, which are not given attention.
- Perceptual constancy that is the tendency to stabilise perception so that contextual changes don't affect them.

Interpreting

Finally, we have the process of interpreting which means forming an idea about a particular object depending upon the need or interest. Interpretation means that the information we have sensed and organised, is finally given a meaning by turning it into something that can be categorised. It includes stereotyping, halo effect etc.

Importance of Perception in OB

We need to understand what the role of perception in an organisation is. It is very important in establishing different role of perceptions like:

- Understanding the tasks to be performed.
- Understanding associated importance of tasks allotted.
- Understanding preferred behaviour to complete respective tasks.
- Clarifying role perceptions.

For example, every member in a group has to be clear regarding the role allotted to them. Programmer writes the code, tester checks it, etc.

LEARNING

Learning can be defined as the permanent change in behaviour due to direct and indirect experience. It means change in behaviour, attitude due to education and training, practice and experience. It is completed by acquisition of knowledge and skills, which are relatively permanent.

Nature of Learning

Nature of learning means the characteristic features of learning. Learning involves change; it may or may not guarantee improvement. It should be permanent in nature, that is learning is for lifelong.

The change in behaviour is the result of experience, practice and training. Learning is reflected through behaviour.

Factors Affecting Learning

Learning is based upon some key factors that decide what changes will be caused by this experience. The key elements or the major factors that affect learning are motivation, practice, environment, and mental group.

Coming back to these factors let us have a look on these factors:

- **Motivation.** The encouragement, the support one gets to complete a task, to achieve a goal is known as motivation. It is a very important aspect of learning as it acts gives us a positive energy to complete a task. *Example.* The coach motivated the players to win the match.

- **Practice.** We all know that "Practice makes us perfect". In order to be a perfectionist or at least complete the task, it is very important to practice what we have learnt. *Example.* We can be a programmer only when we execute the codes we have written.
- **Environment.** We learn from our surroundings, we learn from the people around us. They are of two types of environment – internal and external. *Example.* A child when at home learns from the family which is an internal environment, but when sent to school it is an external environment.
- **Mental group.** It describes our thinking by the group of people we chose to hang out with. In simple words, we make a group of those people with whom we connect. It can be for a social cause where people with the same mentality work in the same direction. *Example.* A group of readers, travelers, etc.

These are the main factors that influence what a person learns, these are the root level for our behaviour and everything we do is connected to what we learn.

How Learning Occurs?

Learning can be understood clearly with the help of some theories that will explain our behaviour. Some of the remarkable theories are:

1. Classical Conditioning Theory

The classical conditioning occurs when a conditioned stimulus is coupled with an unconditioned stimulus. Usually, the conditioned stimulus (CS) is an impartial stimulus like the sound of a tuning fork, the unconditioned stimulus (US) is biologically effective like the taste of food and the unconditioned response (UR) to the unconditioned stimulus is an unlearned reflex response like salivation or sweating.

After this coupling process is repeated (for example, some learning may already occur after a single coupling), an individual shows a conditioned response (CR) to the conditioned stimulus, when the conditioned stimulus is presented alone. The conditioned response is mostly similar to the unconditioned response, but unlike the unconditioned response, it must be acquired through experience and is nearly impermanent.

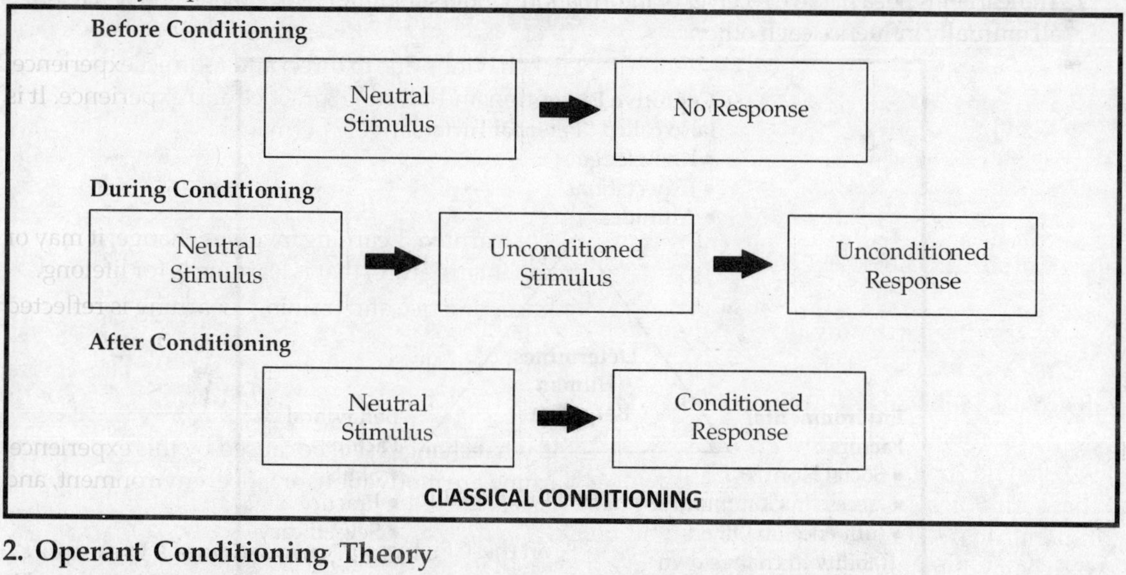

CLASSICAL CONDITIONING

2. Operant Conditioning Theory

Operant conditioning theory is also known as instrumental conditioning. This theory is a learning process in which behaviour is sensitive to, or controlled by its outcomes.

Let's take an example of a child. A child may learn to open a box to get the candy inside, or learn to avoid touching a hot stove. In comparison, the classical conditioning develops a relationship between a stimulus and a behaviour. The example can be further elaborated as the child may learn to salivate at the sight of candy, or to tremble at the sight of an angry parent.

In the 20th century, the study of animal learning was commanded by the analysis of these two sorts of learning, and they are still at the core of behaviour analysis.

OPERANT CONDITIONING

	Reinforcement **Increase Behaviour**	**Punishment** **Decrease Behaviour**
Positive Stimulus (Something added)	Positive Reinforcement Add something to increase behaviour	Positive Punishment Add something to decrease behaviour
Negative Stimulus (Something Removed)	Negative Reinforcement Remove something to increase behaviour	Negative Punishment Remove something to decrease behaviour

3. Social Learning Theory

The key assumptions of social learning theory are as follows:

- Learning is not exactly behavioural, instead it is a cognitive process that takes place in a social context.
- Learning can occur by observing a behaviour and by observing the outcomes of the behaviour (known as vicarious reinforcement).
- Learning includes observation, extraction of information from those observations, and making decisions regarding the performance of the behaviour (known as observational learning or modeling). Thus, learning can occur beyond an observable change in behaviour.
- Reinforcement plays an important role in learning but is not completely responsible for learning.
- The learner is not a passive receiver of information. Understanding, environment, and behaviour all mutually influence each other.

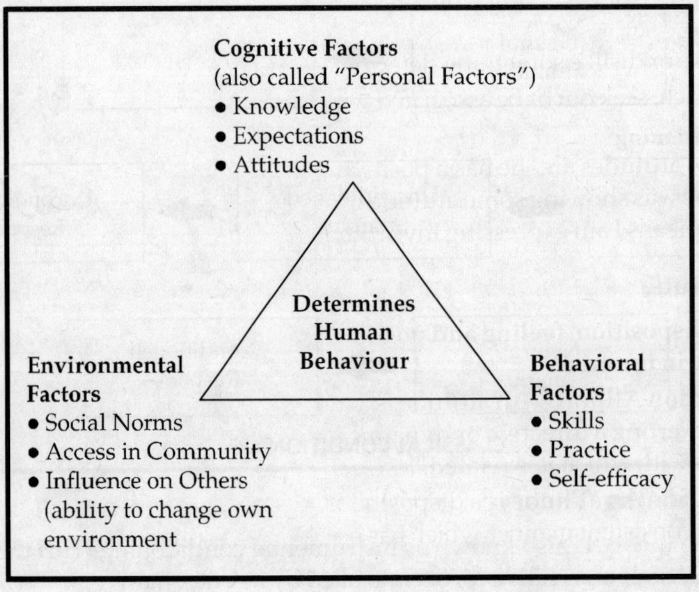

4. Cognitive Learning Theory

Cognition defines a person's ideas, thoughts, knowledge, interpretation, understanding about himself and environment.

This theory considers learning as the outcome of deliberate thinking on a problem or situation based upon known facts and responding in an objective and more oriented manner. It perceives that a person learns the meaning of various objects and events and also learns the response depending upon the meaning assigned to the stimuli.

This theory debates that the learner forms a cognitive structure in memory which stores organised information about the various events that occurs.

Learning & Organisational Behaviour

An individual's behaviour in an organisation is directly or indirectly affected by learning.

Example. Employee skill, manager's attitude are all learned.

Behaviour can be improved by following the listed tips:

- Reducing absenteeism by rewarding employees for their fair attendance.
- Improving employee discipline by dealing with employee's undesirable behaviour, drinking at workplace, stealing, coming late, etc. by taking appropriate actions like oral reprimands, written warnings and suspension.
- Developing training programs more often so as to grab the trainees' attention, provide required motivational properties etc.

ATTITUDE

An attitude is a positive; negative or mixed evaluation of an object that is expressed at some level of intensity.

It is an expression of a favorable or unfavorable evaluation of a person, place, thing or event. These are fundamental determinants of our perceptions of, and actions toward all aspects of our social environment.

Attitudes involve a complex organisation of evaluative beliefs, feelings, and tendencies toward certain actions.

How much we like or dislike something determines our behaviour towards that thing.

We tend to approach, seek out or be associated with things we like; we avoid, shun or reject things we do not like.

Some examples of attitudes are- he has a positive attitude about the changes, she is friendly and has a good attitude, he was showing some attitude during practice today, so the coach benched him, I like my friends that means I am expressing my attitudes towards my friends, etc.

Definition of Attitude

Attitude is manner, disposition, feeling and position with regard to a person or thing, tendency or orientation especially in the mind.

According to **Gordon Allport**, "An attitude is a mental and neural state of readiness, organised through experience, exerting a directive or dynamic influence upon the individual's response to all objects and situations with which it is related."

Frank Freeman said, "An attitude is a dispositional readiness to respond to certain institutions, persons or objects in a consistent manner which has been learned and has become one's typical mode of response."

Thurstone said, "An attitude denotes the sum total of man's inclinations and feelings, prejudice or bias, preconceived notions, ideas, fears, threats, and other any specific topic."

Anastasi defined attitude as, "A tendency to react favorably or unfavorably towards a designated class of stimuli, such as a national or racial group, a custom or an institution."

According to **N.L. Munn**, "Attitudes are learned predispositions towards aspects of our environment. They may be positively or negatively directed towards certain people, service or institution."

Characteristics of Attitude

Attitude can be described as a tendency to react positively or negatively to a person or circumstances.

Thus the two main elements of attitude are this tendency or predisposition and the direction of this predisposition.

It has been defined as a mental state of readiness; organise to through experience which exerts a directive or dynamic influence on the responses.

These can also be explicit and implicit.

Explicit attitudes are those that we are consciously aware of and that clearly influence our behaviours and beliefs. Implicit attitudes are unconscious, but still, have an effect on our beliefs and behaviours.

As said by psychologists Thomas which imposes limits as a level attitude trend is positive and negative, associated with the object of psychology.

Object psychology here include symbols, words, slogans, people, institutions, ideas and so on.

Characteristics of Attitude are:

1. Attitudes are the complex combination of things we tend to call personality, beliefs, values, behaviours, and motivations.
2. It can fall anywhere along a continuum from very favorable to very unfavorable.
3. All people, irrespective of their status or intelligence, hold attitudes.
4. An attitude exists in every person's mind. It helps to define our identity, guide our actions, and influence how we judge people.
5. Although the feeling and belief components of attitude are internal to a person, we can view a person's attitude from his or her resulting behaviour.
6. Attitude helps us define how we see situations, as well as define how we behave toward the situation or object.
7. It provides us with internal cognitions or beliefs and thoughts about people and objects.
8. It can also be explicit and implicit. Explicit attitude is those that we are consciously aware of an implicit attitude is unconscious, but still, have an effect on our behaviours.
9. Attitudes cause us to behave in a particular way toward an object or person.
10. An attitude is a summary of a person's past experience; thus, an attitude is grounded in direct experience predicts future behaviour more accurately.
11. It includes certain aspects of the personality as interests, appreciation and social conduct.
12. It indicates the sum total of a man's inclinations and feelings.
13. An attitude is a point of view, substantiated or otherwise, true or false which one holds towards an idea, object or person.
14. It has aspects such as direction, intensity, generality or specificity.
15. It refers to one's readiness for doing Work.

16. It may be positive or negative and may be affected by age, position, and education.

Attitude may be defined as a feeling or disposition to favor or to be against objects, persons, and situations.

It is a well-defined object of reference. It may be defined as 'an enduring predisposition or readiness to react or behave in a particular manner to a given object or situation, idea, material or person'.

It describes and evaluates the action with respect to an object or a situation, with each belief having a cognitive effect and behavioural components.

Each of these beliefs is a predisposition that results in some preferential response towards the object or the situation.

Actually, it is frequently used in describing people and explaining their behaviour.

For example:

"I like her attitude", "He has a good attitude" etc. Actually, it is characterised by the tendency to feel and behave in a particular way toward some object.

Components of Attitude

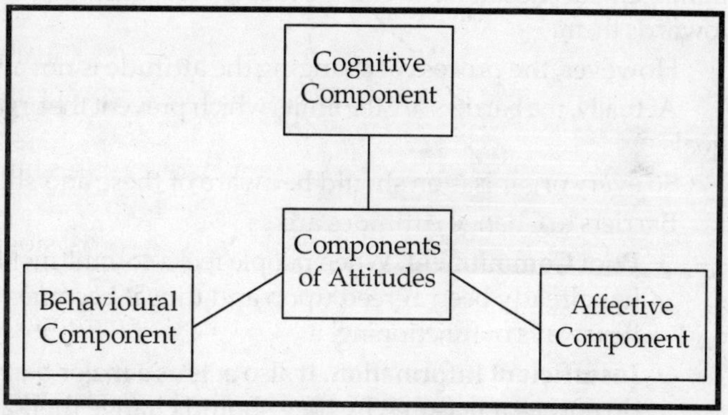

Attitudes are simply expressions of much we like or dislike various things. Attitudes represent our evaluations, preferences or rejections based on the information we receive.

Three components of attitude are: (1) Cognitive Component, (2) Affective Component and (3) Behavioural Component.

Factors Influencing Attitudes

By attitudes, we mean the beliefs, feelings, and action tendencies of an individual or group of individuals towards objects, ideas, and people.

Attitudes involve some knowledge of a situation.

However, the essential aspect, of the attitude is found in the fact that some characteristic feeling or emotion is experienced and, as we would accordingly expect, some definite tendency to action is associated.

Subjectively, then, the important factor is the feeling or emotion.

There are a number of different factors that can influence how and why attitudes form. These are:

- Social Factors.
- Family.
- Personal Experience.
- Educational and Religious Institutions.
- Economic Status and Occupations.
- Direct Instruction.
- Prejudices.
- Media.
- Physical Factors.

Types of Attitudes

Attitude is something that lies between emotions and thought processing. It may be positive or negative.

In organisational behaviour; three types of attitudes are :

1. Job Satisfaction,
2. Job Involvement, and
3. Organisational Commitment.

Functions of Attitudes

The most important function of an attitude can only be ascertained by considering it in relation to the person who holds it and the environment in which they operate.

Daniel Katz outlines four functions of attitude areas:

1. Adjustment Function.
2. Ego-Defensive Function.
3. Value-Expressive Function.
4. Knowledge Function.

Barriers to Change Attitudes

Employees' attitudes can be changed and sometimes it is in the best interests of management to try to do so.

For example, if employees believe that their employer does not look after their welfare, the management should try to change employees' attitude and help to develop a more positive attitude towards them.

However, the process of changing the attitude is not always easy.

Actually, the barriers are the limits which prevent the organisation from achieving its predetermined goals.

So every organisation should be aware of these and should take corrective actions.

Barriers to Change Attitudes are:

- **Prior Commitment.** When people feel a commitment towards a particular course of action that has already been agreed upon and thus it becomes difficult for them to change or accept the new ways of functioning.
- **Insufficient Information.** It also acts as a major barrier to change attitudes. Sometimes people do not see a reason why they should change their attitude due to unavailability of adequate information.

  Sometimes people do not see a reason why they should change their attitude due to unavailability of adequate information.
- **Balance and Consistency.** Another obstacle to a change of attitude is the attitude theory of balance and consistency.

  That is human beings prefer their attitudes about people and things to be in line with their behaviours towards each other and objects.
- **Lack of Resources.** If plans become excessively ambitious, they can sometimes be obstructed by the lack of resources on the part of a company or organisation.

  So, in this case, if the organisation wants to change the attitude of the employees towards the new plan, sometimes it becomes impossible for the lack of resources to achieve this.
- **Improper Reward System.** Sometimes, an improper reward system acts as a barrier to change attitude.

  If an organisation places too much emphasis on short-term performance and results, managers may ignore longer-term issues as they set goals and formulate plans to achieve higher profits in the short term.

  If this reward system is introduced in the organisation, then the employees are not motivated to change their attitude.
- **Resistance to Change.** Another barrier is resistance to change.

Basically, change is a continuous process within and outside the organisation to achieve the set goal.

When the authority changes a plan of the organisation the employees have to change themselves. But some of them do not like this. If their attitude regarding the change of plan cannot be changed, the organisation will not be successful.

Ways of Changing Attitudes

Attitude can be changed if we differentiate negative attitude from a positive attitude.

A positive attitude can bring positive change in life, It is difficult to change attitudes but with some effort, it can be done.

The individual from a culturally deprived environment who holds an array of hostile attitudes may change often he is given opportunities for education.

A person from a privileged subculture, who has always held to a democratic attitude, may become negative towards some group because of one unfortunate experience.

Well established attitudes tend to be resistant to change, but others may be more amenable to change.

Attitudes can be changed be a variety of ways.

Ways of Changing Attitude

- New information will help to change attitudes.
- Negative attitudes are mainly formed owing to insufficient information.
- Attitudes may change through direct experience.
- Another way in which attitudes can be changed is by resolving discrepancies between attitudes and behaviour.
- Change of attitude can come through the persuasion of friends or peers.
- Attitudes may change through legislation.
- Since a person's attitudes are anchored in his membership group and reference groups, one way to change the attitude is to modify one or the other.
- Fear can change attitude. If low levels of fear are used, people often ignore them.
- Changing the attitude differs with reference to the situation also.

Workplace and Attitudes

Taking this a step further, we can assemble some ideas of how these three components can impact the workplace.

The challenge in the workplace is that now these components are tied to work functions, policy, procedures and organisational structure, as well as the people and individuals present in the organisation.

For example, we could have thoughts or beliefs (cognitive) about managers in general, and those thoughts or beliefs could manifest themselves is not trusting a manager (effective), and thus we would never want to develop a close relationship with a manager (behavioural).

It is important to make the point here that these are attitudes – and yes, they can be wrong. Just because we have an attitude that does not mean it is correct. It is just how we feel about a person or situation.

Obviously not every manager is trustworthy, but if we let our negative attitudes dictate how we view and react to managers, we will never be able to see if some are really good people and can be trusted.

Certainly having a good relationship based on trust with the manager is a great thing to have in the workplace.

Attitude Surveys

The concept of an "attitude" comes from Social psychology.

The term "attitude" is defined as "a psychological tendency that is expressed by evaluating a particular entity with some degree of favor or disfavor"

It provides an understanding of how the employee perceives the organisation and workgroups.

The preceding review indicates that knowledge of employee attitudes can be helpful to managers in attempting to predict employee behaviour.

The most popular method is through the use of attitude surveys.

Often an **essential component of organisational training and development,** Employee Attitude surveys provide a picture of the organisation's needs.

These surveys often contain a series of multiple-choice items grouped along one or more dimensions of the organisation.

The surveys of this type provide an understanding of how the employee perceives the organisation.

Employee attitude surveys measure the employee's opinions on most of the aspects of a workplace including:

- Overall satisfaction.
- Corporate culture.
- Compensation.
- Recognition and rewards.
- Training.
- Safety concerns.
- Management/employee relations.
- Career development.
- Benefits.
- Working conditions.
- Staffing levels.
- Policies and procedures.

Organisations are increasingly interested in retaining right talents while targeting for new talents; measuring employees attitude provides an indication of how successful the organisation is in fostering a conducive environment which nurtures great attitude among employee's towards their job and company.

The usual measures of employee attitude involve an employee attitude survey with a set of statements or scale.

The employee is asked to evaluate each statement in terms of their perception of the performance of the organisation being measured.

Uses of Employee Attitude Survey

Employee opinion surveys are about improvement and providing the authority with the information they need to be successful.

The use of regular attitude surveys can alert management to potential problems and employees' intentions early so that action can be taken to prevent repercussions.

Uses for Employee Attitude Surveys include:

- Focusing on employee development programs.
- Enhancing management/employee relations.
- Training needs assessment.
- Evaluation of training.
- Organisational climate survey.
- Facilitating the development and organisational change.

- Getting employee feedback on the internal health of the organisation.
- Measuring the impact of current programs, policies, and procedures.
- Motivating employees and improve job satisfaction.
- Customer satisfaction survey.
- Increase employee retention.

Attitudes and Beliefs

An attitude is a relatively enduring organisation of beliefs, feelings, and behavioural tendencies towards socially significant objects, groups, events or symbols.

It is a learned predisposition to respond in a consistently favorable or unfavorable manner with respect to a given object.

It is an expression of evaluation toward a person, place, thing or event. It will always have a positive and negative element and have a tendency to behave in a certain way.

Attitudes are formed primarily based on underlying values and beliefs.

While attitude is the predisposition to act in a particular way towards an object or situation, opinion is the expression of the judgment of an individual about a particular set of facts.

It is an evaluation of the circumstances presented to an individual.

Beliefs are acquired through real experiences but the original experience related to a particular belief is mostly forgotten.

It affects the quality of our work and relationships because we experience what we believe and it is not based on reality. They are an important part of our identity.

They may be religious, cultural or moral.

Beliefs reflect who we are and how we live our lives. It is composed of multiple factors tending to family, society and the structure of life. It is the trust that something is true and good without any doubt.

It is an internal feeling that something is true, even though that belief may be unproven or irrational.

I believe that walking under a ladder brings bad luck.

Attitudes vs. Behaviour

Attitude refers to feelings, beliefs and behaviour predispositions directed towards people, groups, ideas or objects.

It influences the behaviour of the individuals. It decides how to act or behave in a particular situation.

Attitude is a kind of habit. It is the usual way of doing things.

Everything in an organisation will get better if the attitude of everyone gets better. Successes and failures in life depend upon the attitude of the individuals.

If attitudes are positive, then human relations will be positive. It is internal and very difficult to change.

Behaviour is the way a person responds to his attitude. This response is either positive or negative, depending on how that views his position.

For example, an employee who disagree?

With his supervisor may ignore office protocol.

In addition, an employee who dislikes another coworker or has little respect for a coworker may display this attitude by speaking harshly to this individual.

Behaviour can be influenced by a number of factors beyond attitude, including preconceptions about self and others, monetary factors, social influences, and convenience.

It is the actions or reactions of a person or animal in response to external or internal stimuli. It indicates the manner in which something functions or operates.

MOTIVATION

The term motivation is derived from the word 'motive', which means an active form of a desire, craving or need that must be satisfied. Or in other words motive is anything that initiates or sustains activity. Motivation is the key to organisational effectiveness. The manager in general has to get the work done through others. These 'others' are human resources who need to be motivated to attain organisational objectives.

According to **E.F.L. Brech**, "Motivation is a general inspirational process which gets the members of the team to pull their weight effectively, to give their loyalty to the group, to carry out properly the tasks that they have accepted and generally to play an effective part in the job that the group has undertaken. Motivation is the process of steering a person's inner derives and actions towards certain goals and committing his energies to achieve these goals. It involves a chain reaction starting with felt needs, resulting in motives which give rise to tension (unfulfilled desires) which causes action towards goals. It is the process of stimulating people to strive willingly towards the achievement of organisational goals.

Definition

- According to **Encyclopedia of Management,** "Motivation refers to the degree of readiness of an organism to pursue some designated goals and implies the determination of the nature and locus of force inducing a degree of readiness."
- According to **George R. Terry**, "Motivation is the desire within an individual that stimulates him or her to action."
- According to **Robert Dubin,** it is "the complex of forces starting and keeping a person at work in an organisation". Par. [M.P.S. II] Viteles defines motivation as "an unsatisfied need which creates a state of tension or disequilibrium, causing the individual to move in a goal directed pattern towards restoring a state of equilibrium, by satisfying the need."
- In the basis of above definitions, the following observations can be made regarding motivation:
- Motivation may be positive as well as negative. Positive motivation includes incentives, rewards and other benefits while negative motivation implies some punishment, fear, use of force etc.
- The motivation procedure contributes to and boosts up the morale of the employees. A high degree of motivation may lead to high morale.
- A highly motivated employee works more efficiently and his level of production tends to be higher than others.
- Motivation originates from the needs and wants of an individual. It is a tension of lacking something in his mind, which forces him to work more efficiently.
- Motivation is also a process of stimulating and channelising the energy of an individual for achieving set goals.
- Motivation is an inner psychological force, which activates and compels the person to behave in a particular manner.
- The motivation process is influenced by personality traits, learning abilities, perception and competence of an individual.
- Motivation also plays a crucial role in determining the level of performance. Highly motivated employees get higher satisfaction, which may lead to higher efficiency.

- Motivating force and its degree, may differ from individual to individual depending on his personality, needs, competence and other factors.
- The process of Motivation helps the manager in analysing and understanding human behaviour and finding but how an individual can be inspired to produce desirable working behaviour.

Nature of Motivation

1. Motivation is a Personal and Internal Feeling.
2. Motivation Produces Goal - directed Behaviour.
3. Motivation is a Continuous Process.
4. Motivation is Complex.
5. Motivation is System-oriented.
6. Motivation can be Eithcs Positive or Negative.
7. Motivation is Different from Job satisfaction.

Features of Motivation

The following are the features of motivation:

- It is an internal feeling and forces a person to action.
- It is a continuous activity.
- It varies from person to person and from time to time.
- It may be positive or negative.

Importance of Motivation

Motivation is an important part of managing process. A team of highly qualified and motivated employees is necessary for achieving objectives of an organisation because of the following reasons:

- Motivated employees make optimum use of available resources for achieving objectives.
- Motivation is directly related to the level of efficiency of employees.
- Motivated employees make full use of their energy and other abilities to raise the existing level of efficiency.
- Motivated employees make goal-directed efforts. They are more committed and cooperative for achieving organisational objectives.
- Motivated employees are more loyal and sincere to an organisation. These factors help to reduce absenteeism and labour turnover.
- Motivation is considered as a backbone of good industrial relations.
- Effectively motivated employees get more job satisfaction and possess high morale.
- Motivation also helps in improving the image of an organisation.

The motivation process begins with identification of individual needs. For example, when an employee feels underpaid then what, then he tries to fulfil his needs by asking for a raise or by working harder to earn a raise or by seeking a new job. He then chooses to pursue one or more of these options for instance, working harder while simultaneously looking for a job. If his hard work resulted in a pay rise, he probably feels satisfied and will continue to work hard. But if no raise has been provided he is likely to try another option. Since people have many different needs, the satisfaction of one need or set of needs is likely to give rise to the identification of other needs. Thus, the cycle of motivation is constantly repeated.

Understanding human motivation is crucial for managing people. Extensive research has been performed to find out what makes people work and how to motivate them. This includes managers, social scientists, behaviourists and psychologists. A number of theories have been developed, even though there is no universally acceptable motivation theory. Understanding these theories facilitates the managers to get a better insight into the human behaviour.

Need-based Theories to Motivation

Need-based theories try to answer the question, "what factor(s) motivate people to choose certain behaviours?" Some of the widely known need-based theories are as follows:

(a) Maslow's Hierarchy of Needs

Maslow Abraham proposed his theory in the 1940s. This theory, popularly known as the Hierarchy of Needs assumes that people are motivated to satisfy five levels of needs: physiological, security, belongingness, esteem and self-actualisation needs. The figure shows Maslow's hierarchy of needs.

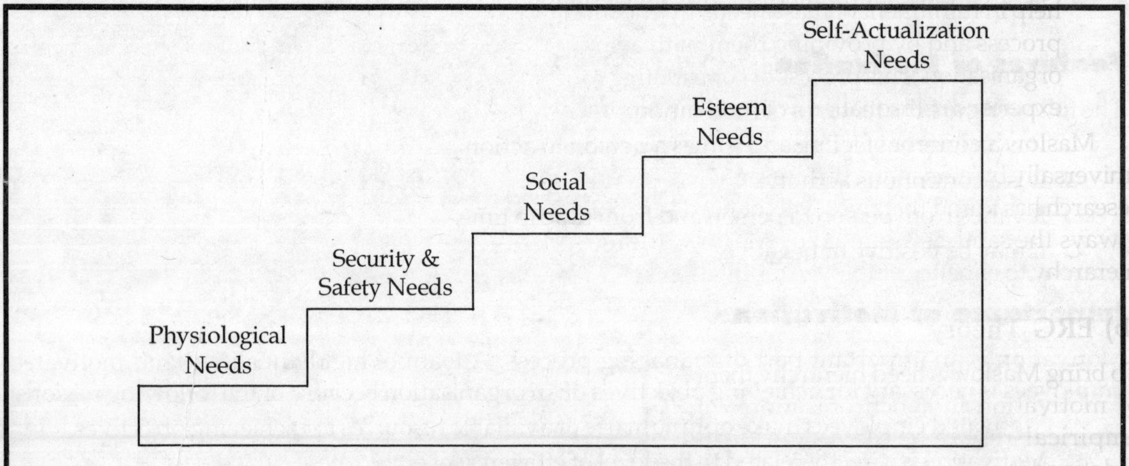

Maslow's Hierarchy of Needs

Maslow suggested that the five levels of needs are arranged in accordance with their importance, starting from the bottom of the hierarchy. An individual is motivated first and foremost to satisfy physiological needs. When these needs are satisfied, he is motivated and 'moves up' the hierarchy to satisfy security needs. This 'moving up' process continues until the individual reaches the self-actualisation level.

1. **Physiological needs** - represents the basic issues of survival such as food, sex, water and air. In organisational settings, most physiological needs are satisfied by adequate wages and by the work environment itself, which provides employees with rest rooms, adequate lighting, comfortable temperatures and ventilation.
2. **Security or safety needs** - refer to the requirements for a secure physical and emotional environment. Examples include the desire for adequate housing and clothing, the need to be free from worry about money and job security and the desire for safe working conditions. Security needs are satisfied for people in the work place by job continuity, a grievance resolving system and an adequate insurance and retirement benefit package.
3. **Belonging or social needs** - are related to the social aspect of human life. They include the need for love and affection and the need to be accepted by one's peers. For most people these needs are satisfied by a combination of family and community relationships and friendships on the job. Managers can help to ensure the satisfaction of these important needs by allowing social interaction and by making employees feel like part of a team or work group.

4. **Esteem needs** - actually comprise of two different sets of needs:
   The need for a positive self-image and self-respect.
   The need for recognition and respect from others.
   Organisations can help address esteem needs by providing a variety of external symbols of accomplishment such as job titles and spacious offices. At a more fundamental level, organisations can also help satisfy to esteem needs by providing employees with challenging job assignments that can induce a sense of accomplishment.
5. **Self-actualisation -** At the top of the hierarchy are those needs, which Maslow defines the self-actualisation needs. These needs involve realising one's potential for continued: growth and individual development. Since these needs are highly individualised and personal, self-actualisation needs are perhaps the most difficult for managers to address. Therefore, an employee should try to meet these needs on his own end. However, an organisation can help his employee by creating a climate for fulfillment of self-actualisation needs. For instance, an organisation can help in fulfillment of these needs by encouraging employee's participation in decision-making process and by providing them with an opportunity to learn new things about their jobs and organisation. This process of contributing to actual organisational performance helps employees experience personal growth and development associated with self-actualising.

Maslow's concept of the need hierarchy possesses a certain intuitive logic and has been accepted universally by managers. But research has revealed several shortcomings of the theory such as some research has found that five levels of needs are not always present and that the order of the levels is not always the same as assumed by Maslow. Moreover, it is difficult for organisations to use the need hierarchy to enhance employee motivation.

(b) ERG Theory

To bring Maslow's need hierarchy theory of motivation in synchronisation with empirical research, Clayton Alderfer redefined it in his own terms. His rework is called as ERG theory of motivation. He recategorised Maslow's hierarchy of needs into three simpler and broader classes of needs:

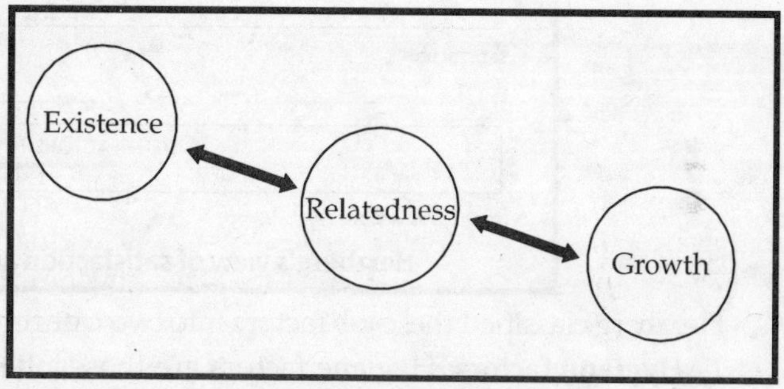

- **Existence needs.** These include need for basic material necessities. In short, it includes an individual's physiological and physical safety needs.
- **Relatedness needs.** These include the aspiration individual's have for maintaining significant interpersonal relationships (be it with family, peers or superiors), getting public fame and recognition. Maslow's social needs and external component of esteem needs fall under this class of need.
- **Growth needs.** These include need for self-development and personal growth and advancement. Maslow's self-actualisation needs and intrinsic component of esteem needs fall under this category of need.

The significance of the three classes of needs may vary for each individual.

Difference between Maslow Need Hierarchy Theory and Alderfer's ERG Theory

- ERG Theory states that at a given point of time, more than one need may be operational.

- ERG Theory also shows that if the fulfillment of a higher-level need is subdued, there is an increase in desire for satisfying a lower-level need.
- According to Maslow, an individual remains at a particular need level until that need is satisfied. While according to ERG theory, if a higher- level need aggravates, an individual may revert to increase the satisfaction of a lower- level need. This is called frustration- regression aspect of ERG theory. For instance when growth need aggravates, then an individual might be motivated to accomplish the relatedness need and if there are issues in accomplishing relatedness needs, then he might be motivated by the existence needs. Thus, frustration/ aggravation can result in regression to a lower-level need.
- While Maslow's need hierarchy theory is rigid as it assumes that the needs follow a specific and orderly hierarchy and unless a lower-level need is satisfied, an individual cannot proceed to the higher-level need; ERG Theory of motivation is very flexible as he perceived the needs as a range/ variety rather than perceiving them as a hierarchy. According to Alderfer, an individual can work on growth needs even if his existence or relatedness needs remain unsatisfied. Thus, he gives explanation to the issue of "starving artist" who can struggle for growth even if he is hungry.

(c) The Dual–Structure Approach to Motivation /Herzberg two Factors Theory of Motivation

In 1959, Frederick Herzberg, a behavioural scientist proposed a two-factor theory or the motivator-hygiene theory. According to Herzberg, there are some job factors that result in satisfaction while there are other job factors that prevent dissatisfaction. According to Herzberg, the opposite of "Satisfaction" is "No satisfaction" and the opposite of "Dissatisfaction" is "No Dissatisfaction".

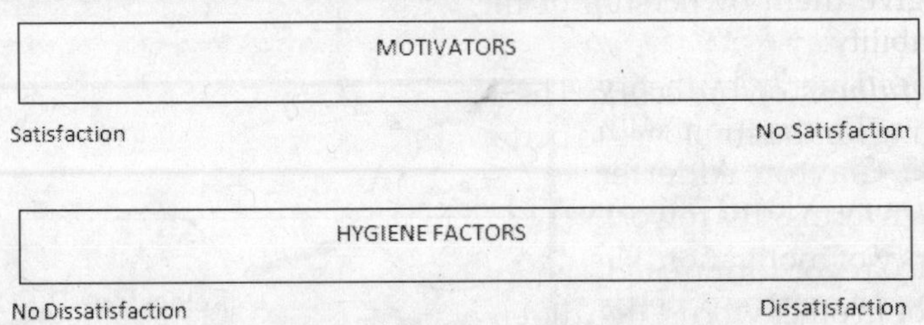

Herzberg's view of satisfaction and dissatisfaction.

Herzberg classified these job factors into two categories :

1. **Hygiene factors.** Hygiene factors are those job factors which are essential for existence of motivation at workplace. These do not lead to positive satisfaction for long-term. But if these factors are absent / if these factors are non-existent at workplace, then they lead to dissatisfaction. In other words, hygiene factors are those factors which when adequate / reasonable in a job, pacify the employees and do not make them dissatisfied. These factors are extrinsic to work. Hygiene factors are also called as **dissatisfies or maintenance factors** as they are required to avoid dissatisfaction. These factors describe the job environment / scenario. The hygiene factors symbolised the physiological needs which the individuals wanted and expected to be fulfilled. Hygiene factors include:
   - ***Pay.*** The pay or salary structure should be appropriate and reasonable. It must be equal and competitive to those in the same industry in the same domain.
   - ***Company Policies and administrative policies.*** The company policies should not be too rigid. They should be fair and clear. It should include flexible working hours, dress code, breaks, vacation, etc.

- *Fringe benefits.* The employees should be offered health care plans (mediclaim), benefits for the family members, employee help programmes, etc.
- *Physical Working conditions.* The working conditions should be safe, clean and hygienic. The work equipments should be updated and well-maintained.
- *Status.* The employees' status within the organisation should be familiar and retained.
- *Interpersonal relations.* The relationship of the employees with his peers, superiors and subordinates should be appropriate and acceptable. There should be no conflict or humiliation element present.
- *Job Security.* The organisation must provide job security to the employees.

2. **Motivational factors.** According to Herzberg, the hygiene factors cannot be regarded as motivators. The motivational factors yield positive satisfaction. These factors are inherent to work. These factors motivate the employees for a superior performance. These factors are called satisfiers. These are factors involved in performing the job. Employees find these factors intrinsically rewarding. The motivators symbolised the psychological needs that were perceived as an additional benefit. Motivational factors include:
   - *Recognition.* The employees should be praised and recognised for their accomplishments by the managers.
   - *Sense of achievement.* The employees must have a sense of achievement. This depends on the job. There must be a fruit of some sort in the job.
   - *Growth and promotional opportunities.* There must be growth and advancement opportunities in an organisation to motivate the employees to perform well.
   - *Responsibility.* The employees must hold themselves responsible for the work. The managers should give them ownership of the work. They should minimise control but retain accountability.
   - *Meaningfulness of the work.* The work itself should be meaningful, interesting and challenging for the employee to perform and to get motivated.

(d) McGregor Theory X and Theory Y

In 1960, Douglas McGregor formulated Theory X and Theory Y suggesting two aspects of human behaviour at work, or in other words, two different views of individuals (employees): one of which is negative, called as Theory X and the other is positive, so called as Theory Y. According to McGregor, the perception of managers on the nature of individuals is based on various assumptions.

Assumptions of Theory X

- An average employee intrinsically does not like work and tries to escape it whenever possible.
- Since the employee does not want to work, he must be persuaded, compelled, or warned with punishment so as to achieve organisational goals. A close supervision is required on part of managers. The managers adopt a more dictatorial style.
- Many employees rank job security on top, and they have little or no aspiration/ ambition.
- Employees generally dislike responsibilities.
- Employees resist change.
- An average employee needs formal direction.

Assumptions of Theory Y

- Employees can perceive their job as relaxing and normal. They exercise their physical and mental efforts in an inherent manner in their jobs.

- Employees may not require only threat, external control and coercion to work, but they can use self-direction and self-control if they are dedicated and sincere to achieve the organisational objectives.
- If the job is rewarding and satisfying, then it will result in employees' loyalty and commitment to organisation.
- An average employee can learn to admit and recognise the responsibility. In fact, he can even learn to obtain responsibility.
- The employees have skills and capabilities. Their logical capabilities should be fully utilised. In other words, the creativity, resourcefulness and innovative potentiality of the employees can be utilised to solve organisational problems.

Comparison between Theory X and Theory Y

Theory X	Theory Y
1. Inherent dislike for work.	1. Work is natural like rest or play.
2. Unambitious and prefer to be directed by others.	2. Ambitious and capable of directing their own behaviour.
3. Avoid responsibility	3. Accept and seek responsibility under proper conditions.
4. People lack self-motivation	4. People are self-motivated.
5. External control and close supervision required to achieve organisational objectives.	5. Self-direction and self-control.
6. Centralisation of authority and autocratic leadership.	6. Decentralisation and participation in decision making. Democratic leadership.

(e) McClelland's Need Theory of Motivation

David C. McClelland and his associate Atkinson have contributed to an understanding of motivation by identifying three types of basic motivating needs.

These needs have been classified as:

1. **Need for Power.** According to this theory the need for power, which might be defined as the desire to be influential in a group and to control one's environment is an important motivation factor. Research suggests that people with a strong need for power, are likely to be superior performers and occupy supervisory positions. Such types of individuals generally look for positions of leadership, they act effectively, are outspoken, have a stubborn character and exert authority.
2. **Need for Affiliation.** The need for affiliation means the desire for human companionship and acceptance. Those with a high need for affiliation often behave the way they think other people want them to, in an effort to maintain friendship. They prefer a job that entails a good deal of social interaction and offers opportunities to make friends. The principal characteristics of such peoples' traits are as follows:
   - Desire to like and be liked.
   - Enjoy company and friendship.
   - Prefer cooperative situation.
   - Excel in group task.
   - Star attraction in gathering.
   - Leadership qualities.

This need is closely associated with the "social-type" of personality, who are sociable, friendly, cooperative and understanding. Persons with high motivation for power and affiliation have better chances of becoming good managers.

3. **Need for Achievement.** People with a high need for achievement, always feel ambitious to be successful; are ever prepared to face challenging situations and set arduous goals for themselves. They are prone to take calculated risks; and possess a high sense of personal responsibility in getting jobs done. These people are concerned with their progress, and feel inclined to put in longer hours of work. Failures never dishearten them and they are always ready to put in their best efforts for excellent performance.

Process-based Theories to Motivation

The field of organisational behaviour has generally moved away from the needs theories of motivation. Needs theories are content-oriented - that is, they explain what the causes are leading to motivated behaviours. They do not explain why or how motivated behaviour occurs. These questions relate to behaviours or actions, goals and feelings of satisfaction. These concepts are addressed by various process-based theories to motivation.

Process-based theories to motivation are concerned with how motivation occurs. They focus on why people choose to enact certain behavioural options to fulfil their needs and how they evaluate their satisfaction after they have attained these goals. Two of the most useful process-based approaches to motivation are expectancy theory and equity theory.

(1) Expectancy Theory of Motivation

Expectancy theory of motivation was developed by: Victor Vroom. Basically, Vroom's expectancy theory views motivation as a process of governing choices. The expectancy theory tries to explain how and why people choose a particular behaviour over an alternative. The theory suggests that motivation depends on two things: how much an individual desires a particular goal and how likely he thinks he can get it. For instance, a person is looking for a job and reads an advertisement for a position of Marketing Executive with a starting salary of Rs. 3 lakh per year. Even though he might want the job, he probably does not apply because he is aware that there is little chance of getting it. Next he sees an advertisement is for Field Supervisor for a salary of Re. 1 lakh per year. In this case he realises that he can probably get the job, but still doesn't apply simply because he doesn't want it. Then he comes across another advertisement for a Management Trainee in a big organisation with a starting salary of Rs. 2 lakh per year. He chooses to apply for this job because he wants it and also thinks that he has a reasonable chance of getting it.

The expectancy theory rests on four assumptions:

- The theory assumes that behaviour is determined by a combination of forces in the individual and in the environment.
- It assumes that people make decisions about their own behaviour in organisations.
- It assumes that different people have different types of needs, desires and goals.
- It assumes that people make choices from among alternative plans of behaviour based on their perceptions of the extent to which a given behaviour will lead to desired outcomes.

The above model suggests that motivation leads to efforts and that effort, when combined with individual ability and environmental factors, result in performance. Performance, in turn, leads to various outcomes—each of which has an associated value called its 'valence'. According to this model, individuals develop some sense of these expectations before they exhibit motivated or non-motivated behaviour.

Effort-to-Performance Expectancy. The effort-to-performance expectancy refers to an individual's perception of the probability that effort will result in high performance. When an individual believes that effort will lead directly to high performance, expectancy is quite strong, that is close to 1.00. For instance, if one feels sure that studying hard for an examination (effort) will result in scoring high marks (performance), then his effort-to-performance expectancy is high, that is close to 1.0. When an individual believes that effort and performance are unrelated, the effort-to-performance expectancy is very weak, that is close to 0.0. Usually we are not sure about our expectations, so they fall somewhere between 0.0 and 1.0 with a moderate expectancy.

- **Performance-to-Outcome Expectancy.** The performance-to-outcome expectancy means an individual's perception of the probability that performance will result in a specific outcome. For example, an individual who believes that high performance will lead to a pay raise has a high performance-to-outcome expectancy, approaching to 1.00. An individual who believes that high performance may possibly lead to a pay raise has a moderate expectancy between 1.00 and 0. And an individual who believes that performance has no relationship to rewards has a low performance-to-outcome expectancy that is close to 0.
- **Outcomes and Valences.** Expectancy theory recognises that an individual may experience a variety of outcomes as a consequence, of behaviour in an organisational environment. A high performer, for example, may get big pay raises, fast promotions and praise from the boss. However, he may also be subject to a lot of stress and incur resentment from co-workers. Each of these outcomes has an associated value or valence that is an index of how much an individual desires a particular outcome. If an individual wants an outcome, its valence is positive. If an individual does not want an outcome, its valence is negative. If an individual is indifferent to an outcome, its valence is zero. It is this advantage of expectancy theory that goes beyond the need-based approaches to motivation.

Thus, for motivated behaviour to occur on the part of any individual, three conditions must be met, which are as follows:

- First, the effort-to-performance expectancy must be greater than zero.
- Second, the performance-to-outcome expectancy must also be greater than zero.
- Third, the sum of the valences for all relevant outcomes must be greater than zero.

Expectancy theory maintains that when all of these conditions are met, the individual is motivated to expand effort. The expectancy theory also has several other important practical implications, which managers should keep in mind. The managers can perform the following activities in relation to this:

- Determine what outcomes employees prefer.
- Define, communicate and clarify the level of performance that is desired.
- Establish attainable performance goals.
- Link desired outcomes to performance goal achievement.

The Porter-Lawlerz Extension. Porter and Lawler have proposed an interesting extension to the expectancy theory. The human religionists assumed that employee satisfaction causes good performance but research has not supported such relationship. Porter and Lawler suggest that there may indeed be a relationship between satisfaction and performance but that it goes in the opposite direction, that is, superior performance can lead to satisfaction.

Porter-Lawler Model. First, an individual's initial effort is influenced by his perception regarding the value of reward and the likelihood that the effort will yield a reward. The probability that increased effort will lead to improved performance is affected by an individual's traits, abilities and perception of his role in an organisation. The model also distinguishes between intrinsic and extrinsic rewards. Finally, the Porter-Lawler model borrows from equity theory the idea that the employee's satisfaction depends on the perceived equity of the rewards relative to the effort expended and the level of performance attained.

Implications for Managers. Expectancy theory can be useful for organisations attempting to improve the motivation of their employees. Nadler and Lawler suggest a series of steps for managers in applying the basic ideas of the theory.

1. They should determine the primary outcomes that each employee likely desires.
2. They should decide what kind and levels of performance are needed to meet organisational goals.
3. They should ascertain that the desired levels of performance are attainable.
4. They should ensure that desired outcomes and performance are linked.
5. They should also analyze the complete work situation for conflicting expectancies.
6. They should make sure that the rewards are large enough.
7. They should make sure that the overall system is equitable for everyone.

The expectancy theory has also its limitations. It is quite difficult to apply, for example, application of this theory in the work place would require to identify all the potential outcomes for each employee, to determine all relevant expectancies and then to balance everything somehow to maximise employee motivation. Expectancy theory also assumes that people are rational - therefore, they will systematically consider all the potential outcomes and their associated expectancies before selecting a particular behaviour. However, few people actually make decisions in such a precise and rational manner

(2) Equity Theory of Motivation

J. Stacy Adams developed equity theory of motivation. The equity theory argues that motivations arise out of simple desire to be treated fairly. Equity can be defined as an individual's belief that he is being treated fairly relative to the treatment of others.

A person's perception of equity develops through a four-step process as shown below:

1. First an individual evaluates the way he is being treated by an organisation.
2. The next step is for an individual to choose a co-worker who seems to be in a roughly similar situation and to observe how an organisation treats him.
3. In the crucial step of equity theory an individual 'compares' the two treatments.
4. In the fourth step he evaluates a sense of equity to see if the two treatments seem similar or if they are different.

Adam suggests that employees make these comparisons by focusing on input and outcome ratios. An employee's contributions or input to an organisation include time, education, effort, experience and loyalty. Outcomes are what an individual receives from an organisation such as, pay, recognition and social relationships. The theory suggests that people view their outcomes and inputs as ratio and then compare their ratio to the ratio of someone else. This other 'person' may be someone in the work group. The comparison may result in three types of attitudes:

- The individual may feel equitably rewarded,
- Under-rewarded.
- Over-rewarded.

An individual will experience a feeling of equity when the two ratios are equal. If an individual has the feeling of equity then he should maintain the status quo. If he has a feeling of inequity then he is likely to change the input.

The single most important idea for managers to remember about equity theory is that if rewards are to motivate employees, they must be perceived as being equitable and fair. However, managers must remember that different employees have different sense towards basis for a reward and this may result in problems. Hence, the best way to avoid such problems is to make all employees aware of the basis for rewards.

Reinforcement Based Approaches to Motivation. A final approach to the motivation process focuses on why some behaviour are maintained and changed overtime. Reinforcement-based approaches explain the role of those rewards as they cause behaviour to change or remain the same over time. Specifically, reinforcement theory is based on the fairly simple assumption that behaviours that result in rewarding consequences are likely to be repeated, whereas behaviour that result in punishing consequences are less likely to be repeated. There are similarities between expectancy theory and reinforcement theory. Both consider the processes by which an individual chooses behaviours in a particular situation. However, the expectancy theory focuses more on behaviour choices and the latter is more concerned with the consequences of those choices.

Reinforcement Contingencies. Reinforcement contingencies are the possible outcomes that an individual may experience as a result of his or her behaviours. The four types of reinforcement contingencies that can affect individuals in an organisational setting are positive reinforcement, avoidance, punishment and extinction.

Positive Reinforcement is a method of strengthening behaviour. It is a reward or a positive outcome after a desired behaviour is performed. When a manager' observes an employee is doing a good job and offers praise then this praise helps in positive reinforcement of behaviour. Other positive reinforces include pay, promotions and awards.

The other reinforcement, contingency that can strengthen desired behaviour is avoidance. This occurs when an individual chooses certain behaviour in order to avoid unpleasant consequences. For instance, an employee may come to work on time to avoid criticism.

Punishment is used by some managers to weaken undesired behaviours. The logic is that the unpleasant, consequence will reduce an undesirable behaviour again, for example, punishing with fine for coming late.

Extinction can also be used to weaken behaviour especially that has previously been rewarded. When an employee tells a vulgar joke and the boss laughs, the laughter reinforces the behaviour and the employee may continue to tell similar jokes. By simply ignoring this behaviour and not reinforcing it, the boss can cause the behaviour to subside which eventually becomes 'extinct'.

Positive reinforcement and punishment are the most common reinforcement contingencies practiced by organisations. Most managers prefer a judicious use of positive reinforcement and punishment. Avoidance and extinction are generally used only in specialised circumstances.

New Approaches to Motivation in Organisations

New approaches are emerging to supplement the established models and theories of motivation. Two of the most promising are Goal-Setting Theory and the Japanese Approach.

(A) Goal Setting Theory to Motivation

This approach to motivation has been pioneered in the USA by Edwin Locke and his associates in 1960s and refined in 1980s. Goal-setting theory suggests that managers and subordinates should set goals for an individual on a regular basis, as suggested by MBO. These goals should be moderately difficult and very specific and of type that an employee will accept and make a commitment to accomplishing them. Rewards should be tied directly to accomplished goals. When involved in goal-settings, employees see how their effort will lead to performance, rewards and personal satisfaction. The mere act of goal setting does not ensure higher levels of motivation among employees. In fact, there seem to be three important criteria that goals must meet if they are to influence the behaviour of organisation members. They are goal specificity, goal difficulty and goal acceptance.

Goal Specificity. Goals must be stated in specific terms if they are to motivate effective performance. Goals must be set in terms of measurable criteria of work performance, *i.e.*, number of units produced, new sales etc. and must specify a time period within which the goal is to be attained. It also gives a sense of personal satisfaction and accomplishment to workers if he is able to meet the specific goal.

Goal Difficulty/Challenge. There exists a relationship between goal difficulty and work motivation. The more difficult and challenging the goal is, the higher the level of motivation and performance. However, it is essential that goals are set at realistic levels. Goals that are very difficult to achieve are unable to motivate since it is beyond the capacity of the concerned individual.

Goal Acceptance. In order to influence motivation and performance, a goal must be internalised by an individual. In other words, the person has to feel some personal ownership of the goal and must have commitment to achieve it.

Goal Setting in Practice. The most obvious implication of goal-setting theory is that managers should be helping subordinates to set goals that are specific and reasonably difficult so that subordinates accept and internalise them as their own goals. Besides this, there are a number of issues that arise in implementing goal setting in practice.

- Though specificity of goal is essential and measurability is desirable, it should not affect in identifying meaningful and valid objective of goal attainment.
- The manager can stimulate goal acceptance in at least three ways:
  - By involving subordinates in goal-setting process.
  - By demonstrating a supportive attitude and approach toward his subordinates.
  - By assigning various rewards to the achievement of goals.

Management by Objectives (MBO) is a managerial technique for improving motivation and performance using goal-setting principles.

Cognitive Evaluation Theory. A researcher 'Charms' reported in 1960 that extrinsic motivation like pay or rewards for a job, which has an intrinsic-motivation content, which is prior to such rewards. It tends to decrease overall level of motivation. This proposal is called, "Cognitive Evaluation Theory" which has been supported by a large number of research studies conducted subsequently.

(B) Japanese Approach to Motivation

The Japanese approach to motivation has gained increasing popularity around the world during the past few years. This approach is rather a philosophy of management than a theory or model. The basic tenet of the Japanese approach is that managers and workers should perform together as partners. Since both of them see themselves as one group, all members are committed and motivated to work in the best interests of an organisation. No one is called an employee; instead everyone is a team member, team leader or coach and everyone owns the 'share' of an organisation. Like goal-setting meow, the Japanese approach is likely to become more common in businesses throughout the world.

Integration of Motivation Theories. Thus several theories complicate our understanding. Some of these theories are compatible and some are not. The real challenge that a researcher has to face is integration of all or at least some of these together so that their inter and intra-relationships are established. This will also improve the understanding of motivation. Certain attempts are made in USA and elsewhere.

Enhancing Motivation in Organisations. Managers trying to enhance the motivation of their employees can, of course, draw on any of the theories described above. They may in practice adopt specific interventions derived from one or more theories or they may influence motivation through the organisation's reward system. The organisation can enhance motivation in following ways:

- ***Promote from within.*** It's great for morale and simplifies hiring procedures.
- ***Use incentive programs.*** Inducing the feeling that 'if you're creative enough, you won't have to rely on expensive financial bonuses.'
- ***Don't whitewash unpleasant assignments.*** Prepare subordinates for unpleasant assignments well in advance and offer what support you can.

- ***Establish appropriate deadlines.*** Every project should have a deadline.
- ***Publicise both short and long-term organisational goals.*** Encourage personal and departmental goal setting.
- ***Admit mistakes.*** People will respect you for it and will be less likely to hide their own mistakes.
- ***Humanise the work environment.*** Respect the need to treat each employee as an individual.
- ***Be liberal with praise.*** It's almost impossible to over praise and easy to under praise.
- Be consistent in your own work and in your relations with others.
- ***Show a personal interest in the people who work for you.*** Relations are always smoother between people who know each other on a personal basis than relations between people who merely want something from each other.

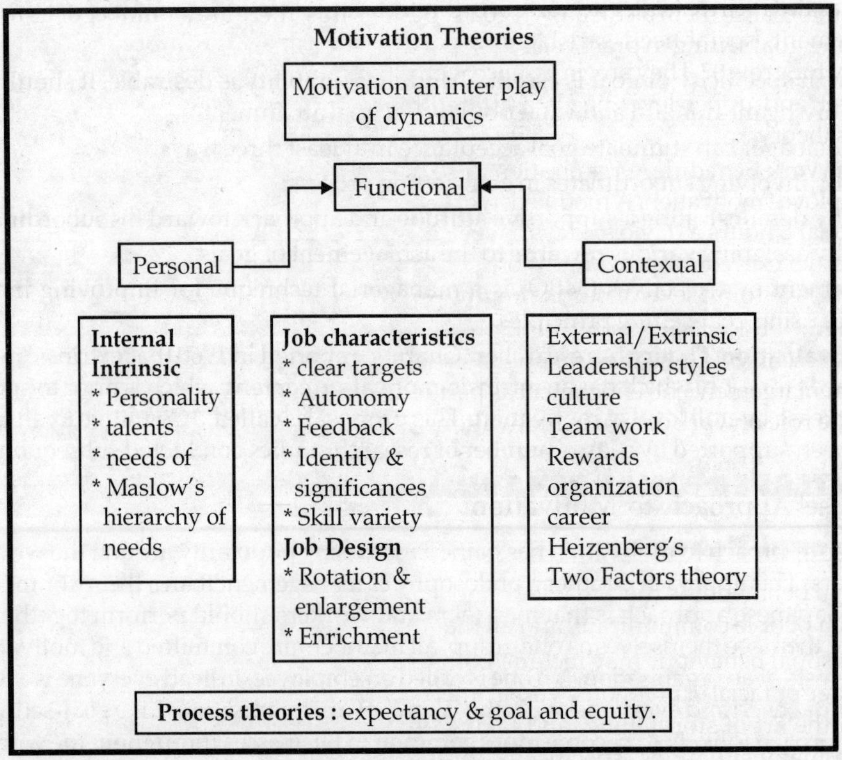

Managerial Approaches for Improving Motivation

A number of approaches can help managers motivate workers, to perform more effectively. The following steps promote intrinsic motivation:

- Workers Participation in Management (WPM)
- Management by Objectives (MBO)
- Organisation Behaviour Modification
- Job-Redesign
- Alternative Work Schedules.

Two approaches, however, have been especially effective: linking pay to job performance and quality of work-life programs.

Pay and Job Performance. Pay often can be used to motivate employee performance. But a pay plan also must be able to do the following tasks:

- Create the belief that good performance leads to high levels of pay;
- Minimise the negative consequences of good performance; and
- Create conditions in which rewards other than pay are evaluated as related to good performance.

Quality of Work Life Programs. Quality of Work Life (QWL) is defined as an attempt through a formal program to integrate employee needs and well being with the intention of improved productivity, greater worker involvement and higher levels of job satisfaction.

Programs for QWL improvements range from those requiring minor changes in an organisation to those requiring extensive modifications in structure, personnel and the utilisation of resources. There are three types of QWL programs, which are as follows:

Quality Circles. Quality Circles (QC) is small groups of workers who meet regularly with their supervisor as their 'circle leader' to solve work-related problems. QCs give employee an opportunity for involvement, social-need satisfaction, participation in work improvement, challenge and opportunity for growth. They are, in essence, vehicles for providing employees with opportunities to satisfy lower and upper-level needs as stated by Maslow, through the motivators described in 'Herzberg's theory.

Alternative Work Schedule. Organisations also frequently use the modified 'work-week' as a way to increase employee motivation. A modified 'work-week' can be any work schedule that does not conform to a traditional 8 hours a day or 5 days a week format. The modified 'work-week' helps individual satisfy higher-level needs by providing more personal control over one's work schedule. It also provides an opportunity to fulfill several needs simultaneously.

Job-Redesign. Job-Redesign or changing the nature of people's job is also being used more as a motivational technique. The idea pursued here is that managers can use any of the alternatives job rotation, job enlargement, job enrichment as part of motivational programme. Expectancy theory helps to explain the role of work design in motivation.

INTERPERSONAL BEHAVIOUR & INTERPERSONAL SKILLS

Interpersonal Behaviour

Interpersonal behaviour is the behaviour and actions that are present in human relationships. The way in which people communicate, and all that this entails, is considered interpersonal behaviour.

Interpersonal behaviour may include both verbal communication and nonverbal cues, such as body language or facial expressions. Verbal interpersonal behaviour consists of joking, relating to one another via the art of storytelling, and taking or following orders. Interpersonal skills are highly desirable in many situations, specifically careers that rely on personal relationships such as the health care industry or sales.

Interpersonal Behaviour is basically how "two persons" interact in any setting. It is extremely important in organisations or even schools and other education institutions to strengthen interpersonal relationships. When at a basic level, that is, between two people the relationship is strong and pleasant, it will lead to proper behaviour. This behaviour will result in productive work which is ultimately what organisations are looking for. At the employee level if trust and passion for work exists, the unity between them can achieve great results. These results would be in terms of reduction in the time lag, better quality work, and excellence in working procedures. Even in an educational institution such behaviours have a chain reaction. If two people do not get together and are forced together in a group assignment, it might just be completed half-heartedly by the two and not achieve desired results. This will have two consequences. First, it will affect the other group members and their grades. Second, it will foster hatred and mistrust within which will have long term effects on those two and those surrounding them.

Intrapersonal communication is a type of communication that a person carries with him or herself. That does not mean talking loudly and crazily in the literary context but figuratively it is a methodology of communicating to oneself that is important in the psychological development of a person, for developing openness to his/ her ideas and gaining access into the psychodynamic dimension of the personality. Its purpose is to think, reason, analyze and reflect the thought procedure.

The skills that are required for effective intrapersonal communication are include enhancing self-esteem, along with increasing the extent of self-awareness (meaning knowing yourself well enough and being sensitive to your attributes). It also requires improving problem-solving skills and analyzing abilities. Moreover the need for increasing self-control and reducing the level of stress is a vital one. Lastly the effective management of intrapersonal conflicts (quagmires in general) is important in the carriage of a smooth intrapersonal communication.

Interpersonal behaviour is a topic that is widely studied by many academics. Basically, the term 'interpersonal' focuses on the bond between two people, and the behaviour between these two individuals will depend on the context of their relationship. For example, the way that a boyfriend and a girlfriend behave with one another will be different to the communication between a mother and a daughter.

Of course, interpersonal behaviour isn't just explored in the environment of friends and family, as it is widely believed that a strong partnership between an employer and their staff can result in higher levels of efficiency in the workplace. This is why character building courses have become a key part of business, as it allows interpersonal behaviour to become stronger as co-workers trust one another further.

There are different theories that surround interpersonal behaviour, and it's widely believed that the more people collaborate with each other, the better they will be at appreciating each other's skills. It doesn't just benefit the results that companies can publish, but it improves levels of happiness in the workplace. Because people are working with their friends and enjoying one another's company, they are going to be chirpier and less likely to get involved with conflict that can damage overall productivity.

Interpersonal Skills

Interpersonal skills are the qualities and behaviours a person uses to interact with others properly. In the business domain, the term refers to an employee's ability to work well with others while performing their job. Interpersonal skills range from communication and listening to attitude and deportment. Strong interpersonal skills are a prerequisite for many positions in an organisation.

Interpersonal skills cannot be learned solely from a textbook. They come naturally to some people, while other people have to work at cultivating them. In many organisations, employees with strong interpersonal skills are valued for their pleasant demeanor and positive, solution-oriented attitude. These employees are team players, who work well with others to achieve a goal.

Interpersonal skills relate to the knowledge of social expectations and customs. Individuals with these skills consider others' reactions to adjust tactics and communication as needed. Some describe interpersonal skills as social intelligence, which relies on paying attention to the actions and speech of others and interpreting them correctly as part of forming a response. While these skills are based, in part, on an individual's personality and instincts, they also develop with experience and knowledge.

Improving Interpersonal Skills

While many people believe interpersonal skills are, to some extent, innate in each person or acquired at an early age, job seekers and those looking for promotions can take steps to improve their interpersonal skills and make themselves more valuable to an organisation.

Steps for improving interpersonal skills include expressing appreciation for team members and support staff, practicing empathy, moderating disputes quickly to contain them, and planning rather than saying or writing the first item that comes to mind. Active listening can be practiced by repeating back to a speaker what they said to make sure true communication is taking place. There are also classes and training that teach these skills.

Interpersonal Skills in the Workplace

In this competitive marketplace, businesses seek to employ those who not only have the proper experience and knowledge but have strong interpersonal skills that fit well within a company's culture. Strong interpersonal skills, such as negotiating, problem-solving and knowledge-sharing, are the main job requirement, as employees must be able to work well with others to achieve company objectives. Interpersonal skills may also include:

- Teamwork
- Verbal and written communication
- Dependability
- Responsibility
- Empathy

GROUP DYNAMICS

Types of Groups: Formal and Informal

What is a group? A group is a collection of individuals who interact with each other such that one person's actions have an impact on the others. In organisations, most work is done within groups. How groups function has important implications for organisational productivity. Groups where people get along, feel the desire to contribute to the team, and are capable of coordinating their efforts may have high performance levels, whereas teams characterised by extreme levels of conflict or hostility may demoralise members of the workforce.

In organisations, you may encounter different types of groups. Informal work groups are made up of two or more individuals who are associated with one another in ways not prescribed by the formal organisation. For example, a few people in the company who get together to play tennis on the weekend would be considered an informal group. A formal work group is made up of managers, subordinates, or both with close associations among group members that influence the behaviour of individuals in the group. We will discuss many different types of formal work groups later on in this chapter.

Stages of Group Development

Forming, Storming, Norming, and Performing

American organisational psychologist Bruce Tuckman presented a robust model in 1965 that is still widely used today. Based on his observations of group behaviour in a variety of settings, he proposed a four-stage map of group evolution, also known as the forming-storming-norming-performing model. Later he enhanced the model by adding a fifth and final stage, the adjourning phase. Interestingly enough, just as an individual moves through developmental stages such as childhood, adolescence, and adulthood, so does a group, although in a much shorter period of time. According to this theory, in order to successfully facilitate a group, the leader needs to move through various leadership styles over time. Generally, this is accomplished by first being more directive, eventually serving as a coach, and later, once the group is able to assume more power and responsibility for itself, shifting to a delegator. While research has not confirmed that this is descriptive of how groups progress, knowing and following these steps can help groups be more effective. For example, groups that do not go through the storming phase early on will often return to this stage toward the end of the group process to address unresolved issues. Another example of the validity of the group development model involves groups that take the time to get to know each other socially in the forming stage. When this occurs, groups tend to handle future challenges better because the individuals have an understanding of each other's needs.

STAGES OF THE GROUP DEVELOPMENT MODEL

Forming

In the forming stage, the group comes together for the first time. The members may already know each other or they may be total strangers. In either case, there is a level of formality, some anxiety, and a degree of guardedness as group members are not sure what is going to happen next. "Will I be accepted? What will my role be? Who has the power here?" These are some of the questions participants think about during this stage of group formation. Because of the large amount of uncertainty, members tend to be polite, conflict avoidant, and observant. They are trying to figure out the "rules of the game" without being too vulnerable. At this point, they may also be quite excited and optimistic about the task at hand, perhaps experiencing a level of pride at being chosen to join a particular group. Group members are trying to achieve several goals at this stage, although this may not necessarily be done consciously. First, they are trying to get to know each other. Often this can be accomplished by finding some common ground. Members also begin to explore group boundaries to determine what will be considered acceptable behaviour. "Can I interrupt? Can I leave when I feel like it?" This trial phase may also involve testing the appointed leader or seeing if a leader emerges from the group. At this point, group members are also discovering how the group will work in terms of what needs to be done and who will be responsible for each task. This stage is often characterised by abstract discussions about issues to be addressed by the group; those who like to get moving can become impatient with this part of the process. This phase is usually short in duration, perhaps a meeting or two.

Storming

Once group members feel sufficiently safe and included, they tend to enter the storming phase. Participants focus less on keeping their guard up as they shed social facades, becoming more authentic and more argumentative. Group members begin to explore their power and influence, and they often stake out their territory by differentiating themselves from the other group members rather than seeking common ground. Discussions can become heated as participants raise contending points of view and values, or argue over how tasks should be done and who is assigned to them. It is not unusual for group members to become defensive, competitive, or jealous. They may even take sides or begin to form cliques within the group. Questioning and resisting direction from the leader is also quite common. "Why should I have to do this? Who designed this project in the first place? Why do I have to listen to you?" Although little seems to get accomplished at this stage, group members are becoming more authentic as they express their deeper thoughts and feelings. What they are really exploring is "Can I truly be me, have power, and be accepted?" During this chaotic stage, a great deal of creative energy that was previously buried is released and available for use, but it takes skill to move the group from storming to norming. In many cases, the group gets stuck in the storming phase.

There are several steps you can take to avoid getting stuck in the storming phase of group development. Try the following if you feel the group process you are involved in is not progressing:

- **Normalise conflict.** Let members know this is a natural phase in the group-formation process.
- **Be inclusive.** Continue to make all members feel included and invite all views into the room. Mention how diverse ideas and opinions help foster creativity and innovation.
- **Make sure everyone is heard.** Facilitate heated discussions and help participants understand each other.
- **Support all group members.** This is especially important for those who feel more insecure.
- **Remain positive.** This is a key point to remember about the group's ability to accomplish its goal.
- **Don't rush the group's development.** Remember that working through the storming stage can take several meetings.

Once group members discover that they can be authentic and that the group is capable of handling differences without dissolving, they are ready to enter the next stage, norming.

Norming

"We survived!" is the common sentiment at the norming stage. Group members often feel elated at this point, and they are much more committed to each other and the group's goal. Feeling energised by knowing they can handle the "tough stuff," group members are now ready to get to work. Finding themselves more cohesive and cooperative, participants find it easy to establish their own ground rules (or *norms*) and define their operating procedures and goals. The group tends to make big decisions, while subgroups or individuals handle the smaller decisions. Hopefully, at this point the group is more open and respectful toward each other, and members ask each other for both help and feedback. They may even begin to form friendships and share more personal information with each other. At this point, the leader should become more of a facilitator by stepping back and letting the group assume more responsibility for its goal. Since the group's energy is running high, this is an ideal time to host a social or team-building event.

Performing

Galvanised by a sense of shared vision and a feeling of unity, the group is ready to go into high gear. Members are more interdependent, individuality and differences are respected, and group members feel themselves to be part of a greater entity. At the performing stage, participants are not only getting the work done, but they also pay greater attention to *how* they are doing it. They ask questions like, "Do our operating procedures best support productivity and quality assurance? Do we have suitable means for addressing differences that arise so we can preempt destructive conflicts? Are we relating to and communicating with each other in ways that enhance group dynamics and help us achieve our goals? How can I further develop as a person to become more effective?" By now, the group has matured, becoming more competent, autonomous, and insightful. Group leaders can finally move into coaching roles and help members grow in skill and leadership.

Adjourning

Just as groups form, so do they end. For example, many groups or teams formed in a business context are project oriented and therefore are temporary in nature. Alternatively, a working group may dissolve due to an organisational restructuring. Just as when we graduate from school or leave home for the first time, these endings can be bittersweet, with group members feeling a combination of victory, grief, and insecurity about what is coming next. For those who like routine and bond closely with fellow group members, this transition can be particularly challenging. Group leaders and members alike should be sensitive to handling these endings respectfully and compassionately. An ideal way to close a group is to set aside time to debrief ("How did it all go? What did we learn?"), acknowledge each other, and celebrate a job well done.

The Punctuated-Equilibrium Model

As you may have noted, the five-stage model we have just reviewed is a linear process. According to the model, a group progresses to the performing stage, at which point it finds itself in an ongoing, smooth-sailing situation until the group dissolves. In reality, subsequent researchers, most notably Joy H. Karriker, have found that the life of a group is much more dynamic and cyclical in nature. For example, a group may operate in the performing stage for several months. Then, because of a disruption, such as a competing emerging technology that changes the rules of the game or the introduction of a new CEO, the group may move back into the storming phase before returning to performing. Ideally, any regression in the linear group progression will ultimately result in a higher level of functioning. Proponents of this cyclical model draw from behavioural scientist Connie Gersick's study of punctuated equilibrium.

The concept of punctuated equilibrium was first proposed in 1972 by paleontologists Niles Eldredge and Stephen Jay Gould, who both believed that evolution occurred in rapid, radical spurts rather than gradually over time. Identifying numerous examples of this pattern in social behaviour, Gersick found that the concept applied to organisational change. She proposed that groups remain fairly static, maintaining a certain equilibrium for long periods of time. Change during these periods is incremental, largely due to the resistance to change that arises when systems take root and processes become institutionalised. In this model, revolutionary change occurs in brief, punctuated bursts, generally catalyzed by a crisis or problem that breaks through the systemic inertia and shakes up the deep organisational structures in place. At this point, the organisation or group has the opportunity to learn and create new structures that are better aligned with current realities. Whether the group does this is not guaranteed. In sum, in Gersick's model, groups can repeatedly cycle through the storming and performing stages, with revolutionary change taking place during short transitional windows. For organisations and groups who understand that disruption, conflict, and chaos are inevitable in the life of a social system, these disruptions represent opportunities for innovation and creativity.

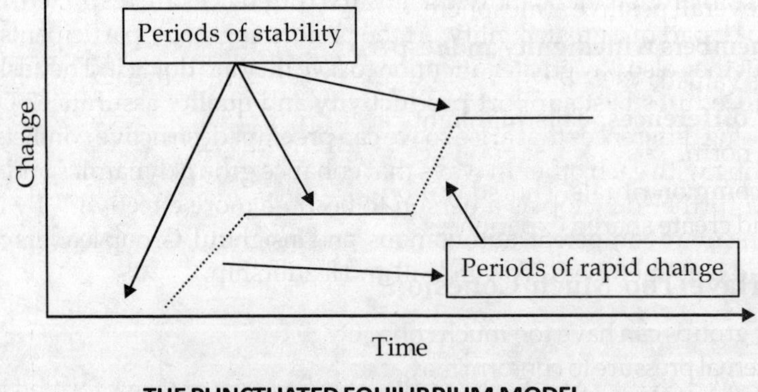

THE PUNCTUATED EQUILIBRIUM MODEL

Cohesion

Cohesion can be thought of as a kind of social glue. It refers to the degree of camaraderie within the group. Cohesive groups are those in which members are attached to each other and act as one unit.

Generally speaking, the more cohesive a group is, the more productive it will be and the more rewarding the experience will be for the group's members. Members of cohesive groups tend to have the following characteristics: They have a collective identity; they experience a moral bond and a desire to remain part of the group; they share a sense of purpose, working together on a meaningful task or cause; and they establish a structured pattern of communication.

The fundamental factors affecting group cohesion include the following:

- **Similarity.** The more similar group members are in terms of age, sex, education, skills, attitudes, values, and beliefs, the more likely the group will bond.
- **Stability.** The longer a group stays together, the more cohesive it becomes.
- **Size.** Smaller groups tend to have higher levels of cohesion.
- **Support.** When group members receive coaching and are encouraged to support their fellow team members, group identity strengthens.
- **Satisfaction.** Cohesion is correlated with how pleased group members are with each other's performance, behaviour, and conformity to group norms.

As you might imagine, there are many benefits in creating a cohesive group. Members are generally more personally satisfied and feel greater self-confidence and self-esteem when in a group where they feel they belong. For many, membership in such a group can be a buffer against stress, which can improve mental and physical well-being. Because members are invested in the group and its work, they are more likely to regularly attend and actively participate in the group, taking more responsibility for the group's functioning. In addition, members can draw on the strength of the group to persevere through challenging situations that might otherwise be too hard to tackle alone.

- **Align the group with the greater organisation.** Establish common objectives in which members can get involved.
- **Let members have choices in setting their own goals.** Include them in decision making at the organisational level.
- **Define clear roles.** Demonstrate how each person's contribution furthers the group goal—everyone is responsible for a special piece of the puzzle.
- **Situate group members in close proximity to each other.** This builds familiarity.
- **Give frequent praise.** Both individuals and groups benefit from praise. Also encourage them to praise each other. This builds individual self-confidence, reaffirms positive behaviour, and creates an overall positive atmosphere.
- **Treat all members with dignity and respect.** This demonstrates that there are no favorites and everyone is valued.
- **Celebrate differences.** This highlights each individual's contribution while also making diversity a norm.
- **Establish common rituals.** Thursday morning coffee, monthly potlucks—these reaffirm group identity and create shared experiences.

Can a Group Have Too Much Cohesion?

Keep in mind that groups can have too much cohesion. Because members can come to value belonging over all else, an internal pressure to conform may arise, causing some members to modify their behaviour to adhere to group norms. Members may become conflict avoidant, focusing more on trying to please each other so as not to be ostracised. In some cases, members might censor themselves to maintain the party line. As such, there is a superficial sense of harmony and less diversity of thought. Having less tolerance for deviants, who threaten the group's static identity, cohesive groups will often excommunicate members who dare to disagree. Members attempting to make a change may even be criticised or undermined by other members, who perceive this as a threat to the status quo. The painful possibility of being marginalised can keep many members in line with the majority.

The more strongly members identify with the group, the easier it is to see outsiders as inferior, or enemies in extreme cases, which can lead to increased insularity. This form of prejudice can have a downward spiral effect. Not only is the group not getting corrective feedback from within its own confines, it is also closing itself off from input and a cross-fertilisation of ideas from the outside. In such an environment, groups can easily adopt extreme ideas that will not be challenged. Denial increases as problems are ignored and failures are blamed on external factors. With limited, often biased, information and no internal or external opposition, groups like these can make disastrous decisions. Groupthink is a group pressure phenomenon that increases the risk of the group making flawed decisions by allowing reductions in mental efficiency, reality testing, and moral judgment. Groupthink is most common in highly cohesive groups.

Cohesive groups can go awry in much milder ways. For example, group members can value their social interactions so much that they have fun together but spend little time on accomplishing their assigned task. Or a group's goal may begin to diverge from the larger organisation's goal and those trying to uphold the organisation's goal may be ostracised (e.g., teasing the class "brain" for doing well in school).

In addition, research shows that cohesion leads to acceptance of group norms. Groups with high task commitment do well, but imagine a group where the norms are to work as little as possible? As you might imagine, these groups get little accomplished and can actually work together against the organisation's goals.

	Low task commitment	High task commitment
Low group cohesion	Low performance	Performance ranges depending on a number of factors
High group cohesion	Low performance	High performance

GROUPS WITH HIGH COHESION AND HIGH TASK COMMITMENT TEND TO BE THE MOST EFFECTIVE.

Social Loafing

Social loafing refers to the tendency of individuals to put in less effort when working in a group context. This phenomenon, also known as the Ringelmann effect, was first noted by French agricultural engineer Max Ringelmann in 1913. In one study, he had people pull on a rope individually and in groups. He found that as the number of people pulling increased, the group's total pulling force was less than the individual efforts had been when measured alone.

Why do people work less hard when they are working with other people? Observations show that as the size of the group grows, this effect becomes larger as well. The social loafing tendency is less a matter of being lazy and more a matter of perceiving that one will receive neither one's fair share of rewards if the group is successful nor blame if the group fails. Rationales for this behaviour include, "My own effort will have little effect on the outcome," "Others aren't pulling their weight, so why should I?" or "I don't have much to contribute, but no one will notice anyway." This is a consistent effect across a great number of group tasks and countries. Research also shows that perceptions of fairness are related to less social loafing. Therefore, teams that are deemed as more fair should also see less social loafing.

When designing a group project, here are some considerations to keep in mind:

- **Carefully choose the number of individuals you need to get the task done.** The likelihood of social loafing increases as group size increases (especially if the group consists of 10 or more people), because it is easier for people to feel unneeded or inadequate, and it is easier for them to "hide" in a larger group.
- **Clearly define each member's tasks in front of the entire group.** If you assign a task to the entire group, social loafing is more likely. For example, instead of stating, "By Monday, let's find several articles on the topic of stress," you can set the goal of "By Monday, each of us will be responsible for finding five articles on the topic of stress." When individuals have specific goals, they become more accountable for their performance.
- **Design and communicate to the entire group a system for evaluating each person's contribution.** You may have a midterm feedback session in which each member gives feedback to every other member. This would increase the sense of accountability individuals have. You may even want to discuss the principle of social loafing in order to discourage it.
- **Build a cohesive group.** When group members develop strong relational bonds, they are more committed to each other and the success of the group, and they are therefore more likely to pull their own weight.
- **Assign tasks that are highly engaging and inherently rewarding.** Design challenging, unique, and varied activities that will have a significant impact on the individuals themselves, the organisation, or the external environment. For example, one group member may be responsible for crafting a new incentive-pay system through which employees can direct some of their bonus to their favorite nonprofits.
- **Make sure individuals feel that they are needed.** If the group ignores a member's contributions because these contributions do not meet the group's performance standards, members will feel discouraged and are unlikely to contribute in the future. Make sure that everyone feels included and needed by the group.

Collective Efficacy

Collective efficacy refers to a group's perception of its ability to successfully perform well. Collective efficacy is influenced by a number of factors, including watching others ("that group did it and we're better than them"), verbal persuasion ("we can do this"), and how a person feels ("this is a good group"). Research shows that a group's collective efficacy is related to its performance. In addition, this relationship is higher when task interdependence (the degree an individual's task is linked to someone else's work) is high rather than low.

LEADERSHIP

Meaning

Simply stated, leadership is the process of influencing the behaviour of others towards the accomplishment of goals in a given situation. Leadership is an integral part of management and plays a vital role in managerial operations. It provides direction, guidance, and confidence to the employees and helps in the attainment of goals in much easier way. In business and industrial organisations, managers play the role of leader and acquire leadership of subordinates, their efforts towards the achievement of organisational goals and activate the individuals of an organisation to make them work. Leadership influences behaviour of the individuals. It has an ability to attract others and potential to make them follow the instructions. Individuals can be induced to contribute their optimum towards the attainment of organisational goals through effective leadership. Leadership acquires dominance and the followers accept the directives and control of a leader. Leadership provides direction and vision for future to an organisation.

Definition

Leadership is the art of influencing and inspiring subordinates to perform their duties willingly, competently and enthusiastically for achievement of groups objectives.

- According to **Louis A. Allen**, "A leadership is one who guides and directs people and gives their efforts, direction and purpose."
- According to **George R. Terry,** "Leadership is the activity of influencing people to strive willingly for mutual objectives."
- According to **Robert Appleby**, "Leadership is a means of direction. It is the ability of management to induce subordinates to work towards group ideas with confidence and keenness."
- According to **Wendell French**, "Leadership is the process of influencing the behaviour of others in the direction of a goal or set of goals or, more broadly, toward a vision of the future."
- According to **Keith Davis**, "Leadership is the process of encouraging and helping others to work enthusiastically towards objectives".
- According to **Koontz and O'Donnell**, "Leadership is the art or process of influencing people so that they will strive willingly towards the achievement of group goals".
- According to **Peter Drucker**, "Leadership means the lifting of man's visions to higher sights, the raising of man's performance to higher standard, the building of man's personality beyond its normal limitations".
- According to **Grey and Starke**, "Leadership is both a process and a property. As a process, it is used for non-coercive influence to shape up the goals of a group or organisation, to motivate behaviour toward the achievement of those goals and to help define group or organisational culture. As a property, leadership is the set multi characteristics attributed to those who are perceived to be leaders".

Features of Leadership

The features of leadership are as follows:

- Leadership is the process of influencing behaviour of individuals of an organisation.
- Leadership uses non-coercive methods to direct and coordinate the activities of the individuals of an organisation.
- Leadership directs the individuals to attain the tasks assigned to them by following the instructions of their leaders.
- A leader possesses qualities to influence others.
- Leadership gives the individuals, a vision for future.
- Leadership is a group activity. Leader influences his followers and followers also exercise influence over his leader.
- Leadership is meant for a given situation, given group for a pre-determined period of time.
- Leadership is continuous process of influencing behaviour. It encourages liveliness in the group.

Importance of Leadership

The following points can judge the importance of leadership:

- A leader should act as a friend of the people whom he is leading.

- A leader must have the capacity to recognise the potentials of the individuals and transform them into realities.
- A leader should have the confidence of the individuals of the organisation.
- A leader must be able to unite the people as a team and build up team spirit.
- A leader should be able to maintain discipline among his group and develop a sense of responsibility.
- A leader must be able to build up a high morale among the individuals of the organisation.
- A leader should motivate his people to achieve goals.
- A leader should try to raise the morale of the individuals and should maintain ethical standards among the individuals.
- A leader should act as a link between the work groups and the forces outside the organisation.

Difference Between Leadership and Management

Leading and managing go together but some differences exist between the two. The following are the differences between the leadership and the management:

- Management takes rational and logical decisions while leadership takes decision on expectations of the followers. Leadership has an emotional appeal while management acts on rationality.
- The management establishes relationship through a lawful authority while leadership establishes relationship through power.
- Managers have formal authority but the leaders have no such authority.
- All leaders are not managers and all managers are leaders.
- Management is a process of planning, organising, directing and controlling the activities of others to attain the organisational objectives. Leadership on the other hand, is a process of influencing the behaviour of the people to attain their assigned tasks. A successful manager must possess both the managerial and leadership qualities.

Types of Leadership

Following are the main types of leadership:

- **Autocratic or Authoritarian Leadership.** In this type of leadership, there is a complete centralisation of authority in the leader, *i.e.,* authority is centred in the leader himself. He has all the powers to make decisions. He uses coercive measures and adopts, negative method of motivation. He wants immediate obedience of his orders and instructions. Any negligence on the part of subordinates results in punishment. There is no participation from the subordinates in decision-making. A leader thinks that he is the only competent person in the organisation. According to Edwin B. Filippo, there are following three types of leaders in autocratic:

  1. ***Hard Boiled or Strict Autocrat.*** Leader, under such type uses negative influence and expects that the employees should obey his orders immediately. Non-compliance of his orders results in punishment. He makes all decisions and does not disclose anything to anyone. He is quite rigid on performance.
  2. ***Benevolent Autocrat.*** Benevolent autocrat leader uses positive influences and develops effective human relations. He is known as paternalistic leader. He praises his employees if they follow his orders and invites them to get the solutions of the problems from him. He feels happy in controlling all the actions of his subordinates.
  3. ***Manipulative Autocrat.*** Leader, under such type is manipulative in nature. He creates a feeling in the minds of his subordinates and workers that they are participating in decision-making processes. But he makes all decisions by himself. Non-compliance of his orders also results in punishment.

- **Democratic or Participative Leadership.** Democratic or Participative leadership is also known as group centered or consultative leadership. In this type of leadership, leaders consult their groups and consider their opinion in the decision-making process. Leaders encourage discussion among the group members on the problem under consideration and arrive at a decision depending on their consent. Participation or involvement of the employees in the decision-making process is also rewarded. Exchange of ideas among subordinates and with the leader is given encouragement. Leaders give more freedom to their group members, who feel that, their opinions are honored and they are given importance. It develops a sense of confidence among subordinates and they derive job satisfaction. It improves quality of decision as it is taken after due consideration of valued opinions of the talented group members.
  - The demerit of this type of leadership is that it takes more time to arrive at a decision, as a lot of time is wasted while taking the views from the employee. It is, therefore, very time consuming.
- **Laissez-faire or Free Rein Leadership.** In this type of leadership, there is virtual absence of direct leadership. It is, therefore, known as "no leadership at all". There is complete delegation of authority to subordinates so that they can make decisions by themselves. Absence of leadership may have both positive and negative effects. Free rein leadership may be effective if members of the group are highly committed to their work. The negative aspect shows that the leader is not competent enough to lead his group effectively. Members may feel insecure and develop frustration for lack of decision-making authority Bureaucratic. This type of leadership emphasizes the rules and regulations of an organisation. The behaviour of a leader is determined by the rules, regulations and procedure to be followed under his leadership. The leader and the subordinates both follow these rules and regulations. Therefore, there is no difference between the management and the administration in this type of leadership. The employees, themselves cannot do anything in this regard. It is the rules that determine their performance.
- **Manipulative.** This type of leadership manipulates the employees to attain their assigned tasks. A manipulative leader is quite selfish and exploits the aspirations of the employees for his gains. He knows very well the needs and desires of the employees but he does very little to fulfill them. Due to such attitude, he has to face the hatred of the employees at times.
- **Paternalistic.** The paternalistic leadership believes in the concept that the happy employees work better and harder. It maintains that the fatherly altitude is the right one for better relationship between the manager and the employees. Everyone within the organisation should work together like a family.
- **Expert Leadership.** The expert leadership emerged as a result of complex structure of modern organisations. This type of leadership is based on the ability, knowledge and competence of the leaders. He handles the situation skillfully with his talent. The employees feel relieved as they are working under a person who is expert and can handle the situation without any problem.

In modern organisations, human resources vary in terms of skill, knowledge and competencies. They differ in quality, determination and their attitude towards the organisation. They exhibit different behaviours as they differ in attitude and outlook also. The leader must understand their behaviour and accordingly can make use of the various types leadership. The manager should assess the situation and adopt that type of leadership, which suits that situation. He should remember that leadership is situational. If situation changes, the use of leadership among its various types also changes. A successful leader is the one who assesses the situation, studies the psychology of the subordinates and adopts the most useful type of leadership to lead the people at work to accomplish the organisational goals.

Comparison between Leadership Style.

S. No.	Points of Comparison	Autocratic Style	Democratic Style	Free-rein Style
1.	Decision-making	Leader sole decision-maker	Leader makes decisions in consultation with subordinates.	Subordinates themselves make decisions.
2.	Motivation Technique	Fear and punishment (negative incentives)	Rewards & involvement (positive incentives)	Self direction and self-control
3.	Communication	one-way (down ward) communication.	Two-way communication	Free flow of communication.
4.	Nature of discipline	Implicit obedience of orders and instructions.	Interchange of ideas and recognition of human values.	Self-discipline or control.
5.	Opportunity to Subordinates	No scope for initiative and creativity I style.	Scope for initiative creativity 'we' style.	Full scope for initiative and creativity 'you' style.

Theories of Leadership

A number of theories and approaches to study leadership have been developed. There are broadly three theories of leadership.

(A) Trait Theory

This theory of studying leadership is taken into consideration to analyze the personal, psychological and physical traits of strong leaders. The assumption made in this theory was that some basic traits or set of traits differentiates leaders from non-leaders. For example, the leadership traits might include intelligence, assertiveness, above average height, self-confidence, initiative and understanding of interpersonal human relations. The existence of these traits determines the importance of leadership. Possession of these traits helps the individuals to gain possession of leadership. Since all individuals do not have these qualities, only those who have them would be considered potential leaders.

Some of the weakness of this theory is:

- All the traits are not identical with regard to essential characteristics of a leader.
- Some traits may not be inherited, but can only be acquired by training.
- It does not identify the traits that are most important and that are least important for a successful leader.
- It does not explain the leadership failures, in spite of the required traits.
- It has been found that many traits exhibited by leaders are also found among followers without explaining as to why followers could not become leaders.
- It is difficult to define traits in absolute terms.
- Thus, the trait theory has been criticised for lack of conclusiveness and predictability.

(B) Behaviour Theory

The behavioural theory assumed that effective leaders behaved differently from ineffective leaders. It also identified the need of consistency of behaviour of good leaders. This theory can be more clearly understood with the help of following case studies.

The Michigan Studies

Researchers at the University of. Michigan, led by Rensis Likert, began studying leadership in the late 1940s. Depending on broad discussions with both the managers and sub-ordinates, the Michigan studies identified two forms of leadership behaviour.

They are discussed as below:

1. ***Job-centred leadership behaviour.*** The first was called job-centred leadership behaviour, which focuses on performances and efficient completion of the assigned tasks. A job-centred leader interacts with group members to explain task procedures and oversee their work.
2. ***Employee centred leadership behaviour.*** The second behaviour was identified as employee centred leader behaviour, which focuses on, high performance standards to be accomplished. This can be done by developing a cohesive work group and ensuring that employees are satisfied with their jobs. Thus, the leader's primary concern is the welfare of the ordinates. The Michigan researchers thought a leader could show signs of one kind of behaviour, but not both.

The Ohio State Studies

At about the same time, a group of researchers at Ohio State also began studying leadership. The Ohio State leadership studies also identified two major kinds of leadership behaviours or styles, which are as follows:

1. ***Initiating-structure behaviour.*** In initiating-structure behaviour, the leader clearly defines the leader-subordinate roles so that everyone knows what is expected. The leader also establishes formal lines of communication and determines how tasks will be performed.
2. ***Consideration behaviour.*** In consideration behaviour, the leader shows concern for subordinates feelings' and ideas. He attempts to establish a warm, friendly and supportive.

The most obvious difference between Michigan and Ohio State studies is that the Ohio State researchers did not position their two forms of leader behaviour at opposite ends of a single continuum. Rather, they assumed the behaviours to be independent variables, which means that a leader could exhibit varying degrees of initiating structure and consideration at the same time *i.e.* a particular leader could have higher ratings on both measures, low ratings on both or high ratings on one and low on the other.

The Ohio State researchers found that a leader's behaviour remains consistent over a period of time, if the situation also remains same. But the researchers could not come up with one best combination of behaviour suitable to all the situations. The researchers used to believe that the leaders in possession of both types of behaviour are most effective. However, their studies at International Harvester found that leaders rated highly on initiating structure behaviour have higher performing but dissatisfied sub-ordinates, whereas leaders rated highly on consideration structure had lower-performing sub-ordinates who showed signs of higher satisfaction.

Most experts now agree that no single set of traits or behaviours appears to be common to all good leaders. The universal approaches to leadership can help managers examine their own leadership characteristics and match them against the traits most commonly identified with good leaders. In order to understand the full complexity of leadership, contingency theory is to be studied.

(C) Contingency Theory

The main assumption of contingency theory is that the behaviour of an appropriate leader varies from one situation to another. The motive of a contingency theory is to identify key situational factors and to specify how they interact to determine appropriate behaviour of a leader.

The three most important and widely accepted contingency theories of leadership are as follows:

The LPC theory. The first contingency theory of leadership is Fred Fielder's Least Preferred Co-worker (LPC) Model. Fielder identified two types of leadership: task-oriented and relationship-oriented. Fielder believes that a leader's tendency to be task-oriented or relationship oriented remains constant. In- other words, a leader is either task-oriented or relationship-oriented while leading his group members. Fielder used the Least Preferred Co-worker (LPC) scale to measure the type of leadership. A leader is asked to describe characteristics of the person with whom he or she is least comfortable while working. They can do this by marking in a set of sixteen scales at each end, by a positive or negative adjective. For example, three of the scales Fielder uses in the LPC are:

Helpful	————————————	Frustrating	8 7 6 5 4 3 2 1
Tense	————————————	Relaxed	1 2 3 4 5 6 7 8
Boring	————————————	Interesting	1 2 3 4 5 6 7 8

The leader's LPC score is then calculated by adding up the numbers below the line checked on each scale. A high total score is assumed to reflect a relationship orientation and a low score, a task orientation by the leader. The LPC measure is controversial because researchers disagree about its validity. This is because some of the LPC measures show whether the score is an index of behaviour, personality or some other unknown factor.

According to Fielder, the contingency factor favours the situation from the leader's point of view. This factor is determined by leader-member relations, task-structure and position-power, which are discussed as below:

- **Leader-member relations.** A Leader-member relation refers to the nature of relationship between the leader and his work group. If the leader and the group enjoy mutual trust, respect, confidence and they like one another, relations will remain good. If there is little trust, respect or confidence and if they do not like one another, relations will remain bad. Good relations are assumed to be favourable and bad relations unfavourable.
- **Task-structure.** Task-structure is the degree to which the group's task is clearly defined. When the task is routine, easily understood, and unambiguous and when the group has standard procedures, the structure is assumed to be high. When the task is non-routine, ambiguous, complex, with no standard procedures and precedents, structure is assumed to be low. High structure is more favourable for the leader and low structure is unfavourable. If the task structure is low, the leader will have to play a major role in guiding and directing the group's activities. If the task structure is high, the leader will not have to pay much attention.
- **Position-power.** Position-power is the power vested in the position of a leader in an organisation. If the leader has the power to assign work, administer rewards and punishment, recommend employees for promotion or demotion, position-power is assumed to be strong. If the leader does not have required powers, the position-power is weak. From the leader's point of view, strong position power is favourable and weak position power is unfavourable. Fielder and his associates conducted various studies highlighting if a situation favours the leadership and group effectiveness or not. When the situation includes good relations, high structure and strong power, a risk-oriented leader to lie most effective. However, when relations are good but task structure is low and position-power is weak, relationship-oriented leader is considered to be most effective.
- A final point about LPC theory is that, Fielder argues that any particular type of leadership, which is measured by the LPC is inflexible and cannot be changed. In other words a leader cannot change his behaviour to fit a particular situation. Fielder's contingency theory has been criticised on the ground that LPC measure lacks validity and that the assumption about the inflexibility of the leader's behaviour is unrealistic.

(D) The Path Goal Theory

The path-goal model of leadership was introduced by Martin Evans and Robert House. Path-goal theory says that a leader can motivate subordinates by influencing their expectations. Leaders can motivate sub-ordinates by making clear what they have to do to get the reward they desire. The path-goal model assumes that leaders can change their style or behaviour to meet the demands of a particular situation. This model identifies four kinds of leader behaviour: directive, supportive, participative and achievement-oriented. According to this model managers can adjust their behaviour to include any four kinds of leadership behaviour mentioned above. For instance, while leading a new group of sub-ordinates, the leader may be directive in giving guidance and instructions to them. He may also adopt supportive behaviour to encourage group cohesiveness, to look after their needs and ensuring that they get the rewards and benefits. As the group becomes more familiar with the task and as new problems are taken into consideration, the leader may use participative behaviour by which he can participate with employees in making decisions and take their suggestions as well. Finally, the leader may use achievement-oriented behaviour to encourage continued high performance of sub-ordinates.

(E) The Vroom-Yetton –Jago Theory (VYJ)

The Vroom-Yetton-Jago model was first introduced by Vroom and Yetton in 1973 and was revised by Vroom and Jago in 1988, this model has a much less focus than the path-goal theory. It helps a leader to determine the extent, to which employees should participate in the decision-making processes,

The VYJ theory argues that decision-effectiveness is best judged by the quality of decision and by the acceptance of that decision on the part of employees. Decision acceptance is the extent to which employees accept and are loyal to their decisions.

To maximise decision effectiveness, the VYJ theory suggests that leaders adopt one of five decision-making leaderships. The appropriate leadership depends on the situation. As summarised in the following table, there are two autocratic types of leadership, which are AI and All, two consultative types of leadership, which are CI and CII and the other one is group GII.

Decision-Making Styles in the VYJ Model

Decision Style	Description
AI	Manager makes the decision alone.
AII	Manager asks for information from subordinates but makes (he decision alone. Sub-ordinates may or may will be informed about what the situation is.
CI	Manager shares the situation with individual sub-ordinates and asks for information and evaluation. Subordinates do not meet as a group and the manager alone makes the decision.
C II	Manager and subordinates meet as a group to discuss the situation but the manager makes the decision.
G II	Manager and subordinates meet as a group to discuss the situation and the group makes the decision.

A = Autocratic; C = Consultative; G = Group

The situation is defined by a series of questions about the characteristics or attributes of the problem under consideration. To address the questions, the leader uses one of the four decisions. Two of them are used when the problem affects the entire group. For example, a decision about the facilities to be given to employees in a new office affects the entire group and the other two are appropriate when the decision affects a single individual only, e.g., a new office for that individual only.

Moreover, one of each is to be used when the decision has to be made quickly because of some urgency and the others are to be used when the decision can be made more slowly and the leaders wants to use the opportunity to develop subordinates decision-making abilities.

The VYJ model was criticised because of its complexity. Computer software has been developed to aid leaders in defining the situation, answering the questions about the problem attributes and developing a strategy for decision-making participation.

Although the VYJ model is too new to have been thoroughly tested, evidence so far indicates that this model can help leaders to choose the most effective way to include the sub-ordinates in decision-making.

Other Contingency Approaches

In addition to these three major theories, there are other contingency models or theories developed in recent years. The other models are as follows:

- **Vertical Dyad Linkage Model.** This model stresses the fact that leaders actually have different kinds of working relationship with different subordinates. Each manager-subordinate relationship represents one vertical dyad. The Vertical Dyad Linkage model suggests that leaders establish special working relationships with some subordinates based on some combination of respect, trust and liking. These people constitute the 'in-group'. Other subordinates remain in the 'out-group's, who receive less of leader's time and attention. Those in the 'in-group' receive more of the manager's time and attention and are better performers. Research shows that people in the 'in-group' are more productive and more satisfied with their work than 'out group' members.
- **Life Cycle Model.** The life cycle model suggests that appropriate leader behaviour depends on the maturity of the followers. In this context, maturity includes motivation, competence and experience. The model suggests that as followers become more mature, the leader needs to move gradually from high to low task orientation. Simultaneously, the leader's employee-oriented behaviour should start low, increase at a moderate rate and then decline again.

  Many leaders are familiar with the life cycle theory because it is both simple and logical. However, it has received little scientific support from researchers.

Emerging Perspectives on Leadership in Organisations

The new perspectives that have attracted attention are the concepts of substitutes for leadership and transformational leadership.

Substitutes for Leadership. The existing leadership theories and models try to specify what kind of leader's behaviour is appropriate for different situations. They do not take into consideration, the situations where the leadership is not needed. The substitute concept identifies the situations where the characteristics of the subordinates, the task and the organisation replace leaders' behaviours. For example, when a patient is admitted to an emergency room in a hospital, nurses, doctors and attendants act immediately without waiting for directive or supportive behaviours of leaders in an emergency ward.

Several characteristics of the sub-ordinate may serve to replace or change the behaviour of the leaders. For example, employees with much ability and experience may not need to be told what to do. Similarly, a strong need for independence by the sub-ordinate may result in ineffectiveness of leaders' behaviour.

Characteristics of the task that may substitute the leadership include, the availability of feedback and intrinsic satisfaction. For example, when the job is routine and simple, the subordinate may not need direction. When the task is challenging, the subordinate may not need or want support.

Organisational characteristics that may substitute for leadership include formalisation group cohesion, inflexibility and a rigid reward structure. For example, when policies are formal and rigid, leadership may not be needed.

Transformational Leadership. Another new concept of leadership goes by a number of labels: charismatic leadership, inspirational leadership, symbolic leadership and transformational leadership. This is a leadership that transmits a sense of mission, increases teaming experiences and inspires new ways of thinking.

Charisma is a form of interpersonal attraction. Charismatic people attract followers and this type of leader has great power over his or her followers. Charismatic leaders are self-confident and can influence others. The followers of a charismatic leader identify with the leader's beliefs, accept, trust and obey the leader without questioning him and thereby contribute toward the success of the organisational goals.

Leadership Skills. There is now recognition in both leadership theory and practice of the importance of skills, how leaders should behave and perform effectively. Although there are many skills, such as cultural flexibility, communication, HRD, creativity, and self-management of learning, the research-based skills identified by *Whitten and Cameron seem* to be most valuable. Their personal skills model, involving developing self-awareness, managing stress and solving problems creatively; the interpersonal skills model, involving communicating supportively, gaining power and influence, motivating others and managing conflict, are especially comprehensive and useful. Finally, the widely recognised organisational behaviour techniques such as, training, job design and leaders can also effectively use behavioural management.

COMMUNICATION

Definition

- **Allen.** "Communication is the sum of all the things one person does when wants to create understanding in the mind of other be. It is a bridge of meaning. It involves a systematic and continuous process of telling, listening and understanding".
- **Fred G. Meyer.** "Communication is the intercourse by words, letters or messages".
- **G.G. Brown.** "Communication is transfer of information from one person to another, whether or not it elicits confidence. But the information transferred must be understandable to the receiver.
- **Keith Davis.** "The process of passing information and understanding from one person to another". Communication is a vital part of direction function. Through communication messages are sent and received. To communicate is to inform to show or to spread information. It is the means by which management gets its job done.
- **William Scott.** "It is a process which involves the transmission and accurate replication of ideas ensured by feedback for the purpose of eliciting actions which will accomplish organisational goals".

Meaning

The process of passing any information from one person to the other person with the aid of some medium is termed as **communication**. The first party who sends the information is called the **sender** and the second party who receives the information, decodes the information and accordingly responds is called the **receiver or the recipient**. Thus in simpler terms communication is simply a process where the sender sends the information to the receiver for him to respond.

Sender ------------------------------- Receiver
Information

In an organisation, your boss will never give you your share of credit, unless and until you present your work in a well defined manner. How will one present his/her work- by communication? Parents will never understand that their child is hurt unless and until, the child cries or shows his wounds. What is crying? A form of communication. What does showing of wounds mean-The child wants to communicate to his parents that he needs to be immediately attended by the doctor.

Communication Process

Communication is a process of exchanging verbal and non verbal messages. It is a continuous process. Pre-requisite of communication is a message. This message must be conveyed through some medium to the recipient. It is essential that this message must be understood by the recipient in same terms as intended by the sender. He must respond within a time frame. Thus, communication is a two way process and is incomplete without a feedback from the recipient to the sender on how well the message is understood by him.

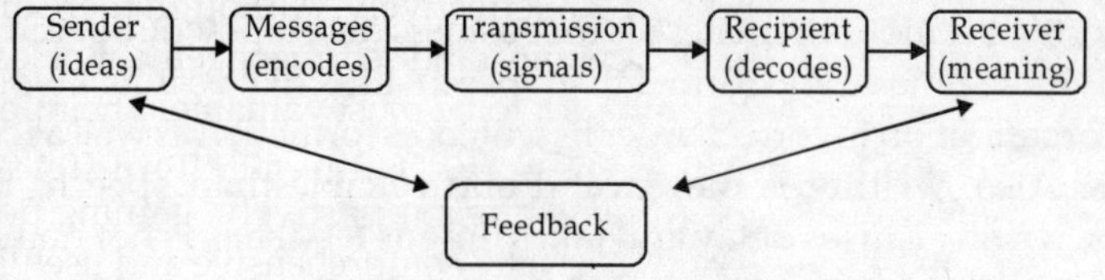

Communication Process

The Main Components of Communication Process

Communication is affected by the context in which it takes place. This context may be physical, social, chronological or cultural. Every communication proceeds with context. The sender chooses the message to communicate within a context.

1. **Sender.** Sender is a person who sends the message. A sender makes use of symbols (words or graphic or visual aids) to convey the message and produce the required response. For instance – a training manager conducting training for new batch of employees. Sender may be an individual or a group or an organisation. The views, background, approach, skills, competencies, and knowledge of the sender have a great impact on the message. The verbal and non verbal symbols chosen are essential in ascertaining interpretation of the message by the recipient in the same terms as intended by the sender.
2. **Message.** Message is a key idea that the sender wants to communicate. It is a sign that elicits the response of recipient. Communication process begins with deciding about the message to be conveyed. It must be ensured that the main objective of the message is clear.
3. **Transmission or Medium.** Medium is a means used to exchange / transmit the message. The sender must choose an appropriate medium for transmitting the message else the message might not be conveyed to the desired recipients. The choice of appropriate medium of communication is essential for making the message effective and correctly interpreted by the recipient. This choice of communication medium varies depending upon the features of communication. For instance - Written medium is chosen when a message has to be conveyed to a small group of people, while an oral medium is chosen when spontaneous feedback is required from the recipient as misunderstandings are cleared then and there.
4. **Recipient/Decoder.** Recipient/Decoder is a person for whom the message is intended / aimed/ targeted. The degree to which the decoder understands the message is dependent upon various factors such as knowledge of recipient, their responsiveness to the message, and the reliance of encoder on decoder.
5. **Feedback.** Feedback is the main component of communication process as it permits the sender to analyze the efficacy of the message. It helps the sender in confirming the correct interpretation of message by the decoder. Feedback may be verbal (through words) or non-verbal (in form of smiles, signs, etc.). It may take written form also in form of memos, reports, etc.

Types of Business Communication

- **Oral Communication.** Meaning Oral communication implies communication through mouth. It includes individuals conversing with each other, be it direct conversation or telephonic conversation. Speeches, presentations, discussions are all forms of oral communication. Oral communication is generally recommended when the communication matter is of temporary kind or where a direct interaction is required. Face to face communication (meetings, lectures, conferences, interviews, etc.) is significant so as to build a rapport and trust.

- **Written Communication.** Written communication has great significance in today's business world. It is an innovative activity of the mind. Effective written communication is essential for preparing worthy promotional materials for business development. Speech came before writing. But writing is more unique and formal than speech. Effective writing involves careful choice of words, their organisation in correct order in sentences formation as well as cohesive composition of sentences. Also, writing is more valid and reliable than speech. But while speech is spontaneous, writing causes delay and takes time as feedback is not immediate.
- **Non Verbal Communication.** Nonverbal communication is behaviour, other than spoken or written communication, that creates or represents meaning. In other words, it includes facial expressions, body movements, and gestures. Nonverbal communication is talking without speaking a word. It is very effective, maybe even more so than speech. Remember the saying, "Actions speak louder than words Nonverbal communication usually understood as the process of communication through sending and receiving wordless messages. Such messages can be communicated through gesture; body language or posture; facial expression and eye contact; object communication such as clothing, hairstyles or even architecture; symbols and info graphics. Speech may also contain nonverbal elements known as para-language, including voice quality, emotion and speaking style, as well as pro-sodic features such as rhythm, intonation and stress. Likewise, written texts have nonverbal elements such as handwriting style, spatial arrangement of words, or the use of emotions.

In an organisation, communication flows in five main directions :

1. Downward
2. Upward
3. Lateral
4. Diagonal
5. External

- **Downward Flow of Communication.** Communication that flows from a higher level in an organisation to a lower level is a downward communication. In other words, communication from superiors to subordinates in a chain of command is a downward communication. This communication flow is used by the managers to transmit work-related information to the employees at lower levels. Employees require this information for performing their jobs and for meeting the expectations of their managers.
- **Upward Flow of Communication.** Communication that flows to a higher level in an organisation is called upward communication. It provides feedback on how well the organisation is functioning. The subordinates use upward communication to convey their problems and performances to their superiors.

  The subordinates also use upward communication to tell how well they have understood the downward communication. It can also be used by the employees to share their views and ideas and to participate in the decision-making process.

  Upward communication leads to a more committed and loyal workforce in an organisation because the employees are given a chance to raise and speak dissatisfaction issues to the higher levels. The managers get to know about the employees feelings towards their jobs, peers, supervisor and organisation in general. Managers can thus accordingly take actions for improving things.
- **Lateral/Horizontal Communication.** Communication that takes place at same levels of hierarchy in an organisation is called lateral communication, *i.e.*, communication between peers, between managers at same levels or between any horizontally equivalent organisational member.

- **Diagonal Communication.** Communication that takes place between a manager and employees of other workgroups is called diagonal communication. It generally does not appear on organisational chart. For instance - To design a training module a training manager interacts with an Operations personnel to enquire about the way they perform their task.
- **External Communication.** Communication that takes place between a manager and external groups such as - suppliers, vendors, banks, financial institutes etc. For instance - To raise capital the Managing director would interact with the Bank Manager.
- **Multi-Directional Communication.** Multi-directional communication is the integration of horizontal, upward and downward communication. Through this kind of communication, organisations achieve more accurate feedback. Business can uses it to motivate employees and generate a feeling of inclusion to all people on all levels of a company. It also helps to promote understanding within an organisation.

Grapevine Communication (Informal Business Communication)

Grapevine is an informal channel of business communication. It is called so because it stretches throughout the organisation in all directions irrespective of the authority levels. Man as we know is a social animal. Despite existence of formal channels in an organisation, the informal channels tend to develop when he interacts with other people in organisation. It exists more at lower levels of organisation. Grapevine generally develops due to various reasons. One of them is that when an organisation is facing recession, the employees sense uncertainty. Also, at times employees do not have self-confidence due to which they form unions. Sometimes the managers show preferential treatment and favor some employees giving a segregated feeling to other employees. Thus, when employees sense a need to exchange their views, they go for grapevine network as they cannot use the formal channel of communication in that case. Generally during breaks in cafeteria, the subordinates talk about their superior's attitude and behaviour and exchange views with their peers. They discuss rumors about promotion and transfer of other employees. Thus, grapevine spreads like fire and it is not easy to trace the cause of such communication at times.

Pros & Cons of Grapevine Communication

Advantages of Grapevine Communication

1. Grapevine channels carry information rapidly. As soon as an employee gets to know some confidential information, he becomes inquisitive and passes the details then to his closest friend who in turn passes it to other. Thus, it spreads hastily.
2. The managers get to know the reactions of their subordinates on their policies. Thus, the feedback obtained is quick compared to formal channel of communication.
3. The grapevine creates a sense of unity among the employees who share and discuss their views with each other. Thus, grapevine helps in developing group cohesiveness.
4. The grapevine serves as an emotional supportive value.
5. The grapevine is a supplement in those cases where formal communication does not work.

Disadvantages of Grapevine Communication

1. The grapevine carries partial information at times as it is more based on rumours. Thus, it does not clearly depict the complete state of affairs.
2. The grapevine is not trustworthy always as it does not follows official path of communication and is spread more by gossips and unconfirmed report.
3. The productivity of employees may be hampered as they spend more time talking rather than working.

4. The grapevine leads to making hostility against the executives.
5. The grapevine may hamper the goodwill of the organisation as it may carry false negative information about the high level people of the organisation.

A smart manager should take care of all the disadvantages of the grapevine and try to minimise them. At the same time, he should make best possible use of advantages of grapevine.

Feedback Communication

Receivers are not just passive absorbers of messages; they receive the message and respond to them. This response of a receiver to sender's message is called Feedback. Sometimes a feedback could be a non-verbal smiles, signs etc. Sometimes it is oral, as when you react to a colleague's ideas with questions or comments. Feedback can also be written like - replying to an e-mail, etc. Feedback is your audience's response; it enables you to evaluate the effectiveness of your message. If your audience doesn't understand what you mean, you can tell by the response and then refine the message accordingly. Giving your audience a chance to provide feedback is crucial for maintaining an open communication climate. The manager must create an environment that encourages feedback. For example after explaining the job to the subordinated he must ask them whether they have understood it or not. He should ask questions like "Do you understand?", "Do you have any doubts?" etc. At the same time he must allow his subordinated to express their views also.

Feedback is essential in communication so as to know whether the recipient has understood the message in the same terms as intended by the sender and whether he agrees to that message or not. There are lot of ways in which company takes feedback from their employees, such as : Employee surveys, memos, e-mails, open-door policies, company news letter etc. Employees are not always willing to provide feedback. The organisation has to work a lot to get the accurate feedback. The managers encourage feedback by asking specific questions, allowing their employees to express general views, etc. The organisation should be receptive to their employee's feedback.

Communication Barriers – Reason for Communication Breakdown

Following are the main communication barriers:

- **Perceptual and Language Differences.** Perception is generally how each individual interprets the world around him. All generally want to receive messages which are significant to them. But any message which is against their values is not accepted. A same event may be taken differently by different individuals. For example : A person is on leave for a month due to personal reasons (family member being critical). The HR Manager might be in confusion whether to retain that employee or not, the immediate manager might think of replacement because his teams productivity is being hampered, the family members might take him as an emotional support. The linguistic differences also lead to communication breakdown. Same word may mean different to different individual.
- "**Value**" means different in different sentences. Communication breakdown occurs if there is wrong perception by the receiver.
- **Information Overload.** Managers are surrounded with a pool of information. It is essential to control this information flow else the information is likely to be misinterpreted or forgotten or overlooked. As a result communication is less effective.
- **Inattention.** At times we just not listen, but only hear. For example a traveler may pay attention to one "NO PARKING" sign, but if such sign is put all over the city, he no longer listens to it. Thus, repetitive messages should be ignored for effective communication. Similarly if a superior is engrossed in his paper work and his subordinate explains him his problem, the superior may not get what he is saying and it leads to disappointment of subordinate.

- **Time Pressures.** Often in organisation the targets have to be achieved within a specified time period, the failure of which has adverse consequences. In a haste to meet deadlines, the formal channels of communication are shortened, or messages are partially given, *i.e.*, not completely transferred. Thus sufficient time should be given for effective communication.
- **Distraction/Noise.** Communication is also affected a lot by noise to distractions. Physical distractions are also there such as, poor lightning, uncomfortable sitting, unhygienic room also affects communication in a meeting. Similarly use of loud speakers interferes with communication.
- **Emotions.** Emotional state at a particular point of time also affects communication. If the receiver feels that communicator is angry he interprets that the information being sent is very bad. While he takes it differently if the communicator is happy and jovial (in that case the message is interpreted to be good and interesting).
- **Complexity in Organisational Structure.** Greater the hierarchy in an organisation (*i.e.* more the number of managerial levels), more is the chances of communication getting destroyed. Only the people at the top level can see the overall picture while the people at low level just have knowledge about their own area and a little knowledge about other areas.
- **Poor retention.** Human memory cannot function beyond a limit. One can't always retain what is being told specially if he is not interested or not attentive. This leads to communication breakdown.

There are several barriers that affect the flow of communication in an organisation. These barriers interrupt the flow of communication from the sender to the receiver, thus making communication ineffective. It is essential for managers to overcome these barriers. The main barriers of communication are summarised below.

Overcoming Communication Barriers

There are a lot of communication barriers faced these days by all. The message intended by the sender is not understood by the receiver in the same terms and sense and thus communication breakdown occurs. It is essential to deal and cope up with these communication barriers so as to ensure smooth and effective communication. As, in the previous section we have discussed the major barriers of communication. Let's talk about **how to overcome these barriers of communication**.

1. **Eliminating differences in perception.** The organisation should ensure that it is recruiting right individuals on the job. It's the responsibility of the interviewer to ensure that the interviewee has command over the written and spoken language. There should be proper Induction program so that the policies of the company are clear to all the employees. There should be proper trainings conducted for required employees (for e.g.: Voice and Accent training).
2. **Use of Simple Language.** Use of simple and clear words should be emphasized. Use of ambiguous words and jargons should be avoided.
3. **Reduction and elimination of noise levels.** Noise is the main communication barrier which must be overcome on priority basis. It is essential to identify the source of noise and then eliminate that source.
4. **Active Listening.** Listen attentively and carefully. There is a difference between "listening" and "hearing". Active listening means hearing with proper understanding of the message that is heard. By asking questions the speaker can ensure whether his/her message is understood or not by the receiver in the same terms as intended by the speaker.
5. **Emotional State.** During communication one should make effective use of body language. He/she should not show their emotions while communication as the receiver might misinterpret the message being delivered. For example, if the conveyer of the message is in a bad mood then the receiver might think that the information being delivered is not good.

6. **Simple Organisational Structure.** The organisational structure should not be complex. The number of hierarchical levels should be optimum. There should be a ideal span of control within the organisation. Simpler the organisational structure, more effective will be the communication.
7. **Avoid Information Overload.** The managers should know how to prioritise their work. They should not overload themselves with the work. They should spend quality time with their subordinates and should listen to their problems and feedbacks actively.
8. **Give Constructive Feedback.** Avoid giving negative feedback. The contents of the feedback might be negative, but it should be delivered constructively. Constructive feedback will lead to effective communication between the superior and subordinate.
9. **Proper Media Selection.** The managers should properly select the medium of communication. Simple messages should be conveyed orally, like: face to face interaction or meetings. Use of written means of communication should be encouraged for delivering complex messages. For significant messages reminders can be given by using written means of communication such as : Memos, Notices etc.
10. **Flexibility in meeting the targets.** For effective communication in an organisation the managers should ensure that the individuals are meeting their targets timely without skipping the formal channels of communication. There should not be much pressure on employees to meet their targets.

Seven C's of Effective Communication

There are **7 C's of effective communication** which are applicable to both written as well as oral communication.

These are as follows:

- **Completeness.** The communication must be complete. It should convey all facts required by the audience. The sender of the message must take into consideration the receiver's mind set and convey the message accordingly.
- **Conciseness.** Conciseness means wordiness, *i.e.*, communicating what you want to convey in least possible words without forgoing the other C's of communication. Conciseness is a necessity for effective communication.
- **Consideration.** Consideration implies "stepping into the shoes of others". Effective communication must take the audience into consideration, *i.e.*, the audience's view points, background, mind-set, education level, etc. Make an attempt to envisage your audience, their requirements, emotions as well as problems. Ensure that the self-respect of the audience is maintained and their emotions are not at harm. Modify your words in message to suit the audience's needs while making your message complete.
- **Clarity.** Clarity implies emphasizing on a specific message or goal at a time, rather than trying to achieve too much at once. Clarity in communication has following features:
  - It makes understanding easier.
  - Complete clarity of thoughts and ideas enhances the meaning of message.
  - Clear message makes use of exact, appropriate and concrete words.
- **Concreteness.** Concrete communication implies being particular and clear rather than fuzzy and general. Concreteness strengthens the confidence. Concrete message has following features:
  - It is supported with specific facts and figures.
  - It makes use of words that are clear and that build the reputation.
  - Concrete messages are not misinterpreted.

- **Courtesy.** Courtesy in message implies the message should show the sender's expression as well as should respect the receiver. The sender of the message should be sincerely polite, judicious, reflective and enthusiastic. Courteous message has following features:
  - Courtesy implies taking into consideration both viewpoints as well as feelings of the receiver of the message.
  - Courteous message is positive and focused at the audience.
  - It makes use of terms showing respect for the receiver of message.
  - It is not at all biased.
- **Correctness.** Correctness in communication implies that there are no grammatical errors in communication. Correct communication has following features:
  - The message is exact, correct and well-timed.
  - If the communication is correct, it boosts up the confidence level.
  - Correct message has greater impact on the audience/ readers.
  - It checks for the precision and accurateness of facts and figures used in the message.

It makes use of appropriate and correct language in the message. Awareness of these 7 C's of communication makes you an effective communicator.

POWER AND AUTHORITY

Power

Power is the potential or actual ability of a person to affect the behaviour of others. This ability can be based on a number of factors, such as knowledge, personality, and even on authority. When power receives formal recognition and backing by the organisation, it will be called authority. In other words, power is a larger concept than authority and indeed, subsumes it as a formal power relationship. Power can also be seen as the influence that is not based on organisational positions. Because of this, power applies to any interpersonal influence that exists either within or outside the bounds of formal organisational relationship. The brief explanation below throws more light on the difference between power and authority. If a supervisor issues directives to subordinates on how to carry out a normal work routine, these directives will be considered by both the supervisor and the subordinates to be official. Here, the supervisor can be said to have used power in the form of position authority which attaches to his or her role as a manager and which has been delegated to him or her by a superior officer in order to get certain organisational goals accomplished. If a supervisor directs a subordinate to do a personal errand for him or her, this errand is clearly outside the official relationship between the supervisor and the subordinate and therefore, the instruction cannot be founded on authority. This instruction, then, is an attempt to use power as the basis of influence. The extent to which an individual can exercise power can be viewed as a function of the dependency relationship that exists between the parties. The higher the dependency ratio; other things being equal, the higher the power and vice versa.

Forms of Power

Influence that is based on power has many forms and in our discussion here, we shall try as much as possible to explain how power gains its support and potency in organisation as the base for our classification.

1. **Rational or Legal Power.** This is a type of power that is recognised and accepted by subordinates as being in agreement with the laid down rules and regulations that are considered legitimate by both parties. Here, there is little or no question about whether its use is considered proper or not. Whatever its source might be, whether through ability or knowledge, once the members of

the society or organisation consider it legitimate to accept a given type of influence, that influence will be properly classified as rational power.

2. **Reward Power.** This is a form of power that comes from one's ability to control and dispense benefits to others. The controller of the benefits has the ability to shape the behaviour of others by the simple act of dispensing or withholding these benefits. The strength of this type of power is primarily determined by two major forces and these are the size of the reward and the belief that it will be dispensed. This proposition is based on the assumption that other things being equal, a large reward gives greater power than a small reward.
3. **Coercive Power.** This is a kind of power that emanates from a person's ability to punish others. This ability to punish others is often strong motivation and can, in many ways, be viewed as the obverse of reward power.
While reward power relies on dispensing of rewards for its strength, coercive power depends on the meting out of punishment for its effectiveness. The effectiveness of coercive power depends on the definition of the punishment, its perceived impact, the probability that it will be used, and the measurement of desired behaviour. For example, if the possible punishment is not defined as such by the offender, if it is seen to be relatively mild, or if the chances of its being used is slight, coercive power will be less effective and vice versa.
4. **Referent Power.** This is a form of power that exists when one has influence over another because the other identifies with him or her. For instance, if "A" has influence over "B" because "B" identifies with "A", that power or influence will be called referent power. This identification will give "A" the power to influence the behaviour of "B" even though "A" may not be aware of the identification. For example, star athletes are worshipped by aspiring youngsters who see that their own abilities can be enhanced by emulating the star's behaviour. At times, people with whom others identify might not be aware of their own referent power. Because of this, it is often difficult to completely trace power relationship in referent power.
5. **Charismatic Power.** This is a kind of power that occurs as a result of one's magnetic quality of personality. The possessor of the personality uses it to influence the behaviour of others. For example, Hitler exercised this type of power in Germany before and during World War II. Those who possess' charismatic powers find it relatively easy to influence their followers. One of the dimensions of charismatic power that helps explain its potency is that charismatic leaders also help their followers attain personal goals. By following such leaders, the followers can realise their own objectives.
6. **Expert Power.** Expert power exists where one exerts influence over others because of one's possession of knowledge or special skill. This skill attracts respect for the expert. For example, Nobel Scientists are respected for their skills and because of this; they are said to posses' expert power. Those who admire the skill or who need it to solve problems are willing to subordinate themselves in return for the expert's assistance. A student who needs a teacher's help in solving a problem is an example. The student attributes the power of knowledge to the teacher and behaves in a manner that will enable him or her to have the advantage of the teacher's knowledge in solving the problem. A successful use of expert power within its sphere of influence tends to increase its potency while its use outside its sphere tends to weaken its strength.

Sources of Power

In the work environment just like the general society, there are numerous sources through which managers and leaders or anybody in authority can enrich himself or herself with power. These sources all revolve around the dependency of one actor on another. The ability to create and manage dependency relationship is among the most important determinants of the amount of power any actor can wield. Some of these sources of power are discussed below:

1. **Power through the Control of Resources.** This is one of the most important sources of power in the organisations and even in our society. Those that possess resources exert tremendous influence on the behaviour of others. Naturally, resources such as money and materials are not equitably distributed and because of this, those who possess them command respect and wield influence which enables them to influence the behaviour of others. This is in line with the general notion in commerce that money commands variety. The word "variety" here includes respect and influence.
2. **Position Power.** This source of power is attached to offices in organisation. Various offices have powers emanating from them and the higher the office in the organisation chart, the higher the power that comes from it. Organisation chart generally depicts the hierarchy of formal authority through which position power gains its potency and recognition.
3. **Personal Qualities.** Personal qualities are another good source of power to some managers and leaders. These qualities consist of knowledge, charisma, and possession of special skills. These qualities enable the individuals that possess them to influence the behaviour of others and therefore enhance their ability to manage and control their subordinates.
4. **Professionalism.** Professionalism as a source of power in organisation comes as a result of an increase in professional expertise through professional examinations and training. In the organisation, those people that passed professional examinations and equally had some training usually possess more power than those that did not pass any professional examination and did not even attend any training.

Authority

The word authority probably brings to our mind a picture of a parent scolding a child or a military officer giving a command to a troop or a manager guiding or altering the behaviour of subordinates. Well, all these are aspects of authority. Authority is a formal right to make decision based on formal organisational relationships. Authority is also seen as the right to command others to act or not to act in a manner deemed by the possessor of the authority to further organisation objectives. Directing the behaviour of others is based on two sub-rights: (a) the right to decide, and (b) the right to issue appropriate implementing instructions. Without the right to decide, no manager could be a successful planner, and without the right to issue orders and instructions, the manager's plans would be worthless. This is because there could be no assurance of the implementation of the plans. Authority is the corner-stone of every organisation. It gives every organisation the characteristic of hierarchy that establishes a defined chain of command. Authority establishes the relationship between the job to be done and the people that will do the job. Thus, authority is fundamental to every organisation because the nature of managerial responsibility involves decision making and influence.

Forms of Authority

There is no general consensus among management writers and researchers on what constitute the forms/ types of authority. Although different writers and researchers give different names to the forms of authority in obedience to the angle from which each of them looks at it, a careful analysis of the different forms shows that the actual meaning which they attach to the forms if summed together goes to the same direction. The difference is only in the connotation and nomenclature and not on the facts. In this article, we adopt the following forms of authority and the aim is to treat the components and uses of authority in order to demonstrate how they affect organisational behaviour and therefore its performance.

1. **Managerial Authority.** This is the form of authority given to managers of formal organisations because they are responsible for acquiring, deploying, and controlling resources needed to accomplish objectives. Managerial authority is composed of the right to enforce those choices

based on official position. Without these components, no manager, can successfully carryout responsibilities. This is true because all managers, regardless of their positions in the organisation structure, are charged with the responsibility of making decisions and ensuring that they are carried out. Thus, managerial authority is the key means for executing managerial responsibility. The exact nature and amount of managerial authority required at any given location in the organisation structure should be a function of the responsibility there. Consequently, the manager's responsibility should be a determining factor in deciding the amount of authority that the manager is granted. This balance between responsibility and authority is in keeping with the principle of parity of authority and responsibility – a long recognised guide to building and maintaining a sound organisation structure.

2. **Staff Authority.** This is a kind of authority given to all staff of an organisation to make suggestions and recommendations about the solution to problems, procedural changes or how their jobs could be made easier or more attractive. Even though we normally associate this type of authority with experts or professional personnel, it is actually possessed by every member of the organisation. This is because everyone in an organisation whether superior or subordinate has the right to recommend, to suggest, and to advice. One possible confusing aspect of the use of staff authority is the fact that subordinates often do not elect to use their staff authority for one reason or the other. In addition, some superiors discourage their subordinates from using it. This situation can be compared to the right to vote. In voting situation, there are those who voluntarily choose not to exercise their voting rights, and there might be occasions where they are virtually prohibited from doing so by others. Whether they are used or not, voting rights are possessed by all qualified citizens and so it is with staff authority.

3. **Situational Authority.** This is a form of authority that has both the elements of managerial authority and that of staff authority. Generally, this kind of authority is delegated to a staff expert who is restricted in the areas of organisation structure and functions in which it can be exercised. This expert is given the right to make binding decisions about a given function in the organisation structure. This type of organisation relationship often begins as a staff authority relationship.

   As time passes and the expert's superior gains confidence in the quality of advice, the expert might be given a grant of situational authority that is approved by the officer who supervises the chief accountant. This means that the accountant can now issue decisions that have the prior approval of the superior through the grant of situational authority. Therefore, it is not necessary to involve the superior in every decision. In practice, situational authority can be quite disruptive to the organisation if it is misused but if properly used, it can be an effective managerial aid. Situational authority is a potent right and should only be delegated after careful consideration and it should have some safeguards about over what activities it can be exercised.

4. **Operative Authority.** This is a type of right given to members of an organisation to take certain decisions about how, in what order, and with which tools they will carry out their assignments. Also included here is the right to work without undue supervision. Some people do not include the operative authority in their list of forms of authorities but here, we deemed it necessary to include it in order to give a complete explanation of the rights of organisation members. For example, at times a worker may be asked to take a decision about work priorities, schedules, and tools and materials to be used for the work. The decision is outside the scope of the managerial, staff, and situational authority and because of that, the decision will be made by using operative authority. Operative authority is made up of two basic rights – the right to carry out responsibility and the right to determine, within reason, how and when it will be done. Whether one is a manager, a technician, or an unskilled labourer, one has these minimum rights. Without them, it would not be possible to plan and carry out one's personal responsibility.

STRESS

Defining Stress

Stress is defined in terms of its physical and physiological effects on a person, and can be a mental, physical, or emotional strain.

Stress is defined in terms of how it impacts physical and psychological health; it includes mental, physical, and emotional strain. Stress occurs when a demand exceeds an individual's coping ability and disrupts his or her psychological equilibrium. Stress occurs in the workplace when an employee perceives a situation to be too strenuous to handle, and therefore threatening to his or her well-being.

Stress at Work

While it is generally agreed that stress occurs at work, views differ on the importance of worker characteristics versus working conditions as its primary cause. The differing viewpoints suggest different ways to prevent stress at work. Different individual characteristics, like personality and coping skills, can be very important predictors of whether certain job conditions will result in stress. In other words, what is stressful for one person may not be a problem for someone else.

Stress-related disorders encompass a broad array of conditions, including psychological disorders (e.g., depression, anxiety, post-traumatic stress disorder) and other types of emotional strain (e.g., dissatisfaction, fatigue, tension), maladaptive behaviours (e.g., aggression, substance abuse), and cognitive impairment (e.g., concentration and memory problems). Job stress is also associated with various biological reactions that may ultimately lead to compromised physical health, such as cardiovascular disease.

Categories of Work Stress

Four categories of stressors underline the different causal circumstances for stress at work:

1. **Task Demands.** This is the sense of not knowing where a job will lead you and whether the activities and tasks will change. This uncertainty causes stress that manifests itself in feelings of lack of control, concern about career progress, and time pressures.
2. **Role Demands.** Role conflict happens when an employee is exposed to inconsistent or difficult expectations. Examples include: interole conflict (when there are two or more expectations or separate roles for one person), intrarole conflict (varying expectations of one role), person-role conflict (ethics are challenged), and role ambiguity (confusion about their experiences in relation to the expectations of others).
3. **Interpersonal Demands.** Examples include: emotional issues (abrasive personalities, offensive co-workers), sexual harassment (directed mostly toward women), and poor leadership (lack of management experience, poor style, cannot handle having power).
4. **Physical Demands.** Many types of work are physically demanding, including strenuous activity, extreme working conditions, travel, exposure to hazardous materials, and working in a tight, loud office.

Causes of Workplace Stress

Work stress is caused by demands and pressure from both within and outside of the workplace.

Work-Related Stress

Problems caused by stress have become a major concern to both employers and employees. Symptoms of stress can manifest both physiologically and psychologically. Work-related stress is typically caused by demands and pressure from either within or outside of the workplace; it can be derived from uncertainty over where the job will take the employee, inconsistent or difficult expectations, interpersonal issues, or physical demands.

Although the importance of individual differences cannot be ignored, scientific evidence suggests that certain working conditions are stressful to most people. Such evidence argues that working conditions are a key source of job stress and job redesign should be used as a primary prevention strategy.

Studies of Work-Related Stress

Large-scale surveys of working conditions—including conditions recognized as risk factors for job stress—were conducted in member states of the European Union in 1990, 1995, and 2000. Results showed a time-related trend that suggested an increase in work intensity. In 1990, the percentage of workers reporting that they worked at high speeds for at least one-quarter of their working time was 48%; this increased to 54% in 1995 and 56% in 2000. Similarly, 50% of workers reported that they worked against tight deadlines at least one-fourth of their working time in 1990; this increased to 56% in 1995 and 60% in 2000. However, no change was noted in the period from 1995 to 2000 in the percentage of workers reporting sufficient time to complete tasks (data was not collected in 1990 for this category).

A substantial percentage of Americans work very long hours. By one estimate, more than 26% of men and more than 11% of women worked 50 hours or more per week (outside of the home) in 2000. These figures represent a considerable increase over the previous three decades—especially for women. According to the Department of Labor, there has been an upward trend in hours worked among employed women, an increase in work weeks of greater than forty hours by men, and a considerable increase in combined working hours among working couples, particularly couples with young children.

Power and Stress

A person's status in the workplace can also affect levels of stress. Stress in the workplace has the potential to affect employees of all categories, and managers as well as other kinds of workers are vulnerable to work overload. However, less powerful employees (those who have less control over their jobs) are more likely to experience stress than employees with more power. This indicates that authority is an important factor complicating the work stress environment.

Economics and Stress

Economic factors that employees are facing in the 21st century have been linked to increased stress levels as well. Researchers and social commentators have pointed out that advances in technology and communications have made companies more efficient and more productive than ever before. This increase in productivity has resulted in higher expectations and greater competition, which in turn place more stress on employees.

The following economic factors can contribute to workplace stress:

- Pressure from investors who can quickly withdraw their money from company stocks.
- Lack of trade and professional unions in the workplace.
- Inter-company rivalries caused by global competition.
- The willingness of companies to swiftly lay off workers to cope with changing business environments.

Social Interactions and Stress

Bullying in the workplace can also contribute to stress. Workplace bullying can involve threats to an employee's professional or personal image or status, deliberate isolation, or giving an employee excess work.

Another type of workplace bullying is known as "destabilization." Destabilization can occur when an employee is not given credit for their work or is assigned meaningless tasks. In effect, destabilization can create a hostile work environment for employees, negatively affecting their work ethic and therefore their contributions to the organization.

Stress Outside of the Workplace

Non-work demands can create stress both inside and outside of work. Stress is inherently cumulative, and it can be difficult to separate our personal and professional stress inducers. Examples of non-work stress that can be carried into the workplace include:

- **Home demands.** Relationships, children, and family responsibilities can add stress that is hard to leave behind when entering the workplace. The Academy of Management Journal states that this constitutes "an individual's lack of personal resources needed to fulfill commitments, obligations, or requirements."
- **Personal demands.** Personal demands are brought on by the person when he or she takes on too many responsibilities, either inside or outside of work.

Consequences of Workplace Stress

Stress can impact an individual mentally and physically and so can decrease employee efficiency and job satisfaction.

Stress

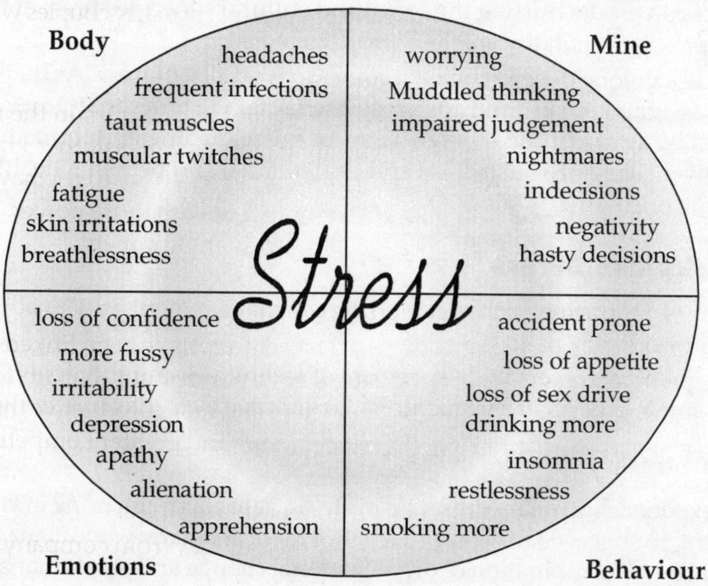

SYMPTOMS OF STRESS. STRESS CAN MANIFEST AS VARIOUS SYMPTOMS AFFECTING ONE'S BODY, MIND, BEHAVIOUR, AND/OR EMOTIONS.

Negative or overwhelming work experiences can cause a person substantial distress. Burnout, depression, and psychosomatic disorders are particularly common outcomes of work-related stress. In general, individual distress manifests in three basic forms: psychological disorders, medical illnesses, and behavioural problems.

Psychological Disorders

Psychosomatic disorders are a type of psychological disorder. They are physical problems with a psychological cause. For example, a person who is extremely anxious about public speaking might feel extremely nauseated or may find themselves unable to speak at all when faced with the prospect of presenting in front of a group. Since stress of this type is often difficult to notice, managers would benefit from carefully monitoring employee behaviour for indications of discomfort or stress.

Medical Illnesses

Physiological reactions to stress can have a long-term impact on physical health. In fact, stress is one of the leading precursors to long-term health issues. Backaches, stroke, heart disease, and peptic ulcers are just a few physical ailments that can arise when a person is under too much stress.

Behavioural Problems

A person can also exhibit behavioural problems when under stress, such as aggression, substance abuse, absenteeism, poor decision making, lack of creativity, or even sabotage. A stressed worker may neglect their duties, impeding workflows and processes so that the broader organization slows down and loses time and money. Managers should keep an eye out for such behaviours as possible indicators of workplace stress.

Organizational Effects of Stress

Stress in the workplace can be, so to speak, "contagious" – low job satisfaction is often something employees will discuss with one another. If stress is not noted and addressed by management early on, team dynamics can erode, hurting the social and cultural synergies present in the organization. Ultimately, the aggressive mentality will be difficult to remedy.

Managers are in a unique position when it comes to workplace stress. As they are responsible for setting the pace, assigning tasks, and fostering the social customs that govern the work group, management must be aware of the repercussions of mismanaging and inducing stress. Managers should consistently discuss job satisfaction and professional and personal health with each of their subordinates one on one.

Reducing Workplace Stress

A combination of organizational change and stress management is a productive approach to preventing stress at work.

Stress management refers to a wide spectrum of techniques and therapies that aim to control a person's levels of stress, especially chronic stress, to improve everyday functioning.

Preventing Job Stress

If employees are experiencing unhealthy levels of stress, a manager can bring in an objective outsider, such as a consultant, to suggest a fresh approach. But there are many ways managers can prevent job stress in the first place. A combination of organizational change and stress management is often the most effective approach. Among the many different techniques managers can use to effectively prevent employee stress, the main underlying themes are awareness of possibly stressful elements of the workplace and intervention when necessary to mitigate any stress that does arise.

Specifically, organizations can prevent employee stress in the following ways:

Intentional Job Design

- Design jobs that provide meaning and stimulation for workers as well as opportunities for them to use their skills.

- Establish work schedules that are compatible with demands and responsibilities outside the job.
- Consider flexible schedules – many organizations allow telecommuting to reduce the pressure of being a certain place at a certain time (which enables people to better balance their personal lives).
- Monitor each employee's workload to ensure it is in line with their capabilities and resources.

Clear and Open Communication

- Teach employees about stress awareness and promote an open dialogue.
- Avoid ambiguity at all costs – clearly define workers' roles and responsibilities.
- Reduce uncertainty about career development and future employment prospects.

Positive Workplace Culture

- Provide opportunities for social interaction among workers.
- Watch for signs of dissatisfaction or bullying and work to combat workplace discrimination (based on race, gender, national origin, religion, or language).

Employee Accountability

- Give workers opportunities to participate in decisions and actions that affect their jobs.
- Introduce a participative leadership style and involve as many subordinates as possible in resolving stress-producing problems.

Stress Prevention Programs

St. Paul Fire and Marine Insurance Company conducted several studies on the effects of stress prevention programs in a hospital setting. Program activities included educating employees and management about workplace stress, changing hospital policies and procedures to reduce organizational sources of stress, and establishing of employee assistance programs. In one study, the frequency of medication errors declined by 50% after prevention activities were implemented in a 700-bed hospital. In a second study, there was a 70% reduction in malpractice claims among 22 hospitals that implemented stress prevention activities. In contrast, there was no reduction in claims in a matched group of 22 hospitals that did not implement stress prevention activities.

ORGANISATIONAL CHANGE AND DEVELOPMENT

Organisational Change

Change simply refers to alteration in the existing conditions of an organisation. Even in most stable organisations change is necessary to maintain stability. The economic and social environment is so dynamic that without adapting to such change even the most successful organisations cannot survive in the changed environment. Therefore, management must continuously monitor the outside environment and be sufficiently innovative and creative to implement these changes effectively.

Organisations encounter different forces for change. These forces come from external and internal sources of the organisation.

External Forces

External forces for change originate outside an organisation. There are four key external forces for change:

Demographic Characteristics. These include age, education, skill level and gender of employees. Organisations need to effectively manage these characteristics in order to receive maximum contribution and commitment from their employees.

Technological Advancements. Both manufacturing and service organisations are increasingly using technology as a means to improve productivity and market competitiveness.

Market Changes. The emergence of a global economy is forcing Indian organisations to change the way they do business. Organisations are entering into new partnerships with their suppliers in order to deliver higher quality products at lower prices.

Social and Political Pressures. These forces are created by social and political events. Personal values affect employees' needs, priorities and motivation. Therefore, managers need to adjust their managerial style according to the changing employee values. Political events also create substantial change in an organisation. Although it is difficult for organisations to predict changes in political forces, many organisations hire lobbyists and consultants to help them detect and respond to social and political changes.

Internal Forces

Internal forces for change come from inside the organisation. This may come from both human resource problems and managerial behaviour.

Human Resource Problems. These problems stem from employee perceptions about their work environment and conflict between an employee and organisation needs. Organisations might respond to these problems by using the various approaches to job design by implementing realistic job previews and by reducing employees' role conflict, stress, work overload and ambiguity.

Managerial Behaviour. Excessive interpersonal conflict between managers and their subordinates is a sign of implementing an immediate change. Inappropriate leader behaviour such as inadequate direction and support are the cause of conflict between managers and their subordinates.

Nature of Change. Organisations introduce changes through people. Unless the people are willing to accept the need and responsibility for organisational change, intended changes can never be translated into reality. In addition, individuals have to learn to adapt their attitudes and behavioural patterns to constantly changing environments.

Management of change involves both individual and organisational change. Individual change is behavioural change, which is determined by individual characteristics of members such as their knowledge, attitudes, beliefs, needs, expectations and skills. It is possible to bring about a total change man organisation by changing behaviours of individual members through participative and educative strategies. Although, the degree of difficulty involved in the change and the time taken to bring about the change will depend on the target of change. The attitudes towards change are largely dependent on the nature of the situation and the manner in which changes are initiated and executed.

Changing individual behaviour is more time consuming and a difficult task. The linkage between attitude and behaviour is not direct and therefore changing behaviour is more difficult than changing attitudes. One's attitude does not necessarily get reflected in one's behaviour. For example, we know that honesty is the best policy and we have favourable altitudes towards people - who are honest but in certain situations, we may still act in a less honest way. Changing group behaviour is usually a more prolonged and harder task. Every group has its own dynamics of push and pull that attempt to neutralise the change that may have taken place in an individual. Due to this group dynamics, individual member's 'changed behaviour' may revert to earlier normative behaviour in order to maintain the change in the existing conditions. However, due to the same reasons of a group's over-riding influence on individual members, sometimes it may be easier to tackle the group as a whole rather than trying to change the behaviour of members one by one.

Approaches to Organisational Change

As **organisational change is a complex process**, therefore managers must approach it systematically and logically. Some organisational changes are planned whereas other changes are reactive. Planned change is designed and implemented by an organisation in an orderly and timely fashion in the anticipation of future change.

Reactive change results from a reaction of an organisation to unexpected events. In contrast to planned change, it is a piece-meal response to circumstances as they develop. External forces that the organisation has failed to anticipate or interpret always bring about reactive change. Since reactive change may have to be carried out hastily, it increases the likelihood of a poorly conceived and poorly executed Program.

Planned change is always preferable to reactive change. Managers who sit back and respond to change only when they can no longer avoid it are likely to waste a lot of time and money trying to patch together a last-minute solution. The more effective approach is to anticipate the significant forces for change working in an organisation and plan ways to address them. To accomplish this, managers must understand the steps needed for effective change.

A Comprehensive Model of Change

The comprehensive model of change shown in the figure shows seven steps that can lead to effective change. This model is useful for both planned and reactive change.

The Seven Steps of Comprehensive Model of Change

Recognise need for change. The first step in this model is recognising need for change. For marketing managers who anticipate needed. Change, recognition is likely to come much earlier, as a result of marketing forecasts indicating new market potential, expert indications about impending socio-economic change or a perceived opportunity to capitalise on a key technological breakthrough. These managers tend to 'initiate change because they expect it to be necessary in the near future in any case'.

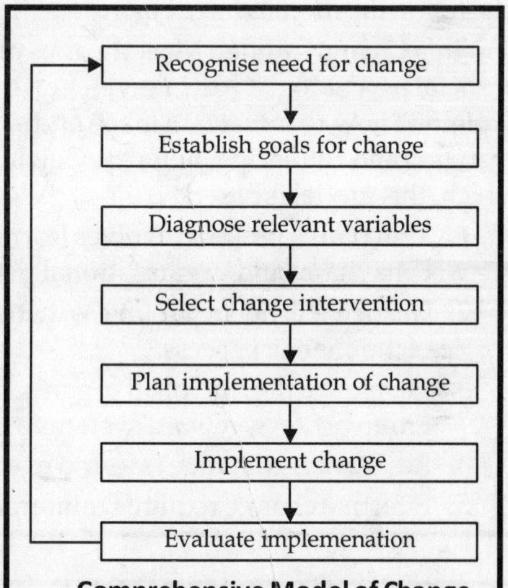

Comprehensive Model of Change

Establish goals for change. The manager must then set goals for the proposed change. It is important for the manager to specify goals that the change is supposed to accomplish. The goals can be set to maintain or increase the market standing, to enter new markets, to restore employee morale, to reduce turnover, to settle a strike and to identify good investment opportunities.

Diagnose relevant variables. An important next step is diagnosing organisational variables that have brought about the need for change. Turnover, for example, may be caused by a variety of factors such as low pay, poor working conditions, poor supervision, better alternatives in the job market or employee job dissatisfaction etc. Thus, if turnover is the recognised stimulus for change, the manager must understand what has caused it in a particular situation in order to make the right changes. To carry out this diagnosis, the manager may discuss the situation with employees and other managers.

Select change intervention. After the manager has developed an understanding of the problem and its causes then he must select a change intervention that will accomplish the intended goal. An intervention is a specific change induced in an organisation with the intention of solving a particular problem or accomplishing a specific objective. For example, if turnover is caused by low pay, then a new reward system is required and if the cause is poor supervision then interpersonal skills and training for supervisors is required.

Plan implementation of change. The manager must then carefully plan the implementation of change. Planning the implementation of change involves consideration of the cost of the change, how the change will affect other areas of the organisation and the degree to which employees should participate in bringing about the change. Hastily implemented change can result in more harm than benefit. For example, if the change involves the use of new equipment, the manager should not make any changes that rely on the use of new equipment until it has arrived and been installed and workers know how to use it. Moreover, if change is thrust upon them too quickly, their resistance may stiffen.

Implement change. A systematically implemented change is more likely to proceed smoothly and to encounter fewer obstacles than is a change that is implemented too quickly and without adequate preparation.

Evaluate implementation. Finally, after the change has been implemented, the manager should verify that it has accomplished its intended goals. A change may fail to bring about the intended results. This may be due to inappropriate goals or inaccurate diagnosis of the situation or wrong selection of intervention.

Models and Dynamics of Planned Change

Managers are criticised for emphasising short-term, quick fix solutions to organisational problems. Quick-fix solutions do not really solve underlying problems and they have little staying power. Researchers and managers have thus tried to identify effective ways to manage the change process. The following models have been developed to effectively manage change:

Lewin's Change Model. Most theories of organisational change originated from the landmark work of social psychologist Kurt Lewin. Lewin developed a three-stage model of planned change, which explained how to initiate, manage and stabilise the change process. The three stages are unfreezing, changing and refreezing. Before reviewing each stage, it is important to highlight the assumptions on which, this model is based:

1. The change process involves learning something new, as well discontinuing current attitudes, behaviours and organisational practices.
2. Change will not occur unless there is motivation to change. This is often the most difficult part of the change process.
3. People are the hub of all organisational changes. Any change, whether in terms of structure, group process, reward systems or job design requires individuals to change.
4. Resistance to change is found even when the goals of change are highly desirable.
5. Effective change requires reinforcing new behaviours, attitudes and organisational practices.

ACTION OF CHANGE

The Following are the Three Stages of Change:

1. **Unfreezing.** The focus of this stage is to make organisation open to change. In doing so individuals are encouraged to replace old behaviours and attitudes with those desired by management. Managers also need to devise ways to reduce the barriers to change during this stage.
2. **Changing.** The focus of this stage is in providing employees with new information, new behavioural models, or new ways of looking at things. The purpose is to help employees learn new concepts to implement change. Role models, mentors, experts, benchmarking organisation against world-class organisations and training are useful mechanisms to facilitate change.
3. **Refreezing.** The focus of this stage is stabilising the change during refreezing by helping employees integrate the changed behaviour or attitude into their normal way of doing things. This is accomplished by first giving employees the chance to exhibit the new behaviours or attitudes. Once exhibited, positive reinforcement is used to reinforce the desired change. Additional coaching and modelling are also used at this point to reinforce the stability of the change.

Expanded Process Model. Lewin's model is very simple and straightforward and virtually all models of organisational change use his approach. However, it does not deal with several important issues. This model looks at planned change from the perspective of top management. The model incorporates Lewin's concept as part of the implementation phase.

Resistance to Change

Although organisations initiate changes in order to adjust to the changes in their environments but people sometimes resist them. Therefore, managers need to recognise the manifestations of resistance both in themselves and in others, if they want to be more effective in supporting change. For example, managers can use the list given in following table:

Acceptance	❍ Enthusiasm
	❍ Cooperation
	❍ Cooperation under pressure from management
	❍ Acceptance
	❍ Passive resignation
	❍ Indifference
Indifference	❍ Apathy: loss of interest in the job
	❍ Doing only what is ordered
	❍ Regressive behaviour
Passive Resistance	❍ Non-learning
	❍ Protests
	❍ Working to rule
	❍ Doing as little as possible
Active Resistance	❍ Slowing down
	❍ Personal withdrawal (increased time off the job)
	❍ Committing "errors"
	❍ Spoilage
	❍ Deliberate sabotage

The sources of resistance to change within organisations are classified into organisational sources of resistance and individual sources of resistance.

Organisational Sources of Resistance. According to **Daniel Katz** and **Robert L Khan**, organisational sources of resistance can be divided into following six general groups.

- Over determination or structural inertia refers to the tendency of an organisation's rules, policies and structure to maintain the existing conditions and therefore resist change even when change would benefit the organisation more than stability.
- When an organisation tries to change one of its division or part of the division without recognising the interdependence of the division with other divisions of the organisation, then it is said to have a narrow focus of change. Often a part of division cannot be changed without changing the whole division.
- Group inertia may weaken an individual's attempt to bring about change.
- Resistance may also take the form of threatened expertise if the change lends to weaken special expertise built after years of experience. Organisational restructuring that involves reducing the number of job categories often meets this kind of resistance.
- Any change that may alter the power relationships within an organisation may meet the form of resistance known as 'threatened power'.

- Resistance may occur when a change threatens quantum of resource allocation from one part of the organisation to another.

Individuals Sources of Resistance. According to researchers, individuals have the following reasons for resisting change:

- Simple habits create a lot of resistance. Most people prefer to do their work the way they did it last week rather than learn a new approach.
- Perhaps the biggest cause of employee resistance to change is uncertainty. In the face of impending change, employees are likely to become anxious and nervous. They worry about their ability to meet new job demands therefore, leading to feeling of job insecurity.
- Some people resist change to avoid feeling of loss. For example, many organisations change interventions and alter work arrangements, thus disrupting existing social networks. Social relationships are important to most people, so they resist any change that might adversely affect those relationships. Change may also threaten people's feelings of familiarity and self-confidence.
- People may resist change because their perceptions of underlying circumstances differ from the perceptions of those who are promoting the change.

Overcoming Resistance to Change

Managers need not abandon planned change in the face of resistance. Before recommending specific approaches to overcome resistance, there are three key conclusions that should be kept in mind. First, an organisation must be ready for change. Second, the top management should inform the employees about the process of change. Third, the employees' perceptions or interpretations of a change should be considered.

The following methods of overcoming-resistance to change are as follows:

- ***Participation.*** Participation is generally considered the most effective technique for overcoming resistance to change. Employees who take part in planning and implementing change are better able to understand the reasons for the change than those who are not involved. They become committed to the change and make it work. Employees who have the opportunity to express their own ideas and to understand the perspectives of others are likely to accept change gracefully. It is a time consuming process.
- ***Education and Communication.*** Educating employees about the need for and the expected results of an impending change help to reduce their resistance. Managers should maintain an open channel of communication while planning and implementing change. However, it is also a time consuming process.
- ***Facilitation of Change.*** Knowing ahead of time that employees are likely to resist change then the manager should do as much as possible to help them cope with uncertainly and feeling of loss. Introducing change gradually, making only necessary changes, announcing changes in advance and allowing time for people to adjust to new ways of doing things can help reduce resistance.
- ***Force-Field Analysis.*** In almost any situation where a change is being planned, there are forces acting for and against the change. In force-field analysis, the manager list each set of forces and then try to remove or minimise some of the forces acting against the change.
- ***Negotiation.*** Where someone or some group will clearly lose out in a change and where that group has considerable power to resist, there negotiation is required. Sometimes it is a relatively easy way to avoid major resistance.
- ***Manipulation and Cooperation.*** This is followed when other tactics will not work or are too expensive. It can be quick and inexpensive; However, it can lead to further problems if people feel manipulated.

- *Explicit and Implicit Coercion.* This is adopted where speed is essential and where the change initiators possess considerable power. It is speedy and can overcome resistance.

Organisational Development

Organisational Development (OD) is a systematic, integrated and planned approach for launching and diffusing change in organisations. Organisation development is a long-range effort to improve an organisations problem-solving and renewal processes, particularly through a more effective and collaborative management of organisation culture with special emphasis on the culture of formal work teams with the assistance of a change agent, or catalyst, and the use of the theory and technology of applied behavioural science, including action research.

The term Organisational Development (OD) refers to a broad range of behavioural science based strategies used to diagnose the need for change in organisations and to implement changes when necessary. OD can be defined as a technique for bringing change in the entire organisation, rather than focusing attention on individuals to bring change easily in the entire organisation.

Nature of Organisational Development

OD is a general strategy or approach to organisational change that is employed to analyze and diagnose the sources of organisational problems and to develop and implement action plans for their solution. According to Bennis, OD has the following characteristics;

- It is an educational strategy for bringing planned change.
- It relates to real problems of an organisation.
- Laboratory training methods based on experienced behaviour are primarily used to bring change.
- Change agent applying OD technique for change is external to the forms of consultants.
- There is a close working relationship between change agents and the people who are being changed. The relationships involve mutual trust, joint goals, means, and mutual influence.
- The change agents share social philosophy about human value. They are humanists seeking to get a humanistic philosophy in organisation.

Process of Organisational Development

The Organisational Development (OD) process is complicated and it takes long time to complete the process. It takes minimum of one year and sometimes continues indefinitely. There are different approaches to OD process but the typical process consists of seven steps, viz., initial diagnosis, data collection, data feedback and confrontation, action planning and problem solving, team building, inter group development and evaluation and follow-up.

1. **Initial Diagnosis.** If executives recognise that there are inadequacies within organisation which can be corrected by OD activities, it is necessary to find out the professional and competent people within the organisation to plan and execute OD activities. If competent people are not available within the organisation the services activities are to be taken. The consultants adopt various methods including interviews, questionnaires, direct observation, analysis of documents and reports for diagnosing the problem.
2. **Data Collection.** Survey method is used to collect the data and information for determining organisational climate and identifying the behavioural problems.
3. **Data Feedback and Confrontation.** Data collected are analyzed and reviewed by various work groups formed from this purpose in order to mediate in the areas of disagreement or confrontation of ideas or opinions and to establish priorities.

MAIN FEATURES OF OD
1. Long-range Effort
2. Broad Based
3. Systems view
4. Dynamic Process
5. Research Based
6. Normative Educational Strategy.

4. **Selection and Design of Interventions.** The interventions are the planned activities that are introduced into the system to accomplish desired changes and improvements. At this stage the suitable interventions are to be selected and designed.
5. **Implementation of Intervention.** The selected intervention should be implemented. Intervention may take the form of workshops, feedback of data to the participants, group discussions, written exercises, on-the-job activities, redesign of control system etc. Interventions are to be implemented steadily as the process is not a one-short, quick cure? for organisational malady. But it achieves real and lasting change in the attitudes and behaviour of employees.
6. **Action planning and problem Solving.** Groups prepare recommendations and specific action planning to solve the specific and identified problems by using data collected.
7. **Team Building.** The consultants encourage the employees throughout the process to form into groups and teams by explaining the advantages of the teams in the OD process, by arranging joint meetings with the managers, subordinates etc.
8. **Inter group Development.** The consultants encourage the inter group meetings, interaction etc., after the formation of groups/teams.

Interventions of Organisational Development

OD interventions refer to various activities which consultant and client organisation perform for improving organisational functioning by enabling organisation members to better manage their team and organisation cultures. French and Well have defined OD interventions as "sets of structured activities in which selected organisational units (target groups or individuals) engage with a task or a sequence of tasks where the task goals are related directly or indirectly to organisational improvement. Interventions constitute the action thrust of organisation development; they make things happen and are what is happening."

These interventions can be clubbed into 15 groups and they are diagnostic, team-building, inter-group activities, survey feedback methods, education and training programmes, techno-structural activities, process consultation, the management grid, meditation and negotiation activities, coaching and counselling and planning and goal setting activities.

1. **Survey Feedback.** It recounts to an approach survey through well planned assessment or Interviews. It covers the feedback to the customer organisation. It has a demand and significance in a genuine situation. The attitude survey can have a purpose to measure the process; for instance, communication, decision making and leadership at different levels. The data produced under this system is perceptual and attitudinal.. A review of the product is prepared in a group discussion. Generally feedback of results is specific to the group which prepares the data. As a result strategies are planned to resolve the organisational problems. Consequently, the process of survey feedback includes: collection of data, feedback, development of action plan and follow-up. Therefore, to ensure authentic results, the survey should be applicable and dependable.
2. **Management Grid.** The method urbanised by Robert Blake and Jane S. Mouton is a step to move toward. This Grid represents a rational support of managing people. Growth of management skills from beginning to end grid program involves wide range of included and instrumented activities are the ways having investigational and planned conditions. The members are secondary to be pleased about the advances to integrate people and their invention.
3. **Team Building.** Team building is an attempt to assist the work group to identify, diagnose and solve its own problems. Actually groups develop their own norms of behaviour which pressurize

the persons and group behaviour. Organisation is a system to interconnect with groups. OD considers that work groups are the teams which are spinning around to introduce changes in the organisation. Team building actions are taken to develop a range of groups in an organisation like permanent work teams, task forces, committees etc. Team building actions focus on finding, task achievement, team relationships and organisational process. The component groups in team building activity are: the external advisors, the group leader and member of the group. In team building movement, associates meet and talk about troubles connecting to their course-work. It obtain sincere and courageous argument. In the team building movements, the associate adds the sequence relating to their personal observation of issues, problems and task relationship.

4. **Sensitivity Training.** Sensitivity training is a small-group interaction under stress in an unstructured encounter group, which requires people to become sensitive to one another's feelings in order to develop reasonable group activity. In sensitivity training, the actual technique employed is T-group. T-group has several characteristic features:
   - The T-group is generally small, from ten to twenty members
   - The group begins its activity with no formal agenda
   - The primary role of trainer is to call attention of members from time to time to the ongoing process within the group
   - The procedure lends to develop introspection and self-examination, with emotional levels of involvement and behaviour.

   The objectives of such training are increased openness with others, more concern for others, increased tolerance for individual differences, less ethnic prejudice, understanding of a group process, enhanced listening skills and increased trust and support.
5. **Four System Management.** Rensis Likert's four System Management has given four stage to represent the organisational values to include the essential collection of job bearing According to Likert management philosophy can be classified into four systems they are:
   (i) Exploitative Autocratic (ii) Benevolent Autocratic
   (iii) Consultative Democratic (iv) Participative Democratic

   This theory explains that three basic concepts of system has four management which will help making the organisation effective they are:
   (a) To use the principle of supportive relationship in the organisation
   (b) To use the group decision making and group methods of supervision in the organisation,
   (c) To emphasize more on the high performance goals.
6. **Management by Objectives (MBO).** It is another important tool of O.D. and involves the process of educating the concerned persons about M.B.O., agreement upon clear cut quantifiable objectives, evaluation of objectives and feedback for deviation and coercive action. . M.B.O. is wide-ranging overall managerial philosophies that focuses upon joint goal setting and synthesise the individual's goal to organisational goals. The entire organisation will have the feeling of unity as all levels of management of an organisation are involved in goal setting. The programmes relating to M.B.O. can be effective if they are properly implemented and needs the support of the top management
7. **Process Consultation.** It can be described as the set of activities on the part of the consultant that helps the client to perceive, understand and act upon the process events that take place in the client's environment. Process consultation concentrates on the analysis of process of activities like communication, leadership etc. It also aims to attempts to develop initial contacts, define relationships, selecting the method of work, collection of data and diagnosis. Process consultation is a method of intervening in an on going system and is designed to change attitudes, values, interpersonal skills, group norms, and cohesiveness and other process variables.

8. **Contingency Approach.** This approach was given by P. Lawrence and J. Lorseh. It is based on the principle that an organisation is a multifaceted social system. Its behaviour must be included into a united effort to enable it to cope with the environment. Theoretically individuals in different departments have different orientations related to the tasks they perform. Genuinely, the organisational units in their regular operations they are differentiated along with their direction. It appears that with the task discrimination coordination is not possible. According to contingency approach separation and combination are possible for total organisation's effectiveness with the help of integrative devices. To sum up, high organisational presentation is well-suited with the existence of both separation as well as combination which are required as per the stress of their immediate environment. The contingency approach can be useful as an OD intervention in industrial organisations in the form of inter group argument meetings of concerned departmental persons.
9. **Role Analysis.** In the presentation of their individual roles persons manifest certain behaviour which may upset team efficiency. At times it is established that the persons are unambiguous about their own expected behaviour from the view point of other members of the team. In these circumstances the role analysis procedure is used to clarify the role expectations and obligations of the members of a team. The ensuing role requirements and the expected behavioural mechanism of each other help the member to enjoy an equally acceptable behaviour in the team work. In this technique, the individual role players analyze the focal role of the individuals.
10. **Inter-group Activity.** Interpersonal relations are not unusual features in organisational performance . Under these circumstances, inter-group motion spotlights to improve the relationships between the groups. It helps in the interaction and communication between the work groups which eventually avoids dysfunctional inimical competitiveness among them. Inter-group team building entails the procedure of discrimination and combination.
11. **Organisation Monitoring.** It monitors the activities of group of members and gets the feedback from the members of several other groups about how is it being professed. Organisational monitoring is used when there is complexity with other department in the organisation. A meeting is called and response is sought from other department. During the meeting the correct picture emerges which will determine many mistakes committed between two groups.
12. **Third Party Peace Making Intervention.** This intervention is the foundation of the thoughts to understand the conflicts and their resolutions at the interpersonal level. It helps to confront the method of resolving the conflicts takes place between two parties who are aware of the existence of the conflicts and want to confront the issues. The advisor as a third party must be accomplished in the art of identifies the conflicts and use confrontation as technique.
13. **Job Design/Redesign.** It is task -technology connected approach and aims at making changes in the work procedure of the groups of employees. Job design occupies a well planned reorganisation of a job. On the whole it focuses to develop worker's motivation, commitment, performance, job satisfaction etc., through job enrichment, job engineering, job rotation, job enlargement and socio-technical system.
14. **Quality Circles.** Quality Circles are semi-autonomous work groups with six persons who volunteer to talk about and solve feature related problems during working hours. It has impact on working conditions, employee's commitment and self development of employees.
15. **Counselling.** Counselling is the method to extend the help by a manager to his assistant to enhance his prospective. It plans at hypothesising and empathize with the workers. It assists to bring about self consciousness in the worker about his capability. Single or group of interventions may be used to resolve the issues.

MULTIPLE CHOICE QUESTIONS

1. What is the definition of Organisational Behaviour?
   (1) The study of how people interact with each other within an organisation
   (2) The study of how organisations are structured
   (3) The study of financial performance within an organisation
   (4) The study of marketing strategies within an organisation
2. What is the scope of Organisational Behaviour?
   (1) Employee motivation, communication, and leadership
   (2) Human resource management
   (3) Organisational structure and design
   (4) All of the above
3. What is the importance of Organisational Behaviour?
   (1) To improve employee performance and job satisfaction
   (2) To increase profitability and competitive advantage
   (3) To promote organisational effectiveness and efficiency
   (4) All of the above
4. What are the three levels of analysis in Organisational Behaviour?
   (1) Individual, group, and organisational
   (2) Cultural, financial, and structural
   (3) Marketing, human resources, and operations
   (4) Strategic, tactical, and operational
5. What is the concept of Job Enlargement?
   (1) The process of expanding the scope of a job to include additional tasks and responsibilities
   (2) The process of reducing the scope of a job to make it more specialized
   (3) The process of outsourcing certain job functions to external organisations
   (4) The process of automating certain job functions through technology
6. What is the concept of Job Enrichment?
   (1) The process of adding more responsibilities to a job to increase the employee's control and autonomy
   (2) The process of reducing the number of responsibilities in a job to alleviate workload
   (3) The process of assigning additional tasks to employees without changing their job title or pay
   (4) The process of outsourcing certain job functions to external organisations
7. What is the focus of Maslow's Hierarchy of Needs Theory?
   (1) The theory that human needs are arranged in a hierarchy from basic physiological needs to self-actualization
   (2) The theory that human needs can be met through social interactions and relationships
   (3) The theory that human motivation is driven solely by financial rewards
   (4) The theory that human motivation is driven solely by the desire for power and influence
8. What is the focus of Herzberg's Two-Factor Theory?
   (1) The theory that employee motivation is driven by hygiene factors such as pay and working conditions, and motivational factors such as job satisfaction

and opportunities for growth
(2) The theory that employee motivation is driven solely by financial rewards
(3) The theory that employee motivation is driven by the desire for power and influence
(4) The theory that employee motivation is driven by social interactions and relationships

9. What is the focus of McClelland's Theory of Needs?
(1) The theory that human needs can be classified into three categories: power, affiliation, and achievement
(2) The theory that human needs are arranged in a hierarchy from basic physiological needs to self-actualization
(3) The theory that human motivation is driven solely by financial rewards
(4) The theory that employee motivation is driven by hygiene factors and motivational factors

10. What is the focus of Vroom's Expectancy Theory?
(1) The theory that employee motivation is driven by the belief that effort will lead to performance, performance will lead to rewards, and that the rewards will be valuable
(2) The theory that employee motivation is driven solely by financial rewards
(3) The theory that employee motivation is driven by social interactions and relationships
(4) The theory that employee motivation is driven by hygiene factors and motivational factors

11. What is the focus of Equity Theory?
(1) The theory that employee motivation is driven by their perception of fairness and equity in the rewards and treatment they receive compared to others in the organisation
(2) The theory that employee motivation is driven solely by financial rewards
(3) The theory that employee motivation is driven by social interactions and relationships
(4) The theory that employee motivation is driven by hygiene factors and motivational factors

12. What is the definition of Perception?
(1) The process of interpreting and organising sensory information to make it meaningful
(2) The process of organising and analyzing financial data within an organisation
(3) The process of managing the flow of goods and services within an organisation
(4) The process of managing employee relationships and interactions within an organisation

13. What are the factors that influence Perception?
(1) Past experiences, motivation, expectations, context, and culture
(2) Education, financial status, job title, and gender
(3) Age, race, nationality, and religion
(4) Political affiliation, social status, and language proficiency

14. What is the definition of Personality?
(1) The sum total of ways in which an individual reacts to and interacts with others
(2) The social, cultural, and economic characteristics that define a person or group
(3) The process of motivating employees through financial rewards and incentives
(4) The process of managing employee performance and training opportunities

15. What is the focus of the Big Five Personality Traits Model?
(1) The theory that personality is determined by five broad dimensions: openness, conscientiousness, extraversion, agreeableness, and neuroticism

(2) The theory that personality is determined by environmental factors such as socialization and cultural norms

(3) The theory that personality is determined by inherited genetic traits

(4) The theory that personality is determined solely by an individual's past experiences and interactions

16. What is the focus of the Myers-Briggs Type Indicator (MBTI)?

(1) The theory that personality is determined by four dichotomies: extraversion vs introversion, sensing vs intuition, thinking vs feeling, and judging vs perceiving

(2) The theory that personality is determined by inherited genetic traits

(3) The theory that personality is determined by environmental factors such as socialization and cultural norms

(4) The theory that personality is determined solely by an individual's past experiences and interactions

17. What is the definition of Motivation?

(1) The process by which a person's efforts are energized, directed, and sustained towards achieving a goal

(2) The process of managing employee performance and training opportunities

(3) The process of managing the flow of goods and services within an organisation

(4) The process of managing employee relationships and interactions within an organisation

18. What is the focus of Goal-Setting Theory?

(1) The theory that specific and challenging goals lead to higher levels of employee performance and motivation

(2) The theory that employee motivation is driven by financial rewards

(3) The theory that employee motivation is driven by social interactions and relationships

(4) The theory that employee motivation is driven by hygiene factors and motivational factors

19. What is the focus of Reinforcement Theory?

(1) The theory that employee behaviour is shaped by the consequences of that behaviour

(2) The theory that specific and challenging goals lead to higher levels of employee performance and motivation

(3) The theory that employee motivation is driven by financial rewards

(4) The theory that employee motivation is driven by social interactions and relationships

20. What is the focus of Expectancy Theory?

(1) The theory that employee motivation is driven by the belief that effort will lead to performance, performance will lead to rewards, and that the rewards will be valuable

(2) The theory that specific and challenging goals lead to higher levels of employee performance and motivation

(3) The theory that employee motivation is driven by social interactions and relationships

(4) The theory that employee motivation is driven by hygiene factors and motivational factors

21. What is the definition of Personality?

(1) The sum total of ways in which an individual reacts to and interacts with others

(2) The social, cultural, and economic characteristics that define a person or group

(3) The process of motivating employees through financial rewards and incentives

(4) The process of managing employee performance and training opportunities

22. Assertion: Chaucer's The Canterbury Tales is a collection of stories told by a diverse group of pilgrims on their way to the cathedral at Canterbury.

Reason: The tales are written in Middle English and provide a glimpse into the social and cultural norms of medieval England.

(1) Both assertion and reason are true and the reason is the correct explanation of the assertion.
(2) Both assertion and reason are true but the reason is not the correct explanation of the assertion.
(3) Assertion is true but reason is false.
(4) Assertion is false but reason is true.

23. Assertion: Shakespeare's plays often explore universal themes such as love, power, and betrayal.

Reason: Shakespeare was a master of the human condition, and his works continue to be relevant and influential today.

(1) Both assertion and reason are true and the reason is the correct explanation of the assertion.
(2) Both assertion and reason are true but the reason is not the correct explanation of the assertion.
(3) Assertion is true but reason is false.
(4) Assertion is false but reason is true.

24. Assertion: Shakespeare's Hamlet is considered one of the greatest works of English literature.

Reason: Hamlet is a philosophical exploration of revenge, mortality, and the human psyche.

(1) Both assertion and reason are true and the reason is the correct explanation of the assertion.
(2) Both assertion and reason are true but the reason is not the correct explanation of the assertion.
(3) Assertion is true but reason is false.
(4) Assertion is false but reason is true.

25. Assertion: Shakespeare's Macbeth is a tragedy that explores themes of ambition, guilt, and the corrupting influence of power.

Reason: The play was written during the reign of King James I of England, and may have been intended as a cautionary tale about the dangers of regicide.

(1) Both assertion and reason are true and the reason is the correct explanation of the assertion.
(2) Both assertion and reason are true but the reason is not the correct explanation of the assertion.
(3) Assertion is true but reason is false.
(4) Assertion is false but reason is true.

26. Assertion: Chaucer's The Canterbury Tales is written in Middle English, a precursor to modern English.

Reason: Chaucer's use of vernacular language helped to establish English as a literary language and contributed to the development of a distinct English culture.

(1) Both assertion and reason are true and the reason is the correct explanation of the assertion.
(2) Both assertion and reason are true but the reason is not the correct explanation of the assertion.
(3) Assertion is true but reason is false.
(4) Assertion is false but reason is true.

27. What is the definition of Perception?

(1) The process of interpreting and organising sensory information to make it meaningful
(2) The process of organising and analyzing financial data within an organisation
(3) The process of managing the flow of goods and services within an organisation
(4) The process of managing employee relationships and interactions within an organisation

28. What are the factors that influence Perception?

(1) Past experiences, motivation, expectations, context, and culture
(2) Education, financial status, job title, and gender

(3) Age, race, nationality, and religion
(4) Political affiliation, social status, and language proficiency

29. What is the difference between Stereotyping and Halo effect?
(1) Stereotyping is making a generalization about a group or individual while Halo effect is a bias where we focus on one positive trait of a person and make a generalized assumption about their overall character.
(2) Stereotyping is usually positive while Halo effect is usually negative
(3) Stereotyping is a cognitive process while Halo effect is an emotional process
(4) Stereotyping is a behaviour while Halo effect is an attitude

30. What is the definition of Attribution Theory?
(1) The process of explaining the causes of behaviour or events
(2) The process of managing and motivating employees within an organisation
(3) The process of analyzing financial statements and data
(4) The process of managing customer relationships and experiences

31. What are the dimensions of Attribution Theory proposed by Bernard Weiner?
(1) Internal vs external and stable vs unstable
(2) Positive vs negative and group vs individual
(3) Cognitive vs emotional and social vs personal
(4) Formal vs informal and authoritative vs democratic

32. What is the definition of Learning?
(1) The process of acquiring knowledge or skills through experience or study
(2) The process of managing and organising resources within an organisation
(3) The process of managing financial investments and portfolios
(4) The process of managing human resources and employee relations

33. What are the different types of learning?
(1) Classical conditioning, operant conditioning, and observational learning
(2) Cognitive learning, emotional learning, and social learning
(3) Formal learning, informal learning, and experiential learning
(4) Kinesthetic learning, auditory learning, and visual learning

34. What is Classical Conditioning?
(1) A type of learning where a new response is learned through the process of reinforcement or punishment
(2) A type of learning where an individual learns to associate a neutral stimulus with a meaningful stimulus
(3) A type of learning where an individual learns to imitate the behaviour of a role model
(4) A type of learning where an individual learns new information through the process of observation

35. What is Operant Conditioning?
(1) A type of learning where an individual learns to associate a neutral stimulus with a meaningful stimulus
(2) A type of learning where a new response is learned through the process of reinforcement or punishment
(3) A type of learning where an individual learns to imitate the behaviour of a role model
(4) A type of learning where an individual learns new information through the process of observation

36. What is Observational Learning?
(1) A type of learning where an individual learns new information through the process of observation
(2) A type of learning where a new response is learned through the process of reinforcement or punishment
(3) A type of learning where an individual learns to associate a neutral stimulus with a meaningful stimulus

(4) A type of learning where an individual learns to imitate the behaviour of a role model

37. What is the definition of Attitude?

(1) A predisposition to react in a particular way to a particular object or situation
(2) A set of norms and values that guide behaviour in an organisation
(3) A set of financial data and statements used to analyze business operations
(4) A set of regulations and policies used to guide decision making in an organisation

38. What are the components of Attitude?

(1) Cognitive, affective, and behavioural
(2) Social, cultural, and economic
(3) Formal, informal, and experiential
(4) Kinesthetic, auditory, and visual

39. What is the difference between Implicit and Explicit Attitudes?

(1) Implicit attitudes are unconscious while explicit attitudes are conscious.
(2) Implicit attitudes are positive while explicit attitudes are negative
(3) Implicit attitudes are emotional while explicit attitudes are cognitive
(4) Implicit attitudes are specific while explicit attitudes are general

40. What is Cognitive Dissonance Theory?

(1) The theory that individuals are motivated to reduce the discomfort caused by inconsistent beliefs or behaviours
(2) The theory that individuals are motivated by their social needs and relationships
(3) The theory that individuals are motivated by financial incentives and rewards
(4) The theory that individuals are motivated by their own personal goals and aspirations

41. What is the difference between Stereotype, Prejudice, and Discrimination?

(1) Stereotype is a generalization about a group or individual, Prejudice is a negative attitude towards a group or individual, and Discrimination is an unfair treatment towards a group or individual based on their perceived characteristics.
(2) Stereotype is a positive attitude towards a group or individual, Prejudice is a positive generalization about a group or individual, and Discrimination is a fair treatment towards a group or individual based on their actual characteristics.
(3) Stereotype is a cognitive process, Prejudice is an emotional process, and Discrimination is a social process.
(4) Stereotype is a behaviour, Prejudice is a value, and Discrimination is a personality trait.

42. What are the different types of Motivation?

(1) Intrinsic and extrinsic
(2) Positive and negative
(3) Cognitive and emotional
(4) Social and personal

43. What is the difference between Intrinsic and Extrinsic Motivation?

(1) Intrinsic motivation comes from within the individual while extrinsic motivation comes from external sources.
(2) Intrinsic motivation is positive while extrinsic motivation is negative
(3) Intrinsic motivation is emotional while extrinsic motivation is cognitive
(4) Intrinsic motivation is personal while extrinsic motivation is social

44. What is the Self-Determination Theory?

(1) The theory that individuals are motivated by their basic needs for autonomy, competence, and relatedness
(2) The theory that individuals are motivated by financial incentives and rewards
(3) The theory that individuals are motivated by their social needs and relationships

(4) The theory that individuals are motivated by their own personal goals and aspirations

45. What is the Goal-Setting Theory?

(1) The theory that individuals are motivated by specific and challenging goals
(2) The theory that individuals are motivated by their basic needs for autonomy, competence, and relatedness
(3) The theory that individuals are motivated by financial incentives and rewards
(4) The theory that individuals are motivated by their social needs and relationships

46. Assertion: Perception is the process by which individuals organise and interpret their sensory impressions in order to give meaning to their environment.

Reason: Perception is an objective process, with little influence from individual attitudes and experiences.

(1) Both assertion and reason are false.
(2) Assertion is true but reason is false.
(3) Assertion is false but reason is true.
(4) Both assertion and reason are true, but reason is not the correct explanation of the assertion.

47. Assertion: Attitudes are predispositions to react in a particular way to a particular object or situation, and are influenced by both internal and external factors.

Reason: Attitudes are relatively stable over time, and are difficult to change.

(1) Both assertion and reason are true and the reason is the correct explanation of the assertion.
(2) Both assertion and reason are true but the reason is not the correct explanation of the assertion.
(3) Assertion is true but reason is false.
(4) Assertion is false but reason is true.

48. Assertion: Extrinsic motivation refers to behaviour that is driven by internal rewards, such as personal satisfaction or a sense of accomplishment.

Reason: Extrinsic motivation is typically more effective than intrinsic motivation in driving behaviour.

(1) Both assertion and reason are false.
(2) Assertion is true but reason is false.
(3) Assertion is false but reason is true.
(4) Both assertion and reason are true, but reason is not the correct explanation of the assertion.

49. Assertion: The Self-Determination Theory proposes that individuals are motivated by their basic needs for autonomy, competence, and relatedness.

Reason: The Self-Determination Theory is an example of an extrinsic motivation theory.

(1) Both assertion and reason are false.
(2) Assertion is true but reason is false.
(3) Assertion is false but reason is true.
(4) Both assertion and reason are true, but reason is not the correct explanation of the assertion.

50. Assertion: The Goal-Setting Theory proposes that individuals are motivated by specific and challenging goals, which can lead to higher levels of performance.

Reason: The Goal-Setting Theory is an example of an intrinsic motivation theory.

(1) Both assertion and reason are false.
(2) Assertion is true but reason is false.
(3) Assertion is false but reason is true.
(4) Both assertion and reason are true, but reason is not the correct explanation of the assertion.

51. What is the definition of Interpersonal Behaviour?

(1) The actions and interactions of individuals within groups and organisations
(2) The process of analyzing financial data and statements
(3) The process of managing customer relationships and experiences

(4) The process of organising and managing resources within an organisation

52. What are the different types of Interpersonal Behaviour?

(1) Task-oriented and relationship-oriented
(2) Formal and informal
(3) Cognitive and emotional
(4) Kinesthetic, auditory, and visual

53. What is the definition of Communication?

(1) The process of exchanging information and ideas
(2) The process of managing financial investments and portfolios
(3) The process of managing and organising resources within an organisation
(4) The process of interacting and managing customer relationships within an organisation

54. What are the different types of Communication?

(1) Verbal, nonverbal, and written
(2) Positive and negative
(3) Formal and informal
(4) Cognitive and emotional

55. What is the difference between Intra-Personal and Interpersonal Communication?

(1) Intra-Personal communication is the communication with oneself while Interpersonal Communication is the communication between two or more individuals.
(2) Intra-Personal communication is verbal while Interpersonal Communication is non-verbal
(3) Intra-Personal communication is formal while Interpersonal Communication is informal
(4) Intra-Personal communication is cognitive while Interpersonal Communication is emotional

56. What is the definition of Group Dynamics?

(1) The study of the processes involved in groups and their interactions
(2) The process of managing and organising financial resources within an organisation
(3) The process of interacting and managing customer relationships within an organisation
(4) The process of organising and managing resources within an organisation

57. What are the different stages of Group Development?

(1) Forming, Storming, Norming, Performing, and Adjourning
(2) Cognitive and emotional
(3) Positive and negative
(4) Formal and informal

58. What is the difference between a Group and a Team?

(1) A Group is a collection of individuals that interact and share a common goal while a Team is a group that works together to achieve a common goal.
(2) A Group is informal while a Team is formal
(3) A Group is cognitive while a Team is emotional
(4) A Group is positive while a Team is negative

59. What is the definition of Leadership?

(1) The ability to influence a group towards achieving a vision or set of goals
(2) The process of managing and organising financial resources within an organisation
(3) The process of interacting and managing customer relationships within an organisation
(4) The process of organising and managing resources within an organisation

60. What are the different styles of Leadership?

(1) Autocratic, Democratic, and Laissez-faire
(2) Cognitive leadership, Emotional Leadership and Formal Leadership

(3) Verbal Leadership, Non-verbal Leadership and written Leadership

(4) Kinesthetic Leadership, Auditory Leadership and Visual Leadership

61. What is Group Cohesiveness?

(1) The degree to which group members are attracted to one another and share group goals

(2) The process of managing and organising financial resources within an organisation

(3) The process of interacting and managing customer relationships within an organisation

(4) The process of organising and managing resources within an organisation

62. What is Social Loafing?

(1) The tendency for individuals to put forth less effort in a group than when working alone

(2) The process of managing and organising financial resources within an organisation

(3) The process of interacting and managing customer relationships within an organisation

(4) The process of organising and managing resources within an organisation

63. What is the difference between Groupthink and Groupshift?

(1) Groupthink is the tendency of group members to conform by adopting a common viewpoint while Groupshift is the tendency of group members to shift their opinions to an extreme position.

(2) Groupthink is the tendency of group members to shift their opinions to an extreme position while Groupshift is the tendency of group members to conform by adopting a common viewpoint.

(3) Groupthink is a cognitive process while Groupshift is an emotional process

(4) Groupthink is a positive outcome while Groupshift is a negative outcome

64. What is the difference between Conformity and Compliance?

(1) Conformity is the process of yielding to group pressure while maintaining personal beliefs while Compliance is the process of yielding to group pressure by adopting group norms and beliefs.

(2) Conformity and Compliance are the same thing

(3) Conformity is a positive outcome while Compliance is a negative outcome

(4) Conformity is an emotional process while Compliance is a cognitive process

65. What is the difference between Perception and Attribution?

(1) Perception is the process of interpreting and organising sensory information to make it meaningful while Attribution is the process of explaining the causes of behaviour or events.

(2) Perception is an emotional process while Attribution is a cognitive process

(3) Perception is a positive process while Attribution is a negative process

(4) Perception is a behaviour while Attribution is a personality trait

66. What is the definition of Conflict?

(1) The process by which two or more parties perceive a difference or goals or opinions

(2) The process of managing and organising financial resources within an organisation

(3) The process of interacting and managing customer relationships within an organisation

(4) The process of organising and managing resources within an organisation

67. What is the difference between Collaboration and Accommodation?

(1) Collaboration is a conflict resolution strategy where both parties work together to create a win-win solution while Accommodation is a conflict reso-

lution strategy where one party gives in to the other party's demands.

(2) Collaboration is a negative outcome of conflict while Accommodation is a positive outcome of conflict

(3) Collaboration is a cognitive process while Accommodation is an emotional process

(4) Collaboration is an informal process while Accommodation is a formal process

68. What is the definition of Power?

(1) The ability to influence or control the behaviour of others

(2) The process of managing and organising financial resources within an organisation

(3) The process of interacting and managing customer relationships within an organisation

(4) The process of organising and managing resources within an organisation

69. What are the different types of Power?

(1) Formal and Informal

(2) Cognitive and Emotional

(3) Positive and Negative

(4) Kinesthetic, Auditory, and Visual

70. What is the difference between Legitimate Power and Coercive Power?

(1) Legitimate Power is the power derived from an individual's formal position or authority while Coercive Power is the power to punish or threaten to punish.

(2) Legitimate Power and Coercive Power are same

(3) Legitimate Power is a positive power while Coercive Power is a negative power

(4) Legitimate Power is an emotional power while Coercive Power is a cognitive power

71. What is the difference between Task Conflict and Relationship Conflict?

(1) Task Conflict is conflict over the content and goals of the work while Relationship Conflict is conflict over personal relationships and communication.

(2) Task Conflict is an emotional process while Relationship Conflict is a cognitive process

(3) Task Conflict is a positive outcome while Relationship Conflict is a negative outcome

(4) Task Conflict is a behaviour while Relationship Conflict is a personality trait

72. What is the definition of Social Identity Theory?

(1) The theory that individuals define themselves by their group memberships and want to feel positively about their groups.

(2) The theory that individuals are motivated by their basic needs for autonomy, competence, and relatedness

(3) The theory that individuals are motivated by financial incentives and rewards

(4) The theory that individuals are motivated by their own personal goals and aspirations

73. What is the difference between Inductive and Deductive Reasoning?

(1) Inductive Reasoning is a type of reasoning that involves generalizing from specific observations or instances while Deductive Reasoning is a type of reasoning that involves starting with a general argument and drawing specific conclusions.

(2) Inductive Reasoning and Deductive Reasoning are the same thing

(3) Inductive Reasoning is a cognitive process while Deductive Reasoning is an emotional process

(4) Inductive Reasoning is a positive outcome while Deductive Reasoning is a negative outcome

74. What is the definition of Social Influence?
(1) The process by which individuals change their attitudes, beliefs, or behaviours in response to the real or imagined influence of others.
(2) The process of managing and organising financial resources within an organisation
(3) The process of interacting and managing customer relationships within an organisation
(4) The process of organising and managing resources within an organisation

75. What is the difference between Obedience and Conformity?
(1) Obedience is the process of yielding to group pressure by following orders or instructions while Conformity is the process of yielding to group pressure by adopting group norms and beliefs.
(2) Obedience is a negative outcome of social influence while Conformity is a positive outcome of social influence
(3) Obedience is a cognitive process while Conformity is an emotional process
(4) Obedience is a personality trait while Conformity is a behaviour

76. What is the definition of Personality?
(1) The relatively stable set of characteristics that influences an individual's behaviour and interactions with others.
(2) The process of managing and organising financial resources within an organisation
(3) The process of interacting and managing customer relationships within an organisation
(4) The process of organising and managing resources within an organisation

77. What are the different approaches to Personality?
(1) Trait, Biological, Psychoanalytic, Humanistic, and Behavioural
(2) Cognitive, Emotional, and Social
(3) Formal and Informal
(4) Kinesthetic, Auditory, and Visual

78. What is the difference between Self-Esteem and Self-Efficacy?
(1) Self-Esteem is the individual's overall self-worth or sense of value while Self-Efficacy is the individual's belief in their ability to accomplish a specific task.
(2) Self-Esteem is an emotional process while Self-Efficacy is a cognitive process
(3) Self-Esteem is an informal process while Self-Efficacy is a formal process
(4) Self-Esteem is negative while Self-Efficacy is positive

79. How do Emotions influence Interpersonal Behaviour?
(1) Emotions can influence perception, motivation, and interaction with others.
(2) Emotions have no influence on Interpersonal Behaviour
(3) Emotions only influence cognitive processes
(4) Emotions only influence emotional processes

80. What is the difference between Attitude and Values?
(1) Attitude is a predisposition to react in a particular way to a particular object or situation while Values are beliefs or ideals that an individual or group holds as important.
(2) Attitude is a cognitive process while Values are an emotional process
(3) Attitude is an informal process while Values are a formal process
(4) Attitude is an individual trait while Values are a group trait

81. What is the difference between Transformational and Transactional Leadership?
(1) Transformational Leadership is the process by which a leader inspires and motivates followers to achieve the organisation's vision while Transactional Leadership is the process by

which a leader uses rewards and punishments to achieve desired behaviour.

(2) Transformational Leadership and Transactional Leadership are the same thing

(3) Transformational Leadership is a negative outcome of leadership while Transactional Leadership is a positive outcome of leadership

(4) Transformational Leadership is a cognitive process while Transactional Leadership is an emotional process

82. What is the difference between Formal and Informal Group?

(1) A Formal Group is a designated work group defined by the structure, organisation, and tasks while an Informal Group is a social group that forms spontaneously around common interests, values, or social networks.

(2) A Formal Group is cognitive while an Informal Group is emotional

(3) A Formal Group is a positive outcome while an Informal Group is a negative outcome

(4) A Formal Group is a behaviour while an Informal Group is a personality trait

83. What is the definition of Group Cohesion?

(1) The degree to which group members are attracted to one another and share group goals

(2) The process of managing and organising financial resources within an organisation

(3) The process of interacting and managing customer relationships within an organisation

(4) The process of organising and managing resources within an organisation

84. What is the difference between Positive and Negative Interdependence?

(1) Positive Interdependence is a situation where individuals or groups perceive that they can achieve their goals if and only if all group members work together while Negative Interdependence is a situation where individuals or groups perceive that they can achieve their goals if and only if other group members fail.

(2) Positive Interdependence and Negative Interdependence are the same thing

(3) Positive Interdependence is a cognitive process while Negative Interdependence is an emotional process

(4) Positive Interdependence is a negative outcome while Negative Interdependence is a positive outcome

85. What is the definition of Social Facilitation?

(1) The tendency for people to perform better on simple tasks when in the presence of others than when alone

(2) The process of managing and organising financial resources within an organisation

(3) The process of interacting and managing customer relationships within an organisation

(4) The process of organising and managing resources within an organisation

86. What is the definition of Motivation?

(1) The process of energizing, directing, and sustaining behaviour to achieve goals

(2) The process of managing and organising financial resources within an organisation

(3) The process of interacting and managing customer relationships within an organisation

(4) The process of organising and managing resources within an organisation

87. How do needs influence Motivation?

(1) Needs are the internal desires that drive behaviour and motivation.

(2) Needs have no influence on Motivation

(3) Needs only influence emotional processes

(4) Needs only influence cognitive processes

88. What is the difference between Maslow's Hierarchy of Needs Theory and Alderfer's ERG Theory?
   (1) Maslow's Hierarchy of Needs Theory proposes that needs are arranged in a hierarchy from physiological needs to self-actualization while Alderfer's ERG Theory proposes that needs are arranged in three core categories: Existence, Relatedness, and Growth.
   (2) Maslow's Hierarchy of Needs Theory and Alderfer's ERG Theory are the same thing
   (3) Maslow's Hierarchy of Needs Theory is a positive outcome while Alderfer's ERG Theory is a negative outcome
   (4) Maslow's Hierarchy of Needs Theory is a cognitive process while Alderfer's ERG Theory is an emotional process

89. What is the definition of Goal-Setting Theory?
   (1) The theory that individuals are motivated by specific and challenging goals, which can lead to higher levels of performance.
   (2) The process of managing and organising financial resources within an organisation
   (3) The process of interacting and managing customer relationships within an organisation
   (4) The process of organising and managing resources within an organisation

90. What is the difference between Equity Theory and Expectancy Theory?
   (1) Equity Theory proposes that individuals are motivated when they perceive fair treatment while Expectancy Theory proposes that individuals are motivated by the belief that their effort will lead to high performance and favorable outcomes.
   (2) Equity Theory and Expectancy Theory are the same thing
   (3) Equity Theory is an emotional process while Expectancy Theory is a cognitive process
   (4) Equity Theory is a negative outcome while Expectancy Theory is a positive outcome

91. What is the definition of Conflict Resolution?
   (1) The process of resolving differences and disputes between individuals or groups
   (2) The process of managing and organising financial resources within an organisation
   (3) The process of interacting and managing customer relationships within an organisation
   (4) The process of organising and managing resources within an organisation

92. What are the different styles of Conflict Resolution?
   (1) Competing, Collaborating, Compromising, Accommodating, and Avoiding
   (2) Cognitive, Emotional, and Social
   (3) Formal and Informal
   (4) Kinesthetic, Auditory, and Visual

93. What is the definition of Group Decision-Making?
   (1) The process by which a group of individuals make a decision together.
   (2) The process of managing and organising financial resources within an organisation
   (3) The process of interacting and managing customer relationships within an organisation
   (4) The process of organising and managing resources within an organisation

94. What are the different types of Group Decision-Making?
   (1) Authority rule, Minority rule, Majority rule, Consensus, and Unanimity
   (2) Cognitive, Emotional, and Social
   (3) Formal and Informal
   (4) Kinesthetic, Auditory, and Visual

95. What is the difference between Group Polarization and Social Comparison Theory?
   (1) Group Polarization is the phenomenon of group decision-making where group

members shift their opinions to an extreme position while Social Comparison Theory is the theory that individuals evaluate their own abilities and opinions by comparing themselves to others.
(2) Group Polarization and Social Comparison Theory are the same thing
(3) Group Polarization is an emotional process while Social Comparison Theory is a cognitive process
(4) Group Polarization is a positive outcome while Social Comparison Theory is a negative outcome

96. What is the definition of Groupthink?
(1) The tendency for group members to seek agreement instead of critically evaluating information relevant to a decision
(2) The process of managing and organising financial resources within an organisation
(3) The process of interacting and managing customer relationships within an organisation
(4) The process of organising and managing resources within an organisation

97. What is the difference between Integration and Fragmentation?
(1) Integration is a group decision-making strategy where the group tries to maximize the differences between alternatives while Fragmentation is a group decision-making strategy where the group tries to minimize the differences between alternatives.
(2) Integration is a negative outcome while Fragmentation is a positive outcome
(3) Integration is an emotional process while Fragmentation is a cognitive process
(4) Integration is a behaviour while Fragmentation is a personality trait

98. What is the definition of Empathy?
(1) The ability to understand and share the feelings of others.
(2) The process of managing and organising financial resources within an organisation
(3) The process of interacting and managing customer relationships within an organisation
(4) The process of organising and managing resources within an organisation

99. What is the difference between Perspective-Taking and Empathic Concern?
(1) Perspective-Taking is the cognitive ability to put oneself in someone else's shoes while Empathic Concern is the emotional response to feeling compassion for someone else's suffering.
(2) Perspective-Taking and Empathic Concern are the same thing
(3) Perspective-Taking is a negative outcome while Empathic Concern is a positive outcome
(4) Perspective-Taking is an emotional process while Empathic Concern is a cognitive process

100. What is the difference between Trust and Distrust?
(1) Trust is the willingness to rely on another person or group in a situation of risk or vulnerability while Distrust is a lack of confidence or faith in someone or something.
(2) Trust and Distrust are the same thing
(3) Trust is a negative outcome while Distrust is a positive outcome
(4) Trust is an emotional process while Distrust is a cognitive process

101. What is the difference between Identification and Internalization?
(1) Identification is the process by which an individual adopts the beliefs, values, and norms of a group to achieve social acceptance while Internalization is the process by which an individual fully accepts and integrates the beliefs, values, and norms of a group into their own personal identity.

(2) Identification and Internalization are the same thing
(3) Identification is a positive outcome while Internalization is a negative outcome
(4) Identification is an emotional process while Internalization is a cognitive process

102. What is the definition of Social Role?
(1) The pattern of behaviour expected of an individual in a particular social position.
(2) The process of managing and organising financial resources within an organisation
(3) The process of interacting and managing customer relationships within an organisation
(4) The process of organising and managing resources within an organisation

103. What is the difference between Role Conflict and Role Ambiguity?
(1) Role Conflict is the conflict that occurs when expectations associated with different roles conflict with each other while Role Ambiguity is the uncertainty that arises when the expectations associated with a role are unclear or unspecified.
(2) Role Conflict and Role Ambiguity are the same thing
(3) Role Conflict is an emotional process while Role Ambiguity is a cognitive process
(4) Role Conflict is a negative outcome while Role Ambiguity is a positive outcome

104. What is the definition of Social Identity?
(1) The part of an individual's self-concept that derives from membership in a particular group.
(2) The process of managing and organising financial resources within an organisation
(3) The process of interacting and managing customer relationships within an organisation
(4) The process of organising and managing resources within an organisation

105. Which of the following is not a leadership style?
(1) Autocratic (2) Democratic
(3) Bureaucratic (4) Kinesthetic

106. Which of the following is a trait theory of leadership?
(1) Behavioural Theory
(2) Situational Leadership Theory
(3) Transformational Leadership Theory
(4) Great Man Theory

107. Who developed the Path-Goal Leadership Theory?
(1) Robert House
(2) Max Weber
(3) Douglas McGregor
(4) Abraham Maslow

108. Who developed the Contingency Theory of Leadership?
(1) Fred Fiedler
(2) Max Weber
(3) Douglas McGregor
(4) Abraham Maslow

109. Which of the following is not a characteristic of Transformational Leadership?
(1) Charisma
(2) Idealized Influence
(3) Transactional Reward
(4) Intellectual Stimulation

110. Which of the following is a key aspect of Authentic Leadership?
(1) Vision
(2) Communication
(3) Self-Awareness
(4) Decisiveness

111. Who developed the Full Range Leadership Model?
(1) James MacGregor Burns

(2) Thomas Carlyle
(3) Robert Greenleaf
(4) Warren Bennis

112. Who developed the Servant Leadership Model?
(1) Robert Greenleaf
(2) James MacGregor Burns
(3) Thomas Carlyle
(4) Warren Bennis

113. What is the difference between Transactional and Transformational Leadership?
(1) Transactional Leadership focuses on task completion and rewards, while Transformational Leadership focuses on inspiring and motivating followers towards a vision.
(2) Transactional Leadership and Transformational Leadership are the same thing
(3) Transactional Leadership is a negative outcome while Transformational Leadership is a positive outcome
(4) Transactional Leadership is an emotional process while Transformational Leadership is a cognitive process

114. Which of the following is a disadvantage of the Charismatic Leadership style?
(1) Lack of transparency and accountability
(2) Over-dependency on the leader
(3) Difficult to maintain in a long run
(4) All of the above

115. Which of the following is not a type of communication?
(1) Interpersonal Communication
(2) Public Communication
(3) Formal Communication
(4) Emotional Communication

116. What is the definition of Communication?
(1) The process of exchanging information and ideas
(2) The process of organising and managing resources within an organisation
(3) The process of managing customer relationships and experiences
(4) The process of analyzing financial data and statements

117. What are the different types of Communication?
(1) Verbal, nonverbal, and written
(2) Positive and negative
(3) Formal and informal
(4) Cognitive and emotional

118. What is the difference between Verbal and Nonverbal Communication?
(1) Verbal Communication is the use of words while Nonverbal Communication is the use of body language and facial expressions.
(2) Verbal Communication and Nonverbal Communication are the same thing
(3) Verbal Communication is a cognitive process while Nonverbal Communication is an emotional process
(4) Verbal Communication is a positive outcome while Nonverbal Communication is a negative outcome

119. What is the definition of Active Listening?
(1) The process of fully attending to, understanding, and responding to spoken and nonverbal messages.
(2) The process of organising and managing resources within an organisation
(3) The process of managing customer relationships and experiences
(4) The process of analyzing financial data and statements

120. What is the difference between Interpersonal and Intrapersonal Communication?
(1) Interpersonal Communication is the communication between individuals while Intrapersonal Communication is the communication with oneself.
(2) Interpersonal Communication is verbal while Intrapersonal Communication is non-verbal
(3) Interpersonal Communication is formal while Intrapersonal Communication is informal

(4) Interpersonal Communication is cognitive while Intrapersonal Communication is emotional

121. What is the definition of Communication Flow?

(1) The direction and pattern of communication in an organisation.

(2) The process of organising and managing resources within an organisation

(3) The process of managing customer relationships and experiences

(4) The process of analyzing financial data and statements

122. What is the difference between Downward and Upward Communication?

(1) Downward Communication is the flow of communication from the top-level management to the lower-level employees while Upward Communication is the flow of communication from the lower-level employees to the top-level management.

(2) Downward Communication and Upward Communication are the same thing

(3) Downward Communication is an emotional process while Upward Communication is a cognitive process

(4) Downward Communication is a positive outcome while Upward Communication is a negative outcome

123. What is the difference between Formal and Informal Communication?

(1) Formal Communication follows prescribed rules, standards, and norms while Informal Communication occurs spontaneously between individuals.

(2) Formal Communication and Informal Communication are the same thing

(3) Formal Communication is an emotional process while Informal Communication is a cognitive process

(4) Formal Communication is a negative outcome while Informal Communication is a positive outcome

124. What is the definition of Filtering in Communication?

(1) The intentional distortion or manipulation of information to make it more favorable to the recipient.

(2) The process of organising and managing resources within an organisation

(3) The process of managing customer relationships and experiences

(4) The process of analyzing financial data and statements

125. Assertion: The Trait Theory of Leadership proposes that there are certain innate characteristics that make individuals better suited for leadership roles.

Reason: This theory does not consider the importance of situational factors in determining leadership effectiveness.

(1) Both assertion and reason are true and the reason is the correct explanation of the assertion.

(2) Both assertion and reason are true but the reason is not the correct explanation of the assertion.

(3) Assertion is true but reason is false.

(4) Assertion is false but reason is true.

126. Assertion: Transformational Leadership is associated with a greater employee job satisfaction and increased productivity.

Reason: Transformational Leaders create an inspiring vision of the future and encourage followers to think beyond individual interests and focus on group goals.

(1) Both assertion and reason are true and the reason is the correct explanation of the assertion.

(2) Both assertion and reason are true but the reason is not the correct explanation of the assertion.

(3) Assertion is true but reason is false.

(4) Assertion is false but reason is true.

127. Assertion: Communication is a process of transferring meanings, ideas, information, thoughts, or feelings.

Reason: Communication involves only verbal exchanges of ideas.
(1) Assertion is true but reason is false.
(2) Assertion and reason are both true.
(3) Assertion and reason are both false.
(4) Assertion is false but reason is true.

128. Assertion: Verbal communication involves the use of words, whether spoken, written or signed.
Reason: Nonverbal communication can include facial expressions, body language, gestures or even touch.
(1) Both the assertion and reason are true and the reason is the correct explanation of the assertion.
(2) Both the assertion and reason are true but reason is not the correct explanation of the assertion.
(3) The assertion is true but the reason is false.
(4) The assertion and reason are both false.

129. Assertion: Active Listening is the process of fully attending to, understanding, and responding to spoken and nonverbal messages.
Reason: Active Listening is a passive process where the listener simply hears the speaker's message without responding.
(1) Assertion is true but reason is false.
(2) Assertion and reason are both true.
(3) Assertion and reason are both false.
(4) Assertion is false but reason is true.

130. What is the definition of Situational Leadership?
(1) A leadership theory that suggests that leadership behaviour varies with the situation.
(2) A leadership theory that suggests that leadership is a social influence process between leaders and followers.
(3) A leadership theory that focuses on self-awareness and interpersonal behaviour.
(4) A leadership theory that proposes that some individuals are born with innate leadership characteristics.

131. What is the difference between Laissez-faire Leadership and Transformational Leadership?
(1) Laissez-faire Leadership is a leadership style where the leader is hands-off and allows the group to make decisions while Transformational Leadership is a leadership style where the leader inspires and motivates followers towards a vision.
(2) Laissez -faire Leadership and Transformational Leadership are the same thing.
(3) Laissez-faire Leadership is a leadership style where the leader is very controlling and directive while Transformational Leadership is a leadership style where the leader is hands-off.
(4) Laissez-faire Leadership is a negative outcome while Transformational Leadership is a positive outcome.

132. What is the definition of Authentic Leadership?
(1) A leadership style that involves a leader who acts as a servant to their followers.
(2) A leadership style that values charisma and inspiration to motivate followers.
(3) A leadership style that fosters self-awareness, transparency, and ethical behaviour.
(4) A leadership style that focuses on rule-following and bureaucratic procedures.

133. What is the difference between Transactional and Charismatic Leadership?
(1) Transactional Leadership focuses on task completion and rewards, while Charismatic Leadership focuses on inspiration and motivation through the leader's personality.
(2) Transactional Leadership is a negative outcome while Charismatic Leadership is a positive outcome.

(3) Transactional Leadership is an emotional process while Charismatic Leadership is a cognitive process.

(4) Transactional Leadership and Charismatic Leadership are the same thing.

134. What is the definition of Distributed Leadership?

(1) A leadership model where the leader delegates decision-making authority to subordinates.

(2) A leadership model that identifies specific traits that effective leaders possess.

(3) A leadership model where leadership responsibilities are shared among team members.

(4) A leadership model that focuses on the influence of situational factors on leadership effectiveness.

135. What is the difference between Personal and Professional Communication?

(1) Personal Communication is informal and focuses on relationships while Professional Communication is formal and focuses on tasks.

(2) Personal Communication and Professional Communication are the same thing.

(3) Personal Communication is a negative outcome while Professional Communication is a positive outcome.

(4) Personal Communication is an emotional process while Professional Communication is a cognitive process.

136. What is the difference between Mass Communication and Interpersonal Communication?

(1) Mass Communication is the transmission of information to a large audience while Interpersonal Communication is between individuals.

(2) Mass Communication is an emotional process while Interpersonal Communication is a cognitive process.

(3) Mass Communication is a negative outcome while Interpersonal Communication is a positive outcome.

(4) Mass Communication and Interpersonal Communication are the same thing.

137. What is the definition of Effective Communication?

(1) The ability to transmit information to others in a clear and concise manner that is easily understood.

(2) The ability to speak with authority and control in social situations.

(3) The ability to manipulate others to do what you want.

(4) The ability to dominate a conversation and speak louder than others.

138. What is the difference between Communication Competence and Communication Apprehension?

(1) Communication Competence is the ability to effectively communicate while Communication Apprehension is anxiety about communicating.

(2) Communication Competence and Communication Apprehension are the same thing.

(3) Communication Competence is a negative outcome while Communication Apprehension is a positive outcome.

(4) Communication Competence and Communication Apprehension are emotional processes.

139. What is the definition of Communication Ethics?

(1) The principles and standards that guide behaviour in the situation of communication.

(2) The ability to manipulate others to do what you want.

(3) The ability to speak with authority and control in social situations.

(4) The ability to dominate a conversation and speak louder than others.

140. Assertion: The Overjustification Effect suggests that rewards can decrease intrinsic motivation.

Reason: Intrinsic motivation refers to behaviour that is driven by internal rewards, such as enjoyment or personal satisfaction.

(1) Both assertion and reason are true and the reason is the correct explanation of the assertion.
(2) Both assertion and reason are true but the reason is not the correct explanation of the assertion.
(3) Assertion is true but reason is false.
(4) Assertion is false but reason is true.

141. Assertion: Communication is a two-way process that involves both sending and receiving messages.

Reason: The sender is responsible for the success of the communication process.

(1) Assertion and reason are both false.
(2) Assertion is true but reason is false.
(3) Assertion and reason are both true but the reason is not the correct explanation of the assertion.
(4) Both assertion and reason are true and the reason is the correct explanation of the assertion.

142. Assertion: In order to be an effective communicator, it is important to understand the audience and adjust communication styles accordingly.

Reason: Communicating in the same way with all individuals regardless of their social, cultural or educational background ensures clarity and efficiency.

(1) Both assertion and reason are true and the reason is the correct explanation of the assertion.
(2) Both assertion and reason are true but the reason is not the correct explanation of the assertion.
(3) Assertion is true but reason is false.
(4) Assertion is false but reason is true.

143. Assertion: Feedback is an important aspect of effective communication.

Reason: Feedback provides the recipient with information on how to improve their communication skills.

(1) Both assertion and reason are true and the reason is the correct explanation of the assertion.
(2) Both assertion and reason are true but the reason is not the correct explanation of the assertion.
(3) Assertion is true but reason is false.
(4) Assertion is false but reason is true.

144. Assertion: Empathy is an important component of effective communication.

Reason: Empathy involves understanding the thoughts and emotions of the recipient without necessarily agreeing with them.

(1) Both assertion and reason are true and the reason is the correct explanation of the assertion.
(2) Both assertion and reason are true but the reason is not the correct explanation of the assertion.
(3) Assertion is true but reason is false.
(4) Assertion is false but reason is true.

145. What is the definition of power in organisational behaviour?

(1) The ability to control resources and affect outcomes.
(2) The ability to motivate others towards a goal.
(3) The ability to create a positive work environment.
(4) The ability to solve complex problems.

146. What is the difference between power and authority in organisational behaviour?

(1) Power is the ability to control resources while authority is the formal right to make decisions.
(2) Power and authority are the same thing.
(3) Power is a negative outcome while authority is a positive outcome.
(4) Power is an emotional process while authority is a cognitive process.

147. What is the role of organisational politics in power and authority?

(1) Organisational politics involves the use of power and influence to gain advantages within an organisation.

(2) Organisational politics is a negative outcome.

(3) Organisational politics is an emotional process.

(4) Organisational politics is not relevant in power and authority.

148. What is the definition of charismatic authority?

(1) Authority based on an individual's personal charisma.

(2) Authority based on formal position and hierarchy.

(3) Authority based on expertise and knowledge.

(4) Authority based on coercion and punishment.

149. What is the role of culture in power and authority?

(1) Culture can influence how power and authority are perceived and used within an organisation.

(2) Culture has no effect on power and authority.

(3) Culture is a negative outcome in power and authority.

(4) Culture is an emotional process in power and authority.

150. What is the definition of stress in organisational behaviour?

(1) A psychological response to environmental demands that exceed an individual's resources.

(2) The feeling of being overwhelmed by tasks.

(3) The inability to handle conflicts in the workplace.

(4) The feeling of anxiety or depression.

151. What is the difference between distress and eustress?

(1) Distress is negative stress while eustress is positive stress.

(2) Distress and Eustress are the same thing.

(3) Distress is a positive outcome while Eustress is a negative outcome.

(4) Distress creates an emotional process while Eustress creates a cognitive process.

152. What is the role of personality in stress?

(1) Different individuals may respond differently to the same environmental stressors due to their personality traits.

(2) Personality has no effect on stress.

(3) Personality is a negative outcome of stress.

(4) Personality is an emotional process in stress.

153. What is the definition of cognitive appraisal in stress?

(1) The process by which individuals judge the significance of potential stressors.

(2) The process of reducing negative emotions associated with stress.

(3) The process of eliminating stressors in the environment.

(4) The process of coping with stress.

154. What is the difference between problem-focused coping and emotion-focused coping?

(1) Problem-focused coping involves attempting to change the source of stress while emotion-focused coping involves regulating emotions.

(2) Problem-focused coping involves regulating emotions while emotion-focused coping involves attempting to change the source of stress.

(3) Problem-focused coping and emotion-focused coping are the same thing.

(4) Problem-focused coping and emotion-focused coping are both negative outcomes of stress.

155. What is the definition of work-life balance?

(1) The ability to balance work responsibilities with personal responsibilities.

(2) The ability to prioritize work responsibilities over personal responsibilities.

(3) The inability to separate work from personal life.

(4) The inability to prioritize personal responsibilities over work responsibilities.

156. What is the role of organisational culture in stress?
(1) Organisational culture can create either a positive or negative environment that can impact employee stress levels.
(2) Organisational culture has no effect on stress.
(3) Organisational culture is a negative outcome in stress.
(4) Organisational culture is an emotional process in stress.

157. What is the difference between acute stress and chronic stress?
(1) Acute stress is short-term stress while chronic stress is long-term stress.
(2) Acute stress and chronic stress are the same thing.
(3) Acute stress is a positive outcome while chronic stress is a negative outcome.
(4) Acute stress is an emotional process while chronic stress is a cognitive process.

158. What is the definition of burnout in organisational behaviour?
(1) A state of physical, emotional, and mental exhaustion that results from long-term involvement in emotionally demanding situations.
(2) A feeling of being overwhelmed by tasks.
(3) The inability to handle conflicts in the workplace.
(4) A feeling of anxiety or depression.

159. What is the difference between type A and type B personalities?
(1) Type A personality is competitive and ambitious while type B personality is relaxed and easy-going.
(2) Type A personality is relaxed and easy-going while type B personality is competitive and ambitious.
(3) Type A and type B personalities are the same thing.
(4) Type A personality is a positive outcome while type B personality is a negative outcome of stress.

160. Assertion: Legitimate power is based on an individual's personal charisma.

Reason: Legitimate power is the formal right to make decisions and take actions.
(1) Both assertion and reason are false.
(2) Both assertion and reason are true but the reason is not the correct explanation of the assertion.
(3) Assertion is false but reason is true.
(4) Both assertion and reason are true and the reason is the correct explanation of the assertion.

161. Assertion: Political behaviour in an organisation can involve the use of power and influence to gain advantages.

Reason: Political behaviour in an organisation is always negative.
(1) Both assertion and reason are true and the reason is the correct explanation of the assertion.
(2) Both assertion and reason are true but the reason is not the correct explanation of the assertion.
(3) Assertion is true but reason is false.
(4) Assertion is false but reason is true.

162. Assertion: Stress is a negative outcome in organisational behaviour.

Reason: Stress can be beneficial in motivating individuals and improving performance.
(1) Both assertion and reason are true but the reason is not the correct explanation of the assertion.
(2) Both assertion and reason are false.
(3) Assertion is true but reason is false.
(4) Both assertion and reason are true and the reason is the correct explanation of the assertion.

163. Assertion: Burnout is a type of stress that results from long-term involvement in emotionally demanding situations.

Reason: Burnout has no negative impact on the workplace.

(1) Both assertion and reason are false.
(2) Both assertion and reason are true but the reason is not the correct explanation of the assertion.
(3) Assertion is true but reason is false.
(4) Both assertion and reason are true and the reason is the correct explanation of the assertion.

164. Assertion: Problem-focused coping involves regulating emotions.

Reason: Emotion-focused coping involves attempting to change the source of stress.

(1) Both assertion and reason are false.
(2) Both assertion and reason are true but the reason is not the correct explanation of the assertion.
(3) Assertion is false but reason is true.
(4) Both assertion and reason are true and the reason is the correct explanation of the assertion.

165. Assertion: The cognitive appraisal of a potential stressor can influence the individuals level of stress.

Reason: The level of stress experienced by an individual is unrelated to their cognitive appraisal of a stressor.

(1) Both assertion and reason are false.
(2) Both assertion and reason are true but the reason is not the correct explanation of the assertion.
(3) Assertion is true but reason is false.
(4) Both assertion and reason are true and the reason is the correct explanation of the assertion.

166. Assertion: Type A personality is relaxed and easy-going.

Reason: Type A personality is characterized by competitiveness, ambition, and aggressiveness.

(1) Both assertion and reason are false.
(2) Assertion is false but reason is true.
(3) Both assertion and reason are true but the reason is not the correct explanation of the assertion.
(4) Both assertion and reason are true and the reason is the correct explanation of the assertion.

167. Assertion: Eustress is a positive outcome of stress.

Reason: Eustress is a type of chronic stress that can lead to negative health outcomes.

(1) Both assertion and reason are false.
(2) Assertion is false but reason is true.
(3) Both assertion and reason are true but the reason is not the correct explanation of the assertion.
(4) Both assertion and reason are true and the reason is the correct explanation of the assertion.

168. Assertion: Organisational culture has no effect on employee stress levels.

Reason: Organisational culture can impact the work environment and the demands placed on employees, which can lead to stress.

(1) Both assertion and reason are false.
(2) Both assertion and reason are true but the reason is not the correct explanation of the assertion.
(3) Assertion is true but reason is false.
(4) Both assertion and reason are true and the reason is the correct explanation of the assertion.

169. Assertion: Personality can influence an individual's level of stress.

Reason: Individuals with an extroverted personality are less likely to experience stress than introverted individuals.

(1) Both assertion and reason are false.
(2) Assertion is false but reason is true.
(3) Both assertion and reason are true but the reason is not the correct explanation of the assertion.
(4) Both assertion and reason are true and the reason is the correct explanation of the assertion.

170. What is the definition of organisational change in organisational behaviour?
(1) Any alteration or adjustment in organisational structure or operations.
(2) The ability to resist changes in organisational culture.
(3) The ability to implement changes in organisational culture.
(4) The inability to adapt to changes in the environment.

171. What is the difference between planned and unplanned change in organisational behaviour?
(1) Planned change is change that is intentionally introduced while unplanned change is change that occurs on its own.
(2) Planned change and unplanned change are the same thing.
(3) Planned change and unplanned change are negative outcomes in organisational behaviour.
(4) Planned change and unplanned change are emotional processes.

172. What is the role of resistance to change in organisational behaviour?
(1) Resistance to change is a natural reaction to change and can impact the success of any organisational change effort.
(2) Resistance to change is a positive outcome in organisational behaviour.
(3) Resistance to change is an emotional process.
(4) Resistance to change is irrelevant in organisational behaviour.

173. What is the definition of organisational culture in organisational behaviour?
(1) The shared values, beliefs, and assumptions that shape behaviour within an organisation.
(2) The hierarchy of positions and responsibilities within an organisation.
(3) The set of standard operating procedures within an organisation.
(4) The ability to change behaviour within an organisation.

174. What is the role of organisational communication in organisational change?
(1) Effective communication is critical in ensuring that employees understand the reasons for change and are able to adapt accordingly.
(2) Organisational communication is not relevant in organisational change.
(3) Organisational communication is a negative outcome in organisational change.
(4) Organisational communication is an emotional process.

175. What is the definition of organisational development in organisational behaviour?
(1) A planned process of change that involves the application of behavioural science principles and techniques to improve organisation performance.
(2) An unplanned process that results in changes in organisational culture.
(3) The ability to resist changes in organisational structure.
(4) The ability to adapt to changes in the environment.

176. What is the role of participative management in organisational development?
(1) Participative management involves involving employees in decision-making processes and can enhance employee engagement and motivation.
(2) Participative management is a negative outcome in organisational development.
(3) Participative management is an emotional process.
(4) Participative management is irrelevant in organisational development.

177. What is the difference between job enrichment and job enlargement?
(1) Job enrichment involves creating opportunities for employees to use their skills and expertise while job enlargement involves increasing the number of tasks.
(2) Job enrichment and job enlargement are the same thing.

(3) Job enrichment is a negative outcome while job enlargement is a positive outcome in organisational development.
(4) Job enrichment is an emotional process while job enlargement is a cognitive process.

178. What is the definition of total quality management?
(1) Total quality management involves continuous improvement efforts focused on increasing customer satisfaction.
(2) Total quality management is a negative outcome in organisational development.
(3) Total quality management is an emotional process.
(4) Total quality management is irrelevant in organisational development.

179. What is the role of team building in organisational development?
(1) Team building involves creating a positive work environment and enhancing communication among team members.
(2) Team building is a negative outcome in organisational development.
(3) Team building is an emotional process.
(4) Team building is irrelevant in organisational development.

180. What is the definition of change management in organisational behaviour?
(1) Change management involves the planning and execution of changes in an organisation.
(2) Change management is irrelevant in organisational behaviour.
(3) Change management is a negative outcome in organisational behaviour.
(4) Change management is an emotional process.

181. What is the role of leadership in organisational development?
(1) Leaders play a critical role in driving organisational change efforts and creating a positive work environment.
(2) Leadership is irrelevant in organisational development.
(3) Leadership is a negative outcome in organisational development.
(4) Leadership is an emotional process.

182. What is the definition of learning organisation in organisational behaviour?
(1) A learning organisation is an organisation that actively promotes and supports ongoing learning and development among its employees.
(2) A learning organisation is an organisation that resists change.
(3) A learning organisation is a negative outcome in organisational behaviour.
(4) A learning organisation is an emotional process.

183. What is the difference between adaptive change and transformational change?
(1) Adaptive change involves incremental adjustments to an organisation while transformational change involves significant and radical changes.
(2) Adaptive change and transformational change are the same thing.
(3) Adaptive change is a negative outcome while transformational change is a positive outcome in organisational behaviour.
(4) Adaptive change is an emotional process while transformational change is a cognitive process.

184. What is the role of employee involvement in organisational development?
(1) Employee involvement can enhance employee engagement and motivation and can promote ownership of organisational change efforts.
(2) Employee involvement is irrelevant in organisational development.
(3) Employee involvement is a negative outcome in organisational development.
(4) Employee involvement is an emotional process.

185. **Assertion:** Organisational change is any alteration or adjustment in organisational structure or operations.

Reason: Organisational change can only be planned and intentional.

(1) Both assertion and reason are false.
(2) Both assertion and reason are true but the reason is not the correct explanation of the assertion.
(3) Assertion is true but reason is false.
(4) Both assertion and reason are true and the reason is the correct explanation of the assertion.

186. Assertion: Resistance to change is a natural reaction to change and can impact the success of any organisational change effort.

Reason: Resistance to change is always a negative outcome in organisational behaviour.

(1) Both assertion and reason are false.
(2) Both assertion and reason are true but the reason is not the correct explanation of the assertion.
(3) Assertion is true but reason is false.
(4) Both assertion and reason are true and the reason is the correct explanation of the assertion.

187. Assertion: Total quality management involves continuous improvement efforts focused on increasing customer satisfaction.

Reason: Total quality management is irrelevant in organisational development.

(1) Both assertion and reason are false.
(2) Both assertion and reason are true but the reason is not the correct explanation of the assertion.
(3) Assertion is true but reason is false.
(4) Both assertion and reason are true and the reason is the correct explanation of the assertion.

188. Assertion: Job enrichment involves creating opportunities for employees to use their skills and expertise while job enlargement involves increasing the number of tasks.

Reason: Job enrichment is a negative outcome while job enlargement is a positive outcome in organisational development.

(1) Both assertion and reason are false.
(2) Both assertion and reason are true but the reason is not the correct explanation of the assertion.
(3) Assertion is true but reason is false.
(4) Both assertion and reason are true and the reason is the correct explanation of the assertion.

189. Assertion: Participative management is a negative outcome in organisational development.

Reason: Participative management is a cognitive process.

(1) Both assertion and reason are false.
(2) Both assertion and reason are true but the reason is not the correct explanation of the assertion.
(3) Assertion is true but reason is false.
(4) Both assertion and reason are true and the reason is the correct explanation of the assertion.

190. Assertion: Organisational communication is irrelevant in organisational change.

Reason: Organisational communication is a negative outcome in organisational change.

(1) Both assertion and reason are false.
(2) Both assertion and reason are true but the reason is not the correct explanation of the assertion.
(3) Assertion is true but reason is false.
(4) Both assertion and reason are true and the reason is the correct explanation of the assertion.

191. Assertion: Adaptive change involves incremental adjustments to an organisation while transformational change involves significant and radical changes.

Reason: Adaptive change is a cognitive process while transformational change is an emotional process.

(1) Both assertion and reason are false.
(2) Both assertion and reason are true but the reason is not the correct explanation of the assertion.

(3) Assertion is true but reason is false.
(4) Both assertion and reason are true and the reason is the correct explanation of the assertion.

192. Assertion: Organisational development is the planned process of change that involves the application of behavioural science principles and techniques to improve organisation performance.
Reason: Organisational development is an emotional process.
(1) Both assertion and reason are false.
(2) Both assertion and reason are true but the reason is not the correct explanation of the assertion.
(3) Assertion is true but reason is false.
(4) Both assertion and reason are true and the reason is the correct explanation of the assertion.

193. Assertion: Leadership is irrelevant in organisational development.
Reason: Leadership can impact the success of organisational change efforts.
(1) Both assertion and reason are false.
(2) Both assertion and reason are true but the reason is not the correct explanation of the assertion.
(3) Assertion is true but reason is false.
(4) Both assertion and reason are true and the reason is the correct explanation of the assertion.

194. Assertion: A learning organisation is an organisation that actively promotes and supports ongoing learning and development among its employees.
Reason: A learning organisation is an emotional process.
(1) Both assertion and reason are false.
(2) Both assertion and reason are true but the reason is not the correct explanation of the assertion.
(3) Assertion is true but reason is false.
(4) Both assertion and reason are true and the reason is the correct explanation of the assertion.

ANSWER KEY

1. (1) 2. (4) 3. (4) 4. (1) 5. (1) 6. (1) 7. (1) 8. (1) 9. (1) 10. (1)
11. (1) 12. (1) 13. (1) 14. (1) 15. (1) 16. (1) 17. (1) 18. (1) 19. (1) 20. (1)
21. (1) 22. (1) 23. (1) 24. (1) 25. (1) 26. (1) 27. (1) 28. (1) 29. (1) 30. (1)
31. (1) 32. (1) 33. (1) 34. (2) 35. (2) 36. (1) 37. (1) 38. (1) 39. (1) 40. (1)
41. (1) 42. (1) 43. (1) 44. (1) 45. (1) 46. (4) 47. (1) 48. (4) 49. (4) 50. (2)
51. (1) 52. (1) 53. (1) 54. (1) 55. (1) 56. (1) 57. (1) 58. (1) 59. (1) 60. (1)
61. (1) 62. (1) 63. (1) 64. (1) 65. (1) 66. (1) 67. (1) 68. (1) 69. (1) 70. (1)
71. (1) 72. (1) 73. (1) 74. (1) 75. (1) 76. (1) 77. (1) 78. (1) 79. (1) 80. (1)
81. (1) 82. (1) 83. (1) 84. (1) 85. (1) 86. (1) 87. (1) 88. (1) 89. (1) 90. (1)
91. (1) 92. (1) 93. (1) 94. (1) 95. (1) 96. (1) 97. (1) 98. (1) 99. (1) 100. (1)
101. (1) 102. (1) 103. (1) 104. (1) 105. (4) 106. (4) 107. (1) 108. (1) 109. (4) 110. (3)
111. (1) 112. (1) 113. (1) 114. (4) 115. (4) 116. (1) 117. (1) 118. (1) 119. (1) 120. (1)
121. (1) 122. (1) 123. (1) 124. (1) 125. (1) 126. (1) 127. (1) 128. (1) 129. (1) 130. (1)
131. (1) 132. (1) 133. (1) 134. (1) 135. (1) 136. (1) 137. (1) 138. (1) 139. (1) 140. (1)
141. (1) 142. (1) 143. (1) 144. (1) 145. (1) 146. (1) 147. (1) 148. (1) 149. (1) 150. (1)
151. (1) 152. (1) 153. (1) 154. (1) 155. (1) 156. (1) 157. (1) 158. (1) 159. (1) 160. (4)
161. (1) 162. (4) 163. (4) 164. (4) 165. (4) 166. (4) 167. (4) 168. (4) 169. (4) 170. (1)
171. (1) 172. (1) 173. (1) 174. (1) 175. (1) 176. (1) 177. (1) 178. (1) 179. (1) 180. (1)
181. (1) 182. (1) 183. (1) 184. (1) 185. (4) 186. (4) 187. (4) 188. (4) 189. (4) 190. (4)
191. (4) 192. (4) 193. (4) 194. (4)

UNIT 5

INDUSTRIAL RELATIONS

Syllabus

- Concept, Scope, Evolution, Approaches, Actors and Models, Conflict and cooperation, Bi-partitism, Tri-partitism, Collective Bargaining, Workers' Participation in Management, Grievance Handling and Disciplinary Action, Code of Conduct, Industrial Relations in changing scenario, Employers' organisations.
- **Trade Unions:** Concepts, Evolution, Problems of trade unions in India, Recognition, The Trade Unions Act, 1926. Emerging role of trade unions in India.

INDUSTRIAL RELATIONS

In broader sense industrial relations means all such relationships that a business enterprise maintains with various sections of society including employee, state, customers and public in industries contact.

In narrow sense it refers to all types of relationships between employer and employee, trade union and management, workers and union and between employee and employee. It also includes all sorts of relationships at both formal and informal levels in the organisation.

The parties involved in industrial relations, i.e., employees and the employers have a common purpose of production. They willingly bind themselves to work together. Economic interest brings employees for wages and employers hire their services as a factor of production. It highlights interpersonal relations but ignores conflicts of interest. It is an art which two parties learn by acquiring the skills of adjustment.

Industrial relations has become one of the most delicate and complex problems of modern industrial society. Industrial progress is impossible without cooperation of labours and harmonious relationships. Therefore, it is in the interest of all to create and maintain good relations between employees (labour) and employers (management).

Industrial relation means the relationship between employers and employees in course of employment in industrial organisations. However, the concept of Industrial Relations has a broader meaning. In a broad sense, the term Industrial Relations includes the relationship between the various unions, between the state and the unions as well as those between the various employers and the government. Relations of all those associated in an industry may be called Industrial Relations.

The HR Employee Relations Manager directs the organisation's employee relations function. They develop employee relations policies and ensure consistent application of company policies and procedures. In addition, they are responsible for employee dispute resolution procedures, performing internal audits, and taking appropriate action to correct any employee relations issues.

The School of Industrial and Labour Relations at Cornell University was the world's first school for college-level study in HR located in Ithaca, New York, USA. ILR (Industrial and Labour Relations) specialises in the fields of human resource management, labour relations, and dispute resolution.

So Industrial relation means the relationship between employers and employees in course of employment in industrial organisations. However, the concept of Industrial Relations has a broader meaning. In a broad sense, the term Industrial Relations includes the relationship between the various unions, between the state and the unions as well as those between the various employers and the government. Relations of all those associated in an industry may be called Industrial Relations.

CONCEPT

The term 'Industrial Relations' comprises of two terms: 'Industry' and 'Relations'. "Industry" refers to "any productive activity in which an individual (or a group of individuals) is (are) engaged". By "relations" we mean "the relationships that exist within the industry between the employer and his workmen."

The term industrial relations explain the relationship between employees and management which stem directly or indirectly from union-employer relationship.

Scope and Evolution of Industrial Relations Work

The concept of industrial relation has a very wide meaning and connotation. It means that the employer-employee relationship confines itself to the relationship that emerges out of the day-to-day association of the management and the labour. In its wider sense, industrial relations include the relationship between

DEFINITIONS

The term 'industrial relations' has been variously defined :

- **J.T. Dunlop** defines industrial relations as "the complex interrelations among managers, workers and agencies of the governments".
- **According to International Labour Organisation**, Industrial relations comprise relationships between the state on one hand and the employer's and employee's organisation on the other, and the relationship among the occupational organisations themselves.
- Industrial Relation is a relation between employer and employees, employees and employers and employees and trade unions. –Industrial dispute Act 1947
- According to **Dale Yoder** "industrial relations is the process of management dealing with one or more unions with a view to negotiate and subsequently administer collective bargaining agreement or labour contract".

According to Ordway Teed, Metcalf, Industrial relations are the composite result of the attitudes and approaches of employers and employees to each other with regard to planning, supervision, direction and coordination of the activities of an organisation with a minimum of human effort and friction, with an animating spirit of a cooperation and with proper regard for the genuine will being of all members of the organisation.

- According to **J. Henry Richardson**, "Industrial relations may be referred to as an out of living together for purposes of production."
- According to **Allan Flanders**, "The subject of industrial relations deals with certain regulated institutionalized relationship in industry.
- According to **H.A. Clegg**, "The field of industrials relations includes the study of workers and their trade unions, management employers associations and the state institutions concerned with the regulation of employment.
- According to **R.A. Lester**, "Industrial relations involve attempts at workable solutions between conflicting objectives and values between incentive and economic security between discipline and industrial democracy, between authority and freedom between bargaining and cooperation.
- According to **Bethal and other**, "Industrial relations refer to the part of management which is concerned with the manpower of the enterprise whether machine operator, skilled worker or manager.
- Encyclopedia Britannica defines a industrial relations as, "The concept of industrial relations has been extended to denote the relation of the state with employers workers and their organisations.

employers in the course of running an industry and may project it to spheres which may transgress to the areas of quality control, Marketing, price fixation and disposition of profits among others.

An industry is a social world in miniature. Associations of various persons, workmen, supervisory staff, management and employer in industry create industrial relationships. This affects the economic, social and political life of the whole community. Thus, industrial life creates a series of social relationship which regulate the relations and working of not only workmen and management but also of community and industry.

Industrial relations are therefore part and parcel of industrial life, as such they include:

(a) **Labour relations.** Relations between union-management (Also called Labour-management relations).

(b) **Employer-employee relations.** Relations between Management and employee.

(c) **Group Relations.** Relations between various groups of workmen.

(d) **Community or public relations.** Relations between industry and society.

The main aspect of industrial relation are :

(i) Promotion and development of healthy labour management relations

(ii) Maintenance of industrial peace and avoidance of industrial strife

(iii) Development of industrial democracy

(i) Promotion and development of healthy labour-management relations. The promotion of healthy management labour relation presupposes.

(a) The existence of well organised, democratic and responsible trade union and association of the employer. These organisation enhance the job security of employees help in increased worker participation in management and give labour a dignified society.

(b) The spirit of collective bargaining and willingness to take course to voluntary arbitration.

(c) Welfare work, whether statutory and non statutory, provided by the state, trade union employer create, maintain and improve labour management relations and thereby contribute to industrial peace.

(ii) Maintenance of industrial peace and avoidance of industrial strife. Industrial peace presupposes the absence of industrial strife which is essential for increase productivity and harmonious labour relation.

(a) Machinery should be set up for the prevention and settlement of the industrial disputes.

(b) The government should have the power to refers disputes to adjudication .

(c) The government should enjoy the power of the status quo.

(d) The provision of the bipartite and tripartite forms for the settlement of disputes.

(iii) Development of industrial democracy. The idea of industrial democracy exhorts that the labour should have the right to be associated with the management of an industry. To achieve this objectives, the following techniques are followed

(a) Establishment of the shop council and joint council

(b) Recognition of human right in industry

(c) Increase in labour productivity

(d) The availability of proper work environment is necessary so that the worker can effectively carry out his assignment, as it is this environment which stimulates or depresses, improve or destroy the relation between management and labour.

The functions of the industrial relations staff are:

1. Administration, including overall organisation, supervision and co-ordination of industrial relations policies and programmes.
2. Liaison with outside groups and personnel departments as well as with various cadres of the management staff.
3. The drafting of regulations, rules, laws or orders and their construction and interpretation.
4. Position classification, including overall direction of job analysis, salary and wage administration, wage survey and pay schedules.
5. Recruitment and employment of workers and other staff.
6. Employment testing, including intelligence tests, mechanical aptitude tests and achievement tests.
7. Placement, including induction and assignment.
8. Safety services, including first aid training.
9. Group activities, including group health insurance, housing, cafeteria programmes and social clubs.
10. Research in occupational trends and employee attitudes, and analysis of labor turnover.
11. Training of apprentices, production workers, foremen and executives.
12. Employee counselling on all types of personnel problems-educational, vocational, health or behaviour problems.
13. Suggestion plans and their uses in labour, management and production committees.

14. Public relations.
15. Employee relations, specially collective bargaining with representatives and settling grievances.
16. Medical and health services.
17. Employee records for all purposes.
18. Control of operation surveys, fiscal research and analysis.
19. Benefit, retirement and pension programmes.

APPROACHES

Different theoretical models/approaches to industrial relations given by different scholar are:

1. **The System approach.** John Dunlop develop the system approach. This approach is quite helpful in studying the industrial relation in the sense that it focuses on participants in the process, environmental forces and the output. Further it studies interrelations among different facets of industrial relation system.

   According to Dunlop industrial relations system consists of three agents - management organisations, workers and formal/informal ways they are organised and government agencies. These actors and their organisations are located within an environment - defined in terms of technology, labour and product markets, and the distribution of power in wider society as it impacts upon individuals and workplace .Within this environment, actors interact with each other, negotiate and use economic/political power in process of determining rules that constitute the output of the industrial relations system.

   He proposed that three parties — employers, labour unions, and government — are the key actors in a modern industrial relations system. He also argued that none of these institutions could act in an autonomous or independent fashion. Instead they were shaped, at least to some extent, by their market, technological and political contexts.

   Thus it can be said that industrial relations is a social sub system subject to three environmental constraints- the markets, distribution of power in society and technology.

   Dunlop's model identifies three key factors to be considered in conducting an analysis of the management-labour relationship:

   (a) Environmental or external economic, technological, political, legal and social forces that impact employment relationships.

   (b) Characteristics and interaction of the key actors in the employment relationship: labour, management, and government.

   (c) Rules that are derived from these interactions that govern the employment relationship.

2. **Giri Approach.** Mr. V.V. Giri who was labour minister and later become the president of India was stronger supporter of collective agreement and mutual negotiations for the settlement of industrial disputes. He was of this opinion that "voluntary efforts on the part of the management and the trade union for Binding up their differences is a tonic to the industry and any compulsion form outside the bitter machines."

   Giri approach gave emphasis that industrial peace might be secured through machinery of collective bargaining, the trade union should grow strong and self reliant without the assistant of any outsider. There must be mutual settlement of disputes through collective bargaining and voluntary arbitration and not the compulsory adjudication.

3. **The Pluralist Approach.** Pluralism is a major theory in labour-management relations, which has many powerful advocates. The focus is on the resolution of conflict rather than its generation, or, in the words of the pluralist, on 'the institutions of job regulation.' *Kerr* is one of the important exponents of pluralism. According to him, the social environment is an important factor in industrial conflicts. The isolated masses of workers are more strike-prone as compared to

dispersed groups. When industrial jobs become more pleasant and employees' get more integrated into the wider society, strikes will become less frequent. Ross and Hartman's cross national comparison of strikes postulates the declining incidents of strikes as societies industrialist and develop appropriate institutional framework. They claim that there has been a decline in strike activity all over the world in spite of an increase in union membership. The theories on pluralism were evolved in the mid-sixties and early seventies when England witnessed a dramatic resurgence of industrial conflicts. However, the recent theories of pluralism emanate from British scholars, and in particular from Flanders and Fox. According to Flanders, conflict is inherent in the industrial system. He highlighted the need for a formal system of collective bargaining as a method of conflict resolution. Fox distinguishes between two distinct aspects of relationship between workers and management. The first is the market relationship, which concerns with the terms and conditions on which labour is hired. This relationship is essentially economic in character and based on contracts executed between the parties. The second aspect relates to the management's dealing with labour, the nature of their interaction, negotiations between the union and management, distribution of power in the organisation, and participation of the union in joint decision-making. The major critics of the pluralist approach are the Marxists according to whom exploitation and slavery will continue unabated in the institutional structure of pluralism. The only difference is that in such a social structure, the worker will be deemed to be a better-paid wage slave.

4. **The Social Action Approach.** The social action model has its origin in webrian sociology .The social approach stresses the way in which an individual influence the social structure and makes the society. This approach attempts to study the behavior influences. Behaviour at work gets influences by the quality of human relation management and the nature of technology.

   Some of the major orientations in the Weberian approach have been to analyse the impact of techno-economic and politico-organisational changes on trade union structure and processes, to analyse the subjective interpretation of workers' approaches to trade unionism and finally to analyse the power of various components of the industrial relations environment - government, employers, trade unions and political parties. Thus the Weberian approach gives the theoretical and operational importance to "control" as well as to the power struggle to control work organisations - a power struggle in which all the actors in the industrial relations drama are caught up.

5. **The Human Relations Approach.** In the words of Keith Davies; human relations are "the integration of people into a work situation that motivates them to work together productively, cooperatively and with economic, psychological and social satisfactions." According to him, the goals of human relations are: (a) to get people to produce, (b) to cooperate through mutuality of interest, and (c) to gain satisfaction from their relationships. The human relations school founded by Elton Mayo and later propagated by Roethlisberger, Whitehead, W.F. Whyte, and Homans offers a coherent view of the nature of industrial conflict and harmony.

   The human relations approach highlights certain policies and techniques to improve employee morale, efficiency and job satisfaction. It encourages the small work group to exercise considerable control over its environment and in the process it helps to remove a major irritant in labour-management relations. But there was reaction against the excessive claims of this school of thought in the sixties. Some of its views were criticised by Marxists, pluralists, and others on the ground that it encouraged dependency and discouraged individual development, and ignored the importance of technology and culture in industry. Taking a balanced view, however, it must be admitted that the human relations school has thrown a lot of light on certain aspects such as communication, management development, acceptance of workplace as a social system, group dynamics, and participation in management.

6. **The Gandhian Approach.** Gandhi can be called one of the greatest labour leaders of modern India. His approach to labour problems was completely new and refreshingly human. He held definite views regarding fixation and regulation of wages, organisation and functions of trade unions, necessity and desirability of collective bargaining, use and abuse of strikes, labour indiscipline, workers participation in management, conditions of work and living, and duties of workers. The Ahmadabad Textile Labour Association, a unique and successful experiment in Gandhian trade unionism, implemented many of his ideas. Gandhiji had immense faith in the goodness of man and he believed that many of the evils of the modern world have been brought about by wrong systems and not by wrong individuals. He insisted on recognising each individual worker as a human being. He believed in non-violent communism, going so far as to say that "if communism comes without any violence, it would be welcome."

   Gandhiji laid down certain conditions for a successful strike.

   These are:

   (a) the cause of the strike evolves appropriate strategies that must be just and there should be no strike without a grievance;

   (b) there should be no violence; and

   (c) non-strikers or "blacklegs" should never be molested.

   He was not against strikes but pleaded that they should be the last weapon in the armory of industrial workers and hence should not be resorted to unless all peaceful and constitutional methods of negotiations, conciliation and arbitration are exhausted. His concept of trusteeship is a significant contribution in the sphere of industrial relations. According to him, employers should not regard themselves as sole owners of mills and factories of which they may be the legal owners.

   They should regard themselves only as trustees, or co-owners. He also appealed to the workers to behave as trustees, not to regard the mill and machinery as belonging to the exploiting agents but to regard them as their own, protect them and put to the best use they can. In short, the theory of trusteeship is based on the view that all forms of property and human accomplishments are gifts of nature and as such, they belong not to any one individual but to society.

   Thus, the trusteeship system is totally different from other contemporary labour relations systems. It aimed at achieving economic equality and the material advancement of the "have-nots" in a capitalist society by non-violent means. Gandhiji realised that relations between labour and management can either be a powerful stimulus to economic and social progress or an important factor in economic and social stagnation.

   According to him, industrial peace was an essential condition not only for the growth and development of the industry itself, but also in a great measure, for the improvement in the conditions of work and wages. At the same time, he not only endorsed the workers' right to adopt the method of collective bargaining but also actively supported it.

   He advocated voluntary arbitration and mutual settlement of disputes. He also pleaded for perfect understanding between capital and labour, mutual respect, recognition of equality, and strong labour organisation as the essential factors for happy and constructive industrial relations. For him, means and ends are equally important.

7. **Human Resource Management Approach.** The term, human resource management (HRM) has become increasingly used in the literature of personnel/industrial relations. The term has been applied to a diverse range of management strategies and, indeed, sometimes used simply as a more modern, and therefore more acceptable, term for personnel or industrial relations management.

Some of the components of HRM are:

(i) human resource organisation; (ii) human resource planning; (iii) human resource systems; (iv) human resource development; (v) human resource relationships; (vi) human resource utilisation; (vii) human resource accounting; and (viii) human resource audit. This approach emphasizes individualism and the direct relationship between management and its employees. Quite clearly, therefore, it questions the collective regulation basis of traditional industrial relations.

8. **The industrial sociology Approach.** Industrial sociologists, G. Maregerison, was develop the industrial sociology approach. Margerison hold the views the core of industrial relation is the nature and developments of the conflicts itself. Margerison developed the two concepts level of industrial relation –one at intra plant level and other outside the firm.

   At plant level there could be three types of conflict-distributive, structural and human relations. To resolve these conflict margerison suggested the collective bargaining, human relations management analysis and structural analysis of socio-technical system. At the second level outside the firm, the main concern with is the conflicts not resolved at intra organisational level.

9. **The Marxist Approach.** The class conflict analysis of industrial relations derives its impetus from Marxist social thinking and interpretation. Marxism is essentially a method of social enquiry into the power relationships of society and a way of interpreting social reality. The application of Marxian theory as it relates to industrial relations derives indirectly from later Marxist scholars rather than directly from the works of Marx himself. Industrial relations, according to Marxists, are in the first instance, market-relations. To Marxists, industrial relations are essentially politicised and part of the class struggle. For Marxists industrial and employee relations can only be understood as part of a broader analysis of capitalist society in particular the social relations of production and the dynamics of capital accumulation. As Marx himself put it, "the mode of production in material life determines the general character of the social, political and spiritual process of life." The Marxist approach is primarily oriented towards the historical development of the power relationship between capital and labour. It is also characterised by the struggle of these classes to consolidate and strengthen their respective positions with a view to exerting greater influence on each other. In this approach, industrial relations is equated with a power-struggle. The price payable for labour is determined by a confrontation between conflicting interests. The capitalist ownership of the enterprise endeavors' to purchase labour at the lowest possible price in order to maximise their profits. The lower the price paid by the owner of the means of production for the labour he employs, the greater is his profit. The Marxist analysis of industrial relations, however, is not a comprehensive approach as it only takes into account the relations between capital and labour. It is rather, a general theory of society and of social change, which has implications for the analysis of industrial relations within what Marxists would describe as capitalist societies.

10. **The psychological Approach.** This approach is given by Mason Haire. The psychologist are of the view problem of industrials relations are deeply rooted in the perception and the attitude of focal participants. According to him industrial relation problem arise due to perceptions of the management, union, and the workers. These perception about the person, the situations or the issues involved the conflicts. The perception and the trade union may differs because the same positions may appears the entirely different to other party. Some aspects of the situation are magnified or suppressed or distorted by other party. He studied the different group namely, "union leaders" and "Executive" through a test. For a test of the photographer of an ordinary middle age person served as a input, which both the group ware expected to rate. It is interesting to note that both the groups rated the photograph in different manner, i.e., the union leaders

referred the person in the photograph as manager where the group of executives saw union leaders in the photograph.

ACTORS AND MODELS

Industrial Relations – Models of IR

1. Dunlop's Industrial Relations System Model- Four Interrelated Elements:

i. **Actors**
   (a) Specialised government agencies.
   (b) Management, non-managerial employees and their representatives.

ii. **Shared Ideology**
   (a) Beliefs within the system which not only define the role of each actor or groups of actors but also define the view that they have of the role of other actors in the system. If the view is compatible-stable IR system and other wise.
   (b) Set of ideas and beliefs held by the actors.
   (c) Helps to bind or integrate the system together.

iii. **Contexts.** Influence and constraints on the decisions of the actors which emanate from other parts of society, such as technology, market, budgetary and the locus of power in the society.

iv. **Rules**
   (a) Procedural
   (b) Substantive
   (c) Distributive
   (d) The regulatory framework developed by a range of process and presented in variety of forms which expresses the terms and nature of the employment relationship.

Criticisms of the Dunlop Model
(i) Descriptive
(ii) Lacks ability to predict outcomes/ relationships
(iii) Underestimates importance of power and conflict in employment relationship
(iv) Static.
(v) Cannot explain rapid decrease in unionisation especially in the U.S.

2. Craig's Industrial Relations System Model

(i) Adds an actor- end user
(ii) Elements from the external environment converted into outputs
(iii) Series of conversion mechanisms
(iv) Outputs flow back into the environment through a feedback loop

External Inputs
(i) Legal Subsystem
(ii) Economics Subsystem
(iii) Ecological Subsystem
(iv) Political Subsystem
(v) Socio-cultural Subsystem

Internal Inputs
(i) Goals- Sought by actors

(ii) Strategies- Processes developed and implemented to achieve goals
(iii) Power- The ability to make another actor agree to your terms

Conversion Mechanisms

(i) Processes actors use to convert internal and external inputs into outputs
(ii) Collective bargaining
(iii) Produces a collective agreement
(iv) Grievances
(v) Written complaint by employees
(vi) Alleges collective agreement not been followed
(vii) Day to day relations-communication

Third-Party Interventions

(i) Interest arbitration
(ii) Mediation
(iii) Grievance arbitration
(iv) Conciliation
(v) Fact-finding
(vi) Mediation/arbitration
(vii) strikes/lockouts
(viii) Joint committees

Outputs

(i) Management outcomes
(ii) Productivity, profitability
(iii) Labour outcomes
(iv) Equity issues, ways to achieve fairness in the workplace
(v) Worker perceptions
(vi) Work climate
(vii) Employee morale
(viii) Organisational commitment
(ix) Union satisfaction/commitment
(x) Conflict or conflict resolution

Industrial Relations – Main Aspects of IR

The main aspects of industrial relations are:

(1) Promotion and development of healthy labour management relations;
(2) Maintenance of industrial peace and avoidance of industrial strife; and
(3) Development of industrial democracy.

(1) **Promotion and Development or Healthy Labour-Management Relations.** One of the aspects of industrial relations is to promote and develop healthy relations between the employer and employees and pre-supposes.

(a) Spirit or collective bargaining and willingness to take recourse to voluntary arbitration. The very feeling of collective bargaining makes them assume equal status in the industry. This feeling may further industrial peace.

(b) The existence or strong, well organised, democratic and responsible trade unions and also associations or the employers in the industry which may ensure job security to workers and their participation in the decision-making and give labour a dignified role in the society. These associations, tend to create grounds for negotiations, consultations and discussions on mutual basis leading to good labour- management relations.

(c) Welfare Work. Whether voluntary or statutory provided by the state, trade unions and the employers do create, maintain and improve good and healthy labour-management relations.

(2) **Maintenance of Industrial Peace.** Industrial peace presupposes the absence of industrial strife. Such peace can be established only when the following rights and privileges are enjoyed by the State and facilities for bipartite or tripartite consultation machinery for resolving disputes if any, are provided–

(a) Machinery for the prevention and settlement of industrial disputes should be established through legislative and administrative enactment.

(b) The provision of the bipartite and tripartite forums for the settlement of disputes must be made. Various codes, model standing orders and procedures to resolve disputes are necessary.

(c) Appropriate Government must have sufficient power to refer the disputes to adjudication or arbitration when it feels it necessary in the interest of the industry, or of the country. The Government must not allow any group in the industry to stop production due to strikes or lock-outs.

(d) Implementation Cells and Evaluation committees must be established, having power to look into the implementation of various agreements, settlements and awards and also to violation of statutory provisions under various labour laws.

(3) **Development of Industrial Democracy.** The idea of 'industrial democracy' is that the labour must have the right to associate with the management in running the industry.

In this connection, following techniques are usually adopted:

(a) Establishment of the Shop Councils and Joint Management Councils at the floor and plant level to improve the working and living conditions through mutual consultation and understanding. It will create necessary climate for the development of industrial democracy;

(b) Increase in labour productivity through various means;

(c) Recognising the labour not as a commodity but as a human being in the industry, allowing them a feeling of self-respect and better understanding of their role in the organisation;

(d) The material and social environment to which the worker adjusts and adapts himself while at work, must be available.

According to Lester, "Industrial relations involve attempts to arrive at solutions between the conflicting objectives and values; between profit motive and social gain; between discipline and freedom; between authority and industrial democracy; between bargaining and cooperation; and conflicting interests of the individual, the group and the community."

Industrial Relations – 3 Main Participants in Industrial Unit

Basically there are two parties in the employment relationship, i.e., the labour and the management. Over the years, the Government has come to play a major role in industrial relations and they have established legal and non-legal measures for cordial industrial relations in the country.

These three parties of industrial relations interact with the environment that prevails in the industry at any time. Good industrial relations are the outcome of (a) Healthy labour management relations, (b) Existence of industrial peace and settlement of all disputes in such a manner that there are no strikes or lockouts and (c) Labour participation in industry which is referred as Industrial democracy.

In an industrial unit, different people are performing the different tasks.

We can have three parties or participants or actors in an industrial unit:

1. **Workers and their Unions.** The total work plays an important role in industrial relations. The total work includes working age, educational background, family background, Psychological factors, social background, culture, skills, attitude towards other work, etc. Workers organisation prominently in trade union activities.

   The main purpose of trade unions is to protect the workers economic interest through collective bargaining and by bringing pressure on management through economic and political practices. Trade union factors include leadership, financial, activities, etc.
2. **Managers and their Associations.** The prominent role is of work group, the differences in their sizes, constitutions and the degree of specialisation they press upon. Of course, there is the necessary provision for mutual communications for the structure of status and authority and for such other organisation as trade unions and employer's associations.
3. **Government.** Government plays a balancing role as a custodian of the nation; government exerts its influence on industrial relations through its labour policy, industrial relations policy, implementing labour laws, the process of conciliation and adjudication by playing the role of a mediator, etc. It tries to regulate the activities and behaviour of both employee's organisations and employer organisations.

   Thus the three groups of employees, employers and the government work within the social and economic environment that prevails at a particular time. Whatever industrial relations system may be in vogue, it has in its framework the intricate rules and regulations which enforce the workplace and the working community.

   The various systems might comprise of different forms of such rules and regulations. There might be laws and awards of different courts, committees or tribunals. There might be agreements written or sanctioned by custom, usage, practice or tradition or there might be the outcome of government policies or intervention.

CONFLICT AND COOPERATION

There are two important aspects of the industrial relations scene in a modern industrial society:

1. **Conflict.** The second aspect of the system of industrial relations obtaining today is the existence of conflict, conflict, like cooperation is inherent in the industrial relations set up of today. The prevailing industrial unrest, the frequency of work – stoppages resulting either from strikes or lock-outs, and the slowing down of production, are the occasional expressional of the ever-present and latent conflict between workers and the management.
2. **Cooperation.** Modern industrial production is based upon cooperation between labour and capital. Here labour stands for the workers who man the factories, mines and other industrial establishment or services. Capital stands for the owners of business enterprises who supply the capital and own the final product. The cooperation between the two is one of the basic requirements for the smooth functioning of modern industries and the growth of industrialisation.

BI-PARTISM

The bipartite consultative machinery comprises two important constituents, viz., the works committees and the joint management councils. These are purely consultative, and not negotiating bodies. This consultative joint machinery – with equal representation of the employers and the workers – has been set up exclusively for dealing with disputes affecting the plant or industry.

Bipartism is a system of industrial relations where social and labour issues are discussed Between trade unions and management, usually at the enterprise level.

Evolution of Such Bodies

The importance of bipartite consultative machinery was first recognised as early as in 1920, when a few joint committees were set up in the presses controlled by the Government of India. They were also introduced in Tata Iron and Steel Company at Jamshedpur.

The importance of bipartite consultation was further highlighted by the First-Five-Year Plan which maintained: There should be the closest collaboration, through the consultative committee at all levels, between employers and employees for the purpose of increasing production, improving quality, reducing cost and eliminating waste. The second Plan also stressed the need for joint consultation and progressively associating the workers and technicians, wherever possible, in management.

Bipartite Bodies

The two important constituents of bipartite consultative machinery are: (1) Works Committee, (2) Joint Management Councils. A brief review of these bodies is given here.

1. **Work Committee.** These committees have been regarded as the most effective social institution of industrial democracy and as a statutory body, established within the industrial units with representatives of the management and workmen, for preventing, and settling industrial disputes at the unit level. The works committee can be formed by any enterprise, employing 100 or more workers.

   Its objectives are:

   (i) To remove the causes of friction in the day-to-day work situation by providing an effective grievances-resolving machinery;

   (ii) To promote measures securing amity and good relationship;

   (iii) To serve as a useful adjunct in establishing continuing bargaining relationship; and

   (iv) To strengthen the spirit of voluntary settlement, rendering recourse to conciliation, arbitration and adjudication rather infrequent; for these are achieved by commenting upon matters of concern or Endeavour to compose any material difference of opinion in respect of such matters.

   Meeting and Submission of Return. The work committee should meet at least once in a three month. As per the requirement of the meeting can be held more frequently also, meeting are held during the working hours of the establishment and the representative of workers, attending the meetings are deemed be on duty. The reports and the return are to be submitted not later then the 20th day of the month following the half years.

2. **Joint Management Council.** These committees give labour a greater sense of participation and infuse a spirit of co-operation between the two parties without encroaching upon each other's sphere of influence, rights and prerogatives. They establish a channel of close mutual interaction between labour and management which, keeping tension at a low level, generates a co-operative atmosphere for negotiation and settlement. These committees also aim at making the will of the employees effective in the management; ensure the operation of the private-owned concern in conformity with national interests and provide for a popular agency for supervising the management of nationalised undertakings. In brief, such committees try to promote industrial goodwill and harmonious relations through better understanding of employees by management and of management by workers. To accomplish this goal, the works committees are entrusted with a number of functions which are of benefit to management as well as employees.

The concept of the JMC is implicit in the industrial relation policy resolution of April 1956 in the following statement

"in a socialist democracy, labour is a partner in the common task of development and should participate in it with enthusiasm. There should be joint consultation ;workers and technicians should, wherever possible, be associated progressively in management. Enterprise in the public sector have to set an example in this respect.

Bipartism's Link with Tripartism

Bipartism is complementary to tripartism at national and other levels. Bipartism and tripartism should be seen as the two sides of the same coin. Both mutually reinforce each other. The prerequisites for the success of both bipartism and tripartism-notions about equality among partners, freedom of association, the right to collective bargaining, and democratic decision-making, among others-are similar.

National and centralised tripartite consultations are usually more influenced by political considerations and state support. Bipartism arrangements, particularly in the context of the current trend towards decentralised firm/plant-level bargaining, adjustment to structural and other changes, and economic crisis, are influenced more by economic considerations. The institutional framework for industrial relations influences substantially, the relative role of tripartism and bipartism in responding to economic changes/policies at macro level.

Tripartism's Contribution to Bipartism

Tripartite consultations and agreements can exercise profound influence in directing and shaping collective bargaining and industrial relations. The three-tier frame work of industrial relations proposed by Kochan, (1987) suggests a direct and active role for tripartite consultation at macro level, to be reinforced by bipartite consultations, collective bargaining, communication, information sharing, and employee participation at industry and firm/plant level. Whether it was the arrangements for the avoidance/settlement of disputes, procedures for recognition of unions, grievance redressals, consultations and cooperation at work place, or collective bargaining on a host of matters relating to industrial relations and human resources, tripartite initiatives played a substantial role in setting up international labour standards, enactment of national legislations, and conclusion of national agreements.

In the Indian context, for instance, the following tripartite declaration played a useful role, at least for a number of years, in influencing bipartite relations and agreements relating to union recognition, automation, and modernisation.

1. Code of discipline,
2. Code of Conduct,
3. Automation Without Tears.

Bipartism's Contribution to Tripartism

Bipartism or more importantly, collective bargaining, which is a key instrument of bipartism, may reduce the need for tripartite interventions. In some cases, tripartism begins where bipartism fails. For instance, when bipartite dialogue does not result in dispute avoidance or settlement, tripartite interventions such as conciliation/mediation and arbitration/adjudication become imperative.

Bipartite arrangements can contribute in the following ways to facilitate meaningful and effective tripartite social dialogue at industry and national level:

1. In countries where the representative character of the social partners is very much limited due to the predominant characteristics of an economy (large unorganised, in formal-sector economy),

the outcomes of tripartite discussions do not necessarily reflect the wishes of the large majority of the working population, not to speak of the society at large. In these and similar other situations it is better to adopt a bottom-up approach through bipartite dialogue at enterprise level.

2. The interests of employers and workers are affected by government policies in areas other than industrial relations such as fiscal, monetary, trade, taxation, licensing, etc. The effects of these aspects is ;more closely and effectively reckoned and evaluated in bipartite consultations, particularly collective agreements, than in tripartite dialogue.
3. Consensual approaches are best planned and implemented if they are developed by parties at the grassroots level, that is plant level. The parties/persons directly affected should be involved in consensus-building social dialogue. Externally imposed consensus through tripartite declarations often may not work effectively at industry/enterprise level.

TRI-PARTITISM

Tripartism is a system of labour relations in which the state, employers, and workers are autonomous yet interdependent partners, pursuing common interests and participating in decisions affecting them in a binding spirit of mutuality and reciprocity. This can take place at either or both macro and micro levels.

Tripartite consultation is an important feature of India's industrial relations system. It has a long history in India as it was set up as early as 1942. The Indian Labour Conference (ILC) and the Standing Labour Committee (SLC) are two main forums for Tripartite Consultation. The objectives of Tripartite Consultation could be mentioned as under:

- To promote uniformity in labour legislation.
- To lay down a procedure for settlement of industrial disputes.
- To consider matters of importance to both the managements and labour.
- Tripartite forums evolve norms or standards in the form of guidelines.

There are a number of tripartite bodies which operate at the Central and State levels. The Indian Labour Conference, Standing Labour Committees, Wage Boards and Industrial Committees operate at the Central level and State Labour Advisory Boards operate at the state level. All these bodies play an important role in reaching at voluntary agreements on various labour matters. Though the recommendations of these bodies are only advisory in nature they carry considerable weight with the government, workers and employers. Some important measures agreed to by the Indian Labour conference in past are:

1. Setting up of bipartite works committees, joint consultative and production committees.
2. Adoption by employers and unions of a voluntary code of discipline;
3. Following proper grievance and disciplinary procedures;
4. Deciding norms for fixing need based wages;
5. Rationalising and revising wage structures of important industries through non-statutory wage boards; and
6. Encouraging voluntary arbitration for the settlement of industrial disputes.

Industrial relations in India have been shaped largely by principles and policies evolved through tripartite consultative machinery at the industry and national levels. The aim of the consultative machinery is – to bring the parties together for mutual settlement of differences in a spirit of co-operation and goodwill. The role of the tripartite machinery has been summarised by the Planning Commission thus – Labour policy in India has been evolving in response to the specific needs of the situation in relation to industry and the working class.

Evolution of Tripatite Bodies

The need for consultation on labour matters on the patterns set by the I.L.O. was recommended by the Whitley Commission in 1931. It envisaged a statutory organisation which should be sufficiently large to ensure adequate representation of the various interests involved; but it should not be too large to prevent the members from making individual contributions to the discussion. The representatives of employers, of labour and of government should meet regularly in conference. The commission also recommended that labour members should be elected by registered trade unions and employers' representatives should be elected by their associations.

But the recommendation was not implemented and nothing could be done in this respect till the outbreak of the Second World War, which necessitated the need for maintenance of industrial peace. During the Second World War separate consultations with the representatives of labour and employers were held in 1941 and 1942 by the Government of India to finalise post-war labour programmes. The experience of these consultations highlighted the necessity of holding joint meetings of the representatives of the government, workers and employers, thus, providing a common platform for the resolution of differences between the employers and workers by means of discussion and mutual understanding. Accordingly, the Fourth Labour Conference was held in August 1942. It set up permanent tripartite collaboration machinery and constituted a Preliminary Labour Conference (later named as the Indian Labour Conference – ILC) and the Standing Labour Advisory Committee (which subsequently dropped the word Advisory from its title SLC). Initially the ILC consisted of 44 members whereas the SLC was about half the size of the ILC. The pattern of representation was governed by the obtaining in the International Labour Conference. It ensured:

i. Equality of representation between the government and the non-government representatives;
ii. Parity between employers and workers;
iii. Nomination of representatives of organised employers and labourers was left to the concerned organisations; and
iv. Representation of certain interests (unorganised employers and unorganised workers), where necessary, on an adhoc basis through nomination by government. The delegates are free to bring one official and one non-official adviser with them.

Tripatite Bodies

Tripartite bodies have been set up by the government to provide a forum of discussion and consultation on various labour related issues.

Some of the notable bodies are:

- The Indian Labour Conference (ILC)
- The Standing Labour Committee (SLC)
- The Committee on Conventions
- The Industrial committee

Other bodies of tripartite nature which deals in various aspects of labour problems:

- Steering Committee on Wages
- Central Implementation and Evaluation Machinery
- Central Boards of Workers Education
- National Productivity Council

Tripartism promotes the idea of partnership between the labour and the management. The two main principles of tripartism are:

- Management and workers should share a relationship of partnership rather than that of employer and employee. They should work in synergy towards the building up of the national economy.

- It holds the whole community liable for protecting the interests of workers and ensures that workers are not deprived of their due share in gains of economic development.

1. Indian Labour Conference (ILC)

The first tripartite labour conference, consisting of the representative of the government, employers and workers was held at Delhi in august 1942. The conference was held to discuss labour relations issues, procedure for the settlement of industrial disputes and to promote uniformity in labour legislation.

This conference is consisted in two organisations namely ILC/SLC.

Both ILC and SLC are two important constituents of tripartite bodies. They play a vital role in shaping, the I.R. system of the country.

A brief account of these bodies is discussed here:

The agenda for ILC/SLC meetings was settled by the Labour Ministry after taking into consideration the suggestions sent to it by member organisations. These two bodies worked with minimum procedural rules to facilitate free and fuller discussions among the members. The ILC meets once a year whereas the SLC meets as and when necessary.

The rules and procedures, which characterise the Indian tripartite consultative machinery, are largely in tune with the recommendations of the ILO Committee on consultation and co-operation. (Recommendation No.113).

The objects of the Indian Labour Conference (ILC) are: (a) To promote uniformity in labour legislation; (b) To lay down a procedure for the settlement of industrial disputes; and c. To discuss all matters of all-India importance as between employers and employees. The function of the ILC is to – advise the Government of India on any matter referred to it for advice, taking into account suggestions made by the provincial government, the states and representatives of the organisations of workers and employers.

A detailed account of various resolutions adopted by the ILC's in their last two sessions is presented here:

A. The 30th Session of the Indian Labour Conference

The 30th Session of the ILC was held on September 7-8, 1993 at New Delhi. After deliberations, it arrived at the following conclusions.

1. On the impact of New Industrial Policy, the chairman referred to the assurance by the Prime Minister that it would not lead to any human distress and the legitimate interests of labour would be protected.
2. In regard to retraining and redeployment, the conference desired identification of labour for such retraining and redeployment and a scheme for industry-wise and occupation-wise redeployment. The conference also expressed the view that Government should identify the agency for retraining and their redeployment. The conference also wanted to know how labour of one unit would be redeployed in another unit.
3. For absorption of surplus labour, if any, as for maximising capacity utilisation, the conference suggested diversification and broad-basing by working the units round the clock and on all days of the week.
4. The conference expressed its serious concern at the low productivity of Indian industry and expressed its determination to improve wherever necessary its productivity, enhance its quality and reduce the price of goods to make them internationally competitive. The conference decided to strive for improvement in discipline and attitude to work at all levels. It also decided that bipartite efforts to improve productivity and quality should be institutionalised.

5. The Trade Unions demanded:
   i. The removal of ceiling on bonus both for eligibility and for computation by promulgation of an ordinance;
   ii. The immediate implementation of the DA rate of Rs. 2 per point of the Consumer Price Index (1960 series).
   iii. Permission for the managements of the public sector units to commence negotiations with the unions on their charter of demands immediately.
   iv. Clearance by government to the agreement regarding pension and for the pension scheme for its early introduction.
   v. Enhancement of the rate of interest on Employees' Provident Fund to at least 13 per cent.
   vi. Enhancement of the limits of exemption of income tax substantially.
6. The employers wanted postponement of the decision on removal of ceiling on bonus both for eligibility and computation of bonus by one year so that a well- thought out scheme could be evolved. They also wanted productivity linked bonus as prescribed under the law.
7. The trade unions indicated that the first National Commission on Labour was appointed about 25 years ago and a time had come to set up another National Commission on Labour to examine the issues that labour was facing today in view of the many changes that has occurred in the meantime.
8. The Labour Cell in the Planning Commission may be revived to facilitate consultation with trade unions while formulating policies concerning labour. The view expressed by the participants in the conference with regard to employment policy may be conveyed to the Planning Commission for its consideration and for the consideration of the two Sub-Committees of the Planning Commission/ NDC which are considering strategies for implementation of the employment policy.

B. 31st Session of I.L.C.

This session of I.L.C. was held at Delhi on 3rd-4th January 1995. In this session various problems of industrial relations in the context of changed economic environment were discussed. The various resolutions adopted at the said conference are as under.

1. The institution of the Indian Labour Conference should be strengthened further
2. The Central and State Governments and the social partners should come together in making the comprehensive industrial relations law a reality and an instrument of production, productivity, employment generation and enhancement of living standards.
3. Productivity of economic enterprises as a whole is of paramount importance.
4. The government should give special attention to streamlining the public distribution system, particularly in centers of concentration of working people.
5. The Government should review the situation arising out of the wage negotiations in Central Public Sector Undertakings and should facilitate speedy conclusion of wage negotiations and settlements.
6. The worker's representatives demanded that the eligibility and calculation ceilings under the Payment of Bonus Act should be scrapped, whereas the employers' representatives demanded that a quick decisions should be taken on introduction of DA slabs.
7. The government should introduce the Pension for Provident Fund subscribers on priority basis and there should be tripartite consultations before its introduction. Management of Social Security Funds should be professionally handled so as to maximise the returns on investments.

8. Steps should be taken for speedy and orderly investigation into the rehabilitation of sick industrial enterprises registered with the BIFR, minimising distress for the workers and disabilities for the employers.
9. The constitution and the functioning of the National Renewal Fund should be reviewed such that the Fund truly serves the purpose of industrial renewal and regeneration and creation of employment opportunities.
10. Implementation of training programmes should be undertaken within the framework of a well thought-out plan.
11. The Central and State Governments should give high priority to allocation of resources for elementary and vocational education. Special attention should be given to the education of women.
12. The government should enact, on priority basis, laws for covering agricultural and construction workers.
13. The Labour Ministry should set up an Advisory Body to review, from time to time, the status of women.
14. The Constitution of the Child Labour Advisory Committee should be reviewed to ensure that it is fully representative of the social partners.
15. Representatives from workers' and employers' organisations should be included in the National delegation to the World Sumit for Social Development.
16. The Vocational Training System in the country should be reorganised.
17. The resolutions of the 32nd Session of the Standing Labour Committee in respect of the social clause, child labour elimination and bonded labour were fully endorsed. The social partners should take further follow up action on the resolutions.
18. The new International Economic Order holds out vast opportunities for economic betterment and upgradation of the living standards of the people. The risks involved in formulating and implementing economic policies to avail of these opportunities should be so handled as to minimise human distress.

2. Standing Labour Committee

The second important organisation in the Indian tripartite machinery is standing labour committee (S.L.C.) & like ILC.

The Standing Labour Committee's (SLC) main function is to consider and examine such questions as may be referred to it by the Plenary Conference or the Central Government, and to render advice taking into account the suggestions made by various governments, workers and employer.

The representatives of the workers and employers were nominated to these bodies by the Central Government in consultation with the all-India organisations of workers and employers.

The objects of the SLC is the same as that of ILC

a. To promote uniformity in labour legislation;
b. To lay down a procedure for the settlement of industrial disputes; and
c. To discuss all matters of all-India importance as between employers and employees.

A. The 31st Session of Standing Labour Committee

The 31st session of S.L.C was held in New Delhi on July 25, 1992. The Committee arrived at the following conclusions:

1. It was resolved that future sessions of the Standing Labour Committee (SLC) should carry fewer items on the agenda so that these could be discussed in greater detail.

2. It was resolved that Government may bring specific proposals for new Industrial Relations Law in the ensuring session of Indian Labour Conference which should reflect the needs of the qualitative change in the industrial/economic scenario in the national/global context.
3. It was resolved to set up a tripartite sub-committee to review the implementation of important Labour laws.
4. It was resolved to set up an autonomous Bipartite Productivity Councils at the national, regional, industrial and plant levels.

B. The 32nd Session of Standing Labour Committee

The thirty second session of the Standing Labour Committee was held in New Delhi on October 27, 1994. It discussed various issues concerning employment, vocational training, child labour, bonded labour, labour standards and international trade. It adopted three important resolutions discussed below:

(a) **Social Clause.** It was agreed that the government along with employers and labour organisations would resist in I.L.O. and all other for any attempt to introduce – Social clause, in relation to carrying our marketing at the international level, contingent upon enforcement of labour standards. Further, it advocated sustained national and international action for upgrading labour standards without any trade linkage.

(b) **Child Labour.** With respect to child labour, it remarked that the – Central and State Governments and Organisations of employers and workers should take co-ordinated action for the elimination of child labour in hazardous occupations by the year 2000 and in other employments progressively. It also emphasized that both Central and State Governments should implement time bound and action plans to take away children from work and provide them education, primary vocational training, health and nutrition and concurrently provide to the parents of such children gainful employment.

(c) **Bonded Labour.** It exhorted that all states should take fresh surveys for the identification release and rehabilitation of bonded labour. Besides this, measures shall be initiated to check the relapse of bondage of such labour.

3. Committee on Conventions

This is a three-man tripartite committee set up in 1954. The object was – (i) to examine the ILO conventions and recommendations which have not so far been ratified by India; and (ii) to make suggestions with regard to a phased and speedy implementation of ILO standard.

4. Industrial Committees

The eighth session of the ILC (1947) decided to set up Industrial Committees – to discuss various specific problems special to the industries covered by them and submit their report to the Conference, which would co-ordinate their activities. These committees are tripartite bodies in which the number of workers' representatives is equal to the number of employers' representatives. They do not meet regularly; meetings are considered afresh each time a session is called.

The committees that were set up immediately after independence related to plantations, cotton textiles, jute, coal mining, mines other than coal, cement, tanneries, and leather goods manufactures, iron and steel, building and construction industry, chemical industries, road transport, engineering industries, metal trades, electricity, gas and power, and banking.

A special tripartite committee was constituted by the Ministry of Labour November in 1992 to study the impact of the new industrial policy on various labour and other problems and for making useful recommendations. The committee in its meetings on December 21, 1991 and January 21, 1992 took a note of the analysis of the performance of public sector units made by the department of public enterprises in its monograph on performance status central public sector enterprises and recognised that some of the public sector units are chronically sick required radical treatment. The committee decided setting up of Tripartite Industrial Committees to examine endemically sick units and suggest preventive measures. As per the recommendations of special tripartite committee six industries committees viz... (1) cotton textiles, (2) jute, (3) chemicals, (4) engineering, (5) electricity, (generation and distribution), (6) road transport were revived. On the major conclusion of these tripartite committee was that there should be case by case discussion on sick unit for their revival and before taking a final decision on sick PSUs, BIFR should be urged to consider the views of tripartite committees. Another important conclusion of the tripartite committees was that at the enterprise level workers and management should prepare a joint revival plans on the basis data supplied by the concerned administrative ministry/ management. The revival proposal would then be considered by the Sectorial tripartite committee.

Other Committees

(1) Committee on N.T.C. Turnaround

The Labour Ministry constituted a special committee to consider the turn-around strategy for NTC on June 26, 1993. On the recommendation of this committee, a sub-committee was constituted to consider the implementation of turnaround strategy. It had eight rounds of meetings. This committee led to the final agreement on April 9, 1994 for the modernisation of N.T.C.

(2) Committee on Plantation

For the effective amendment of the Plantation Labour Act, 1951, a Tripartite Committee on Plantation was reconstituted. The first meeting of the committee took place on April 27, 1994. A sub-committee of the tripartite committee also considered the specific issue relating to medical facilities was held on April 27, 1994. The consensus arrived at meetings called for amendment in Plantations Labour (Amendment) Bill 1992 (that was earlier introduced by the government in the Rajya Sabha).

The 41st session of the Labour Ministers conference was held in New Delhi. On August 13, 1992 under the chairmanship of Union Minister of State for Labour. After deliberations on various issues it arrived at the following conclusion:

(i) The Ramanujan Committee report on trade unions was considered by the conference it was decided to place the report before the next I.L.C. (ii) It was decided to appoint a committee of labour ministers to go into the recommendations of National Commission on Rural Labour (NCRL) pertaining to (1) Social Security, (2) Central legislation for agriculture labour, (3) Central legislation for construction workers, (4) Appointment of National Commission on Bonded Labour. (iii) It was decided to convene a labour minister conference to consider the question of improvement of quality of medical services rendered under the E.S.I.C. (iv) It was held that restriction on the employment of outsider and the problem of inter state migrant worker needs serious consideration and therefore be referred to inter state and even to the national integration council.

For safeguarding the interest of child labour it was emphasized that the Child Labour (Prohibition and Regulation) Act, 1986 needs more effective implementation. The conference also called for the amendment of the Act.

(3) Steering Committee on Wages

It was set up in 1956 as a study group on wages and was subsequently reconstituted as the steering committee on wages. It consists of representatives of state governments, employers and workers and an economist. The functions of this committee are: (i) to study trends in wages, production and prices; (ii) to plan collection of material for drawing up a wage map of India; and (iii) to draw up reports from time to time for laying down principles which will guide wage fixing authorities.

(4) Central Implementation and Evolution Machinery

The 18th session of the Standing Labour Committee in 1957 recommended the setting up of a special machinery at the Centre as well as in the states to ensure proper implementation of labour awards, agreements and Code of Discipline. The implementation machinery at the Centre consists of an Evaluation and Implementative Division and a tripartite implementation committee, consisting of 4 representatives each of central employers' and workers' organisations with the union labour minister as chairman.

(5) Central Boards of Workers' Education

Was constituted to encourage the growth of strong and well-informed trade union movement conducted by the workers themselves on responsible and constructive lines. This consists of representatives of employers and workers, and of central and state governments.

(6) National Productivity Council

Consists of representatives of the government, employers' associations, labourers' organisations and certain independent experts. It encourages the productivity in the country.

INDUSTRIAL RELATIONS IN CHANGING SCENARIO

- The rapid automation and adoption of modern technology in industries have dwindled the job opportunities at an alarming rate. Industries on their part are also eager to reduce the manpower and select highly skilled personnel who can perform multifarious functions single-handedly. This has blocked the entry of personnel who have learnt any one skill or opted for specialisation in a particular subject. Secondly, modern educational opportunities have helped a section of upper layer in our society to compete with the less privileged sections and grabbing the top positions in industries.
- In view of the liberalisation and globalisation initiated and implemented by the Central Government has given an impetus in foreign investments in our country. This has brought in a new culture and diluted labour policy as a backroom understanding with the investors by the Government.
- On the one hand, employers are nowadays concentrating on higher output with less manpower and on the other hand employees are unable to adjust with the new work ethics and strings attached to their job, and they are feared about the loss of employment and welfare amenities which they have been enjoying since long. In fact, the pressure of unemployed people who knock the doors everyday is seen as a major factor for the managements in industries to opt for cheap labour which is available easily from outside sources prompt them to adopt harsher measures on the employees working in industrial organisations with a view to extract more output from them. Such tendency in industrial circle started creating friction in industries.
- Considering the influx of cheap foreign goods and cut throat competition between various industrial units manufacturing similar products forced the managements to change their policy towards the workers in order to survive in the competitive world of today. But, nobody is having time to ponder over the attitudinal changes of the employees, especially of middle and lower levels to find remedial measures in the existing work structure. If someone goes to the roots for the search of its cause, it can be found that the distasteful and monotonous work has made them insensitive to the needs of the organisation.
- On an experimental basis, at least there can have a rapport between the shop floor employees and supervisory cadre so as to measure the growing aspirations and frustrations in their work sphere and report the same to the higher management for corrective measures.

- The other important factor is the suppressed aspiration of an employee to climb the ladder of success, which reflects in the form of dissatisfaction in the work allotted to him and expressing his anger and frustration to his immediate boss and co-workers. In order to make attitudinal changes in the employees, there should have a mechanism to understand the rising aspirations of the employees and their attraction towards higher grades and the status of the post in the hierarchy of an organisation. However, the higher echelons of the organisation naturally fail to judge the mood and reluctant to adopt a pragmatic approach by way of better training and human resources development for utilising their skills and knowledge for its prosperity.
- The modern management concept calls for maintaining mutual understanding between the management and employees based on a pre-fixed target of production and marketing so as to share the profits in a congenial atmosphere. Though the idealism is good, its implementation sometime backfires whenever the expected output is not given by the employees due to the unforeseen factors or stagnant market thereby resulting misunderstanding on either part due to the failure of commitment.
- In the beginning of 21st century, the global recession started raising its ugly heads resulting in large scale retrenchments and golden shake hands in many large and medium scale industrial units. The investors became wary about the future due to the incapacity of the buyers on par with the quantum of production and the tendency on the part of the customers to compare the value of similar products available in the market. All these cumulative factors forced the managements in private sector either to close down their enterprises or invest the capital in profit oriented products to survive under the cut throat competition. The half hearted attitude of the industrialists to revive the existing sick units and the failure to investigate the drawbacks in attaining profits after sales demoralised the workforce to a great extent.
- Many of the small scale units which supplied spares and other auxiliaries to medium and large scale units were forced to close down due to the insufficient orders for their products thereby throwing the workers to the streets, where they are now struggling to earn their livelihoods by doing one or other menial jobs.
- There were tremendous pressures from the trade unions against retrenchment of workers and modernisation. This was because of the fear that in our Indian social condition, modernisation in comparison with the developed western countries may mar the prospects of employment opportunities. To some extent, this view of the trade unions is also agreed by the Government and thus there was a reluctant or forced adoption of modern technology in certain sectors.
- At this stage, the bargaining capacity or muscle power of the unions was eroded in view of the insensitiveness to their demands by the managements in private sector. The gradual closure of many giant industries resulted in loss of production and severe unemployment. But, there was justification for such actions on the part of their managements though trade unions blamed mismanagement and misappropriation of working capital. Moreover, the mushroom growth of professional trade unions and self-styled leaders hampered the interest of the workmen at the final stage of bargaining.
- There are allegations that illiteracy and unawareness of the majority of employees have been exploited by some employers, but in some cases, there were high handedness on the part of employees as they demanded excessive benefits/wages without considering its impact on the organisation. Such developments and distrust between the employers and employees ultimately led to the sickness of industries because the managements failed to convince the workmen about the actual strength on which it stands.
- The other factors were the lack of planning in selection of products, method of manufacturing, marketing strategy, appointment of trained personnel and professionalism in management.
- The erosion of the bargaining strength of trade unions resulted in the loss of faith on the leaders. The employees thought that it is because of the collusion between the management and

leaders; they are deprived of their legitimate demands. Moreover, the litigation in industrial courts for fairness and justice does not provide speedy consolation or award and sometimes, such process has taken years together for final award/settlement.

- During such legal battles, employers and employees loss their mutual relationship and hard their attitude towards each other thereby making an adverse impact on the growth and prosperity of the organisations. However, the visionaries in management, who lead certain industries always try to understand the mood of the employees and provide them with fair wages and welfare measures with a string that they must give optimum output as per the demands of the situation. It is seen as a scientific approach in human relations in industries where non-productive persons have no place to stick on for long time.
- The other attraction of such mutual understanding and relationship for the prosperity of the organisation is that each and every employee is responsible for his own work and the guidance of a humanist supervisor. He knows his sincere work leads the organisation on the forefront of others and in turn he is going to get the share of its prosperity.
- The liberalisation process initiated by the Central Government, the end of licence raj, investment of foreign capital and easy import procedures have attached our economy globally, which until recently was protected by various tariff measures and rules and regulations in a closed market condition.

EMERGING TREND IN INDUSTRIAL RELATIONS

1. **International Trends – Role of ILO & WTO in Industrial Relations.** Today most of the Industries are going global & most of the companies are MNC's, *i.e.,* Multinational Companies. Therefore the companies deal in various countries and with various different sets of people culture & beliefs.

   During the global dealing the companies come across various road blocks in trade like unions, regional barriers to trade in certain countries, different legal system & other practices which may bring the businesses to a halt & all we would find is conflicts emerging everywhere.

   There is a feeling that the people from other states ruin the opportunities of the local people. Same are the beliefs throughout the world, were outsiders treated as a problem area & considered as aliens that have arrived to ruin them.

   Therefore in above situations the WTO & ILO *i.e.* World Trade Organisation & International Labour Organisation play a very important role in maintaining the best trade practices in the world so that no countries are exploited, the ILO plays an important role in seeing that the work force in not exploited & have ease of working under different cultures & laws. Also they help in achieving uniformity in the work & trade environment in the world.

2. **Competition on the basis of cheap labour.** Globalisation and increased competition has lead to less strikes, lockouts and less man days lost due to strikes. Also now in the era of knowledge industry employees are educated and thus don't believe in violent activities. They are having responsibilities in cut throat competition and also are aware of their rights well leading to decline in strikes. Employers also avoid lockouts because decline in production for even hours results in heavy losses so forget about days or weeks.

3. **Disinvestment.** It affects IR in following ways :
   - It changes ownership, which may bring out changes not only in work organisation and employment but also in trade union (TU) dynamics.
   - It changes the work organisation by necessitating retaining and redeployment.
   - It affects the right of workers and Trade unions, including job/union security, income security, and social security.

- Trade unions, management and government are responding to these challenges through various types of new, innovative, or model arrangements to deal with different aspects of disinvestment like Making workers the owners through issue of shares or controlling interests (latter is still not in India.
- Negotiating higher compensation for voluntary separations, Safeguarding existing benefits Setting up further employment generating programs, and
- Proposals for setting up new safety nets that not only include unemployment.
- Insurance but also skills provisions for redundant workers.

4. **Deregulation**

   It is tried to ensure that public sector/ government employees receive similar protection as is provided in public/government employment. The worst affected are the pension provisions. This means, usually a reduction in pension benefits and an uncertainty concerning future provision of pension benefit due to:

   - The absence of government guarantees.
   - Falling interest rates.

   Investment of pension funds in stock markets Decentralisation of IR is seen in terms of the shift in consideration of IR issues from macro to micro and from industry to enterprise level. When the coordination is at the national or sectoral level then work in the whole industry can be paralysed because of conflict in IR. But when the dispute is at the bank level, in the absence of centralised coordination by Trade unions only work in that bank is paralyzed and the other banks function normally. This weakens the bargaining power of unions.

5. **New actors and the emerging dynamics.** Earlier IR was mainly concerned with Trade unions, management and government but now consumers and the community are also a part of it. When the right s of consumers and community are affected, the rights of workers and unions and managers/employers take a back seat. Hence there is ban on bandh and restrictions even on protests and dharnas. Increasingly trade-unions are getting isolated and see a future for them only by aligning themselves with the interests of the wider society.
6. **Pro-labour-pro-investor policies.** This leads to decline in strength and power of Trade unions if not in numbers. Unions have to make alliances with the society, consumers and community and various civil society institutions otherwise they will find themselves dwindling.
7. **Declining TU density**

   - In government and public sectors workforce is declining because of non-filling of vacancies and introduction of voluntary / early separation schemes. New employment opportunities are shrinking in these sectors.
   - In the private sectors particularly in service and software sector, the new, young, and female workers are generally less eager to join unions.
   - Workers militancy replaced by employer militancy.
   - Due to industrial conflicts
     - In 1980-81 man days lost = 402.1 million.
     - In 1990-91 man days lost = 210 million.
   - Not because of improved IR but because of the fear of job security, concern about the futility of strikes, and concern to survive their organisation for their income survival. Trade unions have become defensive evident from the fact that there is significant shift from strikes to law suits. Instead of pressing for higher wages and improved benefits, Trade unions are pressing for maintenance of existing benefits and protection and claims over non-payment of agreed wages and benefits.

8. **Collective Bargaining.** Level of collective bargaining is shrinking day by day. Some more information: In India, while labour is in the Concurrent List, state labour regulations are an important determinant of industrial performance. The Survey notes evidences that states that had enacted more pro-worker regulations, had lost out on industrial production in general. However, on the upside, the Survey said there was a secular decline in the number of strikes and lockouts during 2000-04. The total number of strikes and lockouts went down 13.6% from 552 in 2003 to 477 in 2004. The decline was sharper in the number strikes than in lockouts, it noted. While most of the strikes and lockouts were in private sector establishments, overall industrial relations had improved, especially between 2003 and 2004, when there was a decline in the number of man days lost by 6.39 million.

The Role of ILO

- A United Nations affiliate.
- Consists of government, industry, and union representatives.
- Works to promote fair labour standards in health, safety, and working conditions, and freedom of association for workers.

The ILO defines core labour standards:

- The elimination of all forms of forced or compulsory labour.
- The effective abolition of child labour.
- The elimination of discrimination in respect of employment and occupation.
- Declaration on Fundamental Principles & Rights at Work.

The Role of WTO

- A multilateral trade organisation aimed at international trade liberalisation.
- Came into being in 1995, after a 48-year development that started with trade negotiations at the Geneva Conference in 1947.
- Is a relative of the original International Trade Organisation that was proposed there.
- Successor organisation to GATT to administer international trade and investment accords. In 2002, the Doha Round ended the first stage of implementation. The aim is to further hasten implementation of liberalisation to help the impoverished and developing nations.
- The WTO seeks to establish trade policy rules that help to expand trade and improve world living standards. It does this through :
  - Administering Trade Agreements.
  - Serving as the Forum for Trade Negotiations.
  - Settling Trade Disputes.
  - Reviewing National Trade Policies.
  - Assisting Developing Nations on Trade Policy Issues.

FUTURE IN INDUSTRIAL RELATIONS: THE INDIAN SCENARIO

Today, the Indian economy has opened up to face global competition and there is already a rush of foreign capital and industry into this country. This change in the economic environment has affected the entire gamut of structures, styles, and Contents of all those who have a stake in the economic firmament of this country.

The year 1991 heralded for the entire Indian subcontinent changes that were unprecedented and unheard of in post-independent India. Too many crucial economic decisions were pushed through the government by too few and too fast — decisions that had the greatest ever impact on the social, economic, industrial, political and even on the day-to-day life of the average Indian. From a CRP – controlled, regulated, and protected – economy, India made a shift to the LPG – liberal, privatised, and global economy. This paradigm shift had its greatest impact on the Indian industry. All of a sudden, it had to face four hard realities of this shift. They were:

- First generation competition.
- Second generation systems and procedures.
- Third generation technologies and technical knowhow.
- Fourth generation mindset.

For long, the Indian industry had enjoyed the parental affection of the government under various pleas of socialism, welfare state, economic and industrial development, etc. Now it had to fight for itself for its very survival against the global giants on its own.

For long, the Indian industry had enjoyed the parental affection of the government under various pleas of socialism, welfare state, economic and industrial development, etc. Now it had to fight for itself for its very survival against the global giants on its own.

WORKERS' PARTICIPATION IN MANAGEMENT

Workers' participation in management is an essential ingredient of Industrial democracy. The concept of workers' participation in management is based on Human Relations approach to Management which brought about a new set of values to labour and management.

Traditionally the concept of Workers' Participation in Management (WPM) refers to participation of non-managerial employees in the decision-making process of the organisation. Workers' participation is also known as 'labour participation' or 'employee participation' in management. In Germany it is known as co-determination while in Yugoslavia it is known as self-management. The International Labour Organisation has been encouraging member nations to promote the scheme of Workers' Participation in Management.

Workers' participation in management implies mental and emotional involvement of workers in the management of Enterprise. It is considered as a mechanism where workers have a say in the decision-making.

DEFINITIONS

The term 'industrial relations' has been variously defined :

- According to Walpole, Participation in Management gives the worker a sense of importance, pride and accomplishment; it gives him the freedom of opportunity for self-expression; a feeling of belongingness with the place of work and a sense of workmanship and creativity.
- According to Keith Davis, Participation refers to the mental and emotional involvement of a person in a group situation which encourages him to contribute to group goals and share the responsibility of achievement.

The concept of workers' participation in management encompasses the following:

- It provides scope for employees in decision-making of the organisation.
- The participation may be at the shop level, departmental level or at the top level.
- The participation includes the willingness to share the responsibility of the organisation by the workers.

Features of WPM

1. Participation means mental and emotional involvement rather than mere physical presence.
2. Workers participate in management not as individuals but collectively as a group through their representatives.

3. Workers' participation in management may be formal or informal. In both the cases it is a system of communication and consultation whereby employees express their opinions and contribute to managerial decisions.

There can be five Levels of Management Participation or WPM

(a) **Information participation.** It ensures that employees are able to receive information and express their views pertaining to the matter of general economic importance.

(b) **Consultative importance.** Here workers are consulted on the matters of employee welfare such as work, safety and health. However, final decision always rests with the top-level management, as employees' views are only advisory in nature.

(c) **Associative participation.** It is an extension of consultative participation as management here is under the moral obligation to accept and implement the unanimous decisions of the employees. Under this method the managers and workers jointly take decisions.

OBJECTIVES OF WPM
1. To establish Industrial Democracy. 2. To build the most dynamic Human Resources. 3. To satisfy the workers' social and esteem needs. 4. To strengthen labour-management co-operation and thus maintain Industrial peace and harmony. 5. To promote increased productivity for the advantage of the organisation, workers and the society at large. 6. Its psychological objective is to secure full recognition of the workers.

(d) **Administrative participation.** It ensures greater share of workers' participation in discharge of managerial functions. Here, decisions already taken by the management come to employees, preferably with alternatives for administration and employees have to select the best from those for implementation.

(e) **Decisive participation.** Highest level of participation where decisions are jointly taken on the matters relating to production, welfare etc.

Strategies/Methods/Schemes/Forms of WPM

1. **Suggestion schemes.** Participation of workers can take place through suggestion scheme. Under this method workers are invited and encouraged to offer suggestions for improving the working of the enterprise. A suggestion box is installed and any worker can write his suggestions and drop them in the box. Periodically all the suggestions are scrutinised by the suggestion committee or suggestion screening committee. The committee is constituted by equal representation from the management and the workers. The committee screens various suggestions received from the workers. Good suggestions are accepted for implementation and suitable awards are given to the concerned workers. Suggestion schemes encourage workers interest in the functioning of an enterprise.
2. **Works committee.** Under the Industrial Disputes Act, 1947, every establishment employing 100 or more workers is required to constitute a works committee. Such a committee consists of equal number of representatives from the employer and the employees. The main purpose of this committee is to provide measures for securing and preserving amity and good relations between the employer and the employees.

   Functions. Works committee deals with matters of day-to-day functioning at the shop floor level. Works committees are concerned with:
   - Conditions of work such as ventilation, lighting and sanitation.
   - Amenities such as drinking water, canteens, dining rooms, medical and health services.

- Educational and recreational activities.
- Safety measures, accident prevention mechanisms etc.
- Works committees function actively in some organisations like Tata Steel, HLL, etc. but the progress of Works Committees in many organisations has not been very satisfactory due to the following reasons:
  - Lack of competence and interest on the part of workers' representatives.
  - Employees consider it below their dignity and status to sit alongside blue-collar workers.
  - Lack of feedback on performance of Works Committee.
  - Undue delay and problems in implementation due to advisory nature of recommendations.

3. **Joint Management Councils.** Under this system Joint Management Councils are constituted at the plant level. These councils were setup as early as 1958. These councils consist of equal number of representatives of the employers and employees, not exceeding 12 at the plant level. The plant should employ at least 500 workers. The council discusses various matters relating to the working of the industry. This council is entrusted with the responsibility of administering welfare measures, supervision of safety and health schemes, scheduling of working hours, rewards for suggestions etc.

   Wages, bonus, personal problems of the workers are outside the scope of Joint management councils. The council is to take up issues related to accident prevention, management of canteens, water, meals, revision of work rules, absenteeism, indiscipline etc. the performance of Joint Management Councils have not been satisfactory due to the following reasons:

   - Workers' representatives feel dissatisfied as the council's functions are concerned with only the welfare activities.
   - Trade unions fear that these councils will weaken their strength as workers come under the direct influence of these councils.

4. **Work directors.** Under this method, one or two representatives of workers are nominated or elected to the Board of Directors. This is the full-fledged and highest form of workers' participation in management. The basic idea behind this method is that the representation of workers at the top-level would usher Industrial Democracy, congenial employee-employer relations and safeguard the workers' interests. The Government of India introduced this scheme in several public sector enterprises such as Hindustan Antibiotics, Hindustan Organic Chemicals Ltd. etc. However the scheme of appointment of such a director from among the employees failed miserably and the scheme was subsequently dropped.
5. **Co-partnership.** Co-partnership involves employees' participation in the share capital of a company in which they are employed. By virtue of their being shareholders, they have the right to participate in the management of the company. Shares of the company can be acquired by workers making cash payment or by way of stock options scheme. The basic objective of stock options is not to pass on control in the hands of employees but providing better financial incentives for industrial productivity. But in developed countries, WPM through co-partnership is limited.
6. **Joint Councils.** The joint councils are constituted for the whole unit, in every Industrial Unit employing 500 or more workers; there should be a Joint Council for the whole unit. Only such persons who are actually engaged in the unit shall be the members of Joint Council. A joint council shall meet at least once in a quarter. The chief executive of the unit shall be the chairperson of the joint council. The vice-chairman of the joint council will be nominated by the worker members of the council. The decisions of the Joint Council shall be based on the consensus and not on the basis of voting. In 1977 the above scheme was extended to the PSUs like commercial

and service sector organisations employing 100 or more persons. The organisations include hotels, hospitals, railway and road transport, post and telegraph offices, state electricity boards.

7. **Shop councils.** Government of India on the 30th of October 1975 announced a new scheme in WPM. In every Industrial establishment employing 500 or more workmen, the employer shall constitute a shop council. Shop council represents each department or a shop in a unit. Each shop council consists of an equal number of representatives from both employer and employees. The employers' representatives will be nominated by the management and must consist of persons within the establishment. The workers' representatives will be from among the workers of the department or shop concerned. The total number of employees may not exceed 12.

FUNCTION OF SHOP COUNCIL
1. Assist management in achieving monthly production targets.
2. Improve production and efficiency, including elimination of wastage of man power.
3. Study absenteeism in the shop or department and recommend steps to reduce it.
4. Suggest health, safety and welfare measures to be adopted for smooth functioning of staff.
5. Look after physical conditions of working such as lighting, ventilation, noise and dust.
6. Ensure proper flow of adequate two way communication between management and workers.

WPM in India

Workers' participation in Management in India was given importance only after Independence. Industrial Disputes Act, 1947 was the first step in this direction, which recommended for the setting up of works committees. The joint management councils were established in 1950 which increased the labour participation in management. Since July 1975 the two-tier participation called shop councils at shop level and Joint councils were introduced. Workers' participation in Management Bill, 1990 was introduced in Parliament which provided scope for upliftment of workers.

Reason for Failure of Worker Participation Movement in India

1. Employers resist the participation of workers in decision-making. This is because they feel that workers are not competent enough to take decisions.
2. Workers' representatives who participate in management have to perform the dual roles of workers' spokesman and a co-manager. Very few representatives are competent enough to assume the two incompatible roles.
3. Generally Trade Unions' leaders who represent workers are also active members of various political parties. While participating in management they tend to give priority to political interests rather than the workers' cause.
4. Schemes of workers' participation have been initiated and sponsored by the Government. However, there has been a lack of interest and initiative on the part of both the trade unions and employers.
5. In India, labour laws regulate virtually all terms and conditions of employment at the workplace. Workers do not feel the urge to participate in management, having an innate feeling that they are born to serve and not to rule.
6. The focus has always been on participation at the higher levels, lower levels have never been allowed to participate much in the decision-making in the organisations.
7. The unwillingness of the employer to share powers with the workers' representatives, the disinterest of the workers and the perfunctory attitude of the government towards participation in management act as stumbling blocks in the way of promotion of participative management.

Measure for Making Participation Effective

1. Employer should adopt a progressive outlook. They should consider the industry as a joint endeavour in which workers have an equal say. Workers should be provided and enlightened about the benefits of their participation in the management.
2. Employers and workers should agree on the objectives of the industry. They should recognise and respect the rights of each other.
3. Workers and their representatives should be provided education and training in the philosophy and process of participative management. Workers should be made aware of the benefits of participative management.
4. There should be effective communication between workers and management and effective consultation of workers by the management in decisions that have an impact on them.
5. Participation should be a continuous process. To begin with, participation should start at the operating level of management.
6. A mutual co-operation and commitment to participation must be developed by both management and labour.

Modern scholars are of the mind that the old adage "a worker is a worker, a manager is a manager; never the twain shall meet" should be replaced by "managers and workers are partners in the progress of business"

COLLECTIVE BARGAINING

Good relations between the employer and employees are essential for the success of industry. In order to maintain good relations, it is necessary that industrial disputes are settled quickly and amicably. One of the efficient methods of resolving industrial disputes and deciding the employment conditions is *Collective Bargaining*. Industrial disputes essentially refer to differences or conflicts between employers and employees.

Collective Bargaining is a process in which the management and employee representatives meet and negotiate the terms and conditions of employment for mutual benefit. Collective bargaining involves discussion and negotiation between two groups as to the terms and conditions of employment. It is termed Collective because both the employer's negotiators and the employees act as a group rather than individuals. It is known as Bargaining because the method of reaching an agreement involves proposals and counter-proposals, offers and counter offers. There should be no outsiders involved in the process of collective bargaining.

According to Walton and McKersie the process of Collective Bargaining consists of four types of activities:

1. **Distributive Bargaining.** It involves haggling over the distribution of surplus. Various activities involved in this activity are wages, salaries, bonus and other financial issues. In this activity, both the parties face a win/lose situation.
2. **Integrative Bargaining.** Also known as Interest-Based Bargaining, issues which are not damaging to either party are discussed. It is a negotiation strategy in which both the parties collaborate to find a win-win solution to their problems. This strategy focuses on developing mutually beneficial agreements based on the interests of the disputants. Issues brought up may be better job evaluation procedures, better performance appraisal methods or training programmes etc.
3. **Attitudinal structuring.** Attitudinal structuring refers to efforts by negotiators to shape their opponents' perceptions about the nature of the issues to be negotiated. By cultivating an atmosphere of friendliness, mutual respect, trust, and cooperation, negotiators can encourage

their opponents to view issues largely in integrative terms and participate in joint problem solving. This activity involves shaping and reshaping some perceptions like trust/distrust, friendliness/hostility, co-operative/non-cooperative between the labour and management. When there is a backlog of bitterness between both the parties, attitudinal structuring is required to maintain smooth and harmonious industrial relations.

4. **Intra-Organisational Bargaining.** It is a type of manoeuvreing to achieve consensus among the workers and management. Even within the union there may be differences between different groups as may be the case with the management. Intra-organisational consensus is required for the smooth acceptance of the outcome of Collective Bargaining.

OBJECTIVES OF COLLECTIVE BARGAINING

1. To maintain cordial relations between the employer and employees.
2. To protect the interests of the workers through collective action and by preventing unilateral actions from being taken by the employer.
3. To ensure the participation of trade unions in industry.
4. To avoid the need for government intervention as collective bargaining is a voluntary collective process.
5. To promote Industrial democracy.

CHARACTERISTICS OF COLLECTIVE BARGAINING

1. It is a group or collective action as opposed to individual action. It is initiated through the representatives of the employees.
2. It is a flexible and dynamic process where no party adopts a rigid attitude.
3. It is a continuous process, which provides a mechanism for continuous negotiations and discussions between management and the trade unions.
4. It is a voluntary process without any third-party intervention. Both workers and management voluntarily participate in the negotiations, discuss and arrive at a solution. That is why it is known as a bipartite process where workers' representatives and management get an opportunity for clear, face-to-face communication.
5. It ensures industrial democracy at the workplace; it is a self-run government in action.
6. It is a two-way process. It is a mutual give and take rather than a ***take home all*** method of arriving at a solution to a dispute.

Process of Collective Bargaining

1. **Preparation for Negotiation.** Preparation for negotiation in Collective Bargaining is as important as the negotiation process itself. Upto 83% of the outcomes are influenced by pre-negotiation process. Such preparation is required for both management as well as the union representatives. From the management's point of view, pre-negotiation preparation is required as:
   - Management should decide when and how to open the negotiations/dialogue.
   - Management must choose the representatives to negotiate at the negotiation table.
   - Draft for likely decisions should be prepared in advance so that the final agreement draft can be prepared as soon as the negotiation process is over.
   - From the employees' side also, preparation is required for the following reasons:
     (i) The union should collect the information related to the financial position of the company and their ability to pay the employees.
     (ii) The union must also be aware of the various practices followed by other companies in the same region or industry.

(iii) The union must assess the attitudes and expectations of the employees over concerned issues so that the outcome of negotiations does not face any resistance from them.

2. **Identifying issues for Bargaining.** The second step in bargaining process is the determination of issues which will be taken up for negotiations. The different types of issues are:
   - Wage-related issues: Include wage or salary revision, allowance for meeting increased cost of living like Dearness Allowance (D.A.), financial perks, incentives etc.
   - Supplementary economic benefits: These include pension plans, gratuity plans, accident compensation, health insurance plans, paid holidays etc.
   - Administrative issues: Include seniority, grievance procedures, employee health and safety measures, job security and job changes.

   The wage and benefits issues are the ones which receive the greatest amount of attention on the bargaining table.
3. **Negotiation.** When the first two steps are completed, both parties engage in actual negotiation process at a time and place fixed for the purpose. There are two types of negotiations:
   - ***Boulwarism.*** In this method, the management themselves takes the initiative to find out through comprehensive research and surveys the needs of the employees. Based on the analysis of the findings, the company designs its own package based on the issues to be bargained. Thereafter, a change is incorporated only when new facts are presented by the employees or their unions.
   - ***Continuous Bargaining.*** Involves parties to explore particular bargaining problems in joint meetings over a long period of time, some throughout the life of each agreement. The basic logic behind this method is that all persistent issues can be addressed through continuous negotiation over a period of time. The success of negotiations depends on the skills and abilities of the negotiators.
4. **Initial negotiated agreement.** When two parties arrive at a mutually acceptable agreement either in the initial stage or through overcoming negotiation breakdown, the agreement is recorded with a provision that the agreement will be formalised after the ratification by the respective organisations.
5. **Ratification of agreement.** Ratification of negotiated agreement is required because the representatives of both the parties may not have ultimate authority to decide various issues referred to for collective bargaining. The ratification of agreement may be done by the appropriate manager authorised for the purpose in the case of management, or trade executives in the case of the employees. Ratification is also required by the Industrial Disputes Act. It is important that the agreement must be clear and precise. Any ambiguity leads to future complications or other such problems.
6. **Implementation of agreement.** Signing the agreement is not the end of collective bargaining, rather it is the beginning of the process when the agreement is finalised, it becomes operational from the date indicated in the agreement. The agreement must be implemented according to the letter and spirit of the provisions made by the agreement agreed to by both parties. The HR manager plays a crucial role in the day-to-day administration implementation of the agreement.

GRIEVANCE HANDLING AND DISCIPLINARY ACTION

Grievances in Industry

Grievance means any type of dissatisfaction or discontentment's arising out of factors related to an employee's job which he thinks are unfair. A grievance arises when an employee feels that something has happened or is happening to him which he thinks is unfair, unjust or inequitable. In an organisation, a grievance may arise due to several factors such as:

1. Violation of management's responsibility such as poor working conditions
2. Violation of company's rules and regulations
3. Violation of labour laws
4. Violation of natural rules of justice such as unfair treatment in promotion, etc.

Various sources of grievance may be categorised under three heads: (i) management policies, (ii) working conditions, and (iii) personal factors

1. Grievance resulting from management policies include:
   - Wage rates
   - Leave policy
   - Overtime
   - Lack of career planning
   - Role conflicts
   - Lack of regard for collective agreement
   - Disparity between skill of worker and job responsibility
2. Grievance resulting from working conditions includes:
   - Poor safety and bad physical conditions
   - Unavailability of tools and proper machinery
   - Negative approach to discipline
   - Unrealistic targets
3. Grievance resulting from inter-personal factors includes
   - Poor relationships with team members
   - Autocratic leadership style of superiors
   - Poor relations with seniors

Grievances Procedure

Grievance procedure is a Step by step process an employee must follow to get his or her complaint addressed satisfactorily. In this process, the formal (written) complaint moves from one level of authority (of the firm and the union) to the next higher level.

Grievance procedure is a formal communication between an employee and the management designed for the settlement of a grievance. The grievance procedures differ from organisation to organisation.

- **Open door policy.** Under this policy, the aggrieved employee is free to meet the top executives of the organisation and get his grievances redressed. Such a policy works well only in small organisations. However, in bigger organisations, top management executives are usually busy with other concerned matters of the company. Moreover, it is believed that open door policy is suitable for executives; operational employees may feel shy to go to top management.
- **Step ladder policy.** Under this policy, the aggrieved employee has to follow a step by step procedure for getting his grievance redressed. In this procedure, whenever an employee is confronted with a grievance, he presents his problem to his immediate supervisor. If the employee is not satisfied with superior's decision, then he discusses his grievance with the departmental head. The departmental head discusses the problem with joint grievance committees to find a solution. However, if the committee also fails to redress the grievance,

then it may be referred to chief executive. If the chief executive also fails to redress the grievance, then such a grievance is referred to voluntary arbitration where the award of arbitrator is binding on both the parties.

Model Grievance Procedure

The 15th session of Indian Labor Conference held in 1957 emphasised the need of an established grievance procedure for the country which would be acceptable to unions as well as to management. In the 16th session of Indian Labor Conference, a model for grievance procedure was drawn up. This model helps in creation of grievance machinery. According to it, workers' representatives are to be elected for a department or their union is to nominate them. Management has to specify the persons in each department who are to be approached first and the departmental heads who are supposed to be approached in the second step. The Model Grievance Procedure specifies the details of all the steps that are to be followed while redressing grievances. These steps are:

STEP 1. In the first step the grievance is to be submitted to departmental representative, who is a representative of management. He has to give his answer within 48 hours.

STEP 2. If the departmental representative fails to provide a solution, the aggrieved employee can take his grievance to head of the department, who has to give his decision within 3 days.

STEP 3. If the aggrieved employee is not satisfied with the decision of departmental head, he can take the grievance to Grievance Committee. The Grievance Committee makes its recommendations to the manager within 7 days in the form of a report. The final decision of the management on the report of Grievance Committee must be communicated to the aggrieved employee within three days of the receipt of report. An appeal for revision of final decision can be made by the worker if he is not satisfied with it. The management must communicate its decision to the worker within 7 days.

STEP 4. If the grievance still remains unsettled, the case may be referred to voluntary arbitration.

Employee Grievances – Effective Ways of Handling Grievances

The manager should immediately identify all grievances and must take appropriate steps to eliminate the causes of such grievances so that the employees remain loyal and committed to their work. Effective grievance management is an essential part of personnel management. The managers should adopt the following approach to **manage grievance effectively** :

1. **Quick action.** As soon as the grievance arises, it should be identified and resolved. Training must be given to the managers to effectively and timely manage a grievance. This will lower the detrimental effects of grievance on the employees and their performance.
2. **Acknowledging grievance.** The manager must acknowledge the grievance put forward by the employee as manifestation of true and real feelings of the employees. Acknowledgment by the manager implies that the manager is eager to look into the complaint impartially and without any bias. This will create a conducive work environment with instances of grievance reduced.
3. **Gathering facts.** The managers should gather appropriate and sufficient facts explaining the grievance's nature. A record of such facts must be maintained so that these can be used in later stage of grievance redressed.
4. **Examining the causes of grievance.** The actual cause of grievance should be identified. Accordingly remedial actions should be taken to prevent repetition of the grievance.
5. **Decisioning.** After identifying the causes of grievance, alternative course of actions should be thought of to manage the grievance. The effect of each course of action on the existing and

future management policies and procedure should be analyzed and accordingly decision should be taken by the manager.

6. **Execution and review.** The manager should execute the decision quickly, ignoring the fact, that it may or may not hurt the employees concerned. After implementing the decision, a follow-up must be there to ensure that the grievance has been resolved completely and adequately. An effective grievance procedure ensures an amiable work environment because it redresses the grievance to mutual satisfaction of both the employees and the managers. It also helps the management to frame policies and procedures acceptable to the employees. It becomes an effective medium for the employees to express the feelings, discontent and dissatisfaction openly and formally.

EMPLOYEE DISCIPLINE

Discipline is the regulation and modulation of human activities to produce a controlled performance. The real purpose of discipline is quite simple. It is to encourage employees to confirm to established standards of job performance and to behave sensibly and safely at work. Discipline is essential to all organised group action.

Discipline is employee learning that promotes self-control, dedication, and orderly conduct. In relation to employees in the U.S., discipline is generally used in a restricted sense to mean punishment. Consequently, the written procedures used to punish employees for job deficiencies are called disciplinary procedures. Punishment is the process of either administering an unpleasant stimulus, such as a warning letter or a suspension, or withholding a reward, such as not granting a scheduled pay increase because of an employee's job deficiencies. Punishment is only one form of discipline; other forms are positive reinforcement, including commendations and praise, and human resources development.

TOO HIGH - People are insulted. Productivity drops.

TOO LOW - People take liberties. Productivity drops.

Definitions of Discipline

According to the business directory, employee discipline is defined as the regulations or conditions that are imposed on employees by management in order to either correct or prevent behaviours that are detrimental to an organisation. The purpose of employee *discipline* is not to embarrass or degrade an employee.

According to Richard D. Calhoen, "Discipline may be considered as a force that prompts individuals or groups to observe the rules, regulations and procedures which are deemed to be necessary for the effective functioning of an organisation."

According to William R. Spreigel and Edward Schultz, "The force that prompts an individual or a group to observe the rules, regulations and procedures which are deemed to be necessary to the attainment of an objective, it is force or fear of force which restrains an individual or a group from doing things which are deemed to be, destructive of group objectives. If is also the exercise of restraint or the enforcement of penalties for the violation of group regulations."

According to **Ordway Tead**, "Discipline is the order, members of an organisation who adhere to they desire to cooperate harmoniously in forwarding the end which the group has in view."

- Discipline should be viewed as a condition within an organisation whereby Employees know what is expected of them in terms of the organisation's rules, Standards and policies and what the consequences are of infractions. *—Rue & Byars, 1996*

- Discipline is a procedure that corrects or punishes a subordinate because a rule of procedure has been violated.

—*Dessler, 2001*

From the above definitions, you can find the following elements:

- The objective is orderly behaviour.
- Orderly behaviour is a group desire.
- Orderly behaviour assists the attainment of organisational goals
- When members behave appropriately as per rules, there is no need for disciplinary action. This is self discipline.
- When some members violate the rules and regulations, punitive actions are needed to correct them.
- Punishment serves two purposes: first, to directly punish an individual for an offence and secondly, to set an example for others not to violate the rules and regulations.

Those employees who observe the rules and standards are rewarded by praise, by security and often by advancement. Those who cannot stay in line or measure up to performance standards are penalised in such a way that they can clearly learn what acceptable performance and behaviour are. Most employees recognise this system as a legitimate way to preserve order and safety and to keep everyone working towards the same organisational goals and standards. For most employees, self discipline is the best discipline. As often as not, the need to impose penalties is a fault of the management as well as of the individual worker. For that reason alone, a supervisor should resort to disciplinary action only after all else fails. Discipline should never be used as a show of authority or power on the supervisor's part.

Nature of Discipline

Maintenance of discipline is a prerequisite to the attainment of maximum productivity, not only of the firm but also for the entire nation. It is only because of this that.

After all everything is a matter of realisation! No amount of pressure can succeed in the long run unless one is committed to improve or learn.

True discipline is educational because it changes the very attitude of the workers towards their work and workplace. It must, therefore, be understood that discipline must be developed from within.

Another important point that you should note here is that discipline has to be reformative and not punitive. We should aim at development rather than punishing. I am sure that you will adhere to something that is explained to you in a calm and matured way rather than that is ordered!

According to **Megginson,** discipline involves the following three things.

1. Self-discipline. 2. Orderly behaviour. 3. Punishment

Discipline can Either be Positive or Negative

1. Positive Discipline

Positive discipline involves creation of an atmosphere in the organisation whereby employees willingly conform to the established rules and regulations. Positive discipline can be achieved through rewards and effective leadership.

According to **Spiegel,** *"Positive discipline does not replace reason but applies reason to the achievement of a common objective. Positive Discipline does not restrict the individual freedom but enables him to have a greater degree of self-expression in striving to achieve the group objective, which he identifies as his own."*

It means that positive Discipline is not that ideal that it can't be achieved. It also does not imply that an individual's freedom is restricted. Rather it provides better chances to an individual for expressing himself. The individual in this process, is able to bridge the gap between his and the group goals.

It is also to be noted that positive discipline promotes cooperating and coordination with a minimum of formal organisation. It reduces the need for strict supervision required to maintain standards and observe rules and regulations. Everyone is answerable to oneself and therefore one is not answerable to anyone else.

2. Negative Discipline

Under negative discipline, penalties are used to force the workers to obey rules and regulations. In other words, workers try to adhere to rules and regulations out of fear of warnings, penalties and other forms of punishment. This approach to discipline is called negative or punitive approach.

This is an unfavourable state that subjects the employees to frustration, and consequently results in low morale. Let me ask you a question, how will you react if you are punished for a wrong act of yours? Will you welcome it? I am sure it would be much better that an environment is created where one does not commit any wrongful act. If at all there is some indiscipline, it has to be handled in a calm and matured way.

There is another drawback related to negative discipline. An employee goes astray in his behaviour whenever there is a slightest possibility of escaping the punishment or when he believes that his action will go unnoticed.

Progressive and development oriented managers adopt a positive approach to discipline rather than negative approach. In the positive approach, attempts are made to educate the workers the values of discipline. The workers should be taught self-discipline. Disciplinary action should be taken only in exceptional circumstances where no other alternative is left. Disciplinary action should always incorporate consideration of just cause and due process.

Some of the symptoms of general indiscipline can be:

- Absence from work
- Absenteeism
- Abusing customers
- Abusive language toward supervisor
- Assault and fighting among employees
- Causing unsafe working conditions
- Damage to or loss of machinery or materials Dishonesty
- Disloyalty to employer (includes competing with employer, conflict of interest)
- Falsifying company records (including time records, production records)
- Falsifying employment application
- Gambling
- Horseplay
- Incompetence (including low productivity)
- Insubordination
- Leaving place of work (including quitting early)
- Loafing
- Misconduct during a strike
- Negligence
- Obscene or immoral conduct
- Participation in a prohibited strike

- Possession or use of drugs or intoxicants
- Profane or abusive language (not toward supervisor)
- Refusal to accept a job assignment
- Refusal to work overtime
- Sleeping on the job
- Slowdown
- Tardiness
- Theft Threat to or assault of management representative

Factors Necessary for Effective Disciplinary System

Discipline is the key to success. Theodore Roosevelt has said "With self-discipline almost everything is possible". Self discipline makes employee realise what is required at work. Discipline can be positively related to performance. It is the bridge between goals and accomplishments. Effective discipline should be aimed at the behavior, and not at the employee personality. This is because the reason for discipline is to improve performance rather than punishing the employee.

Factors necessary for effective disciplinary system include:

1. **Training of supervisors is necessary.** Supervisors and managers need to be trained on when and how discipline should be used. It is necessary to provide training on counselling skills as these skills are used while dealing with problem employees. Moreover, discipline decisions taken by trained supervisors are considered fair by both employees and managers.
2. **Centralisation of discipline.** Centralised means that the discipline decisions should be uniform throughout the organisation. The greater the uniformity, higher will be the effectiveness of discipline procedure.
3. **Impersonal discipline.** Discipline should be handled impersonally. Managers should try to minimise the ill feelings arising out of the decisions by judging the offensive behavior and not by judging the person. Managers should limit their emotional involvement in the disciplinary sessions.
4. **Notification of conduct that may result in discipline.** Actions that lead to misconduct can be listed and documented so the employees are aware of such actions. This will unable them to claim that they have not been notified, in advance, regarding the same.
5. **Information regarding penalties.** The employer should define the penalties and other actions like warnings, reprimands, discharge and dismissal well in advance. All these action plans must be communicated to the employees.
6. **Discipline shall be progressive.** Discipline system should be progressive in nature. In a progressive discipline approach the severity of actions to modify behavior increases with every step as the employee continues to show improper behavior. The advantage of this approach is that employees can't take it for granted.
7. **Documentation.** Effective discipline requires accurate, written record keeping and written notification to the employees. Thus less chance will be left for the employee to say the he "did not know" about the policy.
8. **Discipline should be fair.** The disciplinary decision should be fair enough for the employee. Both over-penalisation and under-penalisation are considered to be unfair for the problem employee. Moreover, an internal fairness is to be maintained, that is, two employees who have committed the same offense should be equally punished.

9. **Discipline shall be flexible and consistent.** The manager administering discipline must consider the effect of actions taken by other managers and of other actions taken in the past. Consistent discipline helps to set limits and informs people about what they can and cannot do. Inconsistent discipline leads to confusion and uncertainty.
10. **Disciplinary action should be prompt.** The effective discipline should be immediate. The longer time lag between the misconduct offense and the disciplinary action will result in ineffectiveness of the discipline.

Features of an Effective Disciplinary Process

A disciplinary procedure is directed against the worker's behavior rather than the person. Key features of an effective process include the following principles of disciplining workers.

- The length of time between the misconduct and the discipline should be short. For discipline to be most effective, it must be administered as soon as possible, but without making an emotional, irrational decision.
- Disciplinary action should be preceded by advance warning. Noting rule infractions in an employee's record is not sufficient to support disciplinary action. An employee who is not advised of an infraction is not considered to have been given a warning. Noting that the employee was advised of the infraction and having the employee sign a discipline form are both valid employment practices. Failure to warn an employee of the consequences of repeated violations of a rule is a frequently cited reason for overturning a disciplinary action.
- Consistency in the discipline procedure is key. Inconsistency lowers morale, diminishes respect for the supervisor, and leads to grievances. Consistency does not mean that an absence of past infractions, long length of service, a good work record, and other mitigating factors should not be considered when applying discipline. However, an employee should feel that under essentially the same circumstances any other employee would have received the same punishment/penalty.
- Ordinarily, the supervisor should administer discipline in private. Only in the case of gross insubordination or flagrant and serious rule violations is a public reprimand desirable. Then a public reprimand helps the supervisor regain control of a situation. Even in such situations, however, the supervisor's objective should be to regain control, not to embarrass the employee.
- The supervisor should warn the employee of the result of repeated violations. Sometimes suggestions to the employee on ways to correct behaviour are beneficial. Supervisors should be very reluctant to impose disciplinary suspensions and to discharge workers. Usually, discipline of this degree is reserved for higher levels of management. However, even though supervisors usually lack the power to administer disciplinary suspensions or to discharge workers, they are nearly always the ones who must recommend such action to higher management.
- Finally, it is necessary to document the action taken and inform others in the organisation. Any time an organisation takes disciplinary action, it must consider the possibility of an Equal Employment Opportunity complaint. The documentation should be sufficiently detailed that another manager at a similar level in the organisation would come to the same conclusions or least see clearly why the decision was made. Sufficient documentation does not mean that every detail of an individual's work needs to be recorded. Rather, the manager should keep accurate records of those elements that significantly contribute to or hamper the work effort. In addition, this information, both positive and negative, should be communicated to the employee either orally or in writing.

Code of Discipline

To maintain harmonious relations and promote industrial peace, a Code of Discipline has been laid down which applies to both public and private sector enterprises. It specifies various obligations for the management and the workers with the objective of promoting cooperation between their representatives.

The basic objectives of Code of Discipline are to:

- Maintain peace and order in industry.
- Promote constructive criticism at all levels of management and employment.
- Avoid work stoppage in industry.
- Secure the settlement of disputes and grievances by a mutually agreed procedure.
- Avoiding litigation.
- Facilitate a free growth of trade unions.
- Eliminate all forms of coercion, intimidation and violations of rules and regulations governing industrial relations.

The Code is based on the following principles:

- There should be no strike or lockout without prior notice.
- No unilateral action should be taken in connection with any industrial matter.
- Employees should not follow go slow tactic.
- The existing machinery for the settlement of disputes should be utilised.
- Actions that disturb cordial relationships should be avoided.

To ensure better discipline in industry, management and unions agree on not indulging into various actions. These actions can be summarised as follows:

Management and Union(s) agree

- That no unilateral action should be taken in connection with any industrial matter and that should be settled at appropriate level.
- That the existing machinery for settlement of disputes should be utilised with the utmost efficiency.
- That there should be no strike or lock-out without prior notice.
- That neither party will have recourse to coercion, intimidation, victimisation or go –slow tactics.
- That they will avoid litigation, sit-down and stay-in strikes and lock-outs.
- That they will promote constructive co-operation between their representatives at all levels and as between workers themselves.
- That they will establish upon a mutually agreed grievance procedure which will ensure a speedy and full investigation leading to settlement.
- That they will abide by various stages in the grievance procedure and take no arbitrary action which would by-pass this procedure.

Management Agrees

- Not to increase work-loads unless agreed upon or settled otherwise.
- Not to support or encourage any unfair labor practice such as discrimination and victimisation of any employee.
- To take prompt action for settlement of grievances and implementation of settlements, awards, decision and orders.

- To take appropriate disciplinary action against its officers and members in cases where enquiries reveal that they were responsible for precipitate action by workers leading to indiscipline.

Union agrees

- Not to engage in any form of physical duress.
- Not to permit demonstrations which are not peaceful and not to permit rowdyism in demonstrations.
- That their members will not engage or cause other employees to engage in any union activity during working hours, unless as provide for by law agreement or practice.
- To discourage unfair labour practices such as:
  - Negligence of duty
  - Careless operation
  - Insubordination.
- To take prompt action to implement awards, agreements, settlements and decisions.
- To display at conspicuous places in the union offices, the provisions of this code in the local language (s).
- To express disapproval and to take appropriate action against office-bearers and members of the union for indulging in action against the spirit of this code.

The code symbolises the policy of the Government to build up an industrial democracy on voluntary basis. It tries to preserve industrial peace with the help of the employers and the employees.

The Code of Discipline is the basis of non-violent relations between the union and the management. It should be followed in letter and spirit.

Causes of Indiscipline

Various socio-economic and cultural factors play a role in creating indiscipline in an organisation. We wonder if you realise the fact that often indiscipline may arise because of poor management on your part. Insensitive and thoughtless words and deeds from a manager are potent reasons for subordinates to resort to acts of indiscipline. Defective communication by the superiors and ineffective leadership.

The reasons could range anything from poor wages to, poor management and the communication gaps between the union and management.

The common causes of indiscipline are as follows:

1. **Unfair Management Practices.** Management sometimes indulges in unfair practices like:
   - Wage discrimination
   - Non-compliance with promotional policies and transfer policies
   - Discrimination in allotment of work
   - Defective handling of grievances
   - Payment of low wages
   - Delay in payment of wages
   - Creating low quality work life etc.
2. **Absence of Effective Leadership.** Absence of effective leadership results in poor management in the areas of direction, guidance, instructions etc. This in turn, results in indiscipline. I am sure you remember the importance of leadership as studied in the last semester. If you do (which I suppose you do), you can relate the importance of effective leadership with handling indiscipline.

3. **Communication Barriers.** Communication barriers and absence of humane approach on the part of superiors result in frustration and indiscipline among the workers. The management should clearly formulate the policies regarding discipline. These policies should be communicated and the policies should be consistently followed in the organisations. The management should also be empathetic towards the employees.
4. **Varying Disciplinary Measures.** Consistent disciplinary actions must be there in the organisation to provide equal justice to all concerned. At different times and for everyone, the same standard of disciplinary measures should be taken otherwise it may give rise to growing indiscipline in the industry in future *i.e.*, the judicious function on the past of management must be free form may bias, privilege or favoritism.
5. **Defective Supervision.** Supervisor is the immediate boss of the workers and many disciplinary problems have their in faulty supervision. The attitude and behavior of the supervisor may create many problems. As the maintenance of the discipline is the discipline is the core of supervisory responsibilities, indiscipline may spring from the want of the right type of supervision.
6. **Inadequate attention to personnel Problems.** Delay in solving personnel problems develops frustration among individual workers. The management should be proactive so that there is no discontent among the workers. It should adopt a parental attitude towards its employees. However it should be noted that no relationship can continue for long if it is one sided. What I am implying here is that the workers should also live up to their commitments. They should be reasonable in their demands.
7. **Victimisation.** Victimisation of subordinate also results in indiscipline. The management should not exploit the workers. It is also in the long-term interest of the management to take care of its internal customers.
8. **Absence of Code of Conduct.** This creates confusion and also provides chance for discrimination while taking disciplinary action. We will be discussing Code of Discipline in details etc.

   A **code of conduct** is a set of rules outlining the responsibilities of or proper practices for an individual, party or organisation. Related concepts include ethical codes and honor codes.
9. **Divide and Rule Policy.** Many managers in the business obtain secret information about other employees through their trusted assistants. The spying on employees is only productive of a vicious atmosphere and of undesirable in the organisation. Henry Fayol has rightly pointed out that dividing enemy forces to weaken them is clever, but dividing one's own team is grave sin against the business. No amount of management skill is necessary for dividing personnel, but integrating personnel into a team is the challenging task of sound management.
10. **Deferring settlements of Employee Grievances.** The employee grievances cannot be put off by deferring or neglecting their solutions. The grievances should properly be inquired into and settled by the managers in a reasonable period. Neglect of grievances often results in reduced performance, low morale and indiscipline among the employees. Strikes and work stoppages stem in many cases form the utter neglect of employee grievances.
11. **Mis-judgment in Promotion and Placements.** Mis-judgment in personnel matters like promotion and placements contribute to the growth of indiscipline in an enterprise. Cases of mis-judgment are carefully noted, widely circulated, and hotly debated by the employees. Expecting discipline from misruled people is not possible. Sometimes, undesired persons are placed on the jobs which makes the employees discontented, then giving rise to the problem of indiscipline.

Disciplinary Procedure

Disciplinary procedures are a critical tool for management to succeed. Many people associate disciplinary procedures with negative feedback. If implemented properly, these procedures will positively affect the relationship between a manager and their employees. Employees embrace accountability and it actually improves employee job satisfaction. Correcting employee performance issues is a procedure. Effective interpersonal communication, written communication, and your management skills list must be utilised to assist your employees. Poorly implemented procedures may negatively impact workplace performance.

Before starting the process of discipline, it is essential to hold a preliminary inquiry to know if a prima facie case of indiscipline and misconduct exist. After this, the following steps should be followed:

1. **Issue of charge sheet.** Once the prima facie case of misconduct is established, the management should proceed to issue a charge sheet to the employee. Charge sheet is merely a notice of the charge and provides the employee an opportunity to explain his conduct. Therefore, charge sheet is generally known as a slow cause notice. In the charge sheet, each charge should be clearly specified. There should be a separate charge for each allegation and charge should not relate to any matter, which has already been decided upon. I would suggest each one of you to talk to find out how is a charge sheet prepared. We will discuss that in the next class.
2. **Consideration of Explanation.** On getting the answer for the charge sheet served, the explanation furnished should be considered and if it is satisfactory, no disciplinary action needs to be taken. On the contrary when the management is not satisfied with the employee's explanation, it can proceed with full-fledged enquiry. (However, if the worker admits the charge, the employer can warn him or award him punishment without further enquiry.)
3. **Suspension pending Enquiry.** In case the charge is grave that is serious, a suspension order may be served on the employee along with the charge sheet. According to the Industrial Employment (Standing Order) Act, 1946, the suspended worker is to be paid a subsistence allowance equal to one-half of his wages for the first ninety days of suspension and three-fourths of wages for the remaining period of suspension if the delay in the completion of disciplinary proceedings is not due to the worker's conduct.

   What is grave will depend on the discretion of the management. It has to be decided in accordance with the Code Of Discipline.
4. **Holding of Enquiry.** An enquiry officer should be appointed to hold the enquiry and a notice to this effect should be given to the concerned worker. Principle of natural justice must be followed. The worker should not be denied the chance of explaining himself. The enquiry officer should give sufficient notice to the worker so that he may prepare to represent his case and make submission in his defence. The enquiry officer should proceed in a proper manner and examine witnesses. Fair opportunity should be given to the worker to cross-examine the management witnesses.

   The principles of natural justice can be summarised as follows:

   Principle of Natural Justice

   - Tell the person what he has done
   - Hear Him
   - Give Him a Chance to defend himself

   On the conclusion of the enquiry, the enquiry officer should record his findings and the reasons thereof. He should refrain from recommending punishment and leave it to the decision of the appropriate authority. After all he is just an enquiry officer!!

5. **Order of Punishment.** Disciplinary action can be taken when the misconduct of the employee is proved. While deciding the nature of disciplinary action, the employee's previous record, precedents, effects of the action on other employees, etc., have to be considered.
   When the employee feels that the enquiry conducted was not proper and the action taken unjustified, he must be given a chance to make appeal.

Hot Stove Rule

The "Hot-Stove Rule" of Douglas McGregor gives a good illustration of how to impose disciplinary action without generating resentment. This rule draws an analogy between touching a hot stove, and undergoing discipline. When you touch a hot stove, your discipline is immediate, with warning, consistent, and impersonal.

These four characteristics, according to **McGregor,** as applied to discipline are self-serving and may be explained as follows:

1. **When you touch the hot stove,** you burn your hand. The burn was immediate. Will you blame the hot stove for burning your hand? Immediately, you understand the cause and effect of the offense. The discipline was directed against the act not against anybody else. You get angry with yourself, but you know it was your fault. You get angry with the hot stove too, but not for long as you know it was not its fault. You learn your lesson quickly.
2. **You had warning** as you knew the stove was red hot and you knew what would happen to you if you touched it. You knew the rules and regulations previously issued to you by the company prescribing the penalty for violation of any particular rule so you cannot claim you were not given a previous warning.
3. **The discipline was consistent.** Every time you touch the hot stove you get burned. Consistency in the administration of disciplinary action is essential. Excessive leniency as well as too much harshness creates not only dissatisfaction but also resentment.
4. **The discipline was impersonal.** Whoever touches the hot stove gets burned, no matter who he is. Furthermore, he gets burned not because of who he is, but because he touched the hot stove. The discipline is directed against the act, not against the person. After disciplinary action has been applied, the supervisor should take the normal attitude toward the employee.

In applying this Hot Stove rule in disciplinary action, there must be company policies, rules and regulations regarding certain behaviour and conduct which were issued and clearly explained to employees and accepted by them for compliance. Disciplinary action must be directed against the act, not against the person. It must be used by supervisors as a tool to develop the employee and the group. The steps that should be followed are:

- **Immediate investigation** of the offense must be done to determine the facts. If the company is unionised, the investigation must be conducted in the presence of the union steward or one of the representatives of the union. Promptness is necessary in order that the employee will associate the investigation with the offense rather than with his person.
- **Previous warning.** In labour relations, it is important that the company policies, rules and regulations be issued to and explained to all employees upon induction as part of the orientation program. This should be done by the supervisor with the help of the personnel department. In addition, whenever new policies, rules and regulations are promulgated, they must be posted in the company's bulletin board, circulated, and explained to the employees by the supervisor. It is a good practice to have the employees acknowledge receipt of a copy of the said rule or policy so they could not deny knowledge of the rules.
  In some companies, the rules and regulations provide "progressive discipline" whereby penalties are graduated depending upon the gravity and frequency of the violation.

- **Consistency** in the administration of disciplinary action is highly essential so that employees will know what to expect as a consequence of an infraction or violation of the rule or regulation.
- **Disciplinary action** must be impersonal. It should be directed against the act, not the person. It should be institutional, that is, for the protection and interest of the entire organisation and for all employees, and not done to satisfy the personal whim and caprice of the supervisor.

Key Principles to Remember

Hot Stove Rule where discipline is concerned:

- **You had a warning** – you knew what would happen if you touched the stove
- **The penalty was consistent** – everyone gets the same treatment
- **The penalty is impersonal** – a person is burned not because of who he or she is, but because the stove was touched
- **The penalty is not delayed.**
- **So check out the facts first,** follow due process and, if appropriate, apply the discipline as soon after the event as investigations will allow.

CODE OF CONDUCT

A code of conduct is a set of rules outlining the social norms and rules and responsibilities of, or proper practices for, an individual, party or organisation. Related concepts include ethical, honor, moral codes and religious laws.

Objectives of Code of Conduct

- To ensures that the employers and employees recognise each other's rights and obligations.
- To avoid work stoppage.
- To facilitate the free growth of trade unions.
- To maintain discipline in industry.

Principles of Code of Conduct

- Every employee in industry or unit shall have the freedom and right to join a union of his choice. No coercion shall be exercised in this matter.
- There shall be no dual membership of unions.
- There shall be regular and democratic elections of executive bodies.
- Casteism, communalism and provincialism shall be eschewed by all unions.
- There shall be no violence, cocercion, intimidation, or personal vilification in inter – union dealings.
- All Central unions shall combat the formation or continuance of company unions.

What a Code Can Help to Accomplish

- A quality code of conduct can go a long way in improving a company's success. Companies that view a code merely as a way to communicate legal rules miss much of the value that a code can provide. A well-developed code can help a company to:
  - **Prevent legal and regulatory violations.** This is the first objective that most companies attach to a code of conduct. When violations do occur, a code can help to detect them and mitigate their effects.

- **Foster greater employee loyalty and retention.** When employees feel included and engaged in the company's culture and success, they feel more committed.
- **Encourage greater customer loyalty and retention.** When customers learn about and then experience in practice a company's high standards of conduct, customers are more likely to show their appreciation.
- **Build stronger relationships with suppliers and other business partners.** As with employees, the more that they understand what the company expects of them – and what they can expect from the company – the stronger the alliance.

- Strengthen trust and respect of other stakeholders, such as local communities, regulators, NGOs, even from competitors. As codes become publicly available publications, more outside stakeholders are reviewing them and setting their expectations of the company partly based on its code. The more that a company lives up to the expectations that it has established, the greater goodwill it engenders.
- Build a stronger reputation for integrity by helping the company to do what it says it will do.

How a Code Works

- A quality code of conduct helps a company's leadership to accomplish its strident objectives because of how the code functions. As part of an overall code of conduct program, a code works because it:
  - **Articulates leadership's expectations.** Simply establishing these expectations regarding what leadership expects is worthwhile. It provides clarity and transparency so that staff does not have to guess at leadership's expectations.
  - **Establishes leadership's commitment.** Much as been addressed regarding the importance of tone at the top regarding expectations of responsible conduct, this tone rises in importance.
  - **Provides staff with a roadmap and tools for their daily work.** With clarity regarding leadership's expectations that an employee can easily and regularly reference, staff can act with consistency. Further, employees can turn to the code for guidance on questions or concerns. It is especially important to help employees to make good decisions when they face ambiguous situations or other issues that the code does not directly address.
  - **Provides staff with comfort and confidence.** As ethics consultant Frank Navran puts it, a code can provide staff with comfort that the company will support them when they act according to the code and confidence that the decisions they make when they are in line with the code.
  - **Encourages staff to serve the company's aspirations.** A good code can encourage employees to strive to achieve the company's mission, vision and values in a constructive way.

Elements of an Effective Code

A code of conduct publication does not work in a vacuum. Important factors for a successful code include:

- Foundations that support a successful code program.
- Components of a successful code program.
- Dimensions for an effective code publication.

Foundations for a Program

These foundations serve as important considerations for a successful code of conduct program. While not all of the foundations are mandatory – and in fact they will exist in each company in varying forms

– the more firmly that they are established, the more likely that the code (and the larger ethics and compliance initiative) will lead to success.

- **Leadership commitment to the program.** Without senior leadership's commitment, any code initiative is unlikely to truly engage employees and demonstrate to them the tone at the top that is so critical to any business initiative – especially one focused on doing the right thing.
- **Ethics and compliance processes.** Leadership's commitment means so much more when the organisation can point to procedures and processes that support a code standards and expectations. Otherwise, employees are right to wonder about how leadership expects to achieve adherence to the company's standards and address concerns.
- **Company culture.** A company culture focused around an enduring mission or vision and supported by lasting values sets the best foundation for a proper focus on long-term value and success. These core foundations help a code rise about a narrow focus only on the law to other commitments, promises and aspirations that the company seeks to achieve.
- **Understanding of risk.** A company's awareness of the ethics and compliance risks that it faces is central to a code of conduct. With the hundreds of issues that a code could possibly address, a more targeted risk identification and assessment effort helps to focus the code's contents to those issues that are most important to the company's operations and that will provide it with a higher chance of success.
- **Coordination with policies.** A company's policies often provide the detail underlying its expectations. Policies also can provide the initial framework for a new code of conduct and serve as additional resources to support a code's standards. Where policies exist, they provide important context for a code development or revision effort.

Four Parts

Part 1. Contains the duties and responsibilities of employers, workers, and the government in maintaining discipline in industry

Part 2. Enlists the common obligations of Management and unions

Part 3. Deals with obligations of management only

Part 4. Relates to those unions only

Part 1. To maintain Discipline in Industry (Both in public and Private sector)

- Recognition of employers and workers must be defined by laws and agreements.
- Proper and willing discharge by either party of its obligation consequent on such recognition.

Part 2. To Ensure Better discipline in Industry , Management and Union(s) Agree

- No Unilateral action should be taken
- Existing machinery for settlement of dispute.
- No strike or lockout without notice
- Must follow the democracy principles by mutual negotiation, conciliation and voluntary arbitration
- Must promote constructive cooperation
- In Grievance based speedy and full investigation must be followed.
- Educate the Management and workers regarding obligations

Part 3. Management Agrees

- Not to increase workloads

- Not to support or encourage any unfair labor practice as interference, discrimination, victimisation
- To take prompt actions as settlement of grievance Implementation of settlements, awards, decisions and orders
- To take appropriate disciplinary action against officers and members in which they are responsible for indiscipline among employees.
- Warning, reprimand, suspension will appeal through normal grievance procedure.
- Must follow the rules of Indian Labor conference held in May 1958. Part4:Union(s) Agree
- Not to encourage any form f physical duress
- Not to Permit demonstrations
- Unless law, agreement or practice the employee must not engage in any union activity during working hours
- Discourage unfair labour practices as damage to property, careless operation
- To take prompt action to implement awards , agreements and decisions.
- To display the rules in local languages at important places in union offices.
- Moral sections of code of conduct
- To ask the unit to explain the infringement of the code
- To give notice to the unit within specific period
- Not to give countenance to non members who did not observe the code
- A dispute must not be referred for strikes and lockouts.

TRADE UNIONS

Meaning of Trade Unions

A trade union is an organisation of employees formed on a continuous basis for the purpose of securing diverse range of benefits. It is a continuous association of wage earners for the purpose of maintaining and improving the conditions of their working lives. The Trade Union Act 1926 defines a trade union as a combination, whether temporary or permanent, formed primarily for the purpose of regulating the relations between workmen and employers or between workmen and workmen, or between employers and employers, or for imposing restrictive condition on the conduct of any trade or business, and includes any federation of two or more trade unions.

This definition is very exhaustive as it includes associations of both the workers and employers and the federations of their associations. Here, the relationships that have been talked about are both temporary and permanent. This means it applies to temporary workers (or contractual employees) as well. Then this definition, primarily, talks about three relationships. They are the relationships between the:

- workmen and workmen,
- workmen and employers,
- employers and employers.

Trade unions are associations of workers or organisation formed together by labour, workers or employees to achieve their demands for better conditions at their work atmosphere. In the United States, trade unions go by the name labour unions. A labour union, or trade union, is an organisation of workers who have joined together to achieve goals in areas such as wages and working conditions. The union negotiates contracts and conditions with employers, keeping employee satisfaction high and protecting workers from unsafe or unfair working conditions.

These unions exist to deal with problems faced by labourers, these problems may be of any nature such as those concerning the pay, unfair work rules, timings and so on. All the workers working under one particular employer is represented by the worker's union. All the communication that happens in between the employer and the workforce generally takes place through the union. All of the above trade unions are also liable and responsible for maintaining discipline and among the workers, core purpose is to see that proper relations or being maintained in between management and workers and trade union may take disciplinary action against the workers who ever misbehaves, disturbed peace and harmony in the workplace and maintenance indiscipline.

Definition

According to **Webb's**, a Trade Union is a continuous association of wage earners for the purpose of maintaining and improving the conditions of their working lives.

According to **De Cenzo & Robbins** (1993), A more recent and non-legislative definition of a union is "an organisation of workers acting collectively who seek to protect and promote their mutual interests through collective bargaining".

A modern definition by the Australian Bureau of Statistics states that a trade union is 'an organisation consisting predominantly of employees, the principal activities of which include the negotiation of rates of pay and conditions of employment for its members."

Recent historical research by Bob James in Craft, trade or Mystery (2001) puts forward the view that trade unions are part of a broader movement of benefit societies, which includes medieval guilts, Freemasons, Oddfellows, friently societies and other fraternal organisations.

Evolution of Trade Union Movement

Trade unions in India, as in most other countries, have been the natural outcome the modem factory system. The development of trade unionism in India has checkered history and a stormy career.

Early Period

Efforts towards organising the workers for their welfare were made, during the early period of industrial development by social workers, philanthropists and other religious leaders mostly on humanitarian grounds. The first Factories Act, 1881, was passed on the basis of the recommendations of the Bombay Factory Commission, 1875. Due to the limitations of the Act, the workers in Bombay Textile Industry under the leadership of N. M. Lokhande demanded reduced of hours of work, weekly rest days, mid-day recess and compensation for injuries. Bombay Mill owners' Association conceded the demand for weekly holiday. Consequently, Lokhande established the first Workers' Union in India in 1890 in the name of Bombay Mill hands Association. A labour journal called "Dinabandu" was also published.

Some of the important unions established during the period are: Amalgamated Society of Railway Servants of India and Burma (1897), Management the Printers Union, Calcutta (1905) and the Bombay Postal Union (1907), the Kamgar Hitavardhak Sabha (1910) and the Social Service League (1910). But these unions were treated as adhoc bodies and could not serve the purpose of the TU.

Modest Beginning. The beginning of the labour movement in the modest sense started after the outbreak of World War I in the country. Economic, social and political condition of the day influenced the growth of the trade union movement in India. Establishment of the ILO in 1919 helped the formation of trade union of the country. Madras labour union was formed on systematic lines in 1919. A number of trade union was established between 1919 and 1923.

All India Trade Union Congress. The most important year in the history of Indian Trade Union movement is 1920 when the All India Trade Union Congress (AITUC) was formed consequent upon the necessity of electing delegates for the International Labour Organisation (ILO). This is the first all India trade union in the country. The first meeting of the AITUC was held in October, 1920 at Bombay (now Mumbai) under the presidentship of Lala Lajpat Rai. The formation of AITUC led to the establishment of All India Railwaymen's Federation (AIRF) in 1922. Many Company Railway Unions were affiliated to it. Signs of militant tendency and revolutionary ideas were apparent during this period.

(a) **Period of splits and mergers.** The splinter group of AITUC formed All India Trade Union Federation (AITUF) in 1929. Another split by the communists in 1931 led to the formation of All India Red Trade Union Congress. Thus, splits were more common during the period. However, efforts were made by the Railway Federation to bring unity within the AITUC unity. These efforts did bear fruit and All India Red Trade Union Congress was dissolved. Added to this, All India Trade Union Federation also merged with AITUC. The unified AITUC's convention was held in 1940 in Nagpur. But the unity did not last long.

The World War II brought splits in the AITUC. There were two groups in the AITUC, one supporting the war while the other opposing it. The supporting group established its own central organisation called the Indian Federation of Labour. A further split took place in 1947, when the top leaders of the Indian National Congress formed another central organisation.

(b) **Indian National Trade Union Congress.** The efforts of Indian National Congress resulted in the establishment of Indian National Trade Union Congress (INTUC) by bringing the split in the AITUC; INTUC started gaining membership right from the beginning.

(c) **Other Central Unions.** Socialists separated from AITUC had formed Hind Mazdoor Sabha (HMS) in 1948. The Indian Federation of Labour merged with the HMS, Radicals formed another union under the name of United Trade Union Congress in 1949. Thus, the trade union movement in the country was split into four distinct central unions during the short span of 1946 to 1949. Some other central unions were also formed. They were Bharatiya Mazdoor Sangh (BMS) in 1955, the Hind Mazdoor Panchayat (HMP) in 1965 and the Centre of Indian Trade Unions (CITU) in 1970. Thus, splinter group of INTUC formed Union Trade Union Congress, the split in the Congress Party in 1969 resulted in the split in INTUC and let to the formation of National Labour Organisation (NLO).

Present Position

There are over 9,000 trade unions in the country, including unregistered unions and more than 70 federations and confederations registered under the Trade Unions Act, 1926. The degree of unionism is fairly high in organised industrial sector. It is negligible in the agricultural and unorganised sectors.

Though the number of unions has greatly increased in the last four decades, the union membership per union has not kept pace. The National commission on labour has stated that only 131 unions had a membership of over 5,000. More than 70% of the unions had a membership of below 500. Over the years the average membership figures per union have fallen steadily from about 1387 in 1943 to 632 in 1992-93 (Pocket Book of Labour Statistics, 1997). Unions with a membership of over 2000 constitute roughly 4 per cent of the total unions in the country. There is a high degree of unionisation (varying from 30% to over 70%) in coal, cotton, textiles, iron and steel, railways, cement, banking, insurance, ports and docks and tobacco sector. White-collar unions have also increased significantly covering officers, senior executives, managers, civil servants, self employed professions like doctors, lawyers, traders, etc. for safeguarding their interest.

There are as many as 10 central trade union organisations in the country (as against one or two in UK, Japan, USA). The criteria for recognition as Central Trade Union has been that the combined strength should be 5 lakhs numbers with a spread over to at least 4 states and 4 industries as on 31.12.89. Ten such Trade Unions are; (1) BMS (2) INTUC (3) HMS, (4) U.T.U.C - LS (5) AITUC (6) CITUC (7) NLO (8) UTUC (9) TUCC (10) NFITU. As per one survey (Economic Times, 24.9.97) the five leading Trade Unions' strength are as follows:

Trade Union Strength

- BMS - 331 Lakhs
- INTUC - 271 Lakhs
- AITUC - 18 Lakhs
- HMS - 15 Lakhs
- CITU - 3.4 Lakhs

Trade Unions in India

The Indian workforce consists of 430 million workers, growing 2% annually. The Indian labor markets consist of three sectors:

1. The rural workers, who constitute about 60 per cent of the workforce.
2. Organised sector, which employs 8 per cent of workforce, and
3. The urban informal sector (which includes the growing software industry and other services, not included in the formal sector) which constitutes the rest 32 per cent of the workforce.

Recognitions of Trade Union

The underline idea of former trade union is to negotiate and bargain with employers to improve the service and employment conditions of workers on their behalf. This collective bargaining process can be possible only when employer recognises a trade union as bargaining agent and agree to negotiate with it because it is difficult to negotiate with multiple trade unions in a single organisation.

The Trade Union Act, 1926, the only Central Law, which regulates the working of the unions does not have any provision for recognition of trade union. Some attempts were made to include compulsory recognition in the Trade Union Act in 1947, 1950, 1978 and 1988, but it could not be materialised.

There are, however, state legislations like Maharashtra Recognition of Trade Union and Prevention of Unfair Labour Practices Act 1971, Madhya Pradesh Industrial Relations Act, 1960 and other states like Gujarat, Andhra Pradesh and Orissa etc. which have gone for such legislations, of late. The usual methods used to determine union strength, which is the basis of the recognitions are following:

1. **Election by Secret Ballot.** Under which system, all eligible workers of an establishment may vote for their chosen union, elections to be conducted by a neutral agent, generally the Registrar of Unions, in a manner very similar to the conduct of general elections. Once held, the results of the elections would remain valid for a minimum period, usually two years.
2. **Check-Off method.** Under which each individual worker authorises management in writing to deduct union fees from his wages and credit it to the chosen union. This gives management concrete evidence about the respective strengths of the unions. But the system is also prone to manipulation, particularly collision between management and a favoured union. Sometimes, genuine mistakes may occur, particularly when the number of employees is large. It also depends on all unions accepting the method and cooperating in its implementation.
3. **Verification of union membership** method by the labour directorate as adopted as a resolution in the same session of the ILC and used widely in many establishments. This process is carried out by the labour directorate, which on the invitation of unions and management of an organisation or industry, collects particulars of all unions in a plant, with regard to their registration and membership. The claim lists of the unions, their fees books, membership records and account books are scrutinised for duplicate membership. Under a later amendment, unions also with lists of members in order to avoid dual membership. After cross checking of records, physical sampling of workers, particularly in cases of doubt or duplication, a final verified list is prepared for employers, unions and the government.

4. **Rule of Thumb or intelligent guessing by management or general observation** to assess union strength, either by the response at gate meetings, strikes or discussions with employees. This is not a reliable method, particularly in large establishments and can also be subject to change at short intervals.

   Of the above methods the first one is universally accepted method used all over the world but there has been no consensus amount among the trade unions on that in India.

There are three Forms of Trade Unions

Classical. A trade union's main objective is to collectively protect the interests of its members in given socio-economic-political system. Trade Unions are the expressions of the needs, aspirations and wishes of the working class.

Neo-classical. It goes beyond classical objectives and tries to improve up other wider issues like tax-reliefs, raising saving rates etc.

Revolutionary. Change in the system. Establishing the rule of working class even through violence and use of force etc.

Objectives of Trade Unions

A. **Wages and Salaries.** The subject which drew the major attention of the trade unions is wages and salaries. Of course, this item may be related to policy matters. However, differences may arise in the process of their implementation. In the case of unorganised sector the trade union plays a crucial role in bargaining the pay scales.

B. **Working Conditions.** Trade unions with a view to safeguard the health of workers demands the management to provide all the basic facilities such as, lighting and ventilation, sanitation, rest rooms, safety equipment while discharging hazardous duties, drinking, refreshment, minimum working hours, leave and rest, holidays with pay, job satisfaction, social security benefits and other welfare measures.

C. **Discipline.** Trade unions not only conduct negotiations in respect of the items with which their working conditions may be improved but also protect the workers from the clutches of management whenever workers become the victims of management's unilateral acts and disciplinary policies. This victimisation may take the form of penal transfers, suspensions, dismissals, etc. In such a situation the separated worker who is left in a helpless condition may approach the trade union. Ultimately the problem may be brought to the notice of management by the trade union and it explains about the injustice met out to an individual worker and fights the management for justice. Thus, the victimised worker may be protected by the trade union.

D. **Personnel Policies.** Trade unions may fight against improper implementation of personnel policies in respect of recruitment, selection, promotions, transfers, training, etc.

E. **Welfare.** As stated earlier, trade unions are meant for the welfare of workers. Trade union works as a guide, consulting authority and cooperates in overcoming the personnel problems of workers. It may bring to the notice of management, through collective bargaining meetings, the difficulties of workers in respect of sanitation, hospitals, quarters, schools and colleges for their children's cultural and social problems.

F. **Employee-employer relation.** Harmonious relations between the employees and employer is a sine quo non for industrial peace. A trade union always strives for achieving this objective. However, the bureaucratic attitude and unilateral thinking of management may lead to conflicts in the organisation which ultimately disrupt the relations between the workers and management. Trade union, being the representative of all the workers, may carry out continuous negotiations with the management with a view to promote industrial peace.

G. **Negotiating machinery.** Negotiations include the proposals made by one party and the counter proposals of the other party. This process continues until the parties reach an agreement. Thus, negotiations are based on 'give and take' principle. Trade union being a party for negotiations protects the interests of workers through collective bargaining. Thus, the trade union works as the negotiating machinery.

H. **Safeguarding organisational health and the interest of the industry.** Organisational health can be diagnosed by methods evolved for grievance redressal and techniques adopted to reduce the rate of absenteeism and labour turnover and to improve the employee relations. Trade unions by their effective working may achieve employee satisfaction. Thus, trade unions help in reducing the rate of absenteeism, labour turnover and developing systematic grievance settlement procedures leading to harmonious industrial relations. Trade unions can thus contribute to the improvements in level of production and productivity, discipline and improve quality of work life.

Functions of Trade Unions

Trade unions perform a number of functions in order to achieve the objectives. These functions can be broadly classified into four categories:

1. **Militant Functions.** One set of activities performed by trade unions leads to the betterment of the position of their members in relation to their employment. The aim of such activities is to ensure adequate wages secure better conditions of work and employment get better treatment from employers, etc. When the unions fail to accomplish these aims by the method of collective bargaining and negotiations, they adopt an approach and put up a fight with the management in the form of go-slow tactics, strike, boycott, gherao, etc. Hence, these functions of the trade unions are known as militant or fighting functions. Thus, the militant functions of trade unions can be summed up as:
   - To achieve higher wages and better working conditions.
   - To raise the status of workers as a part of industry.
   - To protect labours against victimisation and injustice.
2. **Fraternal Functions.** Another set of activities performed by trade unions aims at rendering help to its members in times of need, and improving their efficiency. Trade unions try to foster a spirit of cooperation and promote friendly industrial relations and diffuse education and culture among their members. They take up welfare measures for improving the morale of workers and generate self confidence among them. They also arrange for legal assistance to its members, if necessary. Besides, these, they undertake many welfare measures for their members, e.g., school for the education of children, library, reading-rooms, in-door and out-door games, and other recreational facilities. Some trade unions even undertake publication of some magazine or journal. These activities, which may be called fraternal functions, depend on the availability of funds, which the unions raise by subscription from members and donations from outsiders, and also on their competent and enlightened leadership. Thus, the fraternal functions of trade unions can be summed up as:
   - To take up welfare measures for improving the morale of workers.
   - To generate self confidence among workers.
   - To encourage sincerity and discipline among workers.
   - To provide opportunities for promotion and growth.
   - To protect women workers against discrimination.
3. **Social Functions.** Besides the main economic functions consisting basically of organising unions and improving their terms and conditions of employment to enable workers to meet their

physical needs, some unions have now started undertaking and organising welfare activities and also providing variety of services to their members and sometimes to the community of which they are a part, which may be grouped under following heads:

(i) **Welfare activities** provided to improve the quality of work life including organisation of mutual fund, cooperative credit societies for providing housing, cooperative stores, cultural programmes, banking and medical facilities and training for women in various crafts to help them to supplement their family income.

(ii) **Education.** Education of members in all aspects of their working life including improving their civic life, awareness in the environment around them, enhancement of their knowledge particularly in regard to issues that concern them, their statutory and other rights and responsibilities, workers' participation in management.

(iii) **Scheme, and procedure for redressing their grievances.** Some central union organisations are also assisting the Government in implementing the Workers' Education Scheme.

(iv) **Publication of periodicals,** newsletters or magazines for establishing communication with their members, making the latter aware of union policy and stand on certain principal issues and personnel matters concerning members, such as births, deaths, marriages, promotion and achievements.

(v) **Research.** Of late, this is gaining importance and is intended mainly to provide updated information to union negotiators at the bargaining table. Such research is to be more practical than academic, concerning problems relating to day-to-day affairs of the union and its activities and union and management relations. Some of the research activities are : (i) collection and analysis of wage data including fringe benefits, and other benefits and services through surveys of comparative practices, data on working conditions and welfare activities; (ii) preparation of background notes for court cases and also position papers for union officials; (iii) collection and analysis of macro data relating to the economy, industry sectors etc. All the above mentioned activities and services are considered normal activities of unions in the Trade Unions Act which stipulates the objectives on which general funds of the union can be spent.

4. **Political Functions.** These functions include affiliating the union with a political party, helping the political party in enrolling members, collecting donations, seeking the help of political parties during the periods of strikes and lockouts.

Theories of Trade Unionism

The Important theories of trade unionism are as follows :

1. **Karl Marx theory of Classless society.** This theory is also called anti-capitalism approach. Karl marx represented trade union as an instrument for destroying the capitalist class. The trade unionism become necessary to bring about revolunatry and fundamental changes in the social order of the workers. Marx considered trade union as an instrument to overthrow capitalism. He Believed that the capitalism develop three tendency.

   (i) The tendency of heavy conservations of wealth in the hands of few of the largest capitalists.

   (ii) The tendency towards a steady depression of wages and growing misery of the wage earners keep revolutionary order alive.

   (iii) The inevitable and frequent economic crisis under capitalism lead the working class towards destruction. In his view, it was imperative for the workers of the world to collects in an international.

2. **Webb's Theory of Industrial Democracy or Non-Revolutionary.** Webb's book 'Industrial democracy' is the Bible of trade unionism. According to Webb, trade unionism is an extension of

democracy from political sphere to industrial sphere. Webb agreed with Marx that trade unionism is a class struggle and modern capitalist state is a transitional phase which will lead to democratic socialism. He considered collective bargaining as the process which strengthens labour.

3. **Cole's Theory of Union Control of Industry.** Cole's views are given in his book "World of Labour" 1913. His views are somewhere in between Webb and Marx. He agrees that unionism is class struggle and the ultimate is the control of industry by labour and not revolution as predicted by Marx. As per cole, the ultimate objective of the trade union is to have control of the workers over the industry, although the immediate objectives may be realisations of higher wages and better condition of employment for the workers.
4. **Perlman's Theory of the "Scarcity Consciousness" of Manual Workers.** He rejected the idea of class consciousness as an explanation for the origin of the trade union movement but substituted it with what he called job consciousness.

   According to him, 'working people in reality felt an urge towards collective control of their employment opportunities, but hardly towards similar control of industry.' Perlman observed that three dominant factors emerged from the rich historical data:
   (i) The capacity or incapacity of the capitalist system to survive as a ruling group in the face of revolutionary attacks (e.g., failure in Russia).
   (ii) The source of the anti-capitalist influences being primarily from among the intellectuals in any society.
   (iii) The most vital factor in the labour situation was the trade union movement. Trade unionism, which is essentially pragmatic, struggles constantly not only against the employers for an enlarged opportunity measure in income, security and liberty in the shop and industry, but struggles also, whether consciously or unconsciously, actively or passively, against the intellectual who would frame its programmes and shape its policies.

   But Perlman also felt that a theory of the labour movement should include a theory of the psychology of the labouring man. For instance, there was a historical continuity between the guilds and trade unions, through their common fundamental psychology; the psychology of seeking a livelihood in the face of limited economic opportunity. It was when manual workers became aware of a scarcity of opportunity, that they banded together into unions for the purpose of protecting their jobs and distributing employment opportunities among themselves equitably, and to subordinate the interests of the individual to the whole labour organism. Unionism was ruled thus by this fundamental scarcity consciousness (Perlman, 1970).
5. **Hoxie's Social psychological approach.** He classified Unionism on the basis of their functions. His classification were Business Unionism for protecting the interest of various **craftsmen**, "Uplift unionism" for the purpose of contributing better life such as association of sales engineers etc. "Revolutionary Unionism" which is eager to replace existing social order, "Predatory Unionism" which rests on these support of others.

   In other words workers are not divergent in temperament and training but are similar situated at economic and social levels, they have common interpretations of their social situation to their problem of living, so that unite into a union.
6. **Tannenbaum's Theory of capitalism approach or Man Vs. Machine.** He traces the rise of union to the industrial revolution and the workers reaction to the philosophy of individualism. He believed that the fundamental cause of exploitation of workers in the use of machines. The machines threatens the security of the individual workers and they react in self defence, through the union, to attempt to control of machines.

   According to him Union is formed in reaction to alienation and loss of community in an individualistic and unfeeling society. In his words, the union returns to the workers his society, which he left behind him when he migrated from a rural background to the anonymity of an urban industrial location. The union gives the worker a fellowship and a value system that he shares with others like him. Institutionally, the trade union movement is an unconscious effort to harness the drift of our time and reorganise it around the cohesive identity that men working together always achieve Reasons for Joining Trade Union.

7. **Common's Environment Theory.** He was sceptical of generalisations and believed only that which could be proved by evidence. He agreed that collective bargaining was an instrument of class struggle, but he summarised that ultimately there will be partnership between employers and employees.
8. **Mitchell's Economic Protection Theory of Trade Unionism.** Mitchell, a labour leader, completely rejected individual bargaining. According to him unions afford economic protection to.
9. **Simons Theory of Monopolistic.** He denounced trade unionism as monopoly founded on violence. And he claimed monopoly power has no use save abuse.
10. **Sarvodaya Approach of Gandhi.** Mahatma gandhi approach to the growth of trade union was contrary to those of karl marx. Gandhiji philosophy is based upon the sarvodaya principle of truth, trusteeship and non violence. He believed trade union as economic institutions in which capital and labour are not antagonistic but are supplementary to each others. In gandhiji words, "My ideals is that capital and labour should supplement and help each other. They should be a great family living in unity and harmony. Capital not only looking material welfare of the labourers but their moral welfare also-capitalist being trustee of the welfare of the labouring classes under them.

Structure of Trade Unions

Trade union have emerged for the protection of common interest of the workers. Different types of trade union have been formed to protect and defend the workers from injustice and encroachment. A wide variety of union have emerged across the globe.

I. On the Basis of Purpose

1. **Reformist union.** These unions aim to retain present structure of the capitalist society. They want to maintain the usual employer and employee relationship by eliminating the competitive system of production. They seek to dignify labour by availing the right of importance and recognition by the society. They never wish to destroy the existing social, economic or political structure of the state.

   Types of Reformist Unions. R.F. Hoxie has divided reformist union into two categories

   (a) **Business Unionism.** Smooth and cordial business relationship are enjoyed between the employer and the employee under business unionism. All their problem conflict are solved by collective bargaining and peaceful means of demonstration.

   (b) **Uplift Unionism.** Also known as friendly or ideal unionism aims to enhance the social and intellectual and moral values of the workers, such unionism put more emphasis on insurance benefit, health, education and welfare measures, it advocates cooperative enterprise, profit sharing and other idealistic norms.

2. **Revolutionary Union.** Revolutionary unionism generally seeks to achieve their objectives by destroying the existing capitalist structure and replacing it with socialist or communist society. They believe in abolishment of the wage system and private property. They also strive to put an end to the competitive society and existence of individual rights. They try to destroy the existing economic system by revoluntary measures.

   Industrial workers of the world (I.W.W.) are the common example of revolutionary trade union in the USA.

The revolutionary union can be divided into four categories :

(i) ***Anarchist unions.*** Such union aims at destroying the present economic system by resorting to revoluntary measures. They seek to abolish the wage system and private property.

(ii) ***Political union.*** Political union seek to redistribute the wealth by giving effective share to the workers. They also enacts new rules to eliminate the capitalist structure of the state. Political unions basically get their powers through political action only.

(iii) ***Predatory Union.*** Predatory union seek their objectives without sticking to any approach, they may adopt business unionism, uplift unionism or revolutionary unionism for the pursuance of their goal.

(iv) ***Guerrilla Union.*** They believe the exploitation, violence and non cooperation. They are generally not democratic the leaders of guerrilla union are ruthless and irresponsible. They do not believe in cooperation with their employers.

II. On the Basis of Membership Structure

1. **Craft union.** When the workers engaged in a single occupation or craft from a union, it is called craft union. Craft union cover all worker engaged in the same craft, irrespective of the industries in which they are employed. They stand for skilled labourers that work in a particular sector or are employed in a particular craft.
2. **Industrial unions.** Unions organised on the basis of an industry rather than craft is called industrial union. All workers skilled and semiskilled and unskilled working in a particular they represent the workers trading in an industry regardless differences in the craft, skill, position or sex from together an industrial union.. All the workers in that industry, not considering which occupation or which job comes under that industry's union.
3. **Staff union.** A combination of both craft union and industrial union is called staff union. It pre-supposes unity and solidarity among the workers of different trades. Staff union is mostly formed by the workers of territory sector like health services, tour and travel industry education etc.
4. **General unions.** General unions represent labourers from all industries and professions irrespective of what sector of the workforce they come from. Workers of different industries and different occupations from general trade union.

THE TRADE UNIONS ACT, 1926

Objectives

- Provides for registration of trade unions with a view to render lawful organisation of labor to enable collective bargaining.

Scope and Coverage

- Extends to whole of India and applies to all kind of unions of workers and associations of employees which aim at regularising the labor management relations.

Meaning

As per section 2(u), a trade union means any combination, whether temporary or permanent, formed primarily to regulate the relations between workmen and employers or workmen and workmen or employers and employers and for imposing any restrictive conditions on the conduct of any trade or business.

Salient Provisions

Registrations of Trade Unions

- Not compulsory but desirable
- Minimum of 7 workers to form a trade union
- Apply to registrar for the registration
- Prescribed format accompanied by prescribed fee, a copy of rules of the union signed by at least 7 members
- Registrar issues a certificate of registration which shall be conclusive evidence of its registration
- Who can be a member
- Any person who has attained the age of 15 years, is eligible to be a member of a registered trade union, subject to the rules of the union
- Appointment of office bearers
- At least 50% of the office bearers of union should be actually engaged or employed in the industry with which trade union is concerned, and the remaining can be outside such as lawyer, politicians, social workers, etc.

Cancellation of registration

Registrar can cancel or withdraw the registration on an application being made for its cancellation or by giving at least 2 months notice

- If registration has been obtained by fraud or mistake
- If the union has ceased to exist
- If it has willfully contravened any of the provision of the act
- If any rule which is required under section (6) has been deleted

Dissolution of trade unions

By sending a notice of dissolution signed by 7 members and a Secretary of the union, to the registrar within 14 days of dissolution

Funds will be divided in the manner prescribed under the rules of the union or as laid down by the government

Obligations and Rights of registered trade unions

- General funds should be spent only for the objects specified under section 15
- Account books and membership should be kept open for inspection
- A copy of every alteration should be sent to the registrar within 15 days

A trade union has a right to:

- Demonstrate
- Appeal against an order of registrar to the court.

TRADE UNIONS MOVEMENT IN INDIA

Structure of Trade Unions in India

In India there are two types of organisation to which trade unions are affiliated :

I. **The National Federations.** The national federations are the apex trade union, that brings coordination in the activities of different trade union. Any trade union can join national federation to have a national character in its policies. Generally the national federation and politically learned and the leadership of such federations and politically learned and the leadership to such federations is provided by politicians. Some of the trade union leaders are MLA, MP, big corporate.

II. **The Federations of union.** Various union combine together to form the federation of unions for the purpose of gaining more solidarity and strength. Such federation can take collective action, when such need arises, without losing their individuality. The federation of unions have local, regional, state, national and international character. In India, many trade union are affiliated to one or the other central organisation.

LIST OF CENTRAL TRADE UNION ORGANISATIONS IN INDIA
1. All India Trade Union Congress (AITUC)
2. Bharatiya Mazdoor Sangh (BMS)
3. Centre of Indian Trade Unions (CITU)
4. Hind Mazdoor Kisan Panchayat (HMKP)
5. Hind Mazdoor Sabha (HMS)
6. United Trade Union Congress (UTUC) and
7. Trade Unions Co-ordination Centre (TUCC)
8. United Trade Union Congress - Lenin Sarani (UTUC - LS)
9. National Labour Organization (NLO)
10. Indian National Trade Union Congress (INTUC)
11. Indian Federation of Free Trade Unions (IFFTU)
12. National Front of Indian Trade Unions (NFITU)

Role of the Trade Unions

Adopting the model of Prof. Clark Kerr unions assume the following roles:

A. **Sectional Bargainers.** Interests of the workers at plant, industry, national level multiplicity of unions, Crafts Unions, white Collar Union etc.

B. **Class Bargainers.** Unions representing the interest of the class as whole as in France Agricultural Unions, Federations of unions, Civil Servants Union.

C. **Agents of State.** As in U.S.S.R., ensuring targets of production at fixed price. In 1974 Railway strike, INTUC stood behind Government and its agent.

D. **Partners in Social Control.** Co-determinate in Germany. Also, some examples are found in Holland, France, Italy and Sweden; some half-hearted attempts are being made in India also.

E. **Unions role** which can be termed as enemies of economic systems, driven by political ideologies than business compulsions. Leftist unions want to change the fundamental structure of economy and want to have control over it. Therefore, they encourage high wages, high bonus etc. without any consideration for the health of the economy.

F. **Business Oriented Role.** Here unions consider the interests of the organisation along with workers. They think that their member's fate is inextricably linked with that of organisation and they swim or sink together.

G. **Unions as Change Agent.** Lead the changes than to be led by them and thus, performing the pioneering role.

Types of Trade Unions

1. **Craft union.** They stand for skilled labourers that work in a particular sector or are employed in a particular craft.
2. **Industrial unions**. They represent the workers trading in an industry. All the workers in that industry, not considering which occupation or which job comes under that industry's union.
3. **General unions.** General unions represent labourers from all industries and professions irrespective of what sector of the workforce they come from.

4. **White collar unions.** They stand for professionals who work from an office such as those who occupy a managerial or administrative chair.

AIM AND OBJECTIVES OF TRADE UNION MOVEMENT IN INDIA
1. To establish a socialist state in India.
2. To socialize and nationalize the means of production, distribution and exchange as far as possible.
3. To ameliorate the economic and social conditions of the working class.
4. The watch promote, safeguard and further the interests, rights and privileges of the workers in all matters relating to their employment.
5. To co-ordinate the activities of the trade unions affiliated to the AITUC.
6. To fight against all forms of atrocities against women and harassment at place of work.

Classification of Trade Unions

Classification of trade unions is based upon ideology, trade and agreement.

1. Classification Based on Ideology

a. **Revolutionary Unions.** Believe in destruction of existing social/economic order and creation of a new one. They want shift in power and authority and use of force - Left Unions.

b. **Reformist or Welfare Unions.** Work for changes and reforms within existing socio-political framework of society - European Model.

c. **Uplift Unions.** Advocate extensive reforms well beyond the area of working condition i.e., change in taxation system, elimination of poverty etc.

2. Classification Based on Trade

At the other extreme in terms of the range of workers represented in the general union, which has members drawn from all trades. Most unions in India and Sri Lanka are in this category.

- Many unions have memberships and jurisdictions based on the trades they represent. The most narrow in membership is the craft union, which represents only members certified in a given craft or trade, such as pipe fitting, carpentry, and clerical work. Although very common in the western world, craft unions are not common in countries like India and Sri Lanka.
- At the other extreme in terms of the range of workers represented in the general union, which has members drawn from all trades. Most unions in India and Sri Lanka are in this category. Another common delineation of unions based on trades or crafts is that between so called blue-collar workers and white-collar workers. Unions representing workers employed on the production floor, or outdoor trades such as in construction work, are called blue-collar unions. In contrast, those employees in shops and offices and who are not in management grades and perform clerical and allied functions are called white-collar workers.
- In addition, trade unions may be categorised on the basis of the industry in which they are employed. Examples of these are workers engaged in agriculture of forestry: hence agricultural labour unions or forest worker unions.

3. Classification Based on Agreement

Another basis on which labour agreements are sometimes distinguished is on basis of the type of agreement involved, based on the degree to which membership in the union is a condition of employment. These are:

A. **Closed Shop.** Where management and union agree that the union would have sole responsibility and authority for the recruitment of workers, it is called a Closed Shop agreement. The worker joins the union to become an employee of the shop. The Taft-Hartley Act of 1947 bans closed shop agreements in the USA, although they still exist in the construction and printing trades. Sometimes, the closed shop is also called the 'Hiring Hall.'

B. **Union Shop.** Where there is an agreement that all new recruits must join the union within a fixed period after employment it is called a union shop. In the USA where some states are declared to be 'right-to-work'.

C. **Preferential Shop.** When a Union member is given preference in filling a vacancy, such an agreement is called Preferential Shop.

D. **Maintenance Shop.** In this type of arrangement no compulsory membership in the union before or after recruitment exists. However, if the employee chooses to become a member after recruitment, his membership remains compulsory right throughout his tenure of employment with that particular employer. This is called maintenance of membership shop or maintenance shop.

E. **Agency Shop.** In terms of the agreement between management and the union a non union member has to pay the union a sum equivalent to a member's subscription in order to continue employment with the employer. This is called an agency shop.

F. **Open Shop.** Membership in a union is in no way compulsory or obligatory either before or after recruitment. In such organisations, sometimes there is no union at all. This is least desirable form for unions. This is referred to as an open shop.

The important forces that make the employees to join a union are as follows :

1. **Greater Bargaining Power.** The individual employee possesses very little bargaining power as compared to that of his employer. If he is not satisfied with the wage and other conditions of employment, he can leave the job. It is not practicable to continually resign from one job after another when he is dissatisfied. This imposes a great financial and emotional burden upon the worker. The better course for him is to join a union that can take concerted action against the employer. The threat or actuality of a strike by a union is a powerful tool that often causes the employer to accept the demands of the workers for better conditions of employment.
2. **Minimise Discrimination.** The decisions regarding pay, work, transfer, promotion, etc. are highly subjective in nature. The personal relationships existing between the supervisor and each of his subordinates may influence the management. Thus, there are chances of favouritisms and discriminations. A trade union can compel the management to formulate personnel policies that press for equality of treatment to the workers. All the labour decisions of the management are under close scrutiny of the labour union. This has the effect of minimising favouritism and discrimination.
3. **Sense of Security.** The employees may join the unions because of their belief that it is an effective way to secure adequate protection from various types of hazards and income insecurity such as accident, injury, illness, unemployment, etc.
4. **Sense of Participation.** The employees can participate in management of matters affecting their interests only if they join trade unions. They can influence the decisions that are taken as a result of collective bargaining between the union and the management.
5. **Sense of Belongingness.** Many employees joins a union because their co-workers are the members of the union. At times, an employee joins a union under group pressure; if he does not, he often has a very difficult time at work. On the other hand, those who are members of a union feel that they gain respect in the eyes of their fellow workers. They can also discuss their problem with' the trade union leaders.
6. **Platform for self-expression.** The desire for self-expression is a fundamental human drive for most people. All of us wish to share our feelings, ideas and opinions with others. Similarly the workers also want the management to listen to them. A trade union provides such a forum where the feelings, ideas and opinions of the workers could be discussed. It can also transmit the feelings, ideas, opinions and complaints of the workers to the management. The collective

voice of the workers is heard by the management and give due consideration while taking policy decisions by the management.

7. **Betterment of relationships.** Another reason for employees joining unions is that employees feel that unions can fulfil the important need for adequate machinery for proper maintenance of employer-employee relations. Unions help in betterment of industrial relations among management and workers by solving the problems peacefully.

Problems and Measures to Strengthen Trade Unions

Over the years, trade unions in India have been taken for a ride by outside, political leaders. In the process, the interests of workers and their aspirations have been totally neglected. The Trade Unions Act, 1926, did not go for recognising a representative union. As a result multiple unions have cropped up, often with blessings from management and outsiders. The union finances have not been very sound in the beginning. The average membership figures for each union remain poor and have not improved. The forces of liberalisation unleashed in early 90s have strengthened the hands of employers in closing down unviable units. The new corporate 'mantras' productivity, performance, efficiency, survival of the fittest have virtually pushed them to the wall-where their very survival looks uncertain. Let's recount the factors responsible for their ever-increasing woes and depreciated status thus as below:

1. Trade Union Leadership

The nature of leadership significantly influences the union-management relations as the leadership is the lynch-pin of the management of trade unions. The leadership of most of the trade unions in India has been outside leadership mainly drawn from political parties.

Reasons for emergence of outside leadership. Outside leadership has been playing a pivotal role in Indian Trade Union Movement due to the inability of insiders to lead their movement. In view of low education standards and poor command over English language which is still the principal language of labour legislation and negotiations, low level of knowledge about labour legislation, unsound financial position, fear of victimisation by the employer and lack of leadership qualities-outside leaders have come to stay. The main reason for this trend is that the Trade Unions Act, 1926, [India] itself provided the scope for outside leadership.

The evil effects of outside leadership. The evil effects of outside leadership analysed by National Commission on Labour are as follows:

1. Outside leadership undermined the purposes of Trade Unions and weakened their authority. Personal benefits and prejudices sometimes weighed more than unions.
2. Outside leadership has been responsible for the slow growth of Trade Unions.
3. Internal leadership has not been developed fully.
4. Most of the leaders cannot understand the worker' problems as they do not live the life of a worker.

Even though outside leadership is permissible in the initial stages it is undesirable in the long run because of many evils associated with it. Political differences of leaders have been inhibiting the formation of one union in one industry. Most of the Trade Union leaders fulfil their personal aspirations with their knowledge and experience gained in the Trade Unions.

Measures to minimise the evil effects of outside leadership. In view of the limitations of outside leadership, it is desirable to replace the outside leaders progressively by the internal leaders. The National Commission on Labour, 1969, also stated that outsiders in the Trade Unions should be made redundant by forces from within rather than by legal means. Both the management and trade unions should take steps in this direction. The steps may be:

- Management should assure that the victimisation will be at zero level, even if the trade unions are led by insiders;
- Extensive training facilities in the areas of leadership skills, management techniques and programmes should be provided to the workers;
- Special leave should be sanctioned to the office bearers.

Union rivalry has been the result of the following factors:

1. The desire of political parties to have their basis among the industrial workers;
2. Person-cum-fractional politics of the local union leader;
3. Domination of unions by outside leaders;
4. Attitude and policies of the management, *i.e.*, divide and rule policy; and
5. The weak legal framework of trade unions.

Measures to minimise union rivalry. In view of the evil effects of inter-union rivalry and the problem of formation of one union in one industry, it may be necessary to consider the recommendations of National Commission on Labour, 1969. The recommendations of NCL to minimise union rivalry are:

1. Elimination of party politics and outsiders through building up of internal leaders;
2. Promotion of collective bargaining through recognition of sole bargaining agents;
3. Improving the system of union recognition;
4. Encouraging union security; and
5. Empowering labour courts to settle inter-union disputes if they are not settled within the organisation.

2. Multiple Unions

Multiple unionisms both at the plant and industry levels pose a serious threat to industrial peace and harmony in India. The situation of multiple unions is said to prevail when two or more unions in the same plant or industry try to assert rival claims over each other and function with overlapping jurisdiction. The multiple unions exist due to the existence of craft unions, formations of two or more unions in the industry. Multiple unionisms is not a phenomenon unique to India. It exists even in advance countries like UK and USA. Multiple unionisms affect the industrial relations system both positively and negatively. It is sometimes desirable for the healthy and democratic health of labour movement. It encourages a healthy competition and acts as a check to the adoption of undemocratic practice, authoritative structure and autocratic leadership. However, the negative impacts of multiple unions dominate the positive impacts. The nature of competition tends to convert itself into a sense of unfair competition resulting in inter-union rivalry. The rivalry destroys the feeling of mutual trust and cooperation among leadership. It is a major cause for weakening the Trade Union Movement in India. Multiple unionisms also results in small size of the unions, poor finances, etc.

3. Union Rivalry

The formal basis for Trade Union Organisation is provided by the Indian Trade Union Act, 1926. The relevant article reads as follows: "Any seven or more members of a trade union may be subscribing their name to the roles of the trade union and by otherwise complying with the provisions of this act with respect to the registration, apply for registration of the trade union under this Act."

This provision has led to the formation of multiple unions and resulted in inter union rivalry in different industries. But the inter-union rivalry breaks the very purpose of the trade unions by weakening the strength of collective bargaining. On the other hand, the existence of a single, strong union not only protects the employee interests more effectively but also halts the various unproductive activities of the unions and forces the leaders to concentrate on the strategic issues. Further, it helps to bring about congenial industrial relations by bringing about a system of orderliness in dealing with the employees and by facilitating expeditious settlement of disputes.

The state of rivalry between two groups of the same union is said to be inter union rivalry. Inter and intra-union rivalries have been a potent cause of industrial disputes in the country. They are responsible for weal bargaining power of trade unions in collective bargaining. These rivalries are responsible for slow growth of trade union movement in the country.

4. Finance

Sound financial position is an essential ingredient for the effective functioning of trade unions, because in the process of rendering services or fulfilling their goals, trade unions have to perform a variety of functions and organise programmes which require enormous financial commitments. Hence, it is imperative on the part of a trade union to strengthen its financial position.

But it is felt that the income and expenditure of trade unions in India over the years is such, with few exceptions, that the financial position of the union is generally weak, affecting their functioning. It is opined that, "trade unions could be more effective, if they paid more attention to strengthening their organisations and achieving higher attention of financial solvency."

The primary source of income to the unions is membership subscription. Their other sources of union finances are donations, sale of periodicals, etc. The items of expenditure include: allowances to office bearers, salaries to office, annual convention/meeting expenses, rents, stationery, printing, postage, telegrams, etc.

Most of the trade unions in India suffer from inadequate funds. This unsound financial position is mostly due to low membership and low rate of membership fee. Trade Union Act, 1926, prescribed the membership fee at 25 paise per member per month. But the National Commission on Labour recommended the increase of rate of membership subscription from 25 paise to Re. 1 in the year 1990. But the Government did not accept this recommendation.

As the National Commission on Labour observes, "an important factor limiting the effective functioning of unions in our country has been their financial weakness.. In most unions, poor finances are the result of inadequate membership strength. This in turn, can be traced to the small size of units. In a majority of unions, the rate of contributions required of members is also small. With a relatively low rate of unionisation, total funds collected are small. The general picture of finances of unions is disappointing."

5. Low Memberships

The average membership figures of each union are quite depressing. In 1992-93 the average membership figure was 632, a steady fall from 3,594 per union from 1927-28. "Because of their small size, unions suffer from lack of adequate funds and find it difficult to engage the services of experts to aid and advise members in times of need". They can't bargain with the employer effectively on their own.

6. Heterogenous Nature of Labour

Since workers come to the factory with varying backgrounds; it is difficult for them to put a joint front in case of trouble. Employers exploit the situation, under the circumstances, by dividing workers on the basis of race, religion, language, caste, etc.

7. Lack of Interest

For a large majority of workers, unionism even today remains a foreign issue. In fact, workers avoid union activities out of sheer disinterestedness. Those who become part of the union do not also participate in the union work enthusiastically. In such a scenario, it is not surprising to find outside political leaders exploiting the situation serve their own personal agenda.

8. Absence of Paid Office Bearer

Weak finances do not permit unions to engage the services of full time, paid office bearers. Union activists, who work on a part time basis, neither have the time nor the energy to take up union activities sincerely and diligently.

9. Other Problem

The other factors responsible for the unsound functioning of trade unions in India are:

(a) **Illiteracy.** Workers in India fail to understand the implications of modern trade unionism. Their illiteracy coupled with ignorance and indifference account for the predominance of outside leadership.

(b) **Uneven growth.** Trade unionism activities are, more or less, confined to major metros in India and traceable only in large scale units (especially cotton textile. The membership fees should be raised as the amount of wages of the workers increased significantly, compared to the situation in 1926 when Trade Union Act provided for the collection of 25 paise per month per member as subscription fee. Even amended Rs. 1/- is not sufficient. Some other source of finance may also explore to make trade union financially healthy.

Measures to Strengthen Trade Union Movement in India

The following are some of the measures to minimise trade union problems and to strengthen the Trade Union Movement of India.

(a) **United Labour Front.** Unions must put a joint front. Splinter groups multiple unions dissipate their energies, dilute their power and reduce their effectiveness. Trade unions should form a sort of labour party and all the trade unions in the country should be affiliated to it. It gives adequate strength to the trade unions both industry and Parliament.

(b) **Efficient Leadership.** Outside political leadership has developed due to the absence of internal leadership. Outside leadership is the main cause for the multiple problems of the trade unions. These problems can be eradicated through the development of leadership talents from within. Management should encourage internal workers to lead their own movement. Management and trade unions should provide educational and training facilities for the development of internal leadership.

(c) **Membership Fees.** In order to make updated trade union must organise continuous training and developmental programme. Future needs smart and responsive trade union, if they have survive and thrive.

(d) The trade union act should be amended in order to avoid dual membership.

(e) There should be legal provision for the recognition of the representative union.

(f) Unions should not interactive in day to day matters. They must focus on important issues affecting workers.

MULTIPLE CHOICE QUESTIONS

1. What is Industrial Relations?
   (1) The relationship between employers and customers.
   (2) The relationships between employers and employees in the workplace.
   (3) The relationship between employees and customers.
   (4) The relationship between employees and the government.
2. Which of the following is a major factor in the emergence of industrial relations as an academic discipline?
   (1) The Industrial Revolution
   (2) The agricultural revolution
   (3) The technological revolution
   (4) The digital revolution
3. Which of the following is a major objective of Industrial Relations?
   (1) To maximise profits of organisations at any cost.
   (2) To minimise costs of production in organisations.
   (3) To improve the economic efficiency of organisations and the welfare of the society.
   (4) To promote individualistic interests of the employees.
4. Which of the following is a primary source of conflict between employers and employees?
   (1) The distribution of rewards and benefits
   (2) The amount of work assigned to employees
   (3) The geographic location of the workplace
   (4) The type of work performed by employees
5. What is the primary role of a trade union in Industrial Relations?
   (1) To represent the interests of employees in collective bargaining.
   (2) To represent the interests of employers in collective bargaining.
   (3) To represent the interests of customers in collective bargaining.
   (4) To represent the interests of the government in collective bargaining.
6. What is the difference between collective bargaining and individual bargaining?
   (1) Collective bargaining and individual bargaining are the same thing.
   (2) Collective bargaining involves representatives of employers negotiating with representatives of employees while individual bargaining involves individual employees negotiating with their supervisors.
   (3) Collective bargaining involves the government negotiating with employers on behalf of employees.
   (4) Collective bargaining involves representatives of employees negotiating with representatives of employers while individual bargaining involves individual employees negotiating with their supervisors.
7. What is the definition of job security in Industrial Relations?
   (1) The level of assurance that an employee will not be terminated from their job without just cause.
   (2) The amount of money an employee is paid for their job.
   (3) The number of hours an employee is required to work per week.
   (4) The location of the workplace.

8. What are the major sources of power for employees in Industrial Relations?
   (1) The ability to go on strike and the ability to withhold labour.
   (2) The ability to increase production and the ability to reduce costs.
   (3) The ability to increase profits and the ability to reduce losses.
   (4) The ability to influence government policy and the ability to influence public opinion.

9. What is the definition of conflict resolution in Industrial Relations?
   (1) The process of promoting conflict between employers and employees.
   (2) The process of resolving disputes between employees and customers.
   (3) The process of resolving disputes between employers and employees.
   (4) The process of promoting conflict between employees and the government.

10. What is the purpose of grievance handling in Industrial Relations?
   (1) To provide a formal mechanism for employers to raise concerns and complaints with their employees.
   (2) To provide a formal mechanism for employees to raise concerns and complaints with their employer.
   (3) To provide a formal mechanism for customers to raise concerns and complaints with their supplier.
   (4) To provide a formal mechanism for the government to raise concerns and complaints with an organisation.

11. What is the primary objective of the pluralist approach in Industrial Relations?
   (1) To balance the interests of employers, employees, and the society.
   (2) To prioritise the interests of employers over employees.
   (3) To prioritise the interests of employees over employers.
   (4) To prioritise the interests of the government over both employees and employers.

12. What is the primary objective of the Marxist approach in Industrial Relations?
   (1) To promote the interests of the working class and reduce the power of the capitalist class.
   (2) To promote the interests of the capitalist class and reduce the power of the working class.
   (3) To promote the interests of the government and reduce the power of both the working class and the capitalist class.
   (4) To promote the interests of employees over employers.

13. Which of the following is a major criticism of the unitarist approach in Industrial Relations?
   (1) It assumes that conflict of interest between employers and employees is necessary for the growth of an organisation.
   (2) It assumes that the government has no role to play in Industrial Relations.
   (3) It assumes that unions are necessary for the resolution of disputes in Industrial Relations.
   (4) It assumes that there is no conflict of interest between employers and employees.

14. What is the primary role of the International Labour Organisation (ILO) in Industrial Relations?
   (1) To promote the interests of individual countries in Industrial Relations.
   (2) To promote the interests of individual organisations in Industrial Relations.
   (3) To promote social justice and promote decent working conditions globally.
   (4) To promote the interests of multinational corporations in Industrial Relations.

15. What is the primary role of the State in Industrial Relations?
   (1) To maintain a balance between the interests of employers, employees, and the society.
   (2) To promote the interests of employers over employees.

(3) To promote the interests of employees over employers.

(4) To act as a mediator in conflicts between employers and employees.

16. What is the primary objective of the human relations approach in Industrial Relations?

(1) To promote the interests of unions over employers and employees.

(2) To promote the well-being of employees and improve their job satisfaction.

(3) To promote the interests of employers over employees.

(4) To promote the interests of employees over employers.

17. Which of the following is a major limitation of the human relations approach in Industrial Relations?

(1) It fails to recognise the role of the government in Industrial Relations.

(2) It fails to address issues of power and conflict between employers and employees.

(3) It assumes that all employees share the same interests and goals.

(4) It assumes that a high level of efficiency in an organisation is independent of employee morale and job satisfaction.

18. What is the definition of the from-enemy-to-partner approach in Industrial Relations?

(1) An approach that seeks to transform the relationship between employers and employees from one of conflict to one of co-operation.

(2) An approach that seeks to maintain the traditional relationship between employers and employees.

(3) An approach that seeks to maintain the traditional hierarchical structure of organisations.

(4) An approach that seeks to eliminate the role of unions in Industrial Relations.

19. Which of the following is a major objective of the strategic choice approach in Industrial Relations?

(1) To maximise profits of organisations at any cost.

(2) To minimise costs of production in organisations.

(3) To identify the most appropriate Industrial Relations strategy for an organisation in a given situation.

(4) To promote individualistic interests of the employees.

20. Which of the following terms refers to the discipline that studies the rules governing employment relationships?

(1) Employment law

(2) Labour economics

(3) Human resource management

(4) Organisational behaviour

21. What is the definition of a trade union in Industrial Relations?

(1) An organisation formed by government to represent their interests in collective bargaining with employers and employees.

(2) An organisation formed by employees to represent their interests in collective bargaining with employers.

(3) An organisation formed by employers to represent their interests in collective bargaining with employees.

(4) An organisation formed by customers to represent their interests in collective bargaining with suppliers.

22. Which of the following is a major issue in International Industrial Relations?

(1) The exploitation of workers in developed countries.

(2) The exploitation of customers in developing countries.

(3) The exploitation of customers in developed countries.

(4) The exploitation of workers in developing countries.

23. What is the primary role of Industrial Relations institutions in an organisation?

(1) To resolve disputes and promote effective communication between employers and employees.

(2) To maximise profits of the organisation.
(3) To minimise costs of production in the organisation.
(4) To promote individualistic interests of employees.

24. What is the primary objective of the employee relations approach in Industrial Relations?
(1) To promote positive relationships between employers and employees by addressing employee concerns and interests.
(2) To promote the interests of employers over employees.
(3) To promote the interests of employees over employers.
(4) To promote the interests of the government over both employees and employers.

25. What is the difference between Industrial Relations and Human Resource Management?
(1) Industrial Relations and Human Resource Management are the same thing.
(2) Industrial Relations is concerned with the management of employees within an organisation while Human Resource Management is concerned with the relationship between employers and employees.
(3) Industrial Relations is concerned with the relationship between employers and employees while Human Resource Management is concerned with the management of employees within an organisation.
(4) Industrial Relations is concerned with the relationship between employees and the government while Human Resource Management is concerned with the management of employees within an organisation.

26. What is the definition of collective bargaining in Industrial Relations?
(1) The process of negotiations between representatives of employers and employees to establish wages, hours, and working conditions.
(2) The process of negotiations between representatives of employers and government to establish wages, hours, and working conditions.
(3) The process of negotiations between representatives of employees and government to establish wages, hours, and working conditions.
(4) The process of individual negotiation between employees and their supervisors.

27. What is the definition of workplace democracy in Industrial Relations?
(1) The involvement of customers in the management of an organisation.
(2) The involvement of government in the management of an organisation.
(3) The involvement of suppliers in the management of an organisation.
(4) The involvement of employees in the management of an organisation.

28. What is the role of Industrial Relations in ensuring social justice?
(1) Industrial Relations plays a critical role in promoting fairness and equality in the workplace and in society.
(2) Industrial Relations is irrelevant to social justice.
(3) Industrial Relations is a negative influence on social justice.
(4) Industrial Relations is a positive influence on economic growth.

29. What is the definition of human capital in Industrial Relations?
(1) The knowledge, skills, and abilities of an organisation's employees.
(2) The financial assets of an organisation.
(3) The physical assets of an organisation.
(4) The intellectual property of an organisation.

30. What is the definition of a collective agreement in Industrial Relations?
(1) A verbal agreement between employers and employees that establishes wages, hours, and working conditions.

(2) An agreement between employers and government that establishes wages, hours, and working conditions.

(3) A written agreement between employers and employees that establishes wages, hours, and working conditions.

(4) An agreement between employees and government that establishes wages, hours, and working conditions.

31. What is the definition of labour market regulation in Industrial Relations?

(1) The rules and regulations that govern the employment relationship.

(2) The rules and regulations that govern the interaction between organisations.

(3) The rules and regulations that govern the interaction between governments.

(4) The rules and regulations that govern the interaction between customers and suppliers.

32. What is the primary role of a mediator in Industrial Relations?

(1) To facilitate negotiations between employers and employees.

(2) To promote the interests of employers over employees.

(3) To promote the interests of employees over employers.

(4) To promote the interests of the government over both employees and employers.

33. Which of the following is a major advantage of a strike in Industrial Relations?

(1) It can increase the profitability of an organisation.

(2) It can improve the efficiency of an organisation.

(3) It can improve the relations between an organisation and its customers.

(4) It can create leverage for employees in negotiations with their employer.

34. What is the definition of a lockout in Industrial Relations?

(1) The permanent closure of a workplace by an employer.

(2) The temporary closure of a workplace by employees as a tactic to pressure an employer in negotiations.

(3) The permanent closure of a workplace by employees.

(4) The temporary closure of a workplace by an employer as a tactic to pressure employees in negotiations.

35. Which of the following factors is a major contributor to the decline of trade unions in recent years?

(1) Globalisation

(2) Technology

(3) Government policies

(4) All of the above

36. Which of the following is a major objective of an employee representative (ER) in Industrial Relations?

(1) To represent the interests of employees in negotiations with their employer.

(2) To represent the interests of employers in negotiations with their employees.

(3) To represent the interests of customers in negotiations with their supplier.

(4) To represent the interests of the government in negotiations with an organisation.

37. What is the definition of an arbitration in Industrial Relations?

(1) The use of an independent third party to resolve disputes between employers and the government.

(2) The use of an independent third party to resolve disputes between employers and employees.

(3) The use of an independent third party to resolve disputes between employees and the government.

(4) The use of a judge to resolve disputes between employers and employees.

38. What is the definition of a labour court in Industrial Relations?

(1) A court that specialises in resolving disputes related to employment relationships.

(2) A court that specialises in resolving disputes between employers and the government.

(3) A court that specialises in resolving disputes between employees and the government.

(4) A court that specialises in resolving disputes between customers and suppliers.

39. What is the primary objective of the conflict resolution approach in Industrial Relations?

(1) To promote the interests of employers over employees.

(2) To promote the interests of employees over employers.

(3) To resolve disputes between employers and employees through negotiation and dialogue.

(4) To promote the interests of the government over both employees and employers.

40. Which of the following is a major limitation of the pluralist approach in Industrial Relations?

(1) It fails to recognise the power imbalance between employers and employees.

(2) It assumes that all employees share the same interests and goals.

(3) It fails to recognise the role of the government in Industrial Relations.

(4) It assumes that a high level of efficiency in an organisation is independent of employee morale and job satisfaction.

41. What is the primary objective of the systems approach in Industrial Relations?

(1) To promote the interests of employers over employees.

(2) To view the employment relationship as a complex system of interrelated parts.

(3) To promote the interests of employees over employers.

(4) To promote the interests of the government over both employees and employers.

42. Which of the following is a major disadvantage of the systems approach in Industrial Relations?

(1) It tends to focus on the structural rather than the behavioural aspects of the employment relationship.

(2) It tends to focus on the behavioural rather than the structural aspects of the employment relationship.

(3) It tends to ignore the complexity of the employment relationship.

(4) It tends to ignore the role of technology in the employment relationship.

43. What is the definition of the functional approach in Industrial Relations?

(1) An approach that seeks to achieve effective and efficient functioning of an organisation by promoting an atmosphere of conflict and competition.

(2) An approach that seeks to promote the power of unions in Industrial Relations.

(3) An approach that seeks to achieve effective and efficient functioning of an organisation by promoting an atmosphere of co-operation and harmony.

(4) An approach that seeks to promote the power of employers in Industrial Relations.

44. What is the primary objective of the feminist approach in Industrial Relations?

(1) To promote the interests of women in the workplace.

(2) To promote the interests of men in the workplace.

(3) To promote the interests of unions in the workplace.

(4) To promote the interests of employers in the workplace.

45. What is the definition of the power resources approach in Industrial Relations?

(1) An approach that analyses the relative power of employers and employees in the employment relationship.

(2) An approach that ignores the relative power of employers and employees in the employment relationship.

(3) An approach that overestimates the relative power of employers in the employment relationship.

(4) An approach that overestimates the relative power of employees in the employment relationship.

46. What is the primary role of a collective bargaining agent in Industrial Relations?

(1) To represent the interests of employers in negotiations with their employees.

(2) To represent the interests of customers in negotiations with their supplier.

(3) To represent the interests of the government in negotiations with an organisation.

(4) To represent the interests of employees in negotiations with their employer.

47. Which of the following is a major criticism of the strategic choice approach in Industrial Relations?

(1) It assumes that the interests of employers and employees are mutually exclusive.

(2) It assumes that the interests of employers and employees are synonymous.

(3) It assumes that the interests of employers and employees are irrelevant in the employment relationship.

(4) It assumes that the role of the government is irrelevant in the employment relationship.

48. What is the definition of employee involvement in Industrial Relations?

(1) The participation of employees in decision-making processes in an organisation.

(2) The participation of customers in decision-making processes in an organisation.

(3) The participation of employers in decision-making processes in an organisation.

(4) The participation of government officials in decision-making processes in an organisation.

49. What is the definition of employee participation in Industrial Relations?

(1) The process of involving employees in the decision-making process within an organisation.

(2) The process of involving customers in the decision-making process within an organisation.

(3) The process of involving employers in the decision-making process within an organisation.

(4) The process of involving government officials in the decision-making process within an organisation.

50. What is the definition of a referee in Industrial Relations?

(1) An independent third party appointed to resolve disputes between employers and the government.

(2) An independent third party appointed to resolve disputes between employers and employees.

(3) An independent third party appointed to resolve disputes between employees and the government.

(4) An independent third party appointed to resolve disputes between customers and suppliers.

51. What is the main objective of an industrial tribunal in Industrial Relations?

(1) To promote the interests of employers over employees.

(2) To promote the interests of employees over employers.

(3) To promote the interests of the government over both employees and employers.

(4) To resolve disputes between employers and employees.

52. What is the definition of a collective labour agreement in Industrial Relations?

(1) An agreement between employers and government that sets out the terms and conditions of employment.

(2) An agreement between employers and employees that sets out the terms and conditions of employment.

(3) An agreement between employees and government that sets out the terms and conditions of employment.

(4) An agreement between employees and their supervisor that sets out the terms and conditions of employment.

53. What is the difference between trade unions and employee associations in Industrial Relations?

(1) Trade unions and employee associations are the same thing.
(2) Trade unions are formed by employees to represent their interests in collective bargaining with employers while employee associations are formed to promote the interests of employees in other ways.
(3) Trade unions are formed by employers to represent their interests in collective bargaining with employees while employee associations are formed to promote the interests of employees in other ways.
(4) Trade unions are formed by government to represent their interests in collective bargaining with employers and employees while employee associations are formed to promote the interests of employees in other ways.

54. What is the definition of a shop steward in Industrial Relations?

(1) An elected representative of a trade union who acts as an intermediary between the union and its members in a particular workplace.
(2) An elected representative of an employer who acts as an intermediary between the employer and its employees in a particular workplace.
(3) An elected representative of the government who acts as an intermediary between government officials and employees in a particular workplace.
(4) An elected representative of customers who acts as an intermediary between customers and suppliers in a particular workplace.

55. What is the difference between distributive bargaining and integrative bargaining?

(1) Distributive bargaining involves dividing a fixed amount of resources while integrative bargaining involves creating value and expanding the resource pool.
(2) Distributive bargaining and integrative bargaining are the same thing.
(3) Distributive bargaining involves expanding the resource pool while integrative bargaining involves dividing a fixed amount of resources.
(4) Distributive bargaining and integrative bargaining are both methods of conflict resolution.

56. What is the definition of a trade union federation in Industrial Relations?

(1) An organisation that represents multiple employers in a particular country or region.
(2) An organisation that represents multiple suppliers in a particular country or region.
(3) An organisation that represents multiple customers in a particular country or region.
(4) An organisation that represents multiple trade unions in a particular country or region.

57. What is the definition of structural adjustment in Industrial Relations?

(1) Economic policies implemented to reduce the role of the state in the economy, often resulting in job losses and reduced job security.
(2) Economic policies implemented to increase the role of the state in the economy, often resulting in increased job security and wage increases.
(3) Economic policies implemented to increase the power of employers over employees.
(4) Economic policies implemented to increase the power of unions over employers.

58. What is the primary objective of a collective labour law in Industrial Relations?

(1) To regulate the relationship between employers and employees.
(2) To promote the interests of employers over employees.
(3) To promote the interests of employees over employers.
(4) To promote the interests of the government over both employees and employers.

59. What is the definition of social dialogue in Industrial Relations?
(1) The process of negotiation, consultation and exchange of information between employers and employees or their respective organisations with a view to regulation of terms of employment or settlement of disputes.
(2) The process of negotiation, consultation and exchange of information between employers and the government with a view to regulation of terms of employment or settlement of disputes.
(3) The process of negotiation, consultation and exchange of information between employees and the government with a view to regulation of terms of employment or settlement of disputes.
(4) The process of negotiation, consultation and exchange of information between customers and suppliers with a view to regulation of terms of employment or settlement of disputes.

60. What is the primary role of an Industrial Relations practitioner in an organisation?
(1) To promote the interests of employers over employees.
(2) To manage the relationship between employers and employees in an organisation.
(3) To promote the interests of employees over employers.
(4) To promote the interests of the government over both employees and employers.

61. Who are the actors involved in Industrial Relations?
(1) Employers, employees, and the government.
(2) Employers, employees, and customers.
(3) Employers, employees, and suppliers.
(4) Employers, employees, and shareholders.

62. How is the employment relationship defined in Industrial Relations?
(1) The relationship between employers and employees in the workplace.
(2) The relationship between employers and customers in the workplace.
(3) The relationship between employees and suppliers in the workplace.
(4) The relationship between employees and the government in the workplace.

63. What is the primary role of the State in Industrial Relations?
(1) To promote the interests of employers over employees.
(2) To promote the interests of employees over employers
(3) To act as a mediator in disputes between employers and employees.
(4) To promote the interests of the government over both employees and employers.

64. What is the main objective of collective bargaining in Industrial Relations?
(1) To impose terms and conditions of employment on employees.
(2) To establish terms and conditions of employment through negotiations between employers and employees.
(3) To impose terms and conditions of employment on employers.
(4) To promote individualistic interests of employees.

65. What is the difference between bi-partite and tri-partite negotiations?
(1) Bi-partite negotiations involve negotiations between employers and employees while tri-partite negotiations involve negotiations between employers, employees, and the government.

(2) Bi-partite negotiations involve negotiations between employers and customers while tri-partite negotiations involve negotiations between employers, employees, and the government.
(3) Bi-partite negotiations involve negotiations between employers and suppliers while tri-partite negotiations involve negotiations between employers, employees, and the government.
(4) Bi-partite negotiations and tri-partite negotiations are the same thing.

66. What are the major sources of conflict between employers and employees?
(1) Distribution of profits, working conditions, and job titles.
(2) Distribution of awards, strikes and lock-outs.
(3) Distribution of rewards and benefits, working conditions, and job security.
(4) Type of work performed, management styles, and geographic location of the workplace.

67. What is the definition of Industrial Democracy?
(1) The involvement of employees in the management of an organisation.
(2) The involvement of trade unions in the management of an organisation.
(3) The involvement of employers in the management of an organisation.
(4) The involvement of government officials in the management of an organisation.

68. What is the primary role of a trade union in Industrial Relations?
(1) To represent the interests of employers in collective bargaining with their employees.
(2) To represent the interests of employees in collective bargaining with their employers.
(3) To represent the interests of suppliers in collective bargaining with their customers.
(4) To represent the interests of the government in collective bargaining with employers and employees.

69. What is the main objective of the human resource management model in Industrial Relations?
(1) To create high-performance work systems.
(2) To maintain traditional hierarchies in organisations.
(3) To promote conflict between employers and employees.
(4) To promote individualistic interests of employees.

70. What is the difference between conflict and cooperation in Industrial Relations?
(1) Conflict involves the resolution of competing interests while cooperation involves the sharing of interests.
(2) Conflict and cooperation are the same thing.
(3) Conflict involves the sharing of interests while cooperation involves the resolution of competing interests.
(4) Conflict involves the promotion of individualistic interests while cooperation involves the promotion of common interests.

71. Which of the following is a major objective of the pluralist approach in Industrial Relations?
(1) To prioritise the interests of employers over employees.
(2) To prioritise the interests of employees over employers.
(3) To balance the interests of employers, employees, and the society.
(4) To prioritise the interests of the government over both employees and employers.

72. What is the definition of an Industrial Relations system?
(1) The formal and informal rules governing the relationship between government and the society.
(2) The formal and informal rules governing the relationship between suppliers and customers.
(3) The formal and informal rules governing the employment relationship.

(4) The formal and informal rules governing the relationship between employees' families and their employers.

73. What is the difference between conflict of interest and convergence of interest in Industrial Relations?

(1) Conflict of interest and convergence of interest are the same thing.

(2) Conflict of interest involves competing interests while convergence of interest involves shared interests.

(3) Conflict of interest involves shared interests while convergence of interest involves competing interests.

(4) Conflict of interest involves the promotion of individualistic interests while convergence of interest involves the promotion of common interests.

74. Which of the following is a major objective of the Marxist approach in Industrial Relations?

(1) To promote the interests of the working class and reduce the power of the capitalist class.

(2) To promote the interests of the capitalist class and reduce the power of the working class.

(3) To promote the interests of the government and reduce the power of both the working class and the capitalist class.

(4) To promote individualistic interests of employees.

75. What is the primary role of an arbitrator in Industrial Relations?

(1) To promote the interests of employers over employees.

(2) To promote the interests of employees over employers.

(3) To promote the interests of the government over both employees and employers.

(4) To resolve disputes between employers and employees through binding decision making.

76. What is the definition of a grievance in Industrial Relations?

(1) A formal complaint by an employee about a problem related to their work.

(2) A formal complaint by an employer about a problem related to their employee.

(3) A formal complaint by a customer about a problem related to a supplier.

(4) A formal complaint by a government official about a problem related to an organisation.

77. What is the primary objective of the unitarist approach in Industrial Relations?

(1) To prioritise the interests of employers over employees.

(2) To prioritise the interests of employees over employers.

(3) To promote organisational harmony and minimise conflict between employers and employees.

(4) To prioritise the interests of the government over both employees and employers.

78. What is the definition of a lockout in Industrial Relations?

(1) The temporary closure of a workplace by an employer as a tactic to pressure employees in negotiations.

(2) The temporary closure of a workplace by employees as a tactic to pressure an employer in negotiations.

(3) The permanent closure of a workplace by an employer.

(4) The permanent closure of a workplace by employees.

79. What is the primary role of a mediator in Industrial Relations?

(1) To facilitate negotiations between employers and employees.

(2) To promote the interests of employers over employees.

(3) To promote the interests of employees over employers.

(4) To promote the interests of the government over both employees and employers.

80. What is the definition of workplace democracy in Industrial Relations?
(1) The participation of employees in the management of an organisation.
(2) The participation of customers in the management of an organisation.
(3) The participation of employers in the management of an organisation.
(4) The participation of government officials in the management of an organisation.

81. What is the difference between collective bargaining and individual bargaining?
(1) Collective bargaining and individual bargaining are the same thing.
(2) Collective bargaining involves negotiations between representatives of employers and employees while individual bargaining involves negotiations between individual employees and their employers.
(3) Collective bargaining involves negotiations between representatives of employees and government while individual bargaining involves negotiations between individual employees and their employers.
(4) Collective bargaining involves negotiations between representatives of employers and government while individual bargaining involves negotiations between individual employees and their employers.

82. What is the definition of a trade union federation in Industrial Relations?
(1) An organisation that represents multiple trade unions in a particular country or region.
(2) An organisation that represents multiple employers in a particular country or region.
(3) An organisation that represents multiple suppliers in a particular country or region.
(4) An organisation that represents multiple customers in a particular country or region.

83. What is the definition of a strike in Industrial Relations?
(1) A work stoppage by employees to protest against their employer.
(2) A work stoppage by employers to protest against their employees.
(3) A work stoppage by customers to protest against their suppliers.
(4) A work stoppage by government officials.

84. What is the primary role of a conciliator in Industrial Relations?
(1) To promote the interests of employers over employees.
(2) To facilitate negotiations and reach a non-binding solution to a dispute.
(3) To promote the interests of employees over employers.
(4) To promote the interests of the government over both employees and employers.

85. What is the definition of a closed shop in Industrial Relations?
(1) A workplace where only union members can be employed.
(2) A workplace where only non-union members can be employed.
(3) A workplace where membership in a specific political party is required.
(4) A workplace where membership in a specific religious group is required.

86. What is the primary objective of industrial relations?
(1) To promote employer interests.
(2) To promote trade unions.
(3) To promote government interests.
(4) To manage the employment relationship.

87. What is collective bargaining?
(1) A process of negotiation between unions and management over the terms and conditions of employment.
(2) A process of negotiation between employees and customers.
(3) A process of negotiation between suppliers and customers.

(4) A process of negotiation between the government and employers.

88. What are the types of collective bargaining?

(1) Distributive, integrative, and attitudinal.
(2) Distributive, integrative and individual.
(3) Distributive, individual and cooperative.
(4) Distributive, integrative and competitive.

89. Who is the principal negotiator in collective bargaining?

(1) The employer
(2) The government
(3) Union representatives.
(4) Non-unionised employees

90. What is the most critical part of collective bargaining?

(1) Being able to influence the negotiators.
(3) Having a strong financial background.
(3) Having political connections.
(4) Identifying the problems and issues to be addressed.

91. Why is collective bargaining important?

(1) It helps to ensure that employees are treated fairly.
(2) It reduces the power of trade unions.
(3) It reduces the power of employees.
(4) It promotes the interests of employers.

92. What is workers' participation in management?

(1) The involvement of employees in decisions regarding their pay.
(2) The involvement of employees in decision making regarding customer service.
(3) The involvement of employees in decision making regarding their work environment, work organisation and work methods.
(4) The involvement of employees in decision making regarding marketing strategies.

93. What are the benefits of workers' participation in management?

(1) It leads to increased dependence on employers.
(2) It leads to increased job satisfaction, improved productivity and innovation.
(3) It leads to decreased job satisfaction, lowered productivity and innovation.
(4) It leads to increased competition and reduced profit margins.

94. What is the difference between joint consultation and workers' participation in management?

(1) Joint consultation is viewed more as an informational process while workers' participation in management is seen more as involving joint problem solving and consideration of alternatives.
(2) Joint consultation and workers' participation in management are the same thing.
(3) Joint consultation is viewed as involving joint problem solving while workers' participation in management is seen as more of an informational process.
(4) Workers' participation in management is seen as involving input from upper management.

95. What is the role of workers' representatives in workers' participation in management?

(1) To represent only the interests of employees without regard to management.
(2) To assert the rights of employees over management.
(3) To provide a link between employees and management and to work together in decision-making.
(4) To advise employees on how to protect themselves from management.

96. What is the role of works committees in workers' participation in management?

(1) To provide a forum for discussions between employees and management.
(2) To represent only the interests of employees without regard to management.
(3) To assert the rights of employees over management.
(4) To advise employees on how to protect themselves from management.

97. What is employee involvement?
(1) A process that encourages employees to participate more actively in decision-making.
(2) A process that discourages employees from participating in decision-making.
(3) A process that empowers only upper management.
(4) A process that favours employers over employees.

98. What is industrial democracy?
(1) A system of management that emphasizes the paramountcy of employer rights.
(2) A system of management that emphasizes the exercise of power by trade unions and employees over employers.
(3) A system of management that emphasizes government intervention in industrial relations.
(4) A system of management that emphasizes the equal participation of all employees in decision-making and problem-solving.

99. What is workers' control?
(1) A system where employers retain full control of the company.
(2) A system where employees have no say in decision making.
(3) A system where employees have proportional ownership and powers of control within a company.
(4) A system where the government has control over the company.

100. What is the difference between workers' control and workers' participation in management?
(1) Workers' control involves a higher degree of direct democratisation by workers in the enterprise than workers' participation in management.
(2) Workers' control and workers' participation in management are the same thing.
(3) Workers' control involves a higher degree of control by management.
(4) Workers' control involves a higher degree of input from upper management.

101. What is the difference between participative management and employee involvement?
(1) Participative management refers to management practices that discourage employee involvement in decision-making.
(2) Participative management refers to management practices that encourage employee involvement in decision-making.
(3) Employee involvement refers to management practices that encourage employee involvement in decision-making.
(4) Employee involvement refers to management practices that discourage employee involvement in decision-making.

102. What is the role of the Works Council in workers' participation in management?
(1) To represent the interests of employees regarding their working conditions.
(2) To represent only the interests of management.
(3) To represent the interests of the government.
(4) To represent the interests of the shareholders.

103. What is the role of the shop steward in workers' participation in management?
(1) To represent only the interests of management.
(2) To represent the interests of the government.
(3) To represent the interests of the shareholders.
(4) To represent the interests of the union's members in a particular workplace.

104. What is industrial conflict?
(1) A process by which the interests of management and employees collide.
(2) A process by which the interests of upper management and employees collide.
(3) A process by which the interests of management and shareholders collide.
(4) A process by which the interests of government and employees collide.

105. What is the role of the mediator in resolving industrial conflicts?

(1) To investigate the issues and make recommendations to the parties to a dispute.

(2) To impose solutions on the parties to a dispute.

(3) To represent the interests of management in a dispute.

(4) To represent the interests of employees in a dispute.

106. What is the role of the arbitrator in resolving industrial conflicts?

(1) To mediate between the parties to a dispute.

(2) To make a binding decision on the issues in dispute.

(3) To make a non-binding decision on the issues in dispute.

(4) To instruct the employees in a dispute.

107. What is the role of the conciliator in resolving industrial conflicts?

(1) To encourage the parties to come to a voluntary settlement.

(2) To impose a solution on the parties in dispute.

(3) To mediate between the parties in dispute.

(4) To instruct the employees in a dispute.

108. What is the role of the strike in industrial conflicts?

(1) A measure taken by management to force employees to accept an agreement.

(2) A measure taken by government to force an agreement between management and employees.

(3) A measure of last resort to force management to come to an agreement with the union.

(4) A measure taken by shareholders to force an agreement between management and employees.

109. What is the role of the lockout in industrial conflicts?

(1) A measure taken by managers to force employees to accept an agreement.

(2) A measure taken by employees to force management to accept an agreement.

(3) A measure taken by government to force an agreement between management and employees.

(4) A measure taken by shareholders to force an agreement between management and employees.

110. What are the benefits of workers' participation in management according to literature?

(1) Lower job satisfaction, decreased productivity, and worse working conditions.

(2) High employee turnover rates and high absenteeism rates.

(3) Increased conflict between management and employees.

(4) Higher job satisfaction, increased productivity, and better working conditions.

111. Assertion: Collective bargaining is the process of negotiation between unions and management over the terms and conditions of employment.

Reason: Collective bargaining is important as it reduces the power of employees.

(1) Both assertion and reason are true, but the reason is not the correct explanation of the assertion.

(2) Both assertion and reason are true, and the reason is the correct explanation of the assertion.

(3) Both assertion and reason are false.

(4) Assertion is true, but the reason is false.

112. Assertion: Participation of employees in management leads to increased job satisfaction, improved productivity and innovation.

Reason: Participation of employees in management does not lead to any positive outcomes.

(1) Both assertion and reason are false.

(2) Assertion is true, but the reason is false.

(3) Both assertion and reason are true, but the reason is not the correct explanation of the assertion.

(4) Both assertion and reason are true, and the reason is the correct explanation of the assertion.

113. Assertion: The role of workers' representatives in workers' participation in management is to represent only the interests of employees.

Reason: Workers' representatives are not concerned with the interests of the organisation.

(1) Both assertion and reason are false.
(2) Assertion is false, but the reason is true.
(3) Both assertion and reason are true, but the reason is not the correct explanation of the assertion.
(4) Both assertion and reason are true, and the reason is the correct explanation of the assertion.

114. Assertion: Industrial democracy emphasizes the equal participation of all employees in decision-making and problem-solving.

Reason: Industrial democracy is a system of management that emphasizes the exercise of power by trade unions and employees over employers.

(1) Both assertion and reason are false.
(2) Assertion is true, but the reason is false.
(3) Both assertion and reason are true, but the reason is not the correct explanation of the assertion.
(4) Both assertion and reason are true, and the reason is the correct explanation of the assertion.

115. Assertion: Workers' control does not involve the presence of management.

Reason: Workers' control involves a higher degree of control by upper management.

(1) Both assertion and reason are false.
(2) Assertion is false, but the reason is true.
(3) Both assertion and reason are true, but the reason is not the correct explanation of the assertion.
(4) Both assertion and reason are true, and the reason is the correct explanation of the assertion.

116. What is a grievance?

(1) A formal complaint made by an employer about an employee's work performance.
(2) A formal complaint made by a union about management decisions.
(3) A formal complaint made by a customer about the quality of a product.
(4) A formal complaint made by an employee about their work situation.

117. What is the first step in the grievance handling process?

(1) Informal discussion between the employee and their immediate supervisor.
(2) Filing of a formal written complaint.
(3) Mediation by a third-party neutral.
(4) Issuance of a disciplinary action.

118. Who is responsible for resolving grievances?

(1) Management and union representatives through joint discussion and cooperation.
(2) The employee who filed the grievance.
(3) The immediate supervisor of the employee who filed the grievance.
(4) A third-party neutral appointed by the government.

119. What is the purpose of a grievance procedure?

(1) To provide a way for employees to file frivolous complaints without repercussions.
(2) To provide a fair and effective method for resolving disputes between employees and management.
(3) To provide a way for management to ignore employees' complaints.
(4) To provide a way for unions to exert control over management decisions.

120. What is the final step in the grievance procedure?

(1) Arbitration by an impartial third-party neutral.
(2) Mediation by a government-appointed mediator.

(3) Disciplinary action against the employee who filed the grievance.
(4) Termination of the employee who filed the grievance.

121. What is disciplinary action?
(1) The process of correcting behaviour that violates company policy through informal warning.
(2) The process of correcting behaviour that violates labour láws through formal punishment.
(3) The process of correcting behaviour that violates company policy through formal punishment.
(4) The process of correcting behaviour that violates labour laws through informal warning.

122. What is the difference between progressive discipline and corrective discipline?
(1) Progressive discipline is a non-punitive action designed to correct behaviour while corrective discipline is a series of increasingly severe penalties.
(2) Progressive discipline is a series of increasingly severe penalties while corrective discipline is a non-punitive action designed to correct behaviour.
(3) Progressive discipline and corrective discipline are the same thing.
(4) Progressive discipline is used for minor offenses while corrective discipline is used for major offenses.

123. What is the purpose of a code of conduct?
(1) To establish ethical principles and behaviour standards for employees.
(2) To establish behaviour standards for management.
(3) To establish behaviour standards for unions.
(4) To establish behaviour standards for customers.

124. What is the difference between a code of conduct and a code of ethics?
(1) A code of conduct sets behavioural standards while a code of ethics sets broader ethical principles.
(2) A code of ethics sets behavioural standards while a code of conduct sets broader ethical principles.
(3) A code of conduct and a code of ethics are the same thing.
(4) A code of conduct is only applicable to management while a code of ethics is applicable to all employees.

125. What is the purpose of an ethics committee?
(1) To establish and enforce a code of conduct.
(2) To establish policies and procedures for disciplinary action.
(3) To serve as a third-party neutral in resolving disputes.
(4) To establish and enforce a code of ethics.

126. What factors should be considered when determining the appropriate disciplinary action?
(1) The severity of the offense, the employee's past record and mitigating circumstances.
(2) The severity of the offense, the employee's age, and the employee's gender.
(3) The severity of the offense, the length of the employee's tenure and mitigating circumstances.
(4) The severity of the offense and the recommendation of the employee's immediate supervisor.

127. What is the difference between dismissal and termination?
(1) Dismissal is the termination of employment for cause while termination is the end of employment due to illness, retirement, or other reasons.
(2) Dismissal is the termination of employment due to illness, retirement, or other reasons while termination is the end of employment for cause.
(3) Dismissal and termination are the same thing.
(4) Dismissal is the termination of employment for disciplinary reasons while termination is the end of employment due to the employee finding a new job.

128. What is the purpose of an alternative dispute resolution mechanism?
(1) To provide a less confrontational and time-consuming way of resolving disputes between employees and management.
(2) To provide a way for management to exert control over employees.
(3) To provide a way for employees to file frivolous complaints without repercussions.
(4) To provide a way for unions to exert control over management decisions.

129. What is the most common alternative dispute resolution mechanism used in labour relations?
(1) Arbitration by a third-party neutral.
(2) Mediation by a third-party neutral.
(3) Litigation in court.
(4) Disciplinary action against the employee who filed the complaint.

130. What is the objective of an alternative dispute resolution mechanism?
(1) To impose a solution on one of the parties.
(2) To find a way to avoid dealing with the complaint.
(3) To arrive at a mutually acceptable solution.
(4) To provide a way for one of the parties to assert control over the other.

131. What is the purpose of a code of conduct?
(1) To establish ethical principles and behaviour standards for employees.
(2) To establish behaviour standards for management.
(3) To establish behaviour standards for unions.
(4) To establish behaviour standards for customers.

132. What is the difference between a code of conduct and a code of ethics?
(1) A code of ethics sets behavioural standards while a code of conduct sets broader ethical principles.
(2) A code of conduct and a code of ethics are the same thing.
(3) A code of conduct sets behavioural standards while a code of ethics sets broader ethical principles.
(4) A code of conduct is only applicable to management while a code of ethics is applicable to all employees.

133. What is the purpose of an ethics committee?
(1) To establish and enforce a code of ethics.
(2) To establish and enforce a code of conduct.
(3) To establish policies and procedures for disciplinary action.
(4) To serve as a third-party neutral in resolving disputes.

134. What is the difference between been open and closed ethical systems?
(1) An open ethical system emphasizes ethical decision-making based on adherence to established rules and regulations while a closed ethical system emphasizes ethical decision-making based on personal values.
(2) An open ethical system emphasizes ethical decision-making based on personal values while a closed ethical system emphasizes ethical decision-making based on adherence to established rules and regulations.
(3) Open ethical systems and closed ethical systems are the same thing.
(4) An open ethical system emphasizes ethical decision-making based on the input of stakeholders while a closed ethical system is focused solely on the interests of management.

135. Why is ethical leadership important?
(1) Ethical leadership fosters a culture of ethical behaviour within the organisation.
(2) Ethical leadership is not important in a modern business environment.
(3) Ethical leadership emphasizes the interests of customers over those of employees.

(4) Ethical leadership emphasizes the interests of shareholders over those of employees.

136. What is the purpose of a whistleblower policy?

(1) To provide employees with a means to report misconduct within the organisation without fear of retaliation.

(2) To provide management with a means to monitor employee behaviour.

(3) To provide unions with a means to assert control over management decisions.

(4) To provide customers with a means to report issues with products or services.

137. What is the objective of a stakeholder analysis?

(1) To identify and prioritise management interests and influence in order to make informed decisions.

(2) To identify and prioritise union interests and influence in order to make informed decisions.

(3) To identify and prioritise stakeholders' interests and influence in order to make informed decisions.

(4) To identify and prioritise customer interests and influence in order to make informed decisions.

138. What is the difference between positive whistleblowing and negative whistleblowing?

(1) Positive whistleblowing refers to reporting misconduct to prevent it from happening while negative whistleblowing refers to reporting misconduct after it has occurred.

(2) Positive whistleblowing refers to reporting misconduct after it has occurred while negative whistleblowing refers to reporting misconduct to prevent it from happening.

(3) Positive whistleblowing and negative whistleblowing are the same thing.

(4) Positive whistleblowing refers to reporting misconduct when it benefits the employee while negative whistleblowing refers to reporting misconduct when it harms the employee.

139. What is the difference between deontological ethics and consequentialist ethics?

(1) Deontological ethics emphasizes the consequences of actions while consequentialist ethics emphasizes adherence to moral principles and rules.

(2) Deontological ethics and consequentialist ethics are the same thing.

(3) Deontological ethics emphasizes the interests of shareholders while consequentialist ethics emphasizes the interests of employees.

(4) Deontological ethics emphasizes adherence to moral principles and rules while consequentialist ethics emphasizes the consequences of actions.

140. What is the role of corporate social responsibility in a code of conduct?

(1) To ensure that the organisation is accountable for its impact on society and the environment.

(2) To ensure that the organisation maximizes profits at all costs.

(3) To ensure that the needs of employees are met before the needs of customers.

(4) To ensure that the organisation is in compliance with all relevant labour laws.

141. What is a black strike?

(1) A strike that involves employees refusing to perform their job duties

(2) A strike that seeks to reduce productivity and force the employer to negotiate

(3) A strike that involves employees wearing black clothing as a symbol of protest or mourning

(4) A strike that seeks to enforce workplace safety regulations

142. Assertion: A code of ethics is more comprehensive than a code of conduct.

Reason: A code of ethics sets out the ethical philosophy of the organisation.

(1) Both assertion and reason are true, and the reason is the correct explanation of the assertion.
(2) Both assertion and reason are true but the reason is not the correct explanation of the assertion.
(3) Assertion is true but reason is false.
(4) Assertion is false but reason is true.

143. Assertion: The purpose of a whistleblower policy is to prevent employees from reporting misconduct within the organisation.

Reason: A whistleblower policy protects employees who report misconduct from retaliation.

(1) Both assertion and reason are false.
(2) Assertion is false but reason is true.
(3) Both assertion and reason are true but the reason is not the correct explanation of the assertion.
(4) Both assertion and reason are true, and the reason is the correct explanation of the assertion.

144. Assertion: Progressive discipline is a series of increasingly severe disciplinary penalties.

Reason: Corrective discipline is a non-punitive action designed to modify employee behaviour.

(1) Both assertion and reason are true, and the reason is the correct explanation of the assertion.
(2) Both assertion and reason are true but the reason is not the correct explanation of the assertion.
(3) Assertion is true but reason is false.
(4) Assertion is false but reason is true.

145. Assertion: Ethical leadership fosters a culture of ethical behaviour within the organisation.

Reason: Ethical leadership promotes the interests of management over the interests of employees.

(1) Both assertion and reason are false.
(2) Assertion is true but reason is false.
(3) Both assertion and reason are true but the reason is not the correct explanation of the assertion.
(4) Both assertion and reason are true, and the reason is the correct explanation of the assertion.

146. What is industrial relations?
(1) The study of economics in the industrial sector
(2) The study of labour relations within the workplace
(3) The study of safety and security in the workplace
(4) The study of production processes within the workplace

147. What is an emotional strike?
(1) Legal strike, certified strike, white strike, bio data strike
(2) Legal strike, certified strike, wildcat strike, bio data strike
(3) Legal strike, uncertified strike, emotional strike, black strike
(4) Legal strike, wildcat strike, uncertified strike, bio data strike

148. Which of the following is a factor that has changed the industrial relations scenario?
(1) Increased unionisation
(2) Decreased outsourcing
(3) Decreased globalisation
(4) Increased job security

149. What is employee engagement?
(1) A measure of employee productivity
(2) A measure of employee satisfaction and commitment to the organisation
(3) A measure of employee absenteeism
(4) A measure of employee turnover

150. What is human resource management?
(1) The management of physical resources within an organisation
(2) The management of financial resources within an organisation
(3) The management of personnel within an organisation
(4) The management of technology within an organisation

151. What is workforce diversity?
(1) The presence of a wide variety of departmental silos

(2) The presence of a wide variety of employees from different backgrounds

(3) The presence of a wide variety of corporate cultures

(4) The presence of a wide variety of employment contracts

152. What is the difference between employee relations and industrial relations?

(1) Employee relations is a subcategory of industrial relations that deals with the relationship between employees and employers.

(2) Industrial relations is a subcategory of employee relations that deals with the relationship between employees and employers.

(3) Employee relations and industrial relations are interchangeable terms.

(4) Employee relations is a term used by unions to describe their interaction with management.

153. What is the impact of information technology on industrial relations?

(1) It has increased the use of contract workers and temporary employees

(2) It has decreased the use of automation and robotics

(3) It has increased the power of unions

(4) It has decreased the need for employers to pay attention to industrial relations

154. What is the difference between industrial democracy and employee participation?

(1) Industrial democracy involves employee representation on the board of directors while employee participation involves employees having a say in the management of the organisation.

(2) Industrial democracy involves employee participation in the management of the organisation while employee participation involves employee representation on the board of directors.

(3) Industrial democracy is a term used by unions to describe their interaction with management while employee participation is a term used by employers to describe their interaction with employees.

(4) Industrial democracy and employee participation are interchangeable terms.

155. What is collective bargaining?

(1) The negotiation of employment contracts between individual employees and employers

(2) The negotiation of employment contracts between a group of employees and employers

(3) The negotiation of employment contracts between a single union representative and employers

(4) The negotiation of employment contracts between the government and employers

156. What is the difference between wage and salary?

(1) Wage is paid per hour worked while salary is paid on a fixed basis.

(2) Salary is paid per hour worked while wage is paid on a fixed basis.

(3) Wage and salary are interchangeable terms.

(4) Wage and salary are paid on a percentage basis of revenue generated.

157. What is the minimum wage?

(1) The lowest wage an employer can pay their employees as mandated by law

(2) A wage set by unions in a collective bargaining agreement

(3) A wage set by the government for high skilled workers

(4) A wage set by the government for low skilled workers

158. What is the purpose of a union?

(1) To represent the interests of individual employees in matters of employment

(2) To represent the interests of employers in matters of employment

(3) To represent the interests of a group of employees in matters of employment

(4) To represent the interests of the government in matters of employment

159. What is the difference between a union shop and an agency shop?
(1) In a union shop, all employees must be members of the union while in an agency shop, employees are required to pay union dues but not become union members.
(2) In a union shop, employees are required to pay union dues but not become union members while in an agency shop, all employees must be members of the union.
(3) Union shop and agency shop are interchangeable terms.
(4) In a union shop, employees are paid a higher wage than in an agency shop.

160. What is the difference between a closed shop and an open shop?
(1) In a closed shop, all employees must be members of the union while in an open shop, employees are not required to join the union.
(2) In a closed shop, employees are not required to join the union while in an open shop, all employees must be members of the union.
(3) Closed shop and open shop are interchangeable terms.
(4) In a closed shop, employees are paid a higher wage than in an open shop.

161. What is an employers' organisation?
(1) An organisation representing the interests of individual employers.
(2) An organisation representing the interests of a group of employers.
(3) An organisation representing the interests of individual employees.
(4) An organisation representing the interests of a group of employees.

162. What is the purpose of an employers' organisation?
(1) To promote the interests of individual employers
(2) To promote the interests of a group of employers
(3) To promote the interests of individual employees
(4) To promote the interests of a group of employees

163. What is the difference between an employers' association and a trade union?
(1) Employers' associations represent the interests of employers while trade unions represent the interests of employees.
(2) Employers' associations and trade unions are the same thing.
(3) Employers' associations represent the interests of employees while trade unions represent the interests of employers.
(4) Employers' associations and trade unions represent the interests of individuals and not groups.

164. What is the difference between an employers' association and a professional association?
(1) Employers' associations represent the interests of employers while professional associations represent the interests of employees.
(2) Employers' associations represent the interests of a group of employers while professional associations represent the interests of a group of employees.
(3) Employers' associations represent the interests of individual employers while professional associations represent the interests of individual employees.
(4) Employers' associations and professional associations are the same thing.

165. What is the difference between a national employers' organisation and an international employers' organisation?
(1) National employers' organisations represent the interests of employers within a particular country while international employers' organisations represent the interests of employers across multiple countries.

(2) National employers' organisations and international employers' organisations represent the same thing.
(3) National employers' organisations represent the interests of employers across multiple countries while international employers' organisations represent the interests of employers within a particular country.
(4) National employers' organisations are not concerned with the interests of employers outside their country while international employers' organisations are concerned with the interests of employers within a particular country.

166. What is the role of an employers' organisation?
(1) To represent the interests of employers in matters of employment relations.
(2) To negotiate employment contracts with individual employees.
(3) To represent the interests of individual employers in matters of employment relations.
(4) To negotiate employment contracts with groups of employees.

167. What is a trade association?
(1) An association of employers in a particular industry or trade.
(2) An association of employees in a particular industry or trade
(3) An association of employers and employees in a particular industry or trade
(4) An association of the government and industry in a particular industry or trade

168. What is the difference between an employers' organisation and a trade association?
(1) Employers' organisations represent the interests of employers across different industries while trade associations represent the interests of employers within a particular industry.
(2) Employers' organisations and trade associations represent the same thing.
(3) Employers' organisations represent the interests of individual employers while trade associations represent the interests of groups of employers.
(4) Employers' organisations represent the interests of groups of employers while trade associations represent the interests of individual employers.

169. What is the role of a business lobby?
(1) To represent the interests of business in matters of public policy and government regulation.
(2) To represent the interests of employees in matters of public policy and government regulation.
(3) To represent the interests of individual employers in matters of public policy and government regulation.
(4) To represent the interests of the government in matters of public policy and government regulation.

170. What is the difference between a business lobby and an employers' organisation?
(1) Business lobbies represent the interests of business in matters of public policy and government regulation while employers' organisations represent the interests of employers in matters of employment relations.
(2) Business lobbies and employers' organisations represent the same thing.
(3) Business lobbies represent the interests of employees in matters of public policy and government regulation while employers' organisations represent the interests of employers in matters of employment relations.
(4) Business lobbies and employers' organisations represent the interests of the government in matters of public policy and government regulation.

171. Assertion: Industrial democracy refers to the participation of employees in the management of the organisation.

Reason: Employee participation refers to the representation of employees on the board of directors.

(1) Both assertion and reason are false.
(2) Assertion is true but reason is false.
(3) Both assertion and reason are true but the reason is not the correct explanation of the assertion.
(4) Both assertion and reason are true, and the reason is the correct explanation of the assertion.

172. Assertion: Industrial relations refer to the relationship between employees and employers within the workplace.
Reason: Industrial relations are not impacted by changes in technology.
(1) Both assertion and reason are false.
(2) Assertion is true but reason is false.
(3) Both assertion and reason are true, but the reason is not the correct explanation of the assertion.
(4) Both assertion and reason are true, and the reason is the correct explanation of the assertion.

173. Assertion: The purpose of an employers' organisation is to promote the interests of individual employers.
Reason: Employers' organisations are not concerned with employee rights.
(1) Both assertion and reason are false.
(2) Assertion is true but reason is false.
(3) Both assertion and reason are true but the reason is not the correct explanation of the assertion.
(4) Both assertion and reason are true, and the reason is the correct explanation of the assertion.

174. Assertion: The minimum wage is the lowest wage an employer can pay their employees as mandated by law.
Reason: The minimum wage varies from industry to industry.
(1) Both assertion and reason are false.
(2) Assertion is true but reason is false.
(3) Both assertion and reason are true but the reason is not the correct explanation of the assertion.
(4) Both assertion and reason are true, and the reason is the correct explanation of the assertion.

175. Assertion: Collective bargaining is the negotiation of employment contracts between a group of employees and their employer.
Reason: In a collective bargaining agreement, employees agree to waive their right to strike.
(1) Both assertion and reason are false.
(2) Assertion is true but reason is false.
(3) Both assertion and reason are true but the reason is not the correct explanation of the assertion.
(4) Both assertion and reason are true, and the reason is the correct explanation of the assertion.

176. What is a trade union?
(1) An organisation of employers that represents their interests
(2) An organisation of employees that represents their interests
(3) An organisation of employees that represents their employers' interests
(4) An organisation of employers and employees that represents their collective interests

177. What is the main objective of a trade union?
(1) To promote the interests of individual employees
(2) To promote the interests of the employer
(3) To promote the interests of a group of employees
(4) To promote the interests of the government

178. Who is the founder of the trade union movement in India?
(1) Mahatma Gandhi
(2) Pandit Jawaharlal Nehru
(3) N.M. Joshi
(4) Sardar Vallabhbhai Patel

179. What is the difference between a trade union and a labor union?
(1) There is no difference; the terms are interchangeable

(2) A trade union represents workers in a specific trade or industry, while a labor union represents workers across multiple trades or industries
(3) A labor union represents only skilled workers, while a trade union represents only unskilled workers
(4) A trade union represents only unionised workers, while a labor union represents non-unionised workers

180. What is the role of a shop steward in a trade union?
(1) To represent the interests of the employer
(2) To represent the interests of the government
(3) To represent the interests of the employees
(4) To manage the daily operations of the trade union

181. What is collective bargaining?
(1) The process of negotiating salary and benefits for a single employee
(2) The process of negotiating salary and benefits for a group of employees
(3) The process of negotiating salary and benefits for the employer
(4) The process of negotiating work hours for a group of employees

182. What is a strike?
(1) A work stoppage by employees to protest poor working conditions or pay
(2) A work stoppage by employers to protest poor working conditions or pay
(3) An agreement between employers and employees on working conditions or pay
(4) An agreement between employers and employees to increase productivity

183. What is a lockout?
(1) A work stoppage by employees to protest poor working conditions or pay
(2) A work stoppage by employers to protest poor working conditions or pay
(3) An agreement between employers and employees on working conditions or pay
(4) An agreement between employers and employees to increase productivity

184. What is a work to rule?
(1) A work stoppage by employees to protest poor working conditions or pay
(2) A work stoppage by employers to protest poor working conditions or pay
(3) A work action where employees strictly follow all safety rules and regulations, slowing down productivity
(4) An agreement between employers and employees on working conditions or pay

185. What is a picket line?
(1) A line of employees who refuse to work due to a labor dispute
(2) A line of employer representatives who refuse to negotiate with employees
(3) A group of people who protest outside of a workplace to support employees who are on strike or locked out
(4) A group of people who protest outside of a workplace to support the employer

186. What is the difference between closed shop and union shop?
(1) In a closed shop, only union members can be hired, while in a union shop, employees must become union members after hiring
(2) In a closed shop, all employees must be union members, while in a union shop, only some employees must be union members
(3) Closed shop and union shop are interchangeable terms
(4) In a closed shop, all employees must be unionised, while in a union shop, only some employees must be unionised

187. Who is a blue-collar worker?
(1) An employee who works in a white-collar profession
(2) An employee who works in an office or administrative profession
(3) An employee who works in a manual labor profession

(4) An employee who works in a managerial profession

188. Who is a white-collar worker?

(1) An employee who works in a blue-collar profession
(2) An employee who works in an office or administrative profession
(3) An employee who works in a manual labor profession
(4) An employee who works in a managerial profession

189. What is a right-to-work law?

(1) A law that prohibits unions from negotiating collective bargaining agreements with employers
(2) A law that requires unions to represent all employees, regardless of whether or not they are union members
(3) A law that prohibits union membership from being a requirement for employment
(4) A law that prohibits employees from striking or picketing

190. What is a union security agreement?

(1) An agreement between an employer and a union that requires employees to become union members within a certain period of time after being hired
(2) An agreement between an employer and a union that allows employees to opt out of joining the union
(3) An agreement between an employer and a union that requires all employees to pay union dues, regardless of whether or not they are union members
(4) An agreement between an employer and a union that prohibits employees from striking or picketing

191. What is a labor contract?

(1) An agreement between an employer and employees that establishes working conditions and pay rates
(2) An agreement between an employer and a union that establishes working conditions and pay rates
(3) An agreement between an employer and employees that prohibits union membership
(4) An agreement between an employer and a union that prohibits employees from striking or picketing

192. What is collective action?

(1) An action taken by an individual employee to address a workplace issue
(2) An action taken by a group of employees to address a workplace issue
(3) An action taken by an employer to address a workplace issue
(4) An action taken by the government to address a workplace issue

193. What is a labor dispute?

(1) A dispute between an employer and employees over working conditions or pay
(2) A dispute between an employer and a union over working conditions or pay
(3) A dispute between employees over working conditions or pay
(4) A dispute between the government and employees over working conditions or pay

194. What is an industrial action?

(1) Any action taken by an employee or union that hinders productivity or operations
(2) Any action taken by an employer that hinders productivity or operations
(3) A collective action taken by employees or unions to address workplace issues, such as strikes or work to rules
(4) An agreement between employers and unions on working conditions and pay

195. What is a wildcat strike?

(1) A strike that is not authorised by the union
(2) A strike that is authorised by both the union and employer
(3) A strike that is organised by the employer
(4) A strike that is organised by the government

196. What is job targeting?
(1) A union activity that involves pressuring employers to hire union members for specific jobs
(2) A union activity that involves pressuring employers to promote union members to higher-paying jobs
(3) An employer activity that involves pressuring unions to represent only its workers
(4) A job search strategy that involves targeting specific employers for potential jobs

197. What is the difference between a union contract and an employment contract?
(1) A union contract is between an employer and the union, while an employment contract is between an individual employee and the employer
(2) A union contract is between an individual employee and the employer, while an employment contract is between the union and the employer
(3) A union contract and an employment contract are interchangeable terms
(4) A union contract and an employment contract are not legally binding

198. What is a grievance procedure?
(1) A procedure used by an employer to terminate an employee's employment
(2) A procedure used by an employee to file a complaint against the employer
(3) A procedure used by a union to negotiate a collective bargaining agreement with an employer
(4) A procedure used by an employer to train new employees

199. What is a labor standards act?
(1) A law that establishes minimum working conditions for employees, such as hours of work and overtime pay
(2) A law that prohibits unions from negotiating collective bargaining agreements with employers
(3) A law that requires employees to become union members within a certain period of time after being hired
(4) A law that prohibits employees from striking or picketing

200. What is a certification mark?
(1) A mark that shows that a product or service has met certain quality standards
(2) A mark that shows that a union has been certified by the government to represent a group of employees
(3) A mark that shows that an employer has met certain labor standards
(4) A mark that shows that a company is unionised

201. **Assertion:** A trade union is an organisation of employees that represents their interests.
Reason: A trade union promotes the interests of individual employees, rather than a group of employees.
(1) Both assertion and reason are false.
(2) Assertion is true but reason is false.
(3) Both assertion and reason are true but the reason is not the correct explanation of the assertion.
(4) Both assertion and reason are true, and the reason is the correct explanation of the assertion.

202. **Assertion:** A lockout is a work stoppage by employees to protest poor working conditions or pay.
Reason: A lockout is a work stoppage by employers to protest poor working conditions or pay.
(1) Both assertion and reason are false.
(2) Assertion is false but reason is true.
(3) Both assertion and reason are true but the reason is not the correct explanation of the assertion.
(4) Both assertion and reason are true, and the reason is the correct explanation of the assertion.

203. **Assertion:** Collective bargaining is the process of negotiating salary and benefits for a single employee.

Reason: Collective bargaining is the process of negotiating salary and benefits for a group of employees.
(1) Both assertion and reason are false.
(2) Assertion is true but reason is false.
(3) Both assertion and reason are true but the reason is not the correct explanation of the assertion.
(4) Both assertion and reason are true, and the reason is the correct explanation of the assertion.

204. **Assertion:** A union security agreement requires all employees to pay union dues regardless of whether or not they are union members.
Reason: A union security agreement requires all employees to be union members regardless of whether or not they want to be.
(1) Both assertion and reason are false.
(2) Assertion is false but reason is true.
(3) Both assertion and reason are true but the reason is not the correct explanation of the assertion.
(4) Both assertion and reason are true, and the reason is the correct explanation of the assertion.

205. **Assertion:** A wildcat strike is a strike that is not authorised by the union.
Reason: A wildcat strike is a strike that is authorised by the employer.
(1) Both assertion and reason are false.
(2) Assertion is true but reason is false.
(3) Both assertion and reason are true but the reason is not the correct explanation of the assertion.
(4) Both assertion and reason are true, and the reason is the correct explanation of the assertion.

206. What is the main objective of a trade union?
(1) To promote the interests of individual employees
(2) To promote the interests of the employer
(3) To promote the interests of a group of employees
(4) To promote the interests of the government

207. What is the role of a shop steward in a trade union?
(1) To represent the interests of the employer
(2) To represent the interests of the government
(3) To represent the interests of the employees
(4) To manage the daily operations of the trade union

208. What is collective bargaining?
(1) The process of negotiating salary and benefits for a single employee
(2) The process of negotiating salary and benefits for a group of employees
(3) The process of negotiating salary and benefits for the employer
(4) The process of negotiating work hours for a group of employees

209. What is a strike?
(1) A work stoppage by employees to protest poor working conditions or pay
(2) A work stoppage by employers to protest poor working conditions or pay
(3) An agreement between employers and employees on working conditions or pay
(4) An agreement between employers and employees to increase productivity

210. What is a lockout?
(1) A work stoppage by employees to protest poor working conditions or pay
(2) A work stoppage by employers to protest poor working conditions or pay
(3) An agreement between employers and employees on working conditions or pay
(4) An agreement between employers and employees to increase productivity

211. What is a white strike?
(1) A strike that involves employees refusing to perform their job duties

(2) A strike that involves employees engaging in public protests or demonstrations
(3) A strike that involves employees wearing white clothing as a symbol of protest or solidarity
(4) A strike that seeks to enforce workplace safety regulations

212. What is a certification strike?
(1) A strike that is called by the government
(2) A strike that is organised by the union leadership
(3) A strike that is called by employees without union approval
(4) A strike that seeks to compel an employer to recognise and bargain with a particular union

213. What is the purpose of a reverse strike?
(1) To show support for workers who are already on strike
(2) To force the employer to accept union demands
(3) To reduce productivity and force the employer to negotiate
(4) To maximise profits for shareholders

214. What is a go-slow strike?
(1) A strike that involves employees refusing to work or perform their job duties
(2) A strike that involves employees slowing down the pace of work or deliberately reducing productivity
(3) A strike that involves employees leaving work early or arriving late
(4) A strike that involves employees engaging in public protests or demonstrations

215. What is a sit-in strike?
(1) A strike that involves employees refusing to leave a particular area of the workplace
(2) A strike that is limited to a single department or location
(3) A strike that involves employees from multiple industries or sectors
(4) A strike that involves employees refusing to work or perform their job duties

216. What is a sympathy strike?
(1) A strike that is called by employees to show support for workers who are already on strike
(2) A strike that is called by employees in response to a specific workplace issue
(3) A strike that is called by the government
(4) A strike that is limited to a single department or location

217. What is a wildcat strike?
(1) A strike that is organised by the union leadership
(2) A strike that is initiated by employees without union approval
(3) A strike that is called by the government
(4) A strike that is limited to a single department or location

218. What is a general strike?
(1) A strike that targets a specific employer or industry
(2) A strike that involves employees from multiple industries or sectors
(3) A strike that is illegal
(4) A strike that is limited to a single department or location

219. What is a bio-data strike?
(1) Legal strike, certified strike, white strike, bio data strike
(2) Legal strike, certified strike, wildcat strike, bio data strike
(3) Legal strike, wildcat strike, uncertified strike, bio data strike
(4) Legal strike, uncertified strike, emotional strike, black strike

220. What is the purpose of a union grievance?
(1) To appeal a decision or action by an employer that violates the collective bargaining agreement
(2) To initiate a strike or other form of labor action
(3) To promote the interests of the union leadership
(4) To generate public awareness around a particular labor issue

221. What is the purpose of a sympathy strike?
(1) To show support for workers who are already on strike
(2) To promote the interests of the employer
(3) To reduce competition between companies
(4) To maximise profits for shareholders

222. Which of the following is not a type of strike action?
(1) Picketing (2) Work-to-rule
(3) Slowdown (4) Emotional

223. What is the purpose of a work-to-contract campaign?
(1) To maximise profits for employers
(2) To promote better working conditions and wages
(3) To reduce the number of employees in the workplace
(4) To exert more bargaining power during negotiations while technically following the rules of the contract

224. Which of the following is not a potential benefit of union representation for workers?
(1) Improved wages and working conditions
(2) Access to financial services such as loans and insurance
(3) Reduced taxes and fees
(4) Reduced job security and stability

225. What is the purpose of union organising?
(1) To promote the interests of the union leadership
(2) To increase union membership and bargaining power
(3) To reduce competition between companies
(4) To maximise profits for employers

226. What is the purpose of a work-to-rule campaign?
(1) To promote better working conditions and wages
(2) To maximise profits for employers
(3) To reduce the number of employees in the workplace
(4) To reduce productivity and exert more bargaining power during negotiations

227. What is a labor contract?
(1) An agreement between an employer and employees that establishes working conditions and pay rates
(2) An agreement between an employer and a union that establishes working conditions and pay rates
(3) An agreement between an employer and employees that prohibits union membership
(4) An agreement between an employer and a union that prohibits employees from striking or picketing

228. What is collective agreement?
(1) A formal agreement between an employer and a trade union that specifies the terms and conditions of employment for a group of employees
(2) An agreement between employers and employees on working conditions or pay
(3) An agreement between employers and employees to increase productivity
(4) An agreement between employers and employees regarding employee benefits

229. Who is a casual worker?
(1) An employee who works on a permanent basis
(2) An employee who works on a temporary or as-needed basis
(3) An employee who works in a managerial profession
(4) An employee who works in a white-collar profession

230. Who is a contract worker?
(1) An employee who works on a permanent basis
(2) An employee who works on a temporary or as-needed basis under a contract
(3) An employee who works in a managerial profession
(4) An employee who works in a white-collar profession

231. What is an apprenticeship?
(1) A program that provides on-the-job training for a skilled trade or craft
(2) A program that provides on-the-job training for a managerial profession
(3) A program that provides on-the-job training for a white-collar profession
(4) A program that provides on-the-job training for an unskilled labor job

232. What are the benefits of joining a trade union?
(1) Increased job security, better pay and working conditions, and access to collective bargaining
(2) Decreased job security, decreased pay and working conditions, and limited access to collective bargaining
(3) Increased job security, lower pay, and limited access to collective bargaining
(4) Decreased job security, better pay and working conditions, and access to collective bargaining

233. What is the difference between a union member and a non-union member?
(1) A union member is an employee who belongs to a trade union, while a non-union member is an employee who does not belong to a trade union
(2) A union member is an employer who belongs to a trade union, while a non-union member is an employer who does not belong to a trade union
(3) Union members and non-union members have no difference in their work status or benefits
(4) Union members and non-union members have different work status, but the same benefits

234. What is union density?
(1) The percentage of employees who are union members in a particular industry or sector
(2) The percentage of employers who are union members in a particular industry or sector
(3) The percentage of employees who are union members across all industries and sectors
(4) The percentage of employers who are union members across all industries and sectors

235. What is the role of the government in regulating trade unions?
(1) The government provides legal regulation of union activities, including recognition of unions and negotiation and enforcement of collective agreements
(2) The government provides financial support to trade unions to help them achieve their objectives
(3) The government prohibits trade unions from forming or engaging in bargaining and other activities
(4) The government is not involved in regulating trade unions in any way

236. What is the difference between compulsory recognition and voluntary recognition of a trade union?
(1) Compulsory recognition is mandated by law, while voluntary recognition is based on an employer's willingness to recognise a trade union.
(2) Both compulsory recognition and voluntary recognition are the same.
(3) Voluntary recognition is mandated by law, while compulsory recognition is based on an employer's willingness to recognise a trade union.
(4) Compulsory recognition is provided to an employer, while voluntary recognition is provided to a trade union.

237. What is the Employee State Insurance Act 1948?
(1) An act that provides for the provision of medical benefits to employees in case of sickness, maternity etc.
(2) An act that regulates employee-employer relations in India
(3) An act that regulates union activities in India

(4) An act that regulates government-employee relations

238. What is the difference between a union and a federation of trade unions?

(1) A union represents employees of a single organisation, while a federation of trade unions represents employees across multiple organisations

(2) A union represents only skilled workers, while a federation of trade unions represents only unskilled workers

(3) A union represents employers and employees, while a federation of trade unions represents only employees

(4) A union represents employers across a specific location, while a federation of trade unions represents only entrepreneurs

239. What is the difference between consensual bargaining and adversarial bargaining?

(1) Consensual bargaining involves both parties working together to find a mutually acceptable solution, while adversarial bargaining involves each party taking a firm stance and trying to "win" the negotiation

(2) Consensual bargaining involves negotiation by an individual, while adversarial bargaining involves negotiation by a group

(3) Consensual bargaining involves oral negotiation, while adversarial bargaining involves communication through written documentation

(4) Consensual bargaining is mandated by law, while adversarial bargaining is left to the discretion of the employers

240. What is the role of an arbitrator in the collective bargaining process?

(1) An arbitrator is a third party who assists in the development of the collective bargaining agreement

(2) An arbitrator is a representative of the union who negotiates with the employer

(3) An arbitrator is a representative of the employer who negotiates with the union

(4) An arbitrator is a neutral third party who imposes a binding decision on both parties

241. What is the difference between a closed shop and a union shop?

(1) In a closed shop, only union members can be hired, while in a union shop, employees must become union members after hiring

(2) In a closed shop, all employees must be union members, while in a union shop, only some employees must be union members

(3) Closed shop and union shop are interchangeable terms

(4) In a closed shop, all employees must be unionised, while in a union shop, only some employees must be unionised

242. What is the difference between union density and union coverage?

(1) Union density measures the percentage of employees who are union members, while union coverage measures the percentage of employees who are subject to a collective bargaining agreement

(2) Union density and union coverage are interchangeable terms

(3) Union density measures the percentage of employers who are union members, while union coverage measures the percentage of employees who are subject to a collective bargaining agreement

(4) Union density measures the minimum number of employees required for a trade union to be recognised, while union coverage measures the maximum number of employees covered by a collective bargaining agreement

243. What is a yellow dog contract?

(1) A contract between an employer and a union that prohibits employees from joining a union

(2) A contract between an employer and a union that prevents the employer from hiring non-union workers

(3) A contract between an employer and an employee that requires the employee to become a union member

(4) A contract between an employer and an employee that prohibits the employee from joining a union

244. What is meant by union busting activities?

(1) The activities aimed to weaken the bargaining power of the trade unions and keep the businesses in the line of their management team.

(2) The activities aimed to keep the employees stay as a member of trade unions and keep the businesses in the line of their management team.

(3) The activities aimed to strengthen the bargaining power of the trade unions and keep the businesses in the line of their management team.

(4) The activities aimed to make trade unions free from any obligation and keep the businesses in the line of their management team.

245. Which of the following is an example of an illegal strike in India?

(1) A strike that occurs during a lockout

(2) A strike without a notice period

(3) A strike that occurs during the duration of an agreement

(4) All of the above

246. Which Indian law confers trade union rights and privileges, and also lays down rules and regulations governing their functioning?

(1) Industrial Employment (Standing Orders) Act 1946

(2) Employees' State Insurance Act 1948

(3) Trade Union Act 1926

(4) Payment of Bonus Act 1965

247. What is meant by the term "right to work"?

(1) The right to work from home

(2) The right to seek employment without being forced to join a union

(3) The right to work for any employer without consultation and getting approval from the trade union.

(4) The right to unionise and negotiate with the employers.

248. What is the Right to Organise Convention?

(1) A convention that mandates employers to participate in collective bargaining

(2) A convention that recognises the right of workers and employers to form and join unions

(3) A convention that lays down rules regarding the conduct of strikes and lockouts

(4) A convention that sets the minimum wage for workers

249. What is an industrial dispute?

(1) A dispute between an employer and employee over the interpretation of the law

(2) A dispute between two or more employers over the allocation of resources

(3) A dispute between an employer and employee over the terms and conditions of employment

(4) A dispute between the government and employees over the terms and conditions of employment

250. Who is an unorganised worker?

(1) A worker who belongs to an unregistered trade union.

(2) A worker who belongs to a registered trade union.

(3) A worker who is not a member of a recognised trade union.

(4) A worker who falls under the category of a skilled or a semi-skilled worker.

251. What is meant by "comparative union research"?

(1) Research that compares the wages and benefits of union vs non-union workers

(2) Research that compares union density and coverage across different countries

(3) Research that compares the unionisation rates of different industries or sectors

(4) Research that compares the effectiveness of different union organising methods

252. What is the role of a Labour Commissioner?

(1) The Labour Commissioner mediates and conciliates in labor disputes between employers and employees.

(2) The Labour Commissioner is responsible for regulating trade union activities.

(3) The Labour Commissioner is responsible for enforcing companies to organise elections for recognising a trade union.

(4) The Labour Commissioner is responsible for negotiating collective bargaining agreements with employers.

253. What is the difference between a union contract and an employment contract?

(1) A union contract is between an employer and the union, while an employment contract is between an individual employee and the employer

(2) A union contract is between an individual employee and the employer, while an employment contract is between the union and the employer

(3) A union contract and an employment contract are interchangeable terms

(4) A union contract and an employment contract are not legally binding

254. What complaints or grievances can an employee raise with the employer?

(1) Wages, hours of work, leave, and working conditions

(2) Race, sex, and religion

(3) Parking concerns

(4) Employee training

255. Which legislation was enacted to provide for the payment of gratuity to employees working in industries or establishments with more than ten workers?

(1) Payment of Bonus Act 1965

(2) The Employees Provident Funds and Miscellaneous Provisions Act, 1952

(3) Industrial Relations Laws (Regulation and Control) Amendment Act, 1971

(4) Payment of Gratuity Act, 1972

256. What are the types of strikes?

(1) Uncertified strike, general strike, sit-in strike, lock-out .

(2) General strike, sit-in strike, legal strike, wildcat strike

(3) Legal strike, wildcat strike, uncertified strike, bio data strike

(4) Legal strike, uncertified strike, emotional strike, black strike

257. What is a general strike?

(1) A strike that targets a specific employer or industry

(2) A strike that involves employees from multiple industries or sectors

(3) A strike that is illegal

(4) A strike that is limited to a single department or location

258. What is a wildcat strike?

(1) A strike that is organised by the union leadership

(2) A strike that is initiated by employees without union approval

(3) A strike that is called by the government

(4) A strike that is limited to a single department or location

259. What is a sympathy strike?

(1) A strike that is called by employees to show support for workers who are already on strike

(2) A strike that is called by employees in response to a specific workplace issue

(3) A strike that is called by the government

(4) A strike that is limited to a single department or location

260. What is a sit-in strike?

(1) A strike that involves employees refusing to leave a particular area of the workplace

(2) A strike that is limited to a single department or location

(3) A strike that involves employees from multiple industries or sectors

(4) A strike that involves employees refusing to work or perform their job duties

261. Assertion: The Novel is a form of literature that emerged during the Modern period

Reason: The Novel is characterised by its long form, complex characters, and focus on individualism and subjectivity

(1) Both assertion and reason are true and the reason is the correct explanation of the assertion.
(2) Both assertion and reason are true but the reason is not the correct explanation of the assertion.
(3) Assertion is true but reason is false.
(4) Assertion is false but reason is true.

262. Assertion: Romeo and Juliet is a tragedy play by William Shakespeare

Reason: Romeo and Juliet's tragic ending is the result of a feud between their families.

(1) Both assertion and reason are true and the reason is the correct explanation of the assertion.
(2) Both assertion and reason are true but the reason is not the correct explanation of the assertion.
(3) Assertion is true but reason is false.
(4) Assertion is false but reason is true.

263. Assertion: The term "Modernism" refers to a literary movement that emerged in the early 20th century

Reason: Modernist writers rejected traditional literary forms and techniques and focused on the subjective experience of the individual.

(1) Both assertion and reason are true and the reason is the correct explanation of the assertion.
(2) Both assertion and reason are true but the reason is not the correct explanation of the assertion.
(3) Assertion is true but reason is false.
(4) Assertion is false but reason is true.

264. Assertion: Fictional prose is a genre of literature that includes both novels and short stories

Reason: Fictional prose is characterised by its use of narrative, characterisation, and plot.

(1) Both assertion and reason are true and the reason is the correct explanation of the assertion.
(2) Both assertion and reason are true but the reason is not the correct explanation of the assertion.
(3) Assertion is true but reason is false.
(4) Assertion is false but reason is true.

265. Assertion: Non-fictional prose includes works such as essays, speeches, and memoirs.

Reason: Non-fictional prose is characterised by its focus on facts, real-life events, and the author's personal perspective.

(1) Both assertion and reason are true and the reason is the correct explanation of the assertion.
(2) Both assertion and reason are true but the reason is not the correct explanation of the assertion.
(3) Assertion is true but reason is false.
(4) Assertion is false but reason is true.

266. When was the Trade Unions Act passed in India?

(1) 1920 (2) 1926
(3) 1930 (4) 1935

267. As per the Trade Unions Act, how many members are required for registration of a trade union?

(1) 5 members (2) 7 members
(3) 10 members (4) 15 members

268. Who is responsible for the registration of a trade union under the Trade Unions Act?

(1) Registrar of Companies
(2) Registrar of Trade Unions
(3) Registrar of Societies
(4) Registrar of Labour

269. Which type of trade union is specifically recognised by the Trade Unions Act?

(1) National Trade Union
(2) Professional Trade Union
(3) Central Trade Union
(4) Regional Trade Union

270. What is the minimum notice required to call a meeting of a registered trade union?

(1) 7 days (2) 10 days
(3) 14 days (4) 21 days

271. Which of the following is not a function of a trade union?
(1) Protecting workers' interests
(2) Enhancing productivity
(3) Maximising profits for shareholders
(4) Bargaining with employers

272. Which of the following is a characteristic of a craft union?
(1) Represents workers from multiple industries
(2) Represents workers from a specific trade or skill
(3) Has a political agenda
(4) Is focused on maximising profits for shareholders

273. What is the purpose of a strike?
(1) To increase productivity
(2) To improve working conditions and wages
(3) To reduce the number of employees
(4) To maximise profits for shareholders

274. Who can participate in a strike called by a trade union?
(1) Only members of the union
(2) All workers in the industry or sector
(3) Only workers at a specific company
(4) No one, as strikes are illegal

275. What is the purpose of collective bargaining?
(1) To increase profits for employers
(2) To ensure fair wages and working conditions for workers
(3) To eliminate competition between companies
(4) To reduce the number of employees in an industry

276. Which of the following is a type of trade union in India that represents employees in the public sector?
(1) Central Trade Union
(2) National Trade Union
(3) Public Sector Trade Union
(4) Regional Trade Union

277. What is the purpose of a lockout?
(1) To improve working conditions and wages
(2) To reduce the number of employees
(3) To close the workplace and prevent workers from entering
(4) To maximise profits for shareholders

278. Which of the following is not a type of strike?
(1) General strike
(2) Slowdown strike
(3) Certification strike
(4) Emotional strike

279. What is the purpose of a boycott?
(1) To reduce competition between companies
(2) To promote fair trade practices
(3) To financially harm a company or industry as a form of protest
(4) To promote a particular brand or product

280. What is the purpose of a picket line?
(1) To monitor the safety and security of a workplace
(2) To physically block workers from entering a workplace during a strike
(3) To promote a particular political agenda
(4) To reduce competition between companies

281. Which of the following is not a type of trade union structure?
(1) Enterprise unions
(2) Regional unions
(3) Craft unions
(4) Industrial unions

282. Which of the following is a challenge faced by trade unions in India?
(1) High membership rates
(2) Lack of government support
(3) Too much government interference
(4) Strong competition from non-unionised workers

283. What is the role of a trade union in promoting social justice?
(1) To ensure fair wages and working conditions for all workers
(2) To promote equality and non-discrimination in the workplace
(3) To maximise profits for shareholders
(4) To increase productivity and economic growth

284. Which of the following is not a benefit of joining a trade union?
(1) Protection of workers' rights and interests
(2) Improved working conditions and wages
(3) Access to financial services such as loans and insurance
(4) Reduced taxes and fees

285. How is the leadership of a trade union typically chosen?
(1) By members voting in a democratic election
(2) Appointed by the government
(3) Appointed by the management of the workplace
(4) Chosen based on seniority within the union

286. Which of the following is not a factor that influences trade union membership?
(1) The benefits of union membership
(2) The availability of alternative employment options
(3) The strength of the union leadership
(4) The working conditions and wages at the workplace

287. Which of the following is not a strategy used by trade unions in negotiations with employers?
(1) Collective bargaining
(2) Lawsuits and legal action
(3) Strikes and lockouts
(4) Public protests and demonstrations

288. What is the purpose of the International Labour Organisation (ILO)?
(1) To ensure international labor standards and promote social justice
(2) To maximise profits for multinational corporations
(3) To eliminate workplace safety regulations
(4) To reduce competition between companies

289. Which of the following is not a challenge faced by trade unions in the current economic climate?
(1) The rise of non-standard employment arrangements
(2) The increasing role of technology and automation in the workplace
(3) The trend towards globalisation and outsourcing
(4) The growth of the gig economy

290. Which of the following is not a characteristic of a successful trade union?
(1) High membership rates
(2) Effective leadership and decision-making
(3) A clear agenda and strategy for achieving its goals
(4) A strong focus on maximising profits for shareholders

291. What is the purpose of a union contract?
(1) To outline the terms and conditions of employment for workers represented by the union
(2) To reduce competition between companies
(3) To promote fair trade practices
(4) To maximise profits for employers

292. Which of the following is not a responsibility of a trade union representative?
(1) Ensuring compliance with labor laws and regulations
(2) Representing the interests of union members during negotiations with employers
(3) Maximising profits for shareholders
(4) Providing support and advice to union members

293. Which of the following is not a strategy used by unions to increase their bargaining power?
(1) Building alliances with other unions and interest groups
(2) Promoting diversity and inclusion within the workplace
(3) Holding strikes and picket lines
(4) Developing more effective communication channels with union members

294. What is the primary goal of a trade union?
(1) To maximise profits for shareholders
(2) To promote economic growth and development
(3) To ensure fair wages and working conditions for workers
(4) To reduce the number of employees in an industry

295. Which of the following is not a factor that contributes to the decline of trade unions in recent years?
(1) Increased government regulation and interference
(2) Changes in the structure of the economy and labor market
(3) Increased competition from non-unionised workers
(4) Decreasing job security and stability

296. Who can file a complaint against a trade union for violation of the Trade Unions Act?
(1) Any individual or organisation
(2) Only members of the trade union
(3) Only employers affected by the trade union
(4) The government

297. Which of the following is not a benefit of having a strong trade union movement?
(1) Improved working conditions and wages
(2) Stronger economic growth and stability
(3) Increased political power and representation
(4) Greater social justice and equity

298. Which of the following is not a type of strike allowed under the Trade Unions Act?
(1) Legal strike
(2) Wildcat strike
(3) Black strike
(4) Certification strike

299. What is the purpose of collective action by trade unions?
(1) To promote the interests of individual union members
(2) To promote the interests of the broader community
(3) To exert collective bargaining power and achieve better working conditions and wages
(4) To promote the agenda of the union leadership

300. Which type of union is specific to a single workplace or company?
(1) Craft union
(2) Industrial union
(3) Enterprise union
(4) Regional union

301. What is the purpose of arbitration in labor disputes?
(1) To force the employer to accept union demands
(2) To encourage compromise and agreement between the union and employer
(3) To eliminate competition between companies
(4) To promote the agenda of the union leadership

302. Which of the following is not a challenge faced by trade unions in emerging industries such as technology and the gig economy?
(1) The lack of traditional workplace structures and clear employee-employer relationships
(2) The rapid pace of technological change and disruption in the industry
(3) The higher levels of education and skill required for employment
(4) The global nature of the industry and the lack of national labor regulations

303. What is the purpose of a lock-in strike?
(1) To prevent the employer from hiring replacement workers during a strike
(2) To physically keep workers inside the workplace during a labor dispute
(3) To promote the interests of shareholders
(4) To achieve a compromise or settlement in labor negotiations

304. How do trade unions support the enforcement of labor laws and regulations?
(1) By taking legal action against employers who violate the law
(2) By promoting greater awareness and understanding of labor laws and regulations among workers
(3) By lobbying the government to introduce new labor laws and regulations
(4) By reducing the number of employees in a given industry or sector

305. What is the role of a trade union in promoting economic growth and development?
(1) To maximise profits for shareholders
(2) To ensure fair wages and working conditions for workers, which in turn promotes consumer spending and economic growth
(3) To reduce competition between companies
(4) To promote the interests of the union leadership

306. Which of the following is not a criticism leveled against trade unions in India?
(1) The lack of effective leadership and decision-making
(2) The high cost of membership fees
(3) The focus on narrow, sectional interests rather than the broader social good
(4) The prevalence of corruption and political interference within the union movement

307. What is the purpose of a secondary strike?
(1) To reduce competition between companies
(2) To boycott a particular industry or sector as a form of protest
(3) To support workers in other industries who are on strike
(4) To maximise profits for shareholders

308. How is the relationship between trade unions and the government in India characterised?
(1) As collaborative and supportive
(2) As highly antagonistic and confrontational
(3) As indifferent and distant
(4) As largely irrelevant and inconsequential

ANSWER KEY

1. (2)	**2.** (1)	**3.** (3)	**4.** (1)	**5.** (1)	**6.** (4)	**7.** (1)	**8.** (1)	**9.** (3)	**10.** (2)
11. (1)	**12.** (1)	**13.** (4)	**14.** (3)	**15.** (1)	**16.** (2)	**17.** (2)	**18.** (1)	**19.** (3)	**20.** (1)
21. (2)	**22.** (4)	**23.** (1)	**24.** (1)	**25.** (3)	**26.** (1)	**27.** (4)	**28.** (1)	**29.** (1)	**30.** (3)
31. (1)	**32.** (1)	**33.** (4)	**34.** (4)	**35.** (1)	**36.** (1)	**37.** (2)	**38.** (1)	**39.** (3)	**40.** (1)
41. (2)	**42.** (1)	**43.** (3)	**44.** (1)	**45.** (1)	**46.** (4)	**47.** (1)	**48.** (1)	**49.** (1)	**50.** (2)
51. (4)	**52.** (2)	**53.** (2)	**54.** (1)	**55.** (1)	**56.** (4)	**57.** (1)	**58.** (1)	**59.** (1)	**60.** (2)
61. (1)	**62.** (1)	**63.** (3)	**64.** (2)	**65.** (1)	**66.** (3)	**67.** (1)	**68.** (2)	**69.** (1)	**70.** (1)
71. (3)	**72.** (3)	**73.** (2)	**74.** (1)	**75.** (4)	**76.** (1)	**77.** (3)	**78.** (1)	**79.** (1)	**80.** (1)
81. (2)	**82.** (1)	**83.** (1)	**84.** (2)	**85.** (1)	**86.** (4)	**87.** (1)	**88.** (1)	**89.** (3)	**90.** (4)
91. (1)	**92.** (3)	**93.** (2)	**94.** (1)	**95.** (3)	**96.** (1)	**97.** (1)	**98.** (4)	**99.** (3)	**100.** (1)
101. (2)	**102.** (1)	**103.** (4)	**104.** (1)	**105.** (1)	**106.** (2)	**107.** (1)	**108.** (3)	**109.** (1)	**110.** (4)
111. (3)	**112.** (1)	**113.** (1)	**114.** (1)	**115.** (1)	**116.** (4)	**117.** (1)	**118.** (1)	**119.** (2)	**120.** (1)
121. (3)	**122.** (2)	**123.** (1)	**124.** (1)	**125.** (4)	**126.** (1)	**127.** (1)	**128.** (1)	**129.** (2)	**130.** (3)
131. (1)	**132.** (3)	**133.** (1)	**134.** (2)	**135.** (1)	**136.** (1)	**137.** (3)	**138.** (1)	**139.** (4)	**140.** (1)
141. (1)	**142.** (1)	**143.** (4)	**144.** (1)	**145.** (4)	**146.** (2)	**147.** (3)	**148.** (2)	**149.** (2)	**150.** (3)
151. (2)	**152.** (1)	**153.** (2)	**154.** (1)	**155.** (2)	**156.** (1)	**157.** (1)	**158.** (3)	**159.** (1)	**160.** (1)
161. (2)	**162.** (2)	**163.** (1)	**164.** (2)	**165.** (1)	**166.** (3)	**167.** (1)	**168.** (1)	**169.** (1)	**170.** (1)
171. (4)	**172.** (3)	**173.** (3)	**174.** (3)	**175.** (4)	**176.** (2)	**177.** (3)	**178.** (3)	**179.** (3)	**180.** (3)
181. (2)	**182.** (1)	**183.** (2)	**184.** (3)	**185.** (3)	**186.** (1)	**187.** (3)	**188.** (2)	**189.** (3)	**190.** (3)
191. (1)	**192.** (2)	**193.** (3)	**194.** (3)	**195.** (2)	**196.** (1)	**197.** (1)	**198.** (3)	**199.** (1)	**200.** (2)
201. (4)	**202.** (4)	**203.** (3)	**204.** (4)	**205.** (4)	**206.** (3)	**207.** (3)	**208.** (2)	**209.** (1)	**210.** (2)
211. (3)	**212.** (2)	**213.** (3)	**214.** (2)	**215.** (2)	**216.** (2)	**217.** (2)	**218.** (2)	**219.** (3)	**220.** (1)
221. (1)	**222.** (4)	**223.** (4)	**224.** (4)	**225.** (2)	**226.** (4)	**227.** (1)	**228.** (1)	**229.** (2)	**230.** (2)
231. (1)	**232.** (1)	**233.** (1)	**234.** (1)	**235.** (1)	**236.** (4)	**237.** (1)	**238.** (1)	**239.** (1)	**240.** (4)
241. (1)	**242.** (1)	**243.** (4)	**244.** (1)	**245.** (4)	**246.** (3)	**247.** (2)	**248.** (2)	**249.** (3)	**250.** (3)
251. (3)	**252.** (1)	**253.** (1)	**254.** (1)	**255.** (4)	**256.** (1)	**257.** (2)	**258.** (2)	**259.** (2)	**260.** (4)
261. (1)	**262.** (1)	**263.** (1)	**264.** (1)	**265.** (1)	**266.** (2)	**267.** (3)	**268.** (2)	**269.** (3)	**270.** (3)
271. (4)	**272.** (2)	**273.** (2)	**274.** (2)	**275.** (2)	**276.** (3)	**277.** (3)	**278.** (4)	**279.** (3)	**280.** (2)
281. (4)	**282.** (2)	**283.** (2)	**284.** (4)	**285.** (1)	**286.** (2)	**287.** (3)	**288.** (1)	**289.** (2)	**290.** (3)
291. (1)	**292** (4)	**293.** (3)	**294.** (3)	**295.** (2)	**296.** (2)	**297.** (3)	**298.** (3)	**299.** (3)	**300.** (3)
301. (2)	**302.** (2)	**303.** (2)	**304.** (2)	**305.** (2)	**306.** (2)	**307.** (3)	**308.** (2)		

UNIT 6

INDUSTRIAL DISPUTES

Syllabus

- Factors, Forms, Trends, Prevention and Settlement, Role of State and Central Labour Administration, Strikes and Lockouts. The Industrial Employment (Standing Orders) Act, 1946. The Industrial Disputes Act, 1947.

INDUSTRIAL DISPUTES

Industrial dispute does not merely refer to difference between labour and capital as is generally thought, but it refers to differences that affect groups of workmen and employers engaged in an industry. Essentially, therefore, the differences of opinions between employers and workmen in regard to employment, non-employment, terms of employment or the conditions of labour where the contesting parties are directly and substantially interested in maintaining their respective contentious constitute the subject-matter of an industrial dispute.

The HR Employee Relations Manager directs the organisation's employee relations function. They develop employee relations policies and ensure consistent application of company policies and procedures. In addition, they are responsible for employee dispute resolution procedures, performing internal audits, and taking appropriate action to correct any employee relations issues. Industrial disputes are organised protests against existing terms of employment or conditions of work.

According to the Industrial Dispute Act, 1947, an Industrial dispute means "Any dispute or difference between employer and employer or between employer and workmen or between workmen and workmen, which is connected with the employment or non-employment or terms of employment or with the conditions of labour of any person."

In practice, Industrial dispute mainly refers to the strife between employers and their employees. An Industrial dispute is not a personal dispute of any one person. It generally affects a large number of workers' community having common interests.

Causes of Industrial Disputes

The causes of industrial disputes are many and varied. The major ones related to wages, union rivalry, political interference, unfair labour practices, multiplicity of labour laws, economic slowdown and others.

Wage Demands

By far, the most important cause for disputes is related to wages. The demand for wages has never been fully met because of inflation and high cost of living. High inflation results in increased cost of living resulting in never-ending demands from unions.

Management and Unions have wage agreement generally valid for three years. Each new agreement is preceded by a prolonged battle between managements and unions, often resulting in strikes and lockouts. Agreement reached in one company will inspire unions in other plants in the locality, and make them pitch tents demanding similar rise in wages.

Closely related to wages are bonus, incentives, and other allowances. Of all these, wages have been a major issue of contention that leads to disputes.

Union Rivalry

Multiplicity of unions leads to inter-union rivalries. If one union agrees to a wage settlement, another union will oppose it. The consequence is never-ending disputes, as has been happening at the Singareni Collieries. The company had 445 strikes in 1990-91 resulting in a loss of production of 3.12 million tonnes and 34.19 lakh man-days. The reason is mainly union rivalry. One union or the other is always on strike and often the demands of rival unions on an issue are conflicting.

Multiplicity of unions poses peculiar problems to managers. One such problem relates to authenticity of memberships. Unions put up respective numbers of members in such a way that when added together the figure exceeds the total number of workers in the organisation. Another problem relates to the selection of a bargaining agent in the process of collective bargaining. Union rivalry leads to large-scale violence.

Political Interference

Major trade unions are affiliated to political parties. Political affiliation is not peculiar to our country alone. Even a cursory assessment of labour movements around the world would show that trade unions are, by their very nature, political, and that politicisation of labour is the rule rather than the exception.

What happens when unions get politicised? In the first place, distant ideological issues divide and fragment unions on party lines. When unions multiply, inter-union rivalry erupts and the consequences are too obvious. Second, inspired by their political ideologies, certain unions refuse to sign an agreement even if it is favourable to all the workers and thus these perpetual dissenters manage to keep the issue alive.

Third, every political party somehow engineers strikes to demonstrate its political strength. Invariably, the political party which is in power favours a union which is affiliated to it, and the result is end less disputes.

Unfair Labour Practices

Majority of disputes are management inspired. The following points two justify the assertion:

1. The management is generally not willing to talk over any disputes with the employees or the representatives, or refer it to 'arbitration' even when trade unions want it so, and this enrages the workers.
2. A management's unwillingness to recognise a particular trade union and the dilatory tactics to which it resorts while verifying the representative character of any trade union have been a source of industrial strife.

Multiplicity of Labour Laws

Labour laws in our country, as in several other countries, have been enacted to create conditions for the protection of labour from unfair employment practices and to provide a legal framework within which Industrial Relations is to be regulated.

Labour legislation is regarded as the most dynamic institution. From a simple restraint on child labour in 1881, labour legislation in our country has become an important agency of the State for the regulation of working and living conditions of workers, as indicated by the rising number and variety of labour acts. This rapid development of labour legislation is an integral part of the modern social organisation.

There are more than 155 Acts, both Central and State, earning our country the dubious distinction of being one of the few highly labour legislated countries in the world. What has been the outcome of all these? Surely, the result has been endless confusion, industrial strife, loss of production and exploitation of labour by the management and of the management by the labour.

What is strange is that in developed countries of the Western world, labour legislation followed the emergence of industrialisation and in response to a demand for economic and social betterment of the workers. We neither experienced an industrial revolution in the true sense of the term, leading to the gradual emergence of a welfare state, nor a socialist revolution which binds the public sector with a sense of performance.

FORMS OF INDUSTRIAL DISPUTES

The industrial disputes are manifested in the following forms:

Strikes

Strike is the most important form of industrial disputes. A strike is a spontaneous and concerted withdrawal of labour from production. The Industrial Disputes Act, 1947 defines a strike as "suspension or cessation of work by a group of persons employed in any industry, acting in combination or a concerted refusal or a refusal under a common understanding of any number of persons who are or have been so employed to continue to work or accept employment".

According to Patterson "Strikes constitute militant and organised protest against existing industrial relations. They are symptoms of industrial unrest in the same way that boils symptoms of disordered system".

Depending on the purpose, Mamoria et. al. have classified strikes into two types: primary strikes and secondary strikes.

(1) **Primary Strikes.** These strikes are generally aimed against the employers with whom the dispute exists. They may include the form of a stay-away strike, stay-in, sit-down, pen-down or tools-down, go-slow and work-to-rule, token or protest strike, cat-call strike, picketing or boycott.

(2) **Secondary Strikes.** These strikes are also called the 'sympathy strikes'. In this form of strike, the pressure is applied not against the employer with whom the workmen have a dispute, but against the third person who has good trade relations with the employer.

However, these relations are severed and the employer incurs losses. This form of strike is popular in the USA but not in India. The reason being, in India, the third person is not believed to have any locus standi so far the dispute between workers and employer is concerned.

General and political strikes and bandhs come under the category of other strikes:

- **Lock-Outs.** Lock-out is the counter-part of strikes. While a 'strike' is an organised or concerted withdrawal of the supply of labour, 'lock-out' is withholding demand for it. Lock-out is the weapon available to the employer to shut-down the place of work till the workers agree to resume work on the conditions laid down by the employer. The Industrial Disputes Act, 1947 defined lock-out as "the temporary shutting down or closing of a place of business by the employer".

  Lock-out is common in educational institutions also like a University. If the University authority finds it impossible to resolve the dispute raised by the students, it decides to close-down (or say, lock-out) the University till the students agree to resume to their studies on the conditions laid down by the University authority. Recall, your own University might also have declared closure sometimes for indefinite period on the eve of some unrest / dispute erupted in the campus.

- **Gherao.** Gherao means to surround. It is a physical blockade of managers by encirclement aimed at preventing the egress and ingress from and to a particular office or place. This can happen outside the organisational premises too. The managers / persons who are gheraoed are not allowed to move for a long time.

  Sometimes, the blockade or confinements are cruel and inhuman like confinement in a small place without light or fans and for long periods without food and water. The persons confined are humiliated with abuses and are not allowed even to answer "calls of nature".

  The object of gherao is to compel the gheraoed persons to accept the workers' demands without recourse to the machinery provided by law. The National Commission on Labour has refused to accept 'gherao' as a form of industrial protest on the ground that it tends to inflict physical duress (as against economic press) on the persons gheraoed and endangers not only industrial harmony but also creates problems of law and order.

Workmen found guilty of wrongfully restraining any person or wrongfully confining him during a gherao are guilty under Section 339 or 340 of the Indian Panel Code of having committed a cognizable offence for which they would be liable to be arrested without warrant and punishable with simple imprisonment for a term which may be extended to one month or with a fine up to Rs. 500, or with both.

Gherao is a common feature even in educational institutions. You might have seen in your own University officers sometimes gheraoed by the employees / students to compel the officers to submit to their demands. Here is one such real case of gherao.

- **Gherao of the vice chancellor.** The non-teaching employees of a Central University in the North-East India had some demands with the University authority for quite some time. Non-confirmation of some of the employees even after completion of six years service was one of the main demands. That the Vice Chancellor was to resign on 31st October was known to all in the University.

  As the last pressure tactic, the employees started Vice Chancellor's gherao on 31st October at 11.00 a.m. They shut down the entrance gate of the administrative building at 3.00 p.m. to block the egress and ingress from and to the office in the administrative building.

  The Vice Chancellor was kept confined in his office chamber. He was humiliated throughout the gherao by using abuses, disconnecting his telephone line, not allowing him food and water and even not allowing him to answer "calls of nature". This scene lasted for 18 hours and was over only by 5 a.m. next day when some 50 C.R.P.F jawans with local police came from the city which is about 20 kms. away from the University Campus.

  They broke the entrance gate of administrative building, rescued the Vice Chancellor and arrested 117 employees confining the Vice Chancellor under Section 340 of the Indian Penal Code and kept them behind bars for a day.

  On 1st November, the Vice Chancellor handed over the charge of his office to the senior most Professor of the University at his residence in the city. In the wee hours on 2nd November, he left for where he came from. The aftermath of gherao created a tuneful atmosphere in the University Campus for about two weeks.

- **Picketing and Boycott.** Picketing is a method designed to request workers to withdraw co-operation to the employer. In picketing, workers through display signs, banners and play-cards drew the attention of the public that there is a dispute between workers and employer.

  Workers prevent their colleagues from entering the place of work and pursuade them to join the strike. For this, some of the union workers are posted at the factory gate to pursuade others not to enter the premises but to join the strike.

  Boycott, on the other hand, aims at disrupting the normal functioning of the organisation. The striking workers appeal to others for voluntary withdrawal of co-operation with the employer. In-stances of boycotting classes and examinations are seen in the Universities also.

Types of Industrial Disputes

The ILO' has classified the industrial disputes into two main types:

They are:

1. Interest Disputes
2. Grievance or Right Disputes.

They are discussed one by one:

1. *Interest Disputes*

These disputes are also called 'economic disputes'. Such types of disputes arise out of terms and conditions of employment either out of the claims made by the employees or offers given by the employers. Such demands or offers are generally made with a view to arrive at a collective agreement. Examples of interest disputes are lay-offs, claims for wages and bonus, job security, fringe benefits, etc.

2. *Grievance or Right Disputes*

As the name itself suggests, grievance or right disputes arise out of application or interpretation of existing agreements or contracts between the employees and the management. They relate either to individual worker or a group of workers in the same group.

That's way in some countries; such disputes are also called 'individual disputes'. Payment of wages and other fringe benefits, working time, over-time, seniority, promotion, demotion, dismissal, discipline, transfer, etc. are the examples of grievance or right disputes.

If these grievances are not settled as per the procedure laid down for this purpose, these then result in embitterment of the working relationship and a climate for industrial strife and unrest. Such grievances are often settled through laid down standard procedures like the provisions of the collective agreement, employment contract, works rule or law, or customs / usage in this regard. Besides, Labour Courts or Tribunals also adjudicate over grievance or interest disputes.

Generally, industrial disputes are considered as 'dysfunctional' and 'unhealthy'. These are manifested in the forms of strikes and lock-outs, loss of production and property, sufferings to workers and consumers and so on. But, sometimes industrial disputes are beneficial as well.

It is the dispute mainly which opens up the minds of employers who then provide better working conditions and emoluments to the workers. At times, disputes bring out the causes to the knowledge of the public where their opinion helps resolve them.

TRENDS IN INDUSTRIAL DISPUTES

(Source: Labour Bureau, Govt of India; published in 2017)

Between 2003 and 2015, the number of industrial disputes have fallen significantly by nearly three-fourth.

During the year 2014, there were 287 industrial disputes (Strikes and Lockouts) in which 1,158,770 workers were involved and 11,095,370 mandays were lost as compared to 258 disputes, 1,838,160 workers involved and 12,645,371mandays lost in 2013. Of the total disputes, 262 (91.29 per cent) involving 277,917 (23.98 per cent) workers resulting in a loss of 9,837,167 (88.66 per cent) mandays were in State Sphere and remaining were in Central Sphere. Of the total disputes (strikes and lockouts), 29 (10.10 per cent) were in the Public Sector which involved 1,011,111(87.26 per cent) workers resulting in a time loss of 1,796,445 (16.19 per cent) mandays. Whereas the number of disputes in Private Sector were 258 (89.90 per cent) which involved 147,659 (12.74 per cent) workers resulting in a time loss of 9,298,925 (83.81 per cent) mandays. As a result of 287 industrial disputes reported during the year 2014, loss of wages was Rs. 2,244,384,369 (in 85 cases) and production loss was Rs. 2,199,213,431 (in 53 cases). Among the states, West Bengal accounted for the highest number of disputes (i.e., 147 or 51.22 per cent) whereas among the industry groups, it was the manufacturing sector (NIC Code 10 to 33) which accounted for the highest share of disputes i.e. 70.03 per cent or 201. Indiscipline' was the main cause which accounted for 40.1 per cent, followed by Wages & Allowances 27.2 per cent and Charter of Demands 13.2 per cent of the total disputes during this period. The temporary work-stoppage has two components – Strikes and Lockouts. Out of total 287 industrial disputes reported during 2014, 119 (41.46 per cent) were strikes and 168 (58.54 per cent) were lockouts which showed an increase of 15.53 per cent & 8.39 per cent respectively over 2013. Among the states, Gujarat accounted for the highest number of strikes i.e. 25 (21.01 per cent) and West Bengal accounted for the highest number of lockouts i.e. 143 (85.12 per cent). The number of work-stoppages due to reasons other than industrial disputes during the year 2014 was 143 in which 27976 workers were involved and 5847327 mandays were lost. All these Disputes were lockouts. During 2014, 34 industrial units were closed affecting 4,726 workers. This showed decrease of 64.21 percent over 2013. Among the States, Tripura accounted for the highest number of closures i.e. 16 (47.06% of the total closures) and their workers affected i.e. 396 (8.38% of the total workers affected) while Telangana accounted for the highest number of workers affected i.e. 2,745 (58.08% of the total workers affected). Manufacturing Division (Industry codes 10-33) accounted for the maximum number of units closed i.e. 26 (76.47 per cent) with an aggregate of 3,921 (82.97 per cent) viii workers affected during the year 2014. Others' was the main cause of closures which accounted for 50.00 per cent of the total closures. The cases of Retrenchments of workers by industrial establishment were 14 affecting 1,798 workers during the year 2014. Out of these, 9 cases were reported from State Sphere and remaining 5 cases were from Central Sphere. The Union Territory Puducherry reported the highest number of retrenchments cases i.e. 5, affecting 35 workers only while the State of Odisha reported the highest number of workers affected i.e. 1,222 (67.96%). Among the industry group Manufacture of wood and products of wood and cork except furniture' accounted for the highest number of retrenchments i.e. 5 (35.71%) with an aggregate of 35 (1.95%) workers affected during the year 2014 while the industry group Mining of metal ores' accounted for the highest number of workers affected i.e. 1,222 (67.96%). There has been a decrease in the number of retrenchment cases and an increase in the number of workers affected during the year 2014 as compared to 2013. During 2014, 21 cases of Lay-off were reported affecting 2,515 workers and resulted in a time-loss of 4,10,639 Mandays. During this period, there has been a decline in the number of layoffs, workers affected and an increase in the number of Mandays lost as compared to 2013. All the cases of Lay-offs reported against the Manufacturing Division (Industry codes 10-33) and cause wise, Others' which accounted for the highest percentage of lay-offs (42.86%).

Effects of Industrial Disputes

Strike

A strike is a very powerful weapon used by trade unions and other labor associations to get their demands accepted. It generally involves quitting of work by a group of workers for the purpose of bringing the pressure on their employer so that their demands get accepted. When workers collectively cease to work in a particular industry, they are said to be on strike.

Strike action, also called **labour strike, on strike, grieve** (of French: *grève*), or simply **strike**, is a work stoppage caused by the mass refusal of employees to work. A strike usually takes place in response to employee grievances. Strikes became important during the industrial revolution, when mass labour became important in factories and mines. In most countries, they were quickly made illegal, as factory owners had far more political power than workers. Most western countries partially legalized striking in the late 19th or early 20th centuries.

No doubt strike is the ultimate weapon in the hands of worker and labour laws also support strikes if it does in accordance with, if we go through the history of strikes and analyze, core reason we find ultimately is **nonpayment of wages** to workers by their employer, followed by irregular payment of wages and then less payment of the wages.

Types of Strike

(1) **Economic Strike.** Under this type of strike, labours stop their work to enforce their economic demands such as wages and bonus. In these kinds of strikes, workers ask for increase in wages, allowances like travelling allowance, house rent allowance, dearness allowance, bonus and other facilities such as increase in privilege leave and casual leave.

(2) **Sympathetic Strike.** When workers of one unit or industry go on strike in sympathy with workers of another unit or industry who are already on strike, it is called a sympathetic strike. The members of other unions involve themselves in a strike to support or express their sympathy with the members of unions who are on strike in other undertakings. The workers of sugar industry may go on strike in sympathy with their fellow workers of the textile industry who may already be on strike.

(3) **General Strike.** It means a strike by members of all or most of the unions in a region or an industry. It may be a strike of all the workers in a particular region of industry to force demands common to all the workers. These strikes are usually intended to create political pressure on the ruling government, rather than on any one employer. It may also be an extension of the sympathetic strike to express generalized protest by the workers.

(4) **Sit down Strike.** In this case, workers do not absent themselves from their place of work when they are on strike. They keep control over production facilities. But do not work. Such a strike is also known as 'pen down' or 'tool down' strike. Workers show up to their place of employment, but they refuse to work. They also refuse to leave, which makes it very difficult for employer to defy the union and take the workers' places. In June 1998, all the Municipal Corporation employees in Punjab observed a pen down strike to protest against the non-acceptance of their demands by the state government.

(5) **Slow Down Strike.** Employees remain on their jobs under this type of strike. They do not stop work, but restrict the rate of output in an organised manner. They adopt go-slow tactics to put pressure on the employers.

(6) **Hunger strike.** In this form of industrial protest, workmen resort to fasting near the workplace in order to demand the employer to redress their grievances.

On **18, July, 2012,** India's leading car manufacturer Maruti Suzuki Udyog Ltd. in Manesar factory workers in an agitation at factory human resource manager burned to death by workers, made severe damage to companies property and hurt severely several other workers. Thereby MSUL (Maruti Suzuki Udyog Ltd.) sacked all of its workers who ever involved in that incident and filed a police complaint against those employees on 8th November, 2012, few workers strike who are dismissed but claims that they were not involved resorted to hunger strike demanding to reinstate them.

(7) **Wild cat strikes.** These strikes are conducted by workers or employees without the authority and consent of unions. In 2004, a significant number of advocated went on wildcat strike at the City Civil Court premises in Bangalore. They were protesting against some remarks allegedly made against them by an Assistant Commissioner.

Legal Prohibitions on Strike on India

According to Industrial Disputes Act 1947, a strike is "a cessation of work by a body of persons employed in an industry acting in combination; or a concerted refusal of any number of persons who are or have been so employed to continue to work or to accept employment; or a refusal under a common understanding of any number of such persons to continue to work or to accept employment".

This definition throws light on a few aspects of a strike. Firstly, a strike is referred to as stoppage of work by a group of workers employed in a particular industry. Secondly, it also includes the refusal of a number of employees to continue work under their employer.

In a strike, a group of workers agree to stop working to protest against something they think is unfair where they work. Labours withhold their services in order to pressurize their employment or government to meet their demands. Demands made by strikers can range from asking for higher wages or better benefits to seeking changes in the workplace environment. Strikes sometimes occur so that employers listen more carefully to the workers and address their problems.

According to Industrial Disputes Act 1947, **Strike [Sec. 2 (q)]**: Strike means "a cessation of work by a body of persons employed in any industry acting in combination or a concerted refusal under a common understanding of any number of persons who are or have been so employed, to continue to work or to accept employment". Mere stoppage of work does not come within the meaning of strike unless it can be shown that such stoppage of work was a concerted action for the enforcement of an industrial demand.

Procedure of Strikes in India

According to Sec. 22(1) Worker should follow the rules mentioned below for doing strike. The rules are as follows :

1. Issue of notice of strike is mandatory;
2. The date of strike must be within 6 weeks from the date of issue of strike notice;
3. The day of strike must not be within 14 days from the date of notice;
4. There should be no strike on any day before the date specified in the strike notice;
5. There should be no strike during the pendency of conciliation proceedings and 7 days after the conclusion of said proceedings;

Methods of Strikes

Lockouts

A lockout may happen for several reasons. When only part of a trade union votes to strike, the purpose of a lockout is to put pressure on a union by reducing the number of members who are able to work. For example, if a group of the workers strike so that the work of the rest of the workers becomes impossible or less productive, the employer may declare a lockout until the workers end the strike. Another case in which an employer may impose a lockout is to avoid slowdowns or intermittent work-stoppages. Occupation of factories has been the traditional method of response to lock-outs by the workers' movement.

Lockouts in India

A lockout is a work stoppage in which an employer prevents employees from working. It is declared by employers to put pressure on their workers. This is different from a strike, in which employees refuse to work. Thus, a lockout is employers' weapon while a strike is raised on part of employees. According to Industrial Disputes Act 1947, lock-out means the temporary closing of a place of employment or the suspension of work or the refusal by an employer to continue to employ any number of persons employed by him.

Picketing

When workers are dissuaded from work by stationing certain men at the factory gates, such a step is known as picketing. If picketing does not involve any violence, it is perfectly legal. Pickets are workers who are on strike that stand at the entrance to their workplace. It is basically a method of drawing public attention towards the fact that there is a dispute between the management and employees.

The purpose of picketing is:

- to stop or persuade workers not to go to work.
- to tell the public about the strike.
- to persuade workers to take their union's side GHERAO.

Gherao in Hindi means to surround. It denotes a collective action initiated by a group of workers under which members of the management are prohibited from leaving the industrial establishment premises by workers who block the exit gates by forming human barricades. The workers may gherao the members of the management by blocking their exits and forcing them to stay inside their cabins.

The main object of gherao is to inflict physical and mental torture to the person being gherao and hence this weapon disturbs the industrial peace to a great extent.

According to Industrial Disputes Act 1947, **Lockout [Sec. 2(1)]**: Lockout means "the temporary closing of a place of employment, or the suspension of work, or the refusal by an employer to continue to employ any number of persons employed by him". Lockout is the antithesis of strike.

- It is a weapon of the employer while strike is that of the workers.
- Just as a strike is a weapon in the hands of the workers for enforcing their industrial demands, lockout is a weapon available to the employer to force the employees to see his points of view and to accept his demands.
- The Industrial Dispute Act does not intend to take away these rights.
- However, the rights of strikes and lockouts have been restricted to achieve the purpose of the Act, namely peaceful investigation and settlement of the industrial disputes.

Procedure of Lockouts

According to Sec. 22(1) Worker should follow the rules mentioned below for doing Lockouts. The rules are as follows:

- Issue of notice of lockout is mandatory;
- The date of lockout must be within 6 weeks from the date of issue of Lockout notice;
- The day of lockout must not be within 14 days from the date of notice;
- There should be no lockout on any day before the date specified in the strike notice;
- There should be no lockout during the pendency of conciliation proceedings and 7 days after the conclusion of said proceedings;

PREVENTION AND SETTLEMENT

Methods and Machinery for the Settlement of Industrial Disputes

Preventions of Industrial Disputes

The consequences of an Industrial dispute will be harmful to the owners of industries, workers, economy and the nation as a whole, which results in loss of productivity, profits, market share and even closure of the plant. Hence, Industrial disputes need to be averted by all means.

Prevention of Industrial disputes is a pro-active approach in which an organisation undertakes various actions through which the occurrence of Industrial disputes is prevented. Like the old saying goes, "prevention is better than cure".

1. **Model Standing Orders.** Standing orders define and regulate terms and conditions of employment and bring about uniformity in them. They also specify the duties and responsibilities

of both employers and employees thereby regulating standards of their behaviour. Therefore, standing orders can be a good basis for maintaining harmonious relations between employees and employers.

Under Industrial Dispute Act, 1947, every factory employing 100 workers or more is required to frame standing orders in consultation with the workers. These orders must be certified and displayed properly by the employer for the information of the workers.

2. **Code of Industrial discipline.** The code of Industrial discipline defines duties and responsibilities of employers and workers. The objectives of the code are:
   - To avoid work stoppage.
   - To secure settlement of disputes by negotiation, conciliation and voluntary arbitration.
   - To promote constructive co-operation between the parties concerned at all levels.
   - To eliminate all forms of coercion, intimidation and violence.
   - To maintain discipline in the industry.
3. **Works Committee.** The Industrial Dispute Act, 1947 has provided for the establishment of works committees. In case of any industrial establishment in which 100 or more workers are employed, a works committee consisting of employees and workers is to be constituted; it shall be the duty of the Works Committee to promote measures for securing and preserving amity and good relations among the employees and workers.
4. **Joint Management Councils.** Under this system Joint Management Councils are constituted at the plant level. These councils were setup as early as 1958. These councils consist of equal number of representatives of the employers and employees, not exceeding 12 at the plant level. The plant should employ at least 500 workers. The council discusses various matters relating to the working of the industry. This council is entrusted with the responsibility of administering welfare measures, supervision of safety and health schemes, scheduling of working hours, rewards for suggestions etc.
5. **Joint Councils.** The joint councils are constituted for the whole unit, in every Industrial Unit employing 500 or more workers; there should be a Joint Council for the whole unit. Only such persons who are actually engaged in the unit shall be the members of Joint Council. A joint council shall meet at least once in a quarter. The chief executive of the unit shall be the chairperson of the joint council. The vice-chairman of the joint council will be nominated by the worker members of the council. The decisions of the Joint Council shall be based on the consensus and not on the basis of voting.
6. **Collective Bargaining.** Collective Bargaining is a process in which the representatives of the employer and of the employees meet and attempt to negotiate a contract governing the employer-employee-union relationships. Collective Bargaining involves discussion and negotiation between two groups as to the terms and conditions of employment.
7. **Labour welfare officer.** The factories Act, 1948 provides for the appointment of a labour welfare officer in every factory employing 500 or more workers. The officer looks after all facilities in the factory provided for the health, safety and welfare of workers. He maintains liaison with both the employer and the workers, thereby serving as a communication link and contributing towards healthy industrial relations through proper administration of standing orders, grievance procedure etc.
8. **Tripartite bodies.** Several tripartite bodies have been constituted at central, national and state levels. The India labour conference, standing labour committees, Wage Boards and Industries Committees operate at the central level. At the state level, State Labour Advisory Boards have been set up. All these bodies play an important role in reaching agreements on various labour-

related issues. The recommendations given by these bodies are however advisory in nature and not statutory.

Machinery for Settlement of Industrial Disputes

1. Conciliation

Conciliation is an important methods for the settlement for the prevention and settlement of the industrials disputes through third party intervention. Conciliation understood as the friendly intervention of a neutral person in a disputes to help the parties to settle tier differences peacefully.

Conciliation refers to the process by which representatives of employees and employers are brought together before a third party with a view to discuss, reconcile their differences and arrive at an agreement through mutual consent. The third party acts as a facilitator in this process. Conciliation is a type of state intervention in settling the Industrial Disputes. The Industrial Disputes Act empowers the Central & State governments to appoint conciliation officers and a Board of Conciliation as and when the situation demands.

(A) **A Work committee.** The work committee is purely consultive body. It is essentially advisory body. It is essentially advisory in nature and their decision are in the form of recommendations section 3(1) and (2) of the industrial disputes act 1947. The Industrial Dispute Act, 1947 has provided for the establishment of works committees. In case of any industrial establishment in which 100 or more workers are employed, a works committee consisting of employees and workers is to be constituted; it shall be the duty of the Works Committee to promote measures for securing and preserving amity and good relations among the employees and workers.

Committee shall meet at least once in a three month and half yearly progress reports of the functioning of the committee is to be submitted in the triplicate to the concerned conciliation officers.

(B) **Conciliation Officer.** According to the industrial disputes act, 1947, the central and the state government can appoints the conciliation officers by a notifications in the official gazette to that effects. The appropriate government may, by notification in the official gazette, appoint such number of persons as it thinks fit to be the conciliation officer. The duties of a conciliation officer are:

(a) To hold conciliation proceedings with a view to arrive at amicable settlement between the parties concerned.

(b) To investigate the dispute in order to bring about the settlement between the parties concerned.

(c) To send a report and memorandum of settlement to the appropriate government.

(d) To send a report to the government stating forth the steps taken by him in case no settlement has been reached at. The conciliation officer however has no power to force a settlement. He can only persuade and assist the parties to reach an agreement. The Industrial Disputes Act prohibits strikes and lockouts during that time when the conciliation proceedings are in progress.

(C) **Board of conciliations.** A board of conciliation constituted as an adhoc body by the appropriate government .The board may be constituted by the appropriate government by notification in the official gazette.

It shall consist of a chairman and two and four members, as the government think fit, who shall be appointed to represent the party.

2. *Arbitration*

Arbitration is a means of securing an award on a conflict issue by reference to a third party. A neutral third party listens to the disputing parties, gathers information about the dispute, and then takes a decision which is binding on both the parties. The conciliator simply assists the parties to come to a settlement, whereas the arbitrator listens to both the parties and then gives his judgement.

The main objective of the arbitration is the adjudication. And hence, there is no place for compromise in awards through both parties are at liberty to do so. Arbitration decision are different from conciliation because decision of arbitration is binding in nature. There is no place for compromise in awards in case of arbitration.

The arbitration is a Quasi judicial process. The arbitrator is not vested with nay judicial power.

Advantages of Arbitration

- It is based on mutual consent of the parties and therefore helps in building healthy Industrial Relations.
- It is established by the parties themselves and therefore both parties have good faith in the arbitration process.
- The process is informal and flexible in nature.

Disadvantages

- Arbitration is an expensive procedure and the expenses are to be shared by the labour and the management.
- Delay often occurs in settlement of disputes.
- Judgment can become arbitrary when the arbitrator is incompetent or biased.

There are two types of arbitration:

(a) **Voluntary Arbitration.** In voluntary arbitration the arbitrator is appointed by both the parties through mutual consent and the arbitrator acts only when the dispute is referred to him.

(b) **Compulsory Arbitration.** Implies that the parties are required to refer the dispute to the arbitrator whether they like him or not. Usually, when the parties fail to arrive at a settlement voluntarily, or when there is some other strong reason, the appropriate government can force the parties to refer the dispute to an arbitrator.

3. *Adjudication*

Adjudication is the ultimate legal remedy for settlement of Industrial Dispute. Adjudication means intervention of a legal authority appointed by the government to make a settlement which is binding on both the parties. In other words adjudication means a mandatory settlement of an Industrial dispute by a labour court or a tribunal. It envisages government references to statutory bodies such as labour court, industrial tribunal and national tribunal.

Adjudication means mandatory settlement of industrial disputes by labour court or industrial tribunal and national tribunal under the disputes act or any other corresponding state statutes.

Three tier of adjudication machinery:

(A) **Labour Court.** The appropriate government may, by notification in the official gazette constitute one or more labour courts for adjudication of Industrial disputes relating to any matters specified in the second schedule of Industrial Disputes Act. They are:

- Dismissal or discharge or grant of relief to workmen wrongfully dismissed.
- Illegality or otherwise of a strike or lockout.
- Withdrawal of any customary concession or privileges.

Where an Industrial dispute has been referred to a labour court for adjudication, it shall hold its proceedings expeditiously and shall, within the period specified in the order referring such a dispute, submit its report to the appropriate government.

(B) **Industrial Tribunal.** The appropriate government may, by notification in the official gazette, constitute one or more Industrial Tribunals for the adjudication of Industrial disputes relating to the following matters:

- Wages
- Compensatory and other allowances
- Hours of work and rest intervals
- Leave with wages and holidays
- Bonus, profit-sharing, PF etc.
- Rules of discipline
- Retrenchment of workmen
- Working shifts other than in accordance with standing orders.

It is the duty of the Industrial Tribunal to hold its proceedings expeditiously and to submit its report to the appropriate government within the specified time.

(C) **National Tribunal.** The central government may, by notification in the official gazette, constitute one or more National Tribunals for the adjudication of Industrial Disputes in :

- Matters of National importance
- Matters which are of a nature such that industries in more than one state are likely to be interested in, or are affected by the outcome of the dispute.

It is the duty of the National Tribunal to hold its proceedings expeditiously and to submit its report to the central government within the stipulated time.

THE INDUSTRIAL EMPLOYMENT (STANDING ORDER) ACT, 1946

Introduction

Earlier, the economic law of supply and demand in the labor market was existed between employers and workers as a mutually beneficial deal. The mutual bargain was treated as such grants, as the terms and conditions of employment for workers are being kept safe. They had an abiding confident in the unity of this law. But as the law work, their faith has proven incorrect. Workers later found that they have not adequately processed fair bargaining power to secure terms and conditions of their service; they organise themselves into trade unions and began to emphasize collective bargaining with the employer. With the advent of trade unions and collective bargaining, new problems began create to maintain industrial peace and production for the society. Workers began to put forth their demands. The recognition that while, such raw a deal been presented to workers by employers , which was not able to define their terms of service, and was sure to be in a situation of industrial conflict, the Legislature stepped sought to introduce a Industrial Employment (Standing Orders) Bill, 1946.

Statement of Objects and Reasons

Experience has shown that 'standing orders' defining the conditions of recruitment, discharge, disciplinary action, holidays, leave, etc., go a long way towards minimising friction between the management and workers in industrial undertakings. Discussion on the subject at the tripartite Indian Labor Conference revealed a consensus of opinion in favor of legislation. The Bill accordingly seeks to provide for the framing of 'standing orders' in all industrial establishments employing one hundred or more workers. In the first instance, the Act will apply to the categories of industrial establishments specified in clause [2(e)], which include, besides factories and railways, mines, quarries and oil fields, tramway or motor, omnibus services, docks, wharves and jetties, inland steam vessels, plantations and workshops.

Government will be competent to extend the Act to other classes of industrial establishments or to grant exemptions where necessary, by notification. Within 6 months from the date on which the Act becomes applicable to an industrial establishment the employer is required to frame draft 'standing orders' and submit them to the Certifying Officer for certification. The draft should cover all the matters specified in the Schedule to the Act and any other matter that Government may prescribe by rules. The Certifying Officer will be empowered to modify or add to the draft standing orders so as to render them certifiable under the Act. It will not be his function (nor of the Appellate Authority) to adjudicate upon their fairness or reasonableness. There will be a right to appeal against the decisions of the Certifying Officers.

List of Amending Act and Adaptation Orders

1. The Indian Independence (Adaptation of Central Acts and Ordinances) Order, 1948.
2. The Adaptation of Laws Order, 1950.
3. The Part B States (Laws) Act, 1951 (3 of 1951).
4. The Industrial Disputes (Amendment and Miscellaneous Provisions) Act, 1956 (36 of 1956).
5. The Industrial Employment (Standing Orders) Amendment Act, 1961 (16 of 1961).
6. The Industrial Employment (Standing Orders) Amendment Act, 1963 (39 of 1963).
7. The Central Labor Laws (Extension to Jammu and Kashmir) Act, 1970 (51 of 1970).
8. The Industrial Employment (Standing Orders) Amendment Act, 1982 (18 of 1982).

It applies to every Industrial establishment wherein 100 or more workmen are employed or were employed on any day of the preceding 12 months.

Matters to be Provided in Standing Orders Under this Act

- Classification of workmen, *e.g.*, whether permanent, temporary, apprentices, probationers, or badlis.
- Manner of intimating to workmen periods and hours of work, holidays, pay-days and wage rates.
- Shift working.
- Attendance and late coming.
- Conditions of, procedure in applying for, and the authority which may grant leave and holidays. Requirement to enter premises by certain gates, an liability to search.
- Closing and reporting of sections of the industrial establishment, temporary stoppages of work and the rights and liabilities of the employer and workmen arising there from.
- Termination of employment, and the notice to be given by employer and workmen.
- Suspension or dismissal for misconduct, and acts or omissions which constitute misconduct.
- Means of redress for workmen against unfair treatment or wrongful exactions by the employer or his agents or servants.
- Any other matter which may be prescribed.

Submission of Draft Standing Orders

Within six months of the application of the Act , to an industrial establishment, the employer shall submit to the Certifying Officer five copies of the draft standing orders proposed by him for adoption in his industrial establishment.

Standing orders to be accompanied by particulars of workmen. The draft standing orders submitted shall be accompanied by a statement giving prescribed particulars of the workmen employed in the industrial establishment including the name of the trade union, if any, to which they belong. Employers in similar establishments may submit a joint draft for their convenience.

Conditions for certification of standing orders. Standing orders shall be certified under this Act if :

(a) provision is made for every matter set out which is applicable to the industrial establishment.

(b) the standing orders are otherwise in conformity with the provisions of this Act; the Certifying Officer is under an obligation to adjudicate upon the fairness or reasonableness of the provisions of any standing orders.

Certification of Standing Orders

- Copy of the draft standing order to be sent to trade union or workmen: On receipt of the draft, the Certifying Officer shall forward a copy to the trade union, if any, of the workmen, or where there is no such trade union, to the workmen ,in the prescribed form requiring objections, if any, which the workmen may desire to make to the draft standing orders to be submitted to him within fifteen days from the receipt of the notice.
- After giving the employer and the trade union or representatives of the workmen an opportunity of being heard, the Certifying Officer shall decide whether or not any modification or addition to the draft submitted by the employer is necessary to render the draft standing orders certifiable under this Act, and shall make an order in writing accordingly.
- The Certifying Officer shall thereupon certify the draft standing orders, after making any modifications and within seven days send copies of the certified standing orders to the employer and to the trade union or other prescribed representatives of the workmen.

Appeals

Any employer, workman, trade union or other prescribed representatives of the workmen aggrieved by the order of the Certifying Officer within 30 days from the date on which copies are sent by the certifying officer, appeal to the appellate authority, and the appellate authority, whose decision shall be final, shall by order in writing confirm the standing orders either in the form certified by the Certifying Officer or after amending the said standing orders by making such modifications or additions as it thinks necessary to render the standing orders certifiable under this Act. The appellate authority shall, within seven days of its order , send copies of the Certifying Officer, to the employer and to the trade union or other prescribed representatives of the workmen.

Date of operation of standing orders. Standing orders shall, unless an appeal is preferred , come into operation on the expiry of thirty days from the date on which authenticated copies are sent or where an appeal is preferred, on the expiry of seven days from the date on which copies of the order of the appellate authority are sent.

Register of standing orders. A copy of all standing orders as finally certified under this Act shall be filled by the Certifying Officer in a register in the prescribed form maintained for the purpose, and the Certifying Officer shall furnish a copy to any person on payment of the prescribed fee.

Posting of standing orders. The text of the certified standing orders shall be prominently posted by the employer in English and in the language understood by the majority of his workmen on special boards maintained for the purpose at or near the entrance through which the majority of the workmen enter the industrial establishment and in all departments where the workmen are employed.

Duration and modification of standing orders. A certified standing orders shall not, except on agreement between the employer and the workmen or a trade union or other representatives of the workmen be liable to modification until the expiry of six months from the date on which the standing orders or the last modifications thereof came into operation. An employer or workman or a trade union or other representative body of the workmen may apply to the Certifying Officer for the modification and such application shall be accompanied by five copies of the modifications proposed to be made, and where such modifications are proposed to be made by agreement between the employer and the workman or a trade union or other representative of the workmen, a certified copy of that agreement shall be filled along with the application.

THE INDUSTRIAL DISPUTES ACT, 1947

The objective of the Industrial Disputes Act is to secure industrial peace and harmony by providing machincry and procedure for the investigation and settlement of industrial disputes by negotiations. This act deals with the retrenchment process of the employees, procedure for layoff, procedure and rules for strikes and lockouts of the company.

Introduction

Industrial Disputes have adverse effects on industrial production, efficiency, costs, quality, human satisfaction, discipline, technological and economic progress and finally on the welfare of the society. A discontent labour force, nursing in its heart mute grievances and resentments, cannot be efficient and will not possess a high degree of industrial morale. Hence, the Industrial Dispute Act of 1947, was passed as a preventive and curative measure.

Scope and Object

The Industrial Dispute Act of 1947, came into force on the first day of April, 1947. Its aim is to protect the workmen against victimisation by the employers and to ensure social justice to both employers and employees. The unique object of the Act is to promote collective bargaining and to maintain a peaceful atmosphere in industries by avoiding illegal strikes and lock outs. The Act also provides for regulation of lay off and retrenchment. The objective of the Industrial Disputes Act is to secure industrial peace and harmony by providing machinery and procedure for the investigation and settlement of industrial disputes by negotiations.

Definitions

Appropriate Government [Sec. 2(a)]. Appropriate Government means the Central Government in relation to any industrial dispute concerning any industry carried on by or under the authority of the Central Government, any industry carried on by a Railway Company, any controlled industry specified by the Central Government, The Unit Trust of India, Corporations under the Central Statutes, Banking company, Insurance company, Mines, Oil field, Cantonment board, Major ports, etc. In relation to any other industrial dispute, the appropriate Government is the State Government.

Award [Sec. 2 (b)] means an interim or a final determination of any industrial dispute or of any question relating thereto by any Labour Court, Industrial Tribunal or National Industrial Tribunal and includes an arbitration award made under section 10A;

Industry [Sec. 2(j)]. Industry means any business, trade, undertaking, manufacture or calling of employers and includes any calling, service, employment, handicraft or industrial occupation or avocation of workmen.

Industrial Dispute [Sec. 2(k)] means any dispute or difference between employers and employers, or between employers and workmen, or between workmen and workmen, which is connected with the employment or non-employment or the terms of employment or with the conditions of labour, of any person.

Settlement [Sec. 2(p)]. Settlement means a settlement arrived at in the course of conciliation proceeding and includes a written agreement between an employer and a workman arrived at otherwise than in the course of conciliation proceeding where such agreement has been signed by the parties thereto in such manner as may be prescribed and a copy thereof has been sent to an officer authorised by the Appropriate Government and the Conciliation Officer.

Wages [Sec. 2(rr)]. Wages mean all remuneration capable of being expressed in terms of money, which would, if the terms of employment, express or implied were fulfilled, be payable to a workman in respect of his employment or of the work done in such an employment and includes:

(i) such allowances (including dearness allowance) as the workman is for the time being entitled to;

(ii) the value of any house accommodation, or of supply of light, water, medical attendance or other amenity or of any service or of any concessional supply of food grains or other articles;

(iii) Any travelling concession. But the following are excluded:

(a) Any bonus.

(b) Any contribution paid or payable to any pension fund or provident fund, or for the benefit of the workman under any law for the time being in force.

(c) Any gratuity payable on the termination of his service.

2(n) "Public utility service" means -

(i) any railway service or any transport service for the carriage of passengers or goods by air;

(ia) any service in, or in connection with the working of, any major port or dock;

(ii) any section of an industrial establishment, on the working of which the safety of the establishment or the workmen employed therein depends;

(iii) any postal, telegraph or telephone service;

(iv) any industry which supplies power, light or water to the public;

(v) any system of public conservancy or sanitation;

(vi) any industry specified in the First Schedule which the appropriate Government may, if satisfied that public emergency or public interest so requires, by notification in the Official Gazette, declare to be a public utility service for the purposes of this Act, for such period as may be specified in the notification.

Dispute Settlement Authorities Under the Act

The I.D. Act provides elaborate and effective machinery for the investigation and amicable settlement of industrial disputes by setting up the various authorities. These are:

1. Works Committee;
2. Conciliation Officer;
3. Conciliation Board;
4. Court of Enquiry;
5. Labour Court;
6. Industrial Tribunal;
7. National Tribunal;
8. Arbitrators;
9. Grievances Settlement Authority.

Dismissal, etc., of an Individual Workman to be Deemed to be an Industrial Dispute. [Sec. 2A]

Difference in between the workman and his employer connected arising out of following activities shall be deemed to the industrial dispute.

- Dismissal of workman
- Discharge of workman
- Retrenchment of the workman
- Termination of workman from his services

[Sec. 2A (2)]. Workman having the disputes can make a application to the conciliation officer to settle the dispute. After the expiry of 3 months of time conciliation officer fails to settle the dispute, workman can make a direct application to labour courts or tribunals for adjudication.

[Sec. 2A (3)]. Workman should make an application to labour courts or tribunals for adjudication before the expiry of 3 years from the date of discharge, dismissal, retrenchment or otherwise termination of service of workman.

Works Committee [Sec. 3]. In the case of an industrial establishment in which 100 or more workmen are employed, the appropriate Government may require the employer to constitute a 'Work Committee'. It consists of equal number of representatives of employers and workmen engaged in the establishment. The representatives of the workmen shall be chosen from amongst the workmen engaged in the establishment and in consultation with the registered trade union, if any. Works committee deals with the workers problem arising day to day in the industrial establishment.

Conciliation Officer [Sec. 4]. The appropriate Government is empowered to appoint any number of persons, as it thinks fit, to be conciliation officers. The conciliation officer having duty of mediating and acts as the mediators in between the parties to resolve the dispute.

In the case of public utility services matters like strikes and lockouts the conciliation officer can initiate the conciliation proceeding and tries to settle the dispute in between the parties.

If the conciliation officer fails to resolve the dispute between the parties, he should report to the appropriate government. If necessary the dispute shall be referred to the Board, Labour Court, Tribunal or National Tribunal, by the appropriate government. [Sec. 12 (5)]

Duties of Conciliation Officers [Sec. 12]

- Hold conciliation proceedings relating to Strikes and lockouts procedural matters of public utility services.
- Investigate the matters of the disputes.
- Conciliation officers shall induce the parties to come to a fair and amicable settlement of the dispute.
- Duty to send the report of settlement of dispute and memorandum of the settlement signed by the parties to the dispute to the government or his superior.
- In case of failure of settlement of dispute in between parties, duty to send them to the government or his superior, report of facts and circumstances relating to the disputes and in his opinion, a settlement could not be arrived at,
- Duty to send the report to the government or his superior within 14 days from the commencement of the proceeding. Or within such shorter period as may be fixed by the appropriate Government.

Conciliation Board [Sec. 5] as occasion arises appropriate Government is also authorised to constitute a Board of conciliation for promoting the settlement of an industrial dispute. It consists of a chairman who shall be an independent person, and two or four other members. The members appointed shall be in equal numbers to represent the parties to the dispute. On the dispute being referred to the Board it is the duty of the Board to do all things as it thinks fit for the purpose of inducing the parties to come to fair and amicable settlement.

If there are many parties relating to or in the dispute the government may appoint the conciliation board consisting of the above said members.

According to [Sec. 10 (2)] when parties in the industrial dispute apply to the government to refer dispute to the Conciliation Board and if government satisfies it shall make the reference to the Conciliation Board.

Duties of Board [Sec. 13]

- It shall be the duty of the Board to endeavor to bring about a settlement of dispute.
- Investigate the matters relating to the dispute between parties and inducing the parties to come to a fair and amicable settlement of the dispute.
- In case of failure of settlement of dispute in between parties, duty to send to the government the report of facts and circumstances relating to the disputes and board opinion, a settlement could not be arrived at,
- The Board shall submit its report under this section within 2 months of the date on which the dispute was referred to it or within such shorter period as may be fixed by the appropriate Government.

Court of Enquiry [Sec. 6] as occasion arises, Government can initiate a Court of Inquiry. This Court of Inquiry was to find out matters connected with or relevant to an industrial dispute. Where a Court consists of two or more members, one of them shall be appointed as the chairman.

A Court of Inquiry looks into only matters which are referred to it by Government and submits its report to the Government ordinarily within certain period from the date of reference.

Adjudication

Labour Court [Sec. 7]. The appropriate Government is empowered to constitute one or more Labour Courts. Its function is the adjudication of industrial disputes relating to any matter specified in the Second Schedule.

Matters within the Jurisdiction of Labour Courts. Second Schedule

1. The propriety or legality of an order passed by an employer under the standing orders;
2. The application and interpretation of standing orders;
3. Discharge or dismissal of workmen including reinstatement of, or grant of relief to, workmen wrongfully dismissed;
4. Withdrawal of any customary concession or privilege;
5. Illegality or otherwise of a strike or lock-out; and

- According to [Sec. 10 (1) (c)] matters specified in THIRD SCHEDULE, dispute not effecting more than 100 workers can be referred to labour court.
- According to [Sec. 10 (2)] when parties in the industrial dispute apply to the government to refer dispute to the labour court and if government satisfies it shall make the reference to the labour courts.
- According to [Sec. 10 (6)] no Labour Court or Tribunal shall have jurisdiction to adjudicate upon any matter which is under adjudication before the National Tribunal.
- A Labour Court consists of one person only. A person is qualified to be appointed as presiding officer of a Labour Court, if:
  - (a) he is, or has been a judge of a High Court, or
  - (b) he has been a District judge or an Additional District judge for at least three years, or
  - (c) he has held the office of the chairman or any other member of the Labour Appellate Tribunal or of any Tribunal for at least two years, or

(d) he has held any judicial office in India for not less than seven years, or

(e) he has been the presiding officer of a Labour Court constituted under any Provincial Act or State Act for at least five years.

(f) he is or has been a Deputy Chief Labour Commissioner (Central) or Joint Commissioner of the State Labour Department , having a degree in law and at least 7 years' experience in the labour department after having acquired degree in law including three years of experience as Conciliation Officer.

(g) as the case may be, before being appointed as the presiding officer; or (g) he is an officer of Indian Legal Service in Grade III with three years' experience in the grade."

Industrial Tribunal [Sec. 7A]. The appropriate Government may, by notification in the Official Gazette, constitute one or more Industrial Tribunals for the adjudication of industrial disputes relating to any matter, whether specified in the Second Schedule or the Third Schedule and for performing such other functions as may be assigned to them under this Act.

Second Schedule

1. The propriety or legality of an order passed by an employer under the standing orders;
2. The application and interpretation of standing orders;
3. Discharge or dismissal of workmen including reinstatement of, or grant of relief to, workmen wrongfully dismissed;
4. Withdrawal of any customary concession or privilege;
5. Illegality or otherwise of a strike or lock-out; and

Third Schedule

1. Wages, including the period and mode of payment;
2. Compensatory and other allowances;
3. Hours of work and rest intervals;
4. Leave with wages and holidays;
5. Bonus, profit sharing, provident fund and gratuity;
6. Shift working otherwise than in accordance with standing orders;
7. Classification by grades;
8. Rules of discipline;
9. Rationalisation;
10. Retrenchment of workmen and closure of establishment; and
11. Any other matter that may be prescribed.

- According to [Sec. 10 (2)] when parties in the industrial dispute apply to the government to refer dispute to the industrial tribunal and if government satisfies it shall make the reference to the industrial tribunal.
- According to [Sec. 10 (6)] no Labour Court or Tribunal shall have jurisdiction to adjudicate upon any matter which is under adjudication before the National Tribunal.

A Tribunal consists of one person only.

For appointment as the presiding officer of a Tribunal

- he is, or has been, a Judge of a High Court; or
- he has, for a period of not less than 3 years, been a District Judge or an Additional District Judge;
- he is or has been a Deputy Chief Labour Commissioner (Central) or Joint Commissioner of the State Labour Department, having a degree in law and at 7 seven years' experience in the labour

department after having acquired degree in law including three years of experience as Conciliation Officer:

Provided that no such Deputy Chief Labour Commissioner or Joint Labour Commissioner shall be appointed unless he resigns from the service of the Central Government or State Government, as the case may he, before being appointed as the presiding officer; or he is an officer of Indian Legal Service in Grade III with three years' experience in the grade."

National Tribunal [Sec. 7 (B)]. The Central Government may, by notification in the Official Gazette, constitute one or more National Industrial Tribunals. Its main function is the adjudication of industrial disputes which involve questions of national importance or affecting the interest of two or more States.

According to [Sec. 10 (1-A)] dispute involves any question of national importance or is of such a nature that industrial establishments situated in more than one State, whether it relates to any matter specified in the Second Schedule or the Third Schedule, the government will order in writing refer to National Tribunal for adjudication.

According to [Sec. 10 (2)] when parties in the industrial dispute apply to the government to refer dispute to the National Tribunal and if government satisfies it shall make the reference to the National Tribunal.

The Central Government shall appoint a National Tribunal consisting of one person only.

- A person to be appointed a presiding officer of a National Tribunal must be, or
- must have been, a judge of a High Court or
- must have held the office of the chairman or
- any other member of the Labour Appellate Tribunal for a period of not less than two years.
- The Central Government may appoint two persons as assessors to advise the National Tribunal.

Arbitration

Voluntary reference of disputes to arbitration. [Sec. 10 (a)]. An arbitrator is appointed by the Government. Whether the dispute is before Labour Court, or Industrial Tribunal or National Tribunal, the parties can go to arbitration by written agreement. The arbitrators conduct the investigation in to the dispute matters and give arbitration award (final decision or settlement or decree) as for making reference of an industrial dispute. If an industrial dispute exists or is apprehended and the employer and the workman agree to refer the dispute to an arbitration, they may refer the dispute to an arbitration. But such reference shall be made before the dispute has been referred under Sec. 19 to a Labour Court or Tribunal or National Tribunal by a written agreement. The arbitrator may be appointed single or more than one in number. The arbitrator or arbitrators shall investigate the dispute and submit to the appropriate Government the arbitration award signed by the arbitrator or all the arbitrators, as the case may be.

Grievance Settlement Authority [Sec. 9 (c)]. This Section is incorporated as a new chapter II B of the Act. As per this Section, the employer in relation to every industrial establishment in which fifty or more workmen are employed or have been employed on any day in the preceding twelve months, shall provide for, in accordance with the rules made in that behalf under this Act, a Grievances Settlement Authority.

[Sec. 9C]. every industrial establishment employing 20 or more workmen shall have one or more Grievance Redressal Committee for the resolution of disputes arising out of individual grievances.

- The Grievance Redressal Committee shall consist of equal number of members from the employer and the workmen.
- The chairperson of the Grievance Redressal Committee shall be selected from the employer and from among the workmen alternatively on rotation basis every year.

- The total number of members of the Grievance Redressal Committee shall not exceed more than 6: Provided that there shall be, as far as practicable, one woman member if the Grievance Redressal Committee has two members and in case the number of members is more than two, the number of women members may be increased proportionately.
- The Grievance Redressal Committee may complete its proceedings within forty-five days on receipt of a written application by or on behalf of the aggrieved party.
- The workman who is aggrieved of the decision of the Grievance Redressal Committee may prefer an appeal to the employer against the decision of Grievance Redressal Committee and the employer shall, within one month from the date of receipt of such appeal, dispose off the same and send a copy of his decision to the workman concerned.
- Nothing contained in this section shall apply to the workmen for whom there is an established Grievance Redressal Mechanism in the establishment concerned."

Awards (decree) [Secs. 16, 17, 17A]

- The award of a Labour Court or Tribunal or National Tribunal shall be in writing and shall be signed by its presiding officer. [Sec. 16(2)].
- Every arbitration award and every award of a Labour Court, Tribunal or National Tribunal shall, within a period of 30 days from the date of its receipt by the appropriate Government, be published in such manner as the appropriate Government thinks fit. [Sec. 17(1)].
- The award published shall be final and shall not be called in question by any Court in any manner whatsoever. [Sec. 17 (2)].
- An award (including an arbitration award) shall become enforceable on the expiry of thirty days from the date of its publication [Sec. 17A (1)].
- Where the award has been given by a National Tribunal, that it will be inexpedient (not advisable or not practicable) on public grounds affecting national economy or social justice to give effect to the whole or any part of the award, the appropriate Government, or as the case may be, the Central Government may, by notification in the Official Gazette, declare that the award shall not become enforceable on the expiry of the said period of thirty days. [Sec. 17A (1) (b)].
- The appropriate Government or the Central Government may, within 90 days from the date of publication of the award under section 17, make an order rejecting or modifying the award, to legislature of sate or parliament [Sec. 17A (2)]. And if no pursuance has made, the order become enforceable after the expiry of 90 days. [Sec. 17A (3)].
- Any award as rejected or modified laid before legislature of state or parliament, shall become enforceable on the expiry of 15 days from the date on which is so laid. [Sec. 17A (3)].
- Award declared becomes enforceable on the specified date if mentioned, if no date mentioned award becomes enforceable according to above rules.

Period of Operation of Settlements and Awards. [Sec. 19]

- A settlement shall come into operation on such date as is agreed upon by the parties to the dispute, and if no date is agreed upon, on the date on which the memorandum of the settlement is signed by the parties to the dispute.
- An award shall remain in operation for a period of one year from the date on which the award becomes enforceable under section 17A: Provided that the appropriate Government may reduce the said period and fix such period as it thinks fit :
  - the appropriate Government may, before the expiry of the said period, extend the period of operation by any period not exceeding one year at a time as it thinks fit, so however, that the

total period of operation of any award does not exceed three years from the date on which it came into operation.

- *E.g:* If the court orders the employer to reinstate the workman in case of unreasonable removal or discharge , the employer is bind over for one year or in some cases, the period specified by the courts.

Unfair Labour Practices - Fifth Schedule

I. On the part of employers and trade unions of employers

1. To interfere with, restrain from, or coerce, workmen in the exercise of their right to organise, form, join or assist a trade union or to engage in concerted activities for the purposes of collective bargaining or other mutual aid or protection, that is to say :
   (a) threatening workmen with discharge or dismissal, if they join a trade union;
   (b) threatening a lock-out or closure, if a trade union is organised; and
   (c) granting wage increase to workmen at crucial periods of trade union organisation, with a view to undermining the efforts of the trade union at organisation.
2. To dominate, interfere with or contribute support, financial or otherwise, to any trade union, that is to say :
   (a) an employer taking an active interest in organising a trade, union of his workmen; and
   (b) an employer showing partiality or granting favour to one of several trade unions attempting to organise his workmen or to its members, where such a trade union is not a recognised trade union.
3. To establish employer-sponsored trade unions of workmen.
4. To encourage or discourage membership in any trade union by discriminating against any workman, that is to say :
   (a) discharging or punishing a workman, because he urged other workmen to join or organise a trade union;
   (b) discharging or dismissing a workman for taking part in any strike (not being a strike which it deemed to be an illegal strike under this Act);
   (c) changing seniority rating of workmen because of trade union activities;
   (d) refusing to promote workmen to higher posts on account of their trade union activities;
   (e) giving unmerited promotions to certain workmen with a view to creating discord amongst other workmen, or to undermine the strength of their trade union;
   (f) discharging office bearers or active members of the trade union on account of their trade union activities.
5. To discharge or dismiss workmen :
   (a) by way of victimisation;
   (b) not in good faith, but in the colourable exercise of the employer's rights;
   (c) by falsely implicating a workman in a criminal case on false evidence or on concocted evidence;
   (d) for patently false reasons;
   (e) on untrue or trumpet up allegations of absence without leave;
   (f) in utter disregard of the principles of natural justice in the conduct of domestic enquiry or with undue haste;
   (g) for misconduct of a minor or technical character, without having any regard to the nature of the particular misconduct or the past record of service of the workman, thereby leading to a disproportionate punishment.

6. To abolish the work of a regular nature being done by workmen, and to give such work to contractors as a measure of breaking a strike.
7. To transfer a workman mala fide from one place to another, under the guise of following management policy.
8. To insist upon individual workmen, who are on a legal strike to sign a good conduct bond, as a precondition to allowing them to resume work.
9. To show favouritis or partiality to one set of workers regardless of merit.
10. To employ workmen as "badlis" casuals or temporaries and to continue them as such for years, with the object of depriving them of the status and privileges of permanent workmen.
11. To discharge or discriminate against any workman for filling charges or testifying against an employer in any enquiry or proceeding relating to any industrial dispute.
12. To recruit workmen during a strike which is not an illegal strike.
13. Failure to implement award, settlement or agreement.
14. To indulge in acts of force or violence.
15. To refuse to bargain collectively, in good faith with the recognised trade unions.
16. Proposing or continuing a lock-out deemed to be illegal under this Act.

II. On the part of workmen and trade unions of workmen

1. To advise or actively support or instigate any strike deemed to be illegal under this Act.
2. To coerce workmen in the exercise of their right to self-organisation or to join a trade union or refrain from joining any trade union, that is to say :
   (a) for a trade union or its members to picketing in such a manner that non-striking workmen are physically debarred from entering the work places;
   (b) to indulge in acts of force or violence or to hold out threats of intimidation in connection with a strike against non-striking workmen or against managerial staff.
3. For a recognised union to refuse to bargain collectively in good faith with the employer.
4. To indulge in coercive activities against certification of bargaining representative.
5. To stage, encourage or instigate such forms of coercive actions as willful "go slow", squatting on the work premises after working hours or "gherao" of any of the members of the managerial or other staff.
6. To stage demonstrations at the residences of the employers or the managerial staff members.
7. To incite or indulge in willful damage to employer's property connected with the industry.
8. To indulge in acts of force or violence or to hold out threats of intimidation against any workman with a view to prevent him from attending work.

Lay-off and Retrenchment

Lay-off [Sec. 2(kkk)]. Lay-off means "the failure, refusal or inability of an employer on account of shortage of coal, power or raw materials or the accumulation of stocks or the breakdown of machinery or for any other reason to give employment to a workman whose name is borne on the muster rolls of his industrial establishment and who has not been retrenched".

Retrenchment [Sec. 2(oo)]. Retrenchment means the termination by the employer of the service of a workman for any reason whatsoever otherwise than as a punishment indicated by way of disciplinary action.

Rights of Workman Laid Off for Compensation [Sec. 25C]

A workman who is laid off is entitled to compensation only if he complies with the following conditions:

(i) He must not be a badli or a casual workman.
"Badli workman" means a workman who is employed in an industrial establishment in the place of another workman whose name is borne on the muster rolls of the establishment.

(ii) His name must be borne on the muster rolls of the industrial establishment.

(iii) He must have completed at least one year of continuous service.

(iv) A worker is entitled to lay-off compensation for the period of his lay off other than for weekly holidays which may intervene.

(v) The rate of compensation must be equal to 50% of the total of the basic wage and dearness allowance that might have been payable to him.

(vi) No compensation can be claimed for more than forty-five days during the period of twelve months.

Workmen Laid Off not Entitled to Compensation [Sec. 25E]

No compensation shall be paid to a workman who has been laid off:

(i) if he refuses to accept any alternative employment in the same or any other establishment belonging to the same employer situated in the same town or village or within a radius of five miles and it does not require any special skill or previous experience, provided the same wages are offered,

(ii) if he does not present himself for work at the appointed time during normal working hours at least once a day,

(iii) if lay off in the consequence of strike or slowing down of production by the workers in another part of the establishment.

Difference Between the Lay-off and Laid-Off

Laid-off	Lay-off
A person who is temporarily stopped for the work being attended	Temporary stoppage of the running factory by the owner of the establishment or factory.
A company which has declared of lay-off, worker shall be laid-off from the work	Lay-off is implemented due to shortage of the raw material, break-down of machinery etc.
The laid-off compensation shall be payable to worker for 45 day only	After 45 days of lay-off, management can retrench worker.

Close Down any Undertaking [Sec. 25FFA]

- An employer who intends to close down an undertaking shall serve, at least 60 days before the date on which the intended closure.
- A notice, is required to give to the appropriate Government stating clearly the reasons for the intended closure of the undertaking.
- Provided that nothing in this section shall apply to – An undertaking in which less than 50 workmen are employed, or less than 50 workmen were employed on an average per working day in the preceding twelve months. An undertaking set up for the construction of buildings, bridges, roads, canals, dams or for other construction work or project.

Retrenchment of Worker Section. 25C

If lay-off exceeds 45 days only the management or owner can retrench the workers by following below said rules.

The reason for compelling and restricting 45 days period of lay-off before doing retrenchment of employee is.

Lay-off is considered to be a unique situation created by reasons beyond the control of employer, it is supposed to be a temporary situation contingent on the grounds mentioned in the definition of layoffs in the section 2(kkk). However if this contingency is prolonging beyond a reasonable time, say 45 days, it will be matter of serious concern both to the employer and to employees because both of them put to a loss of 50% wages by employees and loss of earnings by employer due to temporary stoppage of work, which employer would have earned if there was no laid-off for the reasons mentioned in section 2 (kkk). In the case if an employer is not able to restore the situation which compelled him to lay off employees, he can retrench employees after the expiry of 40 days in stuff continuing layoffs.

Procedure for retrenchment [Sec. 25G]

LIFO (Last in First Out) method should be followed while retrenchment of workers, a workers who has joined last shall be retrenched first. Further explanation junior should be retrenched first.

Conditions precedent to retrenchment of workmen [Sec. 25F]

Worker who has completed one year of service and continuing in service must be retrenched by the owner by following rules.

- One month notice of retrenchment should be given to the worker by the owner.
- Notice should include the reasons for the retrenchment of the concerned worker.

Retrenchment Compensation [Sec. 25F (b)]

Retrenchment worker can claim compensation from the worker under following procedure 15 days of salary drawn for every year of service completed E.g.: last drawn salary of worker = 10000/-

Number of years of service = 5 years

So, retrenchment compensation calculated as follows

Salary drawn is = 10000/-, for 15 days salary is half of the amount = 5000/- × number of service years = 5. = 25000/- is the retrenchment compensation.

Re-employment of Retrenched Workmen [Sec. 25H]

This Section provides priority for a retrenched workman in the case of reemployment. In case the employer proposes to re-employ any person, he is under an obligation to offer first priority to the persons who have been retrenched.

During Pendency of Proceedings [Sec. 33]

During the pendency of any conciliation proceeding before a conciliation officer or a Board or of any proceeding before an arbitrator or a Labour Court or Tribunal or National Tribunal in respect of an industrial dispute, employer should not do the following :

- For any misconduct connected with the dispute, discharge or punish, whether by dismissal or otherwise, any workmen concerned in such dispute.
- Alter the term of contract according to standing orders.
- Take action against the protected workman. If employer wants to take above actions against the employee, employer should makes an application to a conciliation officer, Board, an arbitrator, a Labour Court, Tribunal or National Tribunal.

Penalties

Sec	Reasons	Punishment
25U	unfair labour practice	punishable with imprisonment for a term which may extend to 6 months or with fine which may extend to 1000/- rupees or with both.
26	Illegal Strikes	punishable with imprisonment for a term which may extend to one month, or with fine which may extend to 50/- rupees, or with both.
26	Illegal Lock-Outs	punishable with imprisonment for a term which may extend to one month, or with fine which may extend to one 1000/- rupees, or with both.
27	Any person who instigates or incites others to take part in, or otherwise acts in furtherance of, a strike or lock-out which is illegal under this Act	punishable with imprisonment for a term which may extend to 6 months, or with fine which may extend to one 1000/- rupees, or with both.
28	Giving Financial Aid to Illegal Strikes and Lock-Outs	punishable with imprisonment for a term which may extend to 6 months, or with fine which may extend to 1000/- rupees, or with both.
30	Disclosing Confidential Information	punishable with imprisonment for a term which may extend to 6 months, or with fine which may extend to 1000/- rupees, or with both.
30A	Closure of establishment Without Notice	punishable with imprisonment for a term which may extend to 6 months, or with fine which may extend to 5000/- rupees, or with both.
31	Contravenes the provisions of section 33	punishable with imprisonment for a term which may extend to 6 months, or with fine which may extend to 1000/- rupees, or with both.

MULTIPLE CHOICE QUESTIONS

1. What is a lockout in industrial disputes?
   (1) Forced closure of factories by workers
   (2) Forced closure of factories by authorities
   (3) Forced closure of factories by management
   (4) Forced closure of factories by customers
2. Which of the following is a form of industrial dispute that occurs when workers refuse to work unless their demands are met?
   (1) Boycott (2) Strike
   (3) Picketing (4) Lockout
3. What is the most common cause of industrial disputes?
   (1) Low wage rates
   (2) Lack of job security
   (3) Poor working conditions
   (4) Lack of training
4. What is collective bargaining in industrial disputes?
   (1) Negotiation between the management and the government
   (2) Negotiation between employees and customers
   (3) Negotiation between employees and the management
   (4) Negotiation between employees and labor unions
5. Which act regulates the settlement of industrial disputes in India?
   (1) Industrial Disputes Act, 1947
   (2) Labor Laws Act, 1956
   (3) Minimum Wages Act, 1948
   (4) Payment of Gratuity Act, 1972
6. What is an example of an economic factor that can contribute to industrial disputes?
   (1) Changes in government policies
   (2) Changes in climate
   (3) Changes in population
   (4) Changes in culture
7. Which of the following is NOT a form of industrial dispute?
   (1) Boycott (2) Strike
   (3) Lockout (4) None of these
8. What is the difference between a legal and illegal strike?
   (1) Legal strikes follow the procedures laid down in the Industrial Disputes Act, 1947, whereas illegal strikes do not
   (2) Legal strikes are approved by the government, whereas illegal strikes are not
   (3) Legal strikes are carried out by employees, whereas illegal strikes are carried out by trade unions
   (4) Legal strikes are peaceful, whereas illegal strikes are violent
9. What is the role of the labor court in industrial disputes?
   (1) To mediate between employees and management
   (2) To oversee the implementation of collective bargaining agreements
   (3) To provide legal representation to employees
   (4) To provide legal representation to management
10. What is an example of an environmental factor that can contribute to industrial disputes?
    (1) Changes in labor laws
    (2) Changes in technology
    (3) Changes in demographics
    (4) Changes in consumer preferences

11. What is arbitration in the context of industrial disputes?
(1) An agreement between employees and the management to resolve disputes
(2) A legal proceeding in which a third party is appointed to settle a dispute
(3) An organized protest by employees to demand better working conditions
(4) A negotiation between employees and the management to reach a settlement

12. Who can initiate conciliation proceedings in the context of industrial disputes?
(1) The government
(2) The management
(3) The employees
(4) All of the above

13. Which of the following is NOT a factor contributing to industrial disputes?
(1) Low job satisfaction
(2) Increased productivity
(3) Poor management
(4) Low wages

14. What is picketing in the context of industrial disputes?
(1) A peaceful protest by employees outside their workplace
(2) A violent protest by employees outside their workplace
(3) A protest by customers outside their workplace
(4) A protest by the management outside their workplace

15. What is the role of the labor commissioner in industrial disputes?
(1) To mediate between the employees and the management
(2) To oversee the implementation of collective bargaining agreements
(3) To investigate and report on disputes
(4) To provide legal representation to employees

16. What is the difference between a strike and a sit-in protest?
(1) A strike involves the cessation of work, whereas a sit-in protest involves occupying the workplace
(2) A strike is more violent than a sit-in protest
(3) A sit-in protest is more effective than a strike
(4) There is no difference between a strike and a sit-in protest

17. Which of the following is a form of industrial dispute that occurs when employees continue to work but refuse to meet their targets?
(1) Slowdown (2) Boycott
(3) Strike (4) Lockout

18. What is the difference between a trade union and a labor union?
(1) There is no difference between a trade union and a labor union
(2) A trade union represents employees in a particular trade or profession, whereas a labor union represents all employees in a particular industry
(3) A trade union protests against the government, whereas a labor union protests against the management
(4) A trade union operates at the state level, whereas a labor union operates at the national level

19. What is the difference between a grievance and a dispute?
(1) A grievance is an issue that can be resolved informally, whereas a dispute is an issue that requires formal intervention
(2) A grievance is an issue that requires formal intervention, whereas a dispute is an issue that can be resolved informally
(3) There is no difference between a grievance and a dispute
(4) A grievance and a dispute refer to the same thing

20. Which of the following is an example of an illegal strike?

(1) A strike called by employees without following the procedures laid down in the Industrial Disputes Act, 1947
(2) A strike to demand better working conditions
(3) A strike to demand higher wages
(4) A strike called by the management

21. What is the role of the industrial tribunal in industrial disputes?
(1) To mediate between employees and management
(2) To oversee the implementation of collective bargaining agreements
(3) To provide legal representation to employees
(4) To settle disputes through adjudication

22. Who can refer a dispute to the industrial tribunal in the context of industrial disputes?
(1) The government
(2) The management
(3) The employees
(4) All of the above

23. What is a recognized union in the context of industrial disputes?
(1) A union that has been recognized by the government
(2) A union that has been recognized by the management
(3) A union that has been recognized by the majority of employees
(4) A union that has been recognized internationally

24. Which of the following is an example of a lockout?
(1) A forced closure of a factory by workers
(2) A forced closure of a factory by authorities
(3) A forced closure of a factory by management
(4) A forced closure of a factory by customers

25. Which of the following is NOT a form of economic dispute?
(1) Lockout (2) Strike
(3) Boycott (4) Slowdown

26. What is a slowdown in the context of industrial disputes?
(1) Refusal to work at the normal pace
(2) Refusal to work entirely
(3) Refusal to meet targets
(4) Refusal to work overtime

27. Who can initiate strike proceedings in the context of industrial disputes?
(1) The government
(2) The management
(3) The employees
(4) All of the above

28. What is the difference between a right to work state and an employment at will state?
(1) There is no difference between a right to work state and an employment at will state
(2) A right to work state prohibits unions from requiring employees to join, whereas an employment at will state allows employers to terminate employees for any reason
(3) A right to work state allows employers to terminate employees for any reason, whereas an employment at will state prohibits unions from requiring employees to join
(4) A right to work state allows unions to strike, whereas an employment at will state does not

29. Which of the following is a form of industrial dispute that involves the refusal of employees to handle certain products or services?
(1) Strike (2) Lockout
(3) Boycott (4) Slowdown

30. What is the role of the conciliation officer in industrial disputes?
(1) To mediate between employees and management
(2) To oversee the implementation of collective bargaining agreements
(3) To provide legal representation to employees
(4) To promote settlement of disputes through conciliation

32. Which of the following is a form of industrial dispute that involves the refusal of employees to perform certain duties?
(1) Strike (2) Lockout
(3) Boycott (4) Work-to-rule

32. Who can appoint a conciliation officer in industrial disputes?
(1) The government
(2) The management
(3) The employees
(4) All of the above

33. What is an example of a social factor that can contribute to industrial disputes?
(1) Changes in labor laws
(2) Changes in technology
(3) Changes in cultural norms
(4) Changes in competition

34. What is the difference between an open- and closed-shop agreement?
(1) An open-shop agreement allows employees to choose whether or not to join a union, whereas a closed-shop agreement requires all employees to join
(2) An open-shop agreement requires all employees to join a union, whereas a closed-shop agreement allows employees to choose whether or not to join
(3) There is no difference between an open- and closed-shop agreement
(4) An open-shop agreement operates at the national level, whereas a closed-shop agreement operates at the state level

35. What is an example of a political factor that can contribute to industrial disputes?
(1) Changes in labor laws
(2) Changes in technology
(3) Changes in climate
(4) Changes in government policies

36. What is the difference between a wildcat and official strike?
(1) A wildcat strike is a strike carried out without the approval of the trade union, whereas an official strike is approved by the trade union
(2) A wildcat strike is peaceful, whereas an official strike is violent
(3) A wildcat strike is carried out by the management, whereas an official strike is carried out by employees
(4) There is no difference between a wildcat and official strike

37. What is the role of the settlement officer in industrial disputes?
(1) To mediate between employees and management
(2) To oversee the implementation of collective bargaining agreements
(3) To provide legal representation to employees
(4) To promote settlement of disputes through voluntary arbitration

38. Which of the following is a form of industrial dispute that involves the refusal of customers to purchase products from a particular company?
(1) Strike (2) Lockout
(3) Boycott (4) Slowdown

39. What is the purpose of the Industrial Disputes Act, 1947?
(1) To regulate the settlement of industrial disputes in India
(2) To promote industrial growth in India
(3) To protect the rights of management in India
(4) To protect the rights of employees in India

40. What is the difference between an individual and collective dispute?
(1) An individual dispute involves a single employee, whereas a collective dispute involves a group of employees
(2) An individual dispute is less serious than a collective dispute
(3) There is no difference between an individual and collective dispute
(4) An individual dispute involves a family member of an employee, whereas a collective dispute involves a group of employees

41. Who can appoint an arbitrator in the context of industrial disputes?
(1) The government
(2) The management
(3) The employees
(4) All of the above

42. What is the difference between an industrial dispute and a legal dispute?
(1) An industrial dispute is a labor dispute that must be settled through conciliation, whereas a legal dispute is a dispute that must be settled through litigation
(2) An industrial dispute is a legal dispute that must be settled through arbitration, whereas a legal dispute is a dispute that can be settled through negotiation
(3) An industrial dispute involves management and labor, whereas a legal dispute involves businesses and consumers
(4) There is no difference between an industrial dispute and a legal dispute

43. What is a strike notice in the context of industrial disputes?
(1) A notice issued by the management to employees before a lockout
(2) A notice issued by employees to the management before a boycott
(3) A notice issued by employees to the management before a strike
(4) A notice issued by the government to employees to prevent a strike

44. What is the difference between arbitration and adjudication in the context of industrial disputes?
(1) Arbitration involves a third party who helps to negotiate a settlement, whereas adjudication involves a third party who makes a binding decision
(2) Arbitration involves a court proceeding, whereas adjudication involves an informal process
(3) There is no difference between arbitration and adjudication
(4) Arbitration involves a trial by jury, whereas adjudication involves a trial by jüdge

45. What is a collective bargaining agreement in the context of industrial disputes?
(1) An agreement between employees and the management to resolve disputes
(2) An agreement between employees and labor unions to resolve disputes
(3) An agreement between employees and the management on terms and conditions of employment
(4) An agreement between employees and customers

46. What is the difference between a direct and indirect industrial dispute?
(1) A direct industrial dispute is a dispute between employees and the management, whereas an indirect industrial dispute is a dispute between employees and a third party
(2) A direct industrial dispute is less serious than an indirect industrial dispute
(3) There is no difference between a direct and indirect industrial dispute
(4) A direct industrial dispute involves labor laws, whereas an indirect industrial dispute involves environmental issues

47. Who can initiate adjudication proceedings in the context of industrial disputes?
(1) The government
(2) The management
(3) The employees
(4) All of the above

48. What is the difference between a boycott and embargo?
(1) A boycott is a protest against a particular company, whereas an embargo is a trade restriction by the government
(2) A boycott is a trade restriction by the government, whereas an embargo is a protest against a particular company
(3) There is no difference between a boycott and embargo

(4) A boycott is a peaceful protest, whereas an embargo is violent

49. What is the difference between a compulsory and voluntary adjudication in the context of industrial disputes?

(1) A compulsory adjudication is mandated by law, whereas a voluntary adjudication is not
(2) A compulsory adjudication involves a third party who makes a binding decision, whereas a voluntary adjudication involves a third party who helps to negotiate a settlement
(3) There is no difference between a compulsory and voluntary adjudication
(4) A compulsory adjudication involves labor unions, whereas a voluntary adjudication involves employees

50. What is the role of the labor commission in the resolution of industrial disputes?

(1) To provide legal representation to employees
(2) To mediate between employees and labor unions
(3) To investigate and report on disputes
(4) All of the above

51. Who can refer a dispute to the labor commission in the context of industrial disputes?

(1) The government
(2) The management
(3) The employees
(4) All of the above

52. What is the difference between a support and primary strike?

(1) A support strike is a strike by employees who are not directly involved in the primary dispute, whereas a primary strike is a strike by employees directly involved in the dispute
(2) A support strike is less serious than a primary strike
(3) There is no difference between a support and primary strike
(4) A support strike is carried out by the management, whereas a primary strike is carried out by employees

53. What is the role of the conciliation officer in a strike in the context of industrial disputes?

(1) To mediate between employees and management
(2) To oversee the implementation of collective bargaining agreements
(3) To provide legal representation to employees
(4) To promote settlement of disputes through conciliation

54. How can effective communication be used to prevent industrial disputes in the workplace?

(1) By providing employees with regular feedback and updates on the status of the company
(2) By promoting open communication channels between employees and the management
(3) By resolving disputes in a timely and respectful manner
(4) All of the above

55. What is the role of the collective bargaining agent in the context of industrial disputes?

(1) To negotiate with the management on behalf of employees
(2) To represent employees in disputes
(3) To promote settlement of disputes through arbitration or adjudication
(4) All of the above

56. How can employee training be used to prevent industrial disputes in the workplace?

(1) By providing employees with regular training on labor laws and dispute resolution procedures
(2) By promoting awareness of the benefits of collective bargaining and union membership
(3) By providing employees with training on communication, conflict resolution, and problem-solving skills
(4) All of the above

57. How can effective conflict resolution policies be used to prevent industrial disputes in the workplace?

(1) By providing clear guidelines for resolving disputes
(2) By promoting open communication channels between employees and the management
(3) By encouraging mediation and negotiation as first steps in dispute resolution
(4) All of the above

58. What is the role of the labor union in the context of industrial disputes?
(1) To represent employees in disputes
(2) To negotiate with the management on behalf of employees
(3) To promote collective bargaining and improve working conditions for employees
(4) All of the above

59. How can a culture of trust and respect be used to prevent industrial disputes in the workplace?
(1) By promoting transparency and fairness in decision-making processes
(2) By establishing clear lines of communication between employees and management
(3) By promoting a workplace environment that values and respects all employees
(4) All of the above

60. What is the difference between an economic strike and an unfair labor practices strike?
(1) An economic strike is a strike to demand higher wages and better working conditions, whereas an unfair labor practices strike is a strike to protest against illegal actions by the management
(2) An economic strike is less serious than an unfair labor practices strike
(3) There is no difference between an economic strike and an unfair labor practices strike
(4) An economic strike is carried out by the management, whereas an unfair labor practices strike is carried out by employees

61. What is the role of the conciliation officer in an economic strike context of industrial disputes?
(1) To mediate between employees and management
(2) To oversee the implementation of collective bargaining agreements
(3) To provide legal representation to employees
(4) To promote settlement of disputes through conciliation

62. Who can refer an economic dispute to a labor court?
(1) The government
(2) The management
(3) The employees
(4) All of the above

63. What is the role of the labor court in an economic strike context of industrial disputes?
(1) To mediate between employees and management
(2) To oversee the implementation of collective bargaining agreements
(3) To provide legal representation to employees
(4) To settle disputes through adjudication

64. What is the difference between a strike and a lockout?
(1) A strike is initiated by employees, whereas a lockout is initiated by the management
(2) A strike is initiated by the management, whereas a lockout is initiated by employees
(3) There is no difference between a strike and a lockout
(4) A strike and a lockout both refer to the samething

65. What is the difference between an ordinary and an illegal strike?
(1) An ordinary strike follows the legal procedures laid down in the Industrial Disputes Act, 1947, whereas an illegal strike does not

(2) An ordinary strike is approved by the government, whereas an illegal strike is not
(3) An ordinary strike is carried out by employees, whereas an illegal strike is carried out by the management
(4) An ordinary strike is peaceful, whereas an illegal strike is violent

66. What is the role of the labor officer in the context of industrial disputes?
(1) To enforce labor laws and regulations
(2) To mediate between employees and management
(3) To investigate and report on disputes
(4) To represent management in disputes

67. What is the role of the labor tribunal in the context of industrial disputes?
(1) To oversee the implementation of collective bargaining agreements
(2) To settle disputes through adjudication
(3) To provide legal representation to employees
(4) To promote settlement of disputes through conciliation

68. How can employee engagement be used to prevent industrial disputes in the workplace?
(1) By involving employees in decision-making processes
(2) By promoting a culture of teamwork and collaboration
(3) By promoting employee well-being and work-life balance
(4) All of the above

69. What is an example of a legal strike?
(1) A strike called by employees following the procedures laid down in the Industrial Disputes Act, 1947
(2) A strike to demand better working conditions
(3) A strike to demand higher wages
(4) A strike called by the management

70. What is a work-to-rule in the context of industrial disputes?
(1) A refusal to carry out certain duties
(2) A refusal to work overtime
(3) A strict adherence to rules and regulations
(4) A refusal to meet targets

71. What is the difference between an inter- and intra-union dispute?
(1) An inter-union dispute is a dispute between two or more unions, whereas an intra-union dispute is a dispute within a single union
(2) An inter-union dispute involves management, whereas an intra-union dispute involves only employees
(3) There is no difference between an inter- and intra-union dispute
(4) An inter-union dispute involves labor laws, whereas an intra-union dispute involves environmental issues

72. What is the role of the settlement officer in a lockout context of industrial disputes?
(1) To mediate between employees and management
(2) To oversee the implementation of collective bargaining agreements
(3) To provide legal representation to employees
(4) To promote settlement of disputes through voluntary arbitration

73. What is an example of a constitutional factor that can contribute to industrial disputes?
(1) Changes in labor laws
(2) Changes in technology
(3) Changes in demographics
(4) Changes in government policies

74. What is the difference between a grievance procedure and an arbitration procedure in the context of industrial disputes?
(1) A grievance procedure involves an informal process, whereas an arbitration procedure involves a formal process
(2) A grievance procedure involves a third party who helps to negotiate a settlement, whereas an arbitration procedure

involves a third party who makes a binding decision
(3) There is no difference between a grievance procedure and an arbitration procedure
(4) A grievance procedure involves an investigation, whereas an arbitration procedure involves a trial

75. What is an example of a religious factor that can contribute to industrial disputes?
(1) Changes in labor laws
(2) Changes in technology
(3) Changes in demographics
(4) Changes in cultural norms

76. What is an industrial dispute?
(1) A dispute between two or more companies
(2) A dispute between employees and the management
(3) A dispute between employees and customers
(4) A dispute between the government and the management

77. Which of the following is an example of an economic factor that can contribute to industrial disputes?
(1) Changes in government policies
(2) Changes in weather patterns
(3) Changes in the economic conditions of the industry
(4) Changes in social norms

78. What is the difference between a wildcat and official strike?
(1) A wildcat strike is a strike carried out without the approval of the trade union, whereas an official strike is approved by the trade union
(2) A wildcat strike is peaceful, whereas an official strike is violent
(3) A wildcat strike is carried out by the management, whereas an official strike is carried out by employees
(4) There is no difference between a wildcat and official strike

79. What is picketing?
(1) A peaceful protest by employees outside their workplace
(2) A violent protest by employees outside their workplace
(3) A protest by customers outside their workplace
(4) A protest by the management outside their workplace

80. What is boycott?
(1) A protest by the management outside their workplace
(2) A protest by customers outside their workplace
(3) A refusal by employees to work unless their demands are met
(4) A refusal by customers to purchase goods or services

81. **Assertion:** The Harlem Renaissance was a cultural movement that celebrated African American culture and heritage.
Reason: The Harlem Renaissance occurred during the 1920s and 1930s, when African American artists, writers, and musicians flourished in the Harlem neighborhood of New York City.
(1) Both assertion and reason are true and the reason is the correct explanation of the assertion.
(2) Both assertion and reason are true but the reason is not the correct explanation of the assertion.
(3) Assertion is true but reason is false.
(4) Assertion is false but reason is true.

82. **Assertion:** John Donne's poetry is known for its metaphysical themes and complex interplay of ideas.
Reason: The metaphysical poets of the 17th century saw the world in terms of an interconnected network of ideas and symbols.
(1) Both assertion and reason are true and the reason is the correct explanation of the assertion.
(2) Both assertion and reason are true but the reason is not the correct explanation of the assertion.

(3) Assertion is true but reason is false.
(4) Assertion is false but reason is true.

83. What is a trade union?
(1) An organization that represents all employees in a particular industry
(2) An organization that represents employees in a particular trade or profession
(3) An organization that represents management in the industry
(4) An organization that represents customers in the industry

84. What is an employment at will state?
(1) A state that allows unions to require employees to join
(2) A state that allows employers to terminate employees for any reason
(3) A state that requires all employees to join a union
(4) A state that allows employees to strike at will

85. What is a closed-shop agreement?
(1) An agreement that requires all employees to join a union
(2) An agreement that allows employees to choose whether or not to join a union
(3) An agreement that prohibits unions from requiring employees to join
(4) An agreement that allows management to terminate employees for any reason

86. What is a right to work state?
(1) A state that prohibits unions from requiring employees to join
(2) A state that allows employers to terminate employees for any reason
(3) A state that allows employees to choose whether or not to join a union
(4) A state that does not allow employees to strike

87. What is the role of the labor commissioner in industrial disputes?
(1) To mediate between employees and the management
(2) To oversee the implementation of collective bargaining agreements
(3) To investigate and report on disputes
(4) To provide legal representation to employees

88. What is the role of the industrial tribunal in industrial disputes?
(1) To mediate between management and labor
(2) To oversee the implementation of collective bargaining agreements
(3) To settle disputes through adjudication
(4) All of the above

89. What is a support strike?
(1) A strike by employees directly involved in the dispute
(2) A strike by employees who are not directly involved in the primary dispute
(3) A strike by the management
(4) A strike that involves the government

90. What is collective bargaining?
(1) Negotiation between the management and the government
(2) Negotiation between employees and customers
(3) Negotiation between employees and the management
(4) Negotiation between employees and labor unions

91. What is the difference between a direct and indirect industrial dispute?
(1) A direct industrial dispute is a dispute between employees and the management, whereas an indirect industrial dispute is a dispute between employees and a third party
(2) A direct industrial dispute is less serious than an indirect industrial dispute
(3) There is no difference between a direct and indirect industrial dispute
(4) A direct industrial dispute involves labor laws, whereas an indirect industrial dispute involves environmental issues

92. What is a grievance procedure?
(1) A formal process for resolving disputes between employees and management

(2) An informal process for resolving disputes between employees and management
(3) A formal process for resolving disputes between employees and labor unions
(4) An informal process for resolving disputes between employees and labor unions

93. What is a lockout notice?
(1) A notice issued by employees to the management before a strike
(2) A notice issued by the management to employees before a lockout
(3) A notice issued by the management to the government
(4) A notice issued by the government to employees

94. What is the difference between an economic strike and an unfair labor practices strike?
(1) An economic strike is a strike to demand higher wages and better working conditions, whereas an unfair labor practices strike is a strike to protest against illegal actions by the management
(2) An economic strike is less serious than an unfair labor practices strike
(3) There is no difference between an economic strike and an unfair labor practices strike
(4) An economic strike is carried out by the management, whereas an unfair labor practices strike is carried out by employees

95. What is a settlement officer?
(1) Someone who mediates between employees and the management
(2) Someone who oversees the implementation of collective bargaining agreements
(3) Someone who promotes settlement of disputes through voluntary arbitration
(4) Someone who promotes settlement of disputes through adjudication

96. What is the role of the labor union in the context of industrial disputes?
(1) To represent employees in disputes
(2) To negotiate with the management on behalf of employees
(3) To promote collective bargaining and improve working conditions for employees
(4) All of the above

97. What is the difference between an illegal and an ordinary strike?
(1) An ordinary strike follows the legal procedures laid down in the Industrial Disputes Act, 1947, whereas an illegal strike does not
(2) An ordinary strike is approved by the government, whereas an illegal strike is not
(3) An ordinary strike is carried out by the management, whereas an illegal strike is carried out by employees
(4) An ordinary strike is peaceful, whereas an illegal strike is violent

98. What is the role of the conciliation officer?
(1) To mediate between employees and management
(2) To oversee the implementation of collective bargaining agreements
(3) To provide legal representation to employees
(4) To promote settlement of disputes through conciliation

99. What is compromise settlement?
(1) A settlement that requires both parties to give up something to reach a resolution
(2) A settlement that requires one party to give up something to reach a resolution
(3) A settlement that requires only the management to give up something to reach a resolution
(4) A settlement that requires onlythe employees to give up something to reach a resolution

100. What is the role of the National Industrial Tribunal?

(1) To resolve industrial disputes through adjudication
(2) To investigate and report on disputes
(3) To mediate between employees and management
(4) All of the above

101. What is a sit-down strike?
(1) A strike in which employees refuse to leave the workplace
(2) A strike in which employees refuse to come to work
(3) A strike in which employees refuse to accept the management's offer
(4) A strike that involves violence

102. What is an overtime ban?
(1) Refusal to work during the regular working hours
(2) Refusal to work more than a fixed number of hours in a day
(3) Refusal to work more than a fixed number of hours in a week
(4) Refusal to work on weekends

103. Assertion: Virginia Woolf's novel, Mrs. Dalloway, is an example of stream of consciousness writing.
Reason: Stream of consciousness writing is a literary technique in which the author presents the thoughts and feelings of characters as they occur in real-time.
(1) Both assertion and reason are true and the reason is the correct explanation of the assertion.
(2) Both assertion and reason are true but the reason is not the correct explanation of the assertion.
(3) Assertion is true but reason is false.
(4) Assertion is false but reason is true.

104. Assertion: The Beat Generation was a literary and cultural movement that emerged in the United States in the 1950s.
Reason: The Beat Generation was a response to the prevailing conformity and consumerism of American society at the time.
(1) Both assertion and reason are true and the reason is the correct explanation of the assertion.
(2) Both assertion and reason are true but the reason is not the correct explanation of the assertion.
(3) Assertion is true but reason is false.
(4) Assertion is false but reason is true.

105. What is the difference between a strike and a lockout?
(1) A strike is carried out by employees, whereas a lockout is carried out by the management
(2) A strike is a work stoppage by employees, whereas a lockout is a work stoppage by the management
(3) There is no difference between a strike and a lockout
(4) A strike and a lockout both refer to the same thing

106. What is the difference between a wildcat and an official strike?
(1) A wildcat strike is a strike that is authorized by the trade union, whereas an official strike is not authorized
(2) A wildcat strike is a strike that is carried out by the management, whereas an official strike is carried out by employees
(3) A wildcat strike is a violent strike, whereas an official strike is a peaceful strike
(4) There is no difference between a wildcat and an official strike

107. What is a picket line?
(1) A line of employees who refuse to work
(2) A line of employees who carry banners and placards outside their workplace
(3) A line of management officials who oversee employees
(4) A line of customers who protest outside the workplace

108. What is a boycott?
(1) Refusal to work overtime
(2) Refusal to purchase goods or services
(3) Refusal to work on weekends

(4) Refusal to accept the management's offer

109. What is a closed-shop agreement?

(1) An agreement that allows all employees to join a union
(2) An agreement that requires all employees to join a union
(3) An agreement that prohibits unions from forming
(4) An agreement that allows employees to choose whether or not to join a union

110. What is a right-to-work state?

(1) A state that allows unions to form freely
(2) A state that requires all employees to join a union
(3) A state that prohibits unions from forming
(4) A state that allows employees to choose whether or not to join a union

111. What is the Industrial Employment (Standing Orders) Act, 1946?

(1) An act that regulates the conditions of employment in certain industrial establishments
(2) An act that provides for the settlement of industrial disputes through arbitration
(3) An act that sets up conciliation machinery for the settlement of disputes
(4) An act that regulates the formation and registration of trade unions

112. What is the Industrial Disputes Act, 1947?

(1) An act that regulates the conditions of employment in certain industrial establishments
(2) An act that provides for the settlement of industrial disputes through arbitration
(3) An act that sets up conciliation machinery for the settlement of disputes
(4) An act that regulates the formation and registration of trade unions

113. What is a sympathy strike?

(1) A strike by employees directly involved in the dispute
(2) A strike by employees who are not directly involved in the primary dispute but are supporting the primary strikers
(3) A strike by the management
(4) A strike that involves the government

114. What is a trade union?

(1) An organization formed by employees to represent their interests to the management or the government
(2) An organization formed by the management to represent their interests to the employees or the government
(3) An organization formed by the government to represent the interests of workers
(4) An organization formed by the customers to represent their interests

115. What is the role of the National Industrial Tribunal?

(1) To investigate and report on disputes
(2) To mediate between employees and management
(3) To resolve industrial disputes through adjudication
(4) All of the above

116. What is a grievance?

(1) A formal complaint by an employee against the management regarding any matter relating to the terms and conditions of employment
(2) A formal complaint by the management against an employee regarding any matter relating to the terms and conditions of employment
(3) A formal complaint by the government against an employee regarding any matter relating to the terms and conditions of employment
(4) A formal complaint by customers against an employee regarding any matter relating to the goods and services provided

117. What is a collective bargaining agreement?

(1) An agreement between the trade union and the management regarding the terms and conditions of employment

(2) An agreement between the employees and the government regarding the terms and conditions of employment
(3) An agreement between the management and the government regarding the terms and conditions of employment
(4) An agreement between the customers and the employees regarding the goods and services provided

118. What is a settlement officer?
(1) Someone who mediates between employees and management
(2) Someone who promotes settlement of disputes through conciliation
(3) Someone who promotes settlement of disputes through voluntary arbitration
(4) Someone who oversees the implementation of collective bargaining agreements

119. What is voluntary arbitration?
(1) A form of dispute resolution in which a third party is brought in to help resolve the dispute and the decision of the third party is binding on the parties
(2) A form of dispute resolution in which a third party is brought in to help resolve the dispute but the decision of the third party is not binding on the parties
(3) A form of dispute resolution in which the management and the trade union work together to resolve the dispute
(4) A form of dispute resolution in which the employees and the government work together to resolve the dispute

120. What is compulsory arbitration?
(1) A form of dispute resolution in which the parties are required to accept the decision of the arbitrator
(2) A form of dispute resolution in which the parties are not required to accept the decision of the arbitrator
(3) A form of dispute resolution in which the management and the trade union work together to resolve the dispute
(4) A form of dispute resolution in which the employees and the government work together to resolve the dispute

121. Assertion: A strike can be defined as the refusal of employees to work with an intention to coerce the management.
Reason: Strikes are legal under the Industrial Disputes Act, 1947.
(1) Both assertion and reason are true and the reason is the correct explanation of the assertion.
(2) Both assertion and reason are true but the reason is not the correct explanation of the assertion.
(3) Assertion is true but reason is false.
(4) Assertion is false but reason is true.

122. Assertion: Lockouts are a legitimate means of protest available to the management in the Industrial Disputes Act, 1947.
Reason: The management can lockout employees if there is a labor dispute.
(1) Both assertion and reason are true and the reason is the correct explanation of the assertion.
(2) Both assertion and reason are true but the reason is not the correct explanation of the assertion.
(3) Assertion is true but reason is false.
(4) Assertion is false but reason is true.

123. Assertion: The Closed Shop Agreement is a violation of the freedom of association and the right to work.
Reason: The Closed Shop Agreement forces all employees to join a union.
(1) Both assertion and reason are true and the reason is the correct explanation of the assertion.
(2) Both assertion and reason are true but the reason is not the correct explanation of the assertion.
(3) Assertion is true but reason is false.
(4) Assertion is false but reason is true.

124. Assertion: Overtime ban may lead to a reduction in output.

Reason: Employees may refuse to work beyond their designated hours of work according to the Industrial Employment (Standing Orders) Act, 1946.

(1) Both assertion and reason are true and the reason is the correct explanation of the assertion.

(2) Both assertion and reason are true but the reason is not the correct explanation of the assertion.

(3) Assertion is true but reason is false.

(4) Assertion is false but reason is true.

125. Assertion: The National Industrial Tribunal adjudicates disputes on matters relating to wages, facilities, and work conditions.

Reason: The government of India appoints the National Industrial Tribunal.

(1) Both assertion and reason are true and the reason is the correct explanation of the assertion.

(2) Both assertion and reason are true but the reason is not the correct explanation of the assertion.

(3) Assertion is true but reason is false.

(4) Assertion is false but reason is true.

126. Assertion: William Shakespeare's plays are still performed and studied widely today.

Reason: Shakespeare's plays have universal themes and characters that still resonate with audiences and readers today.

(1) Both assertion and reason are true and the reason is the correct explanation of the assertion.

(2) Both assertion and reason are true but the reason is not the correct explanation of the assertion.

(3) Assertion is true but reason is false.

(4) Assertion is false but reason is true.

ANSWER KEY

1. (3)	**2.** (2)	**3.** (1)	**4.** (3)	**5.** (1)	**6.** (1)	**7.** (1)	**8.** (1)	**9.** (2)	**10.** (1)
11. (2)	**12.** (3)	**13.** (3)	**14.** (1)	**15.** (3)	**16.** (1)	**17.** (1)	**18.** (1)	**19.** (1)	**20.** (1)
21. (4)	**22.** (3)	**23.** (3)	**24.** (3)	**25.** (3)	**26.** (3)	**27.** (3)	**28.** (2)	**29.** (3)	**30.** (4)
31. (4)	**32.** (3)	**33.** (3)	**34.** (1)	**35.** (4)	**36.** (1)	**37.** (4)	**38.** (3)	**39.** (3)	**40.** (1)
41. (4)	**42.** (1)	**43.** (3)	**44.** (1)	**45.** (3)	**46.** (1)	**47.** (4)	**48.** (3)	**49.** (1)	**50.** (4)
51. (4)	**52.** (1)	**53.** (4)	**54.** (3)	**55.** (3)	**56.** (3)	**57.** (3)	**58.** (1)	**59.** (3)	**60.** (1)
61. (4)	**62.** (3)	**63.** (4)	**64.** (1)	**65.** (1)	**66.** (3)	**67.** (2)	**68.** (3)	**69.** (1)	**70.** (3)
71. (1)	**72.** (4)	**73.** (4)	**74.** (1)	**75.** (4)	**76.** (2)	**77.** (3)	**78.** (1)	**79.** (1)	**80.** (4)
81. (1)	**82.** (1)	**83.** (2)	**84.** (2)	**85.** (1)	**86.** (3)	**87.** (3)	**88.** (3)	**89.** (2)	**90.** (3)
91. (1)	**92.** (1)	**93.** (2)	**94.** (1)	**95.** (4)	**96.** (3)	**97.** (1)	**98.** (4)	**99.** (1)	**100.** (4)
101. (1)	**102.** ()	**103.** (1)	**104.** (1)	**105.** (4)	**106.** (1)	**107.** (2)	**108.** (2)	**109.** (2)	**110.** (4)
111. (3)	**112.** (2)	**113.** (2)	**114.** (1)	**115.** (3)	**116.** (1)	**117.** (1)	**118.** (4)	**119.** (1)	**120.** (1)
121. (4)	**122.** (1)	**123.** (3)	**124.** (1)	**125.** (4)	**126.** (1)				

UNIT 7

LABOUR LEGISLATION

Syllabus

- Objectives, Principles, Classification and Evolution. International Labour Organisation, Social Justice and Labour Legislation, Indian Constitution and Labour Laws.
  - The Factories Act, 1948.
  - The Mines Act, 1952.
  - The Inter-state Migrant Workmen (Regulation of employment and conditions of service) Act, 1979.
  - The Contract Labour (Regulation and Abolition) Act, 1970.
  - The Building and other Construction workers (Regulation of employment and conditions of service) Act, 1996.
  - The Child Labour (Prohibition and Regulation) Act, 1986.

LABOUR LEGISLATION

Labour Legislation refers to all laws of the Government which have been enacted to provide social and economic security to the labour or workers. The evils of industrial revolution have led to the labour legislation. Now the state has a direct interest in the industrial peace and prosperity. These acts are aimed at reduction of production losses due to industrial disputes and to ensure timely payment of wages and other minimum amenities of the workers.

The history of labour legislation in India is naturally interwoven with the history of British colonialism. Considerations of British political economic were naturally paramount in shaping some of these early laws. In the beginning it was difficult to get enough regular Indian workers to run British establishments and hence laws for indenturing workers became necessary. This was obviously labour legislation in order to protect the interests of British employers.

Objectives of Labour Legislation

The main objectives for various labour laws are as follows:

1. To protect the workers from profit seeking exploiters.
2. To promote cordial industrial relations between employers and employees.
3. To preserve the health safety and welfare of workers.
4. To product the interests of women and children working in the factories.

Principle of Labour Legislation

PRINCIPLE OF MODERN LABOUR LEGISLATION
1. Principle of protection
2. Principle of social justice
3. Principle of regulation
4. Principle of welfare
5. Principle of social security
6. Welfare legislation

1. **Social Justice.** Ideal condition in which all members of a company have the same basic rights, security, opportunities, obligations and social benefits.
   Social Legislation: Laws aimed at promoting the social functioning of individuals and groups and at protecting their rights.
2. **Social Equity.** Legislation based on social justice prescribes a definite standard for adoption in future. Such standard is forced after taking into consideration the past and present circumstances. Once this standard is fixed by legislation it cannot be changed unless the circumstances and conditions so warrant.
3. **National Economy.** While framing the labour law the general economic situation of the country has to be kept in mind so that object may not be defeated.
4. **International Uniformity.** International uniformity is another principle on which labour laws are based. This important role played by international organisation in this connection is praiseworthy. This organisation aims at securing minimum uniform standard in respect of all labour matters.

Classification of Labour Legislation In India

Labour Laws may be classified under the following heads:

I. **Laws related to Industrial Relations such as:**
   - Trade Unions Act, 1926.
   - Industrial Employment Standing Order Act, 1946.
   - Industrial Disputes Act, 1947.

II. Laws related to Wages such as:

- Payment of Wages Act, 1936.
- Minimum Wages Act, 1948.
- Payment of Bonus Act, 1965.

III. Laws related to Working Hours, Conditions of Service and Employment such as:

- Factories Act, 1948.
- Plantation Labour Act, 1951.
- Mines Act, 1952.
- Working Journalists and other Newspaper Employees' (Conditions of Service and Misc. Provisions) Act, 1955.
- Merchant Shipping Act, 1958.
- Motor Transport Workers Act, 1961.
- Beedi & Cigar Workers (Conditions of Employment) Act, 1966.
- Contract Labour (Regulation & Abolition) Act, 1970.
- Sales Promotion Employees Act, 1976.
- Inter-State Migrant Workmen (Regulation of Employment & Conditions of Service) Act, 1979.
- Dock Workers (Safety, Health & Welfare) Act, 1986.
- Building & Other Construction Workers (Regulation of Employment & Conditions of Service) Act, 1996.

IV. Laws related to Equality and Empowerment of Women such as:

- Maternity Benefit Act, 1961.
- Equal Remuneration Act, 1976.

V. Laws related to deprived and Disadvantaged Sections of the Society such as:

- Bonded Labour System (Abolition) Act, 1976.
- Child Labour (Prohibition & Regulation) Act, 1986.
- Children (Pledging of Labour) Act, 1933.

VI. Laws related to Social Security such as:

- Workmen's Compensation Act, 1923.
- Employees' State Insurance Act, 1948.
- Employees' Provident Fund & Miscellaneous Provisions Act, 1952.
- Payment of Gratuity Act, 1972.

Social Justice Foundations of Labour Law

According to the model, social justice was a central element of the 'Social' globalisation of legal thought between 1900 and 1968. Social justice was important to this model because it represented the idea that justice did not have to be achieved through a set of abstract legal rights which had little to do with the experience of general society. Justice could be achieved through a consideration and involvement of different social groups in the design and application of law. Social justice meant that the law could expand to meet social compromise, and was not constrained by the liberal commitment to non intervention and the free market under the CLT model. This gave a space for the development of labour law to meet the social compromise of the early twentieth century. New legal forms came to the fore, which recognised the interdependent activities of employers and workers and a need to coordinate those activities in the 'public interest' (for example social insurance against industrial accidents and compulsory collective bargaining). To a certain extent, the creation and the development of the ILO is a good example of this social moment. This organisation was formed in 1919 as part of a broader peace project at the end of the First World War. Its Constitution explained the importance of social justice to that mandate, and the importance of the creation of labour standards in the achievement of that social justice. A commentary on the seven policy concerns in the Constitution discerned three priorities in the ILO in terms of 'social justice'. The first was the concern with work as a source of livelihood and fulfilment, the second was the goal of the prevention of exploitation (for example by limiting hours of work and 'taking measures to protect those who might be particularly vulnerable') and the third was the need to protect workers against the difficulties of working in dangerous or inadequate environments. Social justice thus required a redistribution of power from employers to workers, but also meant the recognition of the value of work to both workers and to the social system as a whole. Social justice represented an idea of work quality given the social value of work. It was understood that this recognition guarded against the treatment of labour 'merely as a commodity or an article of commerce' and ensured that (global) industrial peace could be maintained.

At the national level, there was argu ably a similar commitment to 'social justice', but there was a divergence in what was understood by the use of these concepts. In France and Germany for example, the influence of the 'Social' model can be clearly seen, and a 'social law' model of social justice can be discerned in the design of labour law. In Germany, Gierke, a leading theorist in the 'social' movement was very influential in the creation of early labour law. According to his philosophy, the individual could not be viewed separately from society. By entering into a work contract, each worker was entering into a social relationship and therefore should have a particular social status (Tatbestand). This social status should be guaranteed by statute; hence the development of civil law relating to employment. Furthermore, anti discrimination legislation was instigated early on in the development of employment law in this jurisdiction, recognising that the state should be involved in the guarantee of group, as well as individual status. In a similar way, statutes were created in France during the period of the Social movement (1900 1968), which purported to create legal protections for workers on the grounds of public policy (ordre public). As such, worker contracts become 'socialised' and labour law became dominated by role of public (government) power in the regulation of the employment relation.

By contrast, in the UK the focus was on the specific nature of the employment relationship (aside from other social relationships). In particular, labour theorists referred to the particular problems associated with the unequal relationship between employers and employees, and the need to challenge this unequal distribution of power in order to achieve social justice (for workers). This view had clear Marxist foundations. The employment relationship was seen as imbued with elements of 'subordination' and 'exploitation' as a result of the insertion of employers and employees into the capitalist system of production: 'There can be no employment relationship without a power to command and a duty to obey, that is without this element of subordination in which lawyers rightly see the contract of employment'. In the UK, there was initially great scepticism about the role that the government and the law should play in achieving social justice for workers. It was felt that if workers were to challenge the lack of social power (or inequality of bargaining power) in their employment relationship, then this could only be achieved through collective bargaining: the 'spontaneous creation of a social power on the workers' side to balance that of management'.

Evolution of Labour Legislation in India

The History of Labour Legislation

The history of labour legislation in India is naturally interwoven with the history of British colonialism. Considerations of British political economy were naturally paramount in shaping some of these early laws. In the beginning it was difficult to get enough regular Indian workers to run British establishments and hence laws for indenturing workers became necessary. This was obviously labour legislation in order to protect the interests of British employers.

1. **Then came the Factories Act.** It is well known that Indian textile goods offered stiff competition to British textiles in the export market and hence in order to make India labour costlier the Factories Act was first introduced in 1883 because of the pressure brought on the British parliament by the textile magnates of Manchester and Lancashire. Thus we received the first stipulation of eight hours of work, the abolition of child labour, and the restriction of women in night employment, and the introduction of overtime wages for work beyond eight hours. While the impact of this measure was clearly welfares the real motivation was undoubtedly protectionist.

   To date, India has ratified 39 International Labour Organisation (ILO) conventions of which 37 are in force. Of the ILO's eight fundamental conventions, India has ratified four - Forced Labour 1930, Abolition of Forced Labour 1957, Equal Remuneration 1951, and Discrimination (employment and occupation) 1958.

2. **The organised and the unorganised.** An important distinction that is popularly made nowadays in all discussions relating to labour legislation is between workers in the organised/formal sector and those in the informal sector. Many who make this distinction do so with ulterior motives, yet we must reckon with it - especially because out of the total workforce in the country, 92 per cent work in the informal sector while only eight per cent work in the formal sector.

   At the outset it must therefore be remembered that those who were unorganised yesterday are organised today and those who are unorganised today aspire to become the organised tomorrow. Moreover, many rights, benefits, and practices, which are popularly recognised today as legitimate rights of the workers, are those that have accrued as a result of the struggles carried out by the earlier generation of workers. The attempt, prevalent in some circles to pit one section of workers against the others, must therefore be carefully understood and deserves to be rejected outright.

3. **Trade unionism and the Trade Union Act 1926.** There are almost ten major central union organisations of workers based on different political ideologies. Almost every union is affiliated to one of these. These central organisations have state branches, committees, and councils from where its organisation works down to the local level.

   The first central trade union organisation in India was the All India Trade Union Congress (AITUC) in 1920 - almost three decades before India won independence. At about the same time workers at the Buckingham and Cyanotic Mills, Madras went on strike led by B P Wadia. The management brought a civil suit against the workers in the Madras High Court and not only obtained an injunction order against the strike but also succeeded in obtaining damages against the leader for 'inducing a breach of contract'. This was followed by widespread protests that finally yielded in the Trade Union Act 1926 giving immunity to the trade unions against certain forms of civil and criminal action. Apart from this aspect the Trade Union Act also facilitated registration, internal democracy, a role for outsiders and permission for raising a political fund subject to separate accounting requirements.

   The Trade Union Act facilitates unionisation both in the organised and the unorganised sectors. It is through this law that the freedom of association that is a fundamental right under the Constitution of India is realised.

   The right to register a trade union however does not mean that the employer must recognise the union – there is in fact no law which provides for recognition of trade unions and consequently no legal compulsion for employers, even in the organised sector, to enter into collective bargaining.

   Yet in reality because of the strength of particular trade unions there is fairly widespread collective bargaining, especially in the organised sector.

4. **Wage determinations in the unorganised sector.** Wage determination in India has been achieved by various instruments. For the unorganised sector the most useful instrument is the Minimum Wages Act 1948. This law governs the methods to fix minimum wages in scheduled industries (which may vary from state to state) by using either a committee method or a notification method. A tripartite Advisory Committee with an independent Chairman advises the Government on the minimum wage. In practice unfortunately, the minimum wage is so low that in many industries there is erosion of real wage despite revision of the minimum wage occasionally. A feeble indexation system has now been introduced in a few states only.
5. **Collective bargaining in the organised sector.** An important factor that is not much recognised, but which still prevails in many organised sector units is fixing and revising wages through collective bargaining. The course of collective bargaining was influenced in 1948 by the recommendations of the Fair Wage Committee that reported that three levels of wages exist - minimum, fair, and living.

   These three wage levels were defined and it was pointed out that all industries must pay the minimum wage and that the capacity to pay would apply only to the fair wage, which could be linked to productivity. In addition to this the fifteenth Indian Labour Conference, a tripartite body, met in 1954 and defined precisely what the needs-based minimum wage was and how it could be quantified using a balanced diet chart.

   This gave a great boost to collective bargaining; many organised sector trade unions were able to achieve reasonably satisfactory indexation and a system of paying an annual bonus. It is now the law, that a thirteenth month of wage must be paid as a deferred wage to all those covered by the Payment of Bonus Act. The minimum bonus payable is 8.33 per cent and the maximum is 20 per cent of the annual wage.
6. **Strikes and lockouts.** Workers have the right to strike, even without notice unless it involves a public utility service; employers have the right to lockout, subject to the same conditions as a strike. The parties may sort out their differences either bilaterally, or through a conciliation officer who can facilitate but not compel a settlement which is legally binding on the parties, even when a strike or a lockout is in progress. But if these methods do not resolve a dispute, the government may refer the dispute to compulsory adjudication and ban the strike or lockout.
7. **Conciliation, arbitration, and adjudication.** When parties engaging in collective bargaining are unable to arrive at a settlement, either party or the government may commence conciliation proceedings before a government appointed conciliation officer whose intervention may produce a settlement, which is then registered in the labour department and becomes binding on all parties. If conciliation fails it is open to the parties to invoke arbitration or for the appropriate government to refer the dispute to adjudication before a labour court or a tribunal whose decision may then be notified as an award of a binding nature on the parties. Disputes may be settled by collective bargaining, conciliation, or compulsory adjudication.
8. **Colonial dispute settlement machinery.** The Industrial Disputes Act 1947 (IDA) provides for the settlement machinery above. The framework of this legislation, which is the principle legislation dealing with core labour issues, is of colonial origin. This law originated firstly in the Trade Disputes Act 1929, introduced by the British, when there was a spate of strikes and huge loss of person days and secondly through Rule 81A of the Defence of India Rules 1942, when the British joined the war efforts and wanted to maintain wartime supplies to the allied forces. Interestingly the interim government on the eve of formal independence retained this framework by enacting the IDA, which still remains on the statute book.
9. **Developments after independence.** Even though the IDA was primarily meant for industry in the organised sector, its present application has now extended well into the unorganised sector, through judge-made law. Its pro-worker protection clauses and safeguards against

arbitrary job losses have evolved over a period of time both through the process of sustained legislative amendments and through the process of judicial activism spread over more than five decades.

The original colonial legislation underwent substantial modification in the post-colonial era because independent India called for a clear partnership between labour and capital. The content of this partnership was unanimously approved in a tripartite conference in December 1947 in which it was agreed that labour would be given a fair wage and fair working conditions and in return capital would receive the fullest co-operation of labour for uninterrupted production and higher productivity as part of the strategy for national economic development and that all concerned would observe a truce period of three years free from strikes and lockouts.

10. **Regulation of job losses.** Space does not allow a detailed discussion of this transformation in labour policy and consequent amendments to labour law, but provisions that deal with job losses must be noted. Under the present law any industrial establishment employing more than 100 workers must make an application to the Government seeking permission before resorting to lay-off, retrenchment, or closure; employers resorting to any of the said forms of creating job losses, is acting illegally and workers are entitled to receive wages for the period of illegality. The Reserve Bank of India commissioned a study into the causes of sickness in Indian industry and they reported cryptically, 'Sickness in India is a profitable business'. This chapter in the IDA, which has been identified as offering high rigidity in the area of labour redundancy, has been targeted for change under globalisation and liberalisation.
11. **Protection of service conditions.** A feature of the IDA is the stipulation that existing service conditions cannot be unilaterally altered without giving a notice of 21 days to the workers and the union. Similarly if an industrial dispute is pending before an authority under the IDA, then the previous service conditions in respect of that dispute cannot be altered to the disadvantage of the workers without prior permission of the authority concerned. This has been identified as a form of rigidity that hampers competition in the era of the World Trade Organisation.
12. **Removal from service.** A permanent worker can be removed from service only for proven misconduct or for habitual absence - due to ill health, alcoholism and the like, or on attaining retirement age. In other words the doctrine of 'hire and fire' is not approved within the existing legal framework. In cases of misconduct the worker is entitled to the protection of Standing Orders to be framed by a certifying officer of the labour department after hearing management and labour, through the trade union. Employers must follow principles of 'natural justice', which again is an area that is governed by judge-made law. An order of dismissal can be challenged in the labour court and if it is found to be flawed, the court has the power to order reinstatement with continuity of service, back wages, and consequential benefits. This again is identified as an area where greater flexibility is considered desirable for being competitive.
13. **Return to colonial days!** Almost all pro-worker developments that accrued since independence are now identified as areas of rigidity and in the name of flexibility there is pressure on the government of India to repeal or amend all such laws. Interestingly, if such a proposal is fully implemented, labour law, especially for the organised sector, will go back to the colonial framework where state intervention was meant primarily to discipline labour, not to give it protection.
14. **Globalisations.** The most distinctly visible change from globalization is the increased tendency for off-loading or subcontracting. Generally this is done through the use of cheaper forms of contract labour, where there is no unionization, no welfare benefits, and quite often not even statutorily fixed minimum wages. Occasionally the tendency to bring contract labour to the mother plant itself is seen. This is very often preceded by downsizing, and since there is statutory regulation of job losses, the system of voluntary retirement with the 'golden handshake' is

widely prevalent, both in public and private sectors.

15. **Regulation of contract labour.** The Contract Labour (Prohibition and Regulation) Act 1970 provides a mechanism for registration of contractors (if more than twenty workers are engaged) and for the appointment of a Tripartite Advisory Board that investigates particular forms of contract labour, which if found to be engaged in areas requiring perennial work connected with the production process, then the Board could recommend its abolition. A tricky legal question has arisen as to whether the contract workers should be automatically absorbed or not after the contract labour system is abolished. Recently a Constitutional Bench of the Supreme Court held that there need not be such automatic absorption - in effect this 'abolishes' the contract labourer and has given rise to a serious anomaly.
16. **Phase between organised and unorganised.** We are already witnessing a reduction in the organised labour force and an increase in the ranks of the unorganised. The above law is a kind of inter-phase in the process of regulating the transition from regular employment to irregular employment. If contract labour is seen as introducing a form of flexibility, a strict enforcement of this Act could have had a salutary effect on the transition process. Instead the enforceability of the Act is now diluted and consequently even the minimum protection envisaged under this law to contract labourers is in jeopardy. Dominant thinking in relation to globalization is having its effect on the judicial process also, ignoring Directive Principles of State Policy contained in the Constitution of India.
17. **Employment injury, health, and maternity benefit.** The Workman's Compensation Act 1923 is one of the earliest pieces of labour legislation. It covers all cases of 'accident arising out of and in the course of employment' and the rate of compensation to be paid in a lump sum, is determined by a schedule proportionate to the extent of injury and the loss of earning capacity. The younger the worker and the higher the wage, the greater is the compensation subject to a limit. The injured person, or in case of death the dependent, can claim the compensation. This law applies to the unorganised sectors and to those in the organised sectors who are not covered by the Employees State Insurance Scheme, which is conceptually considered to be superior to the Workman's Compensation Act.

    The Employees State Insurance Act provides a scheme under which the employer and the employee must contribute a certain percentage of the monthly wage to the Insurance Corporation that runs dispensaries and hospitals in working class localities. It facilitates both outpatient and in-patient care and freely dispenses medicines and covers hospitalization needs and costs. Leave certificates for health reasons are forwarded to the employer who is obliged to honour them. Employment injury, including occupational disease is compensated according to a schedule of rates proportionate to the extent of injury and loss of earning capacity. Payment, unlike in the Workmen's Compensation Act, is monthly. Despite the existence of tripartite bodies to supervise the running of the scheme, the entire project has fallen into disrepute due to corruption and inefficiency. Workers in need of genuine medical attention rarely approach this facility though they use it quite liberally to obtain medical leave. There are interesting cases where workers have gone to court seeking exemption from the scheme in order to avail of better facilities available through collective bargaining.

    The Maternity Benefit Act is applicable to notified establishments. Its coverage can therefore extend to the unorganised sector also, though in practice it is rare. A woman employee is entitled to 90 days of paid leave on delivery or on miscarriage. Similar benefits, including hospitalization facilities are available under the law described in the paragraph above.
18. **Retirement benefit.** There are two types of retirement benefit generally available to workers. One is under the Payment of Gratuity Act and the other is under the Provident Fund Act. In the first case a worker who has put in not less than five years of work is entitled to a lump sum

payment equal to 15 days' wages for every completed year of service. Every month the employer is expected to contribute the required money into a separate fund to enable this payment on retirement or termination of employment. In the latter scheme both the employee and the employer make an equal contribution into a national fund. The current rate of contribution is 12 per cent of the wage including a small percentage towards family pension. This contribution also attracts an interest, currently 9.5 per cent per annum, and the accumulated amount is paid on retirement to the employee along with the interest that has accrued. Unfortunately the employee is allowed to draw many types of loan from the fund such as for house construction, marriage of children, and education etc. As a result very little is available at the time of retirement. This is also a benefit, which is steadily being extended to sections of the unorganised sector, especially where the employer is clearly identifiable.

19. **Women labour and the law.** Women constitute a significant part of the workforce in India but they lag behind men in terms of work participation and quality of employment. According to Government sources, out of 407 million total workforce, 90 million are women workers, largely employed (about 87 per cent) in the agricultural sector as labourers and cultivators. In urban areas, the employment of women in the organised sector in March 2000 constituted 17.6 per cent of the total organised sector.

    Apart from the Maternity Benefit Act, almost all the major central labour laws are applicable to women workers. The Equal Remuneration Act was passed in 1976, providing for the payment of equal remuneration to men and women workers for same or similar nature of work. Under this law, no discrimination is permissible in recruitment and service conditions except where employment of women is prohibited or restricted by the law. The situation regarding enforcement of the provisions of this law is regularly monitored by the Central Ministry of Labour and the Central Advisory Committee. In respect of an occupational hazard concerning the safety of women at workplaces, in 1997 the Supreme Court of India announced that sexual harassment of working women amounts to violation of rights of gender equality. As a logical consequence it also amounts to violation of the right to practice any profession, occupation, and trade. The judgement also laid down the definition of sexual harassment, the preventive steps, the complaint mechanism, and the need for creating awareness of the rights of women workers. Implementation of these guidelines has already begun by employers by amending the rules under the Industrial Employment Standing Orders Act 1946.

20. **The unorganised sector.** Many of the laws mentioned above apply to the unorganised sector also. In some cases a separate notification may be necessary to extend the application of a particular law to a new sector. It is useful to notice that some pieces of legislation are more general in character and apply across the board to all sectors. The Trade Union Act 1926, The Minimum Wages Act 1948, The Contract Labour (Regulation and Abolition) Act 1970, The Workman's Compensation Act 1923, and The Payment of Wages Act 1936 are examples of this type. In certain cases, even the IDA 1947 would be included.

In addition to the above there are special sectoral laws applicable to particular sectors of the unorganised. Under this category are laws like the Building and Construction Workers Act 1996, the Bonded Labour System (Abolition) Act 1976, The Interstate Migrant Workers Act 1979, The Dock Workers Act 1986, The Plantation Labour Act 1951, The Transport Workers Act, The Beedi and Cigar Workers Act 1966, The Child Labour (Prohibition and Regulation) Act 1986, and The Mine Act 1952.

Broadly speaking these sectoral laws either abolish or prohibit an abominable practice like bonded labour or they seek to regulate exploitative conditions by regulating working hours and conditions of service.

A recent trend has been to seek the creation of a welfare fund through the collection of a levy from which medical benefits or pension provisions are made. Workers and management may contribute and attempt to set up tripartite boards for implementation of welfare benefits. In some states like Kerala a large number of such boards have already been set up to take care of welfare in different sectors of employment.

INTERNATIONAL LABOUR ORGANISATION (ILO)

India is a founder member of the International Labour Organisation, which came into existence in 1919. At present the ILO has 175 Members. A unique feature of the ILO is its tripartite character. The membership of the ILO ensures the growth of tripartite system in the Member countries. At every level in the Organisation, Governments are associated with the two other social partners, namely the workers and employers. All the three groups are represented on almost all the deliberative organs of the ILO and share responsibility in conducting its work. The three organs of the ILO are:

- **International Labour Conferences.** General Assembly of the ILO – Meets every year in the month of June.
- **Governing Body.** Executive Council of the ILO. Meets three times in a year in the months of March, June and November.
- **International Labour Office.** A permanent secretariat.

The work of the Conference and the Governing Body is supplemented by Regional Conferences, Regional Advisory Committees, Industrial and Analogous Committees, Committee of Experts, Panels of Consultants, Special Conference and meetings, etc.

1. International Labour Conferences

Except for the interruption caused by the Second World War, the international Labour Conference has continued, since its first session in 1919 to meet at least once a year. The Conference, assisted by the Governing Body, adopts biennial programme and budget, adopts International Labour Standards in the form of Conventions and Recommendations and provides a forum for discussing social economic and labour related issues. India has regularly and actively participated in the Conference through its tripartite delegations.

The Conference has so far had 4 Indian Presidents viz., Sir. Atul Chatterjee (1927), Shri Jagjivan Ram, Minister for Labour (1950), Dr. Nagendra Singh, President, International Court of Justice (1970) and Shri Ravindra Verma, Minister of Labour and Parliamentary Affairs (1979). There have also been 8 Indian Vice Presidents of the International Labour Conference, 2 from the Government group, 3 from the Employers and 3 from the Workers' Group. Indians have chaired the important Committees of the Conferences like Committee on Application of Standards, Selection Committee and Resolutions Committee.

2. Governing Body

The Governing Body of the ILO is the executive wing of the Organisation. It is also tripartite in character. Since 1922 Indian has been holding a non-elective seat on the Governing Body as one of the 10 countries of chief industrial importance. Indian employers and workers' representatives have been elected as Members of the Governing Body from time to time.

Four Indians have so far been elected Chairman of the Governing Body. They are Sir Atul Chatterjee (1932-33), Shri Shamal Dharee Lall, Secretary, Ministry of Labour (1948-49), Shri S.T. Merani, Joint Secretary, Ministry of Labour (1961-62) and Shri B.G. Deshmukh, Secretary, Ministry of Labour (1984-85).

The Governing Body of ILO functions through its various Committees. India is a member of all six committees of the Governing Body viz. (i) Programme, Planning & Administrative; (ii) Freedom of Association; (iii) Legal Issues and International Labour Standards; (iv) Employment & Social Policy; (v) Technical Cooperation and (vi) Sectoral and Technical Meetings and Related issues.

3. *International Labour Offices*

The International Labour Office, Geneva provides the Secretariat for all Conferences and other meetings and is responsible for the day-to-day implementation of decisions taken by the Conference, Governing Body etc. Indians have held positions of importance in the International Labour Office. Special mention must be made of Shri S.K. Jain who retired as Deputy Director General of the ILO. Shri Gopinath is currently the Director International Institute of Labour Studies, Geneva.

International Labour Standard - ILO Conventions

The principal means of action in the ILO is the setting up the International Labour Standards in the form of Conventions and Recommendations. Conventions are international treaties and are instruments, which create legally binding obligations on the countries that ratify them. Recommendations are non-binding and set out guidelines orienting national policies and actions. Pakistan (34), Japan (45), Australia (57), China (20), Malaysia (14), Sri Lanka (39) and USA (14).

The approach of India with regard to International Labour Standards has always been positive. The ILO instruments have provided guidelines and useful framework for the evolution of legislative and administrative measures for the protection and advancement of the interest of labour.

Core Conventions of the ILO

The eight Core Conventions of the ILO (also called fundamental/human rights conventions) are:

- Forced Labour Convention (No. 29)
- Abolition of Forced Labour Convention (No.105)
- Equal Remuneration Convention (No.100)
- Discrimination (Employment Occupation) Convention (No.111)

(The above four have been ratified by India).

- Freedom of Association and Protection of Right to Organised Convention (No.87)
- Right to Organise and Collective Bargaining Convention (No.98)
- Minimum Age Convention (No.138)
- Worst forms of Child Labour Convention (No.182)

(These four are yet to be ratified by India)

ILO Area Office, New Delhi

An ILO Branch Office was set up in New Delhi in 1929. The work of the Branch Office consisted of collecting and disseminating information and maintaining links with the Government of India and the Organisations of Employers and Workers and generally to publicise the work of ILO among the Indian audience. With the planned programme of decentralisation, the Branch Office became an Area Office of ILO in 1970. The Area Office at New Delhi has been changing in its jurisdiction over the years. It now coordinates technical assistance activities in diverse focus as such as rural Labour, women workers, employment generation, occupational safety and health, population control, family welfare, etc. in India and Bhutan.

ILO Committee of Experts

Prominent Indians have served on the ILO Committee of Experts on Application of Conventions and Recommendations, which is an independent body to oversee the implementation of the ILO Conventions by Member countries. The Members of the Committee of Experts are appointed in their individual capacity from among persons of independent, standing and are drawn from all parts of the world.

Indian who have been members of the Committee include:

- Justice P.N. Bhagwati, Retd. Chief Justice of India - Since 1978.
- Justice P.V. Gajendragadkar - 1972-1977
- Shri A. Ramaswamy Mudaliar - 1959-1970
- Shri R.M. Bannerjee - 1956-1988
- Shri Atul Chatterjee - 1936-1938 & 1945-1955.

ILO and Child Labour

ILO's interest in child labour, young persons and their problems is well known. It has adopted a number of Conventions and Recommendations in this regard. In India, within a framework of the Child Labour (Prohibition and Regulations) Act, 1986 and through the National Policy on Child Labour, ILO has funded the preparation of certain local and industry specific projects. In two vital projects, viz. Child Labour Action and Support Programmes (CLASP) and International Programme on Elimination of Child Labour (IPEC), the ILO is playing a vital role.

The implementation of IPEC programmes in India has certainly created a very positive impact towards understanding the problem of child labour and in highlighting the need to elimination child labour as expeditiously as possible. A major contribution of the IPEC programme in India is that it has generated a critical consciousness among all the 3 social partners for taking corrective measures to eliminate child labour.

Decent Work

The concept of Decent Work is being propagated by the ILO. It encompasses four strategic objectives:

I. **Promotion of Rights at Work.** It calls for renewed attention to ILO's standards, as well as a fresh look at complimentary means and instruments for achieving this goal.

II. **Employment.** Creation of greater employment and income opportunities for women and men as a means to reduce poverty and inequality.

III. **Social Protection.** This section emphasizes expansion of social security schemes.

IV. **Social Dialogue.** This emphasizes examining ways of strengthening the institutional capacity of ILO constituents as well as their contribution to the process of dialogue.

The concept of Decent Work emphasizes that the quantity of employment should not be divorced from quality of work and stresses that a social and economic system should be evolved to ensure basic security and employment without compromising workers' rights and social standards in a highly competitive world.

Linkage Between Trade and Labour Standard

The issue of linkage between trade and labour standards was first raised at the conclusions of the Uruguay Round at Marrakesh in 1994 by the USA. India and other developing countries had taken the position that labour standards at the international levels can be appropriately addressed only in the ILO, not in the WTO. The social clause is not within the mandate of the WTO. In response, India had countered that the relationship between trade and immigration policies may also be examined in the WTO. The issue was not pursued seriously by the US for sometime thereafter.

The issue again came up at the First Ministerial Conference of the WTO in Singapore in 1996. In this Conference, developing countries including India once again rejected the proposal of the US to include labour standards as an agenda in the WTO. The final Ministerial Declaration at Singapore endorsed the stand of the developing countries and reiterated the following:

i. ILO is the competent body to set and deal with core labour standards and WTO affirms its support in promoting such standards.
ii. It rejected the use of labour standards for protectionist purposes and agreed that the comparative advantage of countries, particularly low wage developing countries, must in no way be put into question.
iii. It noted that the WTO and ILO Secretariats would continue their existing collaboration.

Labour Legislation and Indian Constitutions

The Indian constitutions contain important provisions which have a direct bearing on the course of social and labour legislation in the country. These are mainly incorporated the fundamental rights and directive principle of state policy. Fundamental are justifiable. The directive principle through not justifiable, are "fundamental in divergence of the country" and it is "the duty of the state to apply these principle in making laws". These principles lay down that the state should strive to promote welfare of the people by securing and promoting as effectively as it may, a social order in which social, economic and political, shall inform all institutions of national life.

Labour legislation is necessary from the view point of law and order situation and national security of the country. State plays a vital role the continuing production. It helps in the economic development of the country. The idea of Welfare State is embodied in the Directive Principles of the constitution and for reason; various labour laws have been enacted to protect the sections of the society. The fundamental right and directive principle of state policy are discussed below.

Fundamental Rights Part III

Part III of the Indian Constitution(A 12-35) deals with the FR granted to individuals.

Originally seven groups of rights. But now 44th Amendment 'Right to property' deleted.

Classification of Fundamental Rights: The citizens of India enjoy the following fundamental rights:

1. **Right to equality and liberty (Article 14 to 18).** According to this right all citizens of the country are equal in eyes of law. Everyone has the equal opportunity to get the government job. The untouchability has been abolished. All other types of titles also have been abolished except the educational degrees.
   14: Equality before law
   15: Prohibition of discrimination
   16: Equality of opportunity
   17: Abolishes practices of untouchability
   18: Prohibits state from confirming any title
2. **Right to Freedom (Article 19 to 22).** According to this right every Indian citizen enjoys the following seven fundamental freedoms:
   (i) Freedom of speech and expression.
   (ii) Freedom of assembly peacefully and without arms.
   (iii) Freedom to form associations and unions.
   (iv) Freedom of movement.
   (v) Freedom to reside in any part of India.
   (vi) Right to buy, keep and dispose of property.
   (vii) Freedom of profession.
3. **Right against Exploitation (Article 23 to 24).** According to this right no one can sell or purchase any man or woman, no one can take work from others without paying the money for his labour

and children below 14 years cannot be employed in a factory or mine or any other dangerous work.

4. **Right to Freedom of Religion (Article 25 to 28).** India has been declared a secular State. The State itself has no religion. According to this right, freedom of the religion has been granted to every individual. Anyone can follow, practice and preach any religion he likes and has faith in the same.
5. **Cultural and Educational Right (Article 29 to 30).** According to this right the people of any part of India, whose language or culture is separate have the right to protect and develop it. Every citizen has the right to get admission to any government aided educational institution.
6. **Right to Constitutional Remedies.** The right to constitutional remedies is a most important fundamental right for the citizens of India. According to this right all the citizens have the right to move to the Supreme Court or to any of the High Court in India. With this right the citizens are able to protect their all the fundamental rights. While protecting the fundamental rights these courts can issue the following writs:

The Writs:

Habeas Corpus. "To have a body"- An order calling a person who has detained another to produce the letter before the court to let it know, on what ground he has been confirmed.

Prohibition. It is issued by SC or HC to a inferior court forbidding jurisdiction or to usurp a jurisdiction with which it is not legally vested.

Mandamus. "We command" : Commands the person to whom it is addressed to perform some public or quasilegal duty which he has refused to perform.

Certiorary. It is issued to a lower court after a case has been decided by it, quashing the decision or order.

Quo-Warranto. It is a proceeding by which the court enquires into the legality of the claim which a party asserts to a public office.

Distinction between Fundamental Rights and Directive Principles

- Fundamental Rights are justifiable while Directive Principles are not.
- If there is discrepancy between Fundamental Rights and Directive Principles then Fundamental Rights will prevail.
- Fundamental Rights are negative and Directive Principles are positive.
- Fundamental Rights responsible for political democracy while Directive Principles are for establishment of economical and welfare state.

The Directive Principles of State Policy Part IV

(1) Equitable distribution of wealth or the socialist pattern of society and equal pay for equal work for both men and women.

(2) Provision of adequate means of livelihood to all its citizens, men and women.

(3) Provision of employment to all.

(4) Free and compulsory education for children.

(5) Living wage for workers.

(6) Protection of childhood and youth against exploitation and against moral and material abandonment.

(7) Organisation of village panchayats as units of self-government (Article 40).

(8) Prohibition of the consumption except for medical purposes of intoxicating drinks and of drugs injurious to health.

(9) Organisation of agriculture and animal husbandry on modern and scientific lines.

(10) Promotion of international peace and security and maintenance of just and honorable relations between the nations of the world.

The directive principle of state policy are not enforceable by any court, but they are fundamental in the governance of the country and it is the duty of the state to apply them in making laws (Art. 37) the principle having a bearing on social and labour legislation are as follows. Policy in the Constitution of India have been inspired by the Constitution of Ireland. It contains ideals of a Welfare State. The Directive Principles are contained in Part-IV of the Constitution.

(i) The state shall strive to promote the welfare of the people by securing and protecting as effectively as it may a social order in which justice – social, economic and political shall inform all the institutions of the national life. {Art. 38(1)}

(ii) The state shall, in particular direct its policy towards securing (a) that the citizen men and woman, equally have the right to an adequate means of livelihood (b) that there is equal pay for equal work both men and women (c) that the health and strength of workers, men and women and the tender age of children are not abashed and that the citizen are not forced by economic necessity to enter avocations unsuited to their age and their strength and (d) that the children are given opportunities and facilities to develop in healthy manner and in conditions of freedom and dignity and that childhood and youth. Are protected against exploitations and against moral and material and abandonment (Art. 39).

(iii) "The State shall, within the limits of its economic capacity and development, make effective provision for securing the right to work, to education and to public assistance in cases of unemployment, old age, sickness and disablement and in other cases of undeserved want." The custodian of Fundamental Rights is the Supreme Court of India. (Article 41 in Part IV)

(iv) The state shall make provision for securing just humane conditions of work and for maternity reliefs. (Art. 42)

(v) The state shall Endeavour to secure by suitable legislation or economic organisation or in any other ways to all workers –agricultural, industrial otherwise., work, a living wage, conditions, of work ensuring a decent standard of life and full enjoyment of leisure and social and cultural opportunities. (Art. 43)

(vi) The state shall take step, by suitable legislations or in any other ways, to secure the participation of workers in the management of undertaking, establishment or other organisation engaged in any industry. {Art. 43 (A)}

The above principle have a bearing on both labour and social legislation, but there are some other which are related more to social issues. These are as follows :

(i) The state shall Endeavour to provide, within a periods of ten years from the commencement of this constitution, for free and compulsory education for all children until they complete the age of fourteen years. (Art. 46)

(ii) The state shall promote with special care the educational and economic interest of the weaker sections of the people, and, in particular, of the Scheduled castes and scheduled Tribes and shall protect them from social injustice and all forms of exploitations. (Art. 46)

(iii) The state shall regards the raising of the level of nutrition and the standard of living of its people and the improvement of public health as among its primary duties and, in particular, the state shall Endeavour to bring about prohibition of the consumption except for medicinal purposes of intoxicating drinks and drugs which are injurious to health. (Art. 47)

The Constitution which envisages parliamentary form of government is federal in structure with unitary features. President of India is constitutional head of executive of the Union. Article 74 (1) of the Constitution provides that there shall be a Council of Ministers with the Prime Minister as head to aid and advise president who shall in exercise of his functions, act in accordance with such advice. Real executive power thus vests in Council of Ministers with Prime Minister as head. Council of Ministers is collectively responsible to the House of the People (Lok Sabha). Similarly, in states, Governor is head of executive, but it is the Council of Ministers with Chief Minister as head in whom real executive power vests. Council of Ministers of a state is collectively responsible to Legislative Assembly.

Amended Preamble

We, the people of India, having solemnly resolved to constitute India into a Sovereign Socialist Secular Democratic Republic and to secure to all its citizens: JUSTICE, social, economic and political; LIBERTY of thought, expression, belief, faith and worship; EQUALITY of status and of opportunity; and to promote among them all FRATERNITY assuring the dignity of the individual and unity and integration of the Nation; IN OUR CONSTITUENT ASSEMBLY this twenty-sixth day of November, 1949, do HEREBY ADOPT, ENACT AND GIVE TO OURSELVES THIS CONSTITUTION. Added by the 42nd Constitutional Amendment.

THE FACTORIES ACT, 1948

Objective & Applicability

The Factories Act, 1948 has been enacted to consolidate and amend the law regulating the workers working in the factories. It extends to whole of India and applies to every factory wherein 20 or more workers are ordinary employed. Since the aim and object of the Act is to safeguard the interest of workers and protect them from exploitation, the Act prescribes certain standards with regard to safety, welfare and working hours of workers, apart from other provisions.

Factory means any premises including the precincts thereof where ten or more persons are working in any manufacturing process being carried on with aid of power and where twenty or more workers are working without the aid of power.

Employee Health

- Every factory should be kept dean and free from effluvia arising from any drain, privy or other nuisance. {Section 11}
- Effective arrangements should be made in every factory for the treatment and effluents due to the manufacturing process carried on therein, so as to render them innocuous, and for their disposal. {Section 12}
- Effective and suitable provisions should be made in every factory for securing and maintaining in every workroom; adequate ventilation by the circulation of fresh air; and such a temperatures will secure to workers therein reasonable conditions of comfort and prevent injury to health. {Section 13}
- Effective measures should be taken to prevent inhalation of dust to prevent inhalation of dust and fume that may produce in the course of manufacturing process. {Section 14}
- In any factory where the humidity of air is artificially increased, the State Government may make rules prescribing standards of humidification; regulating the methods used for artificially increasing humidity of the air; and directing prescribed test for determining the humidity of the air to be correctly carried out and recorded; and prescribing methods to be adopted for securing adequate ventilation and cooling of the air in the workrooms. {Section 1S}

- No room in any factory should lie overcrowded to an extent injurious to the health of the workers employed therein. {Section 16}
- In every part of a factory where workers are working or passing, there should be provided and maintained sufficient and suitable lighting, natural or artificial, or both. {Section 17}
- In every factory effective arrangements should be made to provide and maintain at suitable points conveniently' situated for all workers employed therein a sufficient supply of wholesome drinking water. {Section 18}
- In every factory sufficient latrine and urinal accommodation of prescribed types should be provided conveniently situated and accessible to workers, separately for male and female workers, at all times while they are at the factory. {Section 19}
- In every factory there should be provided a sufficient number of spittoons in convenient places and they shall be maintained in a clean and hygienic condition. {Section 20}

Employee Safety

- The machinery in every factory should be properly fenced. {Section 21}
- Only the trained adult male worker, wearing tight fitting clothing which should be supplied by the Occupier, should be allowed to work near the machinery in motion. {Section 22}
- No young person shall be employed on dangerous machinery, unless he is fully instructed as to the danger arising in connection with the machine and the precautions to be observed and he has received sufficient training in work at the machine. {Section 23}
- Suitable arrangements should be made to provide striking gear and devices for cutting off power in case of emergencies. {Section 24}
- Sufficient precautions should be taken with regard to self-acting machines to avoid accidents. {Section 25}
- To prevent danger, all machinery driven by power should be encased and effectively guarded. {Section 26}
- Woman worker and children should not be employed in any part of the factory for pressing cotton in which a cotton-opener is at work. {Section 27}
- Hoists and Lifts in a factory should be periodically inspected by the Competent Person. {Section 28}
- Lifting Machines, Chains, Ropes and Lifting Tackles in a factory should be periodically inspected by the Competent Person. {Section 29}
- Where process of grinding is carried on, a notice indicating the maximum safe working peripheral speed of every grind-stone or abrasive wheel etc., should be fixed to the revolving machinery.{Section 30}
- Where any plant or machinery or any part thereof is operated at a pressure above atmospheric pressure, effective measures should be taken to ensure that the safe working pressure of such plant of machinery or part is not exceeded.{Section 31}
- Floors, stairs and means of access should be soundly constructed and properly maintained. {Section 32}
- Pits, sumps opening in floor etc., should be either securely covered or fenced. {Section 33}
- No workman shall be employed in any factory to lift, carry or move any load so heavy as to be likely to cause him injury. {Section 34}
- Necessary protective equipment should be provided to protect the eyes of the workman, where the working involves risk of injury to the eyes. {Section 35}

- Suitable precautionary arrangements should be taken against dangerous fumes, gases etc. {Section 36}
- Every practicable measures should be taken to prevent any explosion where the manufacturing process produces dust, gas, fume or vapour etc. {Section 37}
- Every practicable measures should be taken to prevent the outbreak of fire and its spread, both internally and externally. {Section 38}
- The Inspector of Factories can ask the Occupier or the Manager of the Factory to furnish drawings, specification etc., of any building, machinery or a plant, in case he feels that condition of such building, machinery or the plant may likely to cause danger to human life. {Section 39}
- The Inspector of Factories can suggest suitable measures of steps to take by the Occupier or Manager for implementation, when he feels the condition of any building, machinery or a plant may likely to cause danger to human life. {Section 40}
- Wherein 1000 or more workmen are employed in a factory, the Occupier should appoint a Safety Officer to look after the safety aspects of the factory. {Section 40-B}

Employee Welfare

- Adequate and suitable 'washing facilities' should be provided in every factory. {Section 42}
- Provision should be made to provide suitable places for keeping clothing not worn during working hours and for the drying of wet clothing.{Section 43}
- In every factory, suitable arrangements for sitting should be provided and maintained for all workers obliged to work in a standing position, in order that they may take advantage of any opportunities for rest which may occur in the course of their work.{Section 44}
- First-Aid Boxes with the prescribed contents should be provided and maintained so as to be readily accessible during all working hours at the rate of at least one Box for every 150 workmen. {Section 45}
- In every factory wherein more than 500 workers are employed there should be provided and maintained an Ambulance containing the prescribed equipment and in the charge of such medical and nursing staff. {Section 45(4)}
- The Occupier should provide a canteen for the use of workers in every factory, where the number of workmen employed is more than 250. {Section 46}
- In every factory wherein more than 150 workers are employed adequate and suitable shelters or rest rooms and a suitable lunch room, with provision for drinking water, where workers can eat meals brought by them, should be provided and maintained for the use of the workers. {Section 47}
- In every factory wherein more than 30 women workers are ordinarily employed there should be provided and maintained a suitable room for the use of children under the age of six years of such women. {Section 48}

  The owner of the mill did not provide medical help. Deterioration of their health without medical care has forced them along with other 19 employees at the rice mill to revolt against the mill owner. Based on a plea by one of the workers who escaped from the mill a few day's ago, Kancheepuram collector sent a team of revenue officials and doctors to inspect the mill on Thursday. The team rescued 21 people including 11 children.
- In every factory wherein more than 500 or more workers are employed, the Occupier should employ in the factory such number of Welfare Officers as may be prescribed. {Section 49}

Working Hours of Adult Workers

- Ordinarily, a worker should not be allowed to work in a factory for more than 48 hours in any week. {Section 51}
- The workman should have one holiday for a whole day in a week. Where he was asked to work on his scheduled weekly holiday, he should be given compensatory holiday within three days of his scheduled weekly holiday. {Section 52}
- After obtaining approval from the Inspector of Factories, the workman shall be allowed to avail the compensatory holidays unavailed by him, within that month during which the compensatory holidays are due or within two months immediately following that month. {Section 53}
- Subject to the provisions of Section 51 no worker should be allowed to work more than nine hours in a day. {Section 54}
- The timings of work should be fixed in such a way that no worker should be required to work continuously for more than five hours; and he should be allowed to avail an interval for rest of at least half-an hour during his work in a day. {Section 55}
- The period of work of a workman should be so arranged that inclusive of his interval for rest under Section 55 should not spread over more than ten and a half hours in any day. {Section 56}.
- Worker works in a factory for more than nine hours in any day or for more than forty-eight hours in any week, he shall, in respect of overtime work, be entitled to wages at the rate of twice his ordinary rate of wages. {Section 59}

Further Restrictions on Employment of Women [Section 66]

Women is not allowed to work during the night hours from between 10 P.M. and 5 A.M. Factories act 1948, shall allow women to work in between the hours of 6 A.M. and 7 P.M. only

General Duties of the Occupier

1. Every Occupier should ensure, so far is reasonably practicable the health, safety and welfare of all workers while they are at work in the factory.
2. Without prejudice to the generality of the provisions of sub-section (1), the matters to which such duty extends, include :
   - the provisions and maintenance of plant and systems of work in the factory that are safe and without risks to health;
   - the arrangements in the factory for ensuring safety and absence of risks to health in connection with the use, handling, storage and transport of articles and substance;
   - the provision of such information, instruction, training and supervision as are necessary to ensure, the health and safety of all workers at work;
   - the maintenance of all places of work in the factory in a condition that is safe and without risks to health and the provision and maintenance of such means of access to, and egress from, such places as are safe and without such risks;
   - the provision, maintenance or monitoring of such working environment in the factory for the workers that is safe, without risks to health and adequates, regards, facilities and arrangements for their welfare at work.
   - Except in such cases as may be prescribed, every Occupier should prepare, and, so often as may be appropriate, revise, a written statement of his general policy with respect to the

health and safety of the workers at work and the organisation and arrangements for the time being in force for carrying out that policy, and to bring the statement and any revision thereof to the notice of all the workers in such manner as may be prescribed. {Section 7-A}

THE MINES ACT, 1952

The Mines Act, 1952 came into force on 1st July, 1952. The provisions of the said Act came into force on different dates but not later than 31st December, 1953 as has been mentioned in the Act. The applicability of the Act is extended to the whole of India. Mines Act, 1952 was legislated with the purpose of regulating the health and safety of labourers working in the mines.

Mines Act, 1952 consists of 88 sections divided into 10 chapters. The said act came into existence solely for the safety and health and welfare of workers working in the mines. The act however, defines as to what is a mine. As per clause (j) of section 2 of the Act, mine means the place where any excavation work is carried on for the searching and obtaining of minerals. Minerals as per clause (jj) of section 2 means those substances which can be obtained from the earth by means of digging, dredging, drilling, mining or through other operations. Minerals as per this clause also include mineral oils which mean natural gas and petroleum.

Chapter 2 of the Act deals with Inspectors and Certifying surgeons. Section 5 provides that there should be an appointment of one chief inspector that would be regulating all the territories in which mining is done and an inspector for every mine who would be sub ordinate to the chief inspector. Moreover, the District Magistrate is also empowered to perform the duties of an inspector subject to the orders of the Central Government. However, the Act restricts the District Magistrate from exercising such powers under sections 22, 22A and 61 of the Act.

The chief inspector or any of the inspectors would make such inquiry, at any time whether day or night, in order to check whether the law is being abided in the mines or not. However, they would not exercise their rights in such a way which would obstruct the work in mines. The inspector would inquire about the safety, welfare and health of the persons working in the mine along with the conditions of the mine. While making inquiry and examining the conditions of the mine, the chief inspector or any inspector has reason to believe that any offence is being committed, in that case, the inspector would be empowered to initiate search and seizure as mentioned in the Code of Criminal Procedure, 1973.

The certifying surgeon is appointed under section 11 of the Act. Any medical practitioner can be appointed as certifying surgeon for a group of mines as notified by the Central Government. The certifying surgeon has the power to appoint qualified medical practitioner to exercise such powers which the certifying surgeon would specify. The certifying surgeon and the qualified medical practitioner would examine the persons working in the mine and the exercise of such medical supervision would be prescribed by the Central Government.

Chapter 5 the of the Act deals with health and safety of the workers. Section 19 provides that there should be the facility of safe drinking water in every mine and that each such point should be legibly marked as "Drinking Water" in such languages as is understood by the people working there. There would be accessibility of first aid boxes or the cupboards filled with such contents and a person trained in such first aid treatment should be available during the working hours of the mines. A conveyance should be readily available in cases where there is a need to take any person to the nearest dispensary or hospital. The number of first aid boxes should be such as prescribed by the central government however, in places where there are more than hundred and fifty workers, in such cases, the size of the room should be such which can occupy all the workers along with first aid boxes and required number of nurses.

The mines act, 1952 was amended in 1983 which provided a new law for the mine workers. It provides that the person working in the mine should not be less than eighteen years of age. If in case a child is seen to be working in the mine, in such a case, the owner, manager or agent of such a mine should be held responsible and a penalty of rupees five hundred would be imposed upon him. Since there is a lesser penalty imposed upon the owner, manager or agent, so the parliament has drafted a new amendment bill in 2011 which is still pending. Therefore, the new amendment bill would bring beneficial changes in favour of the workers working in the mines.

INTER STATE MIGRANT WORKMEN ACT, 1979

The Inter-State Migrant Workmen (Regulation of Employment and Conditions of Service) Act, 1979 is an Act of the Parliament of India enacted to regulate the condition of service of inter-state labourers in Indian labour law. The Act's purpose is to protect workers whose services are requisitioned outside their native states in India. Whenever an employer faces shortage of skills among the locally available workers, the act creates provision to employ better skilled workers available outside the state.

In addition to the general labour laws applicable to all workers, the interstate workers are entitled with:

- equal or better wages for the similar nature & duration of work applicable for the local workmen or stipulated minimum wages under the Minimum Wages Act, 1948 whichever is more,
- displacement allowance (Section 14),
- home journey allowance (Section 15) including payment of wages during the period of journey,
- suitable residential accommodation and medical facilities free of charge on mandatory basis.
- Termination of employment after the contract period without any liability.
- Right to lodge compliant with the authorities within three months of any incident, accident, etc.

Registration of all contractors who employs or employed five or more Interstate Migrant Workmen on any day of the preceding 12 months.

- Furnish the details of workmen periodically in such forms as prescribed by state government.
- Maintain the registers indicating the details of interstate workers and make available for scrutiny by the statutory authorities.
- Issue of passbook affixed with a passport-sized photograph of the workman indicating the name and the place of the establishment where the worker is employed, the period of employment, rates of wages, etc. to every inter-state migrant workman.
- Reporting by the contractor the incidence of fatal accident or serious injury of such workman to the specified authorities of both the States and also the next of kin of the workman.
- Liable for the prescribed punishments for violations committed under this Act.

Role of Principal Employers

- Registration of all principal employers who employs or employed directly or indirectly five or more Interstate Migrant Workmen on any day of the preceding 12 months.
- Maintain the registers indicating the details of interstate workers and make available for scrutiny by the statutory authorities.
- Every principal employer shall nominate a representative duly authorized by him to be present at the time of disbursement of wages by the contractor and it shall be the duty of such representative to certify the amounts paid as wages in such manner and may be prescribed.
- Principal employer shall be liable to bear the wages and other benefits to interstate workers in case of failure by the contractor to effect the same.
- Liable for the prescribed punishments for violations committed under this Act.

Role of State Governments

- Appointment of inspectors to oversee implementation of this act.
- Appointment of registration officers to grant and revoke registration of contractors / principal employers / establishments.
- Appointment of licensing officers to grant, suspend and revoke licenses to contractors / principal employers / establishments.
- Making rules for carrying out the purposes of this Act subject to the condition of previous publication.
- Entertaining appeals from the aggrieved parties and disposal of the same as per this Act.

CONTRACT LABOUR ACT, 1970

The Object of the Contract Labour Regulation and Abolition Act, 1970 is to prevent exploitation of contract labour and also to introduce better conditions of work. A workman is deemed to be employed as Contract Labour when he is hired in connection with the work of an establishment by or through a Contractor. Contract workmen are indirect employees. Contract Labour differs from Direct Labour in terms of employment relationship with the establishment and method of wage payment. Contract Labour, by and large is not borne on pay roll nor is paid directly. The Contract Workmen are hired, supervised and remunerated by the Contractor, who in turn, is remunerated by the Establishment hiring the services of the Contractor.

The Act applies to the Principal Employer of an Establishment and the Contractor where in 20 or more workmen are employed or were employed even for one day during preceding 12 months as Contract Labour. For the purpose of calculating the number, contract labour employed for different purposes through different contractor has to be taken into consideration. This Act does not apply to the Establishments where work performed is of intermittent or seasonal nature. If a Principal Employer or the Contractor falls within the vicinity of this Act then, such Principal Employer and the Contractor have to apply for Registration of the Establishment and License respectively. The contractor The Act also provides for Temporary Registration in case the Contract Labour is hired for a period not more than 15 days. Any change occurring in the particulars specified in the Registration or Licensing Certificate needs to be informed to the concerned Registering Officer within 30 days of such change. From combined reading of Section 7 and Rules 17 & 18 of the Contract Labour (Regulation and Abolition) Central Rules, 1971, it appears that the Principal Employer has to apply for registration in respect of each establishment. Other important point to note is that a License issued for One Contract cannot be used for entirely different Contract work even though there is no change in the Establishment.

The Act enjoins Joint and Several responsibity on the Principal Employer and the Contractor. The Principal Employer should ensure that the Contractor does the following:

(a) Pays the wages as determined by the Government, if any, or;

(b) Pays the wages as may be fixed by the Commissioner of Labour.

(c) In their absence pays fair wages to contract labourer.

(d) Provides the following facilities:

   i. Canteen (if employing 100 or more workmen in one place) and if the work is likely to last for 6 months or more.

   ii. Rest rooms where the workmen are required to halt at night and the work is likely to last for 3 months or more.

   iii. Requisite number of latrines and urinals - separate for men and women.

   iv. Drinking water.

iv. Washing.
v. First Aid.

(e) Maintains various registers and records, displays notices, abstracts of the Acts, Rules etc.
(f) Issues employment card to his workmen, etc.

BUILDINGS AND OTHER CONSTRUCTION WORKERS ACT, 1996

The Act provides for regulating the employment and conditions of service of building and other construction workers and also provides for their safety, health and welfare measures and other matters connected therewith or incidental thereto.

The Act applies to every establishment, belonging to or under the control of government, any body corporate or firm, an individual or association or other body of individuals which or who employs building workers in any building and other construction work and includes an establishment belonging to a contractor which employs, or had employed on any day of the preceding 12 months, 10 or more building workers in any building or other construction work, but does not includes an individual who employs such workers in any building or construction in relation to his residence the total cost of such construction not being more than Rs. 10 lakhs.

The Govt. of NCT of Delhi has notified the Delhi Building and Other Construction Workers (Regulation of Employment and Conditions of Service) Rules, 2002 on 10.1.2002

Responsibility and Liability of Employer

- The Act makes it mandatory for every employer to give notice of commencement of any building or other construction work at least 30 days before the commencement with complete details including nature of the work involved, number of workers likely to be employed, approximate duration of the work and the arrangement for the storage of the explosives to be used in the building or other construction work.
- Every employer is required to get its Establishment registered within 60 days from its commencement or from the date on which this Act becomes applicable to such Establishments.
- Employers are also responsible for payment of wages to each Building Worker employed by him providing weekly paid rest wages for overtime basic welfare amenities like creches, first aid, canteen etc, as provided under the Act and the rules framed there after.
- Every employer is required to pay the Cess @ 1 % of the cost of construction to the Delhi Building & Other Construction Workers Welfare Board.

Enforcement

- Labour Commissioner of Delhi Government has been notified as Chief Inspector of Inspections under this Act.
- All Joint, Deputy, Assistant Labour Commissioners, Labour Officers and Inspecting Officers have been notified as Inspectors.
- All Asstt, Labour Commissioners and Labour Officers have been appointed as Registering Officers for respective Districts.

THE CHILD LABOUR ACT, 1986

The Child Labour (Prohibition and Regulation) Act, 1986 is one the most debated acts regarding children in India. It outlines where and how children can work and where they can not. The provisions of the act are meant to be acted upon immediately after the publication of the act, except for part III that discusses the conditions in which a child may work. Part III can only come into effect as per a date appointed by the Central Government (which was decided as 26th of May, 1993).

The act defines a child as any person who has not completed his fourteenth year of age. Part II of the act prohibits children from working in any occupation listed in Part A of the Schedule; for example: Catering at railway establishments, construction work on the railway or anywhere near the tracks, plastics factories, automobile garages, etc. The act also prohibits children from working in places where certain processes are being undertaken, as listed in Part B of the Schedule; for example: beedi making, tanning, soap manufacture, brick kilns and roof tiles units, etc. These provisions do not apply to a workshop where the occupier is working with the help of his family or in a government recognised or aided school.

The act calls for the establishment of a Child Labour Technical Advisory Committee (CLTAC) who is responsible for advising the government about additions to the Schedule lists.

Part III of the act outlines the conditions in which children may work in occupations/processes not listed in the schedule. The number of hours of a particular kind of establishment of class of establishments is to be set and no child can work for more than those many hours in that particular establishment. Children are not permitted to work for more than three hour stretches and must receive an hour break after the three hours. Children are not permitted to work for more than six hour stretches including their break interval and can not work between the hours of 7 p.m. and 8 a.m. No child is allowed to work overtime or work in more than one place in a given day. A child must receive a holiday from work every week. The employer of the child is required to send a notification to an inspector about a child working in their establishment and keep a register of all children being employed for inspection.

If there is a dispute as to the age of the child, the inspector can submit the child for a medical exam to determine his/her age when a birth certificate is not available. Notices about prohibition of certain child labour and penalties should be posted in every railway station, port authority and workshop/establishment.

The health conditions of work being undertaken by children shall be set for each particular kind of establishment of class of establishments by the appropriate government. The rules may cover topics such as cleanliness, light, disposal of waste and effluents, drinking water, bathrooms, protection of eyes, maintenance and safety of buildings, etc.

Section IV of the act outlines various remaining aspects such as Penalties. The penalty of allowing a child to work in occupations/ processes outlined in the schedule which are prohibited is a minimum of 3 months prison time and/or a minimum of Rs. 10,000 in fines. Second time offenders are subject to jail time of minimum six months. Failure to notify an inspector, keep a register, post a sign or any other requirement is punishable by simple imprisonment and/or a fine up to Rs. 10,000. Offenders can only be tried in courts higher than a magistrate or metropolitan magistrate of the first class. Courts also have the authority to appoint people to be inspectors under this act.

Rules of this act must be passed by the respective parliaments (state or central). Any changes or added provisions must be passed by the parliament. The establishment of this act also calls for a change in a number of other acts. The Employment of Children Act of 1938 is repealed. The enactment of this act changes the definition of child to one who has not completed his fourteenth year of age. Hence under provisions of this act the age of a child is also changed in the Minimum Wages Age 1948, the Plantations Labour Act 1951, the Merchant Shipping Act 1958, and the Motor Transport Workers Act 1961.

MULTIPLE CHOICE QUESTIONS

1. Which of the following is not an objective of labour legislation?
   (1) Protecting workers' rights and interests
   (2) Promoting social justice
   (3) Maximizing profits for employers
   (4) Providing better working conditions
2. Which of the following is not a principle of labour legislation?
   (1) Equality and non-discrimination
   (2) Collective bargaining and freedom of association
   (3) Monetary compensation for workers
   (4) Minimum wage and working hours
3. Which of the following is not a classification of labour legislation?
   (1) Industrial relations legislation
   (2) Safety legislation
   (3) Agricultural legislation
   (4) Financial legislation
4. Which of the following is an example of labour legislation?
   (1) The Occupational Safety and Health Act (OSHA)
   (2) The American Declaration of Independence
   (3) The United Nations Convention on the Rights of the Child
   (4) The Magna Carta
5. Which of the following is a provision of the Child Labour (Prohibition and Regulation) Act, 1986 that ensures the welfare of child laborers?
   (1) The provision of payment of wages
   (2) The provision of free education
   (3) The provision of medical facilities
   (4) All of the above
6. Which of the following is not covered under labour legislation?
   (1) Safety and health standards
   (2) Employment discrimination
   (3) Education standards
   (4) Working conditions
7. What is the purpose of the Equal Pay Act?
   (1) To prohibit employment discrimination based on race, color, religion, sex, or national origin
   (2) To establish minimum wage and overtime pay standards
   (3) To ensure that men and women receive equal pay for equal work
   (4) To establish standards for workplace safety
8. What is the purpose of the National Labor Relations Act?
   (1) To establish minimum wage and overtime pay standards
   (2) To establish standards for workplace ethics
   (3) To ensure workers' right to form unions and engage in collective bargaining
   (4) To establish standards for workplace safety
9. What is the purpose of the Family and Medical Leave Act?
   (1) To establish minimum wage and overtime pay standards
   (2) To establish standards for workplace safety
   (3) To ensure that workers have the right to take time off from work for medical reasons or to care for family members
   (4) To establish standards for workplace ethics

10. What is the purpose of the Occupational Safety and Health Act?
   (1) To establish minimum wage and overtime pay standards
   (2) To establish standards for workplace safety
   (3) To ensure that workers have the right to take time off from work for medical reasons
   (4) To establish standards for workplace ethics
11. What is the purpose of the Americans with Disabilities Act?
   (1) To establish minimum wage and overtime pay standards
   (2) To establish standards for workplace ethics
   (3) To prohibit employment discrimination based on disability
   (4) To establish standards for workplace safety
12. What is the purpose of the Wagner Act?
   (1) To establish minimum wage and overtime pay standards
   (2) To establish standards for workplace safety
   (3) To ensure workers' right to form unions and engage in collective bargaining
   (4) To establish standards for workplace ethics
13. What is the purpose of the Civil Rights Act of 1964?
   (1) To establish minimum wage and overtime pay standards
   (2) To establish standards for workplace ethics
   (3) To prohibit employment discrimination based on race, color, religion, sex, or national origin
   (4) To establish standards for workplace safety
14. What is the purpose of the Age Discrimination in Employment Act?
   (1) To establish minimum wage and overtime pay standards
   (2) To establish standards for workplace ethics
   (3) To prohibit employment discrimination based on age
   (4) To establish standards for workplace safety
15. Which of the following is not a federal labor law?
   (1) The Fair Labor Standards Act
   (2) The National Labor Relations Act
   (3) The Employee Retirement Income Security Act
   (4) The Occupational Safety and Health Act
16. What is the purpose of the Walsh-Healey Public Contracts Act?
   (1) To establish minimum wage and overtime pay standards
   (2) To establish standards for workplace ethics
   (3) To require contractors to pay prevailing wages and benefits
   (4) To establish standards for workplace safety
17. What is the purpose of the Davis-Bacon Act?
   (1) To establish minimum wage and overtime pay standards
   (2) To establish standards for workplace ethics
   (3) To require contractors to pay prevailing wages and benefits
   (4) To establish standards for workplace safety
18. What is the purpose of the Taft-Hartley Act?
   (1) To establish minimum wage and overtime pay standards
   (2) To establish standards for workplace ethics
   (3) To restrict the power of labor unions
   (4) To establish standards for workplace safety
19. What is the purpose of the Landrum-Griffin Act?
   (1) To establish minimum wage and overtime pay standards

(2) To establish standards for workplace ethics
(3) To regulate the internal affairs of labor unions
(4) To establish standards for workplace safety

20. What is the purpose of the Railway Labor Act?
(1) To establish minimum wage and overtime pay standards
(2) To establish standards for workplace ethics
(3) To regulate labor relations in the railroad and airline industries
(4) To establish standards for workplace safety

21. What is the purpose of the Norris-LaGuardia Act?
(1) To establish minimum wage and overtime pay standards
(2) To establish standards for workplace ethics
(3) To regulate labor relations and protect collective bargaining rights
(4) To establish standards for workplace safety

22. What is a union shop?
(1) A workplace in which workers are required to join a union
(2) A workplace in which workers are not required to join a union
(3) A workplace in which workers can join a union but are not required to do so
(4) A workplace in which there are no unions

23. What is an agency shop?
(1) A workplace in which workers are required to join a union
(2) A workplace in which workers are not required to join a union but are required to pay union dues
(3) A workplace in which workers can join a union but are not required to do so
(4) A workplace in which there are no unions

24. What is a right-to-work law?
(1) A law that prohibits workers from joining a union
(2) A law that requires workers to join a union
(3) A law that prohibits unions from forming
(4) A law that prohibits unions and employers from requiring workers to join a union as a condition of employment

25. **Assertion:** Labour legislation aims to promote social justice and protect the interests of workers.

Reason: Labour legislation is a response to the exploitation of workers and the unequal bargaining power between workers and employers.
(1) Both assertion and reason are true and the reason is the correct explanation of the assertion.
(2) Both assertion and reason are true but the reason is not the correct explanation of the assertion.
(3) Assertion is true but reason is false.
(4) Assertion is false but reason is true.

26. **Assertion:** Labour legislation has evolved over time in response to changing social and economic conditions.

Reason: Changes in the labor market, demographic shifts, and technological advancements have played a role in shaping labour legislation.
(1) Both assertion and reason are true and the reason is the correct explanation of the assertion.
(2) Both assertion and reason are true but the reason is not the correct explanation of the assertion.
(3) Assertion is true but reason is false.
(4) Assertion is false but reason is true.

27. **Assertion:** The principle of collective bargaining is a cornerstone of labour legislation.

Reason: Collective bargaining allows workers to bargain collectively with their employers for better wages and working conditions.

(1) Both assertion and reason are true and the reason is the correct explanation of the assertion.
(2) Both assertion and reason are true but the reason is not the correct explanation of the assertion.
(3) Assertion is true but reason is false.
(4) Assertion is false but reason is true.

28. **Assertion:** Labour legislation is necessary to protect workers' rights and interests.
Reason: The free market is inherently fair and equitable, and does not require regulation.
(1) Both assertion and reason are true and the reason is the correct explanation of the assertion.
(2) Both assertion and reason are true but the reason is not the correct explanation of the assertion.
(3) Assertion is true but reason is false.
(4) Assertion is false but reason is true.

29. **Assertion:** The principle of equal pay for equal work is enshrined in many labor laws.
Reason: The principle of equal pay for equal work has been fully realized in the modern workplace.
(1) Both assertion and reason are true and the reason is the correct explanation of the assertion.
(2) Both assertion and reason are true but the reason is not the correct explanation of the assertion.
(3) Assertion is true but reason is false.
(4) Assertion is false but reason is true.

30. In which year was the International Labour Organization (ILO) established?
(1) 1899 (2) 1919
(3) 1945 (4) 1964

31. Which of the following is the tripartite structure of the ILO?
(1) Employers, workers, and government representatives
(2) Workers, trade unions, and employers
(3) Government representatives, civil society, and workers
(4) Employers, business associations, and workers

32. What is the primary objective of the ILO?
(1) To promote social justice
(2) To protect workers' rights
(3) To promote decent work for all
(4) All of the above

33. Which of the following is an ILO convention that deals with forced labor?
(1) Convention No. 87
(2) Convention No. 98
(3) Convention No. 29
(4) Convention No. 100

34. Which of the following is an ILO convention that deals with discrimination in employment?
(1) Convention No. 87
(2) Convention No. 98
(3) Convention No. 111
(4) Convention No. 100

35. Which of the following is an ILO convention that deals with freedom of association and the right to collective bargaining?
(1) Convention No. 87
(2) Convention No. 98
(3) Convention No. 29
(4) Convention No. 100

36. Which of the following is an example of a fundamental right protected under ILO conventions?
(1) The right to work
(2) The right to safe working conditions
(3) The right to social security
(4) All of the above

37. What is the role of ILO conventions and recommendations?
(1) To establish binding legal standards for member states
(2) To provide guidelines and recommendations for member states
(3) To monitor compliance with international labor standards
(4) All of the above

38. Which of the following is an ILO program that aims to eliminate child labor?
(1) International Programme on the Elimination of Child Labour (IPEC)
(2) International Labour Standards (ILS)
(3) Better Work
(4) SCORE

39. What is the purpose of the ILO's Decent Work Agenda?
(1) To promote social justice in the workplace
(2) To promote decent work for all
(3) To address fundamental labor issues and promote social progress
(4) All of the above

40. Which of the following is an ILO initiative that aims to reduce poverty and promote economic development?
(1) International Programme on the Elimination of Child Labour (IPEC)
(2) International Labour Standards (ILS)
(3) Better Work
(4) Microinsurance Innovation Facility

41. Which of the following is an ILO initiative that aims to promote gender equality in the workplace?
(1) Women in Informal Employment: Globalizing and Organizing (WIEGO)
(2) International Programme on the Elimination of Child Labour (IPEC)
(3) SCORE
(4) Better Work

42. Which of the following is an ILO initiative that aims to improve working conditions and productivity in small and medium-sized enterprises?
(1) International Programme on the Elimination of Child Labour (IPEC)
(2) Small and Medium Enterprise (SME) Initiative
(3) SCORE
(4) Better Work

43. Which of the following is an ILO initiative that aims to promote social dialogue in the workplace?
(1) Women in Informal Employment: Globalizing and Organizing (WIEGO)
(2) International Training Centre (ITC)
(3) Industrial Relations and Social Dialogue (IRSD)
(4) Better Work

44. Which of the following is an ILO initiative that aims to promote green jobs and sustainable development?
(1) Better Work
(2) Green Jobs Programme
(3) SCORE
(4) International Labour Standards (ILS)

45. Which of the following is an example of a basic principle of ILO conventions?
(1) The right to form and join trade unions
(2) The prohibition of child labor
(3) The establishment of minimum wage rates
(4) All of the above

46. What is the role of the ILO in promoting social justice in the global labor market?
(1) To establish and promote international labor standards
(2) To provide technical assistance and training to member states
(3) To engage in policy advocacy and research on labor issues
(4) All of the above

47. Which of the following is an example of an ILO program that promotes social protection for workers?
(1) SCORE
(2) Better Work
(3) Social Protection Floor Initiative (SPF)
(4) ILO Global Commission on the Future of Work

48. Which of the following is an example of an ILO convention that deals with occupational safety and health?
(1) Convention No. 87
(2) Convention No. 98
(3) Convention No. 147
(4) Convention No. 100

49. Which of the following is an example of an ILO recommendation that deals with occupational safety and health?
(1) Recommendation No. 197
(2) Recommendation No. 87
(3) Recommendation No. 111
(4) Recommendation No. 100

50. Which of the following is an ILO program that aims to promote job creation and entrepreneurship?
(1) SCORE
(2) Better Work
(3) Start and Improve Your Business (SIYB)
(4) Social Protection Floor Initiative (SPF)

51. What is the purpose of the ILO's Global Commission on the Future of Work?
(1) To explore the future of work and its implications for social justice
(2) To develop policy recommendations for member states
(3) To engage in research and analysis on global labor trends
(4) All of the above

52. Which of the following is an ILO program that aims to promote social dialogue in the textile industry?
(1) Better Work
(2) SCORE
(3) Fairwear
(4) Women in Informal Employment: Globalizing and Organizing (WIEGO)

53. What is the purpose of the ILO's Green EnterPrize program?
(1) To promote sustainable development in the agricultural sector
(2) To promote green jobs and energy efficiency in small and medium-sized enterprises (SMEs)
(3) To promote gender equality in the workplace
(4) None of the above

54. Which of the following is an ILO initiative that aims to promote access to finance for SMEs?
(1) Microinsurance Innovation Facility
(2) Start and Improve Your Business (SIYB)
(3) Better Work
(4) Investment for Business Expansion (IBEX)

55. What is the primary objective of labour legislation?
(1) To promote social justice
(2) To protect workers' rights
(3) To maximize profits for employers
(4) All of the above

56. What is the role of labour legislation in promoting social justice?
(1) To ensure fair and equitable treatment of workers
(2) To provide equal opportunities in the workplace
(3) To address historical and systemic inequalities in the labour market
(4) All of the above

57. Which of the following is an example of labour exploitation?
(1) Paying workers less than the minimum wage
(2) Denying workers basic workplace safety standards
(3) Withholding overtime pay from employees
(4) All of the above

58. What is the role of labour legislation in addressing labour exploitation?
(1) To establish minimum wage and overtime pay standards
(2) To establish workplace safety standards
(3) To prohibit child labour
(4) All of the above

59. Which of the following is a fundamental right protected by labour legislation?
(1) The right to form and join a union
(2) The right to a fair wage
(3) The right to safe and healthy working conditions
(4) All of the above

60. What is the purpose of labour standards-setting organizations such as the International Labour Organization?
(1) To establish global labour standards
(2) To promote social justice in the international labour market
(3) To monitor compliance with labour laws and regulations
(4) All of the above

61. Which of the following is an example of a labour dispute?
(1) A strike by workers demanding higher wages
(2) A lockout by employers to break a union
(3) Negotiations between an employer and a union over a collective bargaining agreement
(4) All of the above

62. What is the role of labour legislation in resolving labour disputes?
(1) To establish legal protections for workers and unions
(2) To provide for arbitration and mediation in resolving disputes
(3) To protect the right to strike and engage in collective bargaining
(4) All of the above

63. What is the purpose of labour inspection and enforcement?
(1) To ensure compliance with labour laws and regulations
(2) To promote social justice in the workplace
(3) To monitor working conditions and protect workers' rights
(4) All of the above

64. Which of the following is not a function of labour administration?
(1) Enforcement of labour laws and regulations
(2) Development of new labour policies and programs
(3) Promotion of social justice in the labour market
(4) Provision of job training and retraining programs

65. Which article of the Indian Constitution deals with the right to work?
(1) Article 14
(2) Article 19
(3) Article 21
(4) Article 41

66. Which article of the Indian Constitution prohibits discrimination on the basis of religion, race, caste, sex, or place of birth?
(1) Article 14
(2) Article 15
(3) Article 16
(4) Article 17

67. Which of the following is a fundamental right protected under the Indian Constitution?
(1) The right to work
(2) The right to safe working conditions
(3) The right to education
(4) All of the above

68. Which of the following is not a directive principle of state policy under the Indian Constitution?
(1) Promotion of social justice
(2) Adequate means of livelihood for all citizens
(3) Promotion of free trade and commerce
(4) Protection of workers' rights

69. What is the purpose of the Minimum Wages Act, 1948?
(1) To establish minimum wage rates for workers
(2) To prohibit child labour
(3) To ensure that workers receive overtime pay
(4) All of the above

70. What is the purpose of the Industrial Disputes Act, 1947?
(1) To establish legal protections for workers and unions
(2) To regulate industrial relations and disputes

(3) To establish workplace safety standards
(4) All of the above

71. Which of the following is a trade union right protected under the Industrial Disputes Act, 1947?
(1) The right to strike
(2) The right to collective bargaining
(3) The right to form and join a union
(4) All of the above

72. Which of the following is not a provision of the Factories Act, 1948?
(1) Establishment of a workplace safety committee
(2) Requirement of workers to wear safety equipment
(3) Promotion of equal pay for equal work
(4) Prohibition of hazardous work for women

73. What is the purpose of the Trade Union Act, 1926?
(1) To regulate the formation and functioning of trade unions
(2) To establish minimum wage rates for workers
(3) To provide protection for child workers
(4) All of the above

74. Which of the following is not a provision of the Employees' Provident Funds and Miscellaneous Provisions Act, 1952?
(1) Establishment of a provident fund for workers
(2) Establishment of a pension scheme for workers
(3) Establishment of an insurance scheme for workers
(4) Establishment of a minimum wage rate

75. What is the purpose of the Payment of Bonus Act, 1965?
(1) To require employers to pay a bonus to workers
(2) To establish minimum wage rates for workers
(3) To regulate trade union activities
(4) None of the above

76. Which of the following is a provision of the Contract Labour (Regulation and Abolition) Act, 1970?
(1) Prohibition of hazardous work for women
(2) Requirement of employers to provide food and housing for contract workers
(3) Prohibition of the employment of contract labour in certain industries and establishments
(4) All of the above

77. Which of the following is not a provision of the Maternity Benefit Act, 1961?
(1) Requirement of employers to provide maternity leave to workers
(2) Provision of maternity benefits to workers
(3) Requirement of employers to provide paternity leave to workers
(4) Provision of nursing breaks to workers

78. What is the purpose of the Equal Remuneration Act, 1976?
(1) To prohibit discrimination in pay on the basis of gender
(2) To establish minimum wage rates for workers
(3) To regulate working conditions in hazardous industries
(4) None of the above

79. Which of the following is not a provision of the Industrial Employment (Standing Orders) Act, 1946?
(1) Requirement of employers to issue standing orders to workers
(2) Requirement of employers to display a notice of the standing orders
(3) Prohibition of strike action by workers
(4) Provision of a grievance redressal mechanism for workers

80. **Assertion:** Labour laws play an important role in promoting social justice in the workplace.

Reason: Labour laws establish minimum wage rates, safe working conditions, and protect the rights of workers.

(1) Both assertion and reason are true and the reason is the correct explanation of the assertion.
(2) Both assertion and reason are true but the reason is not the correct explanation of the assertion.
(3) Assertion is true but reason is false.
(4) Assertion is false but reason is true.

81. **Assertion:** Collective bargaining is a fundamental right protected by Indian labour laws.

Reason: Collective bargaining allows workers to negotiate with their employers for better wages and working conditions.

(1) Both assertion and reason are true and the reason is the correct explanation of the assertion.
(2) Both assertion and reason are true but the reason is not the correct explanation of the assertion.
(3) Assertion is true but reason is false.
(4) Assertion is false but reason is true.

82. Which of the following is a provision of the Factories Act, 1948 that ensures the safety of workers?
(1) The provision of drinking water
(2) The provision of first aid
(3) The provision of fire safety measures
(4) All of the above

83. Which of the following is a provision of the Factories Act, 1948 that ensures the welfare of workers?
(1) The provision of canteen facilities
(2) The provision of restrooms
(3) The provision of creches
(4) All of the above

84. What is the purpose of the Mines Act, 1952?
(1) To regulate the working conditions in mines
(2) To promote the mining industry in India
(3) To regulate the prices of minerals
(4) None of the above

85. Which of the following is a provision of the Mines Act, 1952 that ensures the safety of workers?
(1) The provision of ventilation
(2) The provision of lighting
(3) The provision of a medical officer
(4) All of the above

86. Which of the following is a provision of the Mines Act, 1952 that ensures the welfare of workers?
(1) The provision of drinking water
(2) The provision of bathing facilities
(3) The provision of creches
(4) All of the above

87. What is the purpose of the Inter-state Migrant Workmen (Regulation of employment and conditions of service) Act, 1979?
(1) To regulate the employment and working conditions of inter-state migrant workmen
(2) To regulate the employment and working conditions of domestic workers
(3) To regulate the employment and working conditions of agricultural workers
(4) None of the above

88. Which of the following is a provision of the Inter-state Migrant Workmen (Regulation of employment and conditions of service) Act, 1979 that ensures the welfare of workers?
(1) The provision of suitable living conditions
(2) The provision of medical facilities
(3) The provision of accident insurance
(4) All of the above

89. Which of the following is a provision of the Factories Act, 1948 that regulates the employment of women?
(1) The provision of maternity benefits
(2) The provision of suitable work conditions during pregnancy
(3) The provision of nursing breaks
(4) All of the above

90. What is the maximum number of hours that a child worker can work in a day under the Factories Act, 1948?

(1) 4.5 hours (2) 5 hours
(3) 6 hours (4) 7 hours

91. Which of the following is a provision of the Mines Act, 1952 that regulates the employment of women?
(1) The provision of maternity benefits
(2) The provision of suitable work conditions during pregnancy
(3) The provision of nursing breaks
(4) All of the above

92. What is the maximum number of hours that an adult worker can work in a week under the Mines Act, 1952?
(1) 48 hours (2) 50 hours
(3) 52 hours (4) 60 hours

93. What is the maximum number of hours that an adult worker can work in a day under the Mines Act, 1952?
(1) 8 hours (2) 9 hours
(3) 10 hours (4) 12 hours

94. Which of the following is a provision of the Inter-state Migrant Workmen (Regulation of employment and conditions of service) Act, 1979 that regulates the employment of women?
(1) The provision of maternity benefits
(2) The provision of suitable work conditions during pregnancy
(3) The provision of nursing breaks
(4) All of the above

95. What is the purpose of the Contract Labour (Regulation and Abolition) Act, 1970?
(1) To regulate the employment of contract labor in certain establishments
(2) To regulate the employment of casual labor in certain establishments
(3) To regulate the employment of permanent labor in certain establishments
(4) None of the above

96. What is the minimum number of workers that an establishment must employ to be covered under the Contract Labour (Regulation and Abolition) Act, 1970?
(1) 10 workers (2) 20 workers
(3) 30 workers (4) 50 workers

97. Which of the following is a provision of the Contract Labour (Regulation and Abolition) Act, 1970 that ensures the welfare of workers?
(1) The provision of payment of wages
(2) The provision of bridge schools
(3) The provision of identity cards
(4) All of the above

98. What is the purpose of the Payment of Bonus Act, 1965?
(1) To regulate the payment of bonuses to employees
(2) To regulate the payment of salaries to employees
(3) To regulate the payment of overtime to employees
(4) None of the above

99. Which of the following is a provision of the Payment of Bonus Act, 1965?
(1) An employer shall be bound to pay a minimum bonus of 8.33% of the salary or wage earned by the employee during the accounting year.
(2) An employer shall be bound to pay a maximum bonus of 20% of the salary or wage earned by the employee during the accounting year.
(3) Both (1) and (2)
(4) Neither (1) nor (2)

100. What is the purpose of the Employees' Provident Funds and Miscellaneous Provisions Act, 1952?
(1) To regulate the payment of salaries to employees
(2) To regulate the payment of bonuses to employees
(3) To provide for the institution of provident funds for employees in certain establishments
(4) None of the above

101. Which of the following is a provision of the Employees' Provident Funds and Miscellaneous Provisions Act, 1952?
(1) An employer shall contribute 12% of the basic wages, dearness allowance, and

retaining allowance (if any) of an employee to the provident fund.

(2) An employee shall contribute 12% of his basic wages, dearness allowance, and retaining allowance (if any) to the provident fund.

(3) Both (1) and (2)

(4) Neither (1) nor (2)

102. What is the purpose of the Employees' State Insurance Act, 1948?

(1) To regulate the payment of salaries to employees

(2) To regulate the payment of bonuses to employees

(3) To provide for certain benefits to employees in case of sickness, maternity or employment injury

(4) None of the above

103. Which of the following is a benefit provided under the Employees' State Insurance Act, 1948?

(1) Sickness benefit

(2) Maternity benefit

(3) Disablement benefit

(4) All of the above

104. What is the purpose of the Minimum Wages Act, 1948?

(1) To regulate the payment of salaries to employees

(2) To regulate the payment of bonuses to employees

(3) To provide for the fixing of minimum rates of wages for certain employees

(4) None of the above

105. Which of the following is a provision of the Minimum Wages Act, 1948?

(1) An employer shall pay wages higher than the minimum wages fixed under this Act, if he can afford to do so.

(2) An employer shall pay wages at the minimum rate fixed under this Act, even if he can afford to pay higher wages.

(3) Only (2)

(4) Neither (1) nor (2)

106. What is the purpose of the Maternity Benefit Act, 1961?

(1) To regulate the payment of salaries to employees

(2) To provide for the grant of maternity benefits to women employees

(3) To provide for the grant of paternity benefits to male employees

(4) None of the above

107. Which of the following is a provision of the Maternity Benefit Act, 1961?

(1) A woman employee shall be entitled to maternity leave of not less than 12 weeks.

(2) A woman employee shall be entitled to maternity leave of not less than 16 weeks.

(3) A woman employee shall be entitled to maternity leave of not more than 6 weeks.

(4) A woman employee shall not be entitled to any maternity leave.

108. What is the purpose of the Payment of Wages Act, 1936?

(1) To regulate the payment of salaries to employees

(2) To regulate the payment of bonuses to employees

(3) To regulate the payment of wages to certain classes of employed persons

(4) None of the above

109. What is the minimum time period for the payment of wages to employees under the Payment of Wages Act, 1936?

(1) 1 month

(2) 2 weeks

(3) 1 week

(4) 3 days

110. What is the purpose of the Industrial Employment (Standing Orders) Act, 1946?

(1) To regulate the payment of salaries to employees

(2) To regulate the payment of bonuses to employees

(3) To require employers in industrial establishments to define conditions of employment
(4) None of the above

111. What is a standing order under the Industrial Employment (Standing Orders) Act, 1946?
(1) An order regulating the payment of wages to employees
(2) An order regulating the payment of bonuses to employees
(3) An order defining conditions of employment
(4) None of the above

112. What is the purpose of the Industrial Disputes Act, 1947?
(1) To regulate the payment of salaries to employees
(2) To regulate the payment of bonuses to employees
(3) To provide for the settlement of industrial disputes
(4) None of the above

113. Which of the following is a method of settling industrial disputes under the Industrial Disputes Act, 1947?
(1) Conciliation
(2) Adjudication
(3) Arbitration
(4) All of these

114. What is the purpose of the Trade Unions Act, 1926?
(1) To regulate the payment of salaries to employees
(2) To regulate the payment of bonuses to employees
(3) To provide for the registration of trade unions
(4) None of the above

115. What is a trade union under the Trade Unions Act, 1926?
(1) A group of workers who join together to protect their interests
(2) A group of workers who join together to violate the law
(3) Only (1)
(4) Neither (1) nor (2)

116. What is the purpose of the National Rural Employment Guarantee Act, 2005?
(1) To regulate the payment of salaries to employees
(2) To provide for the guarantee of employment to rural households
(3) To provide for the guarantee of employment to urban households
(4) None of the above

117. Which of the following is a provision of the National Rural Employment Guarantee Act, 2005?
(1) The Act provides for the guarantee of 100 days of employment to rural households.
(2) The Act provides for the guarantee of 50 days of employment to rural households.
(3) Only (1)
(4) Neither (1) nor (2)

118. What is the purpose of the Child Labour (Prohibition and Regulation) Act, 1986?
(1) To regulate the employment of child labor in certain establishments
(2) To prohibit the employment of child labor in certain establishments
(3) Both (1) and (2)
(4) None of the above

119. What is a child under the Child Labour (Prohibition and Regulation) Act, 1986?
(1) A person who is below 14 years of age
(2) A person who is below 18 years of age
(3) A person who is below 21 years of age
(4) None of the above

120. Which of the following is a provision of the Child Labour (Prohibition and Regulation) Act, 1986?
(1) The Act prohibits the employment of a child in any occupation or process.
(2) The Act prohibits the employment of a child in only hazardous occupations or processes.

(3) Only (2)
(4) Neither (1) nor (2)

121. What is the purpose of the Employment of Manual Scavengers and Construction of Dry Latrines (Prohibition) Act, 1993?
(1) To regulate the employment of manual scavengers and the construction of dry latrines
(2) To prohibit the employment of manual scavengers and the construction of dry latrines
(3) Only (1)
(4) None of the above

122. What is a manual scavenger under the Employment of Manual Scavengers and Construction of Dry Latrines (Prohibition) Act, 1993?
(1) A person who manually cleans, carries, disposes off human excreta
(2) A person who manually cleans, carries, disposes off household waste
(3) Both (1) and (2)
(4) Only (1)

123. Which of the following is a provision of the Employment of Manual Scavengers and Construction of Dry Latrines (Prohibition) Act, 1993?
(1) The Act prohibits the employment of manual scavengers and the construction of dry latrines.
(2) The Act prohibits only the employment of manual scavengers.
(3) Only (1)
(4) Neither (1) nor (2)

124. What is the purpose of the Bonded Labour System (Abolition) Act, 1976?
(1) To regulate the employment of bonded labor
(2) To prohibit the employment of bonded labor
(3) Only (1)
(4) None of the above

125. What is bonded labor under the Bonded Labour System (Abolition) Act, 1976?
(1) A person who is forced to work in order to pay off a debt
(2) A person who is forced to work without pay
(3) Both (1) and (2)
(4) None of the above

126. Which of the following is a provision of the Bonded Labour System (Abolition) Act, 1976?
(1) The Act prohibits the employment of bonded labor.
(2) The Act provides for the release and rehabilitation of bonded labor.
(3) Both (1) and (2)
(4) None of the above

127. What is the purpose of the Sexual Harassment of Women at Workplace (Prevention, Prohibition and Redressal) Act, 2013?
(1) To regulate the employment of women in certain establishments
(2) To prevent and prohibit sexual harassment of women at workplace
(3) Only (1)
(4) None of the above

128. What is sexual harassment under the Sexual Harassment of Women at Workplace (Prevention, Prohibition and Redressal) Act, 2013?
(1) Any unwelcome act or behaviour (whether directly or by implication) that creates an intimidating, hostile or offensive work environment
(2) Any act or behaviour that is unwelcome and has a sexual connotation
(3) Both (1) and (2)
(4) Neither (1) nor (2)

129. Which of the following is a provision of the Sexual Harassment of Women at Workplace (Prevention, Prohibition and Redressal) Act, 2013?
(1) The Act requires employers to constitute an Internal Complaints Committee (ICC) in every workplace.
(2) The Act requires employers to provide for a workplace harassment policy.

(3) Both (1) and (2)
(4) Neither (1) nor (2)

130. What is the purpose of the Equal Remuneration Act, 1976?
(1) To regulate the payment of salaries to employees
(2) To provide for equal pay for equal work for men and women
(3) Only (1)
(4) None of the above

131. Which of the following is a provision of the Equal Remuneration Act, 1976?
(1) The Act provides for the payment of an equal remuneration to men and women workers for the same work or work of a similar nature.
(2) The Act provides for the payment of more remuneration to women workers than to men workers for the same work or work of a similar nature.
(3) Only (1)
(4) None of the above

132. What is the purpose of the Payment of Gratuity Act, 1972?
(1) To regulate the payment of salaries to employees
(2) To provide for a gratuity payment to employees on the termination of their employment
(3) Only (1)
(4) None of the above

133. Which of the following is a provision of the Payment of Gratuity Act, 1972?
(1) An employer shall pay gratuity to an employee who has completed 5 years of continuous service with him.
(2) An employer shall pay gratuity to an employee who has completed 10 years of continuous service with him.
(3) Only (1)
(4) None of the above

134. What is the purpose of the Industrial Employment (Standing Orders) Central Rules, 1946?
(1) To prescribe the form and content of the standing orders under the Industrial Employment (Standing Orders) Act, 1946
(2) To regulate the payment of salaries to employees
(3) To regulate the payment of overtime to employees
(4) None of the above

135. Which of the following is a provision of the Industrial Employment (Standing Orders) Central Rules, 1946?
(1) The rules require employers in industrial establishments to define conditions of employment in the form of standing orders.
(2) The rules require employers to submit copies of standing orders to the certifying officer.
(3) Both (1) and (2)
(4) Neither (1) nor (2)

136. What is the purpose of the Employees' Compensation Act, 1923?
(1) To provide for the payment of compensation to employees who are injured or disabled in the course of employment
(2) To provide for the regulation of the payment of salaries to employees
(3) To provide for the regulation of the payment of bonuses to employees
(4) None of the above

137. Which of the following is a provision of the Employees' Compensation Act, 1923?
(1) An employer shall pay compensation to an employee who is injured or disabled in the course of employment.
(2) An employer shall pay compensation to an employee who dies in the course of employment and to his dependents.
(3) Both (1) and (2)
(4) Neither (1) nor (2)

138. What is the purpose of the Contract Labour (Regulation and Abolition) Act, 1970?
(1) To regulate the employment of contract labor in certain establishments

(2) To regulate the employment of casual labor in certain establishments
(3) To regulate the employment of permanent labor in certain establishments
(4) None of the above

139. Which of the following is a provision of the Contract Labour (Regulation and Abolition) Act, 1970 that ensures the welfare of workers?
(1) The provision of payment of wages
(2) The provision of bridge schools
(3) The provision of identity cards
(4) All of the above

140. Which of the following is a provision of the Contract Labour (Regulation and Abolition) Act, 1970 that regulates the employment of women?
(1) The provision of maternity benefits
(2) The provision of suitable work conditions during pregnancy
(3) The provision of nursing breaks
(4) All of the above

141. Which of the following is a provision of the Contract Labour (Regulation and Abolition) Act, 1970 that regulates the employment of children?
(1) The Act prohibits the employment of children as contract labor.
(2) The Act permits the employment of children as contract labor but with certain conditions.
(3) The Act does not regulate the employment of children as contract labor.
(4) None of the above.

142. Which of the following is a provision of the Contract Labour (Regulation and Abolition) Act, 1970 that regulates the working conditions of workers?
(1) The provision of drinking water
(2) The provision of restrooms
(3) The provision of canteen facilities
(4) All of the above

143. Which of the following is a provision of the Contract Labour (Regulation and Abolition) Act, 1970 that ensures the safety of workers?
(1) The provision of ventilation
(2) The provision of lighting
(3) The provision of a medical officer
(4) All of the above

144. What is the minimum wage that an employer shall pay to a contract labor under the Contract Labour (Regulation and Abolition) Act, 1970?
(1) The same wage as that of a permanent worker performing the same job in the establishment
(2) A lower wage than that of a permanent worker performing the same job in the establishment
(3) A higher wage than that of a permanent worker performing the same job in the establishment
(4) None of the above

145. Which of the following is a provision of the Contract Labour (Regulation and Abolition) Act, 1970 requiring registration for employers?
(1) Every employer engaging 20 or more workmen on any day of the preceding 12 months shall apply for registration.
(2) Every employer engaging 10 or more workmen on any day of the preceding 12 months shall apply for registration.
(3) Every employer engaging 50 or more workmen on any day of the preceding 12 months shall apply for registration.
(4) Only (1) and (3)

146. What is the purpose of the Building and Other Construction Workers (Regulation of employment and conditions of service) Act, 1996?
(1) To regulate the employment of construction workers in any establishment
(2) To provide for regulation of employment and conditions of service of building and other construction workers
(3) To provide for regulation of employment and conditions of service of industrial workers
(4) None of the above

147. Which of the following workers is covered under the Building and Other Construction Workers (Regulation of Employment and Conditions of Service) Act?

(1) Workers employed in the construction work of buildings, highways, bridges, tunnels, and dams.
(2) Workers employed in the construction work of power stations, refineries, and chemical plants.
(3) Both (1) and (2)
(4) Neither (1) nor (2)

148. What is the minimum wage that an employer shall pay to a construction worker under the Building and Other Construction Workers (Regulation of employment and conditions of service) Act, 1996?

(1) The same wage as that of a permanent worker performing the same job in the establishment.
(2) A lower wage than that of a permanent worker performing the same job in the establishment.
(3) A higher wage than that of a permanent worker performing the same job in the establishment.
(4) None of the above.

149 Who is responsible for ensuring the registration of establishments under the Building and Other Construction Workers (Regulation of employment and conditions of service) Act, 1996?

(1) The construction worker
(2) The employer
(3) Both (1) and (2)
(4) Neither (1) nor (2)

150. What is the maximum number of hours that an adult worker can work in a day under the Building and Other Construction Workers (Regulation of employment and conditions of service) Act, 1996?

(1) 8 hours (2) 9 hours
(3) 10 hours (4) 12 hours

151. Which of the following is a provision of the Building and Other Construction Workers (Regulation of employment and conditions of service) Act, 1996 that ensures the safety of workers?

(1) The provision of clean drinking water
(2) The provision of first aid
(3) The provision of protective equipment
(4) All of the above

152. What is the purpose of the welfare funds under the Building and Other Construction Workers (Regulation of employment and conditions of service) Act, 1996?

(1) To provide for the welfare of construction workers and their families
(2) To provide for the welfare of employers and their families
(3) To provide for the welfare of the government and its employees
(4) None of the above

153. Which of the following is a benefit provided under the Building and Other Construction Workers (Regulation of employment and conditions of service) Act, 1996?

(1) Medical care
(2) Education facilities
(3) Housing
(4) All of the above

154. What is the purpose of the safety committees under the Building and Other Construction Workers (Regulation of employment and conditions of service) Act, 1996?

(1) To provide for the safety of construction workers and their families
(2) To ensure that safety measures are implemented at construction sites
(3) To regulate the employment of construction workers
(4) None of the above

155. Which of the following is a provision of the Building and Other Construction Workers (Regulation of employment and conditions of service) Act, 1996 that regulates the employment of women?

(1) The provision of maternity benefits
(2) The provision of suitable work conditions during pregnancy

(3) The provision of nursing breaks
(4) All of the above

156. What is the purpose of the Child Labour (Prohibition and Regulation) Act, 1986?
(1) To regulate the employment of children in certain establishments
(2) To prohibit the employment of children in certain occupations and processes
(3) Both (1) and (2)
(4) None of the above

157. What is a child under the Child Labour (Prohibition and Regulation) Act, 1986?
(1) A person who is below 14 years of age
(2) A person who is below 18 years of age
(3) A person who is below 21 years of age
(4) None of the above

158. Which of the following states has the highest number of child laborers according to a 2011 census?
(1) Uttar Pradesh (2) Tamil Nadu
(3) Maharashtra (4) Karnataka

159. Which of the following is a provision of the Child Labour (Prohibition and Regulation) Act, 1986 regarding punishment for the employment of a child?
(1) Imprisonment for a term of 3 years to 10 years and a fine of Rs. 50,000 to Rs. 1 lakh.
(2) Imprisonment for a term of 6 months to 2 years and a fine of Rs. 20,000 to Rs. 50,000.
(3) Both (1) and (2)
(4) Neither (1) nor (2)

160. Which of the following is a provision of the Child Labour (Prohibition and Regulation) Act, 1986 that provides for the rehabilitation of child laborers?
(1) The establishment of special schools for working children
(2) The provision of vocational training to adolescent children
(3) Both (1) and (2)
(4) None of the above

161. Which of the following is a provision of the ChildLabour (Prohibition and Regulation) Act, 1986 that regulates the employment of adolescents?
(1) The Act permits the employment of adolescents in certain occupations but with certain conditions.
(2) The Act prohibits the employment of adolescents in all occupations.
(3) The Act does not regulate the employment of adolescents.
(4) None of the above.

162. What is the penalty for contravening the provisions of the Child Labour (Prohibition and Regulation) Act, 1986?
(1) Imprisonment for a term of 3 years to 10 years and a fine of Rs. 50,000 to Rs. 1 lakh.
(2) Imprisonment for a term of 6 months to 2 years and a fine of Rs. 20,000 to Rs. 50,000.
(3) Both (1) and (2)
(4) Neither (1) nor (2)

ANSWER KEY

1. (4)	**2.** (4)	**3.** (4)	**4.** (1)	**5.** (4)	**6.** (4)	**7.** (3)	**8.** (3)	**9.** (3)	**10.** (2)
11. (3)	**12.** (3)	**13.** (3)	**14.** (3)	**15.** (4)	**16.** (3)	**17.** (3)	**18.** (3)	**19.** (3)	**20.** (3)
21. (3)	**22.** (1)	**23.** (2)	**24.** (4)	**25.** (1)	**26.** (1)	**27.** (1)	**28.** (3)	**29.** (2)	**30.** (2)
31. (1)	**32.** (4)	**33.** (3)	**34.** (2)	**35.** (1)	**36.** (4)	**37.** (4)	**38.** (1)	**39.** (4)	**40.** (4)
41. (1)	**42.** (2)	**43.** (3)	**44.** (2)	**45.** (4)	**46.** (4)	**47.** (3)	**48.** (3)	**49.** (1)	**50.** (3)
51. (4)	**52.** (3)	**53.** (2)	**54.** (4)	**55.** (2)	**56.** (4)	**57.** (4)	**58.** (4)	**59.** (4)	**60.** (4)
61. (4)	**62.** (4)	**63.** (4)	**64.** (4)	**65.** (4)	**66.** (1)	**67.** (4)	**68.** (3)	**69.** (4)	**70.** (2)
71. (4)	**72.** (3)	**73.** (1)	**74.** (4)	**75.** (1)	**76.** (3)	**77.** (3)	**78.** (1)	**79.** (3)	**80.** (1)
81. (1)	**82.** (4)	**83.** (4)	**84.** (1)	**85.** (4)	**86.** (4)	**87.** (1)	**88.** (4)	**89.** (4)	**90.** (2)
91. (4)	**92.** (4)	**93.** (2)	**94.** (4)	**95.** (1)	**96.** (2)	**97.** (4)	**98.** (1)	**99.** (3)	**100.** (3)
101. (3)	**102.** (3)	**103.** (4)	**104.** (4)	**105.** (3)	**106.** (2)	**107.** (2)	**108.** (3)	**109.** (3)	**110.** (3)
111. (3)	**112.** (3)	**113.** (4)	**114.** (3)	**115.** (3)	**116.** (2)	**117.** (3)	**118.** (3)	**119.** (1)	**120.** (3)
121. (2)	**122.** (4)	**123.** (3)	**124.** (2)	**125.** (3)	**126.** (1)	**127.** (2)	**128.** (3)	**129.** (3)	**130.** (2)
131. (2)	**132.** (2)	**133.** (2)	**134.** (1)	**135.** (3)	**136.** (2)	**137.** (3)	**138.** (1)	**139.** (4)	**140.** (4)
141. (2)	**142.** (4)	**143.** (4)	**144.** (1)	**145.** (2)	**146.** (3)	**147.** (3)	**148.** (3)	**149.** (2)	**150.** (2)
151. (4)	**152.** (1)	**153.** (4)	**154.** (2)	**155.** (4)	**156.** (1)	**157.** (1)	**158.** (1)	**159.** (3)	**160.** (3)
161. (1)	**162.** (3)								

UNIT 8

WAGES

Syllabus

- Concept, Types, Factors influencing wages, Wage Theories and Wage Differentials
  - The Minimum Wages Act, 1948.
  - The Payment of Wages Act, 1936.
  - The Payment of Bonus Act, 1965.
  - The Equal Remuneration Act, 1976.
  - The Payment of Gratuity Act, 1972.
  - The Employees' Provident Fund and Miscellaneous Provisions Act, 1952.

WAGES

CONCEPT OF WAGES

- **Wages.** Wages may be defined as the aggregate earning of employee for a given period of time such as a day or a week or a month .Wages are basically the price paid for the services of labour in the process of production. They are composed of two parts – the basic wage and other allowances. The allowances include dearness allowances, city compensatory allowances, overtime pay and medical allowances.
- **Salary.** It is compensation to an employee for services rendered on a weekly, monthly or annual basis. It is usually associated with office staff, supervisors, researchers, manager etc.
- **Wage rate**. It is a wage received by a workers for a unit of time or production excluding special payments for overtime, night work and incentive earning. If the wage rate is determined by the job evaluation. It is called standard wage rate.
- **Nominal Wage.** Wage expressed in terms of money are called nominal wages.
- **Real Wages.** The goods and services which could be purchased with the help of money wages are known as real wages. Nominal wages are divided by a cost of living or consumer price index give real wages.
- **Fringe Benefits.** There refers to compensation given to employees, over and above wages, that often is not directly related to output, performance or time worked.
- **Wage and Salary Administration' refers** to the establishment and implementation of sound policies and practices of employee compensation. The basic purpose of wage and salary administration is to establish and maintain an equitable wage and salary structure. Wages and salaries are often one of the largest components of cost of production and such have serious implications for growth and profitability of the company. On the other hand, they are the only source of workers' income.

After the independence and particularly after 1948, some new terms relating to wages began to be used. These are:

1. Statutory Minimum Wages
2. Basic Minimum Wages
3. Minimum Wages
4. Fair Wages
5. Living Wages

6 Need Based Wages

1. **Statutory Minimum Wages.** By it we mean the minimum amount of wages which should essentially be given to the workers as per provisions of the Minimum Wages Act, 1948.
2. **Basic Minimum Wages.** This minimum wage is fixed through judicial pronouncement, awards, industrial tribunals and labour. The employers are essentially to give this minimum wage to the workers.
3. **Minimum Wages.** The concept of minimum wages has developed due to different standards in different countries. In Indian context, minimum wage means the minimum amount which an employer thinks necessary for the sustenance of life and preservation of the efficiency of the worker. According to Fair Wage Committee, the minimum wages must also provide for some measures of education- medical requirements and amenities.

4. **Fair Wages.** In order to bring about improved relations between labour and management an effort has been made in modern times that the labour gets a fair deal at the hands of owners and managers of industries. Various proposals were undertaken at the Industries Conference in 1947 and a resolution known as the Industrial Truce Resolution was passed. It is provided for the payment of fair wages to labour. The government of India appointed a Fair Wages committee in 1948 to determine the principles on which fair wages should be based and to suggest the lines on which those principles should be applied. According to the report on this Committee, Fair Wages is that wages which the labourer gets for his work just near to minimum wages and living wages. Generally, the current rate of wages being paid in the enterprise are known as fair wages.
5. **Living Wages.** According to Fair Wage Committee Report, "The living wage should enable the male earner to provide for himself and his family not merely the bare essentials of food, clothing and shelter, but also a measure of frugal comfort including education for children, protection against ill health, requirements of essential social needs and a measure of insurance against the more important misfortunes including old age." According to the Committee on Fair Wages, the living wages represent the highest level of the wages and include all amenities which a citizen living in a modern civilized society is to expect when the economy of the country is sufficiently advanced and the employer is able to meet the expanding aspirations of his workers. The Living Wage should be fixed keeping in view the National income and the capacity of the industry to pay.
6. **Need Based Wages.** The Indian Labour Conference at its 15th session held at New Delhi in July, 1957 suggested that minimum wage fixation should be need based. Following are the important points of the Resolution of the Conference.
   (a) The standard working class family should include three consumption units for the one earner.
   (b) Calculation of minimum food requirements should be made on the basis of the recommendation of Dr. Aykoroyed *i.e.* 27000 calories for an average Indian adult.
   (c) Calculation of cloth should be made @ 18 yards annually for one member. As such, a family consisting of four members will require 72 yards of cloth.
   (d) The workers should get minimum rent as per guidelines fixed by the government in the industrial housing policy.
   (e) Expenses for fuel, light and so on should be equal to 20% of the entire minimum wages.

State Regulation of Wages

- A potent objectives of legislation on wages is the regulation and fixation of the quantum of wages. Although prior to the intervention in the field of wages, it was accepted that free bargaining between individual bargaining between individual workmen and their employers would result in fixation of such wage rates which would satisfy both. Many inquires reveled that widespread exploitations of woman and child labour existed in those industries which were generally carried on a small scale and in many cases, even in the homes of the employers. In such industries, the Workers did not have and do not have, even now, strong organization to protect them against the excesses of the employers, strong public opinion, however gradually forced the state to adopt legislation for the fixation of minimum wages in such industries .
- As early as 1896, the state of Victoria adopted a legislation to protect workers employed in certain sweated trades requiring special efforts and hard work. These included boot making, shirt making, clothing, underclothing and furniture manufacturing. A similar protective legislation – the minimum wages act was adopted in 1948.

- The purpose of these all minimum wages laws was prevent the exploitation of labour and payment of unduly low wages in those industries where workers were least organized and where employment of woman workers and children are predominated. It was realized the wages of these industries or occupations were so low that worker engaged, therein could not earn enough to meet even the bare necessities of life though they might be continually employed.
- The fixation of minimum wages in the industries and wages in these industries or occupations and the impositions of legal obligations on the employer to pay the wage rate so fixed, have gone a long way towards mitigating the suffering and hardships of labour in the unorganized industries and employment.
- At times, the state intervention to regulate the quantum of wages to control inflationary pressure as happened during the last world war.
- The state has also regulated wages for maintaining the purchasing power of the wage earners and thereby speeding up the pace of economy recovery.
- Finally, The most comprehensive objectives of state regulation of wages which is finding expression in a large number of countries today even in the capitalist societies ones, has been the pursuit of a national income distribution policy and using the wage policy as an instrument of planned economic development.

State regulation of wages seek to achieve the following objectives :

- Prevention of extra hard work and toil and poverty arising from unduly low wages.
- Fixation of just and fair wages for preventing industrial disputes.
- Control of infantry pressures.
- Raising purchasing power with a view to speeding up the pace of economic recovery.
- Wage regulation as a part of national income distribution policy and programmes of planned economic development.

Wage Fixation

- The necessity for fixing the minimum rates of wage was realized in India as early as the beginning of the present century, but no concrete measures were adopted as long. The question of fixation of the minimum rate of wages are considered by the royal commission on labour which, in its report submitted in 1931.
- This reports recommended making investigation in respect of the fixations of minimum rates of wages in small industries like bid making, wool cleaning, mica works etc.
- It also recommended the establishment of a minimum wages fixing machinery in these industries and the adoption of necessary legislation. The commission further setting up of a statutory wage board for fixing minimum wages in plantation in Assam.
- Labour investigation committee known as Rege committee, appointed by the government of India 1944, also made investigation in respects of wage earning in industrial employment and submitted a main report and 35 adhoc survey.
- The report and survey revealed the existence of low level of wages for almost all categories of worker employed in different industries.
- The international labour organization also adopted the conventions and recommendations relating to fixing the wage machinery. The minimum wage fixing machinery convention NO 26, 1928 provides for creation of wage fixing machinery in certain trades.
- The minimum wages fixed by the machinery are binding to the labour and employer.
- India ratified the convention in 1955, after the enactments of the minimum wages act, 1948, the minimum wages fixing machinery recommendation NO 30, 1928 requires such a machinery to

investigate the condition relevant to the trades and to consult the affected interest before fixing minimum wages.

- The question of the fixation of minimum wages was considered by the standing labour committee and the fifth session of the Indian labour conferences in 1943.
- Government of India introduced the minimum wages Bill in the legislative assembly in 1946, which was passed on the 9th February, 1948 and came into force the 15 of the same year.
- The minimum wages act, 1948 is the first labour legislation in the country dealing with the fixation of minimum rates of wages for workers employed in different exacting employment including agriculture.

Wages Theories

Different writers and thinkers have suggested several theories for determination of wages.

WAGES THEORIES
1. Subsistence Theory
2. Wage Fund Theory
3. Residual Claimant Theory
4. Surplus Value Theory of Money
5. Marginal Productivity Theory
6. Bargaining Theory of Wages
7. Compensation theory
8. Expectancy theory
9. Equity Theory
10. Agency theory

1. **Subsistence Theory.** This theory was propounded by David Richardo. Richardo states that "The labourers are paid to enable them to subsist and perpetuate the race without increase or diminution." This theory is also known as **"Iron Law of Wages"**. According to this theory, if the wages fall below the subsistence level, the number of workers would decrease as many of them would die of hunger, disease, malnutrition etc.. This would make the wage rates go up as labour will become scarce. However, if the workers are paid more than the subsistence wages, they would marry and procreate. This would increase their number and bring down the rate of wages.
   This theory is based on two assumptions, namely,
   (i) The law of diminishing return applies to industry.
   (ii) There is a rapid increase in populations.
2. **Wage Fund Theory.** This was propounded by Adam Smith and further expounded by J.S. Mill. He assumed that wealthy persons have funds of surplus wealth, as a result of their savings wages are paid out of these funds. This fund could be utilised for employing labourers for work. If the fund was large, wages would be high if it was small, wages would be low, just enough for the subsistence. Thus, the size of the fund determined the demand for labour and the wages that could be paid.
   The J.S. Mill said that wages mainly depend upon the demand for and supply of labour or proportion between populations and capital available. The amount of wages is fixed. Wages can't be increased without decreasing the numbers of workers and vice versa. It is the wages fund which determine the demand of labour.
3. **Residual Claimant Theory.** This theory was propounded by Francis A Walker. According to Walker, there are four factors of production namely, land, labour, capital and organisation. Wages represent the amount of value created in the production which remains after payment of the other three factors of production namely land, capital and organisation.
   In others words, labour is residual claimant .The wages are equal to the whole production minus rent, interest and profits.
   This theory tries to prove that if the productivity of the workers increases the production will rise as a result there will be increase in the residual means to be distributed as wages. It also recognises that the workers have a stake in the national income of the country.

4. **Surplus Value Theory of Money.** This theory was propounded by Karl Marx. According to Marx, Labour was to be treated as an article of commerce, which could be purchased on payment of subsistence price. The price of any product was determined by the labour time needed for producing it. The labourers were not paid in proportion to the time spent on job, but much less. The surplus, thus created, was utilized for paying other expenses.
5. **Marginal Productivity Theory.** This theory was propounded by Wick steed and Clark. According to this theory wages depend upon the demand for and supply of labour. Wages are based upon the entrepreneur's estimate of the value that will probably be produced by the last or marginal worker. Workers are paid only what they are economically worth. As long as additional worker contributes more to the total value than the cost in wages, it pays the employer to continue hiring. The result is that the employer has a larger share in profits as he doesn't have to pay to non-marginal workers.
6. **Bargaining Theory of Wages.** This theory was propounded by John Davidson. According to him, wages are determined by the relative bargaining power of workers or trade unions and of employers. When a trade union is involved, monetary benefits, incentives, job differentials etc. tend to be determined by the relative strength of the organisation and the trade union. However this is possible in big plant which are earning huge profits and where labour is well organised, the profits earned but the enterprise play an important role in determining the bargaining wages.
7. **Compensation theory.** All researcher agree on the point that pay affects employee satisfaction and this can have behavioural implications. When employees are dissatisfied with their jobs their desire for money increases and attractiveness of the job is increases and attractiveness of the job decreases. As a result of the desire for more money, they are more apt to pursue behaviours which are likely to raise their pay, such as improving their work performance, joining union and looking for better job.
8. **Expectancy theory.** Vroom's expectancy theory focuses on the link between rewards and behaviour motivation, according to the theory is the result of valence, instrumentally and expectancy. Remunerating system differ according to this impact on these motivational component. Remunerating system according to this impacts on these motivational components.
9. **Equity Theory.** Equity theory seek to relate employees behaviour to their perception of equity and inequity in their compensation. Elliott Jacques has been the leading advocate of the equity approach. His analysis leans heavily on his view that the effective rewards system must relate pay to the level of work as defined by the time span discretions. This time span is the maximum periods for which a job holder can be allowed to exercise discretions or self control without the supervisor review.
10. **Agency theory.** The agency theory focuses on the divergent interest and goal of the organisation stake holder and the way employee remunerations can be used to align these interest and goals. Employer and employees are the two stakeholders of a business unit, the former assuming the role of principle and the latter the role of agent. The remuneration is paid to the employee in the agency cost.

Wage Determinant Process

Wage determination is a complex process. However, wage determination process consists of the following steps:

1. **Job Analysis.** Job analysis describes the duties, responsibilities, working conditions and inter-relationships between the job as it is and the other jobs with which it is associated. It attempts to record and analyse details concerning the training, skills, required efforts, qualifications,

abilities, experience, and responsibilities expected of an employee. After determining the job specifications, the actual process of grading, rating or evaluating the job occurs. A job is rated in order to determine its value relative to all the other jobs in the organization which are subject to evaluation. The next step is that of providing the job with a price. This involves converting the relative job values into specific monetary values or translating the job classes into rate ranges.

2. **Wage Survey.** In determining the wages for a specific job it is very necessary to work as to what wages are being given for the same job in other enterprises. If, on the basis of utility, the wages for a specific job are determined below the wages for the same job on other enterprises, following will be its disadvantages:
   1. Good persons and persons of merit will not be available.
   2. If such people are at all obtained for employment, they will shift to another enterprise after some time.

   It is, therefore, necessary to keep in mind the following in wage-survey:
   (i) Term of survey, (weekly or monthly)
   (ii) The whole wage-payment-knowledge of daily working hours or monthly payment.
   (iii) Definition of jobs.
   (iv) Appropriate questionnaire for collecting information.
   (v) Scientific technique of collecting the data.
3. **Group Similar Jobs into Pay Grades.** After the results of job analysis and salary surveys have been received, the committee can turn to the task of assigning pay rates to each job, but it will usually want to first group jobs into pay grades. A pay grade is comprises the jobs of approximately equal difficulty or importance as determined by job evaluation. Pay grading is essential for pay purposes because instead of having to deal with hundreds of pay rates, the committee might only have to focus on a few.
4. **Price Each Pay Grade.** The next step is to assign pay rates to pay grades. Assigning pay rates to each pay grade is usually accomplished with a wage curve. The wage curve depicts graphically the pay rates currently being paid for jobs in each pay grade, relative to the points or ranking assigned to each job or grade by the job evaluation. The purpose of wage curve is to show the relationship between (i) the value of the job as determined by one of the job evaluation methods and (ii) the current average pay rates for the grades.
5. **Fine-Tune Pay Rates.** Fine tuning involves correcting out of line rates and developing rate ranges.
   (i) ***Correcting out of Line Rates.*** The average current pay for a job may be too high or too low, relative to other jobs in the firm. If a rate falls well below the line, a pay rise for that job may be required. If the rate falls well above the wage line, pay cuts or a pay freeze may be required.
   (ii) ***Developing Rate Ranges.*** Most employers do not pay just one rate for all jobs in a particular pay grade. Instead, they develop rate ranges for each grade so that there might be different levels and corresponding pay rates within each pay grade. The rate is usually built around the wage line or curve. One alternative is to arbitrarily decide on a maximum and minimum rate for each grade. As an alternative, some employers allow the rate for each grade to become wider for the higher pay ranges reflecting the greater demands and performance variability inherent in these more complex jobs.
6. **Wage Administration Rules.** The development of rules of wage administration has to be done in the next step. It is considered advisable in the interests of the concern and the employees that the information about average salaries and ranges in the salaries of group should be made

known to the employees concerned; for secrecy in this matter may create dissatisfaction and it may also vitiate the potential motivating effects of disclosure. Finally, the employee is appraised and the wage is fixed for the grade he is found fit.

Types of Wages

Determination of reasonable wages is a difficult task for the management and so they should give adequate attention to this area. However, different types of wage payment can be divided into three parts:

1. **Time wage.** In this type the worker is given remuneration according to time. This type of remuneration may be per hour, per day or per month or per year. There exists no relationship between the quantum of work and the wage. This type is in operation in all industries in India. This plan is very simple to understand. The worker works after due thinking and with convenience. However it encourages the tendency of prolonging or delaying the work unnecessarily. Moreover, it is very difficult to measure the productivity of the workers under this type of plan.
2. **Piece Rate System.** In this type of plan, a worker gets remuneration according to his output irrespective of the time he takes in finishing his job. Here, the payment of remuneration is related to work and not to time. Under this type, the workers are encouraged to earn more and more. The more the output is, the more the remuneration is. The workers are also at liberty for their job with interest and they need not be supervised. However, this type of wage payment is not suitable for commodities of artistic taste. Moreover, the quality of goods goes down.
3. **Wage incentive Plan.** This type of wage payment is the combination of two types the above referred. Efforts have been made here to obtain the advantages of both these types while avoiding their disadvantages. This includes:
   (A) Halsey Premium Scheme. Halsey premium plan is a combination of time and speed bases of payment and the minimum wages are guaranteed to every worker. Under this scheme if a worker gives an output more than the fixed standard job, he is given about 33% to 50% of the remuneration for that job as bonus. Here a standard of output is fixed and a standard of time is also fixed for the completion of that job before hand. If the job of fixed standard is completed with the standard time fixed for the purpose, the worker gets his fixed wages. But, if he completes the job before the fixed standard time and, thereby, saves some time, he gets a fixed percentage of his wages for the time so saved as bonus.
   (B) Rowan Premium Scheme. This plan is an improvement upon Halsey Plan. Under this plan, premium is that proportion of the wages for the time taken which the time saved bears to the standard time. The credit of this incentive premium method goes to Rowan of Scotland. The worker is paid wages at normal rates for the duration he has worked and is paid extra money in the form of premium on the basis of the time he has saved. Under this scheme, the standard work and the standard time both are fixed. The wages for the time saved will increase in the same percentage that is equal to the proportion the time saved bears to standard time. The premium for the time saved cannot be more than the total standard wages. Thus, a worker cannot get cleverly wages more than needed.
   (C) Taylor's Plan. F.W. Taylor suggested differential piece rate plan as an alternative to time rate system which he considered as unscientific and lacks incentive elements. In his, Taylor did not provide for minimum guarantee wage payment to each workers. Taylor plan is based on wages per unit. In other words, a worker is paid wages in accordance with his output. Higher price rate is fixed for the workers who give production over and above the standard workload fixed. The lower rate is fixed for the workers who give production below the standard workload fixed.

(D) Merrick Plan. This plan is somewhat a modified form of Taylor's plan. This plan offers three grade piece rates than the two offered in the Taylor's plan. The workers who produce less than 83% of standard output are paid are basic piece rate. Those producing form 83% to 100% of the standard output are paid 110% of basic rate. Lastly the workers Producing more than 110% of basic piece rate.

I. First limit is for new workers and is very low.

II. Second limit is for workers with average efficiency.

III. Third limit is for very efficient workers.

(E) Gantt Plan. This is also a modified form of Taylor plan. In it, wages are fixed on the basis of time. On the other hand, the efficient workers are given wages per unit. Thus, the workers who give more output get their wages at enhanced rates. If a workers achieves excel it, gets extra wages varying between 25% to 50% of the hourly rate for the time allowed for the task. But if the workers are fail to complete the task within the standard time, he receives the wages only actual time spent at the specified rate.

(F) Emerson Plan. This plan is a combination of Taylor, Merrick and Gantt plans. However, a slight modification in these plans has been made and different rates of bonus have been fixed under this plan. The amount of bonus increases with the increase in efficiency. These percentages are as under:

1% bonus on 67.5% efficiency.

10% bonus on 90% efficiency.

20% bonus on 100% efficiency.

20% + 30% extra on bonus on efficiency more than 100%.

(G) Profit-Sharing Scheme. Under this scheme, workers are given a certain percentage of profits as bonus. But it suffers from one defect. Suppose, there is no profit in a particular year. Workers will also not be given the bonus for that very year. The workers think that they have been deceived by the employers and therefore, clash with them on this very issue. This assumes the form of worker-management unrest and has its bad effect on the production. This scheme is undoubtedly a new and better scheme. But, the trade unions misuse the scheme.

(H) Scanlon Plan. Under this scheme, the workers are paid bonus equal to the percentage of profits earned more than the profits earned last year by the organisation. 15% of the bonus is deducted and this deduction is deposited in the fund which is distributed among the workers in the year to come.

FACTORS INFLUENCING WAGES

Organisation expects efficient performance from their employees in order to contribute to the attainment of organizational objective. It is possible only when employees are paid remuneration in accordance with their contribution. Many people regard compensation as a yardstick for measuring their success in the world of employment.

'Wage and Salary Administration' refers to the establishment and implementation of sound policies and practices of employee compensation. It includes such areas as job evaluation, surveys of wages and salaries, analysis of relevant organisational problems, development and maintenance of wage structure, establishing rules for administering wages, wage payment incentives, profit sharing, wage changes and adjustments, supplementary payments, control of compensation costs and other related items.

The responsibility to properly manage always lies with top management.

This task is given to Wage and Salary Administration, which follows the following guidelines:

(i) A broad policy to determine manner in which the programme of job evaluation and job description is evolved and approved.

(ii) All activities of the salary administration group must be properly checked against the existing company policies.

(iii) Recommendations of top management about the wage policies for the administration of wage programme are given.

(iv) To recommend changes in wage policies and wage level.

(v) To review wages and salary schemes department-wise.

(vi) Proper recommendation to top management for executives above a specified limit need to be given.

Let us briefly examine these factors:

1. **Supply and Demand Factors in the Economy.** These factors in the demand for labour due to new technology, impact of economic growth, and other factors. The supply aspect is created through the growth of educational institutions and students coming out of schools, vocational institutions, colleges, and universities.
2. **Ability to Pay.** In order to draw the best employees, companies are offering better salaries and benefits. Those who can afford to pay competitive wages and salaries are able to draw the best talent.
3. **Provide Promotional Opportunities.** The companies which provide good training and development facilities end up getting better employees. Such employees upgrade themselves and make use of promotional opportunities offered by the company. When they get promoted they enjoy better compensation and benefits.
4. **Performance Assessment Outcome.** Performance assessment carried out in organizations annually or semiannually has impact on compensation. Some companies place heavy stress on the outcome of performance assessment in determining the following year's salary or wage levels. The increments given for an employee who performs well, puts him or her in a different category.
5. **Job Content.** The job makes an impact on the wage and salary levels of certain unusual jobs in an organization. Such jobs may carry high risk. Besides content, there may be other factors which may place them in special categories.
6. **Budget Limitations.** Due to poor economic conditions or market situation, companies may experience financial difficulties and this poses problems in being leaders in employee compensation. Some organizations make provisions for such economic problems in their budgets.
7. **Trade Union Pressure.** Trade Unions place heavy pressure on companies to raise wage and salary levels and benefits which put constraints on their budget allocations. Generally we see Bank Unions going on strike, if their demands are not met. The unions in most of the essential services exercise greater pressure on organizations for higher wages and salaries.
8. **Public Image.** In order to maintain a good public image of being the best pay-master, some companies always maintain higher wage levels than other companies in the industry or in a community. Microsoft, Infosys, and other leading companies in Information Technology field can be cited as some examples.

The strategy of an organization takes some of the above factors into consideration in determining the wage levels for their employees. That may be one of the reasons for being leaders in their industries and communities. When they maintain such an image, potential employees prefer to work for such companies. When such companies experience economic and market difficulties, the wages and salaries are not the first things to be axed.

Factors Influencing Wage and Salary Structure and Administration – Nine Basic Factors

The wage policies of different organisations vary somewhat Marginal units pay the minimum necessary to attract the required number and kind of labour. Often, these units pay only the minimum wage rates required by labour legislation, and recruit marginal labour. At the other extreme, some units pay well above the going rates in the labour market. They do so to attract and retain the highest caliber of the labour force. Some managers believe in the economy of higher wages.

They feel that, by paying high wages, they would attract better workers who will produce more than the average, worker in the industry. This greater production per employee means greater output per man hour. Hence, labour costs may turn out to be lower than those existing in firms using marginal labour. Some units pay high wages because of a combination of favourable product market demand higher ability to pay and the bargaining power of a trade union.

But a large number of them seek to be competitive in their wage programme, i.e. they aim at paying somewhere near the going rate in the labour market for the various classes of labour they employ. Most units give greater weight to two wage criteria's, viz. job requirements and the prevailing rates of wages in the labour market. Other factors, such as changes in the cost of living, the supply and demand of labour and the ability to pay are accorded a secondary importance.

A sound wage policy is to adopt a job evaluation programme in order to establish fair differentials in wages based upon differences in job contents.

Besides the basic factors provided by a job description and job evaluation, those that are usually taken into consideration for wage and salary administration are:

(i) The organisation's ability to pay and the sustaining strengths;
(ii) Supply and demand of labour and levels of skills;
(iii) The prevailing market rate government legislation on wages;
(iv) The cost of living inflation rate;
(v) Living wage concept;
(vi) Productivity;
(vii) Trade Union's Bargaining power and judicial directions;
(viii) Job requirements, working conditions;
(ix) Managerial attitudes;
(x) Psychological and Sociological factors.
(xi) Levels of Skills available in the market.

(i) **The Organisation's Ability to Pay.** Wage increases should be given by those organisations which can afford them. Companies that have good sales and, therefore, high profits tend to pay higher wages than those which are running at a loss or earning low profits because of the high cost of production or low sales. In the short run, the economic influence on the ability to pay is practically nil.

All employers, irrespective of their profits or losses, must pay no less than their competitors and need pay no more if they wish to attract and keep workers. In the long run, the ability to pay is very important.

During the time of prosperity, employers pay high wages to carry on profitable operations and because of their increased ability to pay. But during a period of depression, wages are cut because funds are not available. Marginal firms and non-profit organisations (like hospitals and educational institutions) pay relatively low wages because of low or no profits.

(ii) **Supply and Demand of Labour.** The labour market conditions or supply and demand forces operate at the national, regional and local levels, and determine organisational wage structure and level.

If the demand for certain skills is high and the supply is low, the result is a rise in the price to be paid for these skills. When prolonged and acute, these labour-market pressures probably force most organisations to "reclassify hard-to-fill jobs at a higher level" than that suggested by the job evaluation. The other alternative is to pay higher wages if the labour supply is scarce; and lower wages when it is excessive.

Similarly, if there is great demand for labour expertise, wages rise; but if the demand for manpower skill is minimal, the wages will be relatively low. Mescon says- "The supply and demand compensation criterion is very closely related to the prevailing pay, comparable wage and on-going wage concepts since, in essence, all of these remuneration standards are determined by immediate market forces and factors."

(iii) **Prevailing Market Rate.** This is also known as the 'comparable wage' or 'going wage rate', and is the most widely used criterion. An organisation's compensation policies generally tend to conform to the wage-rates payable by the industry and the community. This is done for several reasons. First, competition demands that competitors adhere to the same relative wage level.

Second, various government laws and judicial decisions make the adoption of uniform wage rates an attractive proposition. Third, trade unions encourage this practice so that their members can have equal pay, equal work and geographical differences may be eliminated.

Fourth, functionally related firms in the same industry require essentially the same quality of employees, with the same skills and experience. This results in a considerable uniformity in wage and salary rates.

Finally, if the same or about the same general rates of wages are not paid to the employees as are paid by the organisation's competitors, it will not be able to attract and maintain a sufficient quantity and quality of manpower.

Belcher and Atchison observe – "Some companies pay on the high side of the market in order to obtain goodwill or to insure an adequate supply of labour, while other organisations pay lower wages because economically they have to, or because by lowering hiring requirements they can keep jobs adequately manned."

(iv) **The Cost of Living.** The cost-of-living pay criterion is usually regarded as an automatic minimum equity pay criterion. This criterion calls for pay adjustments based on increases or decreases in an acceptable cost of living index. In recognition of the influence of the cost of living, "escalator clauses" are written into labour contracts.

When the cost of living increases, workers and trade unions demand adjusted wages to offset the erosion of real wages. However, when living costs are stable or decline, the management does not resort to this argument as a reason for wage reductions. The cost of living index at certain places is higher than other cities or centres.

(v) **Living Wage Concept.** The Living Wage criterion means that wages paid should be adequate to enable an employee to maintain himself and his family at a reasonable level of existence. However, employers do not generally favour using the concept of a living wage as a guide to wage determination because they prefer to base the wages of an employee on his contribution rather than on his need. Also, they feel that the level of living prescribed in a worker's budget is open to argument since it is based on subjective opinion.

(vi) **Productivity.** Productivity is another criterion, and is measured in terms of output per man-hour. It is not due to labour efforts alone. Technological improvements, better organisation and management, the development of better methods of production by labour and management, greater ingenuity and skill by labour are all responsible for the increase in productivity.

Actually, productivity measures the contribution of all the resource factors men, machines, methods, materials and management. No productivity index can be devised which will measure only the productivity of a specific factor of production.

Another problem is that productivity can be measured at several levels job, plant, industry or national, economic level. Thus, although theoretically it is a sound compensation criterion, operationally many problems and complications arise because of definitional measurement and conceptual issues.

(vii) **Trade Union's Bargaining Power.** Trade unions do affect rate of wages. Generally, the stronger and more powerful the trade union, the higher the wages. A trade union's bargaining power is often measured in terms of its membership, its financial strength and the nature of its leadership. A strike or a threat of a strike is the most powerful weapon used by it.

Sometimes trade unions force wages up faster than increases in productivity would allow and become responsible for unemployment or higher prices and inflation. However, for those remaining on the pay roll, a real gain is often achieved as a consequence of a trade union's stronger bargaining power.

(viii) **Job Requirements.** Generally, the more difficult a job, the higher are the wages. Measures of job difficulty are frequently used when the relative value of one job to another in an organisation is to be ascertained. Jobs are graded according to the relative skill, effort, responsibility, and job conditions required.

(ix) **Managerial Attitudes.** These have a decisive influence on the wage structure and wage level since judgement is exercised in many areas of wage and salary administration including whether the firm should pay below average, or above average rates, what job factors should be used to reflect job worth, the weight to be given for performance or length of service, and so forth, both the structure and level of wages are bound to be affected accordingly.

These matters require the approval of the top executives. Lester observes "Top management's desire to maintain or enhance the company's prestige has been a major factor in the wage policy of a number of firms. Desires to improve or maintain morale, to attract high-caliber employees, to reduce turnover, and to provide a high living standard for employees as possible also appear to be factors in management's wage-policy decisions."

(x) **Psychological and Social Factors.** These determine in a significant measure how hard a person will work for the compensation received or what pressures he will exert to get his compensation increased. Psychologically, persons perceive the level of wages as a measure of success in life; people may feel secure; have an inferiority complex, seem inadequate or feel the reverse of all these.

They may not take pride in their work, or in the wages they get. Therefore, these things should not be overlooked by the management in establishing wage rates. Sociologically and ethically, people feel that "equal work should carry equal wages," which "wages should be commensurate with their efforts," that "they cure not exploited, and that no distinction is made on the basis of caste, colour, sex or religion." To satisfy the conditions of equity, fairness and justice, a management should take these factors into consideration.

(xi) **Skill Levels Available in the Market.** With the rapid growth of industries, business trade, there is shortage of skilled resources. The technological development, automation have been affecting the skill levels at a faster rates. Thus the wage levels of skilled employees are constantly changing and an organisation has to keep its level up to suit the market needs.

Factors Influenced Wage and Salary Administration – Top 7 Factors

Ability to Pay, State Regulation, Labour Unions, Demand and Supply of Labour, and a Few Others

Wages and Salaries represent a significant portion of the total costs in most of the organisations. So the control of wage and salary levels is of paramount importance even though the amount of control which can be exerted may vary among organisations and within an organisation from time to time.

The general objectives of compensation management or wage and salary administration are as follows:

i. Control of cost.
ii. Establishment of fair equitable structure of remuneration.
iii. Utilisation of wages and salaries as an incentive to greater employee productivity.
iv. Maintenance of a satisfactory public image.

The responsibility of wage and salary administration usually lies with the top management of the company. The chief executive is expected to develop policies and procedures which will accomplish the company's objectives. The Personnel Manager plays an important role in developing the wage policies and procedures. In many organisations, this task is entrusted to Wage and Salary Committee composed of line and staff executives.

The main factors which influenced wage or salary structure are:

1. **Ability to Pay.** An organisation's ability to pay its employees is an important factor in the determinant of wage level. It is basically depends upon the profit-earning capacity of the organisation. A multinational company pays higher salaries due to their higher profit earning.
2. **State Regulation.** Wage policy and laws of the government exercise a significant influence on wage levels. Government has enacted laws to protect the interest of the working class. And no organisation can violate laws relating to minimum wages, payment of bonus, dearness allowance and other allowances, equal pay for equal work etc.
3. **Labour Unions.** A well organised trade union give pressure for higher wages and allowances. This pressure is exercised through collective bargaining, strikes and other methods. Salary levels in commercial banks are relatively high due to higher bargaining power of bank unions.
4. **Demand and Supply of Labour.** Further, demand and supply of labour determines the wage level. Where supply of labour is more, or there is no scarcity of labour, wage rates are low. On the other hand, executive salaries have increased in India after liberalisation, due to rise in demand for professionally trained managers.
5. **Prevailing Wage Rates.** While fixing wages, prevailing wages in the particular industry are taken in to account. This is necessary to retain and attract qualified workers.
6. **Productivity.** Where there is higher productivity, due to qualified and hardworking employee, wage rate are increased in comparison to lower productivity.
7. **Job Requirement.** Further, wages depend largely on the physical and mental effort required in a particular job. A dangerous and hazardous job requires higher wages than other job.

These above factors influence the general wage rates. In addition some factors influence the individual differences in wages rates.

These specific factors are as follows:

(a) Work experience
(b) Hazards involved in the job
(c) Demand for the product
(d) Worker's age and potential
(e) Industry's role in the economy
(f) Educational qualifications
(g) Promotion possibilities
(h) Stability of employment

Wage Differentials

Wage differentials mean differences or disparities in wages. Wages differ in different employments or occupations, industries and localities and also between persons in the same employment or grade. One, therefore comes across such terms as occupational wage differentials, inter-industry, inter-firm, inter-area or geographical differentials and personal differentials. In other words, wage differentials may be as follows:

(i) **Occupational Differentials.** The reasons for occupational wage differentials can be varying requirements of skill, knowledge, demand supply situation, degree of responsibilities etc. In countries adopting a course of planned economic development, skill differentials play an important role in manpower and employment programmes, for they considerably help in bringing about an adequate supply of labour with skills corresponding to the requirements of product plans.

(ii) **Inter-firm Differentials.** Inter-firm differentials reflect the relative wage levels of workers indifferent plants in the same area and occupation. Differences in technological advancement, managerial efficiency, financial capability, age and size of them, relative advantages and disadvantages of supply of raw materials, power and availability of transport facilities- those are also accounted for considerable disparities in inter-firm wage rates. Lack of co-ordination among adjudication authorities, too, are responsible for such anomalies.

(iii) **Inter-area or Regional Differentials.** Such differentials arise when workers in the same industry and the same occupational group, but living in different geographical areas, are paid different wages. Regional wage differentials may be conceived in two senses. In the first sense, they are merely a part of inter-industry differentials in a particular region. In the second sense, they may represent real geographical differentials, resulting in the payment of different rates for the same type of work. In both cases, regional differentials affect the supply of manpower for various plants in different regions.

(iv) **Inter-industry Differentials.** These differentials arise when workers in the same occupation and the same area but in different industries are paid different wages. Inter-industry differentials reflect skill differentials. The industries paying higher wages have mostly been industries with a large number of skilled workers, while those paying less have been industries with a large proportion of unskilled and semi-skilled workers. Other factors influencing inter-industry differentials are the extent of unionisation, the structure of product markets, the ability to pay, labour-capital ratio, and the stage of development of an industry.

(v) **Inter-personal Wage Differentials.** These differentials are between workers in the same plant and the same occupation. These may be due to differentials in sex, skills, age, knowledge or experience.

THE MINIMUM WAGES ACT, 1948

According to this Act, the Act enables the Central and State Government to fix minimum rates of wages payable to employees in a selected number of 'sweated' industries. There are certain provisions under the Act.

Object and Scope

The main objective of this Act, is fixing a minimum rate of wages in number of industries where the labours are not organised and sweated labours are most dominant. The Act aims at preventing the exploitation of workers or labours in some industries, for which, the appropriate Government is empowered to take steps to prescribe minimum rates of wages in certain employment.

The Minimum Wages Fixing Machinery convention was held at Geneva in the year 1928 by ILO with reference to remuneration of workers in those industries where the, level of wages was substantially low and the labour was vulnerable to exploitation, being not well organised and having less effective bargaining power.

This act may be called the Minimum Wages Act 1948. The Act enables the Central and State Government to fix minimum rates of wages payable to employees in selected number of 'sweated' industries. The act extends to the whole of India.

Definitions

Following are some of the definitions and sections under the Act:

1. **Adolescent [2. (a)].** "adolescent" means a person who has completed his fourteenth year of age but has not completed his eighteenth year.
2. **Adult [2. (aa)].** "adult" means a person who has completed his eighteenth year of age.
3. **Appropriate government [2. (b)].** "appropriate government" means:
   (i) in relation to any scheduled employment carried on by or under the authority of the Central Government or a railway administration or in relation to a mine oil field or major port or any corporation established by a Central Act the Central Government and
   (ii) in relation to any other scheduled employment the State Government;
4. **Child [2. (bb)].** "child" means a person who has not completed his fourteenth year of age.
5. **Competent authority [2. (c)].** "competent authority" means the authority appointed by the appropriate government by notification in its Official Gazette to ascertain from time to time the cost of living index number applicable to the employees employed in the scheduled employments specified in such notification.
6. **Cost of living index number [2. (d)].** "cost of living index number" in relation to employees in any scheduled employment in respect of which minimum rates of wages have been fixed means the index number ascertained and declared by the competent authority by notification in the Official Gazette to be the cost of living index number applicable to employee in such employment.
7. **Employer [2. (e)].** "employer" means any person who employs whether directly or through another person or whether on behalf of himself or any other person one or more employees in any scheduled employment in respect of which minimum rates of wages have been fixed under this Act and includes except in sub-section (3) of section 26:
   i. in a factory where there is carried on any scheduled employment in respect of which minimum rates of wages have been fixed under this Act any person named under clause (f) of sub-section (1) of section 7 of the Factories Act 1948 (63 of 1948) as manager of the factory;
   ii. in any scheduled employment under the control of any government in India in respect of which minimum rates of wages have been fixed under this Act the person or authority appointed by such government for the supervision and control of employees or where no person or authority is so appointed the head of the department;
   iii. in any scheduled employment under any local authority in respect of which minimum rates of wages have been fixed under this Act the persons appointed by such authority for the supervision and control of employees or where no person is so appointed the chief executive officer of the local authority;
   iv. in any other case where there is carried on any scheduled employment in respect of which minimum rates of wages have been fixed under this Act any person responsible to the owner for the supervision and control of the employees or for the payment of wages;

8. **Prescribed [Sec.2 (f)].** "prescribed" means prescribed by rules made under this Act.
9. **Schedule employment [Sec.2 (f)].** "schedule employment" means an employment specified in the Schedule or any process or branch of work forming part of such employment
10. **Wages [Sec.2(h)]** : "wages" means all remuneration capable of being expressed in terms of money which would if the terms of money which would be payable to a person employed in respect of his employment or of work done in such employment and includes house rent allowance but does not include:
    i. the value of:
       (a) any house accommodation supply of light water medical attendance or
       (b) any other amenity or any service excluded by general or special order of the appropriate government;
    ii. any contribution paid by the employer to any person fund or provident fund or under any scheme of social insurance;
    iii. any travelling allowance or the value of any travelling concession;
    iv. any sum paid to the person employed to defray special expenses entailed on him by the nature of his employment; or
    v. any gratuity payable on discharge;
11. **Employee [Sec.2 (i)].** "employee" means any person who is employed for hire or reward to do any work skilled or unskilled manual or clerical in a scheduled employment in respect of which minimum rates of wages have been fixed; and includes an out-worker to whom any articles or materials are given out by another person to be made up cleaned washed altered ornamented finished repaired adapted or otherwise processed for sale for the purposes of the trade or business of that other person where the process is to be carried out either in the home of the out-worker or in some other premises not being premises under the control and management of that other person; and also includes an employee declared to be an employee by the appropriate government; but does not include any member of the Armed Forces of the Union.

Fixation and Revision of Wages (Sec. 3 to Sec. 5)

The fixation and revision of wages falls under the Sec. 3, Sec. 4 and Sec. 5. Sec. 3 deals with, the appropriate government fix the minimum wages that is payable to the employees in any scheduled employment. The Sec. 4 describes on the contents of minimum wages. Sec. 5 lays down the procedure for fixing and revising the minimum rates of wages.

Minimum Number of Employees. The appropriate government can forbear from fixing minimum rate of wages of any scheduled employment in which there are less than 1,000 employees in the organisation. But if the appropriate government find after an inquiry that there are more than 1,000 employees in any scheduled employment, it shall fix the minimum rate of wages payable as soon as after the finding.

1. **Fixing of minimum rates of wages (Sec. 3).** Under Sec. 3, the appropriate Government fix the minimum rate of wages. The appropriate government :
   a. shall fix the minimum rate of wages payable to the employees employed in the employment specified in Part I or part II of the schedule (the schedule is reproduced at the end of the unit) and in an employment to either by notification in official Gazette.
   b. the employees employed in the employment specified in Part II of the schedule (the schedule is reproduced at the end of the unit), fix the minimum rate of wage for apart of the state or for any specified class, instead of fixing the minimum rate of wages for the whole state.

c. shall review the minimum rate of wages so fixed and revise the same, at such intervals not exceeding 5 years.

Minimum rates. The Appropriate Government may fix:

a. minimum rate of wages for time work (hereinafter referred to as "a minimum time rate");
b. minimum rate of wages for piece work (hereinafter referred to as "a minimum piece rate");
c. a minimum rate of remuneration to apply in the case of employees employed on piece work for the purpose of securing to such employees a minimum rate of wages on a time work basis (hereinafter referred to as "a guaranteed time rate");
d. a minimum rate (whether time rate or piece rate) to apply in substitution for the minimum rate which would otherwise be applicable in respect of overtime work done by employees (hereinafter referred to as "over time rate").

Different minimum rates. The different minimum rates of wages may be fixed for:

a. different scheduled employments;
b. different classes of work in the scheduled employment;
c. adults, adolescents, children and apprentice;

2. **Minimum Rate of Wages (Sec. 4).** The appropriate governments fix or revise minimum rate of wages may consists of-
   a. a basic rate of wages and special allowance
   b. a basic rate of wages with or with the cost of living allowance
   c. an all inclusive rate allowing for the basic rate, the cost of living allowance and the cash value of the concessions
3. **Procedure for fixing and revising minimum wages (Sec. 5).** There are two separate modes of procedure for fixing and revising minimum wages under Sec. 5. The main object of both the procedures is to enable the government to reach a balanced conclusion with regard to fixation of a minimum wage. The two modes are as follows:
   a. **Mode one.** Appointment of Committee: The appropriate government should appoint as many committees or sub-committees as to hold necessary inquires for fixation of minimum rates of wages.
   b. **Mode two.** Publication of proposals in the official gazette: The appropriate government shall by notification in the official Gazette, publish its proposals for the information of the person who is likely to be affected by the fixation of minimum rates of wages.

Safeguards Payment of Minimum Wages (Sec. 11 to 18)

The safeguards payments of minimum wages falls under the sec. 11 to sec. 18. The section are as follows:

1. **Wages in kind (Sec. 11).** The minimum wages under the Act shall be paid in cash. But where it has been custom to pay wages wholly or partly in kind, the appropriate Government may, by notification in the official Gazette, authorize the payment of minimum wages either partly or wholly in kind.

   The cash value of wages in kind and of concessions in respect of supplies of any essential commodities at concessional rates shall be estimated in the prescribed manner.
2. **Payment of minimum rate of wages (Sec. 12).** In respect of any scheduled employment where minimum wages have been fixed, the employer shall pay each and every employee wages at a rate not less than the minimum rate of wages fixed for that class of employees. The wages shall be paid without any deductions except as prescribed.

3. **Fixing hours for a normal working day, etc. (Sec. 13).** In respect of any scheduled employment where minimum wages have been fixed, the appropriate government may:
   a. fix the numbers of hour of work which is the normal working day inclusive of one or more intervals;
   b. provide a day of rest in every period of 7 days and for payment of remuneration in respect of such day of rest;
   c. provide for payment for work on a day of rest at a rate not less than the overtime rate.
4. **Rates of overtime (Sec. 14).** Where employee, whose minimum rate of wages is fixed under this Act, by the hour, by the day or by any longer wage-period as prescribed, works overtime, the employer shall pay him for every hour or for part of an hour so worked in excess, wages at the rates fixed for overtime work under the Act or under any law of the appropriate Government in force, whichever is higher.

   let us know

   The provisions of the minimum Wages Act, 1948 shall not prejudice the operation of the provision of sec. 59 of the Factories Act, 1948 in any case where those provisions are applicable Sec. 59 of the Factories Act, 1948 provides that where a worker works in factory for more than 9 hours in any day or for more than 48 hours in any week, he shall, in respect of overtime work, be entitled to wages at the rate of twice his ordinary rate of wages.
5. **Wages of worker who works for less than the normal working day (Sec. 15).** Sometime it may happen that any employee whose minimum rate of wages has been fixed by the day may work on any day on which he has employed the period less than the required number of hours constituting a normal working day. In that case he is entitled to receive wages for the work done by him on that day if he had worked on a full normal working day except:
   (i) if his failure of work is caused by his unwillingness to work and not by omission of the employer to provide him with work;
   (ii) in such other cases and circumstances as may be prescribed.
6. **Wages for 2 or more classes of work (Sec. 16).** Where an employee does 2 or more classes of work to each of which a different minimum rate of wages is applicable, the employer shall pay to such employee in respect of the time respectively occupied in each such class of work, wages at not less than the minimum rate in force in respect of each such class.
7. **Minimum time rate wages for piece work (Sec. 17).** Where an employee is employed on piece work for which minimum time rate and not a minimum piece rate has been fixed under the Act, the employer shall pay such employee wages at not less than the minimum time rate.
8. **Maintenance of registers and records (Sec. 18).** In an organisation who falls under this Act shall maintain registers and records giving the detail information of the employees, the work performed by them, the wages paid to them and such other particulars and in such form as may be prescribed.

Enforcement of the Act (Sec. 19 to Sec. 20)

The Appropriate Government can appoint by notification in the Official Gazette an inspector (section 19). The inspector can within his local limit

(a) enter at all reasonable hours, with such assistant (if any) or any local or other public authority, as think fit any premises or place of premises where employees are employed or for the purpose of examining any register, record of wages or notices required to be kept;

(b) examine any person he find in such premises or depending on any reasonable causes believe is an employee or an employee who given out his work from therein;

(c) require any person giving out work or any out-workers to give any information, which in his power to give with respect to the names and addresses of the persons from or to whom the work is given out or received and with respect to the payment to be made for the work.

(d) seize or takes copies of the register, record of wages or notices in respect of any offence under the Act.

(e) exercise such other powers as may be prescribed.

Within the meaning of section 175 and 176 under Indian Penal Code, any document or information given by the inspector shall be deemed to be legally bound. The inspector shall be deemed to be a public servant within the meaning of Indian Penal Code.

The employee can claims for minimum wages (under section 20):

1. The Appropriate Government may by notification in the Official Gazette, appoint :
   a. any Commissioner for Workmen's Compensation, or
   b. any officer of the Central Government exercising functions as a Labour Commissioner for any region,
   c. any officer of the State Government not below the rank of the Labour Commissioner or, any other officer.

   Such person should have an experience as a judge of a Civil Court or as a stipendiary Magistrate to hear or decide any claims arising out of the payment of less than the minimum rates of wages.
2. Again for any claims of the employees under section 3, the employees himself or any legal practitioner or any official of a registered trade union or inspector can apply to such Authority and the application shall present to them within six month from the date on which the minimum wages became payable.
3. After the necessary enquiry, the Authority shall hear the applicant and the employer and give them opportunity of being heard. If the wages is paid of less than the minimum rates of wages, than the Authority may asked to the employer to pay exceed the actual amount which has to pay in addition with compensation not exceeding ten times the amount of such excess for such act.

   In any other case, if the payment become due than the employee will get together with the payment of such compensation as the Authority may think fit not exceeding ten rupees.
4. If under this section the Authority hearing any claim and found that it was either malicious or vexatious, it may direct penalty not exceeding fifty rupees to the employer by the person presenting the application.
5. Under this section if any amount is directed to be paid than as if it were a fine imposed by the Authority as a Magistrate or if he is not Magistrate than to such person whom the Authority makes application in this behalf as if were a fine imposed by such Magistrate.
6. Every direction is final under this section.
7. Every Authority appointed shall have all powers of a Civil Court under the Code of Civil Procedure, 1908.

THE PAYMENT OF WAGES ACT, 1936

Object of the Act

The Payment of Wages Act regulates the payment of wages to certain classes of persons employed in industry and its importance cannot be under-estimated. The Act guarantees payment of wages on time and without any deductions except those authorised under the Act. The Act provides for the responsibility for payment of wages, fixation of wage period, time and mode of payment of wages, permissible deduction as also casts upon the employer a duty to seek the approval of the Government for the acts and permission for which fines may be imposed by him and also sealing of the fines, and also for a machinery to hear and decide complaints regarding the deduction from wages or in delay in payment of wages, penalty for malicious and vexatious claims. The Act does not apply to persons whose wage is Rs. 10,000 or more per month. The Act also provides to the effect that a worker cannot contract out of any right conferred upon him under the Act.

Definitions

"employed person" [sec. 2 (i)] includes the legal representative of a deceased employed person;

"employer" [sec. 2 (ia)] includes the legal representative of a deceased employer;

"industrial or other establishment" [sec. 2 (i1)] means any :

(a) tramway service or motor transport service engaged in carrying passengers or goods or both by road for hire or reward;

(aa) air transport service other than such service belonging to or exclusively employed in the military naval or air forces of the Union or the Civil Aviation Department of the Government of India;

(b) Dock wharf or jetty;

(c) inland vessel mechanically propelled;

(d) mine quarry or oil-field;

(e) plantation;

(f) workshop or other establishment in which articles are produced adapted or manufactured with a view to their use transport or sale;

(g) establishment in which any work relating to the construction development or maintenance of buildings roads bridges or canals or relating to operations connected with navigation irrigation or to the supply of water or relating to the generation transmission and distribution of electricity or any other form of power is being carried on;

(h) any other establishment or class of establishments which the Central Government or a State Government may having regard to the nature thereof the need for protection of persons employed therein and other relevant circumstances specify by notification in the Official Gazette.

"Wages" [sec. 2 (iv)] means all remuneration (whether by way of salary allowances or otherwise) expressed in terms of money or capable of being so expressed which would if the terms of employment express or implied were fulfilled by payable to a person employed in respect of his employment or of work done in such employment and includes :

(a) any remuneration payable under any award or settlement between the parties or order of a court;

(b) any remuneration to which the person employed is entitled in respect of overtime work or holidays or any leave period;

(c) any additional remuneration payable under the terms of employment (whether called a bonus or by any other name);

(d) any sum which by reason of the termination of employment of the person employed is payable under any law contract or instrument which provides for the payment of such sum whether with or without deductions but does not provide for the time within which the payment is to be made;

(e) any sum to which the person employed is entitled under any scheme framed under any law for the time being in force, but does not include :

(1) any bonus (whether under a scheme of profit sharing or otherwise) which does not form part of the remuneration payable under the terms of employment or which is not payable under any award or settlement between the parties or order of a court;

(2) the value of any house-accommodation or of the supply of light water medical attendance or other amenity or of any service excluded from the computation of wages by a general or special order of the State Government;

(3) any contribution paid by the employer to any pension or provident fund and the interest which may have accrued thereon;

(4) any travelling allowance or the value of any travelling concession;

(5) any sum paid to the employed person to defray special expenses entailed on him by the nature of his employment; or

(6) any gratuity payable on the termination of employment in cases other than those specified in sub-clause (d).

Responsibility for payment of wages [Section 3]

Every employer shall be responsible for the payment to persons employed by him of all wages required to be paid.

- In the case of the factory, manager of that factory shall be liable to pay the wages to employees employed by him.
- In the case of industrial or other establishments, persons responsibility of supervision shall be liable for the payment of the wage to employees employed by him.
- In the case of railways, a person nominated by the railway administration for specified area shall be liable for the payment of the wage to the employees.
- In the case of contractor, a person designated by such contractor who is directly under his charge shall be liable for the payment of the wage to the employees. If he fails to pay wages to employees, person who employed the employees shall be liable for the payment of the wages.

[Sec. 5 (3)]. With the consultation of the central government, state government having power and can change the person responsible for the payment of the wages in Railways, or person responsible to daily-rated workers in the Public Works Department of the Central Government or the State Government.

Fixation of wage-periods. [Section 4]

Every person responsible for the payment of wages under section 3 shall fix periods in respect of which such wages shall be payable. No wage-period shall exceed one month. That means wage can be paid on daily, weekly, fortnightly (for every 15 days) and monthly only. Wage period for payment of wages to employees by employer should not exceed 30 days i.e. one month according to this act.

But wages cannot be paid for quarterly, half yearly or once in a year.

Time of Payment of Wages. [Section 5]

- In railway factory or industrial or other establishment, if there are less than 1000 employees, wages of employees should be paid before the expiry of the 7th day after the last day of the wage period. (*Ex.*: wages should be paid on starting of present month within 7 days *i.e.*, before 7th date if wage is paid on 1st in previous month)
- In other railway factory or industrial or other establishment, if there are more than 1000 employees, wages of employees should be paid before the expiry of the 10th day after the last day of the wage period. (*Ex.*: wages should be paid on starting of present month within 10 days i.e. before 10th date if wage is paid on 1st in previous month)

- For employees of port area, mines, wharf or jetty, wages of employees should be paid before the expiry of the 7th day after the last day of the wage period.

[Sec. 5 (2)]. If the employee is terminated or removed for the employment by the employer the wage of that employee should be paid within 2 days from the day on which he was removed or terminated.

[Sec. 5 (4)]. Except the payment of wage of the terminated employee, all the wages of the employees should be paid by their employer on the working day only.

Wages to be Paid in Current Coin or Currency Notes. All the wages of the employees must be paid in form of currently using currency notes or coins or in both forms. Currently using currency notes are 1000/-, 500/-, 100/-, 50/-, 20/-, 10/-, 5/- and currently using coins are 10/-, 5/-, 2/-, 1/-.

Deductions which may be Made from Wages. At the time of payment of the wage to employees, employer should make deductions according to this act only. Employer should not make deductions as he like. Every amount paid by the employee to his employer is called as deductions.

The following are not called as the deduction

- Stoppage of the increment of employee.
- Stoppage of the promotion of the employee.
- Stoppage of the incentive lack of performance by employee.
- Demotion of the employee
- Suspension of the employee.

The above said actions taken by the employer should have good and sufficient cause.

Deductions [Sec. 7 (2)]

Deduction made by the employer should be made in accordance with this act only. The following are said to be the deductions and which are acceptable according to this act.

- Fines,
- Deductions for absence from duty,
- Deductions for damage to or loss of goods made by the employee due to his negligence,
- Deductions for house-accommodation supplied by the employer or by government or any housing board,
- Deductions for such amenities and services supplied by the employer as the State Government or any officer,
- Deductions for recovery of advances connected with the excess payments or advance payments of wages,
- Deductions for recovery of loans made from welfare labour fund,
- Deductions for recovery of loans granted for house-building or other purposes,
- Deductions of income-tax payable by the employed person,
- Deductions by order of a court,
- Deduction for payment of provident fund,
- Deductions for payments to co-operative societies approved by the State Government,
- Deductions for payments to a scheme of insurance maintained by the Indian Post Office
- Deductions made if any payment of any premium on his life insurance policy to the Life Insurance Corporation with the acceptance of employee,
- Deduction made if any contribution made as fund to trade union with the acceptance of employee,
- Deductions, for payment of insurance premia on Fidelity Guarantee Bonds with the acceptance of employee,

- Deductions for recovery of losses sustained by a railway administration on account of acceptance by the employee of fake currency,
- Deductions for recovery of losses sustained by a railway administration on account of failure by the employee in collections of fares and charges,
- Deduction made if any contribution to the Prime Minister's National Relief Fund with the acceptance of employee,
- Deductions for contributions to any insurance scheme framed by the Central Government for the benefit of its employees with the acceptance of employee,

Limit for Deductions. [Sec. 7 (3)]

The total amount of deductions from wages of employees should not exceed 50%, but only in case of payments to co-operative societies, deduction from wages of employee can be made up to 75%.

Fines. [Sec. 8]

Fine should be imposed by the employer on employee with the approval of the state government or prescribed authority. Employer should follow the rules mentioned below for and before imposing of fine on the employee.

1. Notice board of fines on employee should be displayed in the work premises and it should contain activities that should not be made by employee.
2. Fine should not be imposed on the employee until he gives the explanation and cause for the act or omission he made.
3. Total amount of fine should not exceed 3% of his wage.
4. Fine should not be imposed on any employee who is under the age of 15 years.
5. Fine should be imposed for one time only on the wage of the employee for the act or omission he made.
6. Fines should not be recovered in the way of instalments from the employee.
7. Fine should be recovered within 60 days from the date on which fine were imposed.
8. Fine should be imposed on day act or omission made by the employee.
9. All fines collected from the employee should be credited to common fund and utilise for the benefit of the employees.

Deductions for Absence from Duty. [Sec. 9]

- Deductions can be made by the employer for the absence of duty by the employee for one day or for any period.
- The amount deducted for absence from the duty should not exceed a sum which bears the same relationship to the wage payable in respect of the wage-period as this period of absence does to such wage-period. (*Example:* if the salary of an employee is 6000/- per month and he was absent for duty for one month. Deduction from the salary for absence of duty should not exceed 6000/-)
- Employee present for the work place and refuses to work without proper reason shall be deemed to be absent from duty.
- If 10 or more persons together absent for the duty without any notice and without reasonable cause, employer can make 8 day of wages as deduction from their wage.

Deductions for Damage or Loss. [Sec. 10]

Employer should give an opportunity to the employee to explain the reason and cause for the damage or loss happened and deductions made by employer from the employee wage should not exceed the value or amount of damage or loss made by the employee.

[Sec. 10 (2)]. All such deduction and all realisations thereof shall be recorded in a register to be kept by the person responsible for the payment of wages under section 3 in such form as may be prescribed.

Deductions for Services Rendered. [Sec. 11]

House-accommodation amenity or service provided by the employer should be accepted by the employee, than only the employer can make deduction from the wage of the employee. Deduction should not exceed an amount equivalent to the value of the house-accommodation amenity or service supplied.

Deductions for Recovery of Advances. [Sec. 12]

In case of advance paid to the employees by the employer before employment began, such advance should be recovered by the employer from the first payment of the wages / salary to the employee. But employer should not recover the advance given for the travelling expense for the employee.

Deductions for Recovery of Loans. [Sec. 12A]

Deductions for recovery of loans granted for house-building or other purposes shall be subject to any rules made by the State Government regulating the extent to which such loans may be granted and the rate of interest payable thereon.

Deductions for Payments to Co-operative Societies and Insurance Schemes. [Sec. 13]

Deductions for payments to co-operative societies or deductions for payments to scheme of insurance maintained by the Indian Post Office or with employee acceptance deductions made for payment of any premium on his life insurance policy to the Life Insurance Corporation shall be subject to such conditions as the State Government may impose.

Maintenance of Registers and Records. [Sec. 13A]

Every employer should maintain such registers and records giving such particulars of persons employed by him, the work performed by them, the wages paid to them, the deductions made from their wages, the receipts given by them and such other particulars and in such form as may be prescribed.

Every register and record required to be maintained and preserved for a period of three years after the date of the last entry made therein. It means for every transaction made within employer and employee should have 3 years of record.

Inspectors. [Sec. 14]

The state government may appoint an inspector for purpose of this act. Every Inspector shall be deemed to be a public servant within the meaning of the Indian Penal Code, 1860 [Sec. 14(5)]. The inspector of this act is having powers mentioned below

- Inspector can make enquiry and examination whether the employers are properly obeying the rules mentioned under this act.
- Inspector with such assistance, if any, as he thinks fit, enter, inspect and search any premises of any railway, factory or industrial or other establishment at any reasonable time for the purpose of carrying out the objects of this Act.
- Inspector can supervise the payment of wages to persons employed upon any railway or in any factory or industrial or other establishment.
- Seize or take copies of such registers or documents or portions thereof as he may consider relevant in respect of an offence under this Act which he has reason to believe has been committed by an employer.

Facilities to be afforded to Inspectors. [Sec. 14A]

Every employer shall afford an Inspector all reasonable facilities for making any entry, inspection, supervision, examination or inquiry under this Act.

Claims Arising out of Deductions from Wages or Delay in Payment of Wages and Penalty for Malicious or Vexatious Claims. [Sec. 15] (2005 amendments)

To hear and decide all claims arising out of deductions from the wages, or delay in payment of the wages, of persons employed or paid, including all matters, incidental to such claims, there will be a officer mentioned below appointed by the appropriate government.

(a) any Commissioner for Workmen's Compensation; or

(b) any officer of the Central Government exercising functions as –

(i) Regional Labour Commissioner; or

(ii) Assistant Labour Commissioner with at least two years' experience; or

(c) any officer of the State Government not below the rank of Assistant Labour Commissioner with at least two years' experience; or

(d) a presiding officer of any Labour Court or Industrial Tribunal, constituted under the Industrial Disputes Act, 1947 (14 of 1947) or under any corresponding law relating to the investigation and settlement of industrial disputes in force in the State; or

(e) any other officer with experience as a Judge of a Civil Court or a Judicial Magistrate, as the authority to hear and decide for any specified area all claims arising out of deductions from the wages, or delay in payment of the wages, of persons employed or paid in that area, including all matters incidental to such claims:

Appropriate Government considers it necessary so to do, it may appoint more than one authority for any specified area and may, by general or special order, provide for the distribution or allocation of work to be performed by them under this Act.

[Sec. 15(2)]. If any employer does opposite to the provisions of this act, any unreasonable deduction has been made from the wages of an employed person, or any payment of wages has been delayed, in such case any lawyer or any Inspector under this Act or official of a registered trade union authorised to write an application to the authority appointed by government for direction of payment of wages according to this act. Every such application shall be presented within 12 months from the date on which the deduction from the wages was made or from the date on which the payment of the wages was due to be made. Time of making an application can be accepted if there is reasonable cause.

[Sec. 15(3)]. After receiving of the application the authority shall give an opportunity to hear the applicant and the employer or other person responsible for the payment of wages and conducts the enquiry if necessary. It is found that there is mistake with employer; authority shall order the employer for payment of the wage or refund to the employee of the amount deducted unreasonably or the payment of the delayed wages, together with the payment of such compensation as the authority may think fit. There will not be any compensation payable by employer if there is a reasonable and genuine cause in delay in the payment of wages.

Powers of Authorities Appointed. [Section 18]

Taking evidence and of enforcing the attendance of witnesses and compelling the production of documents.

Single Application in Respect of Claims from Unpaid Group. [Section 16]

There is no necessity of many applications if there are many employees whose wages has not been paid. Such all employees can make one application to the authority for payment of wages according to this act.

Appeal. [Section 17]

In the following situation the parties who ever dissatisfied can appeal to the district court :

- If the application dismissed by above authorities.

- Employer imposed with compensation exceeding 300/- rupees by the authorities.
- If the amount exceeding 25/- rupees withheld by the employer to single unpaid employee 50/- in case of many unpaid employees.

Penalty for Offences Under the Act. [Section 20] (2005 amendments)

Reasons

- Delay in payment of wages.
- Unreasonable deductions.
- Excess deduction for absence of duty.
- Excess deduction for damage or loss to employer.
- Excess deduction for house-accommodation amenity or service.

Punishable with fine which shall not be less than 1000/- rupees but which may extend to 7500/- rupees.

- If Wage period exceed one month.
- Failure in payments of wages on a working day.
- Wages not paid in form of current coin or currency notes or in both.
- Failure to maintain record for collected fines from employee.
- Improper usage of fine collected from employees.
- Failure of employee to display notice containing such abstracts of this Act and of the rules made.

Punishable with fine which may extend 3000/- rupees

- Whoever obstructs an Inspector in the discharge of his duties under this Act.
- Whoever wilfully refuses to produce on the demand of an Inspector any register or other document.
- Whoever refuses or wilfully neglects to afford an Inspector any reasonable facility for making any entry, inspection, examination, supervision, or inquiry authorised by or under this Act.

Punishable with fine which shall not be less than 1000/- rupees but which may extend to 7500/- rupees

Whoever repeats the same offence committed before.

Imprisonment for a term which shall not be less than one month but which may extend to 6 months and fine which shall not be less than 3750/- rupees but which may extend 20,500/- rupees.

EQUAL REMUNERATION ACT, 1976

The Equal Remuneration Act, 1976 aims to provide for the payment of equal remuneration to men and women workers and for the prevention of discrimination, on the ground of sex, against women in the matter of employment and for matters connected therewith or incidental thereto. According to the Act, the term 'remuneration' means "the basic wage or salary and any additional emoluments whatsoever payable, either in cash or in kind, to a person employed in respect of employment or work done in such employment, if the terms of the contract of employment, express or implied, were fulfilled". Nothing in this Act shall apply:- (i) to cases affecting the terms and conditions of a woman's employment in complying with the requirements of any law giving special treatment to women; or (ii) to any special treatment accorded to women in connection with the birth or expected birth of a child, or the terms and conditions relating to retirement, marriage or death or to any provision made in connection with the retirement, marriage or death.

The Central Industrial Relations Machinery (CIRM) in the Ministry of Labour is responsible for enforcing this Act. CIRM is an attached office of the Ministry and is also known as the Chief Labour Commissioner (Central) [CLC(C)] Organisation. The CIRM is headed by the Chief Labour Commissioner (Central).

The main provisions of the Act are:

- No employer shall pay to any worker, employed by him/ her in an establishment, a remuneration (whether payable in cash or in kind) at rates less favorable than those at which remuneration is paid by him/ her to the workers of the opposite sex in such establishment for performing the same work or work of a similar nature. Also, no employer shall, for the purpose of complying with the provisions of this Act, reduce the rate of remuneration of any worker.
- No employer shall, while making recruitment for the same work or work of a similar nature, or in any condition of service subsequent to recruitment such as promotions, training or transfer, make any discrimination against women except where the employment of women in such work is prohibited or restricted by or under any law for the time being in force.
- Every employer shall maintain such registers and other documents in relation to the workers employed by him/ her in the prescribed manner.
- If any employer: (i) makes any recruitment in contravention of the provisions of this Act; or (ii) makes any payment of remuneration at unequal rates to men and women workers for the same work or work of a similar nature; or (iii) makes any discrimination between men and women workers in contravention of the provisions of this Act; or (iv) omits or fails to carry out any direction made by the appropriate Government, then he/ she shall be punishable with fine or with imprisonment or with both.
- Where an offence under this Act has been committed by a company, every person who at the time the offence was committed, was in charge of, and was responsible to the company for the conduct of the business of the company, as well as the company, shall be deemed, to be guilty of the offence and shall be liable to be proceeded against and punished accordingly.

Definitions

In this Act, unless the context otherwise requires,

(a) "appropriate Government" means,

  (i) in relation to any employment carried on by or under the authority of the Central Government or a railway administration, or in relation to a banking company, a mine, oilfield or major port or any corporation established by or under a Central Act, the Central Government, and

  (ii) in relation to any other employment, the State Government.

(b) "commencement of this Act" means, in relation to an establishment or employment, the date on which this Act comes into force in respect of that establishment or employment;

(c) "employer" has the meaning assigned to it in clause (f) of section 2 of the Payment of Gratuity Act, 1972 (39 of 1972);

(d) "man" and "woman" mean male and female human beings, respectively, of any age;

(e) "notification" means a notification published in the Official Gazette;

(f) "prescribed" means prescribed by rules made under this Act;

(g) "remuneration" means the basic wage or salary, and any additional emoluments whatsoever payable, either in cash or in kind, to a person employed in respect of employment or work done in such employment, if the terms of the contract of employment, express or implied, were fulfilled;

(h) "same work or work of a similar nature" means work in respect of which the skill, effort and responsibility required are the same, when performed under similar working conditions, by a man or a woman and the differences, if any, between the skill, effort and responsibility required of a man and those required of woman are not of practical importance in relation to the terms and conditions of employment :

(i) "worker" means a worker in any establishment or employment in respect of which this Act has come into force;

(j) words and expressions used in this Act and not defined but defined in the Industrial Disputes Act, 1947 (14 of 1947), shall have the meanings respectively assigned to them in that Act.

Duty of Employer to Pay Equal Remuneration to Men and Women Workers for Same Work or Work of a Similar Nature.

(1) No employer shall pay to any worker, employed by him in an establishment or employment, remuneration, whether payable in cash or in kind, at rates less favourable than those at which remuneration is paid by him to the workers of the opposite sex in such establishment or employment for performing the same work or work of a similar nature.

(2) No employer shall, for the purpose of complying with the provisions of sub-section (1), reduce the rate of remuneration of any worker.

(3) Where, in an establishment or employment, the rates of remuneration payable before the commencement of this Act for men and women workers for the same work or work of a similar nature are different only on the ground of sex, then the higher (in cases where there are only two rates), or, as the case may be, the highest (in cases where there are more than two rates), of such rates shall be the rate at which remuneration shall be payable, on and from such commencement, to such men and women workers :

Provided that nothing in this sub-section shall be deemed to entitle a worker to the revision of the rate of remuneration payable to him or her with reference to the service rendered by him or her before the commencement of this Act.

No Discrimination to be Made While Recruiting Men and Women Workers.

On and from the commencement of this Act, no employer shall, while making recruitment for the same work or work of a similar nature, or in any condition of service subsequent to recruitment such as promotions, training or transfer, make any discrimination against women except where the employment of women in such work is prohibited or restricted by or under any law for the time being in force :

Provided that the provisions of this section shall not affect any priority or reservation for Scheduled Castes or Scheduled Tribes, ex-servicemen, retrenched employees or any other class or category of persons in the matter of recruitment to the posts in an establishment or employment.

Advisory Committee

(1) For the purpose of providing increasing employment opportunities for women, the appropriate Government shall constitute one or more Advisory Committees to advise it with regard to the extent to which women may be employed in such establishments or employments as the Central Government may, by notification, specify in this behalf.

(2) Every Advisory Committee shall consist of not less than ten persons, to be nominated by the appropriate Government, of which one-half shall be women.

(3) In tendering its advice, the Advisory Committee shall have regard to the number of women employed in the concerned establishment or employment, the nature of work, hours of work, suitability of women for employment, as the case may be, the need for providing increasing employment opportunities for women, including part-time employment and such relevant factors as the Committee may think fit.

(4) The Advisory Committee shall regulate its own procedure.

(5) The appropriate Government may, after considering the advice tendered to it by the Advisory Committee and after giving to the persons concerned in the establishment or employment an opportunity to make representations, issue such directions in respect of employment of women workers, as the appropriate Government may think fit.

Power of Appropriate Government to Appoint Authorities for Hearing and Deciding Claims and Complaints.

(1) The appropriate Government may, by notification, appoint such officers, not below the rank of a Labour Officer, as it thinks fit to be the authorities for the purpose of hearing and deciding -(a) complaints with regard to the contravention of any provision of this Act; (b) claims arising out of non-payment of wages at equal rates to men and women workers for the same work or work of a similar nature; and may, by the same or subsequent notification, define the local limits within which each such authority shall exercise its jurisdiction.

(2) Every complaint or claim referred to in sub-section (1) shall be made in such manner as may be prescribed.

(3) If any question arises as to whether two or more works are of the same nature or of a similar nature, it shall be decided by the authority appointed under sub-section (1).

(4) Where a complaint or claim is made to the authority appointed under sub-section (1) it may, after giving the applicant and the employer an opportunity of being heard, and after such inquiry as it may consider necessary, direct :

(i) in the case of a claim arising out of non-payment of wages at equal rates to men and women workers for the same work or work of a similar nature, that payment be made to the worker of the amount by which the wages payable to him exceed the amount actually paid;

(ii) in the case of complaint, that adequate steps be taken by the employer so as to ensure that there is no contravention of any provision of this Act.

(5) Every authority appointed under sub-section (1) shall have all the powers of a Civil Court under the Code of Civil Procedure, 1908 (5 of 1908), for the purpose of taking evidence and of enforcing the attendance of witnesses and compelling the production of documents, and every such authority shall be deemed to be a Civil Court for all the purposes of section 195 and Chapter XXVI of the Code of Criminal Procedure, 1973 (2 of 1974).

(6) Any employer or worker aggrieved by any order may be an authority appointed under sub-section (1), on a complaint or claim may, within thirty days from the date of the order, prefer an appeal to such authority as the appropriate Government may, by notification, specify in this behalf, and that authority may, after hearing the appeal, confirm, modify or reverse the order appealed against and no further appeal shall lie against the order made by such authority.

(7) The authority referred to in sub-section (6) may, if it is satisfied that the appellant was prevented by sufficient cause from preferring the appeal within the period specified in sub-section (6), allow the appeal to be preferred within a further period of thirty days but not thereafter.

(8) The provisions of sub-section (1) of section 33C of the Industrial Disputes Act, 1947 (14 of 1947), shall apply for the recovery of monies due from an employer arising out of the decision of an authority appointed under this section.

Duty of Employers to Maintain Registers. On and from the commencement of this Act, every employer shall maintain such registers and other documents in relation to the workers employed by him as may be prescribed.

Inspectors.

(1) The appropriate Government may, by notification, appoint such persons as it may think fit to be Inspectors for the purpose of making an investigation as to whether the provisions of this

Act, or the rules made there under, are being complied with by employers, and may define the local limits within which an Inspector may make such investigation.

(2) Every Inspector shall be deemed to be a public servant within the meaning of section 21 of the Indian Penal Code (45 of 1860).

(3) An Inspector may, at any place within the local limits of his jurisdiction : (a) enter, at any reasonable time, with such assistance as he thinks fit, any building, factory, premises or vessel; (b) require any employer to produce any register, muster-roll or other documents relating to the employment of workers, and examine such documents; (c) take on the spot or otherwise, the evidence of any person for the purpose of ascertaining whether the provisions of this Act are being, or have been, complied with; (d) examine the employer, his agent or servant or any other person found in charge of the establishment or any premises connected therewith or any person whom the Inspector has reasonable cause to believe to be, or to have been a worker in the establishment; (e) make copies, or take extracts from, any register or other document maintained in relation to the establishment under this Act.

(4) Any person required by an Inspector to produce any register or other document or to give any information shall comply with such requisition.

Penalties.

(1) If after the commencement of this Act, any employer, being required by or under the Act, so to do:

(a) omits or fails to maintain any register or other document in relation to workers employed by him, or

(b) omits or fails to produce any register, muster-roll or other document relating to the employment of workers, or

(c) omits or refuses to give any evidence or prevents his agent, servant, or any other person in charge of the establishment, or any worker, from giving evidence, or

(d) omits or refuses to give any information, he shall be punishable with simple imprisonment for a term which may extend to one month or with fine which may extend to ten thousand rupees or with both.

(2) If, after the commencement of this Act, any employer -

(a) makes any recruitment in contravention of the provisions of this Act, or

(b) makes any payment of remuneration at unequal rates to men and women workers, for the same work or work of a similar nature, or

(c) makes any discrimination between men and women workers in contravention of the provisions of this Act, or

(d) omits or fails to carry out any direction made by the appropriate Government under sub-section (5) of section 6, he shall be punishable with fine which shall not be less than ten thousand rupees but which may extend to twenty thousand rupees or with imprisonment for a term which shall be not less than three months but which may extend to one year or with both for the first offence, and with imprisonment which may extend to two years for the second and subsequent offences.

(3) If any person being required so to do, omits or refuses to produce to an Inspector any register or other document or to give any information, he shall be punishable with fine which may extend to five hundred rupees.

Offences by Companies.

(1) Where an offence under this Act has been committed by a company, every person who at the time the offence was committed, was in charge of, and was responsible to, the company for the

conduct of the business of the company, as well as the company, shall be deemed, to be guilty of the offence and shall be liable to be proceeded against and punished accordingly : Provided that nothing contained in this sub-section shall render any such person liable to any punishment, if he proves that the offence was committed without his knowledge or that he had exercised all due diligence to prevent the commission of such offence.

(2) Notwithstanding anything contained in sub-section (1), where any offence under this Act been committed by a company and it is proved that the offence has been committed with the consent or connivance of or is attributable to any neglect on the part of any director, manager, secretary or other officer of the company, such director, manager, secretary or other officer shall be deemed to be guilty of that offence and shall be liable to be proceeded against and punished accordingly.

Explanation. For the purposes of this section :

(a) "company" means any body corporate and includes a firm or other association of individuals; and

(b) "director", in relation to a firm, means a partner in the firm.

Cognizance and Trial of Offences.

(1) No court inferior to that of a metropolitan magistrate or judicial Magistrate of the first class shall try any offence punishable under this Act.

(2) No court shall take cognizance of an offence punishable under this Act except upon :

(a) its own knowledge or upon a complaint made by the appropriate Government or an officer authorised by it in this behalf, or

(b) a complaint made by the person aggrieved by the offence or by any recognised welfare institution or organisation.

Power to Make Rules.

(1) The Central Government may, by notification, make rules for carrying out the provisions of this Act.

(2) In particular, and without prejudice to the generality of the foregoing power, such rules may provide for all or any of the following matters, namely: (a) the manner in which complaint or claim referred to in sub-section (1) of section 7 shall be made; (b) registers and other documents which an employer is required under section 8 to maintain in relation to the workers employed by him; (c) any other matter which is required to be, or may be, prescribed.

(3) Every rule made by the Central Government under this Act shall be laid, as soon as may be after it is made, before each House of Parliament, while it is in session, for a total period of thirty days which may be comprised in one session or in two or more successive sessions, and if, before the expiry of the session immediately following the session or the successive sessions aforesaid, both Houses agree in making any modification in the rule or both Houses agree that the rule should not be made, the rule shall thereafter have effect only in such modified form or be of no effect, as the case may be; so, however, that any such modification or annulment shall be without prejudice to the validity of anything previously done under that rule.

Power of Central Government to Give Directions.

The Central Government may give directions to a State Government as to the carrying into execution of this Act in the State.

Act not to Apply in Certain Special Cases.

Nothing in this Act shall apply:

(a) to cases affecting the terms and conditions of a woman's employment in complying with the requirements of any law giving special treatment to women, or

(b) to any special treatment accorded to women in connection with :
   (i) the birth or expected birth of a child, or
   (ii) the terms and conditions relating to retirement, marriage or death or to any provision made in connection with the retirement, marriage or death.

Power to Make Declaration.

Where the appropriate Government is, on a consideration of all the circumstances of the case, satisfied that the differences in regard to the remuneration, or a particular species of remuneration, of men and women workers in any establishment or employment is based on a factor other than sex, it may, by notification, make a declaration to that effect, and any act of the employer attributable to such a difference shall not be deemed to be contravention of any provision of this Act.

Power to Remove Difficulties.

If any difficulty arises in giving effect to the provisions of this Act the Central Government may, by notification, make any order, not inconsistent with the provisions of this Act, which appears to it to be necessary for the purpose of removing the difficulty:

Provided that every such order shall, as soon as may be after it is made, be laid before each House of Parliament.

Repeal and Saving.

(1) The Equal Remuneration Ordinance, 1975 (12 of 1975), is hereby repealed.

(2) Notwithstanding such repeal, anything done or any action taken under the Ordinance so repealed (including any notification, nomination, appointment, order or direction made there under) shall be deemed to have been done or taken under the corresponding provisions of this Act as if this Act were in force when such thing was done or action was taken.

THE PAYMENT OF BONUS ACT, 1965

Introduction

The practice of paying bonus in India appears to have originated during First World War when certain textile mills granted 10% of wages as war bonus to their workers in 1917. In certain cases of industrial disputes demand for payment of bonus was also included. In 1950, the Full Bench of the Labour Appellate evolved a formula for determination of bonus. A plea was made to raise that formula in 1959. At the second and third meetings of the Eighteenth Session of Standing Labour Committee (G.O.I.) held in New Delhi in March/April 1960, it was agreed that a Commission be appointed to go into the question of bonus and evolve suitable norms. A Tripartite Commission was set up by the Government of India to consider in a comprehensive manner, the question of payment of bonus based on profits to employees employed in establishments and to make recommendations to the Government. The Government of India accepted the recommendations of the Commission subject to certain modifications. To implement these recommendations the Payment of Bonus Ordinance, 1965 was promulgated on 29th May, 1965. To replace the said Ordinance the Payment of Bonus Bill was introduced in the Parliament.

The Payment of Bonus Act, 1965 is the principal act for the payment of bonus to the employees which was formed with an objective for rewarding employees for their good work for the organisation.

OBJECTIVES
1. To improve statutory liability to pay bonus [reward for good work] in case of profits or losses.
2. To prescribe formula for calculating bonus
3. To prescribe Minimum & Maximum percentage bonus
4. To provide of set off/set on mechanism
5. To provide redressal mechanism

It is a step forward to share the prosperity of the establishment reflected by the profits earned by the contributions made by capital, management and labour with the employees.

Definitions

(1) "accounting year" means

(i) in relation to a corporation, the year ending on the day on which the books and accounts of the corporation are to be closed and balanced;

(ii) in relation to a company, the period in respect of which any profit and loss account of the company laid before it in annual general meeting is made up, whether that period is a year or not;

(iii) in any other case

(a) the year commencing on the 1st day of April; or

(b) if the accounts of an establishment maintained by the employer thereof are closed and balanced on any day other than the 31st day of March, then, at the option of the employer, the year ending on the day on which its accounts are so closed and balanced.

(4) "allocable surplus" means:

(a) in relation to an employer, being a company (other than a banking company) which has not made the arrangements prescribed under the Income-tax Act for the declaration and payment within India of the dividends payable out of its profits in accordance with the provisions of section 194 of that Act, 67% of the available surplus in an accounting year;

(b) in any other case, 60% of such available surplus;

(11) "corporation" means anybody corporate established by or under any Central, Provincial or State Act but does not include a company or a co-operative society;

(12) "direct tax" means:

(a) any tax chargeable under-

(i) the Income-tax Act;

(ii) the Super Profits Tax Act, 1963 (14 of 1963);

(iii) the Companies (Profits) Surtax Act, 1964 (7 of 1964);

(iv) the agricultural income-tax law; and

(b) any other tax which, having regard to its nature or incidence, may be declared by the Central Government, by notification in the Official Gazette, to be a direct tax for the purposes of this Act;

(13) "employee" means any person (other than an apprentice) employed on a salary or wage not exceeding 10,000/- rupees per month in any industry to do any skilled or unskilled manual, supervisory, managerial, administrative, technical or clerical work for hire or reward, whether the terms of employment be express or implied; (2007 amendment)

(15) "establishment in private sector" means any establishment other than an establishment in public sector;

(16) "establishment in public sector" means an establishment owned, controlled or managed by:

(a) a Government company as defined in section 617 of the Companies Act, 1956 (1 of 1956);

(b) a Corporation in which not less than forty per cent of its capital is held (whether single or taken together) by:

(i) the Government; or

(ii) the Reserve Bank of India; or

(iii) a corporation owned by the Government or the Reserve Bank of India.

Payment of Bonus Act not to apply to certain classes of employees. [Section 32]

- Life Insurance Corporation ,
- The Indian Red Cross Society or any other institution of a like nature,
- Universities and other educational institutions ,
- Institutions (including hospitals, chambers of commerce and society welfare institutions) established not for purposes of profit,
- Employees employed through contractors on building operations,
- Employees employed by the Reserve Bank of India,
- The Industrial Finance Corporation of India,
- Financial Corporations,
- the National Bank for Agriculture and Rural Development,
- the Unit Trust of India,
- the Industrial Development Bank of India.

Eligibility for bonus. [Sec. 8] (2007 amendment)

Every employee (receiving salary or wages up to Rs. 10,000 p.m) engaged in any industry to do any skilled or unskilled manual, supervisory, managerial, administrative, technical or clerical work is entitled to bonus for every accounting year if he has worked for at least 30 working days in that year.

Calculation of bonus with respect to certain employees. [Sec. 12] (2007 amendment)

Where the salary or wage of an employee exceeds 3500/- rupees per month, the minimum (8.33%) bonus payable to Such employee under section 10 or, in case maximum bonus (20%) payable to such employee under section 11, should be calculated as if his salary or wage were 3500/- rupees per month. That means 3500/- as a salary or wage per month will be the fixed limit amount for calculation of payment of bonus to employees those who are drawing the salary or wage more than 3500/- per month but not more than 10,000/- per month. The Government has decided to enhance the eligibility limit for payment of bonus 3500/- per month.

Disqualification for bonus. [Sec. 9]

An employee shall be disqualified from receiving bonus under this Act, if he is dismissed from service for:

- Fraud; or Riotous or violent behaviour while on the premises of the establishment; or
- Theft, misappropriation or sabotage of any property of the establishment.

Payment of minimum bonus. [Sec. 10]

- Bonus should be paid along with the salary.
- Every year, every employer shall be bound to pay bonus to every employee.
- A minimum bonus which shall be 8.33% cent of the salary or wage earned by the employee during the accounting year or 100/- rupees, whichever is higher.
- Bonus shall be payable in case of profits or losses in the accounting year.

Section 36. Power of exemption of bonus payment by government

In certain circumstances payment of minimum bonus can be exempted by the appropriate government by taking consideration into relevant circumstances of concern factory or establishment which is in losses. Payment of bonus exemption by the appropriate government may be given for a certain period only.

Here are the relevant factors may be, the reasons for occurrence of losses to company, reasons and ingenuity in consecutive occurrence of losses, the reasons must be justifiable, there should not be intention to avoid payment of bonus by creating fake losses (mens rea).

Payment of Maximum Bonus [Sec. 11]

- In case the allocable surplus amount [Section 2(4)] exceeds the minimum bonus (8.33%) payable amount to employees, the employer is bound to pay extra percentage of bonus.
- But maximum of 20% of bonus is payable to the every employee on the wage or salary earned during the year.

Proportionate, reduction in bonus in certain cases [Sec. 13]

Where an employee has not worked for all the working days in an accounting year, the minimum bonus of one hundred rupees or, as the case may be, of sixty rupees, if such bonus is higher than 8.33 per cent of his salary or wage for the days he has worked in that accounting year, shall be proportionately reduced.

Computation of number of working days. [Sec. 14]

An employee shall be deemed to have worked in an establishment in any accounting year also on the days on which :

(a) He has been laid off;

(b) He has been on leave with salary or wage;

(c) He has been absent due to temporary disablement caused by accident arising out of and in the course of his employment; and

(d) The employee has been on maternity leave with salary or wage, during the accounting year.

Calculations for Bonus Payment

Computation of Gross Profits [Sec. 4].

There few differences in computation of gross profits in case of banking company and other than banking companies. For accurate computation of the gross profits in case of banking companies refer to First schedule and for other companies but not banking companies refer to Second schedule. But over view for computation of gross profits is mentioned below :

Net profit (P&L a/c) +Add following items

- Income tax.
- Provision for: Bonus to employees, Depreciation, Direct taxes.
- Bonus paid to employees in respect of previous accounting years.
- The amount, if any, paid to, or provided for payment to, an approved gratuity fund.
- The amount actually paid to employees on their retirement or on termination of their employment for any reason.
- Donations.
- Annuity due.
- Capital expenditure (other than capital expenditure on scientific research.
- Capital losses.
- Capital losses (other than losses on sale) of Capital assets on which depreciation has been allowed for income-tax or agricultural income-tax).
- Losses of, or expenditure relating to, any business situated outside India.

Deduct

(a) Capital receipts and capital profits (other than profits on the sale of assets on which depreciation has been allowed for income-tax or agricultural income-tax).

(b) Profits of, and receipts relating to, any business situated outside India.

(c) Income of foreign concerns from investments outside India.

(d) Expenditure or losses (if any) debited directly to reserves, other than:
   i. Capital expenditure and capital losses (other than losses on sale of capital assets on which depreciation has not been allowed for income-tax or agricultural income-tax) ;
   ii. Losses of any business situated outside India.

(e) In the case of foreign concerns proportionate administrative (over head) expenses of Head Office allocable to Indian business.

(f) Refund of any direct tax paid for previous accounting years and excess provision, if any, of previous accounting years relating to bonus, depreciation, taxation or development rebate or development allowance, if written back.

Computation of Available surplus [Section 5]

Available surplus = gross profit [derived as per First Schedule or Second Schedule of this act] - (minus) Depreciation, investment allowance or development allowance [Section 6] - (minus) direct taxes payable [Section 7] - (minus) further sums as are specified in respect of the employer in the Third Schedule of this act consist of dividend payable (preference shares), reserves and % of paid up equity share capital [investment].

Allocable surplus [sec. 2 (4)]. Allocable surplus = 67% of the available surplus (other than banking companies) or 60% of the available surplus (banking companies and companies linked with abroad)

Payment of bonus calculated on the allocable surplus which is derived by the above calculation

Set-On and Set-Off of Allocable Surplus [Sec. 15]

Set-On (In case of huge profits)

Excess allocable surplus remain after paying the maximum bonus of 20% on the wage or salary of the employee, Should be carried forward to the next following year to be utilised for the purpose of payment of bonus in case of the shortage of the allocable surplus or losses occur. This is called as Set-On.

Set-Off (in case of losses occur)

When there are no profits (available surplus or allocable surplus) or the amount falls short or deficiency for payment of minimum bonus to employees 8.33%, such deficiency amount should be adjusted to the current accounting year from the Set-On amount which was carried forward in case of excess allocable surplus in the previous year. This is called as Set-Off.

Illustration:

- In this Schedule, the total amount of bonus equal to 8.33 per cent of the annual salary or wage payable to all the employees is assumed to be Rs.1,04,167.
- Accordingly, Maximum bonus to which all the employees are entitled to be paid (20% of the annual salary or wage of all the employees) would be Rs. 2,50,000.

Minimum: The balance of Rs.1,10,000 set on from Year-2 lapses.

Special provisions [Sec. 16]

- In case of new establishments up to 5 years, employees' bonus is payable only in case of profits only but not in losses by the management or employer.
- Condition that the Profits are remaining amounts after deducting expenses, depreciation and taxes.

Deduction of certain amounts from bonus payable. [Sec. 18]

Employee is found guilty of misconduct causing financial loss to the employer, then, it shall, be lawful for the employer to deduct the amount of loss from the amount of bonus payable by him to the employee under this Act in respect of that accounting year only and the employee shall be entitled to receive the balance, if any.

Time limit for payment. [Sec. 19]

- Bonus should be paid within a period of 8 months from the close of the accounting year.
- Maximum extended period for payment of bonus is 2 years, but with the permission of the government only.

Recovery of bonus due from an employer [Sec. 21]

- If any amount is due to employee as bonus from his employer, he can write and apply to the government for the recovery of the bonus from the employer.
- Application shall be made within one year from the date on which the money became due to the employee from the employer.

Reference of dispute under this Act. [Sec. 22]

Where any dispute arises between an employer and his employees with respect to the bonus payable under this Act such dispute shall be deemed to be an industrial dispute within the meaning of the Industrial Dispute Act, 1947. All disputes shall be referred to the Labour courts or the industrial tribunals.

Maintenance of registers, records, etc. [Sec. 26]

Every employer shall prepare and maintain such registers, records and other documents in such form and in such manner as may be prescribed.

Inspectors. [Sec. 27]

The Government may, by notification in the official Gazette, appoint such persons as it thinks fit to be Inspectors for the purpose of this Act and may define the limits within which they shall exercise jurisdiction.

Powers;

- Inspector can any reasonable time can enter in the premises and inspect or examine the records, accounts, books, registers and any other documents.
- Employer is having duty to furnish any information asked by the inspector.

Offences and Penalties [Sec. 28 & 29]

- For contravention of the provisions of the Act or rules the penalty is imprisonment up to 6 months or fine up to Rs.1000, or both.
- In case of offences by companies, every person who, at the time the offence was committed, was in charge of, and was responsible to, the company for the conduct of business of the company, as well as the company, shall be deemed to be guilty of the offence and shall be liable to be proceeded against and punished accordingly: any such person liable to any punishment if he proves that the offence was committed without his knowledge or that he exercised all due diligence to prevent the commission of such offence.

THE PAYMENT OF GRATUITY ACT, 1972

In India gratuity is a type of retirement benefit. It is a payment made with the intention of helping an employee monetarily after his retirement. It was held by the Supreme Court of India in Indian Hume Pipe Co Ltd v Its Workmen, that the general principal underlying gratuity scheme is that by service over a long period the employee is entitled to claim a certain amount as retirement benefit. The Payment of Gratuity Act was passed by Indian Parliament in 21 August 1972. The act came in force on 16 September 1972.

Application and Extent

The act applies to the whole of India. But according to section 1(2), in so far it relates to plantation or ports, it shall not be extended to State of Jammu and Kashmir. The act applies to all factories, mines, oilfield, plantation, port and railway company. But in case of shops or establishments other than those stated before, it applies to those organisations with 10 or more persons are employed on any day of the preceding 12 months. Under Section 1(3-A), if in case of any shop and establishment to which the act applies the number of employee reduces below 10, it shall continue to be governed by the act irrespective of the number of employee's. Thus no employer can escape liability under this act by reducing the number of employee's. Under Section 2(e), Nothing in this act applies to Apprentices and Persons who hold civil posts under the Central Government or State Government and are subjected to any other act or rule other than this act.

Payment of Gratuity: Eligibility and Calculation

Under Section 4, payment of gratuity is mandatory. Gratuity shall be payable to an employee on termination of employment after he has rendered continuous service for not less than 5 years in a single organisation. The termination can be due to : 1. Superannuation. 2. Retirement or Resignation. 3. On Death or Disablement due to accident or disease.

As per Section 4(1), the completion of continuous service of 5 years is not required where termination of employment is due to death or disablement. In such case mandatory gratuity is payable.

Gratuity is paid at a rate of 15 days wages for every completed year of service or part thereof in excess of Six months. The wages here means wages last drawn by the employee. The "15 Days Wages" will be calculated by dividing the last drawn wages by 26 and multiplying the result with 15. But under section 4(3), the maximum gratuity that is payable is fixed at Rupees 20,00,000 [1].

Formula for Gratuity Calculation = [((Basic Pay + D.A) x 15 days) / 26] x No. of years of service (example of Gratuity Calculation).

THE EMPLOYEES' PROVIDENT FUND AND MISCELLANEOUS PROVISIONS ACT, 1952

Employees Provident Fund was established in 1952 and hence the act is named as Employees Provident Fund & Miscellaneous Provisions Act, 1952, which extend to the whole of India.

Employee Provident Fund (EPF)

Provident fund is a welfare scheme for the benefits of the employees. Under this scheme both the employee & employer contribute their part but whole of the amount is deposited by the employer. Employer deducted the employee share from the salary of the employee. The interest earned on this investment is also credited in pf account of the employees. At the time of retirement, the accumulated amount is given to the employees, if certain conditions are satisfied.

DIVISION OF EMPLOYER'S CONTRIBUTION TO EPF

Purpose of Scheme	Percentage contributed
Employee's Provident Fund Scheme (EPF)	3.67%
Employees Pension Scheme (EPS)	8.33%
Employee Deposit Linked Insurance Scheme (EDLI)	0.5%
Administrative charges for EPF	1.1%
Administrative charges for EDLI	0.01%

Applicability of the Act

It is applicable:

(a) Every factory engaged in any industry specified in Schedule 1 in which 20 or more persons are employed;

(b) Every other establishment employing 20 or more persons or class of such establishments which the Central Govt. may notify;

(c) Any other establishment so notified by the Central Government even if employing less than 20 persons.

Every employee, including the one employed through a contractor (but excluding an apprentice engaged under the Apprentices Act or under the standing orders of the establishment and casual laborers), who is in receipt of wages up to Rs.6,500 p.m., shall be eligible for becoming a member of the funds. The condition of three months' continuous service or 60 days of actual work, for membership of the scheme.

Taxability of PF

Deduction of PF can be claimed under section 80C while calculating Income Tax & when the employee withdraw the amount of PF & Interest after the retirement then, PF amount & Interest amount is not taxable.

Pf can be accumulated withdrawn by the employee if he is unemployed for more than 2 month. 75% PF can be withdrawn after the employment of 1 month & rest 25% PF can be withdrawn after the unemployment of 2 month. It is on the choice of the employee after withdrawn of 75% amount that they should continue with the PF account or want to withdraw the whole amount.

MULTIPLE CHOICE QUESTIONS

1. What are wages?
   (1) Payment made to an employee for the work they have performed.
   (2) Payment made to an employer for the work their employees have performed.
   (3) Payment made to a customer for the products they have purchased.
   (4) Payment made to investors for the profits they have earned.
2. What is the main purpose of wages?
   (1) To provide employees with a means of living.
   (2) To provide employers with a means of reducing costs.
   (3) To provide customers with a means of saving money.
   (4) To provide investors with a means of earning profits.
3. Which of the following is a factor that influences wages?
   (1) Productivity
   (2) Supply and demand
   (3) Cost of living
   (4) All of the above
4. What is the minimum wage?
   (1) The lowest wage that an employer is required to pay their employees by law.
   (2) The highest wage that an employer is required to pay their employees by law.
   (3) The average wage that an employer is required to pay their employees by law.
   (4) The same wage that an employer pays their employees for overtime work.
5. What is piece rate?
   (1) A type of wage system in which employees are paid a certain amount of money for each unit of work completed.
   (2) A type of wage system in which employees are paid a bonus for meeting certain performance targets.
   (3) A type of investment policy provided to employees.
   (4) None of the above.
6. What is a commission?
   (1) A percentage of sales paid to an employee as a wage or bonus.
   (2) A percentage of profits paid to an employee as a wage or bonus.
   (3) A percentage of assets paid to an employee as a wage or bonus.
   (4) None of the above.
7. What is a salary?
   (1) A fixed amount of money paid to an employee on a regular basis, usually monthly.
   (2) A variable amount of money paid to an employee based on their performance.
   (3) A type of bonus paid to employees for meeting certain targets.
   (4) None of the above.
8. What is a bonus?
   (1) An additional payment made to employees on top of their regular wages as a reward for good performance.
   (2) A type of investment policy provided to employees.
   (3) A type of insurance policy provided to employees.
   (4) None of the above.
9. Which of the following is a factor that influences wages?
   (1) Education and skill level
   (2) Job market conditions

(3) Corporate profits
(4) All of the above

10. What is a living wage campaign?
(1) An effort by workers and labor unions to promote raising the minimum wage to a level that workers can live on.
(2) An effort by employers to reduce wages to increase profits.
(3) A campaign to create more jobs.
(4) None of the above.

11. What is the impact of government policies on wage determination?
(1) Government policies can impact the minimum wage.
(2) Government policies can impact the availability of certain jobs.
(3) Government policies can impact the cost of living.
(4) All of the above

12. Which of the following is a factor that determines wages for low-paid workers?
(1) Race and gender
(2) Age
(3) Education
(4) All of the above

13. What is the relationship between productivity and wages?
(1) A higher level of productivity can lead to higher wages.
(2) A higher level of productivity can lead to lower wages.
(3) Productivity has no impact on wages.
(4) None of the above.

14. What is the labor theory of value?
(1) The idea that the value of a product is determined by the amount of labor required to produce it.
(2) The idea that the value of a product is determined by the price it can fetch in the market.
(3) The idea that the value of a product is determined by the cost of production.
(4) None of the above.

15. What is the marginal productivity theory of wages?
(1) The idea that wages are based on the marginal productivity of the worker.
(2) The idea that wages are based on the cost of living.
(3) The idea that wages are based on the profits earned by the employer.
(4) None of the above.

16. What is the market theory of wages?
(1) The idea that wages are determined by supply and demand.
(2) The idea that wages are determined by the cost of living.
(3) The idea that wages are determined by the marginal productivity of the worker.
(4) None of the above.

17. What is the efficiency wage theory?
(1) The idea that higher wages can lead to higher productivity and lower turnover.
(2) The idea that lower wages can lead to higher profits for the employer.
(3) The idea that wages have no impact on productivity.
(4) None of the above.

18. What is the human capital theory of wages?
(1) The idea that education and skill level can impact wages.
(2) The idea that wages are determined by supply and demand.
(3) The idea that wages are determined by the marginal productivity of the worker.
(4) None of the above.

19. What are wage differentials?
(1) Differences in wage rates between different workers or groups of workers.
(2) The difference between the highest and lowest wage rates in an establishment.
(3) The difference between the wages in different industries.
(4) None of the above.

20. What is a gender wage gap?
(1) The difference in wages between men and women.

(2) The difference in wages between workers in different industries.
(3) The difference in wages between workers with different levels of education.
(4) None of the above.

21. What is the race wage gap?
(1) The difference in wages between workers of different races.
(2) The difference in wages between workers in different industries.
(3) The difference in wages between workers with different levels of education.
(4) None of the above.

22. What is a skills-based wage differential?
(1) The difference in wages between workers with different levels of education or skill.
(2) The difference in wages between workers in different industries.
(3) The difference in wages between different employees with the same level of education or skill.
(4) None of the above.

23. What is a union wage differential?
(1) The wage premium that unionized workers earn compared to non-unionized workers.
(2) The difference in wages between unionized workers in different industries.
(3) The wage premium that non-unionized workers earn compared to unionized workers.
(4) None of the above.

24. What is a geographical wage differential?
(1) The difference in wages between workers in different regions.
(2) The difference in wages between workers in different industries.
(3) The difference in wages between workers with different levels of education or skill.
(4) None of the above.

25. What is a firm wage differential?
(1) The difference in wages between employees within the same organization.
(2) The difference in wages between workers in different industries.
(3) The difference in wages based on geographical location.
(4) None of the above.

26. What is a global wage differential?
(1) The difference in wages between workers in different countries.
(2) The difference in wages between workers in different industries.
(3) The difference in wages based on geographical location.
(4) None of the above.

27. What are the factors that contribute to wage differentials?
(1) Skills, experience, education, race, and gender.
(2) Corporate profits, job market conditions, and government policies.
(3) Productivity, marginal productivity, and efficiency wage theory.
(4) None of the above.

28. What is a compensating wage differential?
(1) The difference in wages paid to compensate workers for working under difficult or unpleasant conditions.
(2) The difference in wages between different workers with the same experience and skill level.
(3) The difference in wages based on geographical location.
(4) None of the above.

29. **Assertion:** Education can impact wages.
Reason: Higher levels of education can lead to higher wages.
(1) Both assertion and reason are true and the reason is the correct explanation of the assertion.
(2) Both assertion and reason are true but the reason is not the correct explanation of the assertion.
(3) Assertion is true but reason is false.
(4) Assertion is false but reason is true.

30. Assertion: The labor theory of value states that the value of a product is determined by the cost of production.

Reason: The labor theory of value states that the value of a product is determined by the price it can fetch in the market.

(1) Assertion is false but reason is true.
(2) Assertion is true but reason is false.
(3) Both assertion and reason are false.
(4) Both assertion and reason are true and the reason is the correct explanation of the assertion.

31. Assertion: Different wage rates exist in different sectors of the economy.

Reason: Different sectors of the economy require different levels of education, skills, and experience.

(1) Both assertion and reason are true and the reason is the correct explanation of the assertion.
(2) Both assertion and reason are true but the reason is not the correct explanation of the assertion.
(3) Assertion is true but reason is false.
(4) Assertion is false but reason is true.

32. Assertion: The marginal productivity theory of wages states that wages are based on the cost of living.

Reason: The marginal productivity theory of wages states that wages are based on the productivity of the worker.

(1) Assertion is false but reason is true.
(2) Assertion is true but reason is false.
(3) Both assertion and reason are false.
(4) Both assertion and reason are true and the reason is the correct explanation of the assertion.

33. Assertion: A union wage differential refers to the difference in wages between unionized and non-unionized workers.

Reason: Unionized workers earn higher wages than non-unionized workers because of the collective bargaining efforts of labor unions.

(1) Both assertion and reason are true and the reason is the correct explanation of the assertion.
(2) Both assertion and reason are true but the reason is not the correct explanation of the assertion.
(3) Assertion is true but reason is false.
(4) Assertion is false but reason is true.

34. Assertion: Economic globalization has led to the equalization of wages across the globe.

Reason: Economic globalization has led to an increase in outsourcing of jobs to developing countries where wages are lower.

(1) Assertion is false but reason is true.
(2) Assertion is true but reason is false.
(3) Both assertion and reason are false.
(4) Both assertion and reason are true and the reason is the correct explanation of the assertion.

35. Assertion: The compensating wage differential is the difference in wages paid to compensate workers for working under difficult or unpleasant conditions.

Reason: The compensating wage differential is the difference in wages paid to workers with different levels of education and skills.

(1) Assertion is true but reason is false.
(2) Assertion is false but reason is true.
(3) Both assertion and reason are false.
(4) Both assertion and reason are true and the reason is the correct explanation of the assertion.

36. Assertion: Efficiency wage theory states that higher wages can lead to higher productivity and lower turnover.

Reason: Efficiency wage theory states that lower wages can lead to higher profits for the employer.

(1) Assertion is true but reason is false.
(2) Assertion is false but reason is true.
(3) Both assertion and reason are false.
(4) Both assertion and reason are true and the reason is the correct explanation of the assertion.

37. **Assertion:** Wage differentials are caused by geographical factors.

Reason: Workers in different regions are paid different wages.

(1) Both assertion and reason are true and the reason is the correct explanation of the assertion.
(2) Both assertion and reason are true but the reason is not the correct explanation of the assertion.
(3) Assertion is true but reason is false.
(4) Assertion is false but reason is true.

38. **Assertion:** The marginal productivity theory of wages states that wages are based on the productivity of the worker.

Reason: The labor theory of value states that the value of a product is determined by the price it can fetch in the market.

(1) Assertion is false but reason is true.
(2) Assertion is true but reason is false.
(3) Both assertion and reason are false.
(4) Both assertion and reason are true and the reason is the correct explanation of the assertion.

39. What is the main purpose of the Minimum Wages Act, 1948?

(1) To ensure that workers are paid a fair wage for their work.
(2) To ensure that employers can reduce labor costs.
(3) To ensure that profits earned by employers are maximized.
(4) None of the above.

40. Which of the following is true about the Minimum Wages Act, 1948?

(1) The Act defines the minimum wage for different industries and regions.
(2) The Act stipulates that employers cannot pay wages below the minimum wage level.
(3) The Act provides for penalties for non-compliance with the minimum wage regulations.
(4) All of the above.

41. What is the definition of a "worker" under the Minimum Wages Act, 1948?

(1) A person who is employed for wages in any kind of work.
(2) A person who is employed for a fixed salary.
(3) Only manual workers are considered workers under the Act.
(4) None of the above.

42. What is the definition of a "wage" under the Minimum Wages Act, 1948?

(1) All remuneration paid or payable to a worker for his/her work.
(2) Only basic salary paid to a worker.
(3) Only hourly wages paid to a worker.
(4) None of the above.

43. Who is responsible for fixing and revising the minimum wage under the Minimum Wages Act, 1948?

(1) The Central Government
(2) The State Governments
(3) Both the Central and State Governments
(4) None of the above.

44. What is the current minimum wage rate in India?

(1) Rs. 176 per day
(2) Rs. 186 per day
(3) Rs. 196 per day
(4) Rs. 202 per day

45. What is meant by the term "minimum time rate"?

(1) A minimum wage rate based on the number of hours worked per day.
(2) A minimum wage rate based on the number of hours worked per week.
(3) A minimum wage rate based on the skills and experience of the worker.
(4) None of the above.

46. What is meant by the term "piece rate"?

(1) A minimum wage rate based on the amount of work done or production output.
(2) A minimum wage rate based on the number of hours worked.

(3) A minimum wage rate based on the skills and experience of the worker.
(4) None of the above.

47. What is meant by the term "overtime rate"?
(1) A wage rate paid for work done beyond the usual working hours.
(2) A wage rate paid for work done on weekends and holidays.
(3) A wage rate paid for work done beyond the designated number of hours per day or per week.
(4) None of the above.

48. What is meant by the term "contract rate"?
(1) A wage rate agreed upon between an employer and a specific worker.
(2) A wage rate agreed upon between an employer and a group of workers.
(3) A wage rate agreed upon between an employer and a labor union.
(4) None of the above.

49. What is the significance of the "schedule of employment" under the Minimum Wages Act, 1948?
(1) It specifies the hours of work per day and per week for each industry.
(2) It specifies the holidays and leave entitlements for each industry.
(3) It specifies the minimum wage rates for each industry and region.
(4) All of the above.

50. What is the penalty for non-compliance with the provisions of the Minimum Wages Act, 1948?
(1) Imprisonment for a period of 1 year
(2) Fine of up to Rs. 5,000
(3) Both (1) and (2)
(4) None of the above.

51. Who is responsible for enforcing the provisions of the Minimum Wages Act, 1948?
(1) The Labor Commissioner
(2) The Inspector appointed by the State Government
(3) Both (1) and (2)
(4) None of the above.

52. What is the difference between a "scheduled employment" and a "non-scheduled employment" under the Minimum Wages Act, 1948?
(1) A scheduled employment is one that is mentioned in the Schedule to the Act, whereas a non-scheduled employment is not mentioned in the Schedule to the Act.
(2) A scheduled employment is one that is more important than a non-scheduled employment.
(3) A scheduled employment is one that is classified as skilled work, whereas a non-scheduled employment is classified as unskilled work.
(4) None of the above.

53. What is the importance of the Third Schedule to the Minimum Wages Act, 1948?
(1) It specifies the minimum rates of wages for different categories of workers in different industries.
(2) It specifies the hours of work per day and per week for different categories of workers in different industries.
(3) It specifies the holidays and leave entitlements for different categories of workers in different industries.
(4) None of the above.

54. What does "fair wages" mean under the Minimum Wages Act, 1948?
(1) Wages that are just and reasonable, and sufficient for the basic needs of the worker and his/her family.
(2) Wages that are determined by the employer based on the profitability of the business.
(3) Wages that are determined by the market forces of supply and demand.
(4) None of the above.

55. What is the role of the Central Advisory Board under the Minimum Wages Act, 1948?
(1) To advise the Central Government on matters concerning the fixing and revision of minimum wages.

(2) To inspect establishments to ensure compliance with the minimum wage regulations.

(3) To establish a system of collective bargaining between employers and workers.

(4) None of the above.

56. What is the role of the Minimum Wages Advisory Board under the Minimum Wages Act, 1948?

(1) To advise the State Government on matters concerning the fixing and revision of minimum wages.

(2) To inspect establishments to ensure compliance with the minimum wage regulations.

(3) To establish a system of collective bargaining between employers and workers.

(4) None of the above.

57. What is the role of the Appropriate Government under the Minimum Wages Act, 1948?

(1) To notify the minimum wages for different industries and regions.

(2) To review and revise the minimum wages periodically.

(3) To ensure that employers comply with the minimum wage regulations.

(4) All of the above.

58. What is the difference between the Central Government and the State Government under the Minimum Wages Act, 1948?

(1) The Central Government is responsible for fixing the minimum wage for industries under its control, whereas the State Government is responsible for fixing the minimum wage for industries under its control.

(2) The Central Government is responsible for enforcing the provisions of the Act, whereas the State Government is responsible for advising the Central Government on matters concerning the Act.

(3) The Central Government is responsible for regulating the hours of work for all industries, whereas the State Government is responsible for regulating the leave entitlements for all industries.

(4) None of the above.

59. What is the definition of "contract work" under the Minimum Wages Act, 1948?

(1) Work done through a contractor but under the direct supervision of the principal employer.

(2) Work done through a contractor under the indirect supervision of the principal employer.

(3) Work done through a contractor with no supervision from the principal employer.

(4) None of the above.

60. What is the definition of "inter-state migrant worker" under the Minimum Wages Act, 1948?

(1) A person who is employed in one State but belongs to another State.

(2) A person who is employed in one State but is not a citizen of that State.

(3) A person who is employed in one State but speaks a different language.

(4) None of the above.

61. What is the definition of "piece work" under the Minimum Wages Act, 1948?

(1) Work done by a worker on a piece-rate basis.

(2) Work done by a worker on a time-rate basis.

(3) Work done by a worker on an hourly basis.

(4) None of the above.

62. What is meant by the term "casual worker" under the Minimum Wages Act, 1948?

(1) A worker who is employed for a short duration or intermittently.

(2) A worker who is employed for a specific task or project.

(3) Both (1) and (2).

(4) None of the above.

63. What is the definition of "semi-skilled work" under the Minimum Wages Act, 1948?

(1) Work that requires some training or skill.
(2) Work that requires no training or skill.
(3) Work that requires advanced training or skill.
(4) None of the above.

64. What is the purpose of the Fourth Schedule to the Minimum Wages Act, 1948?
(1) It specifies the deductions that can be made from the wages of the worker.
(2) It specifies the allowances that can be added to the wages of the worker.
(3) It specifies the leave entitlements of the worker.
(4) None of the above.

65. What is meant by the term "agricultural worker" under the Minimum Wages Act, 1948?
(1) A worker who is employed in any kind of agricultural work.
(2) A worker who is employed in any kind of horticultural work.
(3) Both (1) and (2).
(4) None of the above.

66. What is the role of the State Minimum Wages Advisory Board under the Minimum Wages Act, 1948?
(1) To advise the State Government on matters concerning the fixing and revision of minimum wages for employees in various scheduled employments in the State or any part thereof.
(2) To inspect establishments to ensure compliance with the minimum wage regulations.
(3) To establish a system of collective bargaining between employers and workers.
(4) None of the above.

67. What is meant by the term "plantation worker" under the Minimum Wages Act, 1948?
(1) A worker who is employed in any kind of plantation work.
(2) A worker who is employed in any kind of agricultural work.
(3) Both (1) and (2).
(4) None of the above.

68. What is meant by the term "domestic worker" under the Minimum Wages Act, 1948?
(1) A worker who is employed in a household in any capacity.
(2) A worker who is employed in a household as a cook, housekeeper, or nanny.
(3) Both (1) and (2).
(4) None of the above.

69. What is the purpose of the Second Schedule to the Minimum Wages Act, 1948?
(1) It specifies the minimum rates of wages for different categories of workers in different regions.
(2) It specifies the hours of work per day and per week for different categories of workers in different regions.
(3) It specifies the holidays and leave entitlements for different categories of workers in different regions.
(4) None of the above.

70. What is the definition of "skilled work" under the Minimum Wages Act, 1948?
(1) Work that requires specialized training or skill.
(2) Work that requires basic training or skill.
(3) Work that requires no training or skill.
(4) None of the above.

71. What is the difference between the "basic rate of wage" and the "dearness allowance" under the Minimum Wages Act, 1948?
(1) The basic rate of wage is the minimum wage that is fixed for an industry, whereas the dearness allowance is an adjustment made to the basic rate to reflect changes in the cost of living.
(2) The basic rate of wage is the wage paid for skilled work, whereas the dearness allowance is the wage paid for unskilled work.

(3) The basic rate of wage is the wage paid to contract workers, whereas the dearness allowance is the wage paid to permanent workers.

(4) None of the above.

72. What is the purpose of the First Schedule to the Minimum Wages Act, 1948?

(1) It specifies the minimum rates of wages for different categories of workers in different scheduled employments.

(2) It specifies the hours of work per day and per week for different categories of workers in different scheduled employments.

(3) It specifies the holidays and leave entitlements for different categories of workers in different scheduled employments.

(4) None of the above.

73. What is meant by the term "retrenchment" under the Minimum Wages Act, 1948?

(1) The termination of a worker's employment due to disciplinary action.

(2) The termination of a worker's employment due to a change in management.

(3) The termination of a worker's employment due to closure of the establishment.

(4) None of the above.

74. What is the definition of "weekly hours" under the Minimum Wages Act, 1948?

(1) The total number of hours worked per week by a worker.

(2) The number of hours worked per day multiplied by the number of days worked per week.

(3) Both (1) and (2).

(4) None of the above.

75. What is meant by the term "working day" under the Minimum Wages Act, 1948?

(1) Any day on which a worker is required to work.

(2) Any day on which a worker is willing to work.

(3) Both (1) and (2).

(4) None of the above.

76. What is the definition of "contractor" under the Minimum Wages Act, 1948?

(1) Any person who carries out work on behalf of an employer.

(2) Any person who employs workers on behalf of an employer.

(3) Both (1) and (2).

(4) None of the above.

77. What is the definition of "industrial establishment" under the Minimum Wages Act, 1948?

(1) Any establishment in which any industrial, commercial, or agricultural activity is carried on.

(2) Any establishment in which only industrial activity is carried on.

(3) Any establishment in which only commercial activity is carried on.

(4) None of the above.

78. What is the difference between a "skilled worker" and a "semi-skilled worker" under the Minimum Wages Act, 1948?

(1) A skilled worker is one who has specialized training or skill, whereas a semi-skilled worker is one who has some training or skill.

(2) A skilled worker is paid more than a semi-skilled worker.

(3) Both (1) and (2).

(4) None of the above.

79. What is the definition of "hazardous work" under the Minimum Wages Act, 1948?

(1) Work that is likely to cause death or serious physical injury to the worker.

(2) Work that is likely to cause minor physical injury to the worker.

(3) Work that is likely to cause mental stress or emotional harm to the worker.

(4) None of the above.

80. What is meant by the term "overtime work" under the Minimum Wages Act, 1948?

(1) Work done beyond the usual working hours.

(2) Work done on weekends or holidays.

(3) Work done beyond the designated number of hours per day or per week.
(4) None of the above.

81. What is the significance of the "wage period" under the Minimum Wages Act, 1948?
(1) It determines the length of time for which wages are paid or payable.
(2) It determines the number of hours that constitute an average working day.
(3) It determines the minimum wage rate for a particular industry.
(4) None of the above.

82. What is the main objective of The Payment of Wages Act, 1936?
(1) To regulate the payment of wages to certain classes of employed persons.
(2) To regulate the payment of wages to all employed persons.
(3) To ensure that employers can reduce labor costs.
(4) None of the above.

83. Who is responsible for enforcing the provisions of The Payment of Wages Act, 1936?
(1) The Labor Commissioner
(2) The Inspector appointed by the State Government
(3) Both (1) and (2)
(4) None of the above

84. What is the definition of "employer" under The Payment of Wages Act, 1936?
(1) Any person who employs workers for wages.
(2) Any person who has control over the employment of workers.
(3) Both (1) and (2).
(4) None of the above.

85. What is the definition of "deduction" under The Payment of Wages Act, 1936?
(1) Any amount that is paid by the employer to the worker in addition to wages.
(2) Any sum that is paid by the worker to the employer for services rendered by the employer.
(3) Any amount that is subtracted from the wages of the worker.
(4) None of the above.

86. What is the definition of "authorized deductions" under The Payment of Wages Act, 1936?
(1) Deductions that are allowed by law or permitted by the worker.
(2) Deductions that are permitted by the employer.
(3) Deductions that are made without the knowledge or consent of the worker.
(4) None of the above.

87. What is the definition of "unauthorized deductions" under The Payment of Wages Act, 1936?
(1) Deductions that are not allowed by law or not permitted by the worker.
(2) Deductions that are not permitted by the employer.
(3) Deductions that are made with the knowledge and consent of the worker.
(4) None of the above.

88. What is the penalty for non-compliance with the provisions of The Payment of Wages Act, 1936?
(1) Imprisonment for a period of 6 months
(2) Fine of up to Rs. 1,000
(3) Both (1) and (2)
(4) None of the above

89. What is the role of the Inspector appointed under The Payment of Wages Act, 1936?
(1) To authorize deductions from the wages of workers.
(2) To ensure that employers comply with the provisions of the Act.
(3) To review the wage rates of workers.
(4) None of the above.

90. What is meant by the term "delayed payment" under The Payment of Wages Act, 1936?
(1) Payment of wages later than the wage period.
(2) Payment of wages in installments.

(3) Payment of wages in advance.
(4) None of the above.

91. What is the definition of "minimum rates of wages" under The Payment of Wages Act, 1936?
(1) Rates of wages fixed by a competent authority under any law.
(2) Rates of wages fixed by the employer.
(3) Rates of wages negotiated between the employer and the worker.
(4) None of the above.

92. What is the significance of the "wage register" under The Payment of Wages Act, 1936?
(1) It is a record of every person employed in the establishment.
(2) It is a record of all authorized and unauthorized deductions from the wages of workers.
(3) It is a record of the wage period and the amount of wages paid to each worker.
(4) None of the above.

93. What is meant by the term "deductible limit" under The Payment of Wages Act, 1936?
(1) The maximum amount of deduction that can be made from the wages of the worker.
(2) The minimum amount of deduction that can be made from the wages of the worker.
(3) The amount of wages that the worker is entitled to.
(4) None of the above.

94. What is meant by the term "stoppage of work" under The Payment of Wages Act, 1936?
(1) The suspension of work by the employer.
(2) The suspension of work by the worker.
(3) Both (1) and (2).
(4) None of the above.

95. What is meant by the term "advance" under The Payment of Wages Act, 1936?
(1) Payment of wages after the wage period has ended.
(2) Payment of wages in excess of the amount due for the wage period.
(3) Payment of wages before the wage period has ended.
(4) None of the above.

96. What is meant by the term "dismissal" under The Payment of Wages Act, 1936?
(1) The termination of the worker's employment by the employer.
(2) The termination of the worker's employment by the worker.
(3) The voluntary resignation of the worker.
(4) None of the above.

97. What is the definition of "leave wages" under The Payment of Wages Act, 1936?
(1) Wages paid for the period of leave taken by the worker.
(2) Wages paid for overtime work done by the worker.
(3) Wages paid for work done during public holidays.
(4) None of the above.

98. What is the definition of "normal deduction" under The Payment of Wages Act, 1936?
(1) Deductions that are made during the normal course of employment.
(2) Deductions that are made for reasons beyond the control of the employer.
(3) Deductions that are made without the knowledge or consent of the worker.
(4) None of the above.

99. What is the definition of "bonus" under The Payment of Wages Act, 1936?
(1) A sum of money paid in addition to wages.
(2) A reduction in the amount of wages paid.
(3) A payment made to the employer for services rendered.
(4) None of the above.

100. What is the purpose of the Third Schedule to The Payment of Wages Act, 1936?
(1) It specifies the minimum wages for different categories of workers.

(2) It specifies the authorized deductions from the wages of workers.
(3) It specifies the rates of wages for overtime work and work done on public holidays.
(4) None of the above.

101. What is the definition of "overtime work" under The Payment of Wages Act, 1936?
(1) Work done beyond the usual working hours.
(2) Work done on weekends or holidays.
(3) Work done beyond the designated number of hours per day or per week.
(4) None of the above.

102. What is the definition of "public holiday" under The Payment of Wages Act, 1936?
(1) Any day declared by the Central Government to be a public holiday.
(2) Any day declared by the State Government to be a public holiday.
(3) Any day declared by the employer to be a public holiday.
(4) None of the above.

103. What is meant by the term "double wages" under The Payment of Wages Act, 1936?
(1) Payment of wages twice in a month.
(2) Payment of wages at double the usual rate.
(3) Payment of bonus equal to double the usual wages.
(4) None of the above.

104. What is the significance of the "wage slip" under The Payment of Wages Act, 1936?
(1) It is a record of every person employed in the establishment.
(2) It is a record of all authorized and unauthorized deductions from the wages of workers.
(3) It is a record of the wage period and the amount of wages paid to each worker.
(4) It is a record of the amount of wages paid to the worker and the deductions made from the wages.

105. What is the definition of "dismissal for misconduct" under The Payment of Wages Act, 1936?
(1) The termination of the worker's employment due to his/her involvement in criminal activities.
(2) The termination of the worker's employment due to his/her violation of the terms of employment.
(3) The termination of the worker's employment due to his/her poor performance.
(4) None of the above.

106. What is the definition of "wage ceiling" under The Payment of Wages Act, 1936?
(1) The maximum amount of wages that a worker can earn.
(2) The minimum amount of wages that a worker can earn.
(3) The amount of wages that the worker is entitled to according to his/her qualifications and experience.
(4) None of the above.

107. What is the definition of "wages in kind" under The Payment of Wages Act, 1936?
(1) Any payment made by the employer in the form of food, clothing or other goods instead of money.
(2) Any payment made by the employer in the form of money instead of goods or services.
(3) Any payment made by the worker to the employer for services rendered by the employer.
(4) None of the above.

108. What is meant by the term "advance notice" under The Payment of Wages Act, 1936?
(1) Notice given by the worker to the employer before resigning from his/her job.
(2) Notice given by the employer to the worker before terminating his/her employment.
(3) Notice given by the employer to the worker before making any deduction from his/her wages.
(4) None of the above.

109. What is meant by the term "industrial establishment" under The Payment of Wages Act, 1936?

(1) Any establishment in which any industrial, commercial, or agricultural activity is carried on.

(2) Any establishment in which only industrial activity is carried on.

(3) Any establishment in which only commercial activity is carried on.

(4) None of the above.

110. What is the significance of the "register of fines" under The Payment of Wages Act, 1936?

(1) It is a record of every person employed in the establishment.

(2) It is a record of all fines imposed on the workers.

(3) It is a record of the wage period and the amount of wages paid to each worker.

(4) It is a record of the amount of fines imposed on the worker and the deductions made from the wages.

111. What is meant by the term "plaint" under The Payment of Wages Act, 1936?

(1) An application made to the authority for the recovery of unpaid wages.

(2) An application made by the employer for the deduction of wages from the worker's wages.

(3) An application made by the worker for the payment of advance wages.

(4) None of the above.

112. What is the definition of "deferred wages" under The Payment of Wages Act, 1936?

(1) Payment of wages after the worker has left employment.

(2) Payment of wages that have been withheld by the employer for a future date.

(3) Payment of wages that have been earned by the worker but are not paid immediately due to certain circumstances.

(4) None of the above.

113. What is the significance of the "payment of wages slip" under The Payment of Wages Act, 1936?

(1) It is a receipt given to the worker for the wages paid by the employer.

(2) It is a record of all deductions made from the wages of the worker.

(3) It is a document that is required to be produced by the worker for certain purposes such as obtaining a loan or opening a bank account.

(4) None of the above.

114. What is the definition of "wages for overtime work" under The Payment of Wages Act, 1936?

(1) Payment of wages at double the usual rate for work done beyond the usual working hours.

(2) Payment of wages equal to the usual rate for work done beyond the usual working hours.

(3) Payment of wages at a rate not less than twice the usual rate for work done beyond the specified daily or weekly hours.

(4) None of the above.

115. What is the definition of "normal working day" under The Payment of Wages Act, 1936?

(1) A day consisting of 8 hours of work.

(2) A day consisting of 9 hours of work.

(3) A day consisting of 10 hours of work.

(4) None of the above.

116. What is the definition of "dismissal for gross misconduct" under The Payment of Wages Act, 1936?

(1) The termination of the worker's employment due to a serious violation of the terms of employment.

(2) The termination of the worker's employment due to his/her involvement in criminal activities.

(3) Both (1) and (2).

(4) None of the above.

117. What is the main objective of The Equal Remuneration Act, 1976?

(1) To prohibit discrimination in employment on the basis of gender.

(2) To prohibit discrimination in remuneration on the basis of gender.

(3) To regulate the payment of wages to workers.

(4) None of the above.

118. Who is responsible for enforcing the provisions of The Equal Remuneration Act, 1976?

(1) The Labor Commissioner

(2) The Inspector appointed by the State Government

(3) Both (1) and (2)

(4) The Central Government

119. Which of the following constitutes "remuneration" under The Equal Remuneration Act, 1976?

(1) Basic salary (2) Allowances

(3) Bonus (4) All of these

120. Which of the following is a prohibited act under The Equal Remuneration Act, 1976?

(1) To discriminate in remuneration on the basis of gender.

(2) To discriminate in employment on the basis of gender.

(3) Both (1) and (2)

(4) None of the above

121. What is the penalty for non-compliance with the provisions of The Equal Remuneration Act, 1976?

(1) Imprisonment for a period of 6 months

(2) Fine of up to Rs. 10,000

(3) Both (1) and (2)

(4) None of the above

122. What is the definition of "aggrieved person" under The Equal Remuneration Act, 1976?

(1) Any worker who has been discriminated against in remuneration on the basis of gender.

(2) Any person who has been discriminated against in employment on the basis of gender.

(3) Both (1) and (2)

(4) None of the above

123. Which of the following constitutes "discrimination" under The Equal Remuneration Act, 1976?

(1) Any distinction, exclusion or preference made on the basis of gender

(2) Any distinction, exclusion or preference made on the basis of race, caste, religion, or place of birth.

(3) Both (1) and (2)

(4) None of the above

124. What is the significance of the "register of complaints" under The Equal Remuneration Act, 1976?

(1) It is a record of all complaints received from workers.

(2) It is a record of all deductions made from the wages of workers.

(3) It is a record of the wage period and the amount of wages paid to each worker.

(4) None of the above.

125. What is the definition of "worker employed in the same establishment" under The Equal Remuneration Act, 1976?

(1) A worker who is employed in the same establishment as workers of the opposite gender.

(2) A worker who is employed in a different establishment from workers of the opposite gender.

(3) A worker who is not employed in any establishment.

(4) None of the above.

126. What is the definition of "skill, effort and responsibility" under The Equal Remuneration Act, 1976?

(1) The factors that determine the amount of remuneration to be paid to a worker.

(2) The factors that determine the amount of gratuity to be paid to a worker.

(3) The factors that determine the amount of bonus to be paid to a worker.

(4) None of the above.

127. What is the definition of "competent authority" under The Equal Remuneration Act, 1976?

(1) The Supreme Court of India
(2) The High Court of the State in which the establishment is situated
(3) The Central Government or State Government as the case may be
(4) None of the above.

128. What is the definition of "remuneration committee" under The Equal Remuneration Act, 1976?

(1) A committee appointed by the employer to fix the remuneration of workers.
(2) A committee consisting of representatives of workers and management to fix the remuneration of workers.
(3) A committee appointed by the government to regulate the payment of wages to workers.
(4) None of the above.

129. What is the definition of "basic wage" under The Equal Remuneration Act, 1976?

(1) The minimum wage fixed by the government for a particular category of workers.
(2) The wage paid for the time worked by the worker.
(3) The wage paid for the type and volume of work done by the worker.
(4) None of the above.

130. What is the definition of "equal pay for work of equal value" under The Equal Remuneration Act, 1976?

(1) Payment of equal wages to workers who perform the same job.
(2) Payment of equal wages to workers who perform different jobs but the jobs have equal value.
(3) Payment of wages based on the quantity of work done by the worker.
(4) None of the above.

131. What is the definition of "wages for women workers" under The Equal Remuneration Act, 1976?

(1) Payment of wages at a rate not lower than the rate at which men are paid for the same work.
(2) Payment of wages at a rate not more than the rate at which men are paid for the same work.
(3) Payment of wages at a different rate than the rate at which men are paid for the same work.
(4) None of the above.

132. What is the definition of "service conditions" under The Equal Remuneration Act, 1976?

(1) The conditions of employment of a worker including hours of work, leave, and holidays.
(2) The conditions of employment of a worker including remuneration, hours of work, leave, and holidays.
(3) The conditions of employment of a worker including remuneration, work timings, and travel allowances.
(4) None of the above.

133. What is the definition of "equal wages for same work" under The Equal Remuneration Act, 1976?

(1) Payment of equal wages to workers who perform the same job.
(2) Payment of equal wages to workers who perform different jobs but jobs have equal value.
(3) Payment of equal wages to male and female workers for the same work.
(4) None of the above.

134. What is the definition of "historical discrimination" under The Equal Remuneration Act, 1976?

(1) Discrimination on the basis of past performance of the worker.
(2) Discrimination on the basis of caste, religion, or place of birth.
(3) Discrimination on the basis of gender that has existed in the past.
(4) None of the above.

135. What is the definition of "remuneration discrimination" under The Equal Remuneration Act, 1976?

(1) Discrimination on the basis of work timings.
(2) Discrimination on the basis of job role.
(3) Discrimination on the basis of gender in remuneration.
(4) None of the above.

136. What is the definition of "prohibited discrimination" under The Equal Remuneration Act, 1976?
(1) Discrimination on the basis of work timings.
(2) Discrimination on the basis of job role.
(3) Discrimination on the basis of gender in remuneration.
(4) None of the above.

137. What is the definition of "unfair remuneration" under The Equal Remuneration Act, 1976?
(1) Remuneration paid to the worker in advance of the wage period.
(2) Remuneration paid to the worker after the wage period has ended.
(3) Remuneration paid to the worker that is less than the wages paid to a worker of the opposite gender for the same work.
(4) None of the above.

138. What is the definition of "wage equality" under The Equal Remuneration Act, 1976?
(1) Payment of equal wages to all workers in the establishment.
(2) Payment of equal wages to all workers who perform the same job.
(3) Payment of equal wages to male and female workers for the same work.
(4) None of the above.

139. What is the definition of "remuneration complaints" under The Equal Remuneration Act, 1976?
(1) Complaints received by the employer regarding the remuneration of the workers.
(2) Complaints received from workers regarding their remuneration.
(3) Complaints received from other parties such as suppliers or customers regarding the remuneration of the workers.
(4) None of the above.

140. What is the main objective of The Payment of Gratuity Act, 1972?
(1) To regulate the payment of wages to workers.
(2) To regulate the payment of gratuity to workers.
(3) To prohibit discrimination in employment on the basis of gender.
(4) None of the above.

141. Who is responsible for enforcing the provisions of The Payment of Gratuity Act, 1972?
(1) The Labor Commissioner
(2) The Inspector appointed by the State Government
(3) Both (1) and (2)
(4) The Controlling Authority appointed by the appropriate Government

142. Which of the following is a "controlling authority" under The Payment of Gratuity Act, 1972?
(1) The Central Government
(2) The State Government
(3) The Labor Commissioner
(4) All of the above

143. What is the definition of "continuous service" under The Payment of Gratuity Act, 1972?
(1) The period of employment of a worker with an establishment without interruption.
(2) The period of employment of a worker with an establishment with frequent interruptions.
(3) The period of employment of a worker with more than one establishment.
(4) None of the above.

144. Which of the following constitutes "employee" under The Payment of Gratuity Act, 1972?

(1) Any person employed in a factory, shop or establishment.
(2) Any person employed in any kind of work, manual or otherwise.
(3) Both (1) and (2).
(4) None of the above.

145. What is the definition of "employer" under The Payment of Gratuity Act, 1972?
(1) Any person who employs workers for wages.
(2) Any person who has control over the employment of workers.
(3) Both (1) and (2).
(4) None of the above.

146. What is the definition of "gratuity" under The Payment of Gratuity Act, 1972?
(1) A sum of money paid in addition to wages.
(2) A retirement benefit paid to a worker after a fixed period of service.
(3) A payment made to the family of a worker in case of his/her death.
(4) None of the above

147. What is the formula for calculating the amount of gratuity payable to a worker under The Payment of Gratuity Act, 1972?
(1) Basic salary × years of service × 15/26
(2) Basic salary × years of service × 7/12
(3) Basic salary × years of service × 1/2
(4) None of the above

148. What is the maximum amount of gratuity payable to a worker under The Payment of Gratuity Act, 1972?
(1) Rs. 5 lakhs (2) Rs. 10 lakhs
(3) Rs. 15 lakhs (4) There is no limit

149. What is the definition of "family" under The Payment of Gratuity Act, 1972?
(1) The worker's spouse and children.
(2) The worker's parents and siblings.
(3) Both (1) and (2)
(4) None of the above

150. What is the significance of the "gratuity fund" under The Payment of Gratuity Act, 1972?
(1) It is a fund created by the employer to provide gratuity to the workers.
(2) It is a fund created by the government to provide gratuity to workers.
(3) It is a fund created by the employer to contribute towards the gratuity payable to the workers.
(4) None of the above.

151. What is the definition of "retirement" under The Payment of Gratuity Act, 1972?
(1) The cessation of employment of a worker due to age or disability.
(2) The cessation of employment of a worker after a fixed period of service.
(3) Both (1) and (2).
(4) None of the above.

152. What is the definition of "death" under The Payment of Gratuity Act, 1972?
(1) Cessation of life of a worker due to natural causes or accident.
(2) Cessation of life of a worker due to natural causes.
(3) Cessation of life of a worker due to accident.
(4) None of the above.

153. What is the definition of "nominee" under The Payment of Gratuity Act, 1972?
(1) The worker who is entitled to receive gratuity.
(2) The worker's family member who is entitled to receive the gratuity in case of his/her death.
(3) The worker who is entitled to nominate a person to receive the gratuity in case of his/her death.
(4) None of the above.

154. What is the definition of "due date" under The Payment of Gratuity Act, 1972?
(1) The date on which the gratuity is payable to the worker.
(2) The date on which the worker is retired or his/her employment is terminated.
(3) Both (1) and (2).
(4) None of the above.

155. **Assertion:** The Payment of Gratuity Act, 1972 applies only to establishments employing 10 or more persons.

Reason: Smaller establishments do not have the financial capacity to pay gratuity to their workers.

(1) Both assertion and reason are true and the reason is the correct explanation of the assertion.

(2) Both assertion and reason are true but the reason is not the correct explanation of the assertion.

(3) Assertion is true but reason is false.

(4) Assertion is false but reason is true.

156. **Assertion:** The Payment of Gratuity Act, 1972 applies to all employees irrespective of their salary.

Reason: The Act defines "employee" to include all workers employed in any kind of work, manual or otherwise.

(1) Both assertion and reason are true and the reason is the correct explanation of the assertion.

(2) Both assertion and reason are true but the reason is not the correct explanation of the assertion.

(3) Assertion is true but reason is false.

(4) Assertion isfalse but reason is true.

157. **Assertion:** The amount of gratuity payable to a worker under The Payment of Gratuity Act, 1972 is linked to the period of service.

Reason: The longer the period of service, the higher the amount of gratuity.

(1) Both assertion and reason are true and the reason is the correct explanation of the assertion.

(2) Both assertion and reason are true but the reason is not the correct explanation of the assertion.

(3) Assertion is true but reason is false.

(4) Assertion is false but reason is true.

158. **Assertion:** The Payment of Gratuity Act, 1972 provides for the payment of gratuity to a worker's family in case of his/her death.

Reason: The gratuity paid to the worker's family is calculated on the basis of the worker's last drawn salary.

(1) Both assertion and reason are true and the reason is the correct explanation of the assertion.

(2) Both assertion and reason are true but the reason is not the correct explanation of the assertion.

(3) Assertion is true but reason is false.

(4) Assertion is false but reason is true.

159. **Assertion:** An employer is required to obtain a "gratuity card" for each eligible employee.

Reason: The gratuity card is used to record the amount of gratuity paid to the worker.

(1) Both assertion and reason are true and the reason is the correct explanation of the assertion.

(2) Both assertion and reason are true but the reason is not the correct explanation of the assertion.

(3) Assertion is true but reason is false.

(4) Assertion is false but reason is true.

160. The Employees' Provident Fund and Miscellaneous Provisions Act, 1952, provides for the establishment of:

(1) Pension fund for workers

(2) Provident fund for workers

(3) Mutual fund for workers

(4) All of the above

161. What is the main objective of The Employees' Provident Fund and Miscellaneous Provisions Act, 1952?

(1) To regulate the payment of wages to workers

(2) To regulate the payment of gratuity to workers

(3) To provide social security to workers

(4) None of the above

162. In how many states and union territories is The Employees' Provident Fund and Miscellaneous Provisions Act, 1952 applicable?

(1) In all states and union territories

(2) In only a few selected states
(3) In selected industries
(4) None of the above

163. What is the percentage of contribution of the employee towards the provident fund under The Employees' Provident Fund and Miscellaneous Provisions Act, 1952?
(1) 10% of basic salary
(2) 20% of basic salary
(3) 15% of basic salary
(4) None of the above

164. How many members are required to form a provident fund scheme under The Employees' Provident Fund and Miscellaneous Provisions Act, 1952?
(1) Minimum of 5 members
(2) Minimum of 10 members
(3) Minimum of 15 members
(4) None of the above

165. Which of the following is considered as wage under The Employees' Provident Fund and Miscellaneous Provisions Act, 1952?
(1) Basic pay
(2) Dearness allowance
(3) House rent allowance
(4) All of the above

166. Which of the following is considered as an exempted establishment under The Employees' Provident Fund and Miscellaneous Provisions Act, 1952?
(1) An establishment which has its own provident fund trust
(2) An establishment which does not have to contribute towards the provident fund
(3) An establishment which is exempted from the Act by the government
(4) None of the above

167. What is the minimum rate of interest payable on the provident fund contributions under The Employees' Provident Fund and Miscellaneous Provisions Act, 1952?
(1) 7% per annum
(2) 8% per annum
(3) 10% per annum
(4) None of the above

168. Who is responsible for the administration of the Employees' Provident Fund and Miscellaneous Provisions Act, 1952?
(1) The employer
(2) The government
(3) The employee
(4) None of the above

169. What is the definition of an "unexempted establishment" under The Employees' Provident Fund and Miscellaneous Provisions Act, 1952?
(1) An establishment which is not exempted by the government from the provisions of the Act
(2) An establishment which is not required to contribute towards the provident fund
(3) An establishment which is exempted by the government from the provisions of the Act
(4) None of the above

170. What is the definition of "basic wage" under The Employees' Provident Fund and Miscellaneous Provisions Act, 1952?
(1) The total wage earned by the worker including allowances, overtime, and bonuses
(2) The wage paid for the type and volume of work done by the worker
(3) The wage paid to the worker for the time worked by him or her
(4) None of the above

171. What is the penalty for non-compliance with the provisions of The Employees' Provident Fund and Miscellaneous Provisions Act, 1952?
(1) Imprisonment for a period of 6 months
(2) Fine of up to Rs. 10,000 per day of default
(3) Both (1) and (2)
(4) None of the above

172. What is the definition of "wage ceiling" under The Employees' Provident Fund and Miscellaneous Provisions Act, 1952?

(1) The maximum amount of salary on which provident fund contributions can be made

(2) The minimum amount of salary on which provident fund contributions can be made

(3) The average amount of salary on which provident fund contributions can be made

(4) None of the above

173. What is the maximum amount of salary on which provident fund contributions can be made under The Employees' Provident Fund and Miscellaneous Provisions Act, 1952?

(1) Rs. 15,000 per month

(2) Rs. 10,000 per month

(3) Rs. 20,000 per month

(4) None of the above

174. Who is eligible for receiving provident fund benefits under The Employees' Provident Fund and Miscellaneous Provisions Act, 1952?

(1) Only the employee who has completed 5 years of service

(2) Only the employee who has completed 10 years of service

(3) The employee who has completed 5 years of service and the employee who is retiring due to ill-health or disability

(4) None of the above

175. What is the definition of "nominee" under The Employees' Provident Fund and Miscellaneous Provisions Act, 1952?

(1) A person nominated by the employee to receive the provident fund amount in case of his/her death

(2) The family members of the employee who are entitled to the provident fund amount in case of his/her death

(3) The employer who is responsible for the payment of provident fund amount

(4) None of the above

176. What is the definition of "family" under The Employees' Provident Fund and Miscellaneous Provisions Act, 1952?

(1) The spouse and children of the employee

(2) The parents and siblings of the employee

(3) Both (1) and (2)

(4) None of the above

177. What is the definition of a "seasonal establishment" under The Employees' Provident Fund and Miscellaneous Provisions Act, 1952?

(1) An establishment which is operational only during certain seasons of the year

(2) An establishment which is operational throughout the year but the workers are employed on a seasonal basis

(3) Both (1) and (2)

(4) None of the above

178. What is the definition of a "casual worker" under The Employees' Provident Fund and Miscellaneous Provisions Act, 1952?

(1) A worker who is employed on a permanent basis

(2) A worker who is employed for a short period of time with no fixed duration

(3) A worker who is employed on a work-charged basis

(4) None of the above

179. What is the definition of "employee deposit-linked insurance" under The Employees' Provident Fund and Miscellaneous Provisions Act, 1952?

(1) Insurance coverage for the employee that is linked to his/her provident fund account

(2) Insurance coverage for the employee that is not linked to his/her provident fund account

(3) Insurance coverage for the employer

(4) None of the above

180. What is the definition of an "exempted employee" under The Employees' Provident Fund and Miscellaneous Provisions Act, 1952?

(1) An employee who is not eligible for the provident fund benefits
(2) An employee who is eligible but has opted out of the provident fund scheme
(3) An employee who is covered by an exempted establishment
(4) None of the above

181. What is the definition of "exempted employer" under The Employees' Provident Fund and Miscellaneous Provisions Act, 1952?
(1) An employer who is exempted from contributing towards the provident fund
(2) An employer who has set up his own provident fund trust
(3) An employer who is exempted from the provisions of the Act by the government
(4) None of the above

182. What is the definition of "non-exempted employer" under The Employees' Provident Fund and Miscellaneous Provisions Act, 1952?
(1) An employer who is required to contribute towards the provident fund
(2) An employer who is not required to contribute towards the provident fund
(3) An employer who is exempted from the provisions of the Act by the government
(4) None of the above

183. What is the minimum rate of interest payable on the employee deposit-linked insurance under The Employees' Provident Fund and Miscellaneous Provisions Act, 1952?
(1) 8.5% per annum
(2) 7.5% per annum
(3) 9.5% per annum
(4) None of the above

184. What is the definition of a "managing trustee" under The Employees' Provident Fund and Miscellaneous Provisions Act, 1952?
(1) A person appointed by the employer to manage the provident fund trust
(2) A person appointed by the government to manage the provident fund trust
(3) A person who is a trustee and is responsible for the management of the provident fund trust
(4) None of the above

185. What is the definition of a "trustee" under The Employees' Provident Fund and Miscellaneous Provisions Act, 1952?
(1) A person who is responsible for the management of the provident fund trust
(2) A person who is appointed by the government to manage the provident fund trust
(3) Both (1) and (2)
(4) None of the above

186. What is the definition of "complaint" under The Employees' Provident Fund and Miscellaneous Provisions Act, 1952?
(1) A complaint that is initiated by the employer against the employee
(2) A complaint that is initiated by the employee against the employer
(3) A complaint that is initiated by the government against the employer
(4) None of the above

187. What is the definition of a "member" under The Employees' Provident Fund and Miscellaneous Provisions Act, 1952?
(1) A person who is employed with an establishment that is required to contribute towards the provident fund
(2) A person who is employed with an establishment that is not required to contribute towards the provident fund
(3) A person who is retired and is entitled to receive the provident fund amount
(4) None of the above

188. What is the definition of "account number" under The Employees' Provident Fund and Miscellaneous Provisions Act, 1952?
(1) The number assigned to each member for the purpose of identifying his or her provident fund account.
(2) The account number of the employer who is required to contribute towards the provident fund

(3) The account number of the government which is responsible for the administration of the Act
(4) None of the above

189. What is the definition of "inspector" under The Employees' Provident Fund and Miscellaneous Provisions Act, 1952?
(1) A person appointed by the government to ensure compliance with the provisions of the Act
(2) A person appointed by the employer to manage the provident fund trust
(3) Both (1) and (2)
(4) None of the above

190. What is the definition of "competent authority" under The Employees' Provident Fund and Miscellaneous Provisions Act, 1952?
(1) The government
(2) The inspector appointed by the government
(3) The employer
(4) None of the above

191. What is the definition of "inspector-cum-facilitator" under The Employees' Provident Fund and Miscellaneous Provisions Act, 1952?
(1) A person appointed by the government who is responsible for both inspection and facilitation of the employers and workers
(2) A person appointed by the government who is responsible only for inspection of the employers and workers
(3) A person appointed by the employer who is responsible for both inspection and facilitation of the employees
(4) None of the above

192. What is the definition of "establishment" under The Employees' Provident Fund and Miscellaneous Provisions Act, 1952?
(1) Any factory, shop or commercial establishment where employees are engaged for the purpose of producing goods or services
(2) Any establishment where employees are employed for the purpose of producing goods or services other than factories or shops
(3) Any establishment where employees are employed for the purpose of manufacturing goods
(4) None of the above

193. What is the definition of "salary" under The Employees' Provident Fund and Miscellaneous Provisions Act, 1952?
(1) The total salary earned by the worker including allowances, overtime, and bonuses
(2) The salary paid for the type and volume of work done by the worker
(3) The salary paid to the worker for the time worked by him or her
(4) None of the above

194. What is the definition of a "seasonal worker" under The Employees' Provident Fund and Miscellaneous Provisions Act, 1952?
(1) A worker who is employedonly during certain seasons of the year in a seasonal establishment
(2) A worker who is employed for a short period of time with no fixed duration in a non-seasonal establishment
(3) Both (1) and (2)
(4) None of the above

195. What is the definition of a "migrant worker" under The Employees' Provident Fund and Miscellaneous Provisions Act, 1952?
(1) A worker who has migrated from one state to another for the purpose of employment
(2) A worker who is employed in a foreign country
(3) A worker who is employed on a contractual basis
(4) None of the above

196. What is the definition of an "unorganised worker" under The Employees' Provident Fund and Miscellaneous Provisions Act, 1952?

(1) A worker who is employed in an establishment that is not required to contribute towards the provident fund
(2) A worker who is employed in an establishment that is required to contribute towards the provident fund but the establishment has not yet registered under the Act
(3) A worker who is not covered by any social security scheme
(4) None of the above

197. What is the definition of "deemed wages" under The Employees' Provident Fund and Miscellaneous Provisions Act, 1952?
(1) The wages paid to the workers that are not included in the calculation of the provident fund contributions
(2) The wages that are paid to the workers in the form of perquisites such as housing, medical facilities, etc. that are not included in the calculation of the provident fund contributions
(3) The wages that are paid to the workers in the form of tips and gratuities that are not included in the calculation of the provident fund contributions
(4) None of the above

198. What is the definition of "controlling authority" under The Employees' Provident Fund and Miscellaneous Provisions Act, 1952?
(1) The government
(2) The Regional Provident Fund Commissioner
(3) The employer
(4) None of the above

ANSWER KEY

1. (1) **2.** (4) **3.** (4) **4.** (1) **5.** (1) **6.** (1) **7.** (1) **8.** (1) **9.** (4) **10.** (1)
11. (4) **12.** (4) **13.** (2) **14.** (1) **15.** (1) **16.** (1) **17.** (1) **18.** (1) **19.** (1) **20.** (1)
21. (1) **22.** (1) **23.** (1) **24.** (1) **25.** (1) **26.** (1) **27.** (1) **28.** (1) **29.** (1) **30.** (4)
31. (4) **32.** (4) **33.** (1) **34.** (4) **35.** (4) **36.** (4) **37.** (1) **38.** (4) **39.** (1) **40.** (4)
41. (1) **42.** (1) **43.** (3) **44.** (4) **45.** (1) **46.** (1) **47.** (3) **48.** (3) **49.** (4) **50.** (3)
51. (3) **52.** (1) **53.** (1) **54.** (1) **55.** (1) **56.** (1) **57.** (4) **58.** (1) **59.** (1) **60.** (3)
61. (1) **62.** (3) **63.** (1) **64.** (2) **65.** (3) **66.** (3) **67.** (3) **68.** (3) **69.** (1) **70.** (1)
71. (1) **72.** (1) **73.** (3) **74.** (3) **75.** (3) **76.** (3) **77.** (1) **78.** (1) **79.** (1) **80.** (3)
81. (3) **82.** (1) **83.** (2) **84.** (3) **85.** (3) **86.** (4) **87.** (1) **88.** (2) **89.** (2) **90.** (4)
91. (1) **92.** (3) **93.** (4) **94.** (3) **95.** (3) **96.** (1) **97.** (1) **98.** (1) **99.** (1) **100.** (4)
101. (3) **102.** (4) **103.** (4) **104.** (4) **105.** (4) **106.** (4) **107.** (1) **108.** (3) **109.** (4) **110.** (4)
111. (1) **112.** (3) **113.** (3) **114.** (3) **115.** (3) **116.** (3) **117.** (2) **118.** (4) **119.** (4) **120.** (1)
121. (2) **122.** (3) **123.** (3) **124.** (1) **125.** (1) **126.** (4) **127.** (3) **128.** (2) **129.** (3) **130.** (2)
131. (1) **132.** (2) **133.** (3) **134.** (3) **135.** (3) **136.** (3) **137.** (3) **138.** (3) **139.** (2) **140.** (2)
141. (4) **142.** (4) **143.** (1) **144.** (3) **145.** (3) **146.** (3) **147.** (3) **148.** (1) **149.** (3) **150.** (3)
151. (3) **152.** (3) **153.** (2) **154.** (3) **155.** (1) **156.** (1) **157.** (1) **158.** (4) **159.** (1) **160.** (2)
161. (3) **162.** (1) **163.** (1) **164.** (1) **165.** (1) **166.** (1) **167.** (1) **168.** (2) **169.** (1) **170.** (3)
171. (2) **172.** (4) **173.** (1) **174.** (3) **175.** (1) **176.** (1) **177.** (3) **178.** (3) **179.** (1) **180.** (3)
181. (2) **182.** (3) **183.** (1) **184.** (3) **185.** (3) **186.** (3) **187.** (1) **188.** (1) **189.** (4) **190.** (2)
191. (1) **192.** (1) **193.** (3) **194.** (3) **195.** (1) **196.** (3) **197.** (2) **198.** (2)

UNIT

9

LABOUR WELFARE

Syllabus

- Concept, Scope, Types, Theories and Principles, Industrial Health and Hygiene, Industrial Accidents and safety, Occupational Diseases
- **Social Security:** Concept and Scope, Social Assistance and Social assurance.

LABOUR WELFARE

CONCEPT AND SCOPE

Labour welfare is an important dimension of industrial relation, labour welfare includes overall welfare facilities designed to take care of well being of employee's and in order to increase their living standard. It do not generally constitutes monetery benefits nor these are provided by employers alone, it can also be provided by government, non government agencies and trade unions. Industrialization, mechanisation and globalisation has increased important of labour welfare in industries.

The importance of labour in industrialization and economic development has been recognised globally. In global scenario need and importance of labour welfare has been increasingly appreciated.

History of Labour Welfare

In India the labour welfare started sometime during the 1st world war (1914-1918). Till then wellbeing of workers in factories was hardly thought by anybody. Since, 1st world war labour welfare has been expanding on voluntary basis. Industrial Labour Organisation has played a very significant role for labour welfare. Much labour legislation have been formed by Indian central government and state governments for welfare of labours in Industries. Government has laid down minimum standards for employment and working conditions in organisations. Besides the government, the employers, trade unions and various social organisations also function as agencies for implementation of labour welfare measures. A Industrial labour organisation (ILO) is an advisory body so it cannot force any country to introduce any welfare measures. The need of labour welfare was powerfully felt by the Royal Commission of Labour far back in 1931, Indian constitution emphasized this need under its directive principles of state policy.

Labour Welfare Meaning and Definition

Labour welfare is an important dimension of industrial relation, labour welfare includes overall welfare facilities designed to take care of well being of employee's and in order to increase their living standard. It do not generally constitutes monetary benefits nor these are provided by employers alone, it can also be provided by government, non government agencies and trade unions. Industrialisation, mechanisation and globalisation has increased importance of labour welfare in industries.

The importance of labour in industrialisation and economic development has been recognised globally. In global scenario need and importance of labour welfare has been increasingly appreciated.

- According to **Arthur James** Todd:"Labour welfare means anything done for the comfort and improvement, intellectual and social, of the employees over and above the wages paid which is not a necessity of the Industry."
- According to **Industrial Labour Organisation (ILO)**"Labour welfare may be understood and including such services facilities and amenities which may be established in vicinity of undertaking to perform their work in healthy and congenial environment and to avail of facilities which improve their health and bring high morale."

Scope of Labour Welfare

Scope of Labour Welfare is very broad; however we have tried to include some main aspects of it. The following list of labour welfare scope is not exhaustive.

Working Environment

Favourable working environment enhances efficiency of workers and includes proper illumination, safety, temperature, ventilation, sanitation, cleanliness and canteen facilities. Workplace sanitation and cleanliness is very important for making workplace favourable to workers. Following points should be considerdered to make workplace favourable to workers.

- Proper ventilation, lighting, temperature, cleanliness, seating arrangements etc.
- Proper safety measures for workers should be there.
- Sufficient urinals, lavatories and bathing facilities should be provided and cleaned regularly.
- Proper gardening and cleanliness of open spaces.
- Pure drinking water should be provided.
- Subsidized canteen services should be provided.

Health Facilities

- Health centre should be provided within factory.
- Ambulance service should be provided within factory in case of any emergency.
- Free medical checkups of workers and health and diet counselling of workers.
- Availability of Doctor inside the factory for emergency.
- Women and child welfare work.
- Recreation facilities inside the organisation
- Education and library services

General Welfare Programs

- Housing facilities for workers
- Family case work and counselling

Economic Welfare Programs

- Subsidized consumer goods including grains, vegetables, milk, oil and other daily requirements.
- Banking services and credit facilities.
- Health insurance schemes
- Bonus and profit sharing schemes.
- Transportation services in factory

Objectives of Labour Welfare

Several objectives of Labour welfare are mentioned below:

1. Labour welfare provides social comfort to employees.
2. It provides intellectual improvement of employees.
3. To develop sense of responsibility and belongingness among employees.
4. To ensures that the working conditions for employees are of higher standard.
5. To build stable work force.
6. To reduce absenteeism and labour turnover.
7. To make employees lives good and worth living.
8. To boost productivity and efficiency at the workplace.
9. To provide healthy and proper working conditions.
10. To ensure well being of employees and families.

Approaches or Theories of Labour Welfare

There are some theories which constitutes the conceptual framework of the labour welfare, describe these theories. Several theories constituting the conceptual framework of labour welfare have so far been outlined these are :

1. **Policy theory.** This theory is based on the contention that a minimum standard of welfare is necessary for workers. The assumption on which the theory is based without compulsion, supervision and fear of punishment, no employer will provide even the barest minimum of welfare facilities for workers this theory is based on the assumption that man is selfish and self –centered, and always tries to achieve his own ends, even at the cost of the welfare of others. According to this theory, owners and managers of industrial undertakings make use of every opportunity to engage in this kind of exploitation. The sate has therefore to step in to prevent exploitation by enacting stiff laws to coerce industrialists into offering a minimum standard of welfare to their workers. Such interference it is felt is in the interests of the progress and welfare of the state as well. Laws are enacted to compel management to provide minimum wages, congenial working conditions and reasonable hours of work and social security.
   The policy theory involves several stages of implementation
   - Enactments
   - Periodical supervision
   - Punishment
2. **Religious theory.** The religion theory has two connotations, namely, the investment and atonement aspects. The investment aspect of the religion theory implies that the fruits of today's deeds will be reaped tomorrow. Any action, good or bad is therefore treated as an investment. Inspired by this belief, some employers plan and organise canteens and creches. The atonement aspect of the religion theory implies that the present disabilities of a person are the result of the sins committed by him/her previously. He/she should undertake to do good deeds now to atone or compensate for his/her sins. There is the story of a big Jain employer who firmly held the belief that the provision of welfare facilities for workers was outside the duties of the management. Whatever he did provide was under government compulsion and supervision. It so happened, however, that the children born to him died as soon as they were born. Later, his own health suffered. He felt that, as a compensation, or expiration or even as an investment in a good deed (punyam), he should liberally contribute to the creche in the factory (as well as to other child-welfare institutions), and also to medical services for his workers. Consequently, in this particular factory, there came to exist an excellent creche and a well-organised dispensary.
3. **Philanthropic theory.** Philanthropy means affection for mankind. The philanthropic theory of labour welfare refers to the provision of good working conditions, creches and canteens out of pity on the part of the employers who want to remove the disabilities of the workers. Robert Owen of England was a philanthropic employer, who worked for the welfare of his workers. The philanthropic theory is more common in social welfare. Student hostels, drinking water facilities, the rehabilitation of crippled persons, donations to religious and educational institutions, and so forth are examples of philanthropic deeds.
4. **Trusteeship theory.** In this theory it is held that the industrialists or employers holds the total industrial estate, properties and profits accruing from them in trust for the workmen, for himself, and for society. It assumes that the workmen are like minors and are not able to look after their own interests that they are ignorant because of lack of education. Employers therefore have the moral responsibility to look after the interests of their wards, who are the workers.
5. **Paternalistic Theory.** According to the paternalistic theory, also called the trusteeship theory, of labour welfare, the industrialist or the employer holds the total industrial estate, properties and the profits accruing from them, in trust. The property which he/she can use or abuse as he/she likes is not entirely his/her own. He/she holds it for his/her use, no doubt, but also for the benefit of his/her workers, if not for the whole society. For several reasons, such as low wages, lack of education, and so forth the workers are at present unable to take care of themselves. They are, therefore, like minors, and the employers should provide for their well-being out of

funds in their control. The trusteeship is not actual and legal, but it is moral and, therefore, not less real.

6. **Placating theory.** As labour groups are becoming better organised and are becoming demanding and militant, being more conscious of their rights and privileges that even before, their demand for higher wages and better standards increases. The placing theory advocates timely and periodical acts of labour welfare to appease the workers.

> **PRINCIPLES OF LABOUR WELFARE**
>
> - Welfare activities will be carried out at all levels in the organisation.
> - It will be provided over and above regular wages.
> - Adequate and full co-operation shall be provided from management level.
> - Periodic assesment of labour welfare measures is essential.
> - It shall emphasize on physical, mental, moral and emotional well being of employees.
> - It can be a social concept which relates to welfare of employees, their families and community as a whole.

7. **Public Relations Theory.** According to this theory, welfare activities are provided to create a good impression on the minds of the workers and the public, particularly the latter. Clean and safe working conditions, a good canteen, creche and other amenities, make a good impression on the workers, visitors and the public. Some employers proudly take their visitors round the plant to show how well they have organised their welfare activities.
8. **Functional Theory.** Also known as the efficiency theory of labour welfare, the functional theory implies that welfare facilities are provided to make the workers more efficient. If workers are fed properly, clothed adequately and treated kindly, and if the conditions of their work are congenial, they will work efficiently. Welfare work is a means of securing, preserving and increasing the efficiency of labour.
9. **Social Theory.** The social obligation of an industrial establishment has been assuming great significance these days. The social theory implies that a factory is morally bound to improve the conditions of the society in addition to improving the condition of its employees. Labour welfare, as mentioned earlier, is gradually becoming social welfare.

Labour Welfare Types

Some of the major categories of labour welfare are: (1) Intra-mural Facilities (2) Extra-mural Facilities (3) Statutory Facilities (4) Mutual Facilities and (5) Voluntary.

It is very difficult to classify the welfare activities into certain broad categories.

(1) **Intra-mural Facilities.** The facilities provided inside the factory are known as intra-mural facilities. These facilities include activities relating to minimisation of industrial fatigue, provision of safety measures like fencing and covering of machines, good layout of the plant and machinery, sufficient lighting conditions, provision of first aid appliances etc. Provisions of such facilities are also obligatory in all industrial establishments all over the world.

(2) **Extra-mural Facilities.** Facilities offered to the workers outside the factory are known as extra-mural facilities. They include better housing accommodations, indoor and outdoor recreation sports, educational facilities etc. The provision of these facilities is voluntary. Earlier, due attention was not given to the provision of extra-mural facilities to the workers but now it is realised that these facilities are very important for the general welfare and upliftment of the workers.

(3) **Statutory Facilities.** Under this category, welfare facilities are provided according to the labour legislations passed by the Government. The nature and coverage of these facilities vary from

country to country. Again these facilities may be either intra-mural facilities or extra-mural facilities. These facilities must be provided by all the employers and cannot be ignored. Any contravention of the statutory provisions shall render the employer punishable under the Act concerned.

The National Commission of Labour has divided all the statutory measures under two distinct heads:

a. Facilities which have to be provided irrespective of the size of the establishment e.g., drinking water.

b. Facilities which are to be provided subject to the employment of a specified number of persons, e.g., creches.

(4) **Mutual Facilities.** These facilities are usually outside the scope of the statutory facilities. These activities are voluntarily undertaken by the workers themselves for their own interest. As such the employer has no say in it.

(5) **Voluntary.** The facilities which are voluntarily provided by the employers come under this category. Hence these are not statutory. No doubt, the activities under this category ultimately lead to increase in the efficiency of workers.

INDUSTRIAL HEALTH AND HYGIENE

Organizations are responsible for the overall health and safety of the workers they employ, from warehouse workers to the executive suite at their desks. Keeping employees safe and healthy requires knowledge of industrial hygiene, which is the science dedicated to the anticipation, recognition, evaluation, communication, and control of environmental stressors in the workplace that may result in injury, illness, impairment, or otherwise affect the wellbeing of workers and community members.

Because industrial hygienists are trained to evaluate safety concerns and find solutions to problems, it is important that managers at all levels and across functions are able to effectively work with and manage industrial hygienists. Whether you have an industrial hygienist on your team or you have to hire an outside company for an assessment, being able to speak the language of industrial hygienists will allow you to have a deeper understanding of potential health and safety issues. In addition, once an industrial hygienist has recommended a course of action to correct any real or potential issues, you will be the one responsible for ensuring they are implemented in your workplace.

Industrial hygiene, as stated above, is concerned with identifying, evaluating, and controlling real or potential workplace environmental stressors or hazards that can affect the wellbeing of workers and community members. It is sometimes called Occupational Hygiene, Occupational Health or Workplace Health. Ideally, hazards are identified and controlled when a workplace is being planned, when conditions or processes change, or through yearly reviews, before they become an issue for workers.

In order to help ensure proper industrial hygiene and thus the health and safety of your workers, you can employ an industrial hygienist. The role of an industrial hygienist is to "anticipate health and safety concerns and design solutions to prevent them. They are the guardians of workplace safety, applying science to identify and solve health and safety problems. Industrial hygienists also unite management, workers, and all segments of a company behind the common goal of health and safety." The American Board of Industrial Hygiene certifies industrial hygienists, providing a well-respected benchmark in the field.

An industrial hygienist will use rigorous scientific methods to evaluate and control hazards in the workplace, including risk assessment tools and information, such as Safety Data Sheets, which are put together by chemical manufacturers and contain detailed information about each chemical. Industrial hygienists can also conduct a worksite analysis to evaluate all jobs, operations, machinery, and work activities at that site, in addition to problem solving on specific activities or work areas.

After a hazard is identified, an industrial hygienist will work with the company to control or eliminate the hazard. This can include substituting a chemical for a less hazardous one, reducing exposure to hazards, utilization of personal protective equipment such as gloves or goggles, or increasing ventilation.

Key Components of Industrial Hygiene

Industrial hygiene encompasses a wide range of health and safety concerns in the workplace. As a manager, you should be familiar with the basics of most of them. Here are some, though not all, of the key components of industrial hygiene.

- **Ergonomics.** The goal of ergonomics (the study of people at work), is to reduce stress and eliminate injuries associated with bad posture, overuse of muscles, and repeated tasks. For example, proper ergonomics can help prevent carpal tunnel syndrome, tendonitis, and lower back injuries. While performing an ergonomics intervention, it's important to involve workers in the process to ensure tasks are fit to the worker and workers are properly trained on aspects such as how to lift boxes correctly. Ergonomics can be improved through solutions such as changing the chairs or keyboards office workers use, introducing tools to reduce repetitive tasks, or limiting time on certain jobs.
- **Noise.** Long-term exposure to noise – both wanted and unwanted sound – can lead to hearing loss for workers. Noise issues can be addressed in several ways, including designing a facility to minimize noise, separating workers from noisy machinery as much as possible, and using devices, such as ear muffs or ear plugs, to protect workers.
- **Temperature.** Both high and low temperatures can cause problems for workers. If temperatures are too high, workers are vulnerable to heat stroke or heat exhaustion; heat stroke is a medical emergency that requires immediate attention. Workers should be allowed to slowly adapt to the heat (acclimatization) and drink small amounts of water frequently, and air should be cooled whenever possible. Prolonged exposure to low temperatures can lead to hypothermia or frostbite. Workers should be allowed to wear warm clothing, and take breaks in warmer temperatures when possible.
- **Indoor air quality.** Indoor air quality can be impacted by many factors, including pollution from machines or tools inside the building, highway pollution outside the building, dusts from mechanical processes, or gasses. Poor air quality can cause issues ranging from chronic coughs to nausea to severe headaches. Proper ventilation is important to ensure that fresh air is brought into the work area and air filtering in an HVAC system can help remove contaminants from the air.
- **Chemical exposure.** Chemical hazards can take many forms, from liquid to fumes to dusts, and can be absorbed, inhaled, or ingested into a worker's system. Some common chemicals that can potentially be hazardous are cleaning products, gasoline, and pesticides. Many chemicals can be harmless in small doses, but even some common chemicals can cause symptoms in those who are particularly sensitive, and most chemicals can cause adverse effects in large doses or when proper safety precautions are not taken. These precautions include ventilation, personal hygiene such as hand washing, which can reduce the amount of chemicals absorbed by the skin, and maintaining equipment in order to prevent leaks and breakdowns.
- **Radiation.** There are two types of radiation – non-ionizing radiation and ionizing radiation. Ultraviolet (UV) radiation and laser radiation are the types of non-ionizing radiation most likely to cause safety concerns, usually burns, for workers; UV radiation is a particular problem for outside workers, such as gardeners. Ionizing radiation can cause more considerable health risks for workers, and can be found in settings ranging from health care facilities to nuclear reactors

and their support facilities. This type of radiation damages cells, and possible long term effects include cancer and sterility. Exposure to ionizing radiation should be limited as much as possible, and workers should be shielded from radiation by materials such as lead or concrete.

- **Biological hazards.** Living organisms such as fungi, viruses, and bacteria, can enter the body and cause both acute and chronic infections. Workers who deal with plants or animals and laboratory or medical workers are particularly at risk for biological hazards, but all workers can be at risk for hazards such as mold, and bacteria that cause Legionnaire's disease. Proper hygiene such as hand washing, ventilation, personal protective equipment such as gloves or respirators, and in certain cases, isolation of the hazard, can all help minimize the risks associated with biological hazards.
- **Eliminating or Controlling Hazards.** Once hazardous conditions have been identified there is a systematic approach to eliminating or minimizing the potential hazard. This starts with designing the hazard out of the process or operation, providing local exhaust ventilation, establishing proper work practices, providing proper personal protective equipment (PPE) and applicable administrative measures.

Optimizing these components of industrial hygiene through monitoring and analyzing hazards and engineering solutions to minimize those hazards will help control potential health risks that impact both workers and your organization. These hazards can cause a wide range of negative outcomes from disease and injury to lost time and reduced productivity in your organization. Understanding the principles of industrial hygiene will help you control these factors more effectively and thus have a healthier, more productive workplace.

Industrial Safety and Accidents

An accident is an unwanted event that is never scheduled or planned. Many factors contribute to accidents' occurrence; significant losses and even bodily injury can result following each incident. These basic facts are well understood, yet accidents continue to occur, property damage accumulates, work schedules remain interrupted, and injuries reduce personal income.

Are accidents inevitable? Do they occur as a natural consequence of a daily routine? Can they be avoided?

All accidents are caused. They are the result of human error, and they involve unsafe behavior or an unsafe condition, or a combination of both. Process improvement opportunities are always identified following an accident, and prompt corrective measures are scheduled. Unfortunately, the inherent ability of the environment or behavior that initially caused the accident is seldom addressed in its entirety. Thus, we wait for the next accident in order to identify the next required corrective action. Hindsight has future value, but only after the accident occurs. The opposite of hindsight is foresight. With foresight, you identify accident potentials; with hindsight, you investigate accidents. Let us consider the value of each.

The Process of Hindsight: Accident Investigation

Discovering "what happened" and "why" are the objectives of an accident investigation. To ensure standardization in fact gathering, checklists are often used. Supervisor and employee work together to identify causes and remedial actions. The process requires a "questioning attitude."

Everyone involved should know that an accident investigation is not a "fault finding" or "finger pointing" expedition. Meaningful involvement is essential. Employees can provide valuable suggestions when they are regarded as "full partners" in the investigation process.

There are generally five major elements in a good investigation: specifics, procedures, conditions, unsafe elements (acts and/or behavior), and corrective action. How, when, where, and why did the accident occur? What procedures were being followed and why? What conditions existed when the accident occurred? What was the primary cause of the accident? What should be done to prevent similar occurrences? Remember: All accidents are caused and could have been prevented by the identification and removal of one or more of the contributing factors. All possible factors must be discussed and identified. Participants in the investigation should agree with the conclusions.

"Employee tripped and fell while en route to the parking lot" does not provide sufficient details. "Employee should be more careful" is not adequate corrective action. "Repaired the defective equipment" does not identify the root cause of the failure. "Additional training will be provided" does not explain why the unsafe behavior occurred. Anyone reading an accident investigation report should be able to visualize exactly how the accident happened and should know the corrective action needed to prevent recurrence is adequate.

Hindsight is effective only when each accident, regardless of disposition, is treated as a matter of real importance. Reporting must be encouraged, and investigation must be prompt. Supervisor and employee must work as a team to identify accident causes and corrective actions needed to prevent similar incidents.

The Process of Foresight: Identification of Potentials

Each accident results from a breakdown in the safety system. Employee behavior/procedures and/or the condition of equipment/environment are always involved. The ability to monitor and evaluate these elements on a continuous basis can identify work practices and conditions that have the ability to produce accidents.

Employee involvement is critical to the foresight approach. Most injuries involve shop employees who "do the work." Their work practices and attitudes determine the level of safety that exists in the shop.

It is not possible to provide continuous monitoring during a work shift. A representative sample of work routines is usually enough, provided the data collected is quantified and reviewed with supervisors. Behavioral trends must be determined; equipment abuse/misuse must be identified; random adjustments in work procedures must be discovered; and work flow must be evaluated. Whenever the potential to cause an accident/injury is apparent, corrective action must be implemented.

"Foresight Programs" must be a joint effort (supervisor and employee) with objectives that are predetermined. Audit teams must be developed, and observations of work practices in designated areas must be scheduled. Typically, an audit might involve a supervisor and employee visiting a work area other than their own to observe work habits/routines. The actual process would be:

1. Select the workstation or operation to be observed before beginning the audit. Concentrate on a single worker or operation. (The "big picture look" often produces very little meaningful information.)
2. Observe the work habits/procedures/equipment being used to perform work. Determine how accidents/injuries can occur.
3. Identify any behavioral changes that occur during the audit.
4. Evaluate housekeeping conditions and equipment in the work area. Is anything "out of place"? Is unnecessary material or equipment located in the work area?
5. Discuss work routine with the worker. Do not "coach" the worker. Ask questions such as, "Why are you using (a particular method)?""Do you think there is a better method?""Have you ever had an accident?" The worker should identify unsafe practices and/or potential accident causes without assistance. Unsafe behavior should not be criticized.
6. Summarize your observations and provide corrective action not indicated by the worker. The worker should take the initiative in correcting unsafe work practices and should accept responsibility for working safely.

Information collected should be combined with data from other audits to establish trends and to identify accident potentials that are inherent within the work process. Accident source reports should be developed and reviewed with supervision. Appropriate corrective action should be implemented. All workers should know that these "get acquainted audits" are being conducted to evaluate safety practices and to provide improvements that will "make work easier and safer" for all employees.

Foresight is an effective means of preventing accidents when workers embrace the concept, regular audits are conducted, and corrective action is provided. Participation must be encouraged and supported by top management. Considerable benefits, including "before-the-fact" accident prevention, can be derived from a well-run program.

Hindsight vs. Foresight

Hindsight determines why accidents occurred; it does not prevent them. Foresight identifies potential accident conditions and provides corrective action before the incident occurs. It is the difference between being proactive and reactive in your safety philosophy. Both methods require employee involvement and an investment of time. The foresight approach does not involve equipment and/or property damage, injury costs, unscheduled production downtime, or product quality issues.

While there is no guarantee that accidents will not continue to occur when the foresight approach is adopted, there is a "comfortable feeling" about the value of accident prevention efforts.

Occupational diseases

An occupational disease is a disease or disorder that is caused by the work or working conditions.

This means that the disease must have developed due to exposures in the workplace and that the correlation between the exposures and the disease is well known in medical research. Or put in another way, it must not be likely, beyond reasonable doubt, that the disease was caused by factors other than work.

Examples of occupational diseases:

- Tennis elbow
- Hearing loss
- Allergy
- Asthma

Exposures in the workplace that may cause some of the above diseases:

- Repetitive work movements
- Work with arms lifted above shoulder height
- Heavy lifting work
- Work in a very noisy environment
- Work with hazardous substances

Recognition of an occupational disease

In order for you to get compensation and other benefits as a consequence of a disease, the disease must be recognised as an industrial injury.

A disease can be recognised in two different ways:

- If the disease and the exposure causing the disease are on the list of occupational diseases, we recognise the disease as an occupational disease
- If the disease is not on the list of occupational diseases, it is still possible to recognise it as an occupational disease if the Occupational Diseases Committee, in their recommendation, state that it is likely, beyond reasonable doubt, that the disease was caused by special factors in the workplace.

SOCIAL SECURITY

CONCEPT AND SCOPE

A society that provides security for its citizens protects them not only from war and disease, but also from the insecurities related to making a living through work. Social security systems provide for basic income in cases of unemployment, illness and injury, old age and retirement, invalidity, family responsibilities such as pregnancy and childcare, and loss of the family breadwinner. Such benefits are important not only for individual workers and their families but also for their communities as a whole. By providing health care, income security and social services, social security enhances productivity and contributes to the dignity and full realization of the individual. Social security systems also promote gender equality through the adoption of measures to ensure that women who have children enjoy equal opportunities in the labour market. For employers and enterprises, social security helps maintain a stable workforce adaptable to change. Finally, by providing a safety net in case of economic crisis, social security serves as a fundamental element of social cohesion, thereby helping to ensure social peace and a positive engagement with globalization and economic development. Despite these advantages, only 20% of the world's population have adequate social security coverage, while more than half lack any kind of social security coverage at all.

SOCIAL SECURITY FACTS

- Established on Aug. 14, 1935 as an independent agency.
- Its primary responsibilities were for old age insurance, unemployment compensation and public assistance.
- Social Security is financed through payroll taxes. Employer and employees each pay 6.2% of wages up to $118,500 in 2016. The self- employees pay 12.4%.
- The program, as it stands, is expected to be depleted in the 2030s.
- To learn more about Social Security, you can sing up for a "my Social Security account." https://www.ssa.gov/myaccount/
- To learn more about Social Security, or for more questions, visit the agency's website: https//www.ssa.gov/

Further Social Security Instruments

A later generation of conventions expands the scope of protection provided by Convention No. 102. While offering a higher level of protection in terms of scope and level of benefits to be guaranteed, these instruments authorize certain exceptions which ensure flexibility.

The benefits provided under Convention No. 102 and under later conventions are outlined below. This information does not include provisions on the duration and conditions of entitlement to benefits, derogations allowed under these instruments, or higher levels of benefits provided by relevant recommendations.

Medical Care

- provides for preventive care, general practitioner care, including home visits, specialist care, essential pharmaceutical supplies as prescribed, prenatal, confinement and postnatal care by medical practitioners or qualified midwives, and hospitalization where necessary.
- provides the same benefits as Convention No. 102, plus dental care and medical rehabilitation.

Sickness Benefit

- periodical payments, corresponding to at least 45% of the reference wage.
- periodical payments, corresponding to at least 60% of the reference wage. Also provides for funeral expenses in case of death of the beneficiary.

Unemployment Benefit

- periodical payments, corresponding to at least 45% of the reference wage.
- periodical payments, corresponding to at least 50% of the reference wage. Beyond the initial period, possibility of applying special rules of calculation. Nevertheless, the total benefits to which the unemployed may be entitled must guarantee them healthy and reasonable living conditions in accordance with national standards.

Old-age Benefit

- periodical payments, corresponding to at least 40% of the reference wage. The rates of relevant benefits must be revised following substantial changes in the general level of earnings and /or the cost of living.
- periodical payments, corresponding to at least 45% of the reference wage. Same conditions as Convention No. 102 relating to the revision of rates.

Employment Injury Benefit

- medical care, periodical payments corresponding to at least 50% of the reference wage in cases of incapacity for work or invalidity. Benefits for widow and dependent children in case of death of breadwinner with periodical payments corresponding to at least 40% of the reference wage. Possibility of converting periodical payments into lump sums under certain conditions. Except in the case of incapacity for work, obligation to revise the rates of periodical payments following substantial changes in the cost of living.
- same as Convention No. 102, plus certain types of care at the place of work. Periodical payments, corresponding to at least 60% of the reference wage in cases of incapacity for work or invalidity, benefits for widow, the disabled and dependent widower, and dependent children in case of death of breadwinner, with periodical payments corresponding to at least 50% of the reference wage. Obligation to prescribe minimum amount for these payments, possibility of converting payments into a lump sum under certain conditions, and supplementary benefits for disabled persons requiring the constant help of a third person.

Family Benefit

- provides either periodical payments or the provision of food, clothing, housing, holidays or domestic help, or a combination of these.

Maternity Benefit

- medical care including at least prenatal, confinement and postnatal care either by medical practitioners or by qualified midwives and hospitalization where necessary; periodical payments, corresponding to at least 45% of the reference wage.
- medical benefits including prenatal, childbirth and postnatal care, as well as hospitalization care when necessary; cash benefits to ensure that the woman can maintain herself and her child in proper conditions of health and with a suitable standard of living. At least two-thirds of previous earnings or comparable amount.

Invalidity Benefit

- periodical payments, corresponding to at least 40% of the reference wage; the rates of relevant benefits must be revised following substantial changes in the general level of earnings and/or in the cost of living.
- periodical payments corresponding to at least 50% of the reference wage; the rates of relevant benefits must be revised following substantial changes in the general level of earnings and/or in the cost of living.

Survivors' Benefit

- periodical payments, corresponding to at least 40% of the reference wage; the rates of relevant benefits must be revised following substantial changes in the general level of earnings and/or in the cost of living. .
- periodical payments corresponding to at least 45% of the reference wage; the rates of relevant benefits must be revised following substantial changes in the general level of earnings and/or in the cost of living.

YEAR END REVIEW 2019: MINISTRY OF LABOUR AND EMPLOYMENT

Ministry of Labour and Employment has taken a number of initiatives for bringing transparency and accountability through reforms and enforcement of Labour Laws, with the objective of strengthening the safety, security, health, social security for every worker and bringing ease of compliance for running an establishment to catalyze creation of employment opportunities. These initiatives include governance reforms through use of e-governance measures and legislative reforms by simplifying, amalgamating and rationalizing the existing labour laws into 4 labour codes. Two mega pension schemes were launched during the year for old age protection and social security of unorganized workers.

Legislative Initiatives: Labour Law Reforms

Labour Codes. As per the recommendations of the 2nd National Commission on Labour, Ministry has taken steps for codification of existing Central labour laws into 4 Codes by simplifying, amalgamating and rationalizing the relevant provisions of the Central Labour laws. At present, the Ministry has been working on to simplify, amalgamate & rationalize the provisions of the existing Central labour laws into 4 Labour Codes.

(I) **Labour Code on Wages.** The Code on Wages, 2019 subsumes 4 existing Laws, viz. the Minimum Wages Act, 1948; the Payment of Wages Act, 1936; the Payment of Bonus Act, 1965; and the Equal Remuneration Act, 1976. It has been passed by both Houses of the Parliament and assented to by the President on 08.08.2019.

(II) **Labour Code on Industrial Relations.** The draft Labour Code on Industrial Relations subsumes the existing Laws viz. The Trade Union Act, 1926; The Industrial Employment (Standing Orders) Act, 1946; The Industrial Disputes Act, 1947. The Code has been introduced in the Lok Sabha on 28.11.2019.

(III) **Labour Code on Social Security & Welfare.** The draft Code on Social Security subsumes Labour Acts like: The Employees' Compensation Act, 1923, The Maternity Benefit Act, 1961, The Payment of Gratuity Act, 1972, The Unorganized Workers' Social Security Act, 2008 etc.
The Code has been introduced in Lok Sabha on December 11, 2019.

(IV) **Labour Code on Occupational Safety, Health & Working Conditions.** The Occupational Safety, Health & Working Conditions Code, 2019 subsumes the 13 Labour Acts like: The Factories Act,

1948, The Plantation Labour Act, 1951, The Mines Act, 1952, The Building and Other Constructions Workers' (Regulation of Employment and Conditions of Service) Act, 1996 etc.

The Occupational Safety Health & Working Conditions Code, 2019 was introduced in the Lok Sabha on 23.07.2019. Presently, the Code has been referred to the Parliamentary Standing Committee on Labour for examination.

Governance Reforms Through Technology

Shram Suvidha Portal

The Ministry of Labour& Employment has developed a unified Web Portal 'ShramSuvidha Portal', to bring transparency and accountability in enforcement of labour laws and ease complexity of compliance.

Allotment of unique Labour Identification Number (LIN) to Units after registration to facilitate online inspection & compliance was started on the Portal with its launch on 16.10.2014 itself. Unique Labour Identification Number (LIN) has been allotted to 27,81,065 units as on 08.11.2019.

Transparent Labour Inspection Scheme in Central Sphere was started on the Portal with its launch on 16.10.2014 itself. Since the launch of the Labour Inspection Scheme, 5,24,189 inspection reports across the four Central Labour Enforcement Agencies have been uploaded on ShramSuvidha Portal.

ONLINE RETURN. Unified Online Annual Returns have been made mandatory in respect of eight (8) Central Labour Acts, namely, the Payment of Wages Act, 1936, the Minimum Wages Act, 1948, the Maternity Benefit Act, 1961, the Payment of Bonus Act, 1965, the Industrial Disputes Act, 1947. The Contract Labour (Regulation and Abolition) Act, 1970, the Inter-State Migrant Workmen (Regulation of Employment and Conditions of Service) Act, 1979, and the Building and Other Construction Workers (Regulation of Employment and Condition of Service) (BOCW) Act, 1996. These Returns which were half yearly/annually earlier, now need to be filed by all employers annually only and are to be filed online. 1,08,711 online returns have been filed on the ShramSuvidha Portal as on 08.11.2019 Since launch of the Online Annual Return.

31,047 online returns have been filed on the ShramSuvidha Portal till November 08, 2019 under Mines Act, 1952 (Coal Mines Regulations, Metallurgical Mines Regulations and Oil Mines Regulations).

Unified monthly Electronic Challan-cum-Return (ECR) for EPFO and ESIC has been made operational.

COMMON REGISTRATION. Common Registration form for EPFO and ESIC has been made operational. 1,27,544 units have been registered with EPFO & 1,07,681 units have been registered with ESIC as on November 08, 2019.

Common Registration under three Central Acts namely the Building and Other Construction Workers (Regulation of Employment and Condition of Service) Act, 1996, the Inter-State Migrant Workmen (Regulation of Employment and conditions of Service) Act, 1979 and the Contract Labour (Regulation and Abolition) Act, 1970 is being provided online on ShramSuvidha Portal. 6052 registrations have been issued using this facility as on 08.11.2019.

Licenses under two Central Acts, namely, the, Inter-State Migrant Workmen (Regulation of Employment and Conditions of Service) Act, 1979 and the Contract Labour (Regulation and Abolition) Act, 1970 have been made online. 20,316 licenses have been issued using this facility as on 08.11.2019.

State Integration

Integration of States with ShramSuvidha Portal is under way. As on date, Haryana, Gujarat, Rajasthan, Uttar Pradesh, Madhya Pradesh, Maharashtra, Punjab, Uttarakhand and Delhi are being integrated with the Portal. Data is being shared and LIN is being allotted to the establishments covered by the state labour enforcement agencies.

Start Up India

Facility for exemption from Labour Inspections under six (6) Central Labour Acts is being provided to the Start-ups which submit self certified declarations through ShramSuvidha Portal.

State/UT Governments have been advised to regulate the inspections for the Start-Ups, wherever applicable and extend the self-certification compliance regime from 3 years to 5 years. 27 States/UTs have taken action on the advisory dated 12.01.2016 /06.04.2017 issued by this Ministry for self-certification and to regulate inspection under the four (4) labour laws *viz.* the Building & Other Construction Workers (Regulation of Employment and Conditions of Service) Act, 1996, the Inter-State Migrant Workmen (Regulation of Employment and Conditions of Service) Act, 1979, the Payment of Gratuity Act, 1972 and the Contract Labour (Regulation and Abolition) Act, 1970 for the start-ups wherever applicable.

Social Security Schemes

Government of India has launched two pension schemes for old age protection and social security of Unorganised Workers in 2019.

Pradhan MantriShram Yogi Maan-dhan (PM-SYM), a voluntary and contributory pension scheme, was launched in February, 2019 for the benefit of unorganized workers. It is central sector scheme open to unorganised workers, whose monthly income is Rs.15000/- or below and who has an Aadhar number as well as savings bank / jandhan account. The minimum age for joining the scheme is 18 years and the maximum is 40 years. Under the scheme, minimum assured monthly pension of Rs.3000/- will be provided to the beneficiaries from the age of 60 years onwards. Enrolment to the Scheme is done through the Common Service Centres, with its network of 3.50 lakh Centres across the country. In addition eligible persons can also self-enroll through visiting the portal www.maandhan.in. Under the scheme, the subscriber is required to pay the prescribed monthly contribution amount and the Central Government provides equal contribution. Life Insurance Corporation of India (LIC) is the Pension Fund Manager and shall be responsible for pension pay-out. **Total number of 39,00,525 beneficiaries under PM-SYM have been enrolled as on 10.12.2019.**

National Pension Scheme for Traders, Shopkeepers and Self-Employed Persons has been launched on 12.09.2019. It is a voluntary and contributory pension scheme. Enrolment to the Scheme is done through the Common Service Centres, with its network of 3.50 lakh Centres across the country. In addition eligible persons can also self-enroll through visiting the portal www.maandhan.in. The traders in the age group of 18-40 years with an annual turnover, not exceeding Rs.1.5 crore and who are not a member of EPFO/ESIC/NPS/PM-SYM or an income tax payer, can join the scheme. Under the scheme, 50% monthly contribution is payable by the beneficiary and equal matching contribution is paid by the Central Government. Subscribers, after attaining the age of 60 years, are eligible for a monthly minimum assured pension of Rs.3,000/-. **Total number of 20,000 beneficiaries under NPS-Traders have been enrolled as on 10.122019.**

Pension Week was also celebrated in all the States/UTs w.e.f. 30th November to 06th December, 2019 in coordination with Common Service Centres, to increase the enrolments under both the Schemes, i.e. PM-SYM and NPS-Traders. A Central level function was inaugurated on 30.11.2019 by Minister for Labour and Employment launching the Pension Week/Pension Saptah. All the State Governments/UT Governments were requested for popularizing and bringing more awareness about the scheme. The progress of the Scheme is being reviewed regularly in the Ministry for taking initiatives under Mission Mode.

Major Steps taken in EPFO

Three new apps to improve service delivery of subscribers were launched by Shri Santosh Kumar Gangwar, Minister of State (I/C) for Labour and Employment on EPFO Foundation Day. The details of three important digital initiatives of EPFO are as under:

1. **Online Facility for UAN generation by worker.** *Now any workers can obtain Universal Account Number (UAN) directly on EPFO website which enrolls them for PF, Pension and Life Insurance benefits and a worker need not depend on his employer alone for UAN.* This is in the direction of ease of living and ensuring universal social security.
2. **EPS Pensioner's PPO in DigiLocker website/Application (APP)** EPFO integrates with DigiLocker of NeGD to create depository of electronic PPOs which is accessible to individual pensioners. This is a move towards paperless system and ease of living for pensioners.
3. **e-Inspections.** Digital interface of EPFO with employers: The E-Inspection Form would be available in user login of employers not filing ECR which enables employer to inform either closure of business or unpaid dues with proposal for payment. It will nudge employers for compliant behavior and prevent undue harassment of non-willful defaulters and eliminate inspector raj.

Central Board of Trustees, EPF recommends crediting of 8.65% rate of interest on Accumulations in the EPF Member's Account for the year 2018-19:

In 224th meeting of the Central Board of Trustees, EPF under the chairmanship of Union Minister of State for Labour and Employment (I/C) Shri Santosh Kumar Gangwar, the Central Board recommended crediting of 8.65 % rate of interest on the EPF accumulations in the EPF member's account for the year 2018-19.

New Initiatives taken in Central Board of Trustees (CBT) meeting held on 21 August 2019:

1. **Amendment in Employees' pension Scheme 1995.** In a major decision, the Central Board of Trustees (CBT) EPF in a meeting held at Hyderabad on 21 August 2019, approved the proposal to recommend for amendment in Employees' Pension Scheme (EPS) 1995 for restoration of commuted value of pension to the Pensioners after 15 years of drawing commutation which will benefit approx. 6.3 lakhs pensioners. This was a long pending demand of the pensioner
2. **Launch of Revamped EPFIGMS 2.0 Version.** The Chairman CBT also launched the revamped EPFIGMS 2.0 version which will benefit more than 5 crores subscribers and lakhs of employers by speedy and smooth resolution of grievances.

Selection of ETF Manufacturers: The Board approved the decision to choose the Exchange Traded Fund (ETF) manufacturers through public bidding by 30/10/2019, extension of the term of the present ETF manufacturers (SBI MF and UTI MF) till then and also to authorized the Finance Investment & Audit Committee (FIAC) to conduct the exercise of choosing ETF manufacturers.

Allocation of investment in Nifty 50 and Sensex. The Board approved the proposal that the fund allocation between Nifty 50 and Sensex ETFs be divided evenly, i.e. in the ratio of 50% to 50%.

Appointment of a Consultant in addition to M/s. CRISIL Ltd. The Board approved the nomination of members from employer's and employee side in a Committee constituted to select and appoint a separate Agency/Consultant in addition to M/s. CRISIL limited, inter-alia to review the working of the Portfolio Managers (PMs), assist the investment Committee in redemption of ETFs, etc.

Appointment of Portfolio Managers for managing funds of Central Board, EPF. The Central Board approved Request for Proposal (RFP) document for appointment of Portfolio Managers and recommendation of the FIAC on appointment of Portfolio Managers.

Exercise of early redemption options available in DHFL Bonds. The Board approved for early redemption option in DHFL bonds recommended by FIAC.

Major Steps Taken In ESIC

Rate reduction in ESI Contribution. The ESI Corporation has reduced rates of ESI Contribution being paid by employees and employers covered under ESI Scheme from 6.5 % (Employees' share 1.75% & Employers' share 4.75%) to 4% (Employees' share 0.75% & Employers' share 3.25%) with effect from 01.07.2019. This reduction of contribution rates, will ensures financial relief to employers and employees. However, the healthcare *benefits* under the *ESI* scheme *will* remain the *same*. The decision will benefit 36 million workers and 1.28 million employers.

Health Passbook for ESI Beneficiaries. ESIC has introduced a Health Passbook for ESI Beneficiaries in Phased manner. This Health Passbook serves as a user-friendly mechanism for beneficiary identification, recording of clinical finding and consultation advice by the Insurance Medical Practitioner(s). Salient feature of Health Passbook is as under: -

- Separate Passbook with Unique Health ID, QR code and photograph of Insured Persons and his/her family members.
- Serves for beneficiaries identification & recording of clinical findings and consultation advice by ESI Doctors/IMPs.
- Passbook would be issued by the ESIC Branch Offices in a phased manner.

Insured Persons of ESIC from newly implemented area to get treatment under Ayushman Bharat – Pradhan Mantri Jan ArogyaYojana (PMJAY). ESIC has decided to provide cashless medical care services to entitled Insured Persons and Beneficiaries under Ayushman Bharat package rates in newly implemented area of 102 designated Districts through PMJAY empanelled hospitals up to a maximum limit of Rs.5.00 lakh, beyond which individual case will be channelled to ESIC for seeking approval for further expenditure on ESI beneficiaries. Similarly, PMJAY beneficiaries may get in-house medical treatment services as per Ayushman Bharat approved packages from underutilized ESI Hospitals.

ESIC – Chinta Se Mukti app launched. The Corporation has also **launched the ESIC "Chinta Se Mukti" app available** on the UMANG platform to facilitate stakeholders to view contribution details, eligibility for benefits, claim status, etc. in their Mobile Handset.

Extending medical benefits to Non-IPs. The Corporation has extended its medical services to Non-Insured Persons (General Public) in its under-utilized hospitals. Now, Non-IPs can avail medical services from underutilized ESIC Hospital, at Alwar (Rajasthan), Bihta (Bihar), Gulbarga (Karnataka), Bareilly Varanasi, Sarojani Nagar (Lucknow) &Jajmau (Kanpur) on a nominal charge of Rs.10/- for OPD Consultation and at 25% of CGHS package rates for IPD.

Unified Website. In order to maintain the corporate identity of ESIC and to have a repository of common information, and also to have uniformity in design and content, a Unified Website www.esic.nic.in has been launched. All the Regional Offices/Sub-Regional Offices, ESIC Hospitals and ESIC Medical Institutions & Hospitals have been made part of this single unified website.

ESIC- contributing excellence in sports. ESIC had recruited 135 meritorious sports persons including Shri Pramod Bhagat, ace para-shuttler from all across India during the year 2016. Shri Pramod Bhagat, an ESIC employee at Regional Office, Bhubaneswar has received prestigious Arjuna Award for the current year on 29th Aug., 2019. Shri Pramod Bhagat has many tournaments to his credit including five international titles in six tournaments he participated. He won a gold medal in the men's singles SL 3 category at the BWF Para-Badminton World Championships in Basel. Bhagat said he is now focusing to clinch a gold medal in the Olympics.

Strengthening of Medical Infrastructure. In order to provide in-house quality medical services in the major ESIC Hospitals, of late, ESIC has procured state-of-the-art medical equipments viz. MRI, CT Scan etc. for ICU, Secondary & Super Speciality care.

National Career Service Project (NCS). The Ministry is implementing the National Career Service (NCS) Project as a Mission Mode Project for transformation of the National Employment Service to provide a variety of employment related services like career counselling, vocational guidance, information on skill development courses, apprenticeship, internships etc. The services under NCS are available online and can be accessed directly, through Career Centres, Common Service Centres, post offices, mobile devices, cyber cafes etc. The various stakeholders on the NCS platform include job-seekers, industries, employers, employment exchanges (career centres), training providers, educational institutions and placement organizations.

The progress of NCS Portal is given below:

NATIONAL CAREER SERVICE

Sl. No.	Parameters	Number as on 1st February, 2021
1.	Active Jobseekers Registered	1,04,51,862
2.	Active Employers Registered	1,23,234
3.	Total Vacancies Mobilized	1,04550

With the increased focus of Government on Career Counselling, the Ministry proposes to create a network of Career Counsellors where the Career Centres will become the hub of Career Counselling in their area. Under the process, 5645 Active Career Counsellors from various States/UTs have got registered at NCS Portal.

The NCS Project also envisaged setting up of Model Career Centres (MCCs) to be established in collaboration with States and other institutions to deliver employment services. Approval for 146 MCCs has been accorded (including 07 MCCs on non-funding basis). These model centres can be replicated by the States from their own resources. The Government now, keeping in view of the importance of the employment as a thrust area in Government Schemes, and to provide employment related services to maximum job seekers and other stakeholders has decided to establish 100 more Model Career Centres (MCCs) thereby extending the geographical coverage of the scheme increasing number of Government funded MCCs to 200 during 14th Finance commission (2017-2020). Proposals were received from different States. On the recommendations of the Appraisal Committee, Government has approved 171 (including 07 on non-funding basis) Model Career Centres. Further 37 more model career centers have been recommend by the Inter Ministerial Appraisal Committee in the meeting held on November 20, 2019.

National Career Service Centres for Differently Abled (NCSC-DAs). National Career Service Centres for Differently Abled (NCSC-DAs) are functioning in the country under the administrative control of Directorate General of Employment, M/O Labour& Employment. These Centres evaluate residual capacities of Persons with Disabilities, provide Vocational Training, and extend Vocational Rehabilitation assistances etc. to Persons with Disabilities (PWDs). The Services of NCSC-DAs are open to Persons with Disabilities irrespective of the gender and education in the category of Locomotor, Visual & Hearing impaired, Mild Mental Retardation and Leprosy Cured.

6644 Candidates have been rehabilitated upto October 31, 2019 by NCSC-Das.

National Career Service Centre Centres (NCSCs) for SC/STs: Directorate General of Employment is implementing the scheme for "Welfare of SC/ST job seekers through Coaching, Vocational Guidance and Training and Introduction of new courses in existing National Career Service Centre Centres (NCSCs) for SC/STs and Establishment of new NCSCs in the States not covered so far" Under the scheme, National Career Service Centre Centres (NCSCs) for SC/STs has been set up by Govt. of India, Ministry of Labour& Employment, DGE to enhance the employability of SC/ST job seekers through coaching/training. So far 25 National Career Service Centre Centres for SCs/STs have been set up.

67761 candidates have been provided guidance and counselling services, 5621 students were trained in typing and shorthand and 1050 candidates were trained in computer skills by NCSC-SC/STs upto October 31, 2019.

Pradhan Mantri Rojgar Protsahan Yojana (PMRPY). Under the scheme, Government of India is paying Employer's full contribution i.e. 12% towards EPF and EPS both (as admissible from time to time) for a period of three years to the new employees through EPFO.

This scheme has a dual benefit, where, on the one hand, the employer is incentivised for increasing the employment base of workers in the establishment, and on the other hand, a large number of workers will find jobs in such establishments. A direct benefit is that these workers will have access to social security benefits of the organized sector. All the beneficiaries under this scheme are Aadhaar Seeded.

152778 Establishments covering 12165587 Beneficiaries have benefitted till November 25, 2019 under Pradhan Mantri Rojgar Protsahan Yojana (PMRPY).

Brief of Workers Education Scheme

The Dattopant Thengadi National Board for Workers Education & Development (renaming of CBWE), an autonomous body under the Ministry of Labour & Employment, Government of India conducts the Workers Education Programmes of varied nature and duration in the country through its 50 Regional and 7 Sub-Regional Directorates spread Kashmir to Kannyakumari and Leh and laddakh for all categories without making any distinction on the basis of male and female in Organised, Unorganised and Rural Sectors. The DTNBWED training programmes aim at creating desired awareness among the workers in general and unorganized/ rural workers in particular about their rights and entitlements under various welfare schemes of the Central /State government etc.

The Board has organized 1625 training programme organized sector workers, 1120 programme conducted for unorganized and 150 for rural workers.

SOCIAL INSURANCE AND SOCIAL ASSISTANCE

Social security is a very comprehensive term. The two important means of providing social security are social insurance and social assistance. Thus, it may be called to be the two faces of the same coin. Both of these are part of a social security system.

Social Insurance

Social Insurance is one of the devices to prevent individual from falling to the death of poverty, misery and to help him in times of emergencies. Insurance involves the setting aside of some money in order to provide compensation against loss resulting from a particular emergency. Thus, social insurance is a co-operative device which aims at granting adequate benefits to the insured on the compulsory basis in time of unemployment, sickness and other emergencies. Sir William Beveridge has defined social insurance as giving in returns for contribution benefits upto substance level as of right and without means test so that individual may build freely upon it. Thus social insurance implies both that it is compulsory and that men stand together with their fellows.

This is based on the principles of compulsory mutual aid. The principal elements of social insurance are:

(i) Social insurance is financed by contributions which are normally shared between employers and workers, with perhaps, state participation in the form of a supplementary contribution or other subsidy from the general revenue.

(ii) Participation is compulsory with few exceptions.

(iii) Contributions are accumulated in special funds out of which benefits are paid.

(iv) Surplus funds not needed to pay, current benefits are invested to earn further income.

(v) A person's right to benefit is secured by his contribution record without any test of need or means.

(vi) The contribution and benefit rates are often related to what the person is or has been earning.

Social Assistance

Social assistance refers to the assistance rendered by the society to the poor and needy persons voluntarily without placing any obligation on them to make any contribution to be entitled to relief such as workmen's compensation, maternity benefit and old age pension etc. Thus, one may say that a social assistance scheme provides benefits for persons of small means granted as of right in amount sufficient to meet a minimum standard of need and financed from taxation.

Social assistance represents the unilateral obligations of the community towards its dependant group. It is provided by the society or the **government** to the poor and needy individual. The principal feature of social assistance are: (1) the whole cost of the Programme is met by the State and local units of Government (2) benefits are paid as of legal right in prescribed categories of need (3) in assessing need, a person's other income and resources are taken into account certain resources such as a reasonable level of personal savings are disregarded and (4) the benefit grant is designed to bring a person's total income upto a community determined maximum taking into account other factors such as family size and unavoidable fixed obligations such as rent grants are not related to applicant's previous earnings or customary standard of living. The difference between social insurance and social assistance are as follows:

(a) Social assistance is purely a government affair while social insurance is partly financed by the State.

(b) Social assistance is given gratis while social insurance is granted to those persons who pay a contribution.

(c) Besides, a social insurance does not insist upon a means test upon a means test and benefits are granted without it while social assistance is granted only if certain conditions prescribed by the Government are fulfilled.

Social Insurance and Commercial Insurance

Social insurance is fundamentally different from **Commercial** Insurance. The inspiring motive of social insurance is the maintenance of minimum standard of living whereas there exists no such motive in case of Commercial Insurance. Moreover, while commercial insurance provides against an individual's risk only, Social Insurance is undertaken to meet a chain of contingencies of diverse nature and intensity. Besides, in social insurance the benefits received by the beneficiaries are usually much larger than the contribution they are required to pay towards the fund for the purpose whereas in Commercial Insurance, the policy benefits are according to premium paid. The social insurance is generally compulsory while commercial insurance is necessarily voluntary.

MULTIPLE CHOICE QUESTIONS

1. Which of the following is one of the objectives of labour welfare?
   (1) Promoting employer profitability
   (2) Ensuring maximum working hours for employees
   (3) Ensuring employee wellbeing
   (4) All of the above
2. Which of the following are included under labour welfare?
   (1) Education and training
   (2) Employee safety and health
   (3) Workers participation in management
   (4) All of the above
3. Which of the following is not a type of labour welfare?
   (1) Social security
   (2) Health benefits
   (3) Education and training
   (4) Employee termination benefits
4. Which of the following types of labour welfare deals with providing medical care and protection to workers?
   (1) Employee safety and health
   (2) Social security
   (3) Education and training
   (4) Workers participation in management
5. Which of the following types of labour welfare deals with providing retirement benefits, such as pension and gratuity, to workers?
   (1) Employee termination benefits
   (2) Social security
   (3) Education and training
   (4) Workers participation in management
6. Which of the following types of labour welfare deals with providing financial assistance to workers in case of disability or death?
   (1) Social security
   (2) Employee safety and health
   (3) Education and training
   (4) Workers participation in management
7. Which of the following is not a scope of labour welfare?
   (1) Ensuring employee satisfaction
   (2) Enhancing employee productivity
   (3) Promoting employee engagement
   (4) All of the above are scopes of labour welfare
8. Which of the following is not a principle of labour welfare?
   (1) Voluntarism
   (2) Non-discrimination
   (3) Competition
   (4) The right to participation
9. Which of the following is not a benefit of labour welfare?
   (1) Improved employee morale
   (2) Reduced employee turnover
   (3) Increased employee absenteeism
   (4) Enhanced employee loyalty
10. Which of the following is not a challenge of implementing labour welfare?
    (1) Cost
    (2) Cultural diversity
    (3) Resistance to change
    (4) The elimination of job security
11. Which of the following is not a type of maternity benefit under the Maternity Benefit Act, 1961?
    (1) Payment of medical bonus
    (2) Leave for miscarriage
    (3) Leave for adoption
    (4) None of the above

12. Which of the following is the maximum duration of paid maternity leave under the Maternity Benefit Act, 1961?
(1) 12 weeks (2) 16 weeks
(3) 24 weeks (4) 26 weeks

13. Which of the following types of workers is not covered under the Maternity Benefit Act, 1961?
(1) Women employed in mines
(2) Women employed in factories
(3) Women employed in shops
(4) None of the above

14. Which of the following is not a major objective of the Payment of Bonus Act, 1965?
(1) To ensure payment of bonus to employees
(2) To provide for payment of bonus as a minimum right to employees
(3) To promote industrial peace
(4) To regulate the payment of bonus

15. Which of the following is the maximum amount of bonus that can be paid under the Payment of Bonus Act, 1965?
(1) 8.33% of the salary earned during the accounting year
(2) 10% of the salary earned during the accounting year
(3) 20% of the salary earned during the accounting year
(4) None of the above

16. Which of the following types of organizations are exempted from the Payment of Bonus Act, 1965?
(1) Educational institutions
(2) Hospitals
(3) Export-oriented organizations
(4) All of the above are exempted

17. Which of the following is the maximum duration of work hours under the Factories Act, 1948?
(1) 8 hours a day and 48 hours a week
(2) 10 hours a day and 60 hours a week
(3) 12 hours a day and 72 hours a week
(4) None of the above

18. Which of the following is not a type of leave under the Factories Act, 1948?
(1) Annual leave with wages
(2) Casual leave
(3) Paternity leave (4) Sick leave

19. Which of the following types of accidents are covered under the Workmen's Compensation Act, 1923?
(1) Accidents that occur while commuting to work
(2) Accidents that occur during lunch breaks
(3) Accidents that occur during work hours
(4) None of the above

20. Which of the following is the maximum amount of compensation payable for permanent disablement under the Workmen's Compensation Act, 1923?
(1) Rs. 2 lakh (2) Rs. 5 lakh
(3) Rs. 10 lakh (4) None of these

21. Who is liable to pay compensation under the Workmen's Compensation Act, 1923?
(1) The worker (2) The insurer
(3) The employer (4) None of these

22. Which of the following is not required by law to be covered under the Employees' State Insurance Act, 1948?
(1) Employees earning less than Rs. 21,000 per month
(2) Employees employed in hazardous industries
(3) Employees working in establishments that have at least 10 employees
(4) All of the above are required to be covered

23. Which of the following is the maximum percentage of the wage that can be contributed towards the Employees' State Insurance Scheme under the Employees' State Insurance Act, 1948?
(1) 1.75% of the wage (2) 3% of the wage
(3) 6% of the wage
(4) None of the above

24. Which of the following types of medical benefits are provided to workers under the Employees' State Insurance Act, 1948?
(1) Medical treatment
(2) Sickness benefit

(3) Permanent disablement benefit
(4) All of the above

25. Which of the following types of workers are covered under the National Pension System?
(1) Employees of central and state governments
(2) Employees of private organizations
(3) Self-employed individuals
(4) All of the above

26. Which of the following is not a type of welfare activity under the National Pension System?
(1) Retirement planning
(2) Pension fund management
(3) Financial literacy
(4) All of the above are types of welfare activities

27. Which of the following types of workers are covered under the Employee Provident Fund Scheme?
(1) All employees
(2) Only employees of government institutions
(3) Only employees of private organizations
(4) None of the above

28. Which of the following is the percentage of the amount that can be withdrawn from the employee provident fund in case of unemployment for more than 2 months?
(1) 50% of the amount
(2) 75% of the amount
(3) 100% of the amount
(4) None of the above

29. Which of the following is a criterion to be eligible for withdrawal of the amount from the employee provident fund?
(1) The employee should have worked for at least 5 years
(2) The employee should have worked for at least 10 years
(3) The employee should have worked for at least 15 years
(4) None of the above

30. Which of the following is not a type of welfare activity under the Employee Provident Fund Scheme?
(1) Insurance benefits
(2) Pension benefits
(3) Education and training
(4) All of the above are types of welfare activities

31. Which of the following is not a type of labour welfare activity under the Plantations Labour Act, 1951?
(1) Housing facilities
(2) Medical facilities
(3) Pension benefits
(4) All of the above are types of labour welfare activities

32. Which of the following types of workers are covered under the Plantations Labour Act, 1951?
(1) Workers employed in tea, coffee or rubber plantations
(2) Workers employed in automobile manufacturing
(3) Workers employed in information technology sector
(4) None of the above

33. Which of the following is not a type of welfare activity under the Building and Other Construction Workers' Welfare Cess Act, 1996?
(1) Education and training
(2) Social security
(3) Labour welfare fund
(4) All of the above are types of welfare activities

34. Which of the following is not a criterion to be eligible for benefits under the Building and Other Construction Workers' Welfare Cess Act, 1996?
(1) The worker should have worked for a minimum of 90 days in the last 12 months
(2) The worker should be registered under the Act
(3) The worker should be employed in construction industry
(4) None of the above

35. Which of the following is the percentage of cess that needs to be deposited in the labour

welfare fund under the Building and Other Construction Workers' Welfare Cess Act, 1996?

(1) 1% of the cost of construction
(2) 2% of the cost of construction
(3) 3% of the cost of construction
(4) None of the above

36. Which of the following is not a type of labour welfare activity under the Beedi and Cigar Workers Welfare Fund Act, 1976?

(1) Education and training
(2) Housing facilities
(3) Pension benefits
(4) All of the above are types of labour welfare activities

37. Which of the following types of workers are covered under the Beedi and Cigar Workers Welfare Fund Act, 1976?

(1) Beedi and cigar workers
(2) Workers employed in automobile manufacturing
(3) Workers employed in information technology sector
(4) None of the above

38. Which of the following is not a type of welfare activity under the Iron Ore Mines, Manganese Ore Mines and Chrome Ore Mines Labour Welfare Fund Act, 1976?

(1) Health benefits
(2) Education and training
(3) Housing facilities
(4) All of the above are types of welfare activities

39. Which of the following types of workers are covered under the Iron Ore Mines, Manganese Ore Mines and Chrome Ore Mines Labour Welfare Fund Act, 1976?

(1) Workers employed in iron ore mines, manganese ore mines and chrome ore mines
(2) Workers employed in automobile manufacturing
(3) Workers employed in information technology sector
(4) None of the above

40. Which of the following is not a type of labour welfare activity under the Dock Workers (Safety, Health and Welfare) Act, 1986?

(1) Medical facilities
(2) Education and training
(3) Pension benefits
(4) All of the above are types of labour welfare activities

41. Which of the following types of workers are covered under the Dock Workers (Safety, Health and Welfare) Act, 1986?

(1) Dock workers
(2) Workers employed in automobile manufacturing
(3) Workers employed in information technology sector
(4) None of the above

42. Which of the following is not a type of welfare activity under the Mines Act, 1952?

(1) Health benefits
(2) Education and training
(3) Housing facilities
(4) All of the above are types of welfare activities

43. Which of the following types of workers are covered under the Mines Act, 1952?

(1) Workers employed in mines
(2) Workers employed in automobile manufacturing
(3) Workers employed in information technology sector
(4) None of the above

44. Which of the following is not a type of labour welfare activity under the Beedi Workers Welfare Cess Act, 1977?

(1) Education and training
(2) Housing facilities
(3) Social security
(4) All of the above are types of labour welfare activities

45. Which of the following types of workers are covered under the Beedi Workers Welfare Cess Act, 1977?

(1) Beedi workers
(2) Workers employed in automobile manufacturing

(3) Workers employed in information technology sector
(4) None of the above

46. Which of the following is not a duty of an employer under the Contract Labour (Regulation and Abolition) Act, 1970?
(1) Maintaining record of contract labour
(2) Providing adequate working conditions to contract labour
(3) Providing compensation in case of accidents to contract labour
(4) None of the above

47. Which of the following types of workers are covered under the Contract Labour (Regulation and Abolition) Act, 1970?
(1) Contract labour
(2) Workers employed in automobile manufacturing
(3) Workers employed in information technology sector
(4) None of the above

48. Which of the following is the percentage of workers that should be employed through contractors to be covered under the Contract Labour (Regulation and Abolition) Act, 1970?
(1) 20 (2) 30
(3) 40 (4) None of these

49. Which of the following is not a type of welfare activity under the Inter-State Migrant Workmen (Regulation of Employment and Conditions of Service) Act, 1979?
(1) Medical facilities
(2) Education and training
(3) Social security
(4) All of the above are types of welfare activities

50. Which of the following types of workers are covered under the Inter-State Migrant Workmen (Regulation of Employment and Conditions of Service) Act, 1979?
(1) Inter-state migrant workmen
(2) Workers employed in automobile manufacturing
(3) Workers employed in information technology sector
(4) None of the above

51. Which of the following is not a type of welfare activity under the Building and Other Construction Workers (Regulation of Employment and Conditions of Service) Act, 1996?
(1) Medical facilities
(2) Education and training
(3) Housing facilities
(4) All of the above are types of welfare activities

52. Which of the following types of workers are covered under the Building and Other Construction Workers (Regulation of Employment and Conditions of Service) Act, 1996?
(1) Building and other construction workers
(2) Workers employed in automobile manufacturing
(3) Workers employed in information technology sector
(4) None of the above

53. Which of the following is the minimum number of workmen required for registration of a trade union under the Trade Unions Act, 1926?
(1) 7 (2) 10
(3) 15 (4) None of these

54. Which of the following is the maximum number of office bearers that can be elected from among the members of a trade union under the Trade Unions Act, 1926?
(1) 7 (2) 10
(3) 15 (4) None of these

55. Who is not eligible for being an office bearer of atrade union under the Trade Unions Act, 1926?
(1) A person who has been convicted of a crime involving moral turpitude
(2) A person who has been declared insolvent
(3) A person who is not a member of the trade union
(4) All of the above

56. Which of the following rights is not available to a member of a trade union under the Trade Unions Act, 1926?

(1) The right to elect office bearers
(2) The right to hold office
(3) The right to participate in industrial action without notice
(4) The right to call for a general meeting of the union

57. Which of the following is not a function of a trade union?
(1) Collective bargaining
(2) Industrial action
(3) Legal prosecution of members
(4) Social work

58. Which of the following types of industrial action is not legal in India?
(1) Strike (2) Lockout
(3) Wildcat strike (4) None of these

59. Which of the following is not a remedy available to a worker in case of unfair labour practices under the Industrial Disputes Act, 1947?
(1) Reinstatement
(2) Payment of compensation
(3) Termination of employment
(4) None of the above

60. Which of the following is not a type of industrial dispute under the Industrial Disputes Act, 1947?
(1) Strike (2) Lockout
(3) Individual dispute
(4) All of the above are types of industrial disputes

61. **Assertion:** The Employees' State Insurance Act, 1948 provides for medical benefits to workers.
Reason: The Employees' State Insurance Scheme provides for medical treatment to employees and their dependents in case of sickness, maternity and employment injury.
(1) Both assertion and reason are true and the reason is the correct explanation of the assertion.
(2) Both assertion and reason are true but the reason is not the correct explanation of the assertion.
(3) Assertion is true but reason is false.
(4) Assertion is false but reason is true.

62. **Assertion:** The National Pension System provides for retirement benefits to workers.
Reason: The National Pension System is a voluntary defined contribution retirement savings scheme that provides for pension benefits to subscribers.
(1) Both assertion and reason are true and the reason is the correct explanation of the assertion.
(2) Both assertion and reason are true but the reason is not the correct explanation of the assertion.
(3) Assertion is true but reason is false.
(4) Assertion is false but reason is true.

63. **Assertion:** The Employees' Provident Fund Scheme provides for social security benefits to workers.
Reason: The Employees' Provident Fund Scheme is a compulsory defined contribution retirement savings scheme that provides for social security benefits to subscribers.
(1) Both assertion and reason are true and the reason is the correct explanation of the assertion.
(2) Both assertion and reason are true but the reason is not the correct explanation of the assertion.
(3) Assertion is true but reason is false.
(4) Assertion is false but reason is true.

64. **Assertion:** The Workmen's Compensation Act, 1923 provides for compensation to workers in case of injury or death.
Reason: The Workmen's Compensation Act, 1923 is a social security legislation that provides for compensation to workers or their dependents in case of injury or death by accident arising out of and in the course of employment.
(1) Both assertion and reason are true and the reason is the correct explanation of the assertion.
(2) Both assertion and reason are true but the reason is not the correct explanation of the assertion.
(3) Assertion is true but reason is false.
(4) Assertion is false but reason is true.

65. **Assertion:** The Maternity Benefit Act, 1961 provides for maternity benefits to women workers.
Reason: The Maternity Benefit Act, 1961 is a social security legislation that provides for maternity benefits to women workers during pregnancy and after childbirth.
(1) Both assertion and reason are true and the reason is the correct explanation of the assertion.
(2) Both assertion and reason are true but the reason is not the correct explanation of the assertion.
(3) Assertion is true but reason is false.
(4) Assertion is false but reason is true.

66. Which of the following is not a objective of labour welfare?
(1) To improve the health and safety of workers
(2) To improve the economic and social status of workers
(3) To maximize profits for the employer
(4) To ensure social justice for workers

67. In which year was the Factories Act enacted in India?
(1) 1881 (2) 1891
(3) 1911 (4) 1948

68. Which of the following is not a principle of labour welfare?
(1) The principle of universal coverage
(2) The principle of non-discrimination
(3) The principle of cost-effectiveness
(4) The principle of social justice

69. Which of the following Acts provides for pension benefits to employees in India?
(1) The Employees' State Insurance Act, 1948
(2) The Employees' Provident Funds and Miscellaneous Provisions Act, 1952
(3) The National Pension System (NPS)
(4) The Maternity Benefit Act, 1961

70. The concept of the "Welfare State" originated in which country?
(1) Germany (2) France
(3) United Kingdom (4) Sweden

71. The Employees' State Insurance Scheme covers employees earning up to which monthly wage limit?
(1) Rs. 10,000 (2) Rs. 15,000
(3) Rs. 20,000 (4) Rs. 25,000

72. Which of the following Acts provides for payment of bonus to eligible employees?
(1) The Factories Act
(2) The Payment of Wages Act
(3) The Payment of Bonus Act
(4) The Minimum Wages Act

73. Which of the following is not a form of social security benefit provided to workers in India?
(1) Medical benefits
(2) Disability benefits
(3) Retirement benefits
(4) Life insurance benefits

74. Which of the following provides for compensation to workers in case of accidental injury or death during the course of employment?
(1) The Factories Act
(2) The Industrial Employment (Standing Orders) Act
(3) The Workmen's Compensation Act
(4) The Employees' State Insurance Act

75. Which of the following is not a type of leave provided to workers in India?
(1) Maternity leave for female employees
(2) Paternity leave for male employees
(3) Earned leave for all employees
(4) Sick leave for all employees

76. Which of the following institutions is responsible for administering the Employees' Provident Fund Scheme?
(1) The Ministry of Labour and Employment, Government of India
(2) The Employees' Provident Fund Organization
(3) The Pension Fund Regulatory and Development Authority
(4) The National Institute of Open Schooling

77. Which of the following is not considered a part of labour welfare?
(1) Medical assistance
(2) Old age pension
(3) Wage and bonus
(4) Profit sharing

78. The Trade Unions Act, 1926 provides for the registration of trade unions at what level?
(1) National level (2) State level
(3) District level (4) All of these

79. Which of the following institutions is responsible for enforcing the Payment of Bonus Act, 1965?
(1) The Ministry of Labour and Employment, Government of India
(2) The Employees' Provident Fund Organization
(3) The Employees' State Insurance Corporation
(4) The Chief Labour Commissioner (Central)

80. Which of the following Acts provides for the abolition of child labour in certain industries?
(1) The Factories Act
(2) The Mines Act
(3) The Child Labour (Prohibition and Regulation) Act
(4) The Contract Labour (Regulation and Abolition) Act

81. The Employees' Provident Fund Scheme provides for which of the following benefits to subscribers?
(1) Pension benefits
(2) Death benefits
(3) Provident fund benefits
(4) All of the above

82. The National Social Security Scheme provides for which of the following benefits to eligible workers?
(1) Pension benefits
(2) Medical benefits
(3) Life insurance benefits
(4) All of the above

83. Which of the following Acts provides for the prohibition of bonded labour in India?
(1) The Bonded Labour System (Abolition) Act
(2) The Contract Labour (Regulation and Abolition) Act
(3) The Payment of Bonus Act
(4) The Employees' Provident Funds and Miscellaneous Provisions Act

84. The Employees' State Insurance Scheme provides for which of the following benefits to employees and their dependents?
(1) Medical benefits
(2) Disability benefits
(3) Maternity benefits
(4) All of the above

85. Which of the following Acts provides for the regulation of working conditions in shops and commercial establishments?
(1) The Factories Act
(2) The Mines Act
(3) The Shops and Establishments Act
(4) The Industrial Disputes Act

86. Which of the following institutions is responsible for administering the Employees' State Insurance Scheme?
(1) The Ministry of Labour and Employment, Government of India
(2) The Employees' Provident Fund Organization
(3) The Employees' State Insurance Corporation
(4) The Payment of Bonus Authority

87. Which of the following Acts provides for the welfare of plantation workers in India?
(1) The Plantations Labour Act
(2) The Industrial Disputes Act
(3) The Workmen's Compensation Act
(4) The Payment of Bonus Act

88. Which of the following is not a type of social security benefit provided to workers in India?
(1) Provident fund benefits
(2) Maternity benefits
(3) Gratuity benefits
(4) Incentives benefits

89. The Mines Act, 1952 provides for the welfare of workers in which of the following industries?
(1) Mining (2) Textiles
(3) Construction (4) None of these

90. The Contract Labour (Regulation and Abolition) Act, 1970 provides for the regulation of employment of contract labour in which of the following industries?
(1) Manufacturing (2) Construction
(3) Service (4) Mining

91. Which of the following Acts provides for the payment of minimum wages to workers?
(1) The Factories Act
(2) The Shops and Establishments Act
(3) The Minimum Wages Act
(4) The Payment of Bonus Act

92. The Inter-State Migrant Workmen (Regulation of Employment and Conditions of Service) Act, 1979 provides for the welfare of which of the following types of workers?
(1) Migrant workers
(2) Contract labour
(3) Beedi workers
(4) Bonded labourers

93. The Plantations Labour Act provides for the welfare of workers in which of the following industries?
(1) Agriculture (2) Plantations
(3) Service (4) Mining

94. Which of the following is not a type of insurance benefit provided to workers in India?
(1) Medical insurance benefits
(2) Life insurance benefits
(3) Maternity insurance benefits
(4) Pension insurance benefits

95. The Maternity Benefit Act, 1961 provides for which of the following benefits to female employees?
(1) Maternity leave
(2) Maternity benefits
(3) Nursing breaks
(4) All of the above

96. Which of the following institutions is responsible for enforcing the Minimum Wages Act, 1948?
(1) The Ministry of Labour and Employment, Government of India
(2) The Central Board of Direct Taxes
(3) The State Governments
(4) The Employees' State Insurance Corporation

97. The Beedi Workers Welfare Fund Act provides for the welfare of workers in which of the following industries?
(1) Agriculture (2) Plantations
(3) Construction (4) Beedi making

98. Which of the following institutions is responsible for administering the National Pension System (NPS)?
(1) The Ministry of Labour and Employment, Government of India
(2) The Pension Fund Regulatory and Development Authority
(3) The Employees' Provident Fund Organization
(4) The Employees' State Insurance Corporation

99. The Apprentices Act, 1961 provides for the welfare of which of the following types of workers?
(1) Migrant workers
(2) Contract labour
(3) Apprentices
(4) Bonded labourers

100. Which of the following Acts provides for the welfare of unorganized workers in India?
(1) The Unorganized Workers' Social Security Act, 2008
(2) The Payment of Bonus Act, 1965
(3) The Employees' Provident Funds and Miscellaneous Provisions Act, 1952
(4) The Factories Act, 1948

101. Which of the following is not a form of social protection provided under the Unorganized Workers' Social Security Act, 2008?
(1) Pension benefits
(2) Life insurance benefits

(3) Disability benefits
(4) Provident fund benefits

102. The National Social Assistance Programme provides for which of the following types of social assistance?
(1) Old age pension
(2) Disability pension
(3) Family pension
(4) All of the above

103. The National Rural Employment Guarantee Act, 2005 provides for which of the following guarantees to rural workers?
(1) Employment guarantee
(2) Food security guarantee
(3) Social security guarantee
(4) All of the above

104. The Building and Other Construction Workers' Welfare Cess Act, 1996 provides for the welfare of workers in which of the following industries?
(1) Agriculture (2) Plantations
(3) Construction (4) Mining

105. Which of the following institutions is responsible for administering the Building and Other Construction Workers' Welfare Cess Act, 1996?
(1) The Ministry of Labour and Employment, Government of India
(2) The Employees' Provident Fund Organization
(3) The State Governments
(4) The Employees' State Insurance Corporation

106. Which of the following is not a type of social protection provided under the National Social Assistance Programme?
(1) Old age pension
(2) Maternity benefits
(3) Disability pension
(4) Survivor benefits

107. Which of the following institutions is responsible for administering the unorganized sector workers' social security schemes in India?
(1) The Ministry of Labour and Employment, Government of India
(2) The State Governments
(3) The Labour Welfare Organization
(4) The Central Board of Indirect Taxes and Customs

108. The National Rural Health Mission provides for which of the following benefits to rural workers and their families?
(1) Medical benefits
(2) Maternity benefits
(3) Disability benefits
(4) All of the above

109. Which of the following is not a type of welfare activity provided by the Employees' State Insurance Corporation?
(1) Medical care
(2) Maternity benefits
(3) Retirement benefits
(4) Housing benefits

110. The Industrial Disputes Act, 1947 provides for which of the following types of disputes?
(1) Industrial disputes
(2) Trade disputes
(3) Labour disputes
(4) All of the above

111. The Inter-State Migrant Workmen (Regulation of Employment and Conditions of Service) Act, 1979 provides for which of the following benefits to migrant workers and their families?
(1) Medical benefits
(2) Maternity benefits
(3) Disability benefits
(4) All of the above

112. The Beedi Workers Welfare Fund Act, 1976 provides for which of the following benefits to beedi workers and their families?
(1) Medical benefits
(2) Maternity benefits
(3) Death benefits
(4) All of the above

113. The Plantations Labour Act, 1951 provides for which of the following rights and benefits to plantation workers?
(1) Medical care (2) Housing
(3) Education (4) All of these

114. The Building and Other Construction Workers (Regulation of Employment and Conditions of Service) Act, 1996 provides for which of the following benefits to workers?
(1) Medical benefits
(2) Maternity benefits
(3) Death benefits
(4) All of the above

115. Which of the following institutions is responsible for enforcing the Mines Act, 1952?
(1) The Ministry of Mines, Government of India
(2) The Central Pollution Control Board
(3) The State Governments
(4) The National Green Tribunal

116. **Assertion:** Social security systems provide protection against economic and social risks.
Reason: Social security schemes are universally applicable and provide equal benefits to all citizens.
(1) Both assertion and reason are true and the reason is the correct explanation of the assertion.
(2) Both assertion and reason are true but the reason is not the correct explanation of the assertion.
(3) Assertion is true but reason is false.
(4) Assertion is false but reason is true.

117. Which of the following institutions is responsible for administering the Child Labour (Prohibition and Regulation) Act, 1986?
(1) The Ministry of Labour and Employment, Government of India
(2) The National Commission for Protection of Child Rights
(3) The State Governments
(4) The National Human Rights Commission

118. The Contract Labour (Regulation and Abolition) Act, 1970 provides for the regulation of employment of contract labour in which of the following types of industry?
(1) Manufacturing (2) Service
(3) Construction (4) All of these

119. The Payment of Wages Act, 1936 provides for the payment of wages to employees within which time limit?
(1) One week (2) Two weeks
(3) One month (4) Two months

120. Which of the following Acts provides for the welfare of construction workers in India?
(1) The Building and Other Construction Workers' Welfare Cess Act, 1996
(2) The Building and Other Construction Workers (Regulation of Employment and Conditions of Service) Act, 1996
(3) The Mines Act, 1952
(4) The Shops and Establishments Act

121. The Industrial Disputes (Central) Rules, 1957 provide for which of the following forms of dispute resolution?
(1) Conciliation (2) Mediation
(3) Arbitration (4) All of these

122. Which of the following institutions is responsible for enforcing the Factories Act, 1948?
(1) The Ministry of Labour and Employment, Government of India
(2) The State Governments
(3) The National Green Tribunal
(4) The Central Pollution Control Board

123. Which of the following Acts provides for the welfare of beedi workers in India?
(1) The Beedi Workers Welfare Fund Act, 1976
(2) The Contract Labour (Regulation and Abolition) Act, 1970
(3) The Payment of Bonus Act, 1965
(4) The Shops and Establishments Act

124. Which of the following is not a form of welfare activity provided to construction workers by the Building and Other Construction Workers' Welfare Board?
(1) Housing (2) Medical care
(3) Education
(4) Provident fund benefits

125. The National Rural Employment Guarantee Act, 2005 provides for how many days of guaranteed employment per household in a financial year?

(1) 50 days (2) 100 days
(3) 150 days (4) 200 days

126. Which of the following institutions is responsible for administering the Mines Act, 1952?
(1) The Ministry of Mines, Government of India
(2) The Central Pollution Control Board
(3) The State Governments
(4) The National Green Tribunal

127. The Workmen's Compensation Act, 1923 provides for which of the following types of compensation in case of injury or death during the course of employment?
(1) Disability benefit
(2) Pension benefit
(3) Lump sum payment
(4) All of the above

128. Which of the following Acts provides for the welfare of gig workers in India?
(1) The Gig Workers' Welfare Act, 2021
(2) The Unorganized Workers' Social Security Act, 2008
(3) The Industrial Disputes Act, 1947
(4) The Factories Act, 1948

129. The National Rural Health Mission provides for which of the following benefits to rural workers and their families?
(1) Maternity benefits
(2) Childcare benefits
(3) Disability benefits
(4) All of the above

130. Which of the following institutions is responsible for enforcing the Beedi Workers Welfare Fund Act, 1976?
(1) The Ministry of Labour and Employment, Government of India
(2) The State Governments
(3) The National Commission for Protection of Child Rights
(4) The National Human Rights Commission

131. The Contract Labour (Regulation and Abolition) Central Rules, 1971 prescribe the conditions of service for which of the following types of workers?
(1) Migrant workers
(2) Contract labour
(3) Apprentices
(4) Beedi workers

132. The Maternity Benefit (Amendment) Act, 2017 provides for which of the following enhancements to maternity benefits?
(1) Extension of maternity leave from 12 weeks to 26 weeks
(2) Provision of crèche facilities at the workplace
(3) Provision of work from home facility
(4) All of the above

133. The National Food Security Act, 2013 provides for which of the following benefits to eligible households?
(1) Rice (2) Wheat
(3) Pulses (4) All of these

134. The Social Security Code, 2020 provides for which of the following types of social security benefits?
(1) Provident fund benefits
(2) Maternity benefits
(3) Gratuity benefits
(4) All of the above

135. Which of the following institutions is responsible for administering the Mines and Minerals (Development and Regulation) Act, 1957?
(1) The Ministry of Mines, Government of India
(2) The State Governments
(3) The Central Pollution Control Board
(4) The National Green Tribunal

136. The Unorganised Workers' Social Security Act, 2008 provides for which of the following types of social security benefits to unorganised sector workers?
(1) Provident fund benefits
(2) Health and life insurance benefits
(3) Maternity benefits
(4) All of the above

137. Which of the following types of employment is covered under the Employees' State Insurance Scheme?

(1) Casual employment
(2) Part-time employment
(3) Contract employment
(4) All of the above

138. Which of the following institutions is responsible for enforcing the Payment of Gratuity Act, 1972?
(1) The Ministry of Labour and Employment, Government of India
(2) The State Governments
(3) The Employees' Provident Fund Organization
(4) The Chief Labour Commissioner (Central)

139. The Unorganised Workers' Social Security Act, 2008 defines which of the following as an "unorganized worker"?
(1) Any person in the unorganized sector who is not included in the definition of "worker" under the Industrial Disputes Act, 1947
(2) Any person who is self-employed or a home-based worker in the unorganized sector
(3) Any person who is employed in an unorganized sector enterprise or undertaking
(4) All of the above

140. The Gig Workers' Welfare Act, 2021 provides for which of the following benefits togig workers in India?
(1) Health and life insurance benefits
(2) Maternity benefits
(3) Pension benefits
(4) All of the above

141. The National Food Security Act, 2013 provides for which of the following entitlements to eligible households?
(1) Cereals (2) Pulses
(3) Oils (4) All of these

142. The Employees' Provident Funds and Miscellaneous Provisions Act, 1952 provides for which of the following benefits to employees?
(1) Provident fund benefits
(2) Pension benefits
(3) Insurance benefits
(4) All of the above

143. The Mines and Minerals (Development and Regulation) Act, 1957 provides for which of the following measures to regulate mining activities in India?
(1) Grant of mining leases
(2) Regulation of mineral explorations
(3) Conservation and development of minerals
(4) All of the above

144. The Payment of Gratuity Act, 1972 provides for which of the following types of gratuity?
(1) Retrenchment gratuity
(2) Death gratuity
(3) Superannuation gratuity
(4) All of the above

145. The Industrial Disputes Act, 1947 provides for which of the following mechanisms for settlement of industrial disputes?
(1) Conciliation (2) Mediation
(3) Arbitration (4) All of these

146. The Social Security Code, 2020 provides for which of the following types of social security schemes to workers in India?
(1) Provident fund schemes
(2) Pension schemes
(3) Health and life insurance schemes
(4) All of the above

147. The Building and Other Construction Workers' Welfare Cess Act, 1996 provides for the levy and collection of which of the following cesses?
(1) Education cess
(2) Welfare cess
(3) Employment cess
(4) Health cess

148. The Apprenticeship Act, 1961 provides for which of the following benefits to apprentices?
(1) Stipend
(2) Training
(3) Employment after completion of apprenticeship
(4) All of the above

149. The Employees' State Insurance Act, 1948 provides for which of the following benefits to employees and their dependents?
(1) Medical benefits
(2) Disability benefits
(3) Maternity benefits
(4) All of the above

150. The Unorganised Workers' Social Security Act, 2008 provides for which of the following measures to ensure social security to unorganised sector workers?
(1) Accreditation of service providers
(2) Social security schemes
(3) Awareness campaigns
(4) All of the above

151. The National Rural Employment Guarantee Act, 2005 provides for which of the following types of employment to rural workers?
(1) Unskilled manual work
(2) Skilled work
(3) Professional work
(4) All of the above

152. The Gig Workers' Welfare Act, 2021 provides for which of the following rights to gig workers?
(1) Right to minimum wages
(2) Right to social security benefits
(3) Right to collective bargaining
(4) All of the above

153. The Employees' State Insurance Scheme covers employees working in which of the following types of industries?
(1) Agriculture (2) Manufacturing
(3) Service (4) All of these

154. The Payment of Bonus Act, 1965 provides for the payment of bonus to employees whose wages do not exceed which monthly limit?
(1) Rs. 7,000 (2) Rs. 10,000
(3) Rs. 21,000 (4) Rs. 25,000

155. The Plantations Labour Act, 1951 provides for which of the following rights and benefits to plantation workers?
(1) Housing (2) Medical care
(3) Education (4) All of these

156. Which of the following is not a type of occupational hazards?
(1) Physical hazards
(2) Biological hazards
(3) Chemical hazards
(4) Financial hazards

157. Which of the following ladders is preferred for work at heights?
(1) Single ladder
(2) Extension ladder
(3) Step ladder
(4) Platform ladder

158. Which of the following is not a type of respiratory protective equipment?
(1) Air-purifying respirator
(2) Supplied-air respirator
(3) Powered air-purifying respirator
(4) Belt-mounted respirator

159. Which of the following is not a type of personal protective equipment?
(1) Gloves (2) Safety glasses
(3) Uniforms (4) Office chairs

160. Which of the following is not a type of hearing protective equipment?
(1) Earmuffs
(2) Earplugs
(3) Noise-cancelling headphones
(4) Hard hats

161. What is the purpose of workplace hygiene?
(1) To maintain cleanliness and orderliness in the workplace
(2) To prevent occupational health hazards
(3) To ensure that proper sanitation is maintained
(4) All of the above

162. Which of the following is an example of biological hazard?
(1) Exposure to toxic chemicals
(2) High levels of noise
(3) Exposure to infectious bacteria or viruses
(4) Poor lighting conditions

163. Which of the following is not a type of hazard associated with machine operation?
(1) Electrical hazards
(2) Mechanical hazards
(3) Physical hazards
(4) Financial hazards

164. Which of the following is not a type of safety sign used in the workplace?
(1) Warning sign
(2) Caution sign
(3) Stop sign
(4) Go sign

165. Which of the following is an example of thermal hazard?
(1) Exposure to toxic chemicals
(2) High levels of noise
(3) Exposure to heat or cold
(4) Poor lighting conditions

166. Which of the following is not a basic element of a safety program?
(1) Leadership and management commitment
(2) Workplace inspection
(3) Employee participation
(4) Financial compensation

167. Which type of fire extinguisher is used for Class A fires?
(1) Water or foam extinguisher
(2) CO2 extinguisher
(3) Dry chemical extinguisher
(4) Halon extinguisher

168. Which of the following is a common cause of workplace accidents?
(1) Improper training
(2) Proper safety equipment
(3) Well-lit work areas
(4) None of the above

169. Which of the following is not an example of a workplace hazard?
(1) Chemical exposure
(2) Falling objects
(3) Ergonomic factors
(4) Lack of employee motivation

170. Which of the following is not a type of safety equipment commonly used in the workplace?
(1) Safety glasses
(2) Hard hats
(3) Ear plugs
(4) PC monitors

171. Which of the following is not a duty of the employer in ensuring workplace safety?
(1) Providing safety equipment
(2) Properly training employees
(3) Providing financial compensation to injured workers
(4) Providing a safe work environment

172. Which of the following is not a common cause of workplace fires?
(1) Electrical hazards
(2) Chemical exposure
(3) Combustible materials
(4) Lack of employee motivation

173. What is the purpose of a safety inspection?
(1) To identify hazards and unsafe conditions
(2) To identify opportunities for cost-cutting
(3) To increase productivity
(4) All of the above

174. Which of the following is not a characteristic of a safe work environment?
(1) A clean and organized workspace
(2) Adequate lighting
(3) Clear and visible safety signs
(4) Lack of employee supervision

175. Which of the following is not a type of occupational disease?
(1) Musculoskeletal disorders
(2) Cardiovascular diseases
(3) Infectious diseases
(4) Non-communicable diseases

176. Which of the following is not a common risk factor for occupational diseases?
(1) Exposure to physical hazards
(2) Working long hours

(3) Healthy eating habits
(4) Exposure to environmental toxins

177. Which of the following is an example of a non-communicable occupational disease?
(1) Cancer (2) Influenza
(3) Tuberculosis (4) HIV/AIDS

178. Which of the following is not a preventive measure for occupational diseases?
(1) Proper ventilation
(2) Regular health check-ups
(3) Proper use of personal protective equipment
(4) Reduction of exposure to hazardous substances

179. Which of the following is not a characteristic of a healthy work environment?
(1) Adequate ventilation
(2) Safe and ergonomic working conditions
(3) Elimination of hazardous chemicals
(4) Overcrowding and a high noise level

180. Which of the following is a common occupational disease associated with exposure to asbestos?
(1) Mesothelioma (2) Tuberculosis
(3) Malaria (4) Influenza

181. Which of the following is not a common occupational disease associated with exposure to chemicals?
(1) Cancer
(2) Respiratory disorders
(3) Cardiovascular diseases
(4) Malaria

182. Which of the following is not a common occupational disease associated with exposure to noise?
(1) Hearing loss
(2) Tinnitus
(3) Hypertension
(4) Stress and anxiety disorders

183. Which of the following is an example of an infectious occupational disease?
(1) Mesothelioma
(2) Tuberculosis
(3) Cancer
(4) Hypertension

184. Which of the following is not a type of occupational stressor?
(1) Physical demands of the job
(2) Long working hours
(3) Lack of social support at work
(4) High salary and promotions

185. Assertion: High levels of noise can cause hearing loss.
Reason: Exposure to high levels of noise can damage the hair cells in the ears.
(1) Both assertion and reason are true and the reason is the correct explanation of the assertion.
(2) Both assertion and reason are true but the reason is not the correct explanation of the assertion.
(3) Assertion is true but reason is false.
(4) Assertion is false but reason is true.

186. Assertion: Prolonged exposure to asbestos can cause mesothelioma.
Reason: Mesothelioma is a non-communicable occupational disease caused by asbestos exposure.
(1) Both assertion and reason are true and the reason is the correct explanation of the assertion.
(2) Both assertion and reason are true but the reason is not the correct explanation ofthe assertion.
(3) Assertion is true but reason is false.
(4) Assertion is false but reason is true.

187. Assertion: Safety inspections are essential in identifying hazards and maintaining a safe work environment.
Reason: Safety inspections are an unnecessary expense that add little value to a company.
(1) Both assertion and reason are true and the reason is the correct explanation of the assertion.
(2) Both assertion and reason are true but the reason is not the correct explanation of the assertion.
(3) Assertion is true but reason is false.
(4) Assertion is false but reason is true.

188. **Assertion:** Proper use of personal protective equipment is an important preventive measure for occupational diseases.

Reason: Personal protective equipment is expensive and not necessary for most jobs.

(1) Both assertion and reason are true and the reason is the correct explanation of the assertion.
(2) Both assertion and reason are true but the reason is not the correct explanation of the assertion.
(3) Assertion is true but reason is false.
(4) Assertion is false but reason is true.

189. **Assertion:** Occupational stressors can lead to negative health outcomes for workers.

Reason: Occupational stressors are necessary for workplace productivity and cannot be avoided.

(1) Both assertion and reason are true and the reason is the correct explanation of the assertion.
(2) Both assertion and reason are true but the reason is not the correct explanation of the assertion.
(3) Assertion is true but reason is false.
(4) Assertion is false but reason is true.

190. Social security is an important component of welfare state and is defined as

(1) A system of protection provided by the government against economic and social distress
(2) A system of tax benefits provided to the wealthy
(3) A system of subsidies provided to large corporations
(4) A system of direct cash transfers to the poor

191. The Universal Declaration of Human Rights, adopted by the UN in 1948, recognizes the right to social security. Which article is it?

(1) Article 17 (2) Article 22
(3) Article 25 (4) Article 30

192. Which of the following is not an important objective of social security?

(1) To alleviate poverty and ensure social welfare
(2) To encourage economic growth and development
(3) To promote social cohesion and solidarity
(4) To protect against economic and social risks

193. The International Labour Organization (ILO) has identified which areas as critical for social protection systems?

(1) Heathcare, nutrition, education, and income support
(2) Unemployment insurance, pensions, and disability benefits
(3) All of the above
(4) None of the above

194. Which of the following is a social security scheme provided by the government of India?

(1) Pradhan Mantri Jan Dhan Yojana
(2) Mahatma Gandhi National Rural Employment Guarantee Act
(3) Ayushman Bharat Pradhan Mantri Jan Arogya Yojana
(4) Swachh Bharat Abhiyan

195. Which country has the world's largest social security system?

(1) United Kingdom
(2) United States of America
(3) China
(4) Japan

196. Which of the following is considered a contributory social security scheme?

(1) Universal Basic Income
(2) Unemployment Insurance
(3) Food Stamps
(4) Direct Cash Transfer

197. Which of the following is a non-contributory social security scheme provided by the government of India?

(1) National Pension System
(2) Pradhan Mantri Jan Dhan Yojana
(3) Employees State Insurance Scheme
(4) Atal Pension Yojana

198. Which of the following is not a type of social security benefit?
(1) Old age pension
(2) Disability benefits
(3) Free health insurance
(4) Unemployment insurance

199. In India, which ministry is responsible for social security policies and programs?
(1) Ministry of Finance
(2) Ministry of Human Resource Development
(3) Ministry of Labour and Employment
(4) Ministry of Health and Family Welfare

200. Which of the following is a criticism of contributory social security schemes?
(1) They do not provide enough benefits to the poor
(2) They are funded by taxpayers, putting a burden on the working class
(3) They provide incentives to the wealthy to withdraw from public schemes
(4) They are too expensive to maintain

201. Which of the following is a characteristic of a universal social security scheme?
(1) Benefits are provided based on need, not contribution
(2) Benefits are provided only to specific groups, such as the elderly or disabled
(3) Benefits are funded through taxes and contributions from beneficiaries
(4) Benefits are provided only to those who have never received government support

202. In India, which of the following social security schemes is targeted towards rural areas?
(1) Mahatma Gandhi National Rural Employment Guarantee Act
(2) Atal Pension Yojana
(3) Employees State Insurance Scheme
(4) Pradhan Mantri Fasal Bima Yojana

203. Which of the following is a challenge in implementing effective social security policies and programs?
(1) Lack of political will and funding
(2) Inadequate infrastructure and human resources
(3) Lack of awareness and understanding among beneficiaries
(4) All of the above

204. Which of the following is not a category of social risk addressed by social security schemes?
(1) Old age (2) Unemployment
(3) Disability (4) Maternity

205. Which of the following is not a type of social security benefit under India's National Social Assistance Programme?
(1) Old age pension
(2) Widow pension
(3) Self-employment assistance
(4) Disability pension

206. Which of the following is an important component of social security systems in developing countries?
(1) Universal healthcare coverage
(2) Universal basic income
(3) Conditional cash transfers
(4) Subsidies for large corporations

207. Which of the following is not a characteristic of a well-designed social security system?
(1) Sustainability and adequate funding
(2) Universal coverage and equitable access
(3) Flexible and responsive to changing needs
(4) Efficient and cost-effective administration

208. The International Labour Organization (ILO) has identified which of the following as a principle of social security?
(1) Universality (2) Affordability
(3) Adequacy (4) All of these

209. In which year was the Social Security Act of the United States passed?
(1) 1923 (2) 1935
(3) 1945 (4) 1955

210. Which of the following is a benefit provided by India's National Pension System?
(1) Disability pension
(2) Unemployment insurance
(3) Annuity payments on retirement
(4) Free healthcare for senior citizens

211. Which of the following is a type of social security program targeted towards women in India?
(1) Pradhan Mantri Jan Dhan Yojana
(2) Beti Bachao, Beti Padhao Yojana
(3) Sukanya Samriddhi Yojana
(4) Swachh Bharat Abhiyan

212. Which of the following social security schemes provides income support to pregnant women and lactating mothers in India?
(1) Pradhan Mantri Matru Vandana Yojana
(2) Atal Pension Yojana
(3) Rashtriya Swasthya Bima Yojana
(4) Pradhan Mantri Fasal Bima Yojana

213. Which of the following is a criticism of India's National Rural Employment Guarantee Act (NREGA)?
(1) It does not provide enough benefits to the poor
(2) It is too expensive to maintain
(3) It is not well targeted and suffers from corruption
(4) It does not provide long-term solutions to poverty and unemployment

214. Which of the following is a type of social security scheme that provides benefits to families with children?
(1) Child Support
(2) Child Tax Credit
(3) Childcare Vouchers
(4) Universal Credit

215. Which of the following is not an important principle of social security policies and programs?
(1) Flexibility and responsiveness
(2) Political neutrality and independence
(3) Equity and universality
(4) Sustainability and adequacy

216. Which of the following is a social security scheme providing pension benefits to the elderly in India?
(1) Pradhan Mantri Jan Dhan Yojana
(2) Ayushman Bharat Pradhan Mantri Jan Arogya Yojana
(3) Atal Pension Yojana
(4) Indira Gandhi National Old Age Pension Scheme

217. Which of the following is not a type of social security benefit provided by India's Employees State Insurance Scheme?
(1) Sickness benefit
(2) Maternity benefit
(3) Unemployment insurance
(4) Disability benefit

218. Which of the following is an example of a means-tested social security scheme?
(1) Social Security Old Age Pension
(2) Universal Basic Income
(3) Temporary Assistance for Needy Families
(4) Unemployment Insurance

219. Which of the following is an important principle of social security schemes regarding eligibility for benefits?
(1) Means-testing
(2) Age requirements
(3) Residency requirements
(4) All of the above

220. **Assertion:** Social security is an important component of a welfare state.
Reason: Welfare states prioritize the well-being of citizens and provide support and protection against economic and social risks.
(1) Both assertion and reason are true and the reason is the correct explanation of the assertion.
(2) Both assertion and reason are true but the reason is not the correct explanation of the assertion.
(3) Assertion is true but reason is false.
(4) Assertion is false but reason is true.

221. **Assertion:** Universal coverage is an important characteristic of a well-designed social security system.
Reason: Universal coverage ensures that benefits are provided only to those who are in need, rather than to those who can afford them.
(1) Both assertion and reason are true and the reason is the correct explanation of the assertion.

(2) Both assertion and reason are true but the reason is not the correct explanation of the assertion.
(3) Assertion is true but reason is false.
(4) Assertion is false but reason is true.

222. Assertion: A well-designed social security system must be flexible and responsive to changing needs.
Reason: Social security systems that are rigid and inflexible can lead to exclusion of certain groups and inequality in benefit provision.
(1) Both assertion and reason are true and the reason is the correct explanation of the assertion.
(2) Both assertion and reason are true but the reason is not the correct explanation of the assertion.
(3) Assertion is true but reason is false.
(4) Assertion is false but reason is true.

223. Assertion: Contributory social security schemes provide incentives to those who withdraw from public schemes.
Reason: The wealthy can afford to withdraw from public schemes and have their own insurance and pension plans.
(1) Both assertion and reason are true and the reason is the correct explanation of the assertion.
(2) Both assertion and reason are true but the reason is not the correct explanation of the assertion.
(3) Assertion is true but reason is false.
(4) Assertion is false but reason is true.

224. Assertion: Social security systems provide protection against economic and social risks.
Reason: Social security schemes are universally applicable and provide equal benefits to all citizens.
(1) Both assertion and reason are true and the reason is the correct explanation of the assertion.
(2) Both assertion and reason are true but the reason is not the correct explanation of the assertion.
(3) Assertion is true but reason is false.
(4) Assertion is false but reason is true.

225. Social security is an important component of welfare state and is defined as:
(1) A system of protection provided by the government against economic and social distress
(2) A system of tax benefits provided to the wealthy
(3) A system of subsidies provided to large corporations
(4) A system of direct cash transfers to the poor

226. The Universal Declaration of Human Rights, adopted by the UN in 1948, recognizes the right to social security. Which article is it?
(1) Article 17 (2) Article 22
(3) Article 25 (4) Article 30

227. Which of the following is not an important objective of social security?
(1) To alleviate poverty and ensure social welfare
(2) To encourage economic growth and development
(3) To promote social cohesion and solidarity
(4) To protect against economic and social risks

228. The International Labour Organization (ILO) has identified which areas as critical for social protection systems?
(1) Heathcare, nutrition, education, and income support
(2) Unemployment insurance, pensions, and disability benefits
(3) All of the above
(4) None of the above

229. Assertion: Social assistance programs are targeted towards specific groups, while social assurance programs are universal in nature.
Reason: Social assistance programs are designed to provide direct support to individu-

als in need, while social assurance programs are designed to promote economic growth and development.

(1) Both assertion and reason are true and the reason is the correct explanation of the assertion.
(2) Both assertion and reason are true but the reason is not the correct explanation of the assertion.
(3) Assertion is true but reason is false.
(4) Assertion is false but reason is true.

230. Assertion: India's Pradhan Mantri Jan Dhan Yojana is a contributory social security scheme.

Reason: The scheme provides direct cash transfer benefits to low-income individuals.

(1) Both assertion and reason are false.
(2) Both assertion and reason are true but the reason is not the correct explanation of the assertion.
(3) Assertion is true but reason is false.
(4) Assertion is false but reason is true.

231. Which of the following is considered a contributory social security scheme?
(1) Universal Basic Income
(2) Unemployment Insurance
(3) Food Stamps
(4) Direct Cash Transfer

232. Which of the following is a non-contributory social security scheme provided by the government of India?
(1) National Pension System
(2) Pradhan Mantri Jan Dhan Yojana
(3) Employees State Insurance Scheme
(4) Atal Pension Yojana

233. Which of the following is not a type of social security benefit?
(1) Old age pension
(2) Disability benefits
(3) Free health insurance
(4) Unemployment insurance

234. In India, which ministry is responsible for social security policies and programs?
(1) Ministry of Finance
(2) Ministry of Human Resource Development
(3) Ministry of Labour and Employment
(4) Ministry of Health and Family Welfare

235. Which of the following is a criticism of contributory social security schemes?
(1) They do not provide enough benefits to the poor
(2) They are funded by taxpayers, putting a burden on the working class
(3) They provide incentives to the wealthy to withdraw from public schemes
(4) They are too expensive to maintain

236. Which of the following is a characteristic of a universal social security scheme?
(1) Benefits are provided based on need, not contribution
(2) Benefits are provided only to specific groups, such as the elderly or disabled
(3) Benefits are funded through taxes and contributions from beneficiaries
(4) Benefits are provided only to those who have never received government support

237. In India, which of the following social security schemes is targeted towards rural areas?
(1) Mahatma Gandhi National Rural Employment Guarantee Act
(2) Atal Pension Yojana
(3) Employees State Insurance Scheme
(4) Pradhan Mantri Fasal Bima Yojana

238. Which of the following social security schemes provides income support to pregnant women and lactating mothers in India?
(1) Pradhan Mantri Matru Vandana Yojana
(2) Atal Pension Yojana
(3) Rashtriya Swasthya Bima Yojana
(4) Pradhan Mantri Fasal Bima Yojana

239. Which of the following is not a category of social risk addressed by social security schemes?
(1) Old age
(2) Unemployment
(3) Disability
(4) Maternity

240. Which of the following is not a type of social security benefit under India's National Social Assistance Programme?
(1) Old age pension
(2) Widow pension
(3) Self-employment assistance
(4) Disability pension

241. Which of the following social security schemes provides pension benefits to the elderly in India?
(1) Pradhan Mantri Jan Dhan Yojana
(2) Ayushman Bharat Pradhan Mantri Jan Arogya Yojana
(3) Atal Pension Yojana
(4) Indira Gandhi National Old Age Pension Scheme

242. Which of the following is a type of social security program targeted towards women in India?
(1) Pradhan Mantri Jan Dhan Yojana
(2) Beti Bachao, Beti Padhao Yojana
(3) Sukanya Samriddhi Yojana
(4) Swachh Bharat Abhiyan

243. Which of the following is an important component of social security systems in developing countries?
(1) Universal healthcare coverage
(2) Universal basic income
(3) Conditional cash transfers
(4) Subsidies for large corporations

244. Which of the following is an important principle of social security schemes regarding eligibility for benefits?
(1) Means-testing
(2) Age requirements
(3) Residency requirements
(4) All of the above

245. Which of the following is a type of social security scheme that provides benefits to families with children?
(1) Child Support
(2) Child Tax Credit
(3) Childcare Vouchers
(4) Universal Credit

246. Which of the following is an example of a means-tested social security scheme?
(1) Social Security Old Age Pension
(2) Universal Basic Income
(3) Temporary Assistance for Needy Families
(4) Unemployment Insurance

247. The Social Security Act was passed in response to what event?
(1) The Great Depression
(2) World War II
(3) The Cold War
(4) None of the above

248. Which type of social security benefits are directed towards low-income earners?
(1) Social Security Disability Insurance
(2) Supplemental Security Income (SSI)
(3) Social Security Retirement Benefits
(4) Social Security Survivor Benefits

249. Which country provides a universal basic income to its citizens?
(1) Sweden (2) Finland
(3) Norway (4) Denmark

250. **Assertion:** Social security systems must be sustainable and adequately funded to ensure long-term benefits for beneficiaries.
Reason: Underfunded social security systems can lead to reduced benefits or exclusion of certain groups.
(1) Both assertion and reason are true and the reason is the correct explanation of the assertion.
(2) Both assertion and reason are true but the reason is not the correct explanation of the assertion.
(3) Assertion is true but reason is false.
(4) Assertion is false but reason is true.

251. Which of the following is an example of a social assurance policy?
(1) Old age pensions
(2) Unemployment insurance
(3) Social Security Disability Insurance
(4) Universal Basic Income

252. Social assistance programs are typically directed towards which group of people?
(1) Low-income earners
(2) The elderly
(3) The disabled
(4) All of the above

253. Social assurance programs typically provide which type of benefits?
(1) Direct cash transfers to individuals
(2) Subsidies for specific industries
(3) Establishment of universal basic income programs
(4) Provision of free healthcare to all individuals

254. The World Bank defines social protection as a set of policies and programs that promote which of the following?
(1) Economic growth and development
(2) Social welfare and equity
(3) Subsidies for corporations
(4) Austerity measures to reduce government spending

255. **ssertion:** Social security is an important component of a welfare state.
Reason: Welfare states prioritize the well-being of citizens and provide support and protection against economic and social risks.
(1) Both assertion and reason are true and the reason is the correct explanation of the assertion.
(2) Both assertion and reason are true but the reason is not the correct explanation of the assertion.
(3) Assertion is true but reason is false.
(4) Assertion is false but reason is true.

256. **Assertion:** Universal coverage is an important characteristic of a well-designed social security system.
Reason: Universal coverage ensures that benefits are provided only to those who are in need, rather than to those who can afford them.
(1) Both assertion and reason are true and the reason is the correct explanation of the assertion.
(2) Both assertion and reason are true but the reason is not the correct explanation of the assertion.
(3) Assertion is true but reason is false.
(4) Assertion is false but reason is true.

257. **Assertion:** A well-designed social security system must be flexible and responsive to changing needs.
Reason: Social security systems that are rigid and inflexible can lead to exclusion of certain groups and inequality in benefit provision.
(1) Both assertion and reason are true and the reason is the correct explanation of the assertion.
(2) Both assertion and reason are true but the reason is not the correct explanation of the assertion.
(3) Assertion is true but reason is false.
(4) Assertion is false but reason is true.

258. **Assertion:** Contributory social security schemes provide incentives to those who withdraw from public schemes.
Reason: The wealthy can afford to withdraw from public schemes and have their own insurance and pension plans.
(1) Both assertion and reason are true and the reason is the correct explanation of the assertion.
(2) Both assertion and reason are true but the reason is not the correct explanation of the assertion.
(3) Assertion is true but reason is false.
(4) Assertion is false but reason is true.

ANSWER KEY

1. (3) 2. (4) 3. (1) 4. (1) 5. (1) 6. (1) 7. (2) 8. (3) 9. (3) 10. (4)
11. (4) 12. (1) 13. (3) 14. (1) 15. (1) 16. (3) 17. (1) 18. (3) 19. (3) 20. (1)
21. (3) 22. (1) 23. (1) 24. (4) 25. (4) 26. (3) 27. (1) 28. (1) 29. (1) 30. (4)
31. (3) 32. (1) 33. (3) 34. (3) 35. (1) 36. (3) 37. (1) 38. (3) 39. (1) 40. (3)
41. (1) 42. (4) 43. (1) 44. (3) 45. (1) 46. (1) 47. (1) 48. (1) 49. (3) 50. (1)
51. (4) 52. (1) 53. (1) 54. (1) 55. (4) 56. (3) 57. (4) 58. (3) 59. (3) 60. (3)
61. (1) 62. (1) 63. (1) 64. (1) 65. (1) 66. (4) 67. (4) 68. (4) 69. (3) 70. (1)
71. (3) 72. (3) 73. (4) 74. (3) 75. (2) 76. (2) 77. (4) 78. (4) 79. (4) 80. (3)
81. (4) 82. (4) 83. (1) 84. (4) 85. (3) 86. (3) 87. (1) 88. (4) 89. (1) 90. (3)
91. (3) 92. (4) 93. (2) 94. (4) 95. (4) 96. 97. (4) 98. (2) 99. (3) 100. (1)
101. (4) 102. (1) 103. (4) 104. (3) 105. (3) 106. (4) 107. (3) 108. (4) 109. (4) 110. (4)
111. (4) 112. (4) 113. (4) 114. (4) 115. (3) 116. (1) 117. (3) 118. (4) 119. (2) 120. (2)
121. (4) 122. (4) 123. (1) 124. (4) 125. (2) 126. (1) 127. (3) 128. (4) 129. (4) 130. (2)
131. (2) 132. (2) 133. (4) 134. (4) 135. (1) 136. (4) 137. (4) 138. (4) 139. (3) 140. (4)
141. (4) 142. (4) 143. (4) 144. (4) 145. (4) 146. (4) 147. (2) 148. (4) 149. (4) 150. (4)
151. (4) 152. (4) 153. (4) 154. (3) 155. (4) 156. (4) 157. (2) 158. (4) 159. (4) 160. (4)
161. (4) 162. (3) 163. (4) 164. (4) 165. (3) 166. (4) 167. (1) 168. (4) 169. (4) 170. (4)
171. (4) 172. (4) 173. (4) 174. (4) 175. (4) 176. (4) 177. (1) 178. (2) 179. (4) 180. (1)
181. (4) 182. (3) 183. (2) 184. (4) 185. (1) 186. (1) 187. (1) 188. (1) 189. (1) 190. (1)
191. (4) 192. (4) 193. (3) 194. (3) 195. (3) 196. (4) 197. (2) 198. (4) 199. (3) 200. (3)
201. (3) 202. (1) 203. (4) 204. (2) 205. (4) 206. (3) 207. (3) 208. (4) 209. (2) 210. (3)
211. (3) 212. (1) 213. (3) 214. (2) 215. (3) 216. (4) 217. (3) 218. (3) 219. (4) 220. (1)
221. (1) 222. (1) 223. (1) 224. (1) 225. (1) 226. (4) 227. (4) 228. (3) 229. (1) 230. (4)
231. (4) 232. (2) 233. (4) 234. (3) 235. (3) 236. (3) 237. (1) 238. (1) 239. (2) 240. (4)
241. (4) 242. (3) 243. (3) 244. (4) 245. (2) 246. (3) 247. (1) 248. (2) 249. (2) 250. (1)
251. (4) 252. (4) 253. (3) 254. (2) 255. (1) 256. (1) 257. (1) 258. (1)

UNIT 10

LABOUR MARKET

Syllabus

- Features, Demand and Supply of Labour, Nature and Composition of Indian Labour Force, Unemployment and Underemployment, Types of Labour Market,
- Characteristics of Indian Labour Market, New Dynamics of Labour Market in India, Economic Systems and Labor Market, Problems of Labour in India.

LABOUR MARKET

FEATURES

A labour market is the place where workers and employees interact with each other. In the labour market, employees compete to hire the best, and the workers compete for the best satisfying job. In simple words : A labour market in an economy functions with demand and supply of labour. In this market, labour demand is the firm's demand for labour and supply is the worker's supply of labour. The supply and demand of labour in the market is influenced by changes in the bargaining power.

Meaning

The "labour market" refers to the system in which people who want work, find employers who want workers. This system is referred to as a market because it follows to a large extent the laws of supply and demand. When there are many people chasing few jobs, there is downward pressure on wage rates. Workers are forced to accept lower rates of pay in order to get job. But when there are many jobs available and only a few workers who want them, there is upward pressure on wage rates. Employers are forced to pay higher rates of pay to get workers. However the labour market is not a perfect market and there are many other factors that intervene to prevent wage rates from dropping when there is an oversupply of workers for the number of jobs available.

A labour market is defined as a pool of all potential workers who compete for jobs. It also includes the employers who compete for workers. Labour markets are based on the supply and demand of labour in a country or a specific location that are able and willing to work.

Labour Force. Labour force includes all persons classified either as employed or unemployed during a specified period of time, usually a day or a week. Labour force can be categorized as self-employed, wage and salary earners, casual workers and unemployed.

Labour Market Related Terms

1. **Casual Workers.** Casual workers are those workers who are generally employed by small entrepreneurs on daily or weekly basis on a low wage rate. They are not entitled to any paid holiday leave or paid sick leaves.
2. **Unemployed persons.** The persons in the labour market who are without work, that is, without paid employment or self-employment and are currently either available for work or are seeking any work are considered to be unemployed.
3. **Labour force participation rate.** It is the number of persons in the labour force as a percentage of the working-age population. The working-age population is the population above a certain reference age like 15 years old and over or 15–64, etc.
4. **Employment rate.** It is ratio of employed persons to the total labour force. It is the percentage of working age people who have jobs or are employed.
5. **Unemployment rate.** It is the ratio of unemployed people to the total labour force.
6. **Underemployed persons.** Workers who are employed, but not in the desired capacity, whether in terms of compensation, hours, or level of skill and experience. The skills of such persons are underutilised, for example paying low wages to a highly skilled employee. Underemployment also refers to a situation where a major portion of labour force is unemployed.
7. **Underemployment rate.** It is the ratio of underemployed to either total labour force or total employment.

Labour Market Trends

CHARACTERISTICS OF INDIAN LABOUR
1. Migratory character
2. Low level of literacy
3. Indebtedness of labour
4. Heterogeneity of labour
5. High absenteeism
6. High labour turnover
7. Un-united labour force
8. Ill health of labour
9. Low efficiency

Downsizing

- Businesses are downsizing to improve productivity and competitiveness.
- Businesses can downsize by contracting out or outsourcing work normally done by their own employees.

Self-Employment

- The loss of work from the manufacturing sector, the introduction of new technology and the downsizing of businesses has created a tendency towards self-employment.
- There is government assistance available for people to start a business if they qualify.

Contract work. Employers are increasingly prone to hiring employees under fixed term contracts e.g. one year. This gives employers more flexibility to shape the work force when economic conditions are changing.

Training and education. A university education is more commonplace than 30 years ago. University graduates face stronger competition for jobs. Workers need to return to training and education more frequently during their careers. As technology changes, workers have to be updated. Retraining is required when changing careers.

Working from home. Information technology has made it possible for many people to work from home and still be tied into the business computer network. Working from home has advantages for both employer and employee.

Classification of Labour Market

Perfect market is defined by several conditions, collectively called perfect competition. Among these conditions are:

- Perfect market information
- No participant with market power to set prices
- No barriers to entry or exit
- Equal access to production technology

The following assumptions hold:

(a) there is a large number of buyers;
(b) there is a large number of sellers;
(c) the quantity of goods bought by any individual transactor is so small relative to the total quantity traded that individual trades leave the market unaffected;
(d) the units of goods sold by different sellers are the same - the product is homogeneous;
(e) there is perfect information = all buyers and sellers have complete information on the prices being asked and offered in other parts of the market; and
(f) there is perfect freedom of entry to and exit from the market

Main Features of Perfect Competitions

The following are the characteristics or main features of perfect competition :

1. **Many Sellers.** In this market, there are many sellers who form total of market supply. Individually, seller is a firm and collectively, it is an industry. In perfect competition, price of

commodity is decided by market forces of demand and supply, *i.e.*, by buyers and sellers collectively. Here, no individual seller is in a position to change the price by controlling supply. Because individual seller's individual supply is a very small part of total supply. So, if that seller alone raises the price, his product will become costlier than other and automatically, he will be out of market. Hence, that seller has to accept the price which is decided by market forces of demand and supply. This ensures single price in the market and in this way, seller becomes price taker and not price maker.

2. **Many Buyers.** Individual buyer cannot control the price by changing or controlling the demand. Because individual buyer's individual demand is a very small part of total demand or market demand. Every buyer has to accept the price decided by market forces of demand and supply. In this way, all buyers are price takers and not price makers. This also ensures existence of single price in market.
3. **Homogenous Product.** In this case, all sellers produce homogeneous, *i.e.*, perfectly identical products. All products are perfectly same in terms of size, shape, taste, colour, ingredients, quality, trade marks etc. This ensures the existence of single price in the market.
4. **Zero Advertisement Cost.** Since all products are identical in features like quality, taste, design etc., there is no scope for product differentiation. So advertisement cost is nil.
5. **Free Entry and Exit.** There are no restrictions on entry and exit of firms. This feature ensures existence of normal profit in perfect competition. When profit is more, new firms enter the market and this leads to competition. Entry of new firms competing with each other results into increase in supply and fall in price. So, this reduces profit from abnormal to normal level. When profit is low (below normal level), some firms may exit the market. This leads to fall in supply. So remaining firms raise their prices and their profits go up. So again this ensures normal level of profit.
6. **Perfect Knowledge.** On the front of both, buyers and sellers, perfect knowledge regarding market and pricing conditions is expected. So, no buyer will pay price higher than market price and no seller will charge lower price than market price.
7. **Perfect Mobility of Factors.** This feature is essential to keep supply at par with demand. If all factors are easily mobile (moveable) from one line of production to another, then it becomes easy to adjust supply as per demand. Whenever demand is more additional factors should be moved into industry to increase supply and vice versa. In this way, with the help of stable demand and supply, we can maintain single price in the Market.
8. **No Government Intervention.** Since market has been controlled by the forces of demand and supply, there is no government intervention in the form of taxes, subsidies, licensing policy, control over the supply of raw materials, etc.
9. **No Transport Cost.** It is assumed that buyers and sellers are close to market, so there is no transport cost. This ensures existence of single price in market.
   - ***Imperfect market.*** A market where information is not quickly disclosed to all participants in it and where the matching of buyers and sellers isn't immediate. Generally speaking, it is any market that does not adhere rigidly to perfect information flow and provide instantly available buyers and sellers.
   - ***Monopolistic markets.*** Monopoly is a trade market controlled by only one company, hence the prefix mono which means one. Its cause is greed. By being the only supplier of a good or service, the price is not competitive. The company can overcharge and needs not fear losing revenues to competing companies, because there is no competitor.

The two main causes of monopoly are:

1. government regulation that prevent anyone from competing; and
2. declining average costs- so that economies of scale mean that it would be more expensive for two firms to produce the desired amount of a good or service than for two or more (this is known as a 'natural monopoly').

A Purely Competitive Labour Market

- Numerous firms compete with one another to hire a specific type of labour.
- Each of many qualified workers with identical skills supplies that type of labour.
- Individual firms and individual workers are "wage takers;" neither exerts control over the market wage rate:
  1. Market Demand for Labour-market labour demand curve for a particular labour service is the horizontal sum of the labour demand curves of the individual firms.
  2. Market supply of Labour (assuming that workers individually compete for jobs).

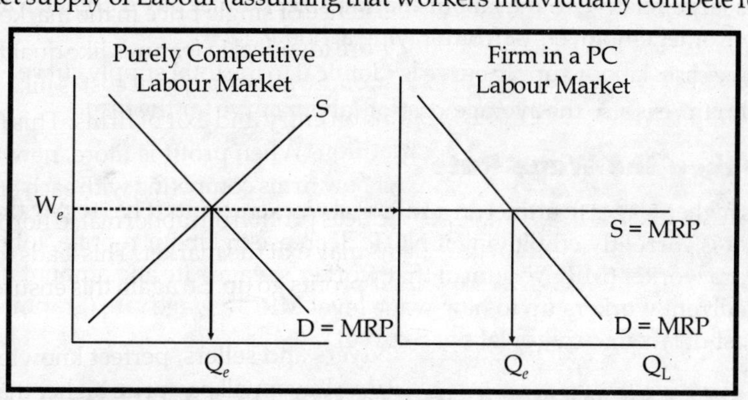

Labour Market Equilibrium

- equilibrium wage rate and level of employment in PC labour market = intersection of market labour D curve and market S curve.
- each individual firm finds it profitable to hire this type of labour up to point at which MRP = MRC.
- The area under the demand curve represents the total costs.

Monopsony Model

PC labour market: employer hires too small an amount of labour to influence the market wage rate :

Monopsony = a market in which a single employer of labour has substantial buying (hiring) power

Characteristics.

- only a single buyer of a particular type of labour
- relatively immobile type of labour, e.g. geographically or backward class workers would have to acquire new skills

Example of pure monopsony power: silver-mining company is the only source of employment in a small town.

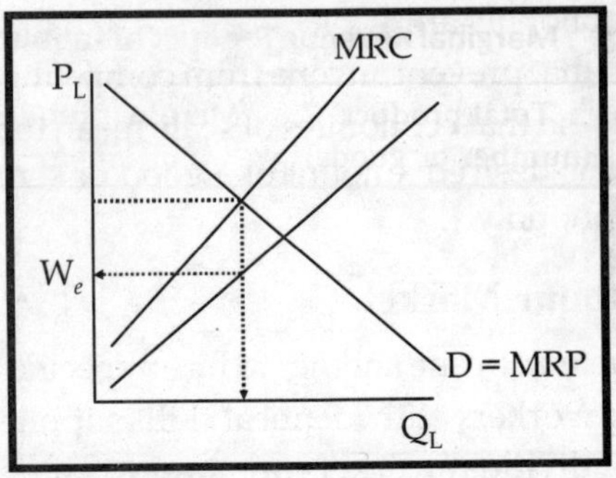

Upward-Sloping Labour Supply to Firm

- When a firm employs most of the available supply of a certain kind of labour, hiring more/less affects the wage rate.
- If a firm is large relative to the labour market size, it must pay a higher wage rate to attract labour from other employers or from staying at home.
- The extreme case: labour supply curve is identical to the total supply curve.
- The supply curve is also the average-cost-of-labour curve for the firm.

MRC Higher then the Wage Rate

Monopolist pays higher wages to attract an additional worker results it has to pay that higher wage to all workers that it is currently employing if NOT, decrease in labour morale, lots of labour unrest paying cost of extra worker (MRC) = sum of that worker's wage rate and amount necessary to bring wage rate of all current workers up to new wage level MRC > wage rate (graphically, MRC line is above average-cost-of labour curve or labour S curve)

DEMAND AND SUPPLY OF LABOUR

Labour Demand and Supply in a Perfectly Competitive Market

In addition to making output and pricing decisions, firms must also determine how much of each input to demand. Firms may choose to demand many different kinds of inputs. The two most common are labour and capital. The demand and supply of labour are determined in the labour market. The participants in the labour market are workers and firms. Workers supply labour to firms in exchange for wages. Firms demand labour from workers in exchange for wages.

The firm's demand for labour. The **firm's demand for labour** is a **derived demand**; it is derived from the demand for the firm's **output.** If demand for the firm's output increases, the firm will demand more labour and will hire more workers. If demand for the firm's output falls, the firm will demand less labour and will reduce its work force.

Marginal revenue product of labour. When the firm knows the level of demand for its output, it determines how much labour to demand by looking at the **marginal revenue product of labour.** The marginal revenue product of labour (or any input) is the *additional revenue* the firm earns by employing *one more unit* of labour. The marginal revenue product of labour is related to the **marginal product of labour.** In a perfectly competitive market, the firm's marginal revenue product of labour is the **value of the marginal product of labour.** For example, consider a perfectly competitive firm that uses labour as an input. The firm faces a market price of $10 for each unit of its output. The total product, marginal product, and marginal revenue product that the firm receives from hiring 1 to 5 workers are reported in table.

Marginal Revenue Product of Labour.

Labour input (workers)	Total product (number of goods)	Marginal product of labour	Marginal revenue product of labour
0	0	—	—
1	9	9	$90
2	17	8	80
3	22	5	50
4	25	3	30
5	26	1	10

The marginal revenue product of each additional worker is found by multiplying the marginal product of each additional worker by the market price of $10. The marginal revenue product of labour is the additional revenue that the firm earns from hiring an additional worker; it represents the **wage** that the firm is *willing* to pay for each additional worker. The wage that the firm *actually* pays is the **market wage rate**, which is determined by the **market demand** and **market supply of labour.** In a perfectly competitive *labour* market, the individual firm is a **wage-taker**; it takes the market wage rate as given, just as the firm in a perfectly competitive product market takes the price for its output as given. The market wage rate in a perfectly competitive labour market represents the firm's **marginal cost of labour**, the amount the firm must pay for each additional worker that it hires.

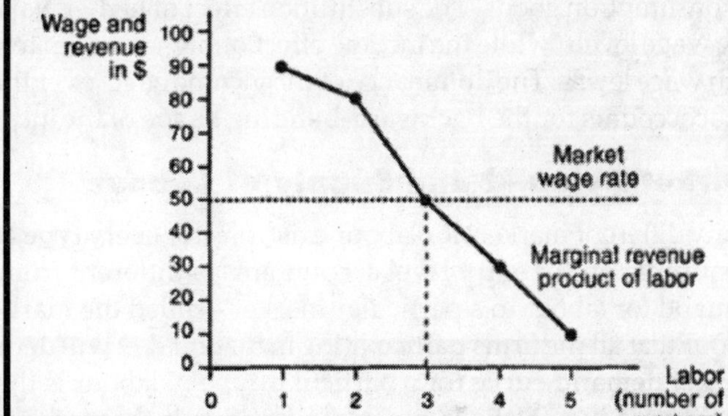

A perfectly competitive firm's profit-maximizing labor-demand decision.

The firm's labour demand curve. The firm's profit-maximizing labour-demand decision is depicted graphically in figure.

This figure graphs the marginal revenue product of labour data from Table along with the market wage rate of $50. When the marginal revenue product of labour is graphed, it represents **the firm's labour demand curve.** The demand curve is downward sloping due to the law of diminishing returns; as more workers are hired, the marginal product of labour begins declining, causing the marginal revenue product of labour to fall as well. The intersection of the marginal revenue product curve with the market wage determines the number of workers that the firm hires, in this case 3 workers.

An individual's supply of labour. An individual's supply of labour depends on his or her **preferences** for two types of "goods": **consumption goods and leisure.** Consumption goods include all the goods that can be purchased with the income that an individual earns from working. Leisure is the good that individuals consume when they are not working. By working more (supplying more labour), an individual reduces his or her consumption of leisure but is able to increase his or her purchases of consumption goods. In choosing between leisure and consumption, the individual faces two constraints. First, the individual is limited to twenty-four hours per day for work or leisure. Second, the individual's income from work is limited by the market wage rate that the individual receives for his or her labour skills. In a perfectly competitive labour market, workers—like firms—are **wage-takers;** they take the market wage rate that they receive as given. **An individual's labour supply curve.** An example of **an individual's labour supply curve** is given in Figure.

As wages increase, so does the **opportunity cost of leisure.** As leisure becomes more costly, workers tend to substitute more work hours for fewer leisure hours in order to consume the relatively cheaper consumption goods, which is the **substitution effect** of a higher wage. An **income effect** is also associated with a higher wage. A higher wage leads to higher real incomes, provided that prices of consumption goods remain constant. As real incomes rise, individuals will demand more leisure, which is considered a **normal good** – the higher an individual's income, the easier it is for that individual to take more time off from work and still maintain a high standard of living in terms of consumption goods. The substitution effect of higher wages tends to dominate the income effect at low wage levels, while the income effect of higher wages tends to dominate the substitution effect at high wage levels. The dominance of the income effect over the substitution effect at high wage levels is what accounts for the **backward-bending shape** of the individual's labour supply curve.

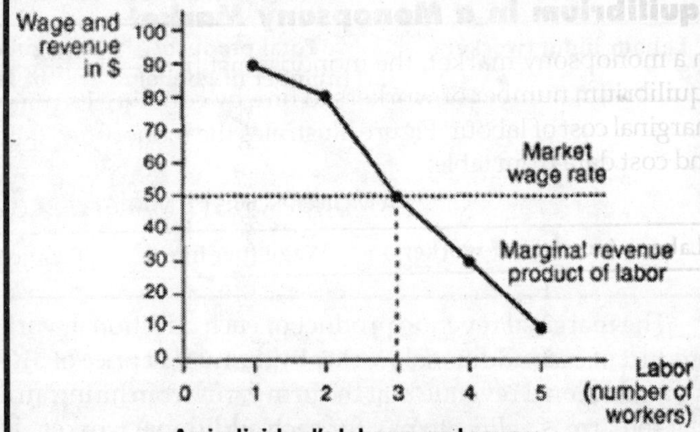

An individual's labor supply curve

Market Demand and Supply of Labour

Many different markets for labour exist, one for every **type and skill level** of labour. For example, the labour market for entry level accountants is different from the labour market for tennis pros. The demand for labour in a particular market - called the **market demand** for labour - is the amount of labour that all the firms participating in that market will demand at different market wage levels. The **market demand curve** for a particular type of labour is the horizontal summation of the marginal revenue product of labour curves of every firm in the market for that type of labour. The **market supply of labour** is the number of workers of a particular type and skill level who are willing to supply their labour to firms at different wage levels. The **market supply curve** for a particular type of labour is the horizontal summation of the individuals' labour supply curves. Unlike an individual's supply curve, the market supply curve is *not backward bending* because there will always be some workers in the market who will be willing to supply more labour and take less leisure time, even at relatively high wage levels.

Labour Demand and Supply in a Monopsony-A labour market in which there is only one firm demanding labour is called a **monopsony.** The single firm in the market is referred to as the **monopolist.** An example of a monopsony would be the only firm in a "company town," where the workers all work for that single firm. **Wage-searching behaviour.** Because the monopsonist is the sole de-mander of labour in the market, the monopsonist's demand for labour is the **market demand for labour.** The supply of labour that the monopsonist faces is the **market supply of labour.** Unlike a firm operating in a perfectly competitive labour market, the monopsonist does not simply hire all the workers that it wants at the equilibrium market wage. The monopsonist faces the *upward-sloping* market supply curve; it is a **wage-searcher** rather than a **wage-taker.** If the monopsonist wants to increase the number of workers that it hires, it must increase the wage that it pays to *all* of its workers, including those whom it currently employs. The monopsonist's **marginal cost of hiring** an additional worker, therefore, will not be equal to the wage paid to that **worker because the monopsonist will have to increase the wage that it pays to all of its workers.**

Equilibrium in a Monopsony Market

In a monopsony market, the monopsonist firm – like any profit-maximising firm – determines the equilibrium number of workers to hire by equating its marginal revenue product of labour with its marginal cost of labour. Figure illustrates the monopsony labour market equilibrium, using the supply and cost data from table.

A MONOPSONIST'S MARGINAL COST OF LABOUR

Labour (number of workers)	Wage (per hour)	Total cost of labour	Marginal cost of labour
1	$10	$10	$10
2	15	30	20
3	20	60	30
4	25	100	40
5	30	150	50

UNEMPLOYMENT AND UNDEREMPLOYMENT

Unemployment

It is important to acknowledge that unemployed labour represents an integral element of the external labour market. People that are out of work but actively Seeking employment, particularly those unemployed over a long period, tell us a great deal about the operation of the labour market. The unemployed or surplus labour in any given market plays a role in determining the cost of employed labour, the terms under which it is engaged and the extent of industrial conflict. For example, where there is a large surplus of labour then this will result in greater competition for jobs, a downward pressure on wages and conditions and a lowered likelihood of employees 'rocking the boat'. Where particular groups are disproportionately affected by unemployment for reasons unconnected to their capabilities (for example, reflecting social group disadvantage) this reflects a distortion of the 'proper' working of the labour market.

There are a number of types of unemployment.

1. **Structural unemployment** exists where there is a fundamental mismatch between the supply and demand for labour. For example, where demand for particular types of skill is low, those in possession of these skills are at a relatively greater risk of being out of work. As such, unemployment can result from a lack of employability and can bead dressed through workers retraining or moving to areas where their skills are in greater demand.
2. **Cyclical unemployment** can also be **cyclical** in that it reflects business or economic cycles. For example, in times of recession the demand for labour in general falls and unemployment rises. Therefore, being out of work is not necessarily associated with one's long-term employability; rather it is linked to a short-term decline in overall demand for labour.
3. **Frictional unemployment** reflects a temporary mismatch in the demand and supply of labour which is always present in an economy. For example, a worker might be unemployed whilst looking for a particular type of job but is yet to identify an appropriate existing vacancy. Therefore, even where supply broadly meets the demand for labour, unemployment temporarily persists.

Underemployment

"**Underemployment**" can mean many things to different people, but when used correctly it means that:

(1) a person is working at a job for they are significantly overqualified (*i.e.* Bill has an MA in Mechanical Engineering and is working as a cashier at Kmart).

Unemployment	Underemployment
Individual is has qualifications, the will and is actively looking for employment but unable to find work.	Individual is employed but does not work for as long they would like to or their qualifications are not fully utilize. They are overqualified.
There is only one type.	Divided into two parts: visible and invisible.
Main causes are rise in the cost of production , drop in the aggregate demand and change in technology.	Caused by a disparity in availability of employment opportunities and corresponding skills availability.
Unemployment rate used to measure.	Distinct measure for underemployment does not exist although can be measured indirectly using brain drain.

(2) a person is working part-time even if he/she wants/needs full-time (*i.e.* Bill is available to work 40 hours a week but can't find a job for more than 20 hours a week).

The classic reason for underemployment is a bad job market. There simply isn't enough work to go around. There can be a glut of applicants for specific occupations (too many assembly line workers after robots take their jobs) or there can be high unemployment levels across the country.

Underemployment refers to an employment situation that is insufficient in some important way for the worker, relative to a standard. Examples include holding a part-time job despite desiring full-time work, and over qualification, where the employee has education, experience, or skills beyond the requirements of the job.

Underemployment has been studied in recent decades from a variety of perspectives, including economics, management, psychology, and sociology. In economics, for example, the term underemployment has three different distinct meanings and applications. All meanings involve a situation in which a person is working, unlike unemployment, where a person who is searching work cannot find a job. All meanings involve under-utilization of labour which is missed by most official (governmental agency) definitions and measurements of unemployment.

Underemployment can Refers to

- "Over qualification" or "over education", or the employment of workers with high education, skill levels, and/or experience in jobs that do not require such abilities. For example, a trained medical doctor who works as a taxi driver would experience this type of underemployment.
- "Involuntary part-time" work, where workers who could (and would like to) be working for a full work-week can only find part-time work. By extension, the term is also used in regional planning to describe regions where economic activity rates are unusually low, due to a lack of job opportunities, training opportunities, or due to a lack of services such as child-care and public transportation.
- "Overstaffing" or "hidden unemployment" (also called "labour hoarding"), the practice in which businesses or entire economies employ workers who are not fully occupied—for example, workers currently not being used to produce goods or services due to legal or social restrictions or because the work is highly seasonal.

Reason for Underemployment

The number of wage employment seekers depends upon the following: the size of the population of working age, the number who, having sufficient unearned incomes, choose to remain idle; the number who, being in command of the requisite means of production, are self-employed; and the prevailing wage-rate and other incentives provided.

Normally, apart from the size of the population of working age, these factors are likely to be more or less stable over short periods. For instance, the span of life regarded as falling within the working age, while subject to variation as, a result of changes in the period of schooling or in the normal age for retirement consequent on changes in health standards and longevity, is likely to remain unchanged in the short period.

Moreover, even when some of these factors change somewhat, the net quantitative effect may not be important. Higher wages, for instance, may induce some of the older workers to postpone their retirement while these may impel some of the married women workers, now that their husbands are better off, to relinquish their jobs. The net effect of a rise in wages will not, therefore, be quantitatively important.

The same applies to other of these factors. The size of the population of working age, too, though not invariant, is measurable as it changes according to definite trends. It follows that the number of wage-seeking population can be determined with a great measure of accuracy. And since the average number of hours of work which each wage-employment seeker wants to put in is likely to be more or less stable in any short period, the total amount of wage employment sought is quite precisely measurable.

Similar observations may be made regarding the permissible allowance for seasonal and frictional unemployment. It will have to vary from season to season, and from year to year, in accordance with the inevitable seasonal variations in employment and in the magnitude of the structural shifts in demand and production that, together with immobility of labour, cause frictional unemployment. It may, therefore, be better defined as a range rather than as a precise figure. Since normally structural shifts in demand and production are unlikely to be violent or spasmodic and since in industrialized countries the incidence of seasonal unemployment is bound to be quite low, the allowance for frictional and seasonal unemployment needs to be very small. A U.N. study has suggested that this allowance need not be beyond a range of 2-4 or 3-5 per cent of the available labour force.

The possibility of measuring the size of the available labour force and inevitable minimum of frictional and seasonal unemployment makes full employment a determinate quantity. As suggested by a U.N. study, as a necessary step in the effective implementation of full-employment policies, each country should fix a full-employment target expressed in terms of the permissible range of frictional and seasonal unemployment. Unemployment in excess of the fixed target would indicate a lapse from full employment calling for remedial action. The fixation of such a target would help to reduce the chances of government inaction or vacillation in the face of growing unemployment. It may also help to maintain confidence among business men whose pessimism ordinarily plays a notable part in magnifying the downswing.

There is, however, the danger of government acting on a false scent. For at times, unemployment may exceed the target due to causes other than insufficient demand. The danger may be minimized by allowing the government the discretion to disregard the signal if it has clear evidence that rise in unemployment is not due to demand deficiency

CHARACTERISTICS OF INDIAN LABAOUR MARKET

India's labour markets are experiencing structural change, but there is a dearth of reliable data to capture these shifts. The debate tends to focus narrowly on the pace of job creation, which itself could be measured more frequently and accurately. We see the need for a new emphasis on the notion of "gainful employment" for India's workforce of 460 million that focuses on improved quality of work and the income derived from it. Gainful employment covers a range of issues, including the quantity and type of work done by people already in employment, growth in labour productivity, higher earnings, and aspects of work quality such as safety, cleanliness, flexibility, income security, and intellectual challenge.

- Surveys showing a three-percentage-point decline in India's overall labour force participation between 2011 and 2015 should not take focus away from the structural shift from agriculture towards the non-farm sector, particularly construction, trade, and transport. During this period, agriculture shrank by 26 million while non-farm jobs rose by 33 million, largely driven by rapid economic growth between 2013 and 2015. More recent trends in aggregate employment cannot be derived from the quarterly enterprise studies available, highlighting the data deficit.

- Labour force participation and the number of employed people do not in themselves measure gainful employment. Declining labour participation may indicate that more young people have stayed in education and/or that more women from households which were once in extreme poverty but have now entered the middle class no longer need to work in low-productivity jobs. Likewise, supplementary income opportunities (such as additional days of work on a construction project or selling home produce through a digital platform) may not increase the number of jobs, but they may raise the income level, choice, flexibility, and security of an underemployed worker engaged in low-productivity work.
- Global trends affecting economies around the world pose challenges to labour but also lead to more opportunities for gainful employment. Three are particularly relevant to India:
  - To bridge India's infrastructure gaps, the government has raised public investment in roads, railways, rural development, power, telecom, housing, and "soft" areas of health care and education, creating work opportunities for an estimated seven million workers, at wages that are 70 percent higher than for average farm workers. In addition to creating jobs, there is some evidence of investment in power and roads infrastructure triggering growth in the non-farm economy in key states.
  - Rapid advances in automation technologies are affecting India's information technology and business process outsourcing sectors. These sectors have remained net job creators, and the industry estimates that companies could hire up to 2.5 to three million more workers by 2025, provided they can acquire the skills to meet changing needs.

NEW DYNAMICS OF LABOUR MARKET

India acutely feels the infrastructure deficit, and the government has moved to close funding gaps. Central government spending (both revenue and capital expenditure) on prioritised sectors rose by 1,080 billion rupees ($17 billion), or 55 percent, between 2014 and 2017, when total spending reached 2,991 billion rupees ($46 billion). Spending was focused particularly on roads, railways, housing, and rural development, as well as in telecom and power, and "soft" infrastructure, such as education and health care (Exhibit 5). Based on average revenue per labour benchmarks in each sector, we estimate that central government spending could translate to employment opportunities for some 6.6 million workers in 2017 (excluding the impact of the Mahatma Gandhi National Rural Employment Guarantee Act, or MGNREGA), or some two million more compared to the level in 2014. A large share of these jobs are in the construction sector, where an average worker earns 70 percent more than an average farm worker, so this trend is good from a gainful employment perspective.

In addition to increased central sector expenditure, direct jobs have also been created through increased spending by states. They spend almost 30 percent more than central government, with a higher share allocated to capital expenditure. Their spending on education, health, and family welfare is also disproportionately higher. More recently, the states' expenditure has been further boosted by the increased devolution of central taxes.

A further boost to work opportunities has come with the government's renewed commitment to MGNREGA since 2015. In addition to enhancing income security in rural areas, this programme aims to build rural infrastructure, such as rural connectivity, water conservation, and land development. Using data from the programme's website, we estimate that it has created an additional 690 million man-days of work in 2017 compared to 2015. Assuming a full-time equivalent job is 300 man-days, this is roughly equal to adding 2.3 million jobs, though in reality, each beneficiary gets about 46 man-days of work, which translates into a total of 51.2 million beneficiary households in 2017, or 10 million more than in 2015. While most of this work may not qualify as a new job (it is considered time spent by an existing daily-wage agricultural worker in construction activities that earns her a wage), it yields income gains that contribute directly to improved wellbeing. Programmes like JAM (Jan Dhan-Aadhaar-Mobile, which gives people access to banking and payments through low-balance bank accounts, Aadhaar-based authentication, and mobile-based payment services) are being implemented to pay wages directly to bank accounts, thereby raising worker bargaining power and contributing further to worker wellbeing. Almost 96 percent of wage and material payments are electronically credited into workers' accounts, according to the Ministry of Rural Development. This has resulted in obvious efficiencies in reducing cost and plugging leakages. Consequently, administrative expenditure has fallen as a percentage of total expenditure from 6.1 percent in 2013-14 to 4.8 percent in 2016-17. A study found that leakage in MGNREGA allocation has fallen by more than 12 percent when payment is made electronically. While evidence about outcomes in terms of asset creation as a result of MGNREGA is less conclusive, the pace of work completed has gained momentum, rising from 2.7 million in 2014 to 6.1 million in 2017

As India's economy continues to grow at 6.5 to 7 percent per year or more, there is room for greater private-sector investment to start flowing into infrastructure, and this could provide an impetus for labour to continue moving into construction. The government's "Housing for All" programme, if well implemented, could provide a further boost. But construction work is becoming more skill intensive, and India's workforce is short of these skills. Sustaining benefits for workers will mean boosting the supply of job-ready skills matched to the types in demand.

ECONOMIC SYSTEMS AND LABOUR MARKET

The Labour Market in Macroeconomic Theory

According to macroeconomic theory, the fact that wage growth lags productivity growth indicates that supply of labour has outpaced demand. When that happens, there is downward pressure on wages, as workers compete for a scarce number of jobs and employers have their pick of the litter. Conversely, if demand outpaces supply, there is upward pressure on wages, as workers have more bargaining power and are more likely to be able to switch to a higher paying job, while employers must compete for scarce labour.

Some factors can influence labour supply and demand. For example, an increase in immigration to a country can grow the labour supply and potentially depress wages, particularly if newly arrived workers are willing to accept lower pay. An aging population can deplete the supply of labour and potentially drive up wages.

These factors don't always have such straightforward consequences, though. A country with an aging population will see demand for many goods and services decline, while demand for healthcare increases. Not every worker who loses his job can simply move into healthcare work, particularly if the jobs in demand are highly skilled and specialized, such as doctors. For this reason, demand can exceed supply in certain sectors, even if supply exceeds demand in the labour market as a whole.

Factors influencing supply and demand don't work in isolation, either. If it weren't for immigration, the U.S. would be a much older, and probably less dynamic society, so while an influx of unskilled workers might have exerted downward pressure on wages, it likely offset declines in demand.

Other factors influencing contemporary labour markets, and the U.S. labour market in particular, include: the threat of automation as computer programs gain the ability to do more complex tasks; the effects of globalization as enhanced communication and better transport links allow work to be moved across borders; the price, quality and availability of education; and a whole array of policies such as the minimum wage.

The Labour Market in Micro-economic Theory

Micro-economic theory analyzes labour supply and demand at the level of the individual firm and worker. Supply, or the hours an employee is willing to work, initially increases as wage increases. No workers will work voluntarily for nothing (unpaid interns are, in theory, working to gain experience and increase their desirability to other employers) and more people are willing to work for $20 an hour than $5 an hour.

Gains in supply may accelerate as wages increase, since the opportunity cost of not working additional hours grows. But supply may then decrease at a certain wage level: The difference between $1,000 an hour and $1050 is hardly noticeable, and the highly-paid worker who's presented with the option of working an extra hour or spending her money on leisure activities may well opt for the latter.

Demand at the micro-economic level depends on two factors, marginal cost and marginal revenue product. If the marginal cost of hiring an additional employee, or having existing employees work more hours, exceeds the marginal revenue product, it will cut into earnings, and the firm would theoretically reject that option. If the opposite is true, it makes rational sense to take on more labour.

Neoclassical micro-economic theories of labour supply and demand have received criticism on some fronts. Most contentious is the assumption of "rational" choice – maximizing money while minimizing work – which to critics is not only cynical but not always supported by the evidence. *Homo sapiens*, unlike *Homo economics*, may have all sorts of motivations for making specific choices. The existence of some professions in the arts and non-profit sector undermines the notion of maximizing utility. Defenders of neoclassical theory counter that their predictions may have little bearing on a given individual, but are useful when taking large numbers of workers in aggregate.

PROBLEMS OF LABOUR IN INDIA

Land is an indispensable but a passive factor production in economics. No production is possible without the use of labour. We cannot expect any production without labour i.e., why it is said to be an indispensable and active factor of production. Labour is one of the main factors which constitute the material foundation of society.

In an economy, where agriculture is the primary occupation and most of the national income is contributed from agriculture, problems related to labour are there but not in a complex form. Labour problems may be considered as social problems which result among different groups where there is absence of cooperative endeavor for the realization of common goal.

In agriculture, labour problems do not arise because of the presence of cooperative mentality. Workers and owners of means of production work together with a sense of cooperation and therefore they do not think in terms of their exact share and the exploitation in the hands of the owners. In agricultural sector mainly family farming prevails where everybody thinks in terms of contributing towards production.

Even if some of the person is removed from this sector, the production remains unaltered and therefore total production is same and the problem of disguised unemployment is faced by this sector. It means agricultural sector does not realise labour problems, however they crop in the system itself.

Things have altogether changed because of the changes in the structure of the economic system. With the development of the society, there is a demand for more goods and services. Agriculture sector cannot meet the rising demand for goods and services. It is the industry sector which can discharge the things at this juncture.

When there is need for large scale production, division of labour and specialisation, machinery, senior skilled labour etc. are automatically on the scene. When normal social relation guided by the existing norms and values are disturbed then problems of social nature automatically emerge. Industries being a substantial change in the society.

Industrial revolution brought a substantial change in our contemporary society. Similarly the economic order which India wants to establish is also changing very fast with the expansion of money supply and credit. The monetary institutions are increasing and the mode of transactions is also changing very fast.

In advanced countries the share of agriculture is low and that of manufacturing and services is high. With the accelerated growth of population in the last few years, the pressure of population on the available land has increased tremendously in the absence of growing industries at the same pace of absorb the new labour force.

The labour ratio being higher, agricultural holdings have become very small and uneconomic. All these factors have brought a radical change in the agrarian Indian society. Consequently various problems are arising out of the new situation e.g. the problem of unemployment; social security and industrial relations etc. are the outcomes of the process of industrialisation.

(1) Wages

Wages are a payment for the service of labour, whether mental or physical. Though in an ordinary language an office executive a minister or a teacher is said to receive a salary, a lawyer or a doctor a fee, and a skilled or unskilled worker a wage, yet in economics no such distinctions are made for different services and all of them are said to receive a wage.

In other words, wages include fees, commissions and salaries. It is another thing that some may be receiving more in the form of real wages and less in terms of money wages and vice versa. Wages may be paid weekly, fortnightly or monthly and partly at the end of the year in the form of bonus.

These are time wages. But the bonus may be a last wage if a work is finished within a specified period or before that. Wages are also paid in accordance with the amount of work done, say in a shoe factory or a tailoring department as per one pair or parts manufactured.

If the rate per pair of shoes or for pants is Rs. 5 a worker will be paid according to the number of pairs of pants manufactured. These will be piece wages. Sometimes, time wages are supplemented by wages earned by working extra time. They are overtime wages.

Sometimes wages are regulated by the State in the interest of the low paid workers in certain or all industries that is minimum wage which ensures a minimum standard of living. In a capitalist society the workmen are exploited. In such a society there are two main classes—the capitalists and the workmen; the former owning the means of production and the latter selling their labour-power.

Owing to the expansion of large scale production with the help of machinery, the number of wage earners increases. Over production is another characteristic of an industrial society. Commodities are produced for the market, and when the market contracts workmen are rendered unemployed.

When demand for commodities increases, their labour power is required again. Such labourers form an industrial reserve army. Even if trusts and cartels are organized, that does not mean that all the workmen will always remain employed. Some of them may still remain unemployed because such industrial organizations close their unremunerated units.

Another contributory cause is the expropriation of the proletariat from land who move to the cities to swell the number of their birth rate. In reality capitalism is the outcome of class struggle which will overthrow the present regime with the result that the expropriators will themselves be expropriated.

Capital is taken to mean money which is used for exploitation. Whereas in pre-capitalist society commodities were produced for their value in use (utility) and their exchange increased utilities, money was not used for exploitation. In a pre-capitalist economy, the equation of exchange was C-M-C in which C stood for commodity and M for money.

Commodity was exchanged for money with the help of money another commodity was purchased. But in a capitalist society since production is undertaken for profit, the question of exchange is M-C-M. The capitalist enters the market with M. M. M the difference being the profit of the capitalists. This shows the degree of exploitation.

While the first process is based on qualitative difference between two goods, the second process must be based, if it is to have any purpose at all, on a qualitative difference between two sums of money. In a slave feudal society exploitation was open; in a capitalist society it is hidden. A worker in any industry works for example 8 hours a day.

It is clear, therefore the exchange value of the product of his labour, will be equal to 8 hours' labour. The wages that he gets are equivalent to 5 hours labour (necessary labour); and the remaining three hours' labour is called surplus labour which creates surplus value, and it goes to the capitalist.

Wages in India are very low. A thorough analysis of the index number of cost of living, money and real earning, may reveal the right of the workers. Effort were made to ameliorate the grievances of workers and the British Government appointed a commission to go into the matters of labour the commission (Royal Commission) suggested exploring the possibilities for fixing up machinery which can look into the matter of the wages but due to certain administrative difficulties the idea was dropped. After Independence, the Minimum Wage Act was passed in 1948 and this Act has been amended subsequently from time to time.

The question of wage is of great significance and importance to the working class. Any one impalpable of maintaining himself and his family out of his income is bound to become discontented.

There will be no peace in his mind and he would always aspire to overthrow the order which compels him to lead a life of poverty, degradation and humiliation inspite of his hard work. It will give rise to industrial unrest. Ultimately the industrial production will suffer. Therefore, a study of wages in different industrial establishments is of paramount importance.

At present, in India, there are three views with regard to wages. The employer's association is trying for fixing a wage which is equivalent to the subsistence wage. The workers unions are striving for a living wage, while Government is considering a middle way approach for fixing fair wage.

The minimum wage is higher than the subsistence wage and the fair wage is something between minimum and living wages. The Fair Wage Committee (1949) stated that, "the state of national income is highly relevant to the problems of wages because no wage policy can be regarded as just or even economically sound unless it encourages increase of the national income and secures to the wage earner a legitimate share in that increase."

We consider that a minimum wage must also provide for some measure of education, medical requirements and amenities. The demand for a living wage is a principal objective of the workers and the pressure for increases in existing wage levels constitutes a problem for economic development.

(2) Unionism

The trade union is a unique organisation in that it explicit, indeed sole, purpose is to protest. The basic fact that has to be firmly grasped is that trade unionism is a system of opposition and not of government, and that unions cannot be responsible for managing anything except their own internal affairs.

Trade unions exist to oppose exploitation in such diverse organisations as factories, banking and insurance companies, government bureaucracies, universities, research institutions and even cooperatives. Inequality is universal to the distribution of money and power in modern industrial society.

Of course, some organisations are economically and politically more exploitative than others. Trade unions have a number of methods open to them to go about the job of protecting against inequality and ensuring a more egalitarian distribution of economic gain and political power. They may negotiate with the management the terms and conditions under which their members are employed.

They may bring pressure to bear on the government to enact legislation that will ensure a better deal to working men. But their most important weapon, and one which unions have fiercely clung to throughout their history, is the collective withdrawal of labour, otherwise called the strike.

The collective withdrawal of labour would be meaning less if the employer were permitted to get others to do the job of striking men. Hence the reliance of unions on picketing, preventing the entry of black-logs and strike breakers of all kinds. Stated boldly disruption of normal industrial production and the provision of essential services is an inevitable consequence of the pursuit of legitimate trade union activity. Unions cannot protest except through disruption.

The problem of collective bargaining and industrial democracy has become most complicated. It has generally found that no solution is equally acceptable to employers as well as to employees. There are strikes and lockouts on account of low wages, long working hours, bad working conditions, non-payment of dues and bonus, absence of security of employment, absence of medical aid and victimisation.

The role of organised labour becomes more significant in the context of present industrialisation and economic development of the country. Hence the study of unionism is very important aspect of the study of labour problems. The agricultural labourers are scattered and are unorganised with the result nothing concrete has been done to ameliorate their grievances.

(3) Employment Security

Lod Keynes diagnosed unemployment in advanced economies to be the result of a deficiency of effective demand. It implied that in such economies machines become idle and demand for labour falls because the demand for the products of industry is no longer there.

Thus Keynesian remedies of unemployment naturally concentrated on measures to keep the level of effective demand sufficiently high so that the economic machine does not slacken the production of goods and services. This type of unemployment caused by economic fluctuations did arise in India during the depression of thirties which caused untold misery.

But with the growth of Keynesian remedies, it has been possible to mitigate cyclical unemployment. Similarly after the Second World War, when wartime industries were being closed there was a good deal of frictional unemployment caused by retrenchment.

These workers were to be absorbed in peace time industries. The process of rationalisation also causes displacement of labour. But more serious than cyclical unemployment or frictional unemployment in an underdeveloped economy like India is the prevalence of chronic under-employment or disguised unemployment in the rural sector and the existence of urban unemployment among the educated classes. It would be worthwhile to emphasise here that unemployment in underdeveloped economies like India is not the result of deficiency of effective demand in the Keynesian sense, but a consequence of shortage of capital equipment or other complementary resources.

The shifting levels of business activity constitute the most important disrupting factor in a capitalistic economy. The seasonal, cyclical and secular changes in activity lead to corresponding variations in the total demand for labour. Loss of jobs may also result from changes in technology or from the inevitable imperfections in the operation of a free labour market.

These various causes interact on each other e.g., technological unemployment tends to be greater during periods of cyclical decline in business activity. The sheer idea of unemployment is prejudicial to a worker's happiness and efficiency, while actual unemployment is the chief source of social maladies and exploitation.

The economic aspect of unemployment is closely related with social, moral and even mental aspect of a worker. An unemployed becomes easy prey of many evil habits and his talents are rusted. For him, all social norms and values appear in a state of dilapidation and ultimately he loses his mental equilibrium.

MULTIPLE CHOICE QUESTIONS

1. What is the term used to describe the willingness and ability of workers to work at a particular wage rate?
   (1) Labour market equilibrium
   (2) Supply of labour
   (3) Demand for labour
   (4) Labour productivity
2. Which of the following is a factor that can increase the demand for labour?
   (1) An increase in the wage rate
   (2) An increase in the price of a substitute good
   (3) An increase in the level of business activity
   (4) An increase in unemployment benefits
3. What type of labour is characterized by high skills, experience, and education?
   (1) Skilled labour
   (2) Unskilled labour
   (3) Semi-skilled labour
   (4) Professional labour
4. Which of the following is a factor that can increase the supply of labour?
   (1) A decrease in the wage rate
   (2) A decrease in the level of business activity
   (3) An increase in the level of education and training
   (4) An increase in the price of a substitute good
5. Which of the following is a factor that can decrease the demand for labour?
   (1) An increase in the level of business activity
   (2) A decrease in the price of a substitute good
   (3) Technological advancements that automate tasks previously done by workers
   (4) An increase in immigration
6. Which type of labour is characterized by a low level of skills and education?
   (1) Skilled labour
   (2) Professional labour
   (3) Unskilled labour
   (4) Semi-skilled labour
7. Which of the following is a factor that can decrease the supply of labour?
   (1) An increase in the wage rate
   (2) A decrease in the level of education and training
   (3) An increase in the retirement age
   (4) An increase in the number of working women
8. Which of the following is a factor that can increase the wage rate in a labour market?
   (1) A decrease in the demand for labour
   (2) An increase in the supply of labour
   (3) An increase in the level of education and training of workers
   (4) A shortage of workers with certain skills or experience
9. What is the term used to describe the number of workers that employers are willing and able to hire at a particular wage rate?
   (1) Labour market equilibrium
   (2) Supply of labour
   (3) Demand for labour
   (4) Labour productivity
10. Which of the following is a factor that can decrease the wage rate in a labour market?
    (1) A decrease in the supply of labour
    (2) An increase in the demand for labour

(3) An increase in the level of business activity
(4) A surplus of workers with certain skills or experience

11. Which of the following is a major source of recruitment for employers in a labour market?
(1) Trade unions
(2) Colleges and universities
(3) Online job boards and social media
(4) Government-run employment agencies

12. What is the term used to describe the total value of goods and services produced by a country's economy in a particular period of time?
(1) Gross Domestic Product (GDP)
(2) Consumer Price Index (CPI)
(3) Unemployment Rate
(4) Interest Rate

13. What is the term used to describe the rate at which the general level of prices for goods and services is rising, and subsequently, purchasing power is falling?
(1) Unemployment Rate
(2) Consumer Price Index (CPI)
(3) Gross Domestic Product (GDP)
(4) Interest Rate

14. Which of the following is a factor that can cause a shift in the supply of labour in a labour market?
(1) A change in the educational qualifications or skills required for a particular job
(2) A change in the level of business activity
(3) Technological advancements that automate tasks previously done by workers
(4) An increase in the number of working women

15. What is the term used to describe the rate at which people are being hired or fired in an economy?
(1) Growth rate
(2) Labour turnover rate
(3) Inflation rate (4) Interest rate

16. What type of unemployment occurs when workers are between jobs because of a change in the labour market, such as technological advancements, changing consumer preferences, or global competition?
(1) Cyclical unemployment
(2) Structural unemployment
(3) Frictional unemployment
(4) Seasonal unemployment

17. What type of unemployment occurs when there is a recession in the economy, and firms have to lay off workers because of a decrease in demand for goods and services?
(1) Structural unemployment
(2) Frictional unemployment
(3) Cyclical unemployment
(4) Seasonal unemployment

18. What type of unemployment occurs when workers are temporarily without work, such as tourism workers in the off-season, seasonal agricultural workers, or construction workers during the winter?
(1) Structural unemployment
(2) Frictional unemployment
(3) Cyclical unemployment
(4) Seasonal unemployment

19. Which of the following is a factor that can cause a shift in the demand for labour in a labour market?
(1) A change in the educational qualifications or skills required for a particular job
(2) An increase in the wage rate
(3) An increase in the level of business activity
(4) An increase in unemployment benefits

20. Which of the following is a factor that can cause a shift in the labour market equilibrium?
(1) A change in the level of business activity
(2) An increase in the retirement age
(3) A shortage of workers with certain skills or experience
(4) All of the above

21. Which of the following is an example of a benefit that employers may offer to attract workers in a competitive labour market?
(1) A retirement plan
(2) Health insurance
(3) Paid time off
(4) All of the above

22. In a labour market, what is the term used to describe the group of workers who are willing and able to work at the current wage rate, but cannot find jobs?
(1) Unemployed workers
(2) Inactive workers
(3) Employed workers
(4) Discouraged workers

23. What is the term used to describe the rate at which unemployed individuals are seeking employment and are available and willing to work?
(1) Unemployment rate
(2) Labour participation rate
(3) Labour turnover rate
(4) Inflation rate

24. Which of the following is an example of a law or regulation that can affect the labour market?
(1) Minimum wage laws
(2) Equal pay laws
(3) Health and safety regulations
(4) All of the above

25. In a labour market, what is the term used to describe the amount of output per hour of work?
(1) Labour force (2) Productivity
(3) Wage rate (4) Employment rate

26. Which of the following is an example of a demand-side policy that can be used to address unemployment in a labour market?
(1) Training programs for workers
(2) Tax incentives for businesses
(3) Government spending on infrastructure projects
(4) Reducing trade barriers

27. Which of the following is an example of a supply-side policy that can be used to address unemployment in a labour market?
(1) Unemployment benefits
(2) Raising the minimum wage
(3) Investing in education and training programs
(4) Government subsidies for businesses

28. Which of the following is a feature of a flexible labour market?
(1) High levels of job security
(2) Rigidity in wage rates and working hours
(3) Easy mobility of workers between industries and occupations
(4) Highly regulated business practices

29. Which of the following is a factor that can increase the productivity of workers in a labour market?
(1) Investing in education and training programs
(2) Providing workers with modern equipment and technology
(3) Increasing the number of working hours per week
(4) Reducing the wage rate

30. According to the law of demand, what is the relationship between the price of labour and the quantity of labour demanded?
(1) There is a positive relationship between the price of labour and the quantity of labour demanded.
(2) There is no relationship between the price of labour and the quantity of labour demanded.
(3) There is a negative relationship between the price of labour and the quantity of labour demanded.
(4) There is an inverse relationship between the price of labour and the quantity of labour demanded.

31. Which of the following is a factor that can increase the labour force participation rate in a labour market?
(1) Reducing the number of working hours per week

(2) Providing workers with childcare facilities
(3) Increasing the retirement age
(4) Reducing the wage rate

32. What is the term used to describe the extent to which skills and abilities are transferable between different industries and occupations?
(1) Transferability of skills
(2) Job specialization
(3) Job design
(4) None of the above

33. Which of the following is a factor that can increase the labour supply in a labour market?
(1) Providing workers with childcare facilities
(2) Implementing policies that encourage immigration
(3) Encouraging women to enter the workforce
(4) Reducing the retirement age

34. Which of the following is a factor that can decrease the labour demand in a labour market?
(1) Increasing the number of working hours per week
(2) Reducing the wage rate
(3) Implementing policies that encourage automation
(4) Increasing the level of business activity

35. Which of the following is an example of a government-run employment agency that provides services to job seekers and employers?
(1) The International Labour Organization (ILO)
(2) The National Trade Union Congress (NTUC)
(3) The United States Department of Labour
(4) The International Trade Union Confederation (ITUC)

36. Which of the following is an example of a factor that can decrease the productivity of workers in a labour market?
(1) Providing workers with modern equipment and technology
(2) Increasing the number of working hours per week
(3) Fostering a hostile work environment
(4) Reducing the wage rate

37. What is the term used to describe the process of reducing the size of a company's workforce?
(1) Downsizing (2) Rightsizing
(3) Upsizing (4) None of these

38. Which of the following is an example of a factor that can cause a shift in the labour demand curve in a labour market?
(1) An increase in the wage rate
(2) Technological advancements that automate tasks previously done by workers
(3) An increase in the level of business activity
(4) An increase in immigration

39. Which of the following is a factor that can increase the labour mobility in a labour market?
(1) Increasing job specialization
(2) Providing workers with housing facilities
(3) Reducing trade barriers
(4) Reducing the retirement age

40. Which of the following is a factor that can decrease the productivity of workers in a labour market?
(1) Providing workers with modern equipment and technology
(2) Increasing the number of working hours per week
(3) Fostering a hostile work environment
(4) Reducing the wage rate

41. What is the term used to describe the process of matching workers with jobs in a labour market?
(1) Workplace diversity
(2) Workplace discrimination
(3) Labour market matching
(4) None of the above

42. Which of the following is a factor that can decrease the labour turnover rate in a labour market?
(1) An increase in the wage rate
(2) Providing workers with opportunities for career advancement
(3) Reducing the number of working hours per week
(4) Fostering a hostile work environment

43. What is the term used to describe the process of offering incentives to workers in a labour market to entice them to stay with a company?
(1) Retention strategy
(2) Recruitment strategy
(3) Downsizing
(4) Rightsizing

44. Which of the following is an example of a non-wage benefit that can be offered to workers in a labour market?
(1) Paid vacation time
(2) Health insurance
(3) Retirement plan
(4) All of the above

45. In a labour market, what is the term used to describe the rate at which jobs are being created or destroyed?
(1) Job growth rate
(2) Job vacancy rate
(3) Job creation rate
(4) Job destruction rate

46. Which of the following is a characteristic of a rigid labour market?
(1) High levels of job security
(2) Fixed wage rates
(3) Difficult mobility of workers between industries and occupations
(4) Reduced levels of unemployment

47. Which of the following is an example of a factor that can decrease the labour mobility in a labour market?
(1) Increasing job specialization
(2) Implementing policies that discourage immigration
(3) Increasing the retirement age
(4) Reducing the number of working hours per week

48. Which of the following is an example of a factor that can cause a shift in the labour supply curve in a labour market?
(1) An increase in the wage rate
(2) An increase in the level of business activity
(3) An increase in the retirement age
(4) Technological advancements that automate tasks previously done by workers

49. Which of the following is an example of a factor that can cause a shift in the labour demand curve in a labour market?
(1) An increase in the wage rate
(2) An increase in the level of business activity
(3) An increase in the price of a substitute good
(4) A decrease in immigration

50. Which of the following is a feature of a flexible labour market?
(1) High levels of job security
(2) Rigidity in wage rates and working hours
(3) Easy mobility of workers between industries and occupations
(4) Highly regulated business practices

51. Which of the following is an example of a benefit that employers may offer to attract workers in a competitive labour market?
(1) A retirement plan
(2) Health insurance
(3) Paid time off (4) All of the above

52. What is the term used to describe the rate at which unemployed individuals are seeking employment and are available and willing to work?
(1) Unemployment rate
(2) Labour participation rate
(3) Labour turnover rate
(4) Inflation rate

53. Which of the following is an example of a law or regulation that can affect the labour market?

(1) Minimum wage laws
(2) Equal pay laws
(3) Health and safety regulations
(4) All of the above

54. Which of the following is a factor that can increase the labour mobility in a labour market?
(1) Increasing job specialization
(2) Providing workers with housing facilities
(3) Reducing trade barriers
(4) Reducing the retirement age

55. What is the term used to describe therate at which the economy is producing goods and services over a period of time?
(1) Economic growth rate
(2) Consumer Price Index (CPI)
(3) Unemployment Rate
(4) Interest Rate

56. Which of the following is a factor that can cause inflation in an economy?
(1) A decrease in the money supply
(2) A decrease in the level of business activity
(3) An increase in the general level of demand
(4) An increase in interest rates

57. What is the term used to describe the rate at which the central bank lends money to other banks in the economy?
(1) Interest rate
(2) Unemployment rate
(3) Inflation rate
(4) Growth rate

58. Which of the following is a factor that can cause a decrease in inflation in an economy?
(1) An increase in the money supply
(2) An increase in the level of business activity
(3) A decrease in the general level of demand
(4) A decrease in interest rates

59. Which of the following is a factor that can cause a decrease in the money supply in an economy?
(1) An increase in government spending
(2) An increase in the level of business activity
(3) A decrease in the interest rates
(4) An increase in immigration

60. Which of the following is a factor that can increase the money supply in an economy?
(1) A decrease in the interest rates
(2) An increase in government spending
(3) A decrease in the level of business activity
(4) An increase in immigration

61. Which of the following is a factor that can increase the inflation rate in an economy?
(1) A decrease in the money supply
(2) A decrease in the general level of demand
(3) An increase in the level of business activity
(4) A decrease in interest rates

62. Which of the following is a factor that can cause a shift in the aggregate demand curve in an economy?
(1) An increase in the money supply
(2) An increase in interest rates
(3) An increase in government spending
(4) A decrease in the level of business activity

63. Which of the following is the term used to describe the phenomenon where prices rise over time, leading to a fall in purchasing power?
(1) Inflation
(2) Interest rate
(3) Growth rate
(4) Unemployment rate

64. Which of the following is an example of a demand-pull factor that can cause inflation in an economy?
(1) A decrease in the money supply
(2) An increase in the level of business activity
(3) An increase in the general level of demand
(4) An increase in interest rates

65. Which of the following is a factor that can cause a decrease in inflation in an economy?
(1) An increase in the money supply
(2) A decrease in the general level of demand
(3) A decrease in the level of business activity
(4) A decrease in government spending

66. What is the term used to describe the willingness and ability of workers to work at a particular wage rate?
(1) Labour market equilibrium
(2) Supply of labour
(3) Demand for labour
(4) Labour productivity

67. Which of the following is a factor that can increase the demand for labour?
(1) An increase in the wage rate
(2) An increase in the price of a substitute good
(3) An increase in the level of business activity
(4) An increase in unemployment benefits

68. What type of labour is characterized by high skills, experience, and education?
(1) Skilled labour (2) Unskilled labour
(3) Semi-skilled labour
(4) Professional labour

69. Which of the following is a factor that can increase the supply of labour?
(1) A decrease in the wage rate
(2) A decrease in the level of business activity
(3) An increase in the level of education and training
(4) An increase in the price of a substitute good

70. Which of the following is a factor that can decrease the demand for labour?
(1) An increase in the level of business activity
(2) A decrease in the price of a substitute good
(3) Technological advancements that automate tasks previously done by workers
(4) An increase in immigration

71. Which type of labour is characterized by a low level of skills and education?
(1) Skilled labour
(2) Professional labour
(3) Unskilled labour
(4) Semi-skilled labour

72. Which of the following is a factor that can decrease the supply of labour?
(1) An increase in the wage rate
(2) A decrease in the level of education and training
(3) An increase in the retirement age
(4) An increase in the number of working women

73. Which of the following is a factor that can increase the wage rate in a labour market?
(1) A decrease in the demand for labour
(2) An increase in the supply of labour
(3) An increase in the level of education and training of workers
(4) A shortage of workers with certain skills or experience

74. Which of the following is a factor that can decrease the wage rate in a labour market?
(1) A decrease in the supply of labour
(2) An increase in the demand for labour
(3) An increase in the level of business activity
(4) A surplus of workers with certain skills or experience

75. Which of the following is a major source of recruitment for employers in a labour market?
(1) Trade unions
(2) Colleges and universities
(3) Online job boards and social media
(4) Government-run employment agencies

76. What is the term used to describe the total value of goods and services produced by a country's economy in a particular period of time?
(1) Gross Domestic Product (GDP)
(2) Consumer Price Index (CPI)
(3) Unemployment Rate
(4) Interest Rate

77. Which of the following is a factor that can cause a shift in the supply of labour in a labour market?
(1) A change in the educational qualifications or skills required for a particular job
(2) A change in the level of business activity
(3) Technological advancements that automate tasks previously done by workers
(4) An increase in the number of working women

78. What is the term used to describe the rate at which people are being hired or fired in an economy?
(1) Growth rate
(2) Labour turnover rate
(3) Inflation rate (4) Interest rate

79. Which of the following is a factor that can cause a shift in the labour market equilibrium?
(1) A change in the level of business activity
(2) An increase in the retirement age
(3) A shortage of workers with certain skills or experience
(4) All of the above

80. Which of the following is an example of a benefit that employers may offer to attract workers in a competitive labour market?
(1) A retirement plan
(2) Health insurance
(3) Paid time off
(4) All of the above

81. What is the term used to describe the rate at which unemployed individuals are seeking employment and are available and willing to work?
(1) Unemployment rate
(2) Labour participation rate
(3) Labour turnover rate
(4) Inflation rate

82. Which of the following is an example of a law or regulation that can affect the labour market?
(1) Minimum wage laws
(2) Equal pay laws
(3) Health and safety regulations
(4) All of the above

83. What is the term used to describe the number of workers who are employed in a particular industry or occupation?
(1) Supply of labour
(2) Demand for labour
(3) Labour force
(4) Unemployment rate

84. Which of the following is a factor that can increase the productivity of workers in a labour market?
(1) Investing in education and training programs
(2) Providing workers with modern equipment and technology
(3) Increasing the number of working hours per week
(4) Reducing the wage rate

85. What is the term used to describe the extent to which skills and abilities are transferable between different industries and occupations?
(1) Transferability of skills
(2) Job specialization
(3) Job design
(4) None of the above

86. Which of the following is a factor that can increase the labour supply in a labour market?
(1) Providing workers with childcare facilities
(2) Implementing policies that encourage immigration
(3) Encouraging women to enter the workforce
(4) Reducing the retirement age

87. Which of the following is a factor that can decrease the productivity of workers in a labour market?
(1) Providing workers with modern equipment and technology

(2) Increasing the number of working hours per week

(3) Fostering a hostile work environment

(4) Reducing the wage rate

88. Which of the following is a major source of recruitment for employers in a labour market?

(1) Trade unions

(2) Colleges and universities

(3) Online job boardsand social media

(4) Government-run employment agencies

89. Which of the following is a factor that can increase the bargaining power of workers in a labour market?

(1) A surplus of workers in the labour market

(2) A decrease in the demand for labour

(3) The presence of a strong trade union

(4) Technological advancements that eliminate jobs

90. Which of the following is a factor that can decrease the bargaining power of workers in a labour market?

(1) An increase in the demand for labour

(2) A decrease in the level of business activity

(3) The absence of a strong trade union

(4) Immigration of workers with similar skills

91. What is a labour market?

(1) A place where workers are bought and sold.

(2) A place where the forces of demand and supply of labour interact to determine the wage rate and the quantity of labour hired.

(3) A place where employers advertise job openings.

(4) None of the above

92. Which type of labour market is characterized by a large pool of interchangeable workers and minimal differences in pay rates?

(1) Monopsonistic labour market

(2) Oligopsonistic labour market

(3) Perfectly competitive labour market

(4) Monopolistic labour market

93. Which type of labour market is characterized by the presence of a single buyer or employer in the market?

(1) Monopsonistic labour market

(2) Oligopsonistic labour market

(3) Perfectly competitive labour market

(4) Monopolistic labour market

94. Which type of labour market is characterized by a few powerful buyers or employers in the market?

(1) Monopsonistic labour market

(2) Oligopsonistic labour market

(3) Perfectly competitive labour market

(4) Monopolistic labour market

95. Which type of labour market is characterized by a single seller or worker in the market?

(1) Monopsonistic labour market

(2) Oligopsonistic labour market

(3) Perfectly competitive labour market

(4) Monopolistic labour market

96. In a monopsonistic labour market, what happens to the wage rate and employment level when the employer reduces the number of workers it hires?

(1) The wage rate increases and the employment level decreases.

(2) The wage rate decreases and the employment level increases.

(3) Both the wage rate and the employment level increase.

(4) Both the wage rate and the employment level decrease.

97. Which type of labour market is characterized by a significant degree of market power held by both buyers and sellers?

(1) Monopsonistic labour market

(2) Oligopsonistic labour market

(3) Monopolistic labour market

(4) Bilateral monopoly labour market

98. What is the term used to describe the process of matching employees with job openings?

(1) Recruitment (2) Selection
(3) Placement (4) Retention

99. Which type of labour market is characterized by a large number of workers with unique and differentiated skills?
(1) Homogeneous labour market
(2) Heterogeneous labour market
(3) Perfectly competitive labour market
(4) Oligopsonistic labour market

100. In a perfectly competitive labour market, what happens to the wage rate and employment level when the demand for labour increases?
(1) The wage rate increases and the employment level decreases.
(2) The wage rate decreases and the employment level increases.
(3) Both the wage rate and the employment level increase.
(4) Both the wage rate and the employment level decrease.

101. In an oligopsonistic labour market, what happens to the wage rate and employment level when the employer reduces the number of workers it hires?
(1) The wage rate increases and the employment level decreases.
(2) The wage rate decreases and the employment level increases.
(3) Both the wage rate and the employment level increase.
(4) Both the wage rate and the employment level decrease.

102. Which of the following is a factor that can cause a shift in the labour supply curve in a labour market?
(1) Changes in population size and demographics
(2) Changes in the price of other goods and services
(3) Changes in production technology
(4) Changes in government policies

103. Which of the following is a factor that can cause a shift in the labour demand curve in a labour market?
(1) Changes in population size and demographics
(2) Changes in the price of other goods and services
(3) Changes in production technology
(4) Changes in government policies

104. What is the term used to describe the percentage of the population that is of working age and is employed?
(1) Unemployment rate
(2) Labour force participation rate
(3) Employment rate
(4) Labour turnover rate

105. Which of the following is a factor that can increase the informal sector in the Indian labour market?
(1) Lack of access to education and training programs
(2) Lack of formal job opportunities
(3) Large multinational corporations setting up in India
(4) Strong trade unions

106. Which of the following is a factor that can increase the formal sector in the Indian labour market?
(1) Weak labour laws and regulations
(2) Low levels of education and training
(3) Investment in infrastructure and industries
(4) Inefficient bureaucracy

107. What is the term used to describe the act of taking a job that is lower in skill, pay, or status than the previous job held?
(1) Labour turnover (2) Deskilling
(3) Job downgrading
(4) Upgrading

108. Which of the following is a factor that can create a mismatch between workers' skills and employers' needs in the Indian labour market?
(1) Rapid economic growth
(2) Investment in education and training programs
(3) Changing market demands
(4) Strong trade unions

109. Which of the following is a sector of the Indian economy that is characterized by a large number of unskilled workers and low wages?
(1) Agricultural sector
(2) Manufacturing sector
(3) Service sector (4) None of the above

110. Which of the following is a factor that can increase labour market segmentation in the Indian labour market?
(1) Investments in infrastructure and industries
(2) Strong trade unions
(3) Caste-based discrimination
(4) Investment in education and training programs

111. What is the term used to describe the percentage of the working age population that is not employed and not seeking employment?
(1) Unemployment rate
(2) Labour force participation rate
(3) Employment rate
(4) Inactive rate

112. Which of the following is a factor that can increase the informal sector in the Indian labour market?
(1) Government incentives for formal sector growth
(2) Strong labour laws and regulations
(3) Lack of formal job opportunities
(4) Investment in education and training programs

113. What is the term used to describe the percentage of the labour force employed in the informal sector of the economy?
(1) Formalisation rate
(2) Informality rate
(3) Employment rate
(4) Labour turnover rate

114. Which of the following is a factor that can decrease the productivity of workers in the Indian labour market?
(1) Investments in education and training programs
(2) Providing workers with modern equipment and technology
(3) Strong trade unions
(4) Low levels of education and training

115. Which of the following is a factor that can create a mismatch between workers' geographical preferences and employers' job locations in the Indian labour market?
(1) Rapid economic growth
(2) High levels of education and training
(3) Unequal distribution of job opportunities
(4) Strong labour laws and regulations

116. Which of the following is a sector of the Indian economy that is characterized by a significant number of skilled workers and high wages?
(1) Agricultural sector
(2) Manufacturing sector
(3) Service sector
(4) None of the above

117. Which of the following is a factor that can decrease the bargaining power of workers in the Indian labour market?
(1) Strong trade unions
(2) Investment in education and training programs
(3) High levels of unemployment
(4) Large informal sector

118. Which of the following is a type of labour market segmentation that is common in the Indian labour market?
(1) Gender-based segmentation
(2) Skill-based segmentation
(3) Geographical segmentation
(4) Age-based segmentation

119. In the Indian labour market, which sector employs the largest percentage of men workers?
(1) Agriculture (2) Manufacturing
(3) Service (4) None of these

120. What is the term used to describe the rate at which workers are laid off from their jobs?
(1) Labour turnover rate

(2) Retrenchment rate
(3) Labour force participation rate
(4) Employment rate

121. Which of the following is a factor that can increase the productivity of workers in the Indian labour market?
(1) Investments in education and training programs
(2) Providing workers with modern equipment and technology
(3) High levels of unemployment
(4) Large informal sector

122. Which of the following is a type of labour market segmentation that is common in the Indian labour market?
(1) Skill-based segmentation
(2) Gender-based segmentation
(3) Age-based segmentation
(4) Geographical segmentation

123. Which of the following is a factor that can increase the bargaining power of workers in the Indian labour market?
(1) High levels of unemployment
(2) Large informal sector
(3) Strong labour laws and regulations
(4) Technological advancements that eliminate jobs

124. **Assertion:** A monopsonistic labour market is characterized by a single buyer or employer in the market.
Reason: A monopsonistic labour market is an example of a perfectly competitive market.
(1) Both assertion and reason are false.
(2) Assertion is true but reason is false.
(3) Both assertion and reason are true but the reason is not the correct explanation of the assertion.
(4) Both assertion and reason are true and the reason is the correct explanation of the assertion.

125. **Assertion:** A heterogeneous labour market is characterized by a large number of interchangeable workers and minimal differences in pay rates.
Reason: A heterogeneous labour market is characterized by a large number of workers with unique and differentiated skills.
(1) Both assertion and reason are false.
(2) Assertion is true but reason is false.
(3) Both assertion and reason are true but the reason is not the correct explanation of the assertion.
(4) Both assertion and reason are true and the reason is the correct explanation of the assertion.

126. **Assertion:** The informal sector of the Indian economy is characterized by low wages and few social protections.
Reason: The informal sector of the Indian economy is the largest sector of the economy.
(1) Both assertion and reason are true and the reason is the correct explanation of the assertion.
(2) Both assertion and reason are true but the reason is not the correct explanation of the assertion.
(3) Assertion is true but reason is false.
(4) Assertion is false but reason is true.

127. **Assertion:** The formal sector of the Indian economy is characterized by high wages and good social protections.
Reason: The formal sector of the Indian economy is larger than the informal sector.
(1) Both assertion and reason are false.
(2) Assertion is true but reason is false.
(3) Both assertion and reason are true but the reason is not the correct explanation of the assertion.
(4) Both assertion and reason are true and the reason is the correct explanation of the assertion.

128. **Assertion:** Geographical segmentation is a type of labour market segmentation that is common in the Indian labour market.
Reason: Geographical segmentation occurs when workers' geographical preferences do not match employers' job locations.
(1) Both assertion and reason are true and the reason is the correct explanation of the assertion.

(2) Both assertion and reason are true but the reason is not the correct explanation of the assertion.
(3) Assertion is true but reason is false.
(4) Assertion is false but reason is true.

129. Assertion: The Indian Labour market is characterized by a large informal sector.

Reason: The informal sector is characterized by low wages, poor working conditions, and fewer social protections.

(1) Both assertion and reason are true and the reason is the correct explanation of the assertion.
(2) Both assertion and reason are true but the reason is not the correct explanation of the assertion.
(3) Assertion is true but reason is false.
(4) Assertion is false but reason is true.

130. Assertion: Low levels of education and training can create a mismatch between workers' skills and employers' needs in the Indian labour market.

Reason: People with higher levels of education and training are more likely to be employed in the formal sector of the Indian economy.

(1) Both assertion and reason are true and the reason is the correct explanation of the assertion.
(2) Both assertion and reason are true but the reason is not the correct explanation of the assertion.
(3) Assertion is true but reason is false.
(4) Assertion is false but reason is true.

131. Assertion: The manufacturing sector of the Indian economy is characterized by a large number of unskilled workers and low wages.

Reason: The manufacturing sector is the largest sector of the Indian economy.

(1) Both assertion and reason are false.
(2) Assertion is true but reason is false.
(3) Both assertion and reason are true but the reason is not the correct explanation of the assertion.
(4) Both assertion and reason are true and the reason is the correct explanation of the assertion.

132. Assertion: Gender-based segmentation is a type of labour market segmentation that is common in the Indian labour market.

Reason: Gender-based segmentation occurs when men and women are employed in different sectors and occupations, with different pay scales and work conditions.

(1) Both assertion and reason are true and the reason is the correct explanation of the assertion.
(2) Both assertion and reason are true but the reason is not the correct explanation of the assertion.
(3) Assertion is true but reason is false.
(4) Assertion is false but reason is true.

133. Assertion: Investment in infrastructure and industries can decrease the labour market segmentation in the Indian labour market.

Reason: Investment in infrastructure and industries creates formal sector job opportunities and reduces reliance on the informal sector.

(1) Both assertion and reason are true and the reason is the correct explanation of the assertion.
(2) Both assertion and reason are true but the reason is not the correct explanation of the assertion.
(3) Assertion is true but reason is false.
(4) Assertion is false but reason is true.

134. Assertion: The agricultural sector of the Indian economy is characterized by a large number of skilled workers and high wages.

Reason: The agricultural sector is the largest sector of the Indian economy.

(1) Both assertion and reason are false.
(2) Assertion is true but reason is false.
(3) Both assertion and reason are true but the reason is not the correct explanation of the assertion.
(4) Both assertion and reason are true and the reason is the correct explanation of the assertion.

135. Assertion: In the Indian labour market, the majority of women workers are employed in the service sector.

Reason: The service sector of the Indian economy is characterized by a large number of unskilled workers and low wages.

(1) Both assertion and reason are false.
(2) Assertion is true but reason is false.
(3) Both assertion and reason are true but the reason is not the correct explanation of the assertion.
(4) Both assertion and reason are true and the reason is the correct explanation of the assertion.

136. Assertion: Skill-based segmentation is a type of labour market segmentation that is common in the Indian labour market.

Reason: Skill-based segmentation occurs when workers with different skills are employed in different sectors and occupations, with different pay scales and work conditions.

(1) Both assertion and reason are true and the reason is the correct explanation of the assertion.
(2) Both assertion and reason are true but the reason is not the correct explanation of the assertion.
(3) Assertion is true but reason is false.
(4) Assertion is false but reason is true.

137. Assertion: The Indian labour market is characterized by a high unemployment rate.

Reason: The Indian labour market is characterized by a large number of workers in the informal sector with low wages and poor working conditions.

(1) Both assertion and reason are true and the reason is the correct explanation of the assertion.
(2) Both assertion and reason are true but the reason is not the correct explanation of the assertion.
(3) Assertion is true but reason is false.
(4) Assertion is false but reason is true.

138. Assertion: Investment in education and training programs can increase the productivity of workers in the Indian labour market.

Reason: Providing workers with modern equipment and technology is the most effective way to increase productivity in the Indian labour market.

(1) Both assertionand reason are false.
(2) Assertion is true but reason is false.
(3) Both assertion and reason are true but the reason is not the correct explanation of the assertion.
(4) Both assertion and reason are true and the reason is the correct explanation of the assertion.

139. Which of the following is a recent development in the Indian labour market?

(1) Increase in formal sector jobs
(2) Decentralization of wage bargaining
(3) Growth of the service sector
(4) Introduction of trade unions

140. What is the term used to describe the practice of hiring workers on a temporary basis?

(1) Contractual labor
(2) Casual labor
(3) Permanent labor
(4) Fixed-term labor

141. Which of the following is a reason for the growth of the informal sector in the Indian labour market?

(1) Technological advancements
(2) Strong trade unions
(3) Weak labor laws and regulations
(4) Investment in education and training programs

142. In the Indian context, what is the term used to describe the employment of a person in a lower-paid and less-skilled occupation or industry than his or her qualifications would merit?

(1) Deskilling (2) Upskilling
(3) Reskilling (4) Multiskilling

143. Which of the following is a cause of migration from rural to urban areas in India?

(1) Decreased population density in rural areas

(2) Increased employment opportunities in rural areas
(3) Increased mechanization of agriculture
(4) Improved infrastructure in rural areas

144. Which of the following is a recent policy initiative to promote formalization of the Indian labor market?
(1) Decentralization of wage bargaining
(2) Simplification of labor laws and regulations
(3) Livelihood promotion programs
(4) Subsidies for informal sector enterprises

145. What is the term used to describe the difference between the wages of workers with similar qualifications and experience but different genders?
(1) The gender pay gap
(2) The experience gap
(3) The skill gap
(4) The qualification gap

146. Which of the following is a cause of the urban-rural wage gap in the Indian labor market?
(1) Differences in education and skills
(2) Differences in work experience
(3) Unequal access to job opportunities
(4) Differences in industry and occupation

147. In the Indian context, what is the term used to describe the hiring of workers for specific projects or tasks on a short-term/limited basis?
(1) Casual labour
(2) Contractual labour
(3) Gig work
(4) Seasonal work

148. Which of the following is a cause of the youth unemployment problem in India?
(1) Lack of education and skills
(2) Inadequate job opportunities
(3) Technological unemployment
(4) All of the above

149. Which of the following is a policy initiative to promote skilling of the Indian workforce?
(1) PM-KISAN scheme
(2) PM-SYM scheme
(3) PMKVY scheme
(4) Ayushman Bharat scheme

150. What is the term used to describe the percentage of individuals who are employed and have adequate wages and social protections?
(1) The decent work rate
(2) The informal work rate
(3) The gig work rate
(4) The underemployment rate

151. Which of the following is a cause of the lack of decent work in the Indian labor market?
(1) Weak labor laws and regulations
(2) High levels of corruption
(3) Unequal access to job opportunities
(4) Inefficient bureaucracy

152. Which of the following is a cause of the increasing income inequality in the Indian labor market?
(1) Differences in education and skills
(2) Technological advancements
(3) Globalization
(4) Decentralization of wage bargaining

153. What is the term used to describe the practice of hiring workers on a full-time basis?
(1) Contractual labor
(2) Casual labor
(3) Permanent labor
(4) Fixed-term labor

154. Which of the following is a recent policy initiative to promote social security in the Indian labor market?
(1) PM-KISAN scheme
(2) PM-SYM scheme
(3) Atal Pension Yojana
(4) PMKVY scheme

155. Which of the following is a policy initiative to promote entrepreneurship in the Indian labor market?
(1) MGNREGA scheme
(2) Startup India scheme
(3) Ayushman Bharat scheme
(4) Stand-Up India scheme

156. In a market economy, how are wages determined?
(1) By negotiations between employers and employees
(2) By government-set minimum wages
(3) By the forces of supply and demand
(4) By labour unions

157. Which of the following is a feature of a command economy?
(1) Decentralized decision-making
(2) Private ownership of businesses
(3) Centralized planning by the government
(4) Competition between businesses

158. Which of the following is a feature of a mixed economy?
(1) Centralized planning by the government
(2) Private ownership of businesses
(3) Government intervention in the economy
(4) Free market competition

159. What is the term used to describe the percentage of individuals who are unemployed and seeking employment?
(1) The job growth rate
(2) The employment rate
(3) The labor force participation rate
(4) The unemployment rate

160. Which of the following is a feature of a traditional economy?
(1) Centralized planning by the government
(2) Private ownership of businesses
(3) Economic decisions based on custom and tradition
(4) Market competition between businesses

161. In a traditional economy, how are wages determined?
(1) By negotiations between employers and employees
(2) By government-set minimum wages
(3) By custom and tradition
(4) By labor unions

162. Which of the following is a feature of a market economy?
(1) Centralized planning by the government
(2) Private ownership of businesses
(3) Government intervention in the economy
(4) Free market competition

163. Which of the following is a feature of a socialist economy?
(1) Decentralized decision-making
(2) Private ownership of businesses
(3) Centralized planning by the government
(4) Competition between businesses

164. Which of the following is a feature of a capitalist economy?
(1) Government intervention in the economy
(2) Decentralized decision-making
(3) Private ownership of businesses
(4) Centralized planning by the government

165. Which of the following is a policy that can reduce income inequality in a mixed economy?
(1) Government regulation of businesses to ensure fair competition
(2) Government provision of public goods and services
(3) Government transfer payments to low-income households
(4) Government subsidies for businesses

166. Which of the following is a factor that can create a labor shortage in a market economy?
(1) High levels of unemployment
(2) Rapid technological advancements
(3) Low birth rate
(4) Increased immigration

167. Which economic system is characterized by a lack of private ownership of businesses and centralized planning by the government?
(1) Market economy
(2) Socialist economy

(3) Capitalist economy
(4) Traditional economy

168. What is the term used to describe the willingness and ability of individuals to work?
(1) Labor demand
(2) Labor supply
(3) Wage rate
(4) Employment rate

169. Which of the following is a factor that can create a surplus of labor in a market economy?
(1) Low levels of unemployment
(2) Rapid technological advancements
(3) High birth rate
(4) Decreased immigration

170. Which of the following is a government policy that can increase labor market flexibility in a mixed economy?
(1) Government provision of public goods and services
(2) Government regulation of businesses
(3) Government investment in education and training programs
(4) Government transfer payments to low-income households

171. In a socialist economy, how are wages determined?
(1) By negotiations between employers and employees
(2) By government-set minimum wages
(3) By central planning by the government
(4) By labor unions

172. Which of the following is a factor that can create a shortage of labor in a market economy?
(1) High levels of unemployment
(2) Rapid technological advancements
(3) Low birth rate
(4) Decreased immigration

173. Which of the following is a government policy that can promote income equality in a mixed economy?
(1) Government provision of public goods and services
(2) Government regulation of businesses to ensure fair competition
(3) Government transfer payments to low-income households
(4) Government subsidies for businesses

174. Which of the following is a factor that can create a surplus of labor in a socialist economy?
(1) Low levels of unemployment
(2) Rapid technological advancements
(3) High birth rate
(4) Decreased immigration

175. Which of the following is a factor that can create a shortage of labor in a socialist economy?
(1) High levels of unemployment
(2) Rapid technological advancements
(3) Low birth rate
(4) Decreased immigration

176. Which of the following is a policy that can increase labor market competition in a mixed economy?
(1) Government provision of public goods and services
(2) Government regulation of businesses to ensure fair competition
(3) Government transfer payments to low-income households
(4) Government subsidies for businesses

177. Which of the following is a factor that can create a surplus of labor in a communist economy?
(1) Low levels of unemployment
(2) Rapid technological advancements
(3) High birth rate
(4) Decreased immigration

178. In a mixed economy, which of the following is a government policy that can promote growth of the formal sector?
(1) Decentralization of wage bargaining
(2) Simplification of labor laws and regulations
(3) Livelihood promotion programs
(4) Subsidies for informal sector enterprises

179. In a communist economy, how are wages determined?
(1) By negotiations between employers and employees
(2) By government-set minimum wages
(3) By central planning bythe government
(4) By labor unions

180. In a market economy, what is the term used to describe the combination of wages and benefits received by an employee in exchange for their labor?
(1) Salary (2) Compensation
(3) Bonus (4) Profit-sharing

181. Which of the following is a factor that can create a surplus of labor in a socialist economy?
(1) Low levels of unemployment
(2) Rapid economic growth
(3) Decreased birth rate
(4) Increased emigration

182. Which of the following is a government policy that can promote skilling and upskilling in a mixed economy?
(1) Decentralization of wage bargaining
(2) Simplification of labor laws and regulations
(3) Investment in education and training programs
(4) Subsidies for informal sector enterprises

183. In a communist economy, what is the term used to describe individuals who work for the government?
(1) Employees (2) Workers
(3) Citizens (4) Laborers

184. What is the term used to describe the practice of hiring workers without regular contracts or benefits?
(1) Casual labor
(2) Permanent labor
(3) Skilled labor
(4) Professional labour

185. Which of the following is a reason for the lack of women in the Indian labor force?
(1) Technological advancements
(2) Social norms and traditions
(3) Access to education and skills training
(4) Lack of job opportunities

186. What is the term used to describe the minimum wage set by the government?
(1) Living wage (2) Market wage
(3) Fair wage (4) Statutory wage

187. Which of the following is a factor that can lead to a skills mismatch in the labor market?
(1) Adequate education and training programs
(2) Rapid technological advancements
(3) Access to job opportunities
(4) Inadequate career guidance and counseling

188. Which of the following is a reason for the prevalence of forced labor and human trafficking in India?
(1) Technological advancements
(2) High levels of poverty
(3) Access to quality healthcare
(4) Strong labor laws and regulations

189. What is the term used to describe the education and skills required to perform a job?
(1) Education level
(2) Skill level
(3) Experience level
(4) Wage level

190. Which of the following is a factor that can create a labor shortage in the Indian labor market?
(1) Low levels of unemployment
(2) Rapid technological advancements
(3) High birth rate
(4) Decreased immigration

191. What is the term used to describe the process of arranging for workers to be trained on the job?
(1) Onboarding (2) Coaching
(3) Mentoring (4) Apprenticeship

192. Which of the following is a reason for the lack of job security in the Indian labor market?

(1) Strong labor laws and regulations
(2) Decentralization of wage bargaining
(3) Lack of social safety net
(4) Government subsidies for informal sector enterprises

193. What is the term used to describe the percentage of individuals in the labor force who are employed?
(1) Unemployment rate
(2) Labor force participation rate
(3) Employment rate
(4) Job growth rate

194. What is the term used to describe the provision of basic income and social services to the most disadvantaged sections of society?
(1) Social safety net
(2) Welfare state
(3) Labor market flexibility
(4) Income redistribution

195. Which of the following is a reason for the lack of formal employment opportunities in the Indian labor market?
(1) Strong labor laws and regulations
(2) Inadequate education and skills training
(3) Access to job opportunities
(4) Decentralization of wage bargaining

196. Which of the following is a policy initiative to promote labor market flexibility?
(1) Decentralization of wage bargaining
(2) Investment in education and skills training
(3) Simplification of labor laws and regulations
(4) Subsidies for informal sector enterprises

197. What is the term used to describe the provision of fair and equal opportunities to all individuals in the labor market?
(1) Labor market flexibility
(2) Labor market equality
(3) Labor market efficiency
(4) Labor market competitiveness

198. What is the term used to describe the minimum wage required for an individual or family to meet their basic needs?
(1) Living wage (2) Minimum wage
(3) Market wage (4) Fair wage

199. Which of the following is a policy initiative to promote formalization of the Indian labor market?
(1) Decentralization of wage bargaining
(2) Simplification of labor laws and regulations
(3) Livelihood promotion programs
(4) Subsidies for informal sector enterprises

200. What is the term used to describe the provision of benefits such as health insurance and retirement benefits to workers?
(1) Social protection
(2) Social welfare
(3) Social safety net
(4) Social inclusion

201. Which of the following is a reason for the lack of job opportunities in the Indian labor market?
(1) Lack of education and skills
(2) High levels of investment in education and skills training
(3) Access to technological advancements
(4) Economic slowdown

202. What is the term used to describe the percentage of the working-age population that is employed or seeking employment?
(1) Unemployment rate
(2) Labor force participation rate
(3) Employment rate
(4) Job growth rate

203. Which of the following is a reason for the lack of social security in the Indian labor market?
(1) Strong labor laws and regulations
(2) Decentralization of wage bargaining
(3) Government subsidies for informal sector enterprises
(4) Lack of government investment in social programs

204. Which of the following is a policy initiative to promote skilling and upskilling of the Indian workforce?

(1) Decentralization of wage bargaining
(2) Simplification of labor laws and regulations
(3) Investment in education and training programs
(4) Subsidies for informal sector enterprises

205. What is the term used to describe the percentage of individuals in the labor force who are underemployed or working below their skill and education level?
(1) Overemployment rate
(2) Underemployment rate
(3) Employment rate
(4) Job growth rate

206. What is the term used to describe the practice of hiring workers from outside the country to work in the domestic labor market?
(1) Outsourcing (2) Globalization
(3) Immigration (4) Offshoring

207. Which of the following is a reason for the lack of job security in the Indian labor market?
(1) Strong labor laws and regulations
(2) Decentralization of wage bargaining
(3) Lack of social safety net
(4) Government subsidies for informal sector enterprises

208. What is the term used to describe the percentage of the working-age population that is employed and has adequate wages and social protections?
(1) The informal work rate
(2) The gig work rate
(3) The decent work rate
(4) The underemployment rate

209. Which of the following is a policy initiative to promote social protection in the Indian labor market?
(1) Decentralization of wage bargaining
(2) Simplification of labor laws and regulations
(3) Investment in public goods and services
(4) Direct cash transfers

210. What is the term used to describe the benefits and compensation received by workers in addition to their wages?
(1) Income support
(2) Social welfare
(3) Fringe benefits
(4) Education and training programs

211. Which of the following is a factor that can lead to a skills mismatch in the labor market?
(1) Adequate education and training programs
(2) Rapid technological advancements
(3) Access to job opportunities
(4) Inadequate career guidance and counseling

212. What is the term used to describe the increase in wages and benefits that follows from the acquisition of additional education and skills?
(1) Wage premium
(2) Skill premium
(3) Compensation premium
(4) Job security premium

213. Which of the following is a reason for the lack of women in the Indian labor force?
(1) Technological advancements
(2) Social norms and traditions
(3) Access to education and skills training
(4) Lack of job opportunities

214. What is the term used to describe the skills and knowledge required to perform a particular job?
(1) Occupational skills
(2) Soft skills
(3) Technical skills
(4) Social skills

215. Which of the following is a factor that can lead to the growth of informal employment in the labor market?
(1) Strong labor laws and regulations
(2) Investment in education and skills training

(3) Technological advancements
(4) Decentralization of wage bargaining

216. What is the term used to describe the percentage of workers who are employed by small and medium-sized enterprises?
(1) The small enterprise employment rate
(2) The informal sector employment rate
(3) The micro, small, and medium enterprises (MSMEs) employment rate
(4) The self-employment rate

217. Which of the following is a policy initiative to promote formal employment in the Indian labor market?
(1) Decentralization of wage bargaining
(2) Simplification of labor laws and regulations
(3) Livelihood promotion programs
(4) Subsidies for informal sector enterprises

218. What is the term used to describe the practice of hiring workers based on their social connections or family background?
(1) Nepotism (2) Cronyism
(3) Meritocracy (4) Oligopoly

219. Which of the following is a reason for the lack of upward mobility in the Indian labor market?
(1) Investment in education and skills training
(2) Access to technological advancements
(3) Economic slowdown
(4) Social discrimination and inequality

220. Assertion: The Indian labour market suffers from low-productivity and low-wage work.
Reason: The lack of education and skill-training programs has made the workforce in India poorly equipped to handle high-skilled work.
(1) Both assertion and reason are true and the reason is the correct explanation of the assertion.
(2) Both assertion and reason are true but the reason is not the correct explanation of the assertion.
(3) Assertion is true but reason is false.
(4) Assertion is false but reason is true.

221. Assertion: The failure to create adequate job opportunities in India has led to the prevalence of informality in labour markets.
Reason: Informality in labour markets is a result of weak labor laws and regulations.
(1) Both assertion and reason are true and the reason is the correct explanation of the assertion.
(2) Both assertion and reason are true but the reason is not the correct explanation of the assertion.
(3) Assertion is true but reason is false.
(4) Assertion is false but reason is true.

222. Assertion: The Indian labour market is characterized by the prevalence of low-paid, insecure jobs and high unemployment among youth.
Reason: Informal employment and mismatched skills in the labour market have created job insecurity and low wages.
(1) Both assertion and reason are true and the reason is the correct explanation of the assertion.
(2) Both assertion and reason are true but the reason is not the correct explanation of the assertion.
(3) Assertion is true but reason is false.
(4) Assertion is false but reason is true.

223. Assertion: The Indian labour market suffers from lack of formal employment opportunities.
Reason: Strong labour laws and regulations have created barriers to the growth of the formal sector in India.
(1) Both assertion and reason are true and the reason is the correct explanation of the assertion.
(2) Both assertion and reason are true but the reason is not the correct explanation of the assertion.
(3) Assertion is true but reason is false.
(4) Assertion is false but reason is true.

224. Assertion: The Indian labour market suffers from low wages and poor working conditions.

Reason: Economic liberalization policies in India have led to an imbalance in labour market power, favoring employers.

(1) Both assertion and reason are true and the reason is the correct explanation of the assertion.
(2) Both assertion and reason are true but the reason is not the correct explanation of the assertion.
(3) Assertion is true but reason is false.
(4) Assertion is false but reason is true.

225. Assertion: The Indian labour market is characterized by the prevalence of unpaid work and work done without contracts or benefits.

Reason: Strong labour laws and regulations have made it difficult for employers to formalize employment arrangements.

(1) Both assertion and reason are true and the reason is the correct explanation of the assertion.
(2) Both assertion and reason are true but the reason is not the correct explanation of the assertion.
(3) Assertion is true but reason is false.
(4) Assertion is false but reason is true.

226. Assertion: The Indian labor market has high rates of female labour force participation.

Reason: Social norms and traditions have made it difficult for women to enter the labour market in India.

(1) Both assertion and reason are true and the reason is the correct explanation of the assertion.
(2) Both assertion and reason are true but the reason is not the correct explanation of the assertion.
(3) Assertion is true but reason is false.
(4) Assertion is false but reason is true.

227. Assertion: The Indian labor market is characterized by a large informal sector.

Reason: Weak labour laws and regulations have contributed to informality in the Indian labor market.

(1) Both assertion and reason are true and the reason is the correct explanation of the assertion.
(2) Both assertion and reason are true but the reason is not the correct explanation of the assertion.
(3) Assertion is true but reason is false.
(4) Assertion is false but reason is true.

228. Assertion: The Indian labor market suffers from a skills mismatch.

Reason: Inadequate education and skills training programs have not kept up with the demands of the labour market in India.

(1) Both assertion and reason are true and the reason is the correct explanation of the assertion.
(2) Both assertion and reason are true but the reason is not the correct explanation of the assertion.
(3) Assertion is true but reason is false.
(4) Assertion is false but reason is true.

229. Assertion: The Indian labor market suffers from a lack of formal employment opportunities.

Reason: Strong labor laws and regulations have created barriers to formalization of employment in India.

(1) Both assertion and reason are true and the reason is the correct explanation of the assertion.
(2) Both assertion and reason are true but the reason is not the correct explanation of the assertion.
(3) Assertion is true but reason is false.
(4) Assertion is false but reason is true.

ANSWER KEY

1. (2) 2. (3) 3. (1) 4. (3) 5. (3) 6. (3) 7. (3) 8. (4) 9. (3) 10. (4)
11. (3) 12. (1) 13. (2) 14. (1) 15. (2) 16. (2) 17. (3) 18. (4) 19. (3) 20. (4)
21. (4) 22. (1) 23. (1) 24. (4) 25. (2) 26. (3) 27. (3) 28. (3) 29. (2) 30. (3)
31. (3) 32. (1) 33. (3) 34. (3) 35. (3) 36. (3) 37. (1) 38. (3) 39. (3) 40. (3)
41. (3) 42. (2) 43. (1) 44. (4) 45. (1) 46. (3) 47. (2) 48. (3) 49. (3) 50. (3)
51. (4) 52. (1) 53. (4) 54. (3) 55. (1) 56. (3) 57. (1) 58. (3) 59. (3) 60. (2)
61. (3) 62. (3) 63. (1) 64. (3) 65. (4) 66. (3) 67. (3) 68. (1) 69. (3) 70. (3)
71. (3) 72. (3) 73. (4) 74. (4) 75. (3) 76. (1) 77. (1) 78. (2) 79. (4) 80. (4)
81. (1) 82. (4) 83. (3) 84. (2) 85. (1) 86. (3) 87. (3) 88. (3) 89. (3) 90. (3)
91. (2) 92. (3) 93. (1) 94. (2) 95. (4) 96. (2) 97. (4) 98. (3) 99. (2) 100. (2)
101. (1) 102. (1) 103. (3) 104. (2) 105. (2) 106. (3) 107. (3) 108. (3) 109. (1) 110. (3)
111. (4) 112. (3) 113. (2) 114. (4) 115. (3) 116. (3) 117. (4) 118. (1) 119. (1) 120. (2)
121. (1) 122. (1) 123. (3) 124. (4) 125. (3) 126. (1) 127. (4) 128. (1) 129. (1) 130. (1)
131. (4) 132. (1) 133. (1) 134. (4) 135. (3) 136. (1) 137. (4) 138. (4) 139. (3) 140. (2)
141. (3) 142. (1) 143. (3) 144. (2) 145. (1) 146. (3) 147. (3) 148. (4) 149. (3) 150. (1)
151. (3) 152. (3) 153. (3) 154. (3) 155. (2) 156. (3) 157. (3) 158. (3) 159. (4) 160. (3)
161. (3) 162. (4) 163. (3) 164. (3) 165. (3) 166. (4) 167. (2) 168. (2) 169. (2) 170. (3)
171. (3) 172. (1) 173. (3) 174. (2) 175. (1) 176. (2) 177. (3) 178. (2) 179. (3) 180. (2)
181. (4) 182. (3) 183. (2) 184. (1) 185. (2) 186. (4) 187. (4) 188. (2) 189. (2) 190. (4)
191. (4) 192. (3) 193. (2) 194. (2) 195. (4) 196. (3) 197. (2) 198. (1) 199. (2) 200. (1)
201. (4) 202. (2) 203. (4) 204. (3) 205. (2) 206. (2) 207. (3) 208. (3) 209. (4) 210. (3)
211. (4) 212. (1) 213. (2) 214. (3) 215. (4) 216. (3) 217. (2) 218. (1) 219. (4) 220. (1)
221. (3) 222. (1) 223. (3) 224. (1) 225. (1) 226. (2) 227. (1) 228. (1) 229. (3)

ADDITIONAL MULTIPLE CHOICE QUESTIONS

1. Examine the following statements about Scientific Management and identify those which are true and false.
   a. The term 'Scientific Management' was not coined by Frederick Winslow Taylor.
   b. Henry R. Towne's 'Engineer as a economist' influenced Taylor's ideas.
   c. 'Shop Management' embodies 'Therbligs'.
   d. Louis D. Brandies heard the case filed against Taylor's Scientific Management by Trade Unions.

   Codes :

   (1) a, b, c are true and d is false.
   (2) a, b, d are true and c is false.
   (3) a, b are true and c, d are false.
   (4) a, c are true and b, d are false.

2. Which of the following statements about open systems as given by Daniel Katz and Robert Khan are true ?
   a. The exportation of energic inputs into the environment.
   b. Transformation of available energy as throughput, so that work is done.
   c. The importation of the output from the environment.
   d. A cycle of events in which the product exported to the environment provides the energy for repetition of the cycle.

   Codes :

   (1) a, b (2) b, c
   (3) b, d (4) a, d

3. Match the following :

List – I (Themes)	**List – II (Propagators)**
a. POSDCORB	i. Henry Fayol
b. Espirit De Corps	ii. George A. Pennock
c. Integration theory	iii. Mary Parker Follette
d. The illumination experiment	iv. Luther Gullick

Codes :

	a	b	c	d
(1)	iv	i	ii	iii
(2)	iv	i	iii	ii
(3)	iii	i	ii	iv
(4)	iv	ii	iii	i

4. Match the following activities (List-I) with the degree of delegation (List-II).

List – I (Activities)	**List – II (Degree of Delegation)**
a. Critical Activity	i. Moderate
b. Needed Activity	ii. High
c. Peripheral Activity	iii. Low

Codes :

	a	b	c
(1)	ii	i	iii
(2)	ii	iii	i
(3)	iii	ii	i
(4)	iii	i	ii

5. The steps in planning process are jumbled up. Arrange them in correct sequence.
   a. Specifying alternatives
   b. Analyzing alternatives
   c. Goal setting
   d. Elaborating plans and specifying details
   e. Establishing standards for measurement
   f. Maintaining communication
   g. Maintaining a time perspective
   h. Planning for unpredictable contingencies
   i. Organising
   j. Implementing
   k. Ensuring Participation
   l. Follow-up, providing for flexibility

   Codes :

   (1) c, e, g, a, b, d, k, f, i, j, l, h
   (2) c, a, g, b, d, k, f, j, i, h, l, e
   (3) d, c, a, f, g, i, b, e, l, h, j
   (4) c, g, e, b, a, k, d, i, f, j, l, h

6. Match the following HRM models (List-I) with their themes (List-II) :

List – I (HRM Models)	List – II (Themes)
a. Long-term Purchase Model	i. Seeks to minimize Labour wage and benefit costs; and Employment levels within organizational boundaries. Outsourcing and externalization of employment are encouraged.
b. Work-force Commitment Model	ii. Different employment models for core and noncore work are adopted.
c. Labour Transactional Model	iii. Firms would employ workers, for as long as they performed well and the company has the capacity to pay.
d. Mixed Model	iv. Employers provide job security in order to elicit long term commitment and organization can develop social and intellectual capital within the boundaries of the firm.

Codes :

	a	b	c	d
(1)	iii	i	iv	ii
(2)	iii	iv	i	ii
(3)	ii	iv	i	iii
(4)	iii	ii	iv	i

7. Which of the following statement/s is/are true ?
   a. Configurational or bundle theorists propose that there are ideal types of configurations of HR practices that promote synergies.
   b. High performance work systems combining information sharing, decentralized decision making via teams; participative management at operational, tactical and strategic levels are, however not part of the configurational framework.

Codes :

(1) only a (2) only b
(3) both a and b (4) neither a and b

8. Read the following statements about 'staffing' as a strategy formation. Identify the ones which are true.
   a. Organisations need to hire 'best' people emphasizing person-organisation fit over person-job fit.
   b. Organisations need to hire people with unique as well as complementary KSAs in order to have the capability to implement flexible and focused business strategies in a fast changing environment.
   c. Organisation need to hire people with talent and creativity to contribute to business strategies in a manner that will take any possible course of action in any direction.

Codes :

(1) only a (2) a, b
(3) b, c (4) a, b, c

9. Which of the following is not a best practice in High Commitment Pay ?
   (1) High wage policies to attract, retain and motivate the best talent, that is based on the belief that, 'You get what you pay for'.
   (2) Employment security is essential to be the 'employer of choice' and it is the bed rock for high quality work and a willingness to be flexible and innovative.
   (3) Encourage employee ownership of the enterprise.
   (4) Non-egalitarian symbols and perquisites.

10. Which of the following may be a possible consequence of inter-group conflict within the involved groups ?

a. Group cohesiveness increases.
b. Group becomes task oriented.
c. Organisation structure becomes more rigid.
d. Leadership becomes more rigid.

Codes :
(1) a, b and d
(2) b, c and d
(3) a, b, c and d
(4) a and b only

11. Assertion (A) : Master-Servant doctrine believed in the inalienable prerogative of Master's will with regard to servant's continuance in employment.

Reason (R) : This prerogative has been granted by the sanction of law made by the State Power.

Codes :
(1) (A) and (R) are wrong.
(2) (A) is wrong and (R) is right.
(3) (A) and (R) are right, but (R) does not justify the Assertion (A).
(4) (A) is right, but (R) is wrong and does not justify the (A).

12. Match the contributors (Behavioural Scientists) List-I with their contributions given in List-II.

List – I	**List – II**
a. Blake R.R. & Mouton J.S.	i. Hawthorne Effect
b. Likert R.	ii. Theory X and Y
c. Mc. Greger	iii. Michigan Study on Leadership Style
d. Mayo E and Rothlisberger F.J.	iv. Managerial Grid Theory

Codes :

	a	b	c	d
(1)	iv	i	ii	iii
(2)	iii	ii	iv	i
(3)	iv	iii	ii	i
(4)	iv	ii	iii	i

13. Which of the following is not a Simulation technique of development ?
(1) Management Games
(2) Case Study
(3) In-basket
(4) Sensitivity Training

14. Which of the following statements is/are true and false ?
a. If motivation is low, monotony (mental fatigue) grips very early.
b. If motivation is high, the will and desire to work increases and both fatigue and monotony decreases.
c. Highly intelligent people are more susceptible to monotony if subjected to repetitive work, because their level of expectations from job towards meaningfulness is low.
d. The anticipation of the end of the work period tends to abolish signs of monotony.

Codes :
(1) a and d are true; b and c are false.
(2) a and c are true; b and d are false.
(3) a, b and d are true; and c is false.
(4) b, c and d are true; and a is false.

15. Consider the following statements :
a. Conflict that supports the goals of the group and improves its performance.
b. Conflict that hinders group performance.
c. Emotional involvement in a conflict creating anxiety, tenseness, frustration, or hostility.
d. Withdrawal from or suppressing conflict.

The above statements, in correct sequence (a, b, c, d) refer to :

Codes :
(1) Dysfunctional, functional, inter-group, and approach-approach conflict respectively.
(2) Functional, Dys functional, Felt conflict and avoidance respectively.
(3) Functional conflict, confrontation strategy, Perceived and manifest conflict respectively.

(4) Inter-group conflict, dysfunctional conflict, Goal Diversity and Containment Strategy.

16. In Transactional Analysis, if the response is by the same ego state as through which the message was received, the transaction is called

(1) Crossed Transaction
(2) Complementary Transaction
(3) Ulterior Transaction
(4) Feed-forward Transaction

17. "Healthy people show the behaviour of maturity, while unhealthy people tend to demonstrate child like immature behaviour." Who among the following behavioural Scientists said this ?

(1) John Berry
(2) Blake and Mouton
(3) F.W. Taylor
(4) Chris Argyris

18. Which of the following statements are true/ false ?

a. Maslow's need theory considers needs to explain human behaviour.
b. Mc Gregor's theory considers opposite perceptions based on managerial assumption of employee behaviour.
c. Vroom's theory considers force, valence, expectancy, and instrumentality to explain motivation.
d. Cognitive evaluation theory classifies persons as intrinsically and extrinsically motivated.

Codes :

(1) a and d are true, c and b are false.
(2) a, b and d are true, c is false.
(3) a, b, c and d are true.
(4) a and c are true, b and d are false.

19. The following three types of tests namely objective tests, projective tests, and situation tests are basically used as tools of

(1) Intelligence tests
(2) Personality tests
(3) Cognitive ability test
(4) Competency mapping

20. 'Alarm Reaction', 'Stage of Resistance' and 'Stage of Exhaustion' are the stages of which of the following syndromes :

(1) Buggy-whip Syndrome
(2) Dissociative Identity Disorder Syndrome
(3) General Adaptation Syndrome
(4) Amoeba Syndrome

21. Who is/are the author (s) of the books titled, 'A History of Trade Unionism' (1897) and 'Industrial Democracy' (1902), the two early writings on Industrial Relations ?

(1) Sidney and Beatrice Webb
(2) Alan Fox and Allan Flanders
(3) Karl Marx (4) H.A. Clegg

22. The Descending Participation i.e., Workers' participation in work was propounded by

(1) The Fabians
(2) The Harvard Group
(3) The Oxford Group
(4) The Tavistock Group

23. Match the themes of the three approaches of industrial relations under contradictions perspective :

Approach	**Theme**
a. The Marxian approach	i. Power struggle to control work organizations.
b. The Socialistic approach	ii. Power struggle to gain political power.
c. The Social Action approach	iii. Power struggle to improve the lot of the working class.

Codes :

	a	**b**	**c**
(1)	i	ii	iii
(2)	ii	iii	i
(3)	iii	ii	i
(4)	ii	i	iii

24. Which of the following is not an industrial union ?

(1) The Engineering Mazdoor Sabha

(2) The Rohtas Workers' Union
(3) The Girni Kamgar Union
(4) The Rashtriya Mill Mazdoor Sangh

25. Who has viewed collective bargaining as a process of social change ?
(1) Neil W. Chamberlain
(2) J.H. Richardson
(3) Arthur D. Butler
(4) H.W. Davey

26. Which of the following is not included in the 'illustrative list of items' approved by the Indian Labour Conference pertaining to the items which the Works Committees will normally deal with ?
(1) Amenities such as drinking water, canteens, creches,medical, and health services.
(2) Quantum of leave and national and festival holidays.
(3) Adjustment of festivals and national holidays.
(4) Safety and accident prevention, occupational diseases and protective equipment.

27. Which of the following was formed in the year 1945 ?
(1) International Federation Chemical, Energy, Mining and General Workers.
(2) International Confederation of Free Trade Unions.
(3) World Federation of Trade Unions.
(4) International Federation of Christian Unions.

28. Who among the following were moderates in the context of trade union movement in India ?
(1) B.T. Ranadive and S.V. Deshpande
(2) Diwan Chamanlal and N.M. Joshi
(3) M.N. Roy and Maniben Kara
(4) H.K. Mehtab and Dattopant Thengadi

29. When a strike is conducted with a view to force an employer to recognise or bargain with a particular trade union instead of another, such strike is called as
(1) Political strike
(2) Ordinary strike
(3) Protest strike
(4) Jurisdictional strike

30. Which of the following pairs is not correctly matched ?

(Name of the Association/ Organisation)	(Year of Establishment /Formation)
(1) Confederation of Indian Indu	- 1895
(2) International Workingmen's Association	- 1864
(3) Central Board for Worker Education	- 1957
(4) Joint Consultative Board of Industry and Labour	- 1951

31. According to William Beveridge which of the following are not part of a comprehensive social security scheme ?
a. Social assistance
b. Compulsory insurance
c. Social insurance
d. Voluntary insurance
e. Voluntary assistance

Codes :
(1) b and e only (2) d and e only
(3) b, d and e only (4) a, b and d only

32. A trade Union has been formed in an establishment employing five hundred employees.
What is the minimum number of members it should have to apply for registering it under the Trade Unions Act, 1926 ?
(1) Seven members
(2) One hundred members
(3) Fifty members (4) Seventy members

33. Under the Industrial Disputes Act, 1947, to which of the following industrial undertakings the provisions relating to lay-off, retrenchment and closure provided under chapter V-B shall be made applicable ?

(1) Industrial establishment in which not less than one hundred workmen were employed on an average per working day for the preceding twelve months.
(2) Industrial establishment in which not less than one hundred workmen were employed on an average per working day in the preceding calendar month.
(3) Industrial establishment in which not less than one hundred workmen were employed on an average per working day during the preceding calendar year.
(4) Industrial establishment in which not less than one hundred workmen were employed on an average for the preceding three months.

34. As per the Government of India notification the wage limit for employees to be covered under the Employees' State Insurance Act, 1948 is proposed to be increased to

(1) Rupees Eighteen thousand
(2) Rupees Twenty-five thousand
(3) Rupees Twenty thousand
(4) Rupees Twenty-one thousand

35. Under the Minimum Wages Act, 1948 what is the extent of representation of Independent persons in the Advisory Committee ?

(1) one-half of its total members.
(2) one-third of its total members.
(3) one-fourth of its total members.
(4) one-half of its total members subject to a maximum of light.

36. If any dispute arises regarding the payment of subsistence allowance to a workman under the provisions of the Industrial Employment (Standing Orders) Act, 1946, then the dispute may be referred to !

(1) Certifying Officer appointed under the Industrial Employment (Standing Orders) Act, 1946.
(2) Enquiry Officer appointed to enquire the allegations framed against the workman.
(3) Chief executive of the industrial establishment in which the workman is employed.
(4) Labour court constituted under the Industrial Disputes Act, 1947

37. What is the minimum period an employee should have worked in an accounting year in an establishment to become eligible for bonus under the payment of Bonus Act, 1965?

(1) Forty five days (2) Thirty days
(3) Sixty days (4) Ninety days

38. Which of the following statements relating to the Constitution of the Advisory Committee under the Equal Remuneration Act, 1976 is true ?

(1) It shall consist of not less than twelve persons of which one-third shall be women.
(2) It shall consist of eight persons of which one-half shall be women.
(3) It shall consist of not less than ten persons nominated by the appropriate Government, of which one-half shall be women.
(4) It shall consist of twelve persons nominated by the Central Government of which one-third shall be women.

39. Match the propounders mentioned in List-I with the theories of wages mentioned in List-II.

List – I	List – II
a. J.S. Mill	i. Marginal Productivity Theory
b. Walker	ii. Wage Fund Theory
c. J.B. Clark	iii. Residual Claimant Theory
d. Ricardo	iv. The Subsistence Theory

Codes :

	a	b	c	d
(1)	iii	iv	i	ii
(2)	ii	iii	iv	i
(3)	i	ii	iii	iv
(4)	ii	iii	i	iv

40. Under which of the following legislations the provision for payment to any trade union fee on a written authorisation from an employee has been provided ?
(1) Industrial Disputes Act, 1947
(2) Trade Unions Act, 1926
(3) Payment of Wages Act, 1936
(4) Industrial Employment (Standing Orders) Act, 1946

41. Match the Principles of Labour Welfare mentioned in List-I with the contents given in List-II.

List – I	List – II
a. Principle of Social Responsibility of Industry	i. Concept of Labour Welfare must spread throughout the hierarchy of an organization.
b. Principle of Responsibility	ii. Industry has an obligation towards its employees to lookafter their welfare.
c. Principle of Totality of Welfare	iii. Both employers and workers are responsible for Labour Welfare.
d. Principle of Repersonalisation	iv. Development of the human personality must be goal of Welfare.

Codes :

	a	b	c	d
(1)	iv	ii	iii	i
(2)	ii	iii	i	iv
(3)	iii	ii	iv	i
(4)	i	iii	ii	iv

42. Which among the following statements is not true is relation to Labour Welfare ?
(1) Labour Welfare is an essential part of Social Welfare.
(2) Labour Welfare Work not only covers the work life of workers in the factory but also extends beyond into his life with his family and community.
(3) Labour Welfare is not concerned with desirable conditions of existence, biologically and Socially determined.
(4) Labour Welfare is a relative concept, relative in time and place.

43. Which one of the following does not constitute to be a direct source of Industrial Jurisprudence in India ?
(1) The Constitution of India
(2) Legislative enactments
(3) International obligations
(4) Judicial decisions

44. Who was the first person to advocate an eight hours working day for workers ?
(1) Robert Owen
(2) John Stuart Mill
(3) George Elliot
(4) August Comte

45. **Assertion (A) :** Welfare is a relative concept, relative in time and place.
Reason (R) : Ideas of Welfare differ with passage of time. Man accepted comparatively less convenient and less sumptuous conditions of existence; for Science and Technology had not made possible better amenities. Then again, meaning and content of Welfare differs from country to country or region to region.
Codes :
(1) (A) is correct, but (R) partially explains (A).
(2) (A) is partially correct and therefore, (R) only partially explains (A).
(3) (A) is correct and (R) explains (A).
(4) (A) is wrong and (R) is partially correct.

46. Labour Welfare Services were divided into two groups by the committee of experts on Welfare facilities for Industrial Workers convened by ILO in 1963. These are (a) Those within the precincts of the establishment and (b) Those outside the precincts of the establishment. The content of Welfare ac-

tivities remained the same as recommended by 1959 study team.

As per the ILO classification, which one among the following is not Welfare and Amenities outside the precincts of the establishment.

(1) Social insurance measures including gratuity, pension and provident fund.
(2) Housing facilities.
(3) Recreation facility.
(4) Arrangement for prevention of fatigue.

47. Which is not true in relation to State Regulation of Wages ?

(1) Internal Wage differentials are regulated by the State.
(2) The ideals of Welfare State necessitate State Regulation of Wages.
(3) It is necessary to raise the efficiency of the workers by ensuring improvements in health, productivity and distribution of income.
(4) It is necessary because of the gap existing between the marginal productivity of labour and the actual level of wages on the average.

48. Twelfth Plan has identified certain sectors that will create large employment. Which among the following sectors has not been identified ?

(1) Textiles and Garments
(2) Leather and Footwear
(3) Gems and Jewellery
(4) Health Care

49. "Marginal productivity, wages and standard of living tend to adjust to one another." What is true in relation to the statement ?

(1) The condition is achieved for short-run only.
(2) The condition never arrives.
(3) The condition is achieved in the long-run.
(4) The condition arrives when high wages are paid.

50. Which among the following is not a factor which will determine the level of demand for any commodity ?

(1) Price
(2) Prices of other commodities
(3) Taste
(4) Social values

51. In his book "The Time Bind : When Home becomes work and work becomes Home", Arlie Hochschild highlights the danger of total integration between work and home leading to either 'workholics' or 'work busters'. The first neglecting the family and realizing it too late. The second 'soldering' on work compromising with efficiency. From the above observation, which of the following inferences can be drawn ?

(a) Home becoming work and work becoming home is an ideal condition.
(b) Home becoming work and work becoming home may create 'workholics' who are good employees and bad home-makers resulting into family break-down.
(c) Employee 'soldering' means taking the job easy leading to inadequate performance.
(d) The passage advocates for work-life balance.

(1) (b), (c), (d) (2) (a), (b), (c)
(3) (a), (c), (d) (4) (a), (b), (c), (d)

52. The National Association of manufacturers in America is a

(1) Purely Advisory Body
(2) Purely Administrative Body
(3) Purely Negotiating Body
(4) Purely Legislative Body

53. The Constitution of India gives its citizens certain fundamental rights. Some of these fundamental rights concerns working class directly. Match the subject matter included in List – 1 with the Articles of the Constitution of India mentioned in List – 2.

List - 1	List - 2
a. The state shall not discriminate against any citizen on grounds only of religion, race, caste, sex, place of birth or any of them.	i. Art. 19(1)
b. There shall be equality of opportunity for all citizens in matters relating to employment or appointment to any office under the state.	ii. Art. 16(1)
c. All citizens shall have the right to freedom of speech and expression and to form associations or Unions and to practice any profession or to carry on any occupation, trade or business.	iii. Art. 15
d. Traffic in human beings and beggar and other forms of forced labour are prohibited.	iv. Art. 23(1)

Codes :

	a	b	c	d
(1)	iii	i	iv	ii
(2)	iii	ii	i	iv
(3)	iv	iii	ii	i
(4)	iv	ii	iii	i

54. The voluntary arbitration in Britain was first introduced under the

(1) Conciliation Act, 1896
(2) Trade Union Act, 1913
(3) The Trade Disputes and Trade Union Act, 1927
(4) The Employment and Protection Act, 1975

55. Assertion (A) : The cause of labour was just but it needed the support of humanitarians and social reformers.

Reason (R) : The need was to preach and persuade people against the powerful social prejudices and barriers.

Codes :

(1) (A) is wrong and, therefore, (R) becomes irrelevant in the context.
(2) (A) is correct and (R) explains (A).
(3) (A) is correct and (R) does not explain (A).
(4) (A) is correct and (R) is wrong.

56. Which of the following statements relating to the Wagner Act is/are not wrong ?

a. It recognizes an employee's right to engage in union activities.
b. It recognizes employees' right to organize and bargain collectively.
c. It has a provision regarding the establishment of a National Labour Relations Board.
d. It has a provision relating to unfair labour practices by employers.

(1) only a (2) only a, and b
(3) a, b and c (4) a, b, c and d

57. From among the following, who focused on the 'soft side of organisation' as a sequel to globalization comprising adhocracy, simple structure, the divisionalized form, the-machine and professional bureaucracy?

(1) Henry Mintzberg
(2) Barlett and Ghosal
(3) Galbraith and Kazanjaam
(4) Burns and Stalker

58. "Marx states that the mass of surplus value is a definite quantum and exists across the system as a whole. It is a product of capitalist mode of production and capitalists compete for a share of this surplus. This surplus can be increased either through a longer working day or by raising productivity of labour. The 'rate of surplus value' is a function of direct labour employed. Constant capital in the form of machinery and raw materials transmits its own value to products but does not create additional value."

Read the passage carefully and answer the question :

(1) Additional Surplus value is created by constant capital.
(2) Additional Surplus value is created by modern technology

(3) Additional Surplus value can only be created by labour.
(4) Labour has no role in creation of Additional Surplus Value

59. Which of the following types of Trade Unions groups the workers' unions horizontally, vertically or on the basis of political ideology with a view to coordinating them ?
(1) Territorial Unions
(2) Occupational Unions
(3) Industrial Unions
(4) General Unions

60. Read the two statements given below :
Statement – I : Marxian Political Economy (MPE) championed the cause of employment, income and social security and kept them within the bargaining power of the working class.
Statement – II : With the onset of globalization, New Institutional Economics (NIE), being driven by market forces, championed the cause of competitiveness, efficiency and cost-effectiveness. It supported the contractual freedom for both the employer and employee to transact on employment and employee cost fundamentals.
Which of the following logics can be inferred ?
(a) The statements take opposing stands.
(b) The statements are explainable in terms of assertion-reasoning compatibility.
(c) The first statement explains the union control on employment and other securities.
(d) The second statement advocates for the imperatives of limited employment security by giving greater freedom to both employers and employees the choice of employment contract severance.
(1) (a) and (b) (2) (b) and (c)
(3) (a), (b) and (c) (4) (a), (c) and (d)

61. Labour welfare, though, is not exactly social work but any welfare is the result of social work. Social work lead to states of welfare both of individuals and groups. And, therefore, it can be derived that labour welfare is an area of social work.
There exists four methods of undertaking social work. Match the subject matter given in List – 1 with the method of social work given in List – 2 :

List – 1	List – 2
a. Situations of lay-off and retrenchment	i. Social Action
b. Collective bargaining contexts	ii. Community Organisation and Development
c. Housing	iii. Social group work
d. Peaceful strike	iv. Social case work

Codes :

	a	b	c	d
(1)	i	ii	iii	iv
(2)	iv	iii	ii	i
(3)	ii	i	iv	iii
(4)	iv	ii	iii	i

62. In which year India became a member of the ILO ?
(1) 1919 (2) 1921
(3) 1926 (4) 1934

63. A situation, which is very serious, has arised and it warrants that the member of the Trade Union be financially assisted. As per the Trade Unions Act, 1926, what is the maximum quantum of benefit which a Trade Union can offer to its member out of the total gross income in the year and the balance of the credit of the preceeding year :
(1) One tenth (2) One sixth
(3) One fourth (4) Half

64. Who said that a trade union is a "continuous association of wage-earners for the purpose of maintaining or improving the conditions of their working lives." ?
(1) G.D.H. Cole (2) Clyde E. Dankert
(3) J. Cunnison
(4) Sydney and Beatrice Webb

65. Which of the following are the four key HR challenges, identified by Deloitte, in its 'Compensation trends Survey Report' for 2012-2013 ?
(a) Reducing operating cost
(b) Retaining critical talent
(c) Reducing capital investment
(d) Hiring of skilled talent
(e) Increasing productivity
(f) Engaging the employees
(g) Restructuring
(h) Training and Developing potential leaders
(1) (a), (c), (e) and (g)
(2) (b), (d), (f) and (h)
(3) (c), (e), (a) and (g)
(4) (d), (f), (g) and (h)

66. Which of the following statements relating to the V.V. Giri National Labour Institute is wrong ?
(1) The institute was set up in the year 1976.
(2) The institute was set up as a registered society.
(3) The institute's affairs are governed by the General Council.
(4) Research occupies a primary place in the activities of the Institute.

67. Members of the Trade Union are required to pay a subscription per annum as per the provisions of the Trade Unions Act, 1926. For workers working in other unorganized sectors, excepting rural workers, the annual rate of subscription should not be less than
(1) Rs. 1 per annum
(2) Rs. 3 per annum
(3) Rs. 12 per annum
(4) Rs. 24 per annum

68. Which of the following is not a characteristic of 'Spaghetti organization structure' adopted by MNCs ?
(1) Paperless organisation
(2) Smart office design
(3) 'Meat Balls' or knowledge centres
(4) Formal communication between people

69. The term 'Social Security' was officially first used in
(1) ILO
(2) The United States of America
(3) The U.S.S.R.
(4) Germany

70. Which of the following conventions of ILO relates to the 'Right of Association' ?
(1) Convention No. 87
(2) Convention No. 90
(3) Convention No. 121
(4) Convention No. 147

71. Examine the following statements about span of control and identify the ones which are true ?
a. More task complexity requires narrower span of control.
b. Routine tasks can have greater span of control than Exceptional tasks.
c. When tasks are dissimilar, then span of control can be larger.
d. Spans of control are generally narrower at the top and broader at the bottom of the hierarchy.
(1) a and b (2) a, c and d
(3) b and d (4) a, b and d

72. As per an amendment of the Employees' State Insurance Act, 1948 in 2010 who among the following have been included for getting medical benefits subject to payment of contribution and such other conditions as may be prescribed by the Central government ?
a. An insured person who has attained the age of superannuation.
b. An insured person who retires under a Voluntary Retirement Scheme.
c. An insured person who takes premature retirement
d. The spouse of the insured person.
(1) c and d only (2) a, b and d only
(3) b, c and d only (4) a, b and c only

73. Examine the following statements and identify the ones which are right and wrong :

a. Industrial relations as an activity is of recent origin.
b. Industrial relations as a field of study is of recent origin.
c. The early writings on industrial relations were mostly reflective of prevailing practices rather than theories and explanations.
d. Initially industrial relations subsumed all aspects of work, including problems and issues affecting both employers' and workers' organizations, and covered only unionized employment relations.

(1) b and d are right, a and c are wrong.
(2) only b is right, a, c and d are wrong.
(3) b, c and d are right and a is wrong.
(4) b and c are right a and d are wrong.

74. The Central Board for Workers' Education was renamed in 2016 as
(1) Sardar Vallabhbhai Patel National Board for Workers' Education and Development
(2) Sardar Vallabhbhai Patel Central Board for Workers' Education
(3) Dattopant Thengadi National Board for Workers' Education and Development
(4) Dattopant Thengadi Central Board for Workers' Education

75. The maximum permissible threshold limits of exposure of chemical and toxic substances in manufacturing processes are provided under which, Schedule of the Factories Act, 1948 ?
(1) The First Schedule
(2) The Second Schedule
(3) The Third Schedule
(4) The Fourth Schedule

76. Based on a series of studies on managerial decision making behaviour. Vroom and Yetton (1973) found evidence in support of which of the following propositions ?
a. Managers tend to be more participative when the quality of the decision is important.
b. Managers tend to be more participative when subordinate acceptance of the decision is critical for its effective implementation.
c. Managers tend to be less participative when they have all the necessary information to make a high quality decision.
d. Managers tend to be less participative when time is limited and immediate action is required.

Codes :
(1) a, b, c and d (2) a, c and d
(3) a, b and c (4) a, b and d

77. Which of the following for the first time made provisions for compulsory rest interval of half an hour each day ?
(1) Factories Act, 1911
(2) Factories Act, 1891
(3) Factories Act, 1934
(4) Factories Act, 1948

78. Which of the following Central Labour Organisations voluntarily adopted the 'Inter-union code of conduct' in 1958 ?
(1) INTUC, AITUC, NFITU
(2) AITUC, NFL, BMS, NLO
(3) INTUC, AITUC, HMS, UTUC
(4) BMS, HMS, CITU, TUCC

79. MBTI is the most widely used instrument for personality analysis. Which of the following statements about MBTI is/are true/false ?
a. MBTI has 108 items
b. Sixteen personality types are generated by the instrument
c. MBTI has 100 items
d. Sixteen personality types are based on a combination of four basic elements of psyche.
e. MBTI was developed by a father-daughter team.
f. MBTI was developed by a mother-daughter team.

Codes :
(1) a, d and e are true
(2) b, c, d and f are true

(3) c, d and e are true
(4) a, b, e and f are true

80. An employee is employed in an industry on a wage of Rupees Eight Thousand and Five Hundred per month, which is fixed as the minimum wage as a scheduled employment by the appropriate Government. What is the amount of bonus he shall be entitled to, if it is to be paid at the minimum rate of 8.33% by the employer under the payment of Bonus Act, 1965 ?
(1) Rupees seven thousand only
(2) Rupees nine thousand only
(3) Rupees eight thousand and five hundred only
(4) Rupees three thousand and five hundred only

81. The inter-union code of conduct aims to
(1) Check Unfair Labour Practices
(2) Control Trade Union Rivalries
(3) Promote Labour Management Cooperation
(4) Promote collective bargaining in India

82. Which of the following are known as 'Big Five' dimensions of personality ?
Dimensions :
a. Extraversion
b. Dominance
c. Sensitivity
d. Agreeableness
e. Conscientiousness
f. Rule-consciousness
g. Self-reliance
h. Emotional Stability
i. Openness to experience
j. Perfectionism
Codes :
(1) a, d, e, h and i
(2) a, e, h, b and j
(3) d, e, f, g and h
(4) a, d, g, i and j

83. Which of the following statements characterize the objectives of labour legislation ?
a. Improve the conditions of labour
b. To protect the rights of labour unions
c. To protect employers
d. To protect the public from possible excess on the part of organized labour
Codes :
(1) a and b only
(2) a, b and c only
(3) a and c only
(4) a, b, c and d

84. In Britain if the Advisory Conciliation and Arbitration Services (ACAS) fails to settle the claims at its level, it must refer the same to
(1) Independent Arbitrator
(2) Board of Arbitration
(3) Central Arbitration Committee
(4) Industrial Tribunal

85. Match the sources of resistance (List – A) and the steps that can be taken to deal with such resistance (List – B) :

List – A (Sources of Resistance)	List – B (Coping Mechanisms)
a. Complacency and Inertia	i. Development of skills
b. Fear of large-scale disturbance	ii. Participation and Involvement
c. Perception of Imposition	iii. Phasing of change
d. Fear of Obsolescence	iv. Fait accompli
e. Fear of loss of power	v. Role re-definition and re-orientation

Codes :

	a	b	c	d	e
(1)	v	iv	iii	ii	i
(2)	i	iii	ii	iv	v
(3)	ii	iv	v	iii	i
(4)	iv	iii	ii	i	v

86. Which of the following Articles of the Indian Constitution deals with "Securing just and humane conditions of work and maternity relief" ?

(1) Article 42 (2) Article 41
(3) Article 46 (4) Article 38

87. Which of the following statements relating to ILO Declaration on Fundamental Principles is not correct ?
(1) The Declaration was adopted at the 86th Session of the International Labour Conference.
(2) The Declaration reiterates the binding nature of the ILO's Philadelphia Declaration.
(3) The Declaration requires compliance of Convention Nos. 88 and 89 even by those countries that have not ratified the same.
(4) The Declaration requires compliance of convention No. 138 even by those countries that have not ratified the same.

88. Match the 'Style of Leadership' with the 'numbers', as they are denoted by, in Managerial Grid :

List – A	List – B
a. Task Management	i. 1, 1
b. Impoverished	ii. 1, 9
c. Team	iii. 5, 5
d. Country Club	iv. 9, 1
e. Middle of the road	v. 9, 9

Codes :

	a	b	c	d	e
(1)	ii	i	iv	v	iii
(2)	ii	i	v	iv	iii
(3)	iv	i	ii	v	iii
(4)	iv	i	v	ii	iii

89. Under the provisions of the Maternity Benefit Act, 1961, nursing breaks are to be provided to every women who returns to duty after delivery of a child, until the child attains the age of
(1) Eighteen months
(2) Fifteen months
(3) Twelve months
(4) Twenty four months

90. The Federation of Indian Chambers of Commerce and Industry was founded by
(1) G.D. Birla and Vallabhbhai Patel
(2) Purushottam Takkar and Mahatma Gandhi
(3) G.D. Birla and Purushottam Takkar
(4) Mahatma Gandhi and Vallabhbhai Patel

91. Process consultation, Confrontation Meetings, Organisational Mirroring and Team Building are commonly used as tools for
(1) Human Resource Accounting
(2) Human Resource Audit
(3) Recruitment Techniques
(4) OD Intervention

92. Under the Employee's Compensation Act, 1923, the minimum amount of compensation payable to an employee suffering from permanent total disablement from the injury is
(1) Rupees one lakh and twenty thousand
(2) Rupees one lakh and ten thousand
(3) Rupees one lakh and forty thousand
(4) Rupees one lakh and seventy thousand

93. An employee working in an organization dies resulting from injury by an accident arising out of and in course of his employment. What is the amount of compensation his dependants are entitled to if his monthly wages was rupees eighteen thousand per month and the relevant factor is 186.90 under the Employees' Compensation Act, 1923 ?
(1) Rs. 7,47,600 (2) Rs. 8,97,120
(3) Rs. 16,82,100 (4) Rs. 7,76,300

94. Who identified the basic elements of work known as 'therbligs' ?
(1) Henry L. Gantt
(2) Frank B. Gilbreth
(3) F.W. Taylor
(4) All of the above

95. Who among the following concluded that the factory was a social system and informal groups at work place play a vital role in industrial affairs ?
(1) Elton Mayo

(2) Henry Fayol
(3) Blake and Mouton
(4) Herzberg

96. Arrange the steps of decision making process in the correct sequence :
a. analysis of alternatives
b. identification of decision criteria
c. implementation of alternative
d. identification of problem
e. selection of alternative
(1) d, b, a, e, c (2) d, a, b, e, c
(3) d, a, b, c, e (4) d, a, e, b, c

97. Departmentation is
a. structuring work to accomplish organisational goals
b. visual display of organisation structure
c. grouping of jobs on some basis
d. arranging jobs in a hierarchy
(1) a and b only
(2) b and c only
(3) a only
(4) c only

98. The tendency of people to expend less effort when working collectively than when working individually is called
(1) Social loafing (3) Socialising
(2) Adjourning (4) Social action

99. Personnel Management is essentially a
(1) Matrix function
(2) Line function
(3) Staff function
(4) Line & staff function

100. Which of the following comes under the scope of line and staff relationship ?
(1) The relationship between works manager and maintenance engineer
(2) The relationship between works manager and personnel manager
(3) The relationship between personnel manager and development engineer
(4) The relationship between the public relation officer and the public

101. Match the following concepts of labour with the relevant theme :

Concept of Labour	**Theme**
a. Commodity concept of Labour	i. Labour regarded by the employer largely as operating organizations in industry.
b. Machinery concept of Labour	ii. Labour has right to be consulted in regard to the terms and conditions under which they are supposed to work.
c. Goodwill concept of Labour	iii. Labour is affected by the law of supply and demand.
d. Citizenship concept of Labour	iv. Paternalistic approach towards labour by the employers.

Codes :

	a	b	c	d
(1)	iii	i	iv	ii
(2)	ii	iv	iii	i
(3)	iv	iii	i	ii
(4)	i	iii	ii	iv

102. Which of the following is not a feature of labour market ?
(1) It is essentially local in character.
(2) It is not monopolistic.
(3) It is less mobile compared to commodity and capital markets.
(4) Monospony in the labour market is less common than monopoly.

103. Which of the following theories of wages is called as the 'Iron Law of Wages' ?
(1) Subsistence Theory
(2) The Standard of Living Theory
(3) The Wage Fund Theory
(4) The Residual Claimant Theory

104. Which of the following is not a factor that creates wage differentials ?

(1) Differences due to existence of non-competing groups.
(2) Non-equalizing differences
(3) Differences in Labour Quality
(4) Labour Market Perfections

105. On what basis the money wage can be converted into real wages ?
(1) Consumer Price Index
(2) Wholesale Price Index
(3) Retail Price Index
(4) Money Exchange Rate

106. When driven by group cohesion, a decision is taken only to be lamented for later is called :
(1) Abilene effect
(2) Placebo effect
(3) Hawthorne effect
(4) Halo effect

107. In which year the Amalgamated Society of Engineers was established in Great Britain ?
(1) 1837 (2) 1850
(3) 1854 (4) 1859

108. Assertion (A) : Workforce diversity requires employers to be more sensitive to the differences that each group brings to the work setting.

Reason (R) : Employees need to be responsive to the values, needs, interests and expectations of fellow employees.

Code :
(1) (A) is right but (R) is wrong.
(2) (A) is wrong but (R) is right.
(3) Both (A) and (R) are right but (R) does not explain (A).
(4) Both (A) and (R) are right and (R) explains (A).

109. A Commercial establishment has engaged one hundred and fifty workmen. If it wants to retrench any workman who has completed one year of continuous service in the establishment, then which of the conditions are to be followed under the Industrial Disputes Act, 1947 ?
(a) It has to serve one month notice in writing in advance or pay in lieu of such notice, wages for the notice period.
(b) It has to serve three months notice in writing in advance or pay in lieu of such notice, wages for the notice period.
(c) Pay retrenchment compensation at the rate of fifteen days average pay for every completed year of continuous service or any part thereof in excess of six months.
(d) Notice in the prescribed manner is served on the appropriate Government.
(e) Prior permission of the appropriate Government has been obtained on an application made in this behalf.

Code :
(1) (a), (c) and (d)
(2) (b), (c) and (e)
(3) (b), (d) and (e)
(4) (a), (c), (d) and (e)

110. The National Association of Letter Carriers was started in USA in the year :
(1) 1887 (2) 1888
(3) 1889 (4) 1890

111. Which one of the following is not a benefit of Total Quality management ?
(1) Maximising cost
(2) Providing greater satisfaction to all concerned
(3) creating quality consciousness
(4) Creating good public image

112. A worker retires from a factory after putting in twenty years of continuous service. His last monthly wages drawn was ₹ 45,500. What is the amount of gratuity the worker is entitled to under the payment of Gratuity Act, 1972.
(1) ₹ 5,75,000 (2) ₹ 5,25,000
(3) ₹ 7,50,000 (4) ₹ 4,55,000

113. Who had given the pluralist approach to industrial relations indicating 'job regulation' drawing from the theories of anomie, collective bargaining and industrial democracy ?

(1) H.A. Clegg (2) Alan Fox
(3) R. Commons (4) Allan Flanders

114. Buzz-Sessions help in :
(a) making workers versatile
(b) making labour become more skilled and hard working
(c) eliminating those employees who sit through the conference session but do not participate
(d) stimulating discussion and participation from each member of group

Code :
(1) (a) and (b) (2) (a), (b) and (c)
(3) (c), and (d) (4) (b), (c) and (d)

115. An employee engaged in an industrial establishment draws wages of ₹ 20,000 per month. What is the amount of bonus he shall be entitled to, if it is to be paid at the rate of 9% by the employer for an accounting year under the provisions of the payment of Bonus Act, 1965 ?
(1) Rupees Seven thousand five hundred sixty only
(2) Rupees Eighteen thousand only
(3) Rupees Eight thousand one hundred thirty only
(4) Rupees Ten thousand six hundred forty only

116. Assertion (A) : Collective bargaining provides for procedural and substantial rules.

Reason (R) : It incorporates mechanism for dealing with interpretations and implementation of agreements as well as resolving conflicts and substantial rules concerning the substance of the agreements in both markets and managerial relationships.

Code :
(1) Assertion (A) is wrong and, thus, Reason (R) fails to explain (A).
(2) Assertion (A) is only partially true and, therefore, the Reason (R) only partially explains (A).
(3) Assertion (A) is correct and Reason (R) explains (A).
(4) Assertion (A) is correct and Reason (R) is wrong.

117. In March 2017, the Government of India in the Ministry of labour and Employment has revised the administrative charges payable by the employers under the Employees Provident Fund Scheme, 1952. Which one of the following statements given is correct ?
(1) 0.65 percent (Zero point six five percent) of the pay subject to a minimum of seventy five rupees per month for every non-functional establishments having no contributory member and five hundred rupees per month for other establishments
(2) 0.67 percent (Zero point six seven percent) of the pay subject to a minimum of one hundred rupees per month for every non-functional establishment having no contributory member and five hundred rupees per month for other establishments
(3) 0.75 percent (Zero point seven five percent) of the pay subject to a minimum of one hundred rupees per month for every non-functional establishment having no contributory member and one thousand rupees per month for other establishments
(4) 0.50 percent (Zero point five zero percent) of the pay subject to a minimum of seventy five rupees per month for every non-functional establishment having no contributory member and one thousand rupees per month for other establishments.

118. Assertion (A) : Both Weber's Bureaucracy and Taylor's scientific management emphasise on rationality, predictability, impersonality, technical competence and authoritarianism.

Reason (R) : Though Weber's writings were less operational than Taylor's, yet 'ideal bureaucracy ' describes many contemporary organisations.

Code:

(1) (A) is right and (R) is wrong.
(2) (A) is wrong and (R) is right.
(3) Both (A) and (R) are right.
(4) Both (A) and (R) are wrong.

119. Which of the following are the trends in International Industrial Relations System?

(a) MNCs try to cultivate centralised ethnocentric approach to the extent of pressurising the national Governments to bring out unprecedented economic and labour reforms.
(b) MNCs aspire for hassle free business climate and for this, adopt the practice of replacing expensive labour with cheap labour through outsourcing.
(c) MNCs promote individual centric Human Resource policies to keep trade unions at bay.
(d) MNCs act like 'octopus'. Nations, trade unions and other actors of Industrial Relations only grapple with the unfathomable strength of MNCs.

Code:

(1) (a) and (c) (2) (b), (c) and (d)
(3) (a), (c) and (d) (4) (a), (b), (c) and (d)

120. Match List - A with List - B and select correct answer by using the code given below:

List - A	List - B
(a) Application of psychology to industry and managament	(i) Henry L. Gantt
(b) Program Evaluation and Review Technique	(ii) Walter Dill Scott
(c) Widely acclaimed first lady of management	(iii) Lillian Gilbreth
(d) Application of psychology to advertising, marketing and personnel.	(iv) Hugo Munsterberg

Codes:

	(a)	(b)	(c)	(d)
(1)	(ii)	(i)	(iv)	(iii)
(2)	(iv)	(i)	(iii)	(ii)
(3)	(iii)	(iv)	(i)	(ii)
(4)	(iii)	(i)	(ii)	(iv)

121. Recently the Government of India has enforced 'the Ease of compliance to Maintain Registers under various Labour Laws Rules, 2017' for maintenance of combined registers provided under various labour legislations. Which of the following legislations is not covered under the above Rules?

(1) Equal Remuneration Act, 1976
(2) Mines Act, 1952
(3) Factories Act, 1948
(4) Minimum Wages Act, 1948

122. According to which one of the following approaches, management is the function of planning, organising, leading and controlling?

(1) Process approach
(2) Systems approach
(3) Quantitative approach
(4) Human behaviour approach

123. Which of the following statements about the definition of 'Trade Union' as given in the Trade Unions Act, 1926 is not true?

(a) A trade union is any combination, whether temporary or permanent.
(b) It regulates the relations between workmen and employer.
(c) It does not regulate the relations between workmen and workmen.
(d) It regulates relations between employers and employers.

Code:

(1) only (a) (2) (a) and (b)
(3) only (c) (4) (b), (c) and (d)

124. Calculate the amount of compensation to be paid to the dependants of a deceased employee, where death results from the injury, under the provisions of Employees, Compensation Act, 1923. (Monthly wages drawn was ₹ 15,000 and Relevant factor is 139.13)

(1) ₹ 1,20,000 (2) ₹ 4,52,400
(3) ₹ 6,50,210 (4) ₹ 5,56,520

125. Which one of the following is not a barrier to communication ?

(1) feedback (2) ambiguity
(3) lack of trust
(4) distortions in communication

126. Which of the following statements relating to the industrial relations policy in India is/are not true ?

(a) Industrial relations in India is highly regulated by state intervention.
(b) Industrial relations policy in India tried to shift from Courts to Codes.
(c) Tripartism was a strong policy shift in industrial relations in India.
(d) Free and compulsory collective bargaining was the chief characteristic feature of industrial relations policy in India.

Code:

(1) only (a) (2) only (b)
(3) (a), (b), (c) (4) only (d)

127. For the first time in India, medical benefit as a non-cash benefit was provided under :

(1) Maternity Benefit Act, 1961
(2) Employees State Insurance Act, 1948
(3) Factories Act, 1948
(4) Mines Act, 1952

128. Who has propagated the bipartite, tripartite and multi-partite aspects of industrial relations with human relations as the invisible energy binding them ?

(1) Sidney and Beatrice Webb
(2) H.A. Clegg
(3) John H. Richardson
(4) Alan Fox

129. In a conflict situation, which of the following errors makes the bargainers assume that their gain must come at the expense of the other party ?

(1) Mythical Fixed Pie
(2) Conflict Dilemma
(3) Winner's Curse
(4) Escalation of Commitment

130. Under the Minimum Wages Act, 1948, which one of the following is not a prescribed wagesperiod for fixation of minimum rate of wages ?

(1) by the hour (2) by the day
(3) by the week (4) by the month

131. Allocable surplus for a banking company under the provisions of the payment of Bonus Act, 1965 means :

(1) Sixty seven percent of the available surplus in an accounting year
(2) Sixty percent of the available surplus in an accounting year
(3) Sixty six percent of the available surplus in an accounting year
(4) Sixty six percent of the available surplus in the financial year

132. Arrange the steps of designing Management Information System in correct sequence :

(a) Analyse information requirements
(b) Aggregate the decisions
(c) Design information processing
(d) Analyse the decision system

Code:

(1) (a), (c), (b), (d) (2) (a), (b), (c), (d)
(3) (d), (a), (b), (c) (4) (a), (d), (b), (c)

133. Which of the following statements relating to primary unions in India is correct ?

(1) These unions fall only under the category of industrial unions
(2) These unions fall only under the category of general unions
(3) These unions fall only under the category of craft unions
(4) These unions fall under all the three categories i.e., industrial unions, general unions and craft unions

134. In which year the National Renewal Fund was abolished by the Government ?

(1) 1992 (2) 1996
(3) 2000 (4) 2004

135. Match the following :

List-I	List-II
(a) Ethnocentric Approach	(i) Primary positions held by nationals from host country
(b) Polycentric Approach	(ii) Qualified people are hired at home and from abroad irrespective of nationality
(c) Regiocentric Approach	(iii) Primary positions are held by citizens of home country
(d) Geocentric Approach	(iv) Primary positions are held by people from same region with similar cultures, experiences and management practices

Codes :

	(a)	(b)	(c)	(d)
(1)	(iv)	(i)	(iii)	(ii)
(2)	(ii)	(iv)	(i)	(iii)
(3)	(iii)	(ii)	(i)	(iv)
(4)	(iii)	(i)	(iv)	(ii)

136. An industrial establishment employing one thousand employees has to pay the wages to the employees within which period after the last day of the wage period in respect of which the wages are payable under the provisions of the payment of Wages Act, 1936 ?

(1) Before the expiry of the seventh day
(2) Before the expiry of the fifth day
(3) Before the expiry of the tenth day
(4) Before the expiry of the eighth day

137. Two distinct schools of thought have emerged in industrial relations. The first one, known as 'Personnel Management School', emphasised the "employers' solution" to labour problems.

The second school of thought, known as 'Institutional Labour Economics School' emphasized the workers' solution of trade unionism and the communities' solution of protective labour legislation and social insurance to labour problems.

Which of the following inferences are right relating to the broad themes of the above two schools ?

(a) The first school takes an "internal" or inside-the-firm perspective on the solution of labour problems.
(b) The second school favoured institutional forms of power balancing and joint governance in the employment relationship.
(c) The first school takes an "external" or outside-the-firm perspective on the solution of labour problems.
(d) The second school emphasized upon building a community of interest between labour and management for which the employer has to take the initiative.

Code :

(1) only (a) and (b)
(2) only (b) and (c)
(3) only (b) and (d)
(4) (b), (c) and (d)

138. Which of the following is not a characteristic of culture according to Hofstede ?

(1) Power distance
(2) Person's relationship with natural world
(3) Masculinity and Femininity
(4) Individualism Vs Collectivism

139. Which of the following facilities is to be provided by an employer employing two hundred fifty workers covered under the Factories Act, 1948 ?

(1) Ambulance Room
(2) Canteen
(3) Shelter and rest rooms
(4) Cooling drinking water

140. Which of the following statements relating to the source of industrial disputes in the Indian context is/are correct ?

(a) Disputes relating to the implementation of labour laws and regulations fall under the category of 'disputes concerning rights'.

(b) Disputes relating to standing orders fall under the category of 'disputes concerning rights.'

(c) Disputes concerning collective agreements and settlements fall under the category of 'disputes concerning rights.'

Code:

(1) only (a) is correct.

(2) only (a) and (b) are correct.

(3) only (b) and (c) are correct.

(4) (a), (b) and (c) are correct.

141. Which of the following are the three dimensions of Mendenhall and Oddou Training Model for expatriates ?

(a) Training Methods

(b) Effectiveness Measurement

(c) Levels of Training

(d) Duration of Training

(e) Selection of Trainer

Code:

(1) (a), (b), (c) (2) (a), (c), (d)

(3) (a), (c), (e) (4) (b), (d), (e)

142. A woman who legally adopts a child below the age of three months shall be entitled to maternity benefit from the date the child is handed over to the adopting mother for a period of how many weeks under the provisions of the Maternity Benefit (Amendment) Act, 2017 ?

(1) Twelve weeks

(2) Twenty six weeks

(3) Eighteen weeks

(4) Eight weeks

143. Which of the following laydown Universal Ethical principles for multinationals ?

(a) The United Nations Declaration of Human Rights

(b) The OECD Guidelines for Multinational Enterprises

(c) The Caux Roundtable Principles of Business

Code:

(1) (a) and (b) only

(2) (b) and (c) only

(3) (a) and (c) only

(4) (a), (b) and (c)

144. Various schemes of workers participation in management were launched in different years and with varied objectives. Match the schemes (List-I) with year of their introduction (List - II) :

List - I	**List - II**
(a) Employees Director in Nationalised banks	(i) 1958
(b) Workers' share in equity	(ii) 1970
(c) Workers participation in industry at the levels of plant and shop floor	(iii) 1985
(d) Joint Management Council	(iv) 1975

Codes:

	(a)	(b)	(c)	(d)
(1)	(ii)	(iii)	(iv)	(i)
(2)	(iv)	(ii)	(iii)	(i)
(3)	(ii)	(i)	(iii)	(iv)
(4)	(iv)	(iii)	(ii)	(i)

145. In which of the following employments the Equal Remuneration Act, 1976 was first enforced ?

(1) Employments under Central and State Governments

(2) Plantations to which the Plantations Labour Act, 1951 applies.

(3) Mines as defined under the Mines Act, 1952

(4) Local Authorities

146. Who has advanced 'coping styles' for role stress combining avoidance and approach to role stress with laws of control of internality and externality ?

(1) Lorsch and Lawrence

(2) Litwin and Stringer

(3) Udai Pareek

(4) T.V. Rao

147. Selig Perlman, whose views are known as 'Job-Consciousness Theory' of trade Unionism, observed that the trade Union is the outcome of pessimistic outlook of a 'manualist' worker.

Which statement is not true in the context of Perlman's theory :

(1) In order to protect one's limited job opportunity, a worker starts uniting with his/her fellow 'manualists'.
(2) Emergence of trade unions mainly from 'Job-Consciousness' is not tenable in all situations.
(3) Genuine Trade Unions are inherently 'bread and butter' trade unions.
(4) After studying the American situation, Perlman observed that during periods of expansion of economy, the American worker had the consciousness of abundance, but this phenomenon existed only for a few years. The optimism of the period of plenty was superseded by pessimism of scarcity. The moment such a situation emerged, trade unions also emerged.

148. Which of the following statements about disciplinary process are true ?

(a) Under Master-Servant doctrine, servant worked at the will of the master, with no subsisting right to continue in employment under laissez fair policy.
(b) Now no workman can be charge sheeted and punished unless one has committed a misconduct as per the relevant standing orders.
(c) Misconduct is not defined in any Act but given under the model standing orders which can be adopted in certified standing orders.

Code :

(1) (b) and (c) (2) (a) and (b)
(3) (a) and (c) (4) (a), (b) and (c)

149. Under the power to make exempting orders of the Factories Act, 1948, the State Government can fix the maximum time of overtime work for any quarter is :

(1) Fifty hours (2) Seventy five hours
(3) Sixty hours (4) Ninety hours

150. Which one of the following statements relating to payment of subsistence allowance under the Industrial Employment (standing orders) Act, 1946 is not correct ?

(1) Subsistence allowance shall be at the rate of fifty percent of the wages which the workman was entitled to immediately preceding the date of such suspension, for the first ninety days
(2) Subsistence allowance shall be at the rate of Seventy-five percent of such wages for the remaining period of suspension if the delay in the completion of disciplinary proceedings against such workman is not directly attributable to the conduct of such workman
(3) If any dispute arises regarding the subsistence allowance payable to a workman, the workman or the employer concerned may refer the dispute to the Labour Court Constituted under the Industrial Disputes Act, 1947
(4) If any dispute arises regarding the subsistence allowance payable to a workman, the appropriate Government may refer the dispute to the Industrial Tribunal constituted under the Industrial Disputes Act, 1947

151. 'Knowledge workers' are :

(a) the workers whose main capital is knowledge
(b) the workers whose jobs are designed around the acquisition and application of information
(c) the workers whose jobs concentrate on routine problems

Code :

(1) (a) only (2) (a) and (b)
(3) (b) and (c) (4) (a), (b) and (c)

152. Which of the following is a statutory workers' participation in management forum ?

(1) Joint Management Council
(2) Shop Council
(3) Joint Council (4) Works Committee

153. 'Pygmalion effect' is associated with :

(1) Self-aggredisement
(2) Self-defence
(3) Self fulfilling prophecy
(4) Self denial

154. An adolescent who has been given a certificate of fitness to work, has worked for 232 days during the calendar year 2016 in a factory. He has been on leave with wages for ten days during the year. How many days of leave with wages he shall be entitled to during the year 2017 ?

(1) Ten days (2) Twelve days
(3) Fifteen days (4) Nil

155. When a union signs an agreement with management for wage revision and other benefits, in most of the cases non-members also get the benefit without either paying subscription or participating in union meetings and other struggles. Such non members are called :

(1) Parasites (2) Fence sitters
(3) Free riders (4) Opportunists

156. Match the following theories of leadership (List-I) with their propagator (List-II) :

List-I	List-II
(a) Leader Member Exchange Theory	(i) Robert House
(b) Path Goal Theory	(ii) Ken Blanchard
(c) Situational Theory	(iii) Fred Fiedler
(d) Contingency Theory	(iv) George Graen

Codes :

	(a)	(b)	(c)	(d)
(1)	(iv)	(i)	(ii)	(iii)
(2)	(iv)	(ii)	(i)	(iii)
(3)	(ii)	(i)	(iii)	(iv)
(4)	(iii)	(ii)	(i)	(iv)

157. Which of the following is the correct set of contingencies identified by William Beveridge in his comprehensive social security scheme ?

(1) Want, sickness, disability, squalor and idleness
(2) Want, disease, old age, squalor and unemployment
(3) Want, disease, ignorance, squalor and idleness
(4) Disease, invalidity, old age, unemployment and ignorance

158. Who is associated with the approaches to Disciplinary action such as judicial approach, human relations approach, human resource approach, group discipline approach and leadership approach ?

(1) N.N. Chatterjee
(2) Mirza S. Saiddain
(3) Arun Monappa
(4) C.B. Mamoria

159. Match phases of change process (List - I) with their propagators (List - II) :

List-I	List-II
(a) Unfreezing, Changing, Freezing	(i) Nadler kand Tushman
(b) Awakening, Mobilising, Reinforcing	(ii) Beckhard & Renbern Harris
(c) Energizing, Envisioning, and Enabling	(iii) Kurt Lewin
(d) Dissatisfaction with the status quo, clear goal, awareness of practical first steps	(iv) Neol Tirchy & Devanna

Codes :

	(a)	(b)	(c)	(d)
(1)	(iii)	(ii)	(i)	(iv)
(2)	(iii)	(iv)	(i)	(ii)
(3)	(iii)	(i)	(iv)	(ii)
(4)	(iii)	(ii)	(iv)	(i)

160. Who among the following shall be the chairperson of the National Security Board constituted under the Unorganised Workers' Social Security Act, 2008 ?

(1) Chief Labour Commissioner (Central)
(2) Director General (Labour Welfare)
(3) Chief Commissioner (Labour Welfare)
(4) Union Minister for Labour and Employment

161. Who defined grievance as, "any discontent or dissatisfaction, whether expressed or not and whether valid or not, arising out of anything connected with the company that an employee thinks, believes or even feels is unfair, unjust, or inequitable" ?

(1) Dale Yoder
(2) Paul Pigors
(3) Michael J. Jucius
(4) Charles A. Myers

162. Who has developed the 'Learning and Performance Wheel' ?
(1) Paul Brenthal et. al
(2) F.J. Roethlisberger et. al
(3) Leonard and Zeace Nadlar
(4) Udai Pareek et. al

163. Match the following List - I with List - II :

List - I	List - II
(a) Malaviya Committee	(i) Minimum wages
(b) B. P. Adarkar Report	(ii) Social security for unorganised labour
(c) D. Aykroid's formula	(iii) Labour welfare
(d) Arjun Sengupta Committee	(iv) Employees' State Insurance

Codes :

	(a)	(b)	(c)	(d)
(1)	(iii)	(ii)	(iv)	(i)
(2)	(iii)	(i)	(iv)	(ii)
(3)	(iii)	(iv)	(i)	(ii)
(4)	(iv)	(iii)	(i)	(ii)

164. A dispute has arisen regarding admission of membership of a union which is a registered and recognised Trade Union. Few workers had filed a joint application for membership of that union. The application was not considered because the application was not in accordance with the procedure laid down by the union. Aggrieved by this, the workers filed a complaint before the Registrar of Trade Unions under Section 28 (1-A). Which one among the following is competent authority to settle the issue ?
(1) Registrar of Trade Unions
(2) Industrial Tribunal
(3) High Court
(4) Civil Court of the competent jurisdiction

165. The HRD matrix linking HRD subsystems to development dimensions has been advanced by :
(1) Dharani P. Sinha (2) D.M. Pestonjee
(3) Udai Pareek (4) T.V. Rao

166. Before the enactment of the Inter-State Migrant Workmen (Regulation of Employment and Conditions of Service) Act, 1979 by the Union Government which of the following States had an exclusive law relating to the migrant labour ?
(1) Odisha (2) Assam
(3) Bihar (4) Tamilnadu

167. The Industrial Disputes Act, 1947 empowers the appropriate Government to constitute a court of inquiry to inquire into any matter appearing to be connected with or relevant to an industrial dispute. It is the duty of the court of inquiry to inquire into matters referred to it and submit its report to the appropriate Government, ordinarily within which period from the commencement of its inquiry :
(1) One month (2) Two months
(3) Four months (4) Six months

168. Associate the following conditions (List-I) with the period in which they prevailed (List-II) :

List-I	List-II
(a) Unbridled individualism, freedom of contract and laissezfaire	(i) Welfarism and Post Welfarism
(b) Rise of Trade Unionism	(ii) Political Liberalism
(c) Rise of socialist and Revolutionary ideas	(iii) Early Industrialism
(d) Rise of Labour Parties	(iv) Marxism

Codes :

	(a)	(b)	(c)	(d)
(1)	(iii)	(i)	(iv)	(ii)
(2)	(iii)	(ii)	(iv)	(i)
(3)	(iii)	(iv)	(i)	(ii)
(4)	(iv)	(ii)	(iii)	(i)

169. Which of the following statements about HR score-card are true ?

(a) Measurement is central to HR score-card

(b) HR architecture inclusive of sum of HR function; the broader HR system and the resulting employee behaviour is crucial to HR scorecard

(c) Measurements generally include total compensation, cost per hire, employee turnover, job satisfaction levels, appraisal categories etc.

(d) Capability, commitment, competencies, learning outcomes are difficult to be measured resulting into a difference between ' What is measured ' and what is important in HR

Code :

(1) (a), (d) (2) (a), (c), (d)
(3) (a), (b), (d) (4) (a), (b), (c), (d)

170. Which one of the following Acts, explains the meaning of "Badli workman" ?

(1) Factories Act, 1948
(2) Industrial Disputes Act, 1947
(3) Industrial Employment (Standing Orders) Act, 1946
(4) Trade Unions Act, 1926

171. Which one of the following is not correct relating to working hours for children under the Factories Act, 1948 ?

(1) Maximum hours of work is four and half hours in any day
(2) No child shall be employed during night
(3) The hours of work including rest should be limited to a maximum spread over period of five and half hours
(4) No female child shall be allowed to work in any factory between 7 pm. to 8 am.

172. Assertion (A) : Between 'hire and fire' policy and VRS, the later is considered as a strategy of less severe severance.

Reason (R) : VRS is conceived as a win-win situation because organisations gain by reducing the surplus and in right sizing the employee structure. Employees, on the other hand may lose jobs, but gain sizeable severance benefits to face post-VRS problems.

Code :

(1) (A) is wrong and (R) is right.
(2) (A) and (R) are right and (R) explains the (A).
(3) (A) and (R) are right but (R) doesn't explain the (A).
(4) (A) is right and (R) is wrong.

173. Michael Porter has given the 'Five Forces' model of strategic management. The sixth force is given by G. Ghemawat and D. Collis called ' COMPLEMENTORS'. Which of the following statements about the 6th force are true ?

(a) Complementors are groups from which buyers purchase complementary services and groups to whom suppliers sell complementary products.

(b) These are different competitive forces from the rest of the 5 forces given by Michael Porter.

(c) Complementors can help both buyers and suppliers to increase their pie by add-on values.

(d) If Complimentors are too Powerful ; then both buyers and suppliers can form coalitions.

Code :

(1) (a), (c), (d) only (2) (a), (b), (d) only
(3) (b), (c), (d) only (4) (a), (b), (c) and (d)

174. Arrange the following Acts in a sequence according to their years of their enactment in USA starting from the earliest to the latest :

(a) Wagner Act
(b) Landrum-Griffin Act
(c) Narris-LaGuaradia Act
(d) Taft-Hartley Act

Code :

(1) (a), (b), (c), (d) (2) (c), (a), (d), (b)
(3) (a), (c), (b), (d) (4) (b), (c), (a), (d)

175. Which one of the following does not find place under the Factories (Amendment) Bill 2016 initiated by the Government ?
(1) Enhance the limit of overtime hours to a maximum of one hundred hours per quarter under section 64.
(2) Enhance the limit of overtime hours to a maximum of one hundred twenty five hours per quarter in public interest under section 65.
(3) Empower the Central Government in addition to the State Governments to make exempting rules and exempting orders in respect of hours of work on overtime in a quarter.
(4) Enhance the limit of total number of hours of work in a week including overtime to a maximum of seventy five hours.

176. Match the following tests (List – A) with the tools used (List – B) for carrying out these tests :

List – A	List – B
a. Thematic Apperception Test (TAT)	i. Ten cards having prints of Ink blots
b. Rosenzweig Test	ii. 45 inkblot cards
c. Rorschach Test	iii. 25 plates, each consisting 3 sketches
d. Holtzman Ink Block Test	iv. Pictures
e. Tomkins-Horn Picture arrangement test	v. Cartoons with balloons above

Codes :

	a	b	c	d	e
(1)	iv	ii	i	iii	v
(2)	v	iii	ii	i	iv
(3)	iv	v	i	ii	iii
(4)	iv	iii	i	ii	v

177. Which of the following statements relating to Industrial Truce Resolution, 1962 is not correct ?
(1) The resolution was passed on December 12, 1962
(2) The Resolution was passed in a joint meeting of employers' and workers' representatives.
(3) Part IV of the Resolution referred to the price stability.
(4) Part V of the Resolution referred to the imperative need for increasing savings, particularly through contribution to the National Defence Fund and / or to investments in Defence Bonds.

178. The bipartite consultative machinery comprises
(1) Works committees and steering committee on wages
(2) Works committees and standing labour committee
(3) Joint management councils and works committees
(4) Joint management councils and standing labour committee

179. Blum and Naylor defined job satisfaction as "the result of various attitudes that the employee holds towards his/her job and organization on account of his/her experience (good or bad) in the organization and a feeling of contentment derived out of these attitudes. Lack of it is job dissatisfaction." Which of the following inferences cannot be considered as logical from the above definition ?
a. The job satisfaction comes out of various attitudes of employees towards their jobs and organisations.
b. The attitudes are formed by the employees' good or bad experience in the organization.
c. The employees shall be content with their experiences in the organization; failing which job satisfaction will result.
d. Job satisfaction will be less if a person becomes an 'isolate' from the group.
(1) a and b
(2) a, b and c
(3) c and d
(4) only d

180. Below given are four figures (List–I). Match them with the communication pattern (List–II).

List – I		List – II
a.	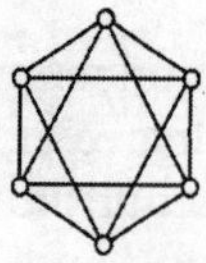	i. Linear vertical
b.	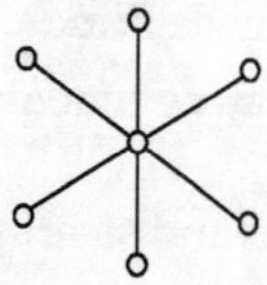	ii. Linear Horizontal
c.		iii. Wheel
d.		iv. All Channel

Codes :

	a	b	c	d
(1)	iii	iv	ii	i
(2)	iv	iii	ii	i
(3)	iv	iii	i	ii
(4)	iii	iv	i	ii

181. The term 'Blackleg' refers to

(1) A worker who forcibly joins those who are on strike.

(2) A worker who continues to work when his/her co-workers in the establishment are on strike.

(3) A worker who wears black shoes while on duty.

(4) A supervisor who breathes on the necks of his/her subordinates.

182. As per the proceedings of the 46th Indian Labour Conference, 2015, the Government of India has proposed to enhance the overtime hours from the present limit of fifty hours, under the Factories Act, 1948 to

(1) Seventy five hours

(2) One hundred ten hours

(3) One hundred hours

(4) Ninety hours

183. Match the following effects List – I with their meanings given in List – II :

List – I	List – II
a. Placebo effect	i. Self fulfilled prophecy
b. Hawthorne effect	ii. Rating error due to attribution to single trait
c. Pygmallion effect	iii. Belief system
d. Halo effect	iv. Controlled behaviour under observation

Codes :

	a	b	c	d
(1)	iii	iv	i	ii
(2)	i	ii	iii	iv
(3)	iv	iii	ii	i
(4)	iii	iv	ii	i

184. Richard P. Calhoon observed that "Grievance procedure is a control necessary for protecting the standards of the employee as discipline is the control necessary for preserving standards of the company".

Which of the following inferences cannot be derived from the above statement ?

(1) Grievance procedure is a control on employer's HR decisions.

(2) Disciplinary actions are control on employee's work related conduct.

(3) Grievance redressal and disciplinary actions are inimical to one another.

(4) Grievance redressal and disciplinary actions as control mechanisms shall be handled through a due, just and judicious process.

185. Recently the Ministry of Labour and Employment, Government of India has drafted a bill for regulating manufacturing factories employing less than 40 workers. The proposed ame of the Bill is

(1) Small Factories (Facilitation and Regulation of Employment and Conditions of Services) Bill, 2015

(2) Small and Medium Factories Bill, 2015

(3) Small Factories (Conditions of services) Bill, 2015

(4) Medium and Small Factories (Regulation of Employment and Conditions of Services) Bill, 2015

186. According to the provisions of the Unorganized Worker's Social Security Act, 2008, which of the following schemes are deemed to be the welfare schemes under the Act ?

a. Janani Suraksha Yojana
b. National Family Benefit Scheme
c. Pradhan Mantri Jan Dhan Yojana
d. Indira Gandhi National Old Age Pension Scheme
e. Grameen Seekho and Kamao Scheme

(1) a, b, c and d (2) a, b and d
(3) c, d and e (4) a, b, d and e

187. Which of the following is/are not a commonly used method of training ?

a. Buzzing b. Regression
c. Role playing d. Rationalisation
e. Brain Storming f. Persuasion

Codes :

(1) b, d, f (2) a, c, e
(3) d, e, f (4) a, c, f

188. Assertion (A) : The MNCs had deeply entrenched themselves by the time unions realised the role of MNCs in spreading capitalism.

Reason (R) : For a pretty long time the international trade unions did not consider the MNCs as their natural opponents.

Codes :

(1) Both (A) and (R) are wrong.
(2) Both (A) and (R) are right and (R) explains (A).
(3) (A) is right and (R) is wrong.
(4) Both (A) and (R) are right, but (R) does not explain (A).

189. Match the provisions given in List – I with the legislations they are covered given in List – II :

List – I	List – II
a. Exempted employee	i. Payment of Bonus Act, 1965
b. Compulsory Insurance	ii. Factories Act, 1948
c. Right of Workers	iii. Payment of Gratuity Act, 1972
d. Development Rebate	iv. Employees' State Insurance Act, 1948

Codes :

	(a)	(b)	(c)	(d)		(a)	(b)	(c)	(d)
(1)	iv	iii	ii	i	(2)	i	ii	iii	iv
(3)	ii	i	iv	iii	(4)	iii	iv	i	ii

190. Assertion (A) : The unilateral HR decision making process partly gave way to negotiated decision making.

Reason (R) : Government norms and market forces imposed HR decisions.

(1) Both (A) and (R) are wrong.
(2) Both (A) and (R) are right, but (R) does not explain (A).
(3) Assertion (A) is right but (R) is wrong.
(4) Both (A) and (R) are right ; and (R) explains (A).

191. In which year the 'Change to Win Federation' was formed in U.S.A. ?

(1) 2002 (2) 2003
(3) 2004 (4) 2005

192. Match the type of Managerial Decisions List – I with the examples given in List – II :

List – I	List – II
a. Judgemental Decisions	i. Daily routines and scheduled activities
b. Adaptive Decisions	ii. Complex production and engineering problems
c. Mechanistic Decisions	iii. Marketing, investment, and personnel problems
d. Analytical Decisions	iv. Research and development and long-term corporate planning

Codes :

	(a)	(b)	(c)	(d)		(a)	(b)	(c)	(d)
(1)	iii	i	iv	ii	(2)	ii	iv	i	iii
(3)	iii	iv	i	ii	(4)	i	ii	iii	iv

193. A workman working in an industry was demoted to a lower grade as a punishment inflicted by way of disciplinary action. If the concerned workman intends to raise an industrial dispute on it, under which of the following conditions it shall be deemed to be an industrial dispute ?

a. If it is supported by a union in the establishment of which he is a member.

b. If it is supported by a minority union of the workmen in the establishment.

c. If it is supported by substantial number of workmen of the establishment in the absence of a union.

(1) Either a or b only
(2) Either a or c only
(3) Either b or c only
(4) a or b or c

194. Which of the following are the characteristic features of 'social assistance' ?

a. It is fully financed by the State.

b. Benefits provided under the scheme is for a short duration.

c. The Financial resources of social assistance scheme is for a short duration of time.

d. Social assistance is substitutive rather than supplemental to social insurance.

(1) a, b and d only (2) b, c and d only
(3) a, b and c only (4) a, b, c and d

195. Match the following inventions / processes in the field of industrial psychology (List – I) with their description (List – II) :

List – I	List – II
a. Ergograph	i. Fatigue related production curve
b. Dynamometer	ii. Sociometry relations
c. Sociogram	iii. Human engineering
d. End-spurt	iv. Single finger muscle activity

Codes :

	(a)	(b)	(c)	(d)		(a)	(b)	(c)	(d)
(1)	iv	iii	ii	i	(2)	i	iii	ii	iv
(3)	iii	i	ii	iv	(4)	iv	i	ii	iii

196. Indian Industrial Relations System can be considered as a mix of which of the following ?

a. North American MNCs' strategic choice for union-free Industrial Relations System.

b. West European MNCs' tradition of encouraging organized trade unions representing the employees' interests.

c. Japanese MNCs' preference for company promoted enterprise unions.

(1) only a (2) a and b
(3) a, b and c (4) a and c

197. What is the full form of 'UBC' in the context of trade union movement in U.S.A. ?

(1) United Brotherhood of Carpenters
(2) Union of Building and Construction workers
(3) Union of Buffalo Construction Inc.
(4) United Brotherhood of construction workers

198. The Deming Prize for Company Wide Quality Control (CWQC) is instituted by the

(1) International Organisation for Standardization (ISO)
(2) The Union of Japanese Scientists and Engineers (JUSE)
(3) CHEA International Quality Group.
(4) Institute of Quality and Control, Israel.

199. What is TQM 'Kitemarks' ?

(1) It is a set of TQM techniques.
(2) It is a set of TQM objectives.
(3) It is a set of TQM philosophies.
(4) It is a set of TQM awards.

200. Who among the following is/are workman under the provisions of the Industrial Disputes Act, 1947 ?

a. A person employed in a technical job draws wages of fifteen thousand rupees per month.

b. A person employed in a supervisory capacity draws wages of sixteen thousand rupees per month.

c. A person employed in a managerial or

administrative capacity draws a salary of ten thousand rupees per month.

d. A person employed in a supervisory capacity draws wages of nine thousand rupees per month.

(1) a, b and d only (2) a and d only
(3) a and b only (4) a, c and d only

201. The overlapping area of the range of two Negotiating parties which indicates the existence of the possibility of settlement, is known as :

(1) Ideals
(2) Negotiating Continuum
(3) Compromising Continuum
(4) Arena

202. Pareto chart represents –

a. most common sources of defects
b. highest occurring type of defect
c. most frequent reason for customer complaints

(1) a and c (2) a and b
(3) b and c (4) a, b and c

203. In making fish bone diagram, causes of problems are identified through

(1) Synetics
(2) Brainstorming
(3) Nominal Grouping
(4) Creative thinking

204. Which of the following is not an objective of workers' education in India ?

(1) To strengthen among all sections of the working class including rural workers, a sense of patriotism, national integrity, unity, communal harmony, secularism and pride in being an Indian.
(2) To equip all sections of workers including rural workers for their intelligent participation in asserting their right through strike.
(3) To develop leadership among the rank and file of workers themselves.
(4) To enable trade unions themselves to take over ultimately the functions of workers' education.

205. Which of the following statements about wage differentials is true ?

a. There are differentials that can be attributed to the imperfections of the employment market.
b. There are wage differentials which originate in social values and prejudices.
c. There will be occupational wage differentials even if employment markets were perfect and social prejudices were absent.

Codes :

(1) Only a (2) a and b
(3) b and a (4) a, b and c

206. Match the stages of Process of Organisational Change (List-A) with their possible descriptions (List-B) given below:

List-A	**List-B**
(a) Diagnosis	(i) The stage for framing a proposal in relation to the problems or issues identified
(b) Stabilisation	(ii) The attempt to search for the main cause underlying the symptoms encountered
(c) Motivation	(iii) The stage where people are involved in detailed consideration of the proposed change
(d) Action Proposal	(iv) The stage of internalizing the change and nuking it a part of the organisation's normal life

Code:

	(a)	(b)	(c)	(d)		(a)	(b)	(c)	(d)
(1)	(iv)	(iii)	(i)	(ii)	(2)	(i)	(iv)	(iii)	(ii)
(3)	(ii)	(iv)	(i)	(iii)	(4)	(ii)	(iv)	(iii)	(i)

207. Match the basic content of the theory (List-I) with the theories (List-II):

List-I

(a) Wages paid are equal to the productivity of the last worker hired
(b) Wages, hours and working conditions are largely a matter of relative bargaining strength of two sides
(c) Wages are residue left over after the other factors of production have been paid
(d) Wages equal the total product of labour of the marginal firm minus the amount discounted by the employer for advance support of the worker

List-II

(i) Taussig's Theory of Wages
(ii) Marginal Productivity Theory
(iii) The Bargaining Theory of Wages
(iv) Residual Claimant Theory

Code:

	(a)	(b)	(c)	(d)		(a)	(b)	(c)	(d)
(1)	(ii)	(iv)	(iii)	(i)	(2)	(iii)	(ii)	(i)	(iv)
(3)	(ii)	(iii)	(iv)	(i)	(4)	(iii)	(i)	(ii)	(iv)

208. Which one of the following is not a fundamental right under the provisions of the constitution of India?

(1) Equality of opportunity in matters of public employment
(2) Prohibition of traffic in human beings and forced labour
(3) Prohibition of employment of children in factories etc.
(4) Just and human condition of work and maternity relief

209. The concept of 'invisible hand theorem' in the context of labour market was put forward by:

(1) Adam Smith (2) Karl Marx
(3) J.S. Mill (4) Ricardo

210. Which of the following statements relating to the Model Grievance procedure is/are correct?

(a) As per the procedure, an aggrieved employee shall first present the grievance verbally (in person) to the officer designated by the management for this purpose.
(b) As per the procedure, an aggrieved worker who is not satisfied with the decision of the officer at the first stage or fails to receive an answer within a stipulated period of 48 hours from the said officer, he/she shall, either in person or accompanied by his/her departmental representative, present his/her grievance to the Head of the Department designated by the management for the purpose of handling grievances.
(c) According to the procedure, if a grievance arises out of an order given by management, the said order shall be complied with before the worker concerned invokes the procedure laid down for redressal of grievances

Code:

(1) (a) only (2) (b) only
(3) (a) and (b) (4) (a), (b) and (c)

211. Match the provisions given in List-A with their respective Articles given in List-B provided under the Constitution of India.

List-A	List-B
(a) Right to work	(i) Article 39
(b) Equal pay for equal work for both men and women	(ii) Article 43
(c) Human Conditions of work	(iii) Article 42
(d) Living wage and decent standard of life	(iv) Article 41

Code:

	(a)	(b)	(c)	(d)		(a)	(b)	(c)	(d)
(1)	(iv)	(i)	(iii)	(ii)	(2)	(i)	(ii)	(iv)	(iii)
(3)	(iii)	(iv)	(ii)	(i)	(4)	(ii)	(iii)	(i)	(iv)

212. Assertion (A): While all programming strategies need to provide for all three phases of individual and organisational learning, they differ according to the training modalities chosen for implementing them.

Reason (R): The chosen modality provides the frame for designing and sequencing training inputs and selecting methods to produce the desired results.

Code:

(1) Assertion (A) is not correct, Reason (R) is correct.
(2) Assertion (A) and Reason (R) both are not correct.
(3) Assertion (A) and Reason (R) both are correct, but Reason (R) does not explain Assertion (A).
(4) Assertion (A) and Reason (R) both are correct, Reason (R) explains Assertion (A).

213. Assertion (A): Occupational Wage differentials provide an incentive to young persons to incur the costs of training and education and encourage workers to develop skills in anticipation of higher earnings in future.

Reason (R): Occupational wage differentials perform a social function by way of determing the social status of workers.

Code:

(1) Assertion (A) is wrong and Reason (R) is right.
(2) Assertion (A) is right and Reason (R) explains Assertion (A).
(3) Assertion (A) is right and Reason (R) fails to explain Assertion (A).
(4) Assertion (A) is right and Reason (R) is wrong.

214. Match List-A: Management Functions with their possible explanation List-B:

List-A	List-B
(a) Controlling/ monitoring	(i) Making optimum use of the resources required to enable successfully carrying out the plans
(b) Leading/ motivating	(ii) Deciding what needs to happen in future and generating plans for action
(c) Organising	(iii) Checking progress against plans, which may need modification based on feedback
(d) Planning	(iv) Getting others to play an effective part in achieving plans

Code:

	(a)	(b)	(c)	(d)		(a)	(b)	(c)	(d)
(1)	(i)	(ii)	(iii)	(iv)	(2)	(iv)	(i)	(iii)	(ii)
(3)	(iii)	(iv)	(ii)	(i)	(4)	(iii)	(iv)	(i)	(ii)

215. Apart from legislations which of the following institutions operate in controlling and directing individual actions into desirable channels?

(a) Religious prescriptions
(b) Social customs, traditions and conventions
(c) Socialist and Revolutionary ideas
(d) Political freedom and Extension of franchise

Code:

(1) (a), (b) and (c) only
(2) (b) and (c) only
(3) (a) and (b) only
(4) (a), (b) and (d) only

216. Who proposed the three-tier structure of industrial relations activity?

(1) John T. Dunlop
(2) Kochan, Katz and McKersie
(3) J.H. Richardson
(4) H.A. Clegg

217. Experienced managers have a simple and effective way to check whether their goals are good or not-they use the acronym "SMART", which stands for:

(1) Specific, Manageable, Attainable, Reasonable, and Timely
(2) Sophisticated, Measurable, Attainable, Relevant, and Targetted
(3) Simple, Measurable, Ambitious, Relative, and Target oriented
(4) Specific, Measurable, Attainable, Relevant, and Timely

218. A worker working in a factory has worked for 225 days during the calendar year 2017.

He has been laid off for 20 days as per the standing order and has also availed 10 days of leave with wages during the said year. How many days of leave with wages he shall be entitled to during the calendar year 2018?

(1) NIL (2) 13 days
(3) 11 days (4) 12 days

219. Which of the following theoretical perspectives implies stewardship without ownership in the context of industrial relations?

(1) The Unitary Perspective
(2) The Pluralist Perspective
(3) The Radical Perspective
(4) The Trusteeship Perspective

220. Assertion (A): The basic planning process always involves setting objectives, forecasting and assessing basic planning "premises" or assumptions, determining alternatives causes of actions, evaluating which options are best, and then choosing and implementing plan.

Reason (R): There is usually a hierarchical aspect to managerial planning. Top management approves a long-term or strategic plan. Then each department creates its own budgets and other plans to fit and to contribute to company's long term plan.

Code:

(1) Assertion (A) is right and Reason (R) is wrong.
(2) Assertion (A) is wrong and Reason (R) is right.
(3) Assertion (A) and Reason (R) both are right, Reason (R) explains Assertion (A).
(4) Assertion (A) and Reason (R) both are right, Reason (R) does not explain Assertion (A).

221. Indifference curves relating to supply of labour have a number of properties some of which are mentioned below:

(a) Indifference curves are downward slopping.
(b) Indifference curves are upward slopping.
(c) Higher indifference curves indicate lower levels of utility
(d) Higher indifference curves indicate higher levels of utility
(e) Indifference curves do not intersect
(f) Indifference curves intersect
(g) Indifference curves are concave to the origin
(h) Indifference curves are convex to the origin

Which among the following properties are not true?

(1) (a), (b), (c), (d) (2) (b), (f), (g), (h)
(3) (a), (c), (e), (g) (4) (b), (c), (f), (g)

222. Under the Employees' Compensation Act, 1923 the list of occupational diseases is provided under which schedule?

(1) Schedule – I (2) Schedule – II
(3) Schedule – III (4) Schedule – IV

223. Assertion (A): In a planned economy a certain degree of wage regulation by the state becomes inevitable as an integral part of planning itself.

Reason (R): It is socially desirable for wage earners to live on a healthy and decent plane and to participate freely in industrial government and that the state should interfere in the economic relationship of its citizens whenever these attainable ideals are not realised.

Code:

(1) Assertion (A) is correct and Reason (R) explains Assertion (A).
(2) Assertion (A) is wrong and Reason (R) is correct.
(3) Assertion (A) is correct and Reason (R) is wrong.
(4) Both Assertion (A) and Reason (R) are correct but Reason (R) fails to explain Assertion (A).

224. Which of the following statements relating to N.M. Lokhande is/are true?

(a) He was instrumental for the establishment of Bombay Mill Hands Association in 1896.

(b) He was a philanthropic promoter of labour legislation and workers' welfare.
(c) He is considered as the Father of Trade Union Movement in India.

Code:

(1) Only (a) (2) (a) and (b)
(3) (b) and (c) (4) (a), (b) and (c)

225. Which one of the following statements is not true as per the provisions of the Employees' State Insurance Act, 1948?

(1) Benefits under the Act are not extended to the apprentices.
(2) Inspectors are re-designated as social security officers.
(3) Medical benefits to the insured person and his spouse have been extended under circumstances where insured person retires under Voluntary Retirement Scheme.
(4) The age limit of the dependants has been enhanced from the age of 18 to 25.

226. A human resource specialist normally collects which of the following information via the Job analysis?

(a) Work Activities
(b) Human Behaviours
(c) Machines, Tools, Equipments, and work aids
(d) Performance Standards
(e) Job Context
(f) Human Requirements

Code:

(1) (a), (b), (d) and (e) only
(2) (a), (b), (c) and (f) only
(3) (a), (b), (c), (d), (e) and (f)
(4) (a) and (e) only

227. Match the following:

Japanese word under the 5S concept	English equivalent
(a) Shitseke	(i) Clearing
(b) Seiton	(ii) Cleanliness
(c) Seiketsu	(iii) Sweeping/washing
(d) Seiri	(iv) Orderliness
(e) Seiso	(v) Discipline

Code:

	(a)	(b)	(c)	(d)	(e)
(1)	(v)	(iv)	(ii)	(i)	(iii)
(2)	(iv)	(iii)	(v)	(ii)	(i)
(3)	(i)	(ii)	(iii)	(iv)	(v)
(4)	(ii)	(i)	(iv)	(v)	(iii)

228. Match the content given in List-I with the Theories of Labour Welfare given in List-II:

List-I

(a) Without compulsion, employers do not provide even the minimum facilities for workers.
(b) Any good work is considered as an investment by which both the benefactor and beneficiary are rewarded.
(c) Man is believed to have an instinctive urge by which he strives to remove the suffering of others and promote their well being.
(d) Employers should provide funds on an on-going basis for the well being of their employees.

List-II

(i) The Trusteeship Theory
(ii) The Philanthropic Theory
(ii) The Religious Theory
(iv) The Police Theory

Code:

	(a)	(b)	(c)	(d)		(a)	(b)	(c)	(d)
(1)	(iv)	(iii)	(ii)	(i)	(2)	(iv)	(ii)	(iii)	(i)
(3)	(i)	(iv)	(iii)	(ii)	(4)	(i)	(iii)	(iv)	(ii)

229. Which of the following correctly explains a 'recruiting yield pyramid'?

(1) Company records showing present performance and promotability of inside candidates for the most important positions.
(2) A forecasting technique for determining future staff needs by using ratios between, for example, sales volume and number of employees needed.
(3) The historical arithmetic relationships between recruitment leads and invitees,

invitees and interviews, interviews and offers made, and offers made and offers accepted.

(4) Finding and/or attracting applicants for the employer's open positions.

230. Which of the following pairs is/are not correctly matched?

Organisation	**Year of Formation**
(a) Trades Union Congress (England)	(i) 1868
(b) Indian National Trade Union Congress	(ii) 1947
(c) International Confederation of Free Trade Unions	(iii) 1948

Code:

(1) (a) and (b) (2) (b) and (c)
(3) (b) only (4) (c) only

231. A Conciliation officer declares an industrial dispute to have ended in failure on 15th October 2017 and submits the failure report to the appropriate Government on 18th October. The said report is being received by the Government on 29th October and the Government refers the dispute to the Labour Court on 5th November 2017. From the above information on which date it is deemed that the conciliation has been concluded?

(1) 15th October (2) 18th October
(3) 29th October (4) 5th November

232. Convention No. 138 of the ILO relates to:

(1) Abolition of Forced Labour
(2) Right to Collective Bargaining
(3) Worst Forms of Child Labour
(4) Minimum Age for Admission to Employment

233. Identify the correct sequence of procedure in creating 'Structured Situational Interview'.

(a) Analyze the job
(b) Appoint the interview panel and conduct interviews
(c) Create interview questions
(d) Create benchmark answers
(e) Rate the job's main duties

Code:

(1) (a), (b), (c), (d), (e)
(2) (a), (c), (b), (e), (d)
(3) (a), (e), (c), (d), (b)
(4) (a), (e), (d), (b), (c)

234. Match the Techniques of Training (List-A) with the possible discriptions there of (List-B) given below:

List-A	**List-B**
(a) Ice Breakers	(i) One Role played alternatively by two participants
(b) Tag Teams	(ii) Listing of alternative solutions to problems
(c) Morphological Analysis	(iii) Games to get team members know each other
(d) Gordon Technique	(iv) Steering a discussion to Crystallise solutions

Code:

	(a)	(b)	(c)	(d)		(a)	(b)	(c)	(d)
(1)	(i)	(iv)	(ii)	(iii)	(2)	(ii)	(iii)	(iv)	(i)
(3)	(i)	(iii)	(iv)	(ii)	(4)	(iii)	(i)	(ii)	(iv)

235. What is the total period of maternity leave admissible for a woman employee having two or more than two surviving children under the provisions of the Maternity Benefit (Amendment) Act, 2017?

(1) Fourteen weeks
(2) Sixteen weeks
(3) Twelve weeks
(4) Twenty six weeks

236. Which of the following is a statutory body?

(1) Indian Labour Conference
(2) Standing Labour Committee
(3) Industrial Committee meant for Plantations
(4) Safety Committee

237. Match the authorities provided under List-A with the respective legislation under which they are covered as provided under List-B:

List-A	List-B
(a) The Controlling Authority	(i) The Mines Act, 1952
(b) Commissioner	(ii) The Payment of Gratuity Act, 1972
(c) Certifying Surgeon	(iii) The Contract Labour (Regulation and Abolition) Act, 1970
(d) Licensing Officer	(iv) The Employees' Compensation Act, 1923

Code:

	(a)	(b)	(c)	(d)
(1)	(ii)	(iv)	(i)	(iii)
(2)	(i)	(ii)	(iii)	(iv)
(3)	(iii)	(i)	(iv)	(ii)
(4)	(iv)	(iii)	(ii)	(i)

238. Identify the correct sequence of steps in developing a BARS (Behaviourally Anchored Rating Scales) as suggested by Gary Dessler:

(a) Scale the incidents
(b) Reallocate incidents
(c) Develop performance dimensions
(d) Write critical incidents
(e) Develop a final instrument

Code:

(1) (c), (b), (d), (a), (e)
(2) (b), (a), (d), (c), (e)
(3) (d), (c), (b), (a), (e)
(4) (a), (b), (c), (d), (e)

239. As per the provisions of the Building and other construction workers (Regulation of Employment and Conditions of Services) Act, 1996. Who among the following is the Ex-officio member in the Central Advisory Committee?

(1) The Chief Inspector
(2) The Chief Labour Commissioner
(3) The Chairperson of the Expert Committee
(4) The Director General

240. 'Welfare implies welfare of man, his family and his community'. Which of the following concepts explains this?

(1) The total concept of welfare
(2) The positive concept of welfare
(3) The social concept of welfare
(4) The relative concept of welfare

241. For which industry the first non-statutory Wage Board was set up in India?

(1) Cotton textile (2) Cement
(3) Iron and Steel (4) Coal mining

242. Assertion (A): It has been suggested that while roles answer the question 'how to be interfaced with other people to reach our goals'? Functions answer the question 'what do you do to accomplish our goals?'

Reason (R): Roles are more relational while functions go beyond interpersonal relations. Functions such as planning, decision-making etc. may not necessarily involve working with others, and several managerial functions can be performed without communication with people.

Code:

(1) Assertion (A) and Reason (R) both are right, Reason (R) explains Assertion (A).
(2) Assertion (A) is true, Reason (R) is not true.
(3) Assertion (A) and Reason (R) both are not true.
(4) Assertion (A) is wrong, hence Reason (R) is not an explanation of Assertion (A).

243. Which of the following statements relating to the second National Commission on Labour is/are not true?

(a) The commission envisaged a system of Labour courts, Lok Adalats and Labour Relations Commissions as the integrated adjudicatory system in labour matters.
(b) The Commission recommended that the Essential Services Maintenance Act should be withdrawn.
(c) The commission was in favour of setting up wage boards for fixing wage rates for workers in any industry.

Code:

(1) Only (a) (2) (a) and (b)
(3) Only (c) (4) (a), (b) and (c)

244. As per the amendment to the Payment of Wages Act, 1936, made in 2017, the Act shall apply to wages payable to an employed person drawing a monthly wage not exceeding:

(1) Rs 28,000 (2) Rs 26,000
(3) Rs 24,000 (4) Rs 30,000

245. Which of the following stages of group development will witness the following trend of group member's behaviour:

'Confront the differences, feel angry or frustrated, result formal leadership, lot of competition, and hostilities'?

(1) Forming (2) Storming
(3) Norming (4) Adjourning

246. For a person employed in a seasonal establishment, what is the rate of gratuity payable under the payment of Gratuity Act, 1972?

(1) Fifteen day's wages for each Season
(2) Seven day's wages for each Season
(3) Ten day's wages for each Year
(4) Ten day's wages for each Season

247. The strikes that are intended to put pressure on the government to do something or desist from doing something are categorised as:

(1) Jurisdictional strikes
(2) Political strikes
(3) General strikes
(4) Quickie strikes

248. Under the provisions of the Payment of Wages Act, 1936, who among the following cannot be appointed as the authority by the appropriate Government to hear and decide claims arising out of deductions from wages or delay in payment of wages and penalty for malicious or Vexacious claims?

(1) Any Commissioner for workmen's Compensation
(2) Regional Labour Commissioner appointed by the Central Government
(3) Any Assistant Labour Commissioner appointed by the State Government
(4) Any other officer with experience as a Judge of a Civil Court or a Judicial Magistrate

249. An organisation structure defines how job, tasks are formally divided, grouped, and coordinated. Managers need to address six key elements when they design their organisation's structure.

Match **List-A** with **List-B** given below:

List-A: Refers to the six key elements encountered by managers in designing their organisation structure.

List-B: Provides possible answer to address the key elements encountered in organisation designing.

List-A

(a) To what degree are activities subdivided into separate jobs?
(b) On what basis will jobs be grouped together?
(c) To whom do individuals and groups report?
(d) How many individuals can a manager efficiently and effectively direct?
(e) Where does decision-making authority lie?
(f) To what degree will there be rules and regulations to direct employees and managers?

List-B

(i) Span of Control
(ii) Centralisation and Decentralisation
(iii) Departmentalization
(iv) Work specialization
(v) Chain of Command
(vi) Formalisation

Code:

	(a)	(b)	(c)	(d)	(e)	(f)
(1)	(ii)	(iv)	(v)	(ii)	(i)	(vi)
(2)	(iv)	(iii)	(v)	(i)	(ii)	(vi)
(3)	(i)	(ii)	(iii)	(iv)	(vi)	(v)
(4)	(ii)	(iii)	(iv)	(vi)	(v)	(i)

250. The need for labour welfare was also emphasized by the constitution of India. There are Articles in Indian Constitution which contain provisions for labour welfare. Which among the following Articles does not contain provision for Labour Welfare?

(1) Article 38 (2) Article 39
(3) Article 40 (4) Article 41

251. Which of the following statements regarding the 'Socialist Manifesto' are true?

(a) It was drafted by Sidney and Beatrice Webb.
(b) It was drafted by Karl Marx and Engels.
(c) It was drafted for converting capitalist Britain into a mixed economy.
(d) It was strongly opposed by the Labour Party in Britain.

Code:
(1) (a) and (b) (2) (b) and (c)
(3) (a) and (c) (4) (c) and (d)

252. In which of the following countries there exists a predominantly adversarial approach to industrial relations?

(1) USA (2) Germany
(3) Sweden (4) Denmark

253. Which of the following statements regarding stress related factors is/are true / false?

(a) Burnout Stress Syndrome (BOSS) is a debilitating psychological condition brought about by unrelieved work tress.
(b) 'Good' and 'bad' stresses are also referred to as 'Distress' and 'Eustress' respectively.
(c) It is natural and healthy to maintain optimal level of stress.
(d) Rustout Stress Syndrome (ROSS) is indicative of stress overload.
(e) Anxiety is a state of emotional tension characterised by Apprehension, fearfulness, and psychic pain.

Code:
(1) (a), (b) and (d) are true. (c) and (e) are false.
(2) (b), (c) and (d) are true. (a) and (e) are false.
(3) (a), (c) and (e) are true. (b) and (d) are false.
(4) (b), (d) and (e) are true. (a) and (c) are false.

254. Which of the following statements relating to the Central Advisory Board under the provisions of the Contract Labour (Regulation and Abolition) Act, 1970 is not correct?

(1) Chairman to be appointed by the Central Government.
(2) The Chief Labour Commissioner (Central) as an ex-officio member.
(3) The Labour Commissioners of all the states as ex-officio member.
(4) Such number of members, not exceeding seventeen but not less than eleven as the Central Government may nominate representing Government, Railways, Coal industry, mining industry, the contractors, the workmen.

255. Which of the following is/are not Team Building Approaches?

(a) Positive Reinforcement
(b) Johari Window
(c) Behaviour modification
(d) Domain Reshuffling

Code:
(1) (a) and (c) (2) (b) and (c)
(3) (c) and (d) (4) (a) and (d)

256. What would be the maximum representation of the independent members in the Central Advisory Board constituted under the Minimum Wages Act, 1948 ?

(A) One-third (B) One-half
(C) Two-third (D) One-fourth

257. Distributive bargaining, as described by Walton and McKersie, is also called:

(1) Win-Win bargaining
(2) Zero sum bargaining
(3) Composite bargaining
(4) Concession bargaining

258. Which of the following statements are true/ false?

(a) Organisation Behaviour (OB) has been influenced by the ; Contingency Approach, and The Interactional Approach.

(b) Hawthorne studies led to Human Relations Movement.

(c) Human Relations Movement's main emphasis was an economic needs i.e. people were more motivated by economic needs rather than Social needs.

(d) Mcgregor and Maslow were not the main proponents and figure heads of the Human Relations movement.

Code:

(1) (a), (b), (c) are true, (d) is false.

(2) (c) and (d) are true, (a) and (b) are false.

(3) (b) and (d) are true, (a) and (c) are false.

(4) (a) and (b) are true, (c) and (d) are false.

259. Labour welfare movement has witnessed some distinctive developments. They are:

(a) Voluntary organisations engaged in labour welfare expanded in number and influences.

(b) State through legislations tried to regulate and improve the lot of labour.

(c) Some enlightened employers took the initiative to improve the working and living conditions of labour.

(d) Trade Unions fought to bring about an improvement in the working conditions of labour and to raise their status socially and economically.

Arrange the developments in correct order from latest to earliest.

Code:

(1) (a), (b), (d), (c) (2) (a), (d), (c), (b)

(3) (b), (c), (d), (a) (4) (b), (d), (a), (c)

260. Assertion (A): It has been observed that the approach to Labour Legislations in India underwent a change after the country became independent.

Reason (R): The basic philosophy has undergone change being influenced by the concepts of social justice and welfare state.

Code:

(1) Assertion (A) is correct and Reason (R) is wrong.

(2) Assertion (A) is correct and Reason (R) fully explains Assertion (A).

(3) Assertion (A) is wrong and Reason (R) is correct.

(4) Assertion (A) is correct and Reason (R) does not explain Assertion (A).

261. The National Labour Relations Board (NLRB) having the responsibility to investigate Unfair Labour Practices and Complaints, was established under:

(1) Industrial Disputes Act, 1947

(2) The Wagner Act, 1935

(3) Trade Unions Act, 1926

(4) The Norris-La Guardia Act, 1932

262. Which one of the following statements relating to protected workman under the Industrial Disputes Act, 1947 is not correct?

(1) A protected workman cannot be discharged or dismissed from the services during the pendency of any such proceeding in respect of an industrial dispute without the express permission in writing from the authority before which the proceeding is pending.

(2) A member of the executive or other office bearer of registered trade union can only be recognised as protected workmen.

(3) The number of protected workman to be recognised shall be within a range of a minimum five to a maximum one hundred.

(4) Two percent of the total workmen can be recognised protected workman.

263. Which of the following statements is/are true/false regarding modes of Conflict Management Styles?

(a) The avoidance modes of Conflict Management aim at avoiding or postponing conflicts.

(b) The compromise mode involves coercion and is likely to fail to reach a solution.

(c) The main objective of the defusion mode of conflict resolution is to buy time for dealing with a conflict.

(d) Withdrawal is a form of approach mode that involves getting away from a conflict situation.

Code:

(1) (a) and (b) are true, (c) and (d) are false.
(2) (a) and (d) are true, (b) and (c) are false.
(3) (a) and (c) are true, (b) and (d) are false.
(4) (b) and (d) are true, (a) and (c) are false.

264. Which among the following statements relating to the features of collective bargaining is/ are correct?

(a) It is a two-way process.
(b) It involves Civilised Confrontation.
(c) It is a Static Process.
(d) It is a Complementary Process.

Code:

(1) (a) and (d) only
(2) (a), (b) and (c) only
(3) (a), (b), and (d) only
(4) (b), (c) and (d) only

265. Hans Selye's (1956) "General Adaptation Syndrome (GAS)" has been widely held as a comprehensive model to explain the stress phenomenon. This three stage model states that when an organism is confronted with a threat, the general physiological response occurs in three stages.

Which of the following stages is not a part of GAS model?

(1) Intrapsychic Disorder stage
(2) Alarm Stage
(3) Exhaustion Stage
(4) Resistance Stage

266. As per the provisions of the Industrial Disputes Act, 1947, under which of the conditions a strike declared by the workmen of public utility service shall be illegal?

(1) Resorting to strike after a lapse of fourteen days of giving a notice of strike.
(2) Resorting to strike within seven days from the conclusion of conciliation proceedings pending before a conciliation officer.
(3) Resorting to strike after seven days of conclusion of such proceedings pending before a Board of Conciliation.
(4) Resorting to strike within two months from conclusion of such proceedings pending before a Labour Court.

267. In which of the following states there exists a legislation having a provision for recognition of Trade Unions?

(1) Odisha (2) Karnataka
(3) Maharashtra (4) Bihar

268. Which of the following statements is/are not true about the "Grid Organisation Development" (Grid OD) Program designed by Robert R. Blake and Jane S. Mouton?

(a) It is a eight phase program lasting about three to five years.
(b) Through this program an organisation can move systematically from the stage of examining managerial behaviour and style to the development and implementation of an "ideal strategic corporate model".
(c) Behavioural science concepts and rigerous business logic are combined in the Grid OD Program's six phases.
(d) The single most significant premise on which Grid OD rests in that the 5, 5 way of doing business which is acknowledged universally by managers as the soundest way to manage to achieve excellence.

Code:

(1) (a) and (b) only (2) (b) and (d) only
(3) (a) and (d) only (4) (b) and (c) only

269. Assertion (A): Labour Welfare Movement acquired new dimensions after independence.

Reason (R): It was realised that Labour Welfare had a positive role to play in increasing productivity and reducing industrial tensions.

Code:

(1) Assertion (A) is correct and Reason (R) is wrong.
(2) Assertion (A) is correct and Reason (R) is fully explains Assertion (A).
(3) Assertion (A) is wrong and Reason (R) is correct.

(4) Both Assertion (A) and Reason (R) are wrong.

270. Who among the following is not a Contractor in relation to an establishment under the provisions of the Contract Labour (Regulation and Abolition) Act, 1970?

(1) Any person who undertakes to produce a given result for the establishment through Contract Labour.

(2) Any person who supplies contract labour for any work of the establishment.

(3) Any person who supplies goods and articles of manufacture to such establishment.

(4) Any person who works as a sub-contractor.

271. Questions relating to the application or implementation of certified standing orders can be referred to which of the following authorities under the Industrial Employment (Standing Orders) Act, 1946 ?

(A) Industrial Tribunals constituted under the Industrial Disputes Act, 1947.

(B) Labour courts constituted under the Industrial Disputes Act, 1947.

(C) Chief Labour Commissioner (Central)

(D) Labour Commissioners of the States

272. Assertion (A): Some of the earliest piece of Labour Legislation in India appear to have been enacted to protect the interest of the employers.

Reason (R): The policy of the Government was to protect the social system rather than to protect workers.

Code:

(1) Assertion (A) is correct and Reason (R) is wrong.

(2) Assertion (A) is correct and Reason (R) explains Assertion (A).

(3) Assertion (A) is wrong and Reason (R) is right.

(4) Assertion (A) is correct and Reason (R) does not explain Assertion (A).

273. Industrial disputes relating to which of the following are within the jurisdiction of the Industrial Tribunal ?

a. Hours of work and rest interval.

b. Withdrawal of any customary concession or privilege.

c. Rules of discipline

d. Leave with wages and holidays

Codes :

(A) a and d (B) b, c and d

(C) a, b and c (D) a, c and d

274. As per the provisions of the Payment of Wages Act, 1936, if deductions are made for payments to co-operative societies, the maximum deductions for any wage period for any employed person shall not exceed:

(1) Fifty percent

(2) Sixty percent

(3) Seventy five percent

(4) Eighty percent

275. Which of the following authorities is not an adjudicatory body under the Industrial Disputes Act, 1947?

(1) Labour Court

(2) Industrial Tribunal

(3) National Tribunal

(4) Arbitration

276. Which of the following countries does/do not figure in the list of Nations of Chief Industrial Importance that hold permanent membership in the Governing Body of ILO?

(a) Sri Lanka (b) Russian Federation

(c) Mexico (d) Brazil

(1) (a) only (2) (b) only

(3) (a) and (c) (4) (c) and (d)

277. In which year the first indication of industrial unrest and earliest work stoppage came to the fore in India at the initiative of weavers of Empress Mills, Nagpur?

(1) 1877 (2) 1878

(3) 1879 (4) 1881

278. Which of the following characteristics of Transactional and Transformational Leaders are not correctly matched?

Leader		Characteristic
(a) Transaction leader	–	Idealised Influence
(b) Transformational leader	–	Management by Exception
(c) Transformational leader	–	Laissez-Faire
(d) Transactional leader	–	Contingent Reward
(e) Transformational leader	–	Intellectual Stimulation

Code:

(1) (a), (b), and (d) only
(2) (c), (d) and (e) only
(3) (a), (b), and (c) only
(4) (a), (d), and (e) only

279. The general pattern of behaviour, shared beliefs and values that organisation members have in common is called:

(1) Organisational Climate
(2) Organisational Culture
(3) Organisational Effectiveness
(4) Organisational Structure

280. What is the maximum aggregate fine that can be imposed on a Trade Union for continuous default in submitting the returns under the provisions of the Trade Unions Act, 1926?

(1) Rs 50 (2) Rs 250
(3) Rs 500 (4) Rs 1000

281. Which of the following is a group incentive plan?

(1) Barth Variable Incentive Plan
(2) Hayne's Incentive Plan
(3) Rowan Incentive Plan
(4) Scanlon Incentive Plan

282. As per the Industrial Disputes Act, 1947, industrial disputes relating the subject matters covered under Second Schedule and Third Schedule are to be adjudicated upon by the Labour Court and Industrial Tribunal. But under which of the following conditions subject matter covered under the Third Schedule can be referred to the Labour Court for adjudication?

(1) If it is not likely to affect more than one hundred workmen.
(2) If the dispute has been raised by a trade union not registered under the Trade Unions Act, 1926.
(3) If it is likely to affect more than one hundred workmen.
(4) If the dispute has been raised by the recognised trade union.

283. Which one of the following methods is not a Behavioural method of performance appraisal?

(1) Balanced score card method
(2) Critical incident method
(3) Assessment centre method
(4) Behavioural check list method

284. Match List – I with List – II and select answer codes given below:

List - I	List - II
(a) Frank B. Gilbreth	(i) Theory of bureaucracy
(b) Max Weber	(ii) Time and Motion studies
(c) F.W. Taylor	(iii) Application of Psychology to Industry and Management
(d) Hugomunsterberg	(iv) Scientific Management

Code:

	(a)	(b)	(c)	(d)		(a)	(b)	(c)	(d)
(1)	(i)	(ii)	(iv)	(ii)	(2)	(ii)	(i)	(iv)	(iii)
(3)	(ii)	(i)	(iii)	(iv)	(4)	(i)	(iii)	(ii)	(iv)

285. A factory has engaged two hundred fifty workers/workmen. If the employer wants to retrench any workman who has completed one year of continuous service in the establishment, then which of the conditions are to be followed by the employer under the Industrial Disputes Act, 1947?

(a) It has to serve three months notice in writing in advance or pay in lieu of such notice, wage for the notice period.
(b) It has to serve one month notice in writing in advance or pay in lieu of such notice, wage for the notice period.

(c) Notice in the prescribed manner is served on the appropriate Government.
(d) Prior Permission of the appropriate Government has been obtained on an application made in this behalf.
(e) Pay retrenchment compensation at the rate of fifteen days average pay for every completed year of continuous service or any part there of in excess of six months.

Code:
(1) (a), (c) and (e) only
(2) (a), (d) and (e) only
(3) (a) and (e) only
(4) (a), (c), (d) and (e) only

286. Which of the following central organisations of labour was not a signatory to the Inter-Union Code of Conduct, 1958?
(1) INTUC (2) BMS
(3) HMS (4) AITUC

287. Which one of the following is not a health provision under the Factories Act, 1948?
(1) Cleanliness
(2) Drinking water
(3) Latrines and Urinals
(4) First-aid appliances

288. Among the following who is known for scientific selection of workers and "Harmonious Co-operation between labour and management":
(1) Gilbreth (2) Elton Mayo
(3) Max Weber (4) Henry L. Gantt

289. An employee engaged in an industrial establishment draws wages of Rs 20,500/- per month. What is the amount of bonus to be paid to him if it is paid at the rate of 10% by the employer for an accounting year under the Payment of Bonus Act, 1965?
(1) Rupees Nine thousand two hundred only.
(2) Rupees Eight thousand four hundred only.
(3) Rupees Ten thousand two hundred fifty only.
(4) Rupees Nine thousand six hundred only.

290. What is the amount of compensation to be paid to an employee suffering from permanent total disablement under the provisions of the Employee's Compensation Act, 1923? (Hintsmonthly wage under drawn was Rs 15,000 and relevant factor 159.80)
(1) Rs 10,38,200 (2) Rs 11,98,500
(3) Rs 6,39,200 (4) Rs 7,67,040

291. Which one of the following falls under 'Dry promotion' category?
(1) responsibilities remain the same but pay increases.
(2) responsibilities increase but there is no increase in the pay.
(3) responsibilities reduce but pay remains the same.
(4) responsibilities reduce but pay increases.

292. The displacement allowance to be paid by the contractor to every inter-state migrant workman at the time of recruitment as per the Inter-State Migrant Workmen (Regulation of Employment and Conditions of Service) Act, 1979 shall be equal to:
(1) Fifty percent of the monthly wages payable to him or seventy five rupees whichever is higher.
(2) Seventy five percent of the monthly wages payable to him or one hundred rupees whichever is higher.
(3) Sixty percent of the monthly wages payable to him or Seventy five rupees whichever is higher.
(4) Fifty percent of the monthly wages payable to him or one hundred rupees whichever is higher.

293. According to which of the following methods of human resource accounting present value of future earning of human resources is taken into account?
(1) Standard cost method
(2) Economic value method
(3) Opportunity cost method
(4) Replacement cost method

294. The record keeping functions for the purpose of the Unorganised Worker's Social Security Act, 2008 shall be performed by:
(1) The Labour Directorate of the State
(2) The District Administration
(3) The State Social Security Board
(4) The Department of Labour of the State

295. The control based on norms, shared values, expected behaviour, and other cultural variables in an organisation is known as:
(1) Bureaucratic Control
(2) System Control
(3) Tailoring Control
(4) Clan Control

296. Multinational Corporations are categorised into four categories namely multidomestic, global, international, and transnational on the basis of their response to two factors namely; global integration and national responsiveness. Keeping this in view match the type of Multinationals given in List-A with their respective characteristics given in List-B.

List-A	List-B
(a) Multidomestic	(i) High national responsiveness, and high global integration
(b) Global	(ii) High national responsiveness and low global integration
(c) International	(iii) High global integration and low national responsiveness
(d) Transnational	(iv) Low to moderate global integration and low to moderate national responsiveness

Code:

	(a)	(b)	(c)	(d)		(a)	(b)	(c)	(d)
(1)	(ii)	(iii)	(iv)	(i)	(2)	(i)	(ii)	(iii)	(iv)
(3)	(iii)	(iv)	(ii)	(i)	(4)	(iv)	(i)	(ii)	(ii)

297. In UK, when the parties to a dispute fail to settle their dispute through collective bargaining and having exhausted all internal procedures available to them in their establishments for settlement of disputes, can seek settlement through __________.
(1) Advisory Conciliation and Arbitration Services.
(2) Central Arbitration Committee
(3) House of Lords
(4) Employment Appeal Tribunals

298. "The state shall take steps, by suitable legislation or in any other way, to secure the participation of workers in the management of undertakings, establishments or other organisations engaged in any industry".
The above statement was provided under:
(1) Article 43A of Constitution (42 Amendment) Act, 1976.
(2) Article 19(C) of the Indian Constitution
(3) Convention No. 11 of I.L.O.
(4) Article 14 of the Indian Constitution

299. Assertion (A): With the evaluation of industrial and employment relations in the face of rapid changes and significant advances in technology among other things, collective bargaining became an instrument of social change.
Reason (R): Shifts in the labour and product markets created pressures as well as opportunities for a new approach.
Code:
(1) Assertion (A) is wrong and Reason (R) is correct.
(2) Assertion (A) is correct and Reason (R) is a proper explanation of Assertion (A).
(3) Assertion (A) is correct but Reason (R) is wrong.
(4) Reason (R) is not an explanation of Assertion (A).

300. Which of the following statements relating to the system of collective bargaining in United Kingdom is true?
(a) It is covered under the Trade Unions and Labour Relations Act, 1974.

(b) It is covered under the Trade Unions and Labour Relations (Consolidation) Act, 1992.

(c) It is covered under the Employment Relations Act, 1999.

(d) It is not covered under any legislation.

Code:

(1) (a) and (b) only (2) (b) and (c) only
(3) (c) only (4) (d) only

301. Who among the following are known for study of work arrangements to eliminate wasteful hand and body motions ?

(1) Henry Gantt and C.I. Barnard
(2) Frank and Lillian Gilbreth
(3) Elton Mayo and H. Emerson
(4) F.W.Taylor and Henry Gantt

302. Which of the following represents the rights inherent in a managerial position to give orders and expect them to be obeyed ?

(1) Power (2) Authority
(3) Influence (4) Responsibility

303. Match the following :

List-I	**List-II**
(a) Robert Owen	(i) Organisations based on group ethics rather than individualism
(b) Hugo Munsterberg	(ii) Social norms and standards of group
(c) Mary Parker Follett	(iii) Employers treat their machines better than workers
(d) Elton Mayo	(iv) Scientific study of human behaviour to identify general patterns and individual differences

Codes :

	(a)	(b)	(c)	(d)
(1)	(i)	(ii)	(iii)	(iv)
(2)	(iii)	(iv)	(i)	(ii)
(3)	(iv)	(iii)	(i)	(ii)
(4)	(iv)	(iii)	(ii)	(i)

304. Which of the following has specialists from different functional departments working on one or more projects that are led by a project manager ?

(1) Functional Organisation
(2) Cross - Functional Team
(3) Matrix Organisation
(4) Product Organisation

305. Which one of the following is related to clan control ?

(1) Relies on administrative rules and regulations
(2) Employee's behaviours are regulated by the shared values, norms, traditions, rituals and beliefs of the organisation
(3) Emphasizes organisational authority
(4) Depends on standardisation activities

306. Which one of the following Acts, deals with the issue of complaints ?

(1) Factories Act, 1948
(2) Payment of wages Act, 1948
(3) Employees' compensation Act, 1923
(4) Industrial Employment (Standing Orders) Act, 1946

307. Job Description implies :

(1) Identification of the qualities required in the job holder
(2) Performance of job in a methodical way
(3) Laying down systematically the duties and responsibilities of the job
(4) Determination of the performance standards of the job

308. The Human Resource Planning is a :

(1) Positive process
(2) Negative process
(3) Reactive process
(4) Pro- active process

309. The degree to which a particular selection device accurately predicts the level of performance is known as :

(1) Construct Validity
(2) Criterion - related validity
(3) Logical validity

(4) Concurrent validity

310. Progressive Discipline is :

(1) For the growth of skills.

(2) A system of warnings and punishments that gradually become more severe.

(3) Discipline to meet future needs.

(4) A system of severe punishments right from the beginning.

311. Read this small passage on HRD and answer questions at the end by chosing appropriate answer from the given alternatives.

HRD is a competence building exercise through which people everywhere (of the world, of the nation, and of the organization) are enabled to recognize their potential so as to utilize their capabilities and available resources and opportunities equitably for not only their own development but also development of their organisations, Nations and the world on a sustainable basis.

Which of the following statements picked up from the passage is/are true or false ?

(a) It talks about Macro and Micro level HRD.

(b) At macro level it encompasses world and national development.

(c) It highlights the contents of HRD vividly.

(d) At all levels, HRD aims at sustainable development.

Code :

(1) (a), (b) are true, (c), (d) are false

(2) (a), (b), (d) are true, (c) is false

(3) (a), (b), (c) are true, (d) is false

(4) All the statements are true

312. Match the following concepts of career planning List - I with their propagators List - II :

List - I	List - II
(a) Career Anchor	(i) Mondy et al
(b) Career Stage Model	(ii) John Holland
(c) Career Path Model	(iii) Edgar Schein
(d) Career Choice Model	(iv) D. T. Hall

Codes :

	(a)	(b)	(c)	(d)
(1)	(iii)	(ii)	(iv)	(i)
(2)	(iii)	(i)	(ii)	(iv)
(3)	(iii)	(ii)	(i)	(iv)
(4)	(iii)	(iv)	(i)	(ii)

313. Quality of work Life is a combination of employee's welfare, working conditions and workplace democracy. Who highlighted the concept of workplace democracy ?

(a) Eric Tryst (b) Udai Pareek

(c) Einar Thorsrud (d) Fred Emery.

Code :

(1) (a) and (b) (2) (a), (c) and (d)

(3) (a) and (d) (4) (a), (b), (c) and (d)

314. 'Bell curve' is represented by which of the traditional methods of performance Appraisal ?

(1) Forced Choice Method

(2) Free from Essay Method

(3) Critical Incidence Method

(4) Forced Distribution Method

315. Match the following approaches of HRD List - I with the person or institution who or which advanced the approach List - II :

List - I	List - II
(a) Human Capital Approach	(i) Human Development Report
(b) Socio/Psychological Approach	(ii) T.U. Schultz
(c) Poverty Alleviation Approach	(iii) David Mc Clelland
(d) World Human Development Approach	(iv) Mahbub Ul Haq.

Codes :

	(a)	(b)	(c)	(d)
(1)	(ii)	(iii)	(iv)	(i)
(2)	(ii)	(i)	(iv)	(iii)
(3)	(ii)	(iii)	(i)	(iv)
(4)	(ii)	(iv)	(i)	(iii)

316. Which of the following statements about the Organisational Behaviour (OB) system is/are true and false ?

(a) OB believes in open system.
(b) It has three sub-systems namely formal Organisation System, Individual System and Social System.
(c) There are no intervening mechanisms to lead Organisational Behaviour towards organisational effectiveness.
(d) OB Mod and reinforcement are outside the purview of OB system.

Code:
(1) (a), (b), (c) are true, (d) is false.
(2) (a), (c), (d) are true, (b) is false.
(3) (a), (c) are true, (b) and (d) are false.
(4) (a) and (b) are true, (c) and (d) are false.

317. What is 'Neotony' as a leadership trait advanced by Bennis and Thomas ?
(1) Calm, confident and predictable under stressful condition
(2) Youthful, curious, playful, fearless, warm and energetic
(3) Encouraging dissent, empathy and obsessive communication
(4) Ambitious, morally strong and competence

318. In which year, in which factory and by whom the first quality circle in India was introduced ?
(1) 1982 ; Bharat Electronics Ltd, S.R. Udpa
(2) 1981 ; Hindusthan Aeronautics Ltd, S.R. Udpa
(3) 1982 ; Hindusthan Machine Tools, R.S. Tarneja
(4) 1982 ; Bharat Heavy Electricals Ltd, S.R. Udpa

319. Which of the following statements relating to 'role' is/are true and false ?
(a) The system of various roles that the individual carries and performs is 'role set'.
(b) The system of various roles of which an individuals role is a part is 'role space'.
(c) Self role integration, proactivity, creativity and confrontation are ingredients of the Role making ' dimension of Role efficacy.
(d) Role stress is caused by both Role space conflict and Role set conflict.

Code:
(1) (a), (c) are true, (b), (d) are false
(2) (a), (b) are true, (c), (d) are false
(3) (a), (b) are false, (c), (d) are true
(4) (a), (d) are true, (b), (c) are false

320. The characteristics of 'Morale' are depicted as (i) The absence of conflict (ii) feeling of happiness (iii) good inter - personal adjustment (iv) involvement in one's job (v) group cohesiveness (vi) Positive job related attitudes (vii) individual's acceptance of the group goals. Who is associated with this explanation ?
(1) Blum and Naylor
(2) Hugo Munsterberg
(3) R.M. Guien (4) J.L. Moreno

321. Who regarded trade unions as "institutions for overcoming managerial dictatorship, to strengthen individual labourers and to give them some voice in the determination of the conditions under which they have to work" ?
(1) Karl Marx (2) Mahatma Gandhi
(3) Sidney and Beatrice Webb
(4) Selig Perlman

322. 'Feather Bedding' refers to :
(1) The prevalence of the work rules which permit employees to be paid for work they do not perform.
(2) The practice of hiring local people as a 'sons-of-the soil' policy.
(3) The practice of providing mattresses as a welfare measure to the employees in the winter season for taking rest at the workplace during the rest intervals.
(4) The practice of hiring people belonging to rural areas only.

323. Which of the following statements relating to the Board for Industrial and Financial Reconstruction is correct ?
(1) It was established in 1986.
(2) It was a non - Statutory body.
(3) It was located in Mumbai.
(4) It was dissolved from December 1, 2016.

324. Who declared that a strike is an "inherent right of the working men for the purpose of securing justice" ?

(1) Mahatma Gandhi
(2) Karl Marx
(3) Sidney and Beatrice Webb
(4) John T. Dunlop

325. In which year, the Calcutta High Court held that a 'gherao' that involved wrongful restraint of a person belonging to the management was a cognizable offence ?

(1) 1964 (2) 1965
(3) 1966 (4) 1967

326. In which year the International Federation of Chemical, Energy, Mining and General Workers formed ?

(1) 1985 (2) 1995
(3) 2005 (4) 2016

327. Who took the initiative of setting up the Joint Consultative Board of Industry and Labour in 1951 ?

(1) V.V. Giri (2) G.L. Nanda
(3) Khandubhai Desai
(4) Babu Jagjiwan Ram

328. In which year, India ratified the ILO Convention concerning the Right of Association for Agricultural Workers ?

(1) 1923 (2) 1924
(3) 1925 (4) 2017

329. The headquarter of Trade Union International of Workers in Building, Wood and Building Materials Industries is located at :

(1) New Delhi (2) Paris
(3) Kolkata (4) Helsinki

330. Which of the following statements relating to ILO Convention No. 182 is wrong ?

(1) The Convention relates to Worst Forms of Child Labour.
(2) It is one of the eight Fundamental Conventions of the ILO.
(3) It was adopted in 1999 by the ILO.
(4) This Convention has not been ratified by India.

331. What is the minimum number of days a woman employee must have actually worked under an employer in the twelve months immediately preceeding the date of expected delivery for becoming eligible for maternity benefit under the Maternity Benefit Act, 1961 ?

(1) Eighty days (2) Ninety days
(3) One hundred twenty days
(4) One hundred days

332. What is the maximum limit of monthly wages to be taken into account for calculation of the compensation under the Employee's Compensation Act, 1923 ?

(1) ₹ 10,000 (2) ₹ 18,000
(3) ₹ 8,000 (4) ₹ 15,000

333. Under which of the following legislation provisions for Rehabilitation and Re-employment are Provided ?

(1) Employees State Insurance Act, 1948
(2) Employees Compensation Act, 1923
(3) Inter - State Migrant Workmen (Regulation of Employment and Conditions of Services) Act, 1979
(4) Contract Labour (Regulation and Abolition) Act, 1970

334. Which one of the following is not covered under Article 39 of the Indian Constitution?

(1) Equal pay for equal work for both men and women
(2) Protection of Childhood and youth against exploitation
(3) Citizens, men and women equally have the right to adequate means of livelihood
(4) Securing just and human conditions of work

335. Living wage, fair wage and minimum wage concepts were adopted by

(1) Committee on fair wages
(2) 15th Indian Labour Conference
(3) Wage Board
(4) Standing Labour Committee

336. Which of the following labour legislations are covered under the category of Protective Labour Legislation ?

(a) Minimum wages Act, 1948

(b) Motor Transport workers Act, 1961
(c) Factories Act, 1948
(d) Trade Unions Act, 1926
(e) Employees compensation Act, 1923

Code:
(1) (a) and (e) only
(2) (a), (c) and (e) only
(3) (a), (b) and (c) only
(4) (b), (c) and (d) only

337. Which one of the following statements is true relating to the composition of the International Labour Conference?
(1) It consists of four delegates nominated by each member state.
(2) It consists of eight delegates nominated by each state.
(3) It consists of six delegates nominated by each state.
(4) It consists of three delegates nominated by each member state.

338. Which one of the statements is true relating to the representation of outsiders as office bearers of any registered Trade Union under the Trade Unions Act, 1926 functioning other than in an unorganised sector?
(1) Not more than one - third of the total number of office bearers or five which ever is more
(2) Not more than one - third of the total number of office bearers or five which ever is less
(3) Not more than one - half of the total number of office bearers or six which ever is less
(4) Not more than one - half of the total number of office bearers.

339. Which of the following are true as per the provisions of the Industrial Employment (Standing Orders) Act, 1946?
(a) Draft standing orders are to be submitted by the employer to the certifying officer within six months from the date on which the Act becomes applicable
(b) Six copies of such draft standing orders are to be submitted to the certifying officer
(c) Draft standing orders are to be prepared in consultation of the workmen employed in the industrial establishment along with the trade unions if any
(d) A statement with particulars of the workmen employed in this industrial establishment including the name of the trade unions, if any to be submitted along with the draft standing order

Code:
(1) (a), (b) and (d) (2) (a), (c) and (d)
(3) (a) and (d) (4) (b) and (c)

340. A commercial establishment has employed two hundred workmen. Then which of the following provisions shall be applicable under the provisions of the Industrial Disputes Act 1947.
(a) Setting up of Grievance Redressal Machinery
(b) Constituting Works Committee
(c) Provisions of chapter V - B
(d) Compulsory reference of disputes to arbitration

Code:
(1) (a), (b) and (c) only (2) (a) and (b) only
(3) (b), (c) and (d) only (4) (a), (b), (c) & (d)

341. Assertion (A): Labour Welfare is a relative concept as it is related to time and space.

Reason (R): Welfare is growing and dynamic. The welfare potential changes as a result of which its content keeps on varying and has to keep pace with the changing times.

Code:
(1) Assertion (A) is wrong and Reason (R) fails to explain (A).
(2) Assertion (A) is correct and Reason (R) fully explains (A).
(3) Assertion (A) is wrong and Reason (R), therefore, cannot explain (A).
(4) Both Assertion (A) and Reason (R) are wrong.

342. Assertion (A): The aims and objectives of Labour Welfare have progressively changed during the last few decades.

Reason (R) : It has gradually moved to the era of paternalism with philanthropic objectives from the primitive policing and placating philosophy of Labour welfare.

Code :

(1) Assertion (A) is correct but Reason (R) fails to explain (A).

(2) Assertion (A) is correct and Reason (R) explains (A).

(3) Assertion (A) is wrong and Reason (R) is correct.

(4) Both Assertion (A) and Reason (R) are wrong.

343. Labour Welfare Services were divided into two groups by the Committee of Experts on Welfare facilities for industrial workers convened by the I.L.O. in 1963. They are within the precincts and outside the establishment. Match the facilities given in List - I with the type provided in List - II :

List - I	List - II
(a) Shift allowance	(i) Outside establishment
(b) Administrative arrangements within a plant for welfare	(ii) Within precincts
(c) Programme for the welfare of women, youth and children	(iii) Outside establishment
(d) Vocational training for dependants of workers	(iv) Within precincts

Codes :

	(a)	(b)	(c)	(d)		(a)	(b)	(c)	(d)
(1)	(ii)	(i)	(iv)	(iii)	(2)	(iii)	(ii)	(iv)	(i)
(3)	(ii)	(iv)	(i)	(iii)	(4)	(iii)	(ii)	(i)	(iv)

344. Work stress is a chronic ailment caused by conditions that negatively affect one's performance and/or overall well being of the body and mind. Employers, these days, are concerned about managing stress.

Which of the following are not the typical symptoms of job related stress ?

(a) Insomnia

(b) Lack of Concentration

(c) Anxiety, depression

(d) Job insecurity

(e) Extreme anger and mood swings

(f) Family conflicts

(g) Strict deadlines

(h) Frustration

Code :

(1) (b) and (h) (2) (d) and (f)

(3) (d) and (g) (4) (g) and (h)

345. Theories of Labour Welfare have been propounded after careful study and observation of the state of affairs prevalent during that particular period of time.

Which theory of labour welfare was propounded after observing " The factories and other industrial workplaces provide ample opportunities for owners and manager of capital to exploit workers in an unfair manner",

(1) Placating Theory

(2) Religions Theory

(3) Policing Theory

(4) Philanthropic Theory

346. Supply - demand framework predicts that termination of any ambitious project depresses a particular segment of Labour market. This type of prediction is an example of

(1) Positive Economics

(2) Equillibrium

(3) Normative Economics

(4) State of Saturation

347. Let us presume that an individual consumes ₹ 500 of consumption of goods and 100 hours of Leisure per week. The utility index would equal 50,000 'utils'. Suppose further that the individual consumes ' 400 worth of goods and 125 hours of Leisure, the utility index would still equal 50,000 'utils'.

Suppose then that we hold utility constant at 50,000 utils, many combinations of utility and Leisure will generate this particular level of utility. The locus of such points is called an indifference curve.

Which among the following is an incorrect property of Indifference curve ?

(1) Indifference curves are downward sloping.

(2) Higher indifference curves indicate higher levels of utility.

(3) Indifference curves do not intersect.

(4) Indifference curves are concave to the origin.

348. Labour is remunerated through payment of wages. There are different methods of wage payment prevalent in different industries in different countries. But the ideal wage system should fulfil certain characteristics. Which among the following is not a characteristic :

(1) It should be conducive to the interest of Labour only.

(2) It should be devised as to avoid industrial conflict.

(3) It should be conducive to the interest of both parties - employer and employee.

(4) It should be fairly simple as well as flexible.

349. Wages of the workers are Normally, the proportionality derived from their efficiency. But the concept of efficiency of labour is itself vague such as amount of physical output, output per man - hour or output per man shift. But output is not the function of man alone. There are other factors which affect the output. Which among the following is/are not the factor(s) that would affect the output directly :

(a) Physical condition of work

(b) Nature of machinery

(c) Technical process

(d) Quality of raw material

(e) System of management

(f) Role of fellow workers

(g) Competitors in the market

Code :

(1) (a) and (e) (2) (e) and (f)

(3) (f) and (g) (4) (d) and (f)

350. Match the following theories of wages List - I with their propagators List - II :

	List - I		**List - II**
(a)	Standard of Living theory	(i)	J.S. Mill
(b)	Wage Fund theory	(ii)	J.B. Clark
(c)	Residual Claimant theory	(iii)	Karl Marx
(d)	Marginal Productivity theory	(iv)	Francis A. Walker

Codes :

	(a)	**(b)**	**(c)**	**(d)**		**(a)**	**(b)**	**(c)**	**(d)**
(1)	(iii)	(i)	(iv)	(ii)	(2)	(iii)	(iv)	(ii)	(i)
(3)	(iii)	(ii)	(iv)	(i)	(4)	(iii)	(i)	(ii)	(iv)

351. Who identified the basic elements of work known as 'therbligs' ?

(1) Henry L. Gantt (2) Frank B. Gilbreth

(3) F.W. Taylor (4) All of the above

352. Who among the following concluded that the factory was a social system and informal groups at work place play a vital role in industrial affairs ?

(1) Elton Mayo

(2) Henry Fayol

(3) Blake and Mouton

(4) Herzberg

353. Arrange the steps of decision making process in the correct sequence :

a. analysis of alternatives

b. identification of decision criteria

c. implementation of alternative

d. identification of problem

e. selection of alternative

(1) d, b, a, e, c (2) d, a, b, e, c

(3) d, a, b, c, e (4) d, a, e, b, c

354. Departmentation is

a. structuring work to accomplish organisational goals

b. visual display of organisation structure

c. grouping of jobs on some basis

d. arranging jobs in a hierarchy

(1) a and b only (2) b and c only

(3) a only (4) c only

355. The tendency of people to expend less effort when working collectively than when working individually is called
(1) Social loafing (2) Socialising
(3) Adjourning (4) Social action

356. Personnel Management is essentially a
(1) Matrix function (2) Line function
(3) Staff function
(4) Line & staff function

357. Which of the following comes under the scope of line and staff relationship ?
(1) The relationship between works manager and maintenance engineer
(2) The relationship between works manager and personnel manager
(3) The relationship between personnel manager and development engineer
(4) The relationship between the public relation officer and the public

358. The broad statement of the duties and responsibilities of a Job or position is called
(1) Job description (2) Job specification
(3) Job analysis (4) Job evaluation

359. The function of attracting, acquiring and inducting Human Resources in an organisation is called
(1) Selection (2) Recruitment
(3) Staffing
(4) Training and Placement

360. Wage Boards Fix wages for employees at
(1) Regional level (2) Plant level
(3) National level (4) Industry level

361. Which of the following is not a Simulation Technique of development ?
(1) In-basket (2) Case study
(3) Sensitivity Training
(4) Management Games

362. Match the following Expression with the Ego states mentioned against them :

Expression	**Ego States**
a. Rationality	i. Parent
b. Fantasizing	ii. Child
c. Demonstrating	iii. Adult

Codes :

	a	b	c		a	b	c
(1)	i	ii	iii	(2)	ii	i	iii
(3)	iii	ii	i	(4)	i	iii	ii

363. Selectivity in responding to information that is in conformity with one's own feeling, is because of
(1) Cognitive Dissonance
(2) Perceptual Defence
(3) Filtering
(4) Mis-perception

364. When one group's performance depends on another group's performance, it may result into inter-group conflict. Such dependence is described as :
(1) Pooled interdependence
(2) Classical interdependence
(3) Reciprocal interdependence
(4) Sequential interdependence

365. The act of an organization which 're-examines its organisational structures, systems and procedures from time to time, even when the organisation is successful and has no problems necessitating such examination' is known as :
(1) Performance Appraisal System
(2) Counteracting system
(3) Self-renewal system
(4) Development system

366. Match the following theories and the scientists who propounded them :

List – A (Theories)	**List – B (Scientists)**
I. Two Factor Theory	a. Adolf Alderfer
II. Achievement Motivation Theory	b. Murray
III. Manifest Need Theory	c. Frederic Hertzberg
IV. ERG Theory	d. David McClelland

Codes :

	I	II	II	IV		I	II	III	IV
(1)	d	c	b	a	(2)	a	b	c	d
(3)	c	d	b	a	(4)	a	d	c	b

367. Which of the following sequence of group development process is correct ?

I. Performing II. Norming
III. Forming IV. Storming
V. Adjourning

Codes :

(1) V I II IV III
(2) III IV III V
(3) III I II V IV
(4) I V III II IV

368. Assertion (A) : The content Theories of Motivation assume a direct relationship between Job Satisfaction and improved performance.

Reason (R) : Job satisfaction does not necessarily lead to work performance.

(1) (A) is true, (R) is false.
(2) (A) is false, (R) is true.
(3) Both (A) and (R) are true. (R) is not the correct explanation of (A).
(4) Both (A) and (R) are false. (R) is the correct explanation of (A).

369. When people give 'Cause and Effect explanation' to their behaviour, it is called

(1) Closure (2) Stereotyping
(3) Attribution (4) Inference

370. The term "Blind Spot" in the Johari Window refers to

(1) The 'Public self' which is known to others as well as to oneself.
(2) The 'self' which is known to others but not to oneself.
(3) The 'self' which is neither known to others nor to oneself.
(4) The motives, feelings, etc. which are known to oneself.

371. Which approach to industrial relations aims to combine social stability with adaptability and freedom ?

(1) Classical approach
(2) Neo-classical approach
(3) Pluralistic approach
(4) Social action approach

372. Which of the following statements about the Marxist approach to industrial relations is not correct ?

(1) It sees industrial conflict as synonymous with political and social conflicts.
(2) It considers pluralism as a mere illusion.
(3) It believes that capitalism cannot continue to maintain itself only by lowering the standard of living of the working class.
(4) It favours transformation of trade unions into revolutionary organisations.

373. Disputes that arise out of deadlocks in negotiations for a collective agreement are popularly known as

(1) Grievance Disputes
(2) Interest Disputes
(3) Recognition Disputes
(4) Unfair Labour Practice Disputes

374. In India, strikes in contravention of the provisions of which section(s) of the Industrial Disputes Act, are illegal ?

(1) Section 22 (2) Section 23
(3) Section 24 (4) All these sections.

375. Which of the following statements about a conciliation officer is not correct ?

(1) He/she has no authority to pass a final order directing the parties to a dispute to act in a particular manner.
(2) He/she shall be deemed to be a public servant within the meaning of Section 21 of the Indian Penal Code.
(3) The appropriate government cannot appoint a conciliation officer for specified industries in a specified area.
(4) It is mandatory for the conciliation officer to hold conciliation proceedings if a dispute relates to a public utility service and a notice has been given.

376. Who emphasised that the trade union movement had emerged as labour's reaction to the dominance of the machine in modern society ?

(1) G.D.H. Cole
(2) Selig Perlman
(3) Karl Marx
(4) Frank Tannenbaum

377. Any Union that caters to all employees working in a variety of industries under one owner located at the same place is categorised as
(1) Primary union of industrial type
(2) Primary union of general type
(3) Primary union of craft type
(4) Region-cum-industrial level union

378. Arrange the following trade union federations on the basis of their year of emergene from the earliest to the latest :
(a) CITU (b) UTUC
(c) AITUC (d) INTUC
(e) BMS
Codes :
(1) c, d, b, e, a (2) a, e, b, d, c
(3) d, c, b, e, a (4) c, b, d, a, e

379. Which of the following statements is/are true about trade unionism in India ?
a. It had moorings in the freedom struggle.
b. It had received patronage from employers.
c. It originated due to workers' demands.
d. It originated due to imperatives of tripartite representation in the ILO.
Codes :
(1) Only a (2) a and b
(3) a, c, d (4) a, b, d

380. The 'Socialist Manifesto' for converting capitalist economy into a mixed economy was developed by
(1) Karl Marx
(2) G.D.H. Cole
(3) William Baveridge
(4) Sidney and Beatrice Webbs

381. The enactment of the Equal Remuneration Act, 1976 is associated with which of the following conventions of the ILO ?
(1) Convention No. 111, 1958
(2) Convention No. 100, 1951
(3) Convention No. 123, 1975
(4) Convention No. 118, 1964

382. The valuation of the assets and liabilities of the ESI corporation shall have to be made at an interval of
(1) Two years (2) Five years
(3) Four years (4) Three years

383. When a conciliation proceeding relating to an industrial dispute ends without reaching a settlement, then under which of the following conditions it is deemed that conciliation proceeding has been concluded?
(1) When the conciliation officer concludes the proceedings.
(2) When the conciliation officer submits the report to the appropriate Government.
(3) When the report of the conciliation officer is received by the appropriate Government.
(4) When the industrial dispute is referred to the Labour Court/Industrial Tribunal.

384. Which of the following statements relating to Labour legislation is not true ?
(1) It seeks to regulate the balance of power in the relationship between the employers and the Government.
(2) It aims to improve living conditions of the workers and their family members.
(3) It has implications for promoting labour efficiency.
(4) It protects minimum labour standards and improves working conditions.

385. Under the provisions of the Payment of Gratuity Act, 1972, employees working in a seasonal establishment and who have not been employed throughout the year, the employers shall be paid gratuity at the rate of
(1) 10 days of wages for every year
(2) 10 days of wags for every season
(3) 15 days of wages for every year
(4) 7 days of wages for every season

386. Under the Factories Act, 1948, the spread over period including rest interval in a day for an adult worker should not normally exceed

(1) 10 ½ hours (2) 11 hours
(3) 12 hours (4) 11 ½ hours

387. Which of the following conditions relating to claims under the Minimum Wages Act, 1948 is not true ?

(1) The authority to hear and decide for all claim cases shall be appointed by the appropriate Government.
(2) Any legal practitioner with a written authorisation from the concerned employee can make a claim application on behalf of the employer.
(3) Any claim application shall have to be presented within one year from the date on which minimum wages became payable.
(4) The Inspector with permission of the Authority appointed under the Act, can make a claim application for an employee.

388. What is the minimum amount of bonus payable to an adult employee during an accounting year ?

(1) Rs. 1000 (2) Rs. 100
(3) Rs. 833 (4) Rs. 750

389. What is the maximum amount of fine that can be imposed on an employee in a wage period under the Payment of Wags Act, 1936?

(1) Three percent of wage
(2) Five percent of wage
(3) Ten percent of wage
(4) Eight percent of wage

390. Who among the following 'relatives' of a deceased employee are dependants under the Employees' Compensation Act, 1923 ?

i. Widowed mother
ii. a widower
iii. a minor child of a predeceased daughter
iv. a paternal grandparent

(1) Both i and iv (2) i, ii and iii
(3) Both ii and iv (4) Both i and ii

391. Assertion (A) : Labour Welfare is not social work being its result but an area of social work.

Reason (R) : As labour too needs the enabling help of social work professional, social work is no trespasses in the realms of labour welfare.

(1) (A) is right, (R) is wrong.
(2) (A) is wrong, (R) is right.
(3) (A) and (R) are wrong.
(4) (A) is right and (R) explains the (A).

392. Which of the following statements about 'housekeeping' is/are true ?

a. It believes in "a place for everything and everything in its place" principle.
b. It is a culture of maintaining cleanliness.
c. It is a system of arranging materials in order of their importance and frequency of use.
d. It talks about the infrastructural facilities provided by the organisation.

Codes :

(1) a, c (2) a, b
(3) a, b, c (4) a, b, c, d

393. Examines the following statements about industrial accidents and safety management. Indicate the one which is not relevant.

(1) Accident Proneness is a behavioural and attitudinal problem that some employees suffer from.
(2) Safety consciousness is not a trainable trait.
(3) Safety in industry can improve if the provisions laid down in the Factories Act, 1948 or any such relevant law are strictly followed.
(4) "Accidents do not just happen but are caused" is only partly true.

394. Match the following principles of labour welfare with the relevant themes :

Principle	**Theme**
a. Principle of coordination	i. Delegation of authority to the committees

b. Principle of association	ii. Avoiding procrastination in welfare work.
c. Principle of responsibility	iii. Avoiding piecemeal approach to labour welfare and adopting a total perspective.
d. Principle of timeliness	iv. Eliciting the participation and collaboration of workers and their representatives.

Codes :

	a	b	c	d
(1)	iii	iv	i	ii
(2)	ii	iv	i	iii
(3)	iii	ii	iv	i
(4)	iv	ii	i	iii

395. Which of the following is an example of 'extra-mural' labour welfare ?

a. Co-operative credit society
b. Recreation facility
c. Library and Reading Rooms
d. Shelters and Rest Rooms

Codes :

(1) b and c (2) a, b and c
(3) b, c and d (4) c and d

396. Match the following concepts of labour with the relevant theme :

Concept of Labour	Theme
a. Commodity concept of Labour	i. Labour regarded by the employer largely as operating organizations in industry.
b. Machinery concept of Labour	ii. Labour has right to be consulted in regard to the terms and conditions under which they are supposed to work.
c. Goodwill concept of Labour	iii. Labour is affected by the law of supply and demand.
d. Citizenship concept of Labour	iv. Paternalistic approach towards labour by the employers.

Codes :

	a	b	c	d
(1)	iii	i	iv	ii
(2)	ii	iv	iii	i
(3)	iv	iii	i	ii
(4)	i	iii	ii	iv

397. Which of the following is not a feature of labour market ?

(1) It is essentially local in character.
(2) It is not monopolistic.
(3) It is less mobile compared to commodity and capital markets.
(4) Monospony in the labour market is less common than monopoly.

398. Which of the following theories of wages is called as the 'Iron Law of Wages' ?

(1) Subsistence Theory
(2) The Standard of Living Theory
(3) The Wage Fund Theory
(4) The Residual Claimant Theory

399. Which of the following is not a factor that creates wage differentials ?

(1) Differences due to existence of non-competing groups.
(2) Non-equalizing differences
(3) Differences in Labour Quality
(4) Labour Market Perfections

400. On what basis the money wage can be converted into real wages ?

(1) Consumer Price Index
(2) Wholesale Price Index
(3) Retail Price Index
(4) Money Exchange Rate

ANSWER KEY

1. (2) 2. (3) 3. (2) 4. (4) 5. (1) 6. (2) 7. (1) 8. (4) 9. (4) 10. (3)
11. (4) 12. (3) 13. (4) 14. (3) 15. (2) 16. (2) 17. (4) 18. (3) 19. (2) 20. (3)
21. (1) 22. (4) 23. (2) 24. (2) 25. (3) 26. (2) 27. (3) 28. (2) 29. (4) 30. (3)
31. (1) 32. (3) 33. (1) 34. (4) 35. (2) 36. (4) 37. (2) 38. (3) 39. (4) 40. (3)
41. (2) 42. (3) 43. (3) 44. (1) 45. (3) 46. (4) 47. (1) 48. (4) 49. (3) 50. (4)
51. (1) 52. (1) 53. (2) 54. (1) 55. (2) 56. (4) 57. (1) 58. (3) 59. (1) 60. (4)
61. (2) 62. (1) 63. (3) 64. (4) 65. (2) 66. (1) 67. (2) 68. (4) 69. (2) 70. (1)
71. (4) 72. (3) 73. (3) 74. (3) 75. (2) 76. (1) 77. (2) 78. (3) 79. (2) 80. (3)
81. (2) 82. (1) 83. (4) 84. (3) 85. (4) 86. (1) 87. (3) 88. (4) 89. (2) 90. (3)
91. (4) 92. (3) 93. (1) 94. (2) 95. (1) 96. (1) 97. (4) 98. (1) 99. (4) 100. (2)
101. (1) 102. (4) 103. (1) 104. (4) 105. (1) 106. (1) 107. (2) 108. (3) 109. (1) 110. (3)
111. (1) 112. (2) 113. (4) 114. (3) 115. (1) 116. (3) 117. (1) 118. (3) 119. (4) 120. (2)
121. (3) 122. (1) 123. (3) 124. (4) 125. (1) 126. (4) 127. (2) 128. (3) 129. (1) 130. (3)
131. (2) 132. (3) 133. (4) 134. (3) 135. (4) 136. (3) 137. (1) 138. (2) 139. (3) 140. (4)
141. (2) 142. (1) 143. (4) 144. (1) 145. (2) 146. (3) 147. (2) 148. (4) 149. (2) 150. (4)
151. (2) 152. (4) 153. (3) 154. (2) 155. (3) 156. (1) 157. (3) 158. (1) 159. (2) 160. (4)
161. (3) 162. (1) 163. (3) 164. (2) 165. (4) 166. (1) 167. (4) 168. (1) 169. (4) 170. (3)
171. (3) 172. (2) 173. (4) 174. (2) 175. (4) 176. (3) 177. (1) 178. (3) 179. (3) 180. (3)
181. (2) 182. (3) 183. (1) 184. (3) 185. (1) 186. (2) 187. (1) 188. (2) 189. (1) 190. (3)
191. (4) 192. (3) 193. (4) 194. (3) 195. (1) 196. (3) 197. (2) 198. (2) 199. (4) 200. (2)
201. (4) 202. (4) 203. (2) 204. (2) 205. (3) 206. (4) 207. (3) 208. (4) 209. (1) 210. (4)
211. (1) 212. (4) 213. (2) 214. (4) 215. (3) 216. (2) 217. (4) 218. (3) 219. (4) 220. (3)
221. (4) 222. (3) 223. (1) 224. (3) 225. (1) 226. (3) 227. (1) 228. (1) 229. (3) 230. (4)
231. (3) 232. (4) 233. (3) 234. (4) 235. (3) 236. (4) 237. (1) 238. (3) 239. (4) 240. (3)
241. (1) 242. (1) 243. (3) 244. (3) 245. (2) 246. (2) 247. (2) 248. (3) 249. (2) 250. (3)
251. (3) 252. (1) 253. (3) 254. (3) 255. (4) 256. (1) 257. (2) 258. (4) 259. (2) 260. (2)
261. (2) 262. (4) 263. (3) 264. (3) 265. (1) 266. (3) 267. (3) 268. (3) 269. (2) 270. (3)
271. (2) 272. (2) 273. (3) 274. (3) 275. (4) 276. (3) 277. (1) 278. (3) 279. (2) 280. (1)
281. (4) 282. (1) 283. (1) 284. (2) 285. (2) 286. (2) 287. (4) 288. (4) 289. (2) 290. (4)
291. (2) 292. (1) 293. (2) 294. (2) 295. (4) 296. (1) 297. (1) 298. (1) 299. (2) 300. (4)
301. (2) 302. (2) 303. (2) 304. (3) 305. (2) 306. (4) 307. (3) 308. (4) 309. (2) 310. (2)
311. (2) 312. (4) 313. (2) 314. (4) 315. (3) 316. (4) 317. (2) 318. (4) 319. (3) 320. (3)
321. (3) 322. (1) 323. (4) 324. (1) 325. (4) 326. (2) 327. (2) 328. (1) 329. (4) 330. (4)
331. (1) 332. (3) 333. (1) 334. (4) 335. (1) 336. (3) 337. (1) 338. (2) 339. (3) 340. (2)
341. (2) 342. (2) 343. (3) 344. (3) 345. (3) 346. (1) 347. (4) 348. (1) 349. (3) 350. (1)
351. (2) 352. (1) 353. (1) 354. (4) 355. (1) 356. (4) 357. (2) 358. (1) 359. (3) 360. (4)
361. (3) 362. (3) 363. (1) 364. (4) 365. (3) 366. (3) 367. (2) 368. (3) 369. (3) 370. (2)
371. (3) 372. (3) 373. (2) 374. (4) 375. (3) 376. (4) 377. (2) 378. (1) 379. (4) 380. (4)
381. (2) 382. (3) 383. (3) 384. (1) 385. (4) 386. (1) 387. (3) 388. (2) 389. (1) 390. (4)
391. (4) 392. (3) 393. (2) 394. (1) 395. (2) 396. (1) 397. (4) 398. (1) 399. (4) 400. (1)

(Revised Pattern)

MODEL PAPERS

SET I

Note : This paper contains **hundred** (100) Objective type questions, each question carrying **two** (2) marks.

Question Numbers : (1 to 5)

Question Label : Comprehension

Biased appraisals have a variety of causes. One study of bias (the tendency for individual differences to affect judgements) focused on rater personality. Raters who scored higher on 'conscientiousness' tended to give their peers lower ratings-they were stricter, in other words; those more 'agreeable' gave higher ratings-they were more lenient. Managers also tend to be more lenient when appraising subordinates for administrative purposes like pay raises than for development purposes. Furthermore, "performance ratings amplify the quality of the personal relationship between boss and employee. Good relationships tender to create good [appraisal] experiences, bad relationships bad ones."

Unfortunately, subordinates' demographic traits (age, race, gender, and so on) also affect ratings. A 36-year-old supervisor ranked a 62-year-old subordinate at the bottom of the department's rankings, and then fired him. The court held that the younger boss's discriminatory motives might have prejudiced the dismissal decision. In one study, promoted women had to have received higher performance ratings than promoted men to be promoted, "suggesting that women were held to stricter standards for promotion." In another study, raters penalized successful women for their success. The point is that the appraisal often says more about the appraiser than about the appraisee. (Or, as one researcher said, "Rater idiosyncratic biases account for the largest percentage of the observed variances in performance ratings") Potential bias is one reason to use multiple raters, have the supervisor's boss review the rating, and/or have 'calibration' meetings where supervisors discuss their reasons for the appraisals they gave each of their subordinates.

Sub questions

1. Two statements are given below. First statement will be called Assertion and the second will be called Reason.

Assertion : Rater's idiosyncratic biases account for the largest percentage of the observed variance in performance rating.

Assertion : Potential bias is one reason to use multiple raters.

Select the alternative that best establishes relationship between Assertion and Reason:

(1) Assertion is not true
(2) Reason is not correct
(3) Reason explains Assertion
(4) Assertion and Reason have no relationship

2. Who are likely to give lower rating to their peer?

(1) Agreeable rater
(2) Liberal rater
(3) Conscientiousness rater
(4) Aged rater

3. A rater has to rate an employee for the purpose of pay increase. The rater will

(1) have liberal approach
(2) have stricter approach
(3) have unchanged approach without being affected by the purpose
(4) refuse the job

4. Choose the correct statement :

(1) Relationship plays no role in rating.
(2) Good relationship leads to lower rating.

(3) Better the relationship, higher is the rating.
(4) Strained relationship leads to higher rating.

5. Which one is the correct statement?
(1) Age of the rater and ratee has nothing to do in rating.
(2) Gender of the ratee is not taken into consideration while rating.
(3) Age of the rater and ratee have bearing on rating.
(4) Demographic traits do not influence rating.

6. Two statements, namely Assertion and Reason, are given below :

Assertion : Organisation involves the grouping of activities necessary to accomplish goals and plans, the assignment of these activities to appropriate departments and the provision for authority delegation and coordination.

Reason : Organisation is an executive function that consists of breaking up the entire Work into different segments, assigning each segment to the qualified individuals and coordinating the efforts of job holders to attain the organisational goals.

Which alternative is most appropriate among the one's given below which exhibits their relationship?
(1) Assertion is incorrect and has no relationship with Reason.
(2) Reason is incorrect and has no relationship with Assertion.
(3) No inter-relationship can be established between the two statements.
(4) Reason appropriately explains Assertion.

7. The function of the management which is associated with measuring results against pre-established standards and taking corrective action for maintaining the system is known as
(1) controlling (2) planning
(3) coordinating (4) directing

8. List-I below gives some names who have contributed for development of different management functions/activities and List-II gives the specific functions they are associated with :

List-I	List-II
(a) Robert Owen	(i) Scientific Management
(b) Henry Fayol	(ii) Modem Personnel Management
(c) F. W. Taylor	(iii) Work Study
(d) H. L. Gantt	(iv) Modem Management Theory

Which of the following gives right match between items of List-I and List-II?
(1) (a)-(ii); (b)-(iii); (c)-(iv); (d)-(i)
(2) (a)-(i); (b)-(ii); (c)-(iii); (d)-(iv)
(3) (a)-(ii); (b)-(iv); (c)-(i); (d)-(iii)
(4) (a)-(iii); (b)-(i); (c)-(ii); (d)-(iv)

9. Process orientation concept of management was developed by numerous authors. Who among the following is not associated with this concept?
(1) McFarland
(2) E. F. L. Breech
(3) Lawrence A. Appley
(4) George R. Terry

10. The Behavioural School of Management has developed many behavioural theories. Arrange the correct sequence of the major contributors to the behavioural school from the earliest to the latest
(a) Mary Parker Follet
(b) Abraham Maslow
(c) Elton Mayo
(d) Douglas McGregor
(e) Chis Argyris

Select the correct options :
(1) (a), (b), (c), (d), (e)
(2) (a), (c), (b), (d), (e)
(3) (a), (c), (d), (b), (e)
(4) (b), (c), (d), (a), (e)

11. Given below are the major contributors in List-I and their contributions in List-II of Behavioural School of Management :

List-I	List-II
(a) Mary Paker Follet	(i) Group influences in the Workplace.
(b) Elton Mayo	(ii) Relates human motivation to a hierarchy of needs.
(c) Abraham Maslow	(iii) Effects of human motivation on productivity and output.
(d) Douglas McGregor	(iv) Emphasizes human characteristics theory X and theory Y and the corresponding style of leadership

Match List-I with List-II and choose the correct match :

(1) (a)-(i); (b)-(iii); (c)-(ii), (d)-(iv)
(2) (a)-(i); (b)-(ii); (c)-(iv); (d)-(iii)
(3) (a)-(i); (b)-(iv); (c)-(iii); (d)-(ii)
(4) (a)-(ii); (b)-(i); (c)-(iii); (d)-(iv)

12. "A horizontal set of divisional reporting relationship is superimposed on a hierarchical structure. This is known as grid organisation or project management organisation." What type of structure it has? Choose the correct one from the functional alternatives given below :

(1) Hybrid structure
(2) Functional structure
(3) Matrix structure
(4) Divisional structure

13. "If the leadership style allows substantial participation by members of the group in the management and decision-making process, subordinates are frequently consulted by the manager on Wide-ranging problems and are allowed sufficient freedom to communicate with the leader and also with their fellow subordinates." It is called

(1) autocratic style of leadership
(2) democratic style of leadership
(3) laissez fair style of leadership
(4) paternalistic style of leadership

14. Harvard model of Human Resource Management centered on four C's of Human Resource Practices. Which among the following has not been described as the HR Practices under Havard model ?

(1) Commitment
(2) Competitiveness
(3) Competence
(4) Cost effectiveness

15. Professor J. Barney and Prof. Patrick Wright have developed a comprehensive model in 1997 to establish Human Resources as a competitive advantage of the firm, which is known as

(1) VRIO Framework
(2) Soft Model of HRM
(3) Multiple Stakeholder Model
(4) Business Process Model

16. Which one of the following is NOT a Human Resource Planning technique?

(1) Predictor variables
(2) Zero-base techniques
(3) Simulation techniques
(4) Managerial Grid Techniques

17. "Take my physical assets, leave my people, and in five years I will have it all back." Who said this?

(1) Alfred Sloan (2) Peter F. Drucker
(3) Bill Gates (4) Rensis Likert

18. Placement aims at placing right man at the right job at right time. It is an attempt to correlate job requirement and individual characteristics. In this context, placement, being a continuous process should come after

(1) recruitment (2) selection
(3) training (4) development

19. Talent management starts with understanding what jobs need to be filled, and the human traits and competencies employee need to do those jobs effectively. Two lists are given below. List-I is term and List-II is their appropriate meaning :

List-I	List-II
(a) Job analysis	(i) A list of job's 'human require-

		ments' that is the requisite education, skills, personality and so on.
(b) Job description	(ii)	A list of job's duties, responsibilities, reporting relationships, working conditions and supervisory responsibilities.
(c) Job specification	(iii)	The procedure for determining the duties and skill requirements of a job and the kind of person who should be hired for it.
(d) Work Flow analysis	(iv)	A detailed study of the flow of work from job to job in a work process.

Which of the following alternatives gives the correct match between List-I and List-II?

(1) (a)-(ii); (b)-(iii)-(c)-(i); (d)-(iv)
(2) (a)-(iii); (b)-(ii); (c)-(i); (d)-(iv)
(3) (a)-(iv); (b)-(ii); (c)-(iii); (d)-(i)
(4) (a)-(i); (b)-(ii); (c)-(iii); (d)-(iv)

20. "A technique by which a new employee is adjusted into the changed surroundings and introduced to the practices, policies and purpose of the organisation" is called

(1) placement (2) induction
(3) training (4) development

21. On-the-job training is based on the principle of 'learning by doing'. Which one of the following is NOT an on-the-job training method?

(1) Coaching (2) Understanding
(3) Role playing (4) Job rotation

22. Performance appraisal means evaluating an employee's current and/or past performance relative to his or her performance standards. Performance appraisal always involves the three steps. Which one of the following is NOT a step of performances appraisal process?

(1) Setting Work standards
(2) Assessing the employee's actual performance relating to those standards
(3) Providing feedback to the employee with the aim of helping him or her to eliminate performance deficiencies or to continue to perform above par.
(4) Grading on a curve predetermined percentages of ratees are placed in various performance categories.

23. Two lists are given below, List-I is related to terms of managing career and List-II is related to their appropriate meaning:

List-I		List-II
(a) Career planning	(i)	The process for enabling employees to better understanding and develop their career skills and interests and to use these skills and interests more effectively
(b) Career management	(ii)	The deliberate process through which some one becomes aware of personal skills, interest, knowledge, motivations and other characteristics and establishes action plan to attain specific goals
(c) Career development	(iii)	The lifelong series of activities that contribute to a person's career exploration, establishment, success and fulfilment

(d) Career coaching	(iv) Focuses on teaching, educating, instructing and training subordinates

Choose the alternative which gives the right match of List-I with List-II :

(1) (a)-(ii); (b)-(i); (c)-(iii), (d)-(iv)
(2) (a)-(i); (b)-(ii); (c)-(iii); (d)-(i)
(3) (a)-(ii); (b)-(i); (c)-(iii); (d)-(iii)
(4) (a)-(iv); (b)-(ii); (c)-(iii); (d)-(iv)

24. There are four new approaches to compensation rewards. Two Lists are given below List-I relates with Approach and List-II relates to appropriate benefits and features

List-I	**List-II**
(a) Skill-based pay	(i) Support for participative organizational structures and improved effectiveness of work teams
(b) Broad banding	(ii) Greater scope for recognising individual differences in employee performance
(c) Variable pay	(iii) Motivation of sustained high performance and better linkages between individual and organizational goals
(d) Team rewards	(iv) Multi-skilled workforce, job assignment, flexibility and higher employee satisfaction and commitment

Match List-I with List-II and choose the correct answer :

(1) (a)-(i); (b)-(iii); (c)-(ii), (d)-(iv)
(2) (a)-(iv); (b)-(ii); (c)-(iii); (d)-(i)
(3) (a)-(iv); (b)-(i); (c)-(iii); (d)-(ii)
(4) (a)-(i); (b)-(ii); (c)-(iii); (d)-(iv)

25. Human Capital Appraisal Approach of HRD function was outlined in 1998. Who among the following has developed the Human Capital Appraisal Approach?

(1) T.V. Rao (2) Udai Pareek
(3) Friedman (4) Ulrich and Lake

26. Values are core of the culture. Both values and belief provide guidelines for employee to follow in their Work. Some organisations have created their own value. Two lists are given below. List-I indicates the name of organisation and List-II indicates their value:

List-I	**List-II**
(a) Caterpillar (USA)	(i) "In 24 hours parts services anywhere in the world."
(b) Larsen and Tubro (India)	(ii) "Faith in youth and tap the youth."
(c) Microsoft (USA)	(iii) "Computer on every desk and every house."
(d) TERI (India)	(iv) "People are prime movers."

Match List-I with List-II and choose the correct answer:

(1) (a)-(i); (b)-(ii); (c)-(iii), (d)-(iv)
(2) (a)-(i); (b)-(iv); (c)-(iii); (d-(ii)
(3) (a)-(ii); (b)-(iii); (c)-(iv); (d)-(i)
(4) (a)-(iii); (b)-(ii); (c)-(i); (d)-(iv)

27. There are different techniques to Human Resource Accounting. Which one of the following is NOT human resource accounting technique?

(1) Historical Cost Method
(2) Replacement Cost Method
(3) Quality Cost Method
(4) Opportunity Cost Method

28. Which one of the following is NOT associated with the three facets of career motivation?

(1) Career resilience
(2) Career insight

(3) Career counselling
(4) Career identity

29. The goal of training is that the trainees learn the task or material presented and the same are retained by them. Which of the following issues influences the retention process?
(1) Contiguity, the law of effect and practice
(2) Task analysis, task achievement and task sequencing
(3) Meaningfulness of material, degree of original learning and interference
(4) Active practice, mental practice and overlearning

30. Who among the following have suggested that learning outcomes can be three types, namely, cognitive, skill based and affective?
(1) Kirkpatrick and Ford
(2) Kraiger, Ford and Salas
(3) Holton and Galvin
(4) Phillips and Brinkerhoff

31. Which of the following factors identified by Dunning in his Eclectic Theory are to be simultaneously met by a company that wishes to set up production unit in a foreign country and wants to operate as a multinational?
(1) Advantages relating to labour, land and capital
(2) Advantages relating to ownership, location and internationalization
(3) Advantages relating to capital, technology and products
(4) Advantages relating to cost, capital and labour

32. Based upon a study on cultural diversity in multinational corporations the following four dimensions emerged that differentiated national cultures in terms of their managerial ideologies :
(i) Organisation as a political system
(ii) Organisation as an authority system
(iii) Organisation as role formalisation system
(iv) Organisation as hierarchical-relation system

Who among the following is associated with the study?
(1) Hofstede (2) Triandris
(3) Laurent (4) Maurice

33. A multinational company appointing a person in a subsidiary, belonging to the country where its subsidiary is located reflects which of the following approaches?
(1) Etlnocentrism (2) Geocenirism
(3) Regiocentrism (4) Polycentiism

34. The competitive strategies for multinational corporations are given in List-I and their features in List-II as below :

List-I	List-II
(a) Multidomesiic strategy	(i) Gives prime importance to efficiency.
(b) Global strategy	(ii) Gives prime importance to development and diffusion of innovations Worldwide
(c) International strategy	(iii) Gives prime importance to global efficiency, national responsiveness and worldwide learning at the same time
(d) Transnational strategy	(iv) Gives prime importance to national responsiveness

From among the following which one gives the right combination between the strategies and their features?
(1) (a)-(iv); (b)-(i); (c)-(ii), (d)-(iii)
(2) (a)-(i); (b)-(ii); (c)-(iii); (d)-(iv)
(3) (a)-(iii); (b)-(iv); (c)-(i); (d)-(ii)
(4) (a)-(ii); (b)-(iii); (c)-(iv); (d)-(i)

35. According to Henry Mintzberg managers perform ten different highly interrelated roles, which are grouped under three broad roles, namely, Interpersonal roles, information roles and decisional roles. From among the following which one is associated with the Interpersonal role?

(1) Monitor and Disseminator
(2) Leader and Figurehead
(3) Spokesperson and Entrepreneur
(4) Negotiator and Resource allocator

36. Three theories of learning are given in List-I and their characteristics in List-II below

List-I	List-II
(a) Classical conditioning	(i) People can learn through observation and direct experience
(b) Operant conditioning	(ii) A type of conditioning in which an individual responds to some stimulus that would not ordinarily produce such a response
(c) Social learning theory	(iii) A type of conditioning in which desired voluntary behaviour leads to a reward or prevents a punishment

Which one of the following gives the correct combination between the theories and their characteristics?

(1) (a)-(i); (b)-(ii); (c)-(iii)
(2) (a)-(iii); (b)-(i); (c)-(ii)
(3) (a)-(i); (b)-(iii); (c)-(ii)
(4) (a)-(ii); (b)-(iii); (c)-(i)

37. As per 'Johari window', the 'closed area' is explained by which one of the following?

(1) An individual's behaviour is known to himself or herself and to those with whom the individual interacts
(2) Those aspects of the person's behaviour and style that others know, but not known to the person himself or herself
(3) The aspects of the person's behaviour and style which are known to the person but not revealed to others
(4) The aspects of behaviour and style neither known to the person nor others

38. A group consisting of members working together to attain a specific objective with which each is concerned, is known as

(1) informal group
(2) task group
(3) friendship group
(4) interest group

39. As per the managerial grid given by Blake and Mouton, the leadership style focussing on low task and high concern for the people is known as

(1) impoverished management
(2) club country management
(3) team management
(4) middle of the road management

40. According to Vroom's expectancy theory of motivation, which of the following refers to the term 'valence'?

(1) Subjective probability of achieving an outcome
(2) Efforts made by an individual for the first level outcome
(3) Relation between the first level and second level outcomes to each other
(4) Strength to an individual's preference for a particular outcome

41. Which one of the following statements are true relating to the Myers-Briggs Type Indicator of personality?

(1) There are sixteen personality types generated on the basis of four basic elements.
(2) There are twenty personality types generated on the basis of five basic elements.
(3) There are ten personality types generated on the basis of four basic elements.
(4) There are eighteen personality types generated on the basis of six basic elements.

42. The term 'grapevine' is associated with which one of the following communication networks of an organisation?
(1) Formal communication
(2) Horizontal communication
(3) Informal communication
(4) Vertical communication

43. The dynamic balance of the driving force and restraining force of change is associated with which of the following'?
(1) Force field analysis model
(2) Force analytical model
(3) Force field balancing model
(4) Force field contingent model

44. The process of change namely coercive, mimetic and normative isomorphisms are associated with which of the following perspectives on organisational change?
(1) Resource dependence perspective
(2) Contingency perspective
(3) Population-ecology perspective
(4) Institutional perspective

45. Which of the following statements relating to Dunlop's industrial relations framework is NOT correct?
(1) Dunlop's framework was designed to broaden the industrial relations horizon from collective bargaining to the full spectrum of present-day industrial relations.
(2) This framework cannot be used for a study of industrial relations within a country as a whole.
(3) Dunlop's industrial relations framework puts emphasis on rule-making by management, workers and specialised government agencies concerned with workers, enterprises and their relationships.
(4) Dunlop's framework focuses on the ideology of the industrial relations system.

46. Which of the following perspectives concerning industrial relations is based on the assumption that conflict is irrational in an organisation?
(1) Unitary perspective
(2) Pluralistic perspective
(3) Trusteeship perspective
(4) Radical perspective.

47. Who among the following is associated with the Human Relations approach to industrial relations?
(1) Charles A. Myers (2) Dale Yoder
(3) Michael Poole (4) Elton Mayo

48. Who is called Sidney Webb in the United States?
(1) John R. Commons
(2) Noel Arnold Levin
(3) Robert F. Hoxie
(4) Frank Tannenbaum

49. The Bombay Mill Hands Association was established under the presidentship of
(1) Bal Gangadhar Tilak
(2) C. F. Andrews
(3) N. M. Joshi
(4) N. M. Lokhande

50. The Bharatiya Mazdoor Sangh was fo ned under the leadership of
(1) S. A. Dange (2) S. V. Ghats
(3) Dattop ant Thengadi
(4) K. N. Joglekar

51. As per the recommendations of the Second National Commission on Labour, what should be the percentage of support of workers, a union should have in an establishment for claiming recognition as a single negotiating agent on the basis of check-off system?
(1) 25 percent (2) 33 percent
(3) 50 percent (4) 66 percent

52. Which of the following statements relating to the 'Participation of Workers in Management Bill' is wrong ?
(1) The Bill was introduced in the Rajya Sabha on May 30, 1990.
(2) The Bill was the first comprehensive legislative effort towards promotion of Workers' participation in management in the country.

(3) It has a provision for constitution of Shop-floor Councils in every establishment.
(4) The Bill does not have any provision regarding the representation of the workers on the Board of Management.

53. The Indian Labour Conference approved 'illustrative lists' of items which the Works Committees should normally deal with and those which they should not. Which of the following items figures in the list of items to be dealt with by the Works Committees?
(1) Bonus and profit-sharing
(2) Rationalization and matters connected with the fixation of workload.
(3) Adjustment of festival and national holidays
(4) Housing and transport services

54. Given below are different statements, some of which are only relevant to productivity bargaining:
(a) Productivity bargaining is a management-initiated process
(b) It has an element of input-output relationship
(c) It is based on the principle of mutuality
(d) It is not a continuous process
From among the following, which alternative presents the relevant features of productivity bargaining?
(1) Only (a) and (b)
(2) Only (b) and (c)
(3) (a), (b) and (c) only
(4) (a), (b), (c) and (d)

55. Which of the following statements relating to the Model Grievance Procedure is correct?
(1) According to the Model Grievance Procedure, an aggrieved worker who is not satisfied with the decision of the departmental head in respect of his grievance, may directly present his grievance to the grievance committee.
(2) The Model Grievance Procedure has a provision regarding reference of a grievance to voluntary arbitration.
(3) According to the Model Grievance Procedure, an aggrieved worker shall have the right to leave the department during working hours without obtaining the prior permission of his superior.
(4) The procedure laid down for the redressal of grievances has to be followed even in the case of any grievance arising out of the dismissal of a worker.

56. The Office of the Director General of Mines Safety is located at
(1) New Delhi (2) Asansol
(3) Dhanbad (4) Kolkata

57. Which of the following is not an attached office of the Ministry of Labour, Government of India?
(1) Office of the Chief Labour Commissioner
(2) Labour Bureau
(3) V.V. Giri National Labour Institute
(4) Office of the Director General, Factory Advice Service and Labour Institutes

58. There are two sets, that are given below. List-I gives the list of terms and List-II indicates their meanings :

List-I	**List-II**
(a) Orbiter dictum	(i) A cursory remark
(b) Puisne	(ii) Subordinate
(c) Mens rea	(iii) Guilty mind
(d) Ultra vires	(iv) Beyond one's powers

Which of the following gives the correct match between the terms and their meanings?
(1) (a)-(i); (b)-(ii); (c)-(iii); (d)-(iv)
(2) (a)-(ii); (b)-(iii); (c)-(iv); (d)-(i)
(3) (a)-(iv); (b)-(i); (c)-(ii); (d)-(iii)
(4) (a)-(iii); (b)-(iv); (c)-(i); (d)-(ii)

59. The ILO's Tripartite Consultation (International Labour Standards) Convention, 1976 was ratified by India in the year
(1) 1978 (2) 1982
(3) 1996 (4) 2016

60. A registered trade union of workmen functioning in an industry having five hundred workmen should have to maintain a minimum of what number of workmen as members in order to continue the registration of the trade union?

(1) Seven (2) Fifty
(3) One hundred (4) Twenty

61. As per the provisions of the Trade Unions Act 1926, who among the following shall not be eligible to be the executive or office bearer of the trade union?

(1) A member of the Legislative Assembly
(2) A member of the Parliament
(3) An elected representative of local body
(4) A minister in the Union Cabinet

62. Under the provisions of the Industrial Disputes Act 1947, the employer of any industry declares lay-off, is required to provide alternate employment to the workmen laid-off in any other industry belongs to him and located at a distance not more than

(1) eight miles (2) six miles
(3) five miles (4) seven miles

63. How many days advance notice is to be given to the affected workmen for change in the conditions of service of workmen, when no proceeding is pending before any adjudicative authorities under the provisions of the Industrial Disputes Act, 1947?

(1) Thirty days
(2) Fourteen days
(3) Twenty-one days
(4) Seven days

64. Under the provisions of the Industrial Disputes Act 1947, the total members of the Grievance Redressal Committee shall not exceed

(1) Ten (2) Six
(3) Eight (4) Twelve

65. Under the provisions of the Industrial Employment (Standing Orders) Act, 1946 who among the following can apply for modifications in the standing orders?

(1) Any employer or the workmen
(2) Any workmen, trade union or representative of workmen
(3) Any employer, workmen, trade union or representative of workmen on agreement
(4) Only trade union

66. As per the provisions of the Industrial Employment (Standing Orders) Act, 1946 the Certifying Officer is required to send copies of the modified standing orders to the employer and the trade union within how many days from the date of notifications?

(1) Five days (2) Seven days
(3) Twelve days (4) Fifteen days

67. As per the provisions of the Factories Act, 1948 a worker of a factory, who quits the employment, shall be paid his wages for the days of unavailed leave before

(1) the expiry of two months from the date of quitting the employment
(2) the expiry of the second working day from the date of quitting
(3) the expiry of one month from the date of quitting
(4) the expiry of his wage period

68. As per provisions of the Factories Act, 1948 under power to make exempting orders, the total number of hours of work in any day for a worker shall not exceed :

(1) Eleven hours (2) Twelve hours
(3) Thirteen hours (4) Ten hours

69. As per the provisions of the Mines Act, 1952 the special officer duly authorised in writing by the Chief Inspector, shall enter into any mine for the purpose of surveying, levelling and measuring after giving notice to the manager of the mine for not less than

(1) Three days (2) Seven days
(3) Ten days (4) Thirty days

70. Who among the following is authorised by the Chief Inspector by a special order in writing to enter the mine for the purpose of surveying, levelling and measuring the mine or part there of as per the provisions of the Mines Act, 1952?

(1) Surveyor (2) Special Officer
(3) Analyst (4) Survey Inspector

71. As per the provisions of the Inter-State Migrant Workmen (Regulation of Employment and Conditions of Service) Act 1979, who is required to issue the passbook duly affixed with a passport size photograph of the workman to the migrant workman?
(1) The Licensing Officer
(2) The Registering Officer
(3) The Contractor
(4) The Inspector

72. The Inter-State Migrant Workmen (Regulation of Employment and Conditions of Service) Act, 197 9 will apply to the establishments employing a minimum of
(1) twenty or more migrant workmen
(2) fifteen or more migrant workmen
(3) ten or more migrant workmen
(4) five or more migrant workmen

73. An employer of an establishment can only employ contract labour, under which one of the following provisions of the Contract Labour (Regulation and Abolition) Act, 1970?
(1) Obtaining a licence from the licensing officer
(2) Obtaining a certificate of registration from the registering officer
(3) Obtaining a written permission from the inspector
(4) Obtaining the permission from the appropriate government

74. Under the provisions of the Building and Other Construction Workers (Regulation of Employment and Conditions of Service) Act, 1996 in order to apply for registration as a beneficiary under the Act, a construction worker must have worked for a minimum period of how many days in the preceding twelve months
(1) Not less than two hundred forty days
(2) Not less than one hundred twenty days
(3) Not less than one hundred eighty days
(4) Not less than ninety days

75. As per the provisions of the Building and Other Construction Workers (Regulation of Employment and Conditions of Service) Act, 1996, because of financial hardship, if a beneficiary under the Act has not paid his contribution, the Board may Waive the contribution at a time for a period
(1) not exceeding three months
(2) not exceeding six months
(3) not exceeding nine months
(4) not exceeding twelve months

76. Child labour shall not be employed or permitted to work in any of the processes in any workshop set forth in which part of the schedule attached to the Child Labour (Prohibition and Regulation) Act, 1986?
(1) Part A (2) Part B
(3) Part C (4) Part D

77. "State to secure a social order for the promotion of welfare of the people" is mentioned in which Article of the Directive Principles of State Policy of the Constitution of India?
(1) Article 43A (2) Article 43
(3) Article 38 (4) Article 42

78. Under the provisions of the Payment of Wages Act, 1936 establishments which are not covered under the Act, the state government after giving how many months notice may extend the provisions of the Act to such establishments?
(1) One month (2) Two months
(3) Three months (4) Six months

79. As per the provisions of the Payment of Wages Act, 1936 'fine' imposed on any employed person cannot be recovered after expiry of how many days from the day the fine was imposed?
(1) Ninety days
(2) One hundred days
(3) One hundred twenty days
(4) One hundred eighty days

80. The appropriate government is empowered under Sec 7 of the Equal Remuneration Act, 1976 to appoint authorities for hearing and deciding claims and complaints, persons not below the rank of
(1) Labour Commissioner

(2) Asst. Labour Commissioner
(3) Labour Inspector
(4) Labour Officer

81. Under the provisions of the Payment of Bonus Act, 1965 in order to determine the bonus of an employee, who is not covered under the Scheduled Employment under the Minimum Wages Act, what amount of monthly wage from the following to be taken into consideration?
(1) Two thousand five hundred rupees
(2) Three thousand five hundred rupees
(3) Five thousand rupees
(4) Seven thousand rupees

82. The representation of the independent members in the Central Advisory Board constituted under the Minimum Wages Act, 1948 shall not exceed what portion of its total members?
(1) One-fourth (2) One-third
(3) One-half (4) Two-third

83. The authority constituted by the Central Government under the Provident Fund and Miscellaneous Provisions Act, 1952 to decide the cases regarding the determination of money due to be recovered from the employers is
(1) Employees' Provident Funds Tribunal
(2) Employees' Provident Fund Organization
(3) Employees' Provident Fund Court
(4) Employees' Provident Funds Appellate Tribunal

84. As per the provisions of the Employees' Provident Fund and Miscellaneous Provisions Act, 1952 the determination of the escaped amount to be recovered from the employer shall be made within which period from the date of communication of the order passed by the authorised officer?
(1) Three years (2) Five years
(3) Seven years (4) Ten years

85. As per the provisions of the Payment of Gratuity Act, 1972 an employee working in a seasonal establishment, shall get his gratuity after superannuation from the employment at the rate for how many days wages for each season, he had worked in that establishment'?
(1) Fifteen days (2) Ten days
(3) Eight days (4) Seven days

86. 'Compulsory Insurance' provision finding its due place under which of the following legislations?
(1) The Employees' Provident Fund Act, 1952
(2) The Employees' Compensation Act, 1923
(3) The Payment of Gratuity Act, 1972
(4) The Employees' State Insurance Act, 1948

87. In order to hear and decide any claims arising out of payment of less than the minimum rate of Wages, under the provisions of the Minimum Wages Act, 1948, the State Governments shall appoint any officer not below the rank of
(1) Chief Inspector under the Minimum Wages Act
(2) Asst. Labour Commissioner
(3) Labour Commissioner
(4) Dy. Labour Commissioner

88. Personal cause of industrial accident is one of the important causes of accident Among the causes given below, which one is not a personal cause of industrial accident?
(1) Neglect in housekeeping
(2) Carelessness, ignorance and inadequate skill
(3) Relationship with supervisor
(4) Improper supervision

89. Labour Welfare is dependent on certain bane principles. Each of these principles has its own content. Two lists are given below. In List-I, principles are given and in List-II content of the principles are given :

List-I	List-II
(a) Principles of adequacy of wages	(i) Welfare is a total concept coordinated approach will promote

	healthy development
(b) Principle of re-personalisation	(ii) Employer should not bargain labour welfare as substitute to wages
(c) Principle of democratic value	(iii) Consultation with and the agreement of Workers in formulation and implementation of welfare services
(d) Principle of integration	(iv) Development of human personality should be the goal of labour welfare

Match the principles with their contents :
(1) (a)-(ii); (b)-(iv); (c)-(iii); (d)-(i)
(2) (a)-(ii); (b)-(i); (c)-(iv); (d)-(iii)
(3) (a)-(iv); (b)-(ii); (c)-(i); (d)-(iii)
(4) (a)-(iv); (b)-(iii); (c)-(ii); (d)-(i)

90. Provisions for ensuring occupational health and safety for workers are contained in Articles 24, 39(e), 39(t) and 42 of the Directive Principles of State Policy of the Constitution of India. Based on the spirit of these, rules have been framed. The subject matter of the rules are both in Union List and Concurrent List. Which among the following is not in Concurrent List?
(1) Conditions of work (2) Safety in mines
(3) Provident funds
(4) Maternity benefits

91. Industrial safety is primarily whose responsibility under the Factories Act, 1948?
(1) Central Government
(2) State Government
(3) Occupier/Management
(4) Safety Committee

92. Occupational diseases are those which arise out of and in the course of employment. Industrial workers fall prey of these occupational diseases.

Two lists are given below. List-I contains the names of the diseases, while List-II contains the type of workers who are likely to suffer from these diseases :

List-I (Name of the disease)	**List-II (Type of workers)**
(a) Mercury poisoning	(i) Barometer worker, refiners of gold and silver
(b) Anthrax	(ii) Workers likely to inhale bagasse or sugarcane dust
(c) Bagassois	(iii) Textile workers
(d) Byssionosis	(iv) Workers engaged in handling wood, hair bristles

Match List-I with List-II :
(1) (a)-(i); (b)-(iii); (c)-(ii); (d)-(iv)
(2) (a)-(i); (b)-(iv); (c)-(ii); (d)-(iii)
(3) (a)-(iv); (b)-(i); (c)-(iii); (d)-(ii)
(4) (a)-(iv); (b)-(iii); (c)-(ii); (d)-(i)

93. Two statements are given below. We will consider the first statement as Assertion and the second one as Reason.

Assertion : Social security has wider aims than prevention or relief of poverty.

Reason : The fundamental purpose of social security is to give individuals and families the confidence that their level of living and quality of life will not be eroded, as far as possible, by any social or economic eventuality.

On the basis of the above given statements, choose the correct answer:
(1) Assertion is wrong
(2) Reason is wrong
(3) Individuals or their families cannot be given confidence
(4) The Reason given justifies Assertion

94. An indifference curve between income and leisure shows
(1) various combinations of income and leisure which give different levels of satisfaction

(2) various combinations of income and leisure which give equal satisfaction
(3) same amount of income and leisure at each point on it which give different levels of satisfaction
(4) same amount of income and leisure which give same amount of satisfaction

95. Whether an individual will supply more work effort or less as a result of the use in the wage rate depends on
(1) income effect only
(2) substitution effect only
(3) the relative strength of income and substitution effects
(4) neither income effect nor substitution effect

96. The term 'management exploitation' was given by
(1) Mrs. John Robinson
(2) Prof. Chamberlin
(3) J. B. Clark (4) J. M. Keynes

97. The demand curve of labour of the monopsonist is given by
(1) the curve of value of the marginal product
(2) the curve of marginal revenue productivity
(3) the average factor cost curve
(4) average wage curve

98. In rural India, which type of unemployment is common?
(1) Educated unemployment
(2) Cyclical unemployment
(3) Disguised unemployment
(4) Voluntary unemployment

99. What is true about Weekly status unemployment?
(a) It is measured in number of persons and shows chronic unemployment
(b) It shows both open and chronic unemployment
(c) It is measured in person, days or years and shows underemployment
(d) It shows only open unemployment

Choose the correct answer :
(1) Only (a) (2) (a), (b) and (c)
(3) Only (b) (4) Only (d)

100. According to Lord Keynes, unemployment in advanced economies was due to
(1) lack of supply
(2) deficiency of effective demand
(3) business cycle
(4) lack of both demand and supply

ANSWER KEY

1. (4)	2. (3)	3. (1)	4. (3)	5. (3)	6. (4)	7. (1)	8. (3)	9. (3)	10. (2)
11. (1)	12. (3)	13. (2)	14. (2)	15. (1)	16. (4)	17. (1)	18. (2)	19. (2)	20. (2)
21. (*)	22. (4)	23. (1)	24. (2)	25. (3)	26. (2)	27. (3)	28. (3)	29. (3)	30. (2)
31. (2)	32. (3)	33. (4)	34. (1)	35. (2)	36. (4)	37. (3)	38. (4)	39. (2)	40. (4)
41. (1)	42. (3)	43. (1)	44. (4)	45. (2)	46. (1)	47. (4)	48. (1)	49. (4)	50. (3)
51. (4)	52. (4)	53. (3)	54. (3)	55. (2)	56. (3)	57. (3)	58. (1)	59. (1)	60. (2)
61. (4)	62. (3)	63. (3)	64. (2)	65. (3)	66. (2)	67. (2)	68. (2)	69. (1)	70. (2)
71. (3)	72. (4)	73. (2)	74. (4)	75. (1)	76. (2)	77. (3)	78. (3)	79. (1)	80. (4)
81. (4)	82. (2)	83. (4)	84. (2)	85. (4)	86. (3)	87. (3)	88. (1)	89. (1)	90. (2)
91. (3)	92. (2)	93. (4)	94. (2)	95. (3)	96. (1)	97. (2)	98. (3)	99. (1)	100. (2)

SET II

Note : This paper contains **hundred** (100) Objective type questions, each question carrying **two** (2) marks.

1. What is the definition of job security in Industrial Relations?

(1) The level of assurance that an employee will not be terminated from their job without just cause.

(2) The amount of money an employee is paid for their job.

(3) The number of hours an employee is required to work per week.

(4) The location of the workplace.

2. How do trade unions support the enforcement of labor laws and regulations?

(1) By taking legal action against employers who violate the law

(2) By promoting greater awareness and understanding of labor laws and regulations among workers

(3) By lobbying the government to introduce new labor laws and regulations

(4) By reducing the number of employees in a given industry or sector

3. Which of the following is not a common employee benefit?

(1) Health insurance

(2) Retirement plan

(3) Job title (4) Paid time off

4. What is the concept of employee wellness?

(1) A focus on providing employees with a high salary and benefits package

(2) A focus on helping employees achieve and maintain physical and emotional health

(3) A focus on employee productivity and efficiency

(4) A focus on compliance with labor laws and regulations

5. Which of the following is a common occupational disease associated with exposure to asbestos?

(1) Mesothelioma (2) Tuberculosis

(3) Malaria (4) Influenza

6. In which year was the Factories Act enacted in India?

(1) 1881 (2) 1891

(3) 1911 (4) 1948

7. Human Resource Planning include

(1) Scenario planning

(2) Action planning

(3) Demand and Supply forecasts

(4) All the above

8. Which one is not a part of recruitment process ?

(1) Determining requirements

(2) Planning recruitment campaign

(3) Attracting candidates

(4) Selecting candidates

9. Which one is not a non-quantitative job evaluation method ?

(1) Ranking method

(2) Grading method

(3) Point rating method

(4) Job-classification method

10. **Assertion:** Lockouts are a legitimate means of protest available to the management in the Industrial Disputes Act, 1947.

Reason: The management can lockout employees if there is a labor dispute.

(1) Both assertion and reason are true and the reason is the correct explanation of the assertion.

(2) Both assertion and reason are true but the reason is not the correct explanation of the assertion.

(3) Assertion is true but reason is false.
(4) Assertion is false but reason is true.

11. Which of the following factors are included in the calculation of human development index ?
(1) Life expectancy
(2) Adult literacy
(3) Decent standard of living
(4) All the above

12. Who is not associated with development of human development index ?
(1) Mahabub-ul-Haq
(2) Manmohan Singh
(3) Meghnad Desai
(4) Sudhir Anand

13. The sequence of human resource development activities according to Leonard Nadler are
(1) Education, training and development
(2) Development, training and education
(3) Training, education and development
(4) Training, development and education

14. Who introduced the concept of quality circles in India ?
(1) P. V. Rao (2) Udai Pareek
(3) Dharani P. Sinha
(4) S. R. Udpa

15. Which of the following is the correct sequence of training evaluation ?
(1) Reaction, learning, behaviour and results
(2) Learning, reaction, behaviour and results
(3) Learning, behaviour, reaction and results
(4) Reaction, learning, results and behaviour

16. Which of the following is the outcome of job satisfaction ?
(1) High employee turnover
(2) High productivity
(3) Absenteeism
(4) All the above

17. Under Alderfer's ERG theory, the three core needs are
(1) Emotional, Relational, and Growth
(2) Emotional, Rational and Growth
(3) Existence, Reliability and Gain
(4) Existence, Relatedness and Growth

18. The group to which a person would like to belong is known as
(1) Primary Group
(2) Membership Group
(3) Reference Group
(4) None of the above

19. The Managerial Grid was given by
(1) Rensis Likert
(2) Kurt Lewin
(3) Hersey Blanchard
(4) Blake and Mouton

20. What is the significance of the "schedule of employment" under the Minimum Wages Act, 1948?
(1) It specifies the hours of work per day and per week for each industry.
(2) It specifies the holidays and leave entitlements for each industry.
(3) It specifies the minimum wage rates for each industry and region.
(4) All of the above.

21. Identify the correct definition of industrial relations
(1) Relations between or among human beings
(2) Relations between employer and employees as individuals
(3) Relations between parties in an employment context
(4) Collective relationship between management and trade unions

22. Who has propounded the system concept of industrial relations ? Find out from the following
(1) L. N. Allen Flander
(2) L. N. Flax
(3) John T. Dunlop
(4) Neil N. Chamberlein

23. Which is the correct order of settlement of industrial disputes ?

a. Industrial Tribunal
b. National Tribunal
c. Conciliation
d. Labour Court

(1) c, a, d, b (2) c, d, a, b
(3) a, d, c, b (4) c, b, d, a

24. Which of the following is not a Tripartite body ?

(1) Works Committee
(2) I. L. O
(3) Indian Labour Conference
(4) Wage Boards

25. The code of discipline was ratified by the Indian Labour Conference to ensure discipline in industry. Identify the year of ratification out of the following

(1) 1957 (2) 1958
(3) 1942 (4) 1962

26. Which of the following is not a characteristics of Trade Union ?

(1) Is an association of employers or the employees or of the independent workers?
(2) Is relatively a permanent combination but not temporary or casual.
(3) Is an association of workers who are engaged in not securing economic benefits for their members.
(4) Is influenced by a member of ideologies.

27. Recognition of trade union is made by the provision of

(1) Trade Unions Act of 1926
(2) Industrial Dispute Act 1947
(3) Code of Discipline
(4) Factories Act of 1948

28. Which is not a structure of Trade Union of Industrial Organisation ?

(1) Craft union
(2) General union
(3) Industrial union
(4) Consumers' union

29. A Trade Union should be registered as per the law must have

(1) 20% of the workers
(2) 150 workmen
(3) Minimum 17 persons
(4) None of the above

30. The founder of Ahmedabad Textile Labour Association was

(1) V. V. Giri (2) M. K. Gandhi
(3) B. P. Wadia (4) N. M. Lokhande

31. If there is wilful removal or disregard by the workman of any safety guard or other device which he knew to have been provided for the purpose of securing safety of workman,

(1) Employer is liable to pay compensation
(2) Employer is not liable to pay compensation
(3) Appropriate government is liable to pay compensation
(4) The Trade Union is liable to pay compensation

32. Who is known for developing the theory of total quality management?

(1) Frederick Taylor
(2) W. Edwards Deming
(3) Elton Mayo
(4) Mary Parker Follett

33. The maternity leave period with full wage is

(1) six months
(2) twelve weeks
(3) four months
(4) sixteen weeks

34. Match the following

(a) Royal Commission on Labour	(i) 1937
(b) Bombay Textile Labour Enquiry committee	(ii) 1946
(c) Second Labour Ministers' Conference	(iii) 1929
(d) Labour Investigation Committee	(iv) 2002
(e) Second National Commission on Labour	(v) 1941

Code :

	(a)	(b)	(c)	(d)	(e)
(1)	(ii)	(i)	(iii)	(iv)	(v)
(2)	(iii)	(ii)	(i)	(v)	(iv)
(3)	(iii)	(v)	(iv)	(i)	(ii)
(4)	(iii)	(i)	(v)	(ii)	(iv)

35. The goal of I LO is

(1) creation of jobs for men and women

(2) not just creation of jobs but the creation of jobs of acceptable quality

(3) not overcoming under employment

(4) not to provide freedom of choice in employment

36. The Payment of Bonus Act, 1965 is applicable to an employee who draws wage or salary of

(1) 3500 in case of apprentice

(2) 5000 in case of apprentice and employee

(3) 7500 in case of employee only

(4) 10,000 in case of employee only

37. Unfair Labour Practices are listed in

(1) the Factories Act, 1948.

(2) the Industrial Employment (Standing Orders) Act, 1946.

(3) the Industrial Disputes Act, 1947.

(4) the Trade Unions Act, 1926.

38. The Minimum Wages Act, 1948 has

(1) one schedule covering different types of industries.

(2) one schedule covering different types of industries, shops and establishments.

(3) one schedule covering shops and establishments.

(4) two schedules covering industrial establishments and agriculture.

39. If deduction is made contrary to the provisions of the Payment of Wages Act, 1936 the aggrieved employee can write to the inspector appointed under the Act within the time period given below from the date on which the deduction from wages was made or the date on which the payment of wages is due

(1) two years (2) one year

(3) twelve weeks (4) six weeks

40. The maximum daily hours of work in a day with normal wage allowed in factories is

(1) 11 hours (2) 10 hours

(3) 9 hours (4) 8 hours

41. What is the difference between a trade union and a labor union?

(1) There is no difference between a trade union and a labor union

(2) A trade union represents employees in a particular trade or profession, whereas a labor union represents all employees in a particular industry

(3) A trade union protests against the government, whereas a labor union protests against the management

(4) A trade union operates at the state level, whereas a labor union operates at the national level

42. What is the role of culture in power and authority?

(1) Culture can influence how power and authority are perceived and used within an organisation.

(2) Culture has no effect on power and authority.

(3) Culture is a negative outcome in power and authority.

(4) Culture is an emotional process in power and authority.

43. Who is the champion of the 'Welfare movement' propagated in mid 19th century ?

(1) Frederick Winslow Taylor

(2) Andrew Ure

(3) Sheebhom Rownlvee

(4) Robert Owners

44. Sequence the following developments by their period of occurrence from earliest to the latest :

(i) The Labour Investigation Committee

(ii) The Whitley Commission

(iii) The Enactment of Factories Act

(iv) The 1st National Commission on Labour

(1) (ii) (i) (iii) (iv) (2) (ii) (iii) (iv) (i)
(3) (i) (ii) (iv) (iii) (4) (iv) (ii) (iii) (i)

45. Which of the following statements relating to Welfare Officer is not true
(1) The provision of Welfare Officer is given in both the Factories Act, 1948 and the Mines Act, 1952.
(2) Welfare Officer's duties and responsibilities are defined and prescribed in the legislation.
(3) Welfare Officer's appointment is tagged to the provision of minimum workforce employed in an organisation
(4) The Welfare Officer's role was designed as a 'Third force'.

46. Which of the following statements about characteristics of labour is not true ?
(1) Labour is a perishable commodity.
(2) Labour cannot be separated from the person.
(3) Workers have no reserve price.
(4) Labour is as flexible and mobile as capital.

47. What is the process of grouping jobs based on similarities in tasks and skills?
(1) Job analysis
(2) Job design
(3) Job classification
(4) Performance appraisal

48. Money Wage is otherwise called as
(1) Real wage (2) Living wage
(3) Nominal wage (4) Fair wage

49. Wage Boards set right
(1) Inter-regional differentials
(2) Inter-sectoral differentials
(3) Intra-industry differentials
(4) Inter-industry differentials

50. Which of the following is not a determinant of wages ?
(1) Prevailing wages
(2) Bargaining strength of Unions
(3) Job Evaluation
(4) Performance Appraisal

51. Match the following

Thinker	**Management Principle**
(a) F.W.Taylor	(i) Authority & Responsibility
(b) Henri Fayol	(ii) Hierarchy
(c) Weber	(iii) Separation of planning from doing
(d) Elton Mayo	(iv) Human relation approach

Codes :

	(a)	(b)	(c)	(d)
(1)	(iii)	(i)	(iv)	(ii)
(2)	(iii)	(iv)	(i)	(ii)
(3)	(iii)	(i)	(ii)	(iv)
(4)	(iii)	(ii)	(i)	(iv)

52. Which of the following is the major element of planning process
(1) Developing leadership abilities
(2) Selecting right people
(3) Perception of opportunities
(4) Motivating people

53. Which principle of management is violated by matrix organisation structure?
(1) Division of labour
(2) Unity of direction
(3) Unity of Command
(4) None of the above

54. Which of the following involves careful analysis of inputs and corrective actions before operations is completed?
(1) Feed forward control
(2) Concurrent control
(3) Feedback Control
(4) All the above

55. Which of the following is not a semantic barrier of communication?
(1) Faulty translation
(2) Ambiguous words
(3) Specialist's Language
(4) Inattention

56. People should be regarded as assets rather than variable costs was emphasised in
(1) Personnel Management
(2) Human Resource Management
(3) Personnel Administration
(4) Public Administration

57. The classical theorists favoured organization based
(1) Civilian model
(2) Strategic Model
(C) Military Model
(4) None of the above

58. Job analysis Includes
(1) Job description and job enlargement
(2) Job enlargement and job enrichment
(3) Job description and job Specification
(4) All the above

59 A test which measures, what it is intended to measures is
(1) Reliable test (2) Standardised test
(3) Objective test (4) Valid test

60. An enquiry that is conducted afresh because of the objections raised by alleged employee is called
(1) Domestic Enquiry
(2) De-novo enquiry
(3) Ex-parte enquiry
(4) None of the above

61. The concept of HRD score-card was introduced in India by
(1) Udai Pareek (2) Rao and Pareek
(3) T.V. Rao
(4) Arun Honappa

62. Performance appraisal by all the following parties is called 360 performance appraisal
(1) Supervisors and peers
(2) Subordinate and employees themselves
(3) Users of services and consultant
(4) All of the above

63. The following is the process of training
(1) Instructional design, validation, needs analysis, implementation and evaluation
(2) Need analysis, Instructional design, validation, implementation and evaluation
(3) Needs analysis, validation, , Instructional design, implementation and evaluation
(4) Instructional design, Needs analysis, implementation, validation, and evaluation

64. Fish bone analysis as a tool of quality circle was advanced by
(1) Edward Deming
(2) Joseph Juran
(3) Kouru Ishikawa
(4) Phillip Crosby

65. Match the following

Book and concept	**Authors**
(a) Games people play	(i) Eric Bernie
(b) I am ok you are ok	(ii) Kurt Lewin
(c) Johri Window	(iii) Thomas A Harris
(d) Force analysis	(iv) Joseph Lufth & Harry Inghams

Codes :

	(a)	(b)	(c)	(d)
(1)	(ii)	(i)	(iv)	(iii)
(2)	(i)	(iii)	(iv)	(ii)
(3)	(iv)	(ii)	(iii)	(i)
(4)	(iii)	(i)	(ii)	(iv)

66. Which of the following decreases group cohesiveness?
(1) Agreement on group goals
(2) Frequency of interaction
(3) Large group size
(4) All the above

67. Mangers subscribing to ______ assumption attempts to structure, control and closely supervise their employees.
(1) Theory "X"
(2) Theory "Y"
(3) Both theory "x" and theory "Y"
(4) Neither Theory "X" nor theory "Y"

68. According to fielder contingency model of leadership ,which one of the following is a situational variable?
(1) Leader-member relationship
(2) Organisational system
(3) Degree of task structure
(4) Leader position power

69. The right sequences of steps in Kurt lewin change procedure is
(1) Unfreezing-Moving -Freezing
(2) Moving, Unfreezing - Freezing
(3) Unfreezing- Freezing- Moving
(4) Freezing, Moving, Unfreezing

70. Which of the following is not a traditional methods of organisational development?
(1) Survey feed back
(2) Sensitivity training
(3) Process consultation
(4) Managerial grid

71. Characteristics of industrial relations do not include
(1) Industrial Relations are outcome of employment relationship in an industrial enterprise.
(2) Industrial relation promote the skill and methods of adjustment and cooperation
(3) IR create complex rules and regulation to maintain Industrial relation
(4) IR system creates environment of distrust and conflict.

72. Who are not the actors of Industrial relation
(1) Workers and their organisation
(2) Employer and their organisation
(3) Community and cultural association
(4) Government

73. Which of the following is a machinery for settlement of ID?
(1) Indian labour conference
(2) Joint management Council
(3) Industrial Tribunal
(4) Government & the role of the state

74. Match the following

List-I	List-II
(a) JMC consisting of representative of workers and Management was considered by the ILC in its 15th session in the year	(i) 1958
(b) Work committee were set up under ID act in the year.	(ii) 1947
(c) ILO was established	(iii) 1919
(d) First commission on labour submitted its report	(iv) 1969

Codes :

	(a)	(b)	(c)	(d)
(1)	(i)	(ii)	(iii)	(iv)
(2)	(iv)	(i)	(iii)	(ii)
(3)	(iii)	(i)	(ii)	(iv)
(4)	(ii)	(iv)	(i)	(ii)

75. Which of the following trends in the employment relation in the new economic era is not correct?
(1) Declining stability and security
(2) Declining labour stability
(3) No shift from contract of service to contact of service
(4) Declining Mutual Commitment.

76. What is the definition of "inspector-cum-facilitator" under The Employees' Provident Fund and Miscellaneous Provisions Act, 1952?
(1) A person appointed by the government who is responsible for both inspection and facilitation of the employers and workers
(2) A person appointed by the government who is responsible only for inspection of the employers and workers
(3) A person appointed by the employer who is responsible for both inspection and facilitation of the employees
(4) None of the above

77. A union may claim recognition for an industry in a local area, if it has membership of
(1) 10% of the worker in that industry
(2) 15% of the worker in that industry
(3) 25% worker in that industry
(4) 30% of the worker in similar industry

78. Who among the following advocated the trusteeship theory of trade union?
(1) N.M. Lokhande (2) B.P. Wadia
(3) G.L. Nanda (4) M.K. Gandhi

79. Inter and Intra union Rivalry in trade union are reduced by
(1) The provision of the Industrial Disputes act, 1947
(2) By Voluntary tripartite code of inter union revelry
(3) By Bipartite mutual agreement at industry level
(4) All of the above

80. Match the following

List-I	List-II
(a) AITUC	(i) 1947
(b) CITU	(ii) 1948
(c) INTUC	(iii) 1920
(d) HMS	(iv) 1970

Codes :

	(a)	(b)	(c)	(d)
(1)	(iii)	(iv)	(i)	(ii)
(2)	(ii)	(iii)	(iv)	(i)
(3)	(iii)	(i)	(ii)	(iv)
(4)	(i)	(ii)	(iii)	(iv)

81. What is a child under the Child Labour (Prohibition and Regulation) Act, 1986?
(1) A person who is below 14 years of age
(2) A person who is below 18 years of age
(3) A person who is below 21 years of age
(4) None of the above

82. Under ESI act, 1948 a member of the corporation ,standing committee or the medical council shall cease to be a member of the body if he fails to attend.
(1) Two consecutive meeting
(2) Three consecutive intermittently
(3) Two consecutive meeting
(4) Two consecutive meeting

83. Under workman compensation act,1923
(1) individual manager subordinate to an employer cannot act as managing agent.
(2) managing agent includes an individual manager subordinate to an employer.
(3) only employer can act as managing agent.
(4) The appropriate government shall appoint managing agent.

84. The workman compensation act 1923, the maternity benefit act, 1965, and the employee state insurance act,1948
(1) Together can be applicable
(2) The maternity benefit act and the employee state insurance act can be applicable at a time
(3) If the workman compensation act and the maternity benefit act are applicable, employee state insurance act can be applicable at a time
(4) and the employee state insurance act can be applicable at a time

85. What is the content of the schedule I of the ESI act, 1948
(1) List of injuries deemed to be result in permanent total disablement
(2) List of injuries deemed to be result in permanent partial disablement
(3) List of occupational diseases
(4) None of the above

86. A person qualified to be chosen as a member of the executive or any other office bearer of the registered trade union if he attained the age of.
(1) Fifteen years
(2) Eighteen years
(3) Twenty one years
(4) Twenty five years

87. The registered trade union can collect political fund from its member as a
(1) General fund
(2) Cannot collect political fund

(3) Separate fund from the interested members
(4) Only from political parties

88. 'Award Under the Industrial Disputes act' 1947 is
(a) Not interim determination of labour court
(b) Not arbitration award under section 10 A
(c) Not final determination of labour court
(d) Not final determination of arbitration award under section 10A
(1) All statements are true
(2) (a) and (b) are true
(3) (b) are true
(D) All statements are wrong

89. What are the components of Attitude?
(1) Cognitive, affective, and behavioural
(2) Social, cultural, and economic
(3) Formal, informal, and experiential
(4) Kinesthetic, auditory, and visual

90. The ceiling on wage or salary under the payment of bonus act 1965 is
(1) Rs 2,500 (2) Rs 3, 500
(3) Rs 4,500 (4) Rs 6,500

91. "A desirable state of existence comprehending physical, mental, moral and emotional health as well being" is the theme of which concept of labour welfare?
(1) Social Concept
(2) Total Concept
(3) Relative concept
(4) Positive concept

92. **Assertion (A) :** Labour welfare is relative to time and space.
Reason (R): It shall be universal and perceptual.
(1) Assertion and Reason are right
(2) Assertion is wrong but Reason is Right
(3) Both Assertion and Reason are wrong
(4) The Assertion is right but Reason is wrong

93. Minimum condition of welfare is explained by
(1) Dr Akykriod formula
(2) Subsistence theory
(3) Both (1) & (2)
(4) None of the above

94. Which of the following is not a principle of labour welfare
(1) The principle of uniformity
(2) The principle of coordination
(3) The principle of coordination and integration
(4) The principle of timeliness

95. Which of the following is the term used to describe the phenomenon where prices rise over time, leading to a fall in purchasing power?
(1) Inflation (2) Interest rate
(3) Growth rate
(4) Unemployment rate

96. Labour is not a commodity"- is the assertion made by
(A) The declaration of Philadelphia adopted by 26th session of ILO
(2) The Magna Carta
(3) The Constitution of India
(4) The International Labour Conference.

97. Match the following

Concept	**Propagators**
(a) Industrial Democracy	(i) Karl MARX
(b) Industrial Citizenship	(ii) Robert Owen
(c) Class Conflict	(iii) Peter. F. Drucker
(d) Welfare Movement	(iv) Sydney and Beatrice Webb

Codes :

	(a)	**(b)**	**(c)**	**(d)**
(1)	(iii)	(i)	(ii)	(iv)
(2)	(iv)	(iii)	(i)	(ii)
(3)	(ii)	(i)	(iv)	(iii)
(4)	(ii)	(iv)	(i)	(iii)

98. **Assertion (A):** Industrial Labour in India has been Migratory
Reason (R): Driving forces in migration comes almost entirely from one end of the channel, that is village end
(1) Both Assertion and Reason are wrong.
(2) Assertion is wrong but Reason is Right
(3) The Assertion is right and Reason is also right
(4) The Assertion is right but Reason is wrong

99. What is the role of labour legislation in promoting social justice?
(1) To ensure fair and equitable treatment of workers
(2) To provide equal opportunities in the workplace
(3) To address historical and systemic inequalities in the labour market
(4) All of the above

100. What is the term used to describe the provision of benefits such as health insurance and retirement benefits to workers?
(1) Social protection
(2) Social welfare
(3) Social safety net
(4) Social inclusion

ANSWER KEY

1. (1)	2. (2)	3. (3)	4. (2)	5. (1)	6. (4)	7. (4)	8. (4)	9. (3)	10. (1)
11. (4)	12. (2)	13. (3)	14. (4)	15. (1)	16. (2)	17. (4)	18. (3)	19. (4)	20. (4)
21. (4)	22. (3)	23. (2)	24. (1)	25. (2)	26. (3)	27. (3)	28. (4)	29. (4)	30. (2)
31. (2)	32. (2)	33. (1)	34. (4)	35. (2)	36. (4)	37. (3)	38. (4)	39. (2)	40. (3)
41. (1)	42. (1)	43. (4)	44. (1)	45. (2)	46. (4)	47. (3)	48. (3)	49. (3)	50. (4)
51. (3)	52. (3)	53. (3)	54. (1)	55. (4)	56. (2)	57. (3)	58. (3)	59. (4)	60. (2)
61. (3)	62. (4)	63. (2)	64. (3)	65. (2)	66. (3)	67. (1)	68. (2)	69. (1)	70. (3)
71. (4)	72. (3)	73. (3)	74. (1)	75. (3)	76. (1)	77. (3)	78. (4)	79. (2)	80. (1)
81. (1)	82. (3)	83. (4)	84. (4)	85. (4)	86. (2)	87. (3)	88. (4)	89. (1)	90. (2)
91. (2)	92. (4)	93. (3)	94. (1)	95. (1)	96. (1)	97. (2)	98. (3)	99. (4)	100. (1)

PREVIOUS YEARS' PAPERS

DECEMBER, 2019

LABOUR WELFARE & INDUSTRIAL RELATIONS, LABOUR & SOCIAL WELFARE, HUMAN RESOURCE MANAGEMENT

PAPER-II

Note : This paper contains **hundred (100)** objective type questions, each question carrying **two (2)** marks.

1. Which one of the following is NOT associated with authority?
(1) Right to issue directions
(2) Obligation to perform the assigned tasks
(3) Delegated from superior to subordinates
(4) Flows from top to bottom

2. Among the following, who is known as the father of Human Relations Approach'?
(1) Henri Fayol (2) F.W. Taylor
(3) J. Woodward (4) Elton Mayo

3. Taylor advocated 'Functional Foremanship' to introduce :
(1) Differential piece-wage plan
(2) Standardisation
(3) Work study
(4) Specialisation

4. Factors with the high probability of impact and high degree of impact are known as :
(1) High priority factors
(2) Low priority factors
(3) Critical factors
(4) Factors to be watched

5. Which one of the following is NOT a principle of coordination?
(1) Direct contact
(2) Early start
(3) Precise and comprehensive programmes and policies
(4) Continuity

6. Who among the following introduced the 'principle of bounded rationality'?
(1) Herbert Simon
(2) Max H. Bazerman
(3) Teresa M. Amabile
(4) Weihrich and Koontz

7. Who described the mechanistic and organic or behavioural organization structures?
(1) Tom Burns and G.M. Stalker
(2) Terry and Franklin
(3) Robert H Miles
(4) Kathryn M. Bartol and David C. Martin

8. Who said that. "Coordination is the orderly arrangement of group efforts to provide unity of action in the pursuit of a common purpose"?
(1) George R. Terry
(2) Ralph C. Davis
(3) Chester Barnard
(4) James D. Mooney

9. A systematic procedure for collecting, storing, maintaining, retrieving and validating data needed by an organization about its human resources is termed as :
(1) Human Resource Forecasting
(2) Human Resource Information System
(3) Human Resource Scanning
(4) Human Resource Succession Planning

10. Which of the following is NOT an item of job description statement'?
(1) Experience
(2) Job summary
(3) Working conditions
(4) Hazards

11. Explaining the relationship between satisfaction and performance, which of the following models suggests that performance leads to satisfaction?

(1) Maslow's Need Hierarchy Model
(2) Herzberg's Two Factor Model
(3) Adam's Equity Model
(4) Porter-Lawler Model

12. From among the following, which one is NOT an avoidance mode of conflict management?
(1) Resignation (2) Appeasement
(3) Negotiation (4) Defusion

13. Which of the following two leadership behaviour patterns were identified by Ohio State Studies?
(1) Employee Orientation and Production Orientation
(2) Initiating Structure and Consideration
(3) Concern for Production and Concern for People
(4) Personalism/Materialism and Opportunism

14. The Propinquity Theory of group formation explains that groups are formed on the basis of :
(1) Spatial or geographical proximity
(2) Similar attitudes towards commonly relevant objects and goals
(3) Activities, interactions and sentiments
(4) Reward-cost outcomes of interactions

15. While staffing a multinational company, if the top management considers national subsidiaries as independent units and allows them to fill management posts themselves with host-country nationals, then the approach is known as :
(1) Etlmocentricity
(2) Polycentricity
(3) Geocentricity
(4) Regiocentricity

16. Dunning's eclectic theory has identified three conditions which must be met by a company that Wishes to set up production in a foreign country and wants to operate as a multinational. Which of the following is NOT included in the three conditions given by Dunning?
(1) Location advantages
(2) Internationalization advantages
(3) Ownership advantages
(4) Quality advantages

17. Taking into consideration the four different layers of culture as suggested by Hofstede identify which one of the following is the first or outermost level?
(1) Rituals (2) Heroes
(3) Symbols (4) Values

18. Edgar Schein has identified different dimensions of organizational roles, one of which is a social dimension. Which one of the following terms is associated with the social dimension?
(1) Inclusionary (2) Functional
(3) Hierarchial (4) Exclusionary

19. In which Section of the Industrial Employment (Standing Orders) Act, 1946, there is a provision for payment of subsistence allowance?
(1) Section 10 (2) Section 10 A
(3) Section 11 (4) Section 12 A

20. Which Article of the Constitution of India deals with the prohibition of Employment of Children in Factories etc.?
(1) Article 17 (2) Article 19
(3) Article 24 (4) Article 25

21. Which of the following is the first convention adopted by the International Labour Organisation in the year 1919?
(1) Hours of Work (Coal Mines) Convention
(2) Hours of Work (Industry) Convention
(3) Hours of Work (Commerce and Offices) Convention
(4) Hours of Work and Rest Periods (Road Transport) Convention

22. The employment of young persons on dangerous machines is prohibited under which Section of the Factories Act. 1948?
(1) Section 21 (2) Section 22
(3) Section 23 (4) Section 24

23. What is the limitation period for filing prosecution from the date on which the alleged commission of offence comes to the knowledge of the Inspector under the provisions of the Contract Labour (Regulation and Abolition) Act. 1970?

(1) Within two months
(2) Within three months
(3) Within six months
(4) Within twelve months

24. What percent of the number of days an employee of a seasonal establishment has to work out of the total number of the days the establishment is operational, in order to claim to be in continuous service under the provisions of the Payment of Gratuity Act. 1972?

(1) Fifty percent
(2) Sixty percent
(3) Seventy five percent
(4) Ninety percent

25. Under the Minimum Wages Act, 1948, a minimum rate of remuneration to apply in the case of employees employed on piece work, for the purpose of securing such employees a minimum rate of wages on a time work basis is known as :

(1) A minimum time rate
(2) A minimum piece rate
(3) A guaranteed time rate
(4) Overtime rate

26. As per the provisions of the Minimum Wages Act, 1948, a claim shall be presented within which time period from the date on which, the minimum wages become payable?

(1) Two months (2) Three months
(3) Six months (4) Twelve months

27. As per the provisions of the Payment of Bonus Act, 1965, set off can be done for next how many accounting years?

(1) Five years (2) Four years
(3) Two years (4) Six years

28. What is the time limit within which the employer is required to pay bonus to the employees, in case of any dispute relating to bonus, on which the award becomes enforceable or the settlement comes into operation as per the provisions of the Payment of Bonus Act. 1965?

(1) One month (2) Two months
(3) Six months (4) Eight months

29. As per the amendment made in the Payment of Wages Act 1936 III the year 2005 who shall appoint inspectors for the purpose of the Payment of Wages Act in respect of all persons employed upon a railway (otherwise than in a factory) to whom the provisions of the Act apply?

(1) The Central Government
(2) The State Government
(3) The appropriate Government
(4) The Chief Inspector

30. As per the provisions of the Industrial Employment (Standing Orders) Act, 1946, a Standing Order finally certified shall not be modified until the expiry of how many days/months'?

(1) Fifteen days (2) Thirty days
(3) Three months (4) Six months

31. Which of the following is NOT included in the definition of 'Wages' as mentioned in the Payment of Wages Act. 1936?

(1) Bonus as a part of salary.
(2) Remuneration payable under any award or settlement between the parties or order of a Court.
(3) Remuneration in respect of overtime work or any leave period.
(4) Any travelling allowances or the value of any travelling concession.

32. Which one of the following matters does NOT fall within the jurisdiction of the 'Industrial Tribunal' constituted under the provisions of the Industrial Disputes Act, 1947'?

(1) Classification by Grades
(2) Rationalisation
(3) Leave with Wages and Holidays

(4) Illegality or otherwise of a strike or lock-out

33. Which one of the following is to be held as an 'Industry', under the definition of 'Industry mentioned in the Industrial Disputes Act, 1947?

(1) Posts and Telegraph Department
(2) Construction and Maintenance of Highways
(3) Central Institute of Fisheries
(4) The Dock Labour Board

34. "Same work or work of a similar nature" is defined under which one of the following legislations?

(1) The Payment of Wages Act
(2) The Minimum Wages Act
(3) The Equal Remuneration Act
(4) The Payment of Bonus Act

35. In which three Articles of the Constitution of India, provisions have been specified for ensuring health and safety of workers?

(1) Articles 24, 25 and 26
(2) Articles 38, 39 (e and f) and 37
(3) Articles 24, 39 (e and f) and 42
(4) Articles 41, 42 and 43

36. Safety departments in industrial units have both Human Resource Unit and Safety Managers. From amongst the functions mentioned below, which is NOT the function of Human Resource Unit in a safety department?

(1) Coordinating health and safety programmes
(2) Investigating accidents
(3) Accidents investigation expertise
(4) Providing technical expertise on accident prevention

37. Based on the statement given below, choose the correct option:

'The strength of the demand for any particular type of labour will depend upon the marginal productivity of labour and the market value of the product'.

(1) The statement is correct
(2) The statement is wrong
(3) Marginal productivity of labour has nothing to do with demand for labour
(4) Market value or price of the product and demand for labour are not related

38. Based on the statement given below choose the correct option:

'For the industry as a whole, the supply of labour is not infinitely elastic'.

(1) The statement is not true
(2) The statement is true
(3) Supply of labour to a given firm is inelastic
(4) The elastic character is not relevant in the context of supply of labour

39. In a developing economy like India, unemployment is the result of:

(1) Deficiency of effective demand in the Keynesian sense
(2) Displacement of workers
(3) Shift from Primary to Tertiary Sector
(4) Shortage of capital equipment or other complimentary resources

40. 'Open Unemployment' is also known as:

(1) Weekly Status Unemployment
(2) Daily Status Unemployment
(3) Usual Principal Status Employment
(4) Seasonal Unemployment

41. Consider the following management theories

(a) Systems theory
(b) Quantitative theory
(c) Behavioural Science theory
(d) Contingency theory

Which of the above are modern management theories"

(1) Only (a) and (b)
(2) Only (a) and (c)
(3) Only (a), (b) and (d)
(4) (a), (b), (c) and (d)

42. Consider the following statements related to HR Audit:

(a) HR Audit is a method of evaluating the current Human Resource Development
(b) HR Audit also helps in calculating the investments made in training and estimating the returns on such investments
(c) HR Audit assesses the training needs and utilization of training as a tool for organizational learning, growth and development

Which of the above is/are correct?

(1) Only (a) (2) Only (b)
(3) Only (a) and (c) (4) (a), (b) and (c)

43. Choose the correct answer regarding the theories of motivation from the following statements:

(a) The concept of ERG theory is similar to Maslow's hierarchy of needs
(b) Theory 'X' and 'Y are similar to each other
(c) Two factor theory is similar to Vroom's theory

Choose the correct option from the following:

(1) Only (a) (2) Only (b)
(3) Only (a) and (b) (4) (a), (b) and (c)

44. Given below are some of the barriers of communication:

(a) Perceptions
(b) Interpersonal sensitivity
(c) Differing frames of reference
(d) Information overload

From among the above identify the barriers, which are considered as sender-related barriers?

(1) (b) and (c) (2) (a) and (b)
(3) (b) and ((d) (4) (c) and (d)

45. Consider the following:

(a) Challenging work
(b) Responsibility
(c) Status
(d) Job security
(e) Recognition

Which of the above are motivators under Herzberg's Two Factor Theory?

(1) (a) and (c) only
(2) (c), (d) and (e) only
(3) (a), (b) and (e) only
(4) (b), (c), (d) and (e) only

46. Given below are some of the terms along with authors associated with them which of the following pairs are correctly matched?

(a) Product Life Cycle — Vernon
(b) Core Competence — Reich
(c) Zero-sum Nationalism — Prahalad and Hamel
(d) Balanced Score Card — Norton

(1) (a) and (b) (2) (b) and (c)
(3) (b) and (d) (4) (a) and (d)

47. Some of the areas relating to organizational change are given below:

(a) Marketing (b) Structure
(c) Strategy (d) Technology
(e) Costs (f) Managing people

Choose the correct option from those given below, which includes the areas relating to the process of change.

(1) (a), (c) and (e) (2) (b), (d) and (f)
(3) (b), (c) and (f) (4) (a), (b) and (c)

48. The four methods of job evaluation are given below:

(a) Ranking Method
(b) Factor Comparison Method
(c) Job Classification Method
(d) Point Rating Method

Choose the correct option from those given below which come under the Quantitative/Analytical methods:

(1) (b) and (d) (2) (a) and (c)
(3) (b) and (c) (4) (a) and (d)

49. Given below are some of the methods of Demand Forecasting relating to Human Resource Planning.

(a) Managerial Judgement
(b) Work-Study Technique
(c) Expert Opinion
(d) Delphi Technique
(e) Group Brainstorming
(f) Nominal Group Technique

Choose the correct option from those given below, which come under the qualitative methods for demand forecasting :

(1) (a), (b) and (e) (2) (c), (d) and (f)
(3) (a), (c) and (d) (4) (b), (c) and (d)

50. Some of the areas relating to organizational change are given below :

(a) Marketing (b) Technology
(c) Quality (d) Structure
(e) Strategy
(f) Managing people

Choose the correct option from those given below, which gives the list relating to content of change.

(1) (a), (b), (e) and (f)
(2) (a), (b) and (c)
(3) (a), (d) and (e)
(4) (b), (c), (d) and (f)

51. Given below are different modes of conflict management.

(a) Resignation (b) Confrontation
(c) Appeasement (d) Negotiation
(e) Defusion

From among the following, choose the alternative, which gives the approach modes of conflict management

(1) (b) and (d) (2) (a) and (e)
(3) (c) and (e) (4) (c) and (d)

52. Which of the following statements relating to the Governing Body of the ILO are correct?

(a) The Governing Body is a non-legislative body
(b) The tenure of the office of the Governing Body is ten years
(c) The Governing Body seeks advisory opinion from the International Court of Justice
(d) It scrutinises the budget of the ILO with the consent of the International Labour Conference

Select the correct option :

(1) (a) and (b) only
(2) (a), (b), (c) and (d)
(3) (a), (c) and (d) only
(4) (b), (c) and (d) only

53. Which of the following statements relating to the Grievance Redressal Machinery envisaged under Chapter II of the Industrial Disputes Act. 1947 are correct?

(a) Every industrial establishment employing twenty or more workmen shall have one or more Grievance Redressal Committee for the resolution of disputes arising out of individual grievances.
(b) The Grievance Redressal Committee shall consist of equal number of members from the employer and the workmen.
(c) The total number of members of the Grievance Redressal Committee shall not exceed more than four.
(d) The Grievance Redressal Committee may complete its proceedings within thirty days of receipt of an application by or on behalf of the aggrieved party.

Select correct option :

(1) Only (a), (b) and (c) are correct
(2) Only (b), (c) and (d) are correct
(3) Only (a), (b) and (d) are correct
(4) Only (a), (c) and (d) are correct

54. Given below are different bodies provided under the Industrial Disputes Act. 1947.

(a) Works Committee
(b) Court of Inquiry
(c) Board of Conciliation
(d) Grievance Redressal Committee

From among the following, which alternative includes the bodies whose functioning is based on the principle of bipartite representation?

(1) Only (a) and (b)
(2) Only (a) and (d)
(3) Only (b) and (d)
(4) Only (a), (b) and (d)

55. Which of the following statements relating to the ILO are correct?

(a) The ILO was established by Versailles Peace Conference on April 12, 1919.

(b) India became member of ILO in 1921.
(c) The ILO became a specialized agency of United Nations in 1946.
(d) The International Labour Conference is the policy making organ of the ILO.

Select the correct option :
(1) (a) and (b) only
(2) (a), (b), (c) and (d)
(3) (b) and (c) only
(4) (c) and (d) only

56. Which of the following matters are specified in Schedule II of 'Participation of Workers in Management Bill, 1990?
(a) Matters relating to operational areas
(b) Matters relating to economic and financial areas
(c) Matters relating to welfare areas
(d) Matters relating to environmental areas

Choose the correct option :
(1) Only (a) and (b)
(2) Only (b) and (c)
(3) Only (a), (b) and (d)
(4) (a), (b), (c) and (d)

57. Which of the following strikes are categorized as 'strikes based on generic purposes'?
(a) Sympathetic strikes
(b) Jurisdictional strikes
(c) Political strikes
(d) General strikes

Choose the correct option :
(1) (a) and (b) only
(2) (a), (b) and (c) only
(3) (b), (c) and (d) only
(4) (a), (b), (c) and (d)

58. The following were some of the developments that took place in the trade union movement in India. Arrange the same in the correct sequence starting from the earliest to the latest.
(a) Formation of National Front of Indian Trade Unions
(b) Formation of Bharatiya Mazdoor Sangh
(c) Formation of Centre of Indian Trade Unions
(d) Formation of Indian Federation of Labour

Choose the correct option :
(1) (a), (b), (c), (d)
(2) (d), (b), (a), (c)
(3) (b), (c), (d), (a)
(4) (c), (a), (b), (d)

59. Arrange in a sequence, the following legislations in the order of years in which those were enacted from the latest to the earliest.
(a) The Mines Act
(b) The Plantation Labour Act
(c) The Beedi and Cigar Workers (conditions of Employment) Act
(d) The Factories Act

Choose the correct option from the following :
(1) (a), (b), (c), (d) (2) (b), (a), (d), (c)
(3) (c), (a), (b), (d) (4) (d), (c), (b), (a)

60. Chronologically arrange the following Chapters which were inserted in the Industrial Disputes Act. 1947 by way of amendments starting from the earliest to the latest"
(a) Chapter II A (b) Chapter II B
(c) Chapter V A (d) Chapter V B

Choose the right option from the following
(1) (a), (b), (c), (d) (2) (c), (a), (d), (b)
(3) (b), (d), (a), (c) (4) (a), (c), (d), (b)

61. Under the provisions of the Mines Act, 1952 an owner or agent of a mine is required to provide which of the following facilities for the persons employed in the mine?
(a) Drinking water
(b) Conservancy
(c) Medical appliances
(d) Recreation facilities

Choose the correct option from the following :
(1) (a), (b) and (d) only
(2) (a), (c) and (d) only
(3) (a), (b) and (c) only
(4) (b), (c) and (d) only

62. Which of the following are considered to be the Principles of Labour Legislation?

(a) Principle of Protection
(b) Principle of Social Justice
(c) Principle of Welfare
(d) Principle of Reasonable Standard of Living

Choose the correct option from the following:

(1) (a), (b) and (d) only
(2) (b), (c) and (d) only
(3) (a), (b) and (c) only
(4) (a), (c) and (d) only

63. There exist certain essential elements of Social Insurance. Which amongst the following are NOT elements of Social Insurance?

(a) Compulsory participation
(b) Contributory finance
(c) No governmental sponsorship
(d) Benefits directly related to contribution

Choose the correct option from the following:

(1) (a) and (b) (2) (c) and (d)
(3) (a) and (c) (4) (b) and (d)

64. Which amongst the following are NOT the characters of labour market in India?

(a) Labour markets lack mobility
(b) Labour markets are perfect markets
(c) Relationship between buyer and seller is expected to continue for sometime barring 'casual labour' market
(d) Monopoly in labour market no more exists today

Choose the correct option:

(1) (a) and (b)
(2) (c) and (d)
(3) (a) and (c)
(4) (b) and (d)

65. Labour Welfare in the present context is the combination of which two of the following theories:

(a) The Police Theory
(b) The Philanthropic Theory
(c) The Placating Theory
(d) The Functional Theory

Choose the correct option from the following:

(1) (a) and (b) (2) (c) and (d)
(3) (a) and (c) (4) (b) and (d)

66. Match List -I with List-II:

List-I (Authors)	**List-II (Books)**
(a) Douglas C McGregor	(i) Functions of the Executive
(b) Elton Mayo	(ii) The New Science of Management Decision
(c) Herbert A. Simon	(iii) The Human Side of Enterprise
(d) Chester Barnard	(iv) Human Problems of an Industrial Civilization

Choose the correct option from those given below:

(1) (a)-(ii), (b)-(iv), (c)-(iii), (d)-(i)
(2) (a)-(iii), (b)-(iv), (c)-(ii), (d)-(i)
(3) (a)-(i), (b)-(iv), (c)-(ii), (d)-(iii)
(4) (a)-(i), (b)-(ii), (c)-(iii), (d)-(iv)

67. Match List-I with List-II

List-I (Training Techniques)	**List-II (Description)**
(a) Skill games	(i) Games to test ability to plan ahead
(b) Mirroring	(ii) Insight into a given interaction
(c) Strategic Planners	(iii) Test to develop analytical skills
(d) Monodrama	(iv) Training with an external perspective

Choose the correct option from those given below:

(1) (a)-(i), (b)-(iii), (c)-(iii), (d)-(iv)
(2) (a)-(iv), (b)-(iii), (c)-(ii), (d)-(i)
(3) (a)-(ii), (b)-(iii), (c)-(iv), (d)-(i)
(4) (a)-(iii), (b)-(iv), (c)-(i), (d)-(ii)

68. Match List-I with List-II

List-I (Performance Appraisal Methods)	List-II (Description)
(a) Alternation Ranking Method	(i) An appraisal method that aims at combining the benefits of narrative critical incidents and quantified ratings by anchoring a quantified scale with specific narrative examples of good and poor performance
(b) Paired Comparison Method	(ii) Keeping a record of uncommonly good or undesirable examples of an employee's work related behavior an reviewing it with the employee at predetermined times
(c) Behaviourally-anchored rating Method	(iii) Ranking employees from best to worst on a particular trait, choosing highest, then lowest, until all are ranked
(d) Critical Incident Method	(iv) Ranking employees by making a chart of all possible pairs of the employees for each trait and indicating which is the better employee of the pair

Incident Method choose the correct option from those given below :

(1) (a)-(iii), (b)-(iv), (c)-(i), (d)-(ii)
(2) (a)-(iii), (b)-(i), (c)-(iii), (d)-(iv)
(3) (a)-(iv), (b)-(iii), (c)-(ii), (d)-(i)
(4) (a)-(ii), (b)-(iii), (c)-(iv), (d)-(i)

69. Adler and Ghadar in their approach of internationalization of HRM activities have identified four phases which are given in List-I and the purpose that is served in each phase given in List II.

List I (Phases)	List II (Purpose)
(a) Domestic	(i) Career and organizational development
(b) International	(ii) Project and career development
(c) Multinational	(iii) Project to get job done
(d) Global	(iv) Reward

Select the alternative from the options given below, giving the correct match between the phases and purpose :

(1) (a)-(iv), (b)-(iii), (c)-(ii), (d)-(i)
(2) (a)-(i), (b)-(ii), (c)-(iii), (d)-(iv)
(3) (a)-(iii), (b)-(iv), (c)-(i), (d)-(ii)
(4) (a)-(ii), (b)-(i), (c)-(iv), (d)-(iii)

70. The three learning outcomes are given in List-I, and the aspects covered under them in List-II.

List I (Learning outcomes)	List II (Aspects Covered)
(a) Cognitive	(i) Knowledge organization
(b) Skill based	(ii) Compilation
(c) Affective	(iii) Attitudinal

Choose the alternative, from the options given below, which gives the right match between

(1) (a)-(ii), (b)-(i), (c)-(iii)
(2) (a)-(i), (b)-(iii), (c)-(ii)
(3) (a)-(ii), (b)-(iii), (c)-(i)
(4) (a)-(i), (b)-(iii), (c)-(iii)

71. Given below are three types of competencies in List-I, and their characteristics in List-II

List I (Competencies)	List II (Characteristics)
(a) Universal competency	(i) Competencies refer to specialized know-how or abilities required within a specific role
(b) Transferrable competency	(ii) Competencies emphasize that all the employees of an organization must reflect the company's value, culture and business imperatives
(c) Unique competency	(iii) Competencies include skills and abilities needed to perform several roles in varying degrees of importance and mastery

Choose the correct alternative, from the options given below, which gives the right match between the competencies and the characteristics

(1) (a)-(i), (b)-(ii), (c)-(iii)
(2) (a)-(iii), (b)-(i), (c)-(ii)
(3) (a)-(i), (b)-(iii), (c)-(ii)
(4) (a)-(ii), (b)-(iii), (c)-(i)

72. Given below are the names of scholars in List-I, and the approaches to industrial relations with which they are associated in List-II

List I (Scholars)	List II (Approaches to Industrial Relations)
(a) John R. Commons	(i) Industrial Sociology Approach
(b) Elton Mayo	(ii) Oxford Approach
(c) Allan Flanders	(iii) Human Relations Approach
(d) G. Margerison	(iv) Economic Approach

Match List-I with List-II, and choose the correct match from the options given below :

(1) (a)-(iv), (b)-(iii), (c)-(ii), (d)-(i)
(2) (a)-(iii), (b)-(iv), (c)-(i), (d)-(ii)
(3) (a)-(ii), (b)-(i), (c)-(iv), (d)-(iii)
(4) (a)-(i), (b)-(ii), (c)-(iii), (d)-(iv)

73. Given below are some of the provisions laid down under the Factories Act, 1948 in List-I and number of workers that should be working in a factory given in List-II for providing those facilities.

List I (Provisions)	List II (Number of workers)
(a) Cool drinking water	(i) More than one hundred fifty
(b) Welfare Officer	(ii) One thousand or more
(c) Shelter Room	(iii) Five hundred or more
(d) Safety Officer	(iv) More than two hundred fifty

Find the correct match between List-I and List-II from the options given below:

(1) (a)-(iii), (b)-(ii), (c)-(iv), (d)-(i)
(2) (a)-(ii), (b)-(i), (c)-(iii), (d)-(iv)
(3) (a)-(iv), (b)-(iii), (c)-(i), (d)-(ii)
(4) (a)-(i), (b)-(iv), (c)-(ii), (d)-(iii)

74. Match List I with List II

List I (Forms of knowledge)	List II (Description)
(a) Shallow knowledge	(i) Information that is directly related to context
(b) Procedural knowledge	(ii) Information that some individuals are not aware of what they know
(c) Casual knowledge	(iii) Information that finds cause-effect relationship
(d) Specific knowledge	(iv) Information that tells people why something occurs

Choose the correct option from those given below :

(1) (a)-(i), (b)-(ii), (c)-(iii), (d)-(iv)
(2) (a)-(ii), (b)-(iii), (c)-(iv), (d)-(i)
(3) (a)-(iv), (b)-(iii), (c)-(i), (d)-(ii)
(4) (a)-(ii), (b)-(i), (c)-(iii), (d)-(iv)

75. Match the themes relating to the definition of labour welfare given in List-I with the scholars/institutions who have put forward the themes given in List-II

List I (Themes)	**List II (Scholars/ Institutions)**
(a) Attitude of mind	(i) A.J. Todd
(b) Improvement in existing industrial system	(ii) Encyclopaedia of Social Sciences
(c) Voluntary efforts beyond what is required by law	(iii) R.R. Hopkins
(d) Comfort and improvement in intellectual and social state	(iv) E.S. Proud

Choose the correct option from those given below :
(1) (a)-(i)- (b)-(iii), (c)-(iv), (d)-(ii)
(2) (a)-(i), (b)-(iv), (c)-(ii), (d)-(iii)
(3) (a)-(iii), (b)-(iv), (c)-(ii), (d)-(i)
(4) (a)-(iii), (b)-(ii), (c)-(iv), (d)-(i)

76. Arrange the following elements of the process of interpersonal communication in sequential order :
(a) the message (b) the channel
(c) feedback (d) the sender
(e) the receiver (f) the encoding
(g) the decoding
Choose the correct option from the following :
(1) (d), (f), (a), (b), (g), (e) and (c)
(2) (a), (d), (e), (g), (b), (c) and (f)
(3) (a), (b), (d), (f), (e), (c) and (g)
(4) (b), (a), (c), (d), (f), (g) and (e)

77. Systematically arrange the five step process of human resource planning given below and choose the correct option :
(a) Forecast of personnel needs and supply
(b) HR Programming
(c) Defining Organisational Objectives and Policies
(d) HRP Implementation
(e) Control and evaluation of programmes
Choose the correct option from the following :
(1) (a), (b), (c), (d), (e)
(2) (b), (a), (b), (d), (e)
(3) (c), (b), (a), (d), (e)
(4) (c), (a), (b), (d), (e)

78. Given below are the steps involved in the selection process
(a) Application Blank
(b) Employment interviews
(c) Physical Examination
(d) Employment tests
(e) Appointment Letter
(f) Reference checks
Choose the alternative from the options given below mentioning the right sequence of the steps starting from the beginning
(1) (a), (d), (c), (b), (f), (e)
(2) (a), (b), (c), (d), (f), (e)
(3) (a), (d), (b), (c), (e), (f)
(4) (a), (d), (b), (f), (c), (e)

79. Given below are different Committees/Commissions set up in India relating to Labour
(a) First National Commission on Labour
(b) Adarkar Committee
(c) Second National Commission on Labour
(d) Rege Committee
Choose the option which gives chronological sequence of their set up starting from the earliest to the latest :
(1) (b), (d), (a), (c) (2) (c), (b), (d), (a)
(3) (a), (c), (b), (d) (4) (b), (a), (c), (d)

80. Given below are the various stages of the conflict process
(a) Cognition and personalisation
(b) Interventions
(c) Potential opposition or incompatibility

(d) Outcomes
(e) Behaviour

Choose the right option which gives the correct sequence of the stages starting from the beginning :

(1) (a), (c), (b), (d), (e)
(2) (b), (a), (c), (e), (d)
(3) (b), (c), (e), (a), (d)
(4) (c), (a), (b), (e), (d)

81. Given below are different stages of group formation :

(a) Storming (b) Norming
(c) Adjourning (d) Forming
(e) Performing

Choose the right option which gives the correct sequence of the steps starting from the beginning:

(1) (a), (d), (e), (b), (c)
(2) (d), (a), (b), (e), (d)
(3) (a), (b), (e), (d), (c)
(4) (c), (a), (b), (e), (d)

82. Arrange the following in correct sequence basing on the years in which they came into force/passed/setup, starting from the earliest to latest :

(a) Board for Industrial and Financial Reconstruction
(b) The Second Industrial Truce Resolution
(c) Code of Discipline
(d) National Institution for Transforming India Aayog

Choose the correct option from the following :

(1) (a), (b), (c) and (d)
(2) (c), (b), (a) and (d)
(3) (b), (c), (a) and (d)
(4) (d), (a), (c) and (b)

83. Arrange the following in a correct sequence basing on the years of their formation starting from the earliest to the latest

(a) Federation of Indian Chamber of Commerce and Industry
(b) Associated Chamber of Commerce
(c) Employers' Federation of India
(d) All India Organisation of Industrial Employers

Choose the correct option from the following

(1) (a), (b), (c), (d) (2) (b), (c), (d), (a)
(3) (b), (a), (d), (c) (4) (a), (c), (b), (d)

84. Arrange in a proper sequence the authorities mentioned in the Industrial Disputes Act, 1947 in resolving grievances or disputes of workmen, starting from the beginning :

(a) Labour court
(b) Grievance Redressal Machinery
(c) Conciliation Officer

Choose the correct option from the following :

(1) (a), (b), (c) (2) (b), (a), (c)
(3) (c), (b), (a) (4) (b), (c), (a)

85. The Government of India has ratified few conventions of ILO relating to child labour. Arrange the conventions in a sequence from the earliest to the latest as per the years of their adoption by ILO :

(a) Night work of Young Persons (Industry) Convention
(b) Medical Examination of Young Persons (Sea) Convention
(c) Night Work of Young Persons (Industry) Convention (Revised)
(d) Minimum Age (Underground Work) Convention

Choose the correct option from the following :

(1) (a), (b), (c) and (d)
(2) (b), (c), (d) and (a)
(3) (d), (c), (b) and (a)
(4) (a), (c), (d) and (b)

86. Given below are two statements – one is labelled as Assertion (A) and the other is labelled as Reason (R) :

Assertion (A) : Management development is one major way for organizations to increase the chances that managers will be effective.

Reasons (R) : While many have believed that ability to manage was primarily an inborn quality, the current view is that capabilities required to be an effective manager can be learned and enhanced

In the light of the above two statements, choose the correct option :

(1) Both (A) and (R) are true and (R) is the correct explanation of (A)
(2) Both (A) and (R) are true and (R) is not the correct explanation of (A)
(3) (A) is true, but (R) is false
(4) (A) is false, but (R) is true

87. Given below are two statements – one labelled as Assertion (A) and the other is labelled as Reason (R) :

Assertion (A) : In the early stages of internationalization of business organizations, it was based on the notion that the logic of industrialism had a homogenizing effect upon business organizations, irrespective of the country they were located in

Reasons (R) : The cultural approach emphasised national differences between the organizations, differences which have cultural factors at their root.

In the light of the above two statements, choose the correct option :

(1) Both (A) and (R) are false
(2) (A) is true and (R) are is false
(3) Both (A) and (R) are true
(4) (A) is false and (R) is true

88. Given below are two statements – one labelled as Assertion (A) and the other labelled as Reason (R) :

Assertion (A) : Trade Unionism in India, as in most other countries, has been the natural outcome of modern factory system

Reasons (R) : In order to counter exploitation, efforts towards organizing the workers for safe-guarding their legitimate position were made by the unions

In the light of the above two statements, choose the correct option :

(1) Both (A) and (R) are true, and (R) is not the correct explanation of (A)
(2) Both (A) and (R) are true, and (R) is the correct explanation of (A)
(3) (A) is true, but (R) is false
(4) (A) is false, but (R) is true

89. Given below are two statements — one is labelled as Assertion (A) and the other is labelled as Reason (R) :

Assertion (A) : Industrial relations constitute one of the most delicate and complex problems of modern industrial society, which is characterized by rapid change, industrial unrest and conflicting ideologies in the national and international spheres

Reasons (R) : It is a dynamic concept which depends upon the pattern of society, economic system and political set-up of a country and changes with the changing economic and social order

In the light of the above two statements, choose the correct option :

(1) Both (A) and (R) are true, and (R) is the correct explanation of (A)
(2) Both (A) and (R) are true, and (R) is not the correct explanation of (A)
(3) (A) is true, but (R) is false
(4) (A) is false, but (R) is true

90. Two statements namely Assertion (A) and Reason (R) are given below :

Assertion (A) : Labour welfare implies the setting up of minimum desirable standards and the provision of facilities

Reasons (R) : Such facilities enable the worker and his/her family to lead a good work, family and social life.

In the light of the above two statements, choose the correct option :

(1) Both (A) and (R-) are true, and (R) is the correct explanation of (A)
(2) Both (A) and (R) are true, and (R) is not the correct explanation of (A)
(3) (A) is true, but (R) is false
(4) (A) is false, but (R) is true

Read the passage carefully and answer the questions :

"A principal fruit of friendship", Francis Bacon wrote in his timeless meditation on the subject 'is the case and discharge of the fullness and swellings of the heart, which passions of all kinds do cause and induce'. For Thoreau, friendship was one of life's great rewards. But in today's cultural landscape of muddled relationship scattered across various platforms for connecting, amid constant debates about whether our Facebook 'friendships' are making us more or less happy, it pays to consider what friendship actually is : That's precisely what 'CUNY' Philosophy Professor Massimo Pigliucci explores in answers for Aristotle : How science and philosophy can lead us to a more meaningful life, which also gave us this provocative read on science of what we call 'intuition.

Philosophers and cognitive scientists agree that friendship is an essential ingredient of human happiness. But beyond the dry academic definitions — like, say, 'voluntary interdependence between two persons overtime, which is intended to facilitate socio-emotional goals of the participants, and may involve varying types and degrees of companionship. Intimacy, affection and mutual assistance' – lies a body of compelling research that sheds light on how, precisely, friendship augments happiness.

The way friendship enhances well-being, it turns out, has nothing to do with quantity and everything to do with quality — researchers confirm that it is not the number of friends or, in case of Facebook, 'friendships'.

Sub questions

91. Which one change effected in the present situation hassled to a re-thinking of the concept of friendship?
(1) Bacon and Thoreau's Theories
(2) The arrival of social media on the scene
(3) There is more interest in science
(4) Friendships are not possible in the real world anymore due to over-competition

92. Whether the views expressed in the passage advocate that friendship is an essential component of well-being? Choose the correct option :
(1) Researches have proved that friendship does lead to happiness
(2) There exists no relationship between passage and happiness
(3) Friends cannot make each other happy
(4) One needs to find one's happiness alone with peace of mind

93. Which of the following is true in the context of Pigliucci's books?
(1) Pigliucc's book discusses science only
(2) The book explains science and philosophy only
(3) The book discusses Aristotle's theories only
(4) Pigliucc's book discusses 'intuition'.

94. In the context of the passage, which of the following is true about friendship?
(1) It is important to have quantity of friends
(2) What is important is comments on social media, not quality of friends
(3) What is important is quality of friends
(4) Quality automatically comes with quantity

95. What is being debated according to the content given in the first paragraph? Choose the correct option.
(1) The debate is centred around whether our facebook friends are helping us become more or less happy.
(2) There are no debates.
(3) The quality of comments on social media is debated.
(4) It is debated that Thoreau's and Aristotle's thinking are at loggerheads.

Question Numbers : (96 to 100)

Question Label : Comprehension

Read the passage carefully and answer the questions that follow :

The International Cricket Council (ICC) announced that the then Pepsico Chairman and CEO Indra Nooyi has been appointed to the ICC

Board as the organisations first independent female Director. Mrs. Nooyi joined the Board in June 2018 to align with the term of ICC Independent Chairman, following the Unanimous confirmation of her appointment at Board's meeting.

The introduction of an independent Director, who must be female, was approved by the ICC full council in June 2017 as part of wide ranging constitutional change aimed at improving the global governance of the sport.

Mrs. Nooyi is a global business leader, consistently ranked by Fortune Magazine among the world's most powerful women. As Chairman and CEO of Pepsico, Mrs. Nooyi was responsible for a global food and beverage portfolio that includes 22 brands generating more than $ 1 billion each in annual retail sales, including Quaker. Tropicana, Gatorade. Frito-lay and Pepsi cola. Mrs. Ncoyi is also the chief architect of performance with purpose. Pepsico's vision to deliver top tier financial performance over the long term by integrating sustainability into company's business strategy. Under her leadership, since 2006 Pepsico has focused on offering more nutrious food and beverages, minimizing their impact on the environment and creating opportunities for their employees and people across the markets they serve.

ICC Chairman Shashank Manohar said : "We are delighted to welcome Indra to ICC. Adding another independent director, particularly a female, is such an important step forward in improving our governance. To have someone of Indra's calibre is fantastic news for the global game. She is frequently recognized as one of the most important and influential people in business today, running one of the world's biggest corporations". "We undertook a global search looking for the right candidate who would complement the existing skills and experience already on our Board. A cricket enthusiast with experience in the commercial sector and independent of ICC, any member or state or associated organization were the primary criteria and in Indra, we have found an exceptional new colleague and we look forward to Working with her in future".

The independent director will be appointed for a two-year term although she may be re-appointed for two further terms with maximum six year consecutive period of service.

In accordance with international standards of good governance, the Independent Ethics Officer for the ICC and Pepsico's General Counsel have reviewed and both formally approved the appointment, providing a clear framework for appropriately managing any potential or perceived conflicts of interest that might arise in the future.

96. Which amongst the following is true in the context of the passage?

(1) Indra Nooyi is the first female chairman of International Cricket Council

(2) She may be reappointed for two further terms resulting in nine years of total service

(3) She may be re-appointed for two further terms with a maximum six years consecutive period of service

(4) Indra Nooyi is ranked number one in the list of most powerful woman by Fortune Magazine

97. What does the writer want to convey by saying 'Mrs. Nooyi is also the chief architect of performance with purpose?

(1) Mrs. Nooyi has started objective based planning in Pepsico

(2) Mrs. Nooyi has driven the concept of corporate social responsibility

(3) Mrs. Nooyi does not want to make profit at the cost of consumer's health

(4) With her vast experience of leadership, Mrs. Nooyi's induction in ICC will improve its global performance

98. What was the purpose of introducing female independent director in International Cricket Council?

(1) To improve global governance of the sport

(2) To prove that Women are better than men

(3) To set an example of gender equality

(4) To fulfill the requirement of constitutional change

99. Which amongst the following confirmed the appointment of Indra Nooyi?

(1) Board of International Cricket Council

(2) General Council of Pepsico

(3) Independent Ethics Officer of ICC

(4) Chairman of ICC

100. Which among the following is NOT true in the context of the passage?

(1) Quaker is a product of Pepsico

(2) Mrs. Nooyi headed over 22 food and beverage brands under the flagship of Pepsico

(3) In order to earn more profit, Pepsico ignores the environment

(4) Mrs. Nooyi was elected unanimously as the Director of ICC

ANSWER KEY

1. (2)	**2.** (4)	**3.** (4)	**4.** (3)	**5.** (3)	**6.** (1)	**7.** (1)	**8.** (4)	**9.** (2)	**10.** (1)
11. (4)	**12.** (3)	**13.** (2)	**14.** (1)	**15.** (2)	**16.** (4)	**17.** (3)	**18.** (1)	**19.** (2)	**20.** (3)
21. (2)	**22.** (3)	**23.** (2)	**24.** (3)	**25.** (3)	**26.** (3)	**27.** (2)	**28.** (1)	**29.** (3)	**30.** (4)
31. (4)	**32.** (4)	**33.** (4)	**34.** (3)	**35.** (3)	**36.** (2)	**37.** (1)	**38.** (2)	**39.** (4)	**40.** (3)
41. (3)	**42.** (4)	**43.** (1)	**44.** (1)	**45.** (3)	**46.** (4)	**47.** (3)	**48.** (1)	**49.** (2)	**50.** (2)
51. (1)	**52.** (3)	**53.** (3)	**54.** (2)	**55.** (4)	**56.** (4)	**57.** (4)	**58.** (2)	**59.** (3)	**60.** (2)
61. (3)	**62.** (3)	**63.** (2)	**64.** (1)	**65.** (2)	**66.** (2)	**67.** (4)	**68.** (1)	**69.** (1)	**70.** (4)
71. (4)	**72.** (1)	**73.** (3)	**74.** (2)	**75.** (3)	**76.** (1)	**77.** (4)	**78.** (4)	**79.** (1)	**80.** (4)
81. (2)	**82.** (2)	**83.** (3)	**84.** (4)	**85.** (1)	**86.** (1)	**87.** (3)	**88.** (2)	**89.** (1)	**90.** (1)
91. (2)	**92.** (1)	**93.** (4)	**94.** (3)	**95.** (1)	**96.** (3)	**97.** (4)	**98.** (4)	**99.** (1)	**100.** (3)

SEPTEMBER, 2020

LABOUR WELFARE & INDUSTRIAL RELATIONS, LABOUR & SOCIAL WELFARE, HUMAN RESOURCE MANAGEMENT

PAPER-II

Note : This paper contains **hundred (100)** objective type questions, each question carrying **two (2)** marks.

1. The statement "I love the company. I am working for, I love my job, I am a learning state and I am growing because of my organisation and so I will give my company the best in return" is associated with

(1) The Eiffel Tower Culture
(2) The Family Culture
(3) The Incubator Culture
(4) The Guided Missile Culture

2. "Minimum requirement about membership of a Trade Union," as Section 9A, inserted by way of an amendment in the Trade Unions Act, 1926, came into force from :

(1) 09th January, 2020
(2) 09th January, 2002
(3) 01st April, 2002
(4) 01st July, 2001

3. Which of the following human resource forecasting techniques is considered as the 'quickest forecasting technique'?

(1) Managerial Judgement
(2) Ratio-Trend Analysis
(3) Delphi technique
(4) Regression analysis

4. Selection criteria for selection of staff for international assignment are broadly categories under two categories namely: individual and situation. Which of the following is covered under the situation criteria?

(1) Language
(2) Family requirements
(3) Technical ability
(4) Cross-Cultural suitability

5. The provision relating to 'Subsistence allowance' finds place under which one of the following legislations?

(1) The Industrial Disputes Act, 1947
(2) The Industrial Employment (Standing Orders) Act, 1946
(3) The Trade Unions Act, 1926
(4) The Plantation Labour Act-. 1951

6. Based on the statement given below, choose the correct option :

'Changes in product demand that increase the product price will raise the marginal revenue product of labour and therefore, increase the demand for labour.'

(1) The statement is wrong
(2) The statement is correct
(3) The demand for product has nothing to do with marginal revenue product of labour
(4) Even if the demand for product increases, the marginal physical product of labour shall remain constant

7. Which among the following is left out while calculating natural rate of Unemployment?

(1) Seasonal Unemployment
(2) Frictional Unemployment
(3) Structural Unemployment
(4) Cyclical Unemployment

8. Under the provisions of the Industrial Employment (standing orders) Act, 1946, a certified standing order shall not be modified until the expiry of which period from the date, the certified standing order came into operation?

(1) Two months (2) Three months
(3) Six months (4) Twelve months

9. Which one of the following subjects is not enumerated in the 'Concurrent List' of Indian Constitution?
(1) Oil fields
(2) Trade Unions
(3) Factories
(4) Vocational and Technical Training of labour

10. Which of the following statement is correct to define 'child' as per the provisions of the child and Adolescent Labour (Prohibition and Regulation) Act, 1986?
(1) A person who has not completed his fourteenth year of age:
(2) A person who has not completed such age as may be specified in the Right of Children to Free and Compulsory Education Act, 2009:
(3) A person who has not completed his fourteenth year of age or such age as may be specified in the Right of Children to Free and Compulsory Education Act, 2009, whichever is more:
(4) A person who has not completed his fourteenth year of age or such age as may be specified in the Right of Children to Free and Compulsory Education Act, 2009, whichever is less.

11. As per the provisions of the Minimum Wages Act, 1948. Which of the following authority advises the appropriate government for fixing and revising minimum wages and coordinating the work of the committees and sub-committees constituted under the Act?
(1) The Advisory Committee
(2) The Central Advisory Board
(3) Advisory Board
(4) The Central Government

12. Shops and Commercial Establishment Legislation comes under which one of the categories of Labour Legislations?
(1) Welfare Legislations
(2) Social Security Legislations
(3) Protective Labour Legislations
(4) Wage Legislations

13. Under the provisions of the Payment of Bonus Act, 1965, an employee of an establishment, shall be entitled for bonus to be paid by the employer provided the employee has worked for a minimum period of how many days in the establishment in a financial year?
(1) Thirty Days
(2) Sixty Days
(3) Ninety Days
(4) Two hundred forty Days

14. Ranking employees from the best to worst on a particular trait, choosing highest then Lowest, until all are ranked is termed as :
(1) Graphic Rating Scale
(2) Alternation Ranking Method
(3) Paired Comparison Method
(4) Forced Distribution Method

15. The process for enabling employees to better understand and develop their career skills and Interests, and to use these skills and interest more effectively is called as
(1) Career Development
(2) Career Management
(3) Career Planning
(4) Career Counselling

16. What percentage of the net profit of the company, the top managers are entitled for their compensation under the Companies Act, 2013?
(1) 4 Percent (2) 11 Percent
(3) 20 Percent (4) 10 Percent

17. Which approach suggests that there is no best way to handle any of the management problems and there is no best organisational structure to suit all situations?
(1) Operational Approach
(2) Contingency Approach
(3) Case/empirical Approach
(4) System Approach

18. Who among the following is called "the father of brainstorming?

(1) Alex F. Osborn
(2) W. Edwards Deming
(3) Frank and William Gilbreth
(4) Thomas Peters

19. A Leader who guide or motivate their followers in the direction of established goals by clarifying role and task requirements is :
(1) Transformational Leader
(2) Charismatic Leader
(3) Transactional Leader
(4) Facilitative Leader

20. Giving employees more authority to make decisions is known as :
(1) Authority
(2) Responsibility
(3) Employee Empowerment
(4) Decentralization

21. As per Vroom's Expectancy Theory of motivation 'Instrumentality' relates?
(1) Efforts to Performance
(2) Efforts with first level outcome
(3) Performance with first level outcome
(4) First level outcome to second level outcome

22. Based on the statement given below, choose the correct option :
'In the case of decrease in product demand, marginal revenue product of labour will decline.'
(1) The statement is wrong
(2) The statement is correct
(3) The demand for product has nothing to do with marginal revenue product of labour
(4) Even if the demand for product decreases, the marginal physical product of labour shall remain constant.

23. System theory of organisation was given by
(1) Max Weber (2) Chester Barnard
(3) Robert Owen (4) F.W. Taylor

24. SOBC model is used to identify the major variables in organisational behaviour and to show how they relate to another. Choose from the following, the alternative that gives the correct terms for the letters SOBC
(1) Structure, Organisation, Behaviour, Cognition
(2) Stimulus, Organisation, Behaviour, Control
(3) Stimulus, Organism, Behaviour, Consequences
(4) Structure, Opportunity, Behaviour, Consequences

25. Revitalising the competitive position of a company through innovativeness learning and strong organisational commitment relating to organisational change is known as :
(1) Re-invention (2) Re-orientation
(3) Strategic Intent (4) Strategic Development

26. Who among the following have distinguished four different phases in the business environment for multinational corporations based on the criteria of price, quality, product line and uniqueness
(1) Bartlett and Ghosal
(2) Heckscher and Ohlin
(3) Adler and Morgan
(4) Bolwijn and Kumpe

27. Who among the following is associated with the Theory of Andragogy relating to Learning?
(1) Edward de Bono
(2) L.S. Vygotsky
(3) G.S. Reynolds
(4) Malcom Knowles

28. According to whom, multiculturalism and geographic dispersion are the two factors that differentiate between domestic and multinational corporations?
(1) N.J. Adler (2) F. Acuff
(3) Robert Reich (4) P.V. Morgan

29. As per the classification of trade unions made by Robert F. Hoxie, the 'Business Unionism' is also known as :
(1) Bread and Butter Unionism

(2) Friendly Unionism
(3) Revolutionary Unionism
(4) Predatory Unionism

30. Who among the following is associated with the idea that human personality progresses along a continuum from immaturity as an infant to maturity as an adult?
(1) Chris Argyris (2) Daniel Levinson
(3) Erik Erikson (4) Sigmund Freud

31. Who among the following has given the concept of the structure of psyche in terms of id, ego and superego?
(1) S. Schachter (2) Carl Yung
(3) Sigmund Freud (4) Eric Berne

32. A method for determining compensation for the international staff, where it takes all costs incurred by the employee in both the home country and host country, is known as :
(1) Balance Sheet System
(2) Budget System
(3) Home-net System
(4) Local going-rate System

33. Based on the statement given below, choose the correct option :
'Man is believed to have an instinctive urge by which he strives to remove the suffering of others and promote their well being.' This concept is imbibed in which theory of labour welfare?
(1) Trusteeship Theory
(2) Public Relations Theory
(3) Philanthropic Theory
(4) The Functional Theory

34. The 'Out Worker' is defined under which of the following legislation?
(1) The Industrial Employment (Standing Orders) Act, 1946
(2) The Contract Labour (Regulation and Abolition) Act, 1970
(3) The Employees' Compensation Act, 1923
(4) The Payment of Wages Act, 1936

35. In which year the committee on conventions was set up in India?
(1) 1924 (2) 1934
(3) 1944 (4) 1954

36. In which year, the Rule S1 (A) was added to the Defence of India Rules?
(1) 1939 (2) 1942
(3) 1945 (4) 1947

37. According to the Trade Unions Act, 1926, a registered trade union can change its name only when it obtains the consent of not less than :
(1) One-fourth of its total number of members
(2) One-third of its total number of members
(3) One-half of its total number of members
(4) Two-thirds of its total number of members

38. Transaction Analysis is associated with
(1) Intrapersonal Conflict
(2) Interpersonal Conflict
(3) Union Management Conflict
(4) Inter Group Conflict

39. Allowing past performance appraisal ratings to unjustifiably influence current ratings is known as :
(1) Rater effect (2) Primacy effect
(3) Spillover effect (4) Status effect

40. Who made the classification of industrial relations systems as :
(a) the Peasant-lord system: (b) the primitive market system: (c) the small manufactory system: (d) the life-time commitment system: (e) the bipartite system: (f) the tripartite system: (g) the corporatist-bureaucratic system: (h) the mobilizing system: and (i) the socialist system?
(1) Richard Peterson
(2) John T. Dunlop
(3) Robert Cox
(4) H.S. Kirkaldy

41. Given below are two statements : One is labelled as Assertion A and the other is labelled as Reason R.

Assertion (A) : Administrative heritage is a barrier to the process of transformation of a domestic company into a multinational corporation.

Reason (R): Proper understanding of the administrative heritage of a company may be the key to initiating the transformation process.

In the light of the above statements, choose the most appropriate answer from the options given below :

(1) Both (A) and (R) are correct and (R) is the correct explanation of (A)
(2) Both (A) and (R) are correct but (R) is NOT the correct explanation of (A)
(3) (A) is correct but (R) is not correct
(4) (A) is not correct but (R) is correct

42. Given below are two statements : One is labelled as Assertion A and the other is labelled as Reason R.

Assertion (A): A person who makes things happen believes in his objectives and he will see to it that they are met regardless of the difficulties.

Reason (R): Such a person is fully alerted to competition and is determined to keep so far in front of the competition that cannot overtake him

In the light of the above statements, choose the most appropriate answer from the options given below :

(1) Both (A) and (R) are correct and (R) is the correct explanation of (A)
(2) Both (A) and (R) are correct but (R) is NOT the correct explanation of (A)
(3) (A) is correct but (R) is not correct
(4) (A) is not correct but (R) is correct

43. Given below are two statements : One is labelled as Assertion A and the other is labelled as Reason R.

Assertion (A): Wages and hours of work, according to Bargaining theory of wages, are ultimately determined by the relative bargaining strength of employers and the workers.

Reason (R): The theory advocates that there is an upper limit and a lower limit of wage rates and the actual rate of wages between these limits are determined by the bargaining power of employers and workers.

In the light of the above statements, choose the most appropriate answer from the options given below :

(1) Both (A) and (R) are correct and (R) is the correct explanation of (A)
(2) Both (A) and (R) are correct but (R) is NOT the correct explanation of (A)
(3) (A) is correct but (R) is not correct
(4) (A) is not correct but (R) is correct

44. Given below are two statements : One is labelled as Assertion A and the other is labelled as Reason R.

Assertion (A): Collective Bargaining provides for procedural and substantial rules. Procedural rules concern mechanism for dealing with interpretations and implementation of agreements as well as resolving conflicts, whereas, substantial rules concern the substance of agreement, in both market and managerial relationships.

Reason (R): Collective Bargaining is viewed as a process of give and take rather than 'giving in'.

In the light of the above statements, choose the most appropriate answer from the options given below :

(1) Both (A) and (R) are correct and (R) is the correct explanation of (A)
(2) Both (A) and (R) are correct but (R) is NOT the correct explanation of (A)
(3) (A) is correct but (R) is not correct
(4) (A) is not correct but (R) is correct

45. Given below are two statements : One is labelled as Assertion A and the other is labelled as Reason R.

Assertion (A): There is a welcome realization about the need to transform the traditional adversarial industrial relations into a cooperative mould to build a new, vibrant and competitive economy/enterprise.

Reason (R): Enterprises have realized that it is essential for their survival in this competitive age.

In the light of the above statements, choose the most appropriate answer from the options given below :

(1) Both (A) and (R) are correct and (R) is the correct explanation of (A)
(2) Both (A) and (R) are correct but (R) is NOT the correct explanation of (A)
(3) (A) is correct but (R) is not correct
(4) (A) is not correct but (R) is correct

46. Given below are some of the conventions adopted by ILO. Arrange those conventions in a sequence from the earliest to latest according to the years of adoption.

(A) The Protection of Wage Convention
(B) The Minimum Wage Fixing Machinery Convention
(C) The Holidays with Pay Convention
(D) The Minimum Wage Fixing Machinery (Agriculture) Convention

Choose the correct answer from the options given below :

(1) (A), (C), (B), (D)
(2) (B), (C), (A), (D)
(3) (B), (D), (A), (C)
(4) (A), (B), (D), (C)

47. Arrange the following steps in proper sequence relating to HR Planning

(A) Forecast of Personnel needs and supplies
(B) Defining organizational objectives and policies
(C) Control and evaluation
(D) H.R. Programming
(E) HRP implementation

Choose the correct answer from the options given below

(1) (A), (B), (D), (E), (C)
(2) (D), (E) (B), (C), (A)
(3) (B), (D), (A), (C), (E)
(4) (B), (A), (D), (E), (C)

48. Given below are the matters provided in different schedules of the Employee's Provident Fund and Miscellaneous Provisions Act, 1952. Arrange them in a sequence from Schedule I to IV as provided in the Act.

(A) Matters for which provision may be made in the Pension Scheme
(B) Matters for which provision may be made in a Scheme
(C) Matters to be provided for in the Employees' Deposit-linked Insurance Scheme
(D) List of Industry notified

Choose the correct answer from the options given below :

(1) (B), (D), (C), (A)
(2) (D), (B), (A), (C)
(3) (B), (A), (C), (D)
(4) (C), (A), (D), (B)

49. Arrange the following components of Guest Model of HRM in proper sequence?

(A) Behavioural Outcomes
(B) HRM Practices
(C) HR outcomes
(D) Performance outcomes
(E) HRM Strategies

Choose the correct answer from the options given below:

(1) (B), (C), (E), (D), (A)
(2) (E), (B), (C), (A), (D)
(3) (A), (B), (C), (E), (D)
(4) (C), (A), (D), (E), (B)

50. Given below the ILO Conventions ratified by the Government of India? Arrange them in a chronological order according to the year of ratification starting from the earliest to the latest.

(A) Hours of work (Industry) Convention
(B) Underground work (Women) Convention
(C) Prevention of Major Industrial Accidents Convention
(D) Labour Inspection Convention

Choose the correct answer from the options given below :

(1) (A), (B), (C), (D)
(2) (A), (B), (D), (C)
(3) (C), (A), (B), (D)
(4) (A), (D), (C), (B)

51. Identify the correct sequence of the following from options in the light of the lowest to the highest level

(A) Living Wage
(B) Minimum Wage
(C) Fair Wage

Choose the correct answer from the options given below :

(1) (C), (A), (B) (2) (B), (C), (A)
(3) (C), (B), (A) (4) (B), (A), (C)

52. The schemes under the Provident Fund Act, 1952 enacted at different years. Arrange those schemes according to their year of enactment from the earliest to the latest.

(A) Employees' Pension Scheme
(B) Family Pension Scheme
(C) Employees' Deposit-linked Insurance Scheme
(D) Employees Provident Fund Scheme

Choose the correct answer from the options given below :

(1) (A), (D), (C), (B)
(2) (A), (C), (B), (D)
(3) (D), (B), (C), (A)
(4) (B), (D), (C), (A)

53. Appreciative Inquiry Process was developed by David Cooperrider and Suresh Srivastava giving four phases. Arrange the four phases from one to four :

(A) Dream
(B) Design
(C) Discovery
(D) Delivery

Choose the correct answer from the options given below :

(1) (B), (C), (A), (D)
(2) (C), (A), (B), (D)
(3) (B), (A), (D), (C)
(4) (D), (A), (C), (B)

54. Given below is a list of organisations. Arrange them in a chronological order starting from the earliest to the latest on the basis of the years of their formation.

(A) Bombay Mill Hands Association.
(B) Amalgamated Society of Railway Servants in India and Burma.
(C) Madras Labour Union.
(D) Indian Federation of Labour

Choose the correct answer from the options given below :

(1) (A), (B), (C), (D)
(2) (A), (C), (B), (D)
(3) (B), (C), (D), (A)
(4) (C), (B), (A), (D)

55. The four steps of frustration cycle is given below. Arrange the correct sequence of frustration cycle.

(A) Adaptive deterioration
(B) Isolation
(C) Defensive Behaviour
(D) Distorted Perception

Choose the correct answer from the options given below

(1) (A), (C), (D), (B)
(2) (A), (B), (D), (C)
(3) (C), (A), (B), (D)
(4) (B), (A), (D), (C)

56. Choose the correct options regarding theories of Motivation :

(A) The concept of ERG theory is similar to Maslow's hierarchy of needs.
(B) Theory 'X' has positive assumptions while theory 'Y' has negative assumptions.
(C) Two factor theory is derived by Mcgregor.

Choose the correct answer from the options given below :

(1) (A) only
(2) (A) and (B) only

(3) (B) and (C) only
(4) (A), (B) and (C) only

57. T.V. Rao has described four indicators, which can be used to arrive at a comprehensive score for HRD maturity. Identify the four indicators from the following :
(A) HRD System Maturity Score
(B) HRD Competence Score
(C) The HRD Innovation Score
(D) Business Linkage Score
(E) The HLRD Culture
Choose the most appropriate answer from the options given below :
(1) (A), (B), (C), (D) only
(2) (A), (B), (D), (E) only
(3) (A), (B), (C), (E) only
(4) (B), (C), (D), (E) only

58. Contingency Theories of leadership were developed by :
(A) Blake and Mouton
(B) Fiedler
(C) Hickson
(D) Vroom and Yetton
Choose the correct answer from the options given below :
(1) (A), (B) and (C) only
(2) (A), (C) and (D) only
(3) (B), (C) and (D) only
(4) (A), (B) and (D) only

59. Trait Theories of Leadership were developed by :
(A) Stogdill
(B) Mc call and Lombardo
(C) Bermis and Thomas
(D) Kurt Lewin
Choose the correct answer from the options given below :
(1) (A) and (B) only
(2) (A), (B) and (C) only
(3) (A), (C) and (D) only
(4) (A), (B), (C) and (D) only

60. Given below are some of the matters Within the jurisdiction of the Industrial Tribunals. As per the provisions of the Industrial Disputes Act, 1947, which option is correct?
(A) Hours of work and rest intervals
(B) Leave with wages and holidays
(C) The application and interpretation of standing orders
(D) Rules of Discipline
Choose the correct answer from the options given below :
(1) (A), (B), (C) only
(2) (B), (C), (D) only
(3) (A), (B), (D) only
(4) (A), (C), (D) only

61. Given below are some of the provisions relating to Strikes and Lockouts in Public Utility services under the I.D. Act, 1947. No person employed in a public utility service shall go on strike :
(A) Without giving to the employer notice of strike within six weeks before striking
(B) Within Forty Five days of giving such notice
(C) Before the expiry of the date of strike specified in any such notice as aforesaid
(D) During the pendency of any conciliation proceeding before a conciliation officer and fifteen days after the conclusion of such proceedings
Choose the correct answer from the options given below :
(1) (A) and (C) only
(2) (A), (B) and (C) only
(3) (A), (C) and (D) only
(4) (A), (B), (C), (D) only

62. Given below are some incentive schemes. Find out the schemes which are covered under the category "Earnings very less proportionately than output"?
(A) Hasley Plan
(B) Emerson's Efficiency Plan
(C) Bath Scheme
(D) Rowan Plan

Choose the correct answer from the options given below :

(1) (A), (B), (C) only

(2) (B), (C), (D) only

(3) (A), (C), (D) only

(4) (A), (B), (D) only

63. Given below are some of the training methods for the executives. Choose the methods which are covered under off-the-job methods.

(A) Special Projects

(B) Programmed Instructions

(C) Committee Assignment

(D) Conference Training

Choose the most appropriate answer from the options given below :

(1) (B) and (C) only

(2) (A), (B) and (C) only

(3) (A) and (D) only

(4) (B) and (D) only

64. As per the provisions of the Payment of Gratuity Act, 1972, the definition of 'family' in relation to an employee includes :

(A) In case of male employee, himself, his wife, his children whether married or unmarried his dependent parents, and children of his predeceased son, if any

(B) In case of female employee, herself, her husband, her children whether married or unmarried, her dependant parents and dependant parents of her husband and the Widow and children of her predeceased son, if any

(C) In case of male employee, himself, his wife, his children, whether married or unmarried, his dependants parents, and the dependant parents of his wife and children of his predeceased son, if any

(D) In case of a male employee, himself, his wife, his children whether married or unmarried and his dependant parents

Choose the correct answer from the options given below :

(1) (A), (B), (D) only

(2) (A), (B), (C) only

(3) (A), (C), (D) only

(4) (B), (C), (D) only

65. Given below are some of the items, which are normally covered under 'Wages. From these items, which of them are included under the definition "basic wages" as per the Employees" Provident Fund and Miscellaneous Provisions Act, 1952?

(A) Cash value of any food concession

(B) Any dearness allowance

(C) House rent allowance

(D) Leave travel concession

Choose the correct answer from the options given below :

(1) (A), (B), (D) only

(2) (A), (B), (C) only

(3) (B), (C), (D) only

(4) (A), (C), (D) only

66. As per the provisions of the Employees Provident Fund and Miscellaneous Provisions Act, 1952, who among the following officers are to be appointed by the Central Government?

(A) Central Provident Fund Commissioner

(B) Chief Accounts Officer

(C) Insurance Commissioner

(D) Financial Adviser

Choose the correct answer from the options given below :

(1) (A), (B), (D) only

(2) (A), (B), (C) only

(3) (A), (C), (D) only

(4) (B), (C), (D) only

67. As per the provisions of the Payment of Gratuity Act, 1972, an employee on termination of employment after continuous period of five years, shall be eligible to receive the Gratuity from employer under which of the following conditions :

(A) On his superannuation

(B) On his retirement or resignation

(C) On his death or disablement due to accident

(D) On dismissal from the employment for gross misconduct

Choose the correct answer from the options given below :

(1) (A), (B), (D) only
(2) (A), (C), (D) only
(3) (A), (B), (C) only
(4) (B), (C), (D) only

68. Given below are some statements relating to payment of Wages/incentives. Choose the statements which are correct?

(A) Time rate system is more suitable where strict supervision is possible
(B) In Halsey's premium plan, time wages are guaranteed
(C) Under the Rowan Plan, incentive paid is fixed
(D) Under the Emerson's Efficiency Plan, the worker gets a normal wage upto 67 percent of efficiency.

Choose the correct answer from the options given below :

(1) (B), (C) and (D) only
(2) (A), (B) and (D) only
(3) (A), (C) and (D) only
(4) (A), (B) and (C) only

69. Which of the following statements relating to the Sachar Committee are true?

(A) It was appointed in 1977.
(B) It submitted its report in 1979.
(C) One of the terms of reference for the Committee was 'to suggest measures by which workers" participation in the share capital and management of companies can be brought about.
(D) The Committee did not recommend any "mandatory participation in equity by the workers"

Choose the correct answer from the options given below :

(1) (A), (B), (C) only
(2) (B), (C), (D) only
(3) (A), (C), (D) only
(4) (A), (B), (D) only

70. Which of the followings are related to steps of Job Analysis?

(A) Gather Information
(B) Questionnaire
(C) Job description
(D) Job specification

Choose the correct answer from the options given below :

(1) (A), (B) and (C) only
(2) (B), (C) and (D) only
(3) (C) and (D) only
(4) (A), (C) and (D) only

71. As per the provisions of the Industrial Disputes Act, 1947, workman who is not a member of the trade union, but is a party to dispute, shall be entitled to be represented by whom?

(A) By any other workman employed in the industry
(B) By any member of the executive of the trade union
(C) By any member of the executive or office bearer of a Federation of Trade Unions
(D) By a Legal Practioner

Choose the correct answer from the options given below :

(1) (A), (B), (C) only
(2) (A), (B), (D) only
(3) (B), (C), (D) only
(4) (A), (C), (D) only

72. Which of the following statements relating to the criteria for Recognition of Unions prescribed in the code of Discipline are true?

(A) Where there is more than one union, a union claiming recognition should have been functioning for atleast one year after registration: where there is only one union, this condition would not apply.
(B) A union may claim to be recognised as a representative union for an industry in a local area if it has a membership of atleast 25 percent of the workers of that industry in that area.

(C) When a union has been recognised, there should be no change in its position for a period of three years.

(D) Where there are several unions in an industry or establishment, the one with the largest membership be recognized.

Choose the correct answer from the options given below :

(1) (A), (B), (C) only
(2) (B), (C), (D) only
(3) (A), (C), (D) only
(4) (A), (B), (D) only

73. Which of the following statements relating to the trade union movement in India are true?

(A) The Indian National Trade Union Congress was formed by Hindustan Mazdoor Sevak Sangh.

(B) There was a rift in the All India Trade Union Congress in 1970.

(C) The first President of the All India Trade Union Congress was Chaman Lal.

(D) The Indian Trade Union Federation was formed in 1930.

Choose the correct answer from the options given below :

(1) (A), (B), (C) only
(2) (B), (C), (D) only
(3) (A), (B), (D) only
(4) (A), (C), (D) only

74. Which among the factors mentioned below are the hidden cost of accident?

(A) Legal issues
(B) Loss of morale
(C) Spoiled work
(D) Training cost of replaced worker
(E) Lost time by fellow employers

Choose the correct answer from the options given below :

(1) (A), (B) and (C) only
(2) (A), (C) and (E) only
(3) (C), (D) and (E) only
(4) (A), (B) and (D) only

75. An employee after completion of one year of service is required to give nomination under the provisions of the Payment of Gratuity Act, 1972. From the statements given below, which are the correct options for nomination by the employee.

(A) If having family, in favour of one or more members of his family.

(B) If the employee at the time of nomination, has no family, in favour of any person or persons of his choice.

(C) If having family, giving nomination in favour of a person, who is not a member of his family.

(D) If the nominee predeceases the employee, giving fresh nomination in favour of a member of the family

Choose the correct answer from the options given below :

(1) (A), (B), (C) only
(2) (A), (B), (D) only
(3) (B), (C), (D) only
(4) (A), (C), (D) only

76. Which among the following services are offered by National Safety Council, a voluntary non profit making body governed by a Board of Directors representing the Government Employers and Trade Union representatives'?

(A) Publication Service
(B) Ambulance Service
(C) Mobile Clinic Service
(D) Safety Training Service

Choose the correct answer from the options given below :

(1) (A) and (D) only
(2) (A) and (B) only
(3) (B) and (C) only
(4) (C) and (D) only

77. The main function of the shop council is to increase production and overall efficiency of the shop or department. Which of the following are the functions of the shop council?

(A) Improvement of physical conditions of working.
(B) To study absenteeism in the shops.
(C) The preparation of schedule of working hours and holidays.
(D) Awarding rewards for valuable and creative suggestions.

Choose the most appropriate answer from the options given below :
(1) (A), (B) and (C) only
(2) (A) and (B) only
(3) (A) and (C) only
(4) (A), (C) and (D) only

78. Which of the following statements relating to the trade union movement in India are true?
(A) The Ahmedabad Textile Labour Association was established in 1920.
(B) The AITUC was established in 1920.
(C) Lala Lajpat Rai was the first General Secretary of the AITUC.
(D) There was a split in the AITUC in 1929.

Choose the correct answer from the options given below :
(1) (A), (B), (C) only
(2) (B), (C), (D) only
(3) (A), (C), (D) only
(4) (A), (B), (D) only

79. Turner and Hodge has proposed four areas of concern in the study of professionalism. They are
(A) Degree of Substantive Theory and Technique
(B) Degree of Monopoly
(C) Degree of External Recognition
(D) Degree of Organisation
(E) Degree of Philosophy

Choose the most appropriate answer from the options given below :
(1) (A), (B), (C), (D) only
(2) (A), (B), (D), (E) only
(3) (A), (B), (C), (E) only
(4) (B), (C), (D), (E) only

80. Which among the following are the essential elements of Social Insurance?
(A) Contributory finance
(B) Benefits prescribed in law
(C) Person's other income and resources are taken into account
(D) Benefits are paid without contribution as legal right in prescribed categories of need

Choose the correct answer from the options given below :
(1) (A) and (D) only
(2) (A) and (C) only
(3) (B) and (D) only
(4) (A) and (B) only

81. Match List I and List II

List I	List II
(A) Reformist Unions	(I) Industrial Workers of the World (IWW)
(B) Revolutionary Unions	(II) Unions affiliated to the American Federation of Labor and Congress for Industrial Organization (AFL-CIO)
(C) Craft Unions	(III) Rashtriya Mill Mazdoor Sangh, Bombay
(D) Industrial Unions	(IV) The Ahmedabad Weavers Union

Choose the correct answer from the options given below :
(1) (A)-(II), (B)-(I), (C)-(IV), (D)-(III)
(2) (A)-(III), (B)-(II) (C)-(I), (D)-(IV)
(3) (A)-(I), (B)-(III) (C)-(II), (D)-(IV)
(4) (A)-(IV), (B)-(III), (C)-(I), (D)-(II)

82. Match List I and List II

List I	List II
(A) Kaizen	(I) Focuses on meeting the customer requirement on time

(B) Value Stream Mapping	(II) Focuses on continuous improvements in manufacturing, engineering or management
(C) 20-Point Programme	(III) Focuses on intense and regular scrutiny of every step in the work processes in an organization
(D) Total Quality Management	(IV) Focuses on specific socio-economic measures

Choose the correct answer from the options given below :

(1) (A)-(I), (B)-(II), (C)-(III), (D)-(IV)
(2) (A)-(II), (B)-(I), (C)-(IV), (D)-(III)
(3) (A)-(III), (B)-(I), (C)-(II), (D)-(IV)
(4) (A)-(IV), (B)-(III), (C)-(I), (D)-(II)

83. Match List I and List II

List I	List II
(A) Subsistence Theory	(I) J.B. Clark
(B) Wage Fund Theory	(II) Walker
(C) Residual Claimant Theory	(III) J.S. Mill
(D) Marginal Productivity Theory	(IV) Ricardo

Choose the correct answer from the options given below :

(1) (A)-(IV), (B)-(III), (C)-(II), (D)-(I)
(2) (A)-(I), (B)-(II), (C)-(III), (D)-(IV)
(3) (A)-(IV), (B)-(II), (C)-(I), (D)-(III)
(4) (A)-(II), (B)-(IV), (C)-(I), (D)-(III)

84. Match List I and List II

List I Training Description	List II Training Technique
(A) Providing a common focus of discussion	(I) Shadowing
(B) Insight into a given interaction	(II) Multiple role playing
(C) Brings out ideas that are not often expressed	(III) Monodrama
(D) Working under a senior to watch and learn	(IV) Doubling

Choose the correct answer from the options given below :

(1) (A)-(II), (B)-(III), (C)-(IV), (D)-(I)
(2) (A)-(III), (B)-(II), (C)-(IV), (D)-(I)
(3) (A)-(IV), (B)-(III), (C)-(I), (D)-(II)
(4) (A)-(II), (B)-(I), (C)-(IV), (D)-(III)

85. Match List I and List II

List I	List II
(A) Discipline	(I) The Payment of Wages Act, 1936
(B) Regulation of Employer-Employees Relations	(II) The Industrial Employment (Standing Orders) Act, 1946
(C) Wage Revision	(III) The Industrial Disputes Act, 1947
(D) Mode and Time of Payment of Wages	(IV) The Minimum Wages Act, 1948

Choose the correct answer from the options given below :

(1) (A)-(II), (B)-(III), (C)-(IV), (D)-(I)
(2) (A)-(III), (B)-(IV), (C)-(I), (D)-(II)
(3) (A)-(III), (B)-(IV), (C)-(II), (D)-(I)
(4) (A)-(III), (B)-(II), (C)-(IV), (D)-(I)

86. Match List I and List II

List I	List II
(A) Frictional Unemployment	(I) Unemployment that varies predictably with season.
(B) Seasonal Unemployment	(II) When people are in transition from one job to another or when they first enter the labour market.
(C) Cyclical Unemployment	(III) In periods of economic change

			when new jobs being created have requirements different from the old jobs being lost.
(D)	Structural Unemployment	(IV)	Associated with a reduction in real outputs during periods of recession.

Choose the correct answer from the options given below :

(1) (A)-(II), (B)-(III), (C)-(I), (D)-(IV)
(2) (A)-(II), (B)-(I), (C)-(IV), (D)-(III)
(3) (A)-(II), (B)-(III), (C)-(IV), (D)-(I)
(4) (A)-(IV) (B)-(I), (C)-(III), (D)-(II)

87. Match List I and List II

List I Commission/ Committee	**List II Chairman**
(A) Royal commission on Labour	(I) Ravindra Verma
(B) First National Commission on Labour	(II) D.V. Rege
(C) Labour Investigation Committee	(III) J.H. Whitley
(D) Second National Commission on Labour	(IV) P.B. Gajendra Gadkar

Choose the correct answer from the options given below :

(1) (A)-(II), (B)-(I), (C)-(IV), (D)-(III)
(2) (A)-(IV), (B)-(III), (C)-(I), (D)-(II)
(3) (A)-(III), (B)-(IV), (C)-(II), (D)-(I)
(4) (A)-(I), (B)-(II), (C)-(III), (D)-(IV)

88. Match List I and List II

List I	**List II**
(A) Group influences in the work place	(I) Max Weber
(B) Administrative theory – Rules of Management	(II) Chester Barnard
(C) Father of Modern Management Theory	(III) Mary Parker Follet
(D) Systems Theory	(IV) Henri Fayol

Choose the correct answer from the options given below :

(1) (A)-(III), (B)-(IV), (C)-(I), (D)-(II)
(2) (A)-(IV), (B)-(I), (C)-(II), (D)-(III)
(3) (A)-(III), (B)-(I), (C)-(IV), (D)-(I)
(4) (A)-(II), (B)-(III), (C)-(IV), (D)-(I)

89. Match List I and List II

List I	**List II**
(A) The other fellow is to be conquered and put at my service	(I) Paternalism
(B) The other fellow should be helped up when down, without too much concern for what got him down	(II) Participation
(C) The other fellow has something to contribute to my efforts and can help me	(III) Welfare
(D) The other person should be cared for, and I will decide to what extent	(IV) Slavery

Choose the correct answer from the options given below :

(1) (A)-(II), (B)-(I), (C)-(II), (D)-(IV)
(2) (A)-(IV), (B)-(III), (C)-(II), (D)-(I)
(3) (A)-(III), (B)-(IV), (C)-(I), (D)-(II)
(4) (A)-(I), (B)-(II), (C)-(IV), (D)-(III)

90. Match List I and List II

List I LEGISLATIONS	**List II PROVISIONS**
(A) The Trade Unions Act, 1926	(I) Retrenched and Protected Workmen
(B) The Code of Discipline	(II) Collection of forms for Political Participation
(C) The Industrial Disputes Act, 1947	(III) Recognition of Trade Unions
(D) The Industrial Employment	(IV) Disciplinary action for

(Standing Orders) misconduct
Act.

Choose the correct answer from the options given below :

(1) (A)-(I), (B)-(II), (C)-(III), (D)-(IV)
(2) (A)-(III), (B)-(III), (C)-(I), (D)-(IV)
(3) (A)-(IV), (B)-(I), (C)-(II), (D)-(III)
(4) (A)-(III), (B)-(IV), (C)-(I), (D)-(II)

Read the passage carefully and answer Q. No. 91 to 95 that follow :

An organisation which is keen to retain good talent must have systems to inform employees that the organization cares for them, belongs to them and it is they who can make it prosper and grow. In other words, people are empowered to consider the organisation as their own. This, to a large extent can be achieved if the employer is sensitive and caring and makes efforts to develop proper systems. This has to be demonstrated through efforts and actions, not merely words. It is important to have systems which seek employees involvement in deciding policy matters, technological upgradation, improving general administration, and productivity etc. instead of thrusting decisions on them. When employees are consulted, two benefits clearly accrue. The first being employees who are well entrenched in operation will normally know the intricacies and will be able to offer valuable suggestions for its improvement. Secondly, once they have participated in the decision making process, acceptance and implementation become much easier since the staff members are in a position to explain to others who may not have participated. Most importantly, seeking participation makes people feel wanted and cater to their esteem needs. They feel respected and recognised. They are empowered to think that they are responsible partners in the process of development and contributing to growth.

91. How can an organisation retain good talent?

(1) By caring of them
(2) By belonging to them
(3) By making them prosper
(4) By making them to feel that the organisation is their own

92. How can the objective of retaining good talent be achieved?

(1) If proper systems are suggested
(2) If the employer is caring and sensitive
(3) If the demands of the employees are met
(4) By imposing decisions on them

93. Which of the following statement is not correct?

(1) Proper systems can be demonstrated through actions
(2) Systems can be made to work through efforts
(3) Systems can become effective through powerful words and dramatic gestures
(4) Systems are needed for employees' involvement.

94. The benefits of consultation are :

(1) Operation and implementation become easier
(2) Production cost goes down
(3) Employees feel proud and superior
(4) Employees do not insist on their rights

95. Participation makes the employees feel that :

(1) their demands are looked into favourably
(2) they are respected and recognised
(3) they have become indispensable
(4) they are saviours of the organisation

Read the passage carefully and answer Q. No. 96 to 100 that follow :

When we look around we see glaring inequalities between man and man. While the constitution and law ensure an ordered society, it is only our hard work and disciplined conduct that will enable us to achieve our social objectives and economic goals that we have set before us. Bapu rightly stressed "Democracy is the art and science of mobilising the entire physical, economic and spiritual resources of all sections of the people in the service of the common good for The purpose of the Government is to achieve this. Our people possess intelligence in abundance, have immense capacity for hard work and they feel for the country. All this is to be mobilised to the best advantage of the nation. Again to quote Gandhi. "Swaraj of a people means the sum total of the Swaraj (Self-rule) of individuals. And such Swaraj comes only by performance of individuals, of their duty as citizens. They come when they are needed for better performance of duty." It is but proper that we remind ourselves of these teachings of the father of the nation.

96. Which of the following will help us to achieve our social goals?
(1) Scientific attitude
(2) Intelligent understanding
(3) Disciplined behaviour
(4) Mobilising the physical resources

97. According to the passage, the Indians are praised for which of the qualities?
(A) Intelligence
(B) Hard work
(C) Patriotism
(D) Service for all
Choose the correct answer from the options given below :
(1) (A), (B) and (C) only
(2) (A), (B) and (D) only
(3) (B), (C) and (D) only
(4) (A), (C) and (D) only

98. According to Gandhiji, people are required to do their duties :
(1) Without thinking of their rights.
(2) Without bothering about others.
(3) Without thinking of the type of government.
(4) Without bothering about the inequalities.

99. Which of the following statement is NOT correct according to the passage?
(1) There are inequalities among the people.
(2) We can achieve our economic objective with hard work.
(3) Democracy is the art, of mobilising all resources.
(4) Indians do not have the capacity for hard Work.

100. As per the passage, what should be the purpose of the government?
(1) To educate people for their betterment.
(2) To provide people adequate source of living.
(3) To mobilise the entire physical, economic and spiritual resources of all sections of people in the service of common good for all.
(4) To mobilise the financial resources of the country for its all round development.

ANSWER KEY

1. (3)	2. (2)	3. (2)	4. (1)	5. (2)	6. (2)	7. (4)	8. (3)	9. (1)	10. (3)
11. (3)	12. (3)	13. (1)	14. (2)	15. (2)	16. (2)	17. (2)	18. (1)	19. (3)	20. (3)
21. (4)	22. (2)	23. (2)	24. (3)	25. (3)	26. (4)	27. (4)	28. (1)	29. (1)	30. (1)
31. (3)	32. (2)	33. (3)	34. (2)	35. (4)	36. (2)	37. (4)	38. (2)	39. (3)	40. (3)
41. (1)	42. (1)	43. (1)	44. (2)	45. (1)	46. (2)	47. (4)	48. (2)	49. (2)	50. (2)
51. (2)	52. (3)	53. (2)	54. (1)	55. (2)	56. (1)	57. (2)	58. (3)	59. (2)	60. (3)
61. (1)	62. (*)	63. (4)	64. (*)	65. (*)	66. (1)	67. (3)	68. (2)	69. (3)	70. (4)
71. (1)	72. (4)	73. (3)	74. (4)	75. (2)	76. (1)	77. (2)	78. (4)	79. (1)	80. (4)
81. (1)	82. (2)	83. (1)	84. (1)	85. (1)	86. (2)	87. (3)	88. (3)	89. (2)	90. (2)
91. (4)	92. (2)	93. (3)	94. (1)	95. (2)	96. (3)	97. (1)	98. (1)	99. (4)	100. (3)

DECEMBER, 2021

LABOUR WELFARE & INDUSTRIAL RELATIONS, LABOUR & SOCIAL WELFARE, HUMAN RESOURCE MANAGEMENT

PAPER-II

Note : This paper contains **hundred (100)** objective type questions, each question carrying **two (2)** marks.

1. Explaining a relationship between satisfaction and performance, which of the following implicitly assumes that "satisfaction leads to improved performance and dissatisfaction detracts from performance"?
(1) Attribution theory of motivation
(2) Content theories of motivation
(3) Vroom's Expectancy theory
(4) Adam's Equity theory

2. The belief that 'conflict is not only a positive force in a group but that it is absolutely necessary for a group to perform effectively' is associated with which of the following?
(1) Unitarist view
(2) Traditional view
(3) Interactionist view
(4) Human Relations view

3. OCTAPACE is an acronym developed by Udai Pareek which identifies eight important values relevant to an organisation's culture. Which one of the following gives the correct expansion of the term OCTAPACE?
(1) Openness, Cooperation, Trust, Authenticity, Proaction, Autonomy, Collaboration, Experimentation
(2) Openness, Confrontation, Trust, Authenticity, Proaction, Autonomy, Collaboration, Experimentation
(3) Openness, Confrontation, Trust, Autonomy, Proaction, Avoidance, Cooperation, Experimentation
(4) Openness, Cooperation, Truthful, Authenticity, Proaction, Authority, Collaboration, Experimentation

4. Consideration and Initiating Structure as the dimensions of leadership were identified by which of the following?
(1) The Iowa leadership studies
(2) Michigan leadership studies
(3) The Ohio State leadership studies
(4) The Harvard leadership studies

5. Who developed the Warwick Model of HRM?
(1) David Guest
(2) Hendry and Pettigrew
(3) Dave Ulrich (4) Harvard

6. Which one of the following is related to on-the-job training?
(1) Committee assignments
(2) Special classes
(3) Case study
(4) Role playing

7. The process of estimating the quantity and quality of people required to meet future needs of the organisation is called
(1) Managerial Judgement
(2) Human Resource audit
(3) Supply forcasting
(4) Demand forcasting

8. Job analysis is the procedure for
(1) Describing about the remuneration
(2) Determining the duties and skill requirements
(3) Fixing the responsibility
(4) Allotment the duties

9. What should be the maximum number of representatives in the Joint Management Council?

(1) Six only
(2) Twelve only
(3) Sixteen only
(4) Twenty only

10. Under which section of the Industrial Disputes Act, 1947, both the Central and State Government have the power to constitute a Court of Inquiry?

(1) Section 6 (2) Section 10
(3) Section 7 (4) Section 5

11. Which country is called 'Home of Collective Bargaining?

(1) Japan
(2) Great Britain
(3) United States of America
(4) Canada

12. An unauthorized strike that is called for without the approval of the union, is commonly known as

(1) Bandh
(2) Quickie strike
(3) Wild-cat strike
(4) Sit-down strike

13. Excluding provisions of Section 22 of the Payment of Bonus Act, 1965, what is the maximum time limit, within which the bonus should be paid by the employer with sufficient reasons?

(1) One year
(2) Two years
(3) Three years
(4) Five years

14. Which one of the following Articles of Fundamental Rights includes Equality of Opportunities for all citizens in matters relating to employment or appointment to any office under the state?

(1) Article 16 (1)
(2) Article 17 (1)
(3) Article 19 (1)
(4) Article 18

15. Which one of the following authorities has the power to prescribe the certificate of fitness to workers in a factory under the provisions of the Factories Act, 1948?

(1) The Certifying Surgeon
(2) The Owner or Occupier of the Factory
(3) The Chief Inspector
(4) The State Government

16. When an employer asks employees to sign a type of loyalty oath stating that "the employee would neither join nor participate in the activities of a union" is known as:

(1) The Conspiracy Doctrine
(2) The Yellow-Dog Contract
(3) Unfair Labour Practices
(4) Collective Bargaining Agreement

17. Under the provisions of the Building and Other Construction Workers' (Regulation of Employment and Conditions of Service) Act 1996, at least how many days before the commencement of the building work is an employer required to send a written notice regarding the construction of building?

(1) Ninety days
(2) Sixty days
(3) Thirty days
(4) Two months

18. "Labour is not a commodity" is the assertion made in which of the following?

(1) The Magna Carta
(2) The Philadelphia Declaration of ILO
(3) The Constitution of India
(4) The Universal Declaration of Human Rights

19. If any question arises as to the application or interpretation of standing orders certified under the provisions of the Industrial Employment (Standing Orders) Act, 1946, either the employer or workmen can refer the same to which one of the following authorities?

(1) Appropriate government
(2) Industrial tribunal
(3) Labour court
(4) Civil court

20. Who viewed "trade unions as a means of representing the interests of workers through the strategies of mutual insurance, collective bargaining, and legal enactments"?

(1) John R. Commons
(2) Sidney and Beatrice Webb
(3) Neil W. Chamberlain
(4) Karl Marx

21. As per the provisions of the Payment of Wages Act, 1936, no fine shall be imposed on any employed person under the age of

(1) Twenty one years
(2) Eighteen years
(3) Sixteen years
(4) Fifteen years

22. "We believe that if these committees (Works Committees) are given proper encouragement and the past errors are avoided, they can play a useful role in the Indian Industrial System".

This statement was given by:

(1) The Whitley Committee of 1916
(2) The Royal Commission on Labour, 1929
(3) The First National Commission on Labour, 1969
(4) The Second National Commission on Labour, 2002

23. As per the provisions of the Payment of Wages Act, 1936, the registers, records relating to the payment of wages shall be preserved for at least how many years after the date of last entry?

(1) Three years
(2) Ten years
(3) Five years
(4) Seven years

24. Which one of the following statements is correct with respect to the Minimum Wages Act?

(1) Only one Schedule covers different types of seasonal industries
(2) Only one Schedule covers different shops and commercial establishments
(3) Three Schedules cover Factories, Plantations, and Mines
(4) One Schedule having two parts covers industries and agriculture

25. Which among the following is NOT a major type of Safety Audits?

(1) Scheduled Audit
(2) Unannounced Audit
(3) Compliance with standards
(4) Promotion of safe behaviour

26. Social Insurance is described as 'giving in return for contribution' and benefits up to the level of

(1) Luxurious living
(2) Fair living
(3) Subsistence living
(4) Descent living

27. Due to the operation of the law of diminishing returns, the demand curve of labour

(1) Slopes down
(2) Moves upward
(3) Remains static
(4) Slopes downward and then moves upward

28. Usual Status (US) unemployment is calculated with reference to the date of the survey to a preceding period of

(1) One day
(2) Seven days
(3) Thirty days
(4) Three hundred sixty five days

29. Full Employment is said to exist, if

(1) The actual rate of unemployment does not exceed the natural rate
(2) The actual rate of unemployment exceeds its natural rate
(3) The actual rate of unemployment is equal to natural rate
(4) All of these

30. Which one of the following is NOT concerned with a Job Description?

(1) Job summary
(2) Experience

(3) Working condition
(4) Supervision given

31. Explaining to understand human behaviour which one of the following emphasizes that, "the person and the environmental situation do not function as independent units but, in conjunction with the behaviour itself, reciprocally interact to determine human behaviour".
(1) Social learning Framework
(2) Behaviouristic Framework
(3) Cognitive Framework
(4) Organizational Development Framework

32. "The labour movement prepares the ground wherein the seed of trade unionism grows." Who said this?
(1) G. D. H. Cole
(2) S. D. Punekar
(3) Karl Marx
(4) Frank Tannenbaum

33. The determination of basic long term objectives of an enterprise and the adoption of courses of action and allocation of resources necessary to achieve these goals is known as
(1) Strategies (2) Policies
(3) Procedures (4) Rules

34. Which one of the following is NOT a principle of coordination laid down by Mary Parker Follett?
(1) Principle of direct contact
(2) Principle of early start
(3) Principle of reciprocal relationship
(4) Principle of completeness

35. Who is also known as 'the father of social system school' of management thought?
(1) Herbert A. Simon
(2) Henri Fayol
(3) Elton Mayo
(4) Chester Barnard

36. In an attempt to integrate individual and organisational goals, who developed the concept of Linking Pin?
(1) Elton Mayo
(2) Rensis Likert
(3) Max Weber
(4) Mary Parker Follett

37. A set of human resource management policies and practices that promote organizational effectiveness is known as
(1) Human Resource Information System
(2) Human Resource Management System
(3) Human Resource Audit System
(4) High Performance Work System

38. Taking into account the characteristics of transnational managers, the three core roles and responsibilities: worldwide, business strategist, architect of an asset and resource configuration and cross-border coordinator and controller are associated with which of the following forms of transnational management?
(1) Worldwide functional management
(2) Geographic subsidiary management
(3) Global business management
(4) Top-level corporate management

39. Who among the following focussed on the soft side of an organization as a sequel to globalization comprising adhocracy, simple structure, the divisionalized form, the machine bureaucracy and the professional bureaucracy?
(1) Burns and Stalker
(2) Henry Mintzberg
(3) J. S. Black
(4) Bartlett and Ghoshal

40. The quantitative gauge of a human resource management activity, such as employee turnover, hours of training per employee, or qualified applicants per position is known as
(1) Human Resource Benchmarking
(2) Human Resource Data Analytics
(3) Human Resource Metrics
(4) Human Resource Appraisal

41. Which of the following are the internal factors of recruitment?

A. Recruitment Policy
B. Sons of the soil
C. Image
D. Human Resource Planning
Choose the correct answer from the options given below:
(1) A, B and C only
(2) A and B only
(3) A and D only
(4) A, C and D only

42. Which among the following are the determinants of the supply of labour?
A. Product demand
B. Preference for Work versus Leisure
C. Number of firms
D. Number of qualified suppliers
Choose the correct answer from the options given below:
(1) A and B only
(2) B and C only
(3) C and D only
(4) B and D only

43. Which among the following are theories of labour welfare?
A. Social Responsibility theory
B. Placating theory
C. Public Relations theory
D. Coordination theory
E. Accountability theory
Choose the correct answer from the options given below:
(1) A and B only (2) B and D only
(3) B and C only (4) D and E only

44. Which among the following are the indirect costs of industrial accidents?
A. Loss of earning power
B. Loss of production
C. Paperwork
D. Legal issues
E. Equipment
Choose the correct answer from the options given below:
(1) A and B only
(2) A and C only
(3) B and D only
(4) D and E only

45. Who among the following are Classical Economists?
A. J. B. Say
B. Marshall
C. Pigou
D. David Ricardo
Choose the correct answer from the options given below:
(1) A and B only
(2) B and C only
(3) A and D only
(4) C and D only

46. Who among the following were the founder members of the Red Trade Union Congress?
A. S. V. Deshpandey
B. G. L. Khandelkar
C. B. T. Ranadiv
D. R. R. Bhalla
Choose the correct answer from the options given below:
(1) A, C and D only
(2) A, B and C only
(3) B, C and D only
(4) A, B and D only

47. Which of the following are the ways of determining a representative union for the purpose of Collective Bargaining in India?
A. Code of Discipline
B. Secret Ballot
C. Check-off System
D. Membership Verification
Choose the correct answer from the options given below:
(1) A and B only
(2) A, B and C only
(3) B, C and D only
(4) A, B, C and D

48. Which three welfare schemes for unorganized workers, the Central Government shall formulate and notify time-to-time under the Unorganized Worker's Social Security Act, 2008?

A. Life and Disability Cover
B. Protection of Employment Cover
C. Health and Maternity Benefit
D. Old Age Protection

Choose the correct answer from the options given below:

(1) A, B and C only
(2) A, C and D only
(3) A, B and D only
(4) B, C and D only

49. By end of 1933, which three all India trade union organizations were in existence?

A. All India Trade Union Congress
B. The Red Trade Union Congress
C. National Trade Union Federation
D. Indian Trade Union Federation

Choose the correct answer from the options given below:

(1) A, B and D only
(2) A, B and C only
(3) B, C and D only
(4) A, C and D only

50. Who among the following took the lead in organizing the Federation of Indian Chamber of Commerce?

A. Sri Purshottamdas Thakurdas
B. Lala Shriram
C. G. D. Birla
D. Dhirubhai Ambani

Choose the correct answer from the options given below:

(1) A, B and D only
(2) A, B and C only
(3) B, C and D only
(4) A, C and D only

51. Which of the following are the key components of a third-generation balanced scorecard?

A. Destination Statement
B. Strategic Objectives
C. Strategic Linkage Model and Perspective
D. Measures and Initiatives

Choose the correct answer from the options given below:

(1) A and B only
(2) C and D only
(3) A, B and C only
(4) A, B, C and D

52. Which two of the following organisations conducted a joint workshop on the subject of defining the informal sector in 1997?

A. The National Commission on Labour
B. National Council for Applied Economic Research (NCAER)
C. The Self-Employed Women's Association (SEWA)
D. The National Commission on Rural Labour

Choose the correct answer from the options given below:

(1) A and B only
(2) B and C only
(3) C and D only
(4) A and D only

53. As per the approved list of Indian Labour Conference, in which of the following three items should the Works Committee not normally deal with?

A. Wages and Allowances
B. Administration of welfare and funds
C. Bonus and profit-sharing schemes
D. Matters connected with the fixation of the standard labour force

Choose the correct answer from the options given below:

(1) A, B and C only
(2) A, C and D only
(3) B, C and D only
(4) A, B and D only

54. Choose the correct options regarding the theories of Motivation

A. Theory 'X' and 'Y' are similar to each other

B. Two factor theory is derived by McGregor
C. The concept of ERG theory is similar to Maslow's hierarchy of needs theory
D. McClelland has identified the need for power, need for achievement and need for affiliation as the motivating needs

Choose the correct answer from the options given below:
(1) A and C only
(2) B and C only
(3) C and D only
(4) A and B only

55. By which three of the following ways can an individual performance be planned?
A. Task analysis or activities analysis
B. Key Result Areas and Goal setting
C. Key Performance Area
D. Key Description Area

Choose the correct answer from the options given below:
(1) A, B and C only
(2) B, C and D only
(3) A, C and D only
(4) A, B and D only

56. Consider the statements relating to the fines under the Payment of Wages Act, 1936
A. No fine shall be imposed on any employed person until he has been given an opportunity of showing cause against the fine
B. The total amount of fine which may be imposed in any one wage period on any employed person shall not exceed an amount equal to three per cent of wages
C. Every fine shall not be deemed to have been imposed on the day of the act or omission in respect of which it was imposed
D. Fine shall not be imposed on any employed person who is under the age of fifteen years
E. All fines and all realisations shall be recorded in a register to be kept by the person responsible for the payment of wages

Choose the correct answer from the options given below:
(1) A, B, C and D only
(2) A, B, C, D and E
(3) A, B, D and E only
(4) A, B, C and E only

57. Consider the statements with respect to the minimum rate of wages fixed or revised, under the Minimum Wages Act, 1948
A. Basic rate of wages with or without the cost of living allowances
B. Basic rate of wages and a special allowance at a rate to be adjusted at such intervals by the appropriate government
C. An all-inclusive rate allowing for the basic rate
D. Basic rate inclusive of house rent allowances and travelling allowances
E. Cash value of concessions, if any

Choose the correct answer from the options given below:
(1) A, B, C and E only
(2) B, C, D and E only
(3) A, B, C, D and E
(4) A, C, D and E only

58. Consider the statements in connection with the Nomination under the provisions of the Payment of Gratuity Act, 1972
A. An employee who has completed one year of service shall require to make the nomination in the prescribed form
B. An employee may, in his nomination, distribute the amount of gratuity payable to him, against more than one nominee
C. An employee is required to make a nomination in favour of one or more member of his family if having family at the time of making the nomination
D. If a nominee predeceases the employee, the interest of the nominee shall not revert to the employee

E. A nomination once made by an employee can be modified by the employee at any time with written notice to the employer

Choose the correct answer from the options given below:

(1) A, B, C and D only
(2) B, C, D and E only
(3) A, B, D and E only
(4) A, B, C and E only

59. Which of the following are the advantages of group activities in accordance with the functions of an enterprise?

A. Logical reflection of functions
B. Maintain power and prestige of major functions
C. Follows principle of occupational specialisation
D. Responsibility for profit is at the top only

Choose the correct answer from the options given below:

(1) A, B and C only
(2) A and C only
(3) A, B and D only
(4) A, C and D only

60. Which of the following factors are given in Porter's Diamond?

A. Factor conditions
B. Related and supporting industries
C. Market conditions
D. Demand conditions
E. Firm strategy and rivalry

Choose the correct answer from the options given below:

(1) A, B, C and D only
(2) B, C and D only
(3) A, C, D and E only
(4) A, B, D and E only

61. The facilities covered under the welfare and health of contract labour as per provisions of the Contract Labour (Regulation and Abolition) Act, 1970 are:

A. Canteens
B. Drinking water facilities
C. Creches
D. Restrooms
E. First-aid facilities

Choose the correct answer from the options given below:

(1) A, B, C, D and E
(2) A, B, D and E only
(3) A, B, C and D only
(4) A, B, C and E only

62. Which two of the following conventions of ILO related to Freedom of Association, Right to Organise and Collective Bargaining have NOT been ratified by India?

A. Convention No 11
B. Convention No 87
C. Convention No 98
D. Convention No 100

Choose the correct answer from the options given below:

(1) A and B only
(2) B and C only
(3) C and D only
(4) A and D only

63. Consider the following statements under the Building and other Construction Workers' (Regulation of Employment and Conditions of Service) Act, 1996

A. A building worker who has been registered as a beneficiary under the Act shall cease to be beneficiary when he attains the age of sixty years
B. A building worker shall cease to be a beneficiary if he has not worked for at least ninety days in a year
C. If the building worker had been a beneficiary for at least three years continuously immediately before attaining the age of sixty years, shall be eligible to get benefits
D. While computing the period of ninety days, the period of absence from the building or other construction work due to any personal injury caused to him by

accident arising out of and in the course of his employment shall be included

Choose the correct answer from the options given below:
(1) A, B and C only
(2) A, B, C and D only
(3) B, C and D only
(4) A, B and D only

64. Which of the following are true relating to Potential Appraisals?
A. Inform employees about their future prospects
B. Help the organization to chalk out a suitable succession plan
C. Update training efforts from time to time
D. Advise employees about what they must do to improve their career prospects

Choose the correct answer from the options given below:
(1) A and B only
(2) B and C only
(3) A, B and C only
(4) A, B, C and D

65. Consider the statements in connection with the liability for payment of wages to an inter-state migrant workman under the provisions of the Inter-state Migrant Workmen (Regulation and Employment and Conditions of Service) Act, 1979
A. The contractor shall be responsible for payment of wages to each inter-state migrant workman
B. The principal employer shall nominate a representative duly authorised by him to be present at the time of disbursement of wages by the contractor
C. It shall be the duty of the contractor to ensure the disbursement of wages in presence of the employers representative
D. In case the contractor fails to make payment of wages, the principal employer shall not be liable to pay wages to the inter-state migrant workman

Choose the correct answer from the options given below:
(1) A, B and C only
(2) B, C and D only
(3) A, B and D only
(4) A, C and D only

66. Match List I with List II

List I Trade Unions	List II Founder President
A. Madras Workers Union	I. B. P. Wadia
B. All India Trade Union Congress	II. V. V. Giri
C. Indian Trade Union Federation	III. Lala Lajpat Rai
D. Indian National Trade Union Congress	IV. Suresh Chandra Bannerjee

Choose the correct answer from the options given below:
(1) A - I, B - III, C - II, D - IV
(2) A - I, B - II, C - III, D - IV
(3) A - II, B - I, C - III, D - IV
(4) A - I, B - IV, C - II, D - III

67. Match List I with List II

List I Provisions given in the schedule	List II Schedule of Industrial Disputes Act
A. Illegality or otherwise of a strike or lock-out	I. Schedule III
B. Shift working otherwise than in accordance with standing orders	II. Schedule V
C. Any changes in contribution paid or payable by the employer to any provident fund or pension fund	III. Schedule II
D. Failure to implement award, settlement, or agreement	IV. Schedule IV

Choose the correct answer from the options given below:

(1) A - III, B - II, C - I, D - IV
(2) A - III, B - I, C - IV, D - II
(3) A - IV, B - II, C - III, D - I
(4) A - I, B - IV, C - II, D - III

68. Match List I with List II

List I	List II
A. Job analysis	I. A list of human requirements of a job
B. Job specification	II. Assigning workers additional activities at the same level
C. Job description	III. Procedure for determining the duties and skill requirements of the job
D. Job enlargement	IV. A list of duties and responsibilities of a job

Choose the correct answer from the options given below:

(1) A - III, B - I, C - IV, D - II
(2) A - I, B - II, C - III, D - IV
(3) A - IV, B - III, C - II, D - I
(4) A - II, B - IV, C - I, D - III

69. Match List I with List II

List I Type of MNC	List II Focus
A. Multinational	I. Home market and export
B. Global	II. Local responsiveness and transfer of learning
C. Domestic	III. Global strategy, low cost and price competition
D. International	IV. Local responsiveness and global integration

Choose the correct answer from the options given below:

(1) A - I, B - II, C - III, D - IV
(2) A - III, B - IV, C - I, D - II
(3) A - IV, B - III, C - II, D - I
(4) A - II, B - I, C - IV, D - III

70. Match List I with List II

List I	List II
A. Committees	I. The Building and Other Construction Worker's (Regulation of Employment and Conditions of Service) Act, 1996
B. Expert Committees	II. The Child and Adolescent Labour (Prohibition and Regulation) Act, 1986
C. Safety Committee	III. The Mines Act, 1952
D. Technical Advisory Committee	IV. The Factories Act, 1948

Choose the correct answer from the options given below:

(1) A - I, B - III, C - IV, D - II
(2) A - II, B - IV, C - III, D - I
(3) A - III, B - I, C - IV, D - II
(4) A - IV, B - III, C - II, D - I

71. Match List I with List II

List I	List II
A. Ivan Pavlov	I. Social learning theory
B. B. F. Skinner	II. S-O-B-C Model
C. Alberta Bandura	III. Classical Conditioning
D. Fred Luthans	IV. Operant Conditioning

Choose the correct answer from the options given below:

(1) A - IV, B - III, C - II, D - I
(2) A - I, B - II, C - IV, D - III
(3) A - III, B - IV, C - I, D - II
(4) A - II, B - I, C - III, D - IV

72. Match List I with List II

List I	List II
A. Product life cycle theory	I. David Ricardo
B. Transaction cost theory	II. R. G. Vernon
C. Comparative Cost Difference theory	III. Dunning
D. Relative Comparative Cost Advantages theory	IV. Heckscher-Ohlin

Choose the correct answer from the options given below:

(1) A - II, B - III, C - IV, D - I
(2) A - I, B - II, C - III, D - IV
(3) A - III, B - I, C - II, D - IV
(4) A - II, B - IV, C - I, D - III

73. Match List I with List II

List I **Training techniques**	List II **Descriptions**
A. Monodrama	I. Training with an external perspective
B. Mirroring	II. Insight into a given interaction
C. Skill games	III. Games to test ability to plan ahead
D. Strategic Planners	IV. Test to develop analytical skills

Choose the correct answer from the options given below:

(1) A - II, B - I, C - IV, D - III
(2) A - III, B - IV, C - II, D - I
(3) A - IV, B - III, C - I, D - II
(4) A - II, B - IV, C - I, D - III

74. Match List I with List II

List I **Theory of group formation**	List II **Characteristics**
A. Propinquity theory	I. Activities interactions and sentiments
B. Balance theory	II. Similar attitudes towards commonly relevant objects and goals
C. Exchange theory	III. Reward-cost outcomes of interaction
D. George Homans' theory	IV. Spatial or geographical proximity

Choose the correct answer from the options given below:

(1) A - I, B - II, C - III, D - IV
(2) A - II, B - IV, C - I, D - III
(3) A - IV, B - II, C - III, D - I
(4) A - III, B - I, C - IV, D - II

75. Match List I with List II

List I	List II
A. Elton Mayo	I. Father of Modern Management Theory
B. F. W. Taylor	II. Hawthorne effect
C. Henri Fayol	III. Comprehensive social system approach
D. Chester Barnard	IV. Principles of scientific management

Choose the correct answer from the options given below:

(1) A - II, B - IV, C - I, D - III
(2) A - II, B - IV, C - III, D - I
(3) A - III, B - IV, C - II, D - I
(4) A - III, B - I, C - IV, D - II

76. Arrange the following in sequential order from the beginning to the end so far as the procedure for implementation of Certified Standing Orders under the provisions of the Industrial Employment (Standing orders) Act, 1941

A. Draft Standing Orders submitted by the Employer to the Certifying Officer

B. Modified copies of the Standing Order submitted before the Certifying Officer if required
C. Copies of the Standing Orders communicated to the Employer and representatives of workmen
D. Implementation of Certified Standing Orders
E. Application of model Standing Orders

Choose the correct answer from the options given below

(1) D, A, C, B, E
(2) E, A, C, B, D
(3) A, C, B, E, D
(4) C, B, A, E, D

77. Given below are the different steps of process of learning. Arrange these from beginning of the process to the end.

A. Assimilation or retention
B. Acquiring knowledge
C. Internalization of new knowledge
D. Application of new learning
E. Self-monitored learning

Choose the correct answer from the options given below

(1) A, B, C, D, E
(2) B, A, C, D, E
(3) B, A, D, C, E
(4) E, A, D, C, B

78. The career management process can be sequenced in five stages. Arrange these stages from the beginning to the end

A. Strategy
B. Assessment
C. Planning
D. Development
E. Evaluation

Choose the correct answer from the options given below

(1) A, C, B, D, E
(2) A, B, C, D, E
(3) B, A, D, E, C
(4) A, C, E, D, B

79. Arrange the four levels of training evaluation from the first to the last as given by Kirkpatrick:

A. Reaction
B. Results
C. Job behavior
D. Learning

Choose the correct answer from the options given below

(1) B, C, D, A
(2) C, B, A, D
(3) D, A, B, C
(4) A, D, C, B

80. Arrange the different phases of strategic planning in multinational firms starting from the beginning to the end :

A. Strategic business units
B. Entry and participation strategy
C. External and internal analysis
D. Organisational structure, control and coordination mechanism

Choose the correct answer from the options given below

(1) C, A, B, D
(2) A, C, D, B
(3) B, D, A, C
(4) D, B, C, A

81. Arrange the following Indian Trade Union/ Organisations on the basis of their founding year from the earliest to the latest

A. United Trade Union Congress
B. The Red Trade Union Congress
C. The Textile Labour Association of Ahmedabad
D. Hind Mazdoor Sabha
E. Self Employed Woman's Association

Choose the correct answer from the options given below

(1) C, B, D, A, E
(2) A, C, D, E, B
(3) B, C, A, D, E
(4) E, D, C, A, B

82. Arrange the following phases of internationalization from the first to the fourth phase as identified by Adler and Ghadar:

A. Domestic
B. Multinational
C. Global
D. International

Choose the correct answer from the options given below

(1) C, D, B, A
(2) A, C, D, B
(3) A, D, B, C
(4) A, B, C, D

83. Arrange the main schemes of Workers Participation in Management according to their year of formation from the earliest to the latest

A. Joint Management Councils
B. Shop Councils
C. Board-Level Participation
D. Institution of Employees' Participation in Management for Public Sector Undertakings
E. Works Committee

Choose the correct answer from the options given below

(1) E, A, C, B, D
(2) E, B, D, C, A
(3) E, C, A, B, D
(4) E, D, C, B, A

84. Arrange in sequence the following legislations in order of their years of enactment from the earliest to the latest

A. The Minimum Wages Act
B. The Payment of Wages Act
C. The Payment of Gratuity Act
D. The Payment of Bonus Act
E. The Equal Remuneration Act

Choose the correct answer from the options given below

(1) A, B, E, D, C
(2) B, A, D, C, E
(3) B, A, E, D, C
(4) E, C, D, A, B

85. Arrange the committees/commission in sequence from the latest to the earliest, as per the year they were set up

A. Royal Commission on Labour
B. National Commission on Labour
C. Standing Labour Committee
D. Labour Investigation Committee
E. Bihar Labour Enquiry Committee

Choose the correct answer from the options given below

(1) C, B, D, E, A
(2) B, D, C, E, A
(3) E, B, C, D, A
(4) A, E, D, B, C

86. Given below are two statements, one is labelled as Assertion A and the other is labelled as Reason R

Assertion A: Financial inclusion is desirable to help the weaker sections of the society in the country

Reason R: Investment activity needs to be promoted to facilitate access to development benefits

In light of the above statements, choose the most appropriate answer from the options given below

(1) Both A and R are correct and R is the correct explanation of A
(2) Both A and R are correct but R is NOT the correct explanation of A
(3) A is correct but R is not correct
(4) A is not correct but R is correct

87. Given below are two statements, one is labelled as Assertion A and the other is labelled as Reason R

Assertion A: Intra-mural and extra-mural welfare facilities in organizations are mutually complimentary

Reason R: The work-life balance needs to be ensured in order to get the best output from an employee

In light of the above statements, choose the most appropriate answer from the options given below

(1) Both A and R are correct and R is the correct explanation of A
(2) Both A and R are correct but R is NOT the correct explanation of A
(3) A is correct but R is not correct
(4) A is not correct but R is correct

88. Given below are two statements, one is labelled as Assertion A and the other is labelled as Reason R

Assertion A: Structural inertia is an organizational resistance process to change because organizations have a built-in mechanism to produce stability

Reason R: People with a high need for security are likely to resist change because it threatens their feeling of safety

In light of the above statements, choose the most appropriate answer from the options given below

(1) Both A and R are correct and R is the correct explanation of A
(2) Both A and R are correct but R is NOT the correct explanation of A
(3) A is correct but R is not correct
(4) A is not correct but R is correct

89. Given below are two statements, one is labelled as Assertion A and the other is labelled as Reason R

Assertion A: It is one thing to hold that the role of the state should be minimal, and quite another to hold that industrial relations should be based only on bilateralism

Reason R: Bilateralism is an essential ingredient of industrial relations and both parties should rely on it as far as possible. But it cannot be denied that there is a role that mediation, arbitration, adjudication or third party intervention can play to ensure industrial peace with justice to both sides and to the society

In light of the above statements, choose the most appropriate answer from the options given below

(1) Both A and R are correct and R is the correct explanation of A
(2) Both A and R are correct but R is NOT the correct explanation of A
(3) A is correct but R is not correct
(4) A is not correct but R is correct

90. Given below are two statements, one is labelled as Assertion A and the other is labelled as Reason R

Assertion A: Attitudes of confrontation must give place to an attitude of genuine partnership

Reason R: Organizations of workers as well as employers, and the state itself, should identify and create the conditions on which harmonious relations that we need can be created and maintained

In light of the above statements, choose the most appropriate answer from the options given below

(1) Both A and R are correct and R is the correct explanation of A
(2) Both A and R are correct but R is NOT the correct explanation of A
(3) A is correct but R is not correct
(4) A is not correct but R is correct

Read the passage carefully and answer question

Following the latest trends and being fashionable is the 'in thing' these days. This fad is not only prevalent in clothes, accessories, home decor and every conceivable thing, but also in attitudes and behaviours. These days being rude, loud, intolerant, and aggressive is 'COOL'. Anyone who is quiet, polite and keeps a low profile is labelled a sissy, simple and regressive.

Increasingly, the world is becoming 'I' centric. Everyone believes and follows the principle of 'ME' and 'MYSELF' above 'YOU' and YOURS'. Checking the phone repeatedly when in company, not listening to others, interrupting a conversation, talking loudly on the phone in a public place, parking the car in the middle of the road and being unmindful of the traffic chaos, being nasty on social media, aggression on the road is all a part of normal behaviour these days.

A 2013 survey found that as social media usage surged over the years, it has given rise to increasing cases of incivility; with 78 per cent of 2698 people reporting an increase in rudeness online. Social media has brought about an increase in bad manners and loss of courtesies, decency and etiquette in society. Perhaps, it is easier to be mean, and rude when one is not in a face to face interaction with somebody. Sadly, appaling behaviour, intolerant views, a good dose of abuse, aggression and expletives thrown in, have become fodder for the soul.

91. In order to be fashionable and cool these days, one has to be:
(1) Dressed in latest fashion
(2) Intolerant, ill-mannered and aggressive
(3) Knowledgeable
(4) Funny and friendly

92. We are becoming increasingly rude because:
(1) We like being rude
(2) Social media encourages such behaviour
(3) We are subjected to modern day stresses
(4) We are not concerned about others' feelings

93. What is NOT included in identification of a low profile individual?
(1) Regressive
(2) Sissy
(3) Attractive
(4) Simple

94. What is NOT considered as a part of normal behaviour these days?
(1) Following the traffic rules
(2) Talking loudly over phone in public place
(3) Being nasty on social media
(4) Not listening to others

95. When is it easier to be nasty?
(1) When one meets the other person
(2) When one is not face to face
(3) When one talks in a group
(4) When one is in a public place

Read the passage carefully and answer questions that follow

'Chanakya Neeti' is synonymous with efficient statecraft around the world, and Chanakya is India's face of political statecraft and the rich political understanding of its ancient heritage. No political efficiency is devoid of understanding Chanakya and his ways of statecraft. In fact, he showed the world that political theory is in practice. Ancient Indian history is incomplete without a reference to his ways of statecraft and politics.

Chanakya amazes any scholar with his multifaceted character, but it had a distinct focused aim. He was more about philosophy and thoughts put into action. He does not bore you with his philosophical theory but engages you to think, act and achieve what you dream of. He overthrew a mighty empire and put in the throne a humble man like Chandragupta Maurya. He identified the potential ruler from a group of children, thus gave the world a great sovereign who united the Indian subcontinent into a political and administrative unit.

For sure, Chanakya's mental capabilities were superb. The modern global diplomacy revolves around his principle of 'saam, daam, dand, bhed' (persuade, purchase/set a price upon, punish, exploit the weakness). His Arthashastra elevates the state to a position where service to it entails imperatives unknown to morality. Chanakya would have been identified as a professor of political science and economics at Takshshila. He was an economic, political and royal adviser and a think tank, and can be credited to have given India its complex united empire.

96. 'Chanakya Neeti' is:
(1) An individual
(2) A political treatise
(3) A philosophy
(4) A complex way of thinking

97. Chanakya amazes scholars because of:
(1) His character
(2) His focused aim
(3) Boring political philosophy

(4) Ability to get people to think, act and achieve their dreams

98. In *Arthashastra*, Chanakya places the interest of the state:

(1) Below moral responsibility
(2) At par with moral responsibility
(3) Above any moral responsibility
(4) The state has nothing to do with moral responsibility

99. The modern day global diplomacy follows the principle of

(1) Reward, request, entreaty and punishment
(2) Request, cajole, threaten and persuade
(3) Purchase, punish, request and accept
(4) Persuasion, exploitation, punishment and purchase

100. Chanakya identified the potential ruler from among which one of the following?

(1) Politicians
(2) Kings
(3) Teachers
(4) Children

ANSWER KEY

1. (2)	**2.** (3)	**3.** (2)	**4.** (3)	**5.** (2)	**6.** (1)	**7.** (4)	**8.** (2)	**9.** (2)	**10.** (1)
11. (2)	**12.** (3)	**13.** (2)	**14.** (1)	**15.** (4)	**16.** (2)	**17.** (3)	**18.** (2)	**19.** (3)	**20.** (2)
21. (4)	**22.** (2)	**23.** (1)	**24.** (4)	**25.** (4)	**26.** (3)	**27.** (1)	**28.** (4)	**29.** (3)	**30.** (2)
31. (1)	**32.** (2)	**33.** (1)	**34.** (4)	**35.** (4)	**36.** (2)	**37.** (4)	**38.** (3)	**39.** (2)	**40.** (3)
41. (3)	**42.** (4)	**43.** (3)	**44.** (1)	**45.** (3)	**46.** (2)	**47.** (4)	**48.** (2)	**49.** (2)	**50.** (2)
51. (4)	**52.** (2)	**53.** (2)	**54.** (3)	**55.** (1)	**56.** (3)	**57.** (1)	**58.** (4)	**59.** (1)	**60.** (4)
61. (2)	**62.** (2)	**63.** (1)	**64.** (4)	**65.** (1)	**66.** (1)	**67.** (2)	**68.** (1)	**69.** (2)	**70.** (3)
71. (3)	**72.** (1)	**73.** (1)	**74.** (3)	**75.** (1)	**76.** (2)	**77.** (2)	**78.** (2)	**79.** (4)	**80.** (1)
81. (1)	**82.** (3)	**83.** (1)	**84.** (2)	**85.** (2)	**86.** (1)	**87.** (1)	**88.** (2)	**89.** (1)	**90.** (1)
91. (2)	**92.** (2)	**93.** (3)	**94.** (1)	**95.** (2)	**96.** (2)	**97.** (4)	**98.** (3)	**99.** (4)	**100.** (4)

JULY, 2022

LABOUR WELFARE & INDUSTRIAL RELATIONS, LABOUR & SOCIAL WELFARE, HUMAN RESOURCE MANAGEMENT

PAPER-II

Note : This paper contains **hundred (100)** objective type questions, each question carrying **two (2)** marks.

1. Who argued that money spent to improving labour was one of the best investments that business executives could make?
(1) Hugo Munsterberg
(2) Elton Mayo
(3) Charles Babbage
(4) Robert Owen

2. Which of the following seeks to determine how a corporation should compete in its business?
(1) Policy (2) Mission
(3) Vision (4) Strategy

3. According to Herzberg, which of the following is a satisfier?
(1) Job Security
(2) Company policy
(3) Recognition
(4) Working conditions

4. Flexible plans that set out general guidelines are
(1) Strategic plans
(2) Single use plans
(3) Directional plans
(4) Long term plans

5. Talent Management relates to
(1) Holistic integrated and result oriented process of planning recruiting selecting, developing, managing and compensating employees.
(2) Result oriented process of manpower planning.
(3) Holistic and integrated process of recruitment, selection and training.
(4) Result oriented training of employees to sharpen talent to prevent obsolescence of human resource.

6. When employees abroad supply services that the company's own employees previously did in house, it is known as
(1) Alternate staffing
(2) Outsourcing
(3) Offshoring
(4) Temporary staffing

7. In which of the following systems employees are paid on the basis of skills and knowledge one is capable of using rather than for the title of the job currently held?
(1) Broadbanding
(2) Competency based pay
(3) Comparable worth
(4) Experience based pay

8. Which of the following is not a direct financial payment to workers?
(A) Wage (B) Incentive
(C) Commission (D) Insurance
Choose the correct answer from the options given below :
(1) B, D and E Only (2) C and E Only
(3) D Only (4) E Only

9. In which of the following approaches, MNCs pay less cash and more benefit compensation package for expatriates?
(1) Cluster System Approach
(2) Buffet Approach
(3) Bargaining Approach
(4) Global Approach

10. 'OCTAPACE' refers to
(1) H.R.D. culture
(2) Human Relations
(3) Human Resource information system
(4) Behaviour Rating

11. Which one of the following categories will not come under the HR outsourcing?
(1) Professional Employer Organization (PEO)
(2) Business Process Outsourcing (BPO)
(3) Application Service Provider (ASP)
(4) Contract Employees (CE)

12. Who among the following said, "Take my physical assets, leave my people, and in five years I will have it all back"?
(1) Bill Gates (2) Rensis Likert
(3) Peter Drucker (4) Alfred Sloan

13. Which one of the following represents the moral values that develop on the basis of influence of role models and other significant persons?
(1) Id (2) Ego
(3) Esteem (4) Superego

14. Under which one of the following styles, a manager is likely to remark that nothing significant can ever be done?
(1) Sulking (2) Withdrawn
(3) Cynical (4) Overindulgent

15. Which one of the following relates to a person's self perceived competence and self image?
(1) Self Esteem
(2) Self Actualisation
(3) Self Efficacy
(4) Self motivation

16. Who gave the operant conditioning theory?
(1) Edward Tolman
(2) Pavlov & Waston
(3) B.N. Skinner (4) Albert Bandurg

17. The book 'Trade Unionism in the New Society' was authored by which of the following?
(1) Harold J. Laski
(2) G.D.H. Cole
(3) Sidney and Beatrice Webb
(4) S.D. Punekar

18. Which of the following is not part of the three tier structure of the Joint Consultative Machinery and Compulsory Arbitration in Govt. Department?
(1) Unit Level
(2) Office/Regional Level
(3) Department bevel
(4) National Level

19. By which convention number of International Labour Organization "Freedom of Association and Protection of the right to organise" has declared as Fundamental rights?
(1) Convention No. 19
(2) Convention No. 87
(3) Convention No. 98
(4) Convention No. 81

20. "Every Class Struggle is a Political Struggle" who said this?
(1) Lenin (2) Karl Marx
(3) G.D.H. Cole (4) Fedrick Engele

21. In which session of the Indian Labour conference the functions of works Committee was discussed and approved a list of functions which could be assigned to the works committee and a list of functions which should not be assigned to the works committee?
(1) 14th Session (2) 16th Session
(3) 17th Session (4) 20th Session

22. Under which Section of the Industrial Disputes (Amendment and Miscellaneous Provisions) Act, 1956, the Central Government is authorized to Constitute the national tribunals?
(1) Section 7 (2) Section 7A
(3) Section 7B (4) Section 10A

23. What shall he the maximum number of members of Grievance Redressal Committee?
(1) Six only (2) Twelve only
(3) Sixteen only (4) Twenty only

24. Which of the following is not a form of Strikes?
(1) Sit-Down (2) Pen-Down
(3) Pickering (4) Wildcat

25. The ______ was the first Act passed to regulate the industrial relations in India.
(1) Apprentice Act
(2) Factories Act
(3) Bombay Trade Disputes Act
(4) Industrial Disputes Act

26. How many parts are there in the Schedule of the Child Labour (Prohibition and Regulation) Act, 1986?
(1) 1 (2) 2
(3) 3 (4) 4

27. The periods of work of adult workers in a factory each day shall be so fixed that no period shall exceed ________ hours and that no worker shall work for more than ______ hours before he has had an interval for rest of at least half an hour.
(1) Five. Five (2) Six. Six
(3) Eight. Eight (4) Nine, Nine

28. The Contract Labour (Regulation & Abolition) Act 1910 shall not apply to establishments in which one of the following?
(1) An intermittent or Casual nature
(2) Permanent Work
(3) Both 1 & 2
(4) None of the above

29. How gratuity is calculated for non seasonable establishment for piece rated employees?
(1) $\frac{\text{Basic wage} \times 15 \times \text{No. of Completed year of Service}}{26}$
(2) $\frac{\text{Last Drawn wages} \times 7 \times \text{No. of Completed Year of Services}}{26}$
(3) $\frac{\text{Basic wage} \times 15 \times \text{No. of Completed year of Service}}{30}$
(4) $\frac{\text{Average of last 3 months wages} \times 1 \times \text{No of Completed Year of Service}}{26}$

30. The Pension scheme of employees is financed by diverting............of ....monthly contribution from the employees provident fund.
(1) 10.33%, Employer's
(2) 10.33%, Employee's
(3) 8.33%, Employer's
(4) 8.33%, Employee's

31. Under Equal Remuneration Act, 1976, "Same work or work of a similar nature means ________ required are the same, when performed under similar working conditions by man or woman.
(1) Skills (2) Efforts
(3) Responsibilities
(4) All of the above

32. Mr. X was terminated by his employer of the factory to which Payment of wages Act is applicable with a reason of non-satisfaction of performance of Mr. X's work. When is the wages earned by Mr. X till the date of termination need to be paid by the employer?
(1) Before expiry of the second working day from the termination.
(2) Within a month's time
(3) Within a weak's time
(4) On the tenth clay from the termination date.

33. When was the Unorganised Workers Social Security Act enacted?
(1) Year 2007 (2) Year 2008
(3) Year 2009 (4) Year 2010

34. Which is NOT a Principle of Labour Welfare?
(1) Adequacy of Wages
(2) Efficiency
(3) Responsibility
(4) Placating

35. Apart from Factories Act, 1948, there exists some Specialised Safety Laws. Which

among the following is NOT a specialised Safety law?

(1) Indian Boilers Act, 1923
(2) Indian Electricity Act, 1910
(3) The Plantation Labour Act, 1951
(4) Indian Explosives Act, 1884

36. Which among the following is a correct statement with respect to Social Insurance?

(1) Social Insurance is Fundamentally different from commercial insurance.
(2) Social Insurance and Commercial Insurance are similar.
(3) Government alone pays for social Insurance.
(4) Employees covered under it are not required to contribute.

37. Some Labour Markets, particularly those in which the sellers of labour are represented by a Union, operate under which one of the following?

(1) Very formal set of rules that partly govern buyer-seller transactions.
(2) An informal environment with no set of formal rules for buyer-seller transactions.
(3) A very formal set of rules that fully govern buyer-seller transactions.
(4) A formal environment with no set of rules for buyer-seller transactions.

38. Isoquant has its particular curvature for which one of the following the reasons?

(1) Labour and Capital are imperfect Substitutes.
(2) Labour and Capital are perfect Substitutes.
(3) Capital and technology are perfect Substitute.
(4) Labour and technology are perfect Substitute.

39. Who confirmed after comprehensive study into the supply curve for Labour that "Variations in the proportion of a city's population in the labour force, that is, its participation rate appear to be inversely associated with variations in its average income per equivalent male worker"?

(1) Paul H. Doughlas
(2) Allan M. Cartter
(3) John Bates Clark
(4) Clarence D. Long

40. When some people are 'between jobs', the unemployment caused is known as which one of the following?

(1) Disguished Unemployment
(2) Seasonal Unemployment
(3) Frictional Unemployment
(4) Cyclic Unemployment

41. Arrange the following steps of test validation process in the correct sequence:

(A) Choose the test
(B) Relate the test scores and criteria
(C) Cross validate and revalidate
(D) Administer the test
(E) Analyse the job and determine predictors

Choose the correct answer from the options given below:

(1) E, A, D, B, C (2) B, A, C, E, D
(3) E, A, B, D, C (4) D, B, C, A, E

42. Which of the following are generally included in the Balanced Scorecard Approach of Control?

(A) Finances
(B) Customers
(C) Internal processes
(D) People and assets

Choose the most appropriate answer from the options given below :

(1) A and C Only (2) A and B Only
(3) B and D Only (4) A, B, C and D

43. Which of the following statements are correct regarding 'mentoring'?

(A) It helps in transfer of knowledge to mentee.
(B) It is good for transmission and sustenance of organisation culture.
(C) It can only be formally organised.
(D) It is an interactive process in which only mentore gives the topic for learning

Choose the correct answer from the options given below :

(1) A and D Only
(2) B and C Only
(3) A and B Only
(4) A and C Only

44. Arrange the following steps of Job Evaluation in ascending order.

(A) Choosing job evaluation committee
(B) Identifying need for job evaluation
(C) Selecting Compensable factors
(D) Identifying bench work jobs
(E) Evaluating worth of each job.

Choose the correct answer from the options given below:

(1) D, B, A, C, E (2) A, B, C, D, E
(3) A, B, E, D, C (4) B, A, D, C, E

45. Arrange the following steps of Job Evaluation in ascending order.

(A) Obtain job information
(B) Compare current pay with what others are paying
(C) Assign a new pay scale
(D) Select jobs and compensable factors
(E) Rank jobs and combine rating

Choose the correct answer from the options given below:

(1) A, E, D, C, B (2) D, B, C, A, E
(3) D, A. B, E, C (4) A, D, E, B, C

46. Which of the following relate to Quality Circles?

(A) Formal organisation
(B) Self-empowered group
(C) Informal organisation
(D) Venture Team

Choose the correct answer from the options given below:

(1) A, B and D only
(2) A, B and C only
(3) B, C and D only
(4) A, C and D only

47. Which of the followings are Human Resource Accounting models?

(A) Flumholtz model
(B) Morris Model
(C) Lev and Schwartz Model
(D) Ogan's Model
(E) Adam's Model

Choose the correct answer from the options given below :

(1) A, B, D Only (2) A, C, D Only
(3) B, C, E Only (4) A, C, E Only

48. Which of the following are the individual Stress coping techniques?

(A) Exercise
(B) Relaxation
(C) Behavioural Self control
(D) Irritability

Choose the correct answer from the options given below:

(1) A and B Only
(2) A, B and E Only
(3) A, B, C and D Only
(4) A, B, C and E Only

49. Which of the following are Human Resource Accounting Models?

(A) Morse Model (B) Likert Model
(C) Ogan's Model (D) Regan's Model
(E) Adam's Model

Choose the correct answer from the options given below:

(1) A, B, D Only (2) A, C, D Only
(3) A, B, C Only (4) A, B, E Only

50. What are the main approaches in the area of international compensation with regard to posting MNCs employees in foreign countries?

(A) Going Rate Approach
(B) Qualitative Approach
(C) Combination Approach
(D) Balance Sheet Approach

Choose the most appropriate answer from the options given below:

(1) A & B Only (2) B & C Only
(3) C & D Only (4) A & D Only

51. Which of the following are the ways of determining representative union for the purpose of Collective Bargaining in India?
(A) Code of conduct
(B) Secret ballot
(C) Check off system
(D) Membership verification
Choose the correct answer from the options given below:
(1) A & B Only (2) C & D Only
(3) C & D Only (4) A, C & D Only

52. Which of the following basic factors were outlined by Selig Perlman in his theory of Labour Movement?
(A) The resistance power of capitalism
(B) The degree of dominance over the labour movement by the intellectuals mentality
(C) The degree of maturity of a trade union's mentality.
(D) The degree of Political Struggle of the workers.
Choose the most appropriate answer from the options given below :
(1) A, B, C Only (2) A, C, D Only
(3) A, B, D Only (4) B, C, D Only

53. Which of the following are non-statutory bodies for prevention & Settlement of Industrial Disputes?
(A) Indian Labour Conference
(B) Standing Labour Committee
(C) Board of Conciliation
(D) State Labour Advisory Boards
(E) Court of Enquiry
Choose the correct answer from the options given below :
(1) B, C Only (2) A, B, D Only
(3) C, E Only (4) D, E Only

54. Which of the following are the autonomous organisations of Labour Ministry?
(A) Employee's State Insurance Corporation
(B) Central Board for Workers' Education
(C) The Directorate General of Mines Safety
(D) V.V. Giri National Labour Institute.
Choose the correct answer from the options given below:
(1) A and B Only (2) B and C Only
(3) A, B, D Only (4) B, C, D Only

55. Given below are the names of Indian Trade Unions / Associations. Arrange the sequence of their establishment year from earlier to later.
(A) Hind Mazdoor Sabha
(B) Madras Labour Union
(C) Indian National Trade Union Congress
(D) Self Employed Women's Association
(E) Hindustan Mazdoor Sevak Sangh
Choose the correct answer from the options given below:
(1) A, E, C, D, B (2) C, A, D, E, B
(3) B, E, C, A, D (4) E, C, D, A, B

56. The Acts belonging to the category of protective legislation are:
(A) Factories Act, 1948
(B) Contract Labour (Regulation and Abolition) Act, 1970
(C) Trade Union Act, 1926
(D) Industrial Disputes Act, 1947
Choose the most appropriate answer from the options given below :
(1) A, B and C Only
(2) A and B Only
(3) C and D Only
(4) A, B and D Only

57. Licences of contractors under the Inter-State Migrant workmen (Regulation of Employment and Condition of Service) Act, 1979 may be revoked under which of the following of situations?
(A) Obtained by misrepresentation or suppression of any material fact.
(B) Without reasonable cause, failed to comply with the conditions subject to which the licence has been granted.
(C) Contravened any of the provisions of the Act.

(D) After receiving an application from the contractors.

Choose the most appropriate answer from the options given below :

(1) A, B and C Only
(2) B, C and D Only
(3) C and D Only
(4) A and B Only

58. Which of the following are the methods of fixing and revising minimum wages under the Minimum Wages Act, 1948?

(A) Committee method
(B) Notification method
(C) Wage Board
(D) Collective Bargaining

Choose the most appropriate answer from the options given below:

(1) A, B, C and D Only
(2) C and D Only
(3) A, C, and D Only
(4) A and B Only

59. Which of the following situations, as per The Employees Provident Fund and Miscellaneous Provision Act, 1952, allow for full withdrawal of provident fund amount?

(A) Death
(B) Superannuation
(C) Retrenchment
(D) Construction of house

Choose the correct answer from the options given below:

(1) A, C and D Only
(2) A, B and C Only
(3) A and B Only
(4) A, B, C, and D Only

60. Wage-periods under The Payment of Wages Act, 1936 can be

(A) 7 days (B) 15 days
(C) 30 days (D) 45 days

Choose the correct answer from the options given below:

(1) B and C Only
(2) A and B Only
(3) B, C and D Only
(4) A, B and C Only

61. Central Government may formulate and notify which suitable welfare schemes for workers under Unorganised Social Security Act, 2008?

(A) Life and Disability cover
(B) Employment protection cover
(C) Health and maternity cover
(D) Old age protection

Choose the correct answer from the options given below:

(1) A, B and C Only
(2) A, C and D Only
(3) A, B and D Only
(4) B, C and D Only

62. Under which Sections of the Factories Act. 1948 as amended, a member the State Government is empowered to constitute a Site Appraisal Committee to examine a factory involving hazardous process?

(A) Section 41 A (1)
(B) Section 41A
(C) Section 41A (2-4)
(D) Section 41A (5)
(E) Section 41 B and C

Choose the most appropriate answer from the options given below :

(1) A and B only (2) A and C only
(3) C and D only (4) B and E only

63. In case of Labour, the Demand Curve illustrates which of the following?

(A) In case of Labour, the Demand Curve illustrates which of the following?
(B) At each possible wage rate, the maximum quantity of labour an employer would be willing to employ per period of time.
(C) At each possible wage rate, the minimum quantity of Labour as employer would be willing to employ per period of time.
(D) At each possible wage rate, quantity of Labour an employer would be willing to employ.

(E) For each possible quantity of Labour, the maximum wage rate at which the employer would be willing to employ that particular quantity.

(F) The Maximum quantity of Labour an employer would employ.

Choose the most appropriate answer from the options given below :

(1) A and B Only (2) A and C Only
(3) A and D Only (4) B and C Only

64. Which are not determinants of Supply of labour among the following?

(A) Preference for work versus leisure.
(B) Prices of other inputs
(C) Other wage rates
(D) Number of Qualified Supplier
(E) Number of firms

Choose the most appropriate answer from the options given below :

(1) A and B Only (2) A and C Only
(3) B and D Only (4) B and E Only

65. The market demand for Labour and the market supply of Labour jointly determine which of the following?

(A) An equilibrium level of wage rate
(B) The maximum level of wage rate
(C) An equilibrium level of employment
(D) The minimum level of employment

Choose the most appropriate answer from the options given below:

(1) A and B Only
(2) B and C Only
(3) A and C Only
(4) C and D Only

66. Given below are two statements :

Statement I: In a Matrix Organisation, specialists from different functional departments work on projects that are led by a project manager.

Statement II: One unique aspect of Matrix organization is that it creates a unity of command managers coordinate and resolve conflicts.

In the light of the above statements, choose the most appropriate answer from the options given below:

(1) Both Statement I and Statement II are correct
(2) Both Statement I and Statement II are incorrect
(3) Statement I is correct but Statement II is incorrect
(4) Statement I is incorrect but Statement II is correct

67. Match List I with List II

List I	List II
(A) Intelligence Test	(I) Preferred Occupation
(B) Personality Test	(II) Memory and Vocabulary
(C) Interest Test	(III) Job knowledge
(D) Achievement Test	(IV) Emotional Stability and Agreeableness

Choose the correct answer from the options given below :

(1) (A)-(IV), (B)-(III), (C)-(I), (D)-(II)
(2) (A)-(II), (B)-(IV), (C)-(I), (D)-(III)
(3) (A)-(I), (B)-(II), (C)-(III), (D)-(IV)
(4) (A-(IV), (B)-(III), (C)-(II), (D)-(I)

68. Match List I with List II

List I Types of Corporations	List II Appropriate Meaning
(A) International Corporation	(I) Subsidiaries operating as stand alone businesses in multiple countries.
(B) Multinational Corporation	(III) Specialised facilities and Complex coordination mechanism provides global integration
(C) Transnational Corporation	(III) Viewing world as a single

	marked and operations controlled centrally from corporate office.
(D) Global Corporation	(IV) Domestic firm using existing capabilities to expand into foreign market.

Choose the correct answer from the options given below:
(1) (A)-(II), (B)-(I), (C)-(III), (D)-(IV)
(2) (A)-(IV), (B), (I), (C)-(II), (D)-(III)
(3) (A)-(I), (B)-(II), (C)-(III), (D)-(IV)
(4) (A)-(IV), (B)-(III), (C)-(I), (D)-(II)

69. Match List I with List II : Given below the theory of Leadership in Lis-I and its Propounder in List-I

List I	List II
(A) Managerial Grid Theory	(I) Mcgreagor
(B) X and Y Theory	(II) Fred E. Fielder
(C) Path-Goal Theory	(III) Robert R. Blake
(D) Contingency Theory	(IV) Martin G. Evans

Choose the correct answer from the options given below :
(1) (A)-(III), (B)-(I), (C)-(IV), (D)-(II)
(2) (A)-(II), (B)-(III), (C)-(I), (D)-(IV)
(3) (A)-(IV), (B)-(I), (C)-(II), (D)-(III)
(4) (A)-(I), (B)-(IV), (C)-(II), (D)-(III)

70. Match List I with List II : Given below four Sub-Process as of Collective Bargaining Negotiations argued by Waltone & Mo Karsic.

List I Sub Process of Bargaining	List II Meaning
(A) Distributive Bargaining	(I) Involves those aspects of negotiation in which one side's gain is the other side's loss. It is win-lose.
(B) Intergrative Bargaining	(II) When there are different goals or preferences of either side (union or management).
(C) Intra-organisational Bargaining	(III) Issues and process in which a solution provides gains to both labour and management leading to join gain or win-win bargaining.
(D) Attitudinal Structuring	(IV) Negotiations often involve a lot of uncertainty, Uncertainty arises from the difficulties the parties face in anticipating how much strikes power they possess and the complication involved in interpreting each other intentions.

Choose the correct answer from the options given below:
(1) (A)-(I), (B)-(II), (C)-(III), (D)-(IV)
(2) (A)-(I), (B)-(III), (C)-(II), (D)-(IV)
(3) (A)-(II), (B)-(III), (C)-(IV), (D)-(I)
(4) (A)-(III), (B)-(II), (C)-(I), (D)-(IV)

71. Match List I with List II : Given below are the negotiation result in List-I and their appropriate meaning in List-II

List I Negotion Result	List II Appropriate Meaning
(A) Win-lose	(I) Both parties get what they want the parties believe in mutual gain.
(B) Lose-Win	(II) Both parties lose or do not get what they want and re-

flect an attitude of take it or leave it.

(C) Lose-Lose (III) The negotioning parties think that wining is every-thing or winning is the only thing.

(D) Win-Win (IV) One party achieves most and the other party loses or gain very little.

Choose the correct answer from the options given below:

(1) (A)-(III), (B)-(IV), (C)-(II), (D)-(I)
(2) (A)-(II), (B)-(III), (C)-(I), (D)-(IV)
(3) (A)-(III), (B)-(II), (C)-(IV), (D)-(I)
(4) (A)-(IV), (B)-(III), (C)-(II), (D)-(I)

72. Match List I with List II

List I **Acts**	**List II** **Years of enactment**
(A) The Factories Act	(I) 1986
(B) The Inter-State Migrant Workmen (Regulation of employment and conditions of services) Act.	(II) 1970
(C) The Contract Labour (Regulation and Abolition) Act	(III) 1979
(D) The Child Labour (Prohibition and Regulation) Act	(IV) 1948

Choose the correct answer from the options given below:

(1) (A)-(IV), (B)-(III), (C)-(II), (D)-(I)
(2) (A)-(IV), (B)-(II), (C)-(I), (D)-(III)
(3) (A)-(IV), (B)-(III), (C)-(I), (D)-(II)
(4) (A)-(II), (B)-(I), (C)-(III), (D)-(IV)

73. Match List I with List II

List I	**List II**
(A) The Payment of Bonus Act, 1965	(I) To remove the suffering of section of the society.
(B) The Payment of Wages Act, 1936	(II) To develop the sense of belongingness among employees
(C) The Minimum Wages Act, 1948	(III) Equal pay for both men and women
(D) The Equal Remuneration Act, 1976	(IV) To ensure regular and timely payment of wages.

Choose the correct answer from the options given below:

(1) (A)-(III), (B)-(I), (C)-(IV), (D)-(II)
(2) (A)-(I), (B)-(III), (C)-(IV), (D)-(II)
(3) (A)-(II), (B)-(IV), (C)-(I), (D)-(III)
(4) (A)-(IV), (B)-(II), (C)-(I), (D)-(III)

74. Given below are two statements :

Statement I: The origin of Labour Welfare activity in India goes back to 1837 when, following the abolition of Slavery in 1833, the British colonies started importing Indian Labour.

Statement II: Labour welfare activities were hardly controlled by legislation during pre-independence period.

In the light of the above statements, choose the correct answer from the options given below:

(1) Both Statement I and Statement II are true
(2) Both Statement I and Statement II are false
(3) Statement I is true but Statement II is false
(4) Statement I is false but Statement II is true

75. Match List I with List II

List I **Propounders**	**List II** **Theory of wages**
(A) John Davidson	(I) Marginal Productivity Theory
(B) John Clark & Hennery Wicksteed	(II) Subsistence Theory

(C) David Ricardo (III) Wage Fund Theory

(D) Adam Smith (IV) Bargaining Theory

Choose the correct answer from the options given below:

(1) (A)-(IV), (B)-(III), (C)-(II), (D)-(I)
(2) (A)-(I), (B)-(II), (C)-(III), (D)-(IV)
(3) (A)-(IV), (B)-(I), (C)-(II), (D)-(III)
(4) (A)-(I), (B)-(IV), (C)-(II), (D)-(III)

76. Given below are two statements : One is labelled as Assertion A and the other is labelled as Reason R.

Assertion (A): Henri Fayol was of the opinion that organizations should be based on group ethic rather than individuals

Reasons (R): Individual potential remains only potential until released through group association

In the light of the above statements, choose the correct answer from the options given below:

(1) Both (A) and (R) are true and (R) is the correct explanation of (A)
(2) Both (A) and (R) are true but (R) is NOT the correct explanation of (A)
(3) (A) is true but (R) is false
(4) (A) is false but (R) is true

77. Given below are two statements : One is labelled as Assertion A and the other is labelled as Reason R.

Assertion (A): In modern times, there is an increase in the number of 'On-demand' workers. These workers can choose when to work, on what to work and how much to work.

Reasons (R): The major worry about 'on-demand' workers is not just about the benefits they receive but about a lack of agency – a future in which computers, rather than humans determine about what you do, when and for how much.

In the light of the above statements, choose the most appropriate answer from the options given below :

(1) Both (A) and (R) are correct and (R) is the correct explanation of (A)
(2) Both (A) and (R) are correct but (R) is NOT the correct explanation of (A)
(3) (A) is correct but (R) is not correct
(4) (A) is not correct but (R) is correct

78. Arrange the following steps of organisational change in the correct sequence from the first to the last:

(A) Action Proposal
(B) Implementation
(C) Initiation
(D) Deliberation
(E) Diagnosis

Choose the correct answer from the options given below:

(1) (E), (B), (C), (D), (A)
(2) (B), (C), (D), (E), (A)
(3) (C), (E), (D), (A), (B)
(4) (A), (B), (E), (D), (C)

79. Arrange the following in the right sequence of Maslow's Hierchy of need starting from the lowest order need

(A) Job security
(B) Achievement
(C) Transforming perception of self into reality
(D) Hunger
(E) Belongings

Choose the correct answer from the options given below

(1) (D), (B), (E), (A), (C)
(2) (A), (D), (B), (E), (C)
(3) (D), (A), (E), (B), (C)
(4) (E), (D), (C), (B), (A)

80. Given below are the names of Indian Trade Union/Associations. Arrange the sequence of their establishment year from earlier to later.

(A) All India Trade Union Congress
(B) The Textile Labour Association of Ahmedabad
(C) United Trade Union Congress

(D) The Hindustan Mazdoor Sevak Sangh
(E) Bharatiya Mazdoor Sangh

Choose the correct answer from the options given below

(1) (B), (A), (D), (C), (E)
(2) (A), (C), (B), (D), (E)
(3) (B), (D), (A), (C), (E)
(4) (C), (E), (A), (D), (B)

81. Given below are two statements : One is labelled as Assertion A and the other is labelled as Reason R.

Assertion (A): Labour Administration in the country has failed to deliver the desired results for protection of labour.

Reasons (R): It has been observed that despite various legislative measures, its ineffective implementation has not given the expected results.

In the light of the above statements, choose the most appropriate answer from the options given below :

(1) Both (A) and (R) are correct and (R) is the correct explanation of (A)
(2) Both (A) and (R) are correct but (R) is NOT the correct explanation of (A)
(3) (A) is correct but (R) is not correct
(4) (A) is not correct but (R) is correct

82. Arrange the following welfare and health provisions of the contract Labour (Regulation and Abolition) Act, 1970 in ascending order of sections:

(A) Rest room
(B) First aid facility
(C) Canteen
(D) Other facility

Choose the correct answer from the options given below

(1) C, A, D, B (2) A, C, B, D
(3) B, A, C, D (4) C, B, D, A

83. Arrange in ascending order the steps of proceedings for fixing or revising minimum wages under the Minimum Wages Act, 1948

(A) Appointing Committee and Sub Committee
(B) Identification of Scheduled Employment
(C) Holding enquiries and making recommendations
(D) Fixing and revising the minimum wages on the case may be

Choose the correct answer from the options given below

(1) (A), (B), (C), (D)
(2) (B), (A), (C), (D)
(3) (C), (A), (B), (D)
(4) (C), (B), (A), (D)

84. Given below are two statements :

Statement I: Labour Welfare, by its very nature, "Must necessarily be elastic; hearing a some what different interpretation in one counting from another, according to the different social custom, the degree of industrialisation and the educational development of the worker."

Statement II: Limits cannot be rigidly laid down for the scope of Labour Welfare for all industries and for all times.

In the light of the above statements, choose the correct answer from the options given below:

(1) Both Statement I and Statement II are true
(2) Both Statement I and Statement II are false
(3) Statement I is true hut Statement II is false
(4) Statement I is false but Statement II is true

85. Given below are two statements : One is labelled as Assertion A and the other is labelled as Reason R.

Assertion (A): A manopsonist in the Labour market is the Sole buyer of a factor of production.

Reasons (R): It is because there is only one demander, there is no distinction between the manopsonist demand for Labour and market demand for Labour.

In the light of the above statements, choose the most appropriate answer from the options given below :

(1) Both (A) and (R) are correct and (R) is the correct explanation of (A)
(2) Both (A) and (R) are correct but (R) is NOT the correct explanation of (A)
(3) (A) is correct but (R) is not correct
(4) (A) is not correct but (R) is correct

86. Given below are two statements :

Statement I: Scanlon Plan is designed to encourage cooperation, Involvement and shaving of benefits.

Statement II: Scanlon Plan divides pay roll expenses by total sales.

In the light of the above statements, choose the mast appropriate answer from the options given below :

(1) Both Statement I and Statement II are correct
(2) Both Statement I and Statement II are incorrect
(3) Statement I is correct but Statement II is incorrect
(4) Statement I is incorrect but Statement II is correct

87. Given below are two statements : One is labelled as Assertion A and the other is labelled as Reason R.

Assertion A: Government intervention in industrial relations system became inevitable when Industrial peace started being threatened.

Reason R: Industrial peace and harmony are essential for industrial development in the country.

In light of the above statements, choose the most appropriate answer from the options given below

(1) Both A and R are correct and R is the correct explanation of A
(2) Both A and R are correct but R is NOT the correct explanation of A
(3) A is correct but R is not correct
(4) A is not correct but R is correct

88. Given below are two statements : One is labelled as Assertion A and the other is labelled as Reason R.

Assertion A: Modem industrialisation has created a new class of industrial proletariat which, with rural background and with very little social and material resources, is in great need of systematised help through social security agencies.

Reason R: Social security is a major aspect of public policy today and the extent of its prevalence is a measure of progress made by the country towards the idea of Welfare State.

In the light of the above statements, choose the correct answer from the options given below :

(1) Both A and R are true and R is the correct explanation of A
(2) Both A and R are true but R is NOT the correct explanation of A
(3) A is true but R is not false
(4) A is not false but R is true

89. Given below are two statements :

Statement I: Under the Child Labour (Prohibition and Regulation) Act, 1986, "family", in relation to an occupier, means the individual, the wife or husband, as the case may be, of such individual and their children, brother or sister of such individual.

Statement II: Duty and obligations of contractors under The Inter State Migrant Workmen (Regulation of Employment and Conditions of Service) Act, 1979, is given in Chapter V of the Act.

In the light of the above statements, choose the correct answer from the options given below :

(1) Both Statement I and Statement II are true
(2) Both Statement I and Statement II are false
(3) Statement I true but Statement II is false
(4) Statement I false but Statement II is true

90. Given below are two statements : One is labelled as Assertion A and the other is labelled as Reason R.

Assertion A: Outside leadership is not appreciable for trade unions.

Reason R: Trade Unions when controlled by outside leadership under political influence, and leadership functions with hidden intention of Serving the political interest of its parent parties. Besides it adversely impacts the growth of internal leadership with the result that the real cause of workers are mostly ignored.

In light of the above statements, choose the most appropriate answer from the options given below:

(1) Both A and R are correct and R is the correct explanation of A
(2) Both A and R are correct but R is NOT the correct explanation of A
(3) A is correct but R is not correct
(4) A is not correct but R is correct

Read the following passage carefully; and answer questions question No. 91-95:

The workmen's Breach of Contract Act, 1859 was a significant piece of legislation at the time. This Act not only demanded fines in cases of employment breaches, but it also provided for orders for specific performance of service. The Government began to intervene in the employment of women and children, as well as the working hours of workers in factories and mines, in the 1880s. The majority of law is the product of various government investigations. However, the legislation was not fairly enforced in these industries working practices, resulting in a very limited and selective effect. For example, the factories Act of 1881 only applied to factories with 100 or more employees using electrical power. The factories Act of 1891 applied to factories with 50 or more employees on the premises.

Several factors mixed the industrial and political environment, including the rise of a strong nationalist movement, the rapid growth of trade unions (which led to the formation of the All India Trade Union Congress in 1920), and the emergence of Communist influence in the labor movement. At that time, the recently formed ILO (International Labour Organization) began to influence the policies in relation to workers.

The Factories Act of 1922, the Mines Act of 1922, and the Workers Compensation Act of 1923 were all protective legislation at the time. With regards to industrial relations, this time saw the advent of a modern outlook, with the formulation of the Trade Union Act of 1926 and the Trade Dispute Act of 1929, both of which are formally still in use by present-by India. Owing to the world economic depression, there was a surge in unemployment. During this period, there was continuous agitation for Indian independence, in which the All India Trade Union Congress played a key role. A wave of strikes accompanied the mass dismissal, which coincided with the economic recession. In 1929, the British government established the Royal Commission on Labour in India. The Indian Labour Movement opposed the commission Unrest in the workplace, wage reductions, and employment losses persisted.

The Industrial Employment (Standing Orders) Act of 1946 required employers to provide employees with transparent terms and conditions of employment as required by the Act's Schedule and the concerned authorities. The Factories Act of 1948 and the Minimum Wage Act of 1948 were also important statutes during this period. Most of these laws has a system similar to the industrial Disputes Act of 1947, which limited their application to specific types of industry establishments.

91. Which of the following is not a correct statement?

(1) The Factories Act of 1881 applied to factories with 100 or more employees using electrical power.
(2) The Factories Act of 1891 applied to factories with 150 or more employees on the premises.
(3) The Factories Act of 1922, the Mine Act of 1922, and the Workmen's Compensation Act of 1923 were all protective legislation at the time.

(4) The Workmen's Breach of Contract Act, 1859 provided for orders for specific performance of service.

92. Which of the following is not associated with Labour Welfare and Industrial Relations?

(1) The industrial Employment (Standing Orders) Act, 1926

(2) The Competition Act, 2002

(3) The Minimum Wages Act, 1947

(4) The Industrial Dispute Act. 1948

93. Who played on important role in agitation against British for Indian Independence?

(1) Bharatiya Mazdoor Sangh

(2) All India Trade Union Congress

(3) Trade Union Coordination Centre

(4) All India Central Council of Trade Unions

94. Royal Labour Commission was :

(1) Set up by the British in UK

(2) Set up by British in India

(3) Set up by the British in Burma

(4) Set up by the Interim Government in Bengal

95. Assertion (A): ILO began influence the policies in relation to workers.

Reasons (R): Several factors mixed the industrial and political environment, including the rise of a strong nationalist movement, the rapid growth of trade unions (which led to the formation of the All India Trade Union Congress in 1920), and the emergence of Communist influence in the labor movement.

(1) (A) and (R) both are correct but (R) is not the right explanation of (A)

(2) (A) and (R) both are correct and (R) is the fight explanation of (A)

(3) (A) and (R) both are incorrect

(4) (A) is correct but (R) is not correct

Read the following passage: and answer question Nos. 96 to 100:

Findings of a survey on stress during COVID times conducted by a global professional network in India during 3rd quarter of 2021, narrated here below: India's overall workforce confidence remained steady with a composite score of +55 from July 31 to September 24, 2021, despite drastic transformations in the world of work. But keeping up with these times of change for the last 18 months has adversely affected the mental health of working professionals in the country. When asked to share their primary reasons for work stress, employed professionals cited 'balancing work with persona] needs' (34%), 'not making enough money' (32%), and 'slow career advancement' (25%) as the top there stressors at work today. Amid such stressful times, 1 in 3 professionals are also seen drawing optimism from the availability of jobs (36%) and improved control over expenses (30%) in today's recovering, yet competitive jobs marketplace. As workforce priorities continue to change in these transformative times, findings go on to indicate that flexibility and work-life balance will serve as critical talent drivers across the Indian professional landscape for years to come. While greater flexibility remains a mutual need across generations, younger professionals found it easier to take a break than their older cohorts. Findings reveal that millennials were 2x more likely to take time-offs, while Gen Z professionals were 1.5x more likely to take breaks during the day, when compared to Baby Boomers. Interestingly, boomers were 1.5x more likely to be open with their colleagues about mental health and stress when compared to millennials as well as Gen Z professionals.

There's a wide gap between what employees need and what employers are offering to cope with stress. While nearly half of (47%) employed professionals wish to end work at reasonable hours, only about one-thirds (36%) were actually able to do so. Also, while 41% planned for time-off, only 30% could take time off in the past two months. 'These alarming statistics reject the urgency for companies to understand how creating a culture that encourages work-life balance and prioritizes wellbeing is critical moving forward' stated by the head of the survey company.

96. We can conclude that:
   (1) Gen Z employees are careless
   (2) Millennials are careful about Baby Boomers
   (3) Baby boomers are more open to discuss their stress issues with others
   (4) Baby Boomers are less careful about Gen Z

97. Which of the following is not a correct statement?
   (1) Gen Z professionals were 1.5x more likely to take breaks during the day.
   (2) Millennials were 2x more likely to take time-offs.
   (3) Baby bommers were 1.5x more likely to be open with their colleagues about mental health and stress when compared to millennials as well as Gen Z professionals.
   (4) Baby boomers were 2.5x more likely to take time-offs.

98. Which of the following is a more suitable statement about the passage?
   (1) The survey is fool-proof and can be used for generalization.
   (2) The state of mental health of Indian employees is at alarming stage.
   (3) There's a wide gap between what employees need and what employers are offering to cope with stress.
   (4) The survey is mainly focused on Baby Boomers.

99. **Statement I:** There's a wide gap between what employees need and what employers are offering to cope with stress.
   Statement II: Nearly 3/4th (74%) of employed professionals wish to end work at reasonable hours.
   (1) Both Statement I and Statement II are correct
   (2) Both Statement I and Statement II are incorrect
   (3) Statement I is correct but Statement II is incorrect
   (4) Statement II is correct but Statement I is incorrect

100. **Assertion (A)** Flexibility and work-life balance will serve as critical talent drivers across the Indian professional landscape for years to come.
   Reasoning (R): Workforce priorities continue to change in these transformative times.
   (1) (A) and (R) both are correct but (R) is not the right explanation of (A)
   (2) (A) and (R) both are correct and (R) is the right explanation of (A)
   (3) (A) and (R) both are incorrect
   (4) (A) is correct but (R) is not correct

ANSWER KEY

1. (4)	**2.** (4)	**3.** (3)	**4.** (3)	**5.** (1)	**6.** (3)	**7.** (2)	**8.** (4)	**9.** (2)	**10.** (1)
11. (4)	**12.** (4)	**13.** (4)	**14.** (3)	**15.** (1)	**16.** (3)	**17.** (1)	**18.** (1)	**19.** (2)	**20.** (2)
21. (3)	**22.** (3)	**23.** (1)	**24.** (3)	**25.** (1)	**26.** (2)	**27.** (1)	**28.** (1)	**29.** (4)	**30.** (3)
31. (4)	**32.** (1)	**33.** (2)	**34.** (4)	**35.** (3)	**36.** (1)	**37.** (1)	**38.** (1)	**39.** (4)	**40.** (3)
41. (1)	**42.** (4)	**43.** (3)	**44.** (4)	**45.** (4)	**46.** (2)	**47.** (2)	**48.** (4)	**49.** (3)	**50.** (4)
51. (3)	**52.** (1)	**53.** (2)	**54.** (3)	**55.** (3)	**56.** (2)	**57.** (1)	**58.** (4)	**59.** (2)	**60.** (4)
61. (*)	**62.** (1)	**63.** (3)	**64.** (4)	**65.** (3)	**66.** (3)	**67.** (2)	**68.** (2)	**69.** (1)	**70.** (2)
71. (1)	**72.** (1)	**73.** (3)	**74.** (2)	**75.** (3)	**76.** (4)	**77.** (1)	**78.** (3)	**79.** (3)	**80.** (1)
81. (1)	**82.** (1)	**83.** (2)	**84.** (1)	**85.** (1)	**86.** (1)	**87.** (1)	**88.** (2)	**89.** (3)	**90.** (1)
91. (2)	**92.** (2)	**93.** (2)	**94.** (2)	**95.** (1)	**96.** (3)	**97.** (4)	**98.** (3)	**99.** (3)	**100.** (2)

MARCH, 2023

LABOUR WELFARE & INDUSTRIAL RELATIONS, LABOUR & SOCIAL WELFARE, HUMAN RESOURCE MANAGEMENT

PAPER-II

Note : This paper contains **hundred (100)** objective type questions, each question carrying **two (2)** marks.

1. According to C. I. Bernard, Zone of Indifference denotes:
(1) The limit where actions are clearly unacceptable and will not be carried out.
(2) The limit where actions are barely unacceptable and have weak chances of being carried out.
(3) The limit within which individuals will respond willingly to the exercise of authority over them.
(4) The limit where no directions are given to carry out actions. A

2. The phenomenon, arising basically from people being "noticed", is known as:
(1) Psychological Effect
(2) Observational Effect
(3) Hawthrone Effect
(4) Mayo Effect

3. Which of the following establishes a required method of handling future activities?
(1) Strategy
(2) Procedure
(3) Programme
(4) Rule

4. Which of the following factors would not lead to narrow span of management?
(1) Inadequate delegation of authority.
(2) Fast changing environment.
(3) Effective interaction between superior and subordinate.
(4) Subordinate's unwillingness to assume responsibility.

5. Which of the following performance appraisal techniques generate critical incidents and develops behavioural dimensions of performance?
(1) Critical Incident Appraisal.
(2) Adjective Rating Scale Appraisal.
(3) Forced Choice Appraisal.
(4) Behaviourally Anchored Rating Scales.

6. An employee development method which was popularized at the Harvard Business School and which focuses on the cases of actual experiences of organizations to make the trainees determine the problems, analyse the causes and develop alternative solutions, is referred as:
(1) Committee Assignment
(2) Simulation
(3) Job Rotation
(4) Outdoor Training

7. Which of the following is not a flexible work arrangement?
(1) Telecommuting
(2) Job sharing
(3) Compressed workweek
(4) Time off

8. Which of the following is one-time payment that some employers pay at the time of terminating an employee?
(1) Supplemental pay
(2) Severance pay
(3) Insurance pay
(4) Disability pay

9. Which of the following is not an organizational level intervention?
(1) Appreciative Inquiry
(2) Parallel Learning Structure

(3) Transformational Leadership
(4) Team Building

10. Which of the following is not an element of knowledge management?
(1) Knowledge creation
(2) Knowledge sharing
(3) Knowledge emigration
(4) Knowledge utilization

11. Which of the following dimensions of Balance Score Card focus on production and operating statistics, such as order fulfilment or cost per order?
(1) Business Process
(2) Financial Performance
(3) Customer Service
(4) Learning and Growth

12. What is the name of the strategy in which MNC's look for innovation and design and produce new products to gain competitive advantage?
(1) Reactors (2) Prospectors
(3) Analysers (4) Defenders

13. Which of the following represent the extent to which group members support and validate one another while at work?
(1) Group Collaboration
(2) Group Functioning
(3) Group Cohesion
(4) Citizenship Behaviour

14. The 'emotional' or 'feeling' aspect of the statement, "I am angry over how little I am paid", represents which component of attitude?
(1) Cognitive component
(2) Affective component
(3) Behavioural component
(4) Normative component

15. Which one of the following is not an organizational factor of stress?
(1) Task structure
(2) Role expectations
(3) Interpersonal variables
(4) Perception

16. Which one of the following is a personality dimension that characterizes someone as calm, self-confident and secure versus nervous, depressed and insecure?
(1) Conscientiousness
(2) Agreeableness
(3) Extra version
(4) Emotional Stability

17. "Industrial Relations is an art, the art of living together for purposes of production", who said this?
(1) Richardson, J. H.
(2) Pigou, A. C.
(3) Dunlop, J. T.
(4) Flanders, A.

18. "The labour movement prepares the ground where in the seed of trade unionism grows", who said this?
(1) G. D. H. Cole (2) S. D. Punekar
(3) Karl Marx
(4) Frank Tannenbaum

19. Which trade union was a laboratory for experiencing ideas about industrial relations as perceived by Gandhiji?
(1) Madras Labour Union
(2) Textile Labour Association of Ahmedabad
(3) All India Trade Union Congress
(4) The Bombay Millhands' Association

20. Who authored the book "Trade Unionism in the New Society?"
(1) Harold J. Laski
(2) G. D. H. Cole
(3) Sidney and Beatrice Webb
(4) S. D. Punekar

21. What would be the maximum compensation to a workmen in case of closure of an organisation on account of unavoidable circumstances beyond the control of employer?
(1) Six months salary
(2) Three months salary
(3) One year salary
(4) 15 day's average pay for every completed year

22. In which of the following Supreme Court Judgement, the two judge bench has delivered a momentous judgement on government servant's right to strike on 6th August 2003?

(1) T. K. Rangarajan Vs. Government of Tamil Nadu
(2) Bharat Kumar K. Palicha Vs. State of Kerala
(3) Kameshwar Prasad Vs. State of Bihar
(4) Meghraj Vs. State of Rajasthan

23. In which session of the Indian Labour Conference, the question of framing standing orders came up for consideration?

(1) The Fifth Indian Labour Conference
(2) The Eighth Indian Labour Conference
(3) The Fifteenth Indian Labour Conference
(4) The Sixteenth Indian Labour Conference

24. In which organisation the schemes of Workers' Participation in Management 1983 were made applicable?

(1) Public Sector Undertakings
(2) Private Sector Undertakings
(3) Central Public Sector Undertakings
(4) State Public Sector Undertakings

25. Who appoints certifying surgeons for the purposes of the Factories Act, 1948?

(1) Central Government
(2) State Government
(3) Chief Inspector
(4) Occupier

26. First Aid room shall be provided and maintained in every mine employing more than:

(1) One hundred (100) Persons
(2) One hundred and fifty (150) Persons
(3) Two hundred and fifty (250) Persons
(4) Five hundred (500) Persons

27. As per the Child and Adolescent Labour Act, 1986, the period of work of adolescent shall be so arranged that inclusive of his interval for rest, it shall not be spread over more than:

(1) Five hours
(2) Five and half hours
(3) Six hours
(4) Ten and half hours

28. Inter-State Migrant Workmen Act, 1979, applies to every establishment in which __________ inter-state migrant workmen are employed or were employed on any day of the preceding twelve months.

(1) Five or more
(2) Ten or more
(3) Twenty or more
(4) One hundred or more

29. Every application to all claims arising out of payment of less than the minimum rates of wages under the Minimum Wages Act, 1948 shall be presented to appropriate authority within which month from the day on which it became payable?

(1) One month
(2) Six months
(3) Twelve months
(4) Twenty-four months

30. When there is a dispute regarding payment of bonus pending before any authority, then the bonus shall be paid within which month from the date on which the award becomes enforceable or the settlement comes into operations?

(1) One month (2) Six months
(3) Eight month (4) Twelve months

31. Who constitutes advisory committee under the Equal Remuneration Act, 1976?

(1) Employer
(2) Occupier
(3) Chief Inspector
(4) Appropriate Government

32. Match List I with List II:

List I (Name of the Laws)	**List II (Authority or Body related to Law)**
a. Minimum Wages Act, 1948	I. Controlling Authority
b. Equal Remuneration Act, 1976	II. Central Board

c.	Payment of Gratuity Act, 1972	III.	Advisory Committee
d.	Employees' Provident Fund & Mics. Provisions Acts, 1952	IV.	Advisory Board

Choose the correct answer from the options given below:

(1) a- IV, b- III, c- I, d- II
(2) a- III, b- IV, c- I, d- II
(3) a- II, b- III, c- I, d- IV
(4) a- II, b- I, c- III, d- IV

33. Which one of the following theories of Labour Welfare assumes that without compulsion and fear of punishment, employers will not provide even the minimum welfare facilities for the workers?

(1) Placating Theory
(2) Trusteeship Theory
(3) Functional Theory
(4) Police Theory

34. What among the following is NOT the internal cause of accidents?

(1) Equipment and other work -related tangibles.
(2) Harmful materials
(3) Human factors
(4) Toxic chemicals

35. Which one of the following is NOT a preventive measure for occupational disease?

(1) Pre-employment and periodic medical examination.
(2) Removal of health hazards to the extent possible.
(3) Provision of first aid and ambulance services.
(4) Education of workers in health and hygiene.

36. Which one of the following principles of Labour Welfare assumes that a combination of social, emotional, and economic welfare together will achieve good results?

(1) Principle of Responsibility
(2) Principle of Adequacy of Wages
(3) Principle of Totality of Welfare
(4) Principle of Efficiency

37. Other factors remaining constant, with decrease in wage rates, what the demand for Labour will show?

(1) An upward trend
(2) A downward trend
(3) Will remain constant
(4) Will show slight downward trend before stabilizing

38. Which one of the following is NOT the characteristic of Indian Labour Market?

(1) Diversity in the work force
(2) Lack of perfect mobility
(3) Productivity of Labour
(4) Monopsony in Labour Market

39. Which one of the following Convention No. adopted at 100th ILO's International Conference in Geneva guarantees "Decent Work for Domestic Workers"?

(1) Convention No. 189
(2) Convention No. 193
(3) Convention No. 200
(4) Convention No. 205

40. Fluctuations occur in the economy due to phases of boom, recession, depression, and recovery in the trade cycle. The Unemployment caused due to these phenomena is called:

(1) Chronic Unemployment
(2) Structural Unemployment
(3) Frictional Unemployment
(4) Cyclical Unemployment

41. Recentralisation is:

(a) a complete reversal of decentralisation.
(b) a complete centralisation of all activities.
(c) a decentralisation of all activities.
(d) a partial centralisation as the authority delegated is not completely withdrawn.

Choose the correct answer from the options given below:

(1) a and b Only

(2) a, b and d Only
(3) c Only
(4) d Only

42. Which of the following statement(s) is / are correct about the classical approach to decision making?
(a) Decision making is completely rational in terms of means and ends.
(b) Man is able to order his preferences so as to get best results.
(c) While choosing the cause of action, man attempts to satisfy or look for the alternative that is good enough.
(d) Decisions are also based on rule of thumb, tricks of trade or force of habit.
Choose the correct answer from the options given below:
(1) a, b and c Only
(2) a and b Only
(3) b and d Only
(4) c and d Only

43. Which of the following are the methods of collecting job analysis information?
(a) Observation
(b) Participant Diary / Logs
(c) Dejobbing
(d) Position Analysis Questionnaire
(e) Reengineering
Choose the correct answer from the options given below:
(1) a and b Only
(2) c and d Only
(3) a, b and d Only
(4) b, c and e Only

44. What is the name of human resource forecasting tool which studies a firm's past employment needs over a period of years to predict future needs?
(1) Ratio Analysis
(2) Trend Analysis
(3) Scatter Plot
(4) Computerized forecast

45. Which of the following are types of human capital?
a. Emotional Capital
b. System Capital
c. Spiritual Capital
d. Project Capital
e. Social Capital
Choose the correct answer from the options given below:
(1) a and b Only
(2) a and c Only
(3) b, c and d Only
(4) a, c and e Only

46. There are specific stages for designing HR Information system. Arrange the stages in ascending order.
a. System Analysis
b. Implementation
c. System Design
d. Project Definition
e. Post Implementation
Choose the correct answer from the options given below:
(1) a, d, e, c, b
(2) b, c, a, e, d
(3) d, a, c, b, e
(4) d, a, b, c, e

47. Which of the following is not the cultural dimension according to the pioneering work of Dutch Scientist Geert Hofstade; around which countries have been clustered, with people in each group exhibiting identical behaviours?
(1) Power distance
(2) Universalism
(3) Uncertainty avoidance
(4) Masculinity

48. Which of the statement(s) is / are correct about legitimate power?
a. It is identical with authority and is closely aligned with reward power and coercive power.
b. It comes from cultural values, social structure and being representative of powerful person or group.

c. It does not create an obligation to accept and be influenced.

Choose the correct answer from the options given below:

(1) a Only (2) a and c Only
(3) b and c Only (4) a and b Only

49. Group Norms help in:

a. Establishing distinctive identity of group.
b. Non-predictable behaviour of group members.
c. Avoiding embarrassing interpersonal problems.
d. Expressing cultural values or goals of group.

Choose the correct answer from the options given below:

(1) a and b Only (2) c and d Only
(3) a, b and d Only (4) a, c and d Only

50. Arrange the following needs of Maslow's Need Hierarchy in right sequence starting from the highest order to the lowest order need.

a. Social Belongingness
b. Physiological
c. Safety-Security
d. Esteem
e. Self-Actualisation

Choose the correct answer from the options given below:

(1) b, c, a, d, e (2) b, a, c, d, e
(3) e, d, a, c, b (4) e, d, c, a, b

51. Which of the following are the objectives of Indian Labour Conference?

a. To promote uniformity in labour legislation.
b. To lay down a procedure for settlement of industrial disputes.
c. To determine and fix the minimum wages for the Industrial Workers.
d. To discuss all matters of all India importance between employers and employees.

Choose the correct answer from the options given below:

(1) a, b and c Only (2) b, c and d Only
(3) a, b and d Only (4) a, c and d Only

52. Which of the following industrial disputes comes under the jurisdiction of Labour Court under section 10 of the Industrial Disputes Act, 1947.

a. Propriety or legality of an order passed by employer under the standing order.
b. Discharge or dismissal of workmen including reinstatement.
c. Leave with wages and holidays.
d. Illegality or otherwise of strike or lockout.

Choose the correct answer from the options given below:

(1) a, b, c Only (2) a, b, d Only
(3) b, c, d Only (4) a, c, d Only

53. Which of the following are the three-tier system for the settlement of grievances under the Model Grievance Procedure?

a. the levels of the immediate supervisor.
b. the departmental or factory head.
c. the bipartite grievance committee.
d. the tripartite grievance committee.

Choose the correct answer from the options given below:

(1) a, b, d Only (2) a, b, c Only
(3) b, c, d Only (4) a, c, d Only

54. Which three of the following was included as unfair labour practices in the amendment of Industrial Disputes Act in 1982?

a. Refusal by the employer to bargain collectively in good faith with recognised trade unions.
b. Refusal by a recognised union to bargain collectively in good faith with the employer.
c. Workers and trade unions of workers indulging in coercive activities against certification of a bargaining representative.
d. Refusal to honour collective agreement.

Choose the correct answer from the options given below:

(1) a, b, c only (2) b, c, d only
(3) a, b, d only (4) a, c, d only

55. Which of the following are related to main aspects of Industrial Relations?

a. Promotion and development of healthy labour-management relations.
b. Maintenance of industrial peace and avoidance of industrial strife.
c. Maintenance and development political democracy in the country.
d. Development of Industrial Democracy.

Choose the correct answer from the options given below:

(1) a, b Only (2) a, b, c Only
(3) a, b, d Only (4) b, c, d Only

56. Which of the following statements are NOT correct?

a. ILO is a tripartite organisation.
b. India is the founder member of ILO.
c. ILO only passes Conventions.
d. ILO adopted the Declaration of Fundamental Principles at its 86th session of International Labour Conference.
e. India has ratified 4 fundamental conventions of ILO till date.

Choose the correct answer from the options given below:

(1) b and d Only (2) b and c Only
(3) c and e Only (4) d and e Only

57. Under the Building and Other Construction Workers Act, 1996, creches shall be provided in every place:

a. Where in more than 30 female building workers are ordinarily employed.
b. Where in more than 50 female building workers are ordinarily employed.
c. For the use of children under the age of 6 years.
d. For the use of children under the age of 5 years.
e. Where in the number of children of women building workers is 25 or more.

Choose the correct answer from the options given below:

(1) a and c Only (2) b and c Only
(3) b and d Only (4) b, c and e Only

58. Which of the following statement is/are NOT correct relating to the Minimum Wages Act, 1948?

a. The appropriate Government shall fix the minimum rates of wages for the employees employed in an employment specified in Schedule I or Schedule II.
b. Different minimum rates of wages may be fixed for different localities.
c. The appropriate Government may review the minimum rates of wages so fixed at such intervals not exceeding three years.
d. The appropriate Government shall appoint committees and sub-committees to advise it in respect of fixation or revision of minimum rates of wages.
e. The minimum wages payable under this act may be paid in kind.

Choose the correct answer from the options given below:

(1) c Only (2) b and c Only
(3) c and e Only (4) a and c Only

59. Which of the following dimensions of work need to be same when performed under similar working condition for considering them as "same work or work of similar nature" as per the Equal Remuneration Act, 1976.

a. Skill b. Knowledge
c. Effort d. Responsibility
e. Difficulty

Choose the correct answer from the options given below:

(1) a, b and c Only
(2) a, c and d Only
(3) b, c and d Only
(4) a, b, d and e Only

60. Which of the following is/are not correct with respect to 'Fine' under the Payment of Wages Act, 1936?

a. No fine shall be imposed on any employed person until he has been give an opportunity of showing cause against the fine.
b. The total amount of fine in any one wage period on any employed person shall not exceed five percent of wages payable to him in that wage period.
c. No fine shall be imposed on any employed person who is under the age of eighteen years.
d. No fine imposed on any employed person shall be recovered from him by instalments.
e. No fine shall be recovered from any employed person after the expiry of ninety days from the day on which it was imposed.

Choose the correct answer from the options given below:
(1) b Only (2) c Only
(3) b and c Only (4) c and e Only

61. Which of the following are NOT welfare and amenities within the precincts of the establishment?
a. Latrines and Urinals
b. Maternity benefits
c. Creches
d. Health
e. Benevolent Fund

Choose the correct answer from the options given below:
(1) a and c Only (2) b and e Only
(3) c and d Only (4) a, c and d Only

62. Which of the following are NOT the indirect cost of industrial accident?
a. Time lost from work by injured employee.
b. Loss in earning power.
c. Damage to tools and equipment.
d. Paperwork.
e. Legal issues.

Choose the correct answer from the options given below:
(1) a and b Only (2) a and c Only
(3) d and e Only (4) b and e Only

63. Which among the following are NOT the unavoidable causes of labour turnover?
a. Resignation and dismissals.
b. Dissatisfaction with wage/salary.
c. Retirement and death.
d. Redundancy
e. Dissatisfaction with working environment.

Choose the correct answer from the options given below:
(1) b and e only (2) a and d only
(3) a and c only (4) a and b only

64. Which among the following are NOT the effect of absenteeism on individual employee?
a. Frequent absenteeism leads to loss in earning.
b. Frequent absenteeism hampers career prospects.
c. Industries suffer loss.
d. Affects organisations efficiency.
e. Affects individual's productivity.

Choose the correct answer from the options given below:
(1) a and b Only (2) d and e Only
(3) c and d Only (4) a, b and e Only

65. Which among the following are NOT the Economic Cause of Labour migration?
A. Better employment opportunities
B. Higher Wages
C. Attraction of better facilities and infrastructure
D. Marriage
E. Social discriminations.

Choose the correct answer from the options given below:
(1) A and B Only (2) A and C Only
(3) A and D Only (4) D and E Only

66. Given below are two statements:

Statement I: Efficiency is the achievement of objectives.

Statement II: Effectiveness is the achievement of the ends with the least amount of resources.

In the light of the above statements, choose the most appropriate answer from the options given below:

(1) Both Statement I and Statement II is correct.

(2) Both Statement I and Statement II is incorrect.

(3) Statement I is correct but Statement II is incorrect.

(4) Statement I is incorrect but Statement II is correct.

67. Given below are two statements:

Statement I: Job rotation is a kind of lateral transfer which allows employees to work at different jobs and it provides good exposure to a variety of tasks.

Statement II: Simulation exercises are learning tasks on the same equipment that one actually will use on the job but in a simulated work environment.

In the light of the above statements, choose the most appropriate answer from the options given below:

(1) Both Statement I and Statement II is correct.

(2) Both Statement I and Statement II is incorrect.

(3) Statement I is correct but Statement II is incorrect.

(4) Statement I is incorrect but Statement II is correct.

68. What is the name of the concept in which organization have local employers abroad w.o do jobs that the firms' domestic employees previously did in house?

(1) Onshoring

(2) Offshoring

(3) Inshoring

(4) Outshoring

69. Given below are two statements:

Statement I: "Social Loafing" is a dysfunction due to pressure to conform and reach consensus in highly cohesive groups and teams.

Statement II: "Groupthink" occurs when members reduce their effort and performance levels while acting in a group.

In the light of the above statements, choose the correct answer from the options given below:

(1) Both Statement I and Statement II is true.

(2) Both Statement I and Statement II is false.

(3) Statement I is true but Statement II is false.

(4) Statement I is false but Statement II is true.

70. Given below are two statements:

One is labelled as Assertion A and the other is labelled as Reason R.

Assertion 'A': Unions, Commonly known as protest organisation, never take up any developmental activities. "Unions are at crossroads. They are on divergent path. One wonders they would like to map the new path early. They have to redefine their social responsibilities in relation to unemployed, contract workers. They may like to explore ways for development of new leadership for new trade unionism appropriate for the global society in the years ahead".

Reason 'R': The consolidation of the workers forces attained in the economic struggle will also have to serve as a Lever in the hands of this class for the struggle against the political power of its exploiters.

In the right of the above statements, choose the most appropriate answer from the options given below:

(1) Both A and R are correct and R is the correct explanation of A.

(2) Both A and R are correct but R is not the correct explanation of A.

(3) A is correct but R is not correct.

(4) A is not correct but R is correct.

71. Given below are two statements:

One is labelled as Assertion A and the other is labelled as Reason R.

Assertion 'A': The scheme of Joint Management Council was evolved on voluntary basis to promote Industrial Peace and harmony between labour and management, to ensure closer association between them, and to increase production and share the responsibility of management.

Reason 'R': The Industrial Policy Resolution 1956 stated, "In a socialist democracy labour is a partner in common task of development and should participate in it with enthusiasm".

In the light of the above statements, choose the most appropriate answer from the options given below:

(1) Both A and R are true and R is the correct explanation of A.
(2) Both A and R are true but R is not the correct explanation of A.
(3) A is true but R is false.
(4) A is false but R is true.

72. Given below are two statements:

Statement I: The provisions relating the hazardous processes under the Factories Act, 1948, is given in the Chapter IV of this Act.

Statement II: The state government may appoint a site appraisal committee for the purposes of advising it to consider the applications for grant of permission for the initial location of a factory involving a hazardous process.

In the light of the above statements, choose the most appropriate answer from the options given below:

(1) Both Statement I and Statement II is correct.
(2) Both Statement I and Statement II is incorrect.
(3) Statement I is correct but Statement II is incorrect.
(4) Statement I is incorrect but Statement II is correct.

73. Given below are two statements:

Statement I: Where the employment of any person is terminated, the wages earned by him shall be paid before the expiry of the 7th day from the day on which his employment is terminated.

Statement II: When the application made to claim arising out of deductions from wages was found either malicious or vexatious, the authority to may direct penalty not exceeding three hundred seventy-five rupees be paid to employer by the person presenting the application.

In the light of the above statements, choose the correct answer from the options given below.

(1) Both Statement I and Statement II is true.
(2) Both Statement I and Statement II is false.
(3) Statement I is true but Statement II is false.
(4) Statement I is false but Statement II is true.

74. Given below are two statements:

Statement I: The term welfare suggests many ideas, meaning and connotations such as the state of well-being, health, happiness, prosperity and the development of human resources.

Statement II: Welfare is called a relative concept, for it is related to time and space.

In the light of the above statements, choose the correct answer from the options given below:

(1) Both Statement I and Statement II is true.
(2) Both Statement I and Statement II is false.
(3) Statement I is true but Statement II is false.
(4) Statement I is false but Statement II is true.

75. Given below are two statements:

Statement I: Neoclassical economics begins from a model of purposive behaviour by individuals. Individuals are assumed to have their own unique tastes, preferences, wants and desires which they attempt to satisfy.

Statement II: Neoclassical economics examines the choices that individuals make in their roles as consumers or as producers.

In the light of the above statements, choose the correct answer from the options given below:

(1) Both Statement I and Statement II is true.
(2) Both Statement I and Statement II is false.
(3) Statement I is true but Statement II is false.
(4) Statement I is false but Statement II is true.

76. Arrange the following on the basis of top-down approach of hierarchy of objectives:

a. Mission
b. Departmental Objectives
c. Individual Objectives
d. Purpose
e. Organisational Objectives

Choose the correct answer from the options given below:

(1) d, a, e, b and c
(2) a, d, b, e and c
(3) a, d, e, c and b
(4) e, a, d, c and b

77. Match List I with List II:

List I (Stages to development of HRM Practices)	List II (Time Period)
a. Scientific Management Era	I. 1980 onwards
b. Human Relations Era	II. 1900-1920's
c. Behavioural Science Era	III. 1930's to 1950's
d. Human Resource Management Era	IV. 1950's to 1960's

Choose the correct answer from the options given below:

(1) a- II, b- III, c- I, d- IV
(2) a-II, b- III, c- IV, d- I
(3) a- I, b- III, c- II, d- IV
(4) a- III, b- II, c- IV, d- I

78. In which of these cultural orientations, the home country's culture is sought to be imposed on subsidiaries?

(1) Polycentric
(2) Geocentric
(3) Ethnocentric
(4) Regiocentric

79. Match List I with List II:

List I	List II
a. Goal	I. Deficiency
b. Drive	II. Defence mechanism
c. Need	III. Fulfilment of deficiencies
d. Frustration	IV. Deficiency with direction

Choose the correct answer from the options given below:

(1) a- II, b- I, c- III, d- IV
(2) a- I, b- III, c- IV, d- II
(3) a- IV, b- II, c- I, d- III
(4) a- III, b- IV, c- I, d- II

80. Arrange the Trade Unions/Associations according to their formation from later to earlier:

a. Bhartiya Mazdoor Sangh
b. The Red Trade Union Congress
c. Hind Mazdoor Sabha
d. Centre of Indian Trade Unions
e. National Council of Central Trade Unions

Choose the correct answer from the options given below:

(1) a, b, c, d, e (2) b, a, c, d, e
(3) e, b, c, d, a (4) e, d, a, c, b

81. Given below are the various authorities under Industrial Disputes Act, 1947. Arrange them in ascending orders of their sections.

a. Industrial Tribunal
b. Voluntary Arbitration
c. Court of Inquiry
d. Board of Conciliation
e. National Tribunals

Choose the correct answer from the options given below:

(1) a, c, b, d, e (2) d, c, a, e, b
(3) b, d, e, a, c (4) c, d, a, b, e

82. Arrange the following provisions relating to health under the Factories Act, 1948, in ascending order of the sections.

a. Artificial humidification
b. Ventilation and temperature
c. Drinking water
d. Lighting
e. Dust and Fume

Choose the correct answer from the options given below:

(1) e, a, b, d, c (2) b, e, a, d, c
(3) e, b, a, c, d (4) b, e, c, a, d

83. Arrange the following deductions under the Payment of Wages Act, 1936, is ascending order of sections.

a. Deductions for services rendered.
b. Deductions for damage or loss.
c. Deductions for absence from duty.
d. Deductions for recovery of loans.
e. Deductions for recover of advances.

Choose the correct answer from the options given below:

(1) b, c, a, d, e (2) c, b, a, e, d
(3) b, c, a, e, d (4) c, a, b, d, e

84. Match List I with List II:

List I (Theory of Labour Welfare)

a. Philanthropic Theory of Labour Welfare
b. Placating Theory of Labour Welfare
c. Public Relations Theory of Labour Welfare
d. Functional or Efficiency Theory of Labour Welfare

List II (Description)

I. Labour groups are becoming demanding and militant and are more conscious.
II. Means to secure, preserve and develop the efficiency and productivity of labour.
III. An atmosphere of goodwill between management and labour and also management and public.
IV. Man's love for man.

Choose the correct answer from the options given below:

(1) a- IV, b- III, c- II, d- I
(2) a- IV, b- I, c- III, d- II
(3) a- IV, b- II, c- III, d- I
(4) a- I, b- II, c- III, d- IV

85. Match List I with List II:

List I	List II
a. Marginal Productivity theory	I. Wages are determined by the bargaining between employers and workers.
b. Exploitation theory of wages	II. Labour is paid according to its marginal productivity under the conditions of perfect competition.
c. Demand and supply theory of wages	III. Wages are determined by the interaction of demand and supply of labour.
d. Bargaining theory of wages	IV. Labour is paid only a part of the share that he produces and the rest is in the hands of capitalist.

Choose the correct answer from the options given below:

(1) a- II, b- IV, c- III, d- I
(2) a- II, b- I, c- III, d- IV
(3) a- II, b- III, c- IV, d- I
(4) a- II, b- I, c- IV, d- III

86. Given below are two statements:
One is labelled as Assertion A and the other is labelled as Reason R.

Assertion 'A': "Dark Triad" is the constellation of negative personality traits consisting of Machiavellianism, Narcissism and Psychopathy.

Reason 'B': An individual in 'narcissism' is pragmatic, maintains emotional distance and believes that ends can justify means.

In the right of the above statements, choose the most appropriate answer from the options given below:

(1) Both A and R are correct and R is the correct explanation of A.
(2) Both A and R are correct but R is not the correct explanation of A.
(3) A is correct but R is not correct.
(4) A is not correct but R is correct.

87. Given below are two statements:

One is labelled as Assertion A and the other is labelled as Reason R.

Assertion 'A': Ingratiation involves agreeing with the recruiters' opinions by the candidate and thus signalling that they share similar beliefs.

Reason 'B': A perceived similarity in attitudes and/or values does not influence how the interviewer rates the applicants competence.

In the right of the above statements, choose the most appropriate answer from the options given below:

(1) Both A and R are correct and R is the correct explanation of A.
(2) Both A and R are correct but R is not the correct explanation of A.
(3) A is correct but R is not correct.
(4) A is not correct but R is correct.

88. Match List I with List II:

Given below the Name of Authors and their authored books.

List I (Authors)	List II (Authored Books)
a. Selig Perlman	I. Trade Unionism in the Unites States.
b. Robert F. Hoxie	II. A Theory of the Labour Movement.
c. Frank Tannenbaum	III. The Mediating Role of the Trade Union in underdeveloped countries.
d. Ashok Mehta	IV. A Philosophy of Labour.

Choose the correct answer from the options given below:

(1) a- I, b- II, c- III, d- IV
(2) a- II, b- I, c- IV, d- III
(3) a- II, b- IV, c- III, d- I
(4) a- III, b- II, c- I, d- IV

89. Match List I with List II:

List I (Article of Indian Constitution)	List II (Meaning of the Article)
a. Article-39	I. Right to work, to education and to public assistance in certain cases.
b. Article-41	II. Endeavour to secure a living wage, conditions of work ensuring a decent standard of life.
c. Article-42	III. Equal pay for equal work for both men and women.
d. Article-43	IV. Provision for securing just and human condition of work and for maternity relief.

Choose the correct answer from the options given below:

(1) a- IV, b- III, c- I, d- II
(2) a- III, b- IV, c- I, d- II
(3) a- III, b- I, c- IV, d- II
(4) a- II, b- IV, c-III, d- I

90. Given below are two statements:

One is labelled as Assertion A and the other is labelled as Reason R.

Assertion 'A': The Constitution of India in the Directive Principles stresses upon the importance of labour welfare.

Reason 'B': Voluntary welfare measures come under welfare work voluntarily carried out by employers and worker's organizations.

In the right of the above statements, choose the most appropriate answer from the options given below:

(1) Both A and R are correct and R is the correct explanation of A.

(2) Both A and R are correct but R is not the correct explanation of A.

(3) A is correct but R is not correct.

(4) A is not correct but R is correct.

Answer Question on the basis of following passage:

During the early period of industrial development, efforts towards workers' welfare were made largely by social workers, philanthropists, religious leaders, mostly on humanitarian grounds. Before the introduction of welfare and other legislation in India, the conditions of labour were miserable. Exploitation of child labour, long hours of work, bad sanitation, absence of safety measures etc., were the regular features of the life. The earliest legislative approach could be tracked back to the passing of the Apprentices Act of 1850. This act was enacted with the objective of helping poor and orphaned children to learn various trades and crafts. The next act was the Fatal Accidents Act of 1853 which aimed at providing compensation to the families of workmen who lost their life as a result of "actionable wrong". Earlier attempts at legislation in this count mainly aimed at regulation of employment.

The movement to improve the working conditions of Indian labour started with the passing of the first Indian Factories Act in 1881. The deplorable conditions in which labour worked in the textile mills in Bombay during those days, as testified by the factory commission of 1875 was the immediate cause for the passing of the Act. Adult labour, however, was not protected in any manner. It was found inadequate in many respects. Anyhow, it recognized the right of the government to safeguard the interests of the workers by means of a suitable legislation. Therefore, the Commission was appointed by the Government of Bombay in 1884 to review the working of the Factories Act of 1881.

The Factories (Amendment) Act 1891 applied to all factories employing 50 persons or more. Provisions relating to better ventilation, and for preventing overcrowding in factories were also made. The hours of work for children were reduced to six per day. Employment of women between 7.00 pm and 5.00 am was prohibited. Women were allowed to work for eleven hours in a day with one-and-a-half-hour rest. Certain provisions were also made for the health and safety of the Industrial workers.

The outbreak of First World War in 1914 led a number of new developments. During the war years (1914 to 1918) the number of factory number of persons employed therein increased. Wages did not keep pace with the rising prices and profits. The establishment of the International Labour Organization (ILO) in 1919 was another important landmark in the history of Labour Welfare Movement in our Country. The formation of AITUC (1920), the first central trade union organization in our country, also helped in furthering the cause of welfare movement.

Another milestone in the field of labour welfare was reached with the appointment of Labour Investigation Committee (Rege Committee) in 1944. The committee was asked to investigate problems relating to wages and earnings, employment, housing and social conditions of workers. It covered different areas in labour welfare such as housing policy, rest and recreation, occupational diseases, relief in the case of old age and death, canteens, medical aid, washing and bathing facilities, educational facilities etc. For the first time in India, this committee highlighted the of welfare measures for workers in improving their social and economic life.

91. What was the number of working hours for children in Indian factories prior to the implementation of the Factories (Amendment) Act, 1891?

(1) 10 hours

(2) 8 hours

(3) The passage does not reveal this fact
(4) 6 hours

92. Which one of the following provisions was not included in the Factories (Amendment) Act 1891?
(1) Ventilation
(2) Cleanliness
(3) Overcrowding
(4) Transportation

93. Who among the following led the Labour Investigation Committee?
(1) Mulock
(2) ILO
(3) Rege
(4) Bombay Presidency Officer

94. Who among the following was not the part of labour welfare reformers during the early period of industrial development in India?
(1) Philanthropists
(2) Religious leaders
(3) Social Workers
(4) Factory Owners

95. Which among the following is not a correct statement?
(1) Wages did not keep pace with the rising prices and profits during the World War-I.
(2) The establishment of the International Labour Organization (ILO) took place in 1919.
(3) The Factories (Amendment) Act 1891 applied to all factories employing 100 persons or more.
(4) The earliest legislative approach could be tracked back to the passing of the Apprentices Act of 1850.

Read the passage carefully and answer the following question:

Indian organizations have traditionally not considered their human resource as a means of distinct competitive advantage. Rather, people management has been a big challenge for the Indian business head. This situation is undergoing a rapid change today; because as Indian organizations are recognizing the need for professional human resource management, simultaneously there is a growing demand for trained human resource professionals. At most of the universities, business schools have begun to offer specialized, customized courses to train the human resource professional. Increasingly, organizations are encouraging line managers to handle human resource responsibilities. Ancient India was known for its occupation-based hierarchy. The ancient Indian text, the Arthashastra refers to the job description of a supervisor and performance linked pay for artisans. It was only after the year 1850 that formal industrial organizations emerged in India. But it was only after India became an independent country in 1947 that significant improvement was witnessed in the personnel management policy of business organisations. After independence, when a mixed economy was encouraged as the Indian growth model, industrial organisations were broadly classified into public sector and private sector. Since the public sector units were the recipients of large investments and became the biggest players, their approach towards personnel management received a lot of attention. The goal of a socialistic society enshrined within the constitution of India implied that the protection of human resource became a significant objective. Many constitutional provisions were created in order to protect workers. Organizations had to appoint welfare officers to take care of all personnel. The next phase of development saw the rise of the trade unions, and manager unions in the Indian business organizations. This further boosted the growth of personnel offices in most of the organizations.

96. Given below are two statements:

Statement I: It was only after the year 1947 that formal industrial organizations emerged in India.

Statement II: Since the public sector units were recipient of limited investments it became centre of industrial disputes.

In the light of the above statements, choose the correct answer from the options given below:

(1) Both Statement I and Statement II is true.
(2) Both Statement I and Statement II is false.
(3) Statement I is true but Statement II is false.
(4) Statement I is false but Statement II is true.

97. Which of the followings are mentioned in the ancient Indian text-Arthashastra?
a. Size of a standard agricultural field.
b. Job description of a supervisor.
c. Wages rates of seasonal workers.
d. Performance linked pay for artisans.
e. Rate of tax applicable on kings revenue.
Choose the correct answer from the options given below:
(1) a and b only
(2) b and c only
(3) b and d only
(4) d and e only

98. Which one of the following factors is responsible for the increased number of personnel office in many organizations in India?
(1) The rise of Unions
(2) Workers friendly policies
(3) Industrial revolution
(4) British influence on Indian Unions

99. After which of the following event, the country has seen significant improvement in the personnel management policy of business organizations?
(1) Independence
(2) Simon Commission
(3) Labore meet of Indian National Congress
(4) Division of Bengal

100. Which one of the following is NOT a correct statement?
(1) Many constitutional provisions were created in order to protect workers.
(2) Industrial organizations were broadly classified into British industries and Indian industries.
(3) Indian organizations have traditionally not considered their human resources.
(4) People management has been a big challenge for the Indian business head.

ANSWER KEY

1. (3)	**2.** (3)	**3.** (2)	**4.** (3)	**5.** (4)	**6.** (2)	**7.** (4)	**8.** (2)	**9.** (4)	**10.** (3)
11. (1)	**12.** (2)	**13.** (3)	**14.** (2)	**15.** (4)	**16.** (4)	**17.** (1)	**18.** (2)	**19.** (2)	**20.** (1)
21. (2)	**22.** (1)	**23.** (1)	**24.** (3)	**25.** (2)	**26.** (2)	**27.** (3)	**28.** (1)	**29.** (2)	**30.** (1)
31. (4)	**32.** (1)	**33.** (4)	**34.** (3)	**35.** (3)	**36.** (3)	**37.** (1)	**38.** (3)	**39.** (1)	**40.** (4)
41. (4)	**42.** (2)	**43.** (3)	**44.** (2)	**45.** (4)	**46.** (3)	**47.** (2)	**48.** (4)	**49.** (4)	**50.** (3)
51. (3)	**52.** (2)	**53.** (2)	**54.** (1)	**55.** (3)	**56.** (3)	**57.** (2)	**58.** (4)	**59.** (2)	**60.** (3)
61. (2)	**62.** (3)	**63.** (1)	**64.** (3)	**65.** (4)	**66.** (2)	**67.** (3)	**68.** (2)	**69.** (2)	**70.** (2)
71. (1)	**72.** (4)	**73.** (4)	**74.** (1)	**75.** (1)	**76.** (1)	**77.** (2)	**78.** (3)	**79.** (4)	**80.** (4)
81. (2)	**82.** (2)	**83.** (2)	**84.** (2)	**85.** (1)	**86.** (3)	**87.** (3)	**88.** (2)	**89.** (3)	**90.** (2)
91. (3)	**92.** (4)	**93.** (3)	**94.** (4)	**95.** (3)	**96.** (2)	**97.** (3)	**98.** (1)	**99.** (1)	**100.** (2)

DECEMBER, 2023

LABOUR WELFARE & INDUSTRIAL RELATIONS, LABOUR & SOCIAL WELFARE, HUMAN RESOURCE MANAGEMENT

PAPER-II

Note : This paper contains **hundred (100)** objective type questions, each carrying **two (2)** marks.

1. Who authored the book 'The Nature of Managerial Work'?
(1) Peter Drucker
(2) Henry Mintzberg
(3) Chester I. Barnand
(4) Henri Fayol

2. According to whom, "management is the art of getting things done through people"
(1) Mary Parker Met
(2) Peter F. Drucker
(3) Elton Mayo
(4) Chester I Barnad

3. Which of the following is a single use plan ?
(1) Program (2) Procedure
(3) Policy (4) Rules

4. Who developed an approach that incorporates the organisation environment into organizational design ?
(1) Joan Woodward
(2) David H. Burnham
(3) Tom Burns and G.M. Stalken
(4) Chester I Barnard

5. The Concept of 'Hard HRM' and 'Soft HRM' has been developed by :
(1) John Storey
(2) Vladmir Pucik
(3) Nina Hatvany
(4) Michael Beer

6. The Online systems that help employers attracts, gather, screen, compile and manage applicants is called ?
(1) Application Service Provider
(2) Application Screening Device
(3) Applicant Tracking Systems
(4) Applicant Recruiting Systems

7. Which of the following is not a method of HR Demand Forecasting ?
(1) Managerial Judgement
(2) Markov dialysis
(3) Scatter plot
(4) Ratio Analysis

8. A group of jobs having similarities in comparable factors or those considered as existing at the same level in terms of their values is called ?
(1) Pay grade (2) Pay range
(3) Pay scale (4) Pay standard

9. Hofstede making a study an national culture identified four dimensions along with managers and employees appear to vary. Which one of the following is not a dimension as identified by him?
(1) Power distance
(2) Relationship to authority
(3) Uncertainty avoidance
(4) Masculinity versus femininity

10. A performance appraisal method which keeps a record of uncommonly good or undesirable and reviewing it with the employee at predetermined times is known as:
(1) Critical incident method
(2) Behaviourally anchored rating scale
(3) Alteration ranking method
(4) Management by objectives

11. If the top management of a multinational corporation, allows the national subsidiaries to fill management posts by themselves with host country national, then the attitude of the management is characterised by :

(1) Polycentricity
(2) Ethnocentricity
(3) Regiocentricity
(4) Geo centricity

12. Which of the following is vestibule training?

(1) On - the job training
(2) Apprenticeship framing
(3) Job rotation training
(4) Off the job training

13. The linking pin model given by Rensis Likert is associated with

(1) Intra - individual behaviour and conflict
(2) Inter personal behaviour and conflict
(3) Intergroup behaviour and conflict
(4) Inter organisational behaviour and conflict

14. Which one of the following is identified as the third dimension in the Reddm's Three Dimensional Model of Leadership?

(1) Effectiveness
(2) Environments
(3) Motivation
(4) Conflict

15. Who among the following had identified the three different skills namely, conceptual skills, human relations skills and technical skills for effective management ?

(1) Robert Blake (2) Robert J. House
(3) Robert Katz (4) Robert Hoxie

16. The S-O-B-C model of organisational behaviour identifies four major variables, which are related to another. Which of the following stands for the letter's?

(1) Structure (2) Stimulus
(3) System (4) Social

17. Who was the main architect of the legislation 'the Bombay Industrial Disputes Act. 1938' being the Parliamentary Secretary in the Bombay Congress Ministry ?

(1) Gulzarilal Nanda
(2) Jaiprakash Narayan
(3) N.M. Joshi
(4) Balgangadhar Tilak

18. "Every class struggle is a political struggle" who said this ?

(1) Lenin (2) Karl Marx
(3) G.D.H Cole (4) Fedrick Engele

19. The criteria for the recognition of trade Unions have been laid down under

(1) The Industrial Disputes Act, 1947
(2) The Trade Unions Act, 1926
(3) Code of Discipline
(4) Industrial Employment (Standing orders) Act, 1946

20. Which pair of Scheme of workers participation and the year of its establishment is inconsistent ?

(1) Works Committee - 1947
(2) Joint Management council - 1958
(3) Shop Council - 1972
(4) Joint Council in Commercial and service Organisation in the public sector - 1977

21. "A strike called by proper authority in a Union and in conforming with the requirement of law" is called ?

(1) Wild cat strike
(2) Authorised strike
(3) Juristicational strike
(4) General Strike

22. Who has developed the "Hot-Stove Rule" for handling discipline ?

(1) Donglas McGregor
(2) Michael J. Jucius
(3) Charles A. Myers
(4) Henri Fayol

23. What are the minimum and maximum numbers prescribed under the Industrial Disputes Act, 1947 for" Protected workmen" ?

(1) Minimum 20 and Maximum 100
(2) Minimum 15 and Maximum 75

(3) Minimum 10 and Maximum 50
(4) Minimum 5 and Maximum 100

24. Which method of settling industrial disputes does not include direct state intervention ?
(1) Statutory Establishment of Bipartite Committee
(2) Adjudication
(3) Collective Bargaining
(4) Compulsory Conciliation

25. The Right of Children to Free and Compulsory Education Act, 2009 was enacted in accordance with which of the following Article of Constitution in India ?
(1) Article 41 (2) Article 38
(3) Article 19 (4) Article 47

26. Which of the Constitution of India provide for the participation of workers in management of industries ?
(1) Article 39 A (2) Article 41
(3) Article 43 A (4) Article 43 B

27. The Site Appraisal Committee is required to submit the report to the state Government after how many days of the receipt of an application for establishment of a factory involving a hazardous process under the Factories Act, 1948 ?
(1) Thirty days
(2) Sixty days
(3) Ninety days
(4) One hundred twenty days

28. The term 'Wages' under the Contract Labour (Regulation and Abolition) Act 1970 has the same meaning assigned to it under which of the following legislations ?
(1) The Industrial Disputes Act
(2) The Payment of Wages Act
(3) The Industrial Employment (Standing Orders) Act
(4) The Minimum Wages Act

29. The Advisory Board constituted under the Minimum Wages Act, 1948 is to:
(1) Advise the employers to pay minimum wages as fixed under the Act
(2) Coordinate the works of committees and sub-committees
(3) Coordinate the work of the advisory committee
(4) Coordinate between the employer and employees to fix minimum wages

30. Under the provisions of the Minimum Wages Act, 1948 the representation of independent members in the Central Advisory Board shall not exceed.
(1) One fourth of the total members
(2) One half of the total members
(3) One third of the total members
(4) Two third of the total members

31. What is the minimum number of persons to be nominated by the appropriate Government to the Advisory Committee constructed under the provisions of the Equal Remuneration Act, 1976 ?
(1) Five (2) Seven
(3) Ten (4) Twelve

32. An exempted establishment formed under the provisions of the Employees Provident Fund and Miscellaneous Provisions Act, 1952 required to establish, which of the following for the administration of the fund ?
(1) Exempted Provident Fund Board
(2) Board of Trustees
(3) An Executive Committee
(4) An Establishment level Committee

33. Who defined Social Welfare as:
'The organised system of social services and institutions designed to aid individuals and groups to attain satisfying standards of life and health, and personal and social relationship which permit them to develop their full capacities and to promote their well being in harmony with the needs of their families and community'.
Choose the correct option;
(1) R.R. Hopkins
(2) Friedlender
(3) Arther James Todd
(4) E.S. Proud

34. Which welfare amenity is NOT included in intra-mural amenity by the committee of exports on welfare facilities for industrial workers constituted by the - International Labour Organisation in the year 1963?
Choose the correct option :
(1) Washing and bathing facilities
(2) Latrines and urinals
(3) Leave travel facilities
(4) Health services including occupational safety

35. Access to social security has become a fundamental human right to which every individual is entitled as a member of the society. This right has been embodied in the Universal Declaration of Human Rights adopted by United Nations General Assembly. In which years, it was adopted?
Choose the correct option:
(1) In the year 1948
(2) In the year 1946
(3) In the year 1950
(4) In the year 1952

36. When was the Royal Commission on Labour was appointed under the Chairmanship of J.H. Whitley?
Choose the correct option:
(1) In the year 1919
(2) In the year 1929
(3) In the year 1938
(4) In the year 1944

37. The shape of supply curve of Individual Labour is
(1) Backward bending
(2) Straight Line
(3) Negatively sloped
(4) Perpendicular to the X axis

38. Advanced capitalist economies generally suffer from which type of unemployment?
(1) Structural Unemployment
(2) Classical Unemployment
(3) Disguised Unemployment
(4) Cyclical Unemployment

39. Which of the following is hue as per modern Economists?
(1) Cut in money wage is the best way to increase Labour demand and bring full employment
(2) Expansionary monetary policy is effective in increasing employment
(3) Flexible wage policy is instrumental in achieving full employment
(4) Money illusion does not affect labour union

40. In an income leisure diagram the wages rate is graphically represented by the
(1) Slope of indifference curve
(2) Curvature of indifference curve
(3) Slope of the budget line
(4) Tangency of budget line with indifference curve

41. Which of the following is/are correct relating to the system approach to management?
(A) A system is an interrelated set of elements punching as a whole
(B) Each system has a boundary that separates it from its environment
(C) Each system interacts with its environment
(D) Feedback is not the key to control the system
Choose the correct answer from the options given below:
(1) (A) and (B) Only
(2) (B) and (C) Only
(3) (A), (B) and (C) Only
(4) (A), (C) and (D) Only

42. Which of the following is/are not the functions of management according to Henri Fayol?
(A) Staffing
(B) Organisation
(C) Controlling
(D) Commanding
(E) Coordinating
Choose the correct answer from the options given below :

(1) (A) Only (2) (D) Only
(3) (E) Only (4) (D) and (E) Only

43. Which of the following are the advantages of group decision making?
(A) More information and knowledge are available
(B) Enhanced communication of decision may result
(C) Undesirable compromises may happen
(D) Groupthink may occur
(E) It is costlier
Choose the correct answer from the options given below :
(1) (A) and (B) Only
(2) (A) and (D) Only
(3) (A), (B) and (D) Only
(4) (A), (B) and (C) Only

44. Which of the following is/are not form of simulation?
(A) Role playing
(B) Coaching
(C) Business game
(D) Conference
(E) In basket exercise
Choose the correct answer from the options given below
(1) (B) and (C) Only
(2) (B) and (D) Only
(3) (A), (B) and (D) Only
(4) (B), (C) and (D) Only

45. Which of the following is/are not the components of direct compensation?
(A) House rent allowance
(B) Pay for vacations
(C) Employer's contribution towards PF
(D) Incentives
(E) Bonus
Choose the correct answer from the options given below :
(1) (B) and (C) Only
(2) (B) and (D) Only
(3) (B), (C) and (D) Only
(4) (C), (D) and (E) Only

46. Which of the following statements are true relating to human personality?
(A) The word personality can be traces to the Latin words 'per sona'
(B) The meaning of the word 'per sona' when translated into English is "to look through"
(C) Human personality' includes the external appearance and behaviour
(D) Human personality includes inner awareness of self as a permanent organising force
Choose the correct answer from the options given below:
(1) (A), (B) and (D) Only
(2) (A), (C) and (D) Only
(3) (A), (B) and (C) Only
(4) (B), C) and (D) Only

47. Which of the following are the Decisional Roles of the managers as identified by Henry Mintzberg?
(A) Figurehead role
(B) Leadership role
(C) Negotiator role
(D) Entrepreneurs role
(E) Disturbance handler role
Choose the correct answer from the options given below :
(1) (C), (D) and (E) Only
(2) (A), (B) and (D) Only
(3) (B), (C) and (D) Only
(4) (A), (B) and (C) Only

48. As per Herzberg's two factor theory of motivation which of the following are the motivators?
(A) Interpersonal relations
(B) Achievement
(C) Advancement
(D) Supervision
(E) Responsibility
Choose the correct answer from the options given below:
(1) (A), (B) and (D) Only
(2) (B), (C) and (E) Only

(3) (B), (C) and (D) Only
(4) (A), (D) and (E) Only

49. Which of the following statements can contribution for developing HRD climates in an organisation ?

(A) Strong belief of the top management on the capabilities of the employees
(B) HRD policies showing high concern for employees
(C) Good HRD sub systems for increasing effectiveness
(D) Presence of strong trade Unions in the organisation

Choose the correct answer from the options given below:

(1) (B), (C) and (D) Only
(2) (A), (C) and (D) Only
(3) (A), (B) and (C) Only
(4) (A), (B) and (D) Only

50. Which of the following factors influence the multi-national corporations to recruit host country nationals ?

(A) They are familiar with the culture
(B) To maintain and facilitate organisational coordination and control
(C) To develop good public relations
(D) The company's conviction that it must maintain a foreign image in the host country

Choose the correct answer from the options given below:

(1) (A), and (D) Only
(2) (B), and (C) Only
(3) (A), and (C) Only
(4) (B), and (D) Only

51. Which of the following factors had played legitimate part in the formation of the Madras Labour Union ?

(A) the status of the labourer as labourer in relation to its employer, affecting the economic and industrial life of the country.
(B) the status of the labourer as a citizen affected by and affecting the political movement and their result.
(C) the status of the labourer in the international world of labour which has been emerging into great importance ever since the Russian revolution.
(D) the status of the Indian crony capitalism that forces the labour to be associated and form trade union.

Choose the correct answer from the options given below:

(1) (A) and (B) Only
(2) (A), B) and (C) Only
(3) (A), (C) and (D) Only
(4) (B), (C) and (D) Only

52. Which of the following three-tier system of participation was recommended by a Tripartite Committee on Worker's Participation in 1977 under the Chairmanship of Shri Ravindra Verma ?

(A) Unit Level
(B) Shop floor Level
(C) Plant Level
(D) Corporate Level

Choose the correct answer from the options given below:

(1) (A), (B) and (C) Only
(2) (A), (C) and (D) Only
(3) (B), (C) and (D) Only
(4) (A), (B) and (D) Only

53. Which of the following All India Trade Union organisations were in existence by the end of 1933 ?

(A) All India Trade Union Congress
(B) The Red Trade Union Congress
(C) National Trade Union Federation
(D) Indian Trade Union Federation

Choose the correct answer from the options given below:

(1) (A) and (B) Only
(2) (B) and (C) Only
(3) (A), (B) and (C) Only
(4) (B),(C) and (D) Only

54. Which of the following statements are correct relating to lockout ?

(A) A lockout is the closure of a place of business or employment or the suspension of work.

(B) A lockout is an antithesis of a strike.
(C) A lockout is the closure of an industrial undertaking because of the existence of or apprehension of an industrial dispute, violence and damage.
(D) A lockout means termination of employment by retrenchment

Choose the correct answer from the options given below:
(1) (A), (B) and (C) Only
(2) (B), (C) and (D) Only
(3) (A), (C) and (D) Only
(4) (C) and (D) Only

55. Which of the following are the role of inspectors appointed by the government under respective labour' legislations ?
(A) Enforce the labour law and related regulations.
(B) Advice employers and workers on how to comply with the laws and regulations.
(C) Issue show cause notice to offending employers for not complying with provisions of the law.
(D) File prosecution in the concerned court if despite show cause notice compliance is not secured in time.
(E) To investigate the dispute as arbitrator and submit the report before the appropriate authority.

Choose the correct answer from the options given below:
(1) (A), (B), (C) and (D) Only
(2) (B), (C), (D) and (E) Only
(3) (A), (C), (D) and (E) Only
(4) (A), (B), (D) and (E) Only

56. As per the provisions of the Inter-State Migrant Workmen (Regulation of Employment and Conditions of Service) Act, 1979, the duties of the contractor includes :
(A) to furnish such particulars in the form prescribed to the specified authority in the state from which, the inter-state migrant workman is recruited.
(B) to issue every inter-state migrant workman, a pass book affixed with a passport size photograph indicating the details of employment, payment of wages, working hours etc.
(C) to provide retention allowance to the inter-state migrant workman when not in employment.
(D) to furnish in respect of every inter-state migrant workman who ceases to be employed, a return in such form and in such manner as prescribed to the specified authority in the state form which, he is recruited.

Choose the correct answer from the options given below :
(1) (A), (B) and (C) Only
(2) (A) and (C) Only
(3) (B), (C) and (D) Only
(4) (A), (B) and (D) Only

57. The certifying surgeon appointed under the provisions of the Mines Act, 1952 shall perform which of the following duties ?
(A) the examination of person engaged in a mine in such dangerous occupation or process.
(B) to conduct medical supervision as may be prescribed for any mine where cases of illness have occurred.
(C) to conduct enquiry into any accident happened in the mine.
(D) for payment of disability allowances to the persons confit to work in the mine

Choose the correct answer from the options given below:
(1) (A), (B) and (D) Only
(2) (A) and (B) Only
(3) (A) and (D) Only
(4) (A), (B), (C) and (D) Only

58. As per the provisions of the Building and other Construction Workers (Regulation of Employment and Conditions of Service) Act, 1996, the appropriate Government may make rules to:

(A) Fix the number of hours of work which shall constitute a normal working day.
(B) Provide for a day of rest in every period of seven days.
(C) Provide for payment of work on a day of rest not less than the average daily wage.
(D) Fix the number of hours of work for a normal working day inclusive of one or more specified intervals.
(E) Payment of full remuneration in respect of such days of rest.

Choose the correct answer from the options given below:
(1) (A) and (C) Only
(2) (A), (B) and (C) Only
(3) (A), (B), (D) and (E) Only
(4) (A), (B), (C) and (E) Only

59. Which of the following statement is/ are not correct with regard to the applicability of the Employees Provident Fund and Miscellaneous Provisions Act 1952 ?
(A) to every establishment which is a factory engaged in manufacture specified in Scheduled of the Act.
(B) to any establishment registered under the cooperative societies Act, 1912 employing less than 50 person working without the aid of power.
(C) to an establishment belonging to or under the control of the Central Government or a State Government whose employees are entitled to the benefit of contributory provident fund.
(D) to any other establishment set up under any Central, Provincial or State Act and where employees are entitled to contributory provident fund and old age pension.

Choose the correct answer from the options given below :
(1) (A) Only
(2) (A) and (B) Only
(3) (A) and (C) Only
(4) (B), (C) and (D) Only

60. As per the provisions of the Employees Provident Fund and Miscellaneous Provisions Act, 1952, a pension fund to be created with which of the followings ?
(A) Such sum from the employers contribution not exceeding eight and one-third percent of the basic wage, dearness allowance and retaining allowances, of any of the concerned employee.
(B) Such sum as are payable by the employers of the exempted establishments.
(C) The net assets of the Employees Family Pension Fund as on the date of the establishment of the Pension Fund.
(D) Such sum from the employees contribution not exceeding one and one-third percent of the basic wage and dearness allowance or retaining allowances, if any
(E) Such sum as the Central Government may, after due appropriation by the parliament by law.

Choose the correct answer from the options given below :
(1) (A), (B) and (C) Only
(2) (A), (B), (C) and (D) Only
(3) (A), (B), (C) and (E) Only
(4) (A), (B), (C), (D) and (E) Only

61. Which is NOT a principle of Labour Welfare ?
(A) Principle of Social Responsibility of Industry
(B) Principle of Re-personalisation
(C) Principle of Trusteeship
(D) Principle of Public Relation
(E) Principle of Totality of Welfare

Choose the correct answer from the options given below
(1) (A) and (E) Only
(2) (B) and (C) Only
(3) (C) and (E) Only
(4) (C) and (D) Only

62. Which among the following is NOT included under Statutory Welfare measure pertaining to canteen facility ?

(A) Section 46 of Factories Act, 1948
(B) Section 11 of Plantation Labour Act, 1951
(C) Section 44 of Factories Act, 1948
(D) Section 12 of Plantation Labour Act, 1951
(E) Section 16 of Contract Labour (Regulation and Abolition) Act, 1970

Choose the correct answer from the options given below:
(1) (A) and (B) Only
(2) (C) and (D) Only
(3) (A) and (E) Only
(4) (B) and (D) Only

63. Which is NOT a theory of Labour Welfare ?
(A) The Police Theory of Labour Welfare
(B) The Theory of Adequacy of Wage
(C) The Philanthropic Theory
(D) The Theory of Efficiency
(E) The Placating Theory

Choose the correct answer from the options given below
(1) (A) and (C) Only
(2) (C) and (E) Only
(3) (B) and (D) Only
(4) (D) and (E) Only

64. Wage-goods strategy of development was propounded by
(A) C.N. Vakil
(B) P.R. Brahmananda
(C) Amartya Sen
(D) Abhijit Sen
(E) A.R. Desai

Choose the correct answer from the options given below :
(1) (A) and (E) Only
(2) (C) and (D) Only
(3) (A) and (B) Only
(4) (B) and (D) Only

65. What are the economic causes of migration?
(A) Better employment opportunities
(B) Marriage
(C) Higher wage
(D) Social discrimination
(E) Attraction of better facilities and infrastructure

Choose the correct answer from the options given below
(1) (A), (B) and (C) Only
(2) (C), (D) and (E) Only
(3) (A), (C) and (E) Only
(4) (B), (C) and (D) Only

66. Arrange the following management concepts in terms of period of evolution from earliest to latest.
(A) Informal organisation
(B) Time and motion study
(C) Six sigma
(D) Need hierarchy model
(E) Management by objectives

Choose the correct answer from the options given below :
(1) (B) → (D) → (A) → (E) → (C)
(2) (B) → (D) → (A) → (C) → (E)
(3) (B) → (A) → (D) → (E) → (C)
(4) (A) → (B) → (D) → (C) → (E)

67. Arrange the following steps in sequential order for designing a structured interview.
(A) Create interview questions
(B) Appoint the interview panel
(C) Analyse the job
(D) Rate the job's main duties
(E) Create benchmark answer

Choose the correct answer from the options given below:
(1) (B) → (D) → (E) → (C) → (D)
(2) (C) → (D) → (A) → (E) → (B)
(3) (C) → (D) → (E) → (A) → (B)
(4) (A) → (E) → (B) → (C) → (D)

68. Arrange the following phases of development of multinational corporations as identified by Alder and Ghadar starting from Phased.
(A) Global (B) Domestic
(C) Multinational (D) International

Choose the correct answer from the options given below :

(1) (B), (C), (A), (D)
(2) (C), (B), (A), (D)
(3) (C), (B), (D), (A)
(4) (B), (D), (C), (A)

69. Arrange the following steps of OB modification in the right sequence starting from the beginning.
(A) Identification of critical behaviours
(B) Measurement of the behaviour's
(C) Evaluation to ensure performance improvement
(D) Functional analysis of the behaviour
(E) Development of an intervention strategy
Choose the correct answer from the options given below:
(1) (A), (B), (E), (D), (C)
(2) (A), (D), (B),(C), (E)
(3) (A), (B), (D), (E), (C)
(4) (A), (B), (C), (D), (E)

70. Arrange the main Government sponsored schemes of Worker's Participation in Management in India from earlier to latest.
(A) Institutions of employees' participation in management for public sector undertakings.
(B) Shop councils and unit councils under the 20-points programme.
(C) Board-Level Participation
(D) Works Committee
(E) Joint Management Councils
Choose the correct answer from the options given below :
(1) (A), (B), (C), (E), (D)
(2) (D), (E), (C), (B), (A)
(3) (B), (C), (D), (E), (A)
(4) (C), (D), (E), (A), (B)

71. Arrange the process of disciplinary action is an industrial undertaking in proper sequence.
(A) Domestic enquiry
(B) Framing of charges
(C) Charge-sheeting
(D) Inflicting punishment
Choose the correct answer from the options given below:
(1) (A), (B), (C), (D)
(2) (B), (C), (A), (D)
(3) (B), (A), (D), (C)
(4) (D), (C), (A), (B)

72. Arrange in a sequence the Committee/Commission set up by the Central Government in the county with regard to the matters concerning labour from the earliest to latest.
(A) Bombay Textile Labour Enquiry Committee.
(B) Royal Commission on Labour.
(C) Health Survey and Development Committee.
(D) First National Commission on Labour.
Choose the correct answer from the options given below :
(1) (A), (B), (C), (D)
(2) (B), (A), (C), (D)
(3) (C), (A), (B), (D)
(4) (B), (A), (D), (C)

73. Arrange the following provisions in the ascending order as mentioned under the Payment of Gratuity Act, 1972.
(A) Determination of the amount of gratuity
(B) Compulsory Insurance
(C) Nomination
(D) Payment of Gratuity
(E) Recovery of Gratuity
Choose the correct answer from the options given below:
(1) (A), (B), (C), (D), (E)
(2) (D), (B), (C), (A), (B)
(3) (B), (C), (D), (A), (E)
(4) (D), (A), (C), (B), (E)

74. Arrange the following welfare facilities provided under the Factories Act 1948 in ascending order as per their sections.
(A) Creche (B) Canteen
(C) Washing
(D) First-aid appliances
(E) Facilities for sitting

Choose the correct answer from the options given below:

(1) (A), (C), (E), (B), (D)
(2) (C), (E), (D), (B), (A)
(3) (B), (A), (C), (E), (D)
(4) (D), (C), (B), (A), (E)

75. Given below are two statements

Statement (I): 'Wages form the pivot round which most of the Labour problems revolve'.

Statement (II): Problems concerning the economic social conditions of wage earners have become topical.

In the light of the above statements, choose the most appropriate answer from the options given below:

(1) Both Statement I and Statement II are correct
(2) Both Statement I and Statement II are incorrect
(3) Statement I is correct but Statement II is incorrect
(4) Statement I is incorrect but Statement II is correct

76. Match List - I with List-II.

List - I	**List - II**
Name	**Concept**
(A) Max Weber	(I) Social systems approach
(B) Chester I. Bamard	(II) Hierarchy
(C) Vilfre Pareto	(III) Unit production
(D) Joan Woodward	(IV) Informal structure

Choose the correct answer from the options given below :

(1) (A)-(II), (B)-(I), (C)-(IV), (D)-(III)
(2) (A)-(II), (B)-(IV), (C)-(I), (D)-(III)
(3) (A)-(III), (B)-(I), (C)-(IV), (D)-(II)
(4) (A)-(II), (B)-(I), (C)-(III), (D)-(IV)

77. Match List - I with List-II.

List - I	**List - II**
Types of Interview	**Meaning**
(A) Situational interview	(I) A series of job-related questions that focus on how the candidate reacted to actual situation in the past
(B) Behavioural interview	(II) A series of job related questions that focus on how the candidate would behave in a given situation
(C) Job-related interview	(III) A series of often rude questions that make the candidate uncomfortable
(D) Stress interview	(IV) A series of job-related questions that focus on relevant past job-related behaviour

Choose the correct answer from the options given below :

(1) (A)-(I), (B)-(II), (C)-(IV), (D)-(III)
(2) (A)-(I), (B)-(III), (C)-(IV), (D)-(II)
(3) (A)-(II), (B)-(I), (C)-(IV), (D)-(III)
(4) (A)-(II), (B)-(IV), (C)-(I), (D)-(III)

78. Match List - I with List-II.

List - I	**List - II**
Development	**Formulater**
(A) The Integrative Framework Approach	(I) T.V. Rao
(B) The Strategic Framework Approach	(II) Friedman
(C) The HRD Scorecard Approach	(III) Ulrich and Lake
(D) The Human Capital Approach	(IV) Young and Berman

Choose the correct answer from the options given below :

(1) (A)-(IV), (B)-(III), (C)-(I), (D)-(II)
(2) (A)-(I), (B)-(II), (C)-(IV), (D)-(III)

(3) (A)-(III), (B)-(II), (C)-(I), (D)-(IV)
(4) (A)-(II), (B)-(I), (C)-(III), (D)-(IV)

79. Match List - I with List-II.

List - I	**List - II**
Theories of motivation	**Propagator**
(A) Expectency theory	(I) J. Stacy Adams
(B) Equity theory	(II) Victor Vroom
(C) ERG theory	(III) Fritz Heider
(D) Attribution theory	(IV) Clayton P. Alderfer

Choose the correct answer from the options given below :
(1) (A)-(IV), (B)-(III), (C)-(II), (D)-(I)
(2) (A)-(III), (B)-(IV), (C)-(I), (D)-(II)
(3) (A)-(I), (B)-(n), (C)-(III), (D)-(IV)
(4) (A)-(II), (B)-(I), (C)-(IV), (D)-(in)

80. Match List - I with List-II.

List - I	**List - II**
Authors	**Books**
(A) Karl Marx	(I) A theory of the labour movement
(B) Selig Perlman	(II) The poverty of philosophy
(C) Robert F. Hoxie	(III) The world of labour
(D) G.D.H. Cole	(IV) Trade unionism in the United States

Choose the correct answer from the options given below :
(1) (A)-(II), (B)-(I), (C)-(IV), (D)-(III)
(2) (A)-(II), (B)-(IV), (C)-(III), (D)-(I)
(3) (A)-(IV), (B)-(III), (C)-(I), (D)-(II)
(4) (A)-(III), (B)-(IV), (C)-(II), (D)-(I)

81. Match List - I with List-II.

List - I	**List - II**
Form of Strikes	**Bask features**
(A) Authorised strike	(I) Restored to for a short period such as day or two to give the employer a warning of the likely wider form of consideration if their demands are not promptly conceded.
(B) Wildcat strike	(II) Such a strike is usefully resorted to in offence, to put pressure on the management.
(C) Sit-down strike	(III) When a section of workmen without authorisation from the union and often in defiance of the direction of the competent authority in a union.
(D) Token strike	(IV) Called by proper authority in a union and in conformity with the requirements of law.

Choose the correct answer from the options given below :
(1) (A)-(III), (B)-(IV), (C)-(II), (D)-(I)
(2) (A)-(IV), (B)-(III), (C)-(II), (D)-(I)
(3) (A)-(I), (B)-(III), (C)-(II), (D)-(IV)
(4) (A)-(IV), (B)-(II), (C)-(III), (D)-(I)

82. Match List - I with List-II.

List - I	**List - II**
Authorities	**Legislations**
(A) Technical Advisory Committee	(I) The Contract Labour (Regulation and Abolition) Act, 1970
(B) Central Advisory Board	(II) The Factories Act, 1948
(C) Export Committee	(III) The Child and Adolescent Labour (Prohibition and Regulation) Act, 1986

(D)	Site Appraisal Committee	(IV)	The Building and other Construction Workers (Regulation of Employment and Conditions of Service) Act 1996

Choose the correct answer from the options given below :

(1) (A)-(III), (B)-(I), (C)-(IV), (D)-(II)
(2) (A)-(IV), (B)-(III), (C)-(II), (D)-(I)
(3) (A)-(I), (B)-(II), (C)-(III), (D)-(IV)
(4) (A)-(III), (B)-(IV), (C)-(I), (D)-(III)

83. Match List - I with List-II.

List - I Legislations	List - II Authorities
(A) The Minimum Wages Act	(I) Advisory Committee
(B) The Equal Remuneration Act	(II) Controlling Authority
(C) The Employees' Provident Fund and Miscellaneous Provision Act	(III) Central Advisory Board
(D) The Payment of Gratuity Act	(IV) Board of Trustees

Choose the correct answer from the options given below :

(1) (A)-II), (B)-(III), (C)-(IV), (D)-(I)
(2) (A)-(I), (B)-(III), (C)-(IV), (D)-(II)
(3) (A)-(III), (B)-(I), (C)-(IV), (D)-(II)
(4) (A)-(IV), (B)-(II), (C)-(III), (D)-(I)

84. Match List - I with List-II.

List - I Occupational Disease	List - II Particulars
(A) Anthrax	(I) Degree of accuracy, speed of work and concentration required for the job
(B) Silicosis	(II) Making of asbestos mattresses
(C) Asbestosis	(III) Caused by inhaling dust containing silica
(D) Telegraphic Cramp	(IV) Disease of animals

Choose the correct answer from the options given below :

(1) (A)-(III), (B)-(IV), (C)-(I), (D)-(II)
(2) (A)-(IV), (B)-(III), (C)-(I), (D)-(II)
(3) (A)-(IV), (B)-(III), (C)-(II), (D)-(I)
(4) (A)-(I), (B)-(II), (C)-(III), (D)-(IV)

85. Match List - I with List-II.

List - I Name of Theory	List - II Propounder
(A) Wage Fund Theory	(I) Ricardo
(B) Residual Claimant Theory	(II) J.B. Clark
(C) Marginal Productivity Theory	(III) J.S. Mill
(D) Subsistence Theory	(IV) Walker

Choose the correct answer from the options given below :

(1) (A)-(III), (B)-(IV), (C)-(II), (D)-(I)
(2) (A)-(III), (B)-(II), (C)-(I), (D)-(IV)
(3) (A)-(I), (B)-(II), (C)-(III), (D)-(IV)
(4) (A)-(II), (B)-(III), (C)-(IV), (D)-(I)

86. Given below are two statements : one is labelled as Assertion (A) and the other is labelled as Reason (R).

Assertion (A) : It is argued that the best way to motivate workers is through job enrichment which comprises of increasing opportunities for the worker to experience feelings of responsibility, achievement growth and recognition.

Reason (R) : Empowered employees would do their jobs well because they realise their responsibilities for providing quality service and towards other dimensions of their work.

In the light of the above statements, choose the most appropriate answer from the options given below :

(1) Both (A) and (R) are true and (R) is the correct explanation of (A)
(2) Both (A) and (R) are true but (R) is not the correct explanation of (A)
(3) (A) is true but (R) is false
(4) (A) is false but (R) is true

87. Given below are two statements: one is labelled as Assertion (A) and the other is labelled as Reason (R).

Assertion (A): It is the employee's perception of a situation that becomes the basis for his/her behaviour.

Reason (R): Individuals behave in a given manner based not on the way their external environment is but, rather on what they see or believe it to be.

In the light of the above statements, choose the most appropriate answer from the options given below:

(1) Both (A) and (R) are true and (R) is the correct explanation of (A)

(2) Both (A) and (R) are true but (R) is not the correct explanation of (A)

(3) (A) is true but (R) is false

(4) (A) is false but (R) is true

88. Given below are two statements:

Statement (I): 'Closed shop' is an industrial or business establishment in which the union security clause in collective agreement provides that a Job seeker must become the member of the union at the time of his employment and continue to do so in order to retain his job.

Statement (II): Closed shop agreements were widely prevalent in the USA and India following the enactment of the Wagner Act (National Labour Relation Act) in 1935 and the Trade Union Act, 1926 respectively.

In the light of the above statements, choose the most appropriate answer from the options given below:

(1) Both Statement I and Statement II are true

(2) Both Statement I and Statement II are false

(3) Statement I is true but Statement II is false

(4) Statement I is false but Statement II is true

89. Given below are two statements : one is labelled as Assertion (A) and the other is labelled as Reason (R).

Assertion (A) : The Factories Act, 1948 is meant to regulate the working conditions and meant to protect workers from exploitation and unhygenic working conditions within the factory premises.

Reason (R) : In the absence of regulated health, safety and welfare provisions along with working hours, leave and restrictions on employment, certain category of workers are likely to be exploited by the greedy business establishment.

In the light of the above statements, choose the most appropriate answer from the options given below :

(1) Both (A) and (R) are correct and (R) is the correct explanation of (A)

(2) Both (A) and (R) are correct but (R) is not the correct explanation of (A)

(3) (A) is correct but (R) is not correct

(4) (A) is not correct but (R) is correct

90. Given below are two statements: one is labelled as Assertion (A) and the other is labelled as Reason (R).

Assertion (A): The main determinants of the general level of wages are the value of the marginal net product of labour, the degree of competition in the markets for the products of industry and the relative bargaining power of the workers and employers.

Reason (R): Most economists now confine their explanation of the determination of wage in the modern free labour market to a combination of marginal productivity theory and bargaining theory.

In the light of the above statements, choose the most appropriate answer from the options given below:

(1) Both (A) and (R) are true and (R) is the correct explanation of (A)

(2) Both (A) and (R) are true but (R) is not the correct explanation of (A)

(3) (A) is true but (R) is false

(4) (A) is false but (R) is true

Read the following passage carefully; and, on the basis of the passage, given answer to question number.

According to recent Survey, India's economic growth in FY23 has been principally led by private consumption and capital formation and they have helped generate employment as seen in the declining urban unemployment rate and in the faster net registration in Employee Provident Fund. Moreover, World's second-largest vaccination drive involving more than 2 billion doses also served to lift consumer sentiments that may prolong the rebound in consumption. Still, private capex soon needs to take up the leadership role to put job creation on a fast track.

It also points out that the upside to India's growth outlook arises from (i) limited health and economic fallout for the rest of the world from the current surge in Covid-19 infections in China and, therefore, continued normalisation of supply chains; (ii) inflationary impulses from the reopening of China's economy turning out to be neither significant nor persistent; (iii) recessionary tendencies in major Advanced Economies (AEs) triggering a cessation of monetary tightening and a return of capital flows to India amidst a stable domestic inflation rate below 6 per cent; and (iv) this leading to an improvements in animal spirits and providing further impetus to private sector investment.

The Survey says, the credit growth to the Micro, Small, and Medium Enterprises (MSME) sector has been remarkably high, over 30.6 per cent, on average during Jan-Nov 2022, supported by the extended Emergency Credit Linked Guarantee Scheme (ECLGS) of the Union government. It adds that the recovery of MSMEs is proceeding apace, as is evident in the amounts of Goods and Services Tax (GST) they pay, while the Emergency Credit Linked Guarantee Scheme (ECGLS) is easing their debt servicing concerns.

Apart from this, increase in the overall bank credit has also been influenced by the shift in borrower's funding choices from volatile bond markets, where yields have increased, and external commercial borrowings, where interest and hedging costs have increased, towards banks. If inflation declines in FY24 and if real cost of credit does not rise, then credit growth is likely to be brisk in FY24.

91. What factor has contributed to the recovery of Micro, Small, and Medium Enterprises (MSME) sector ?
(1) Liberalizing government policies
(2) External Emergency Credit Linked Guarantee Scheme (ECLGS)
(3) Credit creation by the RBI
(4) Boost in industrial export

92. What needs to take a leadership role to accelerate Job Creation, according to the survey ?
(1) Private capital expenditure (capex)
(2) Foreign Direct Investment (EDI)
(3) Public expenditure
(4) Maintaining GDP growth rate

93. What played a role in boosting consumer sentiments and consumption rebound in India ?
(1) Indo-US relationship
(2) GDP Growth Rate
(3) World second largest vaccination drive
(4) Implementation of the Government policies

94. Given below are two statements:
Statement (I): India's economic growth in FY23 has been principally led by boost in agricultural export.
Statement (II): Inflationary impulses from the reopening of China's economy turned out to be neither significant nor persistent.
In the light of the above statements, choose the most appropriate answer from the options given below:
(1) Both Statement I and Statement II are correct
(2) Both Statement I and Statement II are incorrect
(3) Statement I is correct but Statement II is incorrect
(4) Statement I is incorrect but Statement II is correct

95. What were the two main factors contributing to India's economic growth in Financial Year 2023 ?
(1) Public Healthcare initiatives and agriculture reforms
(2) Export growth and technological advancement
(3) EDI and credit formation
(4) Private consumption and capital formation

Read the following passage carefully; and, on the basis of the passage, answer question number.

During the last couple of decades, with the expansion of technology, internet, urbanization and more recently the COVID-19 pandemic, the debate on 'what is the future of work' has been rife among employers, in the 2019 report of the World Bank Group on the 'Changing Nature of Work', it was estimated that less than 0.5% of the active labour force participates in the gig economy globally, with less than 0.3% in developing countries. As per the 2022 report by India's public policy think tank, NITI Aayog, on "India's Booming Gig and Platform Economy' (NITI Report), the share of gig workers in total workers increased from 0.54% in 2011-12 to 1.33% in 2019-20. The advancement of technology has also enabled the emergence of temporary workers using online platforms thereby amplifying the focus on gig work.

The NITI Report considers 'gig workers' as those engaged in work outside the traditional employer-employee arrangement. There are two subsets to gig workers i.e., platform workers and nonplatform workers. When these gig workers use online algorithmic matching platforms i.e., websites or apps like Amazon or Uber to connect with customers, they are known as platform workers. The workers who work outside of these platforms are non-platform workers. These mainly include construction workers, day-job workers and non-technology based temporary workers.

96. Given below are two statements: one is labelled as Assertion (A) and the other is labelled as Reason (R).

Assertion (A): There are two subsets to gig workers, i.e., platform workers and non-platform workers.

Reason (R): The NITI Reports considers 'gig workers' as those engaged in work outside the traditional employer-employee arrangement.

In the light of the above statements, choose the most appropriate answer from the options given below:
(1) Both (A) and (R) are true and (R) is the correct explanation of (A)
(2) Both (A) and (R) are true but (R) is not the correct explanation of (A)
(3) (A) is true but (R) is false
(4) (A) is false but (R) is correct

97. What factors have contributed to the ongoing debate about the future of work ?
(1) Changing demographics, labour strikes, and government policies
(2) Natural disasters, labour unions, and globalization
(3) Economic recession, political instability and social changes
(4) Technological expansion, urbanization, and COVID-19 pandemic

98. According to the 2019 report of the World Bank Group, what percentage of the global active labour force participates in the gig economy?
(1) Less than 0.5% (2) Around 1%
(3) About 5% (4) Over 10%

99. In the context of gig work, what are the platform workers ?
(1) Workers who work exclusively offline
(2) Workers who have traditional employer-employee arrangements
(3) Workers who use online platforms to connect with customers
(4) Workers who engage in temporary

100. Given below are two statements: one is labelled as Assertion (A) and the other is labelled as Reason (R).

Assertion (A): Recently the world has experienced a rise in the number of gig workers.

Reason (R): During the last couple of decades, with the expansion of technology, internet, urbanization and more recently the COVID-19 pandemic, the debate on 'what is the future of work' has been rise among employers.

In the light of the above statements, choose the most appropriate answer from the options given below:

(1) Both (A) and (R) are true and (R) is the correct explanation of (A)

(2) Both (A) and (R) are true but (R) is not the correct explanation of (A)

(3) (A) is true but (R) is false

(4) (A) is false but (R) is true

ANSWER KEY

1. (2)	**2.** (1)	**3.** (1)	**4.** (3)	**5.** (1)	**6.** (3)	**7.** (2)	**8.** (1)	**9.** (2)	**10.** (1)
11. (1)	**12.** (4)	**13.** (3)	**14.** (1)	**15.** (3)	**16.** (2)	**17.** (1)	**18.** (2)	**19.** (3)	**20.** (3)
21. (2)	**22.** (1)	**23.** (4)	**24.** (3)	**25.** (1)	**26.** (3)	**27.** (3)	**28.** (2)	**29.** (2)	**30.** (3)
31. (3)	**32.** (2)	**33.** (2)	**34.** (3)	**35.** (1)	**36.** (2)	**37.** (1)	**38.** (4)	**39.** (2)	**40.** (3)
41. (1)	**42.** (1)	**43.** (1)	**44.** (2)	**45.** (1)	**46.** (2)	**47.** (1)	**48.** (2)	**49.** (3)	**50.** (3)
51. (2)	**52.** (3)	**53.** (3)	**54.** (1)	**55.** (1)	**56.** (4)	**57.** (2)	**58.** (3)	**59.** (1)	**60.** (3)
61. (4)	**62.** (2)	**63.** (3)	**64.** (3)	**65.** (3)	**66.** (3)	**67.** (2)	**68.** (4)	**69.** (3)	**70.** (2)
71. (2)	**72.** (2)	**73.** (2)	**74.** (2)	**75.** (1)	**76.** (2)	**77.** (3)	**78.** (1)	**79.** (4)	**80.** (1)
81. (2)	**82.** (1)	**83.** (3)	**84.** (3)	**85.** (1)	**86.** (1)	**87.** (1)	**88.** (3)	**89.** (1)	**90.** (2)
91. (2)	**92.** (1)	**93.** (3)	**94.** (4)	**95.** (4)	**96.** (2)	**97.** (4)	**98.** (1)	**99.** (3)	**100.** (1)

○○○

SEPTEMBER, 2024

LABOUR WELFARE & INDUSTRIAL RELATIONS, LABOUR & SOCIAL WELFARE, HUMAN RESOURCE MANAGEMENT

PAPER-II

Note : This paper contains **hundred (100)** objective type questions, each question carrying **two (2)** marks.

1. Who has concluded that non- financial incentives are more important than financial incentives.
(1) F.W.Taylor (2) Henri Fayol
(3) Elton Mayo (4) Mary Parker Follet

2. Which approach of management emphasises that "the task of managers is to identify which technique will, in a particular situation, under particular circumstances, and at a particular time, best contribute to the attainment of management goals."
(1) Behavioural approach
(2) System approach
(3) Quantitative approach
(4) Contingency approach

3. The core of planning is-
(1) Objective (2) Decision making
(3) Strategy (4) Forecasting

4. Combining of functional and project or product patterns of departmentation in the same organisation structure is-
(1) Departmentation by time
(2) Customer departmentation
(3) Matrix organisation
(4) Equipment departmentation

5. Which of the following is the correct expansion of PERT?
(1) Programme Evaluation and Review Technique
(2) Performance Evaluation and Report Technique
(3) Progress Evaluation and Review Trend
(4) Programme Evaluation and Research Technique

6. Who among the following is the proponent of theory Z in HRM?
(1) John Storey (2) William G. Ovchi
(3) Vladimir Puick (4) Michael Beer

7. The process of identifying and uncovering of candidates through a proactive recruitment technique is known as
(1) Head hunting (2) Poaching
(3) Candidate sourcing
(4) HR stock taking

8. The 5 S technique is mainly associated with which of the following?
(1) Quality control
(2) Compensation management
(3) Performance appraisal
(4) Shop-floor housekeeping

9. Who has developed/outlined the 'Human Capital Appraisal Approach'?
(1) T. V. Rao (2) Udai Pareek
(3) Friedman
(4) Yeung and Berman

10. Which among the following is not summerised under three Cs Model of Human Resource Development?
(1) Competence (2) Communication
(3) Commitment (4) Culture

11. Reich distinguished three professional categories of the labour force in a global terms. Which of the following does not belong to the categories identified by Reich?
(1) Routine production services
(2) In- Person Services
(3) Symbolic-Analytic Services
(4) High Tech Services

12. In which of the following stages an expatriate suffers from the phenomenon of cultural shock?
(1) During the period of recruitment and selection.
(2) During the period of assignment abroad
(3) During the period of repatriation
(4) During the period of training

13. The theory of personality which is based on physical attributes or psychological factors for categorisation of personalities is known as:
(1) Type theory
(2) Trait theory
(3) Psychometric theory
(4) Social Learning theory

14. An event, repeated several times, evoking desired responses is known as:
(1) Operant conditioning
(2) Instrumental conditioning
(3) Classical conditioning
(4) Cognitive conditioning

15. A leader who is concerned for High Task and High Relationship exhibits which of the following type of leadership?
(1) Supportive style
(2) Autocratic style
(3) Free- Rein style
(4) Participative style

16. In process by which people group stimuli into recognisable pattern so that meaning can be assigned to them, is known as:
(1) Stereotyping
(2) Perceptual organisaation
(3) Perceptual constancy
(4) Perceptual Intigration

17. Who has started the Bengali weekly 'Janawani' in Calcutta?
(1) S.A. Dange
(2) Muzzaffar Ahmed
(3) N.M. Lokhandey
(4) M.N. Roy

18. Who was the founder of 'Madras workers' union?
(1) B. P. Wadia (2) N. M. Joshi
(3) N. M. Lokhandey
(4) Cowasji Namabhoy Davar

19. Under which section of the Trade Union Act. 1926 the formation of separate political fund for promotion of civil and political interest of Trade Union has been provided?
(1) Section 6 (2) Section 12
(3) Section 16 (4) Section 18

20. Who has developed the Technological Theory of Trade Unionism?
(1) Robert T. Hoxie
(2) Frank Tannenbaum
(3) Selig Perlman
(4) John R. Commons

21. What are the minimum and maximum number of 'Protected workmen' prescribed under the Industrial Disputes Act. 1947?
(1) Minimum 20 and Maximum 100
(2) Minimum 15 and Maximum 75
(3) Minimum 10 and Maximum 50
(4) Minimum 5 and Maximum 100

22. In which Convention Number of International Labour Organisation, 'the right to organise and collective bargaining" has been declared as fundamental rights?
(1) Convention No. 19
(2) Convention No.87
(3) Convention No.98
(4) Convention No. 103

23. In which of the following organisations the scheme of workers participation in management 1983 was made applicable?
(1) Public sector undertaking
(2) Private sector undertaking
(3) Central Public sector undertaking
(4) State Public sector undertaking

24. As per the provisions of the Mines Act, 1952, if any owner agent or manager fails to submit within which period a draft bye-law after being called upon by the Chief Inspector or Inspector, the Cliief Inspector or Inspector on his own may propose a draft of such bye- law as appear to him as sufficient?

(1) One month (2) Two months
(3) Six months (4) Twelve months

25. "If a strike is resorted to for a short period such as a day or two to give the employer a warning of the likely wider form of confrontation if their demands are not prompty conceded" is called?
(1) General strike
(2) Particular strike
(3) Token strike
(4) Jurisdictional strike

26. The Certificate of fitness issued by the certifying surgeon to an adolescent worker shall remain valid for which period under the Factories Act, 1948?
(1) Six months (2) Twelve months
(3) One year (4) Two year

27. As per the provisions of the Mines Act, 1952 the special officers after giving not less than how many days notice to the manager of the mine, enter the mine for survey, level or measure the mine.
(1) Thirty Days (2) Fifteen Days
(3) Seven Days (4) Three Days

28. The displacement allowance equal to which of the following to be paid by a contractor to every Inter-state Migrant Workman at the time of recruitment as per the provisions of the Inter-state Migrant Workmen (Regulation of Employment and Conditions of Service) Act, 1979?
(1) Seventy- five percent of monthly wage payable to him or one hundred rupees whichever is higher
(2) Fifty percent of monthly wage payable to him or one hundred rupees whichever is higher
(3) Fifty percent of monthly wage payable to him or seventy five rupees whichever is higher
(4) One month wage to be payable to him or two hundred and fifty rupees whichever is higher

29. The Advisory Committee constituted under the Equal Remuneration Act, 1976 shall consist of how many person nominated by the appropriate government of which one-half shall be women?
(1) Six persons
(2) Eight persons
(3) Ten persons
(4) Fourteen persons

30. As per the provision of the Payment of Bonus Act, 1965, bonus payable to an employee shall be paid with in how many months from the close of the accounting year?
(1) Two months (2) Three months
(3) Six months (4) Eight months

31. Under the provisions of the Employee Provident Fund and Miscellaneous Provisions Act, 1952, a Tribunal may within which period of time from the date of its order can rectify any mistake apparent from record and amend the order?
(1) Within One year
(2) Within Three year
(3) Within Five year
(4) Within Seven year

32. As per the provisions of the Minimum Wages Act. 1948 a worker is required to present his application for less payment of wages before the claim authority within which time from the date on which minimum wages become payable to which he is eligible?
(1) Three months (2) Six months
(3) Sixty days (4) Ninety days

33. When welfare work is used as a means to secure, preserve and develop the efficiency and productivity of labour, it is called :
(1) Philantharopic Theory
(2) Trusteeship Theory
(3) Functional Theory
(4) Placating Theory

34. The Committee of Experts on Welfare facilities for industrial workers constituted by I.LO. in 1963 has divided the welfare services in two groups- intra-mural and extra-mural. What service is not included in extra-mural services?

(1) Maternity benefit
(2) Health service including occupational safety
(3) Library and reading room
(4) Transport to and from the place of work

35. Labour welfare has been defined as "efforts to make life worth living for workers" by:
(1) Oxford Dictionary
(2) Chamber's Dictionary
(3) R. R. Hopkins
(4) James Todd

36. Who has defined social security as "It is a controversial and dynamic subject with various facets- philosophical, theoretical, humanitarian, financial, administrative, social, economic, political, statistical, actuarial, medical and legal."
(1) Fridlander
(2) Lord Beveridge
(3) Weber and Cohen
(4) I.L.O

37. What is not a characteristics of competitive market?
(1) There are many buyer and many sellers in the market.
(2) Goods offered by the various sellers are largely the same.
(3) Buyers and sellers are said to be price takers.
(4) Firms can freely enter the market but cannot exit.

38. The doctrine of conspicuous consumption was propounded by:
(1) Throstein Veblen
(2) Robert Giffin
(3) Paul A. Samuelson
(4) Alfred Marshall

39. In economy, the trade cycle revolves around the phases of boom, recession, depression and recovery. The unemployment caused due to effects of recession and depression is called:
(1) Structural unemployment
(2) Frictional unemployment
(3) Cyclical unemployment
(4) Seasonal unemployment

40. The supply curve of a commodity slops:
(1) Upward in right
(2) Downward in right
(3) In Straight line
(4) Is perpendicular to y-axis

41. Arrange the steps in the process of planning in proper order from earlier to later.
A. Setting objectives
B. Identifying alternative
C. Being aware of the opportunity
D. Choosing an alternative
E. Comparison of alternatives in the light of goals sought.

Choose the ***correct*** answer from the options given below:
(1) C, A, B, E, D
(2) C, B, E, A, D
(3) A, B, C, D, E
(4) B, A, C, D, E

42. Arrange the steps in the process of controlling in proper order from earlier to later.
A. Setting standard
B. Determination of areas of control
C. Comparison of performance against standard
D. Measurement of performance
E. Correction of deviation

Choose the ***correct*** answer from the options given below:
(1) A, B, C, D, E
(2) A, C, D, B, E
(3) B,A, D, C, E
(4) B, C, D, A, E

43. Arrange the following steps of human resource planning in proper sequence starting from the beginning:
A. Plan to modify or adjust the organisational plan.
B. Analysing the organisational plan.
C. Forecasting the demand and supply aspects of human resource.

D. Estimating the net human resource requirements.
E. Plan to manage deficit / surplus of human resources.

Choose the *correct* answer from the options given below:
(1) D, A, E, C, B
(2) A, C, B, D, E
(3) B, C, D, A, E
(4) C, D, A, B, E

44. Arrange the following five career stages starting from the earliest to the latest:
A. Exploration
B. Decline
C. Late-career
D. Mid-career
E. Establishment

Choose the *correct* answer from the options given below:
(1) A, E, D, C, B
(2) A, D, E, C, B
(3) A, C, D, E, B
(4) A, B, D, C, E

45. Arrange the following steps of performance appraisal process from beginning to end.
A. Communicate performance expectations to employees.
B. Establish performance standards
C. Compare actual performance with standards.
D. Measure actual performance.
E. Discuss the appraisal with the employees and. if necessary, initiate corrective actions

Choose the *correct* answer from the options given below:
(1) A, B, D, A, E
(2) B, A, D, C, E
(3) B, C, A, D, E
(4) C, B, A, E, D

46. Arrange the following four types of firms as identified by Bolwijn and Kumpe, in terms of their emergence starting from the earliest to the latest.
A. The quality firm
B. The innovative firm
C. The efficient firm
D. The flexible film

Choose the *correct* answer from the options given below:
(1) A, C, B, D
(2) C, A, D, B
(3) B, D, C, A
(4) D, B, A, C

47. Arrange the following five stages of personality development given by Freud, starting from the earliest to the latest.
A. Phallic stage
B. Genital stage
C. Oval stage
D. Anal stage
E. Latency period

Choose the *correct* answer from the options given below:
(1) C, D, A, E, B
(2) D, C, A, B, D
(3) A, B, D, C, E
(4) B, D, A, E, C

48. Arrange the main provisions of the Trade Unions Act, 1926 according to their sections from earlier to later.
A. Rights and Privileges of a Registered Trade Union.
B. Registration of Trade Union.
C. Incorporation of a registered Trade Union.
D. Power to make regulation.
E. Amalgamation and dissolution of a Trade Union.

Choose the *correct* answer from the options given below:
(1) B, C, A, E, D
(2) B, A, E, C, D
(3) A, B, C, D, E
(4) C, B, A, D, E

49. Arrange the following Trade Unions in proper sequence according to their formation from earlier to later.
A. Hind Mazdoor Sabha
B. The Hindustan Mazdoor Sevak Sangh

C. The Red Trade Union Congress
D. The Textile Labour Association, Ahmedabad
E. Bhartiya Mazdoor Sangh

Choose the *correct* answer from the options given below:

(1) A, C, B, D, E (2) B, C, A, D, E
(3) D, C, B, A, E (4) E, A, B, C, D

50. Arrange the following processes involved in reference of dispute to Voluntary Labour Arbitration from beginning to end.

A. Arbitration agreement
B. Submission of an Award
C. Signing of an Award
D. Choice of Dispute settlement
E. Selection of Arbitrator

Choose the *correct* answer from the options given below:

(1) A, E, D, B, C (2) D, E, A, C, B
(3) C, B, A, D, E (4) A, B, C, D, E

51. Arrange the following in the sequence as mentioned under the Minimum Wages Act, 1948 with regard to fixing and revising minimum rate of wages by the appropriate government.

A. For different localities.
B. For different classes of work in the same schedule employment.
C. For different schedule employment.
D. For adults, adolescent, children and apprentices.

Choose the *correct* answer from the options given below:

(1) A, B, C, D (2) C, B, D, A
(3) D, C, B, A (4) B, C, D, A

52. Arrange the following provisions of the Industrial Disputes Act, 1947 in ascending order in accordance with their years of enactment / amendment.

A. Dismissal etc., of an individual workman to be deemed to be an industrial dispute
B. Setting up Grievance Redressal Machinery
C. Voluntary reference of dispute to arbitration.
D. Payment of full wages of workman pending proceedings in higher courts.
E. Definition of continuous service.

Choose the *correct* answer from the options given below:

(1) E, D, A, B, C (2) A, B, D, E, C
(3) C, E, A, D, B (4) B, C, E, D, A

53. Arrange the following provisions in ascending order from the year of enactment or amendment under the Employees Provident Fund and Misecellanerous Provisions Act, 1952.

A. Employees Provident Fund Scheme
B. Employees' Deposit- linked Insurance Scheme
C. Employees' Pension Scheme
D. Family Pension Scheme

Choose the *correct* answer from the options given below:

(1) A, B, C, D (2) A, D, B, C
(3) A, C, D, B (4) D, C, B, A

54. Arrange the provisions of the Maternity Benefit Act, 1961 according to their section in earlier to later order:

A. Notice of claim for maternity benefits and payment there of
B. Employment of or work by, women prohibited during certain period.
C. No deduction of wages in certain cases.
D. Right to payment of maternity benefit.
E. Dismissal during absence of pregnancy.

Choose the *correct* answer from the options given below:

(1) A, B, C, D, E (2) B, D, A, E, C
(3) B, A, E, C, D (4) A, C, D, B, E

55. Arrange the following poverty elimination alleviation programmes according to the year of their launching in earlier to later order:

A. Swarna Jayanti Gram Swarojgar Yojana
B. Swarna Jayanti Shahri Rojgar Yojana

C. National Rural Employment Guarantee Act
D. Sampoorna Grameen Rojgar Yojana
E. Pradhan Mantri Kaushal Vikas Yojana
Choose the *correct* answer from the options given below:
(1) B, A, D, C, E (2) B, C, D, A, E
(3) A, B, C, E, D (4) A, C, B, E, D

56. Which among the following are the characteristics of Indian Labour Market?
A. Diversity in work place
B. Existence of perfect mobility
C. Monopoly in Labour market
D. Monopsony in labour market
E. Highly competitive in character
Choose the *correct* answer from the options given below:
(1) A, D, E only (2) A, B, C only
(3) B, C, E only (4) C, D, E only

57. As per the provisions of the Payment of Wages Act. 1936 for which of the following industries, the appropriate government is the central government?
A. Railways B. Ports and Docks
C. Mines D. Oilfields
Choose the *correct* answer from the options given below:
(1) A, B, C only (2) A, C, D only
(3) A, B, D only (4) B, C, D only

58. Which among the following are theories of Labour Welfare?
A. Efficiency B. The Police
C. Responsibility D. The Placating
E. The Functional
Choose the *correct* answer from the options given below:
(1) B, D, E only (2) A, C, D only
(3) B, C, D only (4) A, C, E only

59. Which among the following are theories relating to accidents and risk taking behaviour?
A. Psychological theories
B. Economic theories
C. Structural theories
D. Psycho- sociological theories
E. Anthropological theories
Choose the *correct* answer from the options given below:
(1) A, B, C only (2) C, D, E only
(3) A, C, D only (4) B, C, E only

60. Which among the following are classical theories of wages?
A. The Subsistence theory
B. The Standard of Living theory
C. The Marginal Productivity theory
D. The Wage fund theory
E. The Bargaining theory
Choose the *correct* answer from the options given below:
(1) A, B, C only (2) A, B, D only
(3) B, C, E only (4) A, C, D only

61. Which, among the following, are traditional techniques of controlling?
A. Personal observation
B. Management audit
C. Budgeting
D. Responsibility accounting
E. Break- even analysis
Choose the *correct* answer from the options given below:
(1) A, B, C only (2) B, C, D only
(3) C, D, E only (4) A, C, E only

62. Which among the following are process of staffing?
A. Division of activities
B. Manpower planning
C. Selection
D. Training and development
E. Defining authority and resposibility
Choose the *correct* answer from the options given below:
(1) A, B, C only (2) C, D, E only
(3) B, C, D only (4) A, C, E only

63. Which of the following are the on- the- job training methods?
A. Job rotation
B. Vestibule training

C. Role playing
D. Committee assignments
E. Coaching

Choose the *correct* answer from the options given below:
(1) A, B, C only (2) A, D, E only
(3) C, D, E only (4) A, B, D only

64. Which of the following statements are not true relating to grapevine?
A. Information usually travels relatively more slow through grapevine.
B. Grapevines are found in every organisation.
C. The grapevine is a more spontaneous form of communication.
D. The number of people who serve as actual links in the grapevine are generally large.

Choose the *correct* answer from the options given below:
(1) C and D only (2) B and C only
(3) A and D only (4) A and C only

65. Which of the following organisational issues are examined closely in HRD Audit?
A. Long term and short term plans and vision to assess competency requirements.
B. Identification of broad competency requirements for future business goals and objectives
C. Physical and mental conditions, diseases of worker and his family.
D. Examination of adequacies and inadequacies of HRD.

Choose the *correct* answer from the options given below:
(1) A, B, D only (2) A, B, C only
(3) B, C, D only (4) A, C, D only

66. Which of the following culture are associated with OCTAPACE culture of HRD style?
A. Openness B. Collaboration
C. Technology D. Authencity
E. Confrontation

Choose the *correct* answer from the options given below:
(1) A, B, C only
(2) A, B, D, E only
(3) A, C, D, E only
(4) A, B, C, D, E only

67. Which of the following statements relating to transactional analysis are true?
A. There are three different types of transactions namely complimentary, crossed and ulterior occur between the egos.
B. In the crossed transaction there is no scope for conflict.
C. In the ulterior transaction there is high scope of conflict.
D. In the complimentary transection there is no scope of conflict.

Choose the *correct* answer from the options given below:
(1) A, B and C only
(2) B, C and D only
(3) A, B, and D only
(4) A, C and D only

68. According to Herzberg's Two Factor Theory which of the following come under the category of motivater?
E. Achievement B. Supervision
C. Responsibility D. Salary
E. Advancement

Choose the *correct* answer from the options given below:
(1) A, B and D only (2) B, C and D only
(3) A, C and D only (4) A, B and C only

69. Which of the following were recommended by the study group set up by Union Ministry of labour in order to investigate and report the working of the Joint Management Council in 1962?
A. Workers Education and Development
B. Involvement of the middle management personnel.
C. Information sharing
D. 35 percent outsides should be workers representatives in Joint Management Council.

Choose the *correct* answer from the options given below:

(1) A, B and C only
(2) A, C and D only
(3) B, C and D only
(4) A, B and D only

70. Which of the following are core elements of the System Framework of Industrial Relations described by John. T. Dunlop?

E. Certain Actors
B. Certain context
C. Certain habits
D. Certain Ideology
E. Technological context.

Choose the *correct* answer from the options given below:

(1) A, B, C only
(2) A, B, C, D only
(3) A, B, D, E only
(4) B, C, D, E only

71. Which of the following factors had played their legitimate part in building up of the Madras Labour Union?

A. The status of the labourer as labourer in relation to his employer, affecting the economic and industrial life of the country.
B. The status of the labourer as citizen affected by the political movement and their result.
C. The status of the labourer in their international world of labour due to Russian Revolution.
D. The staws of the Indian Crony Capitalism that forces the labour to be associated.

Choose the *correct* answer from the options given below:

(1) A, B, C only (2) A, B, D only
(3) B, C, D only (4) A, C, D only

72. Which of the following organisations are autonomous organisations under Ministry of Labour?

A. Employees State Insurance Corporation
B. Employee Provident Fund Organisation
C. Dattopant Thengadi Board for Workers Education and Development.
D. Labour Bureau
E. V. V. Giri National Labour Institute.

Choose the *correct* answer from the options given below:

(1) A, B, C, D only (2) A, B, C, E only
(3) B, C, D, E only (4) A, B, D, E only

73. The provision for constituting various committees under the Building and Other Construction Worker (Regulation of Employment and Conditions of Service) Act. 1996 are:

A. Technical Advisory Committee
B. Central Advisory Committee
C. State Advisory Committee
D. Safety Committee
E. Expert Committee

Choose the *correct* answer from the options given below:

(1) A, B and C only
(2) A, B, and E only
(3) B, C, D and E only
(4) A, B, C, D, E

74. Select the authorities covered under the provision of the Employees Provident Fund and Miscellaneous Provisions Act. 1952 from the followings.

A. Central Board B. Board of Trustees
C. State Board
D. Advisory Committee
E. Executive Committee

Choose the *correct* answer from the options given below:

(1) A, C, D, E only (2) A, B, C, E only
(3) A, B, C, D only (4) B, C, D, E only

75. Under the provisions of the Inter- state Migrant Worker (regulation of employment and conditions of services) Act. 1979 other facilities to be provided to the migrant workman by his employer includes:

A. To ensure suitable conditions of work.

B. To provide and maintain suitable residential accommodation.

C. To provide education facilities to the children of migrant workmen.

D. To provide the prescribed medical facilities to workmen.

E. To provide such protective clothing to workmen.

Choose the *correct* answer from the options given below:

(1) A, B, C and D only
(2) B, C, D and E only
(3) A, B, D and E only
(4) A, B, C, D, E

76. Match the **List-I** with **List-II**

LIST I Propounders of management thought	**LIST II Explanation**
A. Charles Babbage	I. Development of personnel
B. Robert owen	II. Running organisation in more rational manner instead of traditional authority or charismatic authority
C. Max Weber	III. A system view point may provide the impetus to unify management theory
D. Fred Luthans	IV. Work specialisation

Choose the *correct* answer from the options given below:

(1) A-IV, B-III, C-II, D-I
(2) A-IV, B-I, C-II, D-III
(3) A-I, B-II, C-III, D-IV
(4) A-I, B-III, C-II, D-IV

77. Match the **List-I** with **List-II**

LIST I Formats of organisation	**LIST II Explanation**
A. Project organisation	I. Structured to accomplish specific, task within the constraints of time, money and quality
B. Functional organisation	II. Personnel manager ensures appointment of right people at the right time and place
C. Matrix organisation	III. A hybrid organisational structure which is a combination of functional and project structure
D. Networking organisation	IV. A multinational structural arrangement that combines elements of function, product and geographic design to link worldwide subsidiaries.

Choose the *correct* answer from the options given below:

(1) A-IV, B-III, C-II, D-I
(2) A-II, B-I, C-IV, D-III
(3) A-IV, B-II, C-III, D-I
(4) A-I, B-II, C-III, D-IV

78. Match the **List-I** with **List-II**

LIST I Business Games	**LIST II Utility**
A. Case Study	I. Encountering Skills
B. Role Play	II. Situational judgement and problem solving skill
C. In-basket method	III. Analytical judgemental and decision making skill
D. Simulation	IV. Human Relation Skill

Choose the *correct* answer from the options given below:

(1) A-I, B-II, C-III, D-IV
(2) A-II, B-III, C-IV, D-I
(3) A-III, B-IV, C-II, D-I
(4) A-IV, B-I, C-III, D-II

79. Match the **List-I** with **List-II**

LIST I Methods	LIST II Application
A. Assessment centre	I. Recntmemiit
B. Application blank	II. Performance appraisal
C. Job rotation	III. Selection
D. Employment exchange	IV. Training and development

Choose the *correct* answer from the options given below:

(1) A-II, B-III,C-IV, D-I
(2) A-I, B-II, C-III, D-IV
(3) A-III, B-I, C-II, D-IV
(4) A-IV, B-III, C-II, D-I

80. Match the **List-I** with **List-II**

LIST I Sources of power	LIST II Features
A. Reward power	I. Ability to influence others as a result of being liked and respected
B. Legitimate power	II. Ability to influence other by recognised competencies
C. Expert power	III. Ability to influence others by one's formal position
D. Referrent power	IV. Ability to influence others by giving rewards

Choose the *correct* answer from the options given below:

(1) A-I, B-II, C-III, D-IV
(2) A-II, B-I, C-IV, D-III
(3) A-III, B-IV, C-I, D-II
(4) A-IV, B-III, C-II, D-I

81. Match the **List-I** with **List-II**

LIST I Theories of Motivation	LIST II Propagator
A. Equity Theory	I. Victor Vroom
B. ERG Theory	II. David C. Me Clelland
C. Achievement Theory	III. Clay Alderfer
D. Expectancy Theory	IV. Adams

Choose the *correct* answer from the options given below:

(1) A-I, B-III, C-II, D-IV
(2) A-IV, B-III, C-II, D-I
(3) A-III, B-I, C-IV, D-II
(4) A-II, B-IV, C-I, D-III

82. Match the **List-I** with **List-II**

LIST I HRD Framework	LIST II Developer/ Formulator
A. The strategic framework approach	I. Yeung and Berman
B. The integrative framework approach	II. Ulrich and Lake
C. HRD scorecard approach	III. Curtis and Team
D. The People Capability Matuarity Model (P-CMM) approach	IV. TV. Rao

Choose the *correct* answer from the options given below:

(1) A-II, B-I, C-IV, D-III
(2) A-II, B-III, C-I, D-IV
(3) A-I, B-III, C-IV, D-II
(4) A-III, B-II, C-I, D-IV

83. Match the **List-I** with **List-II**

LIST I Functional classification of trade unions	LIST II Suitable examples
A. Business unionism	I. The knights of labour

B.	Friendly unionism	II. American federation of labour
C.	Revolutionary unionism	III. The brotherhood of teamsters
D.	Predatory unionism	IV. Industrial workers of the world

Choose the *correct* answer from the options given below:

(1) A-II, B-I, C-III, D-IV
(2) A-II, B-I, C-IV, D-III
(3) A-I, B-III, C-IV, D-II
(4) A-III, B-IV C-I, D-II

84. Match the **List-I** with **List-II**

LIST I Provisions	**LIST II Acts**
A. Committees	I. The Contract Labour (Regulation and Abolition) Act, 1970
B. Workers Participation in Safety Management	II. The Child and Adolescent Labour (Prohibition and Regulation) Act, 1986
C. State Advisory Board	III. The Factories Act, 1984
D. Technical Advisory Committee	IV. The Mines Act, 1952

Choose the *correct* answer from the options given below:

(1) A-IV, B-III, C-II, D-I
(2) A-III, B-IV, C-II, D-I
(3) A-IV, B-III, C-I, D-II
(4) A-I, B-II, C-IV, D-III

85. Match the **List-I** with **List-II**

LIST I Forms/ Types of strikes	**LIST II Appropriate meaning**
A. Lightning strike	I. Physical blockade caused by a conflict and organised mostly by employees
B. Gherao	II. Strike suddenly announced without proper notice
C. Picketing	III. An act of posting pickets and implies marching of workmen in front of the premises of the employer
D. Stay in strike	IV. A group of employees take possession of property of the business and stop production and refuse access to the owners desiring to work.

Choose the *correct* answer from the options given below:

(1) A-II, B-III, C-I, D-IV
(2) A-II, B-I, C-III, D-IV
(3) A-III, B-I, C-IV, D-II
(4) A-III, B-IV, C-I, D-II

86. Match the **List-I** with **List-II**

LIST I Provision	**LIST II Laws/Act**
A. Subsistence Allowance	I. The Industrial Disputes Act, 1947
B. Disability Allowance	II. The Inter-state Migrant Workmen (Regulation of Employment and Conditions of Service) Act, 1979
C. Journey Allowance	III. The Industrial Employment (Standing Orders) Act, 1946
D. Notice of change	IV. The Mines Act, 1952

Choose the *correct* answer from the options given below:

(1) A-IV, B-III, C-I, D-II
(2) A-I, B-II, C-IV, D-III
(3) A III, B-IV, C-II, D-I
(4) A-II, B-I, C-III, D-IV

87. Match the **List-I** with **List-II**

LIST I **Laws**	**LIST II** **Underlying Principle**
A. The Factories Act	I. To promote social security
B. The Equal Remuneration Act	II. To regulate the relation
C. The Employees Provident Fund and Miscellaneous Provisions Act	III. To promote welfare and protect from exploitation
D. The Industrial Employment (Standing Orders) Act	IV. To promote social justice

Choose the *correct* answer from the options given below:

(1) A-III, B-IV, C-I, D-II

(2) A-IV, B-III, C-II, D-I

(3) A-II, B-I, C-III, D-IV

(4) A-I, B-II, C-IV, D-III

88. Match the **List-I** with **List-II**

LIST I **Principles of labour welfare**	**LIST II** **Explanation**
A. Adequacy of wages	I. Development of human personality
B. Social responsibility of industry	II. Coordinated effort will promote a healthy development of worker.
C. Re-personalisation	III. Workers have a right to adequate wages
D. Co-ordination	IV. Industry has an obligation, towards its employees to look after their welfare

Choose the *correct* answer from the options given below:

(1) A-I, B-II, C-III, D-IV

(2) A-IV, B-II, C-III, D-I

(3) A-IV, B-I, C-III, D-II

(4) A-III, B-IV, C-I, D-II

89. Match the **List-I** with **List-II**

LIST I **Authorities**	**LIST II** **Acts**
A. Advisory Committee	I. The Payment of Gratuity Act, 1972
B. Controlling Authority	II. The Minimum Wages Act, 1948
C. Advisory Board	III. The Equal Remuneration Act, 1976
D. Central Board	IV. The Employees Provident Fund and Miscellaneous Act, 1952

Choose the *correct* answer from the options given below:

(1) A-III, B-I, C-II, D-IV

(2) A-II, B-III, C-IV, D-I

(3) A-IV, B-II, C-III, D-I

(4) A-IV, B-I, C-II, D-III

90. Match the **List-I** with **List-II**

LIST I Types of unemployment	**LIST II Explanation**
A. Technological	I. When economy faces structural changes like decline in export trade, it occurs.
B. Structural	II. Trade cycle revokes around boom and recession. In periods of depression and recession, demand decreases and leads to this type of unemployment.
C. Frictional	III. Changes in the techniques of production Leads to unemployment
D. Cyclical	IV. Immobility of labour, shortage of raw materials, breakdown of machinery etc causes it

Choose the *correct* answer from the options given below:

(1) A-III, B-IV, C-II, D-I

(2) A-III, B-I, C-IV, D-II
(3) A-II, B-I, C-III, D-IV
(4) A-IV, B-III, C-II, D-I

Read the passage carefully and answer the question:

In the Indian context, the social evils suffered by laboures such as, exploitation, illiteracy, lack of skill training, substance abuse, among many others, are reduced to a greater or lesser extent by the country's welfare policies. During the pre-independence period the industrial relations policy of the British government was generally based on laissez faire and selective intervention. There were hardly any labour welfare schemes. After Independence, labour legislation has been introduced which has shaped industrial relations and social security in contemporary India. The legislations have also provided for the machinery for bipartite and tripartite consultations for the settlement of labour- management disputes.

Soon after independence, the government at a tripartite conference in December 1947 adopted an industrial truce resolution. The following laws were enacted to maintain industrial peace and harmonious labour-management relations: the Factories Act of 1948, the Employees State Insuraance Act of 1948 and the Minimum Wages Act of 1948. Later, the Bonus Act was passed in 1965. The Constitution of India also spells out of the underlying principles of state policy which place an emphasis on labour welfare, especially Articles 38 to 43 of the Constitution. Labour welfare in India is aimed at getting the best out of the worker in the production process by creating the worker conditions required for this outcome.

In the early 1990s, the neoliberal economic reforms that were introduced by the government set in motion a series of measures to reduce state regulation of industries, particularly the larger industries. In general, the country's worker have opposed these economic liberalization policies out of fear of unemployment while the country's entrepreneurs have welcomed it in in hope of obtaining new opportunities to improve India's industries. These new economic policies have directly affected industrial relations in the country.

91. What was the predominant industrial relations policy of the British government in pre-independence India?
(1) Socialist Welfare State
(2) Total State Control
(3) Laissez faire and selective intervention
(4) Free market capitalism

92. The tripartite conference of 1947 adopted which resolution ?
(1) Socialist revolution resolution
(2) Industrial truce resolution
(3) Labour strike resolution
(4) Industrial democracy resolution

93. Which legislation aimed to provide social security benefits to workers in India.
(1) Minimum Wages Act, 1948
(2) Payment of Bonus Act, 1965
(3) Factories Act, 1948
(4) Employees State Insurance Act, 1948

94. How did labour generally react to the neoliberal economic reform in early 1990's?
(1) With concern over potential job loss.
(2) With widespread support and enthusiasm.
(3) With increased demand for higher wage.
(4) With calls for stricter government regulations.

95. What was the primary goal of Labour Welfare Policies in India as stated in the passage?
(1) To promote international trade agreements.
(2) To increase corporate profits.
(3) To enhance worker productivity through improved conditions.
(4) To encourage privatization of industries.

Read the passage carefully and answer the question:

The labour force participation rate (LFPR) and unemployment rate (UR) reflect a combination of whether an individual is looking for job and actually able to get one. The UR is defined as the